WORLD ENCYCLOPEDIA OF

POLITICAL SYSTEMS
AND PARTIES

WORLD ENCYCLOPEDIA OF

POLITICAL SYSTEMS AND PARTIES

THIRD EDITION

EDITED BY George E. Delury

THIRD EDITION EDITED BY
Deborah A. Kaple

VOLUME II

GABON–
NORWAY

Facts On File, Inc.

WORLD ENCYCLOPEDIA OF POLITICAL SYSTEMS AND PARTIES

Copyright © 1983, 1987, 1999 by George E. Delury

Facts On File, Inc.
11 Penn Plaza
New York NY 10001

Library of Congress Cataloging-in-Publication Data

World encyclopedia of political systems & parties / edited by George
   E. Delury. —3rd ed. / supervised by Deborah A. Kaple.
      p. cm.
   Includes bibliographical references and index.
   ISBN 0-8160-2874-5 (set) (alk. paper)
       0-8160-4162-8 (vol. I)
       0-8160-4163-6 (vol. II)
       0-8160-4164-4 (vol. III)
   1. Political parties—Handbooks, manuals, etc. 2. Comparative
government—Handbooks, manuals, etc. I. Delury, George E.
II. Facts on File, Inc. III. Title: World encyclopedia of political
systems and parties.
JF2011.W67   1999
324.2′03—dc21   99-17256

Text design by A Good Thing, Inc.

Printed in the United States of America

VB AGT 10 9 8 7 6 5 4 3 2 1

This book is printed on acid-free paper.

TABLE OF CONTENTS

CONTRIBUTORS TO THE THIRD EDITION

Jon G. Abbink studied history and anthropology in Nijmegen and Leiden (the Netherlands) and has done extensive field research in Israel and Ethiopia on ethnicity, ethnic relations, political change, Ethiopian ethnology, and material culture. He has taught at the Universities of Nijmegen and Amsterdam and is at present a senior researcher at the African Studies Centre, Leiden. He coedited a book on election observation and democratization in Africa that was published in 1999.

As'ad AbuKhalil is associate professor of political science at California State University and Stanislaus and Research Fellow at the Center for Middle Eastern Studies at the University of California at Berkeley. He obtained his Ph.D. in comparative government from Georgetown University. He is the author of *Historical Dictionary of Lebanon* (1998).

Feroz Ahmad is professor of history and University Research Professor at the University of Massachusetts at Boston. He is the author of a number of books and articles on the history and politics of Turkey and the Middle East.

Peter Aimer is an honorary research fellow in the Department of Political Studies at the University of Auckland.

Pooya Alaedini is managing editor of *CIRA Bulletin*, a publication of the Center for Iranian Research and Analysis. He is a doctoral candidate at the School of Planning and Public Policy, Rutgers University, where he is completing his dissertation on the political economy of development in Iran.

Charles Amjad-Ali holds the Martin Luther King, Jr., Chair of Justice and Community at Luther Seminary, St. Paul. Previously he directed the Christian Study Center, Rawalpindi, Pakistan. He has published over 100 articles and edited three journals. His books include *Liberation Ethics* (1985) and *Passion for Change* (1989). He received his Ph.D. from Princeton Theological Seminary.

Thomas D. Anderson earned his Ph.D. from the University of Nebraska and is professor of geography emeritus at Bowling Green State University, Bowling Green, Ohio. He is a cultural geographer, with emphasis on the political geography of the Caribbean. He wrote *Geopolitics of the Caribbean* (1984).

William G. Andrews, Ph.D., is professor emeritus of political science at the State University of New York at Brockport. He was founding executive director of the New York Consortium for European Union Studies and Simulations. He has published numerous books, articles, and scholarly papers on Western European Soviet, and American politics and government.

Kenneth E. Bauzon, Ph.D., Duke University, is assistant professor of political science at Saint Joseph's College in Brooklyn, New York. He is the editor of *Development and Democratization in the Third World: Myths, Hopes, and Realities* (1992). He is preparing a book-length manuscript on the politics of small states in the Euromed.

Craig Baxter is professor emeritus of politics and history at Juniata College. He is the author of *Bangladesh from a Nation to a State* (1997) and coauthor of *Historical Dictionary of Bangladesh* (2d ed., 1996).

Robin Bhatty is an analyst who writes on Caucasian political and security issues.

Thomas Bickford, who received his doctorate in political science from the University of California at Berkeley, is assistant professor at the University of Wisconsin–Oshkosh, where he teaches Asian politics and international relations. His current research is on the role of the military in Chinese politics.

Jan Knippers Black is a professor in the Graduate School of International Policy Studies at the Monterey Institute of International Studies in California and a senior associate member at Saint Antony's College, Oxford. Previously she served as research professor of public administration at the University of New Mexico and as senior research assistant and chair of the Latin American research team in the Foreign Area Studies Division of American University. She has authored or edited and coauthored 10 books, with 3 more scheduled for 1998 publication: *Latin America: Its Problems and Its Promise* (3d ed.), *Recycled Rhetoric and Disposable People*, and *Development in Theory and Practice: Bridging the Gap* (2d ed.). She has also published more than 100 chapters and articles in reference books and anthologies, journals, magazines, and newspapers.

Carlo J. Bonura, Jr., is a doctoral student of political theory in the Department of Political Science, University of Washington. His research focuses on ethnic minorities and questions of nationalism along the Malaysian-Thai border. He is currently pursuing research in these areas in Thailand.

John A. Booth is Regents' Professor of Political Science at the University of North Texas. He is the author of *Costa Rica: Quest for Democracy* (1998) and *The End and the Beginning: The Nicaraguan Revolution* (1985), coauthor of *Understanding Central America* (3d ed.,1999), and coeditor of *Elections and Democracy in Central America, Revisited* (1995). He has published articles and anthology chapters on the political systems of and political participation, culture, violence, elections, and democratization within Central America, Mexico, and Colombia.

Vince Boudreau is assistant professor of political science at the City College of New York and directs its M.A. Program in International Relations. His research interests include Southeast Asian social movements and Philippine politics and culture. He is working on a comparative study of state repression and protest forms in the Philippines, Indonesia, and Burma (now Myanmar).

Kirk Scott Bowman, Ph.D., is assistant professor at the Sam Nunn School of International Affairs, Georgia Institute of Technology. He lived and conducted fieldwork for four years in Belize, Costa Rica, and Honduras. His research has been published in various books and journals, including the *Journal of Peace Research* and *World Development*. Two of the focuses of his present research are the relationship between militarization and development and the political economy of tourism in developing countries.

Mary P. Callahan is assistant professor, Naval Postgraduate School, Monterey, California.

William Crowther is associate professor of political science at the University of North Carolina at Greensboro and codirector of the Parliamentary Documents Center for Central Europe. His research centers on issues of democratization and interethnic relations. He is the author of numerous works on various aspects of Moldovan and Romanian politics.

Richard Dale, who earned his Ph.D. in political science at Princeton University, was present in Botswana for its independence celebration in 1966. He visited the country in 1967, 1970, 1976, 1985, and 1987, and he has published a book, monographs, and articles about Botswana. He taught at the University of New Hampshire, Northern Illinois University, Southern Illinois University at Carbondale, and the U.S. Army School of International Studies at Fort Bragg, N.C. He retired from Southern Illinois University at Carbondale in 1997 and is working on a book dealing with the Namibian war of independence.

Jacob A. Darling is a 1998 honors graduate of Davidson College, receiving a B.A. in political science with an economics minor. He is employed as a financial analyst by First Union Real Estate Capital Markets. He aspires to a career in international development or trade relations.

Robert Dayley is assistant professor at Oglethorpe University in Atlanta. Previously he was visiting assistant professor of government at St. Lawrence University in Canton, N.Y. He holds a Ph.D. in political science from Northern Illinois University. In addition to five years of formal language training in Thai, he lived in Thailand for three years. His doctoral dissertation, "Modeling Chaos: Alternative Explanations of Policy Formulation in Thailand," was based on research conducted as a Fulbright Research Fellow at the National Institute of Development Administration (NIDA) in Bangkok.

Juan del Aguila, who received his doctorate from the University of North Carolina, is associate professor of political science at Emory University. He is the author of *Cuba: Dilemmas of a Revolution* (3d ed., 1994) and of many journal articles, book chapters, and scholarly book reviews focusing on Cuba's government and domestic and foreign policies.

Mark DeLancey is professor of African politics in the Department of Government and International Studies at the University of South Carolina. A former Peace Corps volunteer (Nigeria, 1962–64), he has taught at the University of Nigeria, the University of Yaoundé, Somali National University, and the University of Western Cape. He has published several books and articles on African comparative and international politics.

Edward Dew is professor of politics at Fairfield University, Fairfield, Connecticut. He teaches courses in the politics of Latin America and the Caribbean and is interested in the dynamics of ethnic conflict. He has authored two volumes on Surinamese political history and another on ethnic conflict in the high Andes of Peru.

Yomi Durotoye is visiting associate professor of politics at Wake Forest University in North Carolina. He taught for several years at the Obafemi Awolowo University in Nigeria, where he also served as the chair of the Department of Political Science. He obtained his Ph.D. from Duke University. He writes and works on African politics and policy analysis.

Christine Ehrick is assistant professor of history at the University of Northern Iowa. She received her Ph.D. from the University of California at Los Angeles in 1997. Her dissertation, "*Obrera, Dama, Feminista*: Women's Associations and the Welfare State in Uruguay, 1900–1930, "compares a number of women's political organizations and studies the relationship between Uruguayan feminism and the emerging welfare state. Her publications include "*Madrinas* and Missionaries: Uruguay and the Pan-American Women's Movement," published in *Gender and History* in November 1998.

Neil C. M. Elder is reader emeritus in politics at the University of Hull, UK. He is the author of *Government in Sweden* (1970) and of numerous articles on Swedish and Scandinavian government and politics and coauthor of *The Consensual Democracies* (revised 1988). He is coauthoring a book on government-agency relations in the UK, Sweden, and Germany with Edward Page of the University of Hull history department.

Sheila Elliott is associate professor at Columbia College, Columbia, South Carolina. Her areas of research are women, women's religious association, and social change in Africa. She has traveled extensively in southern Africa and Asia.

Mahmud A. Faksh is professor of political science at the University of Southern Maine. Previously he taught at the University of Connecticut, King Saud University, and Duke University. He has published extensively on Middle Eastern and Islamic affairs. He is the author of *The Future of Islam in the Middle East: Fundamentalism in Egypt, Algeria, and Saudi Arabia* (1997).

Martin F. Farrell is professor of politics and government and director of global studies at Ripon College, Ripon, Wisconsin. He has a doctorate in political science from the University of Chicago.

Karl J. Fields is director of Asian studies and associate professor of politics and government at the University of Puget Sound in Tacoma, Washington. He has published on various topics of East Asian political economy including government-business relations, economic reform, and regional integration. His first book, *Enterprise and the State in Korea and Taiwan* (1995), examines the roles of government and big business in the economic miracles of Taiwan and South Korea. His forthcoming book, *KMT,*

Inc., discusses the stable of enterprises owned and operated by Taiwan's ruling political party.

T. Bruce Fryer (Ph.D., University of Texas–Austin) is professor of Spanish in the Department of Spanish, Italian, and Portuguese at the University of South Carolina. He is editor of Spanish and Portuguese for *Business and the Professions*, published by NTC Contemporary Publishing and the American Association of Teachers of Spanish and Portuguese and is author of numerous books, articles, and reviews on the use of the Spanish language for professional purposes in international cross-cultural contexts. He has conducted research and workshops in Spain, Trinidad and Tobago, Colombia, Mexico, Puerto Rico, and Costa Rica and recently completed a Fulbright project in Cameroon and Equatorial Guinea.

Joel Gordon, assistant professor of history at the University of Nebraska at Omaha, is a specialist in modern Egyptian politics, film, mass media, and popular culture. The author of *Nasser's Blessed Movement: Egypt's Free Officers and the July Revolution* (1992), he is writing a book on popular civic culture in Nasser's Egypt.

Sergei Gretsky is adjunct professor of political science at the Catholic University of America and the Washington editor of *Tsentral'naya Aziya I Kavkaz* (Central Asia and the Caucasus), a journal of social and political studies published in Sweden. He is the author of *Russia's Policy toward Central Asia* (1997) and of a number of book chapters and articles in English, Russian, and Tajik on Islam and various aspects of domestic and foreign policy issues of Central Asian states.

Robert Griffiths is associate professor of political science and director of the International Studies Program at the University of North Carolina at Greensboro. He teaches courses in African politics, politics of development, international law and organization, and international political economy.

Rima Habasch is a doctoral candidate at Boston University. She has several years of work experience with the European Union in Brussels and United Nations agencies in Lebanon.

Olafur Th. Hardarson is associate professor of political science at the University of Iceland and director of the Icelandic Election Studies. He obtained his doctorate from the London School of Economics and Political Science. His publications include *Parties and Voters in Iceland* (1995).

Jeffrey K. Hass earned a Ph.D. from Princeton University. He is studying economic change and market transitions in Eastern Europe (especially Russia) and Latin America and working on a manuscript, "To the Undiscovered Country: Power, Culture, and Building Capitalism in Post-Soviet Russia." His other works and interests include political sociology, economic sociology, social change, organizations, studies of power, and revolutions.

Walter Hawthorne has done graduate work at Stanford University.

Cheryl L. Hendricks is a doctoral student (ABD) at the University of South Carolina.

Alejandro Hope has done graduate work at Princeton University. He lives and works in Mexico City.

Eugene Huskey is professor of political science and director of Russian studies at Stetson University in DeLand, Florida. He has published widely on politics and legal affairs in Kyrgyzstan, Russia, and the Soviet Union. He received his Ph.D. from the London School of Economics and Political Science in 1983.

Paul Hyer received his Ph.D. from the University of California at Berkeley in 1960 and joined the faculty of Brigham Young University as professor of modern Chinese history. He has been a visiting professor at five Chinese universities, including the Central University for Nationalities (Beijing) and the University of Inner Mongolia. His research and publications have focused more particularly on the border lands of the Mongol-China frontier and Tibet.

Pascal James Imperato, a leading authority on Mali, is Distinguished Service Professor at the State University of New York. He is the author of *Quest for the Jade Sea: Colonial Competition around an East African Lake* (1998).

Stephen F. Jones (Ph. D., London School of Economics) is associate professor of Russian and Eurasian studies at Mount Holyoke College. He has written over 60 articles and chapters on Georgian history and current political events in the South Caucasus. He is completing a book on the first independent Georgian republic of 1918–21.

Robert Kadel is visiting assistant professor of education and sociology at Pennsylvania State University. He received his Ph.D. in sociology from Emory University in 1998. He spent considerable time studying and visiting Europe and Scandinavia during college and graduate school and maintains a passion for research in these areas.

Roger Kangas is a specialist on Central Asian politics and economics, having written numerous articles, book chapters, and a book on Central Asian politics, especially that of Uzbekistan. He is a government consultant who coor-

dinates the Central Asia Area Studies Program at the Foreign Service Institute (U.S. Department of State), and is an adjunct instructor at Georgetown University. He previously worked at Johns Hopkins University SAIS, the Open Media Research Institute (OMRI), and the University of Mississippi. He earned his Ph.D. in political science from Indiana University.

Deborah A. Kaple received her Ph.D. in sociology at Princeton University. She is the author of *Dream of a Red Factory: The Legacy of High Stalinism in China* (1994). She works as a freelance editor and writer and teaches writing at Princeton University.

Gershon R. Kieval is senior analyst at the Central Intelligence Agency and was formerly adjunct professor of political science and international affairs at George Washington University. He received his Ph.D. from Johns Hopkins University. He is the author or coeditor of five books on Israel and Israeli national security policy, including, most recently, *Israel: Land of Tradition and Conflict*, 2d ed., with Bernard Reich (1993).

Stanley A. Kochanek is professor of political science at Pennsylvania State University. He has conducted fieldwork in India for the past 35 years and has published several books and numerous research articles. His latest book is the sixth edition of *India: Government and Politics in a Developing Nation* (1993), with Robert L. Hardgrave, Jr.

Roberto Patricio Korzeniewicz, Ph. D., is associate professor of sociology at the University of Maryland–College Park. He is the coeditor of *Latin America in the World Economy* (1996) and *Politics, Social Change, and Economic Restructuring in Latin America* (1997). His articles have appeared in the *American Journal of Sociology*, *Bulletin of Latin American Studies*, *Desarrollo Economico*, *Hispanic American Historical Review*, *Latin American Research Review*, *Political Power and Social Theory*, *Revista Mexicana de Sociologia*, and *Sociological Forum*. He has received grants and fellowships from the Heinz Foundation, the North-South Center at the University of Miami, the Social Science Research Council, and the World Society Foundation. His present research focuses on global patterns of income inequality and on historical and current patterns of political change in Latin America.

Michael R. Kulisheck received his Ph.D. in political science from the University of Pittsburgh in 1998. His research analyzes how political institutions influence patterns of representation and legislative behavior in Latin America. He has been a Fulbright Scholar and a visiting researcher at the Instituto de Estudios Superiores de Administración (IESA) in Caracas, Venezuela. He has published in *Electoral Studies* and is the coeditor of *Reinventing Legitimacy: Democracy and Political Change in Venezuela* (1998).

Michel S. Laguerre is professor of anthropology/Afro-American studies at the University of California at Berkeley. He has published 12 books, among them The *Informal City* (1994), *Diasporic Citizenship* (1998), and *Minoritized Space* (1999). *The Global Ethnopolis: Chinatown, Japantown, and Manilatown in American Society* will be published in the spring of 2000. He is completing another book, *The Global Chronopolis: Diasporic Implosion in American Society.*

Tobias J. Lanz received his Ph.D. from the University of South Carolina in 1997. His area of interest is development theory and environmental politics.

Benjamin N. Lawrance is completing his Ph.D. in African history at Stanford University on nationalism, rights discourse, and Pan-Africanism among the Ewe-speaking population of Togo and Ghana, under the supervision of Richard Roberts. His article "Most Obedient Servants: The Politics of Language in German Colonial Togo" appears in a forthcoming University of Chicago Press volume edited by Jean and John Comaroff.

Fred H. Lawson is professor of government at Mills College in Oakland, California. He is the author of *Bahrain: The Modernization of Autocracy* (1989) and *Why Syria Goes to War* (1996), as well as articles on the political economy of foreign policy in the Arab world.

Christopher J. Lee is a doctoral candidate in African history at Stanford University.

Richard Leitch is assistant professor of political science at Gustavus Adolphus College, St. Peter, Minnesota, where he teaches classes in comparative politics, international relations, and Asian politics. He received his Ph.D. from the University of Illinois and, with Martin E. Weinstein and Akira Kato, wrote *Japan's Role in the Post–Cold War World* (1995).

Timothy Longman is assistant professor of Africana studies and political science at Vassar College and also works as a consultant for Human Rights Watch/Africa. He is the author of numerous articles and book chapters on Rwanda, Burundi, and Congo. He has a forthcoming manuscript on the role of Christian churches in the Rwanda genocide of 1994.

José Antonio Lucero is a visiting researcher at the Center for the Study of Ecuadorian Social Movements (CEDIME) in Quito. He is a Ph.D. candidate in the Department of Politics, Princeton University, and is conducting a comparative study of Indian movements in Bolivia and Ecuador.

Michael Malley is a Ph.D. candidate in political science at the University of Wisconsin and an independent political risk consultant. He holds degrees from Georgetown and Cornell and has conducted research on Southeast Asian politics for more than a decade.

Jon Mandaville, Ph.D., is professor of history and director of the Middle East Studies Center at Portland State University. He specializes in the history and current affairs of the Arabian peninsula. Widely published on the area, he travels there regularly for research. In the early 1980s he served two years as director of the American Institute for Yemeni Studies in San'a.

Stephen C. Markovich, Ph.D. from the University of Virginia in 1968, is professor of political science at the University of North Dakota. He publishes articles and teaches courses on Eastern Europe and the Balkans.

Kristin Marsh is a Ph.D. candidate in sociology at Emory University. Her research encompasses issues of structured inequality and social conflict. Her dissertation, "Compromised Revolution: A Political Economic Explanation of Negotiation," is a cross-national comparative study of rebellion and civil war since 1950. Arguing that both social relations and political processes shape the potential for cooperative resolution to violent conflict, she develops a theoretical explanation of negotiation that combines insights from bargaining theory as well as political science and sociological perspectives on social conflict.

Félix V. Matos Rodríguez, a native of Puerto Rico, is assistant professor of history at Northeastern University. He received his doctorate at Columbia University. He has published on women's history in Puerto Rico, Caribbean historiography, and the Latino community in New England.

Andrei I. Maximenko teaches international relations and comparative politics at the University of South Carolina. His principal areas of interest and expertise are international organization, political economy, and African politics. Born in Kiev, Ukraine, he served as a political analyst in the Soviet Ministry of Foreign Affairs during the 1980s.

Terry M. Mays teaches in the Department of Political Science at the Citadel in Charleston, S.C. His research specialty is African multinational peacekeeping.

Mohamed Mbodj, Ph.D. in history, University of Paris, is associate professor of history at Columbia University. Previously he was professor of history and chair of the history department at the University of Dakar. He has published extensively on the economic and social history of contemporary Africa. He is a former board member of the *Journal of African History* and the *Canadian Journal of African Studies.*

Ken Menkhaus is associate professor of political science at Davidson College in Davidson, North Carolina. He specializes in African and Middle East politics.

B. David Meyers is associate professor of political science at the University of North Carolina at Greensboro. He is the author of numerous articles concerning African politics. In the early 1980s he served as a policy assistant on southern Africa and the southwest Indian Ocean islands in the Office of the Secretary of Defense.

Siamak Namazi is director of Future Alliances International, a private consulting group that concentrates on Iran and the Caspian region. He is also managing editor of *Iran Quarterly Report* and a frequent contributor to *Iran Focus.* He has an M.S. from the School of Planning and Public Policy, Rutgers University.

Richard S. Newell is emeritus professor of history, University of Northern Iowa. He received his Ph.D. from the University of Pennsylvania in South Asia regional studies. He is the author of *The Struggle for Afghanistan* (1981).

Elizabeth Normandy received her Ph.D. from the University of South Carolina. She teaches international relations, comparative politics, and African politics at the University of North Carolina at Pembroke. She has published works on African politics and international relations in *International Studies Notes, Liberian Studies Journal,* and *Journal of Political Science.* She has traveled in Senegal, Mali, Ivory Coast, and Cameroon.

Eugene Ogan is professor emeritus of anthropology, University of Minnesota. He received his Ph.D. from Harvard University and has published widely on the ethnology and history of the Pacific Islands.

Valerie O'Regan, Ph.D., is assistant professor of political science at North Dakota State University. Her main research interests are in European studies and gender politics.

Thomas O'Toole is professor of anthropology at St. Cloud State University, where he is active in the African Studies Program. He remains very interested in Africa and has written extensively about the continent. He is also the author of three editions of the *Historical Dictionary of Guinea* and *The Central African Republic: The Continent's Hidden Heart.* He is the translator of the *Historical Dictionary of the Central African Republic.*

Hun Joo Park is assistant professor of international relations at the Korea Development Institute (KDI) School of International Policy and Management. Among other pursuits, he is the author of *Triumph and Crisis of Dirigisme: The Political Origins of Financial Policy towards Small Business* (forthcoming). His present research project focuses on the impact of globalization on state politics and national identity, especially in the wake of the Asian crisis.

Andrew Parkin is professor of political and international studies at Flinders University in Adelaide, Australia, and a past president of the Australasian Political Studies Association. A graduate of Adelaide and Harvard Universities, he has published extensively on Australian government and politics, immigration and ethnic policy in the Asia-Pacific region, federalism and intergovernmental relations, criminal justice policy, housing policy, urban policy, and liberal-democratic theory.

William D. Pederson is professor of political science at Louisiana State University in Shreveport. Research for his entries (Czech Republic, Slovakia) was done under a grant from the Summer Research Lab of the Russian and East European Center, University of Illinois at Champaign.

Michele Penner is an advanced graduate student in the Department of Politics at Princeton University. She is completing a dissertation entitled "The Differential Evolution of Single-Party Systems in the Middle East: Turkish Democratization and Authoritarian Continuity in Tunisia."

Orlando J. Peréz received his Ph.D. from the University of Pittsburgh in 1996 and is assistant professor in the Department of Political Science at Central Michigan University. He has written chapters on Panamanian politics and voting behavior in Central America for edited volumes. He has completed a book-length manuscript on elite political culture in 20th-century Panama, along with an edited volume on Panamanian politics after the U.S. invasion.

Kenneth J. Perkins is professor of Middle Eastern and North African history at the University of South Carolina in Columbia. His research focuses on the 19th and 20th centuries and particularly on the interactions between the indigenous North African population and the European colonizers. He has traveled to and lived in the region extensively over the past 25 years.

Lawrence G. Potter is deputy director of the Gulf/2000 Project and adjunct assistant professor of international affairs at Columbia University. He holds a Ph.D. in history from Columbia University and is coeditor with Gary Sick of The *Persian Gulf at the Millenium: Essays in Politics, Economy, Security and Religion* (1997).

Bernard Reich is professor of political science and international relations at George Washington University. He received his Ph.D. in foreign affairs from the University of Virginia. A specialist in Middle East politics and foreign relations, he has written or edited many books and articles on those subjects, U.S. Middle East policy, and the Arab-Israeli conflict. With Gershon Kieval, he is the author of *Israel: Land of Tradition and Conflict* (2d ed., 1993).

Jeffrey Rinne is a 1999 Ph.D. candidate at Princeton University. His dissertation is entitled "Redesigning the State in Latin America: Pundits, Policy Makers, and Organized Labor in Argentina and Brazil."

K. Roberts is at present completing a Ph.D. in politics at an Australian university. The thesis deals with political and economic development in Singapore with a special emphasis on the colonial period.

Leo Rose is professor emeritus of political science, University of California at Berkeley. He has conducted research programs in the Himalayan states of Nepal, Sikkim, Bhutan, Arunachal (North East Frontier Area), and Ladakh in India since the mid-1950s. He has published or edited 19 books and innumerable articles on this area.

Curtis R. Ryan, Ph.D., is assistant professor of political science and international affairs at Mary Washington College in Fredericksburg, Virginia. As a Fulbright Scholar (1992–93) to the Hashimite Kingdom of Jordan, he served as guest researcher at the Center for Strategic Studies at the University of Jordan in Amman. His articles on Jordanian and Middle East politics have appeared in the journals *Democratization*, *Middle East Journal*, *Middle East Policy*, and the *Southeastern Political Review*.

Gamini Samaranayake is senior lecturer in the Department of Political Science at the University of Peradeniya, Sri Lanka. He obtained his Ph.D. from the University of St. Andrews, Scotland.

Gregory D. Schmidt, who received his Ph.D. from Cornell, is associate professor of political science at Northern Illinois University in DeKalb. He has published two books and over a dozen journal articles, book chapters, and monographs on political institutions in Peru. He has held fellowships from the Social Science Research Council and the Fulbright Program, served as a consultant to the United States Agency for International Development, and taught at several Peruvian universities.

Robert O. Schneider, Ph.D., is associate professor and chair of the Department of Political Science at the University of North Carolina at Pembroke. He is an expert on the American political process and public policy, and his recent research and publication include work on emergency management policy and implementation at the local level. He has also written on American national politics.

David W. Schodt received his Ph.D. in economics from the University of Wisconsin–Madison. He teaches in the Department of Economics at St. Olaf College, where he is also director of the Hispanic Studies Program. He is the author of two books as well as numerous articles on Ecuadorian political economy. He editor for the Ecuador: Economics section of the *Handbook of Latin American Studies*, published by the Library of Congress.

Reeva S. Simon is assistant director of the Middle East Institute at Columbia University. She is the author of *Iraq between the Two World Wars* (1986) and coeditor of the *Encyclopedia of the Modern Middle East* (1996).

Gordon Smith is emeritus professor of government at the London School of Economics. He specializes in German and European politics and has written extensively on both. He is coeditor of the journal *German Politics* and also of *West European Politics*.

Dale Story is professor and chair in the Department of Political Science at the University of Texas at Arlington. He has written extensively on the political economy of modern Mexico. Among his major works are *Industry, the State, and Public Policy in Mexico* (1986) and *The Mexican Ruling Party* (1986).

Martin Stuart-Fox is professor and head of history at the University of Queensland, Brisbane, Australia. He was previously a correspondent for United Press International for three years in Indochina during the Vietnam War. He has written six books and more than 50 articles and book chapters on Laos. His latest publication is *The Lao Kingdom of lan Xang: Rise and Decline* (1998).

Alastair H. Thomas is professor of Nordic politics in the Department of Social Studies at the University of Central Lancashire, Preston, England. His publications include *Social Democratic Parties in Western Europe* (1977), *The Future of Social Democracy* (1986), *The Consensual Democracies?* (1988), and *The Historical Dictionary of Denmark* (1998). His *Nordic Democracy in the New Europe* is to be published in 2000.

Cris Toffolo, assistant professor in the Department of Political Science at the University of St. Thomas, St. Paul, Minnesota, is also the Pakistan expert of the South Asia Coordination Group of Amnesty International (U.S.A.). Her areas of specialization include South Asian politics (Pakistan, human rights, women's issues, development and democracy) and early liberal and contemporary political theory. She earned her Ph.D. at the University of Notre Dame.

William S. Turley is professor of political science at Southern Illinois University–Carbondale, where he teaches international and comparative politics. He has also taught at Saigon University and Chulalongkorn University. His publications include *The Second Indochina War 1954–1975* (1986), the coedited volume *Reinventing Vietnamese Socialism: Doi Moi in Comparative Perspective* (1993), and the coauthored monograph *The Economics and Politics of Transition to an Open Market Economy: Vietnam* (1999), plus numerous articles dealing with Vietnamese politics, foreign affairs, and political economy.

Aldo C. Vacs, Ph.D. in political science from the University of Pittsburgh, is professor and chair of the Department of Government at Skidmore College. He teaches courses on Latin American politics and relations with the United States, international political economy, and diplomatic negotiations. His research interests are focused on Latin America's international relations and policies, democratization processes, and international political economic issues. With numerous publications since 1984, he has been a research associate at the Center for Latin American Studies of the University of Pittsburgh since 1988 and a contributing editor of the *Handbook of Latin American Studies*, published by the Library of Congress, since 1991, and is a contributor to *Argentina: A Country Study* for the Country Studies Series/ Area Handbook Program sponsored by the Library of Congress.

Alan J. Ward is Class of 1935 Professor of Government at the College of William and Mary in Williamsburg, Virginia. His many publications on Ireland include *Ireland and Anglo-American Relations, 1899–1921* (1969) and *The Irish Constitutional Tradition: Responsible Government and Modern Ireland, 1782–1992* (1994).

Robert Wardhaugh is assistant professor of history at the University of Winnipeg. He is a political and cultural historian whose work focuses on the Canadian Prairie region. He is author of a work that analyzes the relationship between the Canadian federal government and the West, *Mackenzie King and the Prairie West*, expected to appear in 1999.

James Wessman is associate professor of Latin American and Caribbean studies, and anthropology, at The University at Albany, State University of New York. He also serves as associate dean of undergraduate studies. He has been the editor of the Caribbean Studies Association and the Society for Latin American Anthropology.

John Hoyt Williams is Distinguished Professor of Arts & Sciences at Indiana State University–Terre Haute, where he has taught since receiving his Ph.D. from the University of Florida in 1969. His publications include some 40 articles and The *Rise and Fall of the Paraguayan Republic, 1800–1870* (1979), *A Great and Shining Road: The Epic Story of the Transcontinental Railroad* (1988), and *Sam Houston: A Biography of the Father of Texas* (1993). He is working on a social history of Charleston, South Carolina, under siege, 1861–65.

Lauren Yoder is chair and professor of French at Davidson College, where he teaches French and African studies. He has taught at Omar Bongo University in Libreville, Gabon. He has also lived in the Democratic Republic of Congo and in Burundi.

PREFACE TO THE THIRD EDITION

It is hard to imagine a time when the system of political parties was more important than it has been in the last 10 years. During this decade, and since the publication of the second edition of this encyclopedia, many of the world's political systems have come to be defined by democratic competition. Countries and whole regions that have traditionally been associated with one or another form of authoritarianism now hold regular elections. In the place of tanks in the streets, elite factions, or competing warlords, one sees parties of differing ideological stripes representing different sectors of society. Around the world, politics has increasingly become about political parties.

This trend began in Latin America in the 1980s. Led by the collapse of military rule in Argentina and the arrival to power of the Radical Party led by Raúl Alfonsín, Argentina's return to democracy first appeared fragile and even epiphenomenal. Instead, it was merely one of several dramatic returns to peaceful democracy on that continent. Brazil's generals gave up power, Pinochet in Chile accepted a plebiscite, and even Paraguay saw open political competition. For arguably the first time in its history, in the 1990s even the "perfect dictatorship" in Mexico began to crack and the leading party, the PRI, had to behave as a much more traditional political party than a strange beast defying characterization. At the end of the decade, only isolated spots in the Caribbean remain immune to this trend, with Haiti arguably not having a state to compete over and Cuba still ruled by Fidel Castro's unique brand of communism.

In Asia, the long rule of the Congress Party in India appears to be over and a much more competitive if not necessarily positive or peaceful system has taken its place. South Korea and Taiwan, two stalwarts of apparently efficient authoritarian systems, saw a great expansion of democratic rights. In South Korea, an opposition leader ascended to the presidency, and in Taiwan, the Kuomintang became one political party among a group of equals. Even in Singapore, Malaysia, and Pakistan, which are still not democratic, party politics became increasingly important. In Japan, the domination by the LDP essentially ended by middecade, although it is not clear whether this will be replaced by a more open competitive system. The fact that Myanmar (Burma) stands out as the one particularly sad example of a country that has not joined this trend merely highlights how democratic Asia has become. China is perhaps the most important holdout against the democratic wave, yet the 20-year-old transition to the market is already straining the capacity of the Chinese Communist Party (CCP) to dominate political life the way it once did. Whether it be regional and ethnic revolt in the west or the rise of new classes on the coast, it is difficult to imagine the CCP being able to maintain its monopoly over power in the next two decades. At this point, we can only speculate as to whether this change will come about through a dismemberment of China or through the institutionalization of national-level competitive politics. It is even unclear as to whether such a change would bring about a more peaceful and representative rule or lead to a return to the chaos of the first part of the century.

Early hopes for a resurgence of democracy in Africa seem, in retrospect, less well placed, yet there is no denying the symbolic importance of Nelson Mandela's becoming president of South Africa. Even if it was tinged with violence, the competition between the ANC and other political parties at least implied that no single group could again assume political domination. As 1999 began, there was even hope that Nigeria might once again enjoy democratic rule; however, in other parts of the continent, single-party regimes dominate, even if they appear as relatively benign as in Uganda. In other African countries, most notably, Rwanda and Burundi, peaceful political competition remains elusive.

With the exception of Israel and possibly parts of Lebanon, political parties as understood in the West remained rare and weak in the Middle East. Personal rule with the legitimacy through monarch or the control of an official state apparatus is the norm. While much of the West may not like it, the greatest organized voice of opposition has become an assortment of religious fundamentalist parties. How this region will deal with this form of political representation remains a critical challenge.

In Western Europe, many had once predicted long-term domination by conservatives, but by century's end, there appeared to be a practical monopoly of left-of-center parties. For countries that only 50 years before had been torn by war and civil strife, the existence of such long-term, peaceful competitive political rule is nothing short of miraculous. During the last decade, politics in the United States continued to center on single-issue movements or weak coalitions around a group of leaders, instead of strict reliance on one or another political party, although the two-party system is as entrenched as ever. Obviously the most dramatic turn of events occurred in Eastern Europe and the former Soviet Union (FSU). Poland and the Czech Republic are the most hopeful areas, since the shift to the market was accompanied by the successful holding of elections and several peaceful transfers of power. Even if Romania and Bulgaria remain social and economic disasters, opposition parties were able to defeat previously entrenched regimes. In the former Yugoslavia, at least Slovenia achieved what could be called a democratic regime without modifiers, while the situation in Croatia is more ambiguous and that of the rump state of Yugoslavia looks more like its predecessors. In the old Baltic republics of the USSR, debates about citizenship and economic policy made transition to democracy more difficult, but once again, one could argue that democratic regimes were at least developing if not fully achieving consolidation. Ukraine and Belarus faced such difficult economic problems that democracy still remains more of a hope than a reality. In the Central Asian republics, the old apparats and nomenklatura largely replaced the Communist Party with new dictatorships in slightly different clothing. Nevertheless, even these authoritarian regimes now have to step more carefully than their Soviet predecessors. Finally, in Russia, democracy did not bring about a solution to the economic social and political problems associated with the collapse of communism. But a semblance of free press and some islands of democratic competition have made a return to the status quo ante highly improbable.

Even if democracy has not represented the cure-all that many had expected, one has to look at the last decade as an optimistic sign for the development of political rights. If many countries failed to meet the established criteria for democratic regimes, at least those criteria were remotely relevant for many more of them. If one did not particularly like the winners, if the process was often less than clean, nevertheless, the arena of political competition had become more institutionalized and more peaceful. With few exceptions, it has become impossible to deny (at least officially) citizens a role in the definition of who rules them. If democracy is at least a government that recognizes its temporary claim to authority, then the world has become a much more democratic one.

Problems obviously remain. For parts of the world, including Africa and parts of the former Soviet Union, the decision about who will rule the state is almost irrelevant in the absence of a central authority. Increasing inequality, degrading poverty, gender biases, and ethnic hatreds make it unlikely that Westminster democracy will be universal in the 21st century. However, democracy has become the only recognized legitimate system for rule for perhaps the first time in the 20th century, and there are no other important ideological competitors. Of course, issues of defining individual liberty as opposed to collective rights remain, as do managerial problems of how to conduct competitive elections, how to organize transitions, how to respect the rights of those who lose, and how to assure the rule of law definitely remain. But it is not impossible to imagine that the 21st century will see a resolution of these problems and that most citizens of the world can participate in the often-frustrating, yet exhilarating, exercise of democratic rights.

This encyclopedia serves as a guide to the world's countries and where they stand in the spectrum of democracy and party politics. Where relevant we concentrate on the relative power of political parties. In other cases, we attempt to look inside the black box of authoritarian regimes. In all of them we try to always answer a basic question of political studies: Who rules? Our answers are as accurate as possible; we hope you find them useful.

Deborah A. Kaple
Princeton, N.J.
February 11, 1999

INTRODUCTION TO THE FIRST EDITION

The study of politics is a study of conflict. Whenever a few people gather to decide on common aims and means, some degree of conflict appears. Individual ambitions, more or less incompatible social and economic interests, and ideals that are often mutually exclusive compete for the resources of the group. When confined to a small institution—a church, a fraternal order, a business—the means by which such conflict can be pursued are limited and the potential gains and losses are relatively small. When the conduct of a sovereign state is at issue, however, the potential gains in wealth, prestige, and economic and physical power can be immense and the potential losses proportionately severe. Furthermore, the full resources of the state and society can be brought to bear on the conflict—money, people, institutions, and if necessary, weapons. National politics is a serious business, often deadly serious.

The business of politics is conducted within a system of interacting elements that include the state and its government with executive, legislative, and judicial functions and customary and/or written rules of procedure; a variety of social and economic interests that may or may not express themselves through political parties; and processes through which political parties or interests bring their influence to bear on the government. This encyclopedia describes these elements of the political systems of 170 sovereign nations and eight dependent territories in a relatively narrow cross section of time, roughly the summer and fall of 1985.

The standard format of an article begins with an introductory section that provides a basic description of the institutions of government along with the historical background necessary to understand the present political arrangement in the country. This section looks first at the executive functions, the formal locus of policy- and decision-making power in the country. It then outlines the structure and powers of the legislature or any similar body that purports to represent at least some of the population and that discusses, debates, and approves new laws. The judiciary is examined with particular concern for its independence from political pressures or control and its relative power vis-`a-vis the other branches of government. Finally, this section briefly describes regional and local structures of government and tries to assess the degree of local autonomy and political-party activity.

The next section takes up the electoral system. It notes the extent of suffrage, registration and balloting procedures, whether voting is compulsory, and the level of voter turnout for elections. It describes how the country is geographically organized for elections and usually assesses the relative fairness and honesty of elections. Most importantly, this section describes the way in which election winners are determined in the state under consideration; this is important, for there are several systems, which differ markedly from one another. Proportional representation systems, which are used in many countries, require a special explanation.

The simple plurality system now used in most English-speaking countries met with serious objections on the European continent when the suffrage was expanded to include the vast mass of working people who tended to vote socialist. The traditional parties were faced with the possibility that socialist parties could consistently win large parliamentary majorities, even if they did not win a majority of the votes nationwide. It was also noted that a small party that represented an important but scattered minority in the country could be closed out of the legislative process altogether.

To overcome these objections, proportional representation (PR) systems were introduced, beginning with Denmark in 1855. After considerable debate over what constituted a fair system, Victor d'Hondt in 1878 devised a method that is still in common use, although with many variations. At its simplest, the d'Hondt method works as follows. Assume that three parties are competing for nine legislative seats in a multimember district. Voters, who in PR systems usually vote for party lists of candidates rather than for individuals, give Party A 10,000 votes; Party B, 7,000; and Party C, 3,000. The first seat goes to Party A, and its vote is divided by 2. Each time Party A wins another seat, its total vote is divided by the next-highest number—2, 3, 4, and so on. In some countries the process ends there, but in others leftover votes (1,750 for Party B, for example) are pooled at the national level and additional seats are distributed by the same process.

The d'Hondt system tends to favor larger parties at the expense of small ones and can still elect a government that is not supported by a plurality of the voters. To overcome these problems, a variation called the Sainte-Laguë method (developed in 1910) was introduced. The essential difference between the systems is that the Sainte-Laguë method divides the party's total vote by 3, 5, 7, and so on. This makes it progressively harder for a large party to win each successive seat and reduces the advantage of electoral alliances, which in turn discourages the formation of very small parties. The three Scandinavian countries adopted the Sainte-Laguë method, with variations, in the early 1950s.

Another PR system, used in some English-speaking countries, is called the single transferable vote (STV). The STV method requires the setting of a quota—the number of votes needed to win a seat in a multimember district. Sometimes the simple formula—votes divided by number of seats—is used to determine the quota. Most STV systems, however, use "Droop's quota," devised in 1868, which employs the formula $(V \div [S + 1]) + 1$, where V is the total vote and S the number of seats to be distributed. If, for example, the total vote was 10,000 in a race for four seats, a candidate would need 2,001 votes to win a seat. If a candidate gets 5,000 votes, the STV method distributes all the second-preference votes on those ballots to their respective recipients on the basis of the following formula: $(V - Q) \div V$, where V is the total vote for the winning candidate and Q is the quota. [In the example: $(5,000 - 2,001) \div 5,000 = 60\%$.] If a candidate got 1,000 second-preference votes on the winning candidate's ballots, for example, 600 votes would be added to his or her first-preference votes. The advantage of this system is that it allows the voters to vote for individuals and makes nearly every vote count. A variation on the STV system counts second-preference votes only if the voter's first preference fails to get enough votes to get elected.

Articles on countries with multiparty systems turn next to a general description of the system—when and how the parties originated, how they are supported or restricted by law, and their common elements of organiza-tion or lack of it. This section then briefly describes the general tone and methods of election campaigns in the country; it ends, where appropriate, with a look at the issue of voter loyalty to or independence of parties.

Each major party is then described in terms of its history, organization, policy, membership and electoral support, financing, leadership, and prospects for remaining in government or gaining power. The major parties in some of the smaller countries are not treated in quite this detail, not only because of lack of space but also because reliable information was simply not to be found. Even for major and thoroughly studied countries, there is often little or no information on either the sources of funds or the expenditures of political parties. Over most of the world, party financing, the life's blood of politics, is as much of a mystery to political scientists as the circulatory system was to the medical profession in the 16th century.

Reasonably reliable membership figures are also unavailable in many cases. Where such numbers are thought to indicate its basic strength, a party will often inflate them or keep them secret. In other countries, while some or all parties purport to have formal memberships, the rules of enrollment and dues paying are laxly enforced and no accurate counts of members are made. In most one-party states, membership means little or nothing politically; it is simply a means of career advancement.

Following the description of the party in a one-party state, the next section of the article is found only where significant opposition is known to exist either in the country or in exile. Opposition here does not refer to scattered individuals or small groups of like-minded acquaintances—that phenomenon is better labeled dissent. Opposition, in this context, refers to more or less formally organized groups bent either on resisting the power of the one-party state and/or on radically altering the form of government or its leadership.

In many countries, major political roles are played by institutions or social groups that are not primarily political but that have considerable influence in the political system. Chief among these *other political forces* are the

		Party A			Party B			Party C	
Seat 1		10,000	(50%)		7,000	(35%)		3,000	(15%)
Seat 2	÷ 2	5,000			7,000			3,000	
Seat 3		5,000		÷ 2	3,500			3,000	
Seat 4	÷ 3	3,333			3,500			3,000	
Seat 5		3,333		÷ 3	2,333			3,000	
Seat 6	÷ 4	2,500			2,333			3,000	
Seat 7		2,500			2,333		÷ 2	1,500	
Seat 8	÷ 5	2,000			2,333			1,500	
Seat 9		2,000		÷ 4	1,750			1,500	
	5 seats (55%)		3 seats (33%)		1 seat	(12%)			

armed forces, which dominate the political process in many countries. Other such political forces are organized labor, religious institutions, ethnic groups, students, and occasionally foreign governments, international organizations, and even individuals. Each of these groups, where appropriate, is identified, and some indication of their role is provided.

Finally, each article briefly summarizes the nation's prospects for continuing or attaining political stability. These opinions must necessarily be speculative and can only extrapolate from known political facts. The sudden death of a commanding political figure, the rapid rise of a hitherto-little-recognized political group, and unforeseen catastrophe—economic, physical, military—can play no role in such predictions.

The length of the articles is determined more by the importance of the country than by the complexity of its political system. If the complex roles of all elements in a country's political system were clearly understood, two volumes of this size would scarely suffice to deal with it fully.

Because of this complexity and our incomplete understanding, the classification of systems as authoritarian, democratic, multiparty, etc., while useful, must always be regarded critically. The reader is advised to study an article thoroughly before accepting a classification as anything other than a rough indicator of political appearances. A nation with parties and elections is not necessarily a democracy (e.g., Paraguay), nor is a country without those institutions necessarily a dictatorship (e.g., Somalia, Jordan).

Nevertheless, after examining these articles, I have concluded that there are four broad categories in which political systems might be placed more or less accurately. These categories refer not to the political systems themselves but to the common attitudes and expectations—the political ethos—in which these systems function. The four categories can be called "no losers," "winner-take-all," "winner-took-all,"`and "single arbiter."

Perhaps a third of the world's countries have a "no losers" political ethos. Political conflict is channeled into more or less open and effective policy debates and relatively fair electoral processes. Every interested group can bring some degree of influence to bear on the government. Political actors find that it is in their own best interests to pursue moderate aims and to avoid any abuse of power that would seriously threaten the opposition. No single group seeks massive gains, and none faces massive losses. Generally, there is a widespread and deep respect for civil and human rights and for the rule of law. A key element in maintaining a "no losers" ethos is an economic prosperity—or its promise—sufficient to satisfy popular expectations, which can vary from pathetically low to unreasonably high.

The "winner-take-all" political ethos is more common than "no losers." It is found largely, but not exclusively,

in countries numbered among the less economically developed. In this ethos, each contending political force more or less reasonably sees any loss of political or economic power as a threat to its continued existence. Conversely, any gain may be used to further limit or destroy the power of opposing forces. Such systems face the continuing possibility of severe civil strife between ethnic groups (Northern Ireland, South Africa, Lebanon), or classes (El Salvador, Iran), or ideologies (Poland, Chile), or between urban and rural interests (Philippines, Afghanistan). Usually, more than one of these divisive elements are factors in the conflict. Often such conflicts are made virtually unresolvable by religious or ideological dogmas that make the destruction of the opposition a virtuous act. A commonplace solution to the threat of civil strife is the imposition of some form of dictatorial rule by the military, a preeminent political leader, an elite, or even by an outside force. Many states that appear to have developed a "winner-took-all" ethos (some of the "Marxist" states in Africa, for example) are in reality relatively superficial impositions of military or elite power on a political ethos in which the contending forces would otherwise destroy the country.

About 10% of the world's nations seem to fit the "winner-took-all" category, in which there are no apparent bases for major civil conflict, because potential opposition has been destroyed in an earlier "winner-take-all" struggle. Stable, post-revolutionary regimes—the Soviet Union, Cuba, Vietnam—are clear examples.

Finally, the "single arbiter" ethos refers to those societies which accept the more or less benign rule of a traditional authority—a king or an emir—who is the final arbiter of any social conflict. The ruler usually seeks a balance between competing economic and social forces, few of which are threatened with political extinction. Some societies with apparently more "modern" regimes—Egypt, for example—might be seen as continuing the "single arbiter" ethos in a new guise.

When reading about the political system of any country, the reader should keep in mind that the political ethos in which the system functions may not be supportive of that system. Over much of the world, European government and party systems, both democratic and communistic, are often fragile and nearly irrelevant overlays on patterns of social power that are seldom clearly understood even by the participants. A professedly democratic system with regular and apparently open processes of political debate and resolution of conflict can be and often is an oligarchic system in which members of the elite only superficially represent the interests of the otherwise politically impotent groups. On the other hand, a system in which the "winner-took-all" can still retain or develop processes by which social interests effectively compete for influence (Hungary might be an example).

The contributors have demonstrated great commitment to the ideal of knowledge for its own sake. All showed a deep concern to make clear to the general reader the essential political elements operating in each country. Many submitted far more information and expended much greater time and energy on the project than the editor asked for. The editor thanks them heartily for their support, understanding, and patience.

Carol Simon, Muriel Bennet, Tina and A. La Russo, and the editorial staff of Facts On File, Inc., have also contributed to the success of this project. Most particularly, the encouragement and unrelenting demands of Ed Knappman have given this encyclopedia its extra measure of thoroughness.

George E. Delury
January 1983

WORLD ENCYCLOPEDIA OF

POLITICAL SYSTEMS
AND PARTIES

GABONESE REPUBLIC

(La République Gabonaise)

By Lauren Yoder, Ph.D.

THE SYSTEM OF GOVERNMENT

Gabon, a central African nation on the equator with a population of approximately 1.2 million, is a multiparty republic with a presidential form of government. The current president, El-Hadj Omar Bongo, has been in power since 1967. Between 1968 and 1990 the political system centered upon the powerful president who was also head of the only legal political party, the Gabonese Democratic Party (PDG). However, the emergence of illegal opposition parties during the early 1980s and the economic downturn of the late 1980s led to a national debate, the opening of the political system, and a new constitution.

At Gabon's independence in 1960, the government was modeled after the French Fifth Republic. There were two principal parties, the Gabonese Democratic Group (BDG) led by Léon M'Ba and the Gabonese Democratic and Social Union (UDSG) led by J. H. Aubane. In 1966, M'Ba was reelected president and Albert-Bernard (later Omar) Bongo was elected vice president. M'Ba's death later that year elevated Bongo to the presidency. He has been reelected every five years since 1973. The most recent presidential election, in 1993, was marred somewhat by the lack of transparency, but Bongo, one of nine candidates, was declared the winner with 51% of the vote. The strongest opposition candidate, Paul M'Ba Abessole of the Movement for National Regeneration-Woodcutters (MORENA-B) received just over 26%.

Throughout his years as president, Bongo has attempted to maintain the stability of the political system while submerging rivalries and broadening participation. In 1968, he dissolved all existing political parties and announced the formation of a single party, the PDG. In 1975, the office of vice president was abolished along with the right of automatic succession and the office of prime minister was created. Following demands for reform by the Second Extraordinary Congress of the PDG in 1979, Bongo announced several democratizing measures within the party and reshuffled top government officials.

Opposition to the PDG continued throughout the 1980s, however. Student and worker unrest led finally to the convening of a national conference in 1990. Those discussions brought about major changes in the political system, nationwide multiparty parliamentary elections, and a new constitution. The constitution of 1991 and its 1994 revision demonstrate a commitment to liberal democracy and to the guarantee of civil liberties including the freedom to organize political parties. Among the constitution's provisions are a bill of rights, the guarantee of an independent judiciary, and the establishment of a bicameral legislature.

Executive

The president of Gabon is head of state and the commander in chief of the armed forces. The presidency is by far the most powerful political office in the Gabonese political system. According to the constitution, the primary powers of the president are the determination of national policy and the exercise of exclusive executive power. As head of the executive branch, the president may propose legislation as well as executing laws passed by the legislature.

The president appoints the prime minister, Cabinet members proposed by the prime minister, three of the nine judges who sit on the Constitutional Court, and many other officials. The president has the authority to dissolve the National Assembly, to declare a state of emergency (which gives him additional powers), to delay legislation, to submit proposals for vote by referendum, and to appoint and dismiss the prime minister and Cabinet members.

The president is elected by universal suffrage for a term of five years and can be reelected only once. The 1991/94 constitution prescribes that in the event of the president's death or incapacity, the president of the National Assembly serve as chief executive until new elections are held between 30 and 45 days later.

The prime minister as head of government selects the members of the Cabinet (*Conseil des Ministres*), most of whom are members of the National Assembly. Prime Minister Paulin Obame Nguema resigned late in 1998, leaving the post vacant.

Legislature

Legislative power in Gabon is vested in a bicameral Parliament. The National Assembly has 120 members: 111 are directly elected by their constituents for five-year terms in single-seat constituencies, and 9 are appointed by the president. The 91 members of the Senate are elected indirectly and represent local governments. Senators serve six-year terms.

The legislature's role is to make laws and approve taxes, though bills may be initiated by either Parliament or the executive branch. Any bill related to finances or constitutional revision must first be considered by the National Assembly. Any bill related to local government is presented first in the Senate. If the two houses fail to agree on the provisions or the wording of a bill, the prime minister has the authority to call a joint committee to work out an agreement.

Should the president of the republic dissolve the National Assembly, which action is limited to once during any 12-month period, new elections must be held between 30 and 45 days later.

The National Assembly may censure or withdraw its confidence from the government, precipitating the resignation of the prime minister. The current president of the National Assembly, who would replace the president of the republic in the event of the latter's death or incapacity, is Guy Nzouba Ndama.

The first parliamentary elections under the new constitution were held in December of 1996 for the National Assembly and in January and February of 1997 for the Senate.

Judiciary

The judiciary is based on the French civil code and customary law. It ranges from local courts ruling on issues of tribal law to the high courts created by the 1991/94 constitution. The judiciary is unequivocally coequal with the executive and legislative branches, and its independence is guaranteed by the constitution.

The four courts that make up the highest level of the judiciary are the Constitutional Court (*Cour Constitutionnelle*), the Judicial Court (*Cour Judiciaire*), the Administrative Court (*Cours Administrative*), and the Court of Accounts (*Cour des Comptes*). The first oversees elections and interprets the constitution in case of doubts as to its meaning, the second is responsible for civil, commercial, social, and penal questions, the third deals with administrative questions, and the fourth with the use of public monies.

The constitution also provides for a High Court of Justice that would be convened to judge the president of the republic in the event that the Parliament, by a two-thirds majority, should accuse the president of treason or of failing to uphold his oath of office.

Regional and Local Government

Gabon is divided into 9 provinces, which are further divided into 49 departments and 23 districts. Until 1996, all provincial governors, prefects, and subprefects were appointed by the president. A 1996 law provides for the election of municipal and provincial councils on a proportional partisan basis.

THE ELECTORAL SYSTEM

Suffrage in Gabon is universal. All Gabonese nationals 21 years of age or older are eligible electors, and voting is by secret ballot. Elections for local and provincial councils as well as national elections are administered by the newly created (1996) independent National Election Commission.

THE PARTY SYSTEM

Between 1968 and 1990, Gabon was a single-party state. President Bongo was also the head of the *Parti Démocratique Gabonais* (PDG). The 1980s witnessed the formation of illegal opposition parties as well as pressure from the reform wing of the PDG to open the political arena to include opposition parties. After the 1990 conference that addressed the concerns of labor unions and students, Bongo agreed to resign as party head (replaced by Jacques Adiahenot).

In May of 1990 opposition parties were legalized and later that year multiparty parliamentary elections were held. The primary opposition party was the *Mouvement pour le Redressement National* (MORENA), which later split into MORENA-Bûcherons and MORENA-originel.

THE DEMOCRATIC PARTY OF GABON

(Parti Démocratique Gabonais; PDG)

PDG, the party of President Bongo, was founded in 1968 when he convinced the members of the *Bloc Démocratique Gabonais* (BDG) and the *Union Démocratique et Sociale Gabonaise* (UDSG) to merge into a single party in the interest of preventing ethnic and regional conflict. It is still the largest and most powerful political party in Gabon. Following the parliamentary elections of 1996 and 1997, the PDG holds 85 of the 120 seats in the National Assembly and 52 of the 91 seats in the Senate.

OPPOSITION POLITICAL PARTIES

The two opposition parties with the most substantial representation in Parliament are the National Woodcutters

Rally (*Rassemblement National des Bûcherons*; RNB), the former MORENA-B, and the Gabonese Progress Party (*Parti gabonais du progrès*; PGP). The leader of the RNB is Paul M'Ba Abessole, who received strong support in his unsuccessful bid to topple President Bongo during the presidential elections of 1993. The leader of the PGP is Pierre Louis Agondjo-Okawé.

Other opposition parties with more than one seat in parliament include the Convention of Reformist Liberals (*Convention des Libéraux Réformateurs*; CLR), the Union for Gabonese Socialism (*Union pour le socialisme au Gabon*; USG), the Democratic and Republican Alliance (*Alliance Démocratique et Républicaine*; ADERE), and the Rally for Democracy and Progress (*Rassemblement pour la Démocratie et le Progrès*; RDP).

Several additional parties hold only one seat: the Circle for Renewal and Progress (*Cercle pour le renouveau et le progrès*; CRP), the Congress for Democracy and Justice (*Congrès pour la démocratie et la justice*; CDJ), the African Forum for Reconstruction (*Forum Africain pour la Reconstruction*; FAR), the Gabonese Peoples Union (*Union du Peuple Gabonais*; UPG), and the Mouvement pour le Redressement National (MORENA). Several deputies and senators were elected as nonpartisan candidates.

NATIONAL PROSPECTS

It has been encouraging to note Gabon's opening of the political process during the 1990s after the authoritarian regime of the 1970s and 1980s. In spite of some criticism of undue governmental influence during the presidential elections of 1993 on the side of the PDG, most observers feel that substantial progress has been made toward transparency and openness.

Two potential sources of instability need to be addressed. The considerable petroleum-based wealth of the country must be distributed more equitably, and leaders must remain vigilant to the danger of conflict between ethnic groups.

An additional perennial question is the nature of Gabon's relationship to France. Close economic and military ties between the two countries have been a stabilizing force since independence (though some would say that more pressure from France could have brought about multiparty democracy much earlier). Prospects seem good for Gabon to maintain a reasonably open and progressive political system.

Further Reading

Barnes, James F. *Gabon: Beyond the Colonial Legacy.* Boulder, Colo.: Westview Press, 1992.

De Saint Paul, Marc A. *Gabon: The Development of a Nation.* New York: Routledge, 1989.

Gardinier, David E. *Gabon.* World Bibliographical Series, vol. 149. Oxford: Clio Press, 1992.

———. *Historical Dictionary of Gabon*, 2d ed. Metuchen, N.J.: Scarecrow Press, 1994.

Pean, Pierre. *Affaires africaines.* Paris: Fayard, 1983.

Weinstein, Brian. *Gabon: Nation-Building on the Ogooué.* Cambridge, Mass.: MIT Press, 1966.

Yates, Douglas A. *The Rentier State in Africa: Oil Rent Dependency andNeocolonialism in the Republic of Gabon.* Trenton, N.J.: Africa World Press, 1996.

Web Site

Constitution de la République Gabonaise: www.agora.stm.it/politic/gabon.htm

REPUBLIC OF THE GAMBIA

By Steven Metz, M.A.
Revised by Mohamed Mbodj, Ph.D.

THE SYSTEM OF GOVERNMENT

Gambia is a country of 11,295 square kilometers in western Africa. Its main ethnic groups are the Mandinka, 42%; Fula, 18%; Wolof, 16%, Joola, 10%, and Serahuli, 9%. The vast majority of the 1.147 million people (85%) are Muslim, and approximately 10% are Christian.

From 1965, when the nation became independent, until 1970, Gambia was a constitutional monarchy under the British sovereign. The Gambian Republic was declared and the present constitution promulgated in 1970. David Jawara, who was then prime minister, became the first president. The People's Progressive Party (PPP), which Jawara founded in 1959, exercised absolute domination over the new state's politics from 1962 until 1981.

Following an attempt by Marxist rebels to overthrow the government in 1981, a loose confederation was formed with Senegal, which dwarfs Gambia in size and surrounds it geographically. While both nations remained sovereign under this plan, there was a limited integration of security functions, communications, and monetary and economic systems and coordination of foreign policy. The confederation collapsed in 1989 due mainly to Gambia's reluctance to further integrate.

In 1994, an army lieutenant, Yaya Jammeh, staged a successful coup deposing President Jawara. The young officers wanted to rid the country of widespread corruption and the ubiquitous sex tourism, and they hoped to upgrade the country's derelict infrastructure. They saw the PPP as a syndicate of corrupt leaders who have enriched themselves at the expense of their people. After almost two years of military rule, which was marred by several failed coups by former close associates, Jammeh lifted the ban on political activity in August 1996. A new constitution was adopted at the same time.

The new constitution provided for a presidential system and a 49-seat parliament. Since that time, despite the banning of some of the precoup parties and many setbacks, the country has enjoyed a fairly democratic system, which largely protects freedom of the press and respects most human and political rights.

Executive

The primary executive officer in Gambia is the president, who is head of government, head of state, and commander in chief of the security forces. In addition to the usual executive functions dealing with the application of law, the president also has the power to dissolve the legislature and call new elections. Candidates for the presidency must be at least 30 years old and registered voters. The president is chosen by direct election with universal suffrage. A vice president is chosen at the same time as the president. The term of office is five years. Elections were held in September 1996 that returned Jammeh (now a retired colonel) as a civilian president, with 55% of the votes, marking the debut of a new civilian and democratic regime.

Legislature

The unicameral legislature of Gambia is composed of the House of Representatives, with 49 members. Of these, 45 are selected by direct election from single-member districts and 4 are appointed by the president. The president of the republic sets the legislative sessions, but according to the constitution, they may be no more than 12 months apart. The president may also call extraordinary sessions of the legislature.

All laws must be passed by a majority vote in the House of Representatives. A bill that receives majority support is then sent to the president for his signature. If the president chooses not to sign a bill, it can be resubmitted to him within six months if approved by a two-thirds vote of the House. If a bill receives the necessary support and is resubmitted, the president must either sign the bill or dissolve the legislature. The normal term for the House of Representatives is five years.

Judiciary

The highest courts in Gambia are the Supreme Court and the Court of Appeals. Although the president appoints the judges, the constitution gives the courts an independent role. The judiciary is usually strong and independent. Besides lower courts operating under Anglo-Saxon legal rules, indigenous courts have both civil and criminal jurisdictions among the different ethnic groups. Civil actions between Muslims may be heard by special Muslim courts if both parties agree.

Regional and Local Government

The form of local government in Gambia varies. Banjul, the capital and largest city, has an elected council. Many of the rural areas have ruling councils appointed by the head of state. Tribal chiefs retain some authority in these councils, while community leaders representing mostly youth and women hold most of the power.

THE ELECTORAL SYSTEM

Elections in Gambia are direct. Suffrage is universal for Gambian citizens who are at least 18 years old, and secret ballots are used. While voter turnout in local elections is often under 50% of those registered, turnout for national elections is significantly higher (for instance, it was 88% in the September 1996 presidential elections and 73% in the January 1997 legislative contest). The current Gambian electoral system is widely recognized as one of the most open and honest in Africa, with results seldom contested or questioned. This is a change from the 1982 elections when the Progressive People's Party (PPP) was regularly charged with unfair practices, as was the military regime after 1994. A lingering issue remains the use of government resources during electoral campaigns and the heavily progovernment coverage by the state-owned media, especially by the only television channel.

THE PARTY SYSTEM

Gambia has been a working multiparty system throughout its history, except during a brief moment in the wake of the 1994 coup, between late 1994 and mid-1995. However, the exclusive rule of a single party (PPP until 1994, and APRC thereafter) and the overwhelming powers of the head of state frustrated the opponents' hope to win elections. But despite these frustrations, active and vigorous opposition parties seek power within constitutional bounds. Most political parties originally polarize around rural-urban splits, which also have ethnic overtones.

ALLIANCE FOR PATRIOTIC REORIENTATION AND CONSTRUCTION (APRC)

In the wake of the 1994 coup, Jammeh accused the old elite of having colluded to deny power to the people while squandering the country's wealth and betraying African moral values. He then disbanded all the existing parties, saying that he considered them partners in the same plot of deceit. In 1995, following his decision to return to a civilian regime, Jammeh set up the Alliance for Patriotic Reorientation and Construction (APRC). Since the legislative elections of January 1997, it has dominated the political scene with 33 seats out of 49 in the parliament. Its membership crosses all sections of Gambian society, but it is particularly popular among the youth, who are attracted by Jammeh's patriotic, populist, and reform-minded approach.

Party propaganda combined with real achievements make APRC's presence felt everywhere in the country. For example, it was the only party capable of presenting candidates in all the districts during the last elections. Jammeh is part of the small Joola group, but his popularity is deeply rooted among the Mandinka, Wolof, and Fula, the three main ethnic groups. In fact, he seems to represent the neutral figure on a political scene where there is some tension, especially between the Wolof and Mandinka peoples.

OPPOSITION PARTIES

The United Democratic Party (UDP), which has seven seats in the parliament, and the National Reconciliation Party (NRP), which has two seats, are the two main opposition parties. Along with Jammeh's APRC, Ousainou Darbo's UDP is represented throughout the country. The UDP recruits among the moderate and opponents of Jawara and Jammeh, mainly Mandinka who follow Ousainou Darbo, a successful Mandinka lawyer. The UDP is also the watchdog for all who cherish the civil and democratic liberties upheld, however formally, by the previous regime of Jawara. Darbo mustered 35% of the presidential votes against 55% for Jammeh, failing to garner significant support outside the Mandinka, who felt the loss of the supremacy they had enjoyed under Jawara. The smaller People's Democratic Organization for Independence and Socialism (PDOIS) has one seat in the parliament, while two seats are occupied by independents. (Those parties that existed prior to the 1994 coup remain proscribed and their leaders excluded from any political contest.) Young politicians, who often have some radical sympathies, created most of the new parties. Hamat Bah's NRP and Sidia Jatta's PDOIS are more active in the Banjul area, the NRP being more populist while the PDOIS recruits mainly among left-wing radicals.

NATIONAL PROSPECTS

Gambia's political system, which was previously based on compromise, bargaining, and open elections, has evolved into a more polarized and less liberal system. Jammeh has avoided being a dictator, but many see him as a kind of despot. However, his patriotism, a real commitment to reform, and his crusade against corruption and social vices keep his support strong enough to allow him to win over his foes. His achievements in upgrading the infrastructure and social services are real.

One area in which many feared Jammeh would take a more radical approach than previous leaders is foreign relations. After an initial flirtation with Libya, Jammeh has restored a more traditional approach, establishing very good relations with Senegal and Guinea-Bissau. For example, despite being a Joola, he has distanced himself from the Joola-led Casamance separatist rebellion that persists in southwestern Senegal. In fact, his friendly relations with Senegal emphasize security matters and mutual support. Senegal has spearheaded recent efforts to elect a Gambian head of the World Health Organization.

Jammeh keeps the focus on fighting corruption, reducing the country's debt, enhancing self-reliance, stressing morality in the public sphere, and maintaining and upgrading the infrastructure. Such objectives have been laid out in a well-publicized policy document titled "Vison 2000." The document advocates a free-market-oriented agenda, including liberal macroeconomics, private sector–led growth, stabilization of the dalasi, and institutional development. So far, a solid political majority around Jammeh and friendly relations with neighbors have allowed real progress toward such goals.

Further Reading

Daun, Holger. *Change, Conflict Potential and Politics: Two Gambian Case Studies*. Lund, Sweden: Stasvetenskapliga Institutionen, Lunds Unversitet, 1974.

Gailey, Harry A. *Historical Dictionary of the Gambia*. Metuchen, N.J.: Scarecrow Press, 1987.

Nyang, Sulayman S. "Recent Trends in Gambian Politics." *L'Afrique et L'Asie* 109, 1976.

"Ten Years of Gambia's Independence: A Political Analysis." *Présence Africaine* 104, 1977.

Periodicals: *West-Africa* (weekly, London); *Country Profile* and *Country Report* (The Economist Intelligence Unit, London).

GEORGIA

(Sakartvelo)

By Stephen F. Jones, Ph.D.

THE SYSTEM OF GOVERNMENT

Georgia, known to its inhabitants as *Sakartvelo* (Land of the Georgians), is situated in the western half of the Caucasian isthmus. It occupies 27,657 square miles and is approximately twice the size of Belgium. On its northern border lies the Russian Federation. To the south are Turkey and the Republic of Armenia, and to the west and east are the Black Sea and the Republic of Azerbaijan, respectively. Most of Georgia's current territory was annexed by Russia between 1801 and 1811, although Georgia briefly regained its independence in 1918–21 during the Russian civil war. In 1921, it was forcibly incorporated into Soviet Russia (subsequently the USSR) and became one of the Soviet Union's 15 union republics in 1936.

Georgia has undergone a number of political transformations since it regained its independence in April 1991. In January 1992, newly elected Georgian President Zviad Gamsakhurdia was ousted by a coup, and after a brief interregnum under an unelected State Council led by Eduard Shevardnadze, elections in October 1992 established a new republic. It was a cross between a parliamentary and presidential system, with the head of state (there was no president) sharing his considerable powers with the prime minister and Parliament. Shevardnadze, as head of state, was both chairman of the Parliament and head of the executive. A new constitution in 1995 established a presidential system.

The total population of Georgia in 1995 was estimated as between 5 and 5.4 million, of which approximately 55% were urban and 70% ethnically Georgian. According to the 1989 census, the largest minorities are the Armenians (8.1%), Russians (6.3%), Azeris (5.7%), Ossetians (3.0%), Greeks (1.9%), and Abkhazians (1.8%). Political and economic turmoil since independence in 1991 has led to major demographic changes, including ethnic cleansing and emigration, but official or trustworthy statistics on population changes are currently unavailable.

Within Soviet Georgia (1921–91) there were two autonomous republics and an autonomous region that recognized the special needs of religious and ethnic minorities. They were the Abkhazian Autonomous Socialist Republic, the Adjarian Autonomous Socialist Republic, and the South Ossetian Autonomous Region. The autonomous republics, while subject to Georgian central control, had, in theory, significant powers, including their own constitutions, parliaments, and budgets. In reality, almost all political decisions were made in Moscow.

Since Georgian independence, both the Abkhazians—a non-Georgian but indigenous Caucasian people related to the North Caucasian Adyghe and Circassian peoples—and the South Ossetians—a non-Georgian people who speak an Iranian language—have led armed secessionist struggles against the Georgian government. As a result, Georgia has approximately 280,000 internally displaced persons (IDPs), and many more Georgian citizens of Armenian, Greek, Abkhazian, and Russian nationality have fled the conflict zones to Russia, Armenia, and other neighboring states. The status of both Abkhazia and South Ossetia are currently under negotiation. The Adjarian Autonomous Republic, which is an ethnically Georgian but predominantly Muslim region (82.8% of the republic's population are Georgian), has avoided open conflict with Tbilisi. But the Georgian government has limited control over Adjaria and its leader, Aslan Abashidze, who is chairman of the Adjarian supreme council (its parliament). Abashidze has not implemented the democratic reforms introduced by President Eduard Shevardnadze.

The current constitution describes Georgia as democratic (Article 1.2) and federal (Article 73.1). The president is both head of state and head of the executive. Economic and political reform, the growth of organized interest groups, a free press, improved parliamentary competence, and a significant indigenous nongovernmental sector have led to what can be fairly described as a democratic system in Georgia.

Executive

The president has considerable powers, including the appointment of the government and dismissal of ministers, submission of the budget, the setting of parliamentary elections, the convocation of extraordinary parliamentary sittings, and the right to introduce legislation "out of turn." He can call a referendum and in certain cases suspend regional legislative bodies. He has wide powers of nomination or appointment to the Supreme Court, Constitutional Court, armed forces, National Bank, and Chamber of Control (the country's supreme financial supervisory body). He has the power to veto parliamentary bills, although this can be overridden by a parliamentary majority of three-fifths (two-thirds in the case of constitutional laws). He chairs the National Security Council and supervises the State Chancellery, a presidential apparatus staffed with advisers and specialists that, in consultation with the various ministries, generates most of the country's legislative projects. The Cabinet of Ministers, which consists of 20 ministries, is directly responsible to the president, although it is also subject to parliamentary control.

Despite significant powers, the president's authority is subject to checks from Parliament, the judiciary (in particular, the Constitutional Court), and extraparliamentary organizations such as the press and nongovernmental organizations (NGOs). Parliament, for example, can impeach the president by a two-thirds majority if the Supreme Court or Constitutional Court concludes he has committed a crime or violated the constitution. Parliament has to ratify many presidential decrees, appointments, and treaties and can formally question government ministers and members of other executive bodies about their actions.

Parliamentary elections take place once every four years and presidential elections every five years. The latest elections, in October 1995, based on a mixed system of proportional representation and first-past-the-post, reduced the 24 parties and blocs of the 1992–95 Parliament to 3 of any significance. This was due to the introduction of a 5% electoral threshold. The major victor was the Georgian Union of Citizens, which gained 111 seats, an effective working majority for Shevardnadze, a founder of the party who is currently its chair. The two other parties that gained significant parliamentary representation are the National Democratic Party (37 seats), a moderate pro-Western nationalist party distinguished by its official commitment to a role for the Georgian Orthodox Church in state life, and the All-Georgian Revival Union (32 seats), a regional party based in the autonomous republic of Adjaria. Shevardnadze gained 74% of the vote for president. His nearest rival was Jumbar Patiashvili, with 19%.

The next parliamentary elections will take place in 1999. Whether President Shevardnadze will run for a second term as president in the year 2000, when his term expires, is unclear. No obvious rival is apparent. The president is restricted to a maximum of two terms.

Legislature

There have been three democratically elected Parliaments since 1990. The first (1990–92) was dominated by the Round Table–Free Georgia bloc. Under the authoritarian influence of its newly elected parliamentary chairman (and subsequently president), Zviad Gamsakhurdia, it was little more than a rubber-stamp body. The second Parliament (1992–95) was better, but fragmented, inexperienced, and unfamiliar with the rules of parliamentary procedure. Capable of frustrating executive power, it was unable to consolidate parliamentary control over the executive, which took advantage of an ambiguous constitution and an almost constant state of war in the country. The third Parliament, elected in October 1995 (on a 68% turnout), has proved far more effective and disciplined. In 1996, it passed 108 laws, including vital provisions on the privatization and leasing of land and on antimonopoly activities. The most important factor in its increased effectiveness is the creation of 14 powerful parliamentary committees that initiate many, and discuss all, legislative bills.

The current Parliament was elected, like its predecessor, on the basis of party lists (150 members) and single-member districts (85 members). The 5% threshold, which excluded the overwhelming majority of the 54 parties and blocs that competed, left 61% of the population unrepresented by parties of their choice. Elections did not take place in Abkhazia and South Ossetian districts, which are still in conflict zones.

The current Parliament is divided into two chambers, the Council of the Republic (the lower house) and the Senate. The Senate is designed to represent 12 historical-cultural regions in the country, including the autonomous republics of Abkhazia and Adjaria. Due to the unsettled status of Abkhazia and South Ossetia, the Senate has not convened and its role and powers are not yet clear. Members of Parliament have immunity and wide powers of interrogation of officials; they confirm the most important judicial, military, and executive appointments (with the right to remove those who have violated the constitution). They also ratify major agreements and can reject presidential bills. The president, however, provided he has a majority in Parliament, dominates legislative activity. Most of the Union of Citizens, as well as independent members from the regions, support Shevardnadze, who can push through most, but not always all, of his legislative program. (The Union of Citizens, the "presidential party," makes up almost 49% of parliamentary members.)

Shevardnadze is helped by the tendency of Georgian parties to splinter. The Union of Citizens is still unified, although the other two major parties have split. Currently, there are eight official factions in Parliament (a minimum of 10 members must register a faction), but cooperation against President Shevardnadze is rare. The president has enormous powers of patronage, which he uses effectively. The parties, despite their work in parliamentary commissions, are organizationally weak and have little public support.

Judiciary

After the defeat of the Georgian Communists in October 1990, the criminal and civil codes, court structures and procedures, and the constitution were changed in favor of judicial independence. The Supreme Court remained the highest judicial body, although members were now elected for 10 years. The rights of both defense lawyers and defendants were increased; the accusatory bias of court procedure was reduced. Judges were not permitted to belong to any political organization or occupy any state post. Judicial independence remained problematic under President Gamsakhurdia with both the Supreme Court and Constitutional Advisory Commission under his control.

Under Shevardnadze, the situation has improved although occasional abuses still occur. The new constitution advocates the separation of powers and has divided supreme judicial power among a Constitutional Court, Supreme Court, and the Procuracy. Constitutional Court judges are appointed by the president, Parliament, and Supreme Court for 10 years. The new Constitutional Court has supreme and final decision-making power on all constitutional issues, including questions of civil and human rights. It has already reversed a number of government decisions due to their unconstitutionality.

The Supreme Court is the final court of appeal in civil and criminal cases and oversees an extensive system of regional courts, but the whole judicial system is undermined by the poor quality of judges and the absence of proper training. Supreme Court judges and the procurator general are nominated by the president but confirmed by Parliament. Judges have personal immunity and are appointed for not less than 10 years. The new government is currently reviewing the republic's civil and criminal codes. Reforms currently under consideration attempt to further reduce the Procuracy's search and investigatory powers. A jury system is not yet in place. Most cases are still tried by a judge and two assistants.

Regional and Local Government

Before the October 1990 elections, local government in Georgia was administered jointly by elected local councils (*soviets*) and centrally approved Communist Party committees. The councils, organized on city, regional, district, settlement, and village levels, were elected every three years. The councils were not genuine reflections of local democratic control, and after the October 1990 elections, a prefecture system replaced them. Prefects, appointed by the president and jointly responsible to him and to Parliament, had considerable authority over new local electoral assemblies known as *sakrebuloebi*.

Since President Gamsakhurdia's overthrow, the *sakrebuloebi* have remained, but are weak compared with the power held by the district governors and provincial prefects (*gamgeblebi* and *rtsmuneblebi*) appointed by the president. Essentially, the 12 provinces created by presidential decree in 1995, which are subdivided into a further 63 districts, are ruled by decree from the center or through the president's prefects. Until new local government elections planned for 1998 take place, it is hard to talk of democratic local government. Much local government still remains in the hands of superficially transformed Communist Party officials who have inherited the new structures. There are few institutional checks on local officials in the regions (the press, for example, is almost nonexistent), and regional elites exert enormous power through networks of patronage and kinship.

THE ELECTORAL SYSTEM

The electoral system consists of 85 single-mandate electoral districts where elections are "first past the post." The remaining 150 seats are distributed to parties and blocs depending on their total proportion of the national vote. Voters in 1995 had a single nontransferable vote. Parties and blocs could gain a place on the party list ballot after attaining 50,000 signatures, and in the single-mandate districts, candidates required only 1,000. This low requirement for registration meant a profusion of parties and independents participated. The 5% threshold did not encourage, as it was supposed to, the merger and consolidation of smaller parties. Only three parties surpassed the 5% barrier. They were the Union of Georgian Citizens (24%), the National Democratic Party (8%), and the All-Georgian Revival Union (7%). The three Communist Parties between them gained over 9% of the vote, but none of them gained 5% individually.

The 68% turnout surpassed the 50% required minimum. The elections were supervised by a Central Electoral Commission and district and precinct electoral commissions comprised of appointees of the outgoing Parliament and its parties. International observers declared the elections free and fair. The 1995 electoral law provided state media time for the programs of all participating parties and blocs, and all candidates had immunity during the campaign. In contrast to the 1992 elections, if no candidate in the single-member districts received 50% of the vote, there was a run-off. This was to prevent candidates from gaining seats with an extremely small proportion of the vote.

There were five candidates for president. Eduard Shevardnadze received the overwhelming majority (74%). His nearest rival was the Communist candidate, Jumbar Patiashvili.

THE PARTY SYSTEM

Georgian parties first emerged in the late 19th century. The most significant was the Georgian Social Democratic Labor Party, a Marxist party that ruled independent Georgia from 1918 to 1921. With the annexation of Georgia by Soviet Russia in 1921, all parties apart from the Communist Party were banned. Until the October 1990 elections, no other Georgian party could function, except in the political underground. In 1987–88, with the onset of Gorbachev's perestroika, Georgian parties, many of which traced their roots to political antecedents of the 19th and 20th centuries, emerged. They included the Ilia Chavchavadze Society, the Helsinki Union, the National Democratic Party, and the Georgian National Independence Party.

In the October 1990 elections, for the first time since Georgia's annexation, the Communist Party monopoly was ended. Of the six parties and five electoral blocs that took part, the radical-nationalist Round Table–Free Georgia coalition, led by the former dissident Zviad Gamsakhurdia and his Helsinki Union, gained 54% of the vote and 155 of the 250 parliamentary seats. Second came the Georgian Communist Party with 29.6%. The Popular Front was third with 1.93%.

The 1992 elections, which followed the forcible ouster of President Gamsakhurdia, led to a much more fractionalized Parliament. Of the 26 parties that gained parliamentary representation, the most influential (although "influential" did not necessarily reflect electoral support) were the National Democratic Party (with 15 seats, the single largest party), the Republican Party, the Democratic Union, the Greens, the Georgian Popular Front, and the Union of Traditionalists.

There was not much to distinguish party programs, although liberal reformism was best represented by the National Democrats, the Republicans, the Greens, and the Democratic Union. A radical opposition to Shevardnadze's moderate stance toward Russia (negotiation rather than confrontation) formed around the Union of Traditionalists, the National Independence Party, Charter '91, the Merab Kostava Society, and the Ilya Chavchavadze Society. Except possibly for the National Democratic Party, none of the parties had effective national organizations and were essentially parliamentary groups debating among themselves with almost no contact with the voters. Both leadership and financing were erratic as a consequence.

The 1995 elections sent most of these parties to the political wilderness. Of the three largest parties that emerged from the 1995 elections, the Union of Citizens is the most influential. Led astutely by Zurab Zhvania, who is also Speaker of the Parliament, it is becoming, some argue, an "establishment party," although party identity and discipline remain poor. The party is quite youthful, made up of a mixture of Greens, former Communist Party officials, new entrepreneurs, and lawyers. It does not have much contact with the electorate or particularly enthusiastic support among the populace. Its program can hardly be distinguished from the other two parliamentary parties—all share ideas of market reform and welfare provisions for the poorer groups in society. Its current dominant position is bolstered by its links with Shevardnadze and the lack of a coherent rival. Its only potential national rival, the National Independence Party, split into two parliamentary factions after the assasination of its charismatic leader, Gia Chanturia, in late 1994. The parliamentary opposition, when it does coalesce, is made up of National Democrats, independents, and dissident members of the Union of Citizens.

NATIONAL-DEMOCRATIC PARTY OF GEORGIA

This is one of the oldest political parties in Georgia. Founded in 1917, it was reestablished in 1981 as an underground organization. After the collapse of the USSR, the party received in the 1992 elections the largest number of seats for any single party (15), and in 1995, 36 seats made it the second-largest party in Parliament.

Since 1995, it has split into the National Democratic Party led by Irina Chanturia-Sarishvili and the Popular Faction (Social-Democrat) led by Mamuka Georgadze. The program of both factions is essentially the same: full independence, the withdrawal of the Russian army from Georgia, the observance of human rights of ethnic minorities, the defense of Christian values and national traditions, and the acceleration of the process of privatization based on free-market principles.

The party, when it was united, was the best organized and had more support from young people in the provinces. Since it split, it has lost considerable influence but still leads the opposition in Parliament. The National Democratic Party under Chanturia-Sarishvili has links with the Conservative Party in Britain. Both factions jointly have approximately 6,000 members.

CITIZEN'S UNION OF GEORGIA (CUG)

The CUG is the "establishment party" chaired by Shevardnadze himself and has party members in leading parliamentary positions. It was founded in 1995 and claims a membership, very loosely defined, of 100,000. The deputy chairman is Zurab Zhvania, who is also Speaker of the Parliament. The leader of the official parliamentary faction is Giorgi Baramidze.

The party is a strange mixture of former communist-era intellectuals, regional apparatchiks, Greens, and people in business who are united in support for Shevardnadze. In this sense, it is more of a "movement" than a party. Generational and political divisions between former Greens and factory directors or between young Western-trained economists and former Soviet administrators are already apparent within the party.

When Shevardnadze departs, the CUG may splinter, but its high representation in government and executive structures and the absence of an effective opposition place it in a good position to develop into a broad-based institutional party like the Liberal Party in Japan. Many Georgians already view the CUG as a quasi-state structure. Close association with the CUG is an effective way of increasing one's power and status. Its parliamentary majority allows it to control, jointly with the president, crucial appointments to the judiciary, procuracy, army, and media. With its penetration of executive and government structures, it is beginning to resemble the *partitocrazia* ("partocracy") that characterizes Italian and Mexican politics. Currently, party discipline is low, but the CUG chairs all but three of the parliamentary committees and has over 120 of the 233 parliamentary seats. It has enormous potential for political patronage, which may keep it together after Shevardnadze's departure.

THE ALL-GEORGIAN REVIVAL UNION

The All-Georgian Revival Union is a regional party based in the autonomous republic of Adjaria, where it faces no effective opposition. It is led in an authoritarian manner by Aslan Abashidze, the chairman of the supreme council (parliament) of Adjaria. It is the third-largest party in the national Parliament with 31 members in the faction, all of them elected from Adjaria. In the 1995 elections, the party received no seats outside its regional base. The chairman of the parliamentary faction is Jemal Gogitidze. There is no reliable information on its mass membership.

The party split into two factions in August 1997, with the creation of a new group called *Mamuli* (Homeland) led by Vakhtang Shamiladze. The latter split off because of its disagreement with the Revival Union's oppositionist policy in Parliament. *Mamuli* firmly backs the parliamentary majority and considers itself in opposition to Aslan Abashidze, the Adjarian leader. The programs of both factions emphasize a clear delimitation of the functions between supreme state bodies of Georgia and local bodies of power and call for legislation that takes into account distinct regional differences. Both factions want a free economic zone in Adjaria, which Parliament has consistantly rejected. Both factions are secular, although they originate in a predominantly Muslim region.

OTHER POLITICAL FORCES

The transition to the market has led, for the first time, to the rise of independent interest groups and a significant nongovernmental sector. Currently, the most influential interest groups include a Union of Industrialists, which unites many of Georgia's middle-level entrepreneurs, the press (most effectively represented by the Association of the Free Press), private banks, and the various representative organizations of ethnic groups. The Georgian nongovernmental sector, while still small, has played a significant role already in legislative activity, and groups such as the Young Lawyers Association, the International Society for Free Elections, and the League for Protection of the Georgian Constitution are an important check on government activity.

The most powerful transitional organizations, however, remain organizations such as the World Bank and the IMF, which have great power in directing the Georgian economy. Labor issues have not, as yet, mobilized the population, and ethnic problems, particularly in Abkhazia and South Ossetia, continue to dominate Georgian politics.

NATIONAL PROSPECTS

In the fall of 1994, Eduard Shevardnadze introduced, under IMF supervision, systematic economic reform. The lari, a new currency, was introduced in 1994, and in 1996 some sectors of the Georgian economy, in particular, agriculture, transport, communications, and trade, registered growth for the first time. In 1998, the IMF predicts 8% growth in Georgian GDP. Despite the fact that by the government's own statistics, 60% of the population is hovering around the poverty line, public-opinion surveys conducted in 1996 by the European Commission suggest that Georgians are among the most positive in Central and Eastern Europe about economic reform and their own financial future. This paradox probably reflects other factors such as the country's declining rate of crime, the elimination of uncontrolled private militias, an end to secessionist wars, and increasing Western investment following the decision to lay an oil pipeline across Georgia that will link up the oil-rich republic of Azerbaijan with Western European and North American markets.

The biggest problems faced by Georgia are potential ethnic conflict and relations with Russia, both of which are interrelated. Despite the extraordinary political and economic turnaround in the country since 1994–95, Georgia's new-found stability and growth could be upset by a breakdown in negotiations with the Abkhazians and South Ossetians. To ensure that that does not happen, relations with Russia have to be kept on an even keel. Currently, Georgia's economic and political prospects are good: the country is geographically central to the increasingly important trade route that crosses from the Caspian to the Black Sea (known as the Eurasian Corridor) and it has established good relations with all its neighbors, including Turkey, Armenia, Iran, and even with its former imperial master, Russia. Georgia, at this time, can properly be described as the most democratic in the CIS (Commonwealth of Independent States). The big question remains what will happen when President Shevardnadze, who has been central to Georgia's methodical transformation, finishes his presidential term in office.

Further Reading

Gachechiladze, Revaz. *The New Georgia: Space, Society, Politics.* London: University College Press, 1995.

Goldenberg, Susan. *Pride of Small Nations: The Caucasus and Post-Soviet Disorder.* London and New Jersey: Zed Books, 1994.

Hunter, Shireen T. *The Transcaucasus in Transition: Nation-Building and Conflict.* Washington, D.C.: The Center for Strategic and International Studies, 1994.

Jones, Stephen. "Georgia: The Trauma of Statehood." In *New States, New Politics: Building the Post-Soviet Nations.* Ed. Ian Bremmer and Ray Taras. Cambridge: Cambridge University Press, 1997.

———. "Georgia's Return from Chaos." *Current History,* October 1996,. 340–45.

Jones, Stephen, and Robert Parsons. "Georgia and the Georgians." in *The Nationalities Question in the Post-Soviet States.* Ed. Graham Smith. London and New York: Longman, 1996, 291–313.

———. *The Revenge of the Past: Nationalism, Revolution, and the Collapse of the Soviet Union.* Stanford, Calif.: Stanford University Press, 1993.

———, ed. *Transcaucasia: Nationalism and Social Change.* Ann Arbor: University of Michigan Press, 1996.

Suny, Ronald Grigor. *The Making of the Georgian Nation.* London: I.B.Tauris, 1989.

Federal Republic of Germany

(Bundesrepublik Deutschland)

By Gordon Smith, Ph.D.

The System of Government

The Federal Republic of Germany (FRG) came into being in 1949 as a consequence of the division of Germany in 1945. The three western zones of the occupying powers (American, British, and French) made up the new state, with the later addition of the Saarland in 1957. The Basic Law (constitution) established a federal system of 10 states (*Länder*) with a parliamentary system of government.

At the same time as the Federal Republic was founded, a new east German state was created, the German Democratic Republic (GDR). The GDR was formed from the Soviet zone of occupation, and it soon became modeled on the pattern of other Communist states. A Marxist-Leninist party, the Socialist Unity Party of Germany (SED), came to wield sole political and state power in the GDR. The Communist dictatorship was successful in exercising a tight control for a long period, but popular unrest grew with the weakening of Soviet power over East-Central Europe. In the latter part of 1989, the authority and legitimacy of the Communist regime crumbled and the SED was forced to share power with other parties. Free elections were held in March 1990, resulting in the formation of a non-Communist government that was committed to German unification. The *Länder* in the GDR that had earlier been abolished were reestablished, and unification was achieved in October 1990. The process of unification was effected by means of Article 23 of the Basic Law that provided for "other parts" of Germany to accede to the Federal Republic. The enlarged Federal Republic has a population of 82 million (area: 357,000 square kilometers).

As a result of unification, the number of constituent *Länder* rose from 10 to 16, that is, with the addition of the 5 new East German *Länder* plus Berlin; the latter also became the new capital city in place of Bonn.

The West Germany political system had always shown an impressive stability, and this stability persisted after unification. Three parties have been dominant throughout the life of the Federal Republic: the Christian Democrats (CDU/CSU), the Social Democrats (SPD), and the Free Democrats (FDP). The outcome of the first all-German elections in December 1990 confirmed their dominance. Their success in both parts of Germany (with 88.3% of the total vote) was evidence of the overwhelming approval of unification by the electorate throughout Germany. In essence, therefore, both the constitutional order and the political system were unchanged by unification.

The extent of continuity was underlined by the CDU/CSU coalition with the FDP that held office continuously from 1982 until 1998. Helmut Kohl was federal chancellor for the whole period; he was the longest-serving chancellor in the history of the Federal Republic. However, the SPD in coalition with the Greens finally ousted Kohl following the 1998 federal election; the CDU/CSU vote fell to its lowest level since 1949. The shift to a leftist coalition signaled a decisive change of course for Germany.

Executive

Executive authority rests with the federal chancellor, who heads the federal government and appoints and dismisses the federal ministers. He is elected by the members of a new legislative term, and his dismissal can only be be effected by the process of electing a successor. The head of state, federal president, is elected for a five-year term by a Federal Assembly, consisting of the Bundestag and an equal number of representatives from the states. No president may serve more than two consecutive terms of office. The president's powers are very limited and his function is largely ceremonial. The present incumbent is Roman Herzog (born 1929), who was previously a member of the Federal Constitutional Court.

Legislature

Legislative authority is shared between the directly elected Bundestag and a second body, the Bundesrat, which represents the interests of the state governments. All constitutional changes have to be approved by a two-thirds majority in both houses, and the Bundesrat has a power of veto over legislation that affects the powers of the states.

The Bundestag is elected for a maximum life of four years, and because calling new elections is difficult, it has only twice been dissolved early. The Bundestag consists of 656 representatives, but because of the operation of the electoral system its size may be increased, as it was in 1998 with the addition of 13 extra members.

The Bundestag at its first meeting of the legislative term elects a chancellor by secret ballot on the proposal of the president, although the latter has to nominate the person who is likely to secure an absolute majority in the Bundestag, that is, the "chancellor candidate" of the party able to secure a majority by itself or in coalition with another party.

Party discipline in the Bundestag is strong, each party being organized as a party group, or *Fraktion*. The president and four vice presidents of the Bundestag are usually members of the majority coalition. This presidium, together with a further 23 members of the Bundestag selected according to the size of the party groups, make up the Council of Elders (*Ältestenrat*). The Council determines the business agenda of the house and appoints the chairpersons of some 20 specialist committees. The great bulk of legislation is initiated by the federal government, and since the government has a disciplined party majority, its bills invariably pass the Bundestag, although frequently in amended form.

The Bundesrat has a unique composition in that it is not elected directly but consists of government delegations from the individual *Länder* that act on instructions from those governments. *Land* representation varies roughly according to the size of the population. The Bundesrat has a total of 69 seats. Baden-Württemberg, Bavaria, Lower Saxony, and North Rhine-Westphalia each has 6 seats. Berlin, Brandenburg, Hesse, Rhineland-Palatinate, Saxony, Saxony-Anhalt, Schleswig-Holstein, and Thuringia each has 4 seats. The smallest *Länder*, Bremen, Hamburg, Mecklenburg-West Pomerania, and the Saarland, each has 3 seats.

Votes of the delegations must be cast en bloc. The individual delegation—led by the *Land* head of government, the minister-president—is composed of *Land* members of government, although in practice, and especially in committees, they may be replaced by senior civil servants. Unlike the Bundestag, the Bundesrat cannot be dissolved, and its composition alters only with changes of government within the *Länder*.

In the early years of the republic, *Land* governments were controlled by a variety of parties so that clear party blocs did not exist in the Bundesrat. Gradually, the party composition of the Bundesrat has become of leading significance. This was particularly important during the period of CDU/CSU government (1982–98). Because the SPD controlled most *Land* governments, it had a majority in the Bundesrat. The SPD has a large majority in the Bundesrat because it controls most *Land* governments. In some cases the Bundesrat has been used to block government legislation or to secure important amendments. However, around 90% of all federal legislation is uncontested by the Bundesrat. Compromises on legislative variations between the two houses are made in a conciliation committee that consists of equal numbers of members from the Bundestag and Bundesrat.

Judiciary

In addition to the system of federal and *Länder* courts and standing apart from the structure of the ordinary courts, West Germany has a Federal Constitutional Court. The Bundesrat and the Bundestag each appoint half its 16 judges on the nomination of the parties. To be elected a judge requires a two-thirds vote in the Bundestag or in the appropriate Bundesrat committee. A number of appointments are reserved for serving members of the highest federal courts, but otherwise it is only necessary that candidates should have the standard legal qualification. Once appointed for the 12-year term, none of the judges may be removed, except on the motion of the Court itself.

The Federal Constitutional Court, established by the 1949 Basic Law, has unlimited powers of constitutional interpretation. Its ruling on the constitutionality of federal legislation is final. Cases may be referred directly to the Court by the *Land* governments, one-third of the Bundestag deputies, the federal president, or the federal government itself if it is in dispute with a *Land* government. If federal legislation is thought to be in conflict with the constitution, the Court may rule on the issue even before the legislation goes into effect, although it often hears cases from the federal courts where a constitutional issue claimed to be integral to the case. The Constitutional Court also rules on constitutional complaints brought to it by individual citizens who hold that their basic rights have been infringed.

The powers of the Constitutional Court are such that it is bound to become involved in contentious issues, but it has avoided becoming the subject of political controversy. Nor has the mode of appointment of the judges led to an overt political bias in its rulings. The Court's high standing is due, in large part, to the general respect that legal norms enjoy in Germany, a respect which extends to the Basic Law and to the Constitutional Court.

Regional and Local Government

Each *Land* has its own constitution, establishing parliamentary systems very similar to that of the federal government. A *Land* government is headed by a minister-president who is elected by and responsible to the *Land* assembly (*Landtag*). With the exception of Bavaria, the *Land* assemblies are all unicameral. *Landtag* elections take place at four- or five-year intervals. These elections do not coincide with the federal legislative period. As a result, the elections in the *Länder* are taken to be important tests of the federal government's standing with the electorate. They are also significant in altering the party balance in the Bundesrat.

Below the level of the *Länder*, counties, districts, and towns each elect their councils. The local party organizations are very active in these elections. The councils elect the chairpersons or mayors, which means that the parties put forward and promote their best candidates for the job in very much the same manner as the national parties put forward a chancellor candidate. Towns and counties are entitled to set and collect property taxes and also receive a proportion of national and *Land* taxes. Generally, however, these revenues are insufficient to cover the costs of local responsibilities. The localities are thus forced to rely on *Land* revenues with the consequent *Land* control of key elements in local planning and development.

THE ELECTORAL SYSTEM

The electoral system used in the Federal Republic is best described as a form of "personalized" proportional representation. Half of the 656 members of the Bundestag are elected as individuals in local districts by plurality vote and the other half from lists presented by the parties in each *Land*. Each voter has two votes, one to choose the constituency representative and the other, the second vote, or *Zweitstimme*, for the party list.

The second vote is decisive for determining a party's total number of seats in the Bundestag, while the first vote partly influences which members of the party will have seats. The distribution of seats is made on a *Land* basis, and there is no provision for securing overall national proportionality. A small party, such as the Free Democrats (FDP), may not win any district election outright, in which case all its members elected will be drawn from the party list. If, as occasionally happens, a party wins more district seats than it is entitled to on a proportional basis, it keeps the additional seats and the size of the Bundestag is increased accordingly. In that case, of course, none of the party's elected members in that *Land* come from the party list.

Although the electoral system is proportional, a fairly high electoral threshold operates: a party that fails to win 5% of the federal vote (or three district seats) does not share in the proportional distribution at *Land* level (although if it won one or two district seats it would keep them). The 5% barrier operates strongly against small parties; from 1961 until 1983, only three parties were represented in the Bundestag, but since 1990 there have been five. Those that do surpass the barrier benefit from the exclusion of those that do not, so that there is a further distortion of the proportionality principle.

All German citizens 18 years of age and over are eligible to vote, and registration is virtually automatic. Voting is not compulsory, but there are high levels of participation, now usually approaching 80%. However, there is some ignorance as to how the electoral system works: polls show that up to a fifth of all voters are not aware

that it is the "second vote" that is decisive in determining party strength in the Bundestag.

Bundestag Elections, 1998			
	1998 %	1998 Seats	1994 %
SPD	40.9	298	36.4
CDU/CSU	35.1	245	41.5
Greens	6.7	47	7.3
FDP	6.2	43	6.9
PDS	5.1	36	4.4
Others	6.0	—	3.5
Total		669	

THE PARTY SYSTEM

Origins of the Parties

Following the defeat of Germany in May 1945, the occupying forces at first banned all political activity, but from August 1945 those parties judged to be "democratic" (i.e., anti-Nazi) were allowed to operate at a local level. Each party had to be licensed individually, giving rise to the description "democracy under license." Initially, only four party groupings were allowed: the Christian Democrats, Social Democrats, Liberals, and Communists. These parties dominated the first series of *Land* elections within each of the western zones of occupation in 1946 and 1947. As a result, these parties were also the ones to devise the constitutions of the *Länder* and later to be responsible for drawing up the Basic Law, since the Parliamentary Council responsible for that task was composed of representatives from the *Länder* parties. The Christian Democrats—with their Bavarian affiliate, the Christian Social Union (CSU)—and the Social Democrats (SPD) emerged as the most popular parties by far; in the first round of *Land* elections they won some 70% of the total vote.

Although the parties were newly established in 1945, they all drew on important German political traditions; only Christian Democrats represented an entirely new political formation. The SPD and the Communists (KPD) were direct successors of the SPD and KPD in the Weimar Republic (1919–33); the Liberals (later to become the Free Democrats) corresponded to the Liberal parties in the Weimar Republic.

Yet the postwar parties had changed radically from their Weimar counterparts. Whereas in the first republic the parties were strongly ideological in character, in the second they have become pragmatic and much more attuned to the needs of parliamentary government. Whereas in the Weimar Republic the party system had been unstable and fragmented, the new party system was characterized by its stability and by a trend away from multipartism. The impetus for the change came partly from the Allies' method of licensing, but it was reinforced by the imposition of the 5% rule brought in at the insistence of the Allies. Subsequently, it was made more stringent: in the first federal election of 1949 a party was required to obtain only 5% in any one *Land*, but thereafter the threshold was raised to 5% of the national vote.

Eleven parties were represented in the first Bundestag, but the number rapidly declined in the 1950s to three in 1961. The CDU–CSU, SPD, and FDP together won over 99% of the vote in 1976 (as against 72% in 1949), although that aggregate declined in the 1980s because of the rise of the Greens. After unification the former Communists (Party of Democratic Socialism; PDS) further eroded the position of the established parties.

The Parties in Law

As a reaction to the political extremism of the Weimar Republic, the Basic Law was concerned to regulate the position of the parties. Article 21 of the Basic Law declares: "The political parties shall participate in forming the political will of the people." It also places restrictions on their freedom. "Parties which, by reasons of their aims or the behavior of their adherents, seek to impair or abolish the free democratic basis order or to endanger the existence of the Federal Republic shall be unconstitutional." The question of constitutionality is decided by the Constitutional Court, which banned the right-wing Socialist Reich Party in 1952 and the KPD in 1956. However, the clause has not been invoked since then: extreme right-wing parties, such as the Republicans, still compete at elections as does the PDS, which is in a direct line of succession to the old KPD.

The full implementation of Article 21 had to await the passing of a Party Law that was delayed until 1967. The Party Law recognized that since the parties have a public function to perform, they are entitled to financial support from the state. Moreover, it is possible for parties to draw on their state subsidy in advance, although if their vote is lower than expected, the difference has to be repaid.

With the revised Party Law that came into force in 1994, the scale of state subsidy has been reduced, putting greater emphasis on parties raising funds from members' contributions. Previously they received DM 5 for every vote they won. Now they receive DM 1.30 for each vote up to 5 million and DM 1 for each extra vote. In addition they are allocated DM 0.50 from public funds for every mark they receive in the form of members' contributions or from other donations. In any event, there is also an upper limit set on the total of state subsidy of 230 million marks in any year, and contributions made by firms are no longer tax-deductible.

The Party Law also seeks to control the internal organization of the parties to ensure that they are democratically run. It requires the parties to publish accounts and disclose the sources of their income; it provides that there should be a democratic election of officers and that the process of selecting candidates for elections should be open to members, either through a responsible selection committee or by holding a representative party convention.

Party Organization

German parties lay emphasis on securing large mass memberships, but in fact the ratio of members to voters for all parties taken together prior to unification was about 5 per 100, and only a small percentage of members take any active part beyond paying their party dues. Subsequent to unification, the situation has changed: the three "western" parties (CDU, SPD, and FDP) have found it difficult to build up party membership in the new *Länder* of eastern Germany. The SPD has been the worst affected, because both the CDU and FDP benefited to an extent from the existence of similar parties that had been allowed to operate under the Communist regime. The only party to have substantial membership (about 120,000) is the PDS, which relies heavily on the old party cadres of former ruling SED. Membership dues are an important source of party finance, but the advent of state financing of the parties has made them less reliant on membership support. Just as for federal elections, the parties in the *Länder* receive financial support from the *Länder* governments, so they are able to maintain a strong local presence.

A major activity of party members at the local and *Land* level is the selection of candidates for elections to the municipal and district representative body and the *Land* assembly. Candidates are chosen either by conferences of local party members or by a delegate conference. The procedures usually ensure that only party activists will exercise any direct voice.

The parties maintain *Länder* organizations that in many respects function quite independently of the national organizations. This independence arises for two reasons. In the first place, each *Land* is a governing entity in its own right, so that the *Land* parties are geared to winning *Land* office and supplying the ruling minister-president. Delegates from regional organizations, meeting in convention, elect *Land* party chairpersons and also decide on the selection of candidates for the *Landlag* elections. In the second place, the *Länder* parties are responsible for selecting the candidates for the federal elections, and the national party can only use influence and persuasion in the question of the choice of candidates. The selection of candidates for federal elections and, especially, the order in which they appear on the party list are hotly contested. Major party personages will be placed high on the list, and they may also appear as district candidates as well (if successful in the district election, their names will be deleted from the list). While a candidate may be reasonably sure of election if his or her name appears near the head of the list, uncertainty increases the lower down it is, especially since the number of seats the party wins in the districts, an unknown factor until the results are counted, will determine the number of successful list candidates. The voter is not able to change the order in the party list, so that the *Land* convention is the all-important arena for this decision. The party will also seek to place qualified "experts" on its list, since the German political tradition relies heavily on expert knowledge.

Party organization at the federal level is concerned with securing national publicity for the party, with well-endowed research departments in a range of policy areas, with the coordination of the *Länder* parties, and with the formulation of strategy and policy. Party policy itself is decided by national delegate conventions, usually held every other year, with the national party leadership typically in a strong position to carry the convention vote. The convention also elects the party chairperson and an executive committee. For the two major parties, there is also the question of choosing the party's chancellor candidate for the next federal election. While the candidate may be the national party chairperson, that is not necessarily the case. The party convention is a major feature in preparing for a federal election and, in other years, for mobilizing activists and publicity for the party's efforts in *Land* elections.

The national executive elected by the convention is responsible for party organization and policy between conventions. Parties have executives of about 30 members, half of whom will normally be Bundestag deputies, thus facilitating coordination between the membership party and the parliamentary bloc. There is also a smaller party presidium, consisting of a third of the executive. This body makes all the important day-to-day decisions. The relationship between the national leadership and *Länder* parties varies. While the SPD has strong centralist traditions, the *Länder* parties of the CDU and FDP have more independence. For all three parties it is desirable that coalitions at the *Land* level should reflect the lineup of the federal coalition. In the first place, this consideration is important if a party is to put its case convincingly to voters. But also, the nature of *Land* coalitions directly affects the composition of the Bundesrat: a party in federal government naturally wants to see that federal government's policies supported strongly in the Bundesrat, and this will not be the case if the *Land* party opts to go into coalition with a party in federal opposition. However, the arithmetic of coalition building in the *Länder* may force these so-called "cross-coalitions": in several *Länder*, grand coalitions between the CDU and SPD have been formed, since there was no acceptable alternative combination.

For none of the parties would it be correct to regard *Länder* politicians as purely subordinate figures, since recruitment to federal politics takes place principally through the *Länder*. The path to national leadership is most frequently by way of becoming minister-president of a *Land* government. This is the case for Chancellor Kohl who was previously minister-president of the Rhineland Palatinate. The SPD's successful chancellor candidate in 1998, Gerhard Schröder, was also the minister-president of Lower Saxony.

Campaigning

The frequency and importance of *Länder* elections, interspersed as they are throughout the four-year life of the Bundestag, ensures that an atmosphere of continuous election campaigning is maintained. The significance of *Länder* elections means that they will be treated as federal elections in miniature, especially when they directly precede the federal election or when party balance is about equal. There has been a considerable "nationalization" of *Länder* politics as a result, and the elections are usually dominated by national issues with the party leaders actively engaging in the *Länder* campaigns. The normal four-year Bundestag term means that the parties are fairly certain long in advance when the federal election will occur. Campaigning is fairly extensive, although intense activity is restricted to the last four weeks prior to election day. Two factors dominate the buildup to the election. One is the question of the coalition lineup: since one party rarely wins an absolute majority in the Bundestag, it is important to secure a coalition partner. In recent years it has become the practice for the parties to make known their coalition intentions before the election takes place. The consequence is that the campaign is dominated by the claims of the two rival groups for office. After the coalition switch of the FDP to the CDU in 1982, the choice has been between these two parties and the SPD, with the latter looking to the Greens as possible coalition partners on the federal stage. Previously, from 1972 to 1982, the choice was between the CDU–CSU on the one side and the SPD with the FDP on the other.

The second dominant factor relates to this bipolarity: the contest is highly personalized since both of the major parties, the CDU–CSU and the SPD, must produce convincing chancellor candidates. An incumbent chancellor is, of course, already a convincing candidate, unless his government has appeared to fail seriously. The candidates' personalities and electoral appeal are major factors affecting the outcome of the campaign. Television coverage of the party leaders is intensive, and the culmination of the campaign is marked by a marathon television program in which all four major party leaders (SPD, FDP, CDU, and CSU) as well as the Greens discuss and argue their records and policies. Since the west German parties are well endowed with money, they are able to swamp the electorate with posters and campaign literature. The campaigns for the various elections held in 1994 (*Länder*, Bundestag, and for the European Parliament) have been estimated at DM 170 million. The effect of the new Party Law has been to make a greater share paid by the parties rather than the state. As a consequence the parties have cut their campaign expenditures from between 10% and 15% compared with 1990. Although the electorate remains largely passive, interest is keen as shown by the turnout. Even though in actual policy terms not too much separates the parties, partisan commitment is high and the rhetoric of intense conflict is maintained, often accompanied by smear campaigns and personal vilification. That climate quickly changes once the election is over.

Independent Voters

The lack of marked ideological and programmatic differences between the established parties means that party identification is not nearly as strong as it was in the Weimar Republic or in the earlier postwar years. Increasingly, the parties have to compete for the "middle ground" in the electorate, which means taking account of the changing social-class composition of the electorate and the altering occupational structure. Both types of change were particularly in evidence for West Germany, since the country enjoyed exceptionally long periods of almost uninterrupted economic growth. The parties therefore have had to make inroads into the new middle-class and white-collar workers who have no pronounced political affiliation. It is difficult to secure their long-term allegiance, so there is a degree of electoral volatility evident from one election to another.

Unlike the two largest parties, the Free Democrats do not have a reliable "core" vote, and the central position of the FDP in the party system makes the party an acceptable alternative to both the CDU and SPD, attracting better educated and professional people, rather than trade unionists or active church members. The role of the FDP is best exemplified by considering the extent of "ticket splitting" that the German electoral system allows. Since the voter has two votes, one district and one party list, it is possible to vote for the candidate of one party on the first (district) vote but for another party on the second (list) vote. The great majority opt for the same party with both votes, but there is a minority of ticket splitting that predominantly favors the FDP. The high marginal vote the FDP attracts can be seen from the difference between the party's first and second votes. The size of the party's loyal core vote is gauged from the percentage on the first ballot, and in some years there has been a significant difference between the two percentages. Thus, although the party has benefited in terms of Bundestag seats through ticket splitting, it does not represent a stable position. The general point to be made is that the electoral system allows a relatively weak

party identification to be shown and without forcing the voter to make a complete shift in party preference.

CHRISTIAN DEMOCRATIC UNION
(Christlich-Demokratische Union; CDU)

HISTORY
Although the Christian Democratic Union drew on various political traditions of the pre-Nazi period, the formation of the party in 1945 represented a new departure for German politics, and it proved to have an enormous impact on the party system. In the early period of occupation, political activity was restricted, and the CDU came into existence as a loose grouping of independent zonal parties. Nevertheless, they all had a common orientation in seeking to achieve a broadly based party of Christian unity that would bring together Catholics and Protestants into one political organization. It was made easier to achieve after the experience of the Nazi dictatorship, and the pre-Nazi Catholic Center Party provided an organizational model.

In the Weimar Republic, the Catholic population had been a minority, but the division of Germany and the loss of the eastern territories brought about an approximate parity of Catholics and Protestants in western Germany. Parity made it possible for the two camps to base their cooperation on equality, and strenuous attempts were made to ensure that officeholders in the party represented both confessions. As the party increasingly became detached from the CDU in Berlin and the Soviet Zone, so it became more conservative in its outlook and quickly shed its transient flirtation with Christian socialism.

By 1949, the CDU—already the strongest party in many of the *Länder*—was in a position to promote its own brand of economic policy under the title of a "social market economy." The party's later electoral successes can be attributed largely to the prolonged period of economic prosperity in West Germany and the public's perception that CDU policies were responsible. The CDU was also fortunate in having a strong leader, Konrad Adenauer (1876–1967), who became the first West German chancellor in 1949, a post he retained without a break until 1963. Throughout the Adenauer era, the CDU was the dominant party, and in the 1957 election the CDU–CSU won an absolute majority of votes. However, CDU fortunes became too dependent on Adenauer's standing, and as Adenauer's authority declined in the early 1960s, the party's fortunes began to wane. In 1969, the CDU–CSU was forced into opposition for the first time in 20 years. The party had to adapt itself to the role of opposition, and, despite all its efforts, the government coalition of SPD and FDP remained intact until 1982. Only then was the CDU able to get back into office with the aid of the FDP. However, the coalition with the FDP proved exceptionally stable. The CDU–CSU lineup was successful in four successive federal elections (1983, 1987, 1990, and 1994). Nevertheless, in 1994 the coalition only just survived with a narrow margin of 10 seats for an overall majority.

ORGANIZATION

A feature of the CDU since its foundation has been the loose structuring of the party: the CDU still bears the impress of its origins, beginning life in the individual *Länder* rather than as a national party. As long as Adenauer was securely in power as chancellor, the underlying problems were masked, and Adenauer himself saw no reason to create a strong national organization. It is also significant that a federal CDU was not established until 1950, after Adenauer had become chancellor. The long-term consequence has been that CDU leaders in the 16 *Länder* organizations have been able to carve out positions of independent power for themselves, most strikingly in Bavaria where the Christian Social Union exists as a distinct party.

The federal convention of the party is the supreme authority, but in practice the *Land* parties enjoy considerable freedom. This freedom reflects traditional differences, such as between the mainly Protestant northern *Länder* and the Catholic south and west. The new *Länder* of the former GDR are in a different category, since they have no real connection with Christian democratic politics. As a consequence, they have been far more dependent both on the federal CDU organization and on western *Länder* for help and expertise.

National CDU headquarters are at Konrad Adenauer Haus, Friedrich Ebert Alle 73-5, 53113, Bonn.

POLICY

Despite its "Christian" title, the CDU has many of the traits of an orthodox conservative party. The party stands for the rights of private property and is against state intervention. Its belief in the virtues of the "social market economy" is an article of faith, as was its implacable hostility toward communism.

The CDU, of all European parties, is the foremost proponent of European integration. It favors the rapid enlargement of the European Union to include several of the East European states. It supports the creation of a single European single currency by 1999 and moves toward a full political union of a federal nature.

Given its interconfessional character, the Christian emphasis of the party does not mean that the CDU stands particularly close to organized religion, but it does support religious values, stresses the special place of the family in society, and is generally opposed to the further liberalization of abortion laws. The CDU supports the continuation of the "church tax," that is, the collection by the state of contributions by church members (levied as a proportion of income tax) for distribution to the relevant denomination without any cost to the church bodies themselves. The CDU also staunchly defends confessional schooling.

There is no single ideological trend within the CDU. Also the nature of Christian democracy implies that it is an interclass party, which means that the CDU has to avoid siding too openly with the interests of private capital at the expense of organized labor. However, the CDU is opposed to the expansion of social welfare programs, especially since such schemes increase public indebtedness or raise taxation. In fact, the strains of dealing with German unification have forced the CDU government to increase both taxation and public borrowing. Because of these pressures rather than from ideological conviction the CDU is also committed to large-scale privatization of public enterprises, such as Lufthansa, the Bundesbahn, and Telecom.

MEMBERSHIP AND CONSTITUENCY

During its long period in government in the 1950s, the CDU paid relatively little attention to securing a wide mass membership, since its governmental position seemed sufficient to win electoral support. During the 1970s, however, much more effort was made to build up membership. Thus in 1970, membership was only 300,000, but by 1994 it was around 670,000. If CSU membership is added, this total exceeds that of the SPD—historically the mass membership party par excellence.

Electoral support for the CDU is concentrated in the older age groups and in smaller communities. The party is characterized, too, by support from people who are not trade union members and by those, especially Catholics, who are regular churchgoers. On other variables—such as sex, schooling, and occupation—there are no great variations from the SPD, except that the CDU gains more support from farmers, the self-employed, and the professions.

Organized business interests—employers' associations, the Federation of German Industry, and the extremely well organized chambers of commerce and industry operating at local levels—all tend to favor the CDU.

FINANCING

The generous state financing of the parties combined with the size of party membership has meant that the CDU is relatively affluent, and its income has increased at an appreciably faster rate than for the SPD and FDP. Of its current annual income of around DM 15 million (about $6.6 million), some 30% comes from membership dues, 25% from private contributions (mainly from business), and about 30% from the state subsidy. Reliance on membership dues is lower for the CDU than the SPD because of the scale of business funding. Dues are fixed on a sliding scale related to income with a basic annual contribution of DM 36 and an average payment of DM 60 (about $27). The growth in membership and state subsidization has had a beneficial effect in reducing the party's dependence on the paymasters of industry, historically a sinister force in German politics.

LEADERSHIP

Since Adenauer's departure, the CDU long failed to produce a cohesive leadership. The present chancellor, Helmut Kohl (born 1930), was formerly minister-president of the Rhineland-Palatinate and became party chairman in 1973. After the 1976 election, he led the CDU's parliamentary group in the Bundestag. But his position was undermined by his failure to win in 1976 and further weakened prior to the 1980 election when the party opted for Franz-Josef Strauss (CSU) as the CDU/CSU joint chancellor candidate. Strauss's failure to win again opened the question of who would lead the party into the next federal election. The sharp political shift of late 1982, which made Kohl chancellor by a vote in the Bundestag, was confirmed by the outcome of the 1983 election. However, although Kohl won a popular mandate, his performance in government subsequently led to a sharp fall in his political standing. Kohl was anything but a convincing party leader or chancellor, and he was successful in both elections, 1983 and 1987, largely because of the weakness of the SPD.

Kohl's reputation underwent a dramatic transformation from 1989 to 1990 in the course of German unification. He was the first to grasp the possibilities in the collapse of Soviet power and was ideally placed to exploit the opportunity of pushing for unification with eastern Germany (the GDR). As a result, he won the first all-German election of 1990. By the time of the 1994 election he had achieved the status of "the chancellor of German unification" as well as being the foremost statesman promoting European integration.

Kohl's "crown prince," and now successor as DCU leader, is Wolfgang Schäuble. The fact that he is partially paralyzed (after a failed assassination attempt) leads to some doubt whether he will be able to give strong leadership to the party.

PROSPECTS

Despite being (with the CSU) the largest political party, the CDU was in opposition for an exceptionally long period (1969–82). In this situation the party tried various strategies to win back power, but without success. After 1982, the CDU under Chancellor Kohl became the natural party of government, in part because of Kohl's formidable leadership but also because of the inability of the SPD to present a convincing alternative. But that all changed with the CDU's crushing defeat in 1998. Besides the uncertainty of future party leadership, the emergence of a formidable left-leaning bloc of SPD, Greens, and the

PDS means that the weakened CDU may have to spend a lengthy period in opposition with the major task of renewing the basis of Christian democratic appeal.

CHRISTIAN SOCIAL UNION
(Christlich-Soziale Union; CSU)

HISTORY

The Bavarian CSU, the sister party of the CDU, reflects the particularistic traditions of Bavaria, which (along with Saxony) is exceptional in having a direct continuity with a previously independent state, the kingdom of Bavaria. Like its forerunner in the Weimar Republic, the *Bayerische Volkspartei*, which was quite separate from the Catholic Center Party, the CSU has consistently emphasized its independence from the CDU.

The success of the CSU in identifying itself with Bavarian values was shown as early as 1946 when the party won 52.3% of the vote in the first Landtag election. However, it experienced strong competition from the anticlerical Bavarian Party for some years, losing its absolute majority for a time. The failure of the Bavarian Party to maintain a presence in the Bundestag (it was excluded in 1953 when the 5% requirement was extended from a *Land* to a federal base) led to its decline, and from the early 1960s the CSU became the dominant party, controlling an absolute majority from 1962 until the present time. It won an unprecedented 62.1% of the vote in the 1974 Landtag election. Effectively, the CSU has become the "state party" of Bavaria, and consistently wins over 50% of the vote.

ORGANIZATION

Within Bavaria, the CSU is completely free of any obligation to the CDU. Federally, however, there are important constraints. First, the CDU and CSU form a common parliamentary group in the Bundestag, although from 1976 onward the CSU has enjoyed concessions giving the CSU deputies freedom of action. Second, the two parties present a joint chancellor candidate at federal elections (prior to the 1980 election the chancellor candidate had invariably come from the CDU). Third, the CSU is restricted to competing within Bavaria, while the CDU competes in all *Länder* except Bavaria.

The CSU is one of the best organized of all West German parties. There are no fewer than 2,800 local CSU associations, and above these the party is organized at district, provincial, and *Land* levels. The party convention is the party's supreme authority, from which are elected an executive and a party president. The party has its own newspaper, the *Bayernkurier*.

Party headquarters are at Nymphenburger Strasse 64, 8000 Munich.

POLICY

The outlook of the CSU can be best be described as "Christian-conservative." Although generally it subscribes to the main planks of the CDU platform, especially those of a economic nature, the CSU is marked by its clericalism, its virulent antisocialism, and—paradoxically for Bavaria—its uncompromising nationalistic line. Naturally, the CSU is also in the forefront in the defense of *Länder* rights, and it appeals to Bavarian patriotism.

Party policies put the CSU well to the right on the political spectrum, but its confrontational style is just as important in assessing the importance of the CSU in German politics. That style was largely determined by the character of the party's long-term leader and chancellor candidate in the 1980 election, Franz-Josef Strauss (died 1988), a national rather than a merely Bavarian politician whose impact gave the CSU a lasting federal significance.

MEMBERSHIP AND CONSTITUENCY

CSU party membership stands at 185,000, a total that, considering its restriction to Bavaria, compares favorably with other parties. The social makeup of membership differs from the CDU in the much larger proportion of farmers and in the active participation of Catholic priests, who make no secret of their political loyalties. In addition, there are a number of organizations that are closely related to the party and help it to permeate society: the youth movement (*Junge Union*), the women's movement, the Christian Workers' Association, and several others.

The CSU is strongest in the heartland of Upper Bavaria and in the predominantly Catholic areas of Swabia and the Upper Palatinate. It is less powerful in Protestant regions (Upper and Middle Franconia) and in some of the larger cities, such as Munich.

If a party is able to average over 50% of the vote, it is clear that it has considerable interclass appeal, and the CSU—chiefly, though not exclusively, through the Catholic vote—is able to count on support from all sections of the population. It is particularly strong in rural areas, but it also combines urban middle-class support with that of employees. The wide attraction of the CSU in Bavaria is reflected in the weakness of the SPD. In 1994, the SPD won only 30% of the Bavarian vote for the Landtag. Moreover, the CSU has considerable following among young voters, so that its continued hegemony appears assured.

FINANCING

Even though the CSU is an active-membership party, it does not rely disproportionately on membership dues, and its subscription rates are lower than those of other parties, averaging DM 32 per member. The principal source of party funds, about half of an annual income of DM 20 million, comes from state subsidies, federal and *Land*, although this share is falling because of the effects of the 1994 Party Law. In the latter case, the CSU is the major beneficiary of the support provided by the CSU government of Bavaria. The other source of income (somewhat less than 20%) comes under the heading of contributions, a large part of which represents financing from commercial and industrial interests, which are closer to the CSU in Bavaria than they are to the CDU elsewhere.

LEADERSHIP

For many years the fortunes of the CSU were closely identified with the person of Franz-Josef Strauss, who first became party leader in 1961. When the CDU–CSU formed the government in 1982 with the Free Democrats, Helmut Kohl became chancellor. Despite the prominence of Strauss, Kohl refused to give him a ministerial portfolio. Nevertheless, Strauss continued to be a strong influence in federal politics besides being minister-president of Bavaria. The death of Strauss in 1988 left a vacuum in the Bavarian CSU. However, his legacy is still a potent force. Edmund Stoiber, minister-president of Bavaria, has also earned a reputation for upholding traditional Bavarian values. The fact that the CSU held its own in the 1998 election and with the present disarray affecting the CDU means that Stoiber, who favors more conservative policies, will have a greater influence within the CDU/CSU as a whole.

PROSPECTS

After the 1976 election, the CSU made a serious attempt to achieve full freedom from the CDU by declaring the independence of the party group in the Bundestag. That "revolt" failed, and (especially after the departure of Strauss) the party no longer aspires to be an independent force in German politics. Its position has also been weakened as result of German unification: in the enlarged Federal Republic, Bavaria takes a smaller place, since the CSU is restricted to competing within its own *Land*. Its attempt to establish a sister party (the German Social Union) in the new *Länder* failed. However, the CSU, with 6.7% of the vote in the 1998 federal elections, could reasonably be sure of preserving a Bavarian identity at the federal level.

FREE DEMOCRATIC PARTY
(Freie Demokratische Parted; FDP)

HISTORY

The FDP, formed from several liberal parties in the *Länder* of the western zones of occupation in 1948, draws on two types of German liberal tradition: one conservative, nationalist, and close to heavy industry; the other radical, favoring individual liberty and committed to liberal democracy. Both were represented in different parties in imperial

Germany and in the Weimar Republic, but the formation of the FDP brought the two streams together, although the internal politics of the party showed a continuing tension between the conservative and radical wings.

For a long period in the 1950s and 1960s, the FDP was in coalition with the CDU, until the formation of the "grand coalition" between the CDU and SPD in 1966. In 1969, the party joined forces with the SPD, an extremely stable coalition that lasted until 1982. In one sense, the FDP has always been a marginal party compared with the CDU and SPD, since it has never gained more than 12.7% of the vote. On occasion the FDP has been perilously close to the 5% barrier. On the other hand, the FDP has a remarkable record of having a place in government: its total period in office since 1949 exceeds that of the CDU or SPD. The FDP is therefore very much a government-oriented party, and its position between the CDU and SPD makes it an eligible partner for both. Yet it would be incorrect to think of the FDP as being able arbitrarily to switch from one to the other and effectively to be in a position always to determine the nature of the federal government.

In the early years of the republic, the Free Democrats' conservative tradition predominated, and the CDU was their natural ally. Gradually, the outlook of the party changed as a new generation of leaders came to the fore, and a more radical element won control when the party was in opposition from 1966 to 1969. The new leaders saw alliance with the SPD as preferable to a renewal of a CDU–FDP coalition. The shift can be related to changing FDP attitudes toward the *Ostpolitik* and to a greater concern with social and political liberties rather than to any change in thinking about the role of the state in the economy and social welfare.

Once the change in the FDP became evident, the party lost much of its traditional voting support. The continuation of the social-liberal coalition meant that the FDP had to build a new voting base, a fact that may explain the party's modest showing in subsequent elections when it depended on ticket splitting by SPD voters to top the 5% hurdle. The party's switch to the CDU in 1982 alienated support the party had built up in the years of coalition with the SPD. Only ticket splitting by CDU supporters in subsequent elections has ensured its survival in the Bundestag. That was the case for the elections of 1983 and 1987. However, in 1990 (the "unification" election) the fact that the foreign minister, Hans-Dietrich Genscher, was held in high regard in both parts of Germany helped the party win 11% of the vote. In the 1998 elections the FDP vote fell to 6.2%.

ORGANIZATION

As a small, nationwide party, the FDP's organization tends to be weak, especially in *Länder* where the party's support is low, such as Bavaria and all the new *Länder* of eastern Germany. Each *Land* has its own organization, which has a measure of independence from the federal party, especially in the matter of coalition formation. The party convention, meeting yearly, is the supreme organ. Its composition is decided on the basis of two variables: half of the 400 delegates are allocated according to size of party membership in the *Länder* and the other half according to size of the FDP vote in the *Länder* at the previous federal election. All members have a right to attend the convention, though not necessarily to speak. The federal executive, which has been strengthened in recent years, is composed of leading party officials together with members elected by the convention, federal ministers, and the leader of the parliamentary party.

The FDP's youth wing, the Young Democrats (*Jungdemohraten*), was decidedly radical in its orientation, and its membership was quite separate from the parent party. However, it did not survive the rupture of the coalition in 1982. Subsequently a new youth organization, the Young Liberals (*Jungliberalen*), took over. Its outlook is much more in keeping with that of the FDP leadership and the party as a whole.

Federal party headquarters are at Adenauerallee 26, 53113 Bonn.

POLICY

Although in the 1970s the FDP moved toward being a progressive party, its commitments to free enterprise, individual liberties, and historical anticlericalism remain leading traits of the party. In 1971, a new party program was approved that was social-liberal in character and spoke of the "reform of capitalism," without, however, indicating the lines on which reform should proceed. The party was the first to recognize the need for a conciliatory *Ostpolitik*, but its flexibility on this score did not imply any weakening of Western commitments.

Many of the FDP's policy concerns are related to the practical questions of coalition government. Its "moderate" stance between the CDU and SPD implies that the party has had constantly to adjust its policies to harmonize with the coalition partner. It realizes that it will never have a free rein, but is concerned that the "extreme" elements of its coalition partner should be kept in check. In the past the FDP was able to achieve a distinctive policy profile in foreign policy and the *Ostpolitik*, especially with Genscher as the long-serving foreign minister. But since unification, the FDP has been unable to emphasize this aspect. Its main thrust of policy is the prominence it gives to market liberalism, the privatization of state-owned businesses, cutting back on social welfare provision, and generally seeking to contain the escalating public debt caused by financing German unification.

At one time the coalition policies pursued by the FDP in the *Länder* were geared to its national coalition lineup. However, in recent years the FDP has been eliminated from most *Land* assemblies, and coalition strategy in the *Länder* has given way to a simple struggle for survival.

The FDP now has a significant presence only at the national level, and its choice of federal coalition strategy is critical in deciding the party's fate.

MEMBERSHIP AND CONSTITUENCY

For many years the FDP reported a membership of around 80,000, which was probably well on the optimistic side. Immediately after unification, it received a large but temporary boost to its membership in east Germany. That happened because the FDP at first had the benefit of the so-called liberal parties inherited from the GDR, but in fact liberalism in the new *Länder* had no recognizable social base, and support quickly evaporated. There is a striking contrast to the other parties in the FDP's small percentage of manual workers and larger proportion of white-collar workers and public servants. About one-fifth of the membership are women. Support for the FDP comes from Protestants, mainly from larger cities, and from professionals and the self-employed. By far the most important distinguishing feature is the higher level of education of the typical FDP voter. The FDP has always defended the interests of agriculture and industry; the party stands near to a variety of organized industrial and agricultural groups and professional associations. The FDP's almost permanent presence in government has been an attraction for organized economic interests that also work with the CDU.

Yet the FDP is unable to rely on the consistent support of any one social category. The various groups mentioned are far more likely to make the CDU their first choice. It has been estimated that in 1994, for example, less than a third of the party's vote of 7% came from committed FDP supporters.

FINANCING

As a federal party, the FDP fares poorly in comparison with the CDU and SPD because its share of the public subsidy is much smaller; the same applies to subsidies in the *Länder*. From these sources, it obtains about a third of its total income, which is in the region of DM 25 million ($1.13 million). Nor is the party able to rely on membership dues, partly because its membership is low but also because each *Land* party organization is free to set its own dues, a system that tends to depress them. Contributions to the party help fill the gap, accounting for some 40% of the annual budget, relatively much larger than for the other parties. Most such contributions are modest amounts from individual firms or organized groups. For the series of *Länder* elections and those to the Bundestag in 1994, the FDP spent DM 20 million on campaigning.

LEADERSHIP

The FDP has relied heavily on the quality of a small group of federal ministers to enhance its national standing. It was fortunate in being able to supply two presidents of the republic: Theodor Heuss was the first president in 1949 and Walter Scheel from 1974 to 1979. Scheel was the architect of the first SPD–FDP coalition, formed in 1969, and he served as foreign minister and vice chancellor until elected president in 1974. From then onward the leading person, and foreign minister continuously from 1974 until 1990, was Hans-Dietrich Genscher. He was replaced as foreign minister by Klaus Kinkel, who also assumed the party leadership. Kinkel, who had worked alongside Genscher in the foreign office, had only shortly beforehand joined the FDP, and he had difficulty in maintaining the party's strong foreign policy reputation. The sharp reverses in FDP party fortunes in *Land* elections led to Kinkel's being replaced as party leader by Wolfgang Gerhardt.

PROSPECTS

The prospects for the continuing survival of the FDP are not good. Hitherto it has always managed to deny forecasts of impending extinction. But there are two major factors that have worsened its situation in recent years. One is the party's continuing decline in the *Länder* and its increasing reliance on maintaining a federal presence. More serious for the FDP is now the loss of federal office, for this gave the party weight and presence far beyond its modest share of the vote. Its long-term association with the CDU in government also meant that it became virtually a client party of the CDU and relied heavily on CDU voters' splitting their votes in favor of the FDP. The party faces the task of fashioning an independent role for itself in opposition.

THE GREENS
(Die Grunen)

The ecological movement in the Federal Republic is possibly the strongest organized political force of its kind in Western Europe. Although the Green party was only formed as a federal party in 1980, it had had a considerable impact on German politics, especially in putting controversial issues on the political agenda. The Greens arose as a merger of some 250 smaller ecological and related groups that had already been active in *Länder* and communal politics. Prior to the 1980 federal election, the "Green" lists (or the associated "colored" and "alternative" lists) obtained an average of 3.4% of the vote in *Land* elections, winning representation in Bremen and Baden-Wurttemburg. In the 1980 federal election, the new Green party scored only 1.5%. But subsequent *Land* elections showed its underlying strength in mobilizing local support on specific issues (siting of nuclear power stations, housing conditions in Berlin). At a federal level, the party's support has been more diffuse, but the party achieved a breakthrough in 1983 with 5.6% of the national vote. It then had a platform in the Bundestag and was able to focus on national issues: nuclear weapons and the related peace issue, national environmental policies, and the cause of minority and disadvantaged groups.

Support for the Greens is based on a number of factors. One is simply concern with issues such as the environment. Another is the mobilizing of a protest vote against the monopoly of political power wielded by the larger parties and the consensus politics they foster. A third is the advent of idealist politics, appealing particularly to the young and well-educated. A fourth factor concerns the SPD: its long identification with government and the moderate course it has taken in opposition since 1982 have led to dissatisfaction among younger voters who came to see the party as incapable of initiating radical change in German society.

The motivations of those who support the Greens are varied, and the party contains a diversity of ideological views, especially between those who wish to keep to particular issues and those who would like to restructure German society and also have a leftist inclination. Not surprisingly, those who support the Greens also rallied behind the peace movement and campaign against nuclear weapons sites in the Federal Republic.

Party organization and leadership are still loosely structured. That was deliberate and intended to avoid the formation of permanent party elites. The Greens were initially an "antiparty party." Leadership was both collective and rotating so that few people could have a permanent major influence, and Green *Land* organizations were virtually independent.

The Greens have changed considerably since the 1980s and have become a normal party. Unlike earlier years when orthodox politics was rejected, coalitions with other parties at the *Land* level are no longer exceptional. The Greens are still committed to radical change but are prepared to work through the existing institutions to secure them.

In the election of 1990, the Greens fared badly in western Germany, partly because they had been lukewarm on unification. However, the Greens recovered subsequently, thanks to support in the *Länder*. Their vote of 6.7% in 1998 was sufficient to form a coalition with the SPD. The Greens have become a "normal" party, and the party leader, also foreign minister, Joschka Fischer, is a stabilizing and authoritative figure.

Although the Greens have proportionately more younger voters than other parties, the age composition of the party is rising, a process especially evident among the leadership cadre. The Greens will be adversely affected by the operation of the new Party Law that puts a premium on party members' contributions in order to receive state subsidies. The Greens do not aspire to being a membership party, nor can they expect to receive large private donations. Party offices are at Ehrental 2-4, 53332 Bornheim.

PARTY OF DEMOCRATIC SOCIALISM
(Parted des Demokratischen Sozialismus; PDS)

The PDS is the successor party to the Socialist Unity Party of Germany (SED), which wielded sole power in the former German Democratic Republic for 40 years. The peaceful revolution in the GDR swept the Communists from office, and by the time of the first free elections in the GDR held in March 1990, the SED had changed its name to the Party of Democratic Socialism and won 16.4% of the vote, indicating that the Communist system was not entirely discredited. In the all-German election of December 1990 the PDS scored only 2.4% because it had almost no support in western Germany. The PDS has shown that it is not a spent force since it is represented in the *Landtag* of all five new *Länder* and in Berlin. In 1994 the PDS recorded 4.4% of the federal vote. Although it fell below the 5% requirement, the PDS managed to win four district contests (all in Berlin) on the "first vote" and so qualified for its full share of Bundestag seats.

Although the membership of the PDS (at about 120,000) is far lower than for the old SED, it is still larger than that of any other party in the new *Länder* and Berlin. Support for the PDS comes from three main sources: former members of the SED, the unemployed, and (perhaps surprisingly) younger voters. One reason for the PDS's ability to attract a substantial following is that many people in the new *Länder* resent the patronizing attitudes of some west Germans and believe that voting for the PDS is the best way of asserting their identity and furthering their interests. PDS finances come principally from members' contributions, but clearly the party has also had access to the funds and resources of the SED, although it is difficult to assess the party's actual wealth. For the 1994 campaign it spent an estimated 9.5 million marks.

The party's policy is firmly anticapitalist, although playing down its communist ideology, and the PDS commits itself to parliamentary democracy. It particularly emphasizes its role in the new *Länder* and naturally calls for measures to cut unemployment and increase social expenditure. The party demands the disbandment of NATO and does not wish Germany to have a seat on the UN Security Council.

For the future, the PDS appears to have a secure place in the new *Länder* and may win modest support in western Germany. It looks like it has become an established regional party, but it also has a national profile through the strong showing of its young leader, Gregor Gysi. To achieve a breakthrough, the PDS would need to become fully acceptable to other parties, for instance, by participating in *Land* coalitions, but success did come in 1998 when it entered a coalition in Thuringia with the SPD.

SOCIAL DEMOCRATIC PARTY OF GERMANY

(Sozialdemokratische Partei Deutschlands; SPD)

HISTORY

The SPD was founded in 1875 as a merger between Ferdinand Lassalle's General German Workers' Association (formed in 1863 as a moderate, non-Marxist party) and the strongly Marxist Social Democratic Party of August Bebel and Wilhelm Liebknecht. Despite discrimination against it, the SPD became the largest party in the Reichstag in 1912. It formed the new provisional government upon the collapse of the monarchy in 1918. At that time, the left wing of the party split off to become the KPD, and the two parties were mortal enemies throughout the life of the Weimar Republic: the SPD wishing to preserve parliamentary democracy and the KPD dedicated to its destruction. After the collapse of the Third Reich, the SPD was quickly reestablished, since many former party workers enthusiastically rallied to the party. Kurt Schumacher, who had been incarcerated by the Nazis, emerged as the undisputed leader in the western zones, but it soon became apparent that the SPD in the Soviet Zone was to be subject to Soviet pressure. The USSR was not prepared to see the KPD take second place to the SPD. In April 1946, the SPD in East Germany was merged forcibly with the KPD to form the Socialist Unity Party (SED).

The SPD under Schumacher at first appeared to have a claim to undisputed leadership in western Germany, but the rise of the CDU meant that the two parties ran neck and neck in the first *Land* elections as well as in the first federal election in 1949. Excluded from federal government then, the SPD commenced a long spell in opposition. While the CDU went from strength to strength, the SPD stagnated, and its traditional socialism seemed to have little relevance during the period of the "economic miracle" of the 1950s. The SPD reacted by drastically changing the nature of the party with the adoption of the Godesberg Program in 1959. The party committed itself to becoming a party of the whole people rather than a class party and explicitly supported the successful market system. It claimed to be a party with no specific attachment to Marxism and to find its roots in "the Christian ethic, humanism, and classical philosophy." Subsequent to these reforms, the SPD's vote rose gratifyingly in successive elections, but its progress was also due to the personality of Willy Brandt, who in the early 1960s became party leader as well as chancellor candidate. In 1966, the SPD joined the CDU in government, with Brandt as vice chancellor and foreign minister. In 1969 it became the senior governing party in coalition with the FDP, and Brandt was the first SPD chancellor in the postwar period.

Brandt's important contribution was to implement a new *Ostpolitik*. He also appealed to the idealism of younger voters, but without actually bringing about substantial reforms. His resignation in 1974 (over a spy scandal) led to Helmut Schmidt's replacing him as chancellor. Schmidt remained chancellor until he was defeated in the Bundestag in 1982. Brandt retained the party leadership after resigning as chancellor in 1974 and remained the undisputed leader of the party.

The SPD became the largest party in 1972, but subsequently (in 1976 and 1980) the party again had to take second place to the CDU–CSU. For party loyalists, the satisfaction of still having the SPD in government was tempered by the party's stagnating vote and its loss of reforming zeal. Loss of office in 1982 was bitter for the party, but the period of opposition gave the SPD an opportunity to rethink its policies.

ORGANIZATION

The SPD is a centralized party, with authority securely vested in the national leadership, the party convention, and the party's parliamentary group (*Fraktion*) in the Bundestag. Thus although the *Land* leaders and minister-presidents enjoy considerable prestige, there is never any question of their challenging the national leaders.

Each *Land* has a single party organization (except Hesse, which is divided into two). The SPD also emphasizes the contribution of suborganizations. By far the most important is the party's youth movement, the *Jungsozialisten* (Jusos), open to all party members up to the age of 35, although in fact only a small fraction of eligible members participate. The *Jungsozialisten* represented the major ideological challenge to the party leadership, but their influence has declined since the mid-1970s. Over time, the significance of the party's ancillary organizations has declined as a means of integration and mobilization, and consequently the SPD's organization is stronger on paper than it is in practice. Since the German unified trade union movement is by choice (officially) politically neutral, the trade unions do not exist as a suborganization of the party, unlike the situation in the Weimar Republic.

Party headquarters are at Erich Ollenhauer Haus, Ollenhauer Strasse 1, 53173, Bonn.

POLICY

The fount of party policy continues to be the Godesberg Program, although that document is more a statement of principles than a detailed guide to action. It has been supplemented at various times, most notably by the middle-range working programs, which have among other things advocated a larger role for the government in steering and planning the economy. The party also stands for greater social welfare provision, educational reform, and an extension of codetermination in industry. Three policy areas were subject to increasing intraparty conflict when the party was last in government: the position of the Federal Republic with regard to increasing the scale of nuclear armament on its territory; the nuclear power program; and the measures necessary to counter the economic recession, especially the growth in long-term unemployment. The conflicts came to a head in the final years of Schmidt's chancellorship. After years of preparation a supplement to the Godesberg Program was adopted in 1989 (Berlin Basic Program), but this effort was quickly outdated by German unification and anyway was too vague, seeking to please all viewpoints in the party. The 1994 election gave a better idea of the SPD's priorities. On taxation, the SPD proposed to shift the burden to higher income earners and to raise taxes on the use of energy. It also committed an SPD government to "phase out" nuclear energy. The party seeks to improve the status of and chances for women by legislation, and the SPD has already adopted a women's quota (40%) for all its elected offices and candidates. Although the SPD favors closer European integration, it is against the development of a "hardcore" led by France and Germany at the expense of other members of the European Union.

MEMBERSHIP AND CONSTITUENCY

The SPD traditionally has been a mass-membership party; even before 1914 it had no fewer than a million members. Soon after 1945, it reached 800,000, but then declined until the early 1970s when there was a large influx of young people, topping the million mark before declining once more to 890,000 in the early 1990s. The SPD is particularly weak in the new *Länder*, where it has barely 30,000 members. Compared with the early postwar years there has been a massive decline in the proportion of manual workers in the party, only partially reflecting the changing occupational distribution of the labor force: manual workers now account for 25% of members. Members under the age of 30 used to constitute half the total, but the SPD has found it increasingly difficult to attract young voters, many of whom now count themselves as Greens.

Voting support is greatest in the industrial areas and large cities, with a strong concentration among trade union members and among those who are not church members. The SPD benefited from the lowering of the voting age to 18 in 1972 and was then generally attractive to younger voters. This support subsequently declined somewhat, and the Green party has made serious inroads into the first-time and young voters. By far the most important single constituency for the SPD is still the trade union movement, which despite its formally neutral position in politics nevertheless has strong links with the party chiefly through personal connections and overlapping membership. However, German trade union membership, at around 20% of all employees, is on the low side compared with other industrial countries.

FINANCING

The SPD relies heavily on membership dues as a source of party income (36%). There has been a steady rise in personal income and party dues are fixed on a sliding scale according to declared income, an average of DM 46. State subsidies, *Land* and federal, amount to about 31% of income, while the extent of voluntary contributions (10%) is lower than for the CDU and FDP. Annual party income approaches DM 15 million and is comparable with that of the CDU. The inability of the party to rely on contributions makes it especially sensitive to variations in electoral performance (which affect the state subsidy) and to fluctuations in party membership. However, the revised Party Law will benefit large-membership parties such as the SPD, as the state subsidy now tops up members' contributions by 50%. Like other parties, the changed basis of state financing has already had effects on the SPD's campaign spending: in 1994 the party used 75 million marks, a reduction of some 15% from previous campaign years.

LEADERSHIP

During the late 1960s and up to the early 1980s, the SPD was fortunate in its strong leadership, marked especially by the chancellorships of Brandt (1969–74) and Schmidt (1974–82). Subsequently, however, the SPD failed to produce a convincing chancellor candidate and lost four successive federal elections up to 1994. Rudolf Scharping was selected as chancellor candidate for this election by a direct vote of the party membership, and he combined this with the position of party leader. Subsequently, two minister-presidents, Gerhard Schröder (Lower Saxony) and Oskar Lafontaine (Saarland) became contenders for power, with Schröder winning the chancellorship and Lafontaine elected SPD party leader. This split in authority within the SPD could lead to problems for the party, since Schröder is a "modernist," and Lafontaine belongs to the traditional left.

PROSPECTS

Success in the 1998 elections gave the SPD a choice of coalition partners between the center-right and the left. Its choice of the Greens represented a new departure for the Federal Republic. The question is whether it will prove to be a stable formation. There is potential for conflict in matters of foreign policy, defense, and the environment. If the coalition breaks up, the SPD would still have the option of a coalition with the CDU/CSU, or possibly with the FDP.

MINOR POLITICAL PARTIES

No fewer than 41 parties contested the 1998 federal elections. However, besides the major parties already considered, most of the remainder were splinter parties with no hope of electing representatives or winning more than a few thousand votes. Their support also fell in comparison with 1990. The minor parties stand for diverse issues: various kinds of Christian orientation, assorted extreme-left groupings, civil rights, animal welfare. Attracting rather more support were parties such as the Motorists' Party, Natural Law, and The Grays (*Die Grauen*) who represent senior citizens. The Grays won 0.3% of the vote.

Over the past few years, most attention has been focused on the possible threat posed by the extreme right, with three parties contesting *Land* and federal elections: the National Democratic Party (NPD), the German People's Union (DVU), and the Republicans. They gained a significant following in the wake of German unification and more directly over the issue of large-scale migration into Germany, especially because of the large increase of political asylum seekers. However, after the imposition of stricter regulations in 1993 and the consequent fall in numbers, the weight of this issue declined. The Republicans, the only significant party of the extreme right, scored only 1.8% in 1998, and failed to win a seat in the Bundestag. The total share of the extreme right parties was 3.3%. The extreme right has often seemed to be on the brink of making a breakthrough into federal politics, but actual successes have been limited to winning a few seats in several *Land* assemblies.

NATIONAL PROSPECTS

As a consequence of unification, the Federal Republic has become by far the largest country in Western Europe. Germany's economic potential will make it the leading European power once the problems of financing unification have been overcome. Already it is clear that the Federal Republic is intent on providing leadership for Europe, in respect to both pushing for further integration of the European Union and extending it to Eastern Europe.

Nevertheless, political and economic uncertainties affect Germany's prospects. It is unlikely that any successor to Helmut Kohl will be able to provide such determined leadership either in domestic policy or in European matters. Chancellor Schröder may face difficulties with the more radical Greens in the coalition, but also from within his own party.

Of equal concern must be the course of economic development. The Federal Republic is suffering from massive structural unemployment, in part resulting from high labor costs and high social security costs. This threatens to make industry uncompetitive and unattractive for investment. Most affected is eastern Germany: unemployment is higher in the east, and the burden of financing unification is much greater than was expected, which all acts as a deadweight on the more prosperous west. These problems are compounded by the fiscal restraints needed to meet the criteria for the creation of a single European currency. Germany's deserved reputation for political and economy stability since the 1950s will be severely tested in the coming years.

Further Reading

Braunthal, G. *Parties and Politics in Modern Germany.* Lynne Rienner: Boulder, Colo.: 1996.

Conradt, D., et al., eds. *Germany's New Politics: Parties and Issues in the 1990s.* Providence: Pergamon, 1996.

Dalton, R., ed. *Germans Divided: The 1994 Bundestag Election and the Evolution of the Party System.* Washington, D.C., and Oxford: Berg, 1996.

Hancock M., and H. Welsh, eds. *German Unification: Processes and Outcomes.* Boulder, Colo.: Westview Press, 1994.

Merkl, P., ed. *The Federal Republic of Germany at Fifty.* New York: New York University Press, 1998.

Padgett, S., ed. *Adenauer to Kohl: The Development of the German Chancellorship.* London: C. Hurst, 1994.

Pulzer, P. *German Politics, 1945–1995.* New York and Oxford: Oxford University Press, 1995.

Smith, G., W. Paterson, and S. Padgett, eds. *Developments in German Politics 2.* Durham, N.C.: Duke University Press, 1996.

THE REPUBLIC OF GHANA

By Robert J. Griffiths, Ph.D.

THE SYSTEM OF GOVERNMENT

Ghana, a country with a population estimated at 17 million in 1994, lies on the Gulf of Guinea in West Africa. After 10 years of military rule, Ghana returned to a democratic, multiparty political system in 1992 under the constitution of the Fourth Republic. A former flight lieutenant, Jerry Rawlings, is the current president.

Ghana encompasses the territory of the former British colony of the Gold Coast, with the addition of that portion of Togoland administered by Great Britain, first as a League of Nations and then as a United Nations Mandate. On March 6, 1957, Ghana became the first black African country to achieve independence from colonial rule. The independence constitution provided for a parliamentary democracy designed along Westminster lines and headed by a prime minister. In 1960, a new republican constitution was introduced that established a presidential system. In the 1960 plebiscite, which was called to approve the constitutional changes, Kwame Nkrumah, Ghana's first prime minister, was elected president. His party, the Convention People's Party (CPP), attained an overwhelming majority in the National Assembly. The republican constitution transformed Ghana into a de facto one-party state, a condition made formal in 1964. The First Republic, under Kwame Nkrumah, was overthrown in a military coup d'état in February 1966.

Between Nkrumah's ouster and the 1992 elections, Ghanaians experienced two short-lived civilian governments and five military regimes. The National Liberation Council (1966–69), which took over from the First Republic, turned over power voluntarily to a democratically elected government in 1969. The Second Republic, headed by Kofi Busia and the Progress Party, was in turn deposed in a military coup on January 13, 1972. The new military government (first entitled the National Redemption Council and then the Supreme Military Council) was headed by Colonel I. K. Acheampong, who inaugurated a period of ill-fated military reform. Acheampong himself was forced to abdicate in 1978. He was replaced by Lieutenant General Fred Akuffo. Akuffo surrendered in 1979 to Jerry Rawlings's Armed Forces Revolutionary Council. This marked the first appearance of the current leader of Ghana on the political scene. Civilian rule was revived briefly during the Third Republic (1979–81). On New Year's Eve, 1982, Jerry Rawlings once again returned to power, suspended the 1979 constitution, and assumed the chairmanship of the Provisional National Defense Council (PNDC), which ruled Ghana until the 1992 elections.

The Rawlings regime came to power during a period of extreme economic recession and political turmoil. When Rawlings first intervened in 1979, he carried out a self-proclaimed housecleaning exercise aimed at eradicating widespread corruption and abuses on the part of state officials. Although he voluntarily handed over power to Dr. Hilla Limann, the president of the Third Republic, he remained in the country and commented frequently on the inadequacies of his successor. During this period, he called for a thorough revision of the institutional structure of the country and for a code of public accountability for officeholders. He also maintained close links with junior and noncommissioned officers in the army and with student and trade union activists. When Rawlings returned to power, he did so amid reports that members of the Limann government were under investigation for receiving massive bribes from local and foreign firms. Rawlings asserted at the time that he had not led a coup but was only paving the way for ""real democracy, government of the people, by the people, for the people."

To pursue this goal, the PNDC established a series of defense committees, charged with carrying out the aims of the Rawlings revolution. People's Defence Committees (PDCs) were established in each community; Worker's Defence Committees (WDCs) in factories, banks, and major places of wage employment; and Armed Forces Defence Committees (AFDCs) in the armed services. An Interim National Coordinating Committee (later changed to the National Defence Committee) was established to coordinate the activities of the local bodies. By 1984, 20,000 committees, limited in membership to those who supported the precepts of the government, had been created. During the course of 1983, however, the defense committees were increasingly criticized, even by Jerry Rawlings, who decried the overzealousness of some committee activists.

In December 1984, the National Defence Committee was disbanded and PDCs, WDCs, and AFDCs reorganized under the name of Committees for the Defence of the Revolution (CDRs). The CDRs opened membership to all Ghanaians, including chiefs and managers who had been excluded from the previous structures. The switch to CDRs, therefore, introduced a new tone of reconciliation, in contrast to the confrontational style adopted during the early years of PNDC rule.

The system of executive government supported by direct consultation through defense committees stamped Ghanaian governmental structures with an aura of populism, a label frequently attached to the Rawlings regime after 1982.

Rawlings's pursuit of a populist agenda, ideology, and management style allowed his regime to postpone return to civilian rule. However, by 1990, the regime was under domestic and international pressure to democratize. The Movement for Freedom and Justice (MFJ), a loose alliance of previous political groups under the First, Second, and Third Republics headed by Professor Adu Boahen emerged as the leading opposition force to Rawlings's regime. The MFJ demanded a timetable for the return to constitutional rule, an end to the prohibition on political activity, the release of political prisoners, and amnesty for exiles. Rawlings was also pressured by international financial institutions and Western donors to whom his regime had become indebted as a result of his efforts to reverse Ghana's economic decline. In 1990, a National Commission for Democracy was established to convene a series of regional debates on Ghana's political and economic future. In December 1990, Rawlings announced plans for a new constitution to be completed by the end of 1991 and a national consultative body, the Consultative Assembly, which was established in May 1991 with the task of reviewing constitutional recommendations made by the government. The new constitution was finally presented to the Ghanaian people in a referendum in April 1992 and approved by a large margin of those voting.

Preparations for Ghana's elections were overseen by the Interim National Election Committee, established in late 1991. Elections took place November 3, 1992, and Rawlings, who had resigned his military commission to run as a presidential candidate, was elected president with 58.3% of the vote, defeating his closest challenger, Professor Adu Boahen, who got 30.4%. The former president Hilla Limann ran a distant third with 6.7%, Kwabena Darko received 2.8%, and a retired general, E. A. Erskine, got 1.7%.

Although the elections were judged free and fair by the Commonwealth observer group, the opposition charged that there had been widespread voter fraud. Opposition parties boycotted the parliamentary elections in December 1992, giving Rawlings's party, the National Democratic Convention (NDC), an overwhelming 189 seats in the 200-seat Parliament. In the most recent presidential election, held in December 1996, Rawlings was reelected with 57.4% of the vote.

Executive and Legislature

Under the 1992 constitution, the president is elected by universal suffrage of those 18 and over for a term of four years. If no candidate receives over 50% of the vote, a runoff takes place between the top two vote getters. The president is the chief executive, head of state, and commander in chief of the armed forces. The president appoints the vice president and, with the approval of Parliament, also appoints the Council of Ministers. The constitution also provides for a 25-member Council of State made up primarily of presidential nominees and regional representatives and a 20-member National Security Council, both of which advise the president.

The National Parliament is a unicameral legislature consisting of 200 members, who serve four-year terms. Legislation must have the approval of the Parliament and the president in order to become law.

Checks and balances are supposed to prevent any one branch of the government from wielding the preponderance of power.

Judiciary

The legal system is based on the constitution, Ghanaian common law, and parliamentary statutes and contains elements of customary (traditional) law. Under the Courts Act of 1971, the court system consists of the Supreme Court, the Court of Appeal, and the High Court of Justice, which stand at the apex of a complex network of circuit, district, and traditional courts. The PNDC established public tribunals, which tried offenders and meted out justice quickly and, at times, harshly. The Courts Act of 1993 incorporated these public tribunals into the existing court system. The Supreme Court has the power of judicial review over any legislative or executive action. The High Court has both original and appellate jurisdiction. Throughout the postcolonial period, the courts have shown a great deal of resilience and independence.

Regional and Local Government

The country is divided into 10 administrative regions under the administration of regional secretaries. There are also 110 administrative districts, each with a district assembly and a district secretary. There are regional coordinating councils in each of the 10 regions consisting of the regional secretary, the deputy regional secretaries, and all the district secretaries and members of the district assemblies in the region. The 1992 constitution added at least two chiefs to the membership of each council. These councils formulate, implement, and oversee programs in conjunction with the district assemblies and ensure that these programs reflect national policy. Local government consists of submetropolitan district councils, metropolitan assemblies, zonal councils, municipal assemblies, and town and area councils.

THE ELECTORAL SYSTEM

The president and Parliament are elected by universal suffrage of those 18 years of age or older. The 1992 constitution stipulates that in the event that no presidential candidate receives more than 50% of the vote, a runoff election is held within 21 days between the two candidates with the most votes. Both the president and the members of Parliament are elected for four-year terms. The president is limited to two terms in office.

Origins of the Parties

Two major political traditions emerged in Ghanaian politics, and these have endured, despite many changes in name, since independence. The first is associated with Kwame Nkrumah, the independence-era leader, and reflects his socialist, Pan-Africanist ideology. The second is identified with the former prime minister Kofi Busia and one of the founders of the nationalist movement, J. B. Danquah, and has a more conservative, free-enterprise orientation. Over the years, therefore, when electoral opportunities have surfaced, the informal two-party system has been revived under new rubrics.

The Parties in Law

Under the PNDC, political associations were banned in Ghana, reflecting Rawlings's view that political parties were associated with elitism and corruption. In May 1991, the PNDC announced it would support the restoration of a multiparty system, and a year later the Political Parties Law came into effect permitting the formation of political parties. This law was controversial, however, since it outlawed the use of any name, symbol, color, or slogan that had been used by previous political parties contending Ghanaian elections. The law also restricted the size and sources of political contributions for the political parties. Six of the parties that emerged in the aftermath of this legislation were certified to contest the 1992 presidential elections.

Party Organization

There have been a number of changes in Ghana's political parties since the lifting of the ban on party formation in 1992. The National Democratic Congress became the representative of the PNDC, while some other

Rawlings supporters formed the EGLE (Every Ghanian Living Everywhere) Party. The National Convention Party (NCP) originally intended to contest the election with its own candidate, K. N. Arkaah, but eventually entered into an electoral coalition with the NDC and the EGLE Party, with Rawlings as the coalition's presidential candidate and Arkaah as the vice presidential candidate. The People's National Convention Party (PNC) was founded by the former president Hilla Limann as his electoral vehicle. The National Independence Party (NIP) chose a businessman, Kwabena Darko, as its candidate; the People's Heritage Party (PHP) selected the retired lieutenant general E. A. Erskine; and the New Patriotic Party (NPP) candidate was Professor Adu Boahen. The NIP, the PNC, the PHP, and the NCP reflected the Nkrumahist legacy, while the NPP represented the Danquah-Busia tradition.

In the aftermath of their defeat in the 1992 elections, the NPP, PNC, NIP, and PHP formed an alliance known as the Inter-Party Coordinating Committee and announced their intention to act as an opposition to the Rawlings government. When the NPP subsequently accepted the results of the election, the alliance dissolved and a new coalition formed known as the People's Convention Party, consisting of the PHP, NIP, and a faction of the PNC.

In 1994, the NPP, PNC, and the PCP announced their intention to field a single candidate in the 1996 presidential elections. There was also a falling out between Rawlings and his vice president, Arkaah, that led to the NCP's withdrawing from the government coalition. In January 1996, the NCP, PNC, and the People's Party for Democracy and Development (PAD) merged to form the United Convention Party (UCP). In August, the NPP and the PCP announced the Great Alliance, bringing together both of Ghana's political traditions in an effort to defeat Rawlings and the NDC. The Alliance selected J. A. Kufuor as its candidate. In the December 1996 elections, Rawlings received 57.4% of the votes cast to Kufuor's 39.6%. A third candidate, Dr. Edward Mahama, polled 3%. In the parliamentary elections, the NDC won 132 seats, the NPP 60 seats, the PCP 5 seats, and the PNC 1 seat.

OTHER POLITICAL FORCES

Armed Forces

The armed forces consisted of some 6,850 troops in 1994. The army is the largest branch, with 5,000 members. All three branches of the military (the army, the navy, and the air force) are relatively well trained, professional, and ethnically integrated. During the PNDC era elements of the armed forces, especially among the lower ranks, provided Rawlings with important support. He did not, however, enjoy the backing of some veteran army officers and recruits from the central Akan regions. The armed forces have returned to the barracks and appear to have adapted to a reduced role in the internal affairs of the country as well as reductions in strength.

Ethnic Groups

Ghana's population, as that of most African states, is ethnically diverse. The dominant group is the Akan (composed of the Ashanti, Fante, Akim, and Nzima, among others), who in 1991, constituted an estimated 52.4% of the population. Other major groups include the Mossi-Dagomba (15.8%), the Ewe (11.9%), and the Ga-Andagme (7.8%). All told, there are 75 distinct linguistic groups in the country. The Mossi-Dagomba are concentrated in the north, while the other four main groups inhabit the forest and coastal areas of the country and intermingle frequently, especially on the coast. Approximately 43% of the population of Ghana is Christian, and Muslims now constitute about 25%.

Ethnicity remains a factor in Ghanaian politics. Ethnic voting was evident in both the 1992 and the 1996 presidential elections, in which Rawlings, a member of the Ewe ethnic group, received significantly fewer votes in the Ashanti region than elsewhere. In the 1996 elections Ashanti was the only region where Rawlings failed to receive over 50% of the vote.

NATIONAL PROSPECTS

In 1992, President Rawlings successfully transformed his military-backed regime into a civilian government. Democracy was further reinforced by the NDC's adherence to constitutional rule during its first four years and the second round of national elections in 1996. Nevertheless, Ghana still faces important challenges. Although Rawlings won the 1996 presidential elections, opposition parties, which did not contest the 1992 parliamentary elections, won 67 seats in Parliament. The opposition's increased strength in Parliament will make it more difficult for the NDC to implement its programs. Ghana's opposition political parties have been fragmented, however, and they have been unable to seriously challenge the NDC either individually or in coalition. Internal problems in the NDC surfaced prior to the 1996 elections when some 70 NDC parliamentary incumbents were not selected to seek reelection. Furthermore, Rawlings is prohibited from seeking a third term and his successor is unlikely to have as much popular support, making it more difficult to deal with the country's challenges.

Ghana's past political upheavals have been associated with economic problems. The connection between politics and economics remains an important factor in Ghana's political stability. During the 1980s, Ghana adhered to a structural adjustment program that achieved some success and won it the backing of the international financial institutions. In the 1990s, however, Ghana's economic success has faded. The gross domestic product growth rate declined by half a percentage point between 1990 and 1995, and, only twice since 1990 has growth exceeded the 5% average achieved from 1984 to 1989. Although investment has increased, it has been concentrated in the extractive sector with gold overtaking cocoa as the leading export. Agricultural production has suffered from the weather and fluctuations in world cocoa prices. Food production has been affected by a switch to incentives to produce cash crops and increased prices for inputs like fertilizer. Government austerity has also relaxed, including spending prior to both recent elections on popular infrastructure projects, the cost of the elections themselves, and unbudgeted spending to host a Non-Aligned Conference and deploy peacekeepers to Liberia. Economic growth has slowed, inflation has become a concern, and the cedi has lost value, but there have not been incentives to export, unemployment has increased, and there has been little reduction in poverty. Indeed, structural adjustment has imposed significant hardships on Ghana's poorest citizens. Despite the implementation of a Program of Action to Mitigate the Costs of Adjustment (PAMSCAD), the benefits for those most seriously affected by adjustment have been minimal.

Economic problems contributed to Ghana's past political volatility. Although Ghana seems to have embraced democracy, further economic problems and political fragmentation could threaten the country's fragile democratic consolidation process.

Further Reading

Berry, LaVerle. *Ghana: A Country Study*. Washington, D.C. : Federal Research Division, Library of Congress, 1995.

Gyimah-Boadi, E. "Associational Life, Civil Society, and Democratization in Ghana." In *Civil Society and the State in Africa*. Ed. John W. Harbeson, Donald Rothchild, and Naomi Chazan. Boulder, Colo.: Lynne Rienner, 1994.

———. "Ghana's Uncertain Political Opening." *Journal of Democracy* 5, no. 2 (1994): 118–32.

Haynes, Jeff. "Sustainable Democracy in Ghana? Problems and Prospects." *Third World Quarterly* 14, no. 3 (1993).

Herbst, Jeffrey. *The Politics of Reform in Ghana*. Berkeley: University of California Press, 1993.

Jeffries, Richard, and Clare Thomas. "The Ghanaian Elections of 1992." *African Affairs* 92 (1993): 331–66.

Oquaye, Mike. "The Ghanaian Elections of 1992: A Dissenting View." *African Affairs* (1995): 259–75.

Rothchild, Donald, ed. *Ghana: The Political Economy of Recovery*. Boulder, Colo.: Lynne Rienner, 1991.

———. "Rawlings and the Engineering of Legitimacy in Ghana." In *Collapsed States*. Ed. I. William Zartman. Boulder, Colo.: Lynne Rienner, 1995.

GREECE

(Elliniki Demokratia)

By Jeffrey K. Hass, Ph.D.

THE SYSTEM OF GOVERNMENT

Located in southeastern Europe, Greece (formally called the "Hellenic Republic"), the original home to the democratic form of government, has witnessed authoritarianism and a return to stable if constantly shifting and evolving democratic politics in the last 25 years. Military rule, which in 1967 overthrew a formal monarchy in the name of national security and anticommunism, gave way in 1974 to democracy. A constitution was adopted on June 11, 1975, replacing both the monarchical and military systems, and it continues to serve as the basis for Greek political life. One foundation of some political certainty—the two-decades-long rule of the feisty Andreas Papandreou over the hegemonic Pan-Hellenic Socialist Movement and over Greek politics in general—came to an end in 1995, when Papandreou resigned from his post of prime minister due to illness; he died in June 1996. Greece still awaits either another charismatic leader or the institutionalization of stronger formal rules of party life to bring more certainty to the processes of political selection and decision making.

The population of Greece in 1996 was estimated to be over 10.5 million persons, with a growth rate of 0.42% per annum. Life expectancy is 78.1 years for the population as a whole, with 75.6 years for men and 80.78 years for women. Greece is close to ethnic homogeneity, with native Greeks composing 98% of the population; according to the Greek government, there are no ethnic divisions in Greece. (The case of ethnic unrest between Greeks and Turks in Cyprus, which is independent from Greece but still a trouble spot for it, is discussed below.) Greek Orthodoxy claims 98% of openly religious people, with Muslims making up 1.3%. Greek is the majority (and official) language, with English and French the minority spoken languages.

The Greek economy is a mixed system (having both private and public ownership). The public sector, already a major force in economic life under the rule of right-wing parties in the 1950s and 1960s, grew under Papandreou's watch from 1981 to 1989, constituting from 55% of GDP in 1981 to around 70% in 1989 (in spite of austerity measures and attempts after 1985 to curb inflation and macroeconomic stability). This has led to economic stagnation and a public debt of approximately 120%. Government attempts to support a "hard" drachma (Greek currency) and to control wages in the public sector have both helped reign in inflation and brought on economic sluggishness. Prime Minister Kostis Simitis has indicated that he intends to continue pursuing austerity measures and a more technocratic orthodox economic line, although mass privatization is unlikely in the near future, given strong domestic opposition. As would be expected, Greece's main source of foreign revenue is tourism; the country also exports mostly manufactured goods and foodstuffs, while imports include manufactured goods and other forms of foodstuffs and fuels.

The Greek political system is essentially parliamentary. While the political structure in Greece resembles that of most other Western democratic nations—the three-part division of executive, legislative, and judicial branches—the legislative branch is the most powerful, having the most control over policy formulation.

The general ground rules for Greek political life are contained in the 1975 constitution (revised and amended in 1986). The constitution sets procedures for choosing and evicting holders of political positions, defines the right and responsibilities of the different institutional actors, and sets the division of power between the branches. Other rights and rules include setting the voting age (18), recognition of the legitimacy of agreed-upon international agreements, and basic rights such as freedom of speech, print, and assembly. More specific points of Greek political life are defined either by tradition (as in the case of patronage-oriented political parties) or by specific laws (which may introduce slight changes in electoral procedure from election to election).

Executive

The Greek executive has two parts, the presidency and the prime minister and ministries. Presidential powers were much greater before changes to the constitution in 1986 shifted many presidential powers to the prime minister and Parliament. At present the president, as in many European countries, is more a figurehead than a powerful or vital actor in setting policy or shaping the political landscape. The division between president and prime minister follows that of most European countries: the president is the formal head of state and Greece's primary representative in the international arena, while the prime minister heads the state bureaucracy and hence is concerned with domestic matters and implementing policies at home.

The powers of the president are strongest in the realm of diplomacy. Here the president negotiates and concludes international treaties (which require parliamentary approval for implementation) and meets with foreign dignitaries and other heads of state. In this way the president is a "grand ambassador" responsible for international negotiations and presenting the fruits of such negotiations to the Parliament for acceptance. The president also has some powers in declaring war and accepting peace. While the president is nominally the commander in chief of the armed forces and formally has the power to declare war, actual domestic mobilization for war (i.e., actual engagement) can occur only if the Parliament implements a "state of siege." This prevents the president from acting on his own and possibly restricting the ability of another president to stand off against Parliament or call a state of emergency and reintroduce military rule.

Presidential powers in domestic affairs are more restricted. For example, most presidential acts are not valid unless countersigned by the prime minister or by the minister whose sphere of power and competence is most relevant to the presidential act. Only a few presidential acts do not require countersignature: appointing the prime minister, dissolving Parliament in the case of problems with selecting a president (see below, "Electoral System"), returning bills to Parliament for reconsideration (a weak veto), and appointing people to staff positions in the presidential administrative services (although the actual selection of who should fill these offices is decided by others). The president's veto consists of sending bills back to the Parliament for reconsideration; but Parliament may override this presidential veto if an absolute majority again votes in support of the bill. Additionally, the president may proclaim a referendum. In extraordinary circumstances—such as moments of crisis occurring when Parliament is not in session—the president may issue presidential acts that temporarily have the power of legislation. However, this power is also circumscribed. First, the president is supposed to issue such acts only when asked to do so by the Cabinet, and, second, such acts may be subject to parliamentary debate and approval or rejection when Parliament is able to meet once again. The president also has the power to grant pardons and to appoint and dismiss public servants.

Appointment of the prime minister might appear to be the president's greatest domestic power, but even this is a formality: the president, by the constitution, is required to appoint to the position the leader of the party having the absolute majority of seats in Parliament. (If no party has an absolute majority, the president must give the leader of the party with the relative majority an "exploratory mandate," which is the opportunity to ascertain whether a government can be formed that would have majority support in Parliament. If this fails, the president then extends this exploratory mandate to the second-largest party. This process continues either until a government is formed or until the president runs out of parties and either attempts to organize a Cabinet himself or turns to the Supreme Court to do so.) Once the prime minister assumes office, the president appoints those people chosen by the prime minister to fill the basic ministerial posts. If the government loses a vote of no confidence or the prime minister offers his resignation, the president can then remove the prime minister from office. Further, the president does have the power to dissolve Parliament—but only on the suggestion of the government.

In domestic politics the prime minister is far more powerful and important. He selects the ministers who run the government, and only he has the power to dismiss them. The prime minister and the Cabinet retain control over both the state bureaucracy and the formulation and implementation of policy—in essence giving the Cabinet control over day-to-day domestic affairs. The prime minister and the Cabinet have the authority to introduce legislation to the Parliament—in fact, the ministers exercise this power more than the legislature does, which is more concerned with fulfilling political patrons' needs and demands. The exact bounds of the prime minister's power depends also on the structure of power of the party he comes from. For example, if the majority party relies on national-level power, then the prime minister has increased power. But if the party relies on local political patronage machines and bases, then the prime minister is more indebted to these regional allies and will have to go some way to appease them, making it more difficult to control and discipline Cabinet members.

One leading figure in Greek politics and the executive branch for the last 20 years was Andreas Papandreou, leader of the Pan-Hellenic Socialist Movement (PASOK). With the rise to dominance of PASOK in the 1981 parliamentary elections Andreas Papandreou rose to prominence, becoming prime minister. Papandreou's personality (populist and nationalist) and party (ideologically centered and concerned with issues of justice) set the tone for Greek politics in the 1980s. However, illness led Papandreou to resign in late 1995. The PASOK party faction had to vote twice before finally deciding on a successor, Kostis Simitis. Simitis is a former lawyer and economist who served a stint as minister of industry. Simitis's image differs from that of Papandreou; while the latter was more populist and nationalist (especially in his first years as prime minister), Simitis has projected an image as a pragmatist and technocrat more oriented toward European affairs and closer collaboration with the

Continent. Simitis's initial policies included anticorruption drives within the state bureaucracy and an attempt to warm relations between Greece and the European Union and with the United States, with which relations had been rather chilly under Papandreou's watch.

Legislature

At the national level the Greek legislature is the Greek Parliament (*Vouli ton Ellinon*). A full quorum consists of 300 members; a minimum of 200 is needed for a legitimate parliamentary quorum to meet. In theory the legislature shares legislative responsibility with the ministers; in practice, however, the ministers write up and propose most legislation, and the Parliament debates and passes (or rejects) it. Parliamentary members act more as representatives of their home regions than as a nationally minded body (much like the U.S. House of Representatives). Their time is devoted to dealing with the needs and complaints of constituents and to amending legislation to ensure that their constituency receives its share of gain (or reduces its share of pain). In times when Parliament is not in session, some members remain in session as a sort of "mini-Parliament," so that the entire body does not have to be in session for the full calendar year.

Legislation must pass through three readings in Parliament before it is considered passed. In the first vote Parliament considers the general principle of the bill. In the second vote the component parts and divisions of the bill are discussed, debated, and voted on one at a time. In the third reading the Parliament votes on the entire bill itself. While such a system may appear cumbersome—and undoubtedly does suffer from a degree of slowness and inefficiency—it also guarantees closer deliberation of policies and laws. (Such a system also presents ample opportunity for legislators to introduce their own pet changes.)

One additional power Parliament has is the vote of no confidence over the ministries. Once the government is formed, Parliament must table a vote of confidence within 15 days. Additionally, at a later date Parliament may table a vote of confidence in individual ministers or in the government as a whole. Such a motion requires support of one-sixth of members to be introduced. If an absolute majority of deputies supports the measure, the individual or the government as a whole (depending on the target of the vote) must resign. If the vote of no confidence fails, it cannot be introduced for another six months; an exception is if an absolute majority supports a no-confidence motion ahead of time, which would be binding. The probability of a vote of no confidence passing or of another such motion being introduced before the end of the six-month grace period is reduced by the fact that the government is organized by the majority or plurality party. Greek election procedure appears to bring the high probability that one party will have either a majority or a plurality; and because the government will come from this party, only a serious split within party ranks would make a no-confidence vote likely to succeed, guaranteeing a degree of political stability that other countries—such as Italy or many Eastern European countries—can only envy.

Judiciary

The judicial system has three parts. The most important is the Supreme Court, the highest court in Greece. Appeals move their way up from lower courts to this ultimate court. The second court at the top level is the Council of State, which handles administrative issues and the legality of government acts. For example, issues of constitutionality are addressed to the Council of State, which can then rule on and support or reject laws. Because the Council of State rules on constitutionality and because the constitution is the law of the land, decisions by the Council of State are binding on all governmental branches. In this way, the duties of deciding on appeals and on issues of constitutionality—duties fulfilled by a single Supreme Court in many other countries—are split between the Supreme Court and the Council of State. The third high court, the Comptrollers' Council, is responsible for overseeing government accounts and preventing fraud by governmental or administrative personnel. At times a special fourth court, the Special Supreme Court, convenes. The job of this body is to resolve disputes between different courts and to address electoral problems (disputed returns or problematic results of election procedures).

Judges are not directly elected but rather are appointed by special councils made up by judges. Judges work their way up the hierarchy, replacing those above them who die or retire (usually at the age of 65 or 67). In this way the judiciary resembles a professional bureaucracy. While councils of judges recommend the motion up and down the hierarchy, prosecutors have some input in recommending candidates, and the actual appointment and promotion decisions are made by the president.

Regional and Local Government

The constitution provides local administrative organs with a degree of autonomy from the national level, although this autonomy is not total or absolute. At the base Greece is divided into 256 deme (demos in singular) and almost 5,700 communities. (To be considered a demos a community must have at least 10,000 people.) At the next rung up, Greece is divided into 51 local divisions, called nome (nomos in singular). The nomos is run by an agent appointed by the central government, so local administration is not totally free from centralized influence. In fact, many important decisions are made only with input and suggestions from the central government. PASOK has tried to decentralize and increase local autonomy and decision making, but such efforts have had little real impact. For many day-to-day banal cases of decision making, however, local agents handle their own affairs without recourse to central administration—although the local level is dominated by local elites, making local democracy not entirely participatory.

Localities also have legislative councils, elected every four years. If the community has fewer than 5,000 people, the council has five members; more than 5,000 people gives a community a council with as few as 11 to as many as 61 members. Also, a demos is entitled to have a popularly elected mayor.

Politics at the local level is less tied to political parties than is national politics. While national parties may have a presence in major urban areas—especially PASOK and KKE, which have made an effort to extend party organization to the local level—they are less present and important in smaller communities, where particularistic and personal connections and the rule of families and clans are more important. This may change, however, as Greek politics and the Greek economy continue to bureaucratize and centralize.

THE ELECTORAL SYSTEM

Parliamentary elections are crucial to Greek national politics because the processes of selecting both the president and the prime minister go through parliamentary procedure rather than through national ballots. The president is chosen through election within the Parliament and sits for a five-year term and may be chosen for no more than two terms. To stand for the presidency a person must have been a Greek citizen for at least five years, must be at least 40 years old, must be eligible to vote, and must have Greek family heritage through the father's bloodline. By a secret ballot the Parliament votes for the president 1 month before the end of the current president's term. On the first ballot a successful candidate must receive two-thirds of the total number of Parliament members (300—therefore, 200 votes needed). If this majority is not reached, a second round of voting takes place 5 days later, and here again a two-thirds majority is needed. If this round fails, a third round occurs 5 days hence, when a three-fifths majority (180 votes) is needed. If in this third round of parliamentary voting no candidate receives the necessary majority, Parliament is dissolved within 10 days of the failed third round; this acts as an incentive against intraparliamentary infighting. After convocation of the newly elected Parliament, the rules for election become more lenient: first a three-fifths majority; if this fails, a new round of voting takes place within 5 days, and the candidate receiving an absolute majority wins; if even this fails, then the top two vote-receiving candidates continue to another round 5 days later, where whoever receives the relative majority of votes is proclaimed the new president.

Parliamentary elections are held every four years, although it is not unusual for parliamentary elections to be called ahead of schedule. The most recent parliamentary election was such a case, held one year ahead of schedule. PASOK retained its dominant position, garnering almost 42% of the total vote and ending up with 54% of the overall seats in the Parliament, retaining a majority it has held since the 1981 elections.

The system for parliamentary elections is as follows. The Greek nation is divided into 56 constituencies, and the numbers of delegates from each constituency depends on population size. Direct election in these constituencies provides 288 of the 300 seats. An additional 12 seats (called "deputies of state") are reserved for party lists; the proportion of the 12 seats a party receives depends on the proportion of the overall aggregate vote that party obtained.

In 1995 Kostis Stephanopoulos was elected president by the Parliament for a five-year term. The previous president was Constantine Karamanlis.

Parliamentary Composition 1993–96 (election held October 10, 1993)

Party	% of Total Votes	Seats
Pan-Hellenic Socialist Movement (PASOK)	46.9	170
New Democracy (ND)	39.3	111
Political Spring (POLA)	4.87	10
Communist Party of Greece (KKE)	4.54	9
Progressive Left[a]	2.94	—
Independent		1

Source: CIA Factbook, 1996.
[a]Replaced by Coalition of the Left and Progress (SIN).

Parliamentary Election and Composition (election held September 22, 1996)

Party	% of Total Votes	Seats (300)
Pan-Hellenic Socialist Movement (PASOK)	41.5	162
New Democracy (ND)	38.1	108
Communist Party of Greece (KKE)	5.6	11
Coalition of the Left and Progress (SIN)	5.1	10
Democratic Social Movement (DIKKI)	4.4	9
Political Spring (POLA)	2.9	—

Source: "Elections around the World." Ed. Wilfried Derkson: http://www.agora.stm.it/elections/election/greece.htm

---

Overall the electorate has shifted to the left since the end of military rule in 1974 and the rise to prominence of PASOK. New Democracy saw a brief return to power in

1989, but since then both New Democracy and the right wing as a whole have steadily lost support in the last two parliamentary elections. However, the right wing's loss has not translated into PASOK's gains, as PASOK has also lost some support since 1993. The recipients of displaced faith in New Democracy and PASOK have been the Coalition of the Left and Progress and the Democratic Social Movement, both more center-left and less nationalist than PASOK or KKE. In general, then, the polity remains left-leaning but not radical, realizing the need to integrate with Europe and to control macroeconomic problems yet without wanting to give up the Greek welfare system.

THE PARTY SYSTEM

The basis of the Greek political system would appear to be political parties, but this is only partially the case. Political parties arose in Greece after World War II and were given legal support by a right in the 1975 constitution for citizens to organize or join in political parties so long as they did not attempt to break democratic traditions or overthrow democratic institutions (no doubt a legacy of the years of military rule). The number of political parties participating in elections has varied; some parties die out, others are created anew, and other reorganize or split. Forming a political party in Greece is fairly easy. All that is required is registration with the Supreme Court's public prosecutor. There are, however, a few parties that have remained over time and have continued to be players (with varying degrees of power) over the last two decades.

While Greek parties span the political spectrum, left-wing parties have more support and are thus more represented in the legislature. One the one hand, this should not surprising, given the strong history and organization of socialist movements in Greece following World War II. However, there is one caveat: political parties do not adhere intensely to ideology. Rather, like American parties, Greek parties claim to follow an ideology, but the actors within the parties are more pragmatic in outlook. As a result, parties tend to be less highly organized bodies (such as Communist Parties in Eastern Europe) and more like factions under the parliamentary umbrella—that is, parties were more coalitions of political elites or parliamentary deputies, alliances created for political or electoral expediency instead of for the disciplined mobilization of support and resources. This has helped make Greek political party life fluid. Mobilization of support or the rise to power involves the use of political connections and deal making in order to obtain support and votes. As a result, patronage was and remains a central feature of political and party life. Party bosses make it to the top of their parties and into Parliament through deals and alliances, and once in power they have to pay off those who helped their rise.

Such links and chains of patronage from national to local levels, rather than a formal party structure, have been the motor of political action within Greece. One result has been shifting membership: people do not feel themselves to be members of a particular party or organization toward which they should be loyal, but rather they link themselves to individuals on the basis of material gifts in exchange for votes and other forms of political support. Another result of this system is that party movements tend to be personalized, with party organization less bureaucratic and more centered around individuals; because of this, electoral defeats, retirement, or other means of exit from the political stage can lead to the fragmenting of a political party. Adding to this underinstitutionalization of parties has been the fact that parties could not count on home bases, such as workers' movements, middle-class groups, or other such entities, because of Greece's corporatism: the state controlled such bodies and kept them out of the political arena.

Two currents have begun to alter this particularistic party system. First has been changes in Greek economic and social life. The rise of a national media has provided an alternative route to the voter, replacing the development of social networks of patronage and deals. The growth and bureaucratization of the state apparatus have made fulfillment of promises through patronage more difficult, leaving voters and local elites to search for alternative means to achieving political ends. The second current altering this pattern of underinstitutionalization is the Pan-Hellenic Socialist Movement (PASOK), which emerged in the 1974 elections as a unified, organized party able to mobilize support and members for political and electoral action.

Right-wing parties held control of Greek politics from the 1950s until 1977, when PASOK, participating for the second time in national elections, began to gain strength. In 1981, PASOK both took control of Greek politics and had a coattail effect for other left-leaning groups, who benefited and saw an increase in electoral support over the last 20 years. In 1981 the Greek electorate shifted to the left, and while one right-wing party (New Democracy, see below) remains prominent, others have faded and lost much of their political influence and parliamentary power. This left-wing hegemony explains much of the growth of the state sector and other socialist programs in the Greek economy, regardless of the reaction against left-wing economic programs throughout much of the world (especially in the Western Hemisphere but also in Europe) in the 1980s. However, such left-wing politics led to a backlash (perhaps helped by the problems in the communist world in 1988–89). In 1989 power shifted back to the right as PASOK lost ground in the parliamentary elections—due to corruption charges and a publicized affair between Papandreou and a younger woman—and the New Democracy party gained a majority, putting party leader Constantine Mitsotakis into the prime minister post. The New Democracy government introduced austerity measures (reducing social benefits and raising prices) to prepare the Greek economy for integration into the European economy along the lines of the Maastrict Treaty. Privatization measures (for example, of the giant Greek telecommunications networks) were planned but not implemented, as the right-wing victory was short-lived.

After some political turmoil, public reaction against New Democracy's austerity measures and economic programs, and problems within the New Democracy ranks, parliamentary elections were held six months ahead of schedule in 1993, and PASOK stunned the political world with a major comeback, gaining 46.9% of the national vote and, through the Greek system of awarding extra seats to majority parties, gained 171 seats, putting Papandreou back into the position of prime minister.

There are two dominant parties—PASOK and New Democracy—with a third party, the Greek Communist Party, a stable but minority player. Beyond these three parties the picture begins to become more fuzzy, as parties rise, gain seats in an election, and then promptly lose them in the next (or the party reorganizes itself). Thus the political scene is of two protagonists, one important minor player, and several extra stagehands wandering on and off the political stage.

PAN-HELLENIC SOCIALIST MOVEMENT
(Panellino Socialistiko Kinima; PASOK)

HISTORY

Founded in September 1974 by the late Andreas Papandreou and drawing on members of the earlier Center Union Party (headed by George Papandreou, Andreas's father), PASOK initially grew out of the resistance movement against the 1967–74 military regime. Since then PASOK has been gathering strength and, with the exception of the 1989–93 period, has been the majority parliamentary party since 1981.

ORGANIZATION

PASOK's rise to prominence stems from two factors: the organization of the party and from its figurehead, Papandreou. As mentioned earlier, Greek political parties were more like masks for social networks and ties of patronage; while this lent a degree of pragmatism, it also made mobilization for a particular cause, program, or ideology difficult. Under Papandreou PASOK emerged as a more Western-style party: highly organized and hierarchical, disciplined, organizing local-level party cells rather than political personal ties, mobilizing the resources of the mass media to take a political message directly to voters. Organizationally, PASOK's structure resembles a pyra-

mid: a wide base of local-level cells, running up through intermediary levels to the upper-level leaders and the national PASOK congresses. Such an organizational framework brings two results. First, PASOK can convey a sense of "partyness" that other parties do not have, a sense of community and ideology, that one actually belongs to a party. This has helped PASOK energize grassroots support, both for votes and for actual party work. Second, such a framework has allowed PASOK to coordinate political strategies, including spreading political messages and challenging local-level political bosses who still run their bailiwicks through patronage networks to leaders in Parliament or the state bureaucracy. This has helped PASOK recruit young blood away from other parties.

The second advantage PASOK enjoyed in its rise to power was the figure of Andreas Papandreou. Papandreou could count on his father's positive image to boost his own appeal among the electorate. Papandreou was also an outspoken populist: for example, he caused an international stir when entering power with his biting criticisms of the United States. However, he has used his populism to enhance his image in Greece and attract support, implicitly comparing his populist care for the people with the paternalistic patronage of political competitors. Along with his organizational skills and charismatic and political appeal, Papandreou was somewhat mercurial and even dictatorial. As the number one person within the party, Papandreou was not overly tolerant of dissenting views, and at times he expelled people from the party for challenging his authority. While this side of Papandreou's personality may have had its costs (losing members), it also gave Papandreou an aura of authority. (This aura was occasionally tarnished, as before 1989, when corruption, especially ties to corrupt banker Georgios Koskotas and an affair, tarnished Papandreou's image and made him seem out of touch with real political life and more concerned with his own personal affairs.) Finally, Papandreou, unlike his political peers, grasped the importance and centrality of ideology for a modern political party: ideology gives an identity and sense of meaning to a party and can create a political community, holding a party together and making mobilization less costly. Both these factors (organization and personality) have brought results: a PASOK hegemony on parliamentary elections and politics since 1981, when PASOK gained 48% of the vote and thanks to Greek electoral rules ended up with 172 members, its first parliamentary majority.

MEMBERSHIP AND CONSTITUENCY

PASOK's ideology was initially populist, combining leftism and a hint of nationalism; the party united under the slogan "national independence, popular sovereignty, and social liberation." The main policy stance was that Greece had two immediate problems: underdevelopment (and economic dependence on the industrialized world) and social inequality. While still in a minority (following the 1974 and 1977 elections) PASOK hammered this theme home against opponents: New Democracy was not running Greece in the interest of Greece but rather in the interest of domestic elites and international capital. Upon taking power in 1981 PASOK more clearly defined its goals, which focused on reducing inequality and social injustice, developing the Greek economy and gaining some autonomy from international finance, maintaining territorial integrity, and enhancing Greek cultural feelings and overall quality of life. In the arena of international relations, Papandreou stressed nationalist values and concerns; in particular, he was upset with the lack of American support for Greece against Turkey, and PASOK considered withdrawing Greece from NATO and evicting American armed forces from bases on Greek territory. (These demands were dropped soon after, however.) Initial domestic policies sought to address populist issues of injustice and inequality through state intervention and met with some success: income inequality was reduced somewhat, and the underprivileged received legislation giving them more rights in society. However, there was a downside to these policies. Unemployment actually increased, and increased state control of the economy led to spiraling budget deficits and, as a result, inflation. PASOK policies, which thanks to party rhetoric gained an antifinance and antibusiness image, hurt investment from both domestic and foreign sources, adding to economic troubles. As a result, PASOK lost some support in the 1985 elections, although it still held a parliamentary majority (slimmed down from 172 to 161 delegates out of 300). After the 1985 elections PASOK's policies took a more centrist turn, with a stress on attracting investment and implementing austerity measures. This led to unpopularity and hurt PASOK. First, the Communist Party (KKE) tried to mobilize popular discontent and to foment strikes against the austerity policies. Second, as a result of the unpopular (and "unpopulist") measures, PASOK lost its majority in the 1989 elections.

PASOK was not out for long, however; thanks to even harsher neo-orthodox policies and government splits and scandals, New Democracy frittered away its public support (see below), and PASOK returned to power in October 1993. Rather than make a left turn in economic policy, Papandreou and PASOK continued to follow a more neo-orthodox path, albeit with less stress on privatization. Most important was coming to terms with the government deficit and the inflation rate; the Papandreou government adopted spending controls and focused on increasing revenue collection to reduce the deficit and bring down inflation. In 1995 Papandreou left politics due to illness, and died soon after. How PASOK's organization, ideology, policy stance, and fortunes will be affected is unclear at present. His successor, Kostis Simitis, appears to be a more technocratic, less populist, more pragmatic leader. Whether this type of figurehead will have electoral appeal in the new political world of the late 1990s and the 21st century remains to be seen.

FINANCING

While obtaining exact information on membership and finances is difficult, general trends can be discerned. PASOK's actual membership has grown, particularly among younger voters, turning PASOK into a full-fledged mass-mobilizing party. In class respects, PASOK draws support from the middle and lower-middle class, from rural regions, and from the rising managerial class (distinct from capitalist owners or controllers of financial institutions).

NEW DEMOCRACY
(Nea Demokratia; ND)

HISTORY

New Democracy is the standard-bearer for the Greek right wing, remaining as the major player outside the socialist camp to have a sizable number of seats in Parliament. New Democracy was founded in 1974 by Constantine Karamanlis, based on the party he had founded in 1955, National Radical Union. Riding a right-wing wave, New Democracy held parliamentary majorities after the 1974 and 1977 elections but fell out of power until a brief majority after the 1989 elections. In 1980 Karamanlis, who had been prime minister since 1974, was elected president by Parliament and George Rallis became party leader and subsequent prime minister. Under Rallis's leadership New Democracy lost its majority in the 1981 elections, and Rallis was replaced by Evangelos Averoff-Tositsas, who resigned in 1985 and was replaced by Constantine Mitsotakis. As a result of leadership changes, the loss of parliamentary majority, and other debates, New Democracy went into a period of confusion over what its central ideology and programmatic stance should be.

New Democracy briefly returned to power after special June 1989 parliamentary elections. Scandals (including Papandreou's affair with a younger woman, whom he subsequently married), corruption, and the leader's ill health hurt PASOK, and the electorate turned to New Democracy for a sea change. However, ND did not receive a majority and so had to form a coalition—with, surprisingly, KKE (the Communist Party). This coalition ran Greece until the November 1989 elections, when ND gained more seats but was still shy of the majority. (PASOK, in a remarkable comeback, increased its showing over the June 1989 elections.) The KKE refused to join a right-wing coalition, and so the leaders of PASOK, KKE, and ND joined to form a temporary government of national unity. But this "grand coalition" soon broke down, leading to new elections in 1990, at which point

New Democracy finally received a parliamentary majority and could take control of the government. However, as described above, right-wing austerity programs invited a backlash from a population used to some socialist social safety net; responses included strike waves in 1991 and 1992. Further, two other events broke New Democracy's victory: the conflict over the independence of the Yugoslavian Macedonia and the resulting exit of Antonis Samaras. When the Yugoslavian enclave of Macedonia became independent, Greece, especially through its foreign minister, Samaras, issued objections to aspects of Macedonia's independence process. First, Macedonia could not call itself "Macedonia," since this referred to the Greek territory. Second, Samaras and Greek leaders feared that Macedonian independence would have repercussions in the Greek Macedonian territory or that the former Yugoslavian Macedonia might have territorial intentions against Greek sovereign territory. Eventually the Greek leadership gave in when Yugoslavian Macedonia adopted the name "The Former Yugoslav Republic of Macedonia," but this did not suit Foreign Minister Samaras's uncompromising stance. Samaras was forced to resign, but he did not leave quietly. Instead, Samaras formed a right-wing alternative party, Political Spring, and defectors followed Samaras from New Democracy to the new party. As a result, New Democracy lost its slim majority in Parliament and had to call for early elections. Between public bitterness over policies and the spectacle of the Macedonian issue and party fragmentation after Samaras's defection, New Democracy lost its majority position to PASOK in 1993.

ORGANIZATION

New Democracy followed the normal Greek model of party organization, which is a collection of leaders with charisma and/or political connections and backstage deals to stay in power. Such a structure succeeded in winning parliamentary majorities in 1974 and 1977, but it did not help New Democracy beat out PASOK for the majority in 1981. Thus, an attempt was made to transform New Democracy into a more bureaucratic, formally structured organization, with local cells and a formal hierarchy and schedule of meetings and congresses. This process has been difficult, since creating a formal structure contradicts the practices and incentives of parliamentary members who draw power from the network form and would prefer to maintain that system. Also, candidate recruitment and generational turnover have plagued New Democracy (and other parties as well), because the use of networks rather than formal structure makes nomination of younger delegates and their rise to power (à la Britain's Tony Blair) more difficult.

New Democracy did not have a central ideology or political identity; rather, positions and programs espoused by New Democracy tended to reflect the style and substance of party elites, especially Karamanlis and Mit-

sotakis. Karamanlis's legacy was that of an activist state and anticommunism—a fusion of left-wing domestic policies and right-wing rhetoric and identity. Under the National Radical Union, in the 1950s and the 1960s, state activity in the economy expanded (especially in industrial statization and welfare expansion). In the 1970s and early 1980s New Democracy supported a status quo, hoping to build on the memory of stability in the 1950s and 1960s under the National Radical Union's watch. However, this ploy failed, and in the mid-1980s New Democracy rhetoric, under Mitsotakis, turned away from state-led economic policies (which could placate the electorate) to neo-orthodoxy, which under the Thatcher-Reagan banner was sweeping the globe. Such a set of policy positions called for more attention to macroeconomic problems of inflation and budget deficits over concern for welfare and a state-regulated or state-controlled economy. This was the position followed after the 1989 parliamentary victory; however, neo-orthodox prescriptions brought only voter anger in the 1993 elections. New Democracy, then, has moved from the more personalized, politically contingent policies of the National Radical Union legacy to a more neo-orthodox, conservative stance; to call this a party ideology might be a stretch, although this policy stance appears to be gelling as a centerpiece of New Democracy policy and identity. While building a formal party structure has been problematic—although far from defeated—an ideological identity appears to be coming into being, bringing New Democracy closer to the European type of political party.

In foreign policy New Democracy is more consistent: ties to Europe and the United States and continued participation in NATO. Strains appeared, however, after the 1974 Turkish invasion of Cyprus, to which the United States did not strenuously object. As a result Greece moved out of participation in NATO's military procedures and activities, although Greece under New Democracy's watch remained a member. Recent neo-orthodox economic prescriptions from 1989–93 were aimed at further integration in the European economy, continuing a Europe-centered tradition of New Democracy going back to the National Radical Union.

COMMUNIST PARTY OF GREECE

(Kommunistiko Komma Ellados; KKE)

HISTORY

The KKE is currently the third-largest party in Greece, a position it has held since 1981. KKE was originally founded in 1918 in the wave of communism that engulfed Europe following the Bolshevik coming to power in Russia. However, the KKE was not a significant political force before World War II. The KKE gained popularity through its anti-Nazi partisan activities, but the KKE exhausted this support through its insurgent activities in the Greek civil war of 1946–47. After the end of the civil war the KKE was temporarily outlawed; party activists who remained in Greece continued their political operations through the guise of other parties, such as the United Democratic Left (which was disbanded in the 1967 military coup). After the return to democracy in 1974 the KKE was allowed to organize itself into a formal party. However, this did not mean a full return to normal political activity: while KKE is a highly organized and disciplined group, it has also suffered splits, defections, and loss of center-left-leaning support to rivals such as PASOK, the Communist Party of the Interior, or newer groups such as Coalition of the Left and Progress and the Democratic Socialist Movement. The collapse of communism and the East Bloc have also tarnished KKE's image and made it more marginal than earlier.

ORGANIZATION

This attempt to maintain a separate, unique, and attractive identity amidst competition from other left-wing groups has been a major goal and expenditure of effort for KKE. (Another major goal—combating the influence and power of right-wing capitalism and imperialism—was temporarily gained with the turn of the electorate to the left in the 1980s but has been lost somewhat with the return of New Democracy and neo-orthodox policies in the 1990s.) Here KKE has been caught in a bind. On the one hand, PASOK is an ally because it is on the left and identifies with many Communist goals (especially addressing social inequality and injustice and promoting Greek autonomy over outside capitalist forces). However, PASOK is a very popular competitor, and because PASOK has been able to garner parliamentary majorities, KKE does not have much room for negotiating with PASOK over public policy. Hence, while KKE may be satisfied with a left-wing parliamentary majority, it is a majority of another party. Thus, KKE wants both to support and challenge PASOK.

In terms of policy recommendations, KKE still holds to Soviet-style Communist ideology and has made little move to a more post–cold war center-left stance. KKE desires an end to NATO and American military presence in Greece, wishes for Greece to leave the European Economic Community (which would lead to increased foreign financial domination), and calls for more Greek autonomy vis-à-vis the policies of other industrialized nations. In the domestic realm, in addition to policies of social justice, KKE has called for strict regulation or breaking up of monopolies.

MEMBERSHIP AND CONSTITUENCY

While KKE does have a strong grasp on the more extreme left wing of Greek politics and while it appears that KKE's support is not declining (hovering around 4–5% and 10 deputies in Parliament since 1974), KKE also does not appear to be moving up either. PASOK, through its organization and popular appeal of Papandreou, has captured the center-left and left KKE in a marginal position. Further, given PASOK's near-constant majoritarian status, KKE is not needed for forming a coalition of the left and hence does not have the leverage it would need to be a force in national politics. Only an erosion of PASOK power—which still may occur after Papandreou's death—could bring KKE increased influence. Even in such a case, KKE needs to develop tighter organization both to the grassroots level and to springs of resources and support, so that it can mobilize to take advantage of weaknesses in PASOK or New Democracy fortunes.

FINANCING

Figures on KKE's support are difficult to determine, as party membership in Greece is not a strong signal of popularity. KKE claims on membership have fluctuated but in the last decade have hovered around the 600,000-member mark. The majority of Communist support comes from two sources, the working class and Greeks not born in Greece (e.g., Greeks expelled from other countries). KKE also has support from many islands with depressed economic conditions.

MINOR POLITICAL PARTIES

Greek political life is mostly divided between New Democracy and PASOK, with some minor influence by KKE. There are other smaller Greek parties that so far have been marginal, for three reasons. First, many of them are new and need to create a base of recognition, acceptance, and support among the electorate. Second, because Greek politics is still patronage-centered, creating a viable party movement takes time in order to develop personal connections. Third, given possible changes in political structure, party organization may become more important, and creating a viable party structure requires effort, material resources, and a leadership capable of bringing and holding together and disciplining a central core and semiperiphery of activists and supporters. Minor Greek parties still struggle with such problems and with the resulting state of marginalization that hinders further party growth.

Coalition of the Left and Progress (Sinaspismos tis Aristeras ke ti Proodu; SIN),

Greek politics have seen the rise, fall, and reorganization of small left-wing parties. The second Communist Party, KKE-Interior (see below), merged with other left-wing parties to form the Progressive Left (which received only 2.9% of the vote in 1993); the Progresssive Left was again reorganized into the Coalition of the Left and Progress (*Sinaspismos tis Aristeras ke ti Proodu*, SIN), which received 5.1% and 10 seats in the 1996 elections. Some of this gain appears to have come at the expense of

PASOK, whose support declined by more than 5% from 1993 to 1996. SIN is a left-leaning socialist party competing with PASOK for the center-left part of the electorate sympathetic to moderate socialist policies (such as welfare and a state presence in the economy). SIN also is more pro-European than other left-wing groups, and economic platforms are similar to those of 1990s PASOK and New Democracy. SIN's largest problem is that ideologically SIN resembles PASOK and thus must compete with PASOK for the center-left electorate.

Democratic Social Movement
(Dimokratiki Kinoniku Kinima; DIKKI)

The Democratic Social Movement (*Dimokratiki Kinoniku Kinima*; DIKKI) enjoyed entry into parliamentary politics when finally in 1996 it gained 4.4% of the vote and nine parliamentary seats. DIKKI appears to be more European-oriented and less nationalist than other left-leaning parties. Most likely DIKKI gained its electoral support from the same wellspring as SIN: the decline in PASOK fortunes.

Greek Communist Party of the Interior
(Kommunistiko Komma Ellados-Essoterikou; KKE-Interior),

KKE-Interior is another previous left-leaning Greek party, which briefly was a direct competitor to KKE for the left wing; however, KKE-Interior's support was solely from large cities (especially Athens) and stemmed from the popularity of leader Leonidas Kyrkos. KKE-Interior merged with other small leftist groups to form SIN.

Democratic Renewal
(Demokratiki Ananeosi; DA)

On the right wing, the small Democratic Renewal (*Demokratiki Ananeosi*, DA) party, founded in 1985 as a splinter from New Democracy, was formed out of personal rather than ideological differences with ND. Democratic Renewal did not fare well at the polls.

Political Spring
(Politiki Anixi; POLA)

One conservative alternative to New Democracy that enjoyed a moment in the sun and the hopes of survival was Political Spring (*Politiki Anixi*; POLA). Political Spring came into being in 1993 when the former foreign minister Antonis Samaras left New Democracy after disputes over the handling of Yugoslav Macedonian independence. Political Spring ran on a right-wing ticket, but its program was not really different from that of New Democracy—neo-orthodox, technocratic, with slightly more nationalist sentiment than New Democracy—with the exception of taking a hard line on the Macedonian issue and using stronger nationalist rhetoric. After the split Political Spring had a respectable showing for a new small party—4.87% of the vote in the 1993 elections and 10 deputies (with an additional deputy coming from New Democracy some time after the 1993 elections). However, since 1993 Political Spring's fortunes have declined, owing no doubt to the inability of the party to organize itself, to increase its presence, and to attract support away from other right-wing groups; in 1996 Political Spring gained only 2.9% and did not receive a single seat in the Parliament.

OTHER POLITICAL FORCES

The Military

From 1967 to 1974 the Greek military controlled political life, in response to threats from communism. However, blunders in the domestic and international spheres (including a near miss with a war with Turkey) led to the military's turning political control back to a civilian government. Given the collapse of communism internationally, memories of the military intervention, and a subterranean break within the officer corps (with higher-ranking officers in favor of more right-wing politics and younger junior officers closer to PASOK or PASOK-style center-left politics), it is unlikely that the military will venture back into the political realm anytime soon (barring serious political instability or a severe crisis).

In 1996 Greece's armed forces stood at around 188,000 regulars in all three branches combined, plus a paramilitary force of 30,500 men. Almost 2.05 million males are considered fit for potential military service. In 1995 defense expenditures were approximately $4.9 billion, around 4.6% of GDP.

NATIONAL PROSPECTS

Greece does not appear overly troubled by its authoritarian past; unlike the experience in many postauthoritarian nations, legacies of the military period of rule do not appear to have carried over to the present day. The transition to democracy appears complete, and democratic institutions—in spite of the problems of patronage and corruption (familiar to many other democracies)—appear vibrant. The leftist parties in control of politics are not radical and most likely will not lead Greece down a radicalized and unstable path anytime soon (as was the case in Allende's pre-1973 Chile).

One problem for Greece concerns economic change. While Greece hopes to integrate itself into the European Union, its high budget deficit and large state sector make such efforts at further integration troublesome. Further, while anti-inflationary austerity measures have helped ease macroeconomic problems somewhat, additional structural reforms—especially privatization—might have to be the next serious step for Greece to escape economic doldrums. An unemployment rate of around 9.6 %—not the highest in Europe but still high—must also be addressed, especially through promotion of the private sector. Whether Simitis can pull off such structural reforms, especially given the left-leaning composition of the Parliament and the public support for the middle-left, remains to be seen. Privatization and orthodox reform helped oust New Democracy from power in 1993; perhaps the left wing, the providers and defenders of social justice and social provision, can have better luck at economic structural reforms and managing the social pain that might accompany them. For such reforms to work, Greece will have to lock into a healthy European economy; and as the frustrations of Eastern European reformers reveal, such hopes of exporting to happiness via a healthy Western Europe are for the time being problematic.

Another problematic area of Greek politics concerns the fate of Cyprus. This island nation remains divided between Greek and Turkish enclaves, and unification does not appear to be on the immediate horizon. The tension between the two enclaves is exacerbated by economic differences (the Greek enclave is far more prosperous than the Turkish enclave). The lack of American support for Greek claims—difficult for the United States to do, given that both Greece and Turkey are members of NATO and that at present American international interests are stronger in Turkey—helped flame anti-American sentiment, sentiment that only increased with the anti-American and prosocialist rhetoric of Andreas Papandreou and PASOK. The rise of Islamic feelings in Turkey may not help ease the tensions in Cyprus—and hence the tensions between Greece and Turkey and the United States—anytime soon. Until the Cyprus question is settled, Greek foreign policies will continue to revolve around this thorny issue and bring some measure of tension into political relations. Additionally, problems and instability in Yugoslavia—especially the fears that an independent Yugoslav-Macedonia state either may have territorial intentions on Greek Macedonia or may promote internal strife—will make for additional foreign policy headaches in the near future.

The final issue that must be faced is "modernization"—not the modernization of stratospheric social science theory but the industrialization of the economy and its insertion into a wider European economy and the bureaucratization of party politics and the creation of more democratic, maneuverable, and stable political parties. Industrialization, especially via the private path, requires macroeconomic planning. Creating a system of modern parties requires a breakup of older patronage networks. This means changing the incentives of the party elite (who at present would lose in a transformation from patronage-based to bureaucratic party politics) and rooting out corruption (creating negative incentives for patronage and personal networks). Certainly, personal networks are present in all political systems, but a political system firmly founded on and grounded in such a set of networks makes for corruption and difficulty both in mobilizing the public around important issues and in permitting the rise of competent "new blood" into politics. Party reform can only partially be legislated from above; just as important is the morale provided by PASOK's organizational form. If PASOK can use this organizational form to survive the post-Papandreou era, avoiding splits and defections and maintaining its form and procedures, then other parties will likely follow in order to gain the same advantages as PASOK. The only problem could be potential backlash from voters and local elites accustomed to receiving some form of material support, rather than ideological satisfaction, in return for votes. If this transformation does indeed take place, it could be the most important historical legacy left by the mercurial Andreas Papandreou, the enfant terrible of Europe who so colored Greek politics for 20 years.

Further Reading

CIA Factbook, 1996. Washington. D.C.: Government Printing Office, 1996.

Clogg, Richard, ed. *Greece 1981–1989: The Populist Decade.* New York: St. Martin's Press, 1993.

Curtis, Glenn E., ed. *Greece: A Country Study.* Washington, D.C.: Federal Research Division, Library of Congress, 1995.

The Economist.

Web Sites

"Elections in Greece." Ed. Wilfried Derkson: http://www.agora.stm.it/elections/election/greece.htm

The Greek constitution: http://www.agora.stm.it/greece.htm

GRENADA

By Thomas D. Anderson, Ph.D.

THE SYSTEM OF GOVERNMENT

Grenada is an island country of only 340 square kilometers that lies north of the Galleons Passage across from Trinidad-Tobago. The capital is St. Georges. The largely black, English-speaking population of over 94,000 is 98% literate. The island's annual population growth rate is only 0.35%, which is aided by an emigration rate of -20.6 per 1,000 births.

Grenada is a parliamentary democracy that gained independence from Britain in 1974. In 1979, leaders of a bloodless coup d'état proclaimed a one-party socialist state. Murders of the original leaders by more radical members in October 1983 led to an invasion to restore order by a joint U.S.-Caribbean military force. The governor-general then appointed a nine-member Advisory Council that administered the country until general elections were held to restore the parliamentary system in December 1984.

Executive

The chief of state is the British monarch represented by a governor-general who appoints as prime minister the head of the majority party of Parliament. The prime minister holds effective executive power through a Cabinet appointed from members of the legislature.

Legislature

The bicameral legislature consists of a 13-member Senate appointed by the governor-general, 10 upon the advice of the prime minister and 3 on advice of the leaders of the opposition. The 15 members of the House of Representatives serve five-year terms following direct elections. Parliament is empowered to introduce bills and with a two-thirds majority can change the constitution, which dates from December 19, 1973.

The first postindependence legislature was controlled by Eric Gairy's Grenada United Labour Party (GULP), which won nine seats to six for an alliance of opposition parties, despite the fact that Gairy had been removed by the Crown in 1962 for malfeasance as premier. In March 1979, when the New JEWEL Movement seized power, it suspended the constitution and dissolved Parliament. Upon the restoration of democracy in 1984, the New National Party (NNP), a centrist coalition headed by Herbert Blaize, won control of the House.

Judiciary

The judicial system is based on English common law. The law is administered by the Supreme Court of the Judicature, which is composed of the High Court of Justice and a Court of Appeals, the highest court in the land. Further appeals may be sent to the Privy Council of the British Monarch.

Regional and Local Government

Grenada is divided into six parishes and one dependency (the small islands of Carriacou and Petit Martinique in the Grenadines). Although local government structures were effectively eliminated under the arbitrary rule of both Eric Gairy and the NJM, they have been reinstituted following a series of regional discussions by the NNP government.

Grenada has universal suffrage for citizens of 18 years or older. General elections are scheduled every five years. An independent civil servant, the supervisor of elections, oversees voter registration and the conduct of elections.

THE PARTY SYSTEM

From the institution of universal suffrage in 1951 until the NJM coup in 1979, Eric Gairy's GULP dominated Grenadian politics. Gairy was the first political figure to seek support from the previously ignored rural population. By means of his union, the Grenada Manual and Mental Labourers Union (GMMLU), Gairy won higher wages and loyal political support from the workers. His appeal derived less from ideology or program than from his charismatic personality. His formal political party consisted, for example, of only 70 members. As prime minster, Gairy increasingly acted as an autocrat (enforced by his "Mongoose Gang") in an atmosphere of corruption.

Seizure of power by the NJM headed by the magnetic Maurice Bishop in 1979 not only radically altered the exisiting political system and economy but also linked Grenada increasingly closer with the Soviet bloc—and with Cuba in particular—during the cold war. Cuban "volunteers" served as advisers throughout the society, and their work toward completion of a 9,000-foot runway near St. Georges was viewed with geopolitical suspicion in Washington. When in October 1983 Bishop and scores of his supporters were gunned down by an NJM faction (the Revolutionary Military Council, or RMC) headed by Bernard and Phyllis Coard and Hudson Austin, alarm in neighboring island states and the United States led to an invasion by a combined force that quickly restored order and was greeted as liberators by the masses. Seventeen of the conspirators remained in the Richmond Hill Prison in 1998 with little public clamor for their release.

NEW NATIONAL PARTY (NNP)

The NNP is a coalition party formed from three smaller parties in 1984. The impetus for the coalition was the fear by business interests, religious leaders, neighboring governments, and Washington that Gairy's GULP would win again. The agreement was worked out at an August 26, 1984, meeting hosted by the St. Vincent prime minister, James F. Mitchell, and the late Tom Adams of Barbados. Joined were one old party, the Grenada National Party (GNP) of Herbert Blaize, and two new ones, the Grenada National Movement (GDM) of Francis Alexis and the National Democratic Party (NDP) of George I. Brizan. As the oldest and most experienced figure, Blaize was selected as head.

In the December 1984 elections, the NNP won 14 of 15 House seats and moved quickly to draft a new constitution that would provide stronger safeguards against future efforts to overturn the parliamentary system. Despite the winning margin, the NNP's popularity suffered through weak leadership and a stagnant economy, and within its five-year term the party fragmented and lost power. However, in the elections of June 1995, under the leadership of Dr. Keith Mitchell, the NNP again won, with 8 seats in the 15-seat House.

GRENADA UNITED LABOUR PARTY (GULP)

The oldest of the active parties in Grenada, the GULP was Eric Gairy's personal vehicle to power. It won the country's first election, but its corruption and abuses of power contributed to the NJM's forceful takeover in 1979. Gairy went into voluntary exile during that period but returned in 1984 to direct his party in the elections, even though he was not a candidate. His party remained a major contender for the national leadership up to his death, but it never again won control of the House, although in 1995 it did win two seats.

OTHER POLITICAL FORCES

Minor Political Parties

Most successful of the alternative parties has been the National Democratic Congress (NDC) of Nicholas Brathwaite and George Brizan. The NDC leadership pulled its followers out of the NNP coalition prior to the 1990 election, won, and both Braithwaite and Brizan served as prime ministers. In 1995, it won only five seats. The other four parties have slight backing.

The Maurice Bishop Patriotic Movement (MBPM) was formed in May 1984 on what would have been Bishop's 40th birthday by two former ministers in Bishop's government, Kendrick Radix and George Louison. Although some affection for Bishop lingers, both the memory of what he wrought and a lack of confidence in his successors made voters wary of this attempt at revival. Despite advice from Cuba, it has won no seats in two elections.

The oldest of the remaining parties is the National Party (TNP) headed by Ben Jones. It ran 12 candidates in 1995 but received scant support. Two other parties, known as the URP and the GOD, could—according to *Caribbean Week*—be dismissed as "marginal, if not ridiculous."

NATIONAL PROSPECTS

Despite the country's flamboyant recent political history, constitutional government appears to be on firm ground in Grenada. The vigor of the democratic process is attested to by the swirl of political party creation and reformulation, as well as by the lack of dominance of a single figure or party over the past decade. The deaths of both Bishop and Gairy leave personalities less colorful but perhaps more competent. The economy remains largely dependent on exports of mace and nutmeg (Grenada is the world leader) and tourism. The latter is aided greatly by completion of the airport and runway near St. Georges after the invasion by the United States, but the national infrastructure is too weak to provide serious competition to its island neighbors in this activity, despite a recent surge in visitors from Germany. Although the government remains on friendly terms with the United States, it has again resumed closer economic and cultural relations with Cuba.

Further Reading

Alexander, Robert J. *Political Parties of the Americas: Canada, Latin America, and the West Indies*, 2 vols. Westport, Conn.: Greenwood Press, 1982.

Anderson, Thomas D. "Marxists and Non-Marxists in the Caribbean." In *A Critique of Marxist and Non-Marxist Thought*. Ed. Ajit Jain and Alexander J. Matejko. New York: Praeger, 1986, 133–57.

Caribbean Week: The Regional Newspaper of the Caribbean. St. Michael, Barbados.

CIA World Factbook. Washington, D.C.: Government Printing Office, various years.

THE REPUBLIC OF GUATEMALA

(República de Guatemala)

By Kristin Marsh

THE SYSTEM OF GOVERNMENT

Guatemala is a Central American country bordering Mexico to the north and west, Belize to the northeast, and El Salvador and Honduras to the southeast. With 108,430 square kilometers of land area and 11 million people, Guatemala is the largest country in the small but politically significant region. The majority of Guatemalans (56%) are Mayan. The remaining 44% are mestizos, or of mixed Native American and Spanish descent (called Ladino in local Spanish). Spanish, the official language, is spoken by 60% of Guatemalans, and 40% speak 1 of 23 Indian dialects. The religious makeup of the country is approximately 70% Roman Catholic and 30% Protestant. A small minority practice pre-Christian traditions.

Guatemala's recent political history is somewhat of an extreme reflection of the region as a whole and is best characterized as dominated by political instability, social unrest, and repression. Guatemala has been governed under four separate constitutions in the last half century. Under the current constitution, which was passed in 1985 and became effective January 14, 1986, Guatemala's republican form of government is made up of the executive, the legislative, and the judicial branches of government. The Guatemalan economy has benefited a small economic oligarchy, while heightened levels of poverty and inequality increasingly fueled unrest among the indigenous population. Civil war remained a constant backdrop to the political instability for 36 years, finally coming to an end in negotiated settlement between the guerrillas and the government in December 1996.

After gaining independence from Mexico's Central American Federation in 1839, Guatemala had been ruled by a series of dictators through World War II. A popular revolution initiated the socioeconomic reforms of Juan José Arevalo (1945–51) and Jacobo Arbenz Guzmán (1951–54). Reform was to be short-lived, as communist support of Arbenz prompted U.S. Central Intelligence Agency (CIA) sponsorship of Colonel Carlos Castillo Armas's coup d'état. Castillo's short term (1954–57) ended in assassination. The term of his elected successor—Miguel Ydigoras Fuentes (National Democratic Reconciliation Party)—was cut short as well, in 1963.

This time a military junta installed Colonel Enrique Peralta Azurdia.

The 1965 Guatemalan constitution called for presidential elections at four-year intervals. A civilian, Julio César Mendez Montenegro of the moderate leftist Revolutionary Party (PR), was elected to the presidency in 1966. However, real power remained in the hands of the armed forces, and the civilian president held little effective control. When violent political protest escalated in 1966–68, Colonel Carlos Arana Osorio eradicated the guerrilla movement in Zacapa and temporarily quelled the political violence. He went on to win the presidency in 1970 under conditions of electoral terror. Military control of the government would continue to characterize Guatemalan politics through the early 1980s. Because of widespread electoral fraud between 1970 and 1982, voters had little real choice at the polls. Legal parties were conservative allies of the military, and the choice for president represented a strategic alliance between the economically powerful civilian oligarchy and the armed forces high command.

Yet the military was quickly losing its ability to govern in Guatemala. The ruling military-oligarchy alliance was increasingly factionalized and was quickly losing legitimacy within society as a result of the openly fraudulent elections of 1974, 1978, and 1982. From 1978 to 1982, General Romeo Lucas García was able to retain state authority only through extreme repression. And by 1982 outward political reform was needed to return some measure of legitimacy, peace, and stability to the country's military rule. General Efraín Ríos Montt staged a coup d'état, but his extremist "scorched-earth" tactics of indiscriminant killings in rural communities, particularly the Indian highlands of the northwest, eventually lost him the support of the ruling coalition. A second coup d'état in August 1983 saw him replaced by General Oscar Humberto Mejía Víctores. From the standpoint of the leading oligarchy, the goal of both coups was to initiate a return to controlled civilian rule. From the perspective of the military, the goal was both to reestablish the confidence of the bourgeoisie and other sectors of the civilian population and to finally demobilize all leftist opposition.

If the 1982 and 1983 coups represented the outward

initiation of reform, a return to normalized electoral politics was to signal the follow-through of a formally redemocratized, pluralistic Guatemalan government. At first, the rhetoric of political pluralism meant only slight liberalization in practice. The Christian Democratic Party was legalized, and the Social Democratic Party was allowed to participate, but only after renunciation of its leftist leanings. All leftist parties were still excluded from legal participation, and open electoral fraud was replaced by continued political exclusion. In the 1984 election for a constituent assembly that would draft the new constitution and new laws governing elections, exclusion of all but the accepted conservative parties led to a high rate of abstention, and only 43% of the eligible electorate cast valid ballots.

The constitution adopted in 1985 introduced considerable reform and represented a move toward civilian rule. And procedural democratic reform did result in the 1985 election of a civilian president, Vinicio Cerezo. On the other hand, Vinicio Cerezo's government turned out to be weak and ineffectual, and his presidential powers were subordinated to the powers of the armed forces, particularly in the areas of national security and rural development. The military implemented several programs of "security and development" that targeted the rural conflict zones. All adult males were conscribed to newly created Civil Defense Patrols, tens of thousands of displaced civilians were forced to resettle in "model villages," and local government activity was overseen by "interinstitutional coordinators." Electoral reform was thus coupled with the heightened institutionalization of the counterinsurgency activities of the military.

By 1990, public confidence in the Christian Democrats had been fully undermined by the Cerezo administration's corruption and leadership. Also, several high-profile tragedies of the civil war were concentrated in 1990, Cerezo's final year as president: the massacre at Santiago Atitlán, which left 15 dead; the murder of Michael Devine, an American citizen; and the murder of anthropologist Myrna Mack.

Jorge Serrano Elías won the 1991 runoff election as the candidate of the newly formed Solidarity Action Movement (MAS) and with the support of the National Center Union and the Christian Democrats. Corruption charges against Serrano's government, including vote manipulation in Congress, were increasing. Although implicated himself, Serrano argued that congressional and Supreme Court corruption had made it impossible for him to govern. On May 25, 1993, he attempted an *autogolpe*, or self-coup, that involved suspension of the constitution, the Congress, the Constitutional Court, and the Supreme Court of Justice.

The Serrano *autogolpe* proved a critical test of the newly reformed democratic process in Guatemala. In coordinated and quick response, the civilian sectors of Guatemalan society formed the Committee on National Consensus (*Instancia Nacional de Consenso*). Although without legal authority, the *Instancia* acted quickly to return the country to its constitutional order, calling for cleansing of all branches of government. A deal was struck with the Christian Democrats and others opposed to the self-cleansing. Several changes to the constitution were agreed to, as well as procedures for electing a transitional congress and establishing a new Supreme Court.

Understandably, voter turnout in 1994 was low, indicating a lack of confidence in the political system in general, as well as alienation from the established political parties. Voter alienation in 1995 was countered by a widespread call for electoral participation. Even the URNG called a cease-fire for the election and encouraged citizens to participate in support of alternative candidates. While alternatives were few, 1995 marked the first time a participating party represented a platform of the ideological left. The New Guatemalan Democratic Front (FDNG) won six congressional seats on a platform emphasizing land reform, demilitarization, refugee repatriation, and indigenous rights.

Corresponding to the signs of strengthening ideological pluralism and stabilizing constitutional democracy through the first half of the 1990s, the Guatemalan peace process progressed haltingly during the same time period. Working from a framework agreement established in Mexico City in 1991, a series of Accords were signed within the next few years, culminating in the final peace agreement signed in December 1996. Together, the Peace Accords call for substantial reduction of the size and power of the armed forces, elimination of the paramilitary counterinsurgency units, judicial reform, UN verification of respect for human rights, and legal recognition of Guatemala's multiethnic and multilingual population.

Although the settlement has been criticized for lack of accountability of human rights criminals and a neglect of socioeconomic issues such as land reform and unemployment, the 1996 Peace Accords afford the Guatemalan people, at long last, a hope for consolidated peace and the opportunity for stable, institutionalized political participation.

Executive

Guatemala's executive branch of government is made up of the president, the vice president, and the Cabinet (called the Council of Ministers). Under changes made to the constitution in 1994, the president holds the authority of chief of state and head of government and appoints members of the Council of Ministers. Both the president and the vice president are elected to nonrenewable four-year terms. The vice president presides over Congress. The November 1995 general election resulted in a runoff between Alvaro Enrique Arzú Irigoyen (PAN) and Jorge Portillo Cabrera (FRG). Arzú won the election runoff narrowly, with 51.2% of the vote, on January 14, 1996. A rural-urban split characterized the runoff, with support for Arzú concentrated in Guatemala City and other urban areas. The next election is to be held in November 2000.

Legislature

National parliamentary elections are held every four years, and seats of the Congress of the Republic (*Congreso de la Republica*), or National Congress, are filled by proportional representation. In 1993 the Congress approved a reduction of its number from 116 seats to 80. The reduction was approved in a general referendum in January 1994, and a special election was held in August 1994 to elect an interim congress of 80 members to serve until replaced in the November 1995 general election. In the November 1995 elections the National Advancement Party won 43 seats of the 80 total seats, the Guatemalan Republican Front won 21, the New Guatemalan Democratic Front won 6, the Christian Democratic Party won 4, the National Center Union won 3, the Democratic Union won 2, and the National Liberation Movement won only 1 seat.

Judiciary

The Supreme Court of Justice (*Corte Suprema de Justicia*) is Guatemala's highest judicial authority. A minimum of seven judges are elected by the National Congress to six-year terms. In addition, the separate Court of Constitutionality determines the constitutionality of laws and regulations. The Court of Constitutionality is presided over by the president of the Supreme Court.

A lack of separation of powers between the three branches of government in Guatemala has resulted in a continual blurring of judicial and executive roles. Both the executive and the military have influenced judicial functions and decisions. Members of the military, in particular, have been able to act with impunity. Furthermore, the judicial system has historically been characterized by unequal treatment of the indigenous versus nonindigenous population. The 1996 Peace Accords offer some possibilities for change, although the success of judicial reform depends upon successful and complete implementation of the Accords.

A central instrument of the Accords, the Demilitarization Accord (Strengthening of Civilian Power and the Role of the Army in a Democratic Society) calls for extreme limitations to the role and budget of the army, in addition to mandating judicial reform toward the elimination of impunity. The Accord on Identity and Rights of Indigenous Peoples is another instrument that has direct implications for the judicial system. Mandating a constitutional redefinition of Guatemala as multiethnic, multicultural, and multilingual, the Accord on Identity and Rights has the potential to equalize rights and representation of Guatemala's indigenous population.

Regional and Local Government

Guatemala is divided into 22 departments plus the central district of the capital, Guatemala City. A governor traditionally appointed by the president heads each department. The departments are subdivided into 327 municipalities (*municipios*). Each municipality has a mayor who is elected by direct popular vote. In towns of less than 10,000 people, mayors serve $2\frac{1}{2}$-year terms; in large cities the term of office is 5 years. In 1985 the Christian Democrats (DCG) won nearly three-quarters of the mayoralties. In Guatemala City the mayoral contest usually involves candidates loyal to particular localities and from outside the major political parties. The mayor elected in 1985 was Alvaro Arzú, of the conservative Plan of National Advancement (PAN), who ran for president in 1990, then went on to win the presidency in the 1996 runoff. In 1990 the Guatemala City mayoralty again went to the PAN candidate, Oscar Berger.

THE ELECTORAL SYSTEM

The electoral system in Guatemala is based on universal suffrage for all citizens 18 years of age or older. Historically, left and center-left parties have been illegal and were not allowed to participate in elections. In addition, election procedures were consistently fraudulent and elections were held under conditions of terror.

Reform of the electoral system has been slow and minimal but has involved the opening up of the system to include centrist parties, resulting in a slightly broader political spectrum. Nonvoting is punishable by a small fine, though this penalty is rarely imposed. Illiterate citizens (55.6% of the total population over the age of 15 are literate: 62.5% of males and 48.6% of females) are not obliged to vote. Although voting is required and there has been some reform in the electoral system, voter turnout has remained at very low levels. The official abstention rate in 1985 was 34.63%, even lower than in previous elections.

THE PARTY SYSTEM

Guatemala's political party system, in spite of reforms adopted in the 1986 constitution, remained a legacy of the 1954 coup by Colonel Carlos Castillo Armas and the U.S. Central Intelligence Agency through the mid-1990s. The electoral process was continually unsettled, and the Guatemalan left and center-left were consistently excluded from party politics. The military retained considerable control over politics and the party system. After the military coup in 1982, all political parties and organizations were declared illegal and forced to disband. By the mid-1980s, however, the military began to relinquish control of the party system. In the aftermath of Serrano's *autogolpe*, with the 1994 transitional elections, the 1995 general elections, and particularly with the signing of the 1996 Peace Accords, the spectrum of ideological representation via legal party participation has begun to broaden meaningfully.

CHRISTIAN DEMOCRATIC PARTY

(Democracia Christiana Guatemalteca; DCG)

Organized in the late 1950s, the Christian Democratic Party (DCG) was not legally registered as a party until 1968. Today it is considered a center-left party within the Guatemalan political spectrum, although it contains a more conservative faction as well. The DCG claims particular strength among the trade union and peasant-cooperative movements, as well as considerable support among urban middle-class voters. It is closely linked with Christian Democratic Parties elsewhere (Venezuela, Italy, Germany, and El Salvador) and relies on these parties for electoral funding.

In 1974, the DCG ran a strong campaign with Rios Montt as its presidential candidate. While observers considered Rios Montt the winner, the army's candidate, General Kjell Laugerud of the PR/MLN, was declared the winner among widespread charges of electoral fraud. DCG subsequently became a prime target of political repression, and more than 250 Christian Democratic leaders were assassinated under General Romeo Lucas Garcia's presidency between 1978 and 1982. The party leader, Cerezo Vinicio Cerezo Arevalo, managed to survive three assassination attempts during this time.

In 1982, the DCG and the PNR formed an alliance called the Opposition Union (*Union Opositora*) and supported the PNR candidate, Alejandro Maldonado Aguirre, for president, with Roberto Carpio Nicolle as the vice presidential candidate. When both the Opposition Union and the MLN claimed victory, army officers ousted the official (MLN) candidate, and Rios Montt declared himself president.

After the 1983 violent military coup and the subsequent military rule by decree, the Christian Democrats were among participants in the June 1984 election for the constituent assembly to draft the new constitution and electoral laws. Although the largest share of the vote went to the Christian Democrats (21.2%), closely followed by the UCN and a coalition of the MLN and CAN, the DCG was awarded only 20 seats, compared with 23 for the MLN/CAN coalition and 21 for the UCN.

In 1985 the Christian Democratic presidential candidate was Vinicio Cerezo, and he successfully contested the presidential campaign with Roberto Carpio Nicolle as his running mate. In the 1990 elections, the Christian

Democrats had lost popular support due to Cerezo's weak leadership and ineffectual attempt at civilian administration. The party forged an alliance with the Democratic Convergence (DC) toward a renewed progressive image but still achieved only 27 seats in Congress. The 1990 Christian Democratic presidential candidate, Alfonso Cabrera, came in third. The PSD connection with Serrano's administration, and the party's intransigence in the face of the Instancia, further undermined popular support. In 1995 the PSD, in coalition with the National Center Union and the Social Democrats, formed the Grand National Front and supported Andrade Diaz Duran for president. Diaz came in third, and the coalition mustered only three seats in Congress.

DEMOCRATIC UNION

(Unión Democrática; UD)

The Democratic Union (UD) was formed by leader José Luis Chea Urruela in 1994 as a new party of the right. It won only one seat in the transitional congress and earned three seats in the 1995 general election.

GUATEMALAN REPUBLICAN FRONT

(Frente Republicano Guatemalteco; FRG)

Gen. Efraín Rios Montt founded the Guatemalan Republican Front (FRG) as a populist party on the extreme right. The FRG allied with the Democratic Institutionalist Party (PID) and the National Unity Front (FUN) in the 1990 elections under the "No Sellout Platform" (*Plataforma No Venta*; PNV). Rios Montt, who assumed dictatorial powers in 1982, ran as the PNV presidential candidate in 1990, but the party alliance was deregistered on the basis of Montt's participation in the 1982 coup. The FRG managed a strong comeback in the 1994 congressional election, winning 32 of 80 seats and establishing Montt as the president of Congress. In November 1995, FRG's success was less dramatic, with 21 congressional seats. And in the January 1996 runoff presidential election, the FRG candidate (Jorge Portillo Cabrera) came in a close second to Arzú.

NATIONAL ADVANCEMENT PARTY

(Partido por el Adelantamiento Nacional; PAN)

The National Advancement Party (PAN) is currently the leading party force in Guatemala. A center-right party, PAN was founded in 1989 by the then Guatemala City mayor, Alvaro Arzú Irigoyen, to contest the 1990 general election. Arzú received 17.3% of the vote (fourth place) in the November election, and PAN obtained 12 congressional seats as well as the Guatemala City mayoralty. Serrano appointed Arzú foreign minister in the new administration but did not afford him a central role in decision making. As the result of disagreement over the administration's policy on Belize, Arzú resigned as foreign minister in August 1991.

In 1994 elections for an interim congress, PAN won 24 seats (second to the FRG, which won 32 seats). In the 1995 general elections, PAN won 43 congressional seats out of 80. A runoff between Arzú (PAN) and Portillo Cabrera (FRG) resulted in a narrow victory for Arzú, with 51.2% of the vote.

NATIONAL CENTER UNION
(Unión del Centro Nacional; UCN)

The party of the new right, the National Center Union (UCN), was founded as a political vehicle in 1984 by Jorge Carpio Nicolle, owner of the daily newspaper *El Grafico*. UCN presented itself as a new, moderate conservative party in contrast with the traditional parties of the far right, although its rhetoric was sometimes left-wing while its allies often were of the far right. The UCN participated in the June 1984 constituent assembly election and was awarded 21 seats. Support held in 1985, with the UCN coming away with 22 seats in the legislature and Carpio finishing second in the presidential runoff. With Ríos Montt barred from the election in 1990, the presidential vote came down to a runoff between Carpio and Serrano (MAS). Carpio lost the January runoff, despite DCG support. Support for the party dropped dramatically in 1995 when the UCN won only three congressional seats.

The UCN won an impressive 41 congressional seats. After Carpio's assassination in 1993, the party was unable to maintain support. In 1994 and 1995 the UCN won only 8 and 3 congressional seats, respectively.

NATIONAL LIBERATION MOVEMENT
(Movimiento de Liberación Nacional; MLN)

The National Liberation Movement (MLN) was founded in 1960 by Mario Sandóval Alarcón and is one of the two oldest remaining parties in the Guatemalan political system. Traditionally and consistently right-wing, the MLN was strongly critical of the peace process in Guatemala and in Central America more generally, although their stance became more moderate by the early 1990s. The party's spiritual father is considered to be Colonel Carlos Castillo Armas (National Democratic Movement; MDN). Colonel Castillo Armas was leader of the coup that overthrew President Jacobo Arbenz with the aid of the U.S. Central Intelligence Agency in 1954, and he became president from 1954 until his assassination in 1957.

The MLN staged the 1963 coup against Miguel Ydigoras Fuentes, installing the short-lived presidency of Colonel Peralta Azurdia. The MLN lost the 1966 election but regained office from 1970 to 1978. It was during this time that the death squads associated with the MLN were most active.

The MLN participated in the June 1984 constitutional election in alliance with the Authentic Nationalist Central (CAN), winning 23 seats. And for the November 1985 general election, the MLN and PID formed an alliance. The MLN presidential candidate, Sandóval, came in fourth, and the MLN won 6 congressional seats. Support for the MLN was waning, and in the 1990 general election, the MLN allied with the National Advancement Front (FAN) but won only 4 seats in Congress and was fourth in the presidential race. The MLN won only 2 congressional seats in 1994 and a single seat in 1995.

NEW GUATEMALAN DEMOCRATIC FRONT
(Frente Democrático de Nueva Guatemala; FDNG)

Formed in 1995 to take advantage of the broadened political arena, the New Guatemalan Democratic Front (FDNG) was initially a left-wing alliance between the Social Christian Party (PSC) and the Social Reformist Union (URS). The URS withdrew from the coalition shortly before the election, but the Democratic Front nevertheless retained its identity as running a platform most supportive of social reform. While the FDNG was neither formally linked nor self-identified with the URNG, it supported similar interests. The Democratic Front platform called for land reform, demilitarization of the government and civilian patrols, and repatriation of refugees and supported the rights of indigenous peoples. The FDNG won six congressional seats in 1995.

SOCIAL DEMOCRATIC PARTY
(Partido Socialista Democrático; PSD)

A member of the Socialist International, the Social Democratic Party (PSD) was founded in 1978 as a party of the center-left. In response to stepped-up repression in the early 1980s, leaders of the PSD went into exile in Costa Rica. The PSD formed an alliance, the Guatemalan Committee of Patriotic Unity, with other opposition groups and contested the 1982 elections. The coalition called for revolution and boycotted the 1984 elections. With electoral reform imminent in 1985, the party reregistered and gained two congressional seats in coalition with other center-left groups. In the 1990 elections, the PSD allied with the Popular Alliance 5 (AP5) and won one seat in Congress, in addition to earning representation in Serrano's Cabinet. Because of its relationship with the Serrano government, the PSD gained no representation in the 1994 transitional congress. In 1995, the Social Democrats allied with the National Center Union and the Christian Democrats.

SOLIDARITY ACTION MOVEMENT
(Movimiento de Acción Solidaria; MAS)

Newly created in 1990 as a small right-wing political party with its base in the Evangelical Christian community, the Solidarity Action Movement (MAS) fielded Jorge Serrano Elías as its presidential candidate. In the January 1991 runoff election, Serrano beat out the UCN candidate, Jorge Carpio Nicolle. In addition, MAS had won 18 congressional seats.

Serrano's campaign platform combined an emphasis on law and order, human rights, and the peace process. Once in office, Serrano rewarded support he had received in the runoff campaign by forming an alliance between MAS and PAN and by appointing two PAN members to his Cabinet. In the aftermath of Serrano's 1993 *autogolpe*, MAS lost voter confidence, and the party failed to win any representation in the 1995 congressional elections.

MINOR POLITICAL PARTIES AND PARTY COALITIONS

In spite of an exclusionary and ideologically narrow party spectrum, Guatemalan political history has been marked by an unusually high number of political parties and highly tactical (and therefore tenuous) coalition building. A high degree of instability in the party system and coalition building among existing parties emerged amidst the restructuring of the political system in the 1980s. The promised grand coalition of the right never materialized as divisions among right and center-right parties aided the singular DCG. But the Christian Democrats' loss of credibility in the late 1980s and early 1990s necessitated a series of coalitions with other minor parties.

Recent examples of party coalitions include Platform Ninety (*Plataforma No-Venta*; PNV) and the National Front (*Frente Nacionale*; FN). The PNV forged the alliance of the Democratic Institutionalist Party (PID), the Guatemalan Republican Front (FRG), and FAN in the 1994 legislative elections. The FN was established in 1995 as a coalition of the Christian Democrats (DCG), the National Center Union (UCN), and the Social Democrats (PSD). Its presidential candidate, Fernando Andrade Días Durán, came in with 12.9% of the vote in November 1995.

Parties that either have no current representation in Congress or did not participate in the 1995 general election include the following: Citizens for Democracy (*Ciudadanos por Demócracia*; CPD), a recently formed left-wing party; Civic Democratic Front (*Frente Civico Democrático*; FCD), a splinter of the DCG; Democratic Institutionalist Party (*Partido Institucional Democrático*; PID), the official party in 1966 and part of a right-wing alliance thereafter; Democratic Party of National Cooperation (*Partido Democrático de Cooperación Nacional*; PDCN); National Renewal Party (*Partico Nacionalista Renovador*; PNR); National Unity Front (*Frente de Unidad Nacional*; FUN), originally a coalition of the Christian Democrats, the PRA, and the FPP; Nationalist Authentic Central (*Central Auténica Nacionalista*; CAN); Revolutionary Party (*Partido Revolucionario*; PR); Social Christian Party (*Partido Social Cristiano*; PSC); Social Reformist Union (*Unión Reformist Social*; URS), an original member of the New Guatemala Democratic Front electoral alliance; United Revolutionary Front (*Frente Unido Revolucionario*; FUR), the left successor to the Revolutionary Democratic Union; Democratic Alliance (*Alianza Democrática*; AD); Guatemalan Committee of Patriotic Unity (*Comité Guatemalteco de Unidad Patriótica*; CGUP); and Guatemalan Labour Party–National Leadership Nucleus (*Partido Guatemalteco del Trabajo–Nucleo de Dirección Nactional*; PGT–LN), the de facto Guatemalan communist party.

OTHER POLITICAL FORCES

The Guatemalan Oligarchy and Private Business Interests

Historically, Guatemalan business groups have commanded organized political voice. The most powerful and best-known interest group for the private sector is the Coordinating Committee of Commercial, Industrial, and Financial Associations (*Coordinadora de Asociaciones Agrícolas, Comerciales, Industriales, y Financieras*; CACIF). CACIF, representing a broad base of private interests, acts as an umbrella organization for mostly small to medium-sized business organizations. Supporting classical liberalism, CACIF contains the following chambers: commerce, industry, sugar, finances, agriculture, construction, and tourism. CACIF was instrumental in initiating an organized response to Serrano's 1993 *autogolpe*, mobilizing civilian society to form the *Instancia*.

A narrower interest group ideologically, Friends of the Country (*Amigos del Pais*) was founded in 1974 as an ultraconservative lobbying organization. Despite political differences, both CACIF and Amigos del Pais oppose tax and agrarian reform.

The Guatemalan oligarchy has become an increasingly powerful political force in the 1990s. The oligarchy has clearly controlled Guatemala's economy but has also been a powerful political voice even as the members of the armed forces dominated governmental positions throughout the 20th century. More recently, the Guatemalan oligarchy has become an increasingly visible political force in the 1990s—particularly in the aftermath of Serrano's 1993 coup attempt when control of the government has shifted to members of the oligarchy.

Guatemalan National Revolutionary Unity (Unidad Revolucionaria Nacional Guatemalteca; URNG)

The Guatemalan National Revolutionary Unity was formed in 1979 as an insurgent guerrilla alliance of leftist opposition groups. Founding organizations included the Guerrilla Army of the Poor (*Ejército Guerrillero de los Pobres*; EGP), the Rebel Armed Froces (*Fuerzas Armadas Rebeldes*; FAR), and the Guatemalan Labour Party (PGT). The Armed People's Organization (*Organización del Pueblo en Armas*; ORPA) joined the umbrella URNG the following year.

In the late 1980s the URNG began to seek a peace settlement with the government that would lead to eventual participation in institutionalized politics. Initial talks were unproductive, and the peace process was stalled until talks resumed again in Norway in 1990, when Guatemalan political parties and the URNG participated in a series of negotiating meetings, followed by meetings between the URNG and various social sectors, including business. Although the URNG was not legally recognized, this process added legitimacy to the URNG as a central political player and set the stage for formal negotiations in 1991.

In Mexico City, in April of 1991, representatives of the military attended the talks, and a framework agreement was signed that July. With a peace agreement likely in the near future, the URNG supported popular participation in the 1995 elections. The Peace Accords were signed in December 1996, demobilization of nearly 3,000 URNG guerrillas was completed in early May 1997, and the URNG is now forming a political party toward electoral participation in 2000.

The Military

The military in Guatemala has retained control of the state administration through much of the 20th century. Although the 1965 constitution established electoral procedures for presidential selection, the military at that time managed to retain control of the government through formally open elections that in actuality reflected narrow political choices, closely controlled candidate selection by the ruling military-oligarchy alliance, and fraudulent electoral outcome in the face of popular opposition. And even as the 1985 constitution seemed to reestablish standard democratic political rights and guarantees, the same constitution legalized other counterinsurgency institutions. Through the civilian self-defense patrols (*patrullas de autodefensa civil*; PACs), army-controlled "model villages," and other administrative structures, the army was able to retain considerable control throughout the country.

The Demilitarization Accord of September 1996 is a central element of the peace settlement. This accord calls for constitutional reforms to limit the army to the single function of border and territorial defense. In addition, all paramilitary and counterinsurgency units have been eliminated, the size and budget of the army has been reduced by a third, a new civilian police force has been trained and deployed, and judicial reforms are called for to eliminate impunity of members of the military. In contrast with Guatemala's history of militarized and exclusionary politics, full implementation of this aspect of the Peace Accord will represent complete demilitarization of the government and of civilian society.

External Forces

As in neighboring Central American countries, external actors have historically played a key role in shaping Guatemala's political events. The U.S. government has been influential at decisive moments throughout the 20th century. Cold war ideologies led the U.S. Central Intelligence Agency to stage the 1954 coup against Jacobo Arbenz Guzmán, ushering in the series of military-dominated administrations that characterized Guatemala's government for the latter half of the 20th century. And during the 1980s, which opened with the government's 1981–83 "scorched-earth" campaign against guerrilla supporters in the indigenous highlands, the Reagan administration held steadfast to its progovernment position. The level of violence was consistently underestimated, and responsibility for the atrocities was deflected away from the Guatemalan army. Once negotiations had been initiated in the early 1990s, the UN stepped in and played a central role in mediating the negotiations and in implementing portions of the settlement. The Human Rights Accord of March 1994 created a UN Verification Mission (MINUGUA) that ensured an end to the violation of Constitutional human rights guarantees.

NATIONAL PROSPECTS

An estimated 150,000 Guatemalan lives were lost over 36 years of civil war, the longest and costliest civil war in modern Central American history. The December 1996 Peace Accords represent a long-awaited end to the violent conflict. Whether implementation of the terms of settlement will be successful and lead to institutionalized democratization is yet to be seen.

It is too early in the transition period to assess prospects for a lasting, consolidated peace. As with all compromised agreements, the Guatemalan Peace Accords are far-reaching in some respects, timid in others. And because the Accords find malcontents on both sides of the conflict—in the military as well as in leftist groups—implementation of all terms of agreement is proving a slow, conflictual process itself.

Prospects look good for human rights guarantees, which have been monitored since 1994 with the help of the MINUGUA UN verification mission. The Demilitarization Accord signed in September 1996, on the other hand, will be difficult to implement, requiring constitutional reforms to limit the functions of the army, elimination of the paramilitary civilian self-defense patrols, creation of a civilian police force, and reform of the judicial system.

Socioeconomically, it is not likely that the daily lives of Guatemalans will improve with the implementation of peace. Crime is rampant, and the terms of the Peace Accord address neither unemployment nor land reform. Guatemala's high levels of poverty and inequality are likely to continue even as the URNG attempts to bring about socioeconomic reforms through newly institutionalized political channels.

National prospects, while still uncertain, are considerably brighter since the 1996 signing of the Peace Accords. Whether or not competing groups will continue to compromise toward peaceful implementation of the settlement, it is clear that the Accords have provided the minimal conditions to allow Guatemala to finally consolidate ideological pluralism in a peaceful society.

Further Reading

Anderson, Thomas P. *Politics in Central America: Guatemala, El Salvador, Honduras, and Nicaragua.* New York: Praeger, 1988.

Black, George, Milton Jamail, and Normal Stoltz. *Garrison Guatamala.* New York: Monthly Review Press, 1984.

Dominguez, Jorge I., and Abraham F. Lowenthal, eds. *Constructing Democratic Governance: Latin America and the Caribbean in the 1990s.* Baltimore: Johns Hopkins University Press, 1996.

Dosal, Paul J. *Power in Transition: The Rise of Guatamala's Industrial Oligarchy, 1871–1994.* Westport, Conn.: Praeger, 1995.

Goodman, Louis W., William M. LeoGrande, and Johanna Mendelson Forman. *Political Parties and Democracy in Central America.* Boulder, Colo.: Westview Press, 1992.

Handy, Jim. *Gift of the Devil: A History of Revolt.* Boston: South End Press, 1984.

———. *Revolution in the Countryside: Rural Conflict and Agrarian Reform in Guatemala, 1944–1954.* Chapel Hill: University of North Carolina Press, 1994.

Immerman, Richard. *The CIA in Guatemala: The Foreign Policy of Intervention.* Austin: University of Texas Press, 1982.

Jonas, Susanne. *The Battle for Guatemala: Rebels, Death Squads, and U.S. Power.* Boulder, Colo.: Westview Press, 1991.

Lentner, Howard H. *State Formation in Central America: The Struggle for Autonomy, Development, and Democracy.* Westport, Conn.: Greenwood Press.

Seider, Rachel, ed. *Central America: Fragile Transition.* New York: St. Martin's Press, 1996.

Seligson, Mitchell A., and John A. Booth, eds. *Elections and Democracy in Central America, Revisited.* Chapel Hill: University of North Carolina Press, 1996.

Thiesenhusen, William C. *Broken Promises: Agrarian Reform and the Latin American Campesino.* Boulder, Colo.: Westview Press, 1995.

———, ed. *Searching for Agrarian Reform in Latin America.* Boston: Unwin Hyman, 1989.

Yashar, Deborah J. *Demanding Democracy: Reform and Reaction in Costa Rica and Guatemala, 1870s–1950s.* Stanford, Calif.: Stanford University Press, 1997.

REPUBLIC OF GUINEA

(République de Guinée)

By Thomas O'Toole, D.A.

THE SYSTEM OF GOVERNMENT

Guinea, a nation of more than 7 million people, was a one-party presidential regime until the military coup of April 3, 1984. It is now a unitary state with a democratic republic form of government that combines features of both the presidential and the parliamentary systems.

Since gaining independence from France in 1958, the country was led by Sékou Touré. After his death in 1984, a bloodless military coup ousted Touré's Democratic Party of Guinea (PDG) and brought General Lansana Conté to power. Not until the 1990s did Guineans see a constitution that allowed the existence of political parties. On December 19, 1993, the first multiparty presidential elections in more than three decades were held and Conté was elected president, gaining 51.7% of the vote in the final official count. In March 1996 an attempted military coup was put down with considerable bloodshed. Conté was reelected on December 14, 1998, with 54.1% of the vote.

Executive

The president of the republic is the chief of state, elected by an absolute majority of the ballots cast by direct universal suffrage for a five-year term, renewable only once. A second round of voting for the top two candidates is required if a majority is not gained in the first round. The president appoints all ministers and civil servants. Most of the formal business of the executive is transacted in a Council of Ministers chaired by the president. Both the president and the legislature can initiate laws. The president can dissolve the National Assembly once during his term but not before the third year of the legislature.

Legislature

Deputies to the National Assembly are directly elected from slates presented by legally constituted parties by universal direct suffrage for any number of five-year terms unless the Assembly is dissolved. Two-thirds of the deputies are elected from a national list of candidates with proportional representation, and one-third are directly elected from legally defined electoral districts put forth by legally constituted political parties. The president of the National Assembly is elected for the duration of the legislature. The Assembly ordinarily meets in open session for no more than 30 days beginning April 5 and no more than 60 days beginning October 5. The budget for the following year is passed in the second session. The Assembly can be called into special 15-day sessions by the president or by a majority of the deputies a month after the close of a session.

Judiciary

The judiciary includes courts of first instance, two Courts of Appeal (one in Kankan and one in Conakry), and the Supreme Court, the court of final appeal. After 1988 all judgments regarding violations under the penal code were rendered by civilian courts. The constitution affirms the judiciary's independence. However, magistrates are civil servants appointed by the president with no guarantee of tenure. Guinean judicial authorities have often deferred to central authorities in politically sensitive cases. In addition, the administration of justice is plagued by numerous other problems, including a shortage of magistrates (who generally are poorly trained) and lawyers (there are fewer than 50 in the country) and an outdated and overly restrictive penal code. An ethnically based system of justice functions at the village or urban neighborhood level where litigants present their civil cases before a village leader, neighborhood leader, or council of elders. Cases that cannot be resolved to the satisfaction of all parties within this system may be referred to the formal system of adjudication.

Regional and Local Government

Far-reaching changes to regional administrations were introduced in 1994. Instead of the previous four-way divisions (Guinée Maritime, Moyenne Guinée, Haute Guinée, and Guinée Forestière), the country was divided into seven administrative regions. The coastal region, formerly Guinée Maritime, was split into Kindia and Boké regions, with that part of the Futa Jalon bordering Guinea-Bissau now in Boké region. The rest of the Futa, which was in Moyenne Guinée, was split between Labé (to the north) and Mamou regions. The new Faranah region straddles the old boundary between Haute Guinée and Guinée Forestière, with the rumps of the two former regions encapsulated in the new administrative zones of Kankan and N'Zérékoré. Conakry retains its special status as the capital.

THE ELECTORAL SYSTEM

After the elections of December 1993 were verified in January 1994, no fixed timetable for the legislative elections was immediately established. President Conté suggested that a "cooling-off" period before starting new election campaigns was in order. Having undergone the window-dressing democratization demanded by Western donors, President Conté's grip on the reins of power was enhanced by the electoral process. The legislative elections in 1995 were rather anticlimactic, choosing 3 deputies from each of the 38 constituencies in the country under a complex voting procedure, one-third of the deputies elected by a majority vote and the remaining two-thirds by proportional means. The presidential election of 1998 saw Conté improve on the share of the vote he won in 1993.

THE PARTY SYSTEM

The proregime Party of Unity and Progress (*Parti de l'Unité et du Progrès*; PUP) exercises its influence throughout the country by co-opting most state and local administration officials. It is suggested that officials who fail to join the party are reposted or encouraged to find alternative employment. Many of the other 20 parties that offered candidates for the presidential elections of December 1993 were little more than individual initiatives. The PUP has its main strength in the Susu-dominated coastal regions, with some following in most major towns.

OTHER POLITICAL PARTIES

Masses
(DJAMA)

This party offered Mohammed Mansour Kaba, a construction engineer from Kankan, as its candidate on a platform of "hard work and national reconstruction" for the December 1993 elections. He received less than 1% of the total vote.

Party of Unity and Progress
(Parti de l'Unité et du Progrès; PUP)

The presidential party draws most of its support from the Susu ethnic group and holds a dominant position in the electoral process. Its candidate, Lansana Conté, received 51.7% of the vote in the 1993 presidential election and 54.1% in 1998.

Assembly of the Guinean People
(Rassemblement du Peuple de Guinée; RPG)

Drawing most of its support from the Maninka (Malinké) ethnic group and led by the long-term exile and opponent of Sékou Touré, Alpha Condé, this party received 16.9% of the vote in the 1998 presidential election. Condé had supported antigovernment demonstrations from 1990 on. He joined with the PRP to contest the legislative elections.

Union for Progress and Renewal
(Union pour le progrès et le Renouveau; UPR)

This party is a merger of the Union for thes New Republic and the Party of Renovation and Progress. Its presidential candidate in 1998, Mamadou Ba, a former World Bank employee, finished second with 24.6%.

Union for the Progress of Guinea
(Union pour le Progrès de la Guinée; UPG)

This party's Conakry-based leader and candidate for the 1993 presidential election, Jean-Marie Doré, received some support in the forest region but gained less than 1% of the total vote.

National Union for Prosperity
(Union Nationale pour la Prosperité; UNP)

This party is led by a Forécariah-born former military officer under Sékou Touré, Facinet Touré. Facinet Touré also served in Lansana Conté's government. Resigning from Conté's government after a demotion, his campaign for president in 1993 was based largely on his opposition to Conté.

Guinea Progress Party
(Parti Guinéen du Progrès; PGP)

Led by a former member of Sékou Touré's government, Alpha Abdoulaye "Portos" Diallo, who had been jailed for 10 years after the Portuguese invasion in 1970, this party received minimal popular support. In exile Diallo wrote a book critical of the Touré regime and returned to oppose the Conté regime.

Democratic Party of Guinea-African Democratic Assembly
(Parti Démocratique de Guinée-Rassemblement Démocratique Africain; PDG-RDA)

This party takes it name from the original party of independence founded by Sékou Touré. Its leader, El Hadj Ismaila Ghussein, served in the PDG under Touré and was head of the Guinean petroleum office in 1991. Those who had suffered under Touré resented his resurrection of this party name to run against Conté.

OTHER POLITICAL FORCES

France

Under President Conté, relations with France have been fully reactivated. French is once again the language of instruction, French officers train the presidential guard, and many Cabinet ministers have former French civil servants as counsellors. French banks have key roles in the banking sector, French companies have been major participants in the privatization program, and much of Guinea's international trade is controlled by French trading companies. The Bank of Guinea has served notice of its intention to join the French-dominated *Union Monetaire Ouest-Africaine* (UMOA).

International Monetary Fund and World Bank

Like those in more than half the countries in sub-Saharan Africa, the governmental leadership in Guinea adopted IMF- and World Bank–sponsored structural adjustment programs (SAPs) in the 1980s, and their record of implementation has been less than impressive. Coordination efforts were hampered by the weak level of institutional development in the government ministries. The lack of coordination led to confusion and weakened attempts to carry out the reform program.

The experience of government leaders in Guinea today has been characterized by extreme dependence. Insufficient levels of external aid, poor coordination of that aid, a heavy donor presence, and salaries of international experts in ministries amounting to 86% of the entire wage bill for 45,000 Guinean civil servants in 1990 caused widespread anxiety among Guineans. Severing relations with the international financial institutions (IFIs) would result in hardships, which would damage the legitimacy of this leadership, but carrying out the full rigor of the SAPs demanded by the IFIs means cutting subsidies to students, civil servants, and the military, which would also lead to increased civil discontent.

Neighboring States in Turmoil

The continued fighting in Sierra Leone and Liberia has resulted in more than 620,000 refugees from these countries living in Guinea. Most of them are sheltered with members of their own ethnic groups, especially in the southeastern part of Guinea and the Futa Jalon.

NATIONAL PROSPECTS

President Conté won the election in December 1993 only because opposition forces were so divided. Conté is a survivor with a considerable base of popular support, especially in the rural Susu areas, but the political situation of Guinea is far from stable. Budgetary problems are growing, and hopes for substantial new lending or rescheduling of existing debts seems to be fading. Yet, this is a potentially viable country with a wealth of natural resources and a dynamic population.

Further Reading

Kaba, Lansiné, *Guinea*. Boulder, Colo.: Westview Press, forthcoming.

O'Toole, Thomas E., and Ibrahima Bah-Lalya,. *Historical Dictionary of Guinea*, 3d ed. Metuchen, N.J.: Scarecrow Press, 1995.

Yansané, Aguibou. "Guinea: The Significance of the Coup of April 1984 and Economic Issues." *World Development* 18 (1990): 1231–46.

REPUBLIC OF GUINEA-BISSAU

(Republica da Guiné-Bissau)

By Tony Hodges
Revised by Mohamed Mbodj, Ph.D.

Guinea Bissau, a nation of 36,125 square kilometers, is a multiethnic country of 30% Balantas, 20% Fulas, 14% Manjancos, 13% Mandigas, 7% Papels, 4% Mancanhas, 2% Felupes, and 10% other. Some type of African religion is practiced by 65% of the 1.094 million people, while 30% are Muslim and 5% are Christian. The official language is Portuguese.

THE SYSTEM OF GOVERNMENT

For 16 years, since its independence from Portugal in 1974 after a long liberation war, the West African nation of Guinea-Bissau has been a one-party republic under the rule of the African Party for the Independence of Guinea and Cape Verde, or PAIGC. The leader of the PAIGC is automatically the president of the republic. However, since a military coup in 1980, the armed forces have exercised a dominant political influence in the party and the government. The then prime minister, João Bernardo Vieira, a veteran commander of the liberation war, took over from Luiz Cabral as president. The Vieira regime has survived several coup attempts triggered by infighting between rival clans and a deplorable economic situation.

In 1990, the regime decided to allow multiparty politics, which was fully in place by 1994. A new constitution abolished the leading role of the PAIGC as well as that of the militia (groups of veterans and politically involved people who function as a sort of police force and national guard), and it allowed independent trade unions, a free press, and freedom of expression. It also stipulated universal suffrage for the office of president. The 1994 presidential elections were deemed fair and free by foreign observers and Vieira won only after a second round, and with a slim margin. But the opposition, contrary to the observer's views, accused the PAIGC and Vieira of rigging the elections. Three outstanding points remain as impediments to further democratization: the quasi-monopoly exercised over the state-owned media, television in particular; the lack of independence of the small and weak judiciary; and the disproportionate weight of the military and veterans, which shadows the civilian turn the regime has taken reluctantly.

Executive

The authors of the November 1980 coup established a Council of the Revolution (*Conselho da Revolução*), which had nine members, headed by a president, with a vice president and four advisers, all nominated by the PAIGC and elected by the National Assembly. The Council functioned also as the ministerial Cabinet. The secretary-general of the PAIGC was automatically nominated to be president of the Council, head of state, and president of the republic, and election by the National Assembly was a mere formality. Under a transitional constitutional law, published in March 1981, the president of the Council also became commander in chief of the armed forces. Bernardo Vieira, the secretary-general of the PAIGC, held all these offices, and the government was subordinate to the Council of the Revolution.

In May 1984, a new constitution established a 15-member Council of State headed by Vieira and composed of two vice presidents and 12 ministers. All powers remained concentrated in the hands of the president, whose legitimacy came from an unopposed nomination vote by the PAIGC general congress held every four years.

With the advent of multiparty politics after 1990, the new constitution mandated that the president of the republic was to be elected by universal suffrage every four years. All executive powers remain concentrated in his hands, especially the position of commander in chief. Designated candidate by his party, PAIGC, Vieira won the first elections, held in 1994.

Legislature

The country's legislature, the People's National Assembly (*Assembleia Nacional Popular*), was dissolved at the time of the 1980 coup. It was reinstated after the approval of the new constitution and the 1984 elections. It has 180 members elected for four years on a single list of candidates presented by the PAIGC. In addition to legislative powers, it also elects the president and the 15 members of the Council of State, all presented by the PAIGC.

After 1990, the constitution reduced to 100 the number of representatives to be elected by a proportional vote. The first free universal elections held in 1994 allowed six parties to be represented for a four-year mandate. But the National Assembly's powers are not that significant because of the concentration of powers in the president's hands. Under the new constitution, it even loses the power to elect the president and nominate members of his Cabinet.

Judiciary

The judicial system is not independent and still draws from the liberation war and the one-party system eras. It is arguably the weak link of Guinea-Bissau's political institutions. However, recently, human rights watchdog groups have been set up, and they have been active in challenging the state to allow for a truly independent and strong judiciary, along with the opposition parties.

Regional and Local Government

The country is divided into eight regions and one autonomous section (the capital, Bissau), each of which is administered by a state committee and an elected council.

THE ELECTORAL SYSTEM

In the first postindependence elections for the councils, held in December 1976, about 80% of the voters approved the PAIGC slate, though there were significant regional variations. Support for the PAIGC was lowest in the Fula regions of the northeast. The regional councils selected the National Assembly's 150 members. The first elections after the November 1980 coup took place in May 1984. Direct vote and universal suffrage elected eight regional councils. The regional councils in turn elected the National Assembly. After 1990, the elections were open to multiparty competition and election to the National Assembly became direct.

The first truly democratic elections were held in July (parliament) and August (presidential) 1994. The opposition protested massive fraud, despite the fact that international observers pronounced them fair. The next general elections are scheduled for early 1999.

THE PARTY SYSTEM

Since 1994, more than 12 parties have competed in elections, but only three are significant. The dominant party is the old African Party for the Independence of Guinea and Cape Verde, the PAIGC, which is President Vieira's party and has 62 seats in the parliament. Rooted in the rural communities, PAIGC membership is spread throughout the territory. It is the most representative party, garnering some 48 to 50% of the popular votes during the 1994 elections. The fact that President Vieira is from the small Papel ethnic group seems to represent some guarantee of neutrality among the numerous and competing groups. Despite internal dissension, the PAIGC still enjoys a solid lead over its competitors, because of its seniority, its superior organization, and its control of the state's resources.

AFRICAN PARTY FOR THE INDEPENDENCE OF GUINEA AND CAPE VERDE (PAIGC)
(Partido Africano da Independência da Guiné e Cabo Verde)

The PAIGC was founded in 1956 by Amilcar Cabral to lead the independence struggle in both Guinea-Bissau and the Cape Verde Islands. In 1963, the party began a guerrilla war against Portugal in Guinea-Bissau. By 1973, the PAIGC controlled about three-quarters of the country and Portugal retained control of the country's few cities and the northeastern savanna belt inhabited by the Islamic Fula. That same year, the PAIGC proclaimed the Republic of Guinea-Bissau, and, a year later, in September 1974, Portugal recognized the republic and withdrew its troops.

The PAIGC has unlimited control over the state and its citizens. Luiz Cabral, the party's secretary-general, exercises all power. He succeeded his half brother, Amilcar Cabral, the founder of PAIGC who was assassinated while in exile. Soon after the PAIGC took power, however, the new state was beset with problems. Agricultural production fell drastically during the war, and there is no mining and almost no manufacturing. The country has to import all its oil and much of its food, including rice, which is its main staple. The only exports, groundnuts, fish, and palm kernels, together pay for less than 30% of the imports. The foreign debt has grown dangerously large, and there have been prolonged shortages of basic consumer goods, including rice. The shortages did much to undermine popular confidence in Luiz Cabral's regime, as did the widespread corruption especially in the state-run people's shops. There was resentment at the apparent privileges of the Mesticos and Cape Verdians, who were prominent in the urban petty bourgeoisie and the PAIGC leadership. There also was dismay at Cabral's concentration of power and the repression of dissidents, including numerous executions.

Discontent was particularly strong among the largest ethnic group, the Balantas. They had borne the brunt of the struggle and were predominant in the army and the militia but enjoyed little influence in the upper reaches of the PAIGC. They feared attempts to demobilize parts of the war-bloated army and were disillusioned by the economic decline, shortages, and increased taxes.

The 1980 coup enjoyed strong popular support among

Guineans. President Cabral was allowed to go into exile, but the coup was condemned by the Cape Verdian wing of the party, which then changed its name to the African Party for the Independence of Cape Verde (*Partido Africano da Independência de Cabo Verde*; PAICV) and declared its independence. The coup leaders, mainly army veterans, eventually decided to retain the PAIGC organization (and the reference to Cape Verde in its name) and accused Luiz Cabral of betraying the revolutionary principles of his half brother, Amilcar Cabral.

The new Council of the Revolution restructured the PAIGC as purely Guinean, but the people's confidence had been shaken. Since then, there has been substantial instability in the new regime and several unsuccessful coup attempts have followed. The country's consistently poor economic performance continues to cause instability. In particular, the state's inability to provide for most of the demobilized veterans of the army and the militia is a long-standing problem.

OPPOSITION POLITICAL PARTIES

The second-largest party is the Guinea-Bissau Resistance-Bah Fatah Movement, or RGB-MB (*Resistência da Guiné-Bissau-Movimento Ba-Fatah*), which has 19 seats in the parliament. It is a regional party based among the Muslim Fula of the Ba-Fatah and Gabu regions in the northeast who resent Balanta domination and claim to have been left out. The third-largest party is the Social Renovation Party, or PRS (*Partido da Renovacão Social*), which has 12 seats. It is mostly urban-based and is favored by the educated who advocate the end of the veterans' grasp on power. It harbors a radical nationalism and accuses the PAIGC of being a nest of incompetents and profiteers. The leader, Kumba Yala, was the only opposition candidate in the 1994 presidential ballot and garnered 48% in the runoff.

Other opposition parties include Union for Change Coalition (*União para a Mudanca*; UM), 4 seats; Front for the Liberation and Independence of Guinea (*Frente da Libertacão para a Independência Nacional da Guine*; FLING), 1 seat; and Guinean League for the Protection of the Environment (*Liga Guineense de Protecão Ecologica*; LIPE), 1 seat. All opposition parties are united in their rejection of the PAIGC's claim to have liberated the country single-handedly, the overwhelming powers of the president of the republic, the lack of a fair electoral process, and rampant corruption. However, the opposition parties are not a united front, nor are they a stable force. After the 1994 elections, some members left the RGB-MB and formed a new party, the Social Democratic Party (*Partido Social Democratico*; PSD), in protest against RGB-MB's ethnic orientation and its conservatism.

OTHER POLITICAL FORCES

Foreign Relations

Guinea-Bissau remains committed to nonalignment, pragmatically seeking aid from as many sources as possible. In practice, most aid, including food aid, has come from Western countries. Most trade is still with the West, especially the EU. Guinea-Bissau also has established close relations with neighboring Senegal and Guinea-Conakry, despite disputes over maritime borders, which were refereed in the International Court of Justice. Surrounded by French-speaking countries, Guinea-Bissau strongly supports cooperation among the Portuguese-speaking African countries, but without much success. Finally, it joined the African Financial Community (CFA) zone (a monetary zone uniting the former French colonies who share the same currency pegged to the French franc by a fixed exchange rate) in 1997.

Relations with neighbors have been greatly improved, especially with Senegal, despite the accusation that Guinea-Bissau turns a blind eye to the activities of the Casamance separatist guerrillas. These guerrillas are said to launch attacks from Guinea-Bissau and to use refugee camps as rear bases. However, since the mid-1990s, Guinea-Bissau has undertaken the role of mediator and guarantor between the two sides, while restricting the guerrilla movements on its soil. In the meantime, since the 1980 coup, the old goal of unifying Guinea-Bissau and Cape Verde has been abandoned, and integration with the mainland regional system has become the paramount objective. In that regard, Guinea-Bissau has joined the Economic Community of West Africa (ECOWAS), the organizations set up for the exploitation of the Senegal River (OMVS) and of the Gambia River (OMVG), and the West African Monetary Union (UMOA).

Ethnic Groups

Historically, the mixed blood Euro-Africans, Cape Verdians, and local Mesticos have been influential in Guinea-Bissau. Under the colonial regime they enjoyed the enviable status of being considered *assimilados* (nearly Europeans). At that time, they had access to education and economic opportunities and held the little political power left to Africans. By the the 1960s, they constituted the local elite and, under Amilcar Cabral and his PAIGC, led the struggle for independence. Since the 1980 coup, however, they have been excluded from the political forefront, but they remain important as members of the intelligentsia and technocracy. They tend to support Kumba Yala's PRS, the second-largest opposition party.

The Balantas, who constitute about 30% of the population, grow most of the country's rice and account for perhaps 70% of the military. They exercise the decisive role in the ruling PAIGC. The Muslims, mainly the Fula of the Ba-Fatah and Gabu regions, did not play a strong part in the independence war and appear to have little real political influence. Their party, the RGB-MB, is the largest opposition and the second party in the country.

NATIONAL PROSPECTS

The ethnic character of its political parties makes Guinea-Bissau's political scene uncertain and allows the army to play a central role in the country's future. The presence of the army in politics also means that civilians have few prospects for experiencing a genuine, open multiparty system. President Vieira has been nominated by the military and rules largely on its behalf. The necessity to reassess the army's role, to reduce its size, and to involve a new generation in politics is obvious but has yet to be undertaken. The veterans who stand to lose the most are the most active on the political scene, especially in the PAIGC. The obstacles on the road to a true democratic society remain daunting, and Vieira's cautious maneuvering has not been the best solution to the problems facing the country.

The country's very serious economic crisis is unlikely to be resolved in the foreseeable future, but the final integration in the CFA zone (which tied many of the former French colonies' currencies to the French franc), on May 2, 1998, is a step toward liberal economic policies and more financial orthodoxy. The stability of the regime is linked to a stable economy and friendly relations with neighbors. President Vieira has also tried to tackle the economic crisis by scrapping some of the previous regime's prestige projects, curbing corruption, improving transport systems, and channeling more resources into agriculture.

One serious issue that remains is the separatist rebellion in southwestern Senegal, Casamance. Many Senegalese and foreign observers believe that the rebellion is kept active, partially at least, by the Guinea-Bissaun military's connivance and arms trafficking. The refugee camps also attract foreign aid, which is alleged to be diverted by corrupt administration officials. Vieira does not want these short-term minor advantages to block the crucial improvement of his relations with neighbors in the long run. But he has little room to maneuver, since widespread discontent with the regime makes any unlikely alliances possible. In that regard, the most dreaded hypothesis is the junction between chauvinistic nationalists and corrupt, old-style military, which would destabilize the entire subregion.

Further Reading

Aaby, Peter. *The State of Guinea-Bissau, African Socialism or Socialism in Africa?* Uppsala: Scandinavian Institute of African Studies, 1978.

Andreini, J.-C., and M.L. Lambert. *La Guinée-Bissau d'Amilcar Cabral B la Reconstruction Nationale*. Paris: Editions L'Harmattan, 1978.

"Guinea-Bissau: The Black Coup that Ended Amilcar Cabral's Dream." In *Africa Contemporary Record*. Ed. Colin Legum, vol. 13, 1980–81. New York: Holmes and Meier, 1981.

Lobban, Richard, and Peter K. Mendy. *Historical Dictionary of the Republic of Guinea-Bissau*, 3d ed. Lanham, Md.: Scarecrow Press, 1997.

Periodicals: *West-Africa* (weekly, London); *Country Profile* and *Country Report* (The Economist Intelligence Unit, London).

COOPERATIVE REPUBLIC OF GUYANA

By Robert H. Manley, Ph.D.
Revised by James Wessman, Ph.D.

THE SYSTEM OF GOVERNMENT

Guyana, a country of over 700,000 people on the northeast coast of South America, is a multiparty democracy. The population of Guyana contains several ethnic groups. Currently, East Indians make up 51% of the population, Africans 43%, and Amerindians 4%, with Europeans and Chinese accounting for the remainder. About half the population is Christian; a third is Hindu, under 10% is Muslim, and the remaining 8% practice other religions. Guyana is the only English-speaking nation in South America. The population is in a decline of almost 1% per year, due to emigration. Guyana has borders with Venezuela, Suriname, and Brazil and border disputes with the first two countries.

The Guyanese government bears the imprint not only of its colonial past but of neocolonial interference with the project of nation building. Guyana moved toward independence in the 1950s under the leadership of Cheddi Jagan, an Indo-Guyanese, and Forbes Burnham, an Afro-Guyanese, in the People's Progressive Party (PPP). Great Britain, acting under pressure from the United States, suspended Guyana's constitution and landed troops, ostensibly to prevent Guyana from becoming a communist state. The British invasion occasioned a split within the PPP, a socialist party that previously had maintained an alliance between Afro- and Indo-Guyanese, and led eventually to the two-decade-long dictatorship of Burnham, who became leader of the People's National Congress (PNC).

Jagan was imprisoned for a time by the British in 1954, but his party continued to win elections, up to the 1964 elections, when it appeared that Jagan would become prime minister and lead Guyana to independence. That election was marred by race riots that brought on an alliance between the PNC and the United Force, culminating in Burnham's election and independence in 1966. Seven years after Burnham's death in 1985, Jagan became president of Guyana, but died in 1997. He was succeeded by his widow, Janet Jagan, in 1998.

Executive

Under the 1980 constitution, a ceremonial presidency was replaced with a powerful office under the same name that combined responsibilities as head of state, chief executive, and commander in chief of the armed forces. The new post sometimes is referred to as executive president. The position was tailor-made for Forbes Burnham, who ruled from 1964 to the time of his death in 1985. Burnham had been prime minister, and this position was continued but made subsidiary to the presidency, as were other Cabinet positions, including a number of vice presidencies. Appointments to Cabinet positions, including prime minister and vice presidents, are made by the president. The presidency is now an elective rather than an appointive office, and the prime ministership is a kind of senior vice presidency. When President Cheddi Jagan died in 1997, his prime minister, Samuel Hinds, succeeded him, and Jagan's widow, Janet, became prime minister.

Legislature

The constitution vests legislative power (subject to presidential veto) in a National Assembly of 65 elected members. Although the legal system is based largely on English common law, with some features of Roman-Dutch law, Guyana's government combines features of the Westminster and Philadelphia systems. The president may dissolve the National Assembly at any time and must call for new elections within five years of the previous election. Persons appointed to the Cabinet who have not been elected to the Assembly may serve in the Assembly but may not vote.

Judiciary

The constitution provides for a Supreme Court of Judicature, consisting of the Court of Appeal and the High Court. Judges of the Court of Appeal are the chief justice and additional puisne judges as prescribed by the Assembly. The chancellor, chief justice, and other judges are appointed by the president. Critics from many quarters, both within and outside Guyana, have alleged that the courts have not been free from substantial influence by the dominant party.

Regional and Local Government

The constitution provides that the nation is divided into 10 regions, which are further divided into smaller units. A regional democratic council is elected by each region's residents, as well as local democratic organs. The National Congress of Local Democratic Organs, elected by and from the local bodies, is responsible for representing the interests of local governments.

THE ELECTORAL SYSTEM

Of the 65 elected members of the National Assembly, 53 are chosen in an election in which the nation as a whole is one district. Each political party contesting the election presents a list of candidates, and voters cast ballots only for a party list. Seats are allotted to the parties according to the proportion of votes cast for each list. Each party designates one person on the party list as its presidential candidate. Of the 12 remaining seats in the Assembly, 10 are filled in elections by and from the 10 regional democratic councils. The remaining 2 are elected from the National Congress of Local Democratic Organs.

Subject to certain minor disqualifications, all persons may vote who are 18 years of age or older and either citizens of Guyana or Commonwealth citizens domiciled or resident in Guyana for one year. Election of members of the National Assembly is by secret ballot, but many observers have criticized the electoral process as largely rigged and fraudulent.

In the most recent National Assembly elections in 1992, the reported count resulted in the People's Progressive Party (PPP) taking 36 of the 53 seats allocated in the national vote; the People's National Congress (PNC), 26; the United Force (UF), 1; and the Working People's Alliance (WPA), 2.

Allegations of electoral irregularities have accompanied nearly every vote in Guyanian history. The WPA refused to participate in the 1980 elections, claiming that the outcome would be manipulated by the ruling PNC. A report by Lord Avebury called the elections of 1968, 1973, and 1980 fraudulent. The report also questioned the results of the referendum on postponing both new elections and drafting a new constitution. This referendum, initiated by the PNC, was opposed by every other party and all leading civil and religious organizations. Their boycott of the vote rendered the outcome meaningless. By general agreement, the elections of 1992 were the first since 1964 to be free and fair.

THE PARTY SYSTEM

Origins of the Parties

The first major political party of modern times was the People's Progressive Party, founded in 1950. With broad popular support, it pushed for Guyanese independence from Great Britain under the combined leadership of Forbes Burnham and Cheddi Jagan. In the mid-1950s, the party split along ethnic and ideological lines. Burnham formed the PNC with substantial support form African voters in 1957. Shortly thereafter, in 1960, the UF was formed with support from Guyanese of Portuguese and mixed descent. A minority party, the UF threw its support behind Forbes Burnham in 1964, which enabled him to become prime minister and the PNC to control the National Assembly. A movement of protest against corruption and electoral fraud and for a more effective social democratic system developed in the mid-1970s and became the formal WPA party in 1979. The WPA, however, has not been able to break the control of the PPP and the PNC.

The Parties in Law

The right to form political parties and their freedom of action are guaranteed by the constitution. The only stated limitation is that parties "must respect the principles of national sovereignty and democracy." Nevertheless, there are a variety of restraints placed on party activity, including government control of newsprint, which limits publication of opposition newspapers. The opposition parties and their leaders have also been subjected to various forms of harrassment.

Party Organization

The PPP and the PNC aim at being formal membership parties with institutionalized party structures. The PNC is apparently tightly controlled from the top, and the political leadership of the government provides the party's primary organizational scaffolding. The PPP has declared itself to be a Marxist-Leninist party, but it is unclear to what degree it has adopted a thoroughgoing democratic centralist organization. Both parties have been dominated by their respective leaders. There is no reliable information on the size of party memberships or on their finances.

THE PEOPLE'S NATIONAL CONGRESS

The PNC was unable to best the PPP in the first two elections in which the two groups were pitted against each other, in 1957 and 1961. However, in 1964, the first race under a proportional representation system, its vote, when coupled with that of the United Force, surpassed that of the PPP. Accordingly, a PNC–UF coalition government was created, with Forbes Burnham as prime minister and the then UF leader, Peter d'Aguiar, as finance minister. The coalition ended in 1968 when the reported count in the first postindependence elections gave the PNC a majority of National Assembly seats.

Following the end of the coalition with the more conservative United Force, the PNC pushed for measures to bring about a transition to socialism, beginning with the change to cooperative republic status in 1970 and followed in succeeding years by nationalization of all bauxite and of major sugar-producing operations. At the same time, the PNC more and more attempted to present itself and the government as synonymous, raising speculation that a one-party system was its eventual goal.

Linden Forbes Burnham (born 1923) was the undisputed leader of the party from 1966 until his death in 1985. He was of African descent, as are most other major party figures. Hugh Desmond Hoyte, a barrister closely associated with Burnham for two decades, who had served as vice president and as prime minister, became president in August 1985 and won a five-year term in December of that year. Hoyt promptly reversed many of the policies of the Burnham years, defusing a difficult situation and opening the way for a return to democracy. Hoyt remains the leader of the PRN.

PEOPLE'S PROGRESSIVE PARTY (PPP)

At the time of its founding in 1950, the PPP had a broad base of support among both the East Indian and the African populations, the two dominant ethnic groups, in its struggle against British rule in particular and imperialism in general. However, as Guyanese politics polarized ideologically and ethnically from the mid-1950s onward, the PPP became more and more dependent upon East Indian support and, through the years, more and more closely committed to a Marxist-Leninist approach, until in 1969 it made this its official position.

Both Cheddi Jagan (born 1918, died 1997), the PPP leader, and his U.S.-born wife, Janet, were party members at its founding. Mrs. Jagan has edited its daily newspaper, the *Mirror*, and undertaken key organizational tasks during its history. Internationally, the party has maintained warm relations with Cuba and the former Soviet Union. In mid-1975 the PPP undertook a position of "critical support" for the PNC-led government in its asserted goal of achieving socialism and undercutting imperialism. However, it continued outspoken criticism of many aspects of governmental policy and implementation.

The PPP's return to power in 1992 was constructed around an alliance with business and other leaders in Guyana who had opposed the PNC administration of Forbes Burnham but had not embraced the PPP's ideology. This group of leaders, known as "The Civic," was not the result of local initiative but created by the PPP in recognition that alone it could not win the election. Jagan chose Samuel Hinds, a member of The Civic and a political unknown, as his candidate for prime minister. These leaders did not bring in blocks of voters to the PPP but served as examples of the economic and political policies the new PPP stood for. Consequently, the alliance ap-

pealed to independent or uncommitted voters.

In office, President Jagan remained committed to the Marxist principles of his youth but implemented social democratic reforms that had an impact on health and education as well as economic infrastructure. His relations with the business community remained contentious, in part due to Jagan's reputation. He took steps to involve Guyanese of all backgrounds in his government. The Civic is represented by ministers of education, labor, public works, and legal affairs.

Jagan's administration was more pragmatic and developed a climate in which private enterprise expanded greatly. Strained relations with the business community continued, but the United States evidently was satisfied that Guyana's charismatic leader, whose dealings with Cuba early in the 1960s elicited covert operations against him, no longer posed a threat after the fall of the Soviet Union.

The PPP's main decision-making body is its congress, which meets every three years. These delegates determine policy and elect the 35-member central committee. The general secretary of the party is then selected by the central committee. The PPP also features district and regional committees and organizes county conferences in Guyana's three counties. The Progressive Youth Organization (PYO) is the PPP's youth arm, and the Women's Progressive Organization (WPO) is its women's arm. In addition to the *Mirror*, the PPP publishes *Thunder*, a quarterly journal with a theoretical orientation.

UNITED FORCE (UF)

The UF was initially dependent to a considerable degree on support from Portuguese and ethnically mixed Guyanese and has been notably more conservative ideologically than either the PPP or PNC. After Peter d'Aguiar's retirement from active politics in 1969, the United Force leadership fell to Fielden Singh, a barrister. Manzoor Madir currently leads the UF. The party's prospects seem limited to maintaining its very modest minority position.

WORKING PEOPLE'S ALLIANCE (WPA)

The WPA is an ethnically diverse amalgam of opposition forces who are intensely dissatisfied with the incompetence, corruption, and party and ethnic favoritism of the PNC government. Its position is one of eclectic but dedicated socialism. The WPA is widely respected and was increasingly viewed as the force that might end the PNC's dominance. However, in June 1980, its most prominent leader, Walter Rodney, was killed by an explosive device, a death thought by many to have been instigated by the PNC. (The purported assassin was not formally accused until 1996.) The party continues to have creditable leadership in Eusi Kwayana, a widely known political figure, who worked with Jagan and Burnham in the early days of the PPP, and Rupert Roopnarine.

In some of the other political parties can be detected the fragmentation of Guyana's political life. For example, Hamilton Green, once prime minister under Burnham, who maintained close ties to the military, now heads Good and Green Georgetown (GGG). Asgar Ally founded the Guyana Democratic Party (GDP) after he resigned as finance minister of the PPP–Civic government.

OTHER POLITICAL FORCES

Guyana Council of Churches

The Council of Churches has become increasingly important as a focal point for concern about the state of human rights and constitutional legitimacy during a period of evaporating support for the PNC–Burnham government. It has worked with a variety of civic groups to develop better understanding of the political-economic-social system and of alternatives for the future. Its executive secretary is Michal McCormack.

Organized Labor

While some union leadership has been relatively quiescent, leaders and rank and file in a number of unions, notably (but not limited to) those of sugar and bauxite workers, have shown vigor in carrying their demands and complaints to the government and the public. Prior to the national elections held at the end of 1985, trade union militancy increased noticeably.

Guyanese Defense Force (GDF)

Strengthened through the years, partly on the basis of threats posed by Venezuelan and Surinamese claims to Guyanese territory, the GDF has, along with the Guyana police forces, been a key element of PNC internal control. Financing of its operations, along with those of the police, has been a major drain on the nation's resources. The GDF has about 7,000 members in 20 corps, which are involved in development projects.

NATIONAL PROSPECTS

With the death of Cheddi Jagan at age 78 in 1997, Guyana's political scene changed dramatically. Gone are the two "warriors" who dominated Guyanese political life over four decades, first Forbes Burnham in 1985 at age 62 and now Jagan. Others of their generation still are active in national politics, but the overwhelming influence these two figures had has not paved the way for new leadership. The PPP, for example, selected Jagan's widow, Janet Jagan, age 76, a Jewish American nurse from Chicago, as its presidential candidate for the 1998 election. Janet Jagan is the first woman head of state in Guyana and the first Guyanese head of state not born there. Her health has not been good in recent years.

Further Reading

Baber, Colin. *Guyana: Politics, Economics and Society: Beyond the Burnham Era.* New York: Columbia University Press, 1986.

Hintzen, Percy C. *The Costs of Regime Survival: Racial Mobilization, Elite Domination, and Control of the State in Guyana and Trinidad.* New York: Cambridge University Press, 1989.

Premdas, Ralph R. *Ethnic Conflict and Development: The Case of Guyana.* Brookfield, Vt: Ashgate, 1995.

Singh, Chaitram. *Guyana: Politics in a Plantation Society.* New York: Praeger, 1988.

Williams, Brackette. *Stains on My Name, War in My Veins: Guyana and the Politics of Cultural Struggle.* Durham, N.C.: Duke University Press, 1991.

REPUBLIC OF HAITI

(Republique d'Haiti)

By Michel S. Laguerre, Ph.D.

THE SYSTEM OF GOVERNMENT

Haiti, a country with a population of approximately 6.5 million in 1998, occupying one-third (10,850 square miles) of a two-nation Caribbean island, is a parliamentary republic with the seat of government in the capital city of Port-au-Prince. Located on the western side of the island of Hispaniola, it includes as well the following neighboring islets: La Gonâve, la Tortue, l'Ileà-Vache, les Cayemittes, la Navase, la Grande Caye, and smaller ones inside the territorial sea.

In 1986, the three-decade-old dictatorial regime headed first by François "Papa Doc" Duvalier and then by Jean Claude "Baby Doc" Duvalier collapsed under its own weight as a result of street unrest and the unwillingness of the U.S. administration to support the corrupt government. To manage the crisis, the Haitian military stepped in and established a National Council of Government headed by General Henri Namphy. This was the beginning of a turbulent period of political instability, with a succession of nine presidents and eight prime ministers between 1986 and 1996, each spending on average less than a year and half in office.

Following the proclamation of the new constitution of 1987, legislative elections were held to select the senators (*le Sénat*) and representatives of the people (*Chambre des Députés*) in preparation for the 1990 presidential elections. The new president, Jean Bertrand Aristide, a Catholic priest, took the oath of office in February 1991. He was toppled in a military coup the following September. This coup, by unseating a popular president with a national mandate, was seen by the Haitian electorate and the Organization of American States (OAS) as a setback for the installation of democracy in Haiti. It brought about a major constitutional crisis for the nation and much human suffering among the prodemocratic forces and supporters of the fallen regime. From Venezuela, where he was given political asylum, the deposed President Aristide brought the seat of the exiled government to Washington, D.C., to be closer to the mainstream American political scene, the Haitian American diaspora, and human rights activists and grassroots organizations that supported his administration.

In order to return Aristide to Haiti, much negotiation took place among his administration, the General Assembly of the United Nations, the general secretary of the OAS, the Bush and Clinton administrations, and the power brokers of the Haitian armed forces. On July 3, 1993, President Aristide and General Raoul Cédras signed the Governors Island Accord that set in motion President Aristide's return to Haiti. Still unwilling to let Aristide in, the general staff of the Haitian armed forces changed their minds only after it became obvious that they were going to be willingly or unwillingly removed by the U.S. marines. The U.S.-UN Occupation Forces landed in Port-au-Prince in September 1994, and a month later President Aristide ended his exile and was able to return to complete his mandate. Humiliated by the presence of foreign military forces in Haiti and demoralized by the exile of key players among the general staff of the army, many soldiers deserted their barracks and some went into hiding. In 1995, preoccupied with the creation and training of the new civilian police force, and under pressure from the populace to do away with the army, President Aristide disbanded the Haitian armed forces.

On December 17, 1995, René Garcia Préval was elected president with 88% of the vote. Préval appointed Rosny Smarth prime minister in March 1996. However, in June 1997, prime minister Smarth resigned his post, largely over the government's complicity in the electoral fraud committed during and after the April 6, 1997, partial Senate and local government elections. As late as October 1998, the government has been unable to agree on a prime minister and has basically been deadlocked.

Executive

The president of the republic is the head of state while the government is headed by the prime minister. To be elected as president of Haiti, a person must be born in

Haiti, must never have renounced his or her Haitian nationality, must own real estate or practice a profession, must have resided in Haiti for five consecutive years, and must have no criminal background. To become president a person must be 35 years old, and to become prime minister, 30 years old.

The functions of the president and the prime minister are spelled out in the following manner by the constitution: The president is elected for a five-year mandate beginning on the February 7th following the general elections and cannot be reelected at the end of his term in office. However, after an interim period of five years, he may serve an additional term. Under no circumstances can he be elected for a third term.

The powers of the president are multiple. He is responsible for the implementation of constitutional norms, the maintenance of political stability, the functioning of state institutions, and the preservation of the internal and external security of the state. He must select a prime minister from among the majority party in parliament. If no party holds a majority of seats in parliament, he has to confer with the president of the Senate and the Speaker of the House in his selection of a prime minister. He has the right to dismiss the government after he has received a letter of resignation from the prime minister. He promulgates laws voted by the two Houses and enforces judicial decisions. He may pardon or commute sentences if he deems such a practice appropriate. He appoints ambassadors, consuls, and special envoys to foreign countries and receives letters of accreditation of ambassadors from foreign powers. He also presides over the Council of Ministers.

There are also limitations to the powers of the president as set forth by the constitution. He must submit to the Senate his nominees for ambassadorial posts and to the National Assembly (*Assemblé Nationale*) his choice for prime minister and all international treaties, conventions, agreements, and peace treaties. Furthermore, he must deliver his state of the nation address before the parliament at the first annual meeting of that body.

The government is made up of the prime minister, ministers, and secretaries of state. The prime minister has the right to select the members of his Cabinet of Ministers and to appoint or dismiss government officials. His primary role, however, is to run the government smoothly and enforce the laws. He may appear before the upper or lower house to defend the policies of the government. Also, he may serve both as prime minister and minister in charge of a specific ministry; however, he cannot serve as a member of parliament. In the absence of the president, he may preside over the Council of Ministers. In addition to the ministers he is entitled to select, the prime minister may appoint secretaries of state to make the work of the government more efficient.

The primary role of a Cabinet minister is to run his or her ministry efficiently, enforce laws, implement government policies, and cooperate with the prime minister. He or she may appoint government employees in his or her ministry. However, a minister cannot hold another job in the public sector. (An exception is made for those who teach in the public school system or at the university level.) Furthermore, a minister can be dismissed by the executive branch if he or she is censured by the Senate or the House of Representatives.

Legislature

The legislature consists of two bodies that make up the parliament: the Senate (*Sénat*) and the House of Representatives (*Chambre des Députés*). The Senate, the upper house, is a 27-member body, with three senators for each of nine departments. The senators are elected for six-year terms, with one-third up for election every two years. The senators are elected by direct suffrage.

The House of Representatives, or the lower house, has 83 members who are elected for four-year terms. The representatives begin their terms on the second Monday of January, which coincides with the beginning of the first session of parliament. The parliament holds two sessions, the first from the second Monday in January to the second Monday in May and the second from the second Monday in June to the second Monday in September.

The lower house may with a two-thirds majority initiate the process of impeachment of the president, the prime minister, or any of the ministers or secretaries of state. It can do so by simply convoking the accused before the *Haute Cour de Justice* (High Court of Justice, which is not to be confused with the Supreme Court) made up of the president of the Senate and the president and the vice president of the Supreme Court.

Unlike the House of Representatives, which holds two annual sessions, the Senate is permanently in session. In the interim of the legislative sessions, it may adjourn, but it must put in place a permanent committee to handle current businesses. One-third of the Senate is replaced every two years. In addition to its legislative mission, the Senate has the duty to propose to the executive branch of government a list of potential Supreme Court justices and has the right to transform itself into a High Court of Justice to deal with specific legal problems under its jurisdiction.

The National Assembly (*Assemblée Nationale*) is made up of the Senate and the House of Representatives when they meet in a joint legislative session. These two bodies hold joint meetings to open and close each legislative session. The National Assembly administers the oath to the president of the republic, ratifies any decision to declare war before it can take effect, approves or rejects all international treaties and conventions, is an active player in the selection of the Permanent Electoral Council, and is provided at the opening of each session with a report on the government's activities. The National Assembly is headed by the president of the Senate, who serves as its president, and the president of the House of Representatives, who serves as its vice president.

The main role of the legislature is to enact laws for the common good and the welfare of the state. Either house or the executive branch can introduce legislation. Each law or bill must be voted upon and adopted by a majority of legislators present before it can be sent to the executive branch for promulgation. The president reserves the right to veto any laws submitted to his office. The legislature has the legal right to impose disciplinary penalties or even expel members who have not lived up to their constitutional duties.

The number of districts is selected according to the electoral law developed by the Provisional Electoral Council (PEC). However, an electoral district is defined by the constitution as "a collective municipality" whose boundaries are set by the PEC. The last electoral law, issued in 1995, does not spell out how the number of districts is determined.

According to the constitution, any Haitian man or woman who has never renounced his or her Haitian nationality, owns real estate or practices a profession or a trade, and enjoys civil and political rights can be elected to serve in the House of Representatives. He or she must be at least 25 years old and have resided for two consecutive years in the district he or she is to represent. The same requirements hold true for a person to be elected to the Senate; however, he or she must be at least 30 years old and have lived in the department he or she is to represent for at least four consecutive years. Contractors, concessionaires of the state in the operation of public services, and their representatives and agents are not eligible for membership in the legislature.

Judiciary

The mechanisms by which the judiciary functions in Haitian society are set up by the constitution. The judicial branch of government is composed of the following courts: Supreme Court (*Cour de Cassation*), courts of appeals, lower courts (*Tribunaux de Première Instance*), peace courts, and special courts. The judges of the Supreme Court are appointed by the president of the republic from a list of candidates submitted by the Senate. The courts of appeals and lower courts judges are appointed by the president from a list submitted by the departmental assembly concerned, and the peace courts judges are selected by the president from a list submitted by the communal assemblies. While the judges of the Supreme Court and the courts of appeals are appointed for 10-year terms, those of the lower courts are appointed for seven-year terms. Jurisdictions over civil, political, and commercial rights are usually handled by the lower courts and the courts of appeals, while the Supreme Court concentrates its attention on jurisdictional conflicts and the constitutionality of laws.

Regional and Local Government

The department (*département*), the largest territorial division of the republic, is administered by a council of three members elected for four years. The executive branch is represented in each department by a delegate and in each *arrondissement* by a vice delegate. The liaison between the executive branch and the department is made possible by the existence of the interdepartmental council that is made up of representatives designated by departmental assemblies.

Each department is further subdivided into *arrondissements*, and each *arrondissement* has one or more communes and communal sections under its jurisdiction. Any Haitian man or woman who enjoys civil and political rights, has no criminal background, and is at least 25 years old can be elected to serve on the communal section council if he or she has been living in the area for two consecutive years.

The communal section is the smallest administrative territorial entity. A council of three members, who are elected for four-year terms, administers it. These individuals can be reelected. The commune is administered by a municipal council headed by a president who functions as mayor, aided by a municipal assembly made up of representatives of the commune. These officers are elected for four-year terms and can be reelected thereafter.

THE ELECTORAL SYSTEM

On December 8, 1994, President Aristide signed a decree for the creation of a temporary electoral council. This council comprised nine members—three selected by the executive, three by the legislature, and three by the judiciary—with the mission of organizing the presidential, legislative, and mayoral elections of 1995. The council set the electoral guidelines, decided on logistical matters, and made the final decision on eligible candidates, voter turnout, candidate registration, and balloting. The most recent elections were carried out in the presence of delegates from other countries to ensure the fairness of the process and to give more validity to the results.

The legality and authority of this Provisional Electoral Council (PEC) are not recognized by the major opposition parties, which boycotted the last parliamentary elections, in April 1997. As a consequence of low voter turnout and presumed bias of the PEC in favor of Aristide, the parliament rejected these election results. As of late 1998, the country was at a standstill, waiting for a new prime minister to be appointed and for the organization of new municipal and legislative elections.

THE PARTY SYSTEM

During the first six years of the Duvalier dictatorship, all political parties were banned. Not until the 1987 constitution were political parties officially sanctioned in Haiti. While there are many parties and coalitions in existence, one party dominated the last legislative elections, the Lavalas Political Organization (*Organisation politique Lavalas*; OPL), which was also the party of President Préval. Recently renamed Organization of the Struggling People, OPL (*Organisation du Peuple en Lutte*) is headed by Gérard Pierre-Charles. This centrist *Lavalas* ("flood") swept the 1995 Chamber of Representatives election by taking 68 of the 83 seats. Because of internal frictions, the Lavalas family recently broke away from its formal Lavalas Political Organization and created a party known as Lavalas Family (*La Famille Lavalas*) as an alternative, grassroots political party.

The Movement for the Installation of Democracy in Haiti (*Mouvement Pour l'Instauration de la Démocratie en Haiti*) is the next-most-influential party in terms of popularity with the electorate. However, it boycotted the 1995 and 1997 legislative elections.

For the time being, the political system is in a state of paralysis. The disagreement on whether the April 6, 1997, elections were valid and the years of waiting for a prime minister to take office have basically deadlocked Haiti's political process

NATIONAL PROSPECTS

The political situation in Haiti is still very volatile, with a disbanded army, an inexperienced civilian police force, and the vacancy of the prime minister seat. In June 1997, prime minister Rosny Smarth resigned his position and in October vacated the office. At the end of 1998, the country was still without a prime minister and a duly appointed government. President René Préval was running the country with a handful of leftover Cabinet ministers from the fallen government. Although two citizens were chosen consecutively by the president to head the government, the parliament approved neither of them.

This state of affairs came about because of an ongoing conflict between *La Famille Lavalas* (with its populist orientation) and the other political parties, most notably the *Organisation Politique Lavalas* (with its technocratic orientation), over the disputed legislative elections of April 1997. The vast majority of the political parties refused to accept the results of these elections as legitimate because they believed that the transitional electoral committee had favored the newly formed party headed by Jean-Bertrand Aristide. President Préval sided with the Aristide party in this dispute while the opposition still controlled the parliament.

The next presidential elections will be held in 2000, and Jean Bertrand Aristide has already informed the populace that he will run again for the presidency. Although popular among the Haitian electorate and the Haitian American diaspora during the campaigns of 1990, Aristide has lost a good deal of his support because of the collapse of the political coalition that brought him to power and his inability to engineer sustained economic reforms during his first term in office. However, it is still too early to make any realistic predictions on the possible outcome of the forthcoming presidential elections.

Further Reading

Dupuy, Alex. *Haiti in the New World Order: The Limits of the Democratic Revolution*. Boulder, Colo.: Westview Press, 1997.

Laguerre, Michel S. *The Military and Society in Haiti*. Knoxville: University of Tennessee Press, 1993.

———. "National Security, Narcotics Control, and the Haitian Military." In *Security Problems and Policies in the Post-Cold War Caribbean*. Ed. Jorge Rodriguez Beruff and Humberto Garcia Muniz. London: Macmillan, 1996.

Rotberg, Robert I, ed. *Haiti Renewed: Political and Economic Prospects*. Washington, D.C.: Brookings Institution, 1997.

Stotzky, Irwin P. *Silencing the Guns in Haiti: The Promise of Deliberative Democracy*. Chicago: University of Chicago Press, 1997.

THE REPUBLIC OF HONDURAS

(La República de Honduras)

By Kirk Bowman

THE SYSTEM OF GOVERNMENT

Honduras is a constitutional republic in Central America still attempting to consolidate a democratic government and a political culture. The country has been nominally democratic since 1982, but civilian control of the powerful armed forces is still in question and a consolidated full-fledged democracy is still an uncertain goal. While the country has a long history of instability with 14 written constitutions and limited experience with democratic rule, it did not experience the large-scale social upheaval and violence in the 1980s that occurred in neighboring El Salvador, Guatemala, and Nicaragua. Honduras is an extremely poor country, which coupled with a highly unequal distribution of resources leaves the vast majority of the citizenry struggling and many not meeting minimal nutrition and health requirements.

The country of 5.8 million has a land mass of 43,277 square miles, roughly the size of Tennessee. The vast majority of Hondurans live in the western half of the country, while the eastern Caribbean or Mosquito Coast region is sparsely populated. The country has a long northern coastline on the Caribbean and a small opening to the Pacific. Honduras shares a long border with Nicaragua to the south, the site of the U.S.-sponsored contra rebels who fought the Sandinista government in the 1980s. Guatemala is to the west and El Salvador to the southwest. Honduras is largely a Mestizo (mixed-race), Spanish-speaking, and Catholic country, although a small indigenous population exists (7%) as well as a series of Garifuna (of African and Carib Indian descent) communities along the Caribbean (2%).

Executive

Honduras features a presidential system where the chief of state is elected every four years by winning a simple majority of votes. The president must be native-born, at least 30 years old, and not an active member of the armed forces or a pastor or priest. Three vice presidents are elected concurrently with the president. If for any reason the president is unable to continue, the National Assembly selects one of the vice presidents to finish the president's term. The president appoints 14 ministers who form the Cabinet.

In the 1994–98 term, President Carlos Reina created two new ministries (the Public Ministry and the Ministry of Environment). The Public Ministry, which is the Attorney General's Office, is especially important as it coordinates and oversees the police once they leave the jurisdiction of the military, a transition that is in process.

The president has veto power and can both call the Assembly into special session and extend a regular session; a two-thirds vote is required to overturn a veto. The president also has foreign policy and security responsibilities, although there are questions as to where de facto power resides since the military is largely autonomous. While the 1982 constitution gives the National Assembly the power to appoint many government officials, such as Supreme Court justices and the attorney general, in reality the Assembly generally rubber-stamps the wishes of the president (although over time the Assembly is showing greater signs of independence). The president oversees the government bureaucracy of some 70,000 state workers. Government jobs have long been a source of patronage; the civil service lacks professionalism with many positions changing with each election. The president also appoints governors for the country's 18 administrative departments (provinces or *departamentos*).

After decades of military rule, the road to elected executives began in 1980. Legislators were elected and were expected to choose a president, but instead they asked the military president, Policarpo Paz, to stay on until 1982. Roberto Suazo Cordova of the Liberal Party won the 1981 presidential election. In the 1985 elections, Suazo attempted to extend his term and the major parties were unable to select candidates; the military was called on to broker a solution. This solution, known as Option B, was to hold elections that were simultaneously primary and general elections. Multiple candidates for each party appeared on the ballot with the candidate receiving the most votes for each party becoming the nominee. Each party's nominee subsequently received all of the party's combined votes. The final results of the balloting gave

42.6% to Rafael Leonardo Callejas Romero of the National Party and 27.5% to the Liberal Party's José Azcona. However, because the total vote of the combined Liberal candidates was 51.5%, Azcona was declared the victor and assumed office in 1986.

Callejas Romero was victorious in the 1989 elections and a peaceful electoral transfer of power from the Liberals to the Nationals occurred for the first time in Honduran history. Power was transferred back to the Liberal Party with the elections of November 1993, which were won by Carlos Roberto Reina Idiaquez, an attorney with a strong human rights record who ran on an anticorruption and antimilitary platform. President Reina assumed office in January 1994.

The 1997 general elections were the fifth consecutive generally free and competitive elections since the return to democracy in the early 1980s. The Liberal Party candidate was Carlos Roberto Flores Facusse, the former president of the National Congress who had been defeated as the Liberal Party candidate in the presidential election of 1989. Flores studied engineering at Louisiana State University and is the owner of one of the leading newspapers. The National Party standard-bearer was Nora Gunera de Melgar, a former elementary schoolteacher and mayor of Tegucigalpa and the widow of a former president who took power in a military coup in 1975. The campaign was uneventful until early polls showed Flores with a large lead, and the National Party brought in U.S. campaign handler and strategist Dick Morris, who had previously caused a scandal as a consultant to President Clinton. Morris was quick to employ negative campaign tactics, trying to make an issue of the fact that Flores's mother is of Palestinian descent and his wife is American. Melgar began to run ads emphasizing her "100% Honduran roots," and flyers and placards appeared denouncing the Middle Eastern business class in Honduras. Despite these ploys, Flores secured an impressive victory, receiving 52.8% of the vote compared with 42.7% for Melgar.

Legislature

The National Assembly (*Asamblea Nacional*) is a unicameral legislature whose members serve four-year terms concurrently with the president. Congressional members are elected through proportional representation allocated among the 18 departments according to population with each department assured at least one representative. Each deputy is elected with a substitute (*suplente*) who may serve out any vacated office. There are 128 congressional deputies (*diputados*). The largest delegations represent the departments of Morazán (home of Tegucigalpa, the capital) and Cortés (the San Pedro Sula area).

Deputies must be Honduran by birth and over 21 years of age. Religious leaders, members of the military and police forces, and public officials and their spouses and close relatives are barred from becoming deputies. Deputies enjoy personal immunity from most legal and police action. This privilege has become a source of outrage as some 30 officials are currently hiding behind immunity to escape criminal prosecution.

The Assembly elects its own president and appoints a Permanent Commission of nine members that conducts congressional business when the legislature is not in session. The Assembly is in regular session from January 24 to October 31. Extraordinary sessions may be called by the president, by the Permanent Commission, or by a simple majority of members. These extraordinary sessions may only consider matters specifically stated in the convocatory decree.

The powers, duties and responsibilities of the Assembly include the election of the nine Supreme Court Justices and seven alternates, the commander in chief of the armed forces, the comptroller general, and other officials. In practice however, the legislature generally rubber-stamps the recommendations of the president, except in the case of the chief of the armed forces. Then it simply accepts the choice of the armed forces' executive council, although historic reforms of the military institution that would provide greater civilian control are currently under legislative review. The Assembly has the power to make peace and declare war and to approve or disapprove treaties made by the president. The Assembly receives the national budget from the president and has the power to make modifications before formal adoption.

To become law, a bill must pass three readings on three different days. An amendment to the constitution must receive a majority vote of the entire congress, not just of a quorum, in two different years.

The 1997 elections resulted in a congress composed of 67 deputies from the Liberal Party, 54 from the National Party, 5 from the Party for Innovation and Unity, and 2 from smaller parties.

Judiciary

The Honduran judiciary consists of a Supreme Court of Justice, courts of appeal, courts of first instance, and justices of the peace. The Supreme Court has both appellate and original jurisdiction and exercises judicial review in cases involving constitutional questions; it consists of nine justices and seven alternates who are selected by the National Assembly to serve four-year terms concurrent with the election cycle. This leaves the court highly politicized with judges often handpicked by the president. The Supreme Court in turn selects all lower court judges and justices of the peace. These positions are often political rewards, and many of the justices of the peace are of questionable qualifications, often even lacking primary education.

The nine courts of appeal are three-judge panels that hear all appeals from lower courts. Appeal judges must be attorneys and at least 25 years of age. The 64 first-instance courts are trial courts that hear serious civil and criminal cases. Each department capital and municipalities of more than 4,000 inhabitants have two justices of the peace, and municipalities of fewer than 4,000 have one. Justices must be 21, live in the municipality that they serve, and be able to read and write.

While the constitution stipulates that the judiciary receive 3% of the total national budget, this is in practice never followed. The Honduran judiciary is underfunded, politicized, and of questionable effectiveness. Courageous judges have, for example, held trials of military officers for human rights abuses and other crimes, but often the police mock or threaten the judges and ignore orders to capture and imprison convicted soldiers. In addition, women's groups argue that the Penal Code, approved in 1996, is an affront to women. Articles 151 and 152 of the code provide that a man who rapes a girl between the ages of 14 and 18 can go free if he marries the victim and that government prosecutors are prevented from pressing rape charges if the rapist used nonviolent methods—such as drugs or taking advantage of a sleeping or unconscious woman—to commit the crime.

Regional and Local

The nation's 18 departments are headed by presidentially appointed governors, who are essentially dignitaries. The 18 departments are divided into 297 municipalities. Municipalities may contain more than one town within its boundaries and are similar to a counties in the United States. Each municipality (*municipalidad*) has an elected mayor and between 4 and 10 council members, depending on the population. In recent years, there has been a movement toward decentralization and stronger local governments. Beginning with the 1993 elections, municipal officials were elected on a separate ballot from the president and legislature (one vote per ballot). This allows ticket splitting and makes local officials responsible to the electorate. Additionally, this gives the smaller parties much greater opportunities to win local elections. Tegucigalpa, the capital and largest city, also now has an elected mayor and city council. Local governments are highly dependent on the central government for funding.

THE ELECTORAL SYSTEM

The Honduran electoral system is based on universal suffrage (since 1956) for all citizens over the age of 18. Voting is compulsory for those between 18 and 60, though compliance is not enforced. Active members of the armed forces do not vote. The ballot is secret, and since voters merely make a single fingerprint mark on each colored ballot that features symbols of the parties, literacy is not necessary.

For the elections from 1981 through 1989, a single ballot included the name of a presidential candidate and ranked lists of that party's candidates for the National Assembly and the municipal council in the area. Voters cast a single ballot for an entire slate. Beginning in 1993, municipal officials were elected on a separate ballot that allowed ticket splitting between local and national candidates. The 128 seats of the legislature are divided proportionally by votes cast in each department. The president is elected by a simple majority, as are local mayors.

A National Election Tribunal (*Tribunal National de Elecciones*) was created under the 1981 electoral law. The Tribunal is charged with registering all eligible citizens, regulating the registration process of political parties, and overseeing electoral rules. The Tribunal is an independent, autonomous body that has a president chosen by the Supreme Court and one member chosen by each of the registered national parties. In anticipation of the 1997 elections, the Tribunal proposed various changes to electoral rules. The most important was to make a separate ballot for the election of legislative deputies, a proposal that was formally adopted and that benefited the smaller parties. One electoral rule that helps maintain the status quo is that parties are given public campaign funds based on the number of votes received in the previous election.

THE PARTY SYSTEM

Origins of the Parties

Among Central American countries, Honduras has the longest tradition of two dominant parties: the Liberals and the Nationals. The Liberal Party was formed in 1891 by one the country's most successful presidents, Policarpo Bonilla. The National Party was originally a breakaway group of liberals led by Manuel Bonilla. Until 1948, the Nationals and the Liberals were the only official political parties in the country. For many years, the two parties were aligned with rival North American banana companies, the Liberals with Cuyamel and the Nationals with United Fruit. The military has been strongly allied with the National Party. While Hondurans have shown displeasure with the corruption, nepotism, and failure of the principal parties, alternative parties have never captured a significant portion of the electorate.

The Parties in Law

The constitution recognizes the role of legally inscribed political parties in providing for the effective participation of citizens in the political process. Parties are only recognized upon the presentation of petitions bearing the signature of a specified number of voters in each department. Registration traditionally has been difficult due to the challenges in collecting and authenticating the signatures. As would be expected, the two major parties have stopped all movement to more easily facilitate the registration of parties.

At present five parties are legally recognized: the two traditional rivals, the National and Liberal parties; two parties formed in the 1970s, the Party of Innovation and Unity (PINU) and the Christian Democratic Party (PDC); and one party recognized in 1996, the Democratic Unification Party (PUD).

Party Organization

With the exception of the newly formed Democratic Unification Party, all Honduran parties are national in scope. Even departments that are considered National or Liberal strongholds have swung back and forth between the two in national elections. There are no wholly regional parties nor departments entirely in the hands of one or another party.

Political parties have grassroots organizations, student organizations, and dues-paying members with locally selected officials in each department. Many of these groups, in addition to political organization and indoctrination, maintain programs of political education and services such as dental and medical clinics and food distribution at the regional and municipal levels. Local party bosses, especially in the rural areas, are often powerful area chieftains (*caciques*) who still resort to violence to maintain their positions of power and dominance.

Party structures are highly centralized, and power has traditionally been centered in Tegucigalpa. With the rise of San Pedro Sula as the industrial center of the country, this city and the department of Cortés is beginning to challenge the old guard in the capital. The two major parties themselves are divided into bitter factions, and intraparty competition is as bitter and important as that between parties.

Campaigning

The limited size of the country and the concentration of the population in the western half permits personal campaigning by the candidates in all populated areas. The campaign begins a full two years before the national elections when the candidates start their quest for their party's nomination. Candidates visit towns, participate in parades, sponsor barbecues, kiss babies, speak to local groups, and try to garner support from the movers and shakers. Town officials and elites try to line up early behind a successful candidate in order to later receive patronage positions in the government or bureaucracy. The major parties hold national primaries to select their nominees to the presidency. These primaries often involve backroom deals where candidates withdraw and throw their support to another. For the 1993 elections, the National Party's major factions struck a deal and only one candidate ran in the primaries. For the 1997 elections, both the National Party and the Liberal Party primaries featured multiple candidates.

Honduran primaries are held almost a full year before the national election, resulting in a very long campaign season. The country is canvassed with flags, posters, balloons, billboards, wall paintings, hats, and television, radio, and newspaper advertisements featuring the colors and symbols of the parties and the names of the standard-bearer. Even the rocks along the sides of the highways are painted with National blue or Liberal red paint.

While the government provides campaign subsidies based on the number of votes received in the previous election, campaigns are very expensive and expenditures are not limited or reported. Campaign expenses are contributed by wealthy party members, individuals hoping for a patronage position, and merchants and industrialists who are said to hedge their bets by contributing to both major parties.

Independent Voters

Formal party membership, in the sense of paying dues and carrying a membership card, covers a minority of registered voters. Family traditions and party loyalties are strong but declining. The use of a separate ballot to select national legislators resulted in a surprising amount of ticket splitting, resulting in the election of deputies from nontraditional parties, and may lead to a larger number of independent voters in the future.

HONDURAS LIBERAL PARTY
(Partido Liberal de Honduras; PLH)

HISTORY
The oldest political party in the country, the Liberal Party has its roots in the 1890s liberal movement of Policarpo Bonilla whose presidential term (1894–99) marked one of the most successful eras in Honduran political history. During the first half of the 20th century, the Liberal Party was closely allied with Cuyamel, an North American banana company owned by Samuel Zemurray. Zemurray waged land wars against another U.S. company, United Fruit, which was aligned with the National Party. In 1929, Zemurray gave up the battle and sold Cuyamel to United Fruit, leaving the Liberals with a loss of support and on the political sidelines from 1933 to 1957.

In 1957, after years of dictatorship (Tiburcio Carías from 1933 to 1949), the Liberals regained power with Ramón Villeda Morales. While staunchly anticommunist, Villeda was socially progressive and his Liberal administration brought about a new labor code, began discussions on land reform, and started to modernize the country. When it became apparent that an even more progressive liberal, Modesto Rodas Alvarado, would sweep the 1963 elections, the military administered a coup.

The Liberals were not to regain power until the election of Suazo in 1981. A country doctor, Suazo was an incompetent and unpopular executive who attempted to maintain his power beyond his four-year term. In part due to Suazo's machinations, the Liberal Party was unable to select a candidate for the 1985 elections. The military intervened and brokered a plan whereby each party could run multiple candidates in the national election and the party that got the most total votes would win, making the president the candidate who obtained the most votes for said party. This ended in fiasco, with the winning candidate, the Liberal's José Azcona, garnering only 27.5% of the vote. Azcona was forced to make a pact with the National Party in order to govern. Carlos Flores Facussé won the 1988 primary for the Liberals but was defeated in the 1989 elections. In 1993, Carlos Roberto Reina, of the progressive wing of the party, was the party's nominee and ran on a platform of moral revolution (anticorruption) and weakening the power and prerogatives of the military. Reina, an attorney, is a former chancellor of the university and justice on the Interamerican Human Rights Court. The Liberal Party won the 1993 elections in a landslide, and Reina was moderately successful in his attempts to reign in the military. Although there were various attempts on his life and both overt and subtle threats from the military high command, Reina was able to change military service from obligatory to voluntary and to pass a constitutional amendment to transfer the police from military to civilian control. While it is widely accepted that the Reina administration is cleaner than that of its National predecessor, some members in the administration have been accused of corruption. On the economic front, the Reina administration has been unable to ignite the moribund economy and levels of poverty and unemployment remain critically high.

Membership and Constituency

The PLH has a broad base of support throughout the country and strong support in urban areas. Claims of membership are highly suspect, but in open elections it has shown to be the dominant party in the country. The more centrist of the two major parties, the PLH traditionally has had a strong following among organized labor, the educated, and the young.

Financing

The government subsidizes campaigns based on the number of votes received in the previous election. Individual and business donations are not regulated and unreported.

Leadership

Many of the factions in the party are personalistic, and the leaders make deals and campaign vigorously to secure the presidential nomination. The current leader of the party is Carlos Flores Facussé of the New Agenda Movement. He and his opponent in the 1996 primaries, Jaime Rosenthal of the Liberal Renovator Movement, are both wealthy media owners, and both are U.S.-educated.

Prospects

While the party continues to suffer from factionalization, its prospects are good to be a major political force for some time. Its 1997 presidential victory was its fourth in five attempts since electoral democracy was established in 1981.

National Party of Honduras
(Partido Nacional de Honduras; PNH)

History

The National Party, one of two dominant parties in Honduras, was first formed in 1902 as a splinter group of the Liberal Party. It was the party of long-term president and dictator Tiburcio Carías A., who ruled the country with an iron fist from 1932 to 1949, and of his successors, Juan Manuel Gálvez and Julio Lozano. The PNH's candidate, Ramón Cruz, won the 1970 elections, but his weak and aimless administration was toppled by a military coup after only a year in office. The PNH has been an active collaborator in military governments and throughout the cold war was a right-wing, promilitary party with strong ties to the rural landed elite.

During the 1980s, the party was a strong supporter of the militarization of Honduras and cooperation with the United States and U.S.-sponsored contras who used Honduran territory to wage war on the Nicaraguan Sandinistas. In the 1981 elections, which ended years of military rule, the PNH ran Ricardo Zúñiga, an unpopular member of the ultraright wing of the party, who fared poorly in the national elections. In the 1985 elections, the PNH's candidate was Rafael Callejas, a young, U.S.-educated figure who was to put a new face on conservatism in the party. While Callejas won the largest number of votes in the national election, the unusual electoral format of this election gave the victory to the Liberals (see above). Callejas won convincingly in 1989, giving the PNH its first victory in the new era of democracy. Callejas immediately adopted a series of neoliberal economic reforms and structural adjustment programs designed by international lending institutions. This caused widespread protest throughout the country. By the end of his term, unprecedented charges of fraud and abuse were leveled against the administration and against Callejas's family and friends.

In the 1993 elections, the party was taken over by the right wing, which launched the candidacy of Oswaldo Ramos. Ramos's charges that Reina, his presidential opponent, was a communist, fell on deaf ears, and the party lost badly. A host of PNH officials, including Callejas, have been indicted on charges of fraud. In the "Chinazo" case, they are accused of selling Honduran passports to wealthy Hong Kong residents for $100,000 each and keeping the money. In addition, Callejas and his family raided the national petroleum fund. Callejas, like many other elites who face charges in the country, hides behind the immunity that he holds for serving as a member of the Central American Parliament. Instead of rescuing the party, Callejas has further damaged it, thus jeopardizing its chances of winning a national election. The party has splintered recently into eight internal divisions.

ORGANIZATION

The party is nominally run by a convention and executive committee. In practice, various factions battle to gain control. The party has national coverage and party organizations throughout the country. Power runs from the party center in Tegucigalpa out to the grass roots. Patronage and the hope of jobs with winning candidates remain the glue that holds the organization together.

MEMBERSHIP AND CONSTITUENCY

The PNH has traditionally been strong in rural areas and the less-developed departments. The party has a large membership, although it is believed that official membership claims are exaggerated.

FINANCING

The government subsidizes campaigns based on the number of votes received in the previous election. Individual and business donations are not regulated and are unreported.

LEADERSHIP

The 1996 primaries for the 1997 elections featured three strong candidates. Nora de Melgar is the wife of the late Juan Melgar, who was a military president from 1975 to 1978 after a coup against another military leader. Nora was also the mayor of Tegucigalpa. In the primary, Nora defeated the Ramos-wing candidate, Elias Asfura, and the former military officer Hector Fonseca. Nora de Melgar's campaign was backed by both Callejas and Ramos, who were the candidates in the previous two elections. Fonseca attempted to take control of the party as an outsider, having joined the PNH only one year before declaring his candidacy. Educated in the United States, Fonseca is a Protestant and longtime director of the military's wealthy and successful pension fund. PNH rules state

that one must be a member of the party for at least five years to run for the presidential nomination, and the party elite ruled that Fonseca could not participate. A national scandal occurred when Fonseca's wife, a U.S. citizen who had met Fonseca while she worked as a staff member for the ultraconservative U.S. senator Jesse Helms, told a radio interviewer that if the party did not let her husband run, she would use her contacts with Jesse Helms to hold up all aid to the country. Eventually the Supreme Court ruled that Fonseca could run, but he fared poorly and Nora de Melgar was victorious. After the 1997 electoral defeat, the National Party is conspicuously devoid of consensus on leadership.

PROSPECTS

The PNH is facing a difficult challenge. The old faces of the party—the military, the landed elite, Ramos, and Callejas—have been discredited, and dynamic new leaders have not appeared. The National Party faced an uphill battle in the 1997 elections and fared poorly. The party is currently splintered and searching for leadership and features no fewer than eight internal divisions. The PNH has now lost four out of five presidential elections and must reevaluate its strategy, leadership, and organization. The one rising star in the party was Cesar Castellanos, the dynamic mayor of Tegucigalpa and front-runner for the 2001 presidential race, who died in a tragic helicopter accident while surveying the damage from Hurricane Mitch.

MINOR POLITICAL PARTIES

Christian Democrat Party
(Partido Demócrata Cristiano; PDC)

The PDC was formed in 1980 and is a full member of the Christian Democrat International. The party has never won more than two seats in the National Assembly and in the 1993 elections won 1% of the vote and no seats. In 1997 the party recovered slightly, receiving 2.2% of the vote and gaining one seat.

Party of Innovation and Unity
(Partido de Inovación y Unidad; PINU)

The PINU was founded in 1970 and identifies itself as a social democratic party with links to the German Social Democratic Party (SPD). The PINU has consistently won about 2% of the national vote and in the 1993 elections secured two legislative seats. The PINU was the biggest beneficiary of the addition of a separate ballot for the legislature. While earning only 2.1% of the presidential vote, the party received 4.2% of the congressional vote and earned five seats.

Democratic Unification Party
(Partido de Unificación Democrática; PUD)

The latest party to gain recognition from the National Election Tribunal is the PUD, which ran for the first time in the 1997 elections. The PUD's founder and presidential candidate was Matias Funes, a university professor and author. The PUD is the first recognized party of the left. The PUD is antimilitary and anti-neoliberal economic policy and supports humanist and progressive economic and social legislation. The PUD's support in the 1997 elections was a major surprise as the party earned a seat in congress and some municipal positions.

OTHER POLITICAL FORCES

The Military

The strongest alternative political force in the country remains the military. The Honduran military was first professionalized in 1954 with the construction of the Francisco Morazán military academy. By 1956, the military unleashed its first coup. The military played an important role in writing the 1957 constitution, which granted the organization autonomy from elected presidents and freed the head of the armed forces from allegiance to elected officials. The military ruled almost continuously from 1963 to 1982.

In 1982, while power was ostensibly transferred to civilians, the real power in the country lay with the military and its commander in chief, Gustavo Álvarez. Military autonomy was also strengthened in the 1982 constitution. In the Honduran military, leaders are appointed from within—rubber-stamped by the Assembly—and the presidentially appointed defense minister only coordinates. Simultaneously in the early 1980s, the United States was using Honduras as a base for anti-Sandinista contras and sending the Honduran generals unprecedented levels of aid. Commander in Chief Álvarez was staunchly antileft, and during his tenure, human rights abuses increased dramatically. Battalion 3-16, an elite military unit with U.S. training, was responsible for the disappearance of many suspected leftists. The police, totally under military control, also participated in kidnappings, disappearances, and assassinations.

Álvarez was ousted by an internal military coup, and the worst of the human rights abuses disappeared. However, the recent armed forces chiefs Generals Luis Alonso Discua and Mario Hung Pacheco were connected with Battalion 3-16 and have fought to maintain the military's prerogatives and freedom from civilian oversight. Honduras remains the last Central American country where the armed forces chief is selected by the armed forces and not by civilians. Constitutional reforms that would strip the military of autonomy and bring the institution under greater civilian control were approved in 1998 and if passed again in 1999 could greatly advance democratic consolidation.

Reina ran on a platform of controlling the military and has struggled to push through reform. He has successfully changed military service to voluntary from conscription, but with low pay and a discredited image, few are joining the military and the generals are clamoring for a return to conscription. Reina has also made headway in having the military chief selected by the president, and this is scheduled to occur for the first time when Hung's five-year term ends in 2000. Finally, Reina has received constitutional approval to take the police from military control and have it controlled by civilians. The military has not sat by without a fight. There have been several assassination attempts against Reina as well as bombings against the Assembly and Supreme Court, and most observers suspect that the perpetrators were the military. In addition, the military and the police itself, instead of fighting the crime wave in the country, have been implicated in contributing to organized criminal activity. Military officers indicted of serious crimes mock the judicial system by refusing to turn themselves in.

The military has taken much of the windfall money given by the United States during the 1980s and set up a business empire. The Military Pension Institute (IPM) owns banks, a funeral parlor, insurance companies, a credit card company, shrimp farms, and radio stations and in the Honduran version of privatization, purchased the national cement company. With estimated profits of $40 million, the IPM is a major economic actor, and retiring officials are rumored to be receiving $100,000 per year. In a country of misery and poverty, the image of military officers above the law and living in the mansions of Tegucigalpa has produced widespread contempt.

Human Rights Organizations

In recent years, a civil society counterbalance to the military has evolved in the form of domestic human rights organizations. Three major nongovernmental groups exist: the Committee for the Defense of Human Rights in Honduras (CODEH); the Center for the Investigation and Promotion of Human Rights (CIPRODEH); and the Committee of the Families of the Detained and Disappeared in Honduras (COFADEH). CODEH is the largest group and has been harassed and threatened by the military. The group's leader, Ramón Custodio, has been forced to send his family out of the country, and one CODEH regional director was assassinated when scheduled to testify against the military. In 1992, the Callejas government inaugurated the National Commission for the Protection of Human Rights (CONAPRODEH), which gained instant credibility when Dr. Leo Valladares, founder of the CIPRODEH, was named commissioner. Human rights groups stage marches, distribute literature, hold press conferences, provide refuge for those threatened by the military, and have become quite successful in gaining respect and discrediting the military.

NATIONAL PROSPECTS

Honduras is in the midst of the longest period of civilian rule in its history, with five presidents elected in relatively free elections since 1981. There is a strong two-party tradition, and the volatile Central American region appears to have found a permanent peace. However, all is not well for Honduras and Hondurans. The country is poor, its citizens undereducated and underfed, and its industry incapable of competing in the global market. The loss of life and infrastructure resulting from Hurricane Mitch is a devastating setback for the country. The sleaze of the Callejas administration has reinforced the image of the citizenry that politicians are corrupt. The military still wields immense power, and the path to civilian control is still uncertain.

Honduras has one of the most inegalitarian distributions of income in the world, which leads to episodes of violence, especially in the countryside. The end of the U.S.-sponsored Sandinista-contra war left thousands of contras and tens of thousands of weapons idle in Honduras. With massive poverty and unemployment and an oversupply of weapons and mercenaries in the country, crime has escalated out of control. The military and police seem unable and even unwilling to combat lawlessness; indeed they are charged with masterminding the largest crime organizations. Due in part to U.S. pressure, electoral democracy will continue for some time. But the citizenry is becoming increasingly cynical of the promises of democracy, and perpetual crisis will continue as the norm.

Further Reading

Euraque, Dar'o. *Reinterpreting the Banana Republic: Region and State in Honduras, 1870–1972.* Chapel Hill: University of North Carolina Press, 1996.

Merrill, Tim, ed. *Honduras : A Country Study.* Washington, D.C.: Government Printing Office, 1994.

Norsworthy, Kent, and Tom Barry, eds. *Inside Honduras.* Albuquerque: Interhemispheric Press, 1994.

Paz, Ernesto. "The Origin and Development of Political Parties in Honduras." In *Political Parties and Democracy in Central America.* Ed. Louis Goodman et al. Boulder: Colo.: Westview Press, 1992.

Peckenham, Nancy, and Annie Street, eds. *Honduras: Portrait of a Captive Nation.* New York: Praeger, 1985.

Rosenberg, Mark. "Democracy in Honduras: The Electoral and Political Reality." In *Elections and Democracy in Central America, Revisited.* Ed. Mitchell Seligson and John Booth. Chapel Hill: University of North Carolina Press, 1995.

Ruhl, J. Mark. "Doubting Democracy in Honduras." *Current History*, February 1997.

Schulz, Donald E., and Deborah Sundloff Schulz. *The United States, Honduras, and the Crisis in Central America.* Boulder, Colo.: Westview Press, 1994.

HUNGARY

(Magyar Koztarsasag)

By Jeff Hass

With an area of 93,000 square kilometers (smaller than Indiana), Hungary lies in the middle of East-Central Europe, adjacent to traditional "Western Europe" on the west and to former Warsaw Pact members on the east, giving Hungary a prime geopolitical location.

Demographically, Hungary has a population of a little more than 10 million persons, of whom roughly 47.6% are males and 52.4% are females. With a birth rate of 10.72 per thousand, a death rate of 15.06 per thousand, and a net migration rate of –2.48 per thousand, Hungary suffers from a problem common to most former Communist countries, a negative population growth rate. Life expectancy currently is 64.23 years for men and 74.04 years for women (overall 69.02 years for the population). The fertility rate is 1.51 children per woman, and the infant mortality rate is 12.3 deaths per 1,000 live births.

Ethnically, Hungarians are a majority, making up 89.9% of the population. Gypsies make up 4%, Germans 2.6%, Serbs 2%, Slovaks 0.8%, and others 0.7%. Roman Catholicism dominates; 67.5% of the population are nominally Roman Catholic, while 20% follow the Calvinist church, 5% follow Lutheranism, and other religions (and atheists) make up 7.5% of the population. Hungarian is by far the dominant language, spoken by 98.2% of the population.

Hungary's economy was viewed as the potential miracle of Eastern Europe until 1994. Before 1989, Hungary had the most Western-oriented economy of all East bloc countries, with stronger trade ties and with economic reforms—surprising for Soviet-sphere economies (the "New Economic Mechanism")—that allowed for some degree of private enterprise. However, rising external debt made economic reform, especially in the form of privatization and austerity programs, imperative. From 1990 to 1993, economic reforms included financial stabilization and mass privatization. But, with the economic reforms came economic pain: an inflationary spike from price liberalization, rising unemployment, and some social backlash against the rising wealth of the former Communist elite (the nomenklatura) and some economic traders.

In 1994, this pain was translated into an electoral victory for the Hungarian Socialist Party, with slower economic change. Privatization essentially came to a halt, and the state budget and current account deficits rose sharply. In 1995, the Socialists reversed themselves and introduced an austerity package that reduced Hungary's debt and returned to mass privatization. The GDP began to grow in 1994 (2.9%) and 1995 (1.5%), and unemployment began to fall in 1995 (14% to 10%). Inflation, however, has been episodic, with spikes in 1991 and 1995.

Hungary has been one of the more promising countries of Eastern Europe to make the transition from a Communist polity and economy to democracy and market capitalism. While the transition has not been smooth—economic pain paved the way for the Socialists to return to power, and complexities or snags in legislation and procedure have made political institutions run less than smoothly—Hungary still exhibits a successful beginning to institution building. While political actors regularly fight between and within parties and while coalitions and splits have occurred on occasion, there appears to be little threat of political instability, and the Socialists have not tried to turn back the clock on either democracy or the market.

THE SYSTEM OF GOVERNMENT

Hungary's political system at the national level is split into three branches: the executive, headed by the president and the prime minister; the legislative, headed by the Parliament or National Assembly; and the judiciary, headed by the Constitutional Court. The overall political system resembles that of Germany: the prime minister is the most important executive figure and, while autonomous, the executive in the end answers to the legislature, where ultimate political sovereignty resides.

The Executive

The executive branch is headed by two figures, the president and the prime minister. The president is, as in much of Eastern Europe, a figurehead whose powers are mostly in the realm of diplomacy and international affairs. The prime minister derives his or her power from heading the state bureaucracy, and so domestic politics is the sphere of dominance. Both executives, however, are subjugated to the ultimate sovereignty of the National Assembly.

The president, considered in the constitution as the "head of state," is weak. Formally the job of the president is to represent the nation in the international arena and to guard democratic procedure, in essence putting the president above the executive branch and all other branches as well. However, commensurate with this responsibility, the president has few powers. Formally the president can conclude international treaties (which must then be approved by the National Assembly); announce parliamentary and local elections; petition parliament to undertake legislation or other actions; initiate a national referendum; appoint and dismiss the heads of the National Bank, universities, and the armed forces; and grant pardons and bestow citizenship. Most of these acts require the countersignature of the prime minister if they are to be legally valid.

The president also has two forms of a weak veto. First, he can send disagreeable legislation back to the parliament for reconsideration, but the parliament can override this veto with a simple majority vote. Second, the president can refer legislation to the Constitutional Court, which must then rule on its constitutionality.

The president can be removed from office via impeachment if he has violated the constitution (e.g., having a conflict of interest between presidential responsibilities and personal interests, such as side employment) or some other law. A motion for impeachment may be introduced by no less than one-fifth of the parliament and requires a two-thirds majority for impeachment proceedings to begin. At that point the president is suspended from his duties, and the Constitutional Court is called on to rule whether the president did in fact violate the constitution or any other law; the Court then has the final say on the president's guilt. Should the president be found guilty, he must step down. In this case or in any other case when the president cannot execute his or her duties of office, the chain of command runs to the Speaker of the National Assembly (who does not have the power to send legislation back to the parliament or to the Constitutional Court or dissolve the parliament).

The president also has the power to dissolve parliament, but only within strict bounds—either when the parliament has not approved a prime minister 40 days after the first candidate was nominated (e.g., soon after the prime minister resigned) or when the parliament passes a no-confidence motion four times in the course of 12 months. To dissolve parliament the president must request the opinions of the prime minister, the Speaker of the National Assembly, and the parliamentary leaders of the represented parties. The president must be careful when dissolving parliament, however; if he tries to do so beyond these limits, then parliament can consider the president in violation of the constitution and motion for his impeachment.

The prime minister and his deputy ministers run the state bureaucracy and so have great potential power. Ministers do answer to the parliament: they must make reports when asked to do so, and ministerial power to rule by decree is very limited. All ministers except the prime minister are appointed and removed not by parliament but only by the prime minister himself. The prime minister generally comes from the largest parliamentary party and must be approved by majority vote. The National Assembly also has some control over the prime minister through the vote of no confidence; in this way the prime minister can be removed from office.

However, two factors make it more difficult to remove a prime minister in Hungary than elsewhere. First, the prime minister comes from the largest party, and so it would take a major split between the prime minister and his own party before a no-confidence vote could come to pass; and a vote for no confidence cannot come to the floor unless it is brought up with a parallel nomination for another prime minister. This mechanism has made for more stable relations: Hungary does not suffer from as many no-confidence motions and successful votes as do other countries (e.g., Romania, Bulgaria). However, this has not prevented conflict between the two branches, in particular between the prime minister and opposition parties or junior partners in the ruling coalition. (This happened to Jozsef Antall, who in 1992 found himself the target of criticism from the Independent Smallholders' Party, which was a junior member of the ruling coalition.)

Because the executive has two possible heads, conflict between them is a possibility, especially when one member is from the parliamentary opposition. This was the case in the early 1990s, when Antall and Arpad Goncz went head to head over executive prerogative. Goncz had come from the opposition Alliance of Free Democrats as president in a political pact with the Hungarian Democratic Forum, which as the senior member of the ruling coalition had put its own leader, Antall, in the office of prime minister.

In 1991, Goncz and Antall argued over who should represent Hungary at a summit meeting, and later in the year Goncz complained that reorganization of the armed forces had been done without his prior consultation or approval—a contentious issue because the president is the commander in chief. (When asked by Goncz to rule on this dispute, the Constitutional Court claimed that the president "guides" the armed forces, while the government—and thus prime minister—actually runs the military.)

The most impressive confrontation in 1991 was over the appointment of the head of Hungarian Television and Radio. Goncz declined Antall's nominated candidates because of moral objections. Goncz (and opposition parties) argued that the government should not be allowed to place its own people in the leadership of national media. (In this case, the Court once again ruled in Antall's favor and required Goncz to go through with the appointments.) While conflict between the two heads of the executive branch has died down somewhat recently, the institutional grounds for such conflict remains. (While this problem is not unique to Hungary—such intrabranch conflict has occurred in Bulgaria, Romania, and even France—it can destabilize the political process.)

Legislature

The parliament, called the National Assembly (*Orszaggyules*), is a unicameral body and is the most powerful branch of government in Hungary. This resulted from the legacy of communism: because the Communist opposition first came to power within the parliament (and was determined to maintain its power by locating sovereignty in the National Assembly) and because politicians did not want to pave the way for potential dictatorship (which they overthrew in 1989).

The main powers of the parliament are passing legislation, defining policies, approving the budget, approving the government's programs, declaring war or a state of national emergency, calling a national referendum, approving and dismissing the prime minister, and dissolving local assemblies that have violated the law or constitution. Parliamentary approval is reached by simple majority or by two-thirds majority, depending on the situation. For a declaration of war or national emergency, for passing a motion on impeachment, and for altering the constitution, a two-thirds majority is required. In order for parliamentary actions to be binding, a quorum (one-half of delegates) must be present for voting.

Legislation may be initiated by the president, the prime minister, parliamentary committees, or by any member of the National Assembly. If a bill has been passed by a simple majority, the Speaker signs it and sends it to the president, who has 15 days to sign it and promulgate it (5 days if the Speaker has declared the bill an urgent act). Within this period the president may send the bill back to the National Assembly for reconsideration and then to the Constitutional Court. According to the constitution, if the bill is found unconstitutional, the president must send it back to the National Assembly.

The National Assembly, according to the constitution, is the supreme political body in Hungary. All other bodies are subordinate: local government is restrained by national legislation, and the executive branch must report its activities and results of policies to the parliament. Only the Constitutional Court is autonomous from the parliament, and then only in its proceedings; justices must be approved by the National Assembly before entering the bench. Further, the parliament has the power to dismiss the prime minister and government through a vote of no confidence.

The Judiciary

Since 1990, the Hungarian government has been committed to creating an independent judiciary that follows international norms and standards and is able to guarantee the rule of law in the country. Toward this goal the Hungarian government has created the Association of Hungarian Judges, has limited the power of the Ministry of Justice over the judiciary to administrative tasks alone, and has supported the power of the National Judges' Council to approve changes in personnel and judicial budgets. (For example, a judge may be appointed to a position by the Ministry of Justice only after such an appointment has been approved by the National Judges' Council; this helps reduce administrative and political pressure on the judicial branch.)

The Hungarian judicial system follows a continental procedure. This has two practical implications for the functioning of the judiciary. First, contrary to Anglo-American common-law tradition, the Hungarian courts do not follow precedent when deciding cases; instead, each case is decided on the basis of the facts of that case alone and on the relevant laws. Second, and related, the Hungarian courts do not have the power to interpret laws; they have only the power to decide legal outcomes based on the laws themselves. Even the Constitutional Court does not have the power of interpretation, although it can judge the merits of laws.

The judicial hierarchy starts at the lowest level, county tribunals and local courts that oversee decisions in civil disputes and criminal cases. Appeals on rulings may be taken up the judicial hierarchy to the Supreme Court, which is the final arbiter of civil disputes and criminal decisions. Further, courts do have the power to review the *actions* of local authorities. (The Constitutional Court has this power for the national government.) Thus, while the courts themselves cannot interpret the law, they can act as a safeguard against government abuse of the law.

The Constitutional Court stands outside the normal court system. While other courts are concerned with deciding conflicts between civil parties, deciding guilt in criminal cases, or ruling on appeals, the Constitutional Court instead is an overseeing court. Its purpose is to make sure that all branches and organs of government follow the rule of law and remain inside the bounds of power prescribed by law. Since 1990, the Court has reviewed an immense number of laws, petitions, and other documents; included were rulings on abortion and the death penalty (where the Court found Hungary's law unconstitutional), on property distribution, on extending the statute of limitations for crimes committed in the Communist period (which the Court ruled unconstitutional), and on the scope of presidential powers.

According to the constitution, the Constitutional Court consists of 11 justices who are nominated by a Nominating Committee (consisting of one member from each party represented in the National Assembly). The National Assembly as a whole must then approve by two-thirds vote each candidate for justice of the Constitutional Court.

Local and Regional Government

At the local level Hungary is divided into 38 counties (*megyek*), with the capital city, Budapest, equivalent to a county, and each county is composed of cities and communities. Local legislative assemblies are elected for four-year terms; local executives are headed by mayors. Powers of local government include disposal of local government property and funds, levying of local taxes, and passing and implementing of local legislation (which must not violate national laws or the constitution).

Local legislatures are chaired by the mayors. Powers and rights of the local government are constrained by national laws, which may be adopted only by two-thirds majority vote of the National Assembly.

THE ELECTORAL SYSTEM

Origins of the Parties

Hungary's transition to democracy began with political negotiations between the embryonic Hungarian Democratic Forum—the vehicle for rising democratic opposition under communism—and the Hungarian Socialist Workers' Party (the ruling Communist party). The initial steps in the direction of democracy were the revising of the existing constitution in 1989 and the setting of parliamentary elections for 1990. The electoral law was a result of political negotiations, allowing ruling parties to remain in politics but also giving challengers a chance to enter the parliament. The first post-Communist elections gave the most seats to the Democratic Forum and then to other left-leaning social democratic parties and right-leaning (but not nationalist or extremist) parties. After the 1990 elections, a ruling coalition, headed by the Democratic Forum and with the support of the Independent Smallholders' Party (ISP) and the Christian Democratic People's Party (CDPP), was established; while the president was chosen from the Alliance of Free Democrats (Arpad Goncz), the Democratic Forum managed to get its party leader, Jozsef Antall, approved as prime minister.

Governance in Hungary was made more difficult by several political factors. The first was tensions within the ruling coalition, especially between the Forum and the junior member, the ISP. The ISP pushed for land restitution, the return of land to previous owners taken by Communists. Forum members resisted and then wavered, since the ISP was adamant on the issue and the Forum required ISP support to maintain a majority in the National Assembly. A second source of political instability came from tensions between the president and the prime minister. With the separation of powers between the two nominal heads of the executive left vague in the constitution, both actors tried to become the top player; only as disputes emerged did the Constitutional Court begin to delineate the boundaries of power (usually in favor of the prime minister).

The HDF-led government began with the best starting conditions of any former Communist country. Hungary had been tinkering with economic reform, and it had a polity relatively free from nationalist/ethnic or party strife. However, by 1992, Antall came under criticism from opposition parties, especially the Alliance of Free Democrats and the new rising star, the Alliance of Young Democrats, for its inability to take advantage of such conditions and actually reform the economy. Land reform followed the ISP's demands, which did not create a vibrant sector of independent farmers; privatization had bogged down, as the government could not decide among several plans, and what privatization did occur seemed to favor interconnected shareholding between directors of large firms; and the government did not have programs to address unemployment, social support, deficits, and inflation.

In 1994, the HDF-led government's inability to bring quick, effective reform and the pragmatic image propagated by the Socialists led to a victory of the Hungarian Socialist Party. While the HSP achieved a parliamentary majority, it turned to the Alliance of Free Democrats (whose economic and political programs were similar to theirs) to form a coalition; the HSP party leader, Gyula Horn, was approved as prime minister. In 1995, the HSP decided to take action on Hungary's rising deficits and stagnating economy by privatizing state firms and by initiating a fiscal austerity program in order to bring in IMF funding. Such measures have not pleased the electorate, and the HSP has seen its popularity in polls drop to near the bottom of all parties. One proposed measure, a tax on social insurance, led to the resignation of the finance minister. While Hungary has had its share of political scandals and discord, leading to a Cabinet reshuffle and the ouster of several ministers, it has enjoyed relative calm, and the economy has begun to rebound as foreign investment has once again been injected into the country.

Elections

In Hungary the president is elected by the parliament to a five-year term and may repeat himself in office only once. When 30 days remain before the end of the current president's mandate, the Speaker of the National Assembly proclaims the process of selecting a new president, which must be concluded not more than 30 days after the announcement. For a person to become a candidate, at least 50 members of the National Assembly must nominate him or her prior to the announcement of the election. On the day of voting, a candidate receiving two-thirds of all votes cast by parliament is declared the winner. If no candidate receives the two-thirds majority, the voting process is repeated; if this second time no candidate receives two-thirds of the vote, a third round is held, in which the two candidates with the most votes from the second round compete. Only a simple majority is required in the third round. The whole voting process is to take no more than three days, according to the constitution.

The first post-Communist president was Arpad Goncz of the Alliance of Free Democrats—a party that was not in the post-1990 ruling coalition. Goncz received the position in spite of this because of a pact between the AFD and the HDF: an AFD candidate would receive the presidential post (but not a position in the coalition) if the laws were changed so that a two-thirds majority would not be needed for passing legislation (thus making political life easier for the ruling coalition, which consisted of three parties and held only 59% of the vote). The next presidential election was 1995, with the following election scheduled for 1999. In 1995 Goncz was reelected by parliament, receiving 259 of the 335 votes cast.

The National Assembly sits for a period of four years; only Presidential dissolution of parliament may interfere with this period. (Once parliament is dissolved, new elections must occur within three months.) Parliamentary elections in Hungary are extraordinarily complicated owing to the new electoral law. Because various parties wanted to safeguard their ability to enter or remain in the National Assembly, several mechanisms were included that have made the Hungarian electoral difficult to understand; predicting an outcome and the implications of one's vote for different parties is almost impossible.

Delegates enter parliament in one of three ways: through individual races, through local party lists, or through a "national list" based on "fragment votes." (This system is for all practical purposes the same as that in Estonia.) Of the 386 seats in the National Assembly, 176 are set aside for the individual races, 152 are set aside for local county lists (party-based races), and 58 are set aside for the national lists and fragment votes. The two figures of 152 and 58 are only a maximum and a minimum, however; less than 152 seats may be distributed through local party races depending on whether parties receive the necessary votes to garner a mandate, and those seats not determined through the local party races go to the national list. Each voter has two votes: one for a candidate in the individual races and one for a party in the county-level party races.

The individual race is straightforward. For a vote to be valid, more than 50% of registered voters must cast a ballot. To win in the first round, a candidate must receive a majority of votes cast; otherwise, a runoff is held between those candidates who received at least 15% of votes cast, or among the top three candidates if less than three received 15% or more. In the runoff, only 25% participation is required and to win one needs to receive only a plurality (i.e., the highest number of votes) rather than a majority.

The next path is through "county lists," races between parties at the level of the county (not the national level). Parties present lists of potential delegates, and voters cast their votes for a party. To have an opportunity to send candidates to parliament, a party has to overcome a threshold; in 1990 this threshold was 4% of all votes cast, and in 1994 it was 5%. Each county has a number of mandates, depending on the population, and each mandate is a number of votes. A party can receive mandates at the county level, which are translated into parliament seats. A party has to overcome the percentage barrier to have a chance to receive a mandate. For example, if in a certain county there are 10,000 votes per mandate and a party receives 30,000 votes, then that party receives three mandates; the first three candidates on the party list become members of parliament.

Those mandates that are not filled are transferred to

Election Results: Parliamentary Elections, 1990

Party	Individual	Regional	National List	Total
Hungarian Democratic Forum	115	40	10	165
Alliance of Free Democrats	37	34	23	94
Independent Smallholders' Party	11	16	17	44
Hungarian Socialist Party	1	14	18	33
Alliance of Young Democrats	2	8	12	22
Christian Democratic People's Party	3	8	10	21
Independent	7	0	0	7

Ruling Coalition: Hungarian Democratic Forum, Independent Smallholders' Party, and Christian Democratic People's Party, for 230 seats (59.6%).

Source: Laszlo Szarvas, "Parties and Party Factions in the Hungarian Parliament," in *Hungary: The Politics of Transition*, ed. Terry Cox and Andy Furlong » (London: Frank Cass, 1995), 122.

the national list, which is a minimum of 58 but can be augmented by unfilled county mandates. These national-level seats are distributed to the parties that receive overall more than 5% of votes cast nationally. Parties that do not cross the barrier do not get seats from this pool; and those that do cross the barrier receive a number of seats equal to the percentage of votes that party received of all votes cast for parties that break the 5% barrier. (As a consequence, a vote cast for a party that does not cross the 5% barrier is a wasted vote.)

Election Results: Parliamentary Elections, 1994

Party	Individual Seats	Total Seats
Hungarian Socialist Party	149	209
Alliance of Free Democrats	16	69
Hungarian Democratic Forum	5	38
Independent Smallholders' Party	1	26
Christian Democratic People's Party	3	22
Alliance of Young Democrats	—	20

Source: Barnabas Racz and Istvan Kukorelli, "'The Second-Generation' Post-Communist Elections in Hungary in 1994," *Europe-Asia Studies* 47, no. 2 (1995): 266–67.

One must note a slight caveat: once a delegate enters the parliament, he or she is not bound to party discipline and at worst can only be dropped from the party list of candidates in the *next* election. Hence, party strength cannot be based on number of seats alone. For example, the Hungarian Democratic Forum won 165 total seats in the 1990 elections; however, by 1994 the "formal" number of Forum delegates was 136. Of the original 165, 31 had left for other factions (Alliance of Young Democrats or other parties), and the Forum had gained two delegates from two other parties.

Electoral trends in Hungary are similar to those elsewhere in Eastern Europe that have seen a return of Communists to power. As elsewhere, the return of the Socialists can be traced to three factors. The first and most prominent is the economic pain of the market transition. With inflation and rising costs, rising unemployment, lower wages, and scandals and disputes surrounding privatization, average citizens yearned for the social safety net of pre-1989 Hungary once more.

The second factor was strategic. The Hungarian Democratic Forum, Alliance of Free Democrats, Alliance of Young Democrats, and Independent Smallholders' Party focused on anti-Communist slogans rather than on pragmatic solutions to problems or a defense of promarket policies; their slogans sometimes resembled those of a witch hunt. The Socialists, on the other hand, addressed people's economic pain and painted themselves as pragmatic quasi-technocrats able to deal in a impassionate

manner with socioeconomic problems. Finally, the Socialists' party organization allowed them to mobilize grassroots supporters and to create more direct links with the people, especially those in rural areas; other parties, on the other hand, remained organizations for the political elite that tried to appeal to the people from a distance rather than going out among them and organizing support.

THE PARTY SYSTEM

The Hungarian party scene is both stable and unstable. It is stable in that a small group of parties appear to have become constant players, but unstable in that this number will most likely be whittled down. Parties hold to set ideological positions only in a vague sense; tactics often determine what a party believes. Finally, party strength over the long haul is questionable for two reasons. First, parties do not exercise high discipline, and so members can leave and join parliamentary factions; this hurt the Alliance of Young Democrats, for example. Second, with the exception of the Hungarian Socialist Party, parties do not have strong grassroots divisions and do not try to mobilize social support; usually they instead act like groups of political elites making an appeal to the populace from above.

Six parties have taken positions in both the 1990 and 1994 elections. These parties can be grouped along a traditional left-right continuum. However, certain points can be noted at the outset. For one thing, there are no true extremist parties in the parliament. While some parties hold to a more nationalist outlook or promote Christian principles, none take this rhetoric to an extreme, as is the case with Vladimir Zhirinovskii's nationalist party in Russia and Gheorghe Funar's in Romania. Most parties are basically moderate, leaning to one side of the other. Also, Hungary has had only two parliamentary elections; most Eastern European countries had elections in 1990 and have had at least two more since then, allowing for parties to rise and fall more quickly (or for some parties, by surviving all elections, to become more institutionalized players).

HUNGARIAN SOCIALIST PARTY (HSP)
(Magyar Szocialista Part)

On the left is the Hungarian Socialist Party. While the HSP *organizationally* is a direct descendant of the Hungarian Workers' Socialist Party (i.e., the Communist party), *ideologically* the HSP has openly broken all links with the old Communist ideology. The HSP has agreed that a market economy is desirable. Where the HSP differs from other parties is that it supports a slower and more gradual transition that takes into account support for the social safety net (economic support for the population, especially those at risk of poverty) and support for social justice.

However, as 1995 showed, the Socialists realize that the requirements for economic health may contradict party ideology and take precedence. In 1995, the Socialist-led government backed away from a gradualist position and implemented an austerity package that helped lower budget and current account deficits and continued mass privatization of $3 billion worth of state assets. Finally, while the HSP had a majority in the parliament after the 1994 elections, it preferred to build a larger ruling coalition that could embrace other like-minded parties in order to create a larger sense of political community and unity.

ALLIANCE OF FREE DEMOCRATS (AFD)
(Szabad Demokratak Szovetsege)

The Alliance of Free Democrats is a left-leaning liberal party that associates itself with traditional social democracy. The AFD has supported promarket reforms, rejecting historical appeals to a Hungarian third way to economic growth. When calls for increased social responsibility became more pronounced, the AFD stood behind privatization. And while AFD delegates now admit that compensation laws (compensation for property nationalized by the Communists) were faulty, they do not want to correct that situation and prefer to look forward rather than back. Because of its left-leaning sympathies (social justice), the AFD has been able to work with the Socialists while not echoing them; the AFD became part of a larger ruling coalition in 1995.

ALLIANCE OF YOUNG DEMOCRATS FIDESZ (AYD)
(Magyar Polgàri Pàrt)

The Alliance of Young Democrats—as a brief shining star in 1992—was formed that year by young intellectuals and "yuppie"-type political aspirants as a counter to other parties. The AYD, however, has had difficulty finding a platform that both its elite and the population at large support. The party has supported promarket reforms, in particular, rapid privatization and a state economic role reduced to promoting private growth. Early on, the AYD was left-leaning and popular, enabling it to act as an effective opposition party against the HDF-dominated ruling coalition.

However, in preparation for the 1994 elections, party leaders tried to recreate the party's ideological platform, leading to a split between promarket reformers (headed by Viktor Orban) and another group of reformers (headed by Gabor Fodor) who preferred a balance between market reforms and economic and social justice. After the split, in which Orban successfully gained control to define the party platform, Fodor and his followers abandoned the AYD for the AFD—both because the AFD platform was similar and because Orban had the reputation of being a strong-armed political leader who could not well accommodate different views. As a result of the split and defection, the AYD's star dimmed in the 1994 elections.

CHRISTIAN DEMOCRATIC PEOPLE'S PARTY (CDPP)
(Keresztèny Demokrata Nèppàrt)

The Christian Democratic People's Party, one of the members of the 1990–94 ruling coalition, claims to support Christian values and support promarket ideology and reforms. Based in Christian beliefs, the CDPP makes individual freedom a central tenet of its political program. The other basic elements of its program are a state led by Christian ideals, parliamentary democracy, and sovereignty of the people. While CDPP does support some form of social safety net, especially for those most likely to be hurt by economic transformation, it also staunchly supports private property, especially in the agricultural sector, where small private farming should be the foundation.

HUNGARIAN DEMOCRATIC FORUM (HDF)
(Magyar Demokrata Fòrum)

The Hungarian Democratic Forum was the winner of the 1990 parliamentary elections and the center of the ruling coalition from 1990 to 1994. HDF was the group most involved with Hungary's initial transition away from communism, acting as the major opposition to the Hungarian Socialist Workers' Party and forging the creation of parliamentary democratic politics through political negotiation with the Communists. The HDF has supported overall economic and political change, but not through reforms so radical that they would destabilize society and bring social catastrophe. HDF has supported Hungarian traditions and in this way has been democratic, nationalist, and Christian and has opposed all forms of extremism on the left and right. In fact, the HDF supported the idea of gradualist market reform, although gradualism was softened somewhat in the debates with the Independent Smallholders over property compensation.

HDF policies in 1990–94 included slow privatization (privatizing 15% of state-owned enterprises), unemployment support and retraining, encouragement of small business, and attracting foreign investment. Hence, the HDF tempered market reforms with policies of social support. In 1996, after a national convention to decide the party's ideological tone for the future, the HDF split in two—between those who wanted a turn to the right (promarket reform, moderate nationalism, and ties with the smaller and more extremist Hungarian Truth and Life Party) and a more center-right group. The center-right members left the HDF, thus reducing the HDF presence in the National Assembly to 19 deputies, and formed the Hungarian Democratic People's Party.

INDEPENDENT SMALLHOLDERS' PARTY (ISP)
(Független Kisgazda-Füldmunkàs)

Further to the right on the spectrum is the small Independent Smallholders' Party (ISP). The ISP, originally formed after World War II, counts on rural farmers and small entrepreneurs for its support. ISP has championed land reform, in particular returning land to those who owned it before the Communist government nationalized property after World War II. The ISP has stood for Hungarian historical traditions and Christian values, placing the ISP near the Christian Democrats. However, the ISP has stronger support for private property and a thorough repudiation of communism.

In the first instance, the ISP has championed compensation—returning of land to pre-Communist owners or giving a sum of money as compensation. This has been a troublesome policy proposal and has led to tensions within the HDF–CDPP–ISP ruling coalition. Also the ISP has wanted to extend the statute of limitations on crimes committed during the Communist era. The ISP has been hurt by these programs, however, since they have championed either longtime disgruntled anti-Communists or small private farmers; they have not been able (or tried) to extend their base of support. Further, the leader of ISP, Jozsef Torgyan, became the center of political controversy in 1992 when he criticized Antall for timidity in the face of needed radical economic and social reforms. Torgyan's demagoguery, heavy-handed tactics, and behavior in a few situations have not only hurt his own image but led to dissension within ISP's ranks. The result was a poor showing, especially in individual races, in the 1994 elections. Torgyan has maintained vehement criticism of other parties, especially those to the left, marking the ISP as too dangerous for partnership with opposition parties.

NATIONAL PROSPECTS

Relative to other former Communist countries, Hungary seems well on its way to creating a well-functioning democracy and market economy. The legacy of socialist economic reforms made the transformation of the Hungarian economy, particularly the creation of a small entre-preneurial sector, much easier than elsewhere, and the return of Socialists to power did not bring populism and economic decline but the opposite: new economic reforms. Hungary's political system does not suffer from the problems faced elsewhere in the former Communist bloc: ethnic disputes (Romania), overly ambitious leaders holding levers of power (Belarus), institutional bias for one branch that can endanger democracy (Russia), or hatred for the past hindering cooperation in the present (Poland).

Hungary does have one particular problem, however, stemming from its electoral system. A "well-functioning democracy" (as currently understood in the West) fulfills three functions: political justice, chance for negotiations, and some degree of predictability (although not absolute). Voters must be able to have some idea of what outcome their voting will have; political participants must have the possibility to negotiate in order to avoid losses; and voting must bring some degree of justice and legitimacy. This three-way interaction presents the possibility of contradictions, which has happened in Hungary.

To ensure their own continued existence in politics, party elites negotiated an electoral system that through individual races, county lists, and a national list guarantees opportunities to keep from disappearing from the political scene. Such a negotiated electoral contract assuaged the worries of elites; however, the electoral system that resulted has run aground of the other two assumptions of democracy. The electoral system is thoroughly confusing, and so it is nearly impossible for the average (or above-average) Hungarian to figure out just what will happen if he or she and others vote a certain way. Further, such a system has unexpected consequences, making political justice difficult: if voters do not want a certain party to be represented, then that party has no fundamental right to representation, yet the system was created in part to make sure that parties have every chance of returning to parliament.

However, this point aside, Hungary's future prospects are among the brighter of Eastern European countries. The economy remains one of the more attractive to foreign investment, especially given privatization and an orientation both to exports and to integration with the European economy. Hungary's possibility of joining NATO will be a further link to cement relations with the West.

Also, given the absence of strong nationalist or ethnic feeling and the absence of popular and mass-mobilizing nationalist parties, Hungary does not suffer from internal political and ethnic strife, which has been problematic in other countries. Finally, Hungary appears to have turned away from the Communist past in two senses. First, even the Hungarian Socialists have embraced market reforms, much more so than socialist parties elsewhere; while the degree of the human face on capitalism differs from party to party, all appear to be in agreement on the need for a market economy. Second, Hungarian politicians not only appear to be playing by the rules (based on the idea of a rule of law) but also appear to be appealing to a sense of political community. While political criticism has been present and sometimes radical, for the most part Hungarian politics does not have the same degree of polarization as seen in Russia, Romania, or Bulgaria. Before the fall of communism, Hungary was pointed to as the bright star of the Eastern bloc, and in the aftermath of 1989, despite bumps and obstacles on the road to reform, it remains a bright star.

Further Reading

CIA Factbook, 1996. Washington D.C.: Government Printing Office, 1996.

Cox, Terry, and Andy Furlong, eds. *Hungary: The Politics of Transition*. London: Frank Cass, 1995.

Ehrlich, Éva, and Gábor Révész. *Hungary and Its Prospects: 1985–2005*. Trans. András Ottlick. Budapest: Akadémiai Kiadó, 1995.

Oltay, Edith. "Toward the Rule of Law: Hungary." *RFE/RL Research Report*, July 3, 1992, 16–24.

Open Research Media Institute (OMRI).

Pataki, Judith. "Hungarian Government Midway through Its First Term." *RFE/RL Research Report*, June 12, 1992, 18–24.

Web Site

Radio Free Europe/Radio Liberty (RFE/RL): www.RFE/RL.org.

ICELAND

(island)

By Ólafur Th. Hardarson, Ph.D.

THE SYSTEM OF GOVERNMENT

Iceland, an island in the North Atlantic with some 270,000 inhabitants, is a parliamentary republic and a unitary state. The country was settled in the 9th and 10th centuries, mainly from Norway. The settlers founded a commonwealth without a king or executive power. Its central institution, which had legislative and judicial powers, was the *Althingi*, founded in 930. In 1262 the country came under the Norwegian king. When Norway and Denmark united under the Danish Crown in 1380, Iceland became a Danish dependency. The *Althingi* gradually lost its legislative function, and in 1662 the Danish king obtained absolute power. In 1800 the *Althingi* was abolished, having functioned mainly as a judicial body for centuries. It was reestablished in 1845 as a consultative assembly to the Danish king.

In 1874 the king "gave" the Icelanders a constitution, which granted the *Althingi* legislative and financial powers, while the king retained an effective veto. Home rule in 1904 granted the Icelanders authority in most domestic affairs with the establishment of an Icelandic administration headed by a minister, responsible to the *Althingi*. Iceland became a sovereign state in 1918 but remained in a union with Denmark under the king until 1944, when it adopted its present republican constitution.

Executive

The president (*forseti*), who is elected directly by the people every four years, has mainly ceremonial duties. As the potential political power granted to the president in the constitution (e.g., the right to refuse to sign a statute, which then goes to a referendum) has never been used, the major political influence of the office has been in the bargaining process when a new coalition government is formed. The executive power in fact belongs to the Cabinet, which usually represents a majority coalition of two or more parties and is led by the prime minister.

Legislature

The Icelandic parliament, *Althingi*, was made a unicameral parliament in 1991, having previously been divided into an Upper Chamber and a Lower Chamber since 1874. The *Althingi* has 63 members, elected in a general election for a term of four years. During this period the *Althingi* can be dissolved at any given time, and a new election held. This is done by a decree of the president, acting upon the advice of the prime minister, who in practice dissolves the *Althingi* only with the approval of all coalition partners in the Cabinet. Since 1944 there have been 16 general elections, with an average term of around $3\frac{1}{2}$ years.

Formally, the *Althingi* is the most powerful institution in the Icelandic political system. It can make law on any subject it chooses (within the limits set by the constitution), it makes and breaks governments, it can make any changes it likes on the draft budget, and it elects a considerable number of people to various important boards and committees. In practice, however, the political parties are the most important units in the political system, and most policy decisions, as well as major decisions on government coalition formations, are taken by their parliamentary groups rather than the party organizations.

While the Cabinet has increasingly played a major role in policy formation—in 1983–92, 86% of passed bills were government bills—the *Althingi* still retains considerable power vis-à-vis the administration. Government bills are scrutinized by the parliamentary groups of the government coalition before being presented to the assembly, and the *Althingi* interferes more with the budget and the activities of the executive than is the case with most Western European assemblies. Since Iceland became a founding member of the European Economic Area in 1994, an increasing part of legislation stems from Brussels.

Judiciary

The Icelandic court system consists of only two levels of courts, eight district courts (*héradsdómur*) and the Supreme Court (*Haestiréttur*). These courts have jurisdiction in both civil and criminal matters. The rules of procedure are largely based on Scandinavian and German principles.

The Supreme Court, established in 1920, can declare a statute unconstitutional and has done so on a few occasions. The judges are appointed for life by the president, acting upon the advice of the minister of justice.

Two special courts have a limited jurisdiction. The High Court of State (*Landsdómur*) can impeach Cabinet ministers, but this Court has not convened since it was established in 1905. The Labor Court (*Félagsdómur*) tries cases relating to laws on trade unions and employers' associations.

Regional and Local Government

The functions and financial revenues of local governments are mainly decided by law. The basic units are towns (*kaupstadir*) and rural districts (*hreppar*), which elect their own councils (mainly by proportional representation using the d'Hondt formula). The local communes (124 in 1998) vary greatly in size: The capital Reykjavík has some 100,000 inhabitants, while the population in other communes varies from around 50 to 17,000. In recent years, the government has tried to unify communes voluntarily, in order to give local governments increased responsibilities, but with limited success so far. Nevertheless, unification by legislation has been ruled out, while in 1996 the responsibilities of local governments were greatly increased by handing the running of the elementary schools over to them.

THE ELECTORAL SYSTEM

Since mid-1959, the members of *Althingi* have been chosen by direct, proportional election in eight multi-member constituencies. Previously a mixed system of majority representation in single-member constituencies and proportional representation had been in operation. Before the 1987 election, the number of *Althingi* members was increased from 60 to 63. This was accompanied by a change in the rules of the allocation of seats, as well as in the number of seats in several constituencies, while constituency boundaries remained the same. In the present system, all 63 seats are fixed to a particular constituency: the two constituencies in the urban South West (Reykjavík and Reykjanes) receive 19 and 12 members respectively, while the remaining 32 seats go to the six regional five- and six-member constituencies. Of the 63 seats, 50 are allotted to lists according to constituency results, using the "largest remainder" formula. The remaining 13 seats are then allotted to parties that have already obtained at least 1 seat, according to the overall results (their votes/seats ratio, using the d'Hondt formula).

Quite complex and nontransparent rules are used to decide in what constituency the parties have each of these 13 members elected. A party can, for example, obtain an elected member in a particular constituency, while another party obtaining more votes in that constituency does not. The aim of this complex system is to ensure that the number of seats each party obtains is largely pro-

portional to the party's share of votes nationwide; severe regional disproportionality remains, as indicated by the fact that a majority of the *Althingi* members are elected in the six regional constituencies, where only one-third of the electorate lives. While there is an increasing dissatisfaction in the urban South West with this arrangement, a correction would require a constitutional change.

The voter can only cast his vote for a list. While changes in the rank order of candidates on the chosen list are allowed, the rules make it unlikely that such changes, even made by a substantial proportion of the voters, will alter the ranking. Elections take place on a Saturday by secret ballot. With many polling places in each constituency it is easy for the voters to get to the polls. The ballot papers are counted by constituencies. Registration is automatic, and suffrage is universal for adults 18 years of age or older. Absentee ballots can be cast in the eight-week period preceding polling day. Turnout in *Althingi* elections has been stable around 90% in recent decades.

If an elected member cannot attend *Althingi* sessions for at least two consecutive weeks, his place is taken (temporarily, if the member returns) by the next person on the party list. Thus, by-elections are unnecessary.

The president is elected by direct, simple majority vote for a four-year term. The first president, Sveinn Björnsson, was elected by the *Althingi* in 1944. In 1945 and 1949, Björnsson was the only candidate for nationwide direct election, so no actual election was held. When Björnsson died, in 1952, the Independence Party and the Progressive Party together supported one candidate, who was defeated by an *Althingi* member from the small Social Democratic Party, Ásgeir Ásgeirsson, who maintained that the people, not the parties, should choose the president. The political parties never again attempted to put up a candidate or take a stand in presidential elections. In 1968 the director of the National Museum, Kristján Eldjárn, was elected, and in 1980 the director of the Reykjavík Theater, Vigdís Finnbogadóttir, became the first popularly elected female head of state in the world. In 1996 a former leader of the left-socialist People's Alliance, Ólafur Ragnar Grímsson, somewhat surprisingly won the presidential race. His victory was thought clearly based on personal merit, rather than political grounds.

A sitting president who wishes to be reelected has only been opposed once (in 1988), when Finnbogadóttir easily beat a candidate from a fringe political group.

THE PARTY SYSTEM

Origins of the Parties

In the 19th and early 20th century the question of Iceland's relationship with Denmark dominated Icelandic politics. The first political parties emerged at the turn of the century, when home rule and control of the executive were in sight. Those cadre-style parties were mainly based on different attitudes toward tactics in the independence struggle.

The independence question was largely resolved in 1918, and in the 1916–30 period the party system was completely transformed. Economic and class-related issues became the focal point of politics, as four new parties emerged: the Social Democratic Party, the agrarian Progressive Party, the conservative Independence Party, and the Communist Party. The four-party format came to dominate Icelandic politics, but on occasions short-lived minor parties have entered the *Althingi*, especially since the 1970s. Only one of those parties, the Women's Alliance, has however survived more than two terms.

The left-right dimension is still by far the most important in Icelandic politics. While foreign policy also became a major cleavage after the Second World War, those issues are closely related to the left-right spectrum in the minds of voters. In the 1995 election study the voters ranked the six parties that won *Althingi* seats from left to right (on a 0–10 scale) in the following manner: People's Alliance (2.1), People's Movement (3.3), Women's Alliance (3.5), Social Democrats (5.2), Progressive Party (5.7), Independence Party (8.5).

The Parties in Law

The right of association, including the right to form political parties, is guaranteed in the constitution. There is no law on how political parties operate, nor on how they select candidates, and they do not have to disclose their finances. It is easy to get a list on the ballot: all that is needed is a formal recommendation by 100 to 380 registered voters.

Party Organization

Since the 1930s, the major parties have formally been mass parties, organized on a regional basis. The local organizations elect representatives to the party's constituency council and to the party convention. The party convention elects a central national council and usually also the party leader. The institutionalization of the Icelandic parties has however probably always been weaker than among their counterparts in Northern Europe. Criteria for membership have been unclear, as membership fees have rarely been collected on a regular basis and membership files have been inaccurate. The parliamentary groups have been much stronger than the party organizations regarding policymaking, and the position of the leadership is quite strong. Party conferences tend to confirm decisions made by the leadership. Usually that leadership is reelected, although challenges to the leadership, usually by a competing leadership group, have been successful at times.

Since the 1970s, primary elections have been the major method of selecting candidates. Many of these primaries have been open, that is, not confined to party members, as clearly indicated by the fact that on several occasions the number of people taking part in a party's primary in a constituency has greatly exceeded the party's number of votes in the following *Althingi* election. Some primaries, formally confined to party members, have also in fact been open, due to the unclear membership criteria of the parties and the fact that at times people have been able to join the party at the primary polling place. The primaries have clearly weakened party organizations and undermined party cohesiveness.

Campaigning

Election campaigns to a large extent are waged on a national level through the mass media. In an increasingly competitive and nonpartisan media market, candidates from all parties present their views in articles in the national newspapers and take part in discussion programs on television and radio. The impact of local party papers and rallies has decreased. Political advertisements have on the other hand come to play a major role.

Financing

While the parties are not required by law to reveal anything concerning their income and expenditures, only the Independence Party refuses to give any information on party finances. The information the other parties present is, however, often incomplete and can be misleading. Nevertheless it is clear that membership fees have rarely been strictly collected. The parties have instead relied on lotteries and financial support from individuals, interest groups, and firms—some companies are known to donate to all parties. But this kind of fund-raising by the parties has become relatively less important in recent years, as public grants are now the main source of party income, at least in most cases. State support has greatly increased and is proportionally (per vote) much higher than in the neighboring countries. Despite this, at least three parties, the Social Democrats, the Progressives, and the People's Alliance, are heavily in debt. The main reasons for increasing party expenditure are more professional and expensive election campaigns, including extensive political advertising in newspapers, on radio, and—most important—on television since 1987.

Independent Voters

Since the early 1970s electoral volatility has been high. The gains and losses of parties in elections are often quite large. In the elections of 1987, 1991, and 1995 around one-third of the voters claimed to have switched parties between elections. The number of voters claiming no party sympathy whatsoever increased from 19% in 1983 to 27% in 1995.

Althingi Election Results, 1979–95
(percentages of total valid votes and numbers of elected members)

	1979	1983	1987	1991	1995
Independence Party (IP)	35.4 (21)	38.7 (23)	27.2 (18)	38.6 (26)	37.1 (25)
Progressive Party (PP)	24.9 (17)	19.0 (14)	18.9 (13)	18.9 (13)	23.2 (15)
People's Alliance (PA)	19.7 (11)	17.3 (10)	13.3 (8)	14.4 (9)	14.3 (9)
Social Democratic Party (SDP)	17.5 (10)	11.7 (6)	15.2 (10)	15.5 (10)	11.4 (7)
Women's Alliance	—	5.5 (3)	10.1 (6)	8.3 (5)	4.9 (3)
People's Movement	—	—	—	—	7.1 (4)
Citizens' Party	—	—	10.9 (7)	—	—
Social Democratic Alliance	—	7.3 (4)	0.2 (0)	—	—
Others	2.5 (1)	0.5 (0)	4.1 (1)	4.3 (0)	1.9 (0)
Total Number of Seats	60	60	63	63	63
Total Valid Votes	123,751	129,962	152,722	157,769	165,043
Percent Turnout	89.3%	88.3%	90.1%	87.6%	87.4%

INDEPENDENCE PARTY (IP)
(Sjálfstaedisflokkurinn)

HISTORY

The Independence Party (IP) was founded in 1929 with a merger of the Conservative Party (founded 1924) and the Liberal Party (founded 1926). Partly because of Iceland's unusually high degree of ethnic, religious, and linguistic homogeneity, the IP was able to unite the right-of-center opponents of the SDP and the agrarian PP in one party, which has remained the largest party in the country from its foundation, usually polling around 40% of the votes. In the 1930s, the IP's strength among the electorate was however not reflected in seats held in the *Althingi* and the party spent most of its first years in opposition. After a change in the electoral system in 1942, the IP became "the natural party of government" with all of its leaders serving as prime ministers: Ólafur Thors (1942, 1944–47, 1949, 1953–56, 1959–63), Bjarni Benediktsson (1963–70), Jóhann Hafstein (1970–71), Geir Hall-Grímsson (1974–78), Thorsteinn Pálsson (1987–88), and Davíd Oddsson since 1991.

A serious schism emerged in the party in 1980, when the deputy leader, Gunnar Thoroddsen, supported by a few IP members of the *Althingi*, formed a coalition government with the PP and the PA, leaving the bulk of the party, including party leader HallGrímsson, in opposition. Thoroddsen and his supporters remained in the party, however; and in 1983 Thoroddsen left politics, while his supporters were all reelected as *Althingi* members for the IP.

The IP split in 1987, when a popular patronage politician, Albert Gudmundsson, formed the Citizen's Party just before an *Althingi* election. Gudmundsson had been forced to resign as a minister, due to tax evasion while serving as minister of finance. The election results were a disaster for the IP, as the party polled only 27.2% of the votes, while the new Citizen's Party had seven members elected to the *Althingi*. During the next term, however, Gudmundsson left politics for an ambassadorial post in Paris, the Citizen's Party disintegrated, and the IP recovered its previous electoral strength in 1991.

ORGANIZATION

The IP has emphasized that it is a party of independent individuals without strong party discipline, but it has been the best-organized party in Iceland in terms of electoral machinery and national coverage. The party has generally combined strong leadership with a notable tolerance in party discipline. Individual IP members of *Althingi* have—without sanctions—voted against their government on crucial issues (like the Icelandic membership of the European Economic Area in 1993), refused to support a government headed by their party (in 1944), and even formed a coalition government strongly opposed by their party (in 1980).

Separate organizations for women and youth are affiliated to the IP. Separate associations for working-class members have also been organized. The party is a member of the European Democratic Union (EDU) and associated with the Nordic conservative parties. The women's organization is affiliated to the Nordic Association of Conservative Women, while the youth organization is a member of the Democrat Youth Community of Europe (DEMYC), European Young Conservatives, International Young Democrat Union, and Nordic Conservative Youth.

National headquarters are at Sjálfstaedisflokkurinn, Háaleitisbraut 1, 105 Reykjavík.

POLICY

In domestic policy, the IP has combined elements from liberalism and conservatism and emphasized nationalism and opposition to class conflict. In the 1930s, while the party was in opposition, the emphasis in party policy was clearly directed toward economic liberalism and private initiative. After the war the IP became more pragmatic, as the party accepted the welfare state and participated in governments that greatly increased government involvement in the unstable and overpoliticized economy. The IP has quite successfully avoided an anti-working-class image.

In the 1960s, a coalition government of the IP and the SDP abolished strict import controls and introduced free trade as the main principle of external economic policy. Iceland acceded to the General Agreement on Tariffs and Trade and joined the European Free Trade Association, and the government also opened for foreign investment in power-intensive industry. In the 1980s and 1990s the IP has emphasized further liberalization of the economy, following international trends as the other parties have also done to varying degrees. But the IP has been cautious in its approach. Prime Minister Oddsson has for instance led active government involvement in the bargaining process in the labor market, successfully trying to maintain economic stability. In a coalition government with the SDP in 1991–95, the IP resisted SDP demands for liberalizing agricultural imports. While Iceland joined the European Economic Area during that coalition, the IP opposes an application for an Icelandic membership of the European Union.

In security policy the IP has been the most consistent supporter of Icelandic membership in NATO and of the NATO base in Keflavík.

MEMBERSHIP AND CONSTITUENCY

The IP claims around 33,000 members. According to the Icelandic election studies of 1991 and 1995 the number of voters considering themselves IP members is around 20,000. A part of the discrepancy can probably be explained by people who have formally joined the IP in order to participate in primaries but nevertheless do not consider themselves members.

The IP has a remarkably weak class profile for a conservative party. In 1995 the party enjoyed the support of 35% of unskilled workers and 41% of skilled manuals, while only 42% of employers and higher managerials voted for the party. The party's weakest following in any occupational group—by far—was among farmers (20%). In 1995 the party closed a gender gap, as the party's support among men was only 2% higher than among women, while this figure had been 9% and 14% in 1987 and 1991.

The IP has traditionally been stronger in the urban South West (41.1% of the vote in 1995) than in the regions (29.5%).

LEADERSHIP

After the long period (1934–70) of the strong leadership of Ólafur Thors and Bjarni Benediktsson, the IP suffered from rather weak and divided leadership for two decades.

A serious leadership struggle took place in the 1970s and the early 1980s, especially between the party leader, Geir HallGrímsson, and his deputy, Gunnar Thoroddsen. That crisis was solved in 1983, when Thorsteinn Pálsson became leader. Pálsson's leadership was generally considered weak, as exemplified by his short-lived coalition government in 1987–88. He became the first IP leader to lose his post in the leader election at the party convention.

Davíd Oddsson (born 1948), then deputy leader of the IP, successfully challenged Pálsson for the party leadership just before the *Althingi* election of 1991. A few weeks later he became a member of *Althingi* for Reykjavík, as well as prime minister in a coalition he formed with the SDP. After the 1995 election he continued as prime minister, now in a coalition with the PP. Oddsson, educated as a lawyer, had become mayor of Reykjavík in 1982, when the IP regained a majority in the city council, which it lost in 1978, having been in power since the party was founded. The party kept a comfortable majority in the municipal election of 1986, and increased that majority in 1990. Despite winning the party leadership contest in a close vote in 1991, Oddsson quickly obtained a firm grip on the party and is generally considered a strong leader.

Fridrik Sophusson (born 1943), deputy leader of the party in 1981–89 and since 1991, has been a member of *Althingi* for Reykjavík since 1978. Educated as a lawyer, he was minister of industry in 1987–88 and minster of finance in 1991–98.

Geir H. Haarde (born in 1951) has been a member of *Althingi* for Reykjavík since 1987 and was chairman of the parliamentary group in 1991–98. In 1998 he became minister of finance. He studied in the United States and holds master's degrees in economics and international politics.

Björn Bjarnason (born in 1944, son of former IP leader and prime minister Bjarni Benediktsson) entered the *Althingi* for Reykjavík in 1991, having previously been an assistant editor of *Morgunbladid*, specializing in international and security affairs. Bjarnason, educated as a lawyer, has been minister of education since 1995. He is a close ally of party leader Oddsson and is increasingly considered one of the most influential persons in the IP leadership.

PROSPECTS

In a historical perspective, the period between 1971 and 1990 was a difficult one for the IP. The party spent a longer time in opposition than in government, had several bad results at the polls, and suffered from internal disputes and weak leadership. In the 1990s, the party has done rather well at the polls and, more important, has continuously held the premiership since 1991. While considerable policy differences remain within the party, for instance, on liberalizing the economy and Iceland's relationship with Europe, the party nevertheless seems united under Oddsson's strong leadership.

PEOPLE'S ALLIANCE (PA)
(Althydubandalagid)

HISTORY

The People's Alliance (PA) is descended from the Communist Party and other breakaway groups from the SDP. The Communist Party was founded in 1930 by radical SDP members as an orthodox communist party and a member of Comintern. It won its first seats in the *Althingi* in 1937 with 8.5% of the vote. In line with Comintern policy, the Communists demanded that the SDP join it in a Popular Front, but the SDP main body refused. Again, the left wing of the SDP broke off and formed the United Socialist Party with the Communists in 1938. The new party became larger than the SDP in its first election in 1942 with 16.2% of the vote. The United Socialist Party was not a Comintern member, but it was clearly pro-Soviet in foreign policy, and most of its major leaders had been prominent Communists. The party had Cabinet posts in a coalition with the IP and the SDP in 1944–47. In 1956, after another split in the SDP, the PA was created as a loose electoral alliance between the United Socialist Party and the former SDP group. The PA immediately took a role in the government coalition of 1956–58. After a decade out of power, the PA re-created itself as a formal political party in 1968 and the United Socialist Party was dissolved. The PA took part in the governing coalitions of 1971–74, 1978–79, 1980–83, and 1988–91. It has never held the portfolios of prime minister, foreign affairs, or justice, but it was allotted the finance ministry in both 1980 and 1988.

The 1968 reorganization led to a split in the PA, led by former SDP leader Hannibal Valdimarsson and others, who formed the Union of Liberals and Leftists. This group had considerable success in 1971 (8.9% of the vote and five seats), largely at the expense of the SDP. The party lost seats in 1974 and disappeared from the *Althingi* in 1978.

ORGANIZATION

Since 1968, the PA has been organized in a way similar to the other parties. The Communist Party was Leninist in organization, and the United Socialist Party, while formally a branch party like the others, was marked by the Leninist principle of "democratic centralism."

The PA has never been affiliated to any international organizations. It operates a separate organization for youth, but not for women.

Party headquarters are at Althydubandalagid, Austurstraeti 10, 101 Reykjavík.

POLICY

While the PA remains farthest to the left on the Icelandic political spectrum, the party has become more pragmatic in recent years, abandoning its former socialist aims of extensive public ownership and increasingly accepting market solutions. The party—especially when in opposition—has nevertheless been critical of many of the economic liberalization measures carried out in the last decade and generally supports extensive public welfare services. Emphasis on environmental issues has increased in recent years, just as has been the case among left-socialist parties in Scandinavia.

The PA has combined its socialist policies with a strong emphasis on nationalism. For decades, opposition to NATO membership and the U.S. military base in Keflavík was a core of the party program, and those issues were among the most hotly debated in Icelandic politics. Since 1978, however, the PA has taken part in government coalitions without demanding radical changes in security policy, and in the last decade those issues have hardly been raised by the party in the public debate. The PA remains critical of foreign investments and opposes Icelandic membership of the European Union. In 1993 the PA—in opposition—voted against Icelandic membership in the European Economic Area, even though the party had been a member of the previous government that largely negotiated the treaty.

MEMBERSHIP AND CONSTITUENCY

The PA claims 5,000 members, while the election studies of 1991 and 1995 indicate that around 4,000 voters consider themselves PA members. In 1995, the party had a very weak class profile with a similar support among working-class and middle-class voters. It enjoyed strongest support among unskilled manual workers (15%) and the public-sector "caring" professions (17%).

In recent years, the party has been somewhat stronger in the regions (15.3% in 1995) than in the urban South West (13.7%).

LEADERSHIP

In 1987, when party leader Svavar Gestsson had to step down from his post due to term limits in the party rules, a moderate faction, calling itself "the democratic generation," won a leadership contest with the "party owners" when Ólafur Ragnar Grímsson was elected leader. Grímsson's leadership was never seriously challenged—partly because he was willing to make policy compromises with his rivals. Due to the term limits, Grímsson had to step down in 1995, and in 1996 he left politics when he was elected president of the republic. For the first time the new leader was not elected by the party convention in 1995 but in a general election among party members. The first woman to lead one of the four old parties, Margrét Frímannsdóttir, won a close contest with deputy leader Steingrímur Sigfússon.

Party leader Margrét Frímannsdóttir (born 1954) has been a member of *Althingi* since 1987 for the South. She is a moderate within the party and is very keen on closer cooperation of the left parties.

Svavar Gestsson (born 1944) is the chairman of the parliamentary group. He became a member of *Althingi* for Reykjavík in 1978 and was minister of commerce in 1978–79, minister of social affairs, health and insurance in 1980–83, and minister of education in 1988–91. Gestsson was party leader in 1980–87.

Steingrímur J. Sigfússon (born 1955) has been a member of *Althingi* for the North East since 1983 and was minister of agriculture and communications in 1988–91. He has a B.S. degree in geology. Sigfússon was chairman of the parliamentary group in 1987–88 and deputy leader of the party in 1989–95. In 1998 he left the party in order to form a new left-socalist party.

PROSPECTS

In the last three *Althingi* elections, the People's Alliance has obtained 13–14% of the votes, compared with 17–23% in the 1970s and early 1980s. While the party has given up many of its traditional ideological stands, its policies are still perceived by many voters as outdated. There has been growing support within the party for closer cooperation with the other parties of the left (SDP, Women's Alliance, and the People's Movement), and the 1998 party convention decided to form an electoral alliance with those parties, presenting joint lists in the 1999 election. This move has led to a split in the party, as the more traditional elements have left in order to form a new left-socialist/green party.

PROGRESSIVE PARTY, PP
(Framsóknarflokkurinn)

HISTORY

The Progressive Party (PP) was founded as a parliamentary group in 1916. In its first years, the party was almost exclusively a farmer's party, and it had close ties to the cooperative movement. Since 1923, the PP has on average polled around 25% of the vote, which makes it the second-largest party in the country. In the last 20 years, the PP has however polled under 20% in four out of six elections.

Until 1987, the PP was always stronger in the *Althingi* than among the voters, due to the electoral system. This was especially pronounced before 1942 and contributed to the strong position of the party in the coalition system of that period: from 1917 to 1942, it spent only five years in opposition and held the premiership from 1927 to 1942.

In the 1940s, the party lost its role as "the natural party of government" to the IP. Nevertheless, the PP has chaired six coalitions in the postwar period, and since 1971 it has been in opposition for only four years.

ORGANIZATION

While the PP was clearly a cadre party at the beginning, it developed the formal characteristics of a mass party in the 1930s.

The PP is a member of the Liberal International, and it is affiliated to the association of center parties in the Nordic council. The party's youth organization is a member of the International Federation of Liberal and Radical Youth (IFLRY) and the Nordic Youth Center Association (NCF). While the party's women's organization is not a formal member of any international organization, it has informal cooperation with its Nordic counterparts, as well as inside the Liberal International.

Party headquarters are at Framsóknarflokkurinn, Hafnarstraeti 20, Postbox 453, 121 Reykjavík.

POLICY

The PP may be labeled a center or an agrarian party in terms of domestic policy. For decades the party's aims were clearly the defense of the interests of farmers and the more sparsely populated regions. While the PP has supported some of the liberalizing economic measures of recent years, it was critical of foreign investment and EFTA membership in the 1960s and has been the major champion of extensive government programs on rural development. In 1993, half of the party's members of *Althingi* voted against the ratification of the treaty on the European Economic Area, while the other half abstained. The PP opposes an Icelandic application for a membership of the European Union.

The PP has supported Iceland's membership in NATO, but it has been critical of the Keflavík base and, at times, supported its removal.

MEMBERSHIP AND CONSTITUENCY

The PP claims 7,000 members, while the Icelandic election study of 1995 suggests that around 6,000 voters consider themselves party members.

In its early decades, the party's electoral support was almost exclusively in the rural areas. While the PP has been quite successful in broadening its electoral appeal, it nevertheless remains much stronger in the six regional constituencies (34.6% in 1995) than in the urban South West (17.3%).

The class profile of the PP is weak, except that it still enjoys 60% support among farmers, a group that in numbers has however been reduced to electoral insignificance.

LEADERSHIP

Party leader Halldór Ásgrímsson (born 1947) was a university lecturer in business studies before he entered the *Althingi* for the East in 1974. He was minister of fisheries in 1983–91, minster of justice in 1988–89, and became foreign minister in 1995. Ásgrímsson had been deputy leader since 1980 when he took over the leadership post from Steingrímur Hermannsson in 1994. While Hermannsson, who left politics to become one of the three directors of the Central Bank, was widely considered to be opportunistic, anti-European, and leftist, Ásgrímsson is considered more center-right and more pro-European.

Gudmundur Bjarnason (born 1944), was deputy leader of the party in 1994–98 and has been a member of *Althingi* for the North East since 1979. He was minister of health and insurance in 1987–91 and has been minister of environment and agriculture since 1995.

Finnur Ingólfsson (born 1954) holds a university degree in business studies. He has been a member of *Althingi* for Reykjavík since 1991 and was chairman of the parliamentary group in 1994–95. Since 1995 he has been minister of trade and industry. In 1998 he became deputy leader of the party.

Valgerdur Sverrisdóttir (born 1950) has chaired the parliamentary group since 1995. She has been a member of *Althingi* for the North East since 1987.

PROSPECTS

From 1971 to 1991, the PP was continuously (except for a few months) a member of government coalitions. The party performed rather poorly in the elections of 1983–91, receiving less than 20% of the vote. After four years in opposition, the PP fought a highly successful campaign in 1995 under the new leadership of Ásgrímsson, obtained 23.3% of the vote, and joined a coalition with the IP. New candidates, emphasis by Ásgrímsson on a strong government, and continued stability after the election, in addition to some bold election promises, served to improve the standing of the party, especially in the urban South West, where the party has traditionally been weak. The PP now obtained almost half of its total vote in Reykjavík and the surrounding Reykjanes, while—due to the electoral system—only 4 out of the 15 PP members of *Althingi* came from those two constituencies. It may prove difficult for the party to keep the loyalty of the floating urban voters in the next election. A growing tension between the more liberal elements of the party and its traditionalists from the regions can be expected in the next few years.

SOCIAL DEMOCRATIC PARTY (SDP)
(Althyduflokkurinn)

HISTORY

The Social Democratic Party (SDP) was founded in 1916 as the political arm of the labor movement. The party was organizationally tied to the Icelandic Federation of Labor (founded at the same time) until 1942.

The SDP began as a democratic socialist party and was clearly a working-class party. It maintained that politics was about economic distribution and the living conditions of the working class, which was a very radical conception in a period when politics was dominated by the struggle for independence from Denmark.

The SDP grew continously in strength for its first two decades and polled over 20% of the vote in 1934. The party lost some ground in the 1937 election, and since 1942 it has usually been the smallest of the four major parties, receiving 14 to 16% of the vote. This history is in stark contrast to the development of the social democratic parties in Scandinavia. The socialist block in Iceland has been smaller than in the other Nordic countries, and the Icelandic Social Democrats have been the smaller of the two major socialist parties within that block (except in the 1987 and 1991 elections). This can partly be explained by the splits the SDP has suffered, losing its left wing each time.

The SDP first joined a coalition government (with the PP) in 1934, having supported a PP minority government in 1927–31. The party has been in government for around two-thirds of the remaining period, holding the premiership in one coalition (Stefánsson, 1947–49) and two minority cabinets (Jónsson, 1958–59; Gröndal, 1979–80). The SDP has worked with all other major parties in coalitions. Of special interest is the extraordinary long coalition partnership of the SDP with the IP, 1959–71, an unusual political combination by European standards.

Since 1971, the SDP has had mixed fortunes. While the party polled only around 10% of the votes in 1971 and 1974, it won a major victory in 1978 with 22%. After a split leading to the formation of the short-lived Social Democratic Alliance, the SDP was again down to 11.7% in 1983. The party recovered in the elections of 1987 and 1991, receiving over 15%, but after yet another split and the emergence of the People's Movement, the SDP obtained only 11.4% of the vote in 1995.

From 1971 the SDP remained in opposition (except for 1978–80) until 1987. Since then the party was continously a member of various government coalitions until 1995.

ORGANIZATION

The SDP was the first formal mass party and to some extent showed the way toward present party organization and intraparty democratic procedures. The party has suffered more from intraparty disputes than the other parties. Leadership challenges have been common, and the SDP has split five times, in 1930, 1938, 1956, 1983, and 1994.

The SDP is a member of the Socialist International. The party's youth and women's associations are also affiliated to international and Nordic social democratic organizations.

Party headquarters are at Althyduflokkurinn, Hverfisgötu 8-10, 101 Reykjavík.

POLICY

The domestic policy of the SDP has evolved along lines similar to other European social democratic parties: emphasis on nationalization and class struggle has been dropped, while adherence to the principles of the market economy, and a strong welfare state have become core issues of the party program. The fact that the SDP has lost its left wing several times has probably put its mark on party policy, which seems closer to the political center than has been the case with the Scandinavian social democrats. Since 1978, the SDP has increasingly supported radical liberalization measures in the Icelandic economy, long marked by more state involvement and political patronage than has been common in Western Europe. Jón Baldvin Hannibalsson, party leader in 1984–96 and minister of foreign affairs in 1988–95, led the Icelandic negotiations resulting in a membership in the European Economic Area in 1994. Before the 1995 election, the SDP—always the least nationalistic of the major parties—came out in favor of an Icelandic application for a membership of the European Union—so far the only party to do so.

The SDP has been closest to the IP in the foreign policy realm, supporting Icelandic membership in NATO and the base in Keflavík.

MEMBERSHIP AND CONSTITUENCY

The SDP claims 5,500 members, while the Icelandic election study of 1995 suggests that around 4,000 voters consider themselves SDP members. The party has a very weak class profile, except that it has almost no support among farmers. In 1995 the party enjoyed most support among skilled manuals (13%) and employers and higher managerials (16%). The party has traditionally been stronger in the urban South West (13.1% in 1995) than in the regions (8.3%).

LEADERSHIP

Sighvatur Björgvinsson (born 1942) became party leader in 1996 when Hannibalsson chose somewhat unexpectedly to retire. Björgvinsson was a member of *Althingi* for the West Fjords in 1974–83 and since 1987. He was the chairman of the parliamentary group in 1978–83, minister of finance in 1979–80, minister of health and insurance in 1991–93 and 1994–95, and minster of commerce and industry in 1993–95.

Gudmundur Árni Stefánsson (born 1955) was deputy leader in 1994–96. Having been a mayor in the SDP stronghold Hafnarfjördur from 1986, he entered the *Althingi* in 1993 for Reykjanes and immediately became minister of health and insurance. In 1994 he switched over to the ministry of social affairs but resigned from the government a few months later due to allegations of misconduct in office. Stefánsson lost to Björgvinsson in the leadership election at the party convention in 1996 but

nevertheless strengthened his position within the party, as the vote was much closer than expected.

Rannveig Gudmundsdóttir (born 1940) was the chairman of the parliamentary group in 1993–94 and since 1995. She has been a member of *Althingi* for Reykjanes since 1989 and was minister of social affairs in 1994–95. She was the deputy leader of the party in 1993–94.

Össur Skarphédinsson (born 1953) has been a member of *Althingi* for Reykjavík since 1991. Skarphédinsson, who holds a Ph.D. in biology, was the chairman of the parliamentary group in 1991–93 and minister of environment in 1993–95. He was narrowly beaten by Stefánsson in an election for the deputy leadership in 1994.

PROSPECTS

The SDP did badly in the 1995 election, mainly because of the success of the new People's Movement, which obtained 7.1% of the vote and had four members elected. The new party was led by the former SDP minister and deputy leader Jóhanna Sigurdardóttir, criticizing her former party for being too right-wing. Shortly after the election, the People's Movement lost almost all support in the opinion polls, and in 1996 its *Althingi* members joined the SDP in a united parliamentary group.

The SDP has decided to form an electorial alliance with the People's Movement, the PA, and the Women's Alliance in the comming 1999 election, thus hoping to create a broad social democratic party, similar to the large social democratic parties in Scandinavia.

OTHER POLITICAL FORCES

Besides the political parties and the administration, major interest groups—increasingly independent of the political parties—play an important role in the political system. The interests of agriculture and fisheries have traditionally greatly influenced government policy. In recent years, the Federation of Labor (ASÍ) and the Federation of Employers (VSÍ) have increased their influence on policymaking, as governments have tended to offer them certain "policy packages" in return for moderate settlements and peace in the labor market. Interest groups have, for example, influenced legislation on the quota system in fisheries, agricultural policy, indexing of loans, welfare benefits, unemployment measures, mortgages, and taxation—such as the reduction of VAT on food from 24.5% to 14%.

Minor Parties

Challenges to the four-party format of Icelandic politics have become more frequent in recent years. While most minor parties contending elections in the postwar period did not win seats, several short-lived parties have had members elected to the *Althingi*: the National Preservation Party in 1953 (2 members), the Union of Liberals and Leftists in 1971 (5) and 1974 (2), the Social Democratic Alliance in 1983 (4), the Citizen's Party in 1987 (7), and the People's Movement in 1995 (4).

Only one new party, the Women's Alliance, has shown more perseverance as it has had members elected in every election since its initial success in 1983. The party focuses on women's issues and its policies can be termed left-of-center. In 1987 the party doubled its share of the vote with 10.1%. While the party held its own in 1991 (8.4%), it suffered badly in 1995 (4.9%). The party had lost its most prominent leader in the local elections of 1994, when Ingibjörg Sólrún Gísladóttir left her *Althingi* seat in order to become mayor of Reykjavík after the victory of a joint list of all parties except the Independence Party. A feud concerning candidate selection, disagreements on policy, and the fact that the new party on the left wing, the People's Movement, was led by a popular female politician may also have contributed to the party's difficulties. Besides, women have had increasing success in the old parties. In 1998 for instance, 27% of *Althingi* members were female, while the corresponding figure was 5% when the Women's Alliance emerged. In the last few years, the Women's Alliance has been in a deep crisis. A number of prominent members have left the party because of the majority's decision to from a electoral alliance with other left-wing parties in the 1999 election. Regardless of the fortunes of this new alliance, the future of the Women's Alliance as a separate party is very much in doubt.

NATIONAL PROSPECTS

After seven years of recession the economy started to improve in the latter part of 1994 and has been booming since. For the first time in decades, economic stability and low inflation have been maintained for nine years (since 1990), largely due to restraint in the labor market. The cod stocks are recovering after a serious decline: the cod quota in 1994 was down to 155,000 tons as compared with a total cod catch of 350,000 tons in 1989. Foreign investment in power-intensive industry is increasing. While unemployment has increased, it is below 5%.

A balanced budget was achieved in 1997. The economy, long characterized by excessive state involvement by Western European standards, has been greatly liberalized, and some privatization has taken place. Iceland became a founding member of the European Economic Area in 1994. While some structural defects in the economy remain, the economic future looks bright and living standards can be expected to stay among the highest in the world.

In the last decades, the political parties have experi-

enced decreasing power, increasing electoral volatility, and less internal cohesion. The scope for arbitrary decisions of individual politicians has decreased, partly due to increased professionalization of the administration, less state involvement in the economy, and the growth of critical and nonpartisan media. Despite increasing challenges to the old four parties, they have continued to dominate the party system. While numerous attempts to restructure the left wing of the party system have so far been without success, a major restructuring of the left seems likely in the 1999 *Althingi* election.

Further Reading

Grímsson, Ólafur Ragnar. "Iceland: A Multilevel Coalition System." In *Government Coalitions in Western Democracies*. Ed. E.C. Brown and J. Dreijmanis. New York and London: Longman, 1982.

———. "The Icelandic Power Structure 1800–2000." *Scandinavian Political Studies* 11 (1976).

Hardarson, Ólafur Th. "Iceland." *European Journal of Political Reserach* 22 (1992): 429–35; 24 (1993): 451–53; 26 (1994): 327–30; 28 (1995): 369–73; 30 (1996): 367–76; 32 (1997): 391—98.

———. *Parties and Voters in Iceland*. Reykjavík: Social Science Research Institute/University Press, 1995.

Hardarson, Ólafur Th., and Gunnar Helgi Kristinsson. "The Icelandic Parliamentary Election of 1987." *Electoral Studies* 6, no. 3 (1987): 219–34.

Kristinsson, Gunnar Helgi. *Farmers' Parties. A Study in Electoral Adaption*. Reykjavík: Social Science Research Institute, 1991.

———. "The Icelandic Parliamentary Election of April 1991: A European Periphery at the Polls." *Scandinavian Political Studies* 14, no. 4 (1991): 343–54.

———. "The Icelandic Parliamentary Election of 1991." *Electoral Studies* 10, no. 3 (1991): 262–66.

———. "Iceland and Norway: Peripheries in Doubt." In *Prospective Europeans*. Ed. J. Redmond. London: Harvester-Wheatsheaf, 1994.

———. "The Icelandic Parliamentary Election of 1995." *Electoral Studies* 14, no. 3 (1995): 332–36.

———. "The Icelandic Presidential Election of 1996." *Electoral Studies* 15, no. 4 (1996): 533–37.

———. "Parties, States and Patronage." *West European Politics* 19, no. 3 (1996): 433–57.

Kristjánsson, Svanur. "The Electoral Basis of the Icelandic Independence Party 1929–1944." *Scandinavian Political Studies* 2 (new series), no. 1 (1979).

Nordal, Jóhannes, and Valdimar Kristinsson, eds. *Iceland. The Republic*. Reykjavík: Central Bank of Iceland, 1996.

Ólafsson, Stefán. "Variations within the Scandinavian Model: Iceland in a Scandinavian Comparison." In *Welfare Trends in the Scandinavian Countries*. Ed. E. Hansen et. al. New York: M.E. Sharpe, 1993.

Styrkársdóttir, Audur. "From Social Movement to Political Party: The New Women's Movement in Iceland." In *The New Women's Movement*. Ed. D. Dahlerup. London: SAGE, 1986.

REPUBLIC OF INDIA

(Bharat)

By Stanley A. Kochanek, Ph.D.

THE SYSTEM OF GOVERNMENT

India is a federal republic with a British-style parliamentary form of government. Over the past 50 years since independence, the governmental system has evolved from a highly centralized, one-party-dominant state to one that has become increasingly federalized, fragmented, and controlled by unstable multiparty coalitions and alliances.

With a population of 950 million (in 1997), India is one of the poorest, most diverse, and most heterogenous countries in the world. Although Hinduism is the dominant religion, India contains all of the major world religions; it is subdivided into a myriad of castes; and it has 15 major languages plus a vast array of smaller languages, dialects, and tribal tongues. In its diversity and continental size, India is more like the multistate European Community than the more integrated and unified United States federal system.

Though its roots are much deeper, the contemporary Indian political system dates from August 15, 1947, when its long and unique struggle for independence from British rule finally succeeded. Independence brought partition on religious lines between secular but predominantly Hindu India and Muslim Pakistan.

Newly independent India drafted a constitution modeled on the British and other existing constitutions. The constitution, which entered into force on January 26, 1950, provides for a democratic republic, secular, parliamentary, and federal in character. It is one of the longest and most detailed written constitutions in the world and one of the most frequently amended.

Executive

The president of the republic is the head of state and supreme commander of the military forces but exercises the executive power only formally. The president is elected to a five-year term by an electoral college composed of the elected members of both houses of the national Parliament and of the lower houses of the state legislatures. Voting is weighted to allow for population differences between the states. The president is supposed to be a nonpartisan figure, but in practice candidates have been elected only if they were acceptable to the prime minister.

From the beginning, the president was intended to exercise his or her power only with the closest advice of the prime minister and the Cabinet. His primary role was to be symbolic, much in the manner of the British monarch, although there was considerable discussion of the extent of the president's discretionary powers. Any ambiguity was removed by the Forty-Second Amendment to the constitution in 1976 and the Forty-Fourth Amendment in 1978, which explicitly required the president to act in accordance with the advice of the Cabinet.

Thus, effective executive power belongs to the prime minister and the Cabinet (formally the Council of Ministers). The prime minister is appointed by the president and must be able to command majority support in the *Lok Sabha*, the lower house of the Parliament. If there is a recognized leader of a party or coalition that commands a majority in the *Lok Sabha*, the president has no discretion. With the emergence of coalition government, the president's discretionary power to appoint the prime minister has increased.

The prime minister is responsible to the Lok Sabha, which may force the prime minister from office at any time by demonstrating the lack of majority support for him. Since 1979 several Indian prime ministers have been forced to resign in the face of an impending vote of no confidence or failure to maintain majority support.

The president appoints the members of the Council of Ministers on the advice of the prime minister and removes them in the same way. Within the Cabinet, the prime minister has always been the strongest figure; the collective decision-making process of the British system of Cabinet government is much less characteristic of India where the prime minister and his formal and informal advisers (who may or may not be members of the Cabinet) predominate. Cabinet ministers, therefore, mainly are occupied with implementation of policy decisions affecting their governmental ministries and with day-to-day administrative responsibilities.

Ministerial departments are staffed by a powerful and prestigious civil service, the modern successor to the almost legendary Indian Civil Service of British colonial days. At the apex of the modern civil service is the Indian Administrative Service, an elite cadre of highly qualified, competitively selected administrators who exercise wide-ranging power over implementation and administration of government policy subject only to the supervision of politically responsible ministers.

India has had 16 prime ministers in 50 years of independence. Jawaharlal Nehru and his daughter, Indira Gandhi, have governed for 30 of those years. Mrs. Gandhi served from 1966 to 1977, when her Congress Party was defeated by a coalition of opposition parties that took the name Janata (People's) Party after 21 months of authoritarian rule under the draconian emergency provisions of the Indian constitution. The Janata Party formed a government under Prime Minister Moraji Desai, who served from 1977 to mid-1979, when the party split. Charan Singh then became the prime minister. New national elections resulted in Mrs. Gandhi's return to power in January 1980. Mrs. Gandhi was succeeded by her son Rajiv Gandhi following her assassination on October 31, 1984. Rajiv Gandhi led his Congress (I) Party to an overwhelming victory in the December 1984 general elections. Rajiv's policy failures, his centralization of power, and a series of corruption scandals involving defense contracts resulted in his defeat in the November 1989 elections.

Prime Ministers of India, 1947–98

Prime Minister	Party	Dates
Jawaharlal Nehru	Congress	8/15/47–5/27/64
Lal Bahadur Shastri	Congress	6/9/64–1/11/66
Indira Gandhi	Congress	1/24/66–3/24/77
Morarji Desai	Janata	3/24/77–7/8/79
Charan Singh	Janata	7/28/79–1/14/80
Indira Gandhi	Congress	1/14/80–10/31/84
Rajiv Gandhi	Congress	10/31/84–12/1/89
V. P. Singh	National Front	12/2/89–11/10/90
Chandra Shekhar	Samajvadi Janata	11/10/90–6/21/91
P. V. Narasimha Rao	Congress	6/21/91–5/16/96
Atal Behari Vajpayee	BJP	5/16/96–6/1/96
H. D. Deve Gowda	Janata Dal	6/1/96–4/11/97
I. K. Gujral	Janata Dal	4/21/97–3/19/98
Atar Behari Vajpayee	BJP	3/19/98–

The defeat of the Congress Party, however, led to a hung Parliament. For the first time since independence no single party was able to secure a majority and India entered an era of unstable coalition and alliance politics. Following the 1989 elections, the National Front, a loose multiparty coalition, elected V. P. Singh as prime minister. Friction within the National Front, however, led to the downfall of Singh in less than a year. Singh was replaced by Chandra Shekhar, supported by the Congress Party. This unstable alliance lasted only four months, and India was forced to go to the polls for the second time in less

than two years in the midst of major political and economic crises.

The uncertainty that dominated the 1991 *Lok Sabha* elections was further compounded by the assassination of Rajiv Gandhi by a Sri Lankan Tamil during an election meeting in Tamil Nadu. Rajiv's assassination had a dramatic impact on the election results. During the first round of voting that had preceded the assassination, the Congress had suffered severe reverses. However, in the delayed second and third rounds of voting, a significant sympathy vote in favor of the Congress Party enabled the party to win 227 seats—just 29 seats short of a majority. P. V. Narasimha Rao, the newly elected Congress leader, was able to form a minority government that gradually increased its support and survived for a full term of five years.

The Congress revival, however, proved to be short-lived as the party, tainted by charges of corruption, suffered its worst defeat in history in the April–May 1996 elections. The defeat of the Congress, once again, resulted in a hung Parliament that was more fragmented than ever before. Because the Bharatiya Janata Party (BJP) had won the largest number of seats in the election, the president of India asked the party leader, Atal Behari Vajpayee, to form a government. Vajpayee, however, was forced to resign 13 days later when faced by the prospect of losing a no-confidence motion in Parliament. The president then invited the National Front–Left Front, a coalition of 13 regional and national parties, to form a government. The Front elected H. D. Deve Gowda, a former chief minister of Karnataka, to be prime minister. Gowda headed a minority government supported by the Congress Party, which refused to join the coalition Cabinet. Gowda lasted less than a year and was forced to resign when the Congress Party withdrew its support. He was replaced on April 21, 1997, by Inder Kumar Gujral, a candidate more acceptable to the Congress Party. The Gujral government lasted until December, when new parliamentary elections were called. In March 1998, Vajpayee again became prime minister when the BJP cobbled together a coalition of over a dozen and a half regional parties following the 1998 *Lok Sabha* elections.

Legislature

The Indian Parliament is bicameral. The more important lower house is called the *Lok Sabha*, or "house of the people." It has 543 members directly elected from single-member-district constituencies based on population and two seats filled by nomination. Elections are normally held at five-year intervals. The five-year limit has been abridged only once when in 1976, the life of the *Lok Sabha* was extended by one year by Indira Gandhi under the emergency provisions of the constitution. The extension was renewed a year later. Parliamentary elections may be called at less than five-year intervals by the president acting on the advice of the prime minister.

There are 79 *Lok Sabha* seats reserved for members of the Scheduled Castes, or untouchables. Another 40 seats are reserved for members of Scheduled Tribes. These reserved seats are allocated among the states on the basis of the proportion of their populations that fall into the respective Scheduled category. Electorates for the reserved seats are made up of all classes of Indian citizens, but only Scheduled Caste or Scheduled Tribe members may stand for such seats. These provisions for special representation are constitutionally temporary, but they have been regularly extended. In another special category, the president of India is empowered to appoint up to two Anglo-Indians (descendants of mixed British-Indian marriages or liaisons) to the *Lok Sabha*.

By constitution, the *Lok Sabha* must meet at least twice each year with no more than six months between sessions. In practice, it usually meets three times a year.

The upper house of Parliament is the *Rajya Sabha*, or "council of the states." It has 250 members, 12 of whom are appointed by the president from among Indians distinguished in the arts and professions. The remainder are elected by the state legislatures to fixed terms, with approximately one-third retiring every second year. Thus it is possible that the partisan majority in the *Lok Sabha* will not coincide with the majority in the *Rajya Sabha*, which has happened on several occasions.

The two houses of Parliament have the same power over ordinary legislation; both must pass bills in agreed form. However, money bills may be introduced only in the *Lok Sabha*, and the *Rajya Sabha* has only the power of delay. If a money bill is amended or rejected by the *Rajya Sabha*, it needs merely to be repassed by the *Lok Sabha* in the original form to be sent to the president for assent. The *Rajya Sabha* exercises independent jurisdiction in a limited range of issues relating to the states.

Judiciary

India's constitution makers took the notion of parliamentary supremacy from the British model but tried to graft onto it an independent judiciary and judicial review system based largely on the American model. At the apex of an integrated national judicial system is the Supreme Court of India. It consists of a chief justice and not more than 13 other judges appointed by the president. Judges of the Supreme Court serve until they reach the age of 65, unless removed by an elaborate and difficult parliamentary procedure. The chief justice is normally the most senior judge in terms of age, although there have been a few controversial cases of "supersession," i.e., the appointment of a less senior judge as chief justice.

The Supreme Court has broad original and appellate jurisdiction that extends to civil and criminal matters and especially to matters of constitutional interpretation and relations between the Centre (the national government) and the states. The exercise of these powers has led to considerable conflict between governments committed to greater or lesser degrees of social reform and a court equally committed to the protection of fundamental rights outlined in the constitution. The conflict between court and government has been waged in a variety of ways over the years. Many of the 80 amendments to the Indian constitution have been designed to reverse some Supreme Court ruling striking down an act of Parliament. The most substantial attack on the court came in 1976 when Mrs. Gandhi's government pushed through Parliament the very detailed and extensive Forty-Second Amendment Act that, among other things, placed very stringent limitations on the power of the Supreme Court to review acts of Parliament on constitutional grounds. The Supreme Court itself struck down part of this amendment and the Janata Party government further altered it in the Forty-Fourth Amendment in 1978. The fundamental difficulty of reconciling parliamentary supremacy with judicial review remains one of the troublesome issues facing the Indian political system.

One of the most important developments in India in recent years has been the renewal of judicial activism. The Supreme Court has begun to promote public-interest litigation (PIL) based on a reinterpretation of the constitution to include equal treatment under the law and due process. In keeping with this new activism the Supreme Court has encouraged class-action suits, has treated letters written to judges as writ petitions, has acted upon newspaper reports, has appointed committees to investigate the facts of a case, has summoned experts to obtain their views, and has even made public authorities investigating charges of corruption on the part of public officials directly responsible to the Court. The result has been a massive expansion of civil, political, economic, and social rights. Supreme Court activism has also spread to the lower courts. The Court's new role, however, has brought it into conflict with both the executive and the legislature and has led to efforts by both to restrict the Court's action.

Regional and Local Government

Although India is a federation composed of 25 states and 7 union territories, Indian federalism is weighted heavily toward the central government. The union territories are ruled by the central government under a variety of arrangements. The states are organized mainly along language lines. The central government may and occasionally has redrawn state boundaries. The structure of state government is similar to that of the central government. The executive power is vested in a governor who is appointed by the president of India on the advice of the prime minister. The governor is appointed for a five-year term and is largely a figurehead whose powers and role are analogous to those of the national president.

Real political and administrative power is exercised by

a chief minister (analogous to the prime minister at the national level) and his council of ministers who are appointed by the governor and are collectively responsible to the legislative assembly. Most states have a unicameral legislature. The legislative assemblies are composed of between 60 and 500 members chosen by direct election from territorial constituencies based on population. The legislative assemblies function in a manner similar to the *Lok Sabha* at the Centre. Seven states have bicameral legislatures with a smaller legislative council functioning alongside the legislative assembly.

Members of the legislative council are elected indirectly by the assembly or appointed by the governor to fixed terms with approximately one-third retiring every second year.

The Indian constitution divides the functions of government between the states and the central government through three detailed lists. The Union List contains areas exclusively reserved to the national government, including defense and military forces, atomic energy, foreign affairs, railways, shipping, air transport, posts and telegraph, currency, international trade, banking, insurance, mining, and nonagricultural income and corporate taxation. The State List contains items reserved to the states, including public order, police, prisons, local government, public health, agriculture, land and land tenure, property tax, and tax on agricultural income. The Concurrent List contains items on which either the states or the national government may act, including criminal law, preventive detention, marriage and divorce, contracts, economic and social planning, social security, labor, education, and civil procedure. In the event of conflict between the national government and state action on matters on the Concurrent List, the national government position prevails. Moreover, a reserve clause grants the national government exclusive jurisdiction over all areas not enumerated in one of the lists. In periods of emergency or with the concurrence of two-thirds of the *Rajya Sabha*, the national government may act on matters on the State List.

Finally, if the president "is satisfied that a situation has arisen in which the government of the State cannot be carried on in accordance with the provisions of this Constitution," he may, on the advice of the prime minister, suspend the state government and rule directly from Delhi. This is referred to as "president's rule" and has been used with increasing frequency since the 1960s.

THE ELECTORAL SYSTEM

Although the *Rajya Sabha* and the legislative councils are indirectly elected, the more important *Lok Sabha* and the legislative assemblies are elected directly. Since 1967, all electoral constituencies have been single-member. Candidates must be Indian citizens at least 25 years of age.

Most successful candidates are nominated by recognized parties, although a large number of independents (1,900 in 1998) always stand for election. A candidate must put up a deposit of 10,000 rupees (about $236) to run for a *Lok Sabha* seat and 5,000 rupees for a legislative assembly seat. A candidate must poll at least one-sixth of the votes cast in that constituency in order to have his deposit refunded. The candidate receiving a simple plurality of the valid votes cast in the constituency wins.

Vacancies caused by death, resignation, or removal from office are filled through by-elections that are watched carefully as signals of political trends.

Ballots list candidates by party symbol, in English and in the local language(s). Voting is secret and carefully supervised. Although there have been charges of corruption, intimidation, and "booth capturing," most observers agree that Indian elections are remarkably free, fair and orderly.

All Indian citizens 18 years of age or over are eligible to vote. Registration rolls are kept by the Election Commission, an independent agency charged with responsibility for the fair and efficient conduct of elections, and are updated regularly at the initiative of the Commission. To insure against double voting, voters' fingers are marked with indelible ink. Votes are not counted until the final polling day is under way, and returns are not released until all polling is completed.

With approximately 605 million eligible voters, India has the largest democratic electorate in the world. Voter turnout has been relatively high. Since 1952 the average voter turnout has been 57.1% of the eligible voters. The highest turnout was in 1984 following the assassin of Indira Gandhi when 64.1% of the eligible voters turned out. The lowest turnout occurred in the first two elections of 1952 and 1957 when it was only 45.7%.

Lok Sabha Elections, 1998 (voter turnout 62%)

Party	Seats Won	Seats Contested	% Votes
Bharatiya Janata Party (BJP)	179	384	25.47
BJP Allies[a]	73	269	11.94
	252	653	37.41
Congress (I)	141	474	25.88
Congress (I) Allies[b]	26	180	4.06
	167	654	29.94
United Front[c]	97	569	21.80
Other Parties[d]	18	293	6.03
Independents	5	1900	1.98
	539[e]	4069	97.16

[a] BJP allies and numbers of seats: Shiv Sena (6), Samata Party (12), Biju Janata Dal (9), Akali Dal (8), Trinamul Congress (7), Lok Shakti (3), Haryana Vikas Party (1), AIADMK (18), Pattali Makkal Katchi (4), Marumalarchi DMK (3), Tamizhaga Rajiv Congress (1), and Janata Party (1).
[b] Congress (I) allies and numbers of seats: Rashtriya Janata Dal (17), Republican Party of India (4), Muslim League (2) Kerala Congress (M) (1),

United Minorities Front (1), and Rashtriya Janata Party (1).

c United Front and numbers of seats: Janata Dal (6), CPI (M) (32), CPI (9), Tamil Maanila Congress (3), Samajwadi Party (20), Telugu Desam Party (12), Forward Bloc (2), Revolutionary Socialist Party (5), Dravida Munnetra Kazhagam (6), and National Conference (2).

d Other parties and numbers of seats: Bahujan Samaj Party (5), Samajwadi Janata Party (R) (1), Haryana Lok Dal (Rashtriya) (4), Arunchal Congress (2), Manipur State Congress (1), Autonomous State Demand Committee (1), Sikkim Democratic Front (1), Peasants and Workers Party (1), All India Indira Congress (S) (1), and Majlis Ittehadul Muslimeen (1).

e 4 seats are to be filled later.

THE PARTY SYSTEM

Origins of the Parties

Most, but not all, Indian political parties grew out of the independence struggle. The Congress Party, which has held power on the national level for all but 5 of the 50 years since independence, is the direct descendant of the Indian National Congress, the umbrella organization that led the independence struggle from 1885 until independence in 1947. As an umbrella organization, the Congress was highly aggregative, seeking to unite disparate ideologies and personalities in the service of self-rule. With independence at hand, ideological and personal differences led to defections from the Congress.

An early ideological split led to the establishment of the Socialist Party in 1947. Personality differences created a break between Charan Singh and the Congress in Uttar Pradesh, India's largest state, and the establishment of the Bharatiya Kranti Dal in 1967. A combination of ideology and personality led to a major "split" in the Congress in 1969 and the establishment of the Congress (O). Since 1969 the Congress has experienced repeated splits due to personality clashes and factionalism that have considerably weakened the party and filled the ranks of the opposition. Almost all of the Indian parties—except the Communist Party, Bharatiya Janata Party, and some of the regional and state parties—arose from these defections or splits in the Congress Party.

The Parties in Law

Political parties are not given significant treatment in the constitution of India and have little special status in Indian law. Independent candidates have essentially the same legal rights and responsibilities as party candidates: nomination procedures, financial limits, and reporting requirements are the same.

Parties recognized by the Election Commission have reserved symbols. To be recognized a party must meet one of two criteria. It must either exist and participate in political activity for a period of five years or secure at least 4% of the votes cast in the state for the *Lok Sabha* or *Vidhan Sabha* (state assembly) elections. In the (1998)

elections, there were 7 recognized national parties and 40 recognized state parties with reserved symbols.

Party Organization

Most Indian parties profess to be mass organizations based on dues-paying members; in reality, few are. Only the Congress, the Indian People's Party, and the Communist Parties have sustained such a mass character over any length of time. The BJP and the Communists are numerically smaller and confined to a narrower geographical area than Congress. One of the reasons for the relative success of the Congress in the past was that it was a coalition party composed of diverse castes and communities and of disparate groups espousing different emphases in government policy. Over the years, however, the Congress has become less coalitional and more personalistic in character, a process hastened during Indira Gandhi's and her son Rajiv's tenure.

None of the other parties has been of the coalition type, except the Janata briefly during its incumbency from 1977 to 1979. Other parties tend to be ideological, personalistic, or regional.

The main parties maintain national and state organizations. Real power usually is divided between these two sets of organizations in shifting measures. The work of running campaigns rests with the state or local units of the party. While state or local units often carry substantial political power, the national organization usually exerts major influence over the allocation of tickets (nominations). Although the details of party organization differ from party to party and from time to time, all the main national parties are structured to reflect the division of electoral and administrative structures into states and districts.

As in most parliamentary systems, there is a certain amount of tension and conflict between the parliamentary and organizational wings of the parties. Such conflict has been most pronounced in the ruling Congress Party. However, the Janata also experienced major differences when in power from 1977 to 1979, and these resulted in a split of the party in mid-1979. Such differences often have been seen at the state level.

Campaigning

Indian political campaigns have a festive air. People turn out in large numbers of political rallies and other appearances by candidates. Candidates circulate extensively in their constituencies, usually traveling from village to village by jeep, sometimes on foot or by elephant. In urban areas, parties canvass door to door. Signs, banners, and graffiti play a prominent role in campaigns. Party notables move extensively around the state or country making personal appearances in tightly contested constituencies.

Radio and television are government-controlled and

have not played prominent roles in campaigning. However, beginning in 1977 in some state elections and in the 1980 national elections, all recognized parties were provided with campaign time on radio and television.

Campaign expenditures are sharply limited by law. In 1998, each candidate for the *Lok Sabha* was permitted to spend not more than Rs 1,500,000 ($35,461) in election expenses. Each candidate is required to maintain a daily documented account of expenditures that must be submitted to the relevant election official. Failure to comply with these regulations may result in a candidate's being disqualified from serving in either house of Parliament for three years.

However, it is widely agreed that these limits are wholly unrealistic and that Indian elections are vastly more expensive. A well-known Indian news magazine (*India Today*, March 31, 1996) reported a candidate for a seat in the *Lok Sabha* might have to spend anywhere from Rs 500,000 to Rs 50 million ($11,820 to 1,182,033).

Political finances are the subject of much rumor and speculation and little hard data. Parties devote a good deal of effort to raising money. Some of the devices used include the collection of membership dues, the sale of advertisements in party publications, the sale of space and decorations at party functions, requests for direct donations, and, it has been charged, pressures bordering on extortion and solicitation of bribes. The large industrial families—the Birlas, the Tatas, and the like—have a tradition of financial support for political movements that goes back to well before independence. Other sources of funds include small-time traders, local industry lobbies, cooperatives, nonresident Indians, the underworld, government contracting, and various regulatory approvals. The Congress Party has been the main beneficiary of financial support from the business houses, but other parties have increased their share depending on their relative strength. In 1998 it is estimated that the BJP spent more than the Congress Party during the election.

During the cold war Communist Parties were widely believed to have received support from outside India, and there have been repeated charges that other parties, including the Congress, received covert monies from the U.S. Central Intelligence Agency. However, hard evidence about sources of financial support for Indian parties is fragmentary and should be approached with caution. In any event the end of the cold war has sharply reduced incentives by outsiders to fund Indian parties.

Independent Voters

Party membership figures in India are highly unreliable. Personalist parties rarely have any formal membership outside Parliament. Even in mass-based parties, frequent defections, splits, and factional conflicts make available figures highly unreliable. Voting rolls do not indicate party identification, but public-opinion studies indicate that a surprisingly large proportion of the voters expresses identification with parties. Recent elections suggest that party identification may be less indicative of voting behavior than orientation to personalities and issues. Since 1971, *Lok Sabha* and state assembly elections have generally occurred at different times. Therefore, since voters usually cast only one ballot for one member of the *Lok Sabha*, ticket splitting is normally impossible.

INDIAN PEOPLE'S PARTY
(Bharatiya Janata Party; BJP)

HISTORY

The BJP was founded in 1980 after the breakup of the governing Janata Party coalition. It is the current manifestation of the former Jana Sangh (People's) Party with its long tradition of militant Hindu nationalist politics. The Jana Sangh was established in 1950 largely by a cadre of the Rashtriya Swayamsevak Sangh (RSS), or National Volunteer Organization, a paramilitary group and by some figures from the Hindu Mahasabha, a militant Hindu political party. The initiative for a new party was led by Dr. S. P. Mookerjee, a former Hindu Mahasabha leader and former member of Nehru's Cabinet. Beginning with the first general election in 1952, the Jana Sangh gradually replaced the Hindu Mahasabha as the voice of Hindu cultural militancy.

Since its creation the strategy of the Jana Sangh and its successor, the BJP, has oscillated between the propagation of militant Hindu nationalism based on ethnoreligious mobilization and a more pragmatic approach based on moderation and coalition building designed to broaden the movement's electoral appeal. The basic dilemma of the leadership has been to maintain its militant core support based on the paramilitary National Volunteer Organization (RSS) and its cadre and the need to temper that ideology in an effort to develop a more centrist appeal designed to win power. Initially, in the years following its creation in the 1950s the Jana Sangh followed a militant Hindu nationalist strategy. This strategy, however, had a limited impact on the electorate, and the party was marginalized by the strong appeal of the Congress Party and the popularity of its leader, Jawaharlal Nehru.

In an effort to break out of its isolation, the Jana Sangh shifted to a more pragmatic strategy in the 1960s that saw it begin to build electoral support in the Hindi-speaking belt of North and Central India. Its electoral success enabled the party to participate in coalition governments in several states and to gain control of municipal governing bodies. This strategy continued into the 1970s as the Jana Sangh supported the opposition movement led by Jayaprakash Narayan, opposed emergency rule from 1975 to 1977, and joined the broad-based Janata coalition that defeated the Congress Party for the first time since 1947 in the 1977 parliamentary elections. Following the elections, the Jana Sangh became incorporated into the new Janata Party that brought an end to its formal existence.

Following the breakup of the Janata Party, the bulk of the former Jana Sangh members left the Janata Party to form the BJP under the leadership of Atal Bihari Vajpayee, a former Jana Sangh leader who had served as the foreign minister in the Janata government. Under Vajpayee the BJP attempted to build a new Hindu nationalist party that would be more open, centrist, and broadly based than the old Jana Sangh. The party adopted a moderate program based on Gandhian socialism, nationalism, democracy, value-based politics, and positive secularism. This new program, however, upset the party's traditional hard-core supporters in the RSS and generated considerable internal dissent. Members of the RSS became increasingly alienated from the party and began to drift toward the more militant appeals of the Congress Party under Indira Gandhi. The attraction of RSS members to the Congress increased sharply following the assassination of Indira Gandhi by her Sikh bodyguards. The assassination, Sikh separatism, anxiety over isolated incidents of Muslim conversions of low-caste Hindus, and growing insurgencies along India's northern border created a sense of insecurity and a Hindu backlash that resulted in a massive victory for Rajiv Gandhi and a stunning defeat of the BJP in the 1984 elections. Elements of the RSS contributed to this victory by actively working on behalf of Rajiv, and several prominent RSS leaders openly endorsed him.

The defeat suffered by the BJP in the 1984 elections resulted in a change of leadership, policy, and program as the party attempted to return to its roots. The more liberal Vajpayee was replaced as leader of the party by L. K. Advani who had close ties to the RSS. Under Advani the BJP adopted a more militant Hindu nationalist position and a strategy of ethnoreligious mobilization. The shift in BJP policy coincided with a sharp rise in communalism that was heightened by the agitation surrounding the long-simmering dispute over the Babri Masjid (Mosque) in Ayodhya. Hindus claimed that the Babri Masjid had been built by the Mughals on the site of a destroyed Hindu temple that had marked the birthplace of Lord Rama, a Hindu deity. They wanted the mosque demolished and replaced with a new Ramjanmabhoomi temple. The BJP used the religious symbol of the Babri Masjid/Ramjanmabhoomi during the 1989 elections in an effort to mobilize the Hindu vote. This strategy helped the BJP improve its position throughout North India and in the West. Its success was further enhanced by its strategy of election alliance with the newly formed National Front, a coalition composed of the Janata Dal and several regional parties.

Although the 1989 elections resulted in a hung Parliament, V. P. Singh, the leader of the Janata Dal, was elected prime minister with the support of a diverse group of opposition parties including the BJP. The BJP, however, withdrew support in November 1990 in response to Singh's decision to implement the recommendations of the Mandal Commission, which had called for the reservation of 27% of all central government jobs for backward castes.

The fall of the V. P. Singh government and its successor led to the dissolution of the government and new elections in 1991 that were dominated by the twin issues of Mandir (temple) and Mandal (reservations for backward castes). The BJP actively campaigned for the construction of a Hindu temple at Ayodhya and opposed the further reservations based on caste as an attempt to divide the Hindu nation. The BJP's campaign resulted in a major victory for the party across the states of Northern and Western India and significantly increased its strength in the *Lok Sabha*. Although the Congress Party was able to form a government thanks to a wave of sympathy that followed the assassination of Rajiv Gandhi, the BJP appeared destined to become a dominant force in Indian politics. Encouraged by its electoral success, the BJP continued its campaign to build a temple at Ayodhya. The movement peaked when Hindu militants succeeded in destroying the mosque in December 1992. The destruction of the mosque led to the outbreak of the worst communal riots in India since partition.

The seemingly unstoppable success of the BJP in the early 1990s, however, was brought to a crashing halt in the November 1993 state assembly elections in which the party was defeated in North India, its traditional stronghold. The defeat made clear that the BJP's militant strategy of ethnoreligious mobilization had reached its limits. As a result the party was forced to change its militant strategy and adopt a more moderate approach. The BJP began to play down its emphasis on ethnoreligious mobilization and in an effort to broaden its base focused on socioeconomic and national issues. As part of this new strategy the BJP also entered into a series of electoral alliances in preparation for the 1996 parliamentary elections. The 1996 elections, however, ended in another hung Parliament. Although voter support for the BJP increased only marginally, its electoral alliances expanded the number of BJP seats significantly and the party emerged as the largest single party in the *Lok Sabha*. Because of its position as the largest of the 28 parties represented in Parliament, the president of India turned to the BJP and asked it to form a government. The newly formed BJP government, however, lasted only 13 days when the largely secular opposition refused to support it.

Although the 1998 *Lok Sabha* elections produced a highly fractured mandate and another hung Parliament, the BJP again emerged as the largest party, with 179 seats and 25.47% of the vote. In addition, its 12 regional allies won 73 seats for a total of 252 seats that was just 20 seats short of an absolute majority. The BJP was able to cobble together a broad-based unstable coalition government when a combination of independents, small regional parties, and the Telugu Desam Party, a former member of the United Front, agreed to support a BJP-led government.

ORGANIZATION

The party's organizational strength depends on the RSS, a paramilitary cadre group. The RSS provides a tightly knit, well-organized, disciplined body of party workers. The connection, however, has been a mixed blessing for it also creates tension over control of party policy and strategy and has limited efforts to develop electoral alliances.

POLICY

Initially the BJP tried to be more open and liberal than the Jana Sangh. The disastrous defeat of the party at the polls in 1984, however, forced a major change in policy. The party reaffirmed its commitment to the integrity and unity of the county, democracy, value-based politics, positive secularism, Gandhian socialism, and—most important of all—building a polity in India that conformed to Indian culture and traditions. While continuing to emphasize Hindutva (literally, Hindu-ness), a term which has become the equivalent of Hindu/nationalism, the BJP in the 1990s moved away from Gandhian socialism and has become an ardent critic of state intervention in the economy and a strong supporter of the Indian private sector against the forces of globalization and competition from foreign multinationals.

In foreign policy, the Jana Sangh took a militantly anti-Pakistan position, rejecting the legitimacy of the 1947 partition and advocating reunification of the subcontinent by force, if necessary. The responsibilities of office seemed to alter Jana Sangh perspectives, especially those of A. B. Vajpayee, who took a more benevolent approach to neighboring countries including Pakistan, a stance that created some intraparty conflict. Once out of power, some of the old militancy returned to the rhetoric of BJP leaders. The BJP supports a strong national defense, including the development of an effective nuclear capability. BJP made good on this commitment when India conducted five nuclear tests in May 1998 and declared itself to be a nuclear weapons state.

MEMBERSHIP AND CONSTITUENCY

The BJP, like the Jana Sangh before it, draws its main support from upper-caste, middle-class Hindus living in urban areas but has also extended its base to include nonelite intermediate castes. It has proved remarkably attractive to urban youth, and the Vidyarthi Parishad, the student affiliate of the RSS, is India's largest student organization. Geographically, its main strength has been in the Hindi-speaking areas of Northern and Western India, but the party remains weak in the South and East.

FINANCING

Initially the BJP relied heavily on dues and contributions from its ideological supporters. The growing success of the party, however, has begun to attract increased support from Indian industrialists.

LEADERSHIP

The BJP leadership has begun to age. The most prominent leader is A. B. Vajpayee (born 1926), who has been responsible for the strategy of broadening the geographical base of the party. His most important colleague is the former RSS leader and Janata minister, L. K. Advani (born 1927). The next generation of leaders includes the general secretary, G. N. Govindacharya (born 1943), a former president, Murli Manohar Joshi (born 1934), and Promod Mahajan (born 1950). There are also several young leaders working at the state level.

PROSPECTS

Many observers believe that the BJP has the best prospects to become a viable alternative to the Congress (I) among the opposition parties. Its organization, the breadth of its appeal, and strong leadership set it apart from most other Indian parties. The isolation and weakness of the BJP in the South and the East, however, requires a strategy of alliance formation with regional and caste parties. It was this strategy that enabled it to come to power in March 1998. But this strategy also creates a basic dilemma that the party has faced throughout its history. A policy of pragmatism does not appeal to its RSS cadre and core supporters who are committed to the party's more militant ideology. They also oppose the use of caste appeals as contrary to the unity of Hinduism. Yet, given the weakness of its appeal in the South and East, an alliance strategy represents the only hope the party has of coming to power at the national level.

At the state and local level, BJP prospects are somewhat better. The party has become a major political force in the states of the North and the West.

COMMUNIST PARTY OF INDIA (CPI)

HISTORY

Founded in 1925, the Communist Party of India was initially a part of the Communist International and became closely connected with the Communist Party of Great Britain. In the 1930s it collaborated with the Congress in the independence movement. This relationship, however, was never an easy one and broke down completely after Nazi Germany invaded the Soviet Union. Shifting their stance, the Communists advocated collaboration with the British (and the Soviets) in the "antifascist war," while the Congress launched an anti-British noncooperation movement and demanded immediate independence. Legalization of the Communist Party in 1942 gave it the opportunity to broaden its organization while the Congress leaders were immobilized in British jails.

After the war and with the coming of independence, the Communists were divided over the appropriate approach to parliamentary democracy and to the Congress government. This has been a basic issue inhibiting the unity of the Communists throughout the postindependence period.

When the Soviets in 1953 began to woo the international nonaligned movement and its most prominent leader, Nehru, the CPI opted for competitive electoral politics within the parliamentary framework. In 1957, the CPI led a coalition government in the Southern state of Kerala. Congress-led street agitation forced that government from office in 1959.

In 1964, the party split, with the more moderate group under the leadership of S. A. Dange retaining the party label and a close relationship with the Soviet Union. The more militant wing, led by E. M. S. Namboodiripad, a former chief minister of Kerala, and Jyoti Basu, later to become chief minister of West Bengal, left to form the Communist Party of India (Marxist), or CPM. The basic cause of the split was a long-standing difference over how to relate to the ruling Congress. Dange, adhering to the Soviet view, argued that the Congress represented an anti-imperialist force and should be opposed only on domestic issues. Namboodiripad and Basu argued for implacable opposition to the Congress.

The CPI never regained the strength it had possessed before the split, but it did play a prominent role in national politics again in 1969 when its support for Mrs. Gandhi's faction of the Congress provided the necessary parliamentary margin to permit her to retain the prime ministership. The party supported Mrs. Gandhi until the end of the 1975–77 state of emergency. This association with emergency hurt the CPI in the 1977 general elections, and the CPI formally shifted policy and began to take a more critical line.

The relationship to Mrs. Gandhi led to yet another split in the CPI in 1981. The general secretary of the party, C. Rajeswara Rao, argued that the party's support for Mrs. Gandhi during the emergency period had been a mistake. Dange and some of his followers disagreed and left the party to form the All-India Communist Party (AICP).

Since abandoning its cooperation with the Congress (I), the CPI has opposed Congress dominance and the communalism of the BJP and has worked closely with the CPM. Still the CPI has never fully recovered from the 1964 split and its alliance with the Congress (I). The party's electoral support has declined from 23 seats and 5% of the vote in 1967 to 9 seats and 1.75% of the vote in 1998. Unlike the CPM the CPI became part of the United Front government in 1996–98, and its general secretary, Indrajit Gupta, was given charge of the powerful portfolio of home minister.

ORGANIZATION

The CPI claims to have a highly organized structure operating on the basis of democratic centralism. In fact, the state organizations have considerable autonomy, and there is a substantial amount of fragmentation and factionalism. To the extent that power is centralized, it is lodged with the general secretary.

The party has an extensive publication program that includes journals, such as *New Age*, published directly by the party; *Link*, a news magazine that generally follows a Marxist line; and books on technical as well as political subjects. In addition, the party used to distribute subsidized publications from the Soviet Union.

It has acquired control of the All-India Trade Union Congress and operates youth, peasants', and women's organizations.

Party headquarters are at 15 Kotla Marg, New Delhi 110 002.

POLICY

Prior to the collapse of the Soviet Union the CPI always had a close relationship with the Soviets, and Soviet attitudes toward existing Indian governments was often a function of Soviet relations with the particular government. Soviet views, however, were only one among several factors influencing CPI policy and actions.

On domestic issues, the CPI follows classic Marxist policy positions favoring secularism, rapid industrialization, nationalization of large-scale industry, land reform, and collectivized agriculture. In foreign policy, the CPI favored a pro-Soviet position on global issues and an anti-imperialist posture on regional issues.

The collapse of communism in Eastern Europe and the Soviet Union, the breakup of the USSR, and the end of the cold war have accentuated ideological confusion within the CPI and the communist movement in India. The movement has yet to come to grips with these momentous changes. Its policy remains anti-imperialist, anti-American and antimarket. The party has also failed to come to grips with the rise of communalist and xenophobic forces.

MEMBERSHIP AND CONSTITUENCY

The CPI electoral strategy emphasizes a broad rural constituency and the urban working class. In Kerala and Bengal, the CPI has done well among middle peasants and is the dominant Communist influence in the fragmented urban trade union movement. The CPI lost much of the traditional Communist support in West Bengal and Kerala to the CPM.

FINANCING

The CPI uses all the customary devices to raise money. In the past, it apparently raised substantial funds through the sale of subsidized Soviet publications. There were also persistent and generally accepted rumors that the

CPI received substantial direct funding from the Soviet Union.

LEADERSHIP

S. A. Dange's dominant role in the party precluded the rise of other important leaders. His age—he was born in 1899—had already begun to lessen his grip even before he left the party. The present general secretary, Indrajit Gupta, and the former general secretary C. Rajeswara Rao are, like most of the CPI leadership, veterans of union activity.

PROSPECTS

Dange's departure offered an opportunity for the CPI to begin to forge some sort of left unity with the CPM. Although the two parties have actively cooperated with each other, complete unity remains a distant dream. The CPI continues to remain on the fringes of Indian politics, important only in intermittent coalitions in Kerala and West Bengal and its influences in some trade union circles.

COMMUNIST PARTY OF INDIA (MARXIST) (CPM)

HISTORY

The CPM split from the CPI in 1964 over issues of militancy, ideology, and personality. It favored a more militant opposition to the Congress government. It felt the Maoist notion of peasant-based revolution was more relevant to the Indian situation than the worker-based ideas of Marx and Lenin advocated by the CPI.

The CPM gained credibility among Marxist voters when the CPI sided openly with Mrs. Gandhi after 1969. The CPM position of firm opposition to her rule, especially during the emergency period in the mid-1970s, resulted in considerable electoral success among left voters, especially in the election of 1977 when the CPM was allied loosely with the Janata coalition. The CPM has been highly successful in challenging Congress (I) candidates, especially in West Bengal. In state politics, the CPM has been even more successful. It has headed the state government in West Bengal with Jyoti Basu as chief minister since 1977 and has extended its base into Tripura, next door. After leading the Kerala government under E. M. S. Namboodiripad from 1967 to 1969, the CPM continued to be a major factor in that state.

Although the CPM is given the status of a national party by the Indian Election Commission, the party's support is limited to West Bengal, Kerala, and Tripura. In the 1998 *Lok Sabha* elections the CPM won 32 seats and 5.18% of the vote. Unlike the CPI, the CPM refused to join the United Front government in 1996–98 but agreed to give it external support.

ORGANIZATION

The organizational structure of the CPM is similar to that of the CPI—strongly centralized on paper but state-based in practice. In West Bengal, Jyoti Basu has managed to retain a more disciplined control over his party than is usual in India.

Headquarters are at 4 Ashoka Road, New Delhi 110 001.

POLICY

Over the years the CPM has distanced itself from its ideological moorings especially in its stronghold of West Bengal. Many diehard Marxists and Maoists are dismayed at the sellout. While the CPM has opposed the Structural Adjustment Program adopted by the Rao government in 1991, the party in West Bengal has publicly embraced the principles of an open economy and foreign direct investment in the state by foreign multinationals. The party, however, continues to oppose dismantling of the public sector. In foreign policy the CPM supports a strong defense, nonalignment, resistance to American imperialism and cancellation of military cooperation with the United States and opposes attempts to impose the Nuclear Nonproliferation Treaty and the Comprehensive Test Ban Treaty on India.

MEMBERSHIP AND CONSTITUENCY

The CPM has done better than the CPI in the traditional communist strongholds of West Bengal and Kerala, but less well in Uttar Pradesh, Andhra and Bihar. It has targeted landless laborers in rural areas and has done well in that constituency. It has had less success with organized urban workers.

FINANCING

As a participant in the government in West Bengal and Kerala, the CPM has access to traditional sources of funds in these states. In the past there have been occasional rumors of financial support from the People's Republic of China. The CPM has no central treasurer and relies heavily upon mass collection of funds by local party units and trade unions affiliated to the party. All party MLAs and MPs are expected to contribute part of their income, and all card-carrying members must contribute including police and bureaucrats.

LEADERSHIP

With the death of E. M. S. Namboodiripad in March 1998, Jyoti Basu (born 1914) became the last of the old guard. Both were veterans of left-wing and union politics. Basu, trained in law, comes from a prominent elite Bengali family. Namboodiripad was widely regarded as the most intellectually sophisticated of contemporary politicians. Although they had dominated the party since the 1964 split from the CPI, their prominence has attracted a highly competent younger group of leaders.

In the past two decades the CPM has come full circle. Founded as a revolutionary alternative to CPI reformism, the CPM itself has become increasingly reformist. The most radical wing of the party left in 1969 to form the Communist Party of India, Marxist-Leninist. The party has provided land reforms and local government reform to its rural constituency, but in the process it has become increasingly divorced from attempts to revolutionize the masses. The dilution of its ideological position and 20 years of power in West Bengal have had a negative effect on the commitment of its cadre, have resulted in the stagnation of its electoral support, and have obscured the party's transformational agenda. In short, the left in India has become increasingly confused by international developments and has been unable to cope with the rising importance of cultural nationalism, the rise of communalism, and the growing appeal of the BJP.

INDIAN NATIONAL CONGRESS (I)

HISTORY

The Indian National Congress was founded in 1885 as an organization devoted to expanding opportunities for Indians in the colonial regime and incorporating Indian elite opinion in policymaking.

The first two decades of the 20th century brought a deep struggle over philosophy and direction between the early great Congress leaders, B. G. Tilak (1856–1920) and G. K. Gokhale (1866–1915). Gokhale was highly educated in the Western tradition, moderate, elitist, and secular. Tilak was a prominent scholar of the Hindu scriptures, more radical, and wanted to mold the Congress in the Hindu tradition, broaden its mass appeal, and transform it into a more militant organization. Tilak's influence gave the Congress an increasingly Hindu character in spite of continuing professions of secularism.

Mohandas K. Gandhi became the dominant Congress leader in 1920 and remained so until his assassination in 1948. Gandhi was convinced that Congress had to retain its secular character in order to succeed as an umbrella organization. But he also realized that the movement depended on the mobilization of mass participation. Hindu symbolism and philosophical principles provided ready tools for mobilizing the masses. Throughout his years at the helm, Gandhi struggled to balance the commitment to secularism with the necessity of mobilizing the Hindu masses. In the end, however, the predominantly Hindu character of the Congress so frightened significant Muslim elites that independence could only be won at the price of partition.

Gandhi's leadership and philosophy left a profound mark on the postindependence party. He came to be revered as a saint by the Hindu masses. He was univer-sally called Mahatma, "great soul." His philosophy and strategy of nonviolence (ahimsa) and noncooperation based on soul force (satyagraha) and his commitment to secularism, mass participation, village self-sufficiency, and reform of the most discriminatory features of the Hindu caste system continue to be touchstones for the modern Congress party.

The two principal lieutenants of Gandhi, Jawaharlal Nehru and Sardar Vallabhbhai Patel, presided over the transformation of the national movement into a modern political party. As expected, the Congress formed the first independent government under Nehru. Although Congress never won a majority of the popular vote, the electoral system and the fragmentation of the opposition parties ensured that Congress usually would have a majority in the Lok Sabha. Congress has received between 41% and 49% of the vote in each national election, except in 1977 when it polled only 34.5%, 1989 when it polled 39.5%, 1991 when it polled 36.5%, and 1996 and 1998 when it polled only 28.8 and 25.9%. At the state level, Congress was less dominant. It often lost control of state governments to regional parties or to coalitions even before it began to lose power at the center from 1989 onward.

Despite frequent splits and defections, leadership of the party has shown remarkable continuity. Nehru was the dominant leader from 1948 until his death in 1964. Lal Bahadur Shastri was prime minister from 1964 until his sudden death in 1966, but much real power in the party rested with a group of party bosses known as the "Syndicate." The Syndicate played a prominent role in the selection of Nehru's daughter, Mrs. Indira Gandhi (no relation to Mahatma Gandhi), as Shastri's successor and struggled with her for power until a major split occurred in 1969 between pro-Syndicate and pro-Gandhi factions. Her victory was confirmed by the electorate in 1971, and she remained the dominant figure in the party until her death in 1984. In fact, her role was so strong that the party is now officially labeled Congress (I) for Indira.

The combination of a fragmented opposition and a massive wave of sympathy votes following the assassination of Indira Gandhi on October 31, 1984, enabled the Congress Party under the leadership of Rajiv Gandhi to win a massive victory in the 1984 elections. The new prime minister's lackluster performance, his inability to reshape the Congress and a series of corruption scandals weakened Rajiv, and the Congress went down to defeat in the 1989 general elections.

The elections, however, produced a hung Parliament as coalition and alliance politics replaced the era of Congress dominance. Like its predecessor, the Janata Party, the new Janata Dal–led National Front government proved to be weak and unstable and collapsed. As a result, India was forced to go to the polls once more in 1991 only to have tragedy strike again. In the midst of the campaign Rajiv Gandhi, like his mother, was struck down by an assassin. As was the case in 1984, the assassination produced a last-minute wave of sympathy votes in favor of the Congress. Although the party fell just short of a majority, it was able to form a government and returned to power under the leadership of P. V. Narashimha Rao, who was able to survive a full five-year term.

The Rao government came to power in the midst of the most serious economic crisis in postindependence Indian history. Rao's success in handling the economic crisis, however, was undermined by his inept handling of the crisis in Ayodhya when Hindu militants succeeded in destroying the Babri Masjid and communal riots broke out in many parts of India. His leadership was further undermined by charges of corruption.

The Congress Party entered the 1996 elections for the first time without a member of the Nehru-Gandhi dynasty at the helm and plagued by corruption scandals, factionalism, and major defections. The result was the worst defeat of the Congress Party in its history. The party won only 140 seats in the *Lok Sabha* and 28.8% of the vote. Rao was forced to step down as leader of the Congress Party and was replaced by Sitaram Kesri, the longtime party treasurer.

In the 1998 *Lok Sabha* elections, Sonia Gandhi, Rajiv's Italian-born widow, finally decided to officially enter the political arena and campaigned actively on behalf of the Congress. Despite her active role in the campaign, however, the Congress was able to win only 141 seats and 25.88% of the vote. The main impact of the Sonia factor on the elections was to stem the tide of defections from the Congress, boost party morale, and halt the further erosion of Congressional support. Following the elections, control of the party was again placed in the hands of a member of the Nehru-Gandhi dynasty when Sonia was elected president of the party to replace Sitaram Kesri.

ORGANIZATION

Congress (I) is a highly structured party. Basic organizational units exist at the district, the state, and the national levels. The annual conference of the party is composed of the members of the Congress committees at the state and district levels. The conference elects the Congress president to a two-year term and chooses the All-India Congress committee (AICC). Real power, however, is in the Congress working committee (CWC), often called the Congress high command, which has 20 members, 13 of whom are appointed by the Congress president.

The Congress president is usually selected by the prime minister if the Congress is in power. Sometimes, in order to ensure control of the party organization, the prime minister may assume the Congress presidency, as Nehru did in the early 1950s and later Indira and Rajiv Gandhi, and P. V. Narasimha Rao. At other times, the prime minister will ensure that a trusted loyalist holds the position. The two most recent Congress presidents, Sitaram Kesri and Sonia Gandhi, have been elected by the party membership. The Congress (I) Party has an elaborate structure on paper but a weak organizational base. Despite the party's constitution, internal party elections were not held from 1972 until the early 1990s and most committees were ad hoc or nonexistent. Lacking a popular state leadership, the party in most states was forced to rely on the Centre to resolve contentious policy and personnel issues. The result was that issues are often not addressed by the Centre until the problem has reached crisis proportions. Despite the return of some degree of internal party democracy, the Congress organization remains weak, factionalized, and semiparalyzed.

The daily newspaper the *National Herald* was founded by Nehru and is closely tied to the Congress (I). After the CPI gained control of the All-India Trade Union Congress, the Congress Party organized the Indian National Trade Union Congress (INTUC). Congress (I) also has women's and youth organizations.

Headquarters are at 24 Akbar Road, New Delhi 110 001.

POLICY

Until Rao's economic reforms of 1991, Congress (I) had espoused moderate socialism and a planned mixed economy aimed at rapid economic growth, self-sufficiency, and industrialization. It now supports liberalization, deregulation, privatization, and opening up of the Indian economy to foreign direct investment and trade. It also supports a secular state with egalitarian values and special programs for victims of discrimination. Land reform and national integration planks have been consistently incorporated into its party manifestos.

Under Nehru, the Congress developed a foreign policy based on nonalignment, i.e., active participation in international affairs while refraining from alliance with either superpower bloc. Despite the end of the cold war nonalignment continues as the declared policy of the party. At the height of the cold war, American support for Pakistan and the development of warmer relations between the United States and China encouraged a closer relationship between India and the Soviet Union and the USSR became India's chief arms supplier. Although the Congress government signed a long-term Treaty of Friendship with the Soviet Union in 1971 (in the midst of the Bangladesh crisis), the Congress (I) still adhered to a fiercely nationalistic form of nonalignment. Congress (I) favors a strong defense posture with as much self-sufficiency as possible. The Congress favors a nuclear weapons–free world and complete disarmament and refuses to sign the Nuclear Nonproliferation Treaty or the Comprehensive Test Ban Treaty.

Congress (I) has professed a desire for friendly relations with India's neighbors in South Asia but has expected them to acknowledge and accept India's leading role in the area. The party attaches special importance to relations with Pakistan. While desiring more normal relations, Congress (I) clearly expects Pakistan to recognize India's preeminent role in the subcontinent and opposes international military assistance of sophisticated weapons to Pakistan.

MEMBERSHIP AND CONSTITUENCY

In the past, Congress has claimed as many as 10 million primary members and over 300,000 active members, although most observers agree such claims probably overstate the facts. Both membership categories contribute to party finances by payment of dues, although the amount for primary members is nominal. Active members may be assigned specific party duties and are eligible to hold party office.

Congress success had rested on the maintenance of the traditional if incongruous coalition of Muslims, Scheduled Castes, Brahmins, industrialists, landless laborers, and well-to-do landowners. The loss in 1977 was apparently the result of the defection of large numbers of Muslim and Scheduled Caste voters, especially in North India. Minority groups of all sorts, especially religious minorities, have joined the Congress coalition, reflecting the widespread perception that the opposition parties' commitment to secularism is suspect. The Congress electoral defeats of 1996 and 1998 reflect the gradual loss of support among its old constituents to various opposition parties. Some evidence indicates that the Congress is also having difficulty recruiting new support among young voters, who do not remember the Congress role in the independence movement.

Geographically, Congress traditionally has enjoyed strong support in the South except in Tamil Nadu. However, its solid base of support in the Hindi belt of North India has been sharply eroded. Congress also has had to fight more competitively in the Eastern and Western regions of the country.

FINANCING

As the ruling party for most of India's independent history, the Congress has had a decided advantage over other parties in raising funds. Many observers have asserted that Congress fund-raising efforts have sometimes been rather like extortion. In the early days of independent India, Congress enjoyed a near monopoly over political contributions from businesses and still receives substantial support from such sources. Party dues also provide significant funds, and the party is also in a position to command resources from abroad.

LEADERSHIP

The temporary eclipse of the Nehru-Gandhi dynasty saw the emergence of weak, colorless, elderly, old-style Congress leaders. Following the assassination of Rajiv Gandhi the Congress turned to P. V. Narasimha Rao, a loyal supporter of the dynasty. Despite diabetes and heart bypass surgery, Rao at age 69 (born 1921) was the seniormost member of the party leadership and was a compromise candidate. The defeat of the Congress in the April–May 1996 elections and charges of corruption forced the resignation of Rao and the selection of Sitaram Kesri, an 80-year-old compromise candidate.

The persistence of the Nehru-Gandhi legacy is demonstrated by Sonia Gandhi. Following her husband's death, Sonia continued to play a significant behind-the-scenes role in Congress Party affairs, and in mid-1997 she officially became a member of the Congress Party. She actively campaigned for the Congress in the 1998 *Lok Sabha* elections, and following the elections, the 52-year-old Sonia was elected president of the Congress.

Given its long history and extensive governmental experience at the national and state levels, the Congress Party has a large pool of talent and potential leaders. Many of the most prominent, however, have been tainted by charges of corruption. Still, given the Indian contexts, many of these leaders may still be rehabilitated. While Sharad Pawar and Rajesh Pilot see themselves as potential future Congress leaders, there are also a large number of senior leaders who may yet emerge as compromise candidates. The real problem facing Sonia Gandhi and the 112-year party is the need to develop a new generation of local and state leaders capable of coping with the massive challenges India faces as it enters the 21st century.

PROSPECTS

The decline of the Congress has been the most significant political development in the past 50 years of Indian democracy. The party has seen its old coalition of Brahmins, Scheduled Castes and Tribes, Muslims, and other minorities gradually erode as former Congress supporters have drifted away to the BJP, caste, and regional parties. The party's assumption that a return of the Nehru-Gandhi dynasty will result in its return to power may well be wishful thinking. Neither Indira nor Rajiv was able to build or maintain a sustainable party base, and the Italian-born Sonia Gandhi also lacks the charisma, experience, and skills needed. The party needs new leadership and a new program, and it must rebuild its social base for it to return to power as a majority party. In short, while the Congress will continue to play an important role in Indian politics, the days of Congress dominance have passed.

PEOPLE'S PARTY
(Janata Dal; JD)

The Janata Dal was formed in 1988 when a group of centrist parties and factions combined to form a new party led by V. P. Singh, a former minister in Rajiv's government. The Janata Dal then joined with a group of Congress dissidents and the regionally based parties to form the National Front to contest the 1989 general elections.

The National Front won 144 seats in the elections, of which the Janata Dal won 141.

Although the 1989 elections produced a hung Parliament, the results were seen as a mandate for V. P. Singh to become prime minister. The experience of Singh's coalition, however, turned out to be a replay of the Janata experience of 1977 to 1979. Despite his enormous popular support, Singh's leadership of the Janata Dal was challenged by Chandra Shekhar and Devi Lal, two of his chief competitors. In August 1990 in an effort to head off the challenge and strengthen his support, Singh suddenly announced that he had decided to implement the party's electoral pledge to carry out the recommendations of the Mandal Commission and reserve 27% of all central government jobs for members of the backward castes, Devi Lal's chief constituency in the Punjab. The announcement, however, transcended the issue of factional politics within the Janata Dal and touched off a firestorm of protest and criticism throughout India. The action also alienated the BJP, one of the key backers of the National Front, and the party withdrew its support. On November 9, 1990, Singh lost a vote of confidence in the Indian Parliament and was forced to resign. He was replaced by Chandra Shekhar, who split the the JD and was elected prime minister with the support of the Congress Party. Chandra Shekhar's party, the Janata Dal (S), was so dependent on Congress support that it proved to be short-lived and India was forced to go to the polls. Chandra Shekhar's Janata Dal (S) was later converted into the Samajwadi Janata Party (SJP).

As India embarked upon the 1991 elections, a hung parliament appeared to be inevitable. The assassination of Rajiv Gandhi, however, produced a last-minute wave of sympathy votes for the Congress and its new leader, P. V. Narasimha Rao. Rao was able to form a government that lasted the full five-year term of Parliament.

The 1996 elections ended in another hung Parliament, and the Congress Party suffered its worst defeat since 1947. Although the largest bloc of seats was won by the BJP, the party was not able to command a majority in Parliament. In an effort to isolate the BJP, a broad alliance of 13 national and regional parties hammered together a United Front minority government that commanded the support of 180 *Lok Sabha* members. The United Front was supported by the Congress Party, which refused to join the new government. The Janata Dal was the largest constituent in the United Front with 45 seats. The other major components of the United Front were the CPI, the CPM and 10 regional parties. The United Front elected H. D. Deve Gowda, a Janata Dal leader and former chief minister of Karnataka, as prime minister. The new government clearly reflected the anti-upper-caste politics of the post-Mandal era. The coalition, however, proved to be extremely unstable, and Gowda was forced to resign after less than a year in office. The United Front replaced Gowda with I. K. Gujral, a weak compromise candidate

whose government survived until December 1997. Riven by splits and internal factionalism, the Janata Dal suffered a devastating defeat in the 1998 elections, winning only 6 seats and 9% of the vote.

ORGANIZATION

The organization of the Janata Dal at the regional and local level is rudimentary and ad hoc, consisting of little more than the personal followers and clients of its regional leaders and members of Parliament.

POLICY

The Janata Dal advocates the eradication of poverty, unemployment, and wide disparities in wealth, the protection of minorities, and a policy of nonalignment. As leader of the United Front, it was pledged to implement a common minimum program that called for the continuation of the policy of economic liberation begun by Rao in 1991, social justice, and a foreign policy that would stress better relations with India's neighbors.

MEMBERSHIP AND CONSTITUENCY

The Janata Dal, which has been an important force in the states of Bihar, Karnataka, and Orissa, has been almost wiped out in these states. It has lost its Backward Castes (OBCs) and minority vote base to the BJP and breakaway parties that had left the Janata Dal.

FINANCES

The Janata Dal has no central collection system, and each factional leader depends upon his own base of financial support from business houses and industrial lobbies in their respective states. Very little is collected from its membership, and there have been no membership dues for years.

LEADERSHIP

The spiritual leader of the Janata Dal is V. P. Singh, who is no longer active but is consulted during times of crisis. The most important leaders were all regionally based. They were Biju Patnaik of Orissa, who died in 1997, Laloo Prasad Yadav of Bihar and Ramakrishna Hedge, who have since formed their own parties, and H. D. Deve Gowda of Karnataka.

PROSPECTS

Throughout its brief history, the Janata Dal has been plagued by an unending capacity for schism. The Janata Dal (S) left in late 1990, the Samata Party split in 1994, Laloo Prasad Yadav broke away in July 1997 to form the Rashtriya Janata Dal, and Ramakrishna Hedge created the Lok Shakti Party to fight the 1998 elections. Factionalism has all but destroyed the party as a national political force.

The location of the party headquarters is Sardar Patel Bhawan, 7 Jantar Mantar Road, New Delhi 110 001.

MINOR POLITICAL PARTIES

Asom Gana Parishad; (AGP)

The Asom Gana Parishad, or Assam People's Council, was born in 1985 out of the student agitations in Assam against the influx of Bangladeshi refugees in the 1980s. Following the signing by Rajiv Gandhi of the Assam Accord that attempted to settle the refugee issue, the party won a majority of the seats in the 1985 state assembly elections. The failure of the Rajiv government to implement the Accord, however, led to a return of insurgency and president's rule. The AGP was defeated by the Congress in the 1991 *Lok Sabha* elections, and the party split. In the 1996 elections, however, a reunited AGP-led alliance defeated the Congress and was returned to power in the state. The party also won 5 seats in the *Lok Sabha* and became part of the United Front government in June 1996. The AGP was unable to win any seats in the 1998 *Lok Sabha* elections.

Bhujan Samaj Party (BSP)

The Bhujan Samaj Party (literally, "party of society's majority") was founded in 1984 to speak on behalf of India's untouchables or Dalits (oppressed). The party began making its presence felt in the late 1980s but scored its first really big success in the 1993 state elections in Uttar Pradesh when it won 67 seats and 12% of the vote and formed a coalition government with the Samajwadi Party. This Dalit and Backward Caste alliance, however, disintegrated in June 1995, and the BSP formed its own government with the support of various opposition parties. The BSP government, however, lasted only a few months and the state was placed under president's rule.

The BPS won 10 seats in the *Lok Sabha* elections of April–May 1996 and 67 seats in the October 1996 state assembly elections. Since the state assembly elections resulted in a hung Parliament, Uttar Pradesh was again placed under president's rule. Finally in March 1997 the BSP and the BJP agreed upon a unique coalition arrangement whereby the Cabinet would be based on equal representation of each party and the chief ministership would rotate between the two parties. Leadership for the first six months was to be provided by Mayawati, the 42-year-old leader of the BSP in Uttar Pradesh and close confidant of Kanshi Ram, the founder of the party. The BSP won 5 seats and 4.68% of the vote in the 1998 *Lok Sabha* elections. In addition to Uttar Pradesh the BSP also has some support in the Punjab and Madhya Pradesh and sees itself as an All-India voice of the Dalits.

Communist Party of India
(Marxist-Leninist; CPML)

In 1967, an apparently spontaneous peasant revolt broke out in the Naxalbari District of West Bengal. The West Bengal state government, dominated by Communists, adopted a policy of crushing the rebellion. Some leftists—believing the government's actions contrary to the dictates of Marx, Lenin, and Mao—joined forces with the Naxalbari peasants. Dubbed Naxalites, they vowed violent actions against authority, especially in the rural areas of Bengal and Andhra. The central and state governments made determined efforts to stamp out this movement and incarcerate its leaders.

In 1969, several factions of Naxalites came together to form the CPML. The party was banned during the emergency from 1975 to 1977, and factional disputes raged for years over the issue of violent revolutions versus an electoral strategy. The party has now turned to a parliamentary strategy but has not been especially successful at the polls. It has failed to gain any representation at the state or national levels.

Dravida Munnetra Kazhagam (DMK)–Dravidian Progressive Federation & All-India Anna-Dravida Munnetra Kazhagam (AIADMK)

The heir to the anti-Brahmin Dravidian nationalist movement in South India, the DMK was founded in 1949 by C. N. Annadurai to press the claims of Tamil cultural and linguistic autonomy. Its platform of radical populist economics and cultural nationalism bordered on secessionism but served to gain the party control of the Tamil Nadu state government in 1967.

Rivalries that were primarily personal in nature but related to the party's relations with Mrs. Gandhi's Congress followed Annadurai's death in 1969 and led to a split in 1972. Two factions emerged. The old title of DMK was retained by the group led by M. Karunanidhi. A new group, under the leadership of film idol M. G. Ramachandran (universally known as M.G.R.), claimed to be the true followers of Anadurai and called itself the All-India Anna DMK (AIADMK). These two parties have dominated the politics of Tamil Nadu for the last 15 years, with the DMK controlling the state government until 1976 when president's rule was imposed. The AIADMK ruled Tamil Nadu from 1977 to 1989.

Following the death of M.G.R. in 1987, the party split into two factions, one led by his wife, Janaki, and the other by his protege costar Jayalalitha, and lost the 1989 elections to the DMK. The party united again under Jayalalitha and was swept back into power in 1991. The AIADMK began to run into trouble again when Jayalalitha was accused of corruption and using state funds to finance her foster son's wedding in September 1995. The party was defeated in the April–May 1996 elections and replaced by a DMK government led by M. Karunanidhi. At the national level the DMK joined the United Front government in June 1996 and Murasoli Maran of the DMK was allotted the industry portfolio. In the 1998 *Lok Sabha* elections, the AIADMK, in alliance with the BJP, made a remarkable comeback and won 18 seats. The party became a major force in the BJP government and was given 4 seats on the Council of Ministers.

Responsibilities of office have muted whatever secessionist zeal lingered in these parties, though they both continue to champion states' rights and resist the spread of Hindi cultural and linguistic preeminence.

Samajwadi Party (SP)

The Samajwadi (Socialist) Party was formed by a group of Janata Dal dissidents led by Mulayam Singh Yadav, the leader of the Yadav community in Uttar Pradesh, in 1992. The party formed a coalition government with the Bahujan Samaj Party in Uttar Pradesh in 1993 that lasted until June 1995. In the 1996 general elections the SP won 17 seats and became a key component of the United Front government in which Mulayam Singh Yadav served as defense minister. The party won 110 seats in the assembly elections in Uttar Pradesh in October 1997. The SP represents the Backward Castes. In the 1998 *Lok Sabha* elections, the SP won 20 seats and 4.95% of the vote.

Samata Party (SP)

The Samata (Equality) Party was founded in early 1994 following a split with the Janata Dal. The party is led by George Fernandes, a veteran socialist and trade unionist, and Nitish Kumar. The party is based largely in Bihar and in 1996 won 8 seats in the *Lok Sabha*, 6 from Bihar and 1 each in Uttar Pradesh and Orissa. The party had an electoral alliance with the BJP in Bihar and is considered a BJP ally at the national level. In the 1998 *Lok Sabha* elections, the party won 12 seats and Fernandes became the defense minister in the BJP government.

Shiromani Akali Dal (SAD)

The Shiromani Akali Dal is a Sikh communal party confined to the Punjab. Its roots go back to early Sikh nationalism. It has supported greater autonomy for Sikhs. Some even support the notion of Khalistan, an independent homeland. The extremists became increasingly assertive in early 1984, and Indira Gandhi ordered the army to occupy Amritsar's Golden Temple, the major Sikh temple that had become a center for the militant campaign. The attack, resulting in several hundred deaths, angered many Sikhs, as did the bloody anti-Sikh riots that broke out in the wake of Mrs. Gandhi's assassination by two of her Sikh bodyguards.

A moderate Sikh faction of the Akali Dal worked out an agreement with Rajiv Gandhi in July that envisaged returning the state to civil rule. Elections in September 1985 witnessed a victory for the Akali Dal Party, the first time it had won a majority on its own. The militant faction of the Sikhs renounced the agreement, and in early

1986 extremists again seized the Golden Temple and turned it into a center of the Khalistan campaign.

At the height of Sikh militancy the Akali Dal split into a half dozen factions. In the April–May 1996 *Lok Sabha* elections the party faction led by two-time Chief Minister Prakash Singh Badal won 8 seats, and in the February 1997 assembly elections the party won 75 seats in alliance with the BJP. In the 1998 *Lok Sabha* elections, the party again won 8 seats. Stridently anti-Congress, the Akali Dal has become an ally of the BJP and demands a broad-based confederate structure in contrast to militant Sikhs who demand a separate Sikh nation.

Shiv Sena

Founded in the 1960s as an anti-immigrant movement centered in Bombay, the Shiv Sena fostered the building of Maratha pride and demanded that Maharashtrans be given preferences in jobs in the city. The movement expanded its influence in several urban areas outside Bombay in the 1970s and 1980s and increasingly took on a more antiminority, Hindu nationalist color. The Shiv Sena became more prominent in the 1990s as a result of its strong support of the Ayodhya issue and its alliance with the BJP at the state and federal levels. The party won 15 seats in the 1996 *Lok Sabha* elections and supported the short-lived BJP government. In 1998, however, the party won only 6 *Lok Sabha* seats. The Shiv Sena also governs the state of Maharashtra in alliance with the BJP. The party combines religious militancy with regionalism and is led by its founder, Bal Thackeray, a onetime cartoonist.

Tamil Maanila Congress (TMC)

The Tamil Maanila Congress was formed by a group of Congress dissidents in Tamil Nadu who were expelled from the Congress in April 1996. The dissidents opposed P. V. Narasimha Rao's alliance with the AIADMK in the state. The party won 20 of the 39 Tamil Nadu seats in the 1996 *Lok Sabha* elections and 39 seats in the state assembly in alliance with the DMK. In 1998, however, the party won only 3 *Lok Sabha* seats. The party is led by G. K. Moopanar, former general secretary of the Congress, and P. Chidambaram, a former Congress minister. Chidambaram was the finance minister in the United Front government, and the party held 4 other seats on the Council of Ministers.

Telegu Desam Party (TDP)

During the early 1980s, the Centre intervened repeatedly to establish an effective government in Andhra Pradesh, a state ruled by a faction-ridden Congress (I) Party. A succession of chief ministers imposed by the Centre aroused the ire of many voters in the state who were disgusted with the pervasive corruption of Congress (I) politicians and with the Centre's seeming lack of concern for an effective government in the state. On March 21, 1982, the leading matinee idol, N. T. Rama Rao, announced his intention to establish a new party, the Telegu Desam, to restore a clean government that would serve the interests of the common people. In January 1983, state assembly elections were held and the new Telegu Desam won 185 of 261 seats. The Desam resisted the pro–Rajiv Gandhi electoral tide in the 1984 general elections and 1985 assembly vote by winning a large majority of the seats.

N. T. Rama Rao developed a populist program including a number of social welfare schemes such as providing free lunches to all schoolchildren. On the national level, N. T. Rama Rao was a major figure in the unsuccessful move to unify the opposition prior to the general elections in the 1980s.

Andhra switched over to the Congress in 1989 and then back again to Rao in 1994. A rift developed within the family, however, when Lakshmi Parvathi, Rao's biographer, whom he married in August 1993, began playing an active role in party offices. The result was a revolt by Chandrababu Naidu, Rao's son-in-law, who toppled him in August 1995. On Rao's death in January 1996, the leadership of his faction was taken over by his wife. In the 1996 election, however, the TDP-Naidu faction won 16 *Lok Sabha* seats and the Parvathi faction none. Naidu became chief minister and one of the key state leaders responsible for creating the United Front government.

In the 1998 *Lok Sabha* elections, the party won 12 seats. Following the elections, the TDP resigned from the United Front and provided the 12 critical votes that enabled the BJP to win its vote of confidence in March 1998. As a reward for its support of the BJP government, a member of the party was elected Speaker of the *Lok Sabha*.

Muslim League

The remnants of the major Muslim political organization of preindependence days, most of whose leaders went to Pakistan, the Muslim League of today is a small party devoted to the welfare of Muslims in Kerala. It occasionally has participated in coalition governments at the state level. The party won 2 seats in the 1998 *Lok Sabha* elections.

National Conference

The National Conference is the most popular party in Jammu and Kashmir and has been a tool for giving Kashmiri Muslims a special role in their government in a state that Pakistan claims as its territory. The leading figure of the National Conference during the troubled postindependence period was Sheikh Mohammed Abdullah, who served as the state's chief executive until his arrest in 1953. After signing an agreement in 1975 accepting the state's constitutional relationship with India, Abdullah returned as chief minister and retained that post until his death in September 1982. His son, Dr. Farooq Abdullah, was his father's hand-picked successor. Prime Minister Indira Gandhi is believed to have worked to split the National Conference in mid-1984, which brought G. M. Shah, Abdullah's bitter rival, to power. However, Shah's government was unpopular and ineffectual. Following widespread communal riots in early 1986, the prime minister imposed governor's rule.

Although the National Conference was again elected to power in 1987, the government was dismissed in 1990 amid mounting unrest. Despite several efforts, no elections could be held due to an increasingly bloody insurgency by Muslim separatists. The success of the relatively peaceful parliamentary elections in May 1996 led to a decision to hold full-scale state assembly elections in September 1997. Amidst widespread allegations of voter coercion, the National Conference led by Farooq Abdullah won a massive two-thirds majority, enabling the Centre to restore local government in Kashmir for the first time since 1990. In the 1998 *Lok Sabha* elections, the party won 2 seats.

Peasants and Workers Party (PWP)

The Peasants and Workers Party is a radical Marxist party with some influence among landless laborers in Maharashtra. It won 1 seat in the 1998 *Lok Sabha* elections.

OTHER POLITICAL FORCES

Organized Labor

Due to the character of social, economic, and political change, organized labor in India has declined as a political force. Employment in the organized sector has decreased from 9.7% in 1971 to 9% in 1991. This decline has been accompanied by an increasing fragmentation of the working class and deunionization. Of the 27 million Indians employed in the organized sector in 1991, only 6 to 7 million belonged to trade unions. This small group of unionized workers, moreover, is represented by some 50,000 trade unions organized into 12 highly politicized central federations. The top five labor federations and their political affiliations are the Bharatiya Mazdur Sangh with 3.1 million members—BJP; the Indian National Trade Union Congress with 2.7 million members—Congress (I); the Centre of Indian Trade Unions with 1.8 million members—CPM; the Hind Mazdoor Sabha with 1.5 million members—originally socialist now Janata Dal; and the All-India Trade Union Congress with 900,000 members—CPI. While fragmentation has long plagued the Indian trade union movement, the problem has become compounded by the development of sectararianism and criminalization. The only significant effort to organize the unorganized sector in India is being made by nongovernmental organizations (NGOs).

Students

Higher education in India is facing an acute crisis brought on by enrollment pressures, a major resource crunch, increasing privatization, internal stagnation, corruption, apathy, and indifference. Students are increasingly divided on the basis of class, gender, caste, and religion. While Marxism is on the decline and the RSS is on the rise, the majority of students have become increasingly apathetic. The largest student organization is the All-India Students Organization (Akhil Bharatiya Vidyarthi Parishad; ABVP), which is affiliated with the RSS and dominates many of the campuses of North India. It provided an important source of campaign workers for the Jana Sangh and the Janata Party and now provides valuable assistance to the Bharatiya Janata Party. The Congress (I), through the Youth Congress, and the Marxists also have been able to attract periodic activity on their behalf from groups of students.

Business

The Indian business community is the best-organized sector of Indian civil society, and its influence has increased significantly since the beginning of economic liberalization of the Indian economy in 1991. Due to the internal divisions of the business community based on caste, region, and the competition between foreign and indigenous capital, India has three major apex associations that represent business. The largest and most broadly based apex association representing indigenous business is the Federation of Indian Chambers of Commerce and Industry. The Associated Chambers of Commerce and Industry is the oldest, and although it initially represented foreign capital, it now represents indigenous business groups as well. The newest, richest, and most influential apex association is the Confederation of Indian Industry. Since 1991 these associations have increasingly been consulted by government on major issues involving economic policy. The business-government relationship, however, still remains strained and the Indian equivalent of Japan Inc. remains a distant dream.

Farmers and Peasants

Following the green revolution of the 1960s, Indian farmers, began to organize movements under a variety of non-party banners to fight for rural interests against a perceived urban, industrial bias. These new farmers' movements were organized by cultivating landowners producing commercial crops in irrigated areas located largely in the North and West. Farmers' movements began to play a major role in pressing their demands on government in the 1980s but declined in the 1990s as they attempted to play a more direct political role. The vast majority of the peasantry, however, especially landless labor, remains unorganized, and attempts by political parties to develop peasant movements have had limited success. Although each major party has a peasant organization, these organizations have had much less influence on policy than the more articulate and organized farmers' movements. The major new farmers' movements in India are the Bharatiya Kisan Union (BKU) Punjab, Bharatiya Kisan Union (BKU) Uttar Pradesh, Bharatiya Kisan Sangh Gujarat, Shetkari Sanghatana Maharashtra, Karnataka State Farmers' Association (Karnataka Rajya Ryota Sangha or KRRS) Karnataka, Tamil Nadu Agriculturalists' Association (Tamilaga Vyavasavavigal Sangham or TVS) Tamil Nadu.

Nongovernmental Organizations

One of the most significant recent developments in India has been the rise of the NGO sector. NGOs began to mushroom in India in the late 1970s as new issues and new forces began to emerge outside the framework of formal politics and government in an attempt to develop new relations with the rural and urban poor. It is estimated that India has some 100,000 NGOs, of which 25,000 to 30,000 are active. Of these some 14,000 are foreign-funded. NGOs have become active in welfare, relief, charity, development, health, education, and local planning. More recently they have become champions of women's rights, civil liberties, ecology, bonded labor, child labor, and alternative development strategies. Though they are far from being characterized as India's fifth estate, they have become an important force. The 1990s, however, have seen a rising tide of criticism of the NGO sector for lack of coordination, proliferation, politicization, nepotism, and lack of accountability.

Caste

Caste is a hierarchical ordering of status groups, membership in which is based on birth. Caste groups have been the major institution organizing human relationships and interactions in India for centuries. Inevitably, a system so deeply imbedded in Indian society has influenced and been influenced by the modern political system. No single factor influences politics in India more deeply than caste, but this influence is felt most fully at the local level.

Caste groupings and more formal Caste Associations have ecome mediating and mobilizing institutions in Indian politics. They use and are used by political parties at the local level. They interpret political issues and positions to their members and convey caste political interests to the parties and administration. They mobilize voters, workers, and sometimes money and candidates.

Scheduled Castes

Historically the most economically and socially disadvantaged groups in Indian society, the Scheduled Castes are separate castes grouped together for legal and administrative purposes. The Indian constitution outlaws the most extreme forms of discrimination against untouchability and provides special protections in parliamentary representation, civil service employment, and education. Untouchability, however, is still widely practiced in rural India, and members of the Scheduled Castes remain heavily overrepresented among the poorest, least employed, and most illiterate in Indian society.

Until recently, untouchables generally have looked to the Congress (I) Party as the source of protection for their interests. However, while there have always been significant untouchable political movements, the Dalits, as they now prefer to call themselves, are beginning to seek political power on their own. The most important untouchable movement, the Scheduled Caste Federation founded in 1942 by Dr. B. R. Ambedkar, the most prominent untouchable leader of the modern period, was largely confined to Maharashtra and central Uttar Pradesh.

Attempting to broaden its appeal to Non-Scheduled oppressed groups, the Scheduled Caste Federation took the name Republican Party of India (RPI) in 1956. It achieved considerable success at the state level in Maharashtra and at the municipal level in Agra City in the late 1950s and 1960s, but factionalism has reduced its importance in more recent times.

A more militant student-based group called the Dalit (oppressed) Panthers emerged in Maharashtra in the 1960s and developed some influence by forging links between rural and urban groups.

In the late 1970s, another organization, the All-India Backward and Minority Communities Employees Federation (BAMCEF), began to organize the Scheduled Castes and other oppressed groups on a broader geographical basis. It used the now-significant number of Scheduled Caste government employees—holders of reserved posts in the civil service—as an organizing base. Led by Kanshi Ram, the BAMCEF has been transformed into the Bahujan Samaj Party.

Muslims

The most prominent minority in India is the Muslim minority. With over 115 million Muslims, India has the fourth-largest Muslim population in the world. Yet, Muslims are only about 12% of the Indian population. At the time of the partition of British India, many of the Muslim elite migrated to Pakistan. The Muslim population, geographically scattered and without its traditional leadership, turned to the Congress Party for protection. That support began to erode during the 1975–77 emergency when many Muslims felt themselves the victim of overzealous bureaucrats seeking to implement the government's slum removal and sterilization programs. Since then, Muslims have been more selective in their support of various political parties.

Muslim confrontations with the police and with other social groups have become more frequent as the Muslim community has become more assertive politically and socially. This assertiveness is a sign of its growing self-confidence and owes much to the openness of the democratic political system and to a growing middle class more willing to speak out on the community's behalf. Some Muslims support the Jamaat-e-Islami, a tightly organized paramilitary organization, which is roughly the counterpart of the Hindu RSS.

NATIONAL PROSPECTS

Fifty years of independence have produced a mixed picture of success and failure for India. Among the developing countries of the world, India has been generally recognized as a political success but a near economic failure. Despite a variety of problems, Indian democracy has served the country well. Its great socialist experiment, however, has produced neither growth nor equity as the country remains plagued by poverty, illiteracy, disease, massive unemployment, and despair. As India enters its second 50 years of freedom, however, there is considerable hope that its new policy of economic liberalization and globalization will transform the country into an important economic and political force.

Perhaps India's most important success has been the resilience of its democratic order. The basic political framework based on mass franchise, parliamentary government, and an independent judiciary have withstood the test of time and have acquired increased legitimacy. These institutions have played a major role in helping to reconcile India's diverse social, economic, and cultural interest. Dormant institutions like the courts and the election commission have become revitalized and have come to play an increasingly important role.

While India's institutional system has remained intact, its party system has been transformed significantly. The party system has been marked by the gradual decline of the once-dominant Congress (I) Party, repeated failure of centrist alternatives parties to survive, the stagnation of the Communist left, the rise of the Hindu nationalism of the BJP, and the regionalization of parties. None of the national political formations is capable of governing without relying on the votes of regionally based parties that draw their support from caste and religious groups that have become electorally powerful. As a result of the transformation of the party system, India is faced by an era of weak, unstable coalition and alliance governments. These weak governments may not be in a position to make the kind of tough choices that face the country in the coming years, especially in the economic sphere.

The Indian economy has not been an especially notable success. India's most important economic achievement has been in feeding its vast population, warding off famine, and avoiding the horrors of mass starvation that occurred during the British period and in Mao's China. Slow growth, however, has left 320 million people, or 37% of the population, in poverty, and low social expenditures have left half the adult population illiterate. In the industrial sphere, India's vibrant private sector has been overshadowed by a massive, inefficient public sector that remains a major legacy of India's socialist past. The liberalization policies of the Rao government have only begun the process of reducing state intervention in the economy, ending protection, and joining the global economy.

The collapse of the Soviet Union and the end of the cold war have totally undermined the cornerstone of India's foreign policy of nonalignment. Indian leaders and foreign policy officials, however, continue to insist that nonalignment remains relevant and have failed to engage in a fundamental review of India's future role in the post–cold war world. Another legacy of the past is the continued dominance of Indo-Pakistan relations in Indian foreign policy and the problem of its relations with its neighbors. Indo-American policy also remains prickly due to differences over nuclear weapons and missile development and deployment. The May 1998 explosions of five nuclear devices have further complicated India's political, economic, and foreign policy future.

These various economic, political, and foreign policy problems will continue to strain the capabilities of India's political system. India's biggest challenge will center on its ability to deal with the problems of globalization, the development of cultural nationalism, and the need to maintain political stability and effective government in an era of coalition and alliance politics.

Further Reading

Barnett, Marguerite Ross. *The Politics of Cultural Nationalism in South India*. Princeton, N.J.: Princeton University Press, 1976.

Bava, Noorjahan, ed. *Non-Governmental Organizations in Development: Theory and Practice*. Delhi: Kanishka, 1997.

Brass, Paul R. *The Politics of India since Independence*. Cambridge: Cambridge University Press, 1994.

Brass, Tom. *New Farmers' Movements in India*. London: Frank Cass, 1995.

Butler, David, Ashok Lahiri, and Prannoy Roy. *India Decides: Elections 1952–1995*. New Delhi: Books & Things, 1995.

Drèze, Jean, and Amartya Sen. *India: Economic Development and Social Opportunity*. Delhi: Oxford University Press, 1996.

Frankel, Francine. *India's Political Economy, 1947–77*. Princeton, N.J.: Princeton University Press, 1978.

Gould, Harold, and Sumit Ganguly ed. *India Votes: Alliance Politics and Minority Governments in the Ninth and Tenth General Elections*. Boulder, Colo.: Westview Press, 1993.

Graham, Bruce. *Hindu Nationalism and Indian Politics: The Origins and Development of the Bharatiya Jana Sangh*. Cambridge: Cambridge University Press, 1990.

Hardgrave, Robert L. Jr., and Stanley A. Kochanek. *India: Government and Politics in a Developing Nation*, 6th ed. New York and London: Harcourt Brace Jovanovich, 2000.

Jaffrelot, Christopher. *The Hindu Nationalist Movement*. New Delhi: Penguin Books India, 1996.

Joshi, Vijay, and I.M.O. Little. *India's Economic Reforms: 1991–2001*. Delhi: Oxford University Press, 1997.

Kochanek, Stanley A. *Business and Politics in India*. Los Angeles and London: University of California Press, 1974.

———. *The Congress Party of India: The Dynamics of One-Party Democracy*. Princeton, N.J.: Princeton University Press, 1968.

Lewis, John P. *India's Political Economy and Reform*. Delhi: Oxford University Press, 1995.

Mallick, Ross. *Development of a Communist Government: West Bengal since 1977*. Cambridge: Cambridge University Press, 1993.

———. *Indian Communism: Opposition, Collaboration and Institutionalization*. Oxford: Oxford University Press, 1994.

Malik, Yogendra K., and V.B. Singh. *Hindu Nationalists in India: The Rise of the Bharatiya Janata Party*. Boulder, Colo.: Westview Press, 1994.

Omvedt, Gail. *Reinventing Revolution: New Social Movements and the Socialist Tradition in India*. Armonk, N.Y.: M.E. Sharpe, 1993.

Panandiker, V.A. Pai, and Ajay Mehra. *The Indian Cabinet: A Study in Governance*. Delhi: Konark, 1996.

Ray, Rabindra. *The Naxalites and Their Ideology*. Delhi: Oxford University Press, 1988.

Sen Gupta, Bhabani. *Problems of Governance*. New Delhi: Konark, 1996.

REPUBLIC OF INDONESIA

(Republik Indonesia)

By Michael Malley, M.A.

THE SYSTEM OF GOVERNMENT

Indonesia is a unitary state with a presidential system of government. The constitution vests sovereignty in the People's Consultative Assembly and establishes a People's Representative Council, a Supreme Advisory Council, a State Audit Board, and a Supreme Court. However, the constitution provides few checks and balances on executive power. More than three decades of rule by President Soeharto's authoritarian New Order regime (1966–98) institutionalized executive domination over all other branches of government. Following Soeharto's resignation in May 1998, a change in regime as well as government is under way.

The New Order regime claimed legitimacy as the upholder of the 1945 constitution and the national ideology, *Pancasila*, which is contained in the document's preamble. The brief, hurriedly written constitution was adopted at the beginning of the revolution against Dutch colonialism (1945–49) but replaced by a provisional constitution in 1950 that instituted a system of parliamentary democracy. Amid regional rebellions and parliamentary instability, President Soekarno declared martial law in 1957. Two years later, under army pressure, he disbanded the elected Constitutional Assembly and restored the 1945 constitution. In 1966, the army forced Soekarno to cede power to its commander, General Soeharto. Soeharto became acting president in 1968 and remained president until 1998, when massive demonstrations and the defection of key military and bureaucratic supporters led him to resign. His vice president, B. J. Habibie, assumed the presidency and began to grapple with widespread pressures for political reform. He acknowledged that he was a transitional leader and promised to revise the country's electoral laws and hold elections in 1999.

An archipelagic country of 200 million people, Indonesia stretches 3,000 miles along the equator from the Indian Ocean to the Pacific. Although it consists of more than 13,000 islands, only about 6,000 are inhabited. Its population is the fourth-largest in the world. Nearly 60% of the country's people crowd onto the island of Java, which accounts for just 7% of the country's land area.

The rest is spread mostly among Sumatra, Sulawesi, Maluku, Bali, and the Indonesian parts of Borneo and New Guinea. Nearly 90% of the population professes Islam, making it home to more Muslims than any other country. Christian, Hindu, and Buddhist minorities are prominent in certain regions.

The census does not record ethnic identity, but it is estimated that about 40% of Indonesians are ethnically Javanese, traditionally found in eastern and central Java. Other major ethnic groups include the Sundanese in western Java; the Acehnese, Minangkabau, and Batak in Sumatra; the Dayak and Banjar in Borneo; the Bugis in Sulawesi; and the Balinese in Bali. Indonesians of Chinese descent, numbering fewer than 10 million, live mostly in urban areas and control many major economic activities.

Executive

The 1945 constitution declares the president head of state, head of government, and commander of the armed forces. It empowers him to declare domestic states of emergency and to appoint and dismiss Cabinet ministers. The president can make laws, declare war, and conclude treaties only with the agreement of the People's Representative Council. However, the constitution also grants the president authority to issue all regulations necessary to implement laws approved by the legislature. In practice, the government operates according to presidential and ministerial decrees more than legislation.

The People's Consultative Assembly elects the president and vice president to five-year terms. The constitution does not set any limit on the number of terms an individual may serve in these capacities. President Soeharto was elected to his seventh term in March 1998. When he resigned two months later, he was the second-longest-serving head of state in the world (behind Cuba's Fidel Castro). His long tenure encouraged debate about amending the constitution to limit future presidents to two terms. No vice president has been elected to more than one term.

As the regime aged, Soeharto concentrated power ever more in his own hands. Members of the regime who had independent political power bases were gradually eased out, usually into private business. Until the early 1980s, military officers of his own generation occupied important positions and dissident officers occasionally challenged him. Civilian technocrats who helped restore the economy to health in the late 1960s continued to hold high posts until the late 1980s. By the early 1990s, most high-ranking civilian and military officials owed their positions more to their personal ties to Soeharto than to their own political accomplishments. However, even personal relationships between the president and his chief advisers became more distant, as the most senior military officers as well as most Cabinet ministers were at least 20 years younger than he. Future presidents are unlikely to wield as much power as he accumulated.

Legislature

There are two national legislative bodies in the Indonesian political system. The higher body is the People's Consultative Assembly (*Majelis Permusyarawatan Rakyat*), and the lower one is the People's Representative Council (*Dewan Perwakilan Rakyat*). Even academic specialists frequently refer to the Council as a "parliament," since a body of the same name existed during the period of parliamentary democracy in the 1950s. However, under the current system there is no prime minister, the president is elected by the Assembly, and the Council cannot vote to change the executive. The Council's role is more similar to that of the American House of Representatives than the British Parliament.

The constitution does not fix the number of members in either body, the length of their terms, or even how they are to be chosen. It says simply that these bodies shall exist and that the Assembly shall comprise all members of the Council as well as "delegates from regional territories and groups." Under the New Order, the executive appointed as many delegates to the Assembly as there were Council members, and members of both houses served five-year terms. There is no limit on the number of terms members may serve. Since 1987, the Council has had 500 members and the Assembly 1,000; prior to that the Council had 460 and the Assembly 920.

Membership in the Council is partly by election and partly by appointment. Typically about 80% of the members have been elected. President Soeharto increased this to 85% for the Council elected in 1997. During the regime's early years, both civilians and military officers were appointed to fill the remainder, but in recent years all appointed members have been from the military, whose members are not permitted to vote in the general elections.

The constitution assigns to the Assembly the tasks of electing the president and setting "the broad outlines of state policy." Under the New Order, this was an official document that the executive submitted to the Assembly for its approval once every 5 years during the same session in which it elected the president and vice president. Power to amend the constitution is also vested in the Assembly. The body is required to meet only once in 5 years, and though it is not legally precluded from meeting more often, it has not done so in more than 25 years.

During the New Order era, the Council was divided into 11 committees until 1997 when the number was reduced to 10. Since members may serve on only one committee and must include representatives of all parties, the number had to be reduced to accommodate one party's poor showing in that year's election. There are no permanent subcommittees. Though the constitution grants the Council the right to propose legislation, it has not done so during the New Order. In fact, it has made only minor changes to legislation proposed to it by the executive. In public sessions, it permits only tightly controlled discussions, though more debate takes place in intraparty talks behind the scenes. The Council has a limited budget that allows for few staff members and deters it from conducting oversight or independent investigations. In consequence, the legislative branch of government remains far weaker than the executive.

Judiciary

The members of the Supreme Court (*Mahkamah Agung*) are appointed by the president. The Court has both original and appellate jurisdiction but no power of judicial review. It has never played a significant autonomous political role, and the doctrine of separation of powers is not legally recognized. The New Order regime tended to fill high-level posts in the Department of Justice as well as seats on the Supreme Court with military lawyers and judges. Indonesians widely regard the courts as subject to political influence and bribery.

The legal system that the courts attempt to administer is based on the Napoleonic Code, which Indonesia inherited from the Dutch and has revised only slightly.

Regional and Local Government

Indonesia is divided into 27 provinces, more than 300 districts, thousands of subdistricts, and tens of thousands of villages. The law on regional government (Law No. 5 of 1974) permits regional self-government within the framework of a unitary state only at the provincial and the district levels; lower levels are purely administrative. Under the village government law (Law No. 5 of 1979), rural village headmen remain legally autonomous of the state, but urban village headmen are state officials. Revision of these laws to permit greater regional government autonomy is a chief demand of the proreform, anti-Soeharto forces.

Regional governments consist of a legislature and an executive, and the work of both is tightly governed by the national Department of Home Affairs. As in the case of the national Council, only 80% of regional legislators are elected; the others are appointed by the armed forces. The elective share of regional legislatures was not increased in 1997 as it was for the national Council. Regional executives are nominated by the regional legislatures, but the list of nominees must be approved by the national government. Moreover, though the legislature must vote for the regional executive, its vote is not binding on the president, who may appoint either of the two highest vote getters to the post. The justification for this arrangement is that legally regional executives are both the leaders of their regions as well as representatives of the central government in the regions. Hence, their selection must reflect the interests of both national and regional governments.

The government party (Golkar) has won a majority of votes in every province since 1987, but this has not always been the case at the district level. In some cases, Golkar has not even managed to secure a plurality. Nevertheless, the government's hold on those districts remains strong because of the large amount of discretion it has granted the Department of Home Affairs to intervene in regional governmental matters. Members of minority parties have never been named governors, and only until the early 1970s did any serve as district executives.

In recent years, the government has taken modest steps to decentralize regional administration. In 1995, it began a pilot program to shift administrative responsibilities from the provincial level to the districts; in 1997, the program was expanded to include about one-quarter of all districts. Also in 1997, the national legislature approved a new law on regional government finance, replacing a law passed in 1956 but never implemented. These are primarily efforts to achieve fiscal decentralization. However, they compel regional governments, comprised largely of bureaucrats, to implement measures that require negotiation with the major social and economic groups in their regions. Such compromises are inherently political and foreshadow long-term changes in regional politics and center–region relations.

THE ELECTORAL SYSTEM

New Order officials proudly claimed that they held elections six times in 30 years. In contrast, during the country's first two decades of independence, national elections were held just once, in 1955. However, those elections are also widely regarded as the only truly fair elections in the country's history. Under the New Order, elections were used as instruments to legitimate the regime, not to change the government. To this end, electoral rules were made to appear scrupulously fair, but the political system as a whole was structured to produce a predictable outcome—victory for the ruling party.

Elections have been held in 1971, 1977, and every five years thereafter. The same electoral system has been used each time. Elections for members of the national People's Representative Council and the two levels of regional legislatures are held simultaneously. The provinces are multimember electoral districts for the national Council, and provinces and districts are constituted as single multimember electoral districts for their own legislatures.

All citizens aged 18 or older (or married) are eligible to vote, except for members of the armed forces, persons involved in the 1965 "thirtieth of September movement" (which resulted in the kidnapping and murder of six senior army officers on October 1), and other categories such as convicted criminals and the mentally incompetent. Registration is conducted several months before the election by local government officials and is virtually universal. Shortly before the election, each registered voter receives an authorization card that he or she presents to election officials at the polling place on election day in exchange for ballots.

Voting is by party list. Each voter is given three paper ballots containing the parties' names and ballot symbols, one ballot for each legislative level. In the secrecy of the voting booth, the voter punches a hole in the symbols of the party of his or her choice, then deposits the ballots in boxes, labeled with the three legislative levels, placed in front of the election officials and in full view of the public. At the end of balloting, ballot boxes are emptied and counted in the presence of representatives from each party and in full public view. Seats in national and provincial legislatures are distributed according to the percentage of votes each party receives—a simple system of proportional representation. There is no minimum percentage of votes a party must attain in order to earn seats.

Other rules undermine the fairness of the system. Most important is the government's implementation of a rule permitting it to screen all candidates for election. Legislators who have grown too vocal during their time in office are not permitted to run in subsequent elections or are placed low on the party list. Moreover, the same government officials who hold high national and regional Golkar posts also occupy the top positions on the national and regional election boards. For example, the minister of home affairs also serves as the head of the General Election Institute. This has afforded Golkar ample opportunity to manipulate all aspects of the electoral process, particularly the counting of ballots.

According to official data, voter turnout has always exceeded 90%. However, opposition and dissident groups dispute that claim. Since the first election under the New Order in 1971, critics of the regime have advocated not voting or spoiling the paper ballot as forms of protest. In 1997, such groups organized to observe the elections and reported that in some areas, particularly on Java, as many as 20 to 30% of voters stayed away from the polls or purposely cast invalid ballots.

THE PARTY SYSTEM

Origins of the Parties

Legally, the New Order permitted only three parties to exist: Golkar, Development Unity, and Indonesian Democracy. In recent years, dissidents have announced the creation of alternative parties, but since these were considered illegal they have remained tiny and were not allowed to contest elections. The most prominent is the Democratic People's Party, many of whose young founders were jailed on government charges of inciting violence and disrupting the electoral process.

The army founded Golkar in 1964 as a political federation of labor unions and veterans' cooperatives that it sponsored. The army aimed to compete with Communist and radical nationalist parties and their affiliated organizations that dominated politics at that time and opposed the army. When President Soeharto decided in 1969 to hold elections to legitimate his new government, he instructed his associates to transform Golkar into the government's own electoral vehicle.

The other two parties are amalgams of parties that flourished in the country's brief period of multiparty democracy in the early 1950s. Dozens of parties existed during that era, but four dominated. In the 1955 election, the Indonesian Nationalist Party earned 22%, the modernist Muslim party Masyumi took 21%, the traditionalist Muslim party Nahdlatul Ulama won 19%, and the Communist Party carried 16%. After taking power in 1966, Soeharto banned the Communist Party for its alleged involvement in the assassination of several officers on October 1, 1965. He also permitted members of Masyumi, which Soekarno had banned in 1960 for its alleged role in regional rebellions, to form a successor known as Muslimin Indonesia.

When elections were finally held in 1971, Golkar faced nine opponents and defeated them handily. It received 63%, while its nearest competitor, Nahdlatul Ulama, gained just 19%. Despite this massive victory, the new government was not satisfied with its ability to dominate the political system. In 1973, it forced the nine minority parties to "fuse" into just two. The four Muslim parties were incorporated into the Development Unity Party, and the five nationalist and Christian parties into the Indonesian Democracy Party.

In 1977 and 1982, Development Unity garnered more than a quarter of the votes, while Indonesian Democracy failed to reach even 10% and Golkar took 62 to 64%. In 1987 and 1992, Development Unity sank to 16 to 17% and Indonesian Democracy peaked at 15% in 1992. Indonesian Democracy's rise came entirely at Golkar's expense, driving its share of the vote down from 73% in 1987 to 68% in 1992. Fearful of Indonesian Democracy's growing strength, the government undermined the party's leadership in the run-up to the 1997 elections. As a result, Golkar achieved a record 74%, Development Unity improved to 22%, and Indonesian Democracy plunged to a mere 3%.

Party Organization

The New Order's efforts to control the political parties did not stop with their forced consolidation. Additional measures, written into law in the mid-1970s and the mid-1980s, aimed further to depoliticize society and ensure that political parties could not obstruct Golkar's efforts to control society. Proreform forces now target these laws for revision or replacement. This set of laws recognizes only Golkar and the two minority parties, requires that each adopt the same ideology (*Pancasila*), and dictates how all must organize. At the core of these measures is the concept of the "floating mass," which reflects the Soeharto regime's view that politics should be restricted to elites. The masses should be mobilized every five years to vote in general elections but otherwise be left to "float" above politics.

Until the mid-1980s, the parties were formally cadre parties, in recognition of the fact that each was merely a loose federation of previous parties and social organizations, each of which continued to exist as a nonpolitical association. Thus, party membership was indirect. In 1985 a new political parties law (Law No. 3 of 1985) required them to permit direct membership and forbade them from having direct affiliations with other associations.

However, this law has had little impact, and the parties remain federations of cadres divided according to their membership in outside organizations. Intraparty conflicts frequently center on the appropriate distribution of positions among factions representing the old parties. Golkar even explicitly recruits legislative candidates from organizations with which it claims (disingenuously) no longer to be affiliated. In the brief period since Soeharto's resignation, fissures along traditional lines have already begun to emerge.

One of the principal obstacles to becoming mass membership parties is a provision in the political parties law that prohibits the parties from having branches except in provincial and district capitals. Though they are allowed to place representatives in all subdistricts, they are forbidden from organizing at the subdistrict and the village levels. In practice, this means that only Golkar, through its control of the bureaucracy, has direct access to rural dwellers, still about two-thirds of the population.

Preventing political party organization at the village level has sharply reduced the frequency and intensity of rural political conflict and has prevented elite conflicts from spilling over into rural areas—both very common in the pre–New Order era. However, it has not depoliticized village politics. Instead, it has created a near monopoly for Golkar, since local bureaucrats can use loyalty to Golkar as a criterion for doling out favors and disloyalty as an excuse for withholding services.

Village leaders who affiliate with either of the non-government parties in practice cannot become village heads, let alone subdistrict chiefs. And whether such leaders are allowed to remain in these local positions often depends on their ability to produce massive Golkar victories in their localities. The governors of East and Central Java extended the terms of thousands of village heads in 1997 until after that year's general election in order to ensure those officials' loyalty and avoid creating local political conflicts that could backfire on Golkar at election time, as happened in 1992.

The result of the implementation of these rules has been the creation of strongly centralized parties, easily controlled by the national government. Each party has a Central Leadership Board (*Dewan Pimpinan Pusat*), and Regional Leadership Boards (*Dewan Pimpinan Daerah*) at the provincial and district levels. At the national level, these are led by a general chairman and a secretary-general, as well as several assistant chairmen and secretaries-general. These leaders are chosen at infrequent national congresses, funded and supervised closely by the government.

Government intervention in party leadership struggles—and in general elections—was most blatant during the 1970s when members of the security and intelligence forces played direct roles in selecting party leaders. The government again resorted to direct coercion in 1996 to depose the popular head of the Indonesian Democracy Party, Megawati Sukarnoputri, in preparation for the 1997 elections.

Campaigning

During New Order, the government attempted to exert as much control over campaigning as it did over other aspects of the electoral process. A successful campaign was one that proceeded, in the jargon of government officials and military officers, in a manner that was "safe, orderly, and smooth" (*aman, tertib, lancar*).

To ensure that the campaign proceeded this way, parties had to comply with many restrictive rules. Campaigning was permitted for only about four weeks and then had to cease during a "quiet period" (five days in 1997) immediately prior to the polls. During the campaign, the parties were required to obtain police permits to hold rallies, and the content of their speeches and other campaign materials had to be vetted by the national office of the General Election Institute before being disseminated to regional party branches. Parties were forbidden to criticize each other or government policies, and under no circumstances could they question the state ideology, *Pancasila*.

Campaigns were centrally coordinated affairs, largely because the government insisted on maintaining centralized control over the parties and the electoral process. The General Election Institute determined when and where each party could campaign, ostensibly to prevent conflict between rival parties and competition for venues. Typically, national party leaders traversed the country to appear with local officials at large public rallies. To attract the largest possible crowds, nationally known entertainers were flown from Jakarta to regional campaign sites. However, a party's ability to attract large crowds during its campaign has not been a useful indicator of electoral support, as Indonesian Democracy discovered in 1992, and Development Unity found out in 1997.

Violence was a feature of all election campaigns under the New Order, since the regime readily resorted to the use of security forces to manipulate the minority parties and secure overwhelming electoral victories. However, violence seems to have increased in the 1990s, particularly on Java. The causes of campaign violence are complex but are clearly related to two factors. One is the accumulation of minority parties' political grievances, especially the impossibility of effecting real political change through elections. The second factor is the growing number of unemployed urban youth who seek opportunities to protest the economic injustices they attribute to the government. Such people gravitated to Indonesian Democracy in 1992, and then to Development Unity in 1997.

In 1997, the government attempted to institute a "dialogical" style of campaigning in order to avert the potential for mass violence that surfaced in 1992. It forbade motorcades and parades and encouraged party spokespersons to discuss platforms on television rather than at large rallies. These restrictions failed, partly because Golkar supporters insisted on staging their own parades, which provoked a cycle of conflict, counterparades, and further violence.

Independent Voters

Because Indonesian parties are essentially cadre parties, most voters are technically independents. Why and how much these voters identify with the party they choose in an election is unknown. Research on party identification is almost completely lacking and does not support any firm conclusions about independent voters.

However, large swings in the percentage of votes each party has received over the past 20 years suggest that slightly more than 10% of Indonesian voters are not committed to any one party. The share of the national vote that Development Unity lost in 1987 is almost identical to that which Indonesian Democracy lost in 1997. Though Golkar was the chief beneficiary of Development Unity's troubles, both Golkar and Development Unity benefited from Indonesian Democracy's downfall. The independent voters behind these swings are found mostly on Java and in urban areas.

FUNCTIONAL GROUPS
(Golongan Karya; Golkar)

HISTORY

Golkar was the centerpiece of the New Order regime's effort to create a democratic facade for its authoritarian rule. When President Soeharto decided in 1969 to hold elections in an effort to legitimate his grip on power, he instructed close associates to transform Golkar from a small army-sponsored political federation of labor unions and veterans' groups into the regime's electoral vehicle. Its name means "functional group(s)," by which is meant organizations of teachers, fishermen, farmers, youth, women, and so forth. The name was adopted to draw a contrast with the political parties, which seemed to army leaders in the 1960s to represent only narrow interests. (Though it makes no practical difference, it should be noted that legally Golkar is not a political party. Indonesian law distinguishes between functional groups and political parties, though it permits only one Golkar and two parties.)

Since it was founded in 1964, Golkar has attempted to present itself as representing all major social groups. In practice, it has been used more to co-opt, control, and silence diverse groups than to ensure that they are represented in the political arena. In order to give content to its claims to represent a wide variety of "functional groups," Golkar's founders also established or brought under its control a wide variety of social organizations. On important political occasions, these groups turn out to pledge their support for Golkar.

In each of the six elections held during the New Order, Golkar won overwhelming majorities. Its weakest showing was in 1977, when it gained a bit less than 62%; its best performance was in 1997, when it received slightly over 74%. Prior to the first election in 1971, Soeharto appointed some ministers who were not from Golkar, but thereafter he selected only Golkar members. In 1998, Habibie appointed three non-Golkar Cabinet ministers as a gesture of inclusiveness. In 1997, Golkar won 325 of the 425 elective seats in the 500-member Representative Council. It also enjoys the support of the Council's 75 appointed military members. The 500 delegates who join the 500 Council members to comprise the 1,000-member Consultative Assembly are either Golkar members or people approved by Golkar.

ORGANIZATION

Golkar was created by army officers who used their influence within the government to compel civil servants to join and support it. Golkar divides itself into three membership "channels," including the military, the bureaucracy, and nonbureaucrat civilians. Since the late 1970s, the military's role in the bureaucracy gradually has declined. In consequence, the civilian bureaucracy's role has expanded. Only in 1993, however, was a civilian picked to run the party, and that occurred only as a result of direct intervention by President Soeharto. Military officers have continued to dominate most of the regional Golkar boards.

Though military influence in Golkar remains strong, the party is staffed primarily by bureaucrats, and Golkar's structure parallels that of the state. Like the state, it is highly centralized. Its reach extends from the top of the bureaucracy to the bottom, and from the center of the country to its farthest point. Its leadership boards at the national, provincial, and district levels are made up of high-ranking officials, including active-duty military officers. Though Golkar legislators represent the entire spectrum of civilian and military agencies, they generally vote as a unified progovernment bloc.

In addition to the civilian-military tensions, one of the principal tensions within Golkar appears to be between the national and regional leadership boards. Until 1988, the national convention was held, and the national party leadership elected, prior to holding the provincial- and district-level conventions and leadership elections. But in 1987, the national leadership agreed to reverse the order. This has led to more intense competition at regional levels as military and bureaucratic factions attempt to consolidate their positions in preparation for the national convention.

Regional Golkar officials are drawn from regional bureaucracies, and regional bureaucrats are recruited within their own region. As a result, regional Golkar organizations occasionally come to represent regional interests in opposition to national interests. Golkar attempts to mitigate these tensions by providing opportunities for regional bureaucrat-politicians to ascend to more lucrative and prestigious posts in the national government, including the Representative Council. Conflicts arise most often when the central leadership denies regional leaders the opportunity to fill high regional posts in order to grant those posts to higher-ranking officials as rewards for service elsewhere.

MEMBERSHIP AND CONSTITUENCY

Until its third national congress in 1983, membership in Golkar was only through membership in other organizations, since Golkar is ostensibly a federation of "functional groups." Since then, membership has been open to individuals. Nevertheless, it remains primarily a cadre party. Its chief cadres are civil servants who, since 1970, have been required to belong to a civil servants corps that, at government direction, pledges its members' support to Golkar. Civil servants may join one of the minority parties, but only with the permission of their superior; the result is an effective ban on doing so. Following Golkar's setback in 1992, when its share fell to 68% from 73% in 1987, its new head, information minister

Harmoko, instituted an ambitious campaign of cadre development that paid dividends in 1997.

Over the course of six general elections, patterns in electoral support for Golkar are readily apparent. Support is greater in rural areas than urban. As a consequence, support is also greater off Java than on Java. On Java, Golkar has had difficulty gaining much more than 60% of the vote, but off Java it generally does extremely well. In 1997, its best year, Golkar received 67% of the votes cast in Java's 5 provinces. In nine of the 22 remaining provinces, Golkar secured more than 90%, and in 9 others it obtained between 80% and 89%. Its best showing came in Southeast Sulawesi, where it claimed more than 97%. The urban-rural difference is partly attributable to the New Order's record in improving rural living standards but is also due to the bureaucracy's greater capacity to regulate and control rural politics.

Golkar is weakest in those regions where ethnic identity is closely linked to strict adherence to Islamic teachings, whether these regions are on or off Java. Since the 1980s, however, it has succeeded in undermining devout Muslims' support for Development Unity. Not since 1982 has Golkar failed to win a majority in every province.

POLICY

The government and, therefore, Golkar have espoused a consistent set of policy goals since taking power 30 years ago. Their main goal is to achieve rapid economic growth while maintaining political stability. How they have sought to achieve economic growth has varied. In the late 1960s and early 1970s, foreign aid from the United States, Japan, and other anticommunist countries played a key role. For a decade beginning in the early 1970s, oil exports fueled economic growth and encouraged the government to pursue state-led industrialization strategies.

An economic crisis occurred in the mid-1980s as oil prices plunged, and the government then adopted a series of economic liberalization policies to promote export-oriented, labor-intensive industrialization. Industrialization has proceeded rapidly but has been concentrated on Java and in parts of Sumatra. Elsewhere economic change has occurred, often dramatically, but has been concentrated in forestry, plantation agriculture, and mining. Both labor-intensive (e.g., textiles) and natural resource–intensive (e.g., plywood) exports are critical to the economy, but oil and natural gas exports continue to play large roles, too.

The government's failure to respond quickly to the economic crisis of 1997 initiated the process that led to Soeharto's resignation in 1998. Economic deterioration highlighted the "corruption, collusion, and nepotism," as protesters charged, that characterized his rule and placed Golkar's future in serious doubt.

The government's foreign policy has been pragmatic, but in recent years Soeharto sought to chart a more "active and independent" course, as Indonesians say. In large part this is due to confidence born from the success of his domestic policies. In 1985, Soeharto won a United Nations award for achieving self-sufficiency in rice production, and in 1990 another UN award for successful population planning. By the early 1990s, the World Bank recognized Indonesia's success in restructuring its economy by placing it in a category with other "high-performing Asian economies." However, in the aftermath of the cold war, Western countries have become more vocal critics of Indonesia's record on human and political rights, and this, too, has contributed to Soeharto's interest in charting a more independent foreign policy course.

Indonesia's increasingly active foreign policy has spanned a wide range of initiatives. In the early 1990s, it played a key role in brokering an end to Cambodia's civil war. In 1991, it took over the chairmanship of the Non-Aligned Movement, and since the early 1990s it has hosted annual informal meetings among countries engaged with China in territorial disputes in the South China Sea. In 1994, it hosted the annual summit of the Asia Pacific Economic Cooperation forum, at which Soeharto successfully pressed the other members to agree to a timetable for achieving free trade in the region.

FINANCING

Golkar receives its funding from budgetary and nonbudgetary state sources. The government allocates funds to each of the parties for operating expenses, election campaigning, and quinquennial party congresses. Off-budget resources are far more important.

In 1985, President Soeharto established the Dakab Foundation, which he personally controls. Under Indonesian law, foundations do not have to make public financial disclosures. However, it is known that this foundation has serves as the principal conduit of funds from the business community to Golkar.

Dakab stands as a signal example of how Soeharto both personalized and regularized political power. On the one hand, he alone determined how much money the foundation should raise and how that money should be spent. The only link between Golkar and Dakab is Soeharto, as leader of both. On the other hand, Dakab's emergence replaced ad hoc efforts to skim money from various state-owned companies, which are subject to public audit, with regular contributions from the private sector, which grew richer under the government's economic deregulation policies since the mid-1980s. Soeharto's demise almost certainly spells an end to this source of revenue for Golkar.

LEADERSHIP

Until mid-1998, Soeharto himself was the most important Golkar official, and during the 1990s two of his children acquired important roles in the party. The first civilian to serve as party general chairman, Harmoko, was appointed in 1993 over strenuous military objections only because he was Soeharto's choice.

In July 1998, Golkar held an extraordinary congress at which some Soeharto supporters, especially those from the army, lost their party leadership positions to allies of the new president, Habibie.

The party's new general chairman is Akbar Tandjung, a civilian minister in Soeharto's Cabinet since 1993 and holder of the powerful post of minister state secretary under Habibie. He aims to reform the party while maintaining its grip on power. To that end, he has acknowledged that the new Golkar would consider forming coalitions with other parties. Given Habibie's past involvement with Indonesian Muslim Intellectuals Association, and links between Habibie and leaders of new Islamic parties, the most likely coalition is with Muslim parties that represent urban, middle-class Muslims.

PROSPECTS

Since its founding, the bureaucracy and the military have had to employ their coercive resources to ensure Golkar's electoral success. This has left a record of fraud and injustice that undermines even many members' conviction that it rules at the people's will. For more than 30 years, however, political and bureaucratic success has required cooperation with the regime and participation in Golkar. As a result, many talented people and many who disagreed with their party's leadership remained part of it. Moreover, as the regime evolved, Golkar became more and more intimately bound up with the bureaucracy and consequently enjoyed institutional support beyond the means of any other organization.

The result is that members lack loyalty to the organization but enjoy structural power by virtue of their membership in it. Change is likely to follow two paths—reformation of the party and division into separate parties. Both tendencies are already evident. In neither case is it clear that successors will be able to command access to the private sources of capital that Soeharto did.

DEVELOPMENT UNITY PARTY
(Partai Persatuan Pembangunan)

HISTORY

The Development Unity Party is a creation of the New Order regime that, in its own words, sought to "simplify" the political system by "fusing" the four Islamically based political parties into one in 1973. In 1984, the party was forced to give up Islam as one of its "core principles" and accept only *Pancasila* in its place. In that same year, the largest of its four founding members, Nahdlatul Ulama, withdrew from the party to concentrate on its educational and religious missions and to es-

cape the persistent efforts of government security and intelligence agencies to penetrate it.

Despite government attempts to limit its Islamic appeal, Development Unity remains an unmistakably religious party and the only one of the two legal minority parties to enjoy consistent and widespread electoral support. Since the pivotal changes of 1984, it has not managed to achieve the same level of electoral support it enjoyed previously. Its best performance came in 1977 when it won nearly 30% of the vote nationally, as well as a majority in Aceh province and a plurality in the capital region of Jakarta. In 1997 it garnered 22% of the vote and 89 of the 425 elective seats in the 500-member Representative Council.

ORGANIZATION

Though many Muslim leaders had long sought Islamic political unity, government-imposed unity in 1973 simply transformed interparty conflicts into intraparty controversies. Each of the original parties continued to exist as a nonpolitical association. Tensions were greatest between the party's two largest constituent organizations, Muslimin Indonesia and Nahdlatul Ulama (NU). They came into conflict most often over the distribution of party positions and seats in the legislature. Nahdlatul Ulama had a larger electoral and organizational base, but Muslimin Indonesia, itself a government creation, enjoyed stronger government backing.

In 1984, following a deep internal split, Nahdlatul Ulama withdrew from Development Unity. Those who led its withdrawal believed that the party was too constrained by political conditions to achieve any important goals and also feared that government penetration of Development Unity was spreading into Nahdlatul Ulama's nonpolitical religious and educational branches. Since then, NU members have been permitted to remain active in the party, but many were pushed aside by their Muslimin Indonesia rivals.

In contrast to Golkar, Development Unity does not have a network of affiliated organizations of so-called functional groups. Nahdlatul Ulama's withdrawal was a serious blow to the party's electoral performance in large part because it provided the party with the support of its network of Koranic schools as well as its large youth and women's organizations.

MEMBERSHIP AND CONSTITUENCY

As the product of a forced marriage, Development Unity remains a cadre party that draws on the memberships of the nonpolitical associations of the same names as the parties that were amalgamated to create Development Unity. There is little research on the demographic composition of party cadres, and less on the party's constituencies.

It can be observed, however, that the party has received most of its votes in regions where its constituent organizations have their bases. Though the party was badly hurt in the 1987 elections by Nahdlatul Ulama's withdrawal three years earlier, it has done very well since then in regions where Nahdlatul Ulama is strongest, especially the provinces of East Java, Central Java, and South Kalimantan. Muslimin Indonesia has never had the same grassroots organizational basis as Nahdlatul Ulama, and the modernist Muslims it represents have often been more inclined than Nahdlatul Ulama's traditionalists to vote for Golkar. However, the greatest erosion of electoral support has occurred in the eight provinces of Sumatra, Indonesia's most populous island after Java. In nearly every Sumatran province, Golkar has cut Development Unity's share of the vote in half since 1977. The national improvement it has enjoyed in the past two elections has been minimal in Sumatra and Sulawesi.

In addition to attracting votes from devout Muslims, Development Unity has often attracted voters who simply wish to cast a protest vote. Such voters seem to have switched to Indonesian Democracy in 1992 and back to Development Unity in 1997. However, the party has done nothing to diminish its Islamic image and consequently has done poorly in regions that are largely Christian or Hindu. Nonetheless, its electoral support is far broader and deeper than that of Indonesian Democracy.

In 1997, the party won more than 10% of the vote in 16 of 27 provinces, and more than 20% in 8 of those provinces. On Java, 30% of the voters chose Development Unity.

POLICY

During the New Order regime's early years, Soeharto took a series of steps to limit the role of Islam in Indonesian politics and to promote social legislation that ignored the interests of many Muslims. At that time, Development Unity's factions often united to oppose, albeit unsuccessfully, the initiatives that Golkar championed. During the past 10 years, as Soeharto adopted a more accommodating position toward the country's politically active Muslim community, Development Unity has had even less impact on the policymaking process.

In recent years, its principal demand has been that the government change the laws that restrict the rights of political parties in order to permit the party to compete more fairly against Golkar. On economic policy, it often calls for measures that would enhance equity more than growth and criticizes the corruption and collusion that characterize relations between the bureaucracy and the private sector. These issues are important to the party, since the wealthiest Indonesians are largely non-Muslims of Chinese descent, many of whom have got rich because of their closeness to Soeharto. In general, however, the party does not propound or advance a clear set of policies.

FINANCING

Development Unity has few sources of financing. Its principal source is the government, which pays equivalent monthly stipends to each party to cover their operating expenses. However, the amounts are small. In addition, the government provides funds to cover the costs of holding quinquennial national and regional congresses and to support the party's election campaigns.

Little is known of the party's nongovernmental funding sources. In the past, the party could count on support from small businesspeople and landowners affiliated with Nahdlatul Ulama. However, these groups have not done well under New Order economic policies, and Nahdlatul Ulama's withdrawal from the party has made them less willing to contribute to the party. One of the party's largest sources reportedly is a charge the party levies on members who wish to be nominated as legislative candidates and on the salaries of members who are elected to the national and regional legislatures.

LEADERSHIP

Development Unity's top leaders are chosen at a national convention every five years. Under political pressure to prepare for fresh legislative elections planned for mid-1999, the party held a special convention in December 1998 to select new leaders one year ahead of schedule.

Hamzh Haz was elected general chairman, replacing Hasan Ismail Matereum, who had led the party since 1989. Haz is a member of Nahdlatul Ulama but hails from the province of West Kalimantan rather than NU's principal base on Java. He has served in the Representative Council since 1971 and joined President Habibie's Cabinet in May 1998 as minister of investment.

Under Haz, Nahdlatul Ulama regained the influence with the party that it had enjoyed until the early 1980s. Although the executive committee accommodated all four factions within the party, NU received the largest number of positions.

PROSPECTS

The New Order created the Development Unity Party primarily as a vehicle to accommodate and control Muslim political elites, and it has been effective in doing so. Over the last quarter century, those elites have become more distant from their constituents and more attentive to government wishes. In consequence, the party never had a chance to take power. As long as Soeharto remained president and the army backed Golkar, it lacked the capacity to mobilize public support for specific objectives. For all its weaknesses, the party has remained the principal minority voice in government and has retained very strong support in several regions. Its fate in the post-Soeharto era is uncertain. New Islamic parties have been formed that will compete with Development Unity for the same constituency. Untainted by association with the old regime, these new parties may have broader appeal to voters seeking change.

MINOR POLITICAL PARTIES

Indonesian Democracy Party (Partai Demokrasi Indonesia)

For most of its history, the Indonesian Democracy Party has been on the brink of extinction. It has stayed alive primarily through government support. Like the Development Unity Party, it is the product of a forced marriage, but unlike Development Unity its constituent parties did not share a common ideology. They were united only by the fact that they were not based on Islam. Moreover, they could count on little popular support. Its core member, the once-powerful Indonesian Nationalist Party, had drawn most of its support from the bureaucracy, but the New Order required all bureaucrats to support Golkar. The Catholic and Protestant parties had only small regional constituencies, and neither had much prospect of attracting many votes in a largely Muslim country.

Indonesian Democracy's poor performance in the first two elections it contested worried many Golkar officials. They feared the party might disappear and leave it to face a single opponent. Worse, that opponent would be a party identified with Islam. The prospect that Golkar might then be seen as the adversary of the country's largest religious community provoked some segments of the government to lend support to Indonesian Democracy in hopes that it would strengthen enough to maintain a three-party system. Indonesian Democracy exploited this opportunity. By creating a populist image and attributing the country's social and economic inequities to the regime's policies, it doubled its share of the vote between 1982 and 1992.

The regime's efforts to manipulate Indonesian Democracy had backfired, and it spent the next three years seeking a way to weaken the party. It began by trying to oust the party's leader, Soerjadi, but ended up with an even less desirable outcome—former president Soekarno's daughter, Megawati Sukarnoputri, as the party's charismatic head. In 1996, the government engineered her ouster by providing military support for an emergency national party congress at which Soerjadi was reinstalled. Several weeks later, tension between the government-backed Soerjadi faction and Megawati's supporters exploded in the worst violence to occur in Jakarta in almost 25 years.

As a result of such blatant government intervention, the party was discredited and suffered its worst defeat ever. It won more than 10% of the vote in just small two provinces (West Kalimantan and East Timor). Party chief Soerjadi did not win reelection even though he was at the top of his party's list for Jakarta. In the previous two elections, Jakarta had given more than 20% of its votes to the party, but in 1997 it gave less than 2%. Seven other provinces also gave less than 2% of their votes to the party.

In the wake of Soeharto's resignation, each faction of the party held a separate convention to select its leaders. Little reconciliation is likely at the national level, but some has occurred at the local level. The breakaway faction attracted hundreds of thousands of supporters to Bali in October 1998 for a peaceful meeting that reelected Megawati without opposition as party chairperson The officially sanctioned faction met in a remote province, but even there its leaders were beset by security problems arising from popular opposition to them. Despite her low profile in the protests that drove Soeharto from office, Megawati retains broad public support and is one of the leading candidates for president in 1999.

OTHER POLITICAL PARTIES

Since Soeharto's fall, more than 100 political parties have been formed. Religious identity, far more than economic policy, has defined the differences among the major parties. Few of the new parties will be able to garner many votes. The most prominent are based on the country's two major Islamically based social welfare and educational organizations. The leader of Nahdlatul Ulama, Abdurahman Wahid, has formed the National Awakening Party. He is close to Megawati Sukarnoputri, who leads the breakaway faction of the Indonesian Democracy Party. Amien Rais stepped down from his postion as head of Muhammadiyah to form the National Mandate Party. He led many of the demonstrations that brought down Soeharto, but he also has ties to many of Habibie's associates. Both men, despite their role as leaders of the country's two largest religious organizations, have founded ostensibly nonsectarian parties.

NATIONAL PROSPECTS

The nature of elections under the New Order was delegitimating precisely because it prevented political change. The regime's legitimacy declined because of the increasingly evident contradiction between the fairness with which the government claimed to administer the system and the reality of fraud, manipulation, and coercion that political parties, opposition groups, and the mass media documented.

This is Soeharto's legacy and the target of proreform social forces. The chief question is no longer whether major political change will occur but how extensive it will be. Nearly all aspects of political organization are under debate. The close, personalized ties Soeharto developed among the army, the bureaucracy, and Golkar are already dissolving. The possibility that Habibie or anyone else will be able to control the political system as Soeharto did is very small.

Conservative social, military, and bureaucratic forces retain organizational resources that the popular social forces still lack. How much the next government looks like the last depends on proreform groups' ability to enhance their organizational capacity, expand their bases of support from urban to rural areas, and maintain pressure on the government to adopt significant changes to the laws that curb political parties and skew electoral outcomes.

Further Reading

Bresnan, John. *Managing Indonesia: The Modern Political Economy*. New York: Columbia University Press, 1993.

Crouch, Harold. *The Army and Politics in Indonesia*, rev. ed. Ithaca, N.Y.: Cornell University Press, 1988.

Liddle, R. William. "A Useful Fiction: Democratic Legitimation in New Order Indonesia." In *The Politics of Elections in Southeast Asia*. Ed. R.H. Taylor. London and New York: Woodrow Wilson Center Press and Cambridge University Press, 1996.

———. "Indonesia: Suharto's Tightening Grip." *Journal of Democracy* 7, no. 4 (October 1996): 58–72.

———. "Indonesia's Democratic Past and Future." *Comparative Politics*, July 1992, 443–62.

Mackie, Jamie, and Andrew MacIntyre. "Politics." In *Indonesia's New Order: The Dynamics of Socio-economic Transformation*. Ed. Hal Hill. St Leonards, NSW: Allen and Unwin, 1994.

Schwartz, Adam. *A Nation in Waiting: Indonesia in the 1990s*. St. Leonards, NSW: Allen and Unwin, 1994.

Vatikiotis, Michael R.J. *Indonesian Politics under Suharto: Order, Development and Pressure for Change*. London: Routledge, 1993.

ISLAMIC REPUBLIC OF IRAN

(Jomhuri-ye Eslami-ye Iran)

By Pooya Alaedini, Siamak Namazi, and Lawrence G. Potter

THE SYSTEM OF GOVERNMENT

Iran, a country of 64 million people, serves as the nexus between the Caspian Sea and the Persian Gulf and connects the steppes of central Asia to Anatolia and continental Europe. To the north, Iran is bound by the Republic of Azerbaijan, the Caspian Sea, and Turkmenistan, to the east by Afghanistan and Pakistan, to the south by the Sea of Oman and Persian Gulf, and to the west by Iraq and Turkey. Covering some 1.648 million square kilometers, Iran's topography is often likened to that of a bowl with the Alborz Mountains creating the northern rim and the Zagros Mountains the western and southern rims. The center of the country is arid and dry for the most part, while the Alborz Mountains have created a fertile crescent around the Caspian Sea. Most of Iran's major cities, including Tehran, Tabriz, Shiraz, and Mashhad, were built along the foothills of mountains where a traditional system of irrigation canals, *qanats*, delivered needed water.

While the majority of Iran's population is considered to be Persian, the country is diverse in terms of ethnicity and language. Most of the population is Twelver Shi'a Moslem, while religious minorities include Sunni Moslem, Zoroastrian, Jewish, Christian, and Bahai. In addition, Iran is the largest host to refugees in the world and currently shelters close to 3 million displaced persons from Afghanistan and Iraq. The country is undergoing rapid urbanization, and the urban areas now claim 60% of the total population, compared with only 31% in the 1950s. Iran possesses one of the youngest populations in the world with 40% of the people 15 years old or younger.

The country's urban population was largely responsible for the overthrow of the monarch, Shah Mohammad Reza Pahlavi (reigned 1941–79, died July 27, 1980, in exile). A coalition of the clergy, the merchants (*bazaris*), the liberal reformists, students, and the leftists united behind Ayatollah Ruhollah Musavi Khomeini and ended monarchy in Iran on February 11, 1979. This broad coalition fell apart shortly after victory, and the clergy (*olama*), under the leadership of Khomeini, managed to consolidate power by pushing out the liberal reformists and carrying out mass arrests and executions of the various leftist groups between 1980 and 1982.

Iran is officially an Islamic Republic following the vote of 98.2% of eligible voters for a carefully worded referendum on March 29 and 30, 1979; the only two choices given were "Yes" and "No" to this system of government. Modeled after Khomeini's ideas of *velayat-e faqih* (rule of the jurisprudence), in this conception of Islamic government, the state is to be guided by a learned religious jurist who rules in the absence of the Twelfth Imam. This Imam, a descendant of the Prophet Muhammad, went into "concealment" in the 9th century and is expected to return at the end of the world to establish a golden age. Until that time, the Imam's will is transmitted through ayatollahs (*mojtahids*) to the people. Ayatollah Khomeini ruled Iran as the Leader with unique popular and religious authority up to his death in June of 1989.

After Khomeini's death, there has been no absolute source of authority in Iran. While there is no problem identifying the head of different political institutions of authority—such as the leadership, presidency, and judiciary—it is often difficult to tell which institution holds the main cards on a particular issue.

Leadership

The 1979 constitution maintained that the highest political and religious authority of Iran is the Leader (*faqih*). The Leader has very extensive powers: he appoints the religious jurists on the Council of Guardians, appoints the highest judicial authorities, and is designated commander in chief of the country's armed forces. He can declare war. He must sign the order formalizing the election of the president and can dismiss the president if the Supreme Court finds him politically incompetent (a fate that befell Abolhasan Bani Sadr, the first president of the Islamic Republic, in June 1981).

The description of the Leader's power was largely designed to fit the persona of Ayatollah Khomeini, who enjoyed unparalleled popular and religious legitimacy. He was a grand ayatollah and a source of emulation (*marja'-e taqlid*) in the Shi'a religious hierarchy. His unique attributes led the drafters of the original 1979 constitution to marry the positions of highest political and religious authorities in Iran. Not surprisingly, the issue of succession was always on the minds of the clerical rulers of Iran. Originally, Ayatollah Montazeri was designated as Khomeini's successor, but after a series of disagreements between the two over the powers of the leadership in late 1988 and early 1989, Montazeri was dismissed as the future Leader. Khomeini failed to recommend a new figure before his death in June of 1989.

After Khomeini's death no grand ayatollah in Iran had the ambitions to take over the political reins. In fact, the *olama* of Iran traditionally eschewed direct political involvement and saw their mandate as constructive criticism of the system. According to the constitution, "the task of appointing the Leader shall be vested with the experts elected by the people," that is, the Council of Experts. Should there be no decisive majority of the people in favor of one *faqih*, three to five candidates are to be appointed by the Council of Experts to serve on a Leadership Council.

Consequently, in June 1989, the first debate the Council of Experts faced was whether to opt for a single person or a group of *faqihs* to take over Khomeini's position. With the support of Ali Akbar Hashemi Rafsanjani, then Speaker of the *Majles* (the Iranian parliament) and one of Khomeini's most trusted advisers, Hojjatoleslam Hosein Ali Khamenei was nominated as a compromise candidate and won majority support. The government and the media then began referring to him as ayatollah and he was proclaimed Leader of the Islamic Republic, but later his authority was downgraded and his function as the highest religious authority was delegated to Grand Ayatollah Araki.

Khamenei, too young and lacking in religious eminence, has striven to increase his religious authority by appeasing the conservative *olama* of Qom. However, his ambition to become the religious source of emulation was hindered following the death of Grand Ayatollah Araki in 1995, when Iran was left with no grand ayatollahs and the country's high-ranking clergy were forced to announce new sources of emulation among the *olama*. Khamenei's candidacy was rejected, and he was told that he lacked the needed religious credentials, though in an apparent face-saving compromise, he was included on a list of 10 ayatollahs who had the potential to become *mojtahids* in the future.

Notwithstanding, Khamenei is still the highest-ranking official of the Islamic Republic, and the Leadership as an institution maintains a great deal of power and authority. However, the Leadership is increasingly coming under the attack of critics who claim that Khamenei is out of touch with the needs of the country and the Iranian people.

Executive

The Leadership was not the only body of government severely affected by the death of Ayatollah Khomeini. Under the original constitution of 1979, the president of the Islamic Republic was elected by a majority of the votes cast, for a four-year term, and he could be reelected only once. He would preside over a Cabinet of 26 members and would appoint the prime minister, who remained in power unless he lost the confidence of the parliament. The Leader has the power to dismiss the president.

Concurrent with the appointment of Ali Khamenei as the new leader, Rafsanjani was elected the new president of the republic and the post of prime minister was eliminated. In effect, the political authority of Khomeini was now embodied in a Khamenei-Rafsanjani dyad. This arrangement attested to the political skills of Rafsanjani, who has proved himself adept at increasing the power of the political institution he controls.

In many ways, the arrangement was also ideal for the purposes of maintaining the clerical regime. One of the most complex tasks that Ruhollah Khomeini had mastered in his ascent to power was the difficult act of balancing conservative and Islamic leftist forces. To retain both pillars of support, Khomeini often resorted to contradictory messages in various speeches, one day praising the concept of ownership as one that is guaranteed and encouraged by Islam, and the next speaking to the grievances of the *mostaz'afan* (oppressed and poor masses). Similarly, in the duet comprised of Khamenei and Rafsanjani, the responsibility to appease the different power centers was divided: Khamenei was to maintain good relations with the conservative clergy and the powerful merchant class, while Rafsanjani took a moderate position, appealing to the Iranian technocrats and intellectuals. Meanwhile, the Islamic leftists were to be gradually pushed out of the country's political scene.

The official powers and responsibilities of the president are rather vague in the Iranian constitution. Article 113 states: "After the office of Leadership, the president is the highest official in the country. He is the responsibile for implementing the constitution and acting as the head of the executive, except in matters directly concerned with [the office of] the Leadership." The real power of the executive branch, however, rests in its control over Iran's oil revenues, which account for nearly three-quarters of the country's foreign exchange income. The executive also has vast authority over government expenditures.

During his eight years in power, Rafsanjani filled executive seats with his supporters. Key Cabinet positions were given to moderates and technocrats close to him, with few compromises to the conservatives. He further bypassed the legislative checks and balances by often appointing candidates ousted or rejected by the *Majles*' special advisers and vice presidents—positions not subject to parliamentary censor.

While such maneuvers were extremely effective in helping Rafsanjani retain credibility among his supporters, it further complicated the political landscape of the Islamic Republic and created institutions with vague and overlapping mandates. However, the Rafsanjani legacy also paved the way for the prominence of technical expertise as the basis for filling government offices, rather than strictly revolutionary and Islamic credentials. Hence, the number of moderates in key Cabinet positions increased.

In May 1997, Mohammad Khatami won the presidential elections with nearly 70% of the total votes. While only four candidates were allowed to run, Nateq Nuri, the conservative leader of the legislature, was widely viewed as invincible given the support he enjoyed from the strongholds of power, including the Leader himself. Khatami has continued, and expanded upon, the move toward technocracy begun by his predecessor.

Legislature

The *Majles-e Shura-ye Eslami* (Islamic Consultative Assembly), commonly referred to as the *Majles*, is composed of 270 members elected for four-year terms. There are 265 geographical seats, plus 5 seats reserved for recognized religious minorities. The *Majles* holds open sessions, barring exceptional conditions. These discussions are made public by radio, and the minutes are readily available in various media. The constitution empowers this body to make laws and approve international agreements, as well as to conduct investigations into all the affairs of the country.

The *Majles* is by no means a rubber stamp for the government. There is often spirited debate, and the *Majles* has frequently asserted its independence by refusing to confirm some of the choices of the president for Cabinet posts. In fact, when Mohammad Khatami was elected president, analysts immediately evaluated his political skills by how he passed his moderate Cabinet through a conservative legislature. In addition to veto power over the Cabinet, the Iranian legislature has final approval of the five-year plans that set the tone for the country's development and investment approach. The Second Five-Year Plan, which is in effect until March 21, 2000, was originally drafted by the moderates in the executive branch to emphasize industrialization. However, the conservative *Majles* chose to modify the plan and changed its direction to emphasize agricultural development.

The current members of *Majles* began their term following the 1996 elections, when conservatives and moderates competed fiercely for seats. As a result of those elections, 100 of the 270 seats in the *Majles* were clearly connected to the conservative forces led by the current *Majles* Speaker, Hojjatoleslam Nateq Nuri (who was expected to win the presidential election). The groups affiliated with the moderate and Islamic leftist factions won about 90 seats. The remaining 80 deputies were considered independent or having only loose contacts with major political factions. With Nuri expected to win the presidential election, most independent deputies showed support for the conservatives, hence giving them a clear majority. While an independent faction has been formed in the *Majles* as a result of Khatami's election, the conservatives remain more or less in control of the Iranian parliament.

Council of Guardians

This council, known as *Shura-ye Negahban*, is an extremely powerful 12-member group that determines whether laws passed by the parliament conform to Islamic principles and can be ratified. It is responsible for interpreting constitutional law and supervising elections. Of its membership, 6 clergymen are appointed by the *faqih* or Leadership Council; the other 6, whose selection must be confirmed by the *Majles*, are nominated by the High Judicial Council and are laymen lawyers. Members are elected for six-year terms. At times, this group has refused to concur with measures passed by the *Majles*, notably those on land reform. The Council of Guardians is headed by Ayatollah Jannati, an ultraconservative cleric whose followers include the violent group *Ansar-e Hezbollah*.

The Expediency Council

The Council on Determining the System's Expediency (*Majma'-e Tashkhis-e Maslehat-e Nezam*), or the Expediency Council, is one of the key institutions of the Islamic Republic and can be expected to grow in terms of influence and power in the coming years. Created in 1986 by Khomeini's personal decree, the Expediency Council is a mediator and arbitrator between the *Majles* and the Council of Guardians. Originally, this role essentially amounted to mediation between the conservative and Islamic leftist forces in the Islamic Republic.

The Expediency Council's influence and power were increased after Khomeini's death. This move was made to appease the members of the Council of Experts who favored a Leadership Council rather than a single Leader. However, the true potential of this body is yet to be seen. As Rafsanjani neared the end of his second and last term as president under Iranian law, a group of his supporters started a debate over amending the constitution to allow him a third term. Such a move was widely opposed, even by Rafsanjani himself. But the true political prowess of Rafsanjani has always been redefining the political institutions of Iran to suit his needs. Hence, in March 1997, just two months before the presidential elections, it came as no surprise when Ayatollah Khamenei declared that the Expediency Council was to assume increased responsibility. At that time, Khamenei doubled the number of the Leader's appointees to 26, declared that the Expediency Council would serve as his main advisory body, and appointed Rafsanjani as the Council's chairperson.

Council of Experts

The main duties of the Council of Experts have been to draft the constitution, to name the Spiritual Leader, and to make amendments to the constitution. The first Council of Experts was a 75-member group (60 of whom were clergymen) elected in August 1979 to draft the Islamic Republic constitution. These elections were boycotted by opposition groups when it became obvious that dissenting viewpoints would be excluded. When the constitution was completed, that first Council disbanded. A second, 83-member Council of Experts was elected in late 1982 to choose Khomeini's successor, seeking to avoid a political vacuum after his death. In November 1985, it chose Ayatollah Hosein-Ali Montazeri. As outlined earlier, Montazeri was dismissed from that post, and after Khomeini's death in 1989, the Council of Experts formed once again and elected the current Leader, Ali Khamenei.

Judiciary

In principle, the judiciary is an independent force. Its responsibilities are overseen by the five-member High Judicial Council, made up of the head of the Supreme Court, the attorney general, and three judges. They serve for five-year terms, with the possibility of extension for another five. Ayatollah Mohammad Yazdi, a conservative cleric, is currently the chairman of this council and head of the judiciary. The power to appoint and dismiss the head of the judiciary is in the hands of the Leader of the Islamic Republic, and hence the judiciary is fully independent of the executive and legislative powers. Consequently, there have been a number of incidences when the judiciary has stood in the way of the executive branch's policies.

Trials are to be held openly and the public is allowed to attend, unless this is incompatible with public order, which it often is. Judges issue findings on cases, which must be based on Islamic principles. The court system is overloaded due to a scarcity of judges with religious qualifications. In January 1998, a few female judges were allowed to preside over the courts of the Islamic Republic for the first time.

Besides the general courts of the country, a number of "revolutionary courts" were formed in the early days of the revolution. Led by *olama*, these courts were responsible for the execution and imprisonment of the "traitors" in the Pahlavi regime, and wide disparities in sentences for the same crime were common. Although the revolutionary courts were officially merged with the country's general courts in 1984, traces of them still exist.

Regional and Local Government

There has always been a strong tradition of local government in Iran, although power was increasingly centralized in Tehran under the Pahlavis. Provincial heads, as well as the mayor of Tehran, were appointed directly by the shah, and the minister of the interior was the main influence in selecting provincial officials. The only authority elected on a local level was the village headman.

Iran is currently divided into 28 provinces (*ostan*), headed by governor-generals (*ostandar*). However, as a result of rapid population growth and the urban boom, as well as political considerations, these divisions are constantly changing. The cities and suburbs of Qom, Qazvin, and Gorgan have only recently become the provinces Qom, Qazvin, and Golestan, respectively. Soon the province of Khorassan will also be partitioned into two or three provinces. Provinces are divided into districts (*shahrestan*) headed by governors (*farmandar*). Districts are divided into subdistricts (*bakhsh*) administered by lieutenant governors (*bakhshdar*). Subdistricts are divided into townships (*dehestan*) led by sheriffs (*dehdar*). Townships are divided into villages (*deh*), which are led by a headman (*kadkhoda*).

While the Iranian constitution has emphasized the importance of decentralization and local elections, until now this mandate has not been fully realized. For example, Iranian mayors are currently appointed by the minister of the interior, with the exception of the Tehran mayor, who is appointed by the president. The present situation, officially labeled as "for the time being," will change in February 1999 when the local councils elections are held.

THE ELECTORAL SYSTEM

Members of *Majles* are elected by direct and secret ballot. The first elections were held in two rounds, in March and May 1980; the latest elections took place in 1996. A candidate has to have a majority to win on the first ballot; otherwise there are more rounds of voting. This system makes it difficult to fill seats in many constituencies. Also, there have been instances of ballots for entire areas being disqualified and the election process repeated, which certainly adds to voter distrust.

Candidates who wish to run for office must be approved by the Council of Guardians, which pares the list of aspirants drastically. No standard criterion has been declared as the basis of this selection process. Thus, of over 200 candidates who registered to run in the presidential election of 1997, all but 4 were disqualified and no adequate explanation was provided for a person's disqualification.

Suffrage has been universal in the Islamic Republic, an ironic fact given that Khomeini criticized the shah for extending voting rights to women. In 1963, the ayatollah had considered women's suffrage an act against Islamic teachings but apparently changed his mind after ascending to power. The voting age is 15, and assistance in reading the ballot is provided to illiterates. The vote of the youth was a major factor in the victory of Mohammad Khatami who during his campaign had wisely courted the Iranian youth, women, and intellectuals. Around 90% of eligible voters participated in the presidential election. Khatami managed to win the support of 20 million people, or approximately 70% of the total participants.

The results of this latest presidential elections are widely trusted, a phenomenon not experienced since the 1980 election of Abolhasan Bani Sadr, the first president of the Islamic Republic.

The government has been concerned that low voter turnout would tarnish the regime's legitimacy. Hence, Khomeini announced that it is "a divine and religious obligation to vote," a slogan frequently heard at election time. During certain periods, the regime even resorted to using fear to attract people to voting booths, spreading rumors that citizens lacking an election stamp in their identity booklet could be subject to reprisals. Outcomes of elections were easily predictable, and the candidate favored by the establishment was practically guaranteed victory. This legacy, which was largely responsible for the lack of voter enthusiasm, was shattered when Khatami beat Nateq Nuri by a landslide margin.

THE PARTY SYSTEM

Until recently, there were no officially recognized parties in the country, although the 1979 Iranian constitution allowed for their formation provided they did not oppose the principles of Islam or undermine national sovereignty and unity. The Islamic Republic Party, officially sanctioned in the one-party system that was established a few years after the revolution, was disbanded in 1987. As a result of increased polarization within the government and the ruling elite, the formation of new parties out of the existing factions has recently become possible. Two such parties have now been formed whose effectiveness remains to be seen.

POLITICAL FACTIONS WITHIN THE RULING COALITION

While Khomeini was able to defuse disagreements among the ruling coalition, factional fighting has intensified since his death because of real differences among various groups within the regime. At the same time, the survival of the regime has been always at the top of the each faction's agenda, and so far the existence of differences has not resulted in open hostilities. The main actors can be categorized as the conservatives, the moderate pragmatists, and the Islamic leftists.

The Conservatives

The conservatives are mainly identified by their affiliation with a number of Islamic organizations, but mainly with *Jame'eh-ye Ruhaniyyat-e Mobarez* (JRM), or the Society

of Combatant Clergy. Other strongholds of this group include *Jam'iyyat-e Mo'talefeh-ye Eslami* (Society of Islamic Coalition), the Resalat Foundation, and a coalition of organizations known as *Tashakkolat-e Hamsu* (United Formations). Prominent individuals such as Ayatollah Mahdavi Kani (the former secretary of the JRM), Ayatollah Meshkini (chairman of the Assembly of Experts), and Ali Akbar Nateq Nuri (Speaker of *Majles* and presidential hopeful) are among the top figures. This group can rely on national newspapers such as *Qods* and *Jomhuri-ye Eslami* to air their opinions and promulgate their agenda.

The Moderate Pragmatists

The pragmatist faction of the Islamic Republic is formed around the personality and ideas of Hashemi Rafsanjani. In January 1996, a group of Rafsanjani's close aides and advisers created a platform to compete in the *Majles* elections. This group, which is composed of the technocratic elements in the regime, was formally to be known as *Kargozaran-e Sazandegi* (Executives of Construction). It is now an officially recognized party.

Besides Rafsanjani, other members of the Kargozaran include well-known figures in the Islamic Republic such as Gholamhosein Karbaschi (mayor of Tehran), Abdollah Nuri (minister of the interior), and Mohsen Nurbakhsh (governor of the Central Bank of Iran). This faction's ideas and policies are supported by the newspapers *Hamshahri*, *Bahman*, and *Iran*.

The Islamic Leftists

The leftist faction in the Islamic Republic is formed mainly around an organization known as *Majma'-e Ruhaniyyun-e Mobarez* (MRM), or the Assembly of Combatant Clerics—a group that split from the conservative JRM in 1987. This faction is also known to dominate *Sazman-e Mojahedin-e Enqelab-e Eslami*, the Organization of the Crusaders of the Islamic Revolution.

Mohammad Khatami, the current president of Iran, is no doubt now the best-known figure affiliated with this faction. Other prominent figures include Mir Hosein Musavi (former prime minister), Behzad Nabavi (former minister), Musavi Ardebili (former head of the judiciary), and Mehdi Karrubi (former *Majles* Speaker).

The pro-Khatami faction has recently announced the formation of a new political party, called the Islamic Iran Participation Party. The newspaper *Khordad* seems to be publishing the views of this group.

OPPOSITION INSIDE THE COUNTRY

With the total absence of political parties until recently, no opposition party is recognized in Iran today. While a few political groups are tolerated, the rest are in exile. Those with some activity inside Iran include the Liberation

Movement of Iran (*Nahzat-i Azadi-ye Iran*) and circles close to it, as well as the National Front of Iran (*Jebhe-ye Melli-ye Iran*) and the Iranian Nation Party (*Hezb-e Mellat-e Iran*). A major part of opposition activity in Iran has been carried out by intellectual circles gathered around a few relatively independent journals and magazines and by independent writers, clergy, artists, and lawyers.

Liberation Movement of Iran (Nahzat-e Azadi-ye Iran)

The LMI, led by Ebrahim Yazdi (a minister in the postrevolutionary transitional government) has remained active since the revolution. It was founded by Mehdi Bazargan, the late Ayatollah Mahmud Taleqani, and others in 1957. They hoped the party, influenced by Shi'a Islam and European socialism, would show Islam's relevance to modern politics in a way the traditional *olama* could not. For years, this party and its publications have provided public criticism of Khomeini's policies. In the 1980 elections, Liberation Movement candidates won five seats; the party boycotted the 1984 elections. Bazargan sought to run for president in 1985 but was disqualified by the Council of Guardians. He did not oppose the formation of an Islamic Republic but wanted to reform it by persuasion and public protest, not violent action.

Ebrahim Yazdi became secretary-general of the party after Bazargan's death in 1995. LMI remains tolerated despite its criticism of the government, though several of its leaders have been frequently harassed or arrested. LMI and those circles close to it have tried to participate in different Iranian elections with very little success. Yazdi was arrested in late 1997 but was released on bail shortly thereafter without being charged. While calling for democracy, the rule of law, and free elections, the LMI currently supports the newly elected President Khatami against the conservative faction in the ruling coalition.

National Front of Iran (INF) (Jebheh-ye Melli-ye Iran)

The old National Front was not a political party as such but rather a coalition of parties opposed to the shah, originally formed in 1949 by Dr. Mohammad Mosadeq. Most National Front leaders were arrested after the fall of Mosadeq's government in 1953, and the movement was reconstituted as the National Resistance Movement. This, in turn, was banned by the government in 1956.

The new National Front was established in 1977 and played a relatively important role in the early days of the revolution. It was led by Karim Sanjabi until his death. Its ideology has been seen as secularist and slightly left-of-center; it was opposed to the establishment of an Islamic Republic. Support for the party has been drawn from professionals and the educated middle class. INF was led by the secular supporters of Mosadeq, notably Karim Sanjabi and Shahpur Bakhtiar. There was a rift between the two in the fall of 1978. Sanjabi concluded a pact with Khomeini, then in exile in Paris, to work together for the overthrow of the shah. He went on to become foreign minister in the first postrevolutionary government, although he resigned in April 1979. Bakhtiar, who did not oppose the idea of a constitutional monarchy, served as the last prime minister under the shah. The National Front expelled him from the party, and he left Iran in February 1979 after trying to prevent the return of Khomeini. He was assassinated in France a decade later.

Today, although INF is not officially recognized and is often harassed, the party continues its activities in Iran under the direction of a central council. Supporters of the party are also active in Western Europe and North America, where they publish several periodicals. While in the years following the revolution the party was squeezed out by the more radical groups, there still exists a moderate, centrist constituency for the program of the National Front. With the subsiding of the fervor for radical slogans and the gradual opening of the political arena, INF is expected to enlarge its constituency and increase its activities. Among the prominent members of the National Front coalition who are still close to the party are Daryoush Forouhar and his Iranian Nation Party (*Hezb-e Mellat-e Iran*), which has boycotted the presidential and *Majles* elections in the past.

OPPOSITION IN EXILE

There are many Iranian groups outside the country that oppose the current government in Iran. The opposition in exile remains, however, fragmented and is characterized by constantly shifting alliances. The programs of these groups span the political spectrum: from royalists who want to restore the Pahlavi family to the throne to those who argue for a constitutional monarchy to nationalists and leftists.

The National Iranian Resistance Movement, which aimed to establish a social democratic government, was the first exile group to be formed in Paris (in 1979) and was for a while one of the largest and best-funded groups. It was led by Shahpur Bakhtiar, who had long opposed the Shah, although the Shah chose him to be his last prime minister. Bakhtiar was tragically murdered in 1991 in Paris, following which the group seems to have disintegrated.

Royalist groups are primarily directed by the family of the late shah (who never abdicated) or his former top officials. Some support the return to the throne of the shah's son, who declared himself Reza Shah II upon reaching the age of 20 on October 31, 1980. Reza has pledged that as a constitutional monarch, he would reign but not rule. He has kept a low profile and spends most of his time in the United States and Europe. Many, however, doubt his capacity to lead.

The significance and membership of the once-powerful leftist parties have been severely reduced as a result of both the crackdown on their activities inside Iran and the collapse of the Soviet bloc. There are nevertheless several Iranian leftist groups that have kept presence through their publications in Western Europe and North America. Their platforms cover the entire leftist spectrum, from hard-line Stalinists and Maoists to those believing in socialism through parliamentary means. Many of these groups have been formed through split-offs from the Tudeh Party (the original postwar Communist party of Iran) or Fada'yan (originally *Sazman-e Cherik-ha-ye Fadai-ye Khalq-e Iran*), while others may be considered newer groups.

Organization of the Crusaders of the Iranian People (Sazman-e Mojahedin-e Khalq-e Iran)

With the leftist parties and royalists in disarray, the Mojahedin has become the most cohesive Iranian opposition group in exile. The Mojahedin was formed in 1966 and took up military operations in 1971. The group was a major force in the 1978-79 revolution. Following the revolution, however, the Mojahedin broke decisively with the clerical regime, on June 20, 1981, after authorities fired on a huge demonstration organized by the Mojahedin to protest the dismissal of President Bani Sadr by Khomeini.

The leader of the group Mas'ud Rajavi and President Bani Sadr were forced into exile in France and formed a short-lived coalition. Mojahedin continued its activities from Paris until the French government closed down its headquarters in 1986. Mojahedin's leadership as well as other party members moved to Iraq where they formed an army of several thousand fighters, responsible for unsuccessful attacks on the Iranian soil. Women are reported to constitute a majority in this army, which is under an all-female leadership council with Masud Rajavi's wife, Maryam Azdanlu Rajavi, as commander in chief. The Mojahedin has organized an extensive structure in Western Europe and North America to lobby European governments and members of the U.S. Congress against the clerical regime in Iran.

The Mojahedin was a respected organization in Iran because of its long guerrilla struggle against the shah. Its ideology, emphasizing Shi'a Islam, socialism, and Iranian nationalism, proved to have strong appeal to the lower classes that made the revolution. However, this appeal has been seriously compromised because of disillusionment with the group's leaders who have built personality cults around themselves, its violent tactics that kill civilians, its ties with Iraq, and the apparent lack of a viable platform. The Mojahedin, nevertheless, remains a threat to the clerical regime because of their Iraq-based fighters and its well-organized structure in

Western Europe and North America. The party's prospects are not bright, however, considering the shrinking number of supporters of the Mojahedin inside Iran and the possibility of a real rapprochement between the governments of Iran and Iraq.

OTHER POLITICAL FORCES

Shi'a Clergy

The clerical group has been estimated to include 300,000 persons, a large number of whom are lower-ranking clergy active on a local level, preaching in mosques throughout the country and providing religious leadership and education. Middle- and higher-ranking clerics are called *mojtahids*. The title *hojjatoleslam* ("proof of Islam") is below the rank of ayatollah ("sign of God"), of which there are thought to be about 100 at present. The highest-ranking ayatollahs are called grand ayatollahs, of which there are only a few.

The ranks of the Shi'a clergy, and the number of mosques, have swelled since the revolution. Formerly, low-ranking mullahs were not held in high esteem, but now they have achieved new power and prestige. Before the revolution there were about 10,000 theological students in Iran; today their numbers have increased severalfold, two-thirds of them in Qom.

The image of the Iranian *olama* generally conveyed by the foreign media is that of a fanatically intolerant, monolithic establishment. This image, however, is misleading, for it does not take into account the serious personal and ideological disagreements that characterize intraclergy politics.

Khamenei is not a grand ayatollah and therefore cannot be a *marja'* (source of emulation) for Shi'a Moslems. To justify his position as leader, the constitution was changed in 1989 to separate the office of political leadership from that of the *marja'*. This change, however, goes against the spirit of Khomeini's conception of *Velayat-e Faqih* (the rule of the jurist) that is supposedly the basis of the postrevolutionary government. At the same time as Khamenei was appointed by the Council of Experts to the position of political leadership, Grand Ayatollah Araki was chosen as *marja'* (the highest religious authority).

With the death of Araki and a few other grand ayatollahs in the early 1990s, the problem of *marjaiyyat* (the position of the source of emulation) has been brought to the forefront once again. Of the clerics with credentials to be *marja'*, almost none seems to be on good terms with the low- and middle-ranking clergymen who control Iran.

Recently, Ayatollah Montazeri has challenged the establishment by questioning the credentials of Khamenei as leader. Montazeri's office was attacked in response, and demonstrations against him were staged in front of his residence in Qom. Several high-ranking clerics and several leading political and religious figures support Montazeri. The outcome of this struggle and the inherent contradiction in the present ruling arrangement have important implications for the fate of the regime.

Military

The two shahs of the Pahlavi dynasty were both authoritarian figures closely identified with the military. They pampered it and used it as their primary instrument for modernizing the nation and asserting central control from Tehran. Before the revolution, the shah's armed forces (413,000 men in uniform, plus 300,000 reserves) were equipped with the best military hardware available. This formidable force was, however, impotent during the revolution. Afterward, the officer corps was discredited for having supported the shah, and many high-ranking officers were executed or imprisoned or fled the country, and Iran's military was severely weakened.

The clerical rulers continued to mistrust the army, which they considered foreign-oriented. In order to protect itself from a potential coup d'état, the Islamic regime created the Revolutionary Guards (*pasdaran*) as a counterweight to the army. After Iraq's invasion of Iran and the ensuing eight-year war, the Revolutionary Guards grew enormously. The Leader is the commander in chief and supervises both forces.

Today, the *pasdaran* is structured much like the army with its own ground, air, and naval forces. It has a draft, just like the regular army. All males are required to register for military service at the age of 18 for two years, unless they enter university, in which case they serve after obtaining their degree. At present, the regular armed forces consist of 400,000 men, while the Revolutionary Guards are composed of 120,000 men. Due to demographic changes, Iran's armed forces will be inflated in the future since more men are drafted each year than discharged.

The *pasdaran* also control the *basij* (mobilization) forces, which is a large volunteer force (formed in November 1979) used primarily as unpaid guards. The regime is increasingly trying to transform this group from that of a revolutionary force to a civilian one.

Ironically, the regime at times has had trouble controlling the *pasdaran*. The Revolutionary Guards are known to interfere in politics, usually on the side of the conservatives, despite a clear legal ban on doing so.

Foundations

One of the most powerful political forces of postrevolutionary Iran are the quasi-governmental public foundations (*bonyads*). These parastatal organizations have grown into major political and economic nodes of power in the Islamic Republic. With immense financial means at their disposal, some foundations are known to have created and implemented their own policy agenda, including aiding radical groups outside the country. Two foundations deserve particular attention.

The Foundation of the Deprived and the War Veterans (*Bonyad-e Mostaz'afan va Janbazan*) was created atop a number of prerevolutionary foundations. This organization not only inherited the riches of the Pahlavi Foundation, it also took charge of the properties and businesses confiscated by revolutionary courts. The Foundation of the Deprived is currently Iran's richest financial institution and controls a lion's share of the country's economic activity. Said to be the richest foundation in the world, it is headed by Mohsen Rafiqdust, the former head of the Revolutionary Guards and a powerful ally of the conservative forces in Iran. Numerous charges of corruption have been leveled against this organization, and while no one has yet dared to accuse Rafigdust himself, his brother was tried and convicted for the embezzlement of hundreds of millions of dollars.

The 15th of Khordad Foundation (*Bonyad-e Panzdah-e Khordad*) is best known for having placed a bounty on the head of Salman Rushdie, the famous British author of Indian descent against whom Khomeini issued a *fatwa*. This organization is well known for its militant-Islamic ideology and is led by Hasan Sanei, one of the most radical figures in Iran today. Sanei was recently included in the expanded Expediency Council. Some analysts see this move as an attempt to integrate Sanei and the 15th of Khordad Foundation within the system and essentially make the organization more accountable.

Bazaris

Historically, a significant political force in Iran has been the merchants of the *bazar* (bazaar), or *bazaris*. The *bazar* refers to a nationwide network of merchants and shops that has long played a key role in financing the clerical establishment, including Islamic schools and social welfare activities.

Bazaris played a crucial role in organizing antiregime demonstrations in 1978. Following the success of the revolution, many *bazaris* were able to grab high positions in the newly formed government. Retaining their traditional merchant mentality, they turned many of the state agencies into huge profiteering centers that have been in direct competition with the traditional *bazar*, so that the *bazar* has lost much of its former social and economic importance. The establishment of trading houses within ministries has also accelerated this trend. As a result, the traditional hostility of the *bazar* toward the government, which has persisted for more than a century, may again assert itself.

Intelligentsia

Under the previous regime, a rather large group of modern intelligentsia arose. Such people did not hold the Moslem clergy in esteem, although some were religious (e.g., Mehdi Bazargan). They included those who supported the regime and its modernizing efforts as well as those who opposed it, including the liberals, the leftists, and the religious-liberals. The former group constituted the elite in the country and included top military leaders. While the intelligentsia was instrumental in the revolution, it hoped that the new government would be a liberal, if not secular, regime. As a result, the intelligentsia became a favorite target for removal by the postrevolutionary regime after the failure of the transitional government of Bazargan. Many fled abroad (one estimate places the number at 1 million).

With the presence of general restriction on political activity, the secular and the liberal-religious intelligentsia has directed its activities toward cultural and social issues. Several magazines and journals are published in Iran today by this group. These include *Iran-e Farda*, *Goft-o-Gu*, *Asr-e Ma*, *Jame'e-ye Salem*, and *Kiyan*, as well as a host of others in specialized fields.

In general, as a result of unequal opportunities, liberal-religious intellectuals have been more active in Iran than their secular peers since the revolution. While secular intellectuals have been confined to literary or nonpolitical cultural activities, the liberal-religious intelligentsia has entered into important debates on the role of religion in the government and on the new, liberal interpretations of Islam.

While the liberal-religious intelligentsia has dominated the intellectual scene for now, the importance of secular intellectuals should not be discounted. They have the potential to be much more active once a less-restrictive atmosphere prevails. The secular intelligentsia has nevertheless had a big part in demanding more freedoms of speech and pen.

Organized Labor

Trade unions as such do not now exist in Iran. In the earlier part of the century, workers and employers were united in traditional guilds. Between 1945 and 1953, several trade unions were formed, particularly in Tehran and the oilfields, and there were many strikes. However, from 1953 until 1979, any attempt to organize a labor movement was strongly suppressed. After 1959, the government permitted the formation of "official" trade unions, which were not allowed to strike or engage in political activity (unless it was to support the regime). There were about 1,000 such unions by 1978. They were not industrywide but were confined to single factories.

After the fall of the monarchy, many factory owners fled the country and workers took over the factories, which they ran through workers' councils. The postrevolutionary regime has generally taken an ambivalent position toward the workers' councils. With the worsening of the economic situation, many labor strikes have been recorded in the country and have been crushed by the government to prevent further escalation of labor activity. Today, two government-sanctioned, national labor organizations are present in Iran, the House of Workers and the Islamic Society of Workers, with the latter established to counterbalance the former.

Youth

With the rise of the fertility rate in the years following the revolution, Iran has experienced a drastic demographic change. As a result, over half of the country's population either was born after the revolution or has no recollection of the prerevolutionary period and the revolutionary struggle. While the clerical regime has tried its best to educate the youth to its own liking, this group constitutes a disaffected and potentially antagonistic force. With Iran's high unemployment rate and very unpopular social restrictions placed on youth, the government will not be able to satisfy the demands of this segment of the society. Their aspirations were apparent during Iran's last presidential election, in which those young people who could vote became a major force behind Khatami's victory.

University Students

While students in Iran played a prominent role in the ouster of the shah, the extent of their support for the postrevolutionary regime has been at best uncertain. After the 1978–79 revolution, university campuses remained a major scene of political activity. As a result, all colleges and universities were closed in the spring of 1980 in the wake of rioting. They reopened in 1983 after developing a new "Islamic curriculum." Preference is given for entrance to those with a "correct" political and religious background and to war veterans.

Students in today's Iran constitute a large and disaffected group. There is severe competition to matriculate, and upon acceptance, there are many restrictions on behavior and political activity. The government has responded to the problem of space availability by establishing the semiprivate, low-quality Islamic Open University, which has branches in many large and small towns. Since the only possible line of political activity on Iran's university campuses has been through the Islamic student associations, secular students have been severely restricted.

Islamic student associations themselves have recently become platforms for voices of protest in several cases. Many such organizations have invited liberal-religious intellectuals to deliver speeches. As a result, there have been a number of confrontations between such groups and the conservative, government-sponsored students who, with the help of the mob, have tried to prevent such gatherings. As part of this trend, Heshmat Tabarzadi, the secretary-general of the Union of Students' Islamic Association and the editor of the weekly *Payam-e Daneshju* (Students' Message) was fined and banned from working at any publication for five years. In a recent rally, he called for a curtailment of the powers of the supreme Leader, Ayatollah Ali Khamenei, in line with a democratic society. This provoked a physical attack on him by the proregime mob.

Women

Although Iranian women were a major force in the revolution of 1978–79, they became a main target of restriction once the Islamic regime was established. They were forced to cover their hair and dress modestly in public and were encouraged to limit their role in the society to that of housewives. Some university majors and government positions were rendered off-limits to women. Several laws, which previously protected the rights of women in the family, were revoked or modified.

These major setbacks have not remained unchallenged. The major challenge has come from both the women who essentially believe in the regime and those who have adopted an Islamic discourse to fight for women's rights. Women's magazines such as *Zanan* and *Zan-e Ruz* have increasingly used religious texts to call for a change or a new interpretation of laws. As a result of these and other efforts by women's organizations, female *Majles* deputies, and other women close to the ruling elite, and independent women's rights advocates, some of the mentioned restrictions have been lifted. All academic subjects are now accessible to women, and a better law (although still far from just) to protect the rights of women in marriage was passed in 1992. More recently, a female vice president has been appointed by the newly elected President Khatami and the previous ban on women becoming judges has been lifted. Women were a major force behind the election of Khatami and will, without any doubt, increase their political participation and continue the fight for their rights in the future.

Minority Religious Groups

About 90% of the people of Iran adhere to the Twelver Shi'a branch of Islam. The minority religious groups include Sunni Moslems, Bahais, Christians (of different churches), Jews, Zoroastrians, and a few other sects within Shi'ism. Under the previous regime, there existed a general atmosphere of religious tolerance. As a result, the members of most minority religions were very apprehensive at the prospect of a militant Shi'a regime coming to power following the 1978–79 revolution, and their fears were justified.

According to the new Iranian constitution, Zoroastrians, Jews, and Christians are the only recognized non-Moslem minorities and are to be left free to follow their religious precepts. These minority religions have traditionally been protected in Moslem societies, which regard their members as "People of the Book." In Iran, they are represented in the parliament as follows: Zoroastrians and Jews, as minorities, each have one representative; the Assyrian and Chaldean Christians, together, have one representative, and the Armenian Christians of the north and south each have one representative. There is a provision for a small increase in representation, should their numbers increase.

The Bahais, probably the largest non-Moslem minority (over 300,000), are generally reviled by the regime for being apostates from Islam and are not recognized as a legitimate religious group. They are not mentioned in the constitution and have no seat in the parliament. Since their faith was founded in Iran in 1863, the Bahais were subject to intense persecution. Under the previous regime, however, they enjoyed relative freedom; and many high officials in the government were believed to be Bahais.

Ethnic Groups

As in many other nations, the question of what constitutes a distinct ethnic group in Iran is difficult to answer. A combination of language, religion, and cross-border proximity of similar groups seems to determine a group's self-identification as a distinct ethnicity in Iran. Most Iranians speak an Iranian language (Persian, Kurdish languages and dialects, Luri and Bakhtiari dialects, Caspian coast dialects, and Baluchi dialects), which is a subgroup of the Indo-European family of languages. Persian is the most important member of this subfamily and is the official language of Iran. It is also one of the two official languages of Afghanistan and the official language of Tajikistan. Persian is spoken as a first language by approximately 60% of Iranians. The rest speak either a Turkic tongue (Azerbaijani, Turkoman) or a Semitic language (Arabic, neo-Syriac) or Armenian (a non-Iranian Indo-European language).

Within this plurality, those people who do not speak Persian as a first language, live in bordering areas, or do not adhere to the majority religion, while Iranian, may feel remote from urban Persian culture. Some, in particular Kurdish and Baluchi Iranians, have desired autonomy within Iran, although in most cases not actual independence. They have their own political parties, and both have armed factions in Iran opposing the regime. Government warfare against the Kurdis rebels was carried out at the same time as the war against Iraq.

The main political party supported by the Kurds has been the Kurdish Democratic Party, which was led by Abdorrahman Qasemlu until his assassination. The party slogan is "Democracy for Iran, Autonomy for the Kurds." The other Kurdish group, the Kumala, has been important in urban areas, especially Sanandaj. The Fada'yan has also had a Kurdish section. The Baluch Liberation Movement was also allied with the Fada'yan minority group.

While Turkmans and Arabs may desire some autonomy as well, they have been less organized due to various historical reasons. Azerbaijani-speakers are the largest linguistic group in Iran after Persian-speakers. While speaking a Turkic language, which is similar to the official language of the neighboring republic of Azerbaijan, they are well integrated within the Iranian society and constitute a considerable part of the country's elite.

A significant percentage of ethnic groups still profess some degree of affiliation to an *il*, which can be defined as an organized transhuman or sedentary pastoralist group based on kinship relations, formerly under the leadership of an *Ilkhani*. There are, however, no accurate figures on *ils*' populations, and calculation is difficult because many people who may ethnically belong to an *il* now live in urban areas.

Most *ils* have not played a significant role in national politics since the early part of the 20th century, and this fact does not seem likely to change. They had a long history of hostility toward the Pahlavi regime, which attempted, with some success, to integrate them into a modern state by disarming and settling them and forcing them into the state educational and military systems. The present regime, like the monarchy, represents an urban, centralized Persian government and seeks in similar ways to extend central control to *ili* areas. While the general climate of the first postrevolutionary decade was conducive to the political involvement of the *ils*, with the subsequent consolidation of the regime, most activities of this kind have subsided.

NATIONAL PROSPECTS

After two decades of instability due to revolutionary turmoil and war, the clerical regime has consolidated its control over the country. Early predictions that the regime would collapse as a result of war, isolation, or mismanagement were not realized. Even Khomeini's death did not bring about the fall of the Islamic Republic. However, the clerical establishment is increasingly obliged to open up in order not to give way under its own weight. The increased divisions within the ranks of the ruling coalition have provided fertile ground in which political parties formed by the regime's factions may flourish, and it also has created breathing space for Iran's civil society.

Following the landslide victory of Mohammad Khatami, who was backed by an alliance between the new Islamic leftists and the pragmatists, three competing nodes of power have emerged in the regime. The group with tendencies toward liberalization, the rule of law, reduction of social restrictions, ending Iran's isolation, and technocracy is identified with Khatami. While Khamenei can be considered the leading proponent of conservative ideas

and policies, former president Rafsanjani has placed himself in a mediating and sensitive position. Considering that Rafsanjani has been the most important actor since Khomeini's death, it is expected that the Expediency Council, which he now heads, will grow steadily in power and importance.

Essentially, the Khamenei-Rafsanjani duet, which defined post-Khomeini Iran, is now replaced by a trio consisting of Khatami, Khamenei, and Rafsanjani. Khamenei remains the figure to whom the traditional forces in Iranian society, especially the *bazaris*, can relate. Khatami has given the youth a new ray of hope. Rafsanjani should also keep his appeal to moderate clergy and technocratic elements. However, since many of the supporters of the pragmatists are now drawn to Khatami, we can expect Rafsanjani to move slightly closer to the conservative camp in order to broaden his base of appeal.

While these three figures have emerged as the dominant players, it is less certain which one holds ultimate decision-making powers on any given issue. It remains to be seen how much power Khatami can retain in the executive position and what authorities he can reserve for himself. It is certain that while Khatami maintains overwhelming support of the majority of Iranians, the conservative forces will be careful in dealing with him. That in no way means that the Khatami era spells the end for the conservative forces in Iran; they will remain influential.

A major item on Khatami's agenda has been to reduce Iran's isolation. Since his election, he has tried to foster improved relations with Iran's neighboring countries as well as the nations of Western Europe. He has even taken the bold step of initiating talks with the United States.

On the domestic scene, Khatami has the mandate to establish the rule of law, guarantee freedom of expression as specified in the constitution, and ease cultural restrictions. Any move on Khatami's part to fulfill these promises will, on the one hand, be met with opposition from the conservatives and, on the other hand, provide more space to those who challenge the institution of *velayat-e faqih*. Therefore, we can expect increased factional friction in the future.

The true challenge to the Islamic Republic in the future is the booming population, rapid urbanization, low oil prices, and other major blocks to economic development. The government is currently having difficulty meeting the day-to-day needs of the masses. Unemployment and inflation are rampant. The Islamic regime will feel the full severity of these problems as the population born after the 1979 revolution enter the economy. Coupled with the gradual opening of the political arena, this will result in the reemergence of the forces with nationalist and secular agendas in Iran that can increasingly challenge the country's ruling coalition.

Further Reading

Azimi, Fakhredin. "On Shaky Ground: Concerning the Absence or Weakness of Political Parties in Iran." *Iranian Studies* 30, nos. 1–2 (winter/spring 1997).

Bayat, Asef. *Street Politics: Poor People's Movements in Iran.* New York: Columbia University Press, 1997.

Buroujerdi, Mehrzad. *Iranian Intellectuals and the West: The Tormented Triumph of Nativism.* Syracuse, N.Y.: Syracuse University Press, 1996.

Ehteshami, Anoushiravan. *After Khomeini: The Iranian Second Republic.* New York: Routledge, 1995.

Heiss, Mary Ann. *Empire and Nationhood : The United States, Great Britain, and Iranian Oil, 1950–1954.* New York: Columbia University Press, 1997.

Isfandiyari, Halah. *Reconstructed Lives : Women and Iran's Islamic Revolution.* Baltimore: Johns Hopkins University Press, 1997.

Lyle, Garry, and Sandra Stotksy. *Iran* (Major World Nations). New York: Chelsea House, 1997.

Rahnema, Saeed, and Sohrab Behdad, eds. *Iran after the Revolution: Crisis of an Islamic State.* London and New York: I.B. Tauris, 1995.

Schirazi, Asghar. :*The Constitution of Iran : Politics and the State in the Islamic Republic.* Trans. John O'Keene. London: I.B. Tauris, 1997.

REPUBLIC OF IRAQ

(Al-Jumhuriyya al–'Iraqiyya)

By Reeva S. Simon, Ph.D.

THE SYSTEM OF GOVERNMENT

Iraq, a nation of over 21 million people, is a one-party unitary socialist state. The current regime came to power on July 17, 1968, after a Ba'thist coup led by General Ahmad Hasan al-Bakr. Today Saddam Hussein, president and prime minister of Iraq, rules through the Ba'th Party and members of his family whom he has appointed to key positions in the government and security apparatuses.

Executive

The president of the republic is the head of state and government and the chairman of the Revolutionary Command Council (RCC) of the Ba'th (Renaissance) party—the "supreme organ of the state." He is elected by a two-thirds majority vote of the RCC from among its members. There are no provisions in the constitution for the term of the office of president, but he must be a native-born Iraqi. If the president is absent or incapacitated, his duties are taken over by the vice chairman of the RCC, who (also) is elected from among its members.

In 1979 Saddam Hussein replaced Ahmad Hasan al-Bakr as president. Today, he holds the posts of chairman of the RCC, secretary-general of the Ba'th Party, prime minister, commander in chief of the military, and head of internal security. In 1995 Saddam was confirmed by national referendum as president for seven more years.

The head of state exercises power directly or through a Council of Ministers that he appoints. By convention, this Cabinet has consisted of one-third Ba'th Party members who hold the key portfolios. As a result of the Shi'i uprising in 1991 in the aftermath of the Persian Gulf War, Saddam has appointed more Shi'i to the Cabinet on which he has imposed the function of implementing domestic policy and taking responsibility for those policies in order to deflect popular discontent away from the president. Cabinet positions are reshuffled frequently as military and domestic policies, especially in the economic sector, have not met with success.

First established in July 1968, the Revolutionary Command Council was to be the top decision-making body of the state, whose mission is to carry out the popular will and the tenets of the Ba'th Party: "unity, freedom, and socialism." Individual members of the RCC are answerable only to the Council of Ministers as a whole, which can dismiss an RCC member by a two-thirds vote. It can send to trial any member of the RCC, any deputy to the president, or any Cabinet minister. In September 1977, a constitutional amendment stipulated that all members of the Ba'th Party regional command were to be regarded as members of the RCC, increasing the membership of the RCC from the original 5 members to 22. Since 1979 the number has been changed to fit political circumstance.

The president also operates through the RCC, whose functions are executive and legislative. The RCC approves government recommendations concerning national defense and internal security. It declares war, orders general mobilization, concludes peace, ratifies treaties and agreements, approves the general budget of the state, sets rules for the impeachment of RCC members, and can set up a special court to try the impeached. The RCC can authorize the chairman or the vice chairman to exercise some of its powers, except for legislative ones. The chairman of the RCC, who is also the president, signs all laws and decrees issued by the RCC and supervises the work of the Cabinet ministers and operations of state institutions. Approved by the National Assembly and popular referendum and ratified by the president in 1990, a new constitution allowing for the creation of a Consultative Assembly to assume the duties of the RCC (which would be abolished after the constitution's approval) has not been implemented.

Legislature

The provisional constitution of 1970 provided for the election of the National Assembly, but elections did not take place until 1980. The government amended the constitution in July 1973 to provide for an assembly of 100 members to be selected by the RCC, and again in 1979 to provide for an assembly of 250 members elected by secret ballot every four years. Elections were held in 1980, 1984, 1989, and 1996. In all of them more than half the members elected belonged to the Ba'th Party.

According to the constitution, the National Assembly's members are elected proportionally, one deputy for every 50,000 citizens, to a four-year term. Those elected have tended to be young (approximately 40 years of age), from low socioeconomic backgrounds, and with more than a high school education.

The National Assembly, which technically shares legislative powers with the RCC, can introduce and pass laws, approve treaties and international agreements, and discuss domestic and foreign policy and is empowered to question ministers and propose their dismissal to the RCC. However, it has no veto power, cannot interfere in matters of defense and internal security, and cannot question RCC members. A dispute between the Assembly and the RCC over the Assembly's rejection of an amendment is resolved by a two-thirds majority of the combined membership of the two bodies sitting in a joint session.

The National Assembly provides a semblance of popular participation in government and acts as an agent of legitimization for the one-man rule of Saddam Hussein, who uses it as a platform for his policy announcements. In September 1980, for example, the president used the Assembly to announce the abrogation of the 1975 treaty with Iran, thus initiating the Iraq-Iran War.

Judiciary

The highest court is the Court of Cassation, which is the court of last resort. It has a president, a vice president, no fewer than 15 permanent members, deputized judges, reporting judges, and religious judges. In addition to being the court of last appeal, the Court of Cassation has original jurisdiction over crimes committed by high government officials, including judges. Within its organization, the Penal Body, consisting of 3 judges, is the highest court for criminal matters. It does not try cases of offenses against the state, which are defined as security matters and are tried by the Revolutionary Court.

The Revolutionary Court consists of 3 judges who sit permanently in Baghdad. Crimes against the security of the state include economic and political crimes such as trade in narcotics, rebellion, and espionage. The sessions are held in camera, and there is no appeal. After the attempted coups against the regime in 1970 and in 1973, and after the riots in Najaf and Karbala in 1977, the RCC established temporary tribunals to try large numbers of security offenders. These trials wwere presided over by three or four high government officials who were not bound by the ordinary provisions of criminal law and who meted out swift, severe decisions.

Regional and Local Government

Iraq is divided into 19 administrative provinces, each under a governor appointed by the president. The provinces are divided into districts and districts into subdistricts, headed respectively by district officers and subdistrict officers.

Cities and towns are headed by mayors. All chief administrative officers except those of minor cities and towns are apointed by the president. Baghdad, the capital, has a special status.

Although the government's National Action Charter of November 15, 1971, mentions "popular councils" as a means to narow the gap between the government and the people, by 1979, as far as could be determined, these councils existed only in Baghdad, in other major cities, and in a few of the smaller administrative units. Their members seem to be government-appointed, and their function is to channel popular grievances and needs to the proper authorities, as well as educating and encouraging the people to support Ba'th government policies.

THE ELECTORAL SYSTEM

The June 20, 1980, elections were the first since the 1958 overthrow of the monarchy. A government order of March 1980 authorized the elections to the National Assembly by secret ballot under direct universal suffrage. At least 840 candidates stood for election in 250 electoral districts. Nominations were open to all but Communists and property owners. A special election committee screened the candidates to certify that they were civilian native Iraqis whose father or mother was born in Iraq and were not "bourgeois capitalists." Any military personnel who wished to run had to resign from the military, since the Iraqi government stresses the authority of the civilian sector over the military. Although one of the provisions for candidacy was that a candidate had to believe in the principles of the July 17 Revolution, he or she did not have to be a Ba'th Party member. Of the 250 representatives elected, some 175 were Ba'th Party members; 8 were women. In the elections of 1996, 160 Ba'th Party members were elected to the 220-seat National Assembly.

ARAB SOCIALIST BA'TH (RENAISSANCE) PARTY
(Hizb Al-Ba'th Al-'Arabi Al-Ishtiraki)

HISTORY

The Ba'th Party in Iraq is a regional branch of the Arab Socialist Ba'th Party, which was established in the 1940s in Damascus, Syria, by Michel Aflaq and Salah al-Bitar. Its secular ideology combines socialism with Arab unity—the union of the Arab states into one Arab entity. Iraqi students, inspired by the Syrian leaders, founded a local party in Iraq. Early supporters were primarily high school and college students, with some army officers, most of them urban Sunni Arabs. Some early members who were to play leading political roles in the party were

Ahmad Hasan al-Bakr, Salih Mahdi Ammash, and Saddam Hussein. Ahmad Hasan al-Bakr emerged as head of the military wing of the party, while Saddam Hussein led the civilian wing.

The Iraqi Ba'th played a minor role in the 1958 coup that overthrew the Iraqi monarchy, and the party at first supported the coup leader, Abd al-Karim Qasim. In 1959, however, because of the regime's support of the Communists, Ba'thists participated in an attempted assassination of Qasim. The party was suppressed, and Saddam Hussein, one of the plotters, was exiled. In February 1963, leading members of the party led the Ba'th to power, overthrowing Qasim. Shortly after the coup, the Syrian Ba'thists also came to power in that country. The party's national command and the Syrian regional command were located in Damascus. The Iraqi regional command was seated in Baghdad.

In November 1963, a non-Ba'thist military coup, led by 'Abd al-Salam Arif, ousted the Ba'th government. Arif's coup was possible because of the disintegration of the Ba'th Party; party moderates influenced by Arif—including Talib Shabib and Hazim Jawad—had been expelled. The leader of the Marxist wing of the Ba'th, 'Ali Salah Saadi, also severed ties with the Ba'th and formed the Arab Revolutionary Workers Party.

In early 1966, the radical wing of the Syrian Ba'th overthrew the Syrian government of General Amin al-Hafez, which had been supported by Salah al-Bitar, and established a rival national command in Damascus. Ahmad Hasan al-Bakr and Saddam Hussein remained faithful to the leadership of al-Bitar and Aflaq, who moved to Baghdad in 1966. On July 17, 1968, al-Bakr and Saddam Hussein in conjunction with non-Ba'th army officers overthrew the government of Abd al-Rahman Arif. Three weeks later, the Ba'thists took complete control, purging the non-Ba'thist officers.

Bakr and Saddam dominated the RCC after purging the top echelons of the party in the early 1970s. Additional purges in 1977 left only Saddam's close associates in the Baghdad national command and in the RCC. In 1978 there was an extensive purge of the middle ranks of the party. On July 16, 1979, Bakr resigned for reasons of health and Saddam Hussein took over full control. Following an attempted coup by the military wing of the Ba'th two weeks later, Saddam purged the armed forces and reshuffled the RCC, five of whose members were tried and executed for their alleged involvement in a Syrian Ba'thist plot. Saddam used the abortive coup as a pretext to attempt to concentrate his power by appointing relatives and close friends from his hometown, Tikrit, to nearly all key offices. By the mid-1990s, members of his immediate and extended family held these posts.

From 1979 to 1991 the party became less significant as Saddam devoted his attention to concentrating all power in his own hands. Party membership included approximately 1.5 million in a population of some 17 million Iraqis. Interest in joining the party declined as it became a vehicle for career advancement in the bureaucracy or the military, where most of the growth in membership occurred. In 1991 after the Gulf War, Saddam decided to revitalize the party by providing members with economic benefits, holding party congresses, and publicizing the importance of the Ba'th. It remains a shadowy presence devoid of any real power.

ORGANIZATION

As a political party, the Ba'th is highly structured, disciplined, and elitist. The basic unit of the party is the cell or circle (*khalwa*), followed by the section (*firqa*), the branch (*shu'ba*), and the major branch (*far*). The cell is an urban living quarter or a village. A few sections form a branch, which is usually a small town, while a major branch comprises an entire district or a large city. The districts are represented in the party's regional command, whose 16 members compose the core of the party leadership. Although members of the regional command are supposed to be elected by a regional congress that is to meet annually to discuss and approve policy, they are, in reality, chosen by Saddam Hussein.

Party influence emanates from Baghdad, and the party penetrates into every segment of society. Party cadres are in the government, in rural and urban mass organizations, and in the army. Their role is to educate and indoctrinate, to provide guidance according to the party's principles and policies, to improve the party's image, and to monitor the activities of various groups so that infractions can be corrected. Party members attend regular meetings for ideological discussions and participate in general "popular" activity such as the construction of houses and the eradication of illiteracy. The party is portrayed as the intermediary between the state and people, the true advocate of the people, and the conduit through which grievances are channeled. The party fosters professional organizations for lawyers, doctors, and teachers and has organized peasants, women, and youth.

The daily newspaper, *al-Thawra* (Revolution), is the organ of the Ba'th Party. The English-language daily *Baghdad Observer* is state-sponsored. *Babil*, the only new newspaper to appear in more than two decades of Ba'thi rule, is operated by Saddam's son, 'Uday, the heir apparent. Created ostensibly to provide a critical voice, it operates as a mouthpiece for Saddam and the ruling family.

POLICY

The economic orientation of the Ba'th Party is socialism. Once in power, the party nationalized the Iraq Petroleum Company in June 1972, and by 1975 all foreign interests in the IPC were eliminated. Petroleum revenues were used to finance Iraq's economic plan that emphasized industrialization, agricultural and military self-sufficiency, and social welfare. These programs ceased at the end of the Gulf War with the imposition of the oil embargo and economic sanctions against Iraq. Because of the resulting economic hardship, Saddam has soft-pedaled the socialist content of the party ideology and promoted the institution of a stock market and a more capitalist approach toward agriculture. Shifts of population from rural to urban areas have caused reorientations in the government's agricultural program. Saddam Hussein encourages people to return to the farm, and the government offers plots and subsidies to farmers.

The Ba'th Party is opposed to "imperialism, Zionism, and reactionary forces." It espoused nonalignment, and Baghdad was scheduled to host the nonaligned nations' conference in September 1982 but withdrew when a number of nations said they would boycott the conference in protest over the war with Iran. Of late, there has been less emphasis on Arab unity and more on the uniquely Iraqi nature of the party. Saddam has also incorporated Islamic values and education into party ideology, despite his policies of the 1970s and 1980s that insisted on separation of religion and politics in order to protect his regime from the threats of both Shi'i and Sunni Islamist groups. To that end, the regime created the "Committee on Muslim Youth" and has undertaken to construct new mosques.

Iraq's relations with the Soviet Union have undergone a series of shifts as a result of the protracted war with Iran. Before the war, the April 1972 Treaty of Friendship and Cooperation and another agreement signed between the two countries in December 1978, whereby Iraq received arms and technical aid in return for allowing the Iraqi Communist Party to participate in a National Front, created links between the two nations. However, Saddam did not hesitate to purge Communists from the army. In 1980 Iraq denounced the Soviet invasion of Afghanistan and Soviet activities against "Arab Somalia" in the Horn of Africa. At first the Soviet Union, along with France, was the main supplier of armaments to Iraq for use against Iran. Concerned about its dependence on Soviet aid, Iraq sought increased contacts with the West. With the fall of the Soviet Union, Russia's later support for the coalition in the Gulf War, and the imposed economic and military sanctions against Iraq, the Ba'thist regime has been isolated in the international community.

Trade with the United States and imports from Europe and Japan increased in the mid-1970s. Since 1977 arms sales increased from France, which provided Iraq with Mirage combat aircraft, tanks, and antitank missiles. France provided the nuclear reactor at Osirak that was destroyed by Israel in June 1981. By the end of the decade, concern was registered over an Iraqi arms buildup of chemical and biological weapons with components that were supplied by European companies. Trade

with Europe ceased after the Gulf War in 1991, but pressure is being exerted on the United Nations to lift the economic sanctions against Iraq.

Iraq is a founding member of both the Organization of Petroleum Exporting Countries (OPEC; 1960) and the Organization of Arab Petroleum Exporting Countries (OAPEC; 1968). For many years Iraq advocated higher crude prices, but in 1980 as part of Saddam's moderation policy, Iraq joined Saudi Arabia in its oil policy. In economic straits after the end of the Iraq-Iran War, Iraq protested that Kuwait was exceeding its oil production quotas and occupied the sheikhdom in August 1990, thus sparking the United Nations/United States–led coalition that defeated Iraq in the Persian Gulf War of 1991.

The Camp David Agreement (1978) and the fall of the Shah (1979) catapulted Iraq into a pivotal position in the Persian Gulf and the Arab world. Saddam Hussein saw Iraq as the likely successor to Egypt for leadership in the Arab world because of Iraq's population, wealth, military potential, and consistent espousal of the Palestinian cause. Iraq was a major "rejectionist" power and hosted the Baghdad summit conference against the Camp David Agreement. Since then, however, Iraq has shifted to a more moderate position, withdrawing support from the radical Palestine groups and giving it to Yasir Arafat's Palestine Liberation Organization, which supported Iraq in the Gulf War. Iraq resumed diplomatic relations with the United States in November 1984; they were severed in 1991 during the Gulf War.

Iraqi arms buildup and concerns over its chemical, biological, and nuclear arms production in 1990 led to a deterioration of relations with the West. With Iraqi occupation of Kuwait in August 1990 and deployment of troops on its border with Saudi Arabia, the United States, backed by the United Nations and a multinational coalition, stationed some 500,000 troops on Saudi soil for the defense of Saudi Arabia (Operation Desert Shield). Despite intense diplomatic activity to forestall war, Operation Desert Storm, war with Iraq for the liberation of Kuwait, commenced in January 1991. A full cease-fire was agreed to in April, and economic sanctions were placed on Iraq by the United Nations to force Saddam Hussein to disclose all of Iraq's nuclear, chemical, and biological capabilities.

Relations with Syria have been bitter since 1966. A brief rapprochement, despite conflicts over the use of the headwaters of the Euphrates River and competition for leadership of the national command of the Ba'th Party, began with the unity scheme proposed in October 1978 and ended in July 1979. Once Saddam took full control of the government, he disclosed that the plotters against the regime in July 1979 had contact with a "foreign power," namely Syria. Syria supported Iran during the Iraq-Iran War (1980–89).

The war with Iran was initiated by Iraq in September

1980. A basic cause of the war was attempts by the new Shi'i Muslim regime in Iran to arouse the majority Shi'i population of Iraq against the secular Ba'th government. Baghdad also hoped to take advantage of Iran's domestic turmoil to nullify the 1975 Algiers agreement that gave the two countries an equal share in the Shatt al-Arab waterway located between them. Pursued in phases, the war involved attacks on shipping in the Gulf, bombardment of cities, and mass attacks against enemy territory. In 1984 and 1986, Iran refused to engage in talks unless the Iraqi regime was removed. In July 1988, Iran accepted United Nations Security Council Resolution 598 urging an immediate cease-fire, return to recognized boundaries, and mediation toward achieving a peace settlement. In 1990 Iran and Iraq resumed diplomatic relations.

LEADERSHIP

When they took power, RCC members were in their 30s and 40s. The leaders of the party are Arab Sunni, from lower-middle-class families, whose origins are in the small towns northwest of Baghdad, notably the town of Tikrit. Many RCC members are related by marriage or by tribal origin. Saddam introduced more Shi'i Muslims into the RCC in order to ensure the loyalty of the Shi'i population in the conflict with Iran and to placate the Shi'i after their abortive uprising in 1991.

The two leaders to emerge in control of the Ba'th Party in the early 1970s were Ahmad Hasan al-Bakr and Saddam Hussein. Al-Bakr was born in Tikrit in 1914 and served as president from 1968 until he resigned in July 1979. Hussein was born in Tikrit in 1937. In control for the past two decades, Saddam Hussein has relied on power bases from within the Ba'th Party, the military, tribal affiliates, and, increasingly, his own immediate family despite the defection of his two sons-in-law to Jordan in 1995 and their return and subsequent execution a year later. The assassination attempt against Saddam's son, 'Uday, in December 1996 and his subsequent removal from public view leaves succession in doubt.

SATELLITE ORGANIZATIONS

In 1977 there were 13 trade unions with a total membership of some 900,000 members under the direct control of the Ba'th Party and are organized under a federation of unions. The function of trade unions is to mediate between labor and managment; there have been no strikes in Iraq since 1968. Saddam created the "Saddamist Union" in 1994. Headed by 'Uday, by the end of the year the union had enrolled more than 25,000 members, of whom some 15,000 were military personnel.

The paramilitary organizations are more significant. The People's Militia (al-Jay'ish al-Sha'bi) of the Ba'th Party was formed in 1970. In 1978 its estimated strength was 100,000. The original goal of the regime was a mili-

tia of 200,000 by 1980 to be organized in armed units in every town and village in Iraq. It is estimated that there were more than 500,000 militiamen in March 1981; the number expanded during the Iraq-Iran War.

The militia's functions are to protect the regime, to back up the regular armed forces in war, and to carry political indoctrination to the general population. Personnel are armed with light and medium arms including heavy machine guns and antitank weapons. They are positioned in cities and can be used to thwart any coup attempt. Evidence exists that the militia fought in 1975 against the Kurds and in Lebanon on the side of the Palestiniains. In the early 1980s it was used both on the Iranian and the Kurdish fronts. Before the Iraq-Iran War only party members over the age of 18 who had completed their army service were recruited for service in the militia. With the active participation of the militia in the war, recruitment increased and membership included foreign volunteers. During the political and economic instability that resulted from the Iraqi defeat in 1991, the People's Guard was created to safeguard property and maintain civil security.

The paramilitary youth organization for secondary school students is the *Futuwwah* (Youth Vanguard). Boys and girls from the ages of 14 to 18 are organized into youth platoons. The "Saddam Commando Division" was established in 1994.

OTHER POLITICAL FORCES

Kurds

The Kurds are non-Arab, Kurdish-speaking, Sunni tribesmen living primarily in the Irbil, al-Sulaimaniyya, and Kirkuk areas. Their claim to be a majority in Kirkuk is disputed by the government, which would like to minimize Kurdish claims to this oil area. The estimated 3 million Iraqi Kurds are part of a larger group of Kurds numbering from 10 to 25 million who inhabit an area divided among Turkey, the former Soviet Union, Syria, Iraq, and Iran. Since the emergence of Kurdish nationalism in the 20th century, the Kurds have been working for the establishment of an independent Kurdistan.

Under the Iraqi monarchy (1921–58) there were intermittent Kurdish uprisings against the government. At first, the Kurds supported Abd al-Karim Qasim (1958–63), but in 1961 they formally opposed the government when Qasim turned against them. After 1961 large-scale fighting ensued between the Kurds led by Mulla Mustafa Barzani and his *Pesh Merga* (Those Who Face Death) and the central government.

Ba'th policy has been to recognize Kurdish cultural rights while undertaking military offensives against the tribesmen. In March 1970 Barzani and Saddam Hussein agreed to autonomy for the Kurds; in July, a constitutional amendment recognized two principal nationalities in Iraq: Arab and Kurd. The Autonomy Plan of March 1974 granted the Kurds cultural autonomy, but the government simultaneously issued the Kurds an ultimatum to accept the plan. The Kurds refused, turning again to open rebellion.

The Iraqi army was not able to subdue the Kurds until the Ba'th reached an understanding with the shah of Iran. In March 1975 the two parties signed an agreement in Algiers that, in return for Iraqi concessions including the reestablishment of the Iraq-Iran border in the middle of the Shatt al-Arab waterway, the shah would stop supplying the Kurds. By April, the Iraqi army was able to break the rebellion. The government began a resettlement plan, transferring an estimated one-third of the Kurdish population to the south away from the Iranian frontier. In addition, a "dead" area was established along the border—water sources were filled in and vegetation destroyed—in order to prevent movement across the border. Despite these measures, Kurdish forces engaged Iraqi troops in the north after the outbreak of the Iraq-Iran War, causing Saddam to divert troops from the Iranian front to the north. Negotiations ensued during 1983, but hostilities continued in 1984. As the Iranian threat waned in 1987, Iraq moved more troops to the north where the Kurdish separatist movement claimed control and embarked on a "scorched-earth" policy against Kurdish villages near the Turkish and Iranian borders, allegedly using chemical weapons. This policy and that of population transfer set in motion mass flight and the creation of a refugee probelm, leading the Kurds to appeal to the United Nations.

With the defeat of Iraq in the Gulf War, a full-scale Kurdish rebellion broke out, Iraqi armed forces were redeployed to the north, and refugees began to flood border areas with Turkey and Iran. In order to stem this "Kurdish crisis," in 1991 the United Nations created a "safe haven" in northern Iraq and forbade any Iraqi interference there.

The Kurdish parties, all of which advocate Kurdish autonomy, held elections in 1992. No clear leadership emerged because the two major parties, the Patriotic Union of Kurdistan under Jalal Talibani and the Kurdish Democratic Party under Masoud Barzani drew equal support. Internicine warfare between the two groups ensued, and the Iraqi government sent troops to mediate.

Shi'a

Iraq is often described as a country composed of a Shi'i majority ruled by a Sunni minority. The Shi'i make up approximately 55% of the population and are concentrated in the rural areas south of Baghdad and in certain Baghdad neighborhoods. Since the creation of Iraq in 1921, the Shi'i have had little contact with the state and have not been represented proportionately either in the ruling elite or in the military. Despite their reputation for being underprivileged because of the large numbers of rural Shi'i and urban slum dwellers, the Shi'i constitute a large part of Iraq's middle class and are strongly represented in the professions of the civil service.

The most holy shrines of Shi'i Islam are in the Iraqi cities of Najaf and Karbala, and visits to them are incumbent upon observant Shi'i. There has been constant intermingling between the Shi'i faithful of Iraq and Iran. Followers of Shi'i doctrine see the successor of the Prophet Muhammad or his representatives as more than religous leaders; they are also supposed to be the final arbiters of political policy. By and large they have regarded all non-Shi'i regimes as unworthy of any loyalty.

Shi'i were attracted both to the Communist Party and to the Ba'th. Although the secular regime has tried to recruit Shi'i members by emphasizing its nonsectarian ideology and by stressing the "Arabness" of the Iraqi Shi'i, it remains suspicious of Shi'i loyalties. In 1979 three Shi'a were purged from the RCC because of their alleged complicity in a Syrian plot against the regime. Saddam has deported Iranian residents of Iraq and Iraqis of Iranian origin and arrested more than 10,000 people since the Khomeini regime came to power in Iran. Some 178 Shi'i intellectuals, professionals, and religious functionaries, including the religious leader Ayatallah Muhammad Baqr al-Sadr, have been executed.

In spite of Ba'th policy, during the Iran-Iraq War, the Iraqi Shi'i did not identify with the Iranian Shi'i. With the end of the Gulf War in 1991, armed rebellion broke out in March in the Shi'i areas in the south. The anticipated outside assistance did not materialize, and the revolt was brutally suppressed.

One of the two newly emergent Shi'a parties, the *al-Da`wah al-Islamiyya* (The Islamic Call) was founded in al-Najaf in the late 1960s as an attempt at counteracting Shi'a support for the Communist Party. It is split over doctrine and has carried out assassination attempts against Saddam. The *al-Mujahidin* (Muslim Warriors) was founded in Baghdad in 1979. These groups have formed a loose coalition with other opposition groups outside the country.

NATIONAL PROSPECTS

Saddam continues to maintain control by balancing potential bases of support, providing financial incentives to the military, and keeping the population in line through military suppression and economic deprivation. Domestic crime has increased among a once-core middle-class population now reduced to penury because of the economic sanctions imposed on Iraq since the end of the

Gulf War. A potential united movement in opposition to the current regime is fragmented and has not been effective in changing conditions in Iraq.

Further Reading

Baram, Amatzia. "The June 1980 Elections to the National Assembly in Iraq: An Experiment in Controlled Democracy." *Orient*, September 1981.

———. "Saddam Hussein: A Political Profile," *Jerusalem Quarterly,* no. 17 (fall 1980).

Baram, Amatzia, and Barry Rubin. *Iraq's Road to War.* New York: St. Martin's Press, 1993.

Batatu, Hanna. *The Old Social Classes and the Revolutionary Movements of Iraq: A Study of Iraq's Old Landed and Commercial Classes and of Its Communists, Ba'thists, and Free Officers.* Princeton, N.J.: Princeton University Press, 1978.

The Middle East Contemporary Survey. Tel-Aviv: Shiloah Center for Middle Eastern and African Studies, Tel-Aviv University, annual.

IRELAND

By Alan J. Ward, Ph.D.

SYSTEM OF GOVERNMENT

Ireland is a unitary republic with a parliamentary form of government. It is located in five-sixths of the island of Ireland, on the western edge of Europe. It has an area of nearly 70,000 square kilometers (27,000 square miles) and a population of 3.567 million, approximately 93% of whom identify as Roman Catholics. Of the remainder, 3% are members of the Anglican Church of Ireland.

Irish is the first official language of Ireland and English the second. The English text of the constitution uses Irish terms for certain offices and institutions: *Oireachtas* (Parliament), *Dáil Éireann* (House of Representatives), *Seanad Éireann* (Senate), *taoiseach* (prime minister), and *tánaiste* (deputy prime minister). This use of Irish will be followed in this account, as will the customary use of Irish names for three political parties, *Fianna Fáil, Fine Gael*, and *Sinn Féin*.

When the island of Ireland was partitioned by the United Kingdom in 1921, the 6 counties in the northeast, which contained the majority of the island's Protestants, became a self-governing region of the United Kingdom, known as Northern Ireland. The remaining 26 counties became independent in 1922 as the Irish Free State (*Saorstát Éireann*), with the constitutional status of a British Dominion. In 1936, all references to the British crown were deleted from the Free State constitution (*Bunreacht na hÉireann*), and in 1937 Eamon de Valera's government introduced a new constitution, which was approved by a plebiscite. The state was renamed Ireland (*Éire*). The constitution was wholly republican in form, but Ireland retained the External Relations Act of 1936, which authorized the king of England, as head of the British Commonwealth, to act formally for Ireland in external relations. In this way, the country retained a relationship with Britain until 1949, when the Republic of Ireland Act was implemented and Ireland withdrew from the Commonwealth. The state continues to be called Ireland in the constitution, but the names Irish Republic and Republic of Ireland are also widely used.

Executive

The Irish head of state is the president (*Uachtarán na hÉireann*). The constitution specifies that most of the president's powers are exercised on the direction of others: the *taoiseach*, the Government, or *Dáil Éireann*. These include the power to appoint ministers, summon and dissolve the *Oireachtas*, and assent to bills.

The president has seven discretionary powers, but the advice of the Council of State must be sought on five of these, including the most important, the decision to submit a bill to the Supreme Court for a test of its constitutionality. The statutory members of the Council are the *taoiseach*, *tánaiste*, chief justice, president of the High Court, attorney general, presiding officers of the two houses of the *Oireachtas*, and people who have held office as *taoiseach* or chief justice in the past. The president is not required to seek the Council's advice when appointing up to seven additional members of the Council and deciding to dissolve, or not dissolve, *Dáil Éireann* on the advice of a *taoiseach* who has lost the support of a majority in the *Dáil*.

The president must be at least 35 years of age, serves a seven-year term, and may be reelected only once. Elections are partisan, and all but two of the eight presidents to date (1998) were members of the largest party, Fianna Fáil. Four Fianna Fáil nominees were elected unopposed. Until 1990 presidents conducted the office in a low-key manner, but the Independent Labour president, Mary Robinson (1990–97), may have set new expectations for the office by speaking out on public issues and representing Ireland on frequent overseas visits. President Robinson resigned on September 12, 1997, some months before the completion of her term, to take up a position as UN High Commissioner for Human Rights. A new president had to be elected within 60 days of her resignation. A Presidential Commission, composed of the chief justice of the Supreme Court and the two presiding officers of the *Oireachtas*, performed the essential functions of the office during the vacancy. In November, the Fianna Fáil candidate, Mary McAleese, a native of Northern Ireland, was elected president.

As in all parliamentary countries, the effective executive in Ireland is not the president but a Cabinet, known in Ireland as the Government, which is selected from the majority in the lower house of the *Oireachtas, Dáil Éireann*. The Government must resign if it loses the support of the majority, by custom by losing a vote of no confidence in the Government or a vote on the budget. Ireland adopted this model before independence, when the first *Dáil Éireann* was formed during the War of Independence in 1919. The model was retained when the Irish Free State constitution was adopted in 1922 and was confirmed in the constitution of 1937.

The Irish Government is composed of ministers selected from the *Oireachtas* to head government departments. The constitution limits the number to 15, and no more than 2 may sit in the *Seanad*. The *taoiseach, tánaiste*, and minister for finance must sit in the *Dáil*. The number of departments is set by law at 17, including the Department of the *Taoiseach*, which means that some ministers must supervise more than one department. Seventeen ministers of state, or junior ministers, have been established by ordinary law to support ministers, and these must also sit in the *Oireachtas*.

The constitution recognizes the special role of the *taoiseach*, or prime minister, in various ways. Appointed by the president on the nomination of the *Dáil*, the *taoiseach* alone nominates ministers and ministers of state to the president, as well as the attorney general, who need not sit in the *Oireachtas*. The *taoiseach* alone may request the president to dismiss members of the Government. It is the *taoiseach*'s responsibility to request the president to dissolve the *Dáil* and call for a general election. The request must be granted if the *taoiseach* has the support of a majority in the *Dáil*, but it may be denied if that support has been lost. In practice, no president has ever denied a request for a dissolution. If the *taoiseach* resigns or dies in office, the whole Government is deemed to have resigned. In a coalition, some of the *taoiseach*'s powers may be circumscribed because coalition partners will want a say in the disposition of certain offices.

The *taoiseach* is clearly preeminent in the Government, but the constitution requires the Government to meet and act as a collective body in many matters, including the presentation of appropriations bills to the *Dáil*, the conduct of foreign relations, and most instructions to the president. In 1922 the Government decided that all its decisions would be announced as if taken unanimously, and in 1924 it decided that the appearance of unanimity required all Government proceedings to be confidential. It therefore resisted court subpoenas. A constitutional amendment in 1997 confirms secrecy of proceedings but permits court access to documents in some circumstances.

Ministers represent their own departments in Parliament. The Ministers and Secretaries Act of 1924 recognizes each minister as a "corporation sole," which is to say, as personifying the department in law, and it always acts in the minister's name.

The members of the Government control the executive departments, of course, but party discipline enables them to dominate the legislature as well. Standing Orders, which are the rules of each house, have been written to favor the Government in significant ways. The members of the Government also supervise the large, semistate sector of "state-sponsored bodies." These account for roughly 10% of Ireland's GDP, and they engage in a variety of commercial, marketing, research, and regulatory activities. Their governing boards are appointed by ministers, and the *Oireachtas* has very limited influence over them.

The Supreme Court has the constitutional power to reject legislation as unconstitutional, but other formal checks on the Irish Government are weak. Backbench deputies on the Government's side can influence its policies in the privacy of party meetings, but they are socialized to accept its dominance in the *Oireachtas* itself. Members of opposition parties have very little influence in the *Oireachtas*.

Government dominance is most evident when a single party forms a majority Government, but Irish governments have been formed with four kinds of support, each of which tends toward a different degree of dominance. First, a party may be able to form a single-party, majority Government. This has been done nine times since 1922, seven times by Fianna Fáil, and it gives the Government the greatest degree of control. Second, the Government may be formed by a majority coalition composed of two or more parties, as has happened seven times since 1922. The composition and programs of the Government will be, of necessity, compromises between coalition partners. Third, if no party controls a majority of seats in the *Dáil*, a single party may be able to form a minority Government if it has the support of other parties or independents on votes of confidence and budget votes. This has happened nine times since 1922, and it places the Government in a precarious position. Finally, a coalition may form a minority Government under the same conditions, as was the case with the Fianna Fáil–Progressive Democrat government formed in 1997.

Legislature

The *Oireachtas* is defined by the constitution as a tricameral institution, comprising the president, *Dáil Éireann*, and *Seanad Éireann*, but in practice, the *Oireachtas* is always taken to mean an assembly of two chambers, *Dáil Éireann* and *Seanad Éireann*.

Dáil Éireann has 166 members and is the primary house of the *Oireachtas*. Elections are by popular vote using single transferable votes (STV) in multimember constituencies. The *Dáil* may sit for a maximum of five years but can be dissolved in a shorter period at the request of the *taoiseach*. The *Dáil* elects a chairman (*Cathaoirleach*) and deputy chairman (*Leas-Cathaoirleach*) after each general election, usually from a Government party. The seat of a sitting chairman is not contested at a general election. The *Dáil* has exclusive responsibility for nominating the *taoiseach* and approving his nominees for the Government. The *taoiseach, tánaiste,* and minister for finance must sit in the *Dáil,* and money bills, which deal with taxes, appropriations, and public loans, must be introduced there by the Government. Once approved, a money bill is forwarded to the *Seanad,* which has 21 days to make comments, but it may not offer amendments. The *Dáil* may accept the *Seanad*'s recommendations, or it may vote to send the original bill to the president for signature. Nonmoney bills may be initiated in either house, but in practice very few are introduced in the *Seanad.* That house has 90 days to consider a nonmoney bill sent to it from the *Dáil,* and if it does not return the bill in this period or amends it in ways that are unacceptable to the *Dáil,* the *Dáil* may vote to send the original bill to the president for signature. The 90-day delay may be abridged for reasons of public peace, security, or emergency, as determined by the *taoiseach* with the president's concurrence. In practice, the *Seanad* has rejected only a handful of Government bills, and it almost never amends them in ways that are unacceptable to the Government.

The great majority of bills that become law in Ireland are introduced by the Government in *Dáil Éireann.* A small amount of time is available for private members' bills, but it is dominated by opposition parties rather than individual members. Party members are expected, and in some parties are required, to vote as directed by the party on all bills except votes of conscience.

The *Dáil* sits for fewer than 100 days a year. It appoints standing committees to handle the third, or committee, stage of some noncontroversial bills, but most bills pass through all of their stages in the full house, sitting as itself or as a "committee of the whole." Select committees are established annually to consider specialized topics. Some are reappointed year by year, such the Public Accounts Committee, the Procedure and Privileges Committee, the Joint Committee of *Dáil* and *Seanad* on Commercial State-Sponsored Bodies, and the Joint Committee on Secondary Legislation of the European Union, but they do not consider legislation and there are no committees to review financial estimates.

The *Seanad* has 60 members and is very much a secondary chamber. In addition to the constitutional restrictions on its powers discussed above, the Senate is subjected to party discipline and is invariably dominated by the Government. It sits for fewer days than the *Dáil.*

Judiciary

The Irish judicial system was inherited from Britain. Irish law is derived from British common law, British statutes that applied to Ireland at the time of independence and have not been amended by Irish statutes, and Irish statutes passed subsequent to independence.

The lowest court is the district court, which is divided into 23 districts to hear minor civil and criminal cases. More serious cases go to the circuit court, which is divided into 8 circuits. Next in authority is the High Court, a panel of 17 judges who handle the most serious cases and hear appeals from lower courts in civil cases. When hearing criminal cases the High Court sits as the Central Criminal Court. Criminal appeals are heard by the Court of Criminal Appeal, which includes both High Court and Supreme Court judges. The High Court is permitted by the constitution to consider the constitutionality of laws in its decisions. The Supreme Court is the court of final appeal from decisions of the High Court and the Court of Criminal Appeal, and it is required to consider the constitutionality of bills referred to it by the president before signing them into law. Irish judges are appointed by the president on the recommendation of the Government.

Early Irish Supreme Court justices were trained in the British tradition and practiced typically British judicial restraint, but since the 1960s they have been interpreting the constitution quite broadly to nullify acts of the *Oireachtas.* The Irish constitution includes specific provisions regarding marriage, divorce, the family, and education based upon Catholic teachings that courts must apply, and a 1983 referendum added the prohibition of abortion to this list. In addition, since Ireland joined the European Economic Community (now part of the European Union) in 1972, Irish courts have been bound by European law and European Court decisions.

Regional and Local Government

Ireland is a unitary state. All local governments operate under powers granted by the *Oireachtas* and may only perform tasks permitted by law. Councils have occasionally been suspended by the Government, and local elections have been postponed several times, most recently in 1990.

The major local government functions are public housing, roads and traffic, water supply, sewage, environmental protection, planning and development, and recreation. Expenditures are funded, in order of importance, by central government grants, local government charges for goods and services, and taxes on business and industrial property. The central government exerts considerable influence by making laws with respect to local government, making grants for roads, housing, and other purposes, and coordinating certain activities, such as planning. Local governments spend about 5.5% of Ireland's GNP, approximately 65% for current expenditures and 35% for capital expenditures.

In order of descending levels of responsibility, there are 29 county councils and 5 county borough councils, 49 urban district councils and 6 boroughs, and 30 boards of town commissioners. Elections to five-year terms are by proportional representation and are contested by parties. Each jurisdiction has a manager, a public servant who is appointed by the authority on the recommendation of the Local Appointments Board, a central government agency.

Elected members set general policy, the annual tax rate, and public borrowing. They also enact by-laws to regulate local matters, such as traffic and parking. Managers administer according to these policies, but they are typically experienced sources of advice to local councils. About 25,000 people are employed in local government.

Eight regional authorities were established by law in 1994 composed of representatives from local governments. They coordinate regional public services and advise on the implementation of certain European Union programs. In addition, there are regional tourism organizations, vocational education committees, county enterprise boards, fisheries boards, and harbor authorities.

THE ELECTORAL SYSTEM

The minimum voting age for all elections in Ireland is 18, and balloting is secret. The electoral register is prepared by an annual house-to-house survey. Elections for president are by all registered voters in Ireland using the single transferable vote. Candidates must be nominated by 20 members of the *Oireachtas* or 4 county councils. Voters indicate their preferences among the candidates, and if no candidate wins a majority on the first count, the second preferences of the candidate with fewest votes are redistributed to the remaining candidates, as happened, for example, in 1990.

Candidate	First Count	Second Count
Mary Robinson, Independent Labour	38.9	51.9
Brian Lenihan, Fianna Fáil	44.1	46.4
Austin Currie, Fine Gael	17.0	—

Dáil elections are by proportional representation and secret ballot using the STV system in multimember constituencies. There are 41 constituencies, and the number of seats in each varies between 3 and 5. In the June 1997 general election there were 14 constituencies with 5 seats, 15 with 4, and 12 with 3. Constituencies are revised at least every 12 years, and the boundary commissioners are required by the constitution to maintain a ratio of electors to deputies of between 1:20,000 and 1:30,000. Commissioners are also required to consider county boundaries, geographic features, and continuity in relation to constituencies, which is why permissible variations in constituency size are helpful.

The *Dáil* electoral system operates as follows. On their ballots voters number candidates in their order of preference up to the number of seats to be filled. The minimum number of votes required to elect a member is the "quota," which is determined by the formula: the number of valid ballots votes cast/(number of seats + 1) + 1. By this measure, the quota is 25% + 1 in a 3-seat constituency, 20% + 1 in a 4-seat constituency, and 16.66%

+ 1 in a 5-seat constituency. When the ballots are counted, always by hand, the first preferences for each candidate are sorted. Should a candidate reach the quota at this point, the second preferences of votes that are surplus to the quota are redistributed to other candidates. Should no other candidate reach a quota, the second preferences of the candidate receiving the least number of first preferences are redistributed. This process proceeds at length, redistributing the surplus votes of winners and then the second preferences of the bottom candidates, until all the seats are filled. Parties influence the outcome by directing how their supporters should cast their preferences. Two-thirds of the Irish electorate voted in 1997, down nearly 10 points since 1981 and one of the lowest rates in Europe. From 1997, candidates for the *Dáil* have been subject to spending limits for campaigns, but they may receive up to Ir 5,000 pounds in verifiable expenses from the state if they can secure at least 25% of the quota for their districts.

The *Dáil* electoral system produces a house whose membership approximates quite closely the proportion of votes cast for each party. About 80% of voters usually see their first- or second-preference candidates elected. In Britain, by contrast, a majority of seats are won by candidates who poll less than a majority of votes and only a minority of voters can claim a role in electing a member of Parliament. However, because the quotas in Ireland are very high, by proportional representation standards, the STV system somewhat underrepresents small parties, the Green party and Sinn Féin, for example, and overrepresents the major parties, Fianna Fáil and Fine Gael, particularly. STV also has the effect of making deputies compete against members of their own parties for high preferences, and a deputy may lose a seat to a member of the same party who cultivates the constituency more assiduously. Deputies spend a great deal of time performing constituency service to protect their seats, and a majority of them serve on local councils for this reason.

In the 28th *Dáil*, elected on June 6, 1997, party representation, together with the percentage of the first-preference vote won by each party, was as follows:

Party	Seats	% Vote
Fianna Fáil	77	39.33
Fine Gael	54	27.95
Labour	17	10.40
Democratic Left	4	2.51
Progressive Democrat	4	4.68
Green Alliance	2	2.76
Sinn Féin	1	2.55
Others	7	9.80

Labour and the smaller parties do not offer candidates in all constituencies, which limits the proportion of the nationwide vote they can receive. Sinn Féin, for example, won 7.5% of first preferences in seats it contested but only 2.5% in Ireland as a whole. Twenty-four women were elected to the 28th *Dáil*, 14.5% of the total. Though far from satisfactory, this is a substantial increase over the 8% of November 1982 and 7% of 1989.

Proportional representation makes it difficult in Ireland for a party to form a government alone with a majority of seats in the *Dáil*. This has happened only nine times in the 26 governments formed since 1922, and not once since Fianna Fáil lost office in 1981. Elections are more likely to lead to coalition or minority governments.

The Senate has sixty members, selected in three ways. Two groups are selected by elections, which must be held within 90 days of the dissolution of the *Dáil*, using STV and postal ballots. Forty-three members are elected from five panels representing broad vocational constituencies: agriculture, industry and commerce, labor, culture and education, and administration. The distribution of seats per panel is set by law. Candidates to the panels are nominated by recognized nominating bodies or by members of the *Oireachtas*. The electorate for this group of senators is members of the local councils and deputies from the new *Dáil*, about 1,100 voters. Next, three senators each are elected by graduates of the National University of Ireland and the University of Dublin (Trinity College). The third form of selection is by nomination. Eleven senators are appointed on the nomination of the incoming *taoiseach*.

De Valera did not view the Senate as a chamber in which vocational interests would be represented per se. Rather, he thought that elections in vocational panels would produce senators of distinction who would represent the interests of Ireland as a whole. In the event, however, the *Seanad* has been a disappointment by any standard. The nominations process has always been dominated by political parties, and the *taoiseach*'s nominees ensure that the chamber is always friendly to the Government. The Senate selected in 1997 had the following 49 elected members: Fianna Fáil, 23; Fine Gael, 16; Labour, 4; and Independents, 6.

All 6 independent senators are university members. Of the *taoiseach*'s 11 nominees, 4 were assigned to the Progressive Democrats by the Fianna Fáil–Progressive Democrat coalition agreement.

THE PARTY SYSTEM

Parliamentary systems depend on political parties. Without them, governments would have to construct new majorities issue by issue and would be exposed to defeat, and hence resignation, day by day. Disciplined parties bring stability and have been a feature of the Irish political system since independence. They contest elections at every political level. Parties that are registered by the clerk to *Dáil Éireann* and have no fewer than seven members elected at the previous general election receive subsidies from state funds in proportion to the votes they received. In 1997, a sum of Ir 1.5 million pounds was available for distribution. Each candidate's party, if any, is identified on the ballot, and parties are allocated free TV and radio broadcasts during general elections. They are prohibited by law from television and radio advertising during campaigns.

The present Irish party system reflects the events that accompanied the end of the Irish War of Independence. The war was concluded with the Anglo-Irish Treaty of December 1921, which caused a devastating split in Sinn Féin, the party that had led Ireland in the war. The treaty was accepted as the best they could secure from Britain by the Irish negotiators, led by Michael Collins and Arthur Griffith, but it recognized the Irish Free State as a British Dominion, under the Crown, and left Ireland partitioned. When both the *Dáil Éireann* Executive (Cabinet) and the *Dáil* itself approved the treaty by very narrow margins, the more radical Irish nationalists, led by Eamon de Valera, left the Government and the *Dáil*.

This schism led to the Irish Civil War of 1922–23 and laid the foundations for the Irish party system. The present-day Fine Gael and Fianna Fáil parties, the largest parties in the state, are the descendants of the pro- and antitreaty factions of Sinn Féin in 1922. Because the two major Irish parties were defined by their attitudes to the Anglo-Irish Treaty, rather than by social class or economics, and because the people of the Irish Republic are religiously and culturally homogeneous, Irish party politics has not reflected the class and religious cleavages that are characteristic of continental European parties.

Between 1922 and 1932, treaty supporters, now known as the *Cumann nGaedheal* party, constituted the Government of the Irish Free State, but in 1932, the Fianna Fáil Party, formed by opponents of the treaty, took power for the first time. Between 1932 and 1989, Irish party politics revolved around the question of whether Fianna Fáil or an anti–Fianna Fáil coalition led by the successor to *Cumann nGaedheal*, Fine Gael, would form the Government. Fianna Fáil formed 14 governments and anti–Fianna Fáil coalitions 7 in this period. Since 1989, however, Fianna Fáil itself has led two coalition governments. Coalition building is often a tortuous exercise, but it is possible in Ireland because of the nonideological character of the major Irish parties.

Fianna Fáil and Fine Gael move about on the political spectrum from time to time, and at present both can be identified in the center-right part of the European political spectrum. Ireland has one of the lowest levels of support for left-wing parties of any country in Europe for three major reasons: the treaty split stifled the development of class-based parties; Ireland has a small, industrial working class; and the Roman Catholic Church has been extremely hostile to socialism.

In the 1970s, Fine Gael appeared to move toward European social democracy, and it formed coalition governments with the Labour Party in 1973, 1981, and 1982. In the late 1980s, however, it became quite conservative in its economic policies, and in 1993 Labour formed a coalition with Fianna Fáil, which had taken a centrist position on economic policy. When this government broke up in 1994, Fine Gael formed another coalition with Labour and a small party to Labour's left, the Democratic Left. It appeared to move again in a social democratic direction. After the general election of 1997, Fianna Fáil formed a coalition with the Progressive Democratic Party, which is conservative on economic policy but liberal on social issues. Labour has often been the kingmaker because the traditional political enemies, Fianna Fáil and Fine Gael, have been unable to form coalitions together. But ancient enmities are dying, and there is nothing in the ideologies or policies of these two that would forever preclude such a union. Because of proportional representation, minor parties and independents have always been able to meet the election quotas in some seats, and they have often held the balance of power in the *Dáil*.

With the exception of the small Green Alliance, Irish political parties are hierarchically organized. A small central office staff in Dublin coordinates the activities of the party and reports to the national executive, a body of representatives from local branches and members of the *Oireachtas* that manages the party between annual conferences. There are usually several local branches (or *cumann* in Fianna Fáil) in each constituency, but candidate selection is handled by constituency-level bodies. The national executive may influence selections, but most authority lies at the local level. The centerpiece of the party is an annual or biennial conference (or *Árd Fhéis*) attended by delegates from local branches, members of the *Oireachtas*, and members of the national executive. This meeting features an address by the party leader and is increasingly staged for the benefit of broadcast media. The party leader is typically elected by members of the *Dáil*, but Fine Gael adds senators and members of the European Parliament to the electorate. The Democratic Left leader is elected by the annual conference.

Party policy is officially set by the national conference, but when in office, a Government effectively sets party policy. Even in opposition, the leaders of a party in the *Dáil* have a great influence on policy. The Green party has made an effort to deviate from this model, with a "coordinator" rather than a leader, and it develops policies by consensus.

Irish parties do not publish accounts or the identities of major donors, but it is known that they draw their funds from members' contributions or donations, from private gifts from individuals, corporations, or trades unions, and from annual grants from the state, the largest source of funds.

For a 1996 study, Irish parties reported the following membership, branches, and full-time employees:

Party	Members	Branches	Full-Time Employees
Fianna Fáil	70,000	3,000	10
Fine Gael	20,000	2,000	12
Labour	7,000	450	6
Progressive Democrats	8,000	250	5
Sinn Féin	3,000	200	0
Democratic Left	1,400	111	4
Green Alliance	1,000	26	1
Workers' Party	800	40	1
Total	111,200	6,077	39

Source: Michael Marsh, Rick Wilford, Simon King, and Gail McElroy, "Irish Political Data, 1995," *Irish Political Studies* 11 (1996): 290.

FIANNA FÁIL
(Soldiers of Destiny)

Fianna Fáil has been the largest party in the state since 1932. It was formed by Eamon de Valera in 1926 when he and a majority of treaty opponents abandoned their opposition to the Irish Free State. They entered the *Dáil* for the first time in 1927 and took office in 1932 as a minority government with Labour Party support. Since then Fianna Fáil has been the only party to form a single-party government, on 14 occasions.

Fianna Fáil was led by de Valera until he became president in 1959. The party was more inclined to press for the reunion of Ireland than Fine Gael, more protectionist in trade, less inclined to welcome secular influences from abroad, and more protective of traditional Irish values, including the Irish language. The Catholic hierarchy supported this policy of cultural isolation. The fact of Ireland's partition enabled Fianna Fáil to make electoral capital out of republican nationalism. The party has always been conservative on economic, cultural, and moral issues but has also espoused a brand of social populism that expresses support for the poor and underprivileged. In World War II, de Valera's Fianna Fáil government adopted a policy of neutrality that evolved into abstention from military alliances in the postwar years.

De Valera's successor as party leader and *taoiseach*, Séan Lemass, began the process of modernizing the Irish economy in the 1960s and opened Ireland to foreign trade and investment. His government negotiated Irish entry into the European Economic Community in 1972. Lemass also began to change Fianna Fáil's position on Northern Ireland and twice met the prime minister of Northern Ireland, Terence O'Neill, for talks in Belfast and Dublin. Fianna Fáil now accepts that Irish unification must come about by the decision of the people of Northern Ireland themselves and by reconciling the two communities there. In December 1993, the *taoiseach*, Albert Reynolds, signed a joint declaration on peace with the British government that confirmed these policies.

Fianna Fáil sits in Europe with the European Democratic Alliance, which includes the French Gaullists. The Alliance is customarily placed to the left of the larger European People's Party, the Christian Democrat group in Europe.

FINE GAEL
(Tribe of Irish People)

In 1923 the protreaty Sinn Féin republicans took as their name *Cumann nGaedheal*. The party became Fine Gael in 1933 in an amalgamation with the smaller Center party. Fine Gael is today the second-largest party in Ireland. As *Cumann nGaedheal* it formed the government of the Irish Free State until 1932, under the leadership of William Cosgrave, but since then it has only been in government as the largest party in a number of coalitions.

Fine Gael has been less confrontational to Britain than Fianna Fáil, less committed to republican nationalism, less economic protectionist, less populist, and more committed to a pluralist Ireland, but it was a Fine Gael–led coalition that clarified Ireland's republican status in 1949 and withdrew Ireland from the British Commonwealth. In its early years the party was identified with large farmers and professional classes and had a weak party organization. In the mid-1960s, however, it changed its image and became a socially progressive party. The redefinition was led by Senator Garret FitzGerald, who became leader of the party and subsequently *taoiseach* in Fine Gael–Labour coalitions from June 1981 to February 1982 and November 1982 to 1987. FitzGerald also signed the Anglo-Irish Agreement of 1985 with the British Prime Minister, Margaret Thatcher, that committed both countries to pursue a peace in Northern Ireland based on respect for both the Unionist and Nationalist traditions and the consent of the majority in the province. The agreement created the Inter-Governmental Council, in which representatives of the Irish and British governments meet regularly to consider developments in Northern Ireland.

In a very testing period for the Irish economy, Fine Gael became too conservative in economic matters for its Labour coalition partner and the FitzGerald coalition collapsed in 1987. The party returned to power in 1994 in a Fine Gael–Labour–Democratic Left coalition under *Taoiseach* John Bruton. The party won 54 seats in the *Dáil* in 1997 and went into opposition.

Fine Gael has been the leading Irish supporter of the European Union. It sits with the second-largest group in the European Parliament, the European People's Party, a Christian Democrat coalition.

THE IRISH LABOUR PARTY

The Irish Labour Party was founded in 1912 by the trades union leaders James Connolly, James Larkin, and William O'Brien. The party did not contest the 1918 United Kingdom general election or the 1921 Irish elections for fear of splitting the anti-British vote, and when it did contest the Irish general election in 1922 it found that its class-based politics could not compete with the highly charged politics of the treaty. In addition, Ireland had only a relatively small industrial working class of the kind that supported successful left-wing parties elsewhere in Europe. Because of the abstention of antitreaty deputies from the first Irish Free State *Dáil*, Labour became the official *Dáil* opposition and is credited with playing an important part in the development of Irish parliamentary government. It has consistently taken third place among Irish parties since Fianna Fáil entered constitutional politics in 1927 but has participated in seven coalition governments, most recently the Fianna Fáil–Labour Government of 1993 to 1994 and the Fine Gael–Labour–Democratic Left Government of 1994 to 1997. Its leader, Dick Spring, served as *tánaiste* and minister for foreign affairs in both governments. It polled 19.3% of the first-preference votes in the 1992 general election and won 33 seats, its highest number ever, but saw its support drop to 10.4% and 17 seats in 1997. Spring resigned as party leader after the general election and was succeeded by Ruairí Quinn.

In 1990, the Labour Party nominated the Independent Labour Senator Mary Robinson for president of Ireland. She had resigned from the party in 1985 to protest the Anglo-Irish Agreement, which she thought unfair to Unionists in Northern Ireland. She won the election and served from 1991 to 1997.

Labour is a social democratic party committed to social and economic equality. It has its greatest strength in Dublin, where a majority of its branches are located, and is weakest in the west. It currently has 12 affiliated trades unions, representing about half of Ireland's trades unionists. In the European Parliament, it sits with the Party of European Socialists, the largest group, and it is also a member of the Socialist International.

MINOR POLITICAL PARTIES

A large number of minor parties have come and gone in Ireland since 1922, but the following have figured in recent elections.

The Progressive Democrat Party

The Progressive Democrat Party was founded in 1985 by Desmond O'Malley, a former Fianna Fáil government minister who was expelled from the party in 1984. Though relatively libertarian, by Irish standards, on social and moral issues, it is neoliberal on economic issues and believes in minimizing government intervention in the economy. Its present leader, Mary Harney, was elected to succeed O'Malley in 1993 and is the first woman to lead an Irish political party. The party formed a coalition government with Fianna Fáil in 1989, and its withdrawal was responsible for the collapse of the Government in 1991. In 1997, however, the party formed another coalition government with Fianna Fáil, and Mary Harney became *tánaiste*.

The Democratic Left

Democratic Left was formed in 1985 when the Worker's Party, itself an offshoot of Sinn Féin, divided into two. The stronger of the two factions became the Democratic Left, which won four seats in the *Dáil* in 1997. It lies to the left of the Labour Party but joined Labour and Fine Gael in a coalition government from 1994 to 1997. The Democratic Left is committed to a pluralist, socialist, and democratic Ireland. It rejects associations with trades unions and physical force nationalism. It recognizes two legitimate cultural traditions in Northern Ireland and wants each to have proportional representation in decision making. The leader of the party is Prionsias de Rossa. The party is strongly feminist and requires that at least 40% of its national executive be women.

The Green Alliance

The Green Alliance was founded in 1982 as an environmental protection party but now takes positions on a wide range of issues. It is committed to a participatory political system in which decisions are taken at the lowest effective level. It recognizes world peace as a necessary precondition for environmental protection and supports the redistribution of the world's resources from rich to the poor. It offered 26 candidates in the 1997 general election, mostly in Dublin and Leinster, and won 2 seats. The party operates nonhierarchically, rotating leadership positions annually, and seeks to make policy by consensus.

Sinn Féin
(We Ourselves)

Sinn Féin is the lineal descendant of those members of the antitreaty Sinn Féin who did not follow Eamon de Valera into constitutional politics in 1926 and have survived a number of schisms. It still exists, as the political wing of the Irish Republican Army. It polled 2.5% of national first-preference votes in the 1997 Irish general election but an average of 7.5% in the seats it chose to contest. It won one seat.

Sinn Féin is committed to Britain's withdrawal from Ireland and the reunification of the island under a socialist government. It believes that the Unionist majority in the North will come to accept its place as a minority in Ireland as a whole. Its organization is based on local branches, and it has a very strong international support network, particularly in the U.S.A.

NATIONAL PROSPECTS

The Irish republic is a stable democracy and is likely to remain so. It has one of the healthiest economies in Europe and is firmly committed to membership in the European Union. There are no bitter cleavages in the country, economic, ethnic, or political, and whereas developments in Northern Ireland divided Irish political parties in the past, all the major parties now agree that the reunification of Ireland must depend on reconciliation between the nationalist and Unionist communities and the consent of the majority in the North. With the issue of the North neutralized, the politics of the Irish republic will revolve around social and economic issues. Proportional representation will continue to inhibit the formation of single-party, majority governments, but the pragmatic nature of the major parties will make coalition politics possible.

There are likely to be few changes in Ireland's constitution. The Constitutional Review Group appointed by the Government reported in 1996 in favor of only minor changes, and governments seem uninterested in even these. The Commission did recommend, however, that there should be an independent review of the role and composition of the *Seanad*, and this may come about.

Further Reading

Coakley, J., and M. Gallagher, eds. *Politics in the Republic of Ireland* . Dublin and Limerick: Folens and PSAI Press, 1993.

Chubb, B. *The Government and Politics of Ireland*, 3d ed. New York: Longman, 1992.

Dooney, S., and J. O'Toole. *Irish Government Today* . Dublin: Gill and Macmillan, 1992.

Gallagher, M. *Political Parties in the Republic of Ireland* . Manchester: Manchester University Press, 1985.

Keogh, D. *Twentieth-Century Ireland: Nation and State*. New York: St. Martin's Press, 1995.

Lee, J.J. *Ireland, 1912–1985: Politics and Society*. Cambridge: Cambridge University Press, 1989.

Morgan, D.G. *Constitutional Law of Ireland*, 2d ed., Dublin: Round Hall, 1990.

Ward, A.J. *The Irish Constitutional Tradition: Responsible Government and Ireland*. Washington, D.C.: Catholic University of America Press, 1994.

Web Site

University College, Dublin, Politics Department: <http://hermes.ucd.ie/~politics/irpols.html>

STATE OF ISRAEL

(Medinat Yisrael)

By Bernard Reich, Ph.D., and Gershon R. Kieval, Ph.D.

THE SYSTEM OF GOVERNMENT

Israel is a small country in size and population, located in the Middle East on the eastern shore of the Mediterranean Sea and bordered by Jordan, Syria, Lebanon, and Egypt. It is a multiparty parliamentary republic of some 5.8 million people, of whom 14.5% are Muslim Arabs, 2.9% Christians (mostly Arabs), and 1.7% Druze. In addition to Israel itself, the government administers portions of the West Bank and the Gaza Strip. Under terms of the Declaration of Principles (DOP) signed between Israel and the Palestine Liberation Organization (PLO) in September 1993, Israel is to redeploy its forces in the two territories, relinquishing administrative control over some 96% of the Palestinians living in the West Bank and all who reside in Gaza. In 1981, Israel extended its law and jurisdiction to the Golan Heights (formerly Syrian) with a population of several thousand Druze. Approximately 200 Israeli settlements have been established in the West Bank, 24 in the Gaza Strip, and 42 in the Golan Heights.

Although Israel achieved its independence in May 1948, the origins of the political system predate the founding of the state. During the period of the British Mandate (1922–48), the Jewish community in Palestine (the *Yishuv*, or settlement) established institutions for self-government, including the Assembly of the Elected (*Asefat HaNivcharim*), a representative body chosen by secret ballot. The party system appeared with the first election to the Assembly in 1920, and a system of proportional representation was used to distribute the Assembly's seats.

The Assembly met annually and elected the National Council (*Vaad Leumi*) to exercise administrative responsibility for Jewish communal affairs between Assembly sessions. The National Council functioned alongside the Jewish Agency for Palestine, which was created on the authority of the League of Nations Mandate and which included Jewish organizations sympathetic to the idea of a Jewish national home. The Jewish Agency acted as the international diplomatic representative of the *Yishuv*, conducting negotiations with Great Britain, the mandatory government, and the League of Nations, in addition to fund-raising and establishing a network of communi-

cations with foreign governments. After the United Nations adopted a plan for the partition of Palestine in 1947, a National Council of State was chosen from the National Council and the Jewish Agency executive. This provisional government consisted of a state council (which served as a legislature), a cabinet elected from among the state council's members, and a president elected by the state council. The executive of the National Council became the cabinet. The provisional government functioned from May 14, 1948 (Israel's independence day) until February 14, 1949, at which time the state council's authority was transferred to the first *Knesset* (Assembly), a popularly elected, unicameral parliament.

Although Israel has no formal written constitution, a number of Basic Laws have been passed that are intended in time to form portions of a consolidated constitutional document: The *Knesset* (1958); The Lands of Israel (1960); The President (1964); The Government (1968, amended in 1992); The State Economy (1975); The Army (1976); Jerusalem, The Capital of Israel (1980); The Judiciary (1984); The State Comptroller (1988); Human Dignity and Liberty (1992); and Freedom of Occupation (1994).

Executive

The president is the head of state and is elected by the *Knesset* for a five-year term. He may be reelected. His powers and functions are primarily formal and ceremonial. Prior to the May 1996 *Knesset* elections, the president had the task of selecting a member of the *Knesset* to form a government. The political composition of the *Knesset* in practice determined this selection in most cases. However, the president played a crucial role in determining which person was to form the next Cabinet in 1984 and 1990 in situations in which different combinations of parties could have gained the support of the *Knesset*. Even that limited political power was taken away by the 1992 amendment to the Basic Law: The Government, which provided for the direct election of the prime minister and which went into effect with the 1996 election.

The prime minister as head of government is the chief executive officer and wields considerable power. He or she determines the agenda of Cabinet meetings and has the final word in policy decisions, although such decisions are often arrived at by hard bargaining and compromise among the coalition of parties participating in the government.

One of the purported purposes of Israel's new electoral law was to separate the executive branch of government from the legislative branch and thereby reduce the political clout of the smaller parties. By empowering only the elected prime minister to form a government, parties can no longer maneuver between alternative candidates, thus eliminating the political horse-trading that often characterized the process of assembling coalition governments before 1996. Moreover, unless they are prepared to face new parliamentary elections, parties can no longer exert pressure on the prime minister by threatening to pass a vote of no confidence in the *Knesset* by a simple majority of 61—except in extreme circumstances when the prime minister is convicted of an offense involving moral turpitude. At all other times, if the *Knesset* expresses no confidence in the prime minister by a simple majority of 61, new elections for the prime minister and *Knesset* must be held, which presumably would dampen the enthusiasm of coalition partners to pursue such a strategy and lessen their leverage over the prime minister.

Similarly, the prime minister's ultimate weapon in controlling the coalition is the threat to dissolve the *Knesset*, which would mean the fall of the government and the scheduling of new elections for the *Knesset* as well as prime minister. A more common tool of prime ministerial power is the principle of collective responsibility: once a policy is determined, Cabinet members must support it in the *Knesset* or resign, although exceptions in specific policy areas are sometimes agreed to in advance as the price a minor party exacts for joining the Cabinet and supporting the government.

From the outset, Israel's governments have been coalitions of several political parties. This is the result of the intensity with which political views are held, the proportional representation voting system, and the multiplicity of parties. These factors have made it all but impossible for a party to win an absolute majority of seats in the *Knesset*. Despite the constant need for coalition governments, they have proved to be quite stable; only once, in 1990, has a government been forced from office by a vote of no confidence. A new government is constitutionally established when it receives a vote of confidence from the *Knesset*. The maximum term of a government and the *Knesset* is four years.

The stability of Israel's Cabinets and political life has several bases. Until recently, political life in Israel has been dominated by a small and relatively cohesive elite that has held positions in government and other major institutions since the period preceding independence. The strength of the Israel Labor Party until 1977 helped to stabilize the political situation. Between 1977 and September 1983 Prime Minister Menachem Begin's political skills had the same effect. Benjamin Netanyahu's assumption of the leadership of Likud in 1993 and Ehud Barak's election as chairman of the Labor Party in 1997 marked the arrival of a younger generation of leaders who gained their experience only in the postindependence period. Rigorous party discipline in the *Knesset* has helped to curb irresponsible action by individual *Knesset* members.

The coalition system has resulted in the acceptance of bargaining as a procedure for the allocation of government portfolios and the distribution of power, as well as being a factor in determining government policy. This has permitted the religious parties, particularly the National Religious Party and SHAS (Sephardi Torah Guardians), to play strong roles in government decision making because they are essential components of any parliamentary majority.

Legislature

The *Knesset*, a unicameral body of 120 members, is the supreme authority in the state. The *Knesset*'s main functions are similar to those of other modern parliaments and include votes of confidence or no confidence in the government, legislation, participation in the formulation of national policy, approval of budgets and taxation, election of the president, and generally supervising the activities of the administration. Legislation is usually presented by the Cabinet, although a member of the *Knesset* (MK) can initiate private bills. Bills are drafted by ministerial committees in consultation with the Ministry of Justice, approved by the Cabinet, and sent to the Speaker of the *Knesset*, who sends the bill to the appropriate committee for consideration. The legislation is read and voted on three times and is passed by a simple majority of MKs present at the time of the vote. An absolute majority is required for the election of the president and state comptroller and for changes in the system of proportional representation and the Basic Laws.

The state comptroller's office, which functions as an arm of the *Knesset*, oversees the accounts and operations of government ministries and other state bodies. Critical reports from the comptroller usually bring reforms.

Judiciary

The judiciary consists of two court systems, secular and religious. Judges for both types of courts are appointed by the president upon recommendation by the nominations committee chaired by the justice minister. This committee consists of the president of the Supreme Court and two other Supreme Court justices, two MKs, one other Cabinet member, and two members of the Chamber of Advocates (Israel's bar association). The Supreme Court is the highest court in the land. It hears appeals from lower courts in civil and criminal cases, issues writs of habeas corpus, protects the rights of the Israeli citizen, and protects the individual from arbitrary actions by public officials. The Supreme Court does not have the power of judicial review, but it may invalidate administrative actions and ordinances it regards as contrary to *Knesset* legislation. There are five district courts and numerous municipal and magistrate courts on the local level. The military courts are under the purview of the Military Court of Appeal, which is responsible to the Supreme Court.

Religious courts have jurisdiction over personal matters including marriage and divorce, alimony, inheritance, and so on. The High Rabbinical Court of Appeal is the highest Jewish religious court and is overseen by the Ashkenazic and a Sephardic chief rabbis. Its decisions are final. Christian and Muslim courts function in the same capacity.

All judges are tenured, holding office until death, resignation, mandatory retirement at age 70, or removal for cause.

Regional and Local Government

Israel is divided into six administrative districts under the jurisdiction of district commissioners and 14 subdistricts overseen by district officers. These officials are appointed by and responsible to the interior minister. A district official drafts legislation pertaining to local government, approves and controls local tax rates and budgets, reviews and approves by-laws and ordinances passed by locally elected councils, approves local public works projects, and decides matters of grants and loans to local governments.

Local and regional councils are elected by universal, secret, direct, proportional balloting. Mayors are chosen from among these councilmen with the same sort of coalition bargaining as occurs in the *Knesset*. *Kibbutzim* (collectives), *moshavim* (cooperatives), and other types of settlements are also governed by elected councils. Local governments are responsible for providing education, health and sanitation services, water, road maintenance, park and recreation facilities, firehouses, and setting and collecting local taxes and fees.

THE ELECTORAL SYSTEM

Elections for the *Knesset* are national, general, equal, secret, direct, and proportional. Every citizen 18 years of age or older has the right to vote but must be 21 years old in order to be a candidate for a *Knesset* seat. The same rules apply to local elections. In 1992, the *Knesset* approved an amendment to the Basic Law: The Government (1968), which was implemented in the elections for the 14th *Knesset* (1996), reforming the Israeli electoral system. The legislation provided that the prime minister be elected in a direct, nationwide election that would be held at the same time as, but independent of, general elections to the *Knesset*.

Elections to the *Knesset* were virtually unchanged by the new electoral law. The individual voter casts a ballot for a party list, not for an individual candidate. The list is prepared by each party, which ranks from 1 to 120 candidates on the list. Parties determine their lists by different methods, some by means of primary elections among registered party members and others by means of selection by a party committee or other body. The list stands for the entire country as a single constituency; there are no by-elections. If a seat in the *Knesset* becomes vacant, the next person on that party's list takes the seat. Elections are held by law at least every four years but can occur more frequently if the *Knesset* dissolves itself or is dissolved by the prime minister. Participation is very high, averaging about 80% of eligible voters.

Elections are supervised by the Central Election Committee, composed of representatives of each political party in the outgoing *Knesset* and chaired by a justice of the Supreme Court.

The proportional representation system is based on the d'Hondt system. Parties receiving at least 1.5% of the valid votes cast are entitled to a seat in the *Knesset*. The distribution is determined by dividing the total number of valid votes for all the lists that obtained at least 1.5% of the valid vote by the number of *Knesset* seats, the result being the quota required to obtain one seat. Each list receives the largest number of seats that can be determined by this process. The remaining seats are then distributed to those parties with the largest number of surplus votes. Any leftover seats go to the parties that have already won the greatest number of seats.

THE PARTY SYSTEM

Origins of the Parties

Israel's political parties trace their origins to the 1920s and 1930s when three categories of parties developed in the Yishuv: the labor or socialist left, the center and rightist nationalist grouping, and the religious parties. These formal parties, in turn, grew out of movements, clubs, and other groups that began to develop around the Zionist movement in Europe at the turn of the century. A few new parties, mostly small, have developed directly out of Israel's recent political experiences, e.g., Sephardic parties, parties taking a "dovish" stand on the Arab-Israeli conflict, and parties representing new immigrant communities such as those from the former Soviet Union.

The Parties in Law

The only restriction on the formation of a new party is that its list may be disqualified if its candidates espouse the aim of destroying the state or the state's democratic character or if its program is determined to be racist. New parties must collect signatures of supporters and post a bond before being allowed to campaign. These requirements, which are easily met, have permitted the creation of a large number of parties. The bond is forfeited if the party does not win at least one seat. Access to radio and television is provided by the government in proportion to the parties' strength in the outgoing *Knesset*, with a minimum set aside for each party and each new list. The state also provides some financial assistance to the parties according to the number of seats held in the previous *Knesset*. New parties elected to the *Knesset* receive funding retroactively based on the number of seats won in the election. Campaign expenditures are limited by law. All election expense accounts are audited by the state comptroller but are made public only in aggregate. Campaign donations also are restricted by law.

Party Organization

Political activity in Israel is highly ideological, often personalistic, and often based upon alliances of two or more parties. Charismatic individuals (e.g., David Ben-Gurion, Menachem Begin) often contribute to a party's success, and the formation of electoral alliances (GAHAL, Labor–MAPAM Alignment, Likud–Tzomet–Gesher) help the individual parties maximize their strength and influence on policy without losing their ideological identities. Smaller parties may consist of no more than one or two *Knesset* members and their loyal supporters, who are generally highly organized.

Israeli parties are marked by centralized leadership. The central committee and party oligarchs are chosen by party elections but control the party machinery and in some cases determine the rankings on the party's national election list and thus the candidates' chances of winning a seat in the *Knesset*. This central control extends to the local government level. Party branches are often permitted more flexibility in choosing candidates for local office, but party necessities may also require that such candidates be chosen by the party nominating committee or be imposed by the requirements of an alliance or government coalition agreement. The parties are highly disciplined. All viewpoints may be aired in annual conventions, and intense bargaining can occur between factions. But once a policy is decided upon, members are expected to support it, keep silent, or quit the party.

In addition to campaigning and party business in the *Knesset*, the major parties engage in a great variety of other activities: publishing; housing projects; recreational facilities; various types of cooperatives; banking; and in the case of the religious parties, large educational systems. All the major parties maintain a variety of auxiliary organizations for youth, women, and other special groups.

Israeli party membership as a percentage of eligible voters is unusually high. Membership is not required, but many voters join a party as a matter of civic duty and "fraternal" responsibility and to participate in intraparty elections. There are also some practical advantages to party membership and activity since the parties have considerable patronage to distribute. Their economic activities can provide both employment and security for party members.

Within the major groupings of left, center-right, and religious parties, the life of parties and alignments is fluid. Parties form, merge, split, dissolve, change names, and reform. Many small parties are formed primarily to advocate a special point of view on a narrow subject and have little hope of winning a *Knesset* seat. Others are the personal followings of major political figures who can lead their supporters into and out of alliances and mergers as necessary to further their effect on policy or advance their personal ambitions. Some of these small parties do not clearly fit into the three major groupings (left, right, religious) but from time to time may become aligned with one of them. Many parties form in preparation for national elections and dissolve or merge soon after. In 1996, 21 parties contested the election, while 11 secured the minimum 1.5% of the valid votes to obtain a seat in parliament. The two major blocs were relatively close: Labor secured 818,570 votes (34 seats), while Likud–Tzomet–Gesher secured 767,178 votes (32 seats).

Campaigning

Political campaigning takes place both within the parties and between the parties on the national scene. Within the parties, the goal is to achieve leadership positions and high positions on the election list; nationally, it is to secure as many votes as possible for the party. Campaigning focuses more on parties than on individuals, although at times individuals have been made the focus of opposition efforts. The campaigns involve television and radio appeals, substantial use of newspaper and magazine space, and rallies. Given the small size of the country and its population, extensive appearances of the parties' leading candidates throughout the state are an important aspect of the campaign. Generally, the parties seek to rally their traditional supporters and to sway the small number of uncommitted voters. Foreign and security policy issues have assumed greater saliency over domestic issues in recent elections, and security-related developments have often affected the outcome, such as in 1981 and 1996.

The following political parties are arranged in order: the center-right (includes Likud, Tenuat HaHerut, Gesher, Tzomet, and Molodet); the left (includes Israel Labor Party, MERETZ, Communists); religious parties (includes National Religious Party, SHAS, United Torah Judaism); Arab parties; and new political parties (Third Way, Yisrael Ba'aliya).

Political Parties and Knesset Election Results, 1988–96

Party	1988 %	1988 Seats	1992 %	1992 Seats	1996 %	1996 Seats
Labor Party[a]	30.0	39	34.6	44	26.8	34
MAPAM	2.5	3				
Shinui	1.7	2				
Citizens' Rights Movement	4.3	5				
MERETZ[b]			9.5	12	7.4	9
Likud	31.1	40	24.9	32	25.1	32
National Religious Party	3.9	5	4.9	6	7.8	9
Agudat Israel	4.5	5				
Degel HaTorah[c]	1.5	2				
United Torah Judaism[d]			3.2	4	3.2	4
SHAS	4.7	6	4.9	6	8.5	10
TZOMET[e]	2.0	2	6.3	8		
Tehiya	3.1	3	1.2	—		
Moledet[f]	1.9	2	2.3	3	2.3	2
Arab Dem. Party/United Arab List[g]	1.2	1	1.5	2	2.9	4
Progressive List for Peace	1.5	1	0.9	—		
Dem. Front for Peace and Equality[h]	3.7	4	2.3	3	4.2	5
Yisrael Ba'aliya					5.7	7
The Third Way					3.1	4

[a] Formed 1988—merger of Israel Labor and Yahad.

[b] Formed 1992—merger of MAPAM, Shinui, Citizens' Rights Movement.

[c] Formed 1988—splinter group from Agudat Israel.

[d] Formed 1992—merger of Agudat Israel, Degel HaTorah, Moriah.

[e] Formed 1988—splinter from Tehiya-TZOMET.

[f] Led by Rehavam Zeevi.

[g] Led by Adb el-Wahab Darawshe.

[h] Hadash.

LIKUD
(Union)

Likud was established in 1973, and the alliance crystallized at the time of the 1977 elections. It consisted of the GAHAL alliance (Herut and Liberals); the La'am alliance (the State List and the Free Center); Achdut (a one-man faction in the *Knesset*); and Shlomzion, Ariel Sharon's former party. Likud came to power in Israel in 1977, ousting the Labor government for the first time since Israel became independent. Although it retained its government position after the 1981 elections, its majority in the *Knesset* seldom exceeded two or three votes. In 1984, it lost its plurality and joined with the Labor Alignment to form a Government of National Unity in which it shared power and ministerial positions.

Likud emerged with one more seat than Labor in the 1988 election, and a new Government of National Unity was formed but with somewhat less power sharing. That government fell in 1990 in an unprecedented vote of no confidence, but Likud was able to fashion a new coalition government without Labor's participation. Likud suffered a stunning setback in the 1992 elections and found itself in the opposition for the first time since 1977. In 1996, the new Likud leader, Benjamin Netanyahu, won Israel's first-ever direct election for prime minister, slightly edging Labor candidate Shimon Peres by nine-tenths of 1%. Likud, running in an electoral alliance with the Tzomet and Gesher Parties, won 32 *Knesset* seats compared with Labor's 34, but Netanyahu was able to put together a Likud-dominated coalition commanding 66 seats in parliament with the religious parties and two new centrist parties. Likud is center-right, strongly nationalist, and assertive in foreign policy.

TENUAT HAHERUT
(Freedom Movement)

HISTORY

Herut is descended from the Revisionist movement of Vladimir Zeev Jabotinsky (1880–1940), who settled in Palestine after World War I and is regarded by many as the leading Zionist figure after Theodor Herzl, Zionism's founder. The Revisionists advocated militant ultranationalistic action as the means to achieve Jewish statehood. Revisionism called for the creation of a Jewish state in "Greater Israel" (all of Palestine and Jordan), rapid mass immigration of Jews into Palestine, formation of a free-enterprise economy, rapid industrialization—as opposed to agricultural settlements—to increase employment opportunities, a ban on strikes, and a strong army. In order to effect these policies and because they were outnumbered by leftist and moderate elements in the Zionist Organization, the Revisionists formed the New Zionist Organization in 1935. Their rejection of the socialist and liberal Zionist leadership and its conciliatory policy toward the mandatory power led Revisionists to form two paramilitary groups: Irgun Zvai Leumi (Etzel), founded in 1937, and the even more radical LEHI (Stern Gang), founded in 1939–40. The Irgun was commanded by Menachem Begin after 1943. Betar, the Revisionist youth movement, was founded by Vladimir Jabotinsky in 1920 and continues as the Herut youth wing today. Begin founded Herut in June 1948 to advocate the Revisionist program within the new political context of the State of Israel.

ORGANIZATION

Herut organization is highly complicated, varying from place to place, institution to institution, and election to election. While democratic procedures are used within the party and rank-and-file members can influence minor decisions, a small leadership group determines party policy. Herut and Likud headquarters are at 4 Etzel Street, Tel Aviv.

POLICY

Herut's political orientation has changed little over the years. It advocates the "inalienable" right of Jews to settle anywhere in Israel, in its historic entirety, including Judea and Samaria (the West Bank). Other policies include a minimum of economic controls, a restructured free-enterprise system to attract capital investment, and the right to strike.

MEMBERSHIP AND CONSTITUENCY

Israeli political parties are reluctant to reveal membership figures for fear that changes over the years might reveal negative trends in a party's fortunes. There is no reliable estimate of the numbers of Herut members. Herut's electoral strength comes mainly from the Ashkenazic poor and from the Sephardim. The latter generally have a lower level of education, are more traditional in religion and culture, and are less familiar with socialist theory than most Ashkenazim. It has been suggested that Begin's uncompromising attitude toward the Arabs, his strong leadership qualities, and his personal combination of both the national and religious elements in Judaism have attracted many of Herut's voters.

FINANCING

No reliable information is available on Herut finances or sources of income. Most income derives from membership dues and donations.

LEADERSHIP

Within Herut and Likud, Menachem Begin (born 1913 in Poland) was the primary force from Israel's independence until his retirement in 1983. He was regarded by many as a heroic figure because of his role as a leader of the underground in the Israeli struggle for independence. He was also a skillful politician and a charismatic figure. Upon Begin's retirement, Yitzhak Shamir (born 1915) became prime minister and party leader, although he was challenged within Herut by Ariel (Arik) Sharon (born 1928) and David Levy (born 1937). In 1993, Benjamin Netanyahu (born 1949) was elected Likud leader, and in 1996 he was elected prime minister.

PROSPECTS

Under Netanyahu's leadership, Likud is in a strong position to retain control of the government at least until the next scheduled election in 2000. It is a strong and nominally united party, although Netanyahu continues to face internal opposition and a potential leadership challenge from such Likud stalwarts as Ariel Sharon and Dan Meridor. In the policy arena, the biggest challenge facing Netanyahu and Likud is to keep the peace process going with the Palestinians—and possibly beginning peace talks with Syria—while continuing to insist on no Palestinian state, restricting Palestinian autonomy, and retaining control of the Golan Heights.

GESHER
(Bridge)

Gesher was founded in 1995 by David Levy, a former foreign minister and leader of Likud. Driven by his desire to become the head of Likud and prime minister, Levy, a Sephardi, saw himself blocked time and again by the Likud's Ashkenazi elite—most recently in 1993 when Benjamin Netanyahu was elected to succeed Yitzhak Shamir as party leader. At the time of his defection from Likud, Levy said that the party (under Netanyahu) had ceased to represent the interests of Israel's lower-income groups, still mainly Sephardi, who were the party's base of popular support and the reason why Likud had risen to power in the late 1970s. Levy's rhetoric, however, could not overshadow his fierce personality and leadership clash with Netanyahu. After Netanyahu pushed through a series of internal party electoral reforms designed to consolidate his control over the party, Levy bolted to set up his own Sephardi-based party and lay the groundwork for a run at the prime ministership in 1996. A few months before the May 1996 elections, Levy dropped out of the race for prime minister and agreed to form an electoral alliance with Netanyahu's Likud and the right-wing Tzomet party. Levy became vice prime minister and foreign minister in Prime Minister Netanyahu's government, but tensions continued between the two leaders. Levy left the government with his Gesher party in January 1998.

TZOMET
(Junction/Zionist Renewal)

Tzomet, led by Rafael Eitan, former IDF chief of staff, military leader, and hero, first came to prominence in the early 1980s when it formed an electoral alliance with the Tehiya (Renaissance) party. With an unyielding position on the status of the occupied territories, asserting that Israel's security needs demanded it not give up parts of the West Bank and Gaza Strip, the combined Tehiya-Tzomet won five seats in the 1984 election. Tzomet ran as an independent list under Eitan's leadership in the 1988 election and won two seats. In 1992, Tzomet benefited from the antiestablishment mood of the Israeli electorate, soaring to eight *Knesset* seats. Most pollsters attributed the party's success in large part to Eitan's image as a straight-shooting outsider who grew up on a farm and made the army his life. Eitan appealed to many voters, especially younger ones, because of his opposition to official corruption and a bloated civil service and his support for electoral reform and the draft of Orthodox yeshiva students. Eitan brought his Tzomet party into an electoral alliance with Likud and Gesher for the 1996 election, maintaining the party's independent identity and organization. Eitan became deputy prime minister, minister of agriculture, and minister of the environment in Prime Minister Netanyahu's government.

MOLEDET
(Motherland)

Moledet, a right-wing nationalist party formed and still headed by retired army general Rehavam Zeevi, won two *Knesset* seats in the 1988 election. Zeevi created the new party in reaction to what he and other right-wing nationalists believed was the Government of National Unity's weakness in failing to end the Palestinian uprising (*intifada*) in the West Bank and Gaza Strip. The party's campaign literature called for the "transfer" of all Arabs from the occupied territories. Moledet increased its representation in the *Knesset* to three seats in the June 1992 election but fell back again to two seats in the 1996 election. The party's rejection of the Oslo Accords establishing the basis for peace between Israel and the Palestinians and its continued advocacy of the "transfer" of Arabs out of the territories made the party unsuitable for inclusion in Prime Minister Netanyahu's government.

ISRAEL LABOR PARTY
(Mifleget HaAvodah HaYisraelit)

HISTORY

The Israel Labor Party came into being in 1968 as a result of the merger of three labor parties: MAPAI (*Mifleget Poalei Yisrael*; Israel Workers Party), *Achdut HaAvodah* (Unity of Labor), and Rafi (*Reshimat Poalei Israel*; Israel Labor List). MAPAI originated with the union of two smaller parties in 1930, but the roots of the movement can be traced back to the turn of the century in Europe, especially Russia. MAPAI soon became the dominant party in Israel. The two parties that formed it had established the trade union federation Histadrut in 1920, and under their leadership Histadrut became the embodiment of Jewish Palestine. MAPAI controlled it as well as the National Assembly and the Jewish Agency. Many of the noted figures in the creation of Israel came out of MAPAI—Ben-Gurion, Moshe Sharett (Shertok), Golda Meir (Myerson), Moshe Dayan, and others.

After Israel became independent, MAPAI consistently won the largest number of votes in *Knesset* elections, usually about one-third of the total. It was the leading member of all government coalitions and ordinarily held the key portfolios of defense, foreign affairs, and finance, as well as the prime ministership. The party permeated the government, the bureaucracy, the economy, and most of the other institutions of Israel.

Achdut HaAvodah, originally the party of Ben-Gurion in the 1920s, was militantly class-conscious in its early years. It was merged with MAPAI from 1930 to 1944, when it left in disagreement with MAPAI's gradualist policies, the prohibition of party factions, and the general exclusion of more radical elements from MAPAI leadership. It rejoined MAPAI in 1965.

Rafi appeared in 1965, when Ben Gurion and his protégés Moshe Dayan and Shimon Peres left MAPAI, partly out of dissatisfaction with the leadership of Levi Eshkol. Rafi advocated more technocratic efficiency in government, the transfer of some of the Histadrut's functions to the state, and reform of the electoral system in favor of single-member districts with simple plurality elections. Rafi stood alone for only one election (1965) and gained a respectable 10 seats in the *Knesset*.

In 1969, Labor formed an election Alignment (*Maarach*) with MAPAM, a socialist Zionist party that championed the cause of Israel's Arab population and promoted a solution to the Arab-Israeli conflict. The two parties retained their own organizations and memberships. The Alignment continued MAPAI's dominant position until 1977, when lackluster leadership, corruption scandals, and the founding of the Democratic Movement for Change made way for the Likud victory.

In 1984, the Alignment emerged as the largest party in the *Knesset*, and its leader, Shimon Peres, was given the mandate to form the new government. He formed a Government of National Unity with himself as prime minister for the first two years of the government's tenure and with Likud leader Yitzhak Shamir as prime minister for the last two years. The Alignment was the leading force in the parliament and government. Peres's decision to form a coalition with the rival Likud bloc prompted MAPAM to leave the Alignment. To compensate in part for the loss of MAPAM's six *Knesset* seats, the Alignment co-opted Ezer Weizman and his Yahad faction (three *Knesset* seats) upon entering the 1984 unity coalition. Weizman and Yahad formally joined the Labor Party in 1988. The Labor Party won one less seat than Likud in the 1988 election, and the two parties joined in a new Government of National Unity, albeit dominated by Likud. That government lasted until the spring of 1990 when Labor withdrew over Likud's unwillingness to participate in a United States peace initiative. Labor subsequently engineered a successful vote of no confidence (the first ever in Israel's history) bringing about the government's downfall. Although given the first chance to form a new coalition, Peres was unable to do so, and a new Likud government was eventually fashioned.

Yitzhak Rabin, former chief of staff and hero of the 1967 Six-Day War, led the Labor Party to a decisive victory in the 1992 election, although Labor fell short of a parliamentary majority of its own, and he quickly formed a coalition government. The election victory marked a dramatic personal political comeback for Rabin, who returned to the prime ministership 15 years after having been forced to resign the leadership of Labor and relinquish the position of prime minister because of a financial scandal. But the victory did not represent a return to Labor's political dominance in Israel. Rather, it represented a classic case of voters punishing the incumbents, Likud, for years of "bad government" and other failures. Prime Minister Rabin was assassinated by an Israeli right-wing extremist in November 1995. Shimon Peres was returned to the prime ministership and became his party's candidate to run in Israel's first direct election for prime minister in May 1996. Peres narrowly lost that

election, although Labor won two more seats in the *Knesset* than Likud. In 1997, Ehud Barak, former chief of staff and Rabin's hand-picked successor, was elected to replace Peres as Labor Party chairman.

ORGANIZATION

Labor Party organization, like that of Herut, varies considerably. It too uses highly democratic procedures within the party but is really run by a small leadership group. Its headquarters are at 110 HaYarkon Street, Tel Aviv.

POLICY

Labor's policies are Zionistic and socialistic. They include support for the immigration of Jews to Israel, establishment of a social welfare state, a state-planned and publicly regulated economy with room for the participation of private capital, full employment, minimum wages, and the right to strike. Labor stands for the separation of religion and the state, although it has historically made major concessions to the religious parties in this area. It supports equality for minorities, including the Arabs. Labor believes in a negotiated settlement with the Arab states without prior conditions and accepts the possibility of returning some of the occupied territories to Arab sovereignty in return for peace treaties, normalization of relations, and adequate security arrangements.

MEMBERSHIP AND CONSTITUENCY

No accurate data on the party's membership are available. The party's support comes mainly from lower- and middle-class Ashkenazic Jews with a smattering of Sephardic support. The kibbutz and moshav movements primarily support Labor, and Histadrut remains a Labor Party stronghold.

FINANCING

Data on the party's financing are unavailable. Most income is derived from membership dues and contributions.

LEADERSHIP

Ehud Barak (born 1942) is the party's head. Barak, a former chief of staff, was brought into the government of Prime Minister Rabin in 1995 as minister of the interior. At the time, most observers believed that Rabin was grooming Barak to be his successor as Labor Party leader. Following Rabin's assassination, Barak served as foreign minister in the government of Prime Minister Peres. In June 1997, Barak easily won a four-way contest to succeed Peres as leader of the Labor Party.

PROSPECTS

Ehud Barak and the Labor Party face an uphill battle in their bid to capture the prime minister's position and control of the government. To be successful, Barak and Labor must be able to break down the coalition of anti-Labor forces that helped Likud leader Netanyahu win the 1996 election for prime minister: the disaffected Sephardic working class, Russian immigrants, hawkish religious party voters, and the ultra-Orthodox community.

MERETZ
(Vigor)

MERETZ was formed prior to the 1992 election from the merger of three smaller center and center-left parties: *Shinuy* (Change), RATZ (*HaTenua LeZechuyot HaEzrah UleShalom*; Citizens' Rights Movement), and MAPAM (*Mifleget Poalim Hameuhedet*; United Workers Party).

Shinuy was founded as a small protest group by Professor Amnon Rubinstein (born 1931) of Tel Aviv University in the wake of the 1973 war. It sought to effect changes in the Israeli political system and political life. It developed a party organization but did not have a candidate of imposing stature. In 1976, it joined with others to form the Democratic Movement for Change (DMC), which secured 15 seats in the 1977 election. The DMC was constituted under the leadership of an archeology professor, Yigael Yadin, who served as deputy prime minister under Begin after the 1977 elections. Although composed mostly of elements from the center-left, the DMC could not be neatly classified in terms of traditional Israeli political ideology. It focused on the need for electoral reform and general improvement in the political life of the country. The DMC's initial success was not enough to make it an indispensable element in the new government, and failing to achieve its major goals, it dissolved itself just prior to the 1981 elections. *Shinuy* again emerged as an independent unit and won 2 seats in the 1981 elections and joined the Government of National Unity after securing 3 seats in the 1984 election. *Shinuy* won only 2 seats in the 1988 election and refrained from joining the new Likud-dominated Government of National Unity.

The Citizens' Rights Movement was founded in 1973 by Shulamit Aloni (born 1928), a former Labor Party member and civil rights activist. RATZ did well following the 1973 war when there was substantial discontent with the Israel Labor Party. It won 3 seats in the 1973 elections and joined the government coalition for a brief period in 1974. Its position declined in the 1977 and 1981 elections, and, following the latter, Aloni pledged her party's support to Labor in an effort to block Likud's efforts to form the new government. The party changed character in the 1980s. It became a party whose membership was drawn from a variety of older groups: the historical CRM, including various liberals and secularists, the academics of the "Group of 100" (including former

Peace Now and Labor Party doves), and other disaffected left-wing voters. Its constituency was primarily the "middle-class" Ashkenazi population, and its platform featured full civil rights for all Israelis. Yossi Sarid (born 1940), another former Labor Party activist, assumed a significant role in shaping the party's dovish foreign policy. The CRM's greatest success at the polls came in 1988 when it won 5 *Knesset* seats.

MAPAM was organized in 1948 when *HaShomer HaTzair* merged with radical elements from *Achdut HaAvodah*. From its beginnings, the party was more Marxist than MAPAI. The former *Achdut HaAvodah* members left in 1954 because of MAPAM's pro-Soviet orientation and acceptance of Arabs as party members. Although the party's domestic policy was essentially indistinguishable from MAPAI's, MAPAM's share of the vote in national elections declined steadily before it joined the Alignment for the 1969 elections. MAPAM ended its alliance with Labor in September 1984 over the issue of the formation of the Government of National Unity with Likud. MAPAM ran as an independent party list in the 1988 election, winning 3 seats in the *Knesset*.

In the 1992 election, MERETZ, with Shulamit Aloni at the head of the party list, ran on a platform stressing the need for territorial compromise in order to resolve the Arab-Israeli conflict and a freeze on the expansion of existing settlements and building of new settlements in the occupied territories. It advocated the reform of Israel's electoral system in order to broaden political participation and make parties and *Knesset* representatives more accountable to the public. The party also called for greater pluralism and tolerance in the country's educational system, a strict separation between religion and state, and the conscription of Yeshiva students into the army. The new party won 12 seats in the election, 2 more than the movement's component groups held in the outgoing *Knesset*. MERETZ joined Labor in the government formed by Yitzhak Rabin, with Aloni appointed as education minister. In 1993, Aloni was removed from that post because of her frequent attacks against the Orthodox Jewish community and sidelined in the relatively minor post of minister of communications, science, and culture. At the same time, Yossi Sarid was brought into the Cabinet as environment minister. Sarid replaced Aloni as party head prior to the 1996 election, in which MERETZ won 9 seats.

COMMUNISTS

The Communist movement began during the Palestine mandate and has existed continuously since that time, although it has been plagued by internal divisions and splits. Although they are isolated from the mainstream of political life, Communist parties have been legal in Israel since independence and have been represented in the

Knesset continuously. They generally secure a large portion of their support from Israel's Arab population, not apparently out of ideological commitment but as a form of dissent. On average, the Communists have secured four or five seats in the *Knesset*. The Israel Communist Party (*Miflaga Kommunistit Yisraelit*; MAKI) was founded in 1948 and split in 1965. The splinter group, the New Communist List (most commonly known as Hadash, short for *Reshima Kommunistit HaDasha*, or by its Hebrew acronym, RAKAH), was pro-Moscow, strongly anti-Zionist, and primarily Arab in membership and has come to dominate the Communist movement ever since. The party is also known by the name of its 1977 joint electoral list with the Black Panthers (a 1970s protest movement composed of Jews of North African origin), the Democratic Front for Peace and Equality (DFPE), which won five seats. The DFPE won four seats in each of the elections in 1981, 1984, and 1988.

As with other Communist parties worldwide, the collapse of the Soviet Union led to soul-searching within Hadash in an effort to legitimize the party's continued adherence to Communist ideology. The head of the party's *Knesset* list in 1992 noted during the campaign that the party was not built on the basis of relations with the former Soviet Union and that communism was and still is an ideological inspiration. Hadash won only three seats in the 1992 election. In 1996, under the leadership of Mahameed Hashem (born 1945), Hadash increased its *Knesset* representation to five seats. Its platform called for the total withdrawal of Israel from the occupied territories, including from southern Lebanon; the establishment of a sovereign, independent Palestinian state alongside Israel in the territories occupied by Israel in 1967, with eastern Jerusalem as its capital; and the cancellation of all "strategic" agreements between Israel and the United States.

NATIONAL RELIGIOUS PARTY (NRP)
(Miflaga Datit-leumit; MAFDAL)

HISTORY

Founded in 1956, the NRP was a full merger of *Mizrachi* (short for "spiritual center"), formally established as a party in Palestine in 1918, and *HaPoel HaMizrachi* (Mizrachi Worker), founded in 1922. *HaPoel* retained a degree of independence as the trade union section of the party responsible for immigration and absorption, labor and vocational affairs, housing, settlement, culture, pension funds and economic affairs, and so on. The central NRP organization was responsible for policy, party organization, religion and rabbinical relations, and publications. From its beginning, this party of Orthodox religious Zionists began to have an impact on the movement, electing 19% of the delegates to the 12th Zionist congress in 1921. The NRP has participated within the mainstream of Jewish life and the activities of the state of Israel since independence, has been a significant partner in almost all of Israel's governments, and consequently has wielded substantial political power.

Since the early 1980s, the NRP has suffered from internal differences over issues and leadership that have led to the creation of factions—each with its own leadership and agendas—and breakaway parties. Prior to the 1981 election, Aharon Abuhatzeira, the scion of an important Moroccan rabbinical family, bolted from the NRP and formed TAMI (*Tenuah LeMassoret Israel*; Movement for Jewish Tradition) as a North African–oriented religious party. Abuhatzeira broke away from the NRP in part over the issue of ethnic representation, but he was also upset by the perceived lack of support he received from the NRP leadership during his trial for corruption. His new party list won 3 seats in the 1981 election, drawing support from the Oriental community, and appeared to have a major electoral impact on the NRP, which saw its *Knesset* strength cut in half from 12 to 6 seats. TAMI's political fortunes, however, declined steadily thereafter. In the 1984 election, it won only 1 seat, and in 1988 Abuhatzeira was coopted into Likud and guaranteed a safe slot on its list of *Knesset* candidates.

The NRP further splintered in 1984 when its right-wing faction broke away and joined with several other right-wing politicians to form the *Morasha* (Heritage) party. *Morasha* won 2 seats in the 1984 election, and the NRP again lost ground, falling to 4 seats in parliament. *Morasha* collapsed in 1988 when its former NRP component left to rejoin the NRP. The reintegration of the right-wing faction strengthened the nationalist tendencies within the NRP. Changes within the party leadership also contributed to the party's rightward swing. Yosef Burg, the party's moderate elder statesman, was no longer influential in party affairs and his successor as party leader, Zvulun Hammer, was himself replaced by Avner Shaki. Shaki, a Sephardi, was an ardent supporter of the *Gush Emunim* (Bloc of the Faithful) settlement movement in the West Bank and was committed to retention of all the occupied territories. Shaki also took a less conciliatory position on domestic religious issues, particularly the question of changing the Law of Return to recognize only those conversions to Judaism performed according to Orthodox religious law. Though the NRP suffered a small additional percentage loss in popular vote in the 1988 election, it managed to secure 5 *Knesset* seats.

In response to the NRP's rightward trend, party doves left in 1988 and formed the Meimad (Dimension–Religious Center Camp) party. The new party list fell about 7,000 votes short of the threshold (then 1%) for attaining a seat in the 1988 election.

The NRP won 6 *Knesset* seats in the 1992 election. It reinstated Hammer as head of its list, dropping Shaki to the second slot, and used the double entendre "NRP Right at Your Side" as its campaign slogan. The party's campaign identification with the political right wing, and implicitly with Likud, virtually ruled out any chance that NRP leaders would be able to maneuver after the election to join the new Labor coalition under Prime Minister Rabin.

The NRP fared much better in the 1996 election, winning 9 seats. The party's platform called for applying Israeli sovereignty over greater Jerusalem, including the Gush Etzion settlement bloc and the settlements of Ma'ale Adumim and Givat Ze'ev; strengthening Jewish settlement throughout the West Bank, including Hebron (due to be handed over to Palestinian administrative control under terms of the Oslo accords); and retaining all of the Golan Heights.

ORGANIZATION

The party is overseen by the World Center, a council elected by the world conference of the party. (Despite the word "world," the conference is overwhelmingly Israeli as is the World Center.) The conference also elects the chairman of the World Center, the party leader. Delegates to the conference are elected from local party branches by the party members. The World Center supervises the party's women's and youth organizations. The former has over 50,000 members in Israel and is active in providing nurseries and kindergartens and cultural and vocational education for its members. The best known of the party's youth organizations is *Bnai Akiva*. The NRP also has a sports organization, *Elitzur*. In addition, the United Mizrachi Bank and the Mishav construction company are also NRP enterprises. Bar Ilan University and the Mosad HaRav book publishing house were established by Mizrachi and are a part of the NRP operation. Party headquarters are at 108 Ahad Haam Street, Tel Aviv.

POLICY

The NRP was founded to emphasize the need for legislation based on Judaic religious law (*Halacha*) and protective of a "Torah-true" tradition. It actively supports Jewish immigration, the development of the private sector, and government support of all Halachically necessary religious activities, including a religious school system and rabbinical councils in every city and town. These aims have been constant since the founding of NRP's predecessors, and they have been realized to a large degree. With only some minor intraparty disagreement, the NRP view was that it was organized for religious purposes and had no particular role to play in political, economic, or foreign affairs. It was able to cooperate effectively with MAPAI and Labor primarily because of its willingness to defer to the left on foreign and defense questions in return for support on religious matters.

With the Israeli capture of the West Bank and the Sinai peninsula in 1967, however, NRP attitudes began to change. The capture of ancient Israeli cities—Hebron, Shechem (Nablus), and Old Jerusalem—was seen as a miraculous achievement in fulfillment of the covenant between God and the Jewish people. The NRP believed that the return of any of the territory of historic Israel to Arab control would be a repudiation of that covenant. On that basis, NRP "hawks" sought to focus the party's efforts on the rapid settlement of the new territory with the aim of securing it for Israel in perpetuity.

Although "hawks" are to be found in all of the NRP factions, they appear to be concentrated in the youth faction, which originally sought to reform the party organization, in part to increase the opportunities for newer and younger members in the party and government. They also wanted to increase NRP's independence in the coalition with the Labor Party. After 1967, the youth faction sought to appeal to nontraditional voters with the slogan "no return of any part of Eretz [historic land of] Israel." Largely because both groups are composed of the same people, the youth faction has strong but informal ties with *Gush Emunim*, the leading movement of West Bank settlers. In some respects, the youth faction considers itself the political representation of the *Gush Emunim*. youth faction leaders have come to increasing prominence in both the NRP and the government.

MEMBERSHIP AND CONSTITUENCY

No reliable data on NRP membership are available. Voting support comes primarily from Orthodox Jews (the vast majority of religiously active Jews in Israel, where the U.S. Conservative and Reform movements are barely represented). While some traditional Sephardic Jews also support the party, it is from the Ashkenazic community that the party draws most of its support and its leadership.

FINANCING

No reliable information on NRP financing is available. Membership dues and donations provide the bulk of the party's income.

LEADERSHIP

The factionalism of the NRP reflects both personal conflicts and differing policy perspectives. Yosef Burg (born 1909) was the party leader from its founding until the late 1970s and served in most Israeli Cabinets up until 1977. A man of great political skills, he worked successfully to maintain and expand the religious foundation of the state. His seniority and role as head of the largest faction (*Lamifneh*) secured his dominant position in the party, but he did not dictate its positions or policies. His influence was, in part, the result of his shrewd use of patronage in allocating jobs in the party and the party-controlled institutions. As a government minister, he was also able to distribute many public jobs in the religious and educational establishments and a variety of posts controlled by the Ministry of the Interior. Zvulun Hammer (born 1936), who for many years was also head of the youth faction, served as party leader until his death in January 1998. Hammer was appointed education minister in the 1996 government of Prime Minister Netanyahu.

PROSPECTS

The NRP is firmly entrenched in the right-wing nationalist camp allied with Likud. It will continue to play a key role as a coalition partner for Likud, and its voters will remain a critical voting bloc that will support any Likud candidate for prime minister.

SHAS
(Sephardi Torah Guardians)

SHAS split from the ultra-Orthodox *Agudat Yisrael* (see below) and contested the 1984 election. While ideologically close to *Agudat Yisrael*, the former Sephardi chief rabbi, Ovadia Yosef, and other Sephardi rabbis decided to leave the Ashkenazi-dominated Aguda and set up SHAS after Aguda leaders refused to place enough Sephardi candidates on the party's list for the 1984 election. The founders of SHAS wished to get the funds, political jobs, and other forms of support of which they had felt deprived. Eliezer Schach, an Ashkenazi rabbi and leader of non-Hasidic elements within Aguda, helped in the creation of SHAS. (Hasidism comprises several ultra-Orthodox, somewhat mystical, sects, whose leadership tends to be hereditary.) Schach was troubled by the influence of Aguda's Hasidic trends over its non-Hasidic members and thought the formation of a separate Sephardi ultra-Orthodox party would force Aguda's Hasidic leadership to pay more attention to the non-Hasidic segment of the party. SHAS won 4 *Knesset* seats in 1984.

SHAS's strength increased to 6 *Knesset* seats in the 1988 election. The party's success was largely the result of its participation in the previous Government of National Unity. SHAS controlled the Interior Ministry—traditionally the bastion of the NRP—which enabled it to channel funds through local governments to provide services to its constituency of haredi (pious) Sephardi Jews. SHAS also exploited the Sephardi-Ashkenazi split among Israelis, stressing in its platform the restoration of Oriental culture to a position of prominence in Israeli society.

Although SHAS gained some votes in the 1992 election, it did not manage to increase its *Knesset* representation beyond the 6 seats it already held. During the election campaign, the party's advertisements and statements by its leaders strongly suggested that SHAS intended to throw its lot only with a Likud-led government. When it became clear, however, that Labor had won the election and would be in a position to block a Likud-led coalition, SHAS leaders reconsidered their options and eventually decided to join the new government headed by Yitzhak Rabin.

SHAS made significant gains in the 1996 election, increasing its seats in parliament to 10 and confounding the preelection predictions of pollsters. The party continued to stress to its constituents a combination of ethnic pride and traditional values to compensate for the sense of cultural alienation felt by many of them. SHAS also exploited the strong mystical tendencies among potential SHAS voters, distributing 150,000 amulets blessed by the elderly mystic Rabbi Yitzhak Kadourie. In addition, it benefited from having as its spiritual mentor the former Sephardi chief rabbi, Ovadia Yosef, who was popular even among non-Orthodox Orientals. In the prime minister's race, the party's leaders refused to back either Likud leader Netanyahu or Labor leader Peres and allowed their followers to vote for either candidate. In this way, Yosef left all options open for joining either a Likud- or Labor-led coalition afterward.

ORGANIZATION

SHAS formed a council of sages known as *Moetzet Hachmei Ha-Tora* to guide major policy decisions and its leadership is closely linked to the former Sephardic chief rabbi, Ovadia Yosef. SHAS has built an extensive social service network, including low-fee day care centers and afternoon schools, in the Sephardi neighborhoods of Jerusalem, Tel Aviv, and underdeveloped towns throughout the country.

POLICY

SHAS was founded to promote the interests of Sephardi ultra-Orthodox and traditional Sephardim. It argued that the Torah was its platform and regarded itself as a movement of spiritual awakening. It seeks to ensure government support for the party's network of educational and social bodies. The party's leadership holds generally dovish views on issues associated with the Middle East peace process and future disposition of the occupied territories. In the 1990 successful no-confidence vote in the *Knesset*, for example, SHAS refused to support Likud because Rabbi Yosef wanted Prime Minister Shamir to agree to the U.S. initiative to convene Palestinian-Israeli peace talks in Cairo. The party's rank-and-file, however, is generally more hawkish than the leadership on territorial issues.

MEMBERSHIP AND CONSTITUENCY

No reliable data on SHAS membership are available. The party's supporters generally live either in the poor neighborhoods of Jerusalem and Tel Aviv or in the small, poor development towns.

FINANCING

No reliable information on SHAS financing is available.

LEADERSHIP

The former Sephardi chief rabbi of Israel, Ovadia Yosef, is the spiritual mentor of SHAS. The party is led by Rabbi Aryeh Deri (born 1959), who has been battling corruption charges in a seemingly endless trial.

PROSPECTS

SHAS plays an important role in the center of the religious camp and is a potential partner in any Likud- or Labor-led coalition. The party's supporters, however, likely will continue to support Likud candidates as long as Labor is identified with the secular forces that religious voters see as threatening the Jewishness of the state.

UNITED TORAH JUDAISM
(Achdut HaTorah)

United Torah Judaism (UTJ) was formed prior to the 1992 election as a result of the merger of two ultra-Orthodox parties, *Agudat Yisrael* (Association of Israel) and its offshoot, *Degel HaTorah* (Flag of the Torah), which constitute the united party's two main factions.

Agudat Yisrael, the world organization of Orthodox Jews founded in 1912 by various rabbis and other religious leaders in Europe, was at first opposed to Zionism, believing that Israel should wait for divine redemption and the coming of the Messiah and that the establishment of a political state in Palestine was heretical. Although it boycotted the institutions of the Jewish community in Palestine, it eventually gave partial backing to the Zionist endeavor when it supported the establishment of Israel (but without ascribing any religious significance to it) and, upon becoming a political party in 1948, participated in the institutions of the state. As an independent party until 1992, it was represented in parliament and supported most of the coalition governments, but after 1952 it refused to accept a Cabinet portfolio. Its voting strength lies in Jerusalem and Bnei Brak and consists mostly of Ashkenazim.

In 1984, SHAS broke away from the Ashkenazi-dominated Aguda to contest that year's *Knesset* elections. The defection of the Sephardi wing of the party appeared to cost Aguda some of its support in the election; its *Knesset* representation was cut in half from four to two seats.

Agudat Yisrael was again split in 1988. This time, Rabbi Eliezer Schach, who had helped to engineer the creation of SHAS four years earlier, left Aguda with his followers over what he saw as the growing influence within the party of the Lubavitch Hasidic sect and its leader, Brooklyn-based Rabbi Menachem M. Schneerson. So, on the eve of the 1988 election, Schach formed the rival ultra-Orthodox party *Degel HaTorah*. This development led Schneerson to mobilize his followers to vote for *Agudat Yisrael*, and his efforts were largely responsible for Aguda's success at the polls. It secured nearly three times the number of votes it had in 1984 and increased its *Knesset* seats from two to five. *Degel HaTorah* won two seats.

Degel HaTorah was all but negotiated out of existence prior to the June 1992 election when Rabbi Schach agreed that the party join *Agudat Yisrael* in a unified list called United Torah Judaism. Also joining the bloc was a small breakaway party from SHAS, the Moriah party. Schach accepted the fifth and seventh spots on the joint list for his *Degel HaTorah* representatives, but the new electoral alliance won only four seats in the election, as compared with the seven seats that the three constituent groups had held in the outgoing *Knesset*. The Moriah party representative, who had the number two slot on the party list, was forced by a preelection promise to resign his seat in order to allow *Degel HaTorah* to take up the party's fourth and final seat in the new *Knesset*.

United Torah Judaism retained its four *Knesset* seats in the 1996 election but was the only religious party that failed to increase its representation. The party fell solidly behind Likud leader Benjamin Netanyahu in his bid to become prime minister, heeding the injunction of *Agudat Yisrael*'s council of Torah sages to vote for the candidate who would be more likely "to work in the spirit of religion and Jewish tradition."

All crucial UTJ decisions on policy are made not by the party's *Knesset* members or its membership but by *Agudat Yisrael*'s 12-member council of Torah sages, composed of revered rabbis, heads of yeshivas (religious schools), and members of Hasidic dynasties. Besides the council, the party's central institutions are the great assembly, composed of representatives of the local branches, the central world council, and the world executive committee. It has its own school network in which religious instruction is a major part of the curriculum. The government supplies most of the funds for the school system.

UTJ is primarily concerned with enhancing the role of religion in the state and is opposed to all forms of secularism. Its support for the Netanyahu coalition was secured on the basis of a lengthy coalition agreement containing numerous concessions to the group's religious perspectives, e.g., strict Sabbath laws and revision of legislation to accommodate orthodox Jewish principles. The parliamentary leader is Meir Porush, son of a longtime *Agudat Yisrael* MK, Rabbi Menachem Porush. Party headquarters are at 17 Hadaf HaYomi Street, Tel Aviv.

ARAB PARTIES

Arab political parties have been a part of the Israeli political scene since independence, and Arabs have been represented on a regular basis in the *Knesset*. In the elections for the *Knesset* between 1949 and 1969, the majority of Israeli Arabs supported the dominant Jewish party or the Arab lists affiliated with it. In 1973 and 1977, this support declined; the Communists gained nearly 50% of Arab votes in 1977. To a great extent, this reflected growing Arab nationalism and support for the Palestinians by the Communists. Overall Arab participation in the political process also declined during the same period. In 1981, the Alignment tripled its vote among the Arabs of Israel compared with 1977; this was seen as a vote for the best of the bad alternatives. Much of the turn to Labor was seen as anti-Begin and anti-Likud out of disappointment with Begin's ignoring of the Arab problem in Israel. There was an unexpectedly low turnout of voters and a sharp decline in support for RAKAH.

In 1984 an Arab-Jewish list called the Progressive List for Peace (PLP) was formed to offer Israeli Arabs and ultradovish Jews an alternative. The party openly advocated the creation of an independent Palestinian state alongside Israel and accepted the PLO as the legitimate representative of the Palestinians. The PLP won two seats in the 1984 election and one seat in 1988. The PLP failed to cross the 1.5% threshold in the 1992 election and was not represented in the 13th *Knesset*. A more moderate Arab position was advanced by Abd el-Wahab Darawshe and his Arab Democratic Party (ADP) in 1988. Darawshe, an Arab who was elected to the *Knesset* in 1984 on the Labor list, left Labor in response to the national unity government's handling of the *intifada*. His list of candidates was made up entirely of Arabs, in contrast with RAKAH and the PLP, yet he intended from the outset to make his party acceptable to the center-left Zionist parties in order to be able to exert influence within the political system. Darawshe won one seat in the 1988 election and two seats in the 1992 election. In 1996, the ADP accepted into its ranks two smaller parties, including the Islamic Movement, an Islamist group that had been active for several years at the local level, and renamed itself the United Arab List. Led by Abd al-Malik Dahamshe (born 1945), a lawyer who became more religious while serving a seven-year prison sentence in Israel for recruiting members for the PLO's Fatah faction, the United Arab List won four seats in the 1996 election.

THIRD WAY

The Third Way, a centrist political party, developed from an ideological movement based in the Labor Party. Initially it was seen as a grouping of the "hawks" of the Labor Party who sought to balance the doves on the left side of the party and advocated that party's "centrist" tradition—for control over the Golan Heights, the Jordan Valley, and Greater Jerusalem, including Gush Etzion, but against continued rule over the Palestinians.

It became a political party promoting a "third way"—not that of Labor or Likud—out of the conviction that Labor (under Yitzhak Rabin and later Shimon Peres) had deviated from its 1992 election platform and was prepared to relinquish some or all of the Golan Heights and make other concessions that would deleteriously affect Israel's security. As a party it sees itself as an alternative to the Likud and the right-wing national religious movement on the one hand and left-wing groupings such as MERETZ and Labor Party doves on the other.

It established itself as a separate political party in late 1995 and contested the 1996 election under the leadership of Avigdor Kahalani, a retired general and a Labor Party *Knesset* member.

The party was founded by a group of Labor Party members. Various prominent personalities were initially involved with the group when it was based in the Labor Party, but as it moved to become an independent political party to contest the 1996 *Knesset* election some individuals left the movement. Its prime founders and continuing advocates are Avigdor Kahalani and Yehuda Harel. Yehuda Harel is a former longtime Labor Party stalwart and Golan Heights settler and activist. Avigdor Kahalani was born in Ness Ziona of Yemenite parents. Kahalani was seriously wounded on the Golan Heights in the Six-Day War and commanded the IDF armored brigade that stopped the Syrian breakthrough there in the Yom Kippur War.

The Third Way seeks peace with maximum security. It combines a willingness to compromise with an insistence on keeping areas deemed vital to Israel's security. It also focuses on the integrity of Jerusalem as Israel's capital.

The Golan Heights was the issue that precipitated the breach with Labor. Kahalani and his associates argue that it is a major mistake for Israel to withdraw from the Golan Heights, especially in the near term; in the far future, perhaps—seen as at least two generations. Jewish settlement in the Golan is important: these are the real pioneers who contribute to Israel's security and help to ensure Israel's water resources. Kahalani is determined that the Golan should not fall into Syrian hands, at least not now. Kahalani has proposed that Israel test Assad's intentions over "a few generations" before agreeing to withdraw from the Golan.

YISRAEL BA'ALIYA

Yisrael Ba'aliya was founded in March 1996. Natan Sharansky, former prisoner of Zion in the Soviet Union, became the leader.

Among its primary goals was to promote *aliyah* (immigration) from the Soviet Union. Its campaign slogan for the 1996 election was "Security for Israel, Respect for Immigration." It argued that it would not only focus on immigration issues but also had a clear policy on security, religion and state, society and, economics. Yet a major focus was on immigration and immigrants, and Sharansky argued that the establishment ignored the needs of new immigrants, that its attitude was obtuse, paternalistic, and patronizing.

Despite the fact that its leaders are Russian, its lingua franca is Russian (its founding convention in Jerusalem was conducted in Russian), its interests are the interests of Russian immigrants, and its campaign was conducted primarily in Russian, Yisrael Ba'aliya tried to shed its image as a new immigrants party while focusing extensively on the issues of importance to those new immigrants.

Yisrael Ba'aliya did unexpectedly well in the 1996 *Knesset* election: it was the first "Russian" party to enter the *Knesset* and the first immigrant party ever to win seven seats. A new party, it became also a political power as a consequence of the election results. Sharansky strongly felt the need to open the economy and improve economic development. With Yisrael Ba'aliya joining the government coalition, he was named minister of trade and industry and his colleague Yuli Edelstein minister of absorption.

Yisrael Ba'aliya became an important coalition member because of its size and its commitment to the interests of its constituency.

NATIONAL PROSPECTS

The outcome of the 1996 elections, the 14th parliamentary elections since Israel's independence, was interesting in a number of ways. In the first-ever election for prime minister, Shimon Peres, the incumbent, who campaigned on the theme of continuity and expansion of the peace process, was defeated by Benjamin Netanyahu, who focused on the need for security as the first imperative with peace achievable at the same time. Labor employed the legacy of assassinated Prime Minister Yitzhak Rabin to evoke sympathy for its cause, while Likud used the memory of those killed in suicide bombings to inspire distrust of the Labor government's security and peace policies. The ultra-Orthodox camp fell solidly behind Netanyahu, a secular politician, thereby breaking the taboo in Israeli politics for religious voters to vote for a secular party. One reason for this support for Netanyahu was the shared hard-line views on the peace process. Perhaps more important, however, was the religious parties' loathing of the stridently secularist MERETZ party, which had been Labor's junior partner in the outgoing government, and of the overt secularists within Labor, who also were seen as threatening the Jewishness of the state.

The shift from Labor to Likud brought with it a change in the substance and style of Israel's peace process strategy and tactics. Under the previous Labor government of Prime Ministers Yitzhak Rabin and Shimon Peres, Israel made unprecedented gains in its quest for peace and the normalization of relations with the Palestinians and neighboring Arab countries. Direct bilateral relations were held between Israel and its immediate Arab neighbors—Syria, Lebanon, Jordan, and the Palestinians. Peace agreements were concluded between Israel and the Palestinians and Israel and Jordan. Nevertheless, the outcome of the May 29, 1996, election indicated that the majority of Israelis perceived Labor's peace strategy as riskier than Likud's and, consequently, voted in favor of what was envisioned as a more controlled and balanced approach.

Netanyahu's rhetoric during the campaign and his record as Likud leader during the previous four years suggested that at the very least he would change Israel's approach to the Middle East peace process, if not freeze it altogether. During the campaign, Netanyahu promised Israeli voters that he would make "secure peace" and that while he accepted the reality of the Oslo framework for Israeli-Palestinian negotiations, he would never accept a Palestinian state. At the same time, he said he had no intention of rolling back the peace agreements Israel signed with Egypt in 1979 and Jordan in 1994. Nevertheless, the prospects for peace with the Palestinians appeared bleak as Netanyahu assumed the premiership, and the Arab-Israeli conflict remains the country's most important problem. The political system continues to reflect political diversity and strongly held political views. The growing majority of Israel's Oriental Jewish population presages further changes in the composition of the electorate and in the political parties representing them.

Further Reading

Arian, Alan. *The Choosing People: Voting Behavior in Israel*. Cleveland and London: Case Western Reserve University Press, 1973.

———, ed. *The Elections in Israel—1969*. Jerusalem: Jerusalem Academic Press, 1972.

Arian, Asher, ed. *The Elections in Israel—1981*. Israel: Ramot, 1983.

Arian, Asher, and Michal Shamir, eds. *The Elections in Israel: 1984*. New Brunswick, N.J.: Transaction, 1986.

———, eds. *The Elections in Israel, 1988*. Boulder, Colo.: Westview Press, 1990.

———, eds. *The Elections in Israel, 1992*. Albany: State University of New York Press, 1995.

Aronoff, Myron J. *Power and Ritual in the Israel Labor Party*, rev. ed. Armonk, N.Y.: M.E. Sharpe, 1993.

Elazar, Daniel J., and Howard R. Penniman, eds. *Israel at the Polls 1981*. Bloomington: Indiana University Press, 1986.

Elazar, Daniel J., and Shmuel Sandler, eds. *Israel's Odd Couple: The Nineteen Eighty-Four Knesset Elections and the National Unity Government*. Detroit: Wayne State University Press, 1990.

———, eds. *Who's the Boss in Israel: Israel at the Polls, 1988–89*. Detroit: Wayne State University Press, 1992.

———, eds. *Israel at the Polls, 1992*. Lanham, Md.: Rowman & Littlefield, 1995.

Reich, Bernard. *Historical Dictionary of Israel*. Metuchen, N.J.: Scarecrow Press, 1992.

Reich, Bernard, and Gershon R. Kieval. *Israel: Land of Tradition and Conflict*, 2d ed. Boulder, Colo.: Westview Press, 1993.

———, eds. *Israel Faces the Future*. New York: Praeger, 1986.

———, eds. *Israeli Politics in the 1990s: Key Domestic and Foreign Policy Factors*. Westview, Conn.: Greenwood Press, 1991.

Sager, Samuel. *The Parliamentary System of Israel*. Syracuse, N.Y.: Syracuse University Press, 1985.

Shapiro, Yonathan. *The Road to Power: Herut Party in Israel*. Albany: State University of New York Press, 1991.

Shindler, Colin. *Israel, Likud and the Zionist Dream: Power, Politics, and Ideology from Begin to Netanyahu*. New York: St. Martin's Press, 1995.

REPUBLIC OF ITALY

(Repubblica Italiana)

By Jeffrey K. Hass, Ph.D.

THE SYSTEM OF GOVERNMENT

Italy is a republican unitary state, with a functional constitution dating to 1948. The fundamental political system is parliamentary. As a unified country Italy is, in spite of its long history, a relative newcomer, with unification finalized only in this century. After the dark period of fascism, the Italian polity was restructured along democratic lines. However, due to the particularities of political institutions, Italian politics remains less than stable and for the outsider rather confusing. Recent radical changes both in electoral procedure and the organization of political parties, intended to bring greater stability, has made the Italian political landscape as confusing as it had been previously.

Demographically, Italy has a population of approximately 57.5 million people, with a growth rate of 0.13% per year and a fertility rate of 1.27 children born per woman; females slightly outnumber males. Life expectancy is 78 years, with 74.8 for men and 81.5 for women. Ethnically, Italians are the largest group, although within this ethnic group there are some differences—for example, Germanic or French Italians in the north near Switzerland, Slovene Italians in the northeast. However, these intraethnic differences are minor. Sicilians and Sardinians are ethnic minorities. Roman Catholicism is the largest religion, claiming 98% of the population. Italian is the dominant language, with German, French, and Slovene predominant in small communities near Italy's northwest and northeast borders.

Since World War II, Italy's economy has modernized, from an agricultural to an industrial base, and has brought Italy into the ranks of the industrialized powers. However, Italy's industrial structure is not even, as the north is dominated by smaller private firms and sweatshops links through horizontal ties, while the south retains agricultural roots and industrially is dominated by state-owned firms. Recently the government has attempted to privatize much of this state-owned sector, in order to help control the federal budget deficit and to spur economic growth. Further, political instability has often led to currency instability, with the Italian lira occasionally dropping; recently, however, the lira has been more stable, helping Italy's prospects for joining an integrated European currency. (At present there are still problems of the deficit to be worked out before Italy can join monetary union.)

The Italian governmental system is paradoxical, in that it provides the sources of political instability—Italy has had more than 40 governments in the postwar era—and yet still remains able to provide a basic framework to keep politics from sliding into chaos. The executive has the duty of formulating and implementing policies and for maintaining order within the country. However, because of institutional restrictions and because of the structure of Italy's party landscape—in particular, that there are a plethora of parties—it is difficult for a government to remain in power long. Thus, the Parliament is the ultimate seat of power and sovereignty in Italy.

The Italian system is grounded in a constitution, which provides general rules of political conduct. The constitution provides the rules for selection for powers and for structures of the various branches and levels of government. Further, the constitution guarantees certain political and social rights: the existence of a minimum wage, state-sponsored vocational training, gender equality in the workplace, a welfare safety net (for the unemployed, the disabled, and the unfortunate), the right to form trade unions and to strike, the inviolability of private enterprise and private property (except in cases of "general interest").

However, constitutional rules are broad enough that much of the important political reality is governed by political structure and institutions, in particular the structure of parties and the electoral system that shapes that structure. Electoral rules and party structures shape the resulting political landscape, which in turn accounts for policies and for the political instability that has hampered Italian politics in the postwar era.

Background

Italy is a recent newcomer to the Western European community of nation-states. Originally a peninsula of smaller kingdoms, Italy only became a nation-state, with a constitutional monarchy, in 1861. The impetus to unification was driven by an elite from the Piedmont region. Initially Italy was not a democracy, as only 2% of the population enjoyed suffrage rights until 1919, when all males were given the right to vote. This introduction of universal male suffrage caused a split within society, between the mass electorate and the elite. With growing discontent and economic downturn after World War I, Italian society split along class lines, as the working class turned more and more to emerging socialist and communist parties and movements and the middle class followed the lead of the elites and exchanged power for security with Benito Mussolini's emerging reactionary Fascist Party. Fascism contributed to certain future developments in Italian politics. First, Italy's centralization and unification were completed under Mussolini. Second, through the Lateran Pacts of 1929, the Catholic Church received a privileged position (Catholicism was legally admitted as the national religion), which brought Catholic organizations into politics and eventually gave birth to the powerful Christian Democratic Party. Additionally, fascism gave political legitimacy and moral authority to the Socialists and the Communists, who helped lead the Resistance movement (and, in the case of the Socialist leader, Antonio Gramsçi, suffered martyrdom) and thus emerged from World War II as a contending power along with the Christian Democrats. Third, by siding with the Fascists, the bourgeois elite and middle class traded in future political legitimacy for present security. After World War II and the horrors of fascism (and its ally, Nazism), right-wing elite and middle-class bourgeois parties were dead in the water; a mass electorate remembered how bourgeois interests had sold out the nation, and so until 1994 there was no bourgeois party with any serious political support.

The 1970s and 1980s were less kind to the Italian republic. The 1970s saw the continuation of civil strife from the late 1960s, except that radical right-wing and left-wing groups joined in the fray. One infamous radical left-wing organization was the Red Brigade, which used violence to splinter the political system. The Red Brigade's most daring and successful adventure was the kidnapping and murder of a former prime minister, Aldo Moro, in March–May 1978. Such political violence of the 1970s was soon replaced in the 1980s by organized crime, the Mafia. Historically descendants from the private armies feudal landowners used in the 15th and 16th centuries, the Mafia, through its own penetration into the economy and into politics, had become the new threat to Italian stability. Particularly in the south (especially Sicily), the Mafia could harass and threaten even state officials; judges and prosecutors tracking Mafia activities for legal action were targets of Mafia violence and helped trigger an anticorruption and anticrime wave that began to sweep Italy in the late 1980s. (Pressure from the United States over Mafia drug trafficking certainly helped push the state toward increased anti-Mafia activity.)

One important event was increasing openness about corruption and the rising passion to do something about it. Corruption investigations and scandals led to the fall of leading parties and, in the end, helped with the fall of the First Republic. A 1992 sting operation in Milan uncovered large kickback schemes; resulting plea bargaining led to more investigations and uncovered a trail of scandal and kickbacks leading to high government officials (including the former Socialist prime minister, Bettino Craxi) and members of the Christian Democrats. Additional disclosure revealed officially what many already knew: that a kickback system dubbed *Tangentopoli* permeated Italian politics and society. High-ranking government officials were forced to resign; public sentiment became so strong against the ruling politicians that not only did the electorate turn against them for alternative parties but also mobs at times threatened Parliament.

Political shifts occurred in the 1990s with the collapse of the First Republic, owing to party splits, changes in electoral rules, and the rise of regional and right-wing parties. Left-wing parties, tainted by corruption, also had problems dealing with national problems, such as a sluggish economy and a $1 trillion national debt (one-tenth of which was being channeled to political parties illegally). When the left-wing parties could not handle corruption charges or political problems and when electoral laws and intraparty fighting led to political realignments, the time was ripe for a major change in the political landscape and, as a result, the rise of the right. Briefly in 1993 Central Bank head Carlo Ciampi was asked to become prime minister and form a government; but his government was short-lived. Another short-lived government led President Scalfaro to dissolve Parliament early in 1994 and call for new elections (under new electoral rules).

These elections changed the face of Italian politics. Arguably the most important and controversial actor in this whole scenario was the media millionaire Silvio Berlusconi, whose party owed its existence to its boss's drive and to an existing business network. Berlusconi united his right-wing *Forza Italia* with right-wing *Alleanza Nationale*, the regionalist anticenter, promarket *Lega Nord*, and other smaller parties to bring a right-wing government to power in 1994, riding the wave of anticorruption feeling, the disorganization of former major parties, and the threat of a Communist resurgence (as the reorganized Communist Party, now the Democratic Party of the Left, had taken several mayoral races in 1993). This alliance, called the Freedom Pole (*Polo della Libertà*), obtained a majority of seats in Parliament. Berlusconi became prime minister. However, this alliance proved short-lived, as the *Lega Nord*, under the guidance of its fiery leader Umberto Bossi, soon withdrew its support from the alliance. By the latter half of the year Berlusconi was investigated for conflict of interests (for keeping his businesses in a blind trust that he could still control while prime minister) and Berlusconi's brother Paolo was investigated for kickbacks. Silvio Berlusconi tried to hamper judicial and investigatory power into his brother's affairs (through use of an emergency decree), but this was blocked by the threat of resignation by the anticorruption leader, Antonio Di Pietro. Finally, amid the scandals and squabbling within the Freedom Pole alliance, the Northern League withdrew, and Berlusconi resigned. Lamberto Dini, an economist, became the new prime minister in 1995 and attempted neo-orthodox economic reforms in the face of the Freedom Pole's opposition. Social benefits were cut and legislation was introduced to regulate the media (following allegations that Berlusconi had used his media empire unfairly in his election campaign). In 1995 Berlusconi was indicted for kickbacks to tax inspectors, although he did avoid one possible problem when a referendum supported Berlusconi's right to own three major television networks (which the government claimed was near-monopoly power).

The right-wing alliance that had briefly held power was split apart and now tainted by its own scandals, paving the way for a return in 1996 of a more united left wing in the Olive Tree alliance led by Catholic economist Romano Prodi. Olive Tree won only a plurality, and its edge over the Freedom Pole was only a relative handful of votes. A member of the New Democratic Left, Walter Veltroni, was named prime minister and was able to introduce austerity measures to lower inflation and reduce Italy's national debt.

Executive

The executive in Italy, as in much of Europe, has two parts: a president and a prime minister. The president is mostly an international figurehead representing Italy on the world stage and in international negotiations; however, the president also has some powers that occasionally are of political importance. The first power is symbolic: the president can act as a national figure for uniting and rallying the country. Sandro Pertini, more activist than many presidents, did just this. Such symbolic power and the use of the presidential "bully pulpit" help the president mobilize political forces and common voters. Second, the president does have some official institutional powers. For example, the president can suspend legislation—sending it back to the Parliament for reconsideration, although if the two chambers pass the bill once again with a majority of votes, then the president's weak veto is overturned. Presidential acts are considered valid only if they are countersigned by the prime minister, giving some degree of government (and, indirectly, parliamentary) control over the president. Also, the president nominates the prime minister, which can be real power if Parliament is at loggerheads over just whom to nominate. Finally, after consultation with heads of both parliamentary chambers, the president can dissolve the Parliament and call for early elections. In the case when a president cannot serve out his term, he is replaced by the Speaker of the Senate; new elections are to be held within 15 days except in extreme circumstances.

The real executive power in Italy belongs to the prime minister and the Council of Ministers (*Consiglio dei Ministri*). Ministers are proposed by the president; the government then formulates its political program within 10 days and submits itself and the program to each chamber of Parliament. Both chambers must pass a majority vote of confidence if this new government is to be confirmed (although if only one chamber does not pass a vote of no confidence, this does not mean the new government is not confirmed but means that after changes a new vote must be undertaken).

The government may issue decrees and provisional measures in exceptional cases or other cases of necessity; however, these decrees are good for only 60 days and must be submitted within 5 days to the Parliament, which then debates whether these government decrees should become law. Other powers of the ministers are proposing and implementing policy and overseeing the activities of the state bureaucracy. Recent reform policies—for example, neo-orthodox policies of austerity and privatization, to lower Italy's budget deficit and make the country a viable candidate for membership in the monetary union—are the responsibility of the Cabinet, which must not only formulate these policies but also then make sure they will not face opposition in Parliament and that the state bureaucracy will implement them. One result of the power of ministries and government positions and the link between government and parties is that parties (especially the semidominant Christian Democrats) have used control of the government to place their own members into bureaucratic positions, in essence turning the government into a tool of party patronage; this practice came back to haunt the Christian Democrats in the 1980s with the eruption of anticorruption sentiment and investigations of scandals.

The prime minister and other ministers are assembled by the president, who then presents them to Parliament within 10 days for a vote of confidence; this, then, requires knitting together a parliamentary coalition. Herein lies the weakness of the prime minister and Cabinet—and of the executive and the Italian system in general. Prime ministers do have a great deal of direct power; however, given the parliamentary watchdog power of the vote of no confidence, the prime minister and his Cabinet can find themselves in tenuous positions if a supporting coalition in Parliament breaks down. This means that the parties and party bosses have greater power in influencing the executive than in many other parliamentary democracies in Europe, for a government's support depends on brokering between larger and smaller parties in the politics of coalition building. For example, prime ministers have fallen because of splits within their own party. This has led to one major problem with the Italian executive, the rapid turnover of governments and ministers in the postwar period, because of lack of firm support or a firm coalition within the Parliament. Until 1986 the longest term for any one government was four years (that of Socialist Bettino Craxi, from August 1983 to 1987). From 1945 to 1995 Italy had 55 different governments and ruling coalitions; this was due mostly to instability fostered by two factors. The first was the electoral system, which allowed for a large number of parties to enter Parliament and which, as a result, did not encourage the thinning of the ranks to a few powerful parties that could win majorities outright or lead stable coalitions. A second reason was internal instability of the parties themselves; for example, the Christian Democrats often suffered splits within their own ranks, leading members of the ruling Christian Democratic coalition to levy a vote of no confidence against a prime minister and government headed by other members of their own party.

In general, the office of prime minister has gone to a Christian Democrat, since the Christian Democrats have been the most powerful parliamentary party in the postwar era. The exceptions occurred in the 1980s, when the Christian Democrats were wracked by internal strife and by scandals; in this decade a member of the Republican Party, Giovanno Spadolini, and a member of the Socialist Party, Bettino Craxi, took the mantle of the highest executive position.

As of this writing, the president is Oscar Luigi Scalfaro, a member of the Italian People's Party (conservative), elected May 28, 1992, for a seven-year term; the prime minister is Romano Prodi of the center-left Olive Tree coalition.

Legislature

Italy's national legislature is the Parliament (*Parlamento*), which is composed of two houses, the Chamber of Deputies (*Camera dei Deputati*) and the Senate (*Senato della Repubblica*). The Chamber of Deputies is composed of 630 representatives; the Senate is composed of 326 members, 315 of whom are chosen through elections and 11 of whom (at present) are senators-for-life. Senators-for-life are former presidents (who may refuse the option); and each president may appoint up to 5 people as senators-for-life if they have "brought honor to the nation" through their personal achievements in various fields (science, the arts, and social service). The length of a legislative term is five years, although this term can be ended ahead of time if the Speakers of the two chambers agree to do so and the president, after consulting with them, dissolves Parliament and calls for new elections. This was done most recently in 1996 but has also been done numerous times before (1972, 1976, 1979, 1983), when no stable coalition or political compact on formation and support of a government was forthcoming. Whether the new Parliament will serve out its full term is difficult to judge.

The two chambers open their two annual sessions in February and October, although it is not uncommon for a session to continue into the next session, meaning a continuous convocation. There is no stipulation in the constitution or other laws making one house "upper" and the other "lower"; in principle both have equal legislative powers, and both have the same legal chance to send a member to a ministerial post. Each chamber has special committees (11 to 14 in each), which are where legislation is initially debated before being brought to the floor for a vote. Each committee has a president who has the power to control the committee's agenda, giving this individual certain legislative and procedural power. Legislation is more often than not introduced by the executive (especially the ministers) into both chambers, although members of Parliament, members of parliamentary committees, and regional representatives and councils may introduce bills, and citizens' groups may introduce petitions (if 50,000 signatures are collected in support); while the executive submits many important bills, nonexecutive groups (especially parliamentary members) can be at times active in submitting legislation on their own. After being debated in committees, the bill might (if passed by committee) be sent to the chamber for a floor vote. For a bill to become law it must be passed by majority vote in both houses. There are two cases when this path is not used for legislation. First, a popular referendum (which needs at least 500,000 signatures of registered voters or the formal support of five regional councils to be legitimate) can be called by the public; however, referenda cannot alter or address budgetary laws, amnesties, or international agreements. The second alternative method is for a bill to be passed straight out of the committees without a floor vote; this, however, is rare.

These are the formal powers of the legislature. Just as important are the structure of parties within the legislature and the effect this has had on Italian politics. Previous electoral law allowed for any party to hold a seat in Parliament if it obtained votes; this led to a Parliament made up of numerous parties and deprived larger parties such as the Christian Democrats and Communists of the ability either to rule through majority or to have a commanding enough plurality that creating a coalition would require inviting only a few ideologically close parties. The result has been constantly changing coalitions, as no single group has the power to dominate the Parliament. Further, political shifts within parties have led to intraparty fighting, which also threatens potentially stable coalitions. Such a precarious nature of Italian parties can be seen in the breakup of the larger parties (the Communists and Christian Democrats) in 1993 and 1994 into several smaller groups.

Actual coalitions have changed over time. Until 1963 the coalitions making up the government were centrist and center-right; after 1963, centrist and center-left coalitions began to dominate. The years 1992–93 witnessed instability within the coalition system, as no "stable" coalition (defined broadly in the Italian context) could be created. Recent coalitions (from 1993 on) have turned back to a neo-orthodox center-right type of coalition. This began with economic problems and corruption scandals within the government and the major parties. At the same time, media magnate Silvio Berlusconi, using his media empire to promote his political party *Forza Italia* and its allies the Northern League (*Lega Nord*) and the neofascist *Alleanza Nazionale*, came to prominence on a regionalist platform and a conservative reaction against scandals and instability of the 1992–93 crisis years. Berlusconi's coalition lasted from May to December 1994, when it was replaced (following a scandal involving Berlusconi) with a technocratic government of Lamberto Dini, backed by the Northern League, the *Partito Popolare* (formerly of the Christian Democrats), and the Democratic Party of the Left. This government lasted until February 1996, when it was replaced in April 1996 (following the parliamentary elections, called early) with a return to the center-left and a government led by a coalition of center-left parties (former Socialists and Christian Democrats) called "Olive Tree."

Judiciary

While the Constitutional Court—the highest court in the land—was established in the 1948 constitution, it did not become functional until 1956. This Court is composed of 15 members; the number rises to 31 in cases of impeachment; Parliament appoints the additional 16. Originally, 5 judges are appointed by the president, 5 by a joint session of Parliament, and 5 by the judiciary itself; the constitution now states that 10 are chosen by various levels of judges within the legal system and 5 are chosen by the Parliament, all selections made from a pool of legal academics and lawyers with at least 15 years' experience. Except in extreme cases, "special" judges are forbidden by the constitution (most likely a rejection of fascist policies). The formal powers of the Court include decisions on the constitutionality of policies and laws; mediating disputes between the federal and regional governments; and running impeachment proceedings.

The judicial branch is formally independent from other branches and answerable only to the law; this has given judges some independence and helped them sweep aside fascist policy legacies and, at times, push the battle against organized crime. The overall judicial system in Italy is grounded in civil law; judicial review of laws is reserved for the Constitutional Court, so that the Italian system resembles the Continental rather than the Anglo-American system (where precedent, common law, and judicial interpretation of laws are important political procedures). Judges below the Constitutional Court may become judges only after a rigorous examination, making the judiciary resemble the bureaucratic civil service.

Regional and Local Government

The constitution provides for regional autonomy, with a focus on decentralizing some powers to the local level. The hierarchy of local government runs from the regions (20) to the provinces to the communities. Italy's 20 regions are defined in the constitution as the following: Piedmont; Valle d'Aosta; Lombardy; Trentino-Alto Adige; Venetia; Friuli-Venetia Julia; Liguria; Emilia-Romagna; Tuscany; Umbria; Marches; Latium; Abruzzo; Molise; Campania; Apulia; Basilicata; Calabria; Sicily; Sardinia. Regions have a certain degree of autonomy from the federal government, and some regions enjoy additional political autonomy: Sicily, Sardinia, Trentino-Alto Adige (actually more functionally a province but having autonomy like a region), Friuli-Venetia Julia, and the Valle d'Aosta. Regional powers and responsibilities include organizing local planning, transportation, tourism, hospitals and charities, local police, artisanship, agricultural and forestry issues, vocational training, local fairs and markets, and other local duties. Regions are responsible for collecting their own taxes and providing for part of their own finances (although taxation on exchange between regions, or any other regulation of interregional exchange, is forbidden by the constitution). Local branches of the federal administration are overseen by a federal representative.

The local legislative body is the regional council; its powers include legislation at the local level and the proposal of bills to the national Parliament. Any legislation adopted by the regional councils must be sent to the local federal government representative, who has 30 days to approve the legislation or, in cases of unconstitutionality or incongruity with federal laws, to reject it. The executive branch is the Junta, headed by a president. The duties of the Junta and the president include implementation of local-level laws and representing the region to other regions, to the national administration, and to foreign bodies as well. The regional council is elected by the local population, and deputies of the regional council in turn elect the members of the Junta and select the president of the Junta. The regional council may be dissolved ahead of electoral schedule if the federal government finds it in violation of federal laws or the constitution.

Decentralization has been an important political consideration in Italy in the postwar era, partially in reaction to fascist centralization. Historically, Communists and Social Democrats came into conflict over regional reform and autonomy in the postwar world. Communists favored regional decentralization because, given their power bases in the regions rather than at the national level, such reforms favored the increase of Communist power. The Social Democrats, being more of a national party, opposed regionalization for just this reason.

Provincial and community levels have less power and autonomy than the regional level. However, local elections at the community level do have some importance, as these set the government for the various towns. Communists did well in local elections in the 1970s and early 1980s, but they have witnessed a decline from the late 1980s on.

THE ELECTORAL SYSTEM

Italy's electoral system has certain unique characteristics that mark it off from other Western democracies. Most differences are in parliamentary elections, where major changes occurred in 1993 and 1994. Suffrage is extended to Italian citizens who are 25 years old or older.

The election of the president for a term of seven years is fairly straightforward. The president, who must be at least 50 years old to stand for the office, is selected by the Parliament during a joint session of the two chambers, in which there are an additional three delegates from each region (except Val d'Aosta, which sends only one additional delegate). To win office a candidate must receive two-thirds of delegates' votes. Should no one gain this majority, a second round occurs, where victory also requires a two-thirds majority. If this does not produce a winning candidate (and it usually does not), a third round is undertaken, where a candidate needs only an absolute majority.

The electoral system for the legislature is rather confusing to outsiders used to a more circumscribed procedure. Italy's previous electoral system was of proportional representation without minimum vote barriers; this led to fractured politics as various parties competed and attained seats in the two legislative chambers, yet no party or parties within ideological shouting distance could gain an undisputed majority. In the late 1980s and early 1990s, amid charges and investigations for corruption among the political parties, an attempt was made to streamline Italy's political system, reduce the number of parties, and make the country more governable. Parliament approved a new electoral procedure in 1993.

Italy uses a proportional system for elections to the Parliament. Both the Chamber of Deputies and the Senate have different electoral procedures, but both are based on proportional selection and party lists. To be a Chamber candidate an individual must be 25 years old and have suffrage rights. For Chamber elections Italy is divided into 26 constituencies (plus the Valle d'Aosta region, which has only one seat); the number of seats per constituency is equal to that constituency's percentage of the overall Italian population. Constituencies are further divided into single-seat districts; the number of districts is equal to 75% of that constituency's seats. Thus three-fourths of all seats are from single-member districts, while one-fourth is left for proportional representation on the basis of the entire constituency rather than on dis-

tricts. Voters receive two ballots, one for the single-seat race and one for the proportional list. This allows voters to split their votes between one for a particular person and one for a particular party. For the Chamber of Deputies, 475 members are now elected through a first-past-the-post system from the single-seat constituencies; this is the equivalent of American House of Representative elections, where the candidate with the plurality of votes in his or her constituency wins a seat. The remaining 155 members are selected by a complex proportional system that favors "good losers." Once votes are tabulated nationwide, the proportional seats are distributed. Only parties overcoming a national 4% barrier can receive proportionally allocated seats. Further, the number of seats a party may receive is affected by the *scorporo*, a "price" paid for single-seat victories. In essence, the number of votes a party receives for purposes of proportional counting is diminished by the number of seats the second-place candidate gets in the constituency where a party's candidate has won the single-seat race. Thus, parties that lose in the single-seat races gain some ground in the proportional race, because parties that win in the single-seat races then lose votes they would have received on the second (proportional) ballot. This is a "good loser" system unique to Italy.

The Senate also splits its members by single-seat mandate and proportional representation. To stand as a candidate an individual must be at least 40 years old. A constituency receives a number of Senate seats equal to its proportion of the overall population, although there are two stipulations to this constitutional rule: no constituency will have fewer than 10 senators, and the Molise constituency has only 2 and Valle d'Aosta has only 1. According to the recent electoral law, 232 members win their positions through first-past-the-post systems in their home constituencies; 83 members are selected through a proportional system. Constituencies are divided into 20 single-member districts for the 232 single-member seats, which follow a first-past-the-post system. The remaining 83 are distributed to parties based on the general number of votes they received from the party affiliation of individual candidates; these seats are distributed at the constituency level rather than at the national level (as is the case for the Chamber of Deputies). There is also no minimum percentage barrier, as there is for the Chamber of Deputies. Further, the *scorporo* works somewhat differently for Senate races: a party with a losing candidate receives votes for the proportional seats based on the number of votes its losing candidates received. This complicated and confusing system allows smaller parties a fairer chance at representation (and would seem to promote the continuance of representation of smaller parties, and thus the fragmentation of Parliament).

The accompanying table shows how Italy's regions are divided into constituencies; these data are based on the 1994 election.

Chamber of Deputies

Constituency	Total Seats	Single-Member Seats	Proportional Seats
Valle d'Aosta	1	1	0
Piedmonte 1	25	19	6
Piedmonte 2	23	17	6
Lombardia 1	41	31	10
Lombardia 2	42	32	10
Lombardia 3	15	11	4
Trentino A. A.	10	8	2
Veneto 1	29	22	7
Veneto 2	20	15	5
Friuli V. G.	13	10	3
Liguria	19	14	5
Emilia Rom.	43	32	11
Toscana	39	29	10
Umbria	9	7	2
Marche	16	12	4
Lazio 1	42	32	10
Lazio 2	15	11	4
Campania 1	33	25	8
Campania 2	29	22	7
Puglia	45	34	11
Basilicata	7	5	2
Calabria	23	17	6
Sicilia 1	27	20	7
Sicilia 2	28	21	7
Sardegna	18	14	4
Abruzzo	14	11	3
Molise	4	3	1
Italy Total	630	475	155

Senate

Constituency	Total Seats	Single-Member Seats	Proportional Seats
Valle d'Aosta	1	1	0
Piedmonte	23	17	6
Lombardia	47	35	12
Trentino A. A.	7	6	1
Veneto	23	17	6
Friuli V. G.	7	5	2
Liguria	9	6	3
Emilia Rom.	21	15	6
Toscana	19	14	5
Umbria	7	5	2
Marche	8	6	2
Lazio	28	21	7
Abruzzo	7	5	2
Molise	2	2	0
Campania	30	22	8
Puglia	22	16	6
Basilicata	7	5	2
Calabria	11	8	3
Sicilia	27	20	7
Sardegna	9	6	3
Italy Total	315	232	83

Source: Stefano Bartolini and Roberto D'Alimonte, "Plurality Competition and Party Realignment in Italy: The 1994 Parliamentary Elections," EUI Working Paper SPS No. 95/7 (Italy, 1995): 54.

Chamber of Deputies Elections, April 21, 1996

Party	% Votes	Seats	(Seats in 1994)
L'Ulivo ("Olive Tree," Liberal-Social Democratic)	**41.2**	**284**	**(213)**
Partito Democratico della Sinistra	{21.1}	{156}	
Bloc of Four[a]	{6.8}	{67}	
Rinnovamenta Italiano (Italian Renewal)	{4.3}	{24}	
Federazione dei Verdi (Federation of Greens)	{2.5}	{21}	
Combined Lists		{—}	{16}
Rifondazione Cominsta (Communist Refoundation)	8.6	35	(40)
Polo della Libertà (Freedom Pole, Conservative)	**40.3**	**246**	**(248)**
Forza Italia (Forward Italy)	{20.6}	{123}	
Alleanza Nazionale (National Alliance)	{15.7}	{93}	
Centro Crisiano Democratico/Christiani Democratici Uniti (Christian Democratic Center/Union of Christian Democrats)	{5.8}	{30}	
Lega Nord (Northern League, Regionalist)	9.9	59	(118)

Note: The number in parentheses is the number of seats obtained in the 1994 parliamentary election to the Chamber of Deputies. **Bold** indicates a party bloc or cartel. The number in brackets is that party's votes within the larger bloc.

[a]Group of four parties allied together within the "Olive Tree": Partito Popolare Italiano (Italian People's Party, Christian Democratic); Südtiroler Volkspartei (South-Tyrolean People's Party, regionalist); Unione Democratica (Democratic Union, liberal); Partito Repubblicano Italiano (Italian Republican Party, liberal).

Senate Elections, April 21, 1996

Party/Bloc	% Votes	Seats
L'Ulivo	41.2	157
Rifondazione Cominsta (RC)	2.9	10
Polo Liberta	37.3	116
Lega Nord	10.4	27
Movimento Sociale–Fiamma Tricolore	2.3	1
Lista Pannella Sgarbi	1.6	1
Regional Lists[a]	4.3	3

Source: CIA Factbook, 1996; "Elections around the World," ed. Wilfried Derksen: http://www.agora.stm.it/elections/election/italy.htm.

[a]"regional lists" for the Senate race include the combined parties Lista Socialista (socialists), Lega d'Azione Meridionale (southern regionalist), Partito Sardo d'Azione (Sardinian regionalist), Collegio Vale d'Aosta (not an organized party).

In spite of the confusion and constant governmental changes, general orientation of Italian politics has been fairly stable. The accompanying table below shows the results for selected previous elections. The first number is percentage, with number of parliamentary seats in parentheses.

These trends reflect a common wisdom about Italian postwar politics up until the crises of the late 1980s: the fascist legacy hurt the initial formation of right-wing movements, helping the left and center-left parties establish a stranglehold on politics. Two factors hindered right-wing formation: first, this legacy, which left political domination with the Christian Democrats, Communists, and Socialists and made advancement of center-right parties difficult; second, because of Italy's social structure (a state presence in the economy, bifurcation between industrial north and agricultural south, a small individualist bourgeoisie) organizing and mobilizing potential right-wing support were difficult. In short, no right-wing party could gain ground without some system shock.

This system shock came in the late 1980s and early 1990s, with economic problems, the collapse of leftism in the end of the cold war, and political scandals. This drove many voters away from the left to regionalist or right-wing parties untainted by corruption. Further, entrepreneurship and the growth of a bourgeoisie provided the soil for right-wing groups, so that when Berlusconi entered the political scene, serendipity had provided the opportunity for a major political shift. This occurred in 1994.

The right-wing alliance, *Polo della Libertà*, managed to capture a majority within the Parliament. As noted earlier, the actual political coalition was short-lived, as *Lega Nord* withdrew its support for Berlusconi. Further, center-left parties organized into the *l'Ulivo* (Olive Tree) coalition, which came to power after the 1996 elections. However, this does not mean an end of the right wing and a return to center-left politics. *Forza Italia* managed to gain seats in the Chamber of Deputies between 1994 and 1996, and the right wing, while more splintered than earlier, remains a force to be reckoned with. Italian politics, in the wake of a global move to neo-orthodox politics and away from socialism and state-centered policies, has noticeably shifted to the right and, barring a serious economic downturn due to neo-orthodox market reforms or political scandals, should remain viable after almost 50 years of marginality.

THE PARTY SYSTEM

History

Italy's party system did not begin to take shape until the 20th century. While the Socialist Party was founded in 1892, it remained marginalized, as its support base, the working class, did not have the right to vote. Catholic

Party	1948	1958	1968	1976	1983	1992
DC	48.5 (304)	42.3 (273)	39.1 (265)	38.8 (263)	32.9 (225)	29.7 (206)
PCI/PDS	—	22.7 (140)	27.0 (177)	34.4 (227)	29.9 (198)	16.1 (107)
Far Left/RC	—	—	—	1.5 (6)	1.5 (7)	5.6 (35)
MSI	2.0 (6)	4.8 (24)	4.5 (24)	6.1 (35)	6.8 (42)	5.4 (34)
PRI	2.5 (9)	1.4 (6)	2.0 (9)	3.1 (14)	3.7 (21)	4.4 (27)
PLI	3.8 (19)	3.6 (17)	5.8 (31)	1.3 (5)	2.9 (16)	2.8 (17)

Source: Donald Sassoon, *Contemporary Italy: Economy, Society, and Politics*, 2d ed. (London: Addison-Wesley, 1997), 177.

Key:

PCI = Partito Comunista Italiano (Italian Communist Party), renamed Partito Democratico della Sinistra (PDS, Democratic Party of the Left) in 1992

PSI = Partito Socialista Italiano (Italian Socialist Party)

DC = Democrazia Cristiana (Christian Democrats), split 1994

RC = Rifondazione Comunista (Communist Refoundation), formed upon splitting from the PDS in 1992

MSI = Movimento Sociale Italiano (Italian Social Movement)

PRI = Partito Repubblicano Italiano (Italian Republican Party, liberal party)

PLI = Partito Liberale Italiano (Italian Liberal Party)

1994 Elections: The New Rules Emerge

Cartel/Party	Chamber of Deputies	Senate
Progressisti	213 (33.8)	122 (38.7)
PDS	109 (17.3)	60 (19.0)
RC	39 (6.2)	18 (5.7)
Verdi	11 (1.7)	7 (2.2)
PSI	14 (2.2)	12 (3.8)
Rete	6 (1.0)	6 (1.9)
AD	18 (2.9)	10 (3.2)
CS	5 (0.8)	4 (1.3)
RS	1 (0.2)	1 (0.3)
Independent	10 (1.6)	4 (1.3)
Patto per l'Italia	46 (7.3)	31 (9.8)
PPI	33 (5.2)	30 (9.5)
Patto Segni	13 (2.1)	1 (0.3)
Polo della Libertà	366 (58.1)	156 (49.5)
Forza Italia	99 (15.7)	32 (10.2)
CCD	29 (4.6)	12 (3.8)
UDC	4 (0.6)	3 (1.0)
PLD	2 (0.3)	—
Riformatori	6 (1.0)	1 (0.3)
ÅN	109 (17.3)	47 (14.9)
Lega Nord	117 (18.6)	60 (19.0)
Others	5 (0.8)	6 (1.9)
Total	630	315

Source: Stefano Bartolini and Roberto D'Alimonte, "Plurality Competition and Party Realignment in Italy: The 1994 Parliamentary Elections," ECU Working Paper SPS No. 95/7 (Italy, 1995), 70–72.

Note: Cartels in **bold**, parties normal; number = seats won, percentage of votes in parentheses.

Key:

PDS = Partito Democratico della Sinistra (Democratic Party of the Left)

RC = Rifondazione Comunista (Communist Refoundation)

PSI = Partito Socialista Italiano (Italian Socialist Party)

AD = Alleanza Democatica (Democratic Alliance)

CS = Cristiano-Sociali (Social Christians)

RS = Rinascita Socialista (Socialist Renewal)

PPI = Partito Popolore Italiano (Italian People's Party)

CCD = Centro Cristiano Democratico (Christian Democratic Center)

UDC = Unione di Centro (Union of the Center)

PLD = Polo Liberal-Democratico (Liberal-Democratic Pole)

AN = Alleanza Nazionale (National Alliance)

groups initially remained outside politics, a protest against the Catholic Church's loss of power in the face of secular unification and centralization. However, as the Socialist party began to gain strength, Catholic organizations came together to form in 1919 the Catholic Popular Party. The Socialist and Catholic Parties remained apart from each other, and this helped the rise to power of Mussolini's Fascist Party, which in 1926 outlawed all other political parties. As suggested earlier, the fascist period shaped the following political period: the Lateran Pacts brought Catholicism back into social domination, and helped give Catholic groups a firmer organizational base; and the struggle with fascism gave political legitimacy and capital to the Socialist and Communist organizations (which managed to hurt each other through splits and feuds borne of Stalin's antisocialist policies). Opposition to fascism made a temporary alliance between Socialist and Catholic groups possible, but this alliance fell apart in the postwar era. In the postwar world the Communists were kept out of power but still managed to gain a following among the working classes and certain industrialized northern regions; the Socialists and Christian Democrats became the leading parties but could not gain sufficient dominance to create durable coalitions. Additionally, party splits and an electoral system favorable to small parties led to a plethora of political parties and a consistently fragmented Parliament.

This was the general landscape for most of the postwar era. However, the situation changed in the 1990s. First, investigations into corruption led to shocks within the parties. Second, the changes in the electoral system encouraged and sped up centrifugal tendencies within the parties. Finally was the weakening of the left, and especially of the Communist Party, in the late 1980s, and the rise of regional and conservative forces, led by the mercurial Silvio Berlusconi. The result was splits and realignments and a major reconfiguration of the party landscape.

In postwar Italy political parties have popped up like mushrooms after a storm, although some of these mushrooms have been far larger than others. This is due to two primary factors. The first is Italy's fractured nature: a liberal industrialized north and a conservative agrarian south, with less of a sense of national unity than other European countries. The second is the Italian electoral system, which allowed many small parties into the Parliament and did not weed out these minor parties but instead encouraged their marginal existence. Yet in spite of the plethora of parties, a few parties managed to dominate, in particular the Christian Democrats and the Communists.

Below, the current parties are separated into three groups—the leftists, the moderates, and the conservatives—and placed under the umbrella of the former larger parties of which they once were part. (Note that the realignment is due not only to parties splitting up but also to these factions combining, often across former party lines—for example, one nationalist wing of the Christian Democrats joined the right-wing *Alleanza Nationale*.)

Organization

Before the recent party breakups, political parties in Italy had two important features: they were mass parties, and they centered themselves and their actions around ideolo-

Party Splits, Reformations, Realignments	
Traditional (up to 1990s)	**New (postsplit)**
Christian Democrats	Partito Popolore Italiano (1/94)
	Rete-Movimento Democatico ('91)
	Popolari per la riforma (10/92)–Patto Segni (11/93)
	Cristiano Sociali ('93)
	Centro Cristiano Democratico
	Alleanza Nazionale (1/94)
Communist Party of Italy	Partito Democartico della Sinistra (1/91)
	Rifondazione Comunista (2/91)
	Rete-Movimento Democratico ('91)
Italian Socialist Party	Partito Socialista (1/94)
	Rinascita Socialista (6/93)
	Alleanza Democratica
	Patto Segni (6/93)
	Federazione Liberal Socialista–Unione dei Democratici e dei Socialisti (fall '93)
Italian Social Movement–National Right (MSI–DN)	MSI-Alleanza Nazionale (Italian Social Movement–National Allaince, MSI–AN)
Partito Repubblicano Italiano	Partito Repubblicano Italiano
	Alleanza Democratica
Partito Liberale Italiano	Partito Liberale Italiano–Federazione dei liberali
	Unione di Centro
	Alleanza Democratica
Partito Social Democratico Italiano (Italian Social-Democratic Party)	Unione dei Democratici e dei Socialisti
	Alleanza Democratica

ciety. Parties have cells and formal ties with unions, with movements, with associations, and other political or nonpolitical organizations. These links are partly personal but also partly ideological, bringing political ideology into everyday life to a degree not seen in many other Western democracies. And the personal or clan side makes its way into the party-society structure as well. While many ties are ideological in nature—such as ties between parties and local cultural festivals—other links are patronage. For example, parties with influence in an area will get their people placed in local government, or a party drawing support from a region will use its parliamentary power either to get people from that region jobs in the state bureaucracy or to provide benefits, such as housing, government contracts, and the like.

Internal organization of most parties does not differ from mass parties elsewhere. On the one hand, there are institutions of democracy that promote mass participation. Local cells elect members of sections and section heads, who then select the provincial committees, which select the regional committees, and so on to the top. This provides some local grassroots influence and power. For most parties, national congresses that set the party programs are held every two years. However, as Robert Michels would have predicted, this democracy is dulled by the need for everyday organization, which means the rise of a party elite and a party bureaucracy. This system gives party elites patronage power within the party (similar to patronage through the state) and the ability to reproduce their own power.

The four major parties before the realignments were the Christian Democratic Party (*Partito della Democrazia Cristiana*; DC), the Italian Communist Party (*Partito Communista Italiano*; PCI), the Italian Socialist Party (*Partito Socialista Italiano*; PSI), and the Italian Social Movement (*Movimento Sociale Italiano*; MSI). In the early 1990s, splits and realignments led to the creation of several new and smaller parties. Because of these splits, obtaining accurate information (when available) on membership, finances, and precise party procedures is difficult.

gies and ideological identity. Joining most parties required sponsorship by someone inside the party, in order to test for ideological "purity," and joining a political party was an ideological statement of sorts. And yet in spite of the stress on ideology, Italian parties were notorious for being factionalized. These factions are less based on splinters within the ideological framework than they are centered on personal networks and personalized groups or clans within parties. In this way, ideology served as the glue holding mass parties together, and yet the parties were rent through and through with networks of personal cliques and loyalties that weakened them.

Parties are linked with many other organizations in so-

LEFT-WING PARTIES

Italian left-wing parties made, with the exception of 1994–96, a strong showing in Italian politics. The two basic left-wing camps are the Socialists and the Communists, broken through a Comintern-dictated split in 1921. In the postwar era both camps played on their partisan activities for legitimacy and popularity; the Socialists were able to become a legitimate governing party (although they had only one Socialist prime minister, Craxi) and the Communists remained in opposition.

The Italian Communist Party, formerly the largest Communist Party west of the Iron Curtain, was founded

in 1921 following a Comintern-inspired split between socialists and more radical Communists. During fascism the PCI was illegal and its leaders threatened or jailed; some, such as Palmiro Togliatti, escaped Italy, while others, such as Antonio Gramsçi, went to prison. The persecution under fascism did not, in the end, hurt the party; if anything, the PCI's resistance to fascism provided a certain moral power that helped the PCI survive the period and prosper afterward. Further, the PCI had always maintained some distance from Stalin and the Comintern; therefore, when Stalin's excesses were revealed in the 1956 "secret speech," the Italian Communists did not lose face or legitimacy as other Western European Communist Parties did.

After World War II, the Communists temporarily took part in government in a three-way alliance with the Socialist Party and the Christian Democrats; however, PCI participation in government came to an end with the onset of the cold war. Initially the Socialists supported the Communists, but by the 1960s the Socialists moved closer (tactically) to the Christian Democrats in order to participate in the executive branch. This did not necessarily hurt the PCI; with the Socialists in some way involved in running the country, the PCI could remain an opposition force loyal to its party base (the working class); and indeed the PCI remained until recently not only Italy's second-largest party but also the guardian of the left wing. By the 1970s, with the threats of neofascist parties' growing (although still small) success and the example of right-wing reaction against a left-wing government in Chile, the PCI turned to "strategic alliances" with other prodemocracy parties; this helped raise the PCI's support to over 30% of the electorate. However, this alliance also hurt the PCI, which was now more involved with the government and would lose some of the support among the left-wing dissatisfied elements in society (such as the working class). By the 1980s, with the loss of popular leader Enrico Berlinguer and with the problems of moving closer to the ruling parties, the PCI's support slipped, so that by 1987 PCI was only the third-largest party. Of little comfort was the loss of support among party strongholds—the working class, especially in the industrialized north.

By 1989, some factions within the PCI came to the decision that a change was needed. The PCI had been slowly moving away from more radical policy and opposition tactics to become more of a social-democratic party; further, the fall of the Communist East bloc in 1989 sealed the fate of Communist Parties everywhere. In February 1991 the different tensions within the party over its future came to a head, and PCI split into two parties: the Democratic Party of the Left (*Partito Democratico della Sinistra*; PDS) and more traditional Communists, who broke off to form Communist Refoundation (*Rifondazione Comunista*; RC). The PDS suffered in the early 1990s from its split and from the taints of corruption that all major parties endured. However, in the 1994 elections the PDS regained some lost ground; as a response, Massimo D'Alema, the new head of PDS, organized for the 1996 elections the *l'Ulivo* (Olive Tree) coalition, consisting of the PDS, smaller liberal parties, and small parties from the Christian Democrats.

One last remark should be made about left-wing parties: the lesson of 1994 was that electoral alliances were the key to victory, given that party splits prevented any one party from dominating, as the Christian Democrats and Communists had done throughout the postwar era. The right-wing parties and the Northern League, under Berlusconi's leadership, had united and taken power in 1994 (although the alliance soon split up); in order to regain power for the left, leftist parties could not simply rely on right-wing mistakes (such as rapid economic reform) but had to forge their own unity. The result was the electoral alliance in 1996 Olive Tree (*l'Ulivo*). This coalition was able to install its own government, the Prodi government, in May 1996. While the Olive Tree coalition is not entirely stable, it appears to be more stable than the right-wing coalition.

Democratic Party of the Left (Partito Democratico della Sinistra, PDS)

The PDS moved from its predecessor's radical leftism to a center-left ideology. In response to the fall of communism in 1989–91, PDS rejected Marxism and turned to social democracy. In spite of this move to the center, the PDS still has one advantage: it has only one competitor on the left flank, the RC, which maintains its radicalism. The PDS appeals to the middle class as much as to the working class. Ideologically, while the PDS does not entirely endorse austerity measures and radical market reforms (such as rapid privatization or a full withdrawal of the state from the economy), the party also has not championed strong opposition to these policies; in short, the PDS does not appear to have a set ideological line and wants to turn neither to its outmoded leftism of the past nor to the right wing's policies. Essentially, the PDS (and, perhaps, its *l'Ulivo* coalition) appears to be moving toward a variant of social democracy, which does not oppose capitalist structure or practice per se but focuses on issues of social justice, social support, and welfare.

Communist Refoundation (Rifondazione Comunista; RC)

In contrast to PDS, the Communist Refoundation (RC) remains more radical, mostly because continued dedication to more Marxist leftism is the RC's raison d'être: the RC broke off when the Communist Party changed its name to PDS, essentially an admission to critics that the Communist Party was indeed Communist, with all the sins of postwar Europe that this implied. The RC has been able to hold onto a small leftist segment of society. It has been reluctant to enter into electoral or political coalitions, thus maintaining ideological purity but also electoral marginality.

The Italian Socialist Party (Partito Socialista Italiano)

The Italian Socialist Party emerged from World War II with an antifascist image (although not nearly as strong as the Communists' image and legitimacy). In spite of weaker organization than the Communists, the Socialists quickly became the second-largest party in Italy. Still the Socialists remained a party with a core of cadres and without a more organized mass base. Throughout the postwar era the Socialists remained a moderate left-wing party: forming governments with the Christian Democrats, trying to act as mediator between sides in the tense atmosphere of 1968. The Socialists provided a degree of stability to Christian Democratic governments, supplying the necessary vote count in Parliament to get new governments off the ground (although not being able to sustain them for long periods of time). The Socialists also took a more moderate ideological and policy line than their Communist brethren: the PSI remained pro-NATO and pro–law and order.

One major problem that the Socialists faced was constructing their own "ground" amid a two-front battle with Christian Democrats and the Communists, in essence to build its own identity separate from both the Communists and Christian Democrats and provide a left-wing "alternative." This "alternative" never materialized, and demoralization in the party continued in the 1970s. Bettino Craxi, party leader and briefly prime minister in the 1980s attempted to change the style of the Socialists; Craxi personalized both the Socialist Party and Italian politics, in this way acting as a legitimate forerunner of Berlusconi's brand of personalized politics. Craxi also tried to make the Socialists into a liberal party supporting modernity and reforms but tailored this image to the region of the country. In the north the Socialists appealed to entrepreneurs with a stress on fiscal discipline and support of a privatization program, while in the south they advocated using the public sector and relying on clientelism and a degree of patronage (which brought on charges of corruption in the 1990s). When in the 1990s Craxi was under suspicion for corruption, the Socialist Party fell into disgrace along with its leader and has yet to recover. Given that the PSI became associated with one individual and had not set out its own political space, the Socialists had a difficult time regaining ground (as the Communists could) after 1994. Ironically, the So-

cialist position, which the PSI had tried to form before the 1990s, was taken by the major bloc of the newly reorganized Communists, the PDS.

"Green" Parties

The last set of center-left parties are the various "Green" parties—proenvironmental groups that entered the Parliament following the 1987 elections. While Green parties appear condemned to marginality—averaging around 2.5% of the national vote—they are essential to the center-left Olive Tree coalition, where their small number of votes are crucial for a balance against the right wing. Green parties in Italy, like those in other European countries, focus more on environmental issues than on other political themes; this makes an alliance with center-left parties, which do not support free capitalism, more palatable than an alliance with right-wing parties, which wish to reduce state intervention (thus possibly leading to further unintended market-created environmental problems).

CENTRIST PARTIES

Christian Democrats (Democrazia Cristiana, DC)

While no single party had the power to dominate, the centrist Christian Democrats (*Democrazia Cristiana*; DC) were the most powerful party until the 1990s. The DC came into being when Catholic organizations that had not sided with the Fascists (including the Popular Party, *Partito Popolare Italiano*) came together in 1943. Before this, Catholic organizations had one problem entering political life: as a result of the creation of a secular Italian state and the decentering of the Vatican from temporal power, the Pope had forbidden the participation of Catholics in politics. However, some groups did focus on politics (albeit at a grassroots, rather than institutional, level), addressing mostly issues of social injustice; the Lateran Pacts of 1929 allowed Catholics to begin organizing for political activity. In 1943, Catholics entered politics directly through the DC, which in the 1946 parliamentary elections emerged as the largest party. Drawing on both liberal and conservative Catholics and positioning themselves in opposition to the Communists and Socialists, the DC was able to remain Italy's premier party in the early elections, establishing itself at least for the medium term as an important power broker. The Catholics gained strength from two sources: first from more fervent Catholic workers, who would not support the secular Socialists and Communists, and second from the situation on the right flank, where right-wing parties were discredited by their links to fascism, thus making the centrist DC the legitimate outlet for center-right voters with no parties of their own.

The DC dominated politics, always being involved in creating governments. In the late 1960s and 1970s, when social upheaval disturbed Italian society and the center-left parties made progress on "progressive" issues (such as the issue of divorce laws), the DC lost support and eventually was forced to strike an alliance with the Communists. In the 1980s, the DC lost control of the position of prime minister to the Socialists. In spite of these electoral problems, the DC remained a popular party. Its appeal cut across classes; geographically, the DC was originally popular in the north, but state investment in development in the south, combined with the DC's control of government and hence its command of patronage, led to a shift of geographic support from north to south in the last decades. Additionally, the DC had greater popularity with women and with the more devout Catholic or clerical regions in Italy. These advantages—links to Catholicism and appeal beyond a single class or geographic base—helped the DC remain the largest and most powerful political party until the 1990s.

In terms of policy, the DC was anticommunist, touted democracy and individual freedom, and brought Italy into the European Community and NATO. In the center-left tradition the DC championed social justice, but in a center-right (and traditionally religious) tone it opposed divorce and abortion. On economic issues the DC never developed a well-thought-out ideology, instead relying on a laissez-faire approach to economic policy rather than active support of state intervention or of market domination (although the DC subscribed to the importance of both state and market mechanisms).

The DC did not support nationalization of the economy, as this was communist, and did support bourgeois values; however, because the DC had control over the state and thus over patronage, the party did not fight against increased state investment in industrial or other economic projects. In the 1980s, facing economic troubles stemming from the energy crisis, the DC discussed austerity measures, but these raised opposition inside and outside the party and hurt the DC in 1980s elections. Ideologically, then, the DC had no true identity, short of its Catholic traditions and its anticommunism; this was due in part to the history of the party and its identity (anticommunist) and in part to the fact that it was not a coherent, tightly organized party but rather a collection of factions (from center-right to center-left, with some right-wing groups on the fringes) lumped together into one party.

Scandals and its factional nature led in 1994 to a breakup of the DC into various smaller autonomous parties. First, the DC was "migrating" to the south; northern elites and entrepreneurs began to look negatively on the DC's patronage machine in the south. When the kickback schemes came to light, these entrepreneurs and other northern actors pounced on them and attacked the DC, bringing it into crisis. Second, relations between the factions within the party were becoming tense. One faction, based in Sicily, opened an anti-Mafia agenda. A northern faction, facing rising competition from the local "leagues" (see below), began calling for changes in the electoral system (to the dismay of other factions). One renegade politician took his faction out of the DC and founded the party *Patto Segni*. These factions had debated within the DC over policies and tactics; center-right factions early on held sway, but from the 1950s center-left factions gained the upper hand. The power of the factions was related not only to who held what positions within the party but also to who held what positions (and thus patronage) within the state bureaucracy.

Between factionalization and the corruption scandals, the DC saw its popularity and internal organization decline precipitously. In the 1992 local elections the DC's returns were catastrophic. On January 18, 1994, the DC was officially dissolved in the wake of these two crushing pressures. Soon after, a "new" party was established, drawing on DC tradition by using the name of the largest founding party of the DC, the Italian People's Party (*Partito Popolare Italiano*; PPI).

Italian People's Party (Partito Popolare Italiano; PPI)

The PPI entered the 1994 elections without allies and received only 11% of votes. In spite of claiming the mantle of "pure" (e.g., nonpoliticized and noncorrupt) Christian democracy, the PPI did not fare well. On the one hand, the party was perceived as being too weak to stand up to the left, and so conservative voters were less inclined to automatically throw their support behind PPI. Additionally, unlike earlier years, when the DC could attract a right wing with no where else to go, conservative voters had an alternative in *Forza Italia* and Berlusconi's *Polo* right-wing electoral alliance.

PPI has remained a centrist party, but this has brought problems. First, Italian politics has become polarized in the 1990s, between those supporting left-wing policies and those desiring a turn to right-wing conservative and/or capitalist policies. Second, were the PPI to move to the right or the left, it would confront a larger dominant party, *Forza Italia* on the right and the PDS on the left. In 1995 a pact between the PPI's new leader and Berlusconi led to further splintering, with the minority leaving to join Berlusconi's group and the majority retaining the PPI name and, for the 1996 elections, throwing its weight behind the PDS-led center-left *l'Ulivo* cartel to fend off Berlusconi's group. At present the PPI does not have a developed ideology, a developed organizational structure, or a large following. While the PPI may remain as a centrist party calling on Catholic tradition, it is currently subordinated to the center-left coalition and will need much time to rebuild; as long as a strong right wing remains, PPI will probably remain small and unable to stake out a center ground for itself (especially as the PDS has moved from the left to the center, formerly the DC's political turf).

The PPI was not the only group to emerge from the DC breakup. The Catholic right wing found its voice in the Christian Democratic Center (*Centro Cristiano Democratico*; CCD). In 1994 the CCD joined Berlusconi's *Polo* alliance; in the 1996 elections the CCD combined with the Union of Christian Democrats (*Christiani Democratici Uniti*; CDU). The Sicilian anti-Mafia faction dubbed itself *La Rete* (or *Rete-Movimento democratico*) and politically sided with the left wing of Italian politics. Some more nationalist-oriented supporters and members left to join the newly reorganized *Alleanza Nationale*.

RIGHT-WING PARTIES

The Italian right saw renewed strength in the 1994 elections, owing to Berlusconi's resources and increased right-wing party organization, along with the discrediting of the left-wing and centrist parties through news of scandals and corruption and through economic problems left-wing policies could not solve. Further, the return of the right was enhanced by the rise of Silvio Berlusconi and his *Forza Italia* party.

Forward Italy
(Forza Italia; FI)

The most important right-wing party in the 1990s is also Italy's newest party, Silvio Berlusconi's Forward Italy (*Forza Italia*; FI). The party and its leader, who served a brief stint as prime minister in 1994, are inextricably linked; the party owes its fortunes to the leader, and the leader owes his ability to enter politics to the party network that brought electoral support. Berlusconi owed his rise to prominence to his media empire (three television networks that attained approximately 45% of the audience market), built through competition with inefficient state-run media outlets and through his control of the popular Milan football (soccer) team. Berlusconi himself also enjoyed personal acclaim as an entrepreneur who had built his own entertainment empire through his own hard work and had provided Italians with entertainment outside of that provided inefficiently by the state.

In January 1994, Berlusconi created *Forza Italia* on the basis of his media connections and of the Milan football team's various clubs, which became the equivalent of party cells. Berlusconi and *Forza Italia* rode a wave of antipolitician sentiment in 1994, but this was not the only political force to bring Berlusconi and his party to power. Berlusconi noticed that in spite of the window of opportunity open in the early 1990s, left-wing parties were numerous and could form their own alliances to return to power; hence, the emerging right wing had to form political alliances as well to pool their voters and resources. In 1994 Berlusconi was able to forge an alliance among his party, the right-wing *Alleanza Nationale* (which was popular in the south), and the new party *Lega Nord*, whose more regionalist agenda remained antiinsider and could deliver northern voters.

FI's and Berlusconi's ideological appeal came from two sources: no stain from political scandals (or from a political past) and adherence to neoliberal policies. The first benefited enormously, as Berlusconi could position himself and his party and alliance against the entrenched interests using the state to maintain their own power. The second built on the first, as Berlusconi could emphasize entrepreneurship, individualism, and a neoliberal economic platform that would lower corruption and bring economic growth (as his own personal history testified). He stressed anticommunism as well, although in the 1990s this tactic does not have the power it did in the cold war. Finally, Berlusconi was seen as a strong individual who could set Italian politics right and sweep away the old corruption.

National Alliance
(Alleanza Nationale; AN)

Bringing up a more radical right wing was the Italian Social Movement (MSI), which in 1994 changed its name to MSI-Alleanza Nazionale and in 1995 simply to Alleanza Nationale (AN). Established in 1946, the MSI reflected much of the ideology and worldviews of the discredited (and in 1952 illegal) Fascist Party. In 1972 MSI merged with the Monarchist Party and became known as *Movimento Sociale Italiano–Destra Nazionale* (Italian Social Movement–National Right), but problems after the 1976 elections led moderate members to break off and form their own party, *Democrazia Nazionale* (National Democracy).

AN's policy is anticommunist and right-wing. This has come to hurt AN, which saw its fortunes start to drop until the 1994 elections, when in a party cartel it reversed the decline. The MSI had a strong organizational framework that the AN appeared mostly to have inherited—branches throughout Italy attached to youth and student movements, to women, to war veterans, and to some trade unions. Originally having roots in the north (where fascism had been at its strongest), the MSI slowly "migrated" south, a process helped when MSI "swallowed" the Monarchist Party. MSI tries to appeal in part to disillusioned youth; its rules permit one to join at the age of 14. While MSI had more of a pseudofascist appeal, AN has tried to moderate this image somewhat while remaining a right-leaning party.

AN ideology is problematic, mostly because party platforms and grassroots support do not necessarily meet, and the party's right-wing image is vague enough to attract many right-wing voters who have no other real party to turn to. AN, as MSI before it, took a strong positive view toward some Western ideals, toward corporatism, anticommunism, lower-middle-class populism (which made it difficult, until the 1990s, to espouse right-wing radical free-market reforms), and more conservative social views (such as stances against abortion and divorce). Certain aspects of MSI ideology, such as more open admiration for fascism and hints of anti-Semitism and racism, have been dropped or pushed into the background (along with party leaders espousing these views). Most important in the ideology is a sense of "anti-insider" politics: criticisms of the centrist and left-wing parties that had led Italy for so long.

When one turns to the rank-and-file support, however, the ideological picture of AN gets muddled. While a sizable number of supporters still hold to an AN that is oppositionist and outside the system, more supporters now believe that AN should ally itself with other parties and enter the government. Further, against the traditional views of the party, a majority of supporters favor sexual equality; and a majority are not hostile to Catholicism, which contradicts historical anti-Catholic views of MSI and AN. One surprise on the ideology front—both for official AN views and views of supporters—is the lack of anti-immigrant sentiment. Given the influx of immigrant workers and the rise of anti-immigration right-wing politics throughout Europe (especially in France), one would expect a right-wing protofascist party like MSI/AN to play this card; however, both AN and its supporters have refrained from making anti-immigration policies a centerpiece of party platforms. This does *not* mean that AN will *not* play this card in the future, however.

MSI's biggest problem, which appears to have been overcome in the 1990s with the formation of AN, was the creation of a veil of legitimacy. The MSI had two political stains that it had to wash out: first, its ideological and imagined links with fascism, and second, 1970s right-wing terrorism. In spite of MSI's freedom from corruption scandals, these stains were problematic. Several events helped bring the MSI (and then the AN) into legitimacy and respectability. The first was the collapse of the Christian Democrats and the Communists in 1992; this allowed an opening for new parties to grab up electoral votes. Second was party leader Giafranco Fini's ability to put together a network of political contacts that allowed AN to engage in political alliances in elections—and thus to overcome one of MSI's major problems, political isolation due to lack of political alliances. Third was the political air of 1993–94, when MSI changed its name to AN and when AN linked up with Berlusconi and *Forza Italia*, whose coattails added to AN's increasing popularity. Berlusconi's open support for AN in 1993—when Berlusconi himself was still popular—helped AN in local elections and propelled the party forward in 1994 national elections.

REGIONAL POLITICAL PARTIES

The Northern League (Lega Nord; LN)

Occasionally, small regionalist parties arise and compete in Italian politics, such as the *Union Valdôtaine* (drawing from the small Val d'Aosta) or Sardinia's *Sardo d'Azione*. However, until the 1990s they could not compete with the larger national parties. Only in the 1990s, with the change in electoral rules and the creation and realignment of parties, did one regionalist party arise to play more than a marginal role in politics: the Northern League (*Lega Nord*; LN). The *Lega Nord* began as an association of smaller northern regionalist parties, the most important of which was the *Lega Veneta*, stemming from Venice. The Venetian League surprised observers in the 1980s and refused to die; when it began to lose popularity, Leagues in other northern cities were already established political forces. In the late 1980s these small regional movements and parties unified into the umbrella *Lega Nord*, which in 1990 regional elections scored well, garnering nearly 19% of the vote.

The League's growing popularity was greatly helped by the breaking scandals, especially in 1992. These scandals ended the stranglehold the Christian Democrats and Socialists had held in northern towns and brought the *Lega Nord*, as the remaining important regional party, into prominence in 1993 local elections and then in 1994 national elections.

The basic ideology of the *Lega Nord* is regionalist. The League, rather than taking strong abstract positions, focuses on more concrete issues. One set of issues concerns misuse of public funds by the major parties. The League has supported fiscal reform and lowered taxes; relatedly, the League has voiced the outrage of northern voters that their tax money is drained away to Rome and southern Italy, where it is used in corrupt patronage and never finds its way back to honest development in the north. Another set of issues the League supports is pro-market reforms. This stems from the individualist "Protestant Ethic" views of many northern elites and voters: that, as Berlusconi might suggest, development and growth come from hard work by individuals and not through state-led programs or the welfare state. Yet another set of issues is regionalist identity. Although the League is not secessionist, it does exude an antisouthern sentiment, regarding northern Italy as developed and European while seeing southern Italy as underdeveloped, flooded with immigrants and thieves, controlled by the Mafia, and in general rather immoral. The League is more pro-European than some other parties. One caveat should be mentioned at the end, however. While these are the general sentiments voiced by League leaders and supporters, the *Lega Nord*, unlike many of the pre-1990s parties, does not really have a formal, worked-out party ideology; this purposive vagueness acts, in a sense, as a "big tent" for general discouragement and disillusionment with southern Italy, the welfare state, and the failures of postwar policies. So instead of formal programs, the League champions general issues such as devolution of political power and anticenter sentiment.

In terms of party organization, the League is not a preeminent example of the modern party, as *Forza Italia* or the pre-1990s Communists are. The party has a very loose structure, making it more of an umbrella social movement than a true organized party. It does not have the party machine—cells, a party press—that, for example, *Forza Italia* has. Further, *Lega Nord* has been wary of electoral alliances; while it did ally itself with Berlusconi in 1994, the League proved to be a less-than-charming partner, and its quick break with Berlusconi brought down the Berlusconi government in 1994, not long after it had formed. In 1996, rather than join an electoral alliance with *Forza Italia* and *Alleanza Nationale*, the Northern League decided to go it alone—and its vote count actually increased by a small margin.

The general portrait of the *Lega Nord* supporter is a male, with less-than-average education, either from the working class or from small individual businesses, who lives in a rural locale. However, given the League's loose structure, determining actually party membership and other party procedures is difficult at present.

Other regionalist parties exist. The *Südtiroler Volkspartei* (South-Tyrolean People's Party) is based in German-speaking South Tyrol; before the 1990s it allied itself with the Christian Democrats and in the 1990s has allied itself with center-left parties and recently with the Olive Tree coalition. Another regional group is the *Partito Sarda d'Azione* (Sardinian Action Party). Another southern regionalist group is *Lega d'Azione Meridionale*.

MINOR POLITICAL PARTIES

Since the party breakups and reorganizations there have appeared numerous smaller parties, many of which have short histories and about which there is little available information in English—for example, *Rinnovamenta Italiano* (Italian Renewal), and the alliance of Green (environmentalist) parties, *Federazione dei Verdi* (Federation of Greens). Several other marginal parties are listed below.

Italian Republican Party
(Partito Repubblicano Italiano; PRI)

Founded in 1894, PRI supported the creation of a republican government. From its early years on, PRI was more intellectual than populist or popular—it began to fare well only by the late 1970s and 1980s, raising electoral support from over 2% to over 4%. The Fascist period hurt the PRI's image and thus hurt postwar electoral chances. Yet in spite of its size, because the PRI could garner 2% to 3% of the vote, it could be included in government coalitions to shore up parliamentary support. PRI policies focused on democracy and on efficient government activity; PRI also supported some degree of government intervention to counter social injustices, although it also called for political decentralization and a greater role in social life for local governments.

In the 1990s PRI suffered a split, as PRI became two groups, the PRI (retaining the name) and the *Alleanza Democratica* (AD), which gained membership from center-left members of the defunct DC. The AD gained some splinter members of the Socialist Party and participated in the 1994 elections in a center-left coalition, winning almost 3% of the vote; in 1994 the PRI joined with *Patto Segni* in a centrist coalition that gained 2.1% of the vote. In 1996 PRI ran in a bloc with three other parties, further within the Olive Tree cartel; the "bloc of four" received almost 7% of the vote. Both groups appear slated for marginality, as none can claim the center ground amid competition and a polarized political spectrum.

Italian Liberal Party
(Partito Liberale Italiano, PLI)

In the second half of the 19th century the PLI was the dominant political organization; however, the rise of the DC and the Socialists and Communists drew electoral power away from this elite-centered party. Weak resistance to fascism further hurt PLI strength. Declining political power and internal factionalization led to a breakup even of this small party. In 1993 some members of PLI split off to form *Unione di Centro* (Center Union), a right-wing party that joined Berlusconi's right-wing alliance in 1994 and 1996. The PLI itself has practically disappeared from electoral politics.

Radical Party
(Partito Radicale)

This party was in the past a small but strong supporter and leader of social reforms. Under its leader, Marco Pannella, the Radical Party scored political gains in the 1970s (more than 2% of votes) but also moved more and more to the left and eventually became a small organization oriented toward its leader. The Radicals were libertarian in social views, supporting divorce and abortion rights and the demands of environmentalist groups.

NATIONAL PROSPECTS

Italy has not had one of Europe's more stable political systems—witness the constant changes in governments, the constant dissolutions of Parliament before the end of its five-year term, and the fracturing of parties in the last years—but also has not fallen into the same kind of chaos that has threatened other countries such as Belarus or many underdeveloped nations. Italy's instability is more a threat to policy efficacy and continuity than to the political and social fabric of the nation. On the one hand, such instability did make policy implementation difficult; however, changing coalitions always remained in one part of the political spectrum, so that ruptures were not great and policies could be implemented. On the other hand, recent imperatives, especially European integration, make stability vital for the implementation of reform policies that Italy sorely needs if it is to enter monetary union. Additionally, the social and political fabric could be threatened by other forces in the political and social realms, especially crime.

For Italy to continue its march into prosperity, two issues must be addressed. First, there is the issue of corruption and crime. The political system in the 1980s and 1990s was crippled by scandals of political corruption, in particular by widespread and deep structures of party patronage. While patronage had its positive side—breaking class stratification and helping development of various regions, especially those in the south—it also led to recriminations of political favoritism and to the formation of right-wing reactionary groups, especially in the north. Such corruption, in spite of its ability to funnel resources to often needy patrons, also can lead to abuses of power and distraction of policies.

Corruption is not the only part of the dark underside plaguing Italy's politics: there is also the Mafia, especially prominent in southern Italy and Sicily, where Mafia families dominate and in fact are the real power, literally ousting more ineffectual state structures. These Mafia families are involved in a lucrative drug trade, spurring tensions and conflict between organized crime and the state and leading at times to bloodshed. Mafia control makes further centralization and organization of state power and authority problematic. The Mafia also contributes heavily to the problem of official corruption.

Second, there is the problem of political fragmentation and instability. Certainly Italy is not about to plunge into chaos or civil war; nevertheless, the Italian political system, with its parliamentary rules and abundance of parties, is not conducive to continuity either in leadership or in policies. The new rules do attempt to introduce some winnowing of parties but could also act as a double-edged sword. On the one hand, single-seat mandates might favor parties that can develop large national organizations and support their local-level candidates to defeat less organized parties' candidates; on the other hand, this procedure could also lead to further fragmentation if a few parties cannot help their candidates win in the constituencies. The problem is compounded by the recent breakup of larger parties; the process of winnowing will have to begin anew, and it is not clear that one party can dominate. Further, the resurgence of regionalism and regionalist parties (stemming from Italy's history of decentralized power) has made the emergence of a few national parties that much more difficult.

Thus, it appears that Italy's political scene will remain for many years as it has been—splintered and unstable, perhaps even more so with the fall of the main large parties. This does not threaten civil war, especially since the upheavals of the 1960s and 1970s are behind and the radical left is discredited by the fall of communism. Whether a center-right or center-left coalition will settle into one coherent party able to dominate politics and leave a prime minister in office without the distractions of no-confidence votes remains to be seen, although most likely this will not occur for some time. Further, whether the right wing can sustain its power depends on the ability of its politicians to deliver better social and living conditions without giving in to corruption (which, it appears, some right-wing leaders have been unable to do). For the short term, Italian politics will likely remain the type that requires its chroniclers to read the newspapers at least on a weekly basis.

Further Reading

Bartolini, Stefano, and Roberto D'Alimonte. "Plurality Competition and Party Realignment in Italy: The 1994 Parliamentary Elections." EUI Working Paper SPS No. 95/7, Italy, 1995.

CIA Factbook, 1996. Washington D.C.: Printing Office, 1996.

Collier's Year Book (for the years 1993–97).

The Economist.

Sassoon, Donald. Contemporary Italy: Economy, Society, and Politics, 2d ed. London: Addison-Wesley, 1997.

Smith, Denis Mack. Modern Italy. A Political History. Ann Arbor: University of Michigan Press, 1997.

REPUBLIC OF IVORY COAST

(République de la Côte d'Ivoire)

By Elizabeth L. Normandy, Ph.D.

THE SYSTEM OF GOVERNMENT

Slightly larger than the state of New Mexico, Ivory Coast is located in West Africa between Ghana and Liberia. Its coastline borders the North Atlantic Ocean.

There is no single dominant ethnic group in Ivory Coast. Of the approximately 60 ethnic groups, 4 groups make up over 67% of the 14 million population. They are distributed as follows: Baoule, 23%; Bete, 18%; Senoufou, 15%; Malinke, 11%. About 3 million non-Ivorian Africans reside in the Ivory Coast, including 300,000 Liberians who have taken refuge in the country as a result of the Liberian civil war. There are also sizable French and Lebanese populations. The country's major religious groups are Muslim, 60%; Christian, 12%; and indigenous religions, 25%.

Ivory Coast has a presidential form of government built on a separation of powers. The system is based on the constitution adopted at independence in 1960. For more than three decades, Ivorian politics was dominated by President Félix Houphouët-Boigny, who led the country to independence, wrote the constitution, and governed the country until his death in 1993.

Executive

Most political power lies with the presidency, as stipulated by the constitution. The president has the power to submit a bill to a national referendum or initiate legislation in the National Assembly, where approval is almost automatic. He or she may appoint, dismiss, and outline the functions of the Cabinet members and may appoint most other high-ranking civil, judicial, and military leaders. The president is also commander in chief of the military and may negotiate and ratify certain treaties.

The president is chosen by a direct national election for a five-year term of office. The constitution stipulates that the president be at least 40 years old, an eligible voter, and not the holder of one of several high political offices. The president is elected if he receives a majority of votes cast on the first ballot or, if no candidate receives a majority, through a runoff election between the two top candidates.

In the country's first multiparty elections in 1990, Houphouët-Boigny defeated Laurent Gbagbo, a candidate of the "democratic left" coalition. Houphouët received 81.68% of the vote, and Gbagbo received 18.32%. Alassane Ouattara was named to the newly created post of prime minister by Houphouët-Boigny. Nonetheless, real power remained in the hands of the president, who guided Outtara's decisions from behind the scenes.

On the death of Houphouët-Boigny in 1993, Henri Konan Bédié, Speaker of the National Assembly, assumed the presidency as decreed by law. In the 1995 elections, Henri Bédié retained the presidency, winning 96% of the vote. Outtara, the most serious challenger to Bédié, was forced to withdraw from the race because of a recently enacted restrictive electoral code.

Legislature

Ivory Coast's legislature is the National Assembly, consisting of 175 members. Since 1990, deputies have been selected in multiparty elections, replacing the multicandidate elections established in 1980. Deputies are elected by direct universal suffrage for five-year terms that run concurrently with the term of the president.

According to the constitution, the National Assembly meets in two regular sessions, each lasting about three months. The first session opens in April and the second in October. The primary powers of the National Assembly are the voting of laws and the authorization of taxes. The constitution stipulates that any power not expressly given to the National Assembly is outside its domain. This serves to augment the power of the president, who has fewer constitutional limits on his power. In practice, the National Assembly has little independence from the president. It does not check the president's powers, nor does he consult it. Rather, its role is to ratify executive decisions in order to give them legitimacy.

In the 1990 legislative elections, the Democratic Party

of Ivory Coast (PDCI) won 163 of 175 seats. The Ivorian Popular Front (FPI) won 9 seats, the PIT 1 seat, and independent candidates took 2 seats. In the 1995 legislative elections, the PDCI maintained its dominance in the legislature. It is expected that the presence of opposition legislators will expand public debate on policy if not the role of the legislature in policymaking.

Judiciary

The legal system of Ivory Coast is a mixture of customary and French law. The Supreme Court's constitutional section may rule on the constitutionality of bills that have been proposed or passed by the National Assembly but not promulgated. The Court's administrative section is the court of final appeal for cases dealing with government administration and the bureaucracy, and the audit and control section oversees state expenditures and audits state accounts. The High Court of Justice, composed of deputies to the National Assembly, rules on crimes committed by government officials within the line of duty and on charges of treason against high officials, including the president. The judicial system includes a court of appeals and lower courts. Although nominally independent, the judiciary does not ensure due process and is subject to pressure from the executive in political cases. Reports persist that defendants with ties to the opposition are treated more harshly than those with ties to the government. Freedoms of speech, press, assembly, association, and movement are restricted.

Regional and Local Government

Local government in Ivory Coast is modeled after the French system. The country is divided into 50 departments, each governed by a prefect appointed by the president. There are 135 communes, each headed by a competitively elected mayor. The 37 largest towns and cities are governed by municipal councils that are also elected. In 1985, the number of departments and local councils was increased in order to bring the administration closer to the people and to allow them to have greater participation in the management of resources.

THE ELECTORAL SYSTEM

Elections in Ivory Coast are direct; suffrage is universal for those 21 years of age or older. The electoral process is by secret ballot and follows a campaign limited by law to a two- or three-week period. Elections are held every five years.

Under a multiparty system adopted in 1990, parties are legally free to organize and run candidates for office. However, election law stipulates that candidates must meet stringent parentage, residency, and citizenship require-

ments. Changes to the law in 1995 require candidates to prove that both parents were born in Ivory Coast.

THE PARTY SYSTEM

Prior to 1990, Ivory Coast was in practice a one-party state dominated by the PDCI. The PDCI prevented the rise of a formal opposition by giving prominent persons who might conceivably lead such an opposition high and demanding positions in the government. The total domination of the government by the PDCI helped to make it an unofficial fourth branch of the government. Most important decisions affecting government policy actually were made by the elite of the PDCI.

In 1990, several weeks of strikes and protests of unprecedented scale and intensity revealed intense dissatisfaction with PDCI-controlled government With the party's popularity at an all-time low and opposition parties covering the entire political spectrum forming underground, the government announced that opposition parties would be recognized officially. In the elections that followed later that year, 26 opposition parties contested the elections.

DEMOCRATIC PARTY OF IVORY COAST
(Parti démocratique de la Côte d'Ivoire; PDCI)

HISTORY

The PDCI was formed in the late 1940s as the Ivorian branch of the African Democratic Rally (*Rassemblement Démocratique Africain*; RDA). The RDA was an organization formed to encourage independence for French West Africa. Although the French opposed the efforts of the RDA prior to 1951, after that date the French withdrew their support of other African groups and then allowed the RDA—and its branch, the PDCI—to dominate politics in the region. Both the RDA and the PDCI were founded by Houphouët-Boigny. The PDCI has dominated in every election since independence.

ORGANIZATION

The organization of the PDCI is highly centralized. While party organs exist down to the local level, all policy is formed at the national level. Local party organs serve more to mobilize support than as policymaking bodies.

At the 1990 party congress, the PDCI instituted substantial changes in the party. Some party decision-making structures were abolished or replaced. A renewal manifesto drafted by senior party officials during the campaign period condemned repression of dissidents and opponents; criticized the party for laxity, nepotism, and corruption; and called for a thorough and critical self-examination. Following the 1990 election, the party chose a new general secretary and abolished its student wing.

POLICY

In effect, the PDCI is a nonideological party that deemphasizes political programs and advocates a pragmatic approach to solving current problems. The party's base is predominantly Baoule, and its strength is concentrated in the northern and central regions of the country.

Prior to 1990, Houphouët-Boigny maintained his control of the party and the government through strict repression of violence and co-opting of the opposition. During the 1990 election campaign, the PDCI used its control over political resources, such as the news media and government facilities, to ensure that it won the election. In 1992, the PDCI-controlled government used heavy-handed tactics to suppress the opposition. Prior to the 1995 elections, the government used lethal force to control antigovernment demonstrations that had been banned by decree.

MEMBERSHIP

The party claims universal membership. Through village-level organs of the party, all eligible voters participate in party activity, although this activity is more an expression of support than real input into policymaking.

FINANCING

Although no data are available on party finances, it can be assumed that substantial funds come directly from the government.

LEADERSHIP

From 1960 to 1990, Félix Houphouët-Boigny led the party as well as the government. In 1990, the party chose a new general secretary, but Houphouët-Boigny continued to exercise considerable power in party affairs. Upon the death of Houphouët-Boigny in 1993, Henri Konan Bédié assumed the presidency and with it a significant role in the running of the party. Bédié had been positioned to assume the presidency by having been selected by Houphouët-Boigny to be Speaker of the National Assembly. Alassane Outtara, who had been acting as prime minister when Houphouët-Boigny died, challenged Bédié for the presidency unsuccessfully. In 1995, Bédié again won the presidency.

MINOR POLITICAL PARTIES

Minor parties made their first official appearance in 1990 when multiparty elections were first allowed. In that elec-

tion, only two of the three or four main opposition parties gained seats. Ivorian Popular Front (*Front Populaire Ivorian*; FPT) won 9 seats, and PIT, Ivorian Workers Party (*Parti Ivorian des Travailleurs*; PIT) won 1 seat. The platforms of the opposition parties generally agreed on the need for greater civil liberties but differed in their economic prescriptions.

In the 1995 elections, approximately 80 registered political parties contested the elections. The main opposition parties, including the FPI and the Rally of Republicans (RDR), were grouped under the banner of the Republican Front (RF). Despite a poor showing due to disunity and the failure to present coalition candidates, the RDR captured 25 seats.

NATIONAL PROSPECTS

Historically, much of the stability and efficiency of the Ivorian government has depended on the prosperity of the economy. After experiencing a 7% annual growth rate since independence, Ivory Coast saw its growth rate slow to almost zero in the 1980s because of the decline in the price of coffee and cocoa, the major sources of revenue for the country. Despite austerity measures and structural reforms, the continuing economic crisis has been a constant source of political unrest.

The economy seemed poised to make a comeback in 1994 due to improved prices for cocoa and coffee, offshore oil and gas discoveries, debt rescheduling by multilateral lenders, and a 50% currency devaluation. However, a bloated public sector and large foreign debt continue to constrain development.

Even if the economy improves, it will not solve political problems such as persistent corruption and political manipulation of the electoral and legal systems. Until the political leadership is willing to stand for election under rules that promote rather than inhibit a level playing field, Ivory Coast's progress toward democratization will be impeded.

Further Reading

Cohen, Michael A. *Urban Policy and Political Conflict in Africa: A Study of the Ivory Coast.* Chicago: University of Chicago Press, 1974.

Foster, Philip, and Aristide R. Zolberg. *Ghana and the Ivory Coast.* Chicago: University of Chicago Press, 1971.

Mundt, Robert J. *Historical Dictionary of Côte d'Ivoire*, 2d ed. African Historical Dictionaries Series, vol. 41. Lanham, Md.: Scarecrow Press, 1995.

Widner, Jennifer A. "The 1990 Elections in Côte d'Ivoire." *Issue* 20, no. 1 (winter 1991): 31–40.

JAMAICA

By Thomas D. Anderson, Ph.D.

THE SYSTEM OF GOVERNMENT

Jamaica is one of the Greater Antilles with an area of 10,830 square kilometers lying south of Cuba and west of Haiti in the Caribbean Sea. It is a parliamentary democracy that was granted independence from the British Empire on August 6, 1962. The capital city is Kingston. It has an English-speaking population of about 2.6 million with an annual growth rate of 2.6%, tempered by an emigration of of −5.9 per 1,000 births. Racially the population is 76% black, with another 20% partially black. Whites, Chinese, and others make up the remainder. Although nearly 60% of the population are Christian (largely Protestant), most of the rest identify with various spiritual faiths, the most important of which in Rasta Farianism, which originated in Jamaica. Agriculture is a major feature of the landscape, with about a quarter of the surface devoted to field and tree crops. However, bauxite mining, light manufacturing, and tourism are the most significant sectors of the economy.

Executive

The chief of state is the British monarch, represented by a governor-general appointed by the monarch on the advice of the Jamaican prime minister. The governor-general is advised by the six-member Privy Council. Effective executive power is held by the prime minister, who is leader of the majority party in the House of Representatives, to which the prime minister and Cabinet are responsible.

Legislature

The bicameral Parliament consists of the House of Representatives and the Senate. The House has 60 members elected by direct suffrage to five-year terms. The 21-member Senate is appointed by the governor-general: 13 members on the advice of the prime minister and 8 on the advice of the leader of the opposition. Cabinet members may be appointed from either the House or the Senate. Although the Parliament is the preeminent legal authority, it is effectively under the control of the prime minister.

Bills may be introduced by either body, except for money bills, which must originate in the House. Although the Senate may delay passage of a bill by voting it down, the House may override the action by passing the bill a second time. Senate approval is required for constitutional amendments. Parliamentary standing committees handle legislative business under direction of the prime minister and his Cabinet. On advice from the prime mnister, the governor-general may dissolve the parliament and call for new elections at any time. Otherwise elections are held at five-year intervals.

Judiciary

The judicial system is based on English common law and practices. The high courts are the Supreme Court and the Court of Appeal. The Supreme Court consists of the chief justice and other judges. The chief justice is appointed by the governor-general on the advice of the prime minister and in consultation with the leader of the opposition. The other judges also are appointed by the governor-general on the advice of the Judicial Service Commission, which is chaired by the chief justice. Appeals from the Supreme Court go to the Court of Appeals, which is the highest court in Jamaica. Further appeals may be sent to the Privy Council in London, which is the ultimate court of appeal. Judges retire after 65 years of age but otherwise can only be removed on the request of the governor-general to the Privy Council in London and after investigation by that body.

Regional and Local Government

For administrative purposes, Jamaica is divided into 14 parishes and the Kingston and St. Andrew Corporation, which includes the principal metropolitan area. Each parish has an elected council that administers local affairs.

THE ELECTORAL SYSTEM

National elections have been held since 1944. Suffrage is universal for citizens 18 years old or older. Elections to the House of Representatives are held at least every five years, and seats are won by simple plurality in single-member constituencies. A nominal cash deposit is required for those who stand for office and is forfeited should the candidate receive less than 12.5% of the constituency vote. The boundaries of the constituencies are reviewed periodically by a standing committee in the Parliament. In general, elections have been fair, although allegations of fraud were widespread after the election of 1976.

THE PARTY SYSTEM

The first open demand for greater self-government in the British West Indian possession came in 1936, when Jamaican expatriates in New York City founded the Jamaican Progressive League. This period was one of growing labor strife in the British West Indies. It began when an attempt to organize sugar workers on St. Kitts was suppressed. Two years later a general strike began in Trinidad, and related strikes and demonstrations spread to other British territories. London's reaction was to legalize unions and widen the franchise. What next evolved was a hybrid political structure peculiar to the British Caribbean.

Although conditions differed, those that developed in Jamaica were somewhat archetypical: a two-party, two-union system with labor and political elements intertwined but still distinguishable. The pairings were the Jamaica Labour Party (JLP) and the Bustamante Industrial Trades Union, arrayed against the Peoples National Party (PNP) and the National Workers Union. The unions were very similar in composition. The leaders of each normally serve in Parliament, and both unions were blanket types in that a wide cross section of worker categories was represented. A significant event in 1952 was the expulsion from the PNP of the "Four H's"—Ken Hill, Frank Hill, Arther Henry, and Richard Hart—for exposing Marxist doctrines in violation of party rules. The policies of the PNP have varied little since that time. External influences have helped to shape the distinctive non-Marxist union/party forms, such as U.S. and Western European governments and labor unions. Especially important was the Scandinavian example of worker participation in control of an industry's operation rather than its ownership. Two towering figures had major roles in these events. Alexander Bustamante first gained national stature when he was arrested and imprisoned following labor unrest in 1938. His defense lawyer was Norman Manley.

The party system is open and well developed. There are no barriers to the entry of new parties or independent candidates, but none of the former and few of the latter have fared well in competition with the disciplined organizations of the two major parties. Both the PNP and the JLP are organized by constituency. Since the early years, the party structures have been more influential than those of the unions. Both parties maintain youth organizations that provide the core of their forces during campaigns as well as training for the leadership of the future. Campaign expenditures are limited by law, but few details are pubic knowlege. It is generally assumed that both parties receive major contributions from business and industrial enterprises.

Election campaigns are well organized and fiercely contested—unfortunately in recent years this has included serious violence. In the 1980 campaign, an estimated 500 people died in campaign-related incidents. Much of the violence is attributed to youth wings of the parties, which attempt to control sections of Kingston and exclude campaigning by their opponents in these sectors.

Most violence occurs in the poorest neighborhoods where each party competes strongly for a sector of the vote that had been a deciding factor in a recent election. The 1972 and 1976 successes of the PNP were attributed to Manley's left-wing appeals to the urban poor, whereas his failure to improve their lot and a 30% unemployment rate was decisive in the rout of the PNP in 1980.

In 1983, the ruling JLP called a snap election that the PNP decided not to contest. Prime Minister Edward-Seaga sought to capitalize on a wave of popular support for his role in backing the invasion of Grenada in order to reaffirm his leadership. The opposition boycotted on the grounds that the voter lists had not been updated to include 100,000 new voters. As a result, the JLP won all 60 seats in Parliament, leaving Jamaica without an offical opposition for the first time. It was feared that such one-party rule would harm the political system, but the PNP remained active and because the JLP permitted public participation in the House of Assembly, a lively exchange of views continued.

JAMAICA LABOUR PARTY (JLP)

The JLP was founded by Alexander Bustamante in 1943 after he took his Bustamante Industrial Trade Union (BITU) out of association with the PNP in a dispute over that party's advocacy of Jamaican independence. Most of the JLP's support came from the workers, whereas the leadership was primarily from businesses and professionals. Initially opposed to independence, the JLP first came to power in 1944 when Jamaica was granted self- government. It lost power from 1955 to 1962 but presided over the transfer of sovereignty in 1962. From 1972 to 1980, it again served as an opposition party. The JLP held power again until defeat by the PNP in February 1993. The scale of the loss (the JLP won only eight seats) was such that the JLP contended that the election was the most fraudulent in Jamaican history and that they would refuse to contest any by-elections until electoral reforms were implemented.

They did, however, drop 14 of 16 court challenges in specific constituencies.

In its early years, the party was dominated by Bustamante, but following his retirement in the mid-1960s, the strength of the constituency organizations increased as greater democracy was introduced. The party's political stance has always been right-of-center, with emphasis on free enterprise, foreign investment, and economic expansion as the best strategies to improve conditions for the island's poor. Along with a strong rural base, the JLP also draws strength from the social elite. The 1993 election defeat caused Seaga in 1995 to poll the party delegates regarding his standing. His version of the result (critics had their doubts) was a 78% approval rating, and he remained in the leadership post.

PEOPLES NATIONAL PARTY (PNP)

The PNP was founded in 1939 by Norman Manley. Its early policy thrust was Jamaican independence and an end to the dominance of British capital on theisland. In its early years, it relied heavily on Bustamante's union for support, but after Bustamante split with the party in 1943, it eventually developed an organization that won support both within the middle class and among labor when Manley organized the National Workers' Union in the 1950s.

Despite its early strength among the business and professional community under the leadership of Norman Manley, the party moved sharply to the left after the founder's death in 1969 and his son, Michael Manley (born 1923), took over. The younger Manley had been an NWU organizer and leader, and he increased the appeal of the party to the urban poor and younger voters. As prime minister from 1972 to 1980, Manley pursued a socialist policy that included nationalization of foreign holdings and social progams such as a literacy campaign, agricultural collectivization, and government-funded education through the university level. Manley identified Jamaica with the Third World and Non-Aligned movements and expressed solidarity with the Caribbean Marxist governments in Cuba and Grenada.

During Manley's eight years as prime minister Jamaica experienced a 17% drop in its economy, an increase in unemployment from 20% to 30%, and an accumulation of foreign debt that reached to over a billion U.S. dollars. The reaction of the voters was a resounding defeat of his party, although Manley retained his own seat in the House. An additional factor in this rejection was the attempt by Fidel Castro to provide money and political advice in support of the Manley campaign. Newspaper reports of these activities both swayed some voters and induced a wider turnout by others.

Despite this down period, the PNP retained its traditional solid base of support and took advantage of errors and a stagnant economy during the subsequent terms of Edward Seaga to return to power in the election of February 1988. Ill health induced Manley to give way to P. J. Patterson in March 1992, and he led the PNP to victory in 1993. The party did so in stunning fashion, winning 52 seats to 8 for the JLP. Michael Manley died in March 1997, and plans were made to declare December 10 a day of commemoration of his memory.

NATIONAL DEMOCRATIC MOVEMENT (NDM)

In the context of Jamaica's dominant two-party structure the political alternatives could usually be more accurately termed factions. However, in October 1995, the former JLP chairman and heir apparent to Edward Seaga as party leader, Bruce Golding, formed the National Democratic Movement made up of dissidents from the major parties. Polls taken in September suggested that such an entity would draw as much voter support as either the JLP or the PNP, but that none of the three parties ranked much above 20% in popularity. Nevertheless, Golding's NDM attracted enough "crossover" members to become the opposition in the House. His suggestions for change included a clearer separation of the executive and legislative branches, with a prime minister or president elected separately from the MPs.

OTHER POLITICAL FORCES

Minor Political Parties

The New Beginnings Movement (NBM), with several hundred adherents, is a minor political party with only a slight political impact. The Rasta Farians ("Rastas") of the country, despite their relative informal organizational status, could be a potent political force should they decide collectively to take positions on specific issues. The movement has spread widely throughout the Caribbean as well as into Anglo-America and Britain but remains most influential in its land of origin and especially in the interior highlands (the "Cockpit" country).

NATIONAL PROSPECTS

Jamaican politics has demonstrated a pattern of transfer of party power about every two terms, a characteristic that can be regarded as public frustration with the sluggish pace of economic development. An interpretation of this behavior and the inability of political alternatives to appeal to the general populace is that a stable democracy is in place and that it is likely to continue. With the downturn of the bauxite market and the increasing competition for tourist dollars (especially from Cuba), the prospects for economic growth appear best in the expansion of the manufacturing sector. Expansion of the North American Trade Agreement to Mexico, along with the continued exclusion of the rest of the Caribbean, has raised serious concerns about the likelihood of such expansion. In early 1997 the apparel industry suffered its first downturn in 20 years, with Mexico named as the culprit.

Further Reading

Alexander, Robert J. *Political Parties of the Americas: Canada, Latin America and the Caribbean*, 2 vols. Westport, Conn.: Greenwood Press, 1982.

Anderson, Thomas D. "Marxists and Non-Marxists in the Caribbean." In *A Critique of Marxist and Non-Marxist Thought*. Ed. Ajit Jain and Alexander J. Matejko. New York: Praeger, 1986.

Caribbean Week: The Regional Newspaper of the Caribbean. St. Michael, Barbados.

CIA World Factbook. Washington, D.C.: Government Printing Office, various years.

JAPAN

(Nihon/Nippon)

By Richard Leitch, Ph.D.

THE SYSTEM OF GOVERNMENT

Japan is an island nation-state located in Northeast Asia between the North Pacific Ocean and the Sea of Japan, approximately 450 miles east of China. The Japanese archipelago consists of roughly 3,300 islands, but the four largest islands—Honshu, Kyushu, Hokkaido, and Shikoku— account for 97% of Japan's land area and are home to 98% of Japan's approximately 125 million people.

Executive

Executive authority is vested in a Cabinet, at present numbering 21 members, all of whom must be civilians. The Cabinet consists of the prime minister, the chief Cabinet secretary, 12 ministers of state with portfolio, and seven directors general of agencies, all without portfolio. The constitution stipulates that the prime minister selects and may dismiss other members of the Cabinet and also states that the prime minister, as well as a majority of the Cabinet ministers, must be members of the Diet. Since ministerial appointments are usually made as a reward for political loyalty to the prime minister and/or factions within the ruling party or parties, tradition has held that only under extraordinary circumstances would a member of the Cabinet not also be a member of the Diet. Most often, therefore, for the prime minister Cabinet appointments are considerations of political exigency rather than selections of experts on the policy facing the various ministries and agencies.

A midterm Cabinet shuffle and replacement with new ministers is a common strategy of prime ministers, who attempt to take full advantage of this perquisite during their time in office. With the formation of the third Cabinet of Prime Minister Hashimoto Ryutaro in September 1997, there have been 68 Cabinets in postwar Japan. Generally, these frequent Cabinet reorganizations have not weakened the overall policy continuity of the respective ministries and agencies, for the appointment of a parliamentary minister has always been recognized by the bureaucracy as a political, and not a public policy, decision.

The power of the Cabinet is limited by its relationship to the Diet, especially to the Lower House. Cabinet members are required to attend the sessions of both houses of the Diet and the meetings of the committees relevant to their appointment, and to reply to questions raised in these forums. In policy, the power of the prime minister is checked in legislative matters primarily by party members of the Diet—particularly its leaders—and to a lesser extent by the leaders of the opposition parties in the Diet. Cabinet power is also limited by the role of bureaucrats in the drafting and implementation of legislation: the first because of their relatively greater knowledge of the specifics of a policy issue and the second because of their ability to enforce the law. At the height of bureaucratic involvement in the process of policy formulation, it was estimated that more than 80% of all legislation that reached the floor of the Diet was initiated by civil servants and presented through the Cabinet. However, now that the assumption of Liberal Democratic Party (LDP) dominance has been shaken and citizens are expecting more accountability and response from their elected officials, national policy is no longer assumed to be primarily the domain of the bureaucratic corps.

The most significant check that the legislative branch holds over the Cabinet is the power constitutionally delegated to the Lower House to present no-confidence resolutions against the Cabinet. The Upper House of the legislature is not empowered to present no-confidence motions, and the Cabinet does not have the authority to dissolve the Upper House. If the Lower House passes a no-confidence motion (or rejects a confidence motion), the Cabinet must resign en masse. To date, 36 no-confidence motions have been filed, and only four times in the postwar period has the Lower House passed no-confidence motions against the Cabinet. Only twice have Cabinets resigned en masse on their own accord. Cabinet members may also be impeached by resolution of either house of the Diet, although such an impeachment has yet to occur.

Prior to 1993, a prime minister could expect to serve from two to six years in office, while Cabinet members would, on average, serve for two years total in Cabinet positions throughout their political career, although rarely continuously. Because of the political prestige associated with holding a Cabinet post and the prime minister's ability to fill the posts based on party or personal loyalty, it has not been unusual for any one individual to serve in several different Cabinet positions over the course of multiple administrations. It is from this more exclusive group, comprising those 10% of Cabinet ministers who serve between four and seven years, that most of Japan's postwar prime ministers have been drawn.

Terms in Office of Postwar Prime Ministers

Prime Minister	Term in Office
Higashikuni Naruhiko	August 1945–October 1945
Shidehara Kijuro	October 1945–May 1946
Yoshida Shigeru	May 1946–May 1947
Katayama Tetsu	May 1947–March 1948
Ashida Hitoshi	March 1948–October 1948
Yoshida Shigeru	October 1948–December 1954
Hatoyama Ichiro	December 1954–December 1956
Ishibashi Tanzan	December 1956–February 1957
Kishi Nobusuke	February 1957–July 1960
Ikeda Hayato	July 1960–November 1964
Sato Eisaku	November 1964–July 1972
Tanaka Kakuei	July 1972–December 1974
Miki Takeo	December 1974–December 1976
Fukuda Takeo	December 1976–December 1978
Ohira Masayoshi	December 1978–July 1980
Suzuki Zenko	July 1980–November 1982
Nakasone Yasuhiro	November 1982–November 1987
Takeshita Noboru	November 1987–June 1989
Uno Sosuke	June 1989–August 1989
Kaifu Toshiki	August 1989–August 1991
Miyazawa Kiichi	August 1991–August 1993
Hosokawa Morihiro	August 1993–April 1994
Hata Tsutomu	April 1994–June 1994
Murayama Tomiichi	June 1994–January 1996
Hashimoto Ryutaro	January 1996–July 1998
Obuchi Keizo	July 1998–

As is the case with all parliamentary democracies, Japan's prime minister is chosen from the ranks of the legislative branch. From its creation in 1955 until the general election of October 1993, the Liberal Democratic Party either held a majority of seats in the formerly 511-member Lower House of the legislature (therefore, at least 256 seats) or was able to win the support of minor parties or party independents in the unusual event that it did not win a majority of seats via the ballot box (only between 1976 and 1980 was this the case). Technically, these unusual situations would have made such an arrangement a coalition government, but because of the preponderance of LDP power in the relationship or the subsequent decision of the non-LDP representatives to change their party affiliation to the more powerful and better organized LDP, the instability inherent in a coali-

tion government was virtually eliminated. Therefore, because of this LDP dominance, from 1955 to 1993 all prime ministers of Japan were members of the Liberal Democratic Party.

Conflict between the executive and legislative branches over legislation has traditionally been less frequent than is often the case in those nation-states that have a presidential form of government. Conflict between the legislative and executive branches was also lessened during the LDP reign because of the ritualized opposition role played by other political parties. The tactics of opposition parties were often determined well in advance of the presentation of an issue before the Diet, and as their position was shared with members of the ruling LDP, everyone knew what was expected of the respective parties when the issue was ultimately presented. Conflict between the executive and legislative branches in Japan has also been mitigated because most prime ministers have been weak leaders in terms of innovative or bold policy agendas and have instead arrived at the position as a result of their seniority within the party, their ability to raise funds for the party, or sheer happenstance. In contemporary times, LDP Prime Ministers Takeshita Noboru and Miyazawa Kiichi were notable as skilled fund-raisers (especially so in the case of the former) and elder statesmen who held a number of ministerial posts (especially so in the case of the latter), but both were judged especially ineffective in leading the nation and unifying party members to legislate what the citizenry believed to be needed reform.

The most recent election for the Lower House of the Diet was held in October 1996. As indicated by the table of postwar prime ministers' terms in office, Murayama Tomiichi held the prime minister's post for nearly an additional three months following the 1996 election, although his party was decimated at the polls. In January 1996, LDP stalwart Hashimoto Ryutaro succeeded Murayama as prime minister, and at the 1997 LDP convention, Hashimoto was the first-ever LDP president who was unopposed by other LDP members in his bid to maintain the party presidency.

By law, the next election for the Lower House of the Diet must be no later than October 2000, at which time the issue of the prime ministership would be considered. However, LDP rules state that a party president who has served two terms, totaling four years, cannot be reelected. Since Hashimoto began serving his second term in September 1997, unless LDP rules are revised, he would have to step down in September 1999 and a new prime minister would have to be selected.

Legislature

Legislative authority is vested in a bicameral legislature called the *kokkai* (Diet), consisting of the 252-member Upper House, the *sangiin* (House of Councillors), and the relatively more powerful 500-member Lower House, the *shugiin* (House of Representatives). Members of the House of Representatives are elected for four-year terms, but as Japan is a parliamentary democracy based on the British model, the prime minister has the power to dissolve the Lower House at any time during this four-year term and call for new elections, for a variety of reasons. Foremost among these is that public opinion polls may have been favorable for the ruling party, and its members, believing that they will likely be reelected by an approving electorate, are hopeful of extending their term in office for an additional four years. During the 38-year reign of the Liberal Democratic Party, which spanned from its founding in 1955 until its defeat in the Lower House election of July 1993, dissolution of the Lower House for this reason was not uncommon. Indeed, only once during the postwar period have Lower House members served the duration of their four-year terms (1972–76), with the average term lasting approximately $2\frac{1}{2}$ years.

While "snap elections" called by the prime minister are the most frequent reason for early termination of a representative's term in office, elections are also required following a successful vote of no-confidence (or rejection of a confidence resolution) against the Cabinet by the rank and file of the Lower House, or in the event of a vacancy in the post of the prime minister, or if the Cabinet resigns en masse.

In all three events described above, the composition of the House of Councillors is not affected. Members serve fixed, six-year terms, with half of the body up for election every three years, usually in July. And although relatively weaker than the Lower House as far as powers granted to it by the constitution, the Upper House does have some power to influence the specifics of legislation or to delay the legislative process.

As a result of U.S. influence in drafting Japan's postwar constitution, and similar to the operations of the U.S. Congress, most debate on proposed legislation takes place at the committee level. Both houses of the Diet have standing and special committees, with the Lower House committees approximating the jurisdictions of the various government ministries and agencies and those of the Upper House relevant to national policy rather than to administrative matters. There are 16 standing committees in both houses, each with its counterpart in the other, and two additional standing committees (science and technology, and the environment) in only the Lower House. All are granted the right to conduct investigations of the actions of the government offices relevant to their charges, and the standing committees have their own investigative branches staffed by researchers and policy specialists. Representation on standing committees is apportioned according to the relative strength of each party's representation in the appropriate house, with chairposts traditionally assigned to members of the ruling party or, in the case of a coalition government, ruling par-

ties. Special committees are formed if the issue in question falls outside the scope of the standing committees and are disbanded after their findings have been reported to the Diet.

There are three distinct research offices that assist two distinct parts of policymaking. Both the Lower House Legislative Bureau and the National Diet Library Research and Legislation Office assist Diet members in drafting bills. National Diet Library records indicate that during the period including the 1995 Diet session, Lower House lawmakers presented a total of 2,065 bills and Upper House members 911. Of these, only 36.4% and 16.9%, respectively, became law. On the other hand, the Cabinet Legislation Bureau, through the Cabinet, presented 7,426 bills to the Diet, 87% of which became law. Cabinet bills are rarely the initiative of the Cabinet members themselves but, as the result of bureaucratic initiative and research, are often referred to as "government bills."

This frequency of "bureaucratic lawmaking," especially in the light of relatively far fewer Dietmember bills becoming law, is not to imply that Dietmembers lack knowledge about policy matters. *Zoku* refer to those policy and issue-related realms in which Dietmembers have specialist knowledge or experience, and they act to protect the interests of affected groups by intervening in administrative and legislative matters on their behalf. For example, among others, there is an agriculture and forestry group (*norin-zoku*), a construction group (*kensetsu-zoku*), and a commerce and industry group (*shoko-zoku*). Under the multimember districts of the pre-1996 electoral system, on average, three to five representatives would hail from each district, with there rarely being two *zoku* representatives from the same district. Unless under exceptional circumstances, each representative would establish one *zoku* affiliation, which was coordinated by the LDP.

The *zoku* phenomenon was once seen as reflecting the close ties between members of the LDP, their counterparts in government ministries and agencies, and the special-interest groups that they represented. This collaborative relationship became known as an "iron triangle" or, when it applied to the big-business realm of policymaking, "Japan, Inc." Such a generalized, simplistic view obfuscates the conflict that was often inherent among the three groups, and it seems especially inapplicable in the post-1993, post–economic boom era.

Under Japan's revised, single-seat electoral system, representatives are now expected by the party (or compelled if they want to win a subsequent term) to develop multiple *zoku* affiliations. In contrast to the earlier era when *zoku* representatives could be considered experts on policy relating to that *zoku*, the result under the new system may be that less-than-knowledgeable Diet representatives come to rely on bureaucratic knowledge and assistance on those issues that fall outside of their primary *zoku* expertise even more than they had before. On the other hand, however, the likelihood of collusion among special-interest groups, politicians and bureaucrats—formerly accepted by the electorate as part of politics, but now openly criticized—may likely be mitigated.

It is normally the case that bills and other matters requiring Diet approval are first referred to the appropriate committee or committees for deliberation and then presented to the plenary session for a vote. Exception to this practice is given to those matters deemed so urgently in need of immediate legislative action that they must sidestep the committee channeling process. Following full-house deliberation, these issues are voted upon in the plenary session. Far more frequent than immediate-action cases but again exceptional relative to the number of bills first brought before committees are those significant items over which the ruling party (or parties) and the opposition will clearly be at odds. In these instances, which are termed important or "confrontational" bills, the item is introduced before the plenary session together with an explanation as to why the item is important enough to merit exception from the normal legislative channels. It is sure then to evoke debate during the plenary session. Although such a bill is not acted upon when introduced but is instead referred to the appropriate committee or committees, with an important bill's introduction before the full house, the stage has been set for backroom brokering and negotiations between the parties. Failing an interparty agreement before the bill once again reaches the plenary session for a vote, well-orchestrated, vitriolic harangues and displays of vote-stalling tactics by the party or parties that realize the vote may be against their cause are not uncommon.

The Diet is convened for any of three distinct sessions: regular, extraordinary, and special. By law, regular sessions must be held at least once a year. They are opened in December and last for 150 days. Extraordinary sessions are most often convened when the Cabinet determines the need for such a session or when one-fourth of the membership of either house requests such a session. Special sessions are held in accordance with Article 54 of the constitution, which stipulates that upon dissolution of the House of Representatives, "there must be a general election of members of the House of Representatives within forty days from the date of dissolution, and the Diet must be convoked within thirty days from the date of the election."

The term of an extraordinary or special session is somewhat flexible, as it is decided by agreement of both houses, with the Lower House decision binding if no agreement can be reached. Yet expedience and efficiency are essential during any of these sessions, for a bill that is not approved by both houses during the same session cannot be carried over to the next session unless both houses agree to continue deliberations at the committee level. A Diet session can also be extended, in accordance with the procedure for determining the initial term of an extraordinary or special session, although the number of extensions permitted is limited to one for a regular session and two for extraordinary or special sessions. For the LDP, which from 1955 to 1989 either held an absolute majority in both houses or had the support of smaller parties when it did not, extending sessions or prolonging the life of a bill was a matter of intraparty, not interparty, concern. But once it lost its majority in the Upper House following the July 1989 election, the LDP was forced to consider more seriously the influence of the opposition.

The constitution establishes the primacy of Lower House decisions over those of the Upper House in four areas: enactment of laws, passage of the budget, approval of treaties, and designation of the prime minister. If the two houses vote differently on a bill, a joint committee is convened to create a compromise bill that is returned to both houses for action. In such instances, if the Upper House still votes differently from the Lower House or if agreement cannot be reached through the deliberations of a compromise committee, the decision of the Lower House prevails. Of significance, if the budget is not passed by the Upper House, then the administration continues to operate on a budget equivalent to that of the preceding fiscal year.

Before the LDP's loss of its majority in the House of Councillors following the election of 1989, the convocation of a joint committee was for 33 years a rarity. But since 1989—and especially since 1993—the joint committee is becoming more frequent. The constitution stipulates that if the two houses cannot agree on a compromise version, the measure becomes law if approved by two-thirds or more of Lower House members present (Article 59). Yet since no party has ever held two-thirds of the seats in the Lower House, this scenario is possible only as a result of party alliances. In fact, the only period when these two-thirds alliances were struck was in the early years of LDP rule, and the most recent successful Lower House override of a measure other than those mentioned above (budget, treaties, and designation of the prime minister) was in 1957.

The 1996 election was the first conducted under a new electoral system that eliminated multimember districting in an effort to reduce corruption, decrease party factionalism, and create more cohesive parties in the Diet. It is still too early to judge whether these objectives have been, or will be, realized.

Judiciary

Article 81 of the constitution specifies that the Supreme Court is "the court of last resort with power to determine the constitutionality of any law, order, regulation, or official act." While the Supreme Court has the power of ju-

House of Representatives Election Results
for 1990, 1993, and 1996

	Seats, 1990	Seats, 1993	Seats, 1996
Liberal Democrats	275 (54%)	223 (44%)	239 (48%)
Japan New Party	0	35	
Japan Renewal (Shinseito)	0	55	
New Harbinger (Sakigake)	0	13	2
New Frontier			156
Komeito (Clean Govt. Party)	45	51	
Democratic Socialist	13	15	
United Social Democratic	4	4	
Democratic Party of Japan			52
Japan Socialist Party	136	70	15
Japan Communist Party	16	15	26
Independents and Other Minor Parties	22	30	10
Total	511	511	500

dicial review, with minor exceptions it has rarely been invoked, as the Court has taken a decidedly apolitical stance on issues involving constitutionality. On those infrequent rulings, the Court has generally maintained a status quo, progovernment, propublic stance, in contrast to a confrontational, progressive, or individual rights position. Characteristically, in one 1997 Supreme Court ruling, the government was ordered to pay the historian Ienaga Saburo approximately $3,500 in damages in his suit against the Ministry of Education, for its ordering Ienaga to delete or revise passages dealing with Japan's role in World War II in history textbooks he had authored. But the Court did not rule the system of textbook screening unconstitutional.

Another relatively recent case further reveals the Court's preference for maintaining the status quo, even if its rulings appear contradictory. Claiming that the system of apportionment of electoral districts for the national constituency races in Upper House seats was weighed against them, voters in Osaka filed suit against the government to invalidate the election results for their district. In the Upper House election of 1992, the maximum vote-disparity ratio was calculated at 6.59 to 1, meaning that in one rural region a constituent's single vote had the weight of 6.59 votes of his or her urban counterparts. In an earlier ruling, the Supreme Court had determined that a vote disparity of more than 6 to 1 would constitute voting inequality, yet even while recognizing the inequality in the Osaka case by declaring the vote disparity unconstitutional, the Court did not judge the election itself unconstitutional.

The Supreme Court consists of 15 members, 14 of whom are selected by the Diet from a list provided by the Court itself, while the chief justice of the Court is appointed by the emperor on the recommendation of the Cabinet. Therefore, in theory, the executive, legislative, and judicial branches are responsible for determining who will serve in these 15 posts, but the actual power of appointment rests with the Cabinet (Article 79). The names of justices are brought before the electorate at the first general election of members of the Lower House following the justices' appointment and are reviewed again at the first Lower House election following a lapse of 10 years and every 10 years thereafter in the same manner. A simple majority of those votes cast is needed for both continuity and termination of one's term of office. Yet because the office itself rarely questions the workings and decisions of either the executive or the legislative branch through judicial review, the members of the Supreme Court are nearly anonymous to the general electorate, and never has one who has sought a continuation of service not been returned.

In addition to the Supreme Court, which is at the pinnacle of a hierarchic judicial structure that allows for appeal of decisions, adjudication of criminal and civil matters occurs in Japan's 8 high courts, 50 district courts, 50 family courts, and 452 summary courts. At lower levels of adjudication, however, for reasons of bringing embarrassment to those involved and a lack of willingness to air personal matters in public forums, Japanese have traditionally preferred to settle disagreements through the payment of compensation deemed appropriate by both parties in a dispute or, failing that, through mediation that does not involve the court system. The number of attorneys is therefore low relative to other democracies, especially the United States.

There is a further explanation for the low number of civil proceedings handled by the Japanese court system, and that is the inaccessibility of the system to ordinary citizens. Japan's Civil Proceedings Law, under which civil matters are adjudicated, has not been revised in more than 70 years. The procedures are archaic, as is the language, written in classical, literary Japanese, used to explicate those proceedings.

Adjudication is the purview of the judges themselves, and with the exception of the Supreme Court, in which most hearings involve only 5 of its 15 members, cases at all levels of the judicial system are heard before either 3 judges or 1 judge and 2 subordinates who are considered to be experts in legal matters. There is no jury system in Japan.

Regional and Local Government

In keeping with the occupation authorities' belief that decentralized, local government would strengthen the foundations of democracy in Japan, the constitution provides for local government autonomy and grants these various lower levels of government the right "to manage their property, affairs, and administration and to enact their own regulations within the law (Article 94)." In practice, however, as with all unitary forms of government, Japan's 47 prefectures and other lower levels of municipal government are autonomous of the central government only to the extent that the central government, located in Tokyo, grants them that autonomy. It is a unitary form of government with generally mutual respect of the roles of each successively lower level of government, although each level is dependent to a large degree on the central government for the revenue necessary for it to carry out its functions. The primacy of the central government and its laws are recognized (and rarely have been challenged) by municipalities, either prefectural, city, or village. Nor, with rare exception, has the central government had to overtly use its power to enforce its position and make these lower levels of government conform to the policy of the center.

THE ELECTORAL SYSTEM

Under the revised national-level electoral system, which applies only to elections for the House of Representatives and not to those of the House of Councillors, voters cast two votes, one for a candidate in a single-member district system and the other for a political party in a national proportional representation system. Voting is by secret ballot, and for the Lower House races voters receive two ballots. For the single-seat races voters select from a list of candidates, while on the proportional representation ballot, voters must write in the name of the party. The October 1996 Lower House election was the first national election in Japan conducted under this reformulated electoral districting system that attempts to shift emphasis from individual candidates to political parties. Of the now 500-member Lower House, 300 members are elected with a plurality in single-member districts and another 200 members are selected from ranked lists of

candidates on the basis of their party's proportional share of the vote in 11 electoral regions. As a concession to incumbents whose tenure might have been jeopardized under the new system, a candidate may appear on both the district and regional ballots.

The objective of allowing dual candidacy was to make parties more significant than individual politicians, but critics complained that the system also allows those who could not win election in the single-seat constituencies to have a chance at winning in the broader-based proportional representation districts. In the 1996 election, 566 candidates ran in both races, while 260 of them, which represented approximately 90% of all the party's Lower House candidates, were from the LDP. Of those LDP candidates who lost their single-seat races, 32 won seats in the proportional contest.

In eliminating multimember districts, the new electoral system may have addressed the structural explanation for political corruption in Japan, but it will not cease the demands of constituents on their representatives. Additionally, parties must now maintain a presence in 300 electoral districts compared with the previous 130, increasing the demand for funds.

The new electoral system also decreased the relative number of seats allocated to rural districts, recognizing that overrepresented citizens in these regions had benefited from the LDP's occasional, minor electoral reforms that failed to accurately reflect rural-to-urban population shifts. Yet even the relatively significant reapportionment brought on by the new electoral system has not eliminated the disparity between the value of an urban dweller's vote and that of most rural counterparts. For example, the smallest single-seat constituency (rural Shimane's District 3) has 193,213 eligible voters, while the largest (urban Tokyo's District 22) has 429,857, resulting in a vote-value discrepancy of 2.225 times in favor of the Shimane district voters. The vote-value gap was found to be as wide as 2-to-1 in 47 of the 300 single-seat constituencies, without exception in favor of the rural voter.

To run as a party candidate in a single-seat constituency, a candidate's party must be represented in the

Constituency Representation of
Lower House Members, 1996 Election

	Members Elected	Change	Single-Seat Districts	Proportional Representation
Liberal Democratic Party	239	+28	169	70
New Frontier Party	156	−4	96	60
Democratic Party of Japan	52	0	17	35
Japan Communist Party	26	+11	2	24
Social Democratic Party	15	−15	4	11
Sakigake	2	−7	2	0
Others	10	−6	10	0

Diet by at least 5 party members or have obtained 2% of the votes cast in the previous national election. Of course, it is also possible to run as a party independent, but the prospects for election appear slim.

Voting rights were realized in three distinct periods in Japan: a period of limited male suffrage, from 1890 to 1925, in which voting was restricted to taxpaying male citizens, with qualifications gradually liberalized to increase the size of the eligible electorate; a period of universal male suffrage, from 1925 to 1945, in which male citizens aged 25 or over, with one year prior residence in the municipality and no tax qualification, were eligible to vote; and the present period of universal suffrage, which was established in 1945 and which also reduced the voting age from 25 to 20. The Election Law provides that anyone at least 25 years of age can stand for election to the Lower House. Only those judged legally incompetent or who are serving prison sentences or have violated the election law are prohibited from voting or seeking public office.

Although the intent of the Election Law is to provide a nearly universal opportunity for political hopefuls to seek office, the selection of political candidates is fairly limited, as it is in other nation-states. Three routes are more certain than most in winning election to a national-level post: inheriting the position, having experience in the national-level bureaucracy, and having served as an elected official in lower levels of government (such as local assemblies and municipal offices).

In the hereditary-post scenario, those veteran politicians who retire because of age or illness nominate their successors, with the support of the district's constituents. Oftentimes the successor may be a relative (son, daughter, or even adopted son-in-law), but familial relations are not essential. Through the successor, the retiree can still influence politics to some degree, and the constituents can benefit from the political machine that the retiree developed over the course of several terms. The number of successful hereditary Dietmembers in the 1996 Lower House election totaled 122, almost one-fourth the total number of seats. The practice of hereditary officeholding is most common in the LDP, where 41% of present LDP Dietmembers have inherited their posts.

THE PARTY SYSTEM

Origins of the Parties

The first political parties in Japan were founded in 1874, when several oligarchs split with the other members of Japan's government over the issue of whether or not Korea should be invaded for, among other reasons, its refusal to recognize the legitimacy of the Meiji government. Those who advocated an invasion viewed this as an opportunity to restore pride to the *samurai* class, which had seen its status in society progressively decline. As their

more numerous opponents were concerned that such an endeavor would prove costly to Japan's limited treasury resources, the proinvasion faction of the government lost what has been referred to as the "Great Debate of 1873" and walked away from their government posts. Their subsequent attempts to return to power focused on the betterment of former elite *samurai*, and the organizations they founded advanced a narrow interpretation of popular rights. It is from these early organizations that Japan's political party system was created.

Party Organization

Japan has a multiparty system in which one political party (the LDP) has since its founding in 1955 been clearly predominant at the national level. This dominance has been tempered by the existence of several opposition parties, usually one that can be considered the primary opposition party in terms of its representation at the national level and several smaller parties that can see their relative strength temporally increase if their support is needed on legislative or parliamentary matters. For most of the post-1955 period, this main opposition party was the Japan Socialist Party (*Nihon Shakaito*), but since its founding in 1994, the New Frontier Party (*Shinshinto*) has, to some extent, played this role. A moderate range of liberal and conservative ideologies are represented through this multiparty system, which, with the exception of the Japan Communist Party, lacks the extremist parties found in some nation-states. The result is similar to what is found in most nation-states with an established two-party system characterized by leadership turnover— an appeal by the parties to the priorities and preferences of the mass of moderate voters—although the change in leadership never materialized in Japan until 1993.

Seizing their opportunity to organize at the height of anti-LDP sentiment, these new party leaders established parties that were far too dissimilar in name, platform, and justification to bode well for the long-term survivability of most. Predictably, their party names included words that expressed a sense of newness, freshness, or reform; their platforms espoused the creation of a "true" democracy, increased accountability, and progress; and their justification was based on the anti-LDP, antigovernment cynicism of the electorate.

Campaigning

In principle, contemporary Japanese elections have operated on the basis of a distinction between political activity, or activities that seek to make the public understand the party's policies and programs, on the one hand, and election campaigning, or activity that is intended to secure votes for a particular candidate in a particular election, on the other. *Koenkai*, grassroots support networks for individual politicians, serve a role in achieving both objectives and can be considered the "modern" form of party organization in Japan. A politician forms a *koenkai* or to expand and to some extent institutionalize his support among the electorate. These mass-membership support groups are created and financed by the politician, but the myth is maintained that they are organized by the Diet candidate's supporters. In addition to including ordinary citizens, who make up the majority of the *koenkai*, local officials are given official titles and positions for their support. What makes *koenkai* "modern" is the use of mass membership for supporting candidates, not the appointment of local officials to head them. *Koenkai* also usually have various groups they organize, such as youth groups and women's groups.

Under the revised electoral system, all candidates receive a certain amount of free advertising space in newspapers, which in the 1996 election amounted to five ads, each 9.6 centimeters wide and 2 columns deep. While there are strict limits on how frequently individual candidates may publicize their campaign via the mass media and limits as to how much they may spend in doing so, political parties are not faced with the same degree of regulation. No candidate or party may officially advertise a campaign via the mass media until 12 days before the date of election, which is also reduced from a 14-day period under the former system. Yet within those 12 days, political parties spent an estimated ¥10 billion (approximately $100 million), with the NFP spending approximately ¥3 billion ($30 million) and the LDP ¥2 billion ($20 million).

The recent revisions to the Public Office Election Law maintained the prohibition of house-to-house canvassing by candidates and strengthened publicity limits by not allowing posting of campaign materials from six months before the expiration of one's term of membership or before the day following dissolution of the Lower House. Penalties for campaign violators and those convicted of bribery were also increased, as each can result in a five-year deprivation of the right to seek public office and the right to vote. Under the former system, no such penalty existed. Bribery within the party, for example, by those attempting to become the party nominee in a single-seat district or attempting to improve their relative place on the party list in proportional districts, would result in a prison term of up to three years for the influence wielder and a sentence of up to three years and a fine of up to 1 million yen (approximately $10,000) for the candidate. Depending on the severity of the crime, these penalties could be increased by 2.5 to 4 times the maximum for a less egregious infraction. Again, none of these provisions or penalties existed under the former system. Recent amendments to the 1948 Political Funds Control Law will, in policy at least, ban all political contributions from corporations and other organizations beginning in the year 2000. Additionally, political parties must report

contributions—and their contributors and recipients—of more than ¥50,000 (approximately $500), a change from the earlier level of ¥1 million (approximately $10,000). Failure to report such contributions would result in a five-year imprisonment and a fine of ¥1 million for the party accountant.

A more significant electoral reform was the establishment of the Political Party Subsidies Law. Any political party is eligible to receive public funding, provided that it has a representation of at least five of its members in the Diet or at least some representation if less than five, in which case it must have also obtained at least 2% of the total number of votes cast in the latest Lower House election or in the previous Upper House election or any national election before that. It is clear from such relatively minor requirements that the intent of the reformers was to make public financing the basis for party funds.

The pool of funds is allocated in the government budget and is based on the most recent census figures multiplied by ¥250 per citizen (for a total of approximately ¥31 billion, or $310 million). Half the amount is distributed to parties in proportion to the number of Diet seats it holds, with the remaining half distributed on the basis of the share of votes each party obtained in the most recent national election.

LIBERAL DEMOCRATIC PARTY (LDP)
(Jiminto)

HISTORY

The Liberal Democratic Party was formed by the merger of the Liberal Party and the Democratic Party in 1955, at the initiative of business leaders and in response to the unification of leftist political organizations two weeks before its establishment. Despite its electoral defeat of 1993, which many commentators believed would usher in a system in which political leadership would alternate between two major political parties, a rival to the LDP's degree of organization, connections, and representation has yet to emerge.

ORGANIZATION

The LDP continues to be a group of groups, or factions. Leaders of the then five extant factions (named after their leaders or former leaders, which included the Obuchi, Komoto, Miyazawa, Mitsuzuka, and Watanabe factions) complied with a 1994 order of party bosses that they disband and cease their formal operations in the wake of legislation that created the new electoral system of single-member districts. In theory, this new system would have made the existence of factions superfluous. Indeed, following implementation of the revised law, there was an

FY1997 Political Party Subsidies (Approximate)

Political Party	FY1997	Increase / Decrease from FY1996
Jiminto (Liberal Democratic Party)	¥14.7 billion ($147 million)	+ ¥980 million ($9.8 million)
Shinshinto (New Frontier Party)	¥9.3 billion ($93 million)	– ¥506 million ($5.06 million)
Shaminto (Social Democratic Party)	¥2.7 billion ($27 million)	– ¥1.97 billion – ¥1.97 billion
Minshuto (Democratic Party of Japan)	¥2.7 billion ($27 million)	+ ¥2.29 billion ($22.9 million)
Sakigake (New Party Harbinger)	¥380 million ($3.8 million)	– ¥470 million ($4.7 million)
Komei	¥339 million ($3.39 million)	– ¥89 million ($890,000)
Taiyoto (Sun Party)	¥297 million ($2.97 million)	— —

Note: The Japan Communist Party refused to request government subsidization.

Former LDP Factions, and Their Representation in the
Diet following the 1996 Lower House Election

	Ex-Komoto Faction	Ex-Mitsuzuka Faction	Ex-Miyazawa Faction	Ex-Obuchi Faction	Ex-Watanabe Faction
Lower House Members	17	57	56	49	51
Increase / Decrease	–2	+6	+6	+22	+8
Incumbents	13	44	43	28	39
Nonincumbents with Previous Diet Experience	0	5	5	0	4
First Term Representatives	4	8	8	21	8
Upper House Members	4	25	16	38	16
Total of Upper and Lower House Members	21	82	72	87	67

initial diminution in the role played by the former factions, which have since adopted some variant of the name "policy research groups."

MEMBERSHIP AND CONSTITUENCY

Despite its 1993 electoral defeat, and other relatively minor setbacks that preceded it, in terms of representation in both houses of the Diet the LDP has been the dominant political party in Japan since 1955 and remains so today.

As the LDP was in part formed by the initiative of business leaders worried about a united socialist front, business interests have naturally been a traditional support base for the LDP. Four major economic organizations deserve mention. The Japan Federation of Economic Organizations (*Keidanren*), Japan Federation of Employers Associations (*Nikkeiren*), Japan Chamber of Commerce and Industry (*Nissho*), and the Japan Association for Corporate Executives (*Keizai Doyukai*) have been, to varying degrees, supporters of the LDP. The largest and most influential of the four, *Keidanren*, is a corporation consisting of approximately 120 industrial organizations and 1,000 member companies. When it served as the principal conduit for member firms' contributions to the LDP, *Keidanren* was also a political force. But in 1993, the organization decided to stop collecting political donations from member businesses, limiting their purpose to the LDP. The four groups' influence as a factor to be considered in policymaking and their role as mediators between the government (or, more specifically, the LDP) and the business world have declined with the downturn of the Japanese economy, which began in the early 1990s.

Further LDP support is found in rural areas, among the elderly, and among interest groups that had to develop a relationship with the LDP during its years in office if they wanted their positions considered. In the 1996 election, the LDP received only 19.7% of its total votes for the single-seat contests from those 73 districts classified as urban, while the remaining 80.3% came from those 227 districts classified as nonurban. Not to be overlooked, the same pattern applied to both the NFP and SDP.

POLICY

Historically, the LDP has ardently supported policies that benefit its major support bases, big business and agricultural interests, and, generally, it continues to do so. However, LDP-backed 1994 legislation that provides for a gradual liberalization of Japan's rice market (which had been closed to foreign competition) and other similar agricultural deregulation legislation made some agricultural supporters of the LDP reconsider their party loyalties, and subsequently their support has moved to the NFP. Similarly, as should be expected, both corporate and small business interests are divided about the repercussions of proposed deregulation measures, which the LDP generally supports, particularly those that target the energy, telecommunications, and finance sectors, as well as Japan's distribution system. Thus, one can no longer say that the party's policy interest, or even the prioritization of those interests, is as narrow as it once was.

FINANCING

Traditional financial supporters had been big business (primarily the construction, heavy industry, and automobile sectors), banks, and other financial services companies; but because of the *jusen* (housing loan companies) scandal of 1996, the LDP would not accept political contributions from the more than 20 leading banks that founded the housing loan companies. Political donations from the banking sector, which in 1989 accounted for nearly 30% of LDP contributions, therefore fell from more than $8 million in 1995 to under $300,000 in 1996. Further, in the recent period of protracted economic stagnation, fewer companies than previously are donating more than ¥50,000 (approximately $500) because they do not want their company name revealed, which would be required under the revised Political Funds Control Law. Fund-raising events, for which a fee is usually charged to those who attend, realize nearly as much as the amount contributed by businesses and other organizations. Finally, as the party most represented at the national level, the LDP is also the leading beneficiary of the public subsidization law.

LEADERSHIP

A new procedure for electing the party president was initiated in 1995. A candidate is elected LDP party president if he or she receives a majority of votes, with one given to each LDP Dietmember and one representing every 10,000 party members who vote via mail (at present, there are approximately 1.5 million dues-paying LDP party members). If no candidate garners a majority of votes, LDP Dietmembers will determine the party president in a runoff election between the top two vote earners.

Hashimoto Ryutaro was reelected to the party presidency in 1997, the first time a candidate for the LDP presidency has run unopposed. As previously stated, Hashimoto began serving his second term as party president in September 1997. Unless LDP party rules were revised, Hashimoto would have had to step down in September 1999, leading to the selection of both a new party president and if the LDP maintained a majority in the Lower House, a new prime minister. Because Hashimoto accepted responsibility for the LDP's poor showing in the July 1998 Upper House election, however, he resigned from both posts and was succeeded by Obuchi Keizo as party president and prime minister.

Kato Koichi is serving his third term as secretary-general of the LDP, an unusually long tenure for the post.

PROSPECTS

Although the LDP achieved a near absolute majority in the 1996 Lower House election, this representative strength relative to other parties belies the level of dissatisfaction with LDP politics and policies. The LDP share of the vote was only 39% in single-seat constituencies and 33% in the proportional representation contests, while the party witnessed a decline in support among young and urban voters. In some districts, nearly one-fifth of the electorate who voted for LDP candidates in the single-member races effectively split their tickets and tempered the power of the LDP by casting their ballots for a non-LDP party in the proportional contests.

Low voter turnout for the 1996 election may have been a result of fewer choices and the perception that incumbents are difficult to unseat. The percentage of seats won by first-time candidates was 26.0% in the 1990 election and 26.2% in 1993 and declined to 23.0% in 1996. Nearly half of the successful newcomers ran in districts in which there was no incumbent, and when we consider those races for which there was an incumbent on the ballot, only 11% of first-time candidates were successful. Prospects for the LDP appear strong, if only because they are the party with the most incumbents. Additionally, the LDP remains the only party that can truly qualify as a national party in terms of representation from a variety of districts throughout Japan.

NEW FRONTIER PARTY (NFP)
(Shinshinto)

HISTORY

Shinshinto was founded in December 1994 by the former prime ministers Hosokawa Morihiro (of the Japan New Party, or *Nihon Shinto*) and Hata Tsutomu (of the Japan Renewal Party, or *Shinseito*) and its architect, the former LDP secretary-general Ozawa Ichiro (also *Shinseito*), through an amalgamation of LDP splinter parties and smaller upstarts, most of which were formed prior to the 1993 election and hoped to capitalize on public disfavor with the LDP. In addition to the Japan New Party and the Japan Renewal Party, *Shinshinto* includes former members of the disbanded Clean Government Party (*Komeito*), the Democratic Socialist Party (*Shakai Minshuto*), and several minor political groups.

ORGANIZATION

These smaller pre-*Shinshinto* parties owed their electoral success in the 1993 election to an anti-LDP sentiment rather than to an endorsement of their leaders' lofty, rhetorical, and generally amorphous policy agendas. From the start, the seven-party ruling coalition that included them—with the LDP representatives placed in the unfamiliar role of the opposition force—proved unmanageable. Following the reemergence of LDP leadership with the support of the Social Democratic Party and *Sakigake*, these smaller parties aligned as the *Shinshinto* to form a united front against the power of the LDP.

After *Shinshinto*'s establishment, critics of Japan's one-party dominance and what was perceived as its less-than-democratic system predicted the beginnings of true two-party politics in Japan. The LDP always had the numbers and the better organization, while the sole foundation uniting these disparate political forces in the form of *Shinshinto* has chiefly been its anti-LDP stance.

MEMBERSHIP AND CONSTITUENCY

The support of members of Soka Gakkai, a lay organization that has practiced a strain of Buddhism since it was established in 1930, is the most significant electorate support base for the NFP, as they are thought to control an estimated 6 million votes throughout Japan. This support is not assured, however. Soka Gakkai members have recently been concerned about revisions to the law on religious organizations, which prohibits political activity by religious groups. These revisions were implemented in September 1996 in the wake of the investigation of *Aum Shinrikyo* (Aum Supreme Truth), a religious cult most notorious for its sarin gas attack on the Tokyo subway system in 1995. It is expected that some Soka Gakkai support will shift to the ruling LDP as a way to influence interpretation of the newly amended law.

Although the inaugural election for the NFP presidency was open to all party members and any Japanese citizen of at least 18 years of age (provided that these nonparty members paid a ¥1000 ($10) "participation fee"), the NFP can hardly be called a national party, for it was unable to field candidates in 65 of the 300 single-seat electoral district races in the 1996 election. Further, in single-seat constituency races, the NFP won a plurality of votes prefecturewide in 10 prefectures (out of 47), 5 of which are the home districts of NFP party leaders. On the other hand, the NFP has achieved relatively strong representation in prefectural assemblies.

POLICY

In theory, NFP policy advocates "thoroughgoing reform," including deregulation and decentralization, although its members are divided as to what constitutes these objectives and how to realize them if the NFP is to come to power. Further, considering its creation as an amalgamation party, the NFP is not united about several specific, critical policy matters, including constitutional issues such as collective security and the role of the SDF.

FINANCING

In addition to public subsidization funds, financial support for the NFP comes from groups that wish to unseat the LDP's grip on power and those who are balancing their support of the LDP with simultaneous support of the NFP (including business interests and, to a lesser extent, agricultural groups). It is uncertain whether this support will continue, particularly from the latter group. While some rural voters supported the NFP in the voting booth, paradoxically the rural electorate incorrectly considers the NFP to be primarily a political party based on urban interests.

LEADERSHIP

The president of the NFP is Ozawa Ichiro, who many

present and former NFP members criticize for his reputedly autocratic leadership style.

PROSPECTS

The moment of hope for the NFP may very well have been the 1995 House of Councillors election, in which a majority of NFP members defeated their LDP counterparts. But even in that election, support for the NFP had to be considered in light of the lowest turnout ever for an Upper House election (only 44.5% of eligible voters). Since the 1995 Upper House election, the NFP has been losing ground because of defections (primarily to the DPJ but to a lesser extent to Taiyoto), because of internal conflict, and because of an unclear policy agenda.

Recent remarks by the former prime minister and former NFP member Hosokawa Morihiro that a split of the NFP into smaller, cooperative parties reflecting their pre-NFP merger might be beneficial are characteristic of the difficulties that will beset the NFP. Unless the party can move beyond the superficial basis that brought them together in the first place, which was their proclaimed mutual disrespect of the LDP, it will not survive in its present form beyond the next few elections, if even that far.

DEMOCRATIC PARTY OF JAPAN
(Nihon Minshuto)

HISTORY

The Democratic Party of Japan (DPJ) was established in 1996 by two former high-ranking members of *Shinto Sakigake* (New Party Harbinger), Hatoyama Yukio and Kan Naoto, a former minister of health and welfare. While serving in the ministerial post, Kan had acquired a sudden national reputation as an advocate of the people for his investigation into a Ministry of Health and Welfare policy of the mid- to late 1980s not to inform the public that some blood products used in Japan may have been tainted by the HIV virus.

ORGANIZATION

As a relatively new party to the political arena, the DPJ has not yet established a solid organization at lower levels and remains mostly a national-level party, if only for its representation in the Diet. National-level organization is also weak at this early stage, and party policy does not require members to vote the party line in the Diet.

MEMBERSHIP AND CONSTITUENCY

In contrast to the rural-based support of the LDP, NFP, and even the SDP, in the 1996 election the DPJ garnered significant support from urban areas, with almost 42% of its votes coming from the 73 urban districts. Despite this urban support, however, the party lacks a clearly identifiable, regional base of support, as it failed to win a plurality of votes cast in any of Japan's 47 prefectures for single-seat races in the 1996 election. Additionally, the DPJ has earned the partial endorsement of those unions that have reconsidered their support for the SDP, for example, the All-Japan Prefectural and Municipal Workers' Union (*Jichiro*) and some factions of the Japan Trade Unions Confederation (*Rengo*).

POLICY

Since its founding, the DPJ has advertised itself as a "citizen-oriented network" more often than it has a political party. Its leaders have stated that they will disband the party once its goals, which include an idealistic-sounding creation of a national mood of trust and cooperation, are achieved. Other policy objectives are equally unlikely to be realized, including the establishment of a regional security system. More concrete policy proposals highlight education reform, reform of the tax system, and more local government autonomy. Among other intraparty rifts, there is apparent division between those DPJ members who hailed from the SDP and those who were former NPS members over security issues and administrative reform measures.

Its leaders' and members' record of switching their positions on several issues illustrates the conundrum facing the DPJ, which does not appear certain whether it should support the DPJ or attempt to become a leading force in an anti-LDP alliance.

FINANCING

It is assumed that significant financial support for the party's operations comes primarily from party cofounder Hatoyama Yukio and his brother, Hatoyama Kunio, also a party member. Their grandfather, Hatoyama Ichiro, was the first president of the LDP, and both brothers have amassed sizable personal wealth from their inheritance, securities, and land holdings. Even with the financial support of the Hatoyamas, the party is rumored to be facing a shortage of funds.

LEADERSHIP

Until recently, the party had practiced a policy of dual leadership by two nationally recognized politicians, ostensibly to increase support for the party. However, the two frequently disagreed on policy positions. Kan Naoto was subsequently named the party president, and Hatoyama Yukio the secretary-general.

PROSPECTS

The party lost some legitimacy soon after it was established, following the decision by party founder Kan to maintain his Cabinet post in the LDP–SDP–Sakigake coalition. Political missteps have plagued the party since. More significantly, its policy objectives seem too similarly amorphous to those of other new political parties to make it a distinct, viable political force and challenger for national leadership in the immediate future. On the other hand, there is perhaps a degree of generational appeal to the party's successes, as many leading party members are in their 40s. If the party can cultivate these relatively younger voters by developing clear policy goals and proposing realistic programs to achieve them, the party may continue as a considerable opposition force. If recent experience continues, the party will also benefit from further union abandonment of the SDP.

SOCIAL DEMOCRATIC PARTY (SDP)
(Shaminto)

HISTORY

The original incarnation of the SDP (the JSP, or the Japan Socialist Party, and subsequently the Social Democratic Party of Japan, although for both English language renderings it was known as *Shakaito*) was established in 1955 with a merger of formerly disparate left-wing and right-wing socialist forces. Until its support of the LDP-dominated coalition government in 1993, the SDP had been the LDP's primary opposition for 39 years. The SDP is at present headed by Doi Takako, a law professor who in 1986 was elected by party representatives as the first female leader of a major political party.

The 1993 Lower House election proved to be a disaster for the Social Democrats who, with anti-LDP sentiment among voters at a zenith, lost what was clearly their best chance at national leadership. Doi took responsibility for the party's relatively poor showing at the ballot box, and her successor, 74-year-old Murayama Tomiichi, was selected by his coalition partners—dominated by the overwhelming plurality of LDP representation in the Lower House—as the first Socialist prime minister in Japan since 1947.

However, the minority status of the Socialists in this coalition arrangement and the perception that Murayama was unable to lead the country toward reform became apparent, and in January 1996 the LDP replaced Murayama with one of its own, Hashimoto Ryutaro. On the verge of the SDP's near extinction, Doi was returned as party leader in hopes of recapturing some of the promise that ushered in her first term. Party members and followers are at present engaged in a period of retrospective soul-searching, and even though expectations that it would fold in the mid-1990s were premature, one must wonder what role, if any, the SDP will play in Japan's long-term political future.

ORGANIZATION

Until its collaboration with the LDP from 1994, the JSP was a party divided into left, moderate, and right wings—united more by its perpetual opposition to LDP leadership than by agreement over policy matters. Party policy and leadership selection at the national level were dominated by leftist ideologues, resulting in party positions that made the SDP more radical on some issues than the Japan Communist Party. The party has both national and regional organizations, but, as described below, sustained ties between the center and regional organizations are uncertain.

MEMBERSHIP AND CONSTITUENCY

Until recently, support by unions had always been a significant, nearly assured base of support for the long-term viability of the SDP, for once policy was formulated by union leaders, it was assumed that the union rank and file would follow their directive. One difficulty confronting the SDP, however, is that union membership in Japan has been declining, just as it has in other industrialized democracies. Further, many union leaders felt betrayed by the SDP's participation in the LDP-dominated three-party coalition, particularly since their party's leader was the prime minister of that coalition.

The 8-million-member, leftist-dominated *Rengo* (Japan Trade Unions Confederation) had traditionally been the largest supporting organization for the SDP. *Rengo*'s continued support for the party, as with that of other union-based groups, is now questionable, since labor interests are concerned that the recent poor electoral showings of the SDP will diminish their voice in policymaking. Other leftist-leaning labor organization support is from (among others) the Japan Teachers' Union (*Nikkyoso*) and the All Japan Prefectural and Municipal Workers' Union (*Jichiro*). With the support of *Rengo* now less than secure, *Jichiro*, which has approximately 1 million members is, at least in numerical terms, the largest supporter of the SDP. More moderate labor unions, such as the Japan Postal Workers' Union (*Zentei*) and the All Japan Telecommunications Workers Union (*Zendentsu*), nominally support the SDP, although both broke with other party groups in the 1996 elections because of ideological differences and endorsed candidates from parties who, for example, supported both the existence of the SDF and the United States–Japan Security Treaty. Other distancing from the party can be attributed to its desperate long-term prospects for national leadership and its limited representation at the national level.

POLICY

In keeping with the SDP's history of divisiveness during most of its existence, to this day proclaimed party supporters are divided over party ideology, particularly the constitutionality of the Self Defense Forces (SDF) and the United States–Japan Security Treaty. Those on the left generally advocate an abolition of both. Before the 1989

Upper House election, Doi moderated the party's historical opposition to the security treaty by stating that the arrangement would be "reviewed" instead of summarily abrogated if the SDP were to come to power.

FINANCING

Before the party's most recent spate of electoral misfortunes, financial support had been from dues-paying members, union organizations, and big business concerns (which had developed ties with the SDP in the event that the party might assume leadership at the national level) and the sale of party publications. Since this scenario of true SDP leadership, in distinction to minor coalition leadership, has become less likely, both business and union financial support for the party has declined, as has its share of public subsidization funds. More than any other party, the SDP has relied on dues-paying members for a substantial portion of its finances, now especially so with the decline of financial support from other groups mentioned above. Even when the SDP was a major recipient of funds—whatever the source—it was perpetually facing financial crisis.

LEADERSHIP

The SDP is at present headed by Doi Takako, but as an illustration of the continued turmoil and questions regarding longevity of the party, no one in 1997 stepped forward to file a candidacy for the party presidency.

PROSPECTS

Somewhat ironically, the SDP's only moment of leadership at the national level may have also weakened whatever party cohesion had existed. Only once before, for nine months spanning the 1947–48 administration of Katayama Tetsu, did Socialists ever hold the prime minister's post. Hard-line Socialists who advocate a strengthening of the party's traditional union base cried betrayal at what they perceived as the right-leaning, collaborationist policies of Murayama Tomiichi during his term as prime minister in an LDP-dominated coalition government. Most visible among this faction is the New Socialist Party (*Shin Shakaito*), represented only in the Upper House and formed in January 1996.

The most recent increase in the party's popularity was based on its opposition to a nationwide 3% consumption tax proposed by the then ruling LDP in 1989. But it was during the LDP–SDP–Sakigake coalition, with Murayama serving as prime minister, that an increase of that enacted 3% to a proposed 5% was initiated and legislated, with Doi serving as Speaker of the Lower House at that time.

Considering that union support is essential for the future prospects of the SDP, the prospects of the party do not appear bright unless it can strengthen those present union ties and cultivate other bases of support.

JAPAN COMMUNIST PARTY
(Nihon Kyosanto)

HISTORY

Officially founded in 1922 during Japan's period of post–World War I liberalism, the Japan Communist Party (JCP) is the oldest political party in Japan. But as an organized group that has advocated radical policies, including an end to the imperial institution, the JCP was banned when liberalism took a back seat to Japan's militarist policies of World War II. Postwar occupation authorities released the jailed members of the former JCP and granted the party legal recognition. It is the only major political party that has not been included in any of the four mostly short-lived coalition governments that followed the 1993 defeat of the LDP.

ORGANIZATION

Along with the LDP, the JCP has established itself as a well- organized political party, although, in contrast to the LDP, its grassroots appeal is generally limited to the urban electorate. A 168-member central committee elects the 38-member presidium, and the 14-member presidium standing committee. The standing committee alone determines policy, and once a policy decision is made, the party's belief in the concept of democratic centralism dictates that the decision must be followed by all party members.

MEMBERSHIP AND CONSTITUENCY

Support for the JCP is concentrated in major urban areas, and Communists have served as mayors of some of Japan's largest cities. The JCP has traditionally competed with the SDP for a share of the progressive votes, with (until recently) the SDP attracting relatively more voters. Following the LDP–SDP–Sakigake coalition government, the JCP has since referred to itself as "the only opposition party," a move to attract those leftists in the SDP, moderates in the DPJ, and even some support from alienated former LDP backers.

POLICY

The JCP is the only one of Japan's major political parties that, at least ideologically and rhetorically, could be considered extremist. Among other policies, the JCP advocates a democratic revolution of the Japanese people against the rule of U.S. imperialism and a nationalization of the mass media. In action, however, with exception neither the party nor its members have displayed any radicalism or initiated any violence toward the existing social and political system. It is for this reason more than all others that the JCP is able to appeal to some members of the electorate whose primary party identification (if any) is for moderate or even conservative political parties. For example, in the 1997 Tokyo Assembly election the JCP won the second-most seats, behind the LDP. However, some of the party's most distinctive positions, such as its call for abrogation of the United States–Japan Security Treaty, appear anachronistic and are clearly against the prevailing public sentiment.

FINANCING

At its peak circulation, *Akahata* (Red Flag), the party newspaper, had the ninth largest circulation for newspapers in the country and was a guaranteed source of revenue for the party. Circulation has dropped in the past four years, to less than 170,000 at present, an indication that although support for the party may be widening, the core of party adherents and loyalists is decreasing. Although it is eligible, the party has refused to apply for funds authorized under the Political Party Subsidies Law.

LEADERSHIP

For decades, the head of the JCP had been Miyamoto Kenji, a colorful leader who had been jailed for 12 years during the war for his Communist views. Miyamoto resigned from the post in 1997 at the age of 88. Fuwa Tetsuzo is the present party chairman, while Shii Kazuo is head of the Party Secretariat.

PROSPECTS

While its counterparts have disbanded throughout the world, the JCP is remarkable in the developed world if only because it has almost always had successful candidates in national-level elections and, in recent times, its electoral support has widened at both the national and municipal levels. Nevertheless, it is highly unlikely that the middle mass of the Japanese electorate—including those voters who are uncommitted to a political party— would vote in large numbers for the JCP, even if it is able to gradually increase its representation at all levels of government (but particularly at the national level) and somehow implement even a few of the policies that, in rhetoric at least, its members espouse.

NEW PARTY HARBINGER (NPH)
(Shinto Sakigake)

HISTORY

Launched in 1993 by disenchanted leaders of the LDP, the *Sakigake* (NPH) had its most visible moments as the smallest party in the three party LDP–SDP–Sakigake coalition.

ORGANIZATION

The NPH is not well organized or widely supported throughout Japan, and it has served primarily as a parliamentary party.

MEMBERSHIP AND CONSTITUENCY

The NPH has only two members in the Lower House, Takemura Masayoshi, a former finance minister and former LDP party member who served as the NPH's first president, and the party secretary-general, Sonoda Hiroyuki. In addition to the party's acting president, Domoto Akiko, the NPH has two members in the Upper House.

POLICY

Among other somewhat vague goals, the NPH advocates a move from "bureaucracy-centered politics" to "people-oriented" politics and a role for Japan to serve as the "model of leadership" of an advanced country that confronts and attempts to resolve those issues that are confronting all of humanity.

FINANCING

Income for the initial year of its existence totaled ¥478 million (approximately $4.7 million). But of that amount, half was in the form of a loan from Hatoyama Yukio, who has since left to become the cofounder of the DPJ. An equal amount was loaned by former party president Takemura. Public subsidization funds represent a considerable portion of NPH finances, but continuation of these funds will be jeopardized if the party achieves only nearminimal eligibility requirements and is unable to increase its Diet representation and its share of the national vote.

LEADERSHIP

The acting president is Domoto Akiko, and the party secretary-general is Sonoda Hiroyuki.

PROSPECTS

Unless the assent of its minor number of representatives at the national level is needed for the formation of a near-future coalition government or the passage of a key piece of legislation, prospects for the continued existence of the NPH do not appear bright. It is likely that either present party members will rejoin the LDP or the party may be subsumed by one of the new parties (i.e., the DPJ).

MINOR POLITICAL PARTIES

Sun Party
(Taiyoto)

The Sun Party was formed in December 1996 by former Prime Minister Hata Tsutomu. For most of his political career, Hata had been an LDP loyalist, but, with Ozawa Ichiro, he bolted from the LDP to form the Renewal Party (*Shinseito*) in June 1993. *Shinseito* was a founding party of the NFP (*Shinshinto*), established in December 1994. Suspected disagreements with NFP party head Ozawa were the apparent motivation for Hata's defection from the NFP. *Taiyoto* is represented by 10 members in the Lower House. Considering that many of the party's members, including Hata himself, originally hailed from the LDP, it is possible that some may return to the LDP fold.

The *Taiyoto* party platform advocates "self responsibility and symbiosis (harmonious living together)," and its policy statements favor deregulation, decentralization, information disclosure, and environmental consciousness. The party has not existed long enough for there to be sufficient information regarding its financial support, if any. Long-term prospects for its continued autonomous existence appear highly unlikely, for *Taiyoto* founder and president Hata Tsutomu has already advanced the idea of an alliance with other political parties.

New Party Komei (Komeishinto)

The *Komeishinto* (usually referred to as *Komei*) was formed in December 1994 by those members of the former Clean Government Party (*Komeito*) who refused to join the NFP amalgamation and members of the former Democratic Socialist Party (*Jimin Minshuto*) who held similar sentiments regarding the NFP. *Komei* is represented by 14 members in the Upper House and none in the Lower House but is well represented in municipal assemblies, particularly those in cities, towns, and villages. For the immediate future (if it continues as a viable political party), *Komei* will continue to be a party that emphasizes this local representation.

OTHER POLITICAL FORCES

Gaiatsu

Gaiatsu literally means "pressure from outside" or, in other words, foreign governments applying political pressure on the Japanese government to change its policies. For example, most analysts recognize that *gaiatsu* had some degree of influence on Japan's rice issue, in which Japan was pressured to open its rice market to imported competition (particularly from the United States). These analysts disagree, however, on the extent to which *gaiatsu* contributed to the politicization of the rice issue and to the ultimate decision.

The influence of *gaiatsu* can be measured against the influence of the Japanese government. As far as the rice issue is concerned, some analysts argue that *gaiatsu* was weak and the Japanese government held its position not to open the rice market, and then did so only marginally. One reason that the Japanese government may have acceded is that the issue of food security is no longer so important to a generation that does not remember a Japan

on the brink of starvation after World War II and in whose diet rice does not figure so prominently. On the whole, these commentators believe, the Japanese government seems to be stronger in many cases than is *gaiatsu* and cannot be bulldozed into action.

Other political observers argue that unless the Japanese government was confronted by periodic doses of *gaiatsu*, nothing would have changed in a status quo–seeking Japan. This camp therefore believes that a high degree of landmark legislation is attributable to the *gaiatsu* factor. Included among these significant policy shifts, they argue, were the decisions to liberalize Japan's rice market and to implement administrative and financial market reform (an initiative that, they claim, was the result of repeated foreign criticism of the difficulties of "doing business in Japan")—and even a movement toward understanding and admitting Japan's role in World War II.

Bureaucracy

For most of Japan's postwar history, civil servants—particularly those of the national government—were nearly revered for their abilities, generally beyond reproach for their steadfastness as public servants, and universally respected for the immense power that they commanded. Recently, however, the focus of reporting official corruption has shifted from politicians to civil servants. Together with a prolonged stagnation of Japan's economy, for which the bureaucracy was often attributed credit during economic prosperity, the bureaucracy has lost the public trust and is the target of administrative reform measures proposed at the national level.

The effects of the collapse of Japan's bubble economy of the late 1980s and early 1990s are still being felt. In 1996, the Diet passed legislation authorizing taxpayer funds to underwrite the bailout of seven *jusen* (housing-loan companies) saddled by billions of dollars worth of nonperforming loans. In the course of deliberations, it was revealed that more than a dozen former officials of the Ministry of Finance held leadership posts in these firms. In addition to the "*jusen* scandal," other recent bureaucratic scandals involve the HIV-tainted blood dilemma, numerous cases involving officials at the Ministry of Finance, *amakudari* benefits awaiting civil servants shortly after retirement, and the perception of their less-than-transparent way of going about their duties or of describing their jobs.

Amakudari, literally "descent from heaven," refers to the practice of former civil servants, particularly those upper-ranking members of Japan's central government bureaucracy, receiving prestigious nongovernment posts in exchange for their contacts developed during their government careers. Recent legislation ruled that upon retirement, civil servants are prohibited from accepting employment in companies connected with their former ministries or agencies for two years, although this restriction can be waived if approval is granted by the National Personnel Authority. In 1995, for example, nearly 200 former bureaucrats retired to lucrative corporate jobs, while a 1996 study reported that 35% of Ministry of Finance middle-ranking and higher-level bureaucrats landed postretirement positions in private-sector financial institutions and quasi-governmental corporations (including the Export-Import Bank of Japan, the Japan Development Bank, and the Housing and Urban Development Corporation).

In a May 1996 public-opinion poll that presented a list of admirable qualities interspersed with loathsome qualities, the three characteristics most often cited reflecting the public's view of high-ranking civil servants were "desire for a successful career," "opportunity for *amakudari*," and "collusion with political and industrial circles." It is little wonder, then, that in a 1996 survey, nearly 78% of those polled replied that they held a "feeling of distrust or dissatisfaction toward the bureaucrats of the government ministries and agencies."

Administrative reform is the contemporary buzzword in Japan, and all political parties have advocated it to a certain degree. Yet it is difficult to gauge how much of the drive is based, on the one hand, on a desire to decrease redundancy and inefficiency while increasing accountability and, on the other, on targeting a specific group of people who have found recent disfavor with the public. The most recent recommendations for bureaucratic streamlining, which propose a merger of the present 21 ministries and agencies and the Office of the prime minister into 12 and the Office of the Prime Minister, began in 1996. This is not the first time that such a reform movement has been initiated: there have been three previous Ad Hoc Councils for Promotion of Administrative Reform (1964, 1982, and 1993)—none of their suggestions have been implemented.

It appears that the public distrust of bureaucrats may be the impetus behind this move, and if sustained through revelation of further bureaucratic scandals and/or a continued malaise of the Japanese economy, some of the suggestions of this most recent group may be realized.

NATIONAL PROSPECTS

In many developed-world nation-states, the vitality of democracy is threatened by the cynicism of a postmodern electorate. In contrast to a citizenry of critics who are engaged in the process of reflection, participation, and change, a cynical public tends to believe that it is not a part of the system and hardly has the means to change it. And in a democracy, the most visible and direct way that voters can express their opinions—either for change or for the status quo—is via the ballot box.

The national election of 1993 was preceded by weeks of both planned and spontaneous protests at the gates of the Diet, launched by groups of individuals united in their criticism of the defects that a one-party system had created. Their voices were heard, and their actions produced the opportunity for new leaders to change a system that nearly all agreed needed to be fixed. But that phase of naive idealism, which succeeded the immediate results of the election, was confronted by the reality of politics and the realization that maybe some of the self-proclaimed change agents were instead seekers of the status quo. For the rest, somewhat troubling was the inability of these new leaders to crystallize those anti-LDP sentiments into genuine interest in the political process.

Relative to the nominal revisions to the system that preceded them, the reform measures of the post-1993 Diet sessions have been remarkable, but they have hardly met the expectations of many of those whose first experience in the political process was swept up in the emotionalism of the anti-LDP movement. In retrospect, besides the ambiguous goal of "change," it is not clear what many of those new entrants into the political process sought or how they imagined change would be realized. Nevertheless, in subsequent elections, that momentary activism—superficial though it may have been—has given way to cynicism toward (and withdrawal from) the system.

For example, the July 1997 election for Tokyo's prefectural assembly, which, along with other major prefectural assemblies, has served as a fairly accurate predictor of national voting trends and sentiment of the electorate, drew the lowest turnout ever for a prefectural election (barely 40% of eligible voters). In that election, those who did bother to go to the polls voted for the two parties that, to the electorate, represented stability and a relatively developed agenda, although diametrically opposed ones at that: the reactionary conservatism of the LDP and the revolutionary extremism of the Japan Communist Party. *Shinshinto*, the largest opposition party in the Diet, failed to win even one seat in the Tokyo election.

As practiced, democracies might have different variants throughout the world, but they all share the characteristic of choice for the voter. Yet with their absence from the voting booth, the most clearly absent voter—the young, educated, middle-class urbanite Japanese citizen—has not been making a conscious statement of protest against the system, for such an act would imply knowledge of the system and its defects. Instead, a generation of young, educated, increasingly internationalized Japanese citizens has become more like disinterested subjects rather than active participants in a democracy, a situation that does not bode well for the future of meaningful political parties in Japan or the likelihood of an active, critical electorate.

Further Reading

Allinson, Gary D. *Japan's Postwar History*. Ithaca, N.Y.: Cornell University Press, 1997.

Hrebnar, Ronald J. *The Japanese Party System*, 2d ed. Boulder, Colo.: Westview Press, 1992.

Jain, Purnendra Jain, and Takashi Inoguchi, eds., *Japanese Politics Today: Beyond Karaoke Democracy?* New York: St. Martin's Press, 1997.

Johnson, Chalmers. *Japan: Who Governs? The Rise of the Developmental State*. New York: W.W. Norton, 1995.

Kohno, Masaru. *Japan's Postwar Party Politics*. Princeton, N.J: Princeton University Press, 1997.

Masumi, Junnosuke. *Contemporary Politics in Japan*. Trans. Lonny E. Carlile. Berkeley: University of California Press, 1995.

Muramatsu, Michio. *Local Power in the Japanese State*. Berkeley: University of California Press, 1997.

Ozawa, Ichiro. *Blueprint for a New Japan*. Tokyo: Kodansha International, 1994.

Richardson, Bradley. *Japanese Democracy: Power, Coordination and Performance*. New Haven, Conn.: Yale University Press, 1997.

Tabb, William K. *The Postwar Japanese System*. New York: Oxford University Press, 1995.

HASHEMITE KINGDOM OF JORDAN

(al-Mamlaka al-Urduniyya al-Hashimiyya)
By Curtis R. Ryan, Ph.D.

THE SYSTEM OF GOVERNMENT

Like many other postcolonial states in the Middle East, the Hashemite Kingdom of Jordan has largely artificial boundaries, drawn by European imperial powers as the previous empire, that of the Ottoman Turks, collapsed in the wake of the First World War. But since these inauspicious beginnings, what began as the British Mandate of Transjordan in 1921 evolved into the Emirate of Transjordan at the time of independence from Britain in 1946, and finally into its current form as the Hashemite Kingdom of Jordan since 1949. Jordan has, in short, evolved into a modern state that has long defied predictions of its imminent demise. The British installed two brothers of the House of Hashim, Abdullah and Faisal, respectively in their mandates of Jordan and Iraq as a reward for Hashemite support in the Arab Revolt against the Ottoman Empire during World War I. The Hashimites originally hailed from the Hijaz area in what is today western Saudi Arabia but had been forcibly expelled by their Saudi rivals.

This kingdom of almost 5 million people is situated in southwest Asia and is bounded to the north by Syria, to the east by Iraq, to the south by Saudi Arabia, and to the west by Israel and the Palestinian territories. Given this location, Jordan was from the outset deeply involved in the various dimensions of the Palestinian-Israeli and broader Arab-Israeli conflicts. By the time of Jordanian independence in 1946, tensions were peaking in neighboring Palestine between Jews and Arabs over the issue of Zionist versus Palestinian aspirations to full statehood. The United Nations voted to partition Palestine between the two peoples in 1947, and Israel declared its independence and statehood the following year. Within 24 hours several Arab armies had invaded the new state, joining fighting that had already begun between the two communities. One of these armies was Jordan's Arab Legion.

Following the Israeli victory and the tense peace that followed, Jordan continued to occupy the territory of the West Bank of the Jordan river (including East Jerusalem), formally annexing it in 1950. In July 1951, King Abdullah was assassinated by a Palestinian nationalist as he entered the Al Aqsa Mosque in Jerusalem. Abdullah was succeeded briefly by his son Talal, who was ultimately judged mentally unfit to rule and was in turn succeeded by his own son, Hussein, in 1953. Well over four decades later, King Hussein Ibn Talal remained on the throne of the Hashemite Kingdom of Jordan.

King Hussein's long reign has been marked by a seemingly relentless succession of regional and domestic crises. In regional politics, further Arab-Israeli wars were fought in 1956, 1967, 1973, and 1982. Of these, the devastating Arab defeat in the 1967 Six-Day War was by far the most important for Jordan. For the Jordanians lost not only the war but also the entire territory of the West Bank—including East Jerusalem. In addition, tens of thousands of Palestinian refugees streamed into Jordan, joining those already there from the 1948 war. The large numbers of Palestinians in the kingdom led to recurrent domestic tensions between the Jordanian regular army and Palestinian guerrilla forces linked to the PLO. This spilled over into a bloody civil war in September 1970. King Hussein's bedouin-dominated army ultimately defeated and expelled the PLO forces and also pushed back an invasion force from Syria. But the legacy of tension remained decades later—between radical Arab nationalists and the conservative Hashemite regime and also between the Palestinian and "East Banker" Jordanian communities within the kingdom.

The Hashemite regime had for years maintained its claim to the West Bank and East Jerusalem, but in 1988 it renounced these claims and turned instead toward consolidating its rule east of the Jordan River. The kingdom remained under martial law from the time of the 1967 war until it was lifted in 1992 following the promulgation of a new National Charter in 1991 that aimed at creating more pluralism and political liberalization in Jordan while also ensuring that the country remains a Hashemite monarchy.

Executive

In accordance with the 1952 constitution, the king is head of state and government, with complete authority over the armed forces and power to appoint both the prime minister and Cabinet. The king also has the authority to put laws into effect and to dissolve the legislature and call new elections. The prime minister is at least nominal head of government, appointed by the king, and in practice Jordanian prime ministers have selected their own Cabinets subject to royal approval.

Legislature

Jordan has a bicameral legislature, divided between the 80-member House of Representatives (*Majlis al-Nu'ab*) and the 40-member House of Notables or Senate (*Majlis al-Ayyan*). Members of the lower house are elected by universal suffrage, while members of the Senate—the de facto upper house—are appointed directly by the king. The membership of the House of Notables amounts to a veritable who's who (or who was who) of Jordanian politics.

Although the combined houses of the legislature can legally override the king's veto of any legislation, the fact that the entire Senate is made up of royal appointees effectively nullifies this as a threat to royal privilege.

Judiciary

The highest court in the kingdom is the High Court of Justice, centered in the capital, Amman. The court system includes a series of lower courts including courts of appeal, courts of first instance, and courts of magistrates. In addition, and particularly in social and family matters, there are separate religious courts for the Muslim and Christian religious communities. Finally, in the rural areas of the kingdom, there are additional tribal courts for local bedouin affairs.

Regional and Local Government

The entire country is divided into five provinces or governates: Amman, Balqa, Irbid, Karak, and Ma'an. Each of these is headed by a governor and is further subdivided down to the level of the municipality. At that most local level, most municipalities are governed by town councils or—in the case of rural areas—by local Mukhtars, traditional village or tribal leaders.

THE ELECTORAL SYSTEM

Full national parliamentary elections in Jordan only reemerged in 1989, following a more than two-decade hiatus in the wake of the 1967 war. The trigger event was the imposition of an IMF-sponsored economic austerity plan in April 1989 that led to the outbreak of rioting across the country. The riots, against both economic hardship and political corruption, prompted a shaken regime to respond with promises of elections and political reforms to begin that same year. The first of these elections took place in November 1989 and yielded a lower house of parliament in which both Islamist and secular leftist candidates were well represented.

By the time of the next round of elections, in November 1993, the regime had lifted martial law and its longstanding ban on political parties. More than a dozen newly legalized parties contested the 1993 elections, with the Islamists faring more poorly on their second attempt at national parliamentary power. This was due, in part, to a public backlash against unpopular Islamist legislation in the previous parliament but also to adjustments in the electoral law that limited each voter to one vote.

The previous electoral law had allowed voters to vote up to the number of representatives allotted for their district. Thus voters in Irbid in 1989 could vote for up to nine representatives from their city to the national parliament. In that election the Muslim Brotherhood, as the only organized group at the time, had run lists of candidates up to the exact number of seats for a district. In this way, they were able to exploit the plurality-based electoral system to gain representation well above their proportion of the overall vote. But in the 1993 elections, almost the reverse happened, with the government closing that loophole and replacing it with the one-person–one-vote law and also with adjusted new districts that disproportionately favored traditionally pro-Hashemite areas (such as rural rather than urban districts).

Voting rights in Jordan are universal for adults (aged 20 or older). The franchise was extended to include women in 1973, but since no new elections were held until 1989, women were unable to exercise their right to vote or run for office until that time. The 80 members of the lower house are divided among 21 multimember constituencies. Of that total number, the regime reserved a number of seats for specific minority constituencies, all of which have traditionally been strong supporters of the Hashimite monarchy. These include six seats for the rural bedouin, nine seats for the Christian community, and finally three seats for the Circassian and Chechen communities collectively. In 1993, one of the Circassian seats went to Tujan al-Faysal, the first woman in the House of Delegates. But even before that election, a number of grassroots organizations had formed that aimed to field more women candidates in the future and to mobilize blocs of women voters.

THE PARTY SYSTEM

Jordan's monarchs had in the past experimented in limited ways with party systems, including a brief but fairly vibrant period in the 1950s, but each experiment ended in the state's curbing party activity. In 1957, for example, the state charged that military and party leaders were colluding in an attempt to overthrow King Hussein. This resulted in a ban on political parties that lasted for decades, aside from some brief state-directed experiments with forming loyalist parties. With the beginning of the political liberalization process in 1989, however, a new era emerged that would lead to the restoration of political parties and parliamentary life in Jordan.

With the legalization of political parties in 1992, dozens of new and old parties applied to the Ministry of the Interior for approval. Many of these were approved and went on to contest the 1993 elections. But in many ways the Jordanian party system remains fluid, with parties rising and falling, merging or splitting in two, as a result of electoral campaign fortunes or internal struggles over platform issues and party leadership.

Following is a select list of the main parties that have emerged since 1992. These are organized by their approximate position on the political and ideological spectrum.

LEFTIST AND PAN-ARAB NATIONALIST PARTIES

Jordanian Arab Progressive Ba'th Party (JAPBP)
(Hizb al-Ba'th al-'Arabi al-Taqadumi al-Urduni)

One of two wings of the pan-Arab and socialist Ba'th Party in Jordan, this wing is said to be linked to Syria. Its leader is Mahmud Musa al-Mu'aytah. The JAPBP has not been as successful in electoral politics as its pro-Iraqi counterpart, the Jordanian Arab Socialist Ba'th Party, but still draws support not just from Ba'thist sympathizers but sometimes also from Jordanians who favor stronger ties with Syria in general.

Jordanian Arab Socialist Ba'th Party (JASBP)
(Hizb al-Ba'th al-'Arabi al-Ishtiraki al-Urduni)

This second wing of the Ba'th Party in Jordan is said to be linked to Iraq and was blamed by the government for "inciting" the 1996 bread riots following the imposition of the IMF austerity program. Despite being singled out for such criticism, which had resulted in temporary arrests of numerous party officials, the JASBP did manage to win a seat in the 1997 elections to parliament. The JASBP was therefore one of few leftist opposition parties to actually contest the elections, disregarding the opposition boycott. It is led by Ahmad Najdawi and Khalil Haddadin.

Jordanian Communist Party (JCP)
(Hizb al Shuyu'i al-Urduni)

The Jordanian Communist Party (JCP), recognized by the state in 1993 after an initial rejection, later lost many of its members to the other secular leftist parties such as the Jordanian United Democratic Party. Still, the JCP is one of the oldest parties in the kingdom and dates its roots to the late 1940s. The Communist Party maintains a radical stance toward most socioeconomic and political issues, has ties to its counterpart in Israel, and has openly supported a two-state solution to the Israeli-Palestinian conflict. It is led by Yaqub Zayyadin.

Jordanian Democratic Popular Unity Party (JDPUP)
(Hizb al-Wahda al-Sha'biyya al-Dimuqrati al-Urduni)

A Jordanian secular, leftist, and Arab nationalist party with ties to George Habash's Popular Front for the Liberation of Palestine (PFLP). The JDPUP became a legal party only in the 1990s, in accordance with the 1992 National Charter legalizing political parties, but it had operated as an underground party since the 1960s. Its policy stances closely correspond to those of the PFLP, including its opposition to the Palestinian and Jordanian peace negotiations with Israel. It is led by Azmi al-Khawajah.

Jordanian People's Democratic Party
(Hizb al-Sha'b al-Dimuqrati al-Urduni)

Better know as "Hashd," this secular neo-Marxist party is affiliated with Nayef Hawatmeh's Democratic Front for the Liberation of Palestine (DFLP). Just as the JDPUP corresponds closely to the PFLP, Hashd's policies strongly reflect those of its Palestinian counterpart, the DFLP. Before its legalization as a Jordanian political party in 1993, Hashd had been viewed by the government as virtually inseparable from the DFLP faction within the PLO. While opposed to what it views as the unfavorable terms of the Jordanian-Israeli Peace Treaty and the Israeli-PLO Accords, Hashd has stressed its support for a peace process in general. The party sees the current process, however, as slanted and unfair. Its leader is Taysir al-Zibri.

Jordanian United Democratic Party (JUDP)
(Hizb al-Dimuqrati al-Wahdawi al-Urduni)

In 1995, the JUDP emerged following the merger of several secular leftist and pan-Arab nationalist parties, with strong Palestinian roots. The JUDP is made up largely of pan-Arab nationalists and moderate former members of the Jordanian Communist Party (JCP). The party presents itself as a secular-left opposition force but is considerably more moderate than most other Jordanian leftist parties and has, for example, taken a moderate stance toward the Arab-Israeli peace process. Its leader is Isa Madanat.

CENTRIST, CONSERVATIVE, AND ISLAMIST PARTIES

Future Party
(Hizb al-Mustaqbal)

The Future Party is a pan-Arab nationalist and conservative party, usually well represented in parliament and even in Cabinet posts. The party's leader, Sulayman Arar, was elected Speaker of Jordan's lower house of parliament following the 1989 elections. In the 1997 electoral campaign, however, the Future Party surprised many on the Jordanian political scene by joining the opposition boycott of the elections.

Islamic Action Front (IAF)
(Jabha al-'Amal al-Islami)

The main Islamist party in Jordan, the Islamic Action Front is the political wing of the Muslim Brotherhood (see below). Before creating the IAF as a legal political party in 1992, the Muslim Brotherhood had been by far the kingdom's best-organized and most successful political grouping. In the 1989 elections, Islamists affiliated with the Brotherhood won 22 seats in parliament. They were so successful, in fact, that they prompted the regime to change the electoral law to the current one-person–one-vote system. Despite their protests against this change, the newly formed IAF decided to compete in the 1993 elections, this time winning 16 seats. But in 1997, the IAF was one of the main parties leading the electoral boycott and thereby has no official representation in the 1997–2001 parliament (although several independent Islamists did win seats). The IAF is, in general, critical of the peace process and of Jordan's ties with the United States, but it has maintained a promonarchy stance as a "loyal opposition" party. Its leader is Ishaq Farhan.

National Constitutional Party
(Hizb al-Dusturi al-Urduni)

The NCP emerged only in 1997 following the merger of several other parties such as the Awakening Party (*Hizb al-Yaqazah*). The core of the National Constitutional Party, however, remained that of its main predecessor, the Pledge Party (*Hizb al-'Ahd*). The NCP presents itself as conservative and avowedly "pro-Jordanian" and draws support from Jordan's "tribal" communities as well as from numerous former ministers and army officers. The party advocates a Jordanian nationalism distinct from Jordan's Palestinian community. The NCP, in both its membership and its loyalist platform, is very much an establishment party. Its leader, 'Abd al-Hadi al-Majali, for example, is the brother of Prime Minister 'Abd al-Salam al-Majali. In the 1997 elections, the NCP attempted to take advantage of the opposition electoral boycott to corner a core of parliamentary seats as the self-declared party of the regime. Its electoral performance, however, was less impressive, garnering only 2 of the 10 seats it officially contested.

MINOR POLITICAL PARTIES

Freedom Party
(Hizb al-Huriyya)

Secular and leftist, the party advocates social democracy and a kind of reformed neo-Marxism. The Freedom Party is one of several small parties in Jordan that emerged in 1993 as offshoots of the Jordanian Communist Party. Its leader is Fawaz al-Zu'bi.

Jordanian Arab Democratic Party (JADP)
(Hizb al-'Arabi al-Dimuqrati al-Urduni)

A secular leftist party supportive of Palestinian rights and critical of the peace treaty with Israel. The JADP experienced some electoral success in 1993, winning two seats in parliament, but since then has divided over the peace process. Some of this pro-Palestinian party's members supported the PLO's positions, including its accords with Israel, while others opposed the peace process in general. Its leader is Mun'iz Razzaz.

Jordanian National Alliance Party
(Hizb al-Tajammu al-Watani al-Urduni)

Led by Mijhim al-Khuraysha, this is a conservative, pro-government, pro-Hashemite party with strong roots in Jordan's bedouin communities.

National Party
(Hizb al-Watan)

A conservative and usually proregime party, al-Watan's leaders have been represented in Jordanian Cabinet positions as well as parliament, although the party did oppose the regime's peace treaty with Israel. It is led by Akif al-Fayiz.

Progress and Justice Party
(Hizb al-Taqaddumi wa al-'Adl)

Led by 'Ali Farid al-Sa'ad, this is essentially a progovernment, centrist-to-conservative party that originally billed itself as economically liberal but socially conservative.

OTHER POLITICAL FORCES

Muslim Brotherhood

The Muslim Brotherhood has long been the most organized political opposition group in Jordan. Even during the years when parties were banned, the Muslim Brotherhood was tolerated by the regime. As a result, when parliamentary elections resumed in 1989, the Muslim Brotherhood was the only really organized political force and used this to its advantage in the national elections that year. When the ban on political parties was lifted in 1992, the Islamic Action Front emerged as the political wing of the Muslim Brotherhood and as one of Jordan's most successful political parties. Unlike the mutual hostility that characterizes the relationship between Islamists and the state in neighboring Syria, the Muslim Brotherhood and Hashemite monarchy have had a decades-long relationship of "peaceful coexistence."

Military

As early as the foiled coup attempt of 1957, King Hussein has relied on the loyalty of his armed forces to thwart serious challenges to his rule. The military was then composed almost entirely of bedouin and other "East Bank" Jordanians loyal to the Hashemite regime. Today, the army is still a bedrock constituency for the monarchy but represents a broader range of the population ever since the institution of the draft in the early 1970s.

Palestinians

Estimates of the size of the Palestinian population in Jordan vary widely, anywhere from 30% to 60% of the overall population. Some still live in refugee camps, while others have more fully integrated into Jordanian economic and political life. The rift between Palestinian and Jordanian communities within Jordan tends to be exaggerated, overlooking the many overlaps between families and the number of Jordanians of Palestinian origin who are key parts of the political elite. But some level of difference does remain a source of tension, leading to charges of Jordanian domination of the public sector or of Palestinian domination of the private sector.

Foreign Nations

Throughout its existence as an independent state, the Hashemite Kingdom of Jordan has remained deeply dependent on economic assistance from external patrons. Originally, the kingdom's main ally in this regard was the United Kingdom. But since the 1960s, the role of the United States and of Arab Gulf monarchies became increasingly important to the economic survival of the kingdom. In addition to these critical external aid linkages, the kingdom remains vulnerable to pressures on its domestic politics from its many powerful neighbors—in particular Syria, Iraq, and Israel.

NATIONAL PROSPECTS

The 1990s was a traumatic decade for Jordan, beginning with the Gulf crisis over Iraq's invasion of Kuwait. Even before that, however, the kingdom had been rocked by riots over price increases and political corruption in April 1989. With the onset of the Gulf crisis and the war that followed, Jordan attempted to maintain its political and economic alignment with Iraq, while opposing the annexation of Kuwait and trying to mediate the crisis. As the crisis steadily tumbled toward war, Jordan's fence straddling was viewed as betrayal by Kuwait, Saudi Arabia, and the Western-led coalition—in particular, Jordan's key ally, the United States. The price for Jordan's Gulf crisis stand was the abrupt cutoff in economic aid from the Gulf monarchies and the United States and the expulsion from Saudi Arabia and Kuwait (after the war) of more than 300,000 Palestinians and Jordanians. These Gulf "returnees" put tremendous strain on Jordan's social services and housing sector, but ultimately the kingdom managed to weather the crisis and eventually even restored its diplomatic links (and hence its foreign aid connections) to the United States and the Gulf states.

This diplomatic success was due in part to Jordan's participation in the United States–sponsored Middle East peace negotiations that began in Madrid in 1991. Following the surprise announcement of an Israeli-PLO accord in 1993, Jordan quickly concluded a full peace treaty with Israel in 1994. The regime appeared to rush well ahead of its populace in doing so, possibly banking on an expected financial windfall based on full economic relations with Israel and also on financial rewards from Western states. The windfall, however, never took place, and domestic discontent over the peace treaty mounted steadily, especially following the election of hard-line Prime Minister Benjamin Netanyahu in Israel in 1996.

Domestic anger spilled over into unrest in August 1996, when the regime implemented its second IMF-sponsored austerity program. As in 1989, riots broke out in Karak, Ma'an, and elsewhere. The 1996 riots, however, were not quite as widespread or violent as those of seven years earlier. They did, nonetheless, demonstrate clearly the level of public dissatisfaction over key issues of state policy—from economic reform to the pace of political liberalization to foreign policy issues such as Jordan's relations with Israel.

In response to mounting criticism, the regime backpedaled in the process of political liberalization by issuing a new set of restrictive guidelines for the press. Jordan's print and television media had opened up considerably since the reform process began in 1989, yielding one of the most open societies in the Arab world. For that reason, however, the regime's media restrictions were regarded by many in the kingdom as draconian. As the Oslo peace process began to collapse, domestic disaffection increased within Jordan and 11 opposition parties, led by the Islamic Action Front, organized a boycott of the November 1997 parliamentary elections. The opposition demanded that the electoral law be changed, that press freedoms be restored, and that normalization with Israel cease. None of these demands were met by election day, and so Jordan's 1998–2001 parliament included few members of either the Islamist or leftist opposition. Instead, with most of Jordan's parties sitting out the electoral process, the new parliament was tilted heavily toward conservative proregime figures. Thus although the regime could then expect to deal with a far more pliant parliament, it did so at the cost of setting back the minimal gains that had been made in Jordan's program of political liberalization.

The political liberalization process, along with the economic adjustment program and the peace treaty with Israel, were all meant to erase questions about the political future of Jordan and its monarchy. But as the kingdom entered the 21st century, profound questions remained about each of these areas of concern. In addition, the kingdom also faced the question of what would happen after King Hussein passed from the scene. At least in legal and constitutional terms, there had been no real "question" of succession since the king's brother, Hasan, had been crown prince for more than 30 years and was therefore the designated successor to Hussein. But in January 1999, the king surprised many observers by changing the succession and appointing his first-born son, Abdullah, to be his successor rather than Hasan. Thus what had seemed a relatively clear question of succession had instead become far more controversial. But with the death of King Hussein in February 1999, Abdullah ascended to the throne of Jordan, and in his first official act, appointed his half-brother Hamza crown prince. Yet even with this transition, the dominant questions in Jordanian politics continued to be about economic restructuring, political liberalization, and peace with Israel. In sum, under King Abdullah II, as under King Hussein before him, the main challenges facing the regime and the country remain the same.

Further Reading

Brand, Laurie A. *Jordan's Inter-Arab Relations: The Political Economy of Alliance Making.* New York: Columbia University Press, 1994.

Brynen, Rex. "Economic Crisis and Post-Rentier Democratization in the Arab World: The Case of Jordan." *Canadian Journal of Political Science* 25, no. 1 (1992).

Day, Arthur R. *East Bank/West Bank: Jordan and the Prospects for Peace.* New York: Council on Foreign Relations, 1986.

Nevo, Joseph, and Ilan Pappe. *Jordan in the Middle East 1948–1988: The Making of a Pivotal State.* Portland, Ore.: Frank Cass, 1994.

Robinson, Glenn E. "Defensive Democratization in Jordan." *International Journal of Middle East Studies* 30, no. 3 (August 1998): 387–410.

Ryan, Curtis R. "Elections and Parliamentary Democratization in Jordan." *Democratization* 5, no. 4 (winter 1998): 194–214.

———. "Jordan in the Middle East Peace Process: From War to Peace with Israel." In *The Middle East Peace Process.* Ed. Ilan Peleg. New York: State University of New York Press, 1997.

———. "Peace, Bread, and Riots: Jordan and the I.M.F." *Middle East Policy* 6, no. 2 (fall 1998): 54–66.

Wilson, Mary C. *King Abdullah, Britain and the Making of Jordan.* Cambridge: Cambridge University Press, 1987.

THE KAZAKH REPUBLIC

(Kazakh Respublikasy)

By Roger D. Kangas, Ph.D.

THE SYSTEM OF GOVERNMENT

Kazakhstan is located in the heart of Central Asia, just south of Russia and west of China. It is 2,717,300 square kilometers and has a current population of 16,916,463 (July 1996 estimate). Given the high numbers of Russians, Germans, and Ukrainians who have left the country since independence in 1991, the population is actually smaller now than it was a year ago. Experts note that this trend is decreasing and Kazakhstan should see a population increase in the next couple of years. Kazakhstan is currently a republic with a strong president, as outlined in the 1995 revised constitution.

Executive

Like the other Central Asian states, Kazakhstan possesses a very strong president. Nursultan Nazarbayev has been president since the beginning, making a seamless transition from Communist Party of Kazakhstan's first secretary (appointed in 1989) to independent president. Nazarbayev was elected president of independent Kazakhstan on December 1, 1991, running unopposed. A referendum held on April 30, 1995, extended his mandate until the year 2000, preempting a 1996 scheduled election. The reported support for the referendum was 95% of eligible voters—a figure disputed by international observers. In October 1998, President Nazarbayev revised the constitution, eliminating the age and term limits on presidents and making terms of office seven years. He called for an early election to be held on January 10, 1999, which he promptly won with almost 80% of the vote.

As with the other Central Asian leaders, Nazarbayev has been able to successfully consolidate his authority. According to the most recent constitution (August 1995), the president has the authority to appoint and dismiss judges, Cabinet ministers, senators, regional officials, and other bureaucrats in the government. In addition, he can call referenda at any time, can issue presidential decrees, and is responsible for all treaties and foreign negotiations. In sum, like the other Central Asian states, Kazakhstan has a presidential system.

The other executive is the prime minister, who has, in the past, played an important role in carrying out Nazarbayev's policies. This was especially true when the legislature was not in session, as during the 1995 dissolution of that body. At that time, the prime minister; Akezhan Kazhegeldin, was in charge of implementing the president's domestic policies. It became apparent in 1997 that Nazarbayev was dissatisfied with his prime minister; he replaced him on October 10, 1997, with the former oil and gas minister, Nurlan Balgimbayev. This is representative of the problems facing the "second executive" in Kazakhstan: Kazhegeldin was actually trying to wield his own authority and was also gaining a power base independent of the president. It seems that internal politics, more so than the stated "health reasons," prompted his resignation. Balgimbayev fits more in the mold of a supportive prime minister.

Legislature

Kazakhstan has had three different legislatures in its short existence as an independent state. In 1991, the Soviet-era Supreme Soviet took on the role of legislature in the country, although it was dissolved in 1994 to accommodate the new constitutional arrangement. In that year, elections were held for a 177-seat legislature. These elections were considered multiparty but, because of voting irregularities, not considered free and fair by international observers. In spite of efforts by Nazarbayev to control the elections, his parties failed to gain a majority of the seats and the 1994 legislature quickly began to assert its authority vis-à-vis Nazarbayev.

Because of an instance of "voter irregularity" in one district, the Kazakhstani Constitutional Court declared the entire 1994 election invalid on March 6, 1995. As a result, Nazarbayev dissolved the legislature five days later. A caretaker government under then prime minister Kazhegeldin took over for most of 1995, until a new constitution could be implemented and new elections called. It was at this time that Nazarbayev called for his own term extension and, on August 30, held another referendum on his new constitution. This referendum received slightly less support than the term extension, garnering only 89% of all eligible voters.

The powers of the new bicameral legislature—a 47-member *Senat* (Senate) and a 67-member *Majlis* (Assembly)—are significantly weaker, and it is nothing more than a rubber-stamp organization. While the members can challenge presidential legislation, they cannot address his decrees, effectively allowing the president and his Cabinet to circumvent legislative oversight. In principle, the upper house represents the regions and regional governments, with the lower house representing the people. Surveys conducted by the U.S.-based group IFES (International Foundation for Election Systems) reveal that most Kazakhstani citizens cannot even name their legislator or senator and base their knowledge of politics on Nazarbayev's speeches and policies.

The *Majlis* held its first elections on December 9, 1995, with runoff elections in January and February 1996. The 67 members were selected from single-member districts where a 50%+1 vote was needed in the first round; otherwise, a runoff was required. The party composition of the *Majlis* is as follows: PNEK, 24; Zheltoksan, 12; Kazakhstan Agrarian Union, 5; Confederation of Kazakh Trade Unions, 5; KPK, 2, others, 19. It is important to note that a number of parties did not participate in the elections, protesting the 1995 annulment of the legislature. Furthermore, party representation in the *Senat* is not even recorded, and in the *Majlis*, there is a high number of regional "independents" who are ostensibly supportive of the president.

Judiciary

There is a Supreme Court that oversees the constitutionality of laws and is the highest court of appeal in the country. The Court has not been active enough to give a fair assessment of its independence and position on issues. However, the fact that all justices are appointed by the president for fixed terms means that, most likely, the judiciary is subservient to the president. The 1995 constitutional crisis strongly supports this belief.

Regional and Local Government

Up until 1997, Kazakhstan comprised 19 *oblasts* and the city of Almaty. A number of the *oblasts* have been merged into larger entities, bringing the total number down to 14. Various reasons have been given for this, including the need to control regional clan groups. Most likely, this streamlining is a way to more effectively control regional governments in general, particularly the *oblasts* in the Russian-dominated north, where the mergers have taken place. Each region, or oblast, has its own legislature (*Majlis*) and executive (*Akim*). The former are chosen through regional elections, and the latter are appointed by the president. Each *Akim* is also allowed to appoint a consultative body, much like the president's

Cabinet. Because the planning system is centralized, regional governments are largely dependent upon the central government for financial assistance. Terms are fixed for each of these officeholders at four years, although it is not uncommon for an *Akim* to be replaced more frequently.

Kazakhstan also has a system of *mahallas*, or communal governments, that resemble rural township and urban district politics in the former Soviet system. Like the oblast governments, however, the *mahallas* have little power in the way of budgetary oversight.

THE ELECTORAL SYSTEM

Kazakhstan uses three types of electoral systems in the executive and legislative branches. The presidency is determined through a nationwide election with the winner needing 50%+1 of the votes to win. Failing that, the top two vote getters participate in a runoff election shortly after the first vote. Nazarbayev ran unopposed in the December 1991 election. In the January 1999 race, he did allow three challengers: the Communist Party chief, Serkbolsyn Abdildin, who won 13.5% of the vote, and two minor figures who received 4.3% and less than 1%, respectively. Nazarbayev himself received 78.3% of the vote. As the presidency now has a seven-year term, Nazarbayev does not have to face the voters until the year 2006.

The *Majlis* is based on single-member districts (67) with the same 50%+1 requirement noted above. In addition, for an election to be considered valid, at least 50% of the electorate must participate. The *Senat* races were determined in two ways: 40 seats were selected via indirect elections with the legislatures of the 19 *oblasts* and the city of Almaty each selecting 2 senators; the president was able to appoint 7 on his own. In 1997, Nazarbayev successfully pushed to have several of Kazakhstan's *oblasts* merge into larger units, ostensibly to make them easier to manage. Now, instead of 19, there are only 14 *oblasts*. Because the *Senat* seats are held for four-year terms, with half of the members up for election every two years, the membership has dropped to 42 (35 elected and 7 appointed) and will be further reduced to 37 in 1999 (30 elected and 7 appointed).

THE PARTY SYSTEM

Origins of the Parties

As with the other post-Soviet states, Kazakhstan's party system is a result of two phenomena: the Communist Party and the social organizations that emerged in the late 1980s to counter Communist Party activity. The current Kazakhstani constitution allows for opposition parties, as long as they are registered with the state.

Party Organization

Political parties in Kazakhstan resemble, in most ways, the structure of the former Communist Party of Kazakhstan (KPK), which differentiated between the "nomenklatura" and the masses. The former were/are the political elite within the party that held top offices, while the latter were in shop-floor groups, rural associations, and other local-level structures, called primary party organizations (PPOs). Above this level, the KPK was based on councils (*sovety*) and executive branch associations (*buro*) that operated at the district (*raion*), regional (*oblast*) and republic levels. This top level was seen in the KPK party congress, political bureau, and secretariat, which was headed by the first secretary. The current political parties in Kazakhstan bear a striking resemblance to this structure, particularly the People's Unity of Kazakhstan, the Socialists, and the Communists, which are all, in many ways, the heirs to the defunct KPK.

Campaigning

Campaigning in Kazakhstan has been lackluster at best. The presidential contest of 1991 was a one-candidate affair, so any campaign advertisements and rallies were for Nazarbayev only. The legislative campaign of 1994 did see a brief flurry of activity among the opposition parties. However, the annulment of that legislature and the creation of a new body in 1995 severely weakened any trend in fostering open elections. The combination of a short electoral season in December 1995 and the fact that a number of opposition parties opted not to participate (or could not, because they were not registered) meant that, once again, voters saw little in the way of campaigning.

Independent Voters

Since party identification is still weak in Kazakhstan, it is difficult to assess the role of independent voters in the country. With most votes going to PNEK party members, or "independents" supportive of that party, it can be assumed that the Soviet-era trend of supporting the major political party remains.

PARTY OF PEOPLE'S UNITY OF KAZAKHSTAN

(Partiya Narodnoye Edinstvo Kazakstana; PNEK)

HISTORY

Founded in March 1993 as a vehicle to support President Nursultan Nazarbayev, the PNEK (former known as the Union of People's Unity of Kazakhstan) is, in many ways, the historical successor to the Communist Party of Kazakhstan apparatus also headed by Nazarbayev. As the Soviet Union was breaking up, Nazarbayev remained loyal to the Communist Party of Kazakhstan, although in August 1991, he had the party renamed the "Socialist Party of Kazakhstan." In October 1991, he attempted to merge the various social organizations present in the country into a "People's Congress," which was headed by the writers Olzhas Suleymanov and Mukhtar Shakhanov. However, these individuals often openly expressed their opposition to the president, and eventually this organization ran afoul of Nazarbayev. His third attempt at establishing a propresidential party was the PNEK in 1993.

ORGANIZATION

PNEK, as noted above, parallels the traditional party structure of the former Communist Party of Kazakhstan. There is a central administration based in Almaty—soon to move to Aqmola, the new capital—and oblast headquarters in each region. Given that the PNEK was able to successfully take over the administrative and organizational elements of the former Communist Party, it has a ready-made system in place, needing minor revisions.

MEMBERSHIP

Membership is based on a probationary-status system with required sponsorship of a current member. At present, there are an estimated 40,000 registered members, although some accounts place it as high as 60,000. Perhaps reflecting the post-Soviet reality in the country, party membership is not necessarily viewed as essential to upward mobility. That and the fact that Nazarbayev himself is at least publicly distanced from the party system may be seen as an explanation as to why membership figures are not higher.

POLICY

The PNEK is openly supportive of Nazarbayev's reform agenda and is viewed as the most progovernment party in the political spectrum. On paper, it supports a market economy, state control of the energy export industries, and the maintenance of the social welfare system. In the area of foreign policy, it supports ties with Russia while at the same time exploring relations with other regional states. This is the result of the fact that Kazakhstan shares a lengthy border with Russia and must be on good terms with this neighbor to the north.

FINANCING

Technically, the PNEK gets no funding from the government, raising its money through membership dues.

LEADERSHIP

The current chairman is Kuanysh Sultanov, although most experts consider Nazarbayev himself to be the unofficial leader of the party. Technically, since Article 5 of the constitution prohibits government officials from being party leaders, Nazarbayev is forced to play this shadow role.

PROSPECTS

As long as Nazarbayev remains in power, the PNEK will most likely remain one of the strongest parties in Kazakhstan. Public-opinion polls suggest a strong recognition of the party, as compared with others. In addition, its infrastructural support will ensure continued existence. The only problem it may face is if Nazarbayev further distances himself from the party in an effort to present himself as completely above party politics. This seems unlikely at present, given the valuable support the PNEK gives the president.

MINOR POLITICAL PARTIES

The rest of the party spectrum in Kazakhstan can be considered a collection of minor parties. While there are a number of parties registered, technically making Kazakhstan a multiparty system, these tend to be limited in membership, leadership, and scope. Indeed, some are really nothing more than organizations supporting a particular political leader's opposition to Nazarbayev.

Socialist Party of Kazakhstan (Sotsialisticheskaya Partiya Kazakhstana; SPK)

This party is technically the successor to the Communist Party of Kazakhstan (KPK) of the Soviet era, formed in September 1991 following the failed coup attempt in Moscow. Unlike its predecessor, however, the SPK advocates market reform and political pluralism. President Nazarbayev was a member of this party until he left in the fall of 1991. Its leader is Petr Svoik (chairman).

Communist Party of Kazakhstan (Kommunisticheskaya Partiya Kazakhstana; KPK)

The "other successor" to the Soviet-era KPK, this party was formed in September 1991 by members who opposed the reformist position of the SPK. Legally registered in March 1994, the KPK has had some difficulty in remaining a political force in Kazakhstan. For instance, the Ministry of Justice attempted to have the party banned because it favored reunification of the Soviet Union. Faced with this challenge, the KPK revised its platform to be more supportive of Kazakhstani independence. Nevertheless, it is still seen as a party that favors close ties with the other members of the Commonwealth of Independent States (CIS). In addition, the KPK's platform includes maintaining state control of most of the economy as well as the continuation of the Soviet-era welfare state. Its leader is Serkbolsyn Abdildin.

People's Congress of Kazakhstan (Narodnyi Kongress Kazakhstana; NKK)

This was seen as one of the first real opposition parties to the SPK or KPK when it was founded in the fall of 1991. Headed by the popular writer Olzhas Suleymanov, the NKK at least initially had the backing of President Nazarbayev. However, the party's periodic criticisms of the president, as well as its growing popularity, prompted the president to part ways with Suleymanov. In August 1995, Suleymanov was appointed ambassador to Italy, effectively removing him from Kazakhstani domestic politics. The party won nine seats in the 1994 election, but it did not participate in the 1995 elections and is therefore unrepresented in the *Majlis*.

Agrarian Union

This party's main base of support is the former collective and state farms of Kazakhstan. A single-issue entity, the Agrarian Union sees itself as a force able to protect the rights of Kazakhstan's farmers. It is supportive of Nazarbayev's policies, and its five members who hold seats in the *Majlis* vote with the PNEK.

Confederation of Trade Unions of Kazakhstan

Like the Agrarian Union, the Trade Union Confederation is less of a political party and more of a social/interest group movement. Its base is the industrial workforce of Kazakhstan, and it advocates such positions as industrial development and the payment of wage arrears for Kazakhstani workers. It, too, has five members in the current *Majlis*.

Freedom Civil Movement of Kazakhstan "Azat" (Grazhdanskoye Dvizhenie Kazakhstana Azat; GDK Azat)

This organization predated independence and was one of the national opposition groups advocating greater independence during the Soviet period. Since its founding in 1990, Azat has made several alliances with other political parties, but personality differences have resulted in breakdowns. Its leader is Mikhail Isinaliyev.

December National Democratic Party (Natsionalnaya Demokraticheskaya Partiya Zheltoksan; NDP Zheltoksan)

Founded in May 1990, this organization was another of the Soviet-era nationalist groups in the Kazakh Republic. Under the leadership of Hasan Kozhakhmetov, Zheltoksan has remained a staunch supporter of ethnic Kazakh nationalism and the primacy of the Kazakh language in political discourse. The name of the party commemorates the December 1986 riots that followed Gorbachev's replacement of the then Kazakh first secretary, Dinmukhammed Kunaev, with an ethnic Russian, Gennadi Kolbin. In the December 1995 elections, it won 12 seats.

Republican People's Slavic Movement "Harmony"
(Respublikanskoye Obshestvennoye Slavyanskoye Dvizhenie "Lad")

After independence and in reaction to the Kazakh nationalist parties, ethnic Russians of the former party elite founded Lad in 1993. Like the KPK, Lad supports ties with Russia and the other CIS members, as well as such specific policies as dual citizenship for ethnic Russians and equal status of the Russian language with Kazakh (the "official language" of Kazakhstan). In advocating the rights of Russian-speakers, Lad has successfully garnered the support of other non-Kazakhs in the country, including Ukrainians, Germans, and Koreans. Its chairman is Alexandra Dokuchaeva.

Alash National Freedom Party
(Partiya Natsionalnoi Svobody Alash)

Whereas Lad advocates the rights of ethnic Russians, Alash is openly supportive of ethnic Kazakh rights and views the future of the Kazakhstani state as being inextricably linked with the future of the Kazakh people. This linkage with Kazakh nationalism is the reason for the name: Alash was a political movement that came to prominence during the Russian Civil War and, for a short time, declared a separate nation for the Kazakh people. Under the leadership of Aron Atabek and Rashid Nutushev, Alash has repeatedly run into problems with the government for its hard-line views and Kazakh nationalism. It is currently not represented in the legislature.

Umbrella Organizations

In addition to these individual parties, there are also two umbrella organizations that are attempting to unite the fractionated opposition. It is too early to tell how successful these blocs will be in the next round of elections.

"Republic" Coordinating Council of Public Associations
(Koordinatsionnyi Sovet Obshestvennyih Obyedinenyi Respublika; KSOOR)

This organization was formed in May 1994 to be a "constructive opposition bloc" to the PNEK. It includes a number of political parties that run on a common plat-

form. In principle, this organization will run collectively in the 2000 presidential and legislative elections. The coordinator of this party is Serkbolsyn Abdildin.

"Citizen" (Azamat)

This is yet another organization of political parties in Kazakhstan. Founded in April 1996, it is seen as a legitimate opposition force to the PNEK and, assuming its leaders can stay united, could actually challenge Nazarbayev's party. Its leaders are Murat Auezov, Petr Svoik, and Turegeldy Sharmanov.

OTHER POLITICAL FORCES

Ethnic Minorities

Without question, the strong Russian and non-Kazakh minority in the country will remain a significant force in the near future. To date, Kazakhs are still less than 50% of the total population, a situation that may not be the case much longer, as the administration recently declared that the "unofficial" percentage of Kazakhs is 50.1%. The most significant minority population in Kazakhstan is the Russians, at 35% of the Kazakhstani population. Living primarily along the Russo-Kazakhstani border, the Russians have expressed great concern over being "second-class citizens" in Kazakhstan. In particular, there have been vociferous debates over the language laws, which state that Kazakh is the official language of the republic, as well as the language taught in primary and secondary schools.

Almost a third of Kazakhstan is made up of nearly 100 other listed minority groups, most of them too small to be of political importance. The exceptions are the Uighurs, Uzbek, and Germans. The Uighurs are a Turkic minority that straddles the Sino-Kazakhstani border and is more heavily represented in the People's Republic of China, with estimates ranging from 7 million (official) to 22 million (from nationalist organizations). The Uighurs have been a source of protests and concern in China over the past decade, and as these demonstrations increase in intensity, the PRC has become most concerned over what happens in Kazakhstan. This issue has become so sensitive that President Nazarbayev has banned several Uighur-language newspapers and does not allow political movements advocating Uighur rights to register, although several are reported to exist in Kazakhstan.

Finally, the German population represents a continuing trend for the ethnic minorities in Kazakhstan. The unification of Germany in 1990, combined with the opening of the former Soviet borders the following year, has resulted in a significant outmigration of ethnic Germans to Germany. German immigration to the Kazakh territories actually began during the czarist period, with the most significant inflow taking place in 1944 with the deportation of Volga Germans to Kazakhstan. In 1989, the German population in Kazakhstan was over 1 million. As a result of the outmigration, the population decreased by almost 50%, and it is now estimated that there are fewer than 600,000 ethnic Germans in Kazakhstan. Their importance, as well as that of ethnic Poles and Koreans, is that they are seen as links to these foreign countries and foundations for economic trade in the region. On the other hand, the emigration of these peoples also underscores the problems of Kazakh nationalism and the attempt to build a multiethnic Kazakhstani state.

NATIONAL PROSPECTS

The political future of Kazakhstan is open to some variation, although if Nazarbayev can maintain his hold on power, there should be no change at the top. However, unlike the situation in most other Central Asian states, there are legitimate challengers to his authority and potential coalition partners who would like nothing better than to defeat Nazarbayev in an open and fair election. Nazarbayev's most serious challenger, former prime minister Akezhan Kazhegeldin, was accused of illegal activities and thus prohibited from participating in the January 1999 presidential election. As a result, Nazarbayev was assured of an easy victory.

A good deal of Nazarbayev's authority—and ability to stay in power—will increasingly be linked to his ability to turn the economy around and realize profits from energy exports. While he can pin the blame on others (as with the former prime minister Kazhegeldin), such reasoning will eventually fall on deaf ears. Local protests over wage arrears in Chimkent in 1997 are just one sign that even the Kazakhstani people have a level of tolerance that can be sorely tested.

Further Reading

"Kazakhstan." In *Nations in Transit 1998*. Ed. Adrian Karatnycky et al. Piscataway, N.J.: Transaction, 1999.

Kazakhstan Report on Human Rights 1997. Washington, D.C.: Department of State, 1998.

Olcott, Martha Brill. "Democratization and the Growth of Political Participation in Kazakhstan." In *Conflict, Cleavage, and Change in Central Asia and the Caucasus*. Ed. Karen Dawisha and Bruce Parrott. Cambridge: Cambridge University Press, 1997.

———. *The Kazakhs*. Stanford, Calif.: Hoover University Press, 1987.

REPUBLIC OF KENYA

(Djumhuri ya Kenya)

By Andrei I. Maximenko

THE SYSTEM OF GOVERNMENT

The Republic of Kenya, a nation of more than 28.8 million people according to a 1997 estimate, lies astride the equator on the east coast of Africa. It is a unitary, formally multiparty (from 1992), partially democratic state with a strong president.

Inland, Kenya was formerly a British colony, and along the coast, it was a protectorate. The first significant African nationalist organization was the Kenya African Union (KAU), founded in 1944 and supported mainly by the Kikuyu, the largest ethnic group in Kenya. In 1947 Jomo Kenyatta became president of the KAU and led the Union's active anti-British campaign in the 1950s.

Following general elections in May 1963, Kenya was granted internal self-government in June of the same year. The country became independent on December 12, 1963, and a republic exactly one year later. Kenyatta, then the leader of the Kenya African National Union (KANU), was appointed prime minister in June 1963 and became the country's first president in December 1964.

Through the dominance of KANU (the only party contesting elections to the National Assembly in 1969 and 1974), Kenyatta established some stability in Kenya. However, the assassination in 1969 of Tom Mboya, a Cabinet minister and secretary-general of KANU, led to civil unrest and the banning of the opposition Kenya People's Union.

Following the death of Kenyatta in August 1978, the vice president, Daniel arap Moi, was proclaimed president in October and was the only candidate in the presidential election of November 1979. In June 1982 the National Assembly officially declared Kenya a one-party state. A series of political detentions and increasing press censorship were followed by an attempted coup in August, which was suppressed at the cost of several hundred deaths.

During 1986 and 1987 the government acted to suppress an unofficial left-wing opposition group known as Mwakenya (the Union of Nationalists to Liberate Kenya). By early 1987 more than 100 people (mainly university teachers, students and journalists) had been arrested in connection with the activities of Mwakenya. In July of that year the human rights organization, Amnesty International, published allegations that Kenyan political detainees had been tortured and that two had died in custody.

In May 1990 a broad alliance of intellectuals, lawyers, and clergy under the leadership of Kenneth Matiba began to exert pressure on the government to legalize political opposition to KANU. In July President Moi ordered the arrests of several prominent members of the alliance, including Matiba. Shortly afterward serious rioting erupted in Nairobi and its environs: more than 20 people were killed, and more than 1,000 were reportedly arrested.

In late November international creditors suspended aid to Kenya for 1992, pending the acceleration of both economic and political reforms. In December 1991, a special conference of KANU delegates, chaired by President Moi, acceded to the domestic and international pressure for reform and resolved to permit the introduction of a multiparty political system. Soon afterward the National Assembly approved the necessary legislation.

In December 1992, multiparty presidential and legislative elections were held. Amid accusations of intimidation, fraud, and ethnic clashes aimed at impeding the opposition's election campaign, Moi was reelected as president by a narrow margin and KANU managed to win slightly over 50% of elective seats in the National Assembly. The validity of election results was challenged by the opposition; however, in February 1994, the Court of Appeal rejected the opposition's petition.

During 1994, 1995, and 1997 the government continued to suppress opposition activity. Anti-KANU political meetings were repeatedly dispersed by the security forces, and criticism of the government in the national media was not tolerated. Interethnic violence continued to disrupt national unity.

Kenya's system of government is based on the 1963 constitution as amended in 1964, 1967, 1982, 1988, and 1991. The 1964 amendment, known as the republican constitution, established a republican form of government with a strong executive and a powerful central government. The power of the president was further strengthened by amendments passed in 1988. The 1982 and 1991 amendments, respectively, established and abolished the one-party system.

Executive

Executive power is vested in the president, vice president, and Cabinet. The president is the head of state, head of government, and commander in chief of the armed forces. Both the vice president and the Cabinet are appointed by the president from among members of the National Assembly. The president, who is elected to a five-year term by popular vote, must himself be a member of the National Assembly and at least 35 years of age. The president must command a majority vote in the National Assembly; should he lose a vote of confidence, the president must resign or dissolve the legislature and call for new elections. If a president dies, or a vacancy otherwise occurs during a president's period of office, the vice president becomes interim president for up to 90 days while a successor is elected.

The president, since 1978, has been Daniel Teroitich arap Moi.

Legislature

The national legislature is the unicameral National Assembly. The body consists of 224 members: 210 elected by popular vote for five-year terms, 12 nominated by the president, and the attorney general and Speaker, who are ex officio members. The attorney general may not vote. Unless dissolved before the end of its term, the Assembly sits for five years. The National Assembly may be dissolved by the president at any time or by the body itself on the passage of a no-confidence vote. If the Assembly is dissolved, legislative and presidential elections must be held within 90 days.

Since independence, and especially after 1988, the executive has exerted tremendous political influence over the legislature. Until 1992 nearly all legislation was drafted and introduced by the government. While the opposition after the 1992 elections has sought to play an active role in the legislative process, the government relies on the KANU majority in the Assembly (and often reverts to direct repression) to ensure favorable outcome in important legislative matters.

Judiciary

Kenyan jurisprudence is based on English common law, African customary law, Islamic law, legislative acts of the National Assembly after 1963 and of the British Parliament before independence, and judicial precedent.

A chief justice and 11 puisne (associate) judges make up Kenya's High Court, which sits continuously in Nairobi, Mombasa, Nakuru, Kisumu, and Nyeri. The High Court supervises a system of subordinate courts, including provincial and district magistrates' courts and Muslim district courts, which rule on questions of Islamic law relating to family and domestic affairs. The Court of Appeal issues the final verdict in contested civil and criminal cases. The president has the authority to appoint and dismiss High Court and Court of Appeal judges.

The courts are empowered to review government acts and legislation and to declare laws and acts null and void. However, the Kenyan judiciary's independence has been seriously eroded through the passage of 1988 constitutional amendments affecting the security of tenure of judges and the employment of expatriate judges who work under contracts with the Kenyan government. While Kenya's legal system has been noted for its overall integrity, there have been cases, especially after 1988, when it was used by the ruling regime against its political opponents.

Regional and Local Government

Kenya is divided administratively into provinces, districts, divisions, locations, and sublocations. Provincial commissioners, who answer directly to the president, govern the country's seven provinces (Central, Coast, Eastern, Northeastern, Nyanza, Rift Valley, and Western) and the Nairobi Extra Provincial District. The commissioners are responsible for education, transport, and health in the provinces. Districts and divisions within districts are headed, respectively, by district commissioners and district officers. As of 1988, there were 40 districts and 215 divisions.

Local authorities (councils), elected by popular vote, are divided into five levels: municipal councils, town councils, county councils, urban councils, and area councils. Local councils raise revenue by levying taxes, build and maintain roads and public housing, supervise public health, welfare, and education, and provide various social services. With centralization of political power in Kenya, many of the local councils' functions are being transferred to ministries and regional administrations.

Traditionally, rural people have also participated in local governmental processes through general meetings, called *barazas*, convened by chiefs, subchiefs, or district officers.

While the ruling KANU was never a mass political party, opposition parties, since 1992, have attempted to enlist popular support at local levels. In response, the government has often resorted to repressive measures, including direct violence, against political activists and supporters of the opposition.

THE ELECTORAL SYSTEM

Under Kenya's constitution, regular presidential and legislative elections are held simultaneously every five years. All citizens 18 years or older are eligible to vote. The president and members of the National Assembly are elected through direct popular vote by secret ballot. To be elected president, a candidate must receive more votes than any other single candidate and meet the legal requirement that the winner receive 25% or more of the vote in at least five of the eight provinces (including Nairobi). Candidates to the National Assembly are elected in single-member districts.

Voter turnout in the 1992 elections was under 50% of registered voters. However, no dependable figures are available regarding the percentage of eligible voters who were actually registered. The KANU government has been accused of failing to introduce procedures that would permit free and equal access to registration, party nomination, campaigning, and voting. Many people found it difficult to obtain the voter's cards they needed to register. There were claims of card purchases by KANU. In addition, ethnic tensions, allegedly provoked by the government, seriously impeded the process of registration and voting. Opposition candidates in more than 20 constituencies were physically prevented from presenting their nomination papers. International monitors accessing the degree of freedom and fairness of the elections admitted serious flaws, while stating that the outcome generally reflected "the will of the people."

The trends and controversies of the 1992 campaign largely continued during the 1997 elections.

THE PARTY SYSTEM

A constitutional amendment passed in December 1991 established a multiparty political system. Several new parties have emerged to challenge the dominant KANU, although their success has been marred in part by factionalism.

The 1992 and 1997 election campaigns were politically tense. Few norms and regulations regarding campaigning had been established. KANU's close links to the government gave it a comparative advantage in permits for rallies, money, and time on official radio and TV channels. Reporters covering opposition rallies for newspapers and weekly magazines were harassed, usually at the direction of state or KANU officials. The leading opinion weeklies sometimes found their entire press run impounded and their editors detained.

All political parties, including KANU, are primarily electoral parties with weak formal structures and little top-to-bottom control. Ethnicity and personality play a dominant role in determining party allegiance.

KENYA AFRICAN NATIONAL UNION (KANU)

HISTORY

Founded in 1960 by the late President Jomo Kenyatta, KANU was Kenya's sole legal political party from 1982 to 1991. A successor to the Kenya African Union (KAU), which was originally a Kikuyu organization, KANU broadened its base of support in the early 1960s. After the volun-

tary dissolution of its former rival, Kenya African Democratic Union (KADU), which represented some of the country's smaller ethnic groups, in 1964 KANU became the only political party in Kenya. Many former KADU officials, including Daniel Moi, obtained positions within KANU. The Kenya People's Union (KPU), formed in 1966 by Luo leader Oginga Odinga, was banned in 1969.

ORGANIZATION

Largely because it has never developed an effective, popular political ideology, KANU has failed to become a mass party or to enlist widespread grassroots support. Despite an attempt to expand its popular base in the mid-1980s, it remains principally an electoral party, functioning only in times of stress, turmoil, or elections. KANU's party institutions also are weak. National congresses are rarely held, and most national party officials are appointed by the president. The party's local officeholders are elected by a delegate conference, which includes all KANU members of the National Assembly. There is also a tacit understanding that the seats on KANU's national executive should go to representatives of the country's eight provinces (including Nairobi).

POLICY

KANU's political principles include centralized government, racial harmony, Kenyanization of the economy, economic development on the basis of free enterprise, and "positive nonalignment" in foreign affairs.

MEMBERSHIP AND CONSTITUENCY

It is difficult to determine the true number of KANU members, especially after 1991. The government has sought to inflate KANU membership: at one point, in the late 1980s, as many as 5 to 6 million members were reported. The actual numbers had little significance, because from the mid-1980s to 1992, the government and KANU were virtually indistinguishable from each other, the latter practically subsumed by the former.

FINANCING

Since its inception KANU has been plagued with financial difficulties. Increases in membership dues, "reenrollment" campaigns among KANU life members in 1979, a forced enrollment of civil servants in 1985, and other similar measures proved to be inadequate. It has been reported that since the mid-1980s, state funds have been increasingly diverted to party coffers. Whether the end use was for party finances or personal profit of top party officials is difficult to determine.

LEADERSHIP

KANU's leadership parallels that of the political leadership of Kenya. The party is headed by Daniel Teroitich arap Moi (born in 1924) as party president.

OTHER POLITICAL FORCES

Other Political Parties

The history of Kenya's multipartyism is very short. Previously united by their opposition to President Moi and KANU, new political groupings are still searching for political identities beyond those of their respective leaders. In the 1992 elections three major opposition parties emerged, FORD-Kenya, FORD-Asili, and the Democratic Party (DP), each winning blocks of seats in the new parliament. In the 1997 elections the Social Democratic Party and the National Development Party replaced FORD-Asili as major players.

FORD

The Forum for Restoration of Democracy (FORD) was founded in 1991 as a "discussion group" and became a formal political party when the multiparty system was introduced at the end of that year. The leading figures in FORD were Oginga Odinga (1911–94), the vice president of Kenya at independence, and Kenneth Matiba (born in 1932), a successful businessman formerly appointed by President Moi to the Cabinet. Each took advantage of the lack of organization in FORD to press its case to be its presidential candidate. In October 1992 FORD split into two parties: FORD-Kenya, headed by Odinga (chairman) and Gitobu Imanyara (secretary-general), with strong backing from Luo-speaking politicians; and FORD-Asili, led by Matiba (chairman) and Martin Shikuku (secretary-general), and widely supported among a part of the Gikuyu-speakers in Central Province. In the 1992 elections, FORD-Kenya and FORD-Asili each won 31 seats. In 1997 FORD-Kenya won 18 seats, while FORD-Asili was able to reclaim only 1 seat.

THE DEMOCRATIC PARTY

The Democratic Party was also formed in 1991 by a former minister of health and vice president, Mwai Kibaki (born in 1931), and a group of disgruntled former civil servants. Supported mainly by a large section of Gikuyu-speakers, the party won 23 seats in the 1992 elections and 41 seats in 1997. The Democratic Party is headed by Kibaki, who is president, and John Keen, who is secretary-general.

The three parties focus mainly on the need to curb what they perceive as the "corrupt and authoritarian" practices of the Moi regime and argue for further democratization of Kenya. Ideological differences between the three are not very pronounced. FORD-Kenya and FORD-Asili are more populist in their political orientation, while the Democratic Party is more conservative. Organizationally, the three parties are weak, with no meaningful grassroots structures. It appears that just like KANU, these parties will be primarily electoral organizations, attempting to enlist mass support only occasionally, especially at times of elections. There is no reliable information regarding their sources of finance. It has been reported, however, that financial backing during the last election campaign came chiefly from wealthier representatives of the ethnic groups that have supported the respective candidates.

Since 1992 there have been a number of "splits" and "defections" in all three key opposition parties. After the death of Oginga Odinga in 1994, FORD-Kenya was divided into two factions, led by Raila Odinga and Michael Wamalwa, the official party chairman, respectively. In the same year, a group of FORD-Asili members formed a rival party executive headed by Salim Nsamwe. The Democratic Party has faced similar problems.

In the 1997 elections the National Development Party, chaired by Raila Odinga, and the Social Democratic Party, led by Charity Kaluki Ngilu, won 22 and 16 seats respectively, in the National Assembly.

Minor Political Parties

A number of smaller parties were formed in the wake of the 1991 abolition of the one-party system, among them the Islamic Party of Kenya, The chair of the Islamic Party is Oman Mwinyi, and the secretary-general is Abdoulrahman Wandati. In addition, there are the Kenya National Congress, chaired by Titus Mbaathi; the Kenya National Democratic Alliance party, chaired by Mukaru Ng'ang'a; the Kenya Social Congress, chaired by George Moseti Anyona; the Party for Independent Candidates of Kenya, chaired by Otieno Otoera; the Labour Party Democracy, chaired by Mohamed Ibrahim Noor; the People's Union for Justice and New Order, led by Wilson Owili; and the Rural National Democratic Party, chaired by Sebastian Munene.

More recently, several new political organizations have been created. Among them are Safina (led by Richard Leakey and Muturi Kigano) and Mwazanga (headed by Paul Muite, a former FORD-Kenya vice chairman); their strong opposition to KANU and wide popular orientation have been a source of concern for the government. As a result, the two organizations have become a target of violent government-inspired attacks and have had difficulties with registration.

International Donors

The international community has come to play an important role in promoting political changes in Kenya in the early 1990s. The Moi regime came under serious international criticism, particularly from the United States, for its record on human rights. In August 1990, the U.S. administration suspended military aid of US$5 million to Kenya in protest against the Kenyan government's arrest of opposition leaders in July of that year. In October 1990, Kenya severed diplomatic ties with Norway, following protests by the Norwegian government regarding the arrest on treason charges of a Kenyan dissident who had been exiled in Norway; Norway subsequently suspended aid allocation to Kenya. In mid-November 1991, following protests by several overseas governments against arrests by Kenyan security forces of opposition leaders who had organized a prodemocracy rally, the Moi government accused U.S., German, and Swedish diplomats of assisting Kenyan dissidents (allegations that were strongly denied). Later in the same month, donor countries and organizations agreed to withhold aid to Kenya. Forced to rely increasingly on external sources of finance by growing external debt and problems in its domestic economy, the Moi government had to yield to the international and domestic opposition and initiate some measure of political reform in late 1991. International donors have since maintained their pressure on the Kenyan government on human rights and democracy issues.

Ethnic Groups

Ethnic tensions exploded on a number of occasions in the early 1990s, particularly in the Rift Valley Province. While none of the major political parties in Kenya claim to represent a specific ethnic group, ethnicity has become a significant factor in determining party allegiance. Interparty rivalry is affected by the ongoing conflict between the traditionally economically and politically dominant Kikuyu, Luo, and smaller ethnic groups, such as the Kalenjin and Maasai.

Party officials have blamed their opponents for inciting ethnic violence. While on a number of occasions party (especially KANU) involvement has been evident, it is not clear how much control the parties exercise over some of the more radical ethnic organizations, including militant "youthwingers."

Mwakenya

Emerging in early 1980s, Mwakenya became the most discussed underground opposition group in Kenya. With no clear organization, it was allegedly initially formed by university researchers, whose arrests in 1985 and 1986 first brought the group to public attention. It has been suggested that while the movement is leaderless, it has urban, rural, and exile components. University graduates have been allegedly responsible for drafting Mwakenya's "platform," including the "Draft Minimum Program," with its demands for legalization of political parties, social justice, and human rights. While the message of Mwakenya was quite persuasive in the 1980s, it remains to be seen whether it will be able to play a significant role in the present political situation.

The Church

Church involvement in the protection of civil liberties began in 1986 with the National Council of Churches of Kenya (NCCK) speaking publicly against the government decision to replace the secret ballot with a queuing system during primary elections. Later, the churches broadened their criticisms to include protests against the detention of political opponents of the Moi regime and general opposition to the one-party system.

In 1989 and 1990, churches became vocal in their demands to overhaul the electoral system, attack corruption, and allow more political freedom, including the formation of new political parties. In May 1990 Bishop Henry Okullu criticized the KANU leadership and endorsed a multiparty system. The same year 18 Catholic bishops signed a pastoral letter urging political liberalization.

Church activism provoked virulent government attacks against the clergy. Some priests were arrested. However, given the influence of the church among the Kenyans, the regime could not move decisively to prevent its activity. The church has continued in its new political role as a strong voice for broad civil liberties.

Students

There has been a history of conflict between the government and the student body of the University of Nairobi. On a number of occasions in late 1980s and early 1990s, university students staged meetings protesting government actions against the opposition. The government usually responded by detaining student activists and temporarily closing the university. However, attempts to stop political activity on campus have not been successful, and President Moi once remarked that the university has become "a breeding ground of subversion."

The Urban Poor

Since independence, Kenya's cities, especially Nairobi and Mombasa, have grown at a tremendous rate. Most of the new inhabitants have been peasants forced to move to the city by the poverty in rural areas. A vast majority of these urban residents (almost 80% in Nairobi and more than 70% in Mombasa) live in shantytowns in appalling conditions. Most are unemployed. Dissatisfaction among the urban poor with visible disparities of wealth and the evidence of widespread corruption have made city slums a serious trouble spot for the government. The destruction of shantytowns and expulsion of their dwellers have further antagonized the poor.

Organized Labor

Approximately 630,000 workers (about 47% of all employed) are members of Kenya's 24 labour unions. All unions, with the exception of the Kenya National Union of Teachers (KNUT) are affiliated with the Central Organization of Trade Unions (COTU). The government, through its ministry of labor, controls union registration and has the authority to certify union election results. In 1993, using a split that occurred among the delegates of COTU's national congress, the government practically selected the organization's new leadership by endorsing one of the factions.

NATIONAL PROSPECTS

Economic growth and diversification have made Kenya one of Africa's leaders in per capita income, international investment and technology transfer, industrial and commercial development, and trade. At the same time, rigid class distinctions based on wealth and political power have been evident. A small and well-entrenched elite still dominates the political system and much of the economy. Corrupt practices have proliferated in both business and government. Incessant wooing of foreign investment and aid has outpaced Kenya's ability to absorb new assistance and made it heavily dependant on external financing.

Although Kenya has been traditionally noted for its political stability, the country is currently undergoing a process of fundamental, albeit slow, change to more political pluralism. Consequently, the old political system is facing serious difficulties trying to cope with new pressures. The next few years will be critical in determining whether Kenya is able to deal with its growing economic and political problems without descending into political turmoil, caused by serious ethnic and class conflict. In the same vein, it will be important to see if the country does not follow the example of many of its neighbors and either descend into civil unrest or provoke its currently politically dormant military to intervene in the political process.

Further Reading

Barkan, Joel D., and John J. Okumu. *Politics and Public Policy in Kenya and Tanzania*. New York: Praeger, 1979.

Bevan, David. *Peasants and Governments: An Economic Analysis*. Oxford: Clarendon, 1989.

Godia, George I. *Understanding Nyayo: Principles and Policies in Contemporary Kenya*. Nairobi: Transafrica, 1984.

Hazelwood, Arthur. *The Economy of Kenya: The Kenyatta Era*. London and New York: Oxford University Press, 1979.

Kitching, Gavin. *Class and Economic Change in Kenya: The Making of an African Petite Bourgeoisie*. New Haven, Conn.: Yale University Press, 1980.

Miller, Norman N., and Rodger Yeager. *Kenya: The Quest for Prosperity*, 2d ed. Boulder, Colo.: Westview Press, 1994.

Ndegwa, Stephen N. *The Two Faces of Civil Society: Ngos and Politics in Africa*. West Hartford, Conn.: Kumarian Press, 1996.

Thomas, Barbara P. *Politics, Participation and Poverty: Development through Self-Help in Kenya*. Boulder, Colo.: Westview Press, 1985.

Widner, Jennifer A. *The Rise of a Party-State in Kenya: From "Harambee!" to "Nyayo!"* Berkeley, Los Angeles, and Oxford: University of California Press, 1993.

KIRIBATI

By Eugene Ogan, Ph.D.

The democratic republic of Kiribati was known as the Gilbert Islands until it achieved independence from Great Britain in 1979. Great Britain had administered the Gilbert Islands as part of a protectorate that included the Ellice Islands. In a referendum held in 1974, inhabitants of the latter voted to form a separate nation, now Tuvalu. Kiribati remains within the British Commonwealth.

Kiribati is made up of 33 islands, all of them coral atolls except Banaba, which had been a major producer of phosphate until operations ceased in the year of independence. Total land area is 823 square kilometers, including 103 square kilometers of uninhabited isles. In 1995, there were 77,650 residents, more than one-third of whom live on the single island of South Tarawa. Population pressures have been recognized for decades, and migration to the Solomon Islands was encouraged by the former British administration. When phosphate on Banaba was exhausted and the island was no longer habitable, Banabans were relocated to Rabi, in the Fiji group.

A mixture of parliamentary and presidential systems, the Kiribati government is headed by a president, or *Beretitenti*. He is both head of state and head of government. The Great House of Assembly, or *Maneaba ni Maungatabu*, nominates up to four candidates from its membership, and one is chosen in a national election. The voting age is 18, but candidates for the *Maneaba* and presidency must be at least 21. Presidents are elected to a normal term of four years and may be reelected twice. They can be removed by a no-confidence vote in the House of Assembly, in which case a Council of State serves until a new election can be held. The president selects a vice president, as many as eight ministers, and an attorney general who must be a lawyer and may or may not be an elected member of the *Maneaba*. These constitute the Cabinet and, with the president, the executive authority.

Elections for the *Maneaba* are held every four years. It is a single-chamber legislative body, consisting of 39 members elected from 23 single-member or multimember constituencies and a representative of the Banaban community nominated by the Rabi Council in Fiji. If the at-

torney general is not an elected member, he serves ex officio. Each member must be elected by an overall majority of votes cast, and runoff elections are often necessary. A distinctive feature of the House is that the Speaker is chosen from among persons who are not members. Except for Cabinet ministers, members may be recalled by a petition of a majority of voters in their electorates.

Judicial authority is vested in a High Court, a Court of Appeal, and a system of magistrates' courts. The chief justice of the High Court is appointed by the president with the advice of the Cabinet. There are 24 magistrates' courts serving every inhabited island; each has three magistrates. A primary function of magistrates' courts is dealing with land matters.

There are 19 local government councils, including town or urban councils. Council members are elected for three-year terms, but *Maneaba* members also serve ex officio on councils located in their electorates.

Kiribati's government is notable for its political stability as well as its financial prudence, especially when compared with other Pacific Island nations. However, the country's economic situation remains gloomy. Since the exhaustion of the major phosphate deposits, fishing remains the resource with greatest potential. In 1991, Kiribati received over 20 million U.S. dollars in aid; Japan was the largest donor. This was the equivalent of approximately half the country's gross domestic product.

Even more threatening are predictions of global warming and a consequent rise in sea level. There is much debate about the accuracy of these forecasts, but they represent a real danger for the low-lying atolls of Kiribati. If the worst-case scenario should occur in the next century, this Pacific Island nation might simply disappear.

Further Reading

Van Trease, Howard, ed. *Atoll Politics: The Republic of Kiribati.* Universities of Canterbury (New Zealand) and the South Pacific (Fiji), 1993.

DEMOCRATIC PEOPLE'S REPUBLIC OF KOREA

(Chosun Minjujueui Inmin Konghwaguk)

By Hun Joo Park, Ph.D.

THE SYSTEM OF GOVERNMENT

The Democratic People's Republic of Korea, or North Korea, is a Stalinist single-party state that controls the northern half of the Korean peninsula. Korea was divided between rival governments in the aftermath of the 35 years of Japan's colonial rule and the Second World War. North Korea, with a land mass of 122,370 square kilometers, about 55% of the total land area of the peninsula, shares a 1,025-kilometer border with the People's Republic of China along the Yalu and Tumen Rivers and a 16-kilometer border with Russia at the mouth of the Tumen River. Since the end of the Korean War in July 1953, the demilitarized zone (DMZ), a 4,000-meter-wide "no man's land" along the 38th parallel, has divided the Democratic People's Republic of Korea from the Republic of Korea (South Korea). As of 1993, North Korea's population size was 23 million, which is about half the population of South Korea (44.5 million).

An examination of the history, both ancient and modern, of the Korean peninsula sheds much light on the character and the preoccupations of the North Korean regime. Korea is an ancient country that, like Poland in the West, has been a marching ground for the armies of its more powerful neighbors (China, the Mongols, Japan, the Manchus, and, to a lesser extent, Russia) and yet has managed, with great tenacity, to preserve its national identity. A tragic history has given the Korean people great determination and strength of character and has also made them highly suspicious of outsiders and, at times, rigidly conservative. The Yi dynasty, which despite foreign invasion and bitter internal rivalry between political factions lasted from 1392 to 1910, sought protection by becoming a tributary state of China, assiduously copying its political institutions and social practices. By closing itself off from all other foreign influences, it became what Westerners in the 19th century called the "hermit kingdom."

In 1876, however, Japan forcibly opened the country, in much the same manner as Japan itself was opened by the United States in 1853. The next three decades saw intense rivalry among Japan, China, and, to a far lesser extent, Russia for dominant influence in Korea, but Japan's control of Korea was set after its victories in the Sino-Japanese War of 1894–95. Although the Russo-Japanese War (1904–05) broke out primarily over their rivalry for Manchuria, Japan's victory over Russia sealed Korea's tragic fate. Japan's colonial rule, which officially began in 1910, combined policies of economic exploitation and systematic destruction of the Korean national identity. Koreans bitterly resented the Japanese, and their national resistance continued in various forms throughout the rule. The March 1, 1919, mass uprising was a culmination of such resistance.

The dream of Korean independence after the defeat of Japan in World War II gave way to the tragedy of dismemberment with the occupation of the peninsula by Soviet and American armed forces. Although the United Nations planned for Korea's reunification after nationwide elections, it never materialized. On August 15, 1945, with the early advance of Soviet troops into the peninsula, the United States proposed dividing Korea at the 38th parallel so the Japanese troops in Korea could surrender. Stalin accepted the proposal, but that temporary division ironically hardened into two separate states. The Soviet-backed Democratic People's Republic of Korea, with its own constitution, was established on September 8, 1948, claiming control over the entire peninsula and accusing the rival Republic of Korea, established in August 1948, of being a "puppet" regime.

North Korea initiated the Korean War (June 1950 to July 1953) by invading South Korea. The war, which resulted in the death and dislocation of millions of people and the desolation of the entire peninsula, not only intensified and militarized the cold war but also locked the governments of the North and South into a stance of rigid hostility. For over four decades the peninsula has been one of the most militarized in the world.

Kim Il Sung, born near P'yongyang on April 15, 1912, fought with guerrilla units against the Japanese on the Soviet-Manchuria border between 1932 and 1945. He led the Korean Workers' Party (KWP), the ruling Communist party, since its founding in 1946, was premier after 1948, and, following the adoption of the 1972 constitution, president of the DPRK. By the early 1960s, Kim had established unchallenged control of the Korean

Workers' Party and thereby full state power. Kim could consolidate his position because his Kapsan guerrilla faction successfully purged every rival political faction in the North Korean government one by one. Kim first purged Pak Hon-yong's domestic faction, many of whom were socialist intellectuals of the South who had fled to the North right before the Korean War. He blamed them for the failure of "liberating" the South and executed Pak on charges of spying on the United States. Exploiting the party membership registration issue, Kim then purged the Russian faction that Ho Ka-i led, a group neither well organized nor cohesive. Finally, Kim purged the Yenan faction, which had begun to criticize Kim's personality cult in light of the onset of de-Stalinization that took place in the Soviet Union in 1956.

Kim Il Sung built a monumental personality cult around himself, dwarfing that of Stalin or Mao. Kim then groomed his son Kim Jong Il (born February 16, 1942) as his own successor, and beginning in 1975, he began referring to the younger Kim as the "Party Center." Kim Il Sung died of heart failure at the age of 82 on July 8, 1994, and the process of father-to-son power succession seems to be on track. However, the future of the ruling regime itself looks extremely uncertain as it has been increasingly unable to feed its own people. In any event, North Korea has become a Communist hereditary monarchy, a historically unprecedented phenomenon.

Executive

As in other Communist countries, the state organization of the Democratic People's Republic of Korea is defined as subordinate to the ruling Korean Workers' Party. The state implements policy formulated by the party, which owes its dominant position to its role as representative and "vanguard" of the revolutionary working class. However, in practice, the constitutional changes in 1972 shifted the center of power from the party and its political committee to the presidency and the Central People's Committee (CPC), a kind of supra-Cabinet that directs the large and unwieldy Cabinet of the State Administration Council (SAC). (The SAC has 32 ministries and 13 commissions, or supraministries.)

The head of state is the president. From 1972 when the office was established until his death in 1994, North Korea knew no other president than Kim Il Sung. The creation of this office marked the unrivaled supremacy of Kim, who was at the same time secretary-general of the Korean Workers' Party. Although the president is supposed to be elected for renewable four-year terms by the national legislature, the Supreme People's Assembly (SPA), he is in practice accountable to no one. The president is the commander of the armed forces, chief executive with control over the State Administration Council, and supreme legislator through his power to issue edicts with the force of law and the requirement that all other legislation be approved by him. The president is also responsible for approving treaties and agreements with foreign countries.

At present, the office of the president remains vacant, as Kim Jong Il has as yet to formally assume the position as well as that of KWP secretary-general. The formal titles that the younger Kim holds include supreme commander of the Korean People's Army (KPA) and head of the National Defense Commission (NDC). The NDC was originally set up in 1972 under the executive branch's Central People's Committee, but in 1992 it became a separate and apparently higher military decision-making body. In fact, since Kim Il Sung's death, no CPC meetings have taken place, let alone any of the Supreme People's Assembly (SPA). The Korean Workers' Party congress last convened 18 years ago, in 1980.

Legislature

Delegates to the unicameral Supreme People's Assembly are chosen for four-year terms in direct elections based on universal suffrage. Each delegate represents a constituency of about 30,000 persons. The nominal powers of the SPA include the election of the president, the passing of laws, amendment of the constitution, and approval of the national budget and economic plans. Sessions are supposed to be held twice a year, in spring and late fall. When the SPA is not in session, its standing committee, elected by the deputies, acts in its name. Although the 1972 constitution defines the SPA as the "highest organ of state power," it is, in fact, a rubber-stamp organization.

The Central People's Committee, elected by the SPA for a four-year term, functions essentially as the link between party and state, the great majority of its members being members of the central political bureau (politburo) of the KWP. Its powers and responsibilities are broad, including the definition of domestic and foreign policy lines and control over the State Administration Council and Central People's Commissions dealing with national defense, foreign policy, state control, internal matters, and justice and security.

Judiciary

Central Court judges are elected by the SPA for three-year terms. They thus fall under the control of the state and party and have no independence. Furthermore, the procurator general, appointed by the SPA, exercises supervisory control over the court system down to the provincial and local people's courts.

Regional and Local Government

The country is divided into nine provinces and four "special cities" (the capital, P'yongyang, Kaesong, Namp'o, and Ch'ongjin). Subnational units are divided into urban districts (the special cities and other large cities), regular cities, and some 152 counties. Each of these units has its own local people's assembly, local administration committee, and local people's committee, corresponding to the SPA, the State Administration Council, and the Central People's Committee on the national level. On the village level, there are no formal government organizations. Instead, administrative matters are the responsibility of the chairman of the local agricultural collective.

THE ELECTORAL SYSTEM

Elections are managed by the party's umbrella organization, the democratic front for the reunification of the fatherland. A single slate of candidates approved by the party is presented to the electorate, and their election is automatic. Voter turnout routinely is reported at 100%. Most candidates are KWP members; other political groupings generally receive a few seats.

THE PARTY SYSTEM

The Democratic People's Republic of Korea is one of the most tightly regulated countries on earth, far closer in fact to the model of a totalitarian state than was the Soviet Union or the People's Republic of China. North Korea's small size facilitates efficient surveillance. Its continuing confrontation with South Korea creates a pervasive atmosphere of military discipline and mobilization. The Korean Workers' Party, which monopolizes political and state powers at both the national and the local levels, remains in total control of this isolated society.

THE KOREAN WORKERS' PARTY (KWP)
(Chosun Nodongdang)

HISTORY

The Korean Workers' Party was established in August 1946 as a coalition of diverse elements, including Korean Communists who had been based in the Soviet Union before and during World War II, particularly in the Maritime Province bordering Manchuria and Korea. Others had been in China and were closely associated with the Chinese Communist movement. A third group consisted of underground resistance fighters who had operated within Japanese-occupied Korea. The party structure and principles were modeled after those of the USSR's Communist Party; a number of its most prominent members had been members of the Soviet party. The party's development after 1946, however, was unambiguously in the direction of one-man rule under its secretary-general, Kim Il Sung. In the early years, Kim, who owed his position as KWP leader to Soviet support, had to recognize and deal with the somewhat divergent viewpoints of other party leaders even if no one seriously challenged his supremacy. As briefly discussed earlier, however, a series of purges eliminated other factions, so that by 1956 all sources of potential opposition to the Kapsan faction's dominance were eliminated. Kim reorganized the KWP and subjected it to intense and unremitting doses of ideological remolding. In the 1960s, a campaign to idolize Kim and his revolutionary achievements was initiated and has remained the dominant theme of North Korean political life.

ORGANIZATION

The highest organ of the Korean Workers' Party is its party congress, whose delegates are elected by members of provincial and special city party congresses. Although it is supposed to be convened every four years, the congress has in fact met much less frequently. As is the case in other one-party systems, the congress, meeting so infrequently and with a membership of over 3,000, is not the effective locus of decision making but only a platform for the promulgation of decisions made by a much smaller group of leaders.

Power is concentrated in even smaller concentric circles. The central committee convenes the congress and acts in its name when it is not in session. Technocrats formed the largest single group in the central committee following the 6th party congress in 1980. The political bureau is elected by the central committee. The standing committee of the political bureau is composed of North Korea's most powerful leaders.

The secretariat is a national-level party organ that has nine secretaries heading different party departments, including the inspection committee (responsible for party discipline), an audit committee (responsible for finances), a military committee (which was headed by Kim Il Sung), and a liaison bureau (in charge of relations with underground "revolutionary" elements in South Korea). Other central committee departments deal with a variety of matters such as agriculture, fisheries, science and education, and propaganda and agitation. The party publishes *Nodong Sinmum* (The Workers' News), a daily newspaper, and *Kulloja* (The Laborer), a theoretical journal.

There are party congresses, committees, and secretariats on all subnational levels as well as smaller party units in rural villages. The basic unit of the party on the local level is the cell, to which all party members must belong.

Important mass organizations include the socialist working youth league, which schools future party members, and the young pioneer corps for children. The democratic front for the reunification of the fatherland also comprises a number of groups coordinated by the party. Among them are the general association of Korean residents in Japan, which organizes support for the P'yongyang regime among Japan's more than 600,000 Korean nationals, as well as the Korean social democratic party and the young friends party (*Ch'ondogyo Chongu*). The latter two are permitted a limited existence under the supervision of the KWP, which is the leading force in the democratic front. (*Ch'ondogyo* is a religious movement founded in the 19th century.)

POLICY

Kim Il Sung has been revered not only as the revolutionary leader who liberated Korea from the Japanese (the role of the Soviets being glossed over) but as the creator of the *Juch'e* (self-reliance or independence) ideology, originally conceived of as an adaptation of Marxist-Leninist ideology to the Korean context. *Juch'e* ideology is more consistent with traditional Korean Confucian thoughts or Korean nationalism than proletarian internationalism. *Juch'e* somewhat repudiates Soviet and Chinese models of socialist construction, but it has also over time shown a tendency to depart from the theoretical foundation of the revolution, Marxism-Leninism. While the Chinese Communists have always modestly described "Mao Zedong Thought" as only an application of universal Marxist-Leninist truths, in the DPRK, the thought of Kim is known as "Kim Il Sung *Jueui*," a full-class "ism" equal and perhaps superior to Marxism-Leninism.

To understand the *Juch'e* ideology fully, one must look at the origins of the idea, which was the changing international political context of the 1960s. First, the Sino-Soviet rift became increasingly clear in the early 1960s. Second, once Soviet Communist Party leader Khrushchev's de-Stalinization campaign began in earnest, Kim's autocracy and personality cult began to be criticized. Third, during the Chinese Cultural Revolution in the late 1960s, the Red Guards openly criticized Kim as a bureaucratic revisionist who was indulging in a luxurious, decadent bourgeois lifestyle. It was in this context that Kim advocated *Juch'e* in order to maintain distance from the big Communist brothers. It also came at a time when economic aid from the Soviet Union and China was declining. It goes without saying that the idea of *juch'e* has been stretched too far to justify Kim Il Sung's familial dictatorship and North Korea's extremely isolationist policies.

Kim pursued a policy of self-reliance in the military sphere as well. As a result, the military share of North Korea's government budgets has increased, imposing a serious burden on the country's economy. As of 1993, North Korea's military spending amounted to 8.9% of GDP, while that of South Korea was 3.8%. In that same year, North Korea's GDP per capita was one-tenth of South Korea's.

The militarization of society has increased the importance of the military in North Korean politics, especially after Kim Il Sung's death. Kim Jong Il is still not head of the state or KWP secretary-general, so his official power base lies in his being the chair of the National Defense Commission, the top decision-making body concerning military matters. The appointment of Choe Gwang, the most prominent veteran military man, as defense minister in October 1995 also suggests that the military is increasingly the real locus of power in North Korea.

The great preoccupation of the P'yongyang government since the end of the Korean War has been its hostile and competitive relationship with the Republic of Korea. Technically, the peninsula is still in a state of war. The North Korean leaders, former guerrilla fighters, have turned their country into a tightly disciplined armed camp. No fewer than 1.2 million men are in military uniform in a total population of 23 million, and most of them are deployed offensively close to the de-militarized zone. DPRK actions against the South have included border provocations, armed infiltration of the Republic of Korea, and, most dramatically, terrorist acts such as the attempt to assassinate South Korean President Chun Doo Hwan on October 9, 1983. While on a state visit to Rangoon, Burma, Chun narrowly escaped death when a bomb set off by North Korean agents killed 17 South Koreans, including four Cabinet ministers.

These hostile acts have alternated in a very unpredictable fashion with gestures of conciliation such as the North Korean offers of rice, clothes, and medical supplies to South Korean victims of floods in September 1984. In 1985, people from both the North and the South were allowed to visit family members on the other side of the DMZ for the first time since the Korean War. Variegated, if intermittent, inter-Korean talks have continued since the 1970s. North Korea even signed a wide-ranging agreement on cooperation in 1991, although no real implementation of the agreement has taken place.

Perhaps out of sheer necessity, North Korea played its nuclear card by withdrawing from the Nuclear Nonproliferation Treaty in March 1993. It apparently paid off, since in October 1994 South Korea, Japan, and the United States agreed to give North Korea $5 billion worth of nuclear power stations of the sort that cannot easily be used to make nuclear bombs and 500,000 tons of free fuel per year until the completion of the new reactors. North Korea has agreed to engage in preliminary talks to hold four-party (North and South Korea, the United States, and China) peace talks, as South Korea and the United States jointly proposed in April 1996. North Korea's interests in agreeing to come to the negotiating table seem to lie in its desire to normalize diplomatic relations with the United States as well as to secure more economic aid. North Korea's insistence on the American troop withdrawal from South Korea as a precondition to the four-party talks has been a major stumbling block to further progress thus far.

MEMBERSHIP AND CONSTITUENCY

It is estimated that the number of KWP members could have been as high as 3.2 million at the time of the 6th party congress (1980), a sharp rise from the 2 million announced by the KWP in 1976. This could have been due to the induction of a large number of the "Three Revolution Workteams," a mass political mobilization movement. Overall, about 15% of the total population are party members. Recruits must be recommended by members in good standing and must serve a one-year probationary period.

Criteria for party membership include personal commitment to its ideology, loyalty to Kim Il Sung and now to Kim Jong Il, and proper class background. Former revolutionary fighters, workers, and poor peasants have generally been perceived as the most revolutionary classes and thus most eligible for party membership. In recent years, however, technical and administrative expertise has been seen as important as class background, and such skills play an increasingly central role in the selection of party cadres and management personnel. Schools for the training of KWP cadres include the college of people's economic management, the Kim Il Sung higher party school, and the Kumsong political college.

FINANCING

Information on party financing is unavailable. It can be assumed that as in other Communist states, party members pay a portion of their income in dues and that direct government support is considerable.

NATIONAL PROSPECTS

North Korea finds itself totally ill prepared to adapt to drastic changes that are taking place in the post–cold war era. North Korea's economy is in shambles, in part because the Soviet Union, its biggest aid donor and trade partner, collapsed, and in part because its Stalinist eco-nomic management has utterly failed. Both the Soviet Union in 1990 and China in 1992 normalized their diplomatic relations with South Korea, while the North still has no equivalent ties with the United States or Japan. It joined the United Nations together with South Korea in 1991, only because it became clear that it was no longer able to block the UN from accepting South Korea as a member.

With regard to North Korea's future and the reunification of the two Koreas, various scenarios are conceivable. Any of these variants could materialize: the "big bang" scenario, as in the case of German unification or Romania's collapse; a military confrontation, although it would be suicidal for the North Korean regime; a stalemate; or a smooth transition to reunification. Only time will tell what will actually transpire. But given the fact that the North Korean regime has trouble even feeding its own people, the question of what kind of reunified Korea will be built on the peninsula is critically dependent upon how South Korea responds to this historic challenge.

Further Reading

The Economist. "A Subversive Weapon." *The Economist.* August 23, 1997.

The Economist Intelligence Unit Limited. *North Korea: EIU Country Profile, 1996–97.*

Lee, Chong-Sik. *Korean Workers' Party: A Short History.* Stanford, Calif.: Hoover Institution Press, 1978

Lee, Hong Yung. "The Korean Question in Post–Cold War East Asia." Unpublished typescript, May 1997.

Satterwhite, David H. "North Korea in 1996." *Asian Survey* 37, no. 1 (January 1996).

Scalapino, Robert A., and Chong-Sik Lee. *Communism in Korea*, 2 vols. Berkeley: University of California Press, 1972.

REPUBLIC OF KOREA

(Daehan Minguk)

By Hun Joo Park, Ph.D.

THE SYSTEM OF GOVERNMENT

Background

Since 1987 the Republic of Korea, or South Korea, has been a democracy. It continues to progress toward further political democratization, with a centralized, presidential system of government. The Republic of Korea has become one of the most successful developing countries in the postwar era. Through some 30 years of condensed industrialization and modernization, its per capita GNP dramatically grew from one of the lowest to more than $10,000 by 1996. Its annual export growth rates exceeded 20% in real terms, and South Korea has become the world's 11th-largest trading nation. It controls the southern half of the Korean peninsula, with a land area of 98,477 square kilometers, or about 45% of the total area of the peninsula. South Korea's population in 1993 was 44.5 million (about twice that of North Korea), with Seoul, the capital, one of the largest cities in the world, having over 10 million inhabitants.

The ancient country of Korea, unified since 668 C.E. and with at least 2,000 years of continuous and distinct sociocultural history, has trodden a tough, if tragic, modernization path. Being confronted with colonialism at the end of the 19th century, the 500-year-old Yi dynasty found itself unable to modernize the country and preserve independence. It fell under Japan's exploitative totalitarian rule in 1910, but in reality, Japan's ruthless rule over Korea had already begun after the Sino-Japanese War of 1894–95. At the end of World War II, Japan's rather sudden surrender after the U.S.'s dropping of two nuclear bombs prompted the United States to propose to the Soviet Union the use of the 38th parallel as a temporary dividing line for taking surrender of Japanese troops in Korea. That division hardened into two separate states: the Republic of Korea in the south and the Stalinist Democratic People's Republic of Korea, or North Korea, in the north. (For a brief review of Korean history prior to 1950, see the article on North Korea.)

The Korean War, which began in June 1950 with the invasion of the south by the armed forces of the north in-

tent on "liberating" the entire peninsula, had a formative influence on the development of the political system of the Republic of Korea. Millions of people were dislocated, which was a cause of great social and political instability in the postwar years. The threat of further aggression from the north led political leaders to establish a highly centralized, authoritarian order, under which dissent and opposition were linked with Communist subversion, often without justification. American military support of the Seoul government made South Korea the keystone of the U.S. defense perimeter in East Asia. Even today, after the fall of the Soviet Union, the cold war continues on the Korean peninsula.

During the period from 1948 to 1960, known as the First Republic, Syngman Rhee, a political science Ph.D. from Princeton University, was president of the Republic of Korea. Rhee was one of the most prominent leaders of the struggle for national independence. Having been the first president of the Korean government-in-exile in Shanghai in 1919, he enjoyed quite a bit of prestige. That he was descended from Yi Song-gye, founder of the Yi dynasty, gave him an added aura of legitimacy, particularly among the country's tradition-oriented peasants who made up the majority of the population. His anti-Communist credentials also gave him an edge in getting U.S. backing for his bid to become the country's first president. His administration, however, was marked by pervasive corruption and favoritism, and Rhee himself had no tolerance for critics or political opponents. Rhee was already 73 years old in the first year of his presidency. He refused to support the establishment of a parliamentary system of government in which the legislature would have supreme power, insisting instead on a centralized presidential system that would give him broad powers as chief executive. Rhee's first four-year term was to end in August 1952, and the National Assembly had defeated a constitutional amendment sponsored by him that would allow for a popularly elected president, rather than one chosen by the Assembly. Rhee declared martial law in May 1952 and forced the Assembly to pass the amendment. In 1955, a second constitutional amendment was passed, also through the use of dubious methods, to allow Rhee to succeed himself indefinitely. However, student and popular outrage over his autocratic and often-brutal methods forced him to retire in 1960, after some 142 students were killed by the police during demonstrations early that year.

South Korea experienced a brief period of democratic rule during the Second Republic, which lasted from April 1960 to May 1961. The constitution was revised once again, this time to provide for a parliamentary form of government. Chang Myon, a leader of the opposition Democratic Party, was chosen as prime minister. Bitter struggles between Democratic Party factions and continued instability in the nation as a whole gave a small group of military officers under Major General Park Chung Hee the opportunity to seize power, on May 16, 1961.

Park dissolved the National Assembly and established a junta, called the Supreme Council for National Reconstruction. Military officers took over high-level administrative positions in the government. Under martial law, all political activities were suspended, and many politicians of the Rhee era were "blacklisted." In June 1961, the Korean Central Intelligence Agency (KCIA) was established to carry out surveillance of civilian and military opponents of the new regime. Its founder and first director was Colonel Kim Jong Pil, a member of the junta and nephew of Major General Park through marriage. Kim also played a central role in organizing the government-sponsored Democratic Republican Party. Under the new constitution of the Third Republic, which allowed for popular election of the president, Park retired from the military and ran for election as the Democratic Republican Party candidate, winning narrowly in October 1963 against Yun Po-sun of the opposition New Democratic Party.

Spectacular economic growth during Park's 16-year rule as president transformed South Korea from a predominantly rural, agricultural country into an urbanized, industrial one exporting manufactured products to world markets. The South Korean "miracle" insured support for Park's regime, as individual incomes steadily rose. Close links with Japan were seen as essential for economic development, and thus a South Korea-Japan treaty normalizing relations between the two countries was ratified in June 1965. There had, however, been substantial opposition, particularly among students, given the history of Japanese colonialism, and violent demonstrations led to the imposition of martial law. Park won the presidential elections in 1967 and 1971 with rather narrow margins of votes against New Democratic Party candidates Yun Po-sun and Kim Dae Jung. Like Rhee in his time, Park had the constitution amended in 1969 to allow himself a third term in 1971.

The decade of the 1970s saw Park establish dictatorial authoritarian rule. In October 1972, he proclaimed martial law and dissolved the National Assembly. A month later, he held a national referendum on the *yushin*, or "restoration," constitution that established the Fourth Republic. The new constitution gave absolute power to the president over the executive, legislative, and judiciary branches. The president was to be elected by an electoral college of the National Conference for Unification, a body consisting of some popularly elected 2,359 members, and there were no limits to the number of terms that one person could serve as president. In effect, the *yushin* constitution practically guaranteed Park's lifelong presidency.

Continued popular opposition caused Park to enact Emergency Measure Number Nine (May 1975), which made it a crime to criticize the *yushin* system or advocate its revision. The KCIA became increasingly powerful and feared as it used harsh methods to silence opposition, even among Koreans overseas. The most spectacular example was the KCIA kidnapping of the New Democratic Party leader, Kim Dae Jung, from a Tokyo hotel in August 1973, an event which caused a serious rupture in South Korean–Japanese relations and underlined the regime's increasingly poor human rights record. Thousands of South Koreans were jailed or put under house arrest, including the Second Republic president, Yun Po-sun, and the dissident poet Kim Chi Ha; many were subjected to brutal treatment.

The domestic and international crises of the late 1970s hastened the downfall of Park's rule. By then, there were clear signs of failure of the heavy and chemical industrialization drive, on which President Park staked so much political capital. Inflation was rampant, unemployment soared, and the ruling party for the first time failed to win more popular votes than the opposition in the 1978 National Assembly election, despite the less than perfectly free and fair electoral environment. In 1979, Korean exports experienced a negative growth in real terms, the second oil shock hit, and in 1980, Korea's economy contracted by 4.8%.

As antigovernment demonstrations erupted across the country, Park's lieutenants split into hard-liners and moderates. The head of the hard-liner camp was Cha Ji Chul, chief of the presidential security forces, who argued for harsher repression to crack down on any form of antiregime opposition. Kim Jae Gyu, director of the KCIA, took a more pragmatic stance and advocated dialogue rather than outright confrontation with the opposition and demonstrators. Park generally leaned toward Cha Ji Chul's side. During a secret party in one of the Blue House's "safe houses" on October 26, 1979, Kim Jae Gyu shot both Park and Cha in a desperate plot to change course. The assassination of Park led to the collapse of the *yushin* system and the brief restoration of civilian rule under an acting president, Choi Kyu Ha. In December 1979, Choi abolished Emergency Measure Number Nine and released a large number of political prisoners who had been jailed under its provisions. These included Kim Dae Jung, who had been under house arrest following his kidnapping from Tokyo to Seoul. The political scene was enlivened as both the Democratic Republican Party under Kim Jong Pil and the New Democratic Party under Kim

Young Sam and Kim Dae Jung began jostling in anticipation of presidential and National Assembly elections, which were to follow the promised establishment of a more liberal constitutional order.

Factional struggles within the parties, strikes by workers demanding higher wages and better working conditions, and a wave of student unrest, however, provided the military with yet another opportunity to establish its dominance over the political system. Major General Chun Doo Hwan, head of the Defense Security Command, established his control over the military by leading younger generals in a successful move to oust the chief of staff, General Chung Seung Hwa, and other Park-era senior military officers, on December 12, 1979. On May 17, 1980, Chun reacted to increased student militancy, aimed at removing the military from politics, by proclaiming martial law. His decree banned all forms of political activity, closed the headquarters of political parties, outlawed strikes, and muzzled journalists. The universities were closed, and the National Assembly suspended. Opposition leaders were arrested on charges of corruption and sedition. In Kwangju, the capital of South Cholla province, Kim Dae Jung's home region and long a center of opposition sentiment, the brutal treatment of student demonstrators by the police and army paratroopers sparked a revolt by the general populace that lasted nine days and reportedly resulted in the death of up to 2,000 people. The official death toll was 189.

The junta established the Special Committee for National Security Measures with power in the hands of four men: Generals Chun Doo Hwan, Cha Kyu Hun, Roh Tae Woo, and Chung Ho Yung. A campaign of "social purification" was initiated. Some 9,000 people—members of the National Assembly, government officials, managers of state-run corporations, and educators—were fired from their posts. Nearly 200 magazines and newspapers were closed, and several hundred journalists were sacked for promoting "corrupt influences." Kim Dae Jung and a number of his supporters were tried by a military court; Kim was sentenced to death on charges of subversion in September 1980.

President Choi Kyu Ha resigned on August 16, and Chun, now a five-star general, retired from the military to run for the presidency. With the support of the military, Chun was approved as interim president by the National Conference for Unification, which acted as an electoral college. Chun's new constitution (the Fifth Republic), ratified in a referendum on October 22, 1980, constituted only a slight modification of the *yushin* constitution. The Chun constitution abolished the National Conference for Unification, limited the presidency to a single, nonrenewable seven-year term, and made it more difficult for the president to proclaim martial law and dissolve the National Assembly. Both the Chun and *yushin* constitutions, however, provided for indirect, rather than direct, election of the chief executive.

After three years of harsh repression of all political activities unauthorized by the state, South Korean politics entered a period of softening by 1984. No authoritarian regime can rule by coercion alone. As Korea's economy had recovered its confidence and the GNP growth rates started to pick up again, Chun took a much more conciliatory attitude. By combining carrots and sticks, Chun tried to prolong his own grip of state powers. Despite the pent-up societal demand for democracy and the direct presidential election system, Chun attempted to maintain the existing rules of the game at least until after the election of his hand-picked successor. In April 1987, Chun issued an order to prohibit any discussion of constitutional changes. But 1987 was not 1980.

In the mass demonstrations that followed Chun's order, office workers as well as students and factory workers in Seoul took to the streets to demand democracy. Against such a backdrop came the famous June 29, 1987, declaration by Roh Tae Woo, then the official presidential candidate of Chun's Democratic Justice Party (DJP). The eight points that the declaration contained included the restoration of Kim Dae Jung's political rights and constitutional revision for a directly elected presidential system. Given the ruling party's incumbency premium of about 35% and the popularity of the two Kims (Kim Dae Jung and Kim Young Sam), the DJP's strategy must have been to divide the opposition and rule. No matter what the political calculation behind the June 29th declaration, it laid the groundwork for Korea's transition to democracy.

The outcome of the first presidential election under the Sixth Republic in 1987 turned out to be disastrous not only to the two Kims but to those who wished to see the end of the military domination of the country's politics. Roh, who helped Chun to seize power by illegally bringing his front-line division to Seoul, was elected to the presidency with 36% of the popular vote. Kim Dae Jung and Kim Young Sam split the opposition vote by getting 27% and 28%, respectively. Nonetheless, the process of democratization was now set in motion.

In the National Assembly elections of 1988, the governing party, for the first time in the nation's history, failed to obtain a simple majority. In order to resolve the ruling party's minority dilemma in the legislature, Roh merged the Democratic Justice Party with Kim Young Sam's party to form the Liberal Democratic Party, a grand conservative coalition. Subsequently, Kim Young Sam managed to win the presidential nomination of the ruling party through an open competition and thereby the presidential election in 1992.

On December 18, 1997, the former political prisoner Kim Dae Jung of the National Congress for New Politics party (*Sae Jungchi Kukmin Hoiee*; SJKH) was elected president of South Korea with 40.3% of the vote. Lee Hoi Chang of the Grand National Party came in second with 38.7% of the vote. Rhee In Je of the New

TABLE 1
Presidential Election Results, December 1992 (in thousands, %)

	Total Votes	Kim Young Sam	Kim Dae Jung	Jung Ju Yung
Seoul	6,021	2,167 (35.9)	2,246 (37.3)	1,070 (17.7)
Pusan	2,565	1,551 (60.4)	265 (10.3)	133 (5.1)
Taegu	1,172	690 (58.8)	90 (7.5)	224 (19.1)
Inchon	1,081	397 (36.7)	338 (31.2)	228 (21.0)
Kwangju	685	4 (0.5)	652 (95.1)	8 (1.1)
Taejon	582	202 (34.7)	165 (28.3)	133 (22.8)
Kyonggi	3,502	1,254 (35.8)	1,103 (31.4)	798 (22.7)
Kangwon	834	340 (40.7)	127 (15.2)	279 (33.4)
Chungbuk	750	281 (37.4)	191 (25.4)	175 (23.3)
Chungnam	973	351 (36.7)	271 (27.8)	240 (24.6)
N. Cholla	1,126	63 (5.5)	991 (88.0)	35 (3.1)
S. Cholla	1,285	53 (4.1)	1,170 (88.0)	26 (2.0)
N. Kyongsang	1,559	991 (46.7)	147 (9.4)	240 (15.3)
S. Kyongsang	2,118	1,514 (71.4)	193 (9.1)	241 (11.3)
Cheju	265	104 (31.5)	85 (25.7)	42 (12.7)
Total	24,095	9,977 (42.0)	8,041 (33.8)	3,880 (16.3)

People's Party, with 19.2%, and minor parties garnered the rest of the vote.

Executive

In Korea, power is highly concentrated in Seoul, the capital, in the executive branch, and ultimately in the presidency. In terms of both power concentration and power centralization, the country, in effect, verges on absolutism; accordingly, the degree of centralization in the policymaking process is extremely high.

There has never been a meaningful system of checks and balances in the Korean government. Executive dominance is deeply rooted historically in the conservative, statecentric Confucian tradition, which found strong reinforcement in the Japanese "colonial totalitarianism" and the subsequent military authoritarianism. Under the *yushin* constitution, for example, the president had the power not only to dissolve the National Assembly but also to appoint one-third of its members, which guaranteed an easy majority for the ruling party. The president also appointed—without the legislative branch's approval—the Supreme Court justices, whose terms were limited to six years. Further, the president was empowered to issue emergency decrees "in the whole range of state affairs, including . . . economic, financial, and judicial affairs." As noted earlier, President Chun's Fifth Republic inherited this system and kept it basically intact.

The new constitution of 1987 stripped the president of the power to dissolve or appoint members to the National Assembly, to appoint judges without the legislature's approval, or to issue emergency decrees. The National Assembly, a unicameral body whose elected members serve four-year terms, regained the right to audit and investigate all administrative affairs. The legislature must have at least 200 members and currently has 299; 253 are directly elected on a single-member plurality system and the rest (46) are allocated among the parties in proportion to their share of the total votes.

The Constitutional Court, the supreme organ of judicial review, is beginning to perform its functions. Still, the nine Constitutional Court adjudicators as well as the Supreme Court justices (whose total number may not exceed 14) serve six-year terms, and the chief justice's term is nonrenewable. Thus far, the legislature remains too impotent to balance presidential power, and the judiciary is still not fully independent.

TABLE 2
National Assembly Election Results, April 1996

Party	Total Seats	% Votes Won	Direct	Proportional
NKP	121	18	139	34.5
NCNP	66	13	79	25.3
ULD	41	9	50	16.2
DP	9	6	15	11.2
Independents	16	—	16	12.9
Total	253	46	299	100.0

Notes: NKP, New Korea Party (former Democratic Liberal Party), now Grand National Party; NCNP, National Council for New Politics; ULD, United Liberal Democrats; DP, Democratic Party.

The executive branch writes 80 to 90% of the total legislative bills. With the bills it writes, it makes sure that they get passed in as broad and abstract terms as possible, delegating the authority to work out the details of enforcement to administrative statutes or ordinances. This tactic has been extremely useful in ensuring executive dominance over the legislature and party politicians in the day-to-day execution of rule by decree. With the judiciary perpetually weak and pathetic, the Public Prosecutions Administration (PPA) itself remains a pawn, if effective, to the governing regime. The continuing dominance of the executive is most clear in the arbitrary manner in which the Kim Young Sam administration has carried out top-down reforms such as the anticorruption campaign and the introduction of the real-name financial transaction system in 1993.

The chief executive and his staff have stood above the society throughout the nation's history. The president, much like the traditional king, has looked upon the people as more subjects than citizens. Commerce was successfully stifled during the Yi dynasty, in contrast to Tokugawa Japan, and until recently, there was no tradition of autonomous, voluntarily organized associations in the society. Without the existence of viable *pouvoirs intermediaires* between the president and the people, his exercise of practically unlimited power was often justified on the plebiscitarian principle. In the most immediate sense, plebiscitarianism in Korea has meant the use of referendum as a means to obtain a popular mandate on important public issues like constitutional revisions.

Regional and Local Government

The Republic of Korea is divided into nine provinces and four province-level special cities, Seoul, Pusan, Taegu, and Inchon. The four special cities and other large cities are divided into wards and precincts, while the provinces are divided into cities and counties. Counties are divided into towns, townships, and villages.

The local elections of June 27, 1995, marked the real beginning of a new era of local autonomy in South Korea. (Limited local elections had already taken place in 1991 for the election of members of legislative assemblies and councils of local and provincial governments.) For the first time since 1961, the country's citizens were allowed to elect provincial governors, mayors of big cities, and heads of wards, counties, and towns.

The 1995 election results dealt a major blow to President Kim Young Sam and his Democratic Liberal Party. The ruling DLP won only 5 out of 15 "large-area" leadership races (3 governorships in Kyonggi and the two Kyongsang provinces, and 2 mayorships in Pusan and Inchon) and 2 out of 25 ward headships in Seoul. In December 1995, the DLP changed its name to the New Korea Party (NKP).

THE PARTY SYSTEM

Origins of the Parties

Political parties first appeared in South Korea at the end of the Second World War. The decade of the 1950s was marked by the struggle between the Liberal Party, which Syngman Rhee established in 1951, and the Democratic Party, which originally supported Rhee but opposed his altering of the constitution to establish a strong presidency. The short-lived Second Republic saw the Democratic Party in power, but much weakened by factional infighting. Between 1963 and 1972, the first decade of Park Chung Hee's presidency, the dominant group was the government-sponsored Democratic Republican Party (DRP). During this period, relatively fair and open competition existed between the DRP and the opposition New Democratic Party (NDP). The establishment of the *yushin* system in 1972, however, undercut party politics. The president was now selected by the National Conference for Unification, whose members could not be affiliated with political parties, and the powers of the National Assembly were curtailed. The DRP itself became, in a sense, superfluous, and a battery of emergency regulations put a tight lid on the activities of opposition groups.

The unsettled period between the assassination of Park in October 1979 and Chun Doo Hwan's complete control of state powers in May 1980 saw increased activities by political parties, particularly the NDP, although at this time it was split into rival factions led by Kim Young Sam and Kim Dae Jung. On May 17, 1980, however, Chun Doo Hwan's military extended martial law to the entire nation, dissolved the National Assembly, prohibited all political activities and assembly, imposed tight censorship on press and media, closed universities, made labor strikes illegal, and banned rumors, slanders, or defamation of the government. Chun's harsh political repression continued unabated until 1984.

THE PARTIES IN LAW

Under the Political Party Act as amended on December 27, 1993, a group of 20 or more initiators who are not teachers, public officials, or other persons with the status of public officials can legally start the process of founding a political party. But any political party must have district parties that number one-tenth or more of the total regional election districts for the National Assembly members, which means 26 or more branch chapters. Moreover, any party's registration can be revoked if it does not obtain seats in the general election for the National Assembly members and does not get more than two-hundredths of the total effective votes.

To register as candidates for the election of the National Assembly members, party nominees need nomination letters and a deposit of 10 million won. In addition to the deposit money, independent candidates are required to submit recommendations from 300 to 500 voters.

Despite the Fourth Amendment made to the Political Funds Act on March 16, 1994, the campaign contributions act remains far from perfect. Among other things, virtually all major campaign funds continue to flow to candidates by way of political parties. It is so in part because the law prohibits individuals' direct contributions or "independent" expenditures to affect electoral outcomes, while it does not regulate political parties' expenditures "on behalf of" candidates. Given the lack of regulation on campaign financing information disclosure, the fact that the law imposes no limitations on "party fees" permits the possibility of a small number of big sponsors dominating the party.

The Election for Public Office and Election Malpractice Prevention Act of March 16, 1994, meticulously and strictly regulates the manner in which the elections take place through the Central Election Management Committee. For instance, the law stipulates that the period of the presidential, National Assembly, and local elections be 23 days, 17 days, and 14 days, respectively.

Opposition parties, centering around the New Democratic Party during President Park's rule and its successors created by many of the same leaders following President Chun's political softening in 1984, tended to focus narrowly on political issues like democratization and the constitutional revision. They hardly criticized the government's modernization strategy. Partly because of the experiences of the Korean War and the existence of real and perceived threats from the Communist North, the nation's ideological spectrum had to be narrow, and the opposition parties turned out to be quite conservative on economic issues.

As demonstrated by the 1992 presidential election results, regionalism continued to be the most important factor in voter preference. It was the *yushin* regime that exacerbated the problem of regionalism in South Korean politics by intensifying the socioeconomic cleavages in an effort to bolster the sagging political support base during the 1970s. As a consequence, industrial development took place in an extremely uneven fashion across provinces. By the end of 1985, for example, over 50% of business firms were concentrated in Seoul, and almost 30% of the total in the two Kyongsang provinces, leaving out the Cholla provinces in particular. (Ever since Park Chung Hee's coup in 1961, all the presidents and their close subordinates have come from the Yongnam region, or North and South Kyongsang provinces.)

Regionalism was, once again, decisive in the 1996 National Assembly elections. For instance, the New Korea Party, President Kim Young Sam's party, won all 21 seats contested in Pusan, which is near Kim's hometown; the ruling NKP also picked up 17 out of 23 seats in the president's native province of South Kyongsang. In contrast, the National Council for New Politics, Cholla province–based Kim Dae Jung's party, captured 36 out of 37 seats in Kwangju and the two Cholla provinces. Further, Kim Jong Pil's United Liberal Democrats won 17 out of 21 seats in his native region, the two Ch'ungch'ong provinces.

GRAND NATIONAL PARTY
(Hannara Dang; HD)

Grand National Party is a coalition of the old New Korea Party and the Democratic Party. It is the main opposition party. It was previously known as the New Korea Party.

On January 23, 1990, in order to break from the problem of a "ruling minority and opposition majority" (*yoso yadae*), President Roh Tae Woo merged his ruling Democratic Justice Party with two opposition parties, Kim Young Sam's Reunification and Democracy Party (RDP) and Kim Jong Pil's New Democratic Republican Party (NDRP), into a grand conservative alliance to create the Democratic Liberal Party. The creation of DLP in the image of Japan's Liberal Democratic Party was not well received by the public. However, by taking the chance to merge his party with the ruling DJP, Kim Young Sam, who had perpetually been in the opposition, subsequently won the governing DLP's nomination for the presidency in 1992. After suffering a big loss in the local elections in 1995, President Kim renamed the party the New Korea Party.

During the 1997 presidential campaign, the contender Lee Hoi Chang changed the New Korea Party's name to Grand National Party. This was seen as Lee Hoi Chang's attempt to remake the party in his own image, since he was in the middle of an unsuccessful campaign and the then President Kim had been only lukewarm about supporting his candidacy.

Although figures on party membership are not readily available, both the 1992 presidential election and the 1996 National Assembly election showed that popular support for the party was generally more balanced throughout the nation than for the opposition parties. Because of the government's pro–Kyongsang province development policies that have been in effect since Park Chung Hee seized power in 1961, political support for the ruling party in the two Kyongsang provinces remains pronounced. The rural areas have also been traditionally a progovernment political support base.

Financial support for the parties comes largely from the big business conglomerates known as *chaebol*, which dominate Korea's economy. During the presidential election in December 1992, for example, the Central Election Management Committee (CEMC) set the ceiling for each candidate's total expenditures at US$45 million. The reported total expenditures of the three major candidates were US$20–25 million each. However, some in the *chae-*

bol sector informally estimate that the governing party's total presidential election campaign expenditures in 1992 could range from 500 billion to 1 trillion *won* and that Kim Dae Jung's party's would be one-quarter or one-fifth of that. Although details on the sources of those funds remain unavailable, it is a well-known secret that the *chaebol* provided the bulk of the campaign money.

NATIONAL COUNCIL FOR NEW POLITICS (NCNP)
(Sae Jungchi Kukmin Hoiee; SJKH)

If South Korea's politics is still fundamentally characterized not by the rule of law but by the rule of men, the history of the nation's political parties has not been an exception. The National Council for New Politics has indeed centered around one man, Kim Dae Jung. Although Kim's Democratic Party was the major opposition party in 1992, he resigned his top position and left politics after having lost the presidential election in December of that year. But the NCNP, which Kim created upon his return to politics, became the number one opposition party after the 1996 National Assembly elections. As manifested in the 1992 and 1996 election outcomes, the honam region (two Cholla provinces, including Kwangju) represents the key political support base for the opposition NCNP. The opposition party also has tended to do better in major cities than the governing party.

UNITED LIBERAL DEMOCRATS (ULD)
(Jayu Minju Yonmaeng)

Shortly before the 1995 local elections, Kim Jong Pil broke with President Kim and his Democratic Liberal Party and created the United Liberal Democrats. The ULD did surprisingly well in the 1996 National Assembly elections and thereby solidified its position as a major opposition party second only to NCNP. As the election results showed, the ULD's main political support base lay in Chungchong provinces, Kim Jong Pil's hometown (the ULD won 24 of the 28 Assembly seats up for popular voting in the Taejon and Chungchong provinces).

OTHER POLITICAL FORCES

Military

Military officers, both active and retired (often occupying powerful and lucrative civilian posts), have been the most critical power base for the ruling military regime since 1961. The dominant role of the military in the political system has been a feature that the Republic of Korea shares with many developing countries; yet in light of Korea's long history, it is something of an aberration. Traditionally, it has been civilian scholar-officials versed in the Confucian classics, rather than military officers, who have held political power. Popular disapproval of the military, particularly among students and intellectuals, grew out of the conviction that military rule per se was illegitimate, no matter what its accomplishments. Yet the ruling military circle saw itself as the only group in society with the training, discipline, and organization needed to run the state in an efficient manner. It has taken credit, with much justification, for the spectacular modernization of South Korea in the post-1961 period.

Under the Japanese, Korea had no armed forces of its own, and the United States occupation authorities had to build up a military establishment virtually from scratch. A small number of Korean officers had served in the Japanese army or had led anti-Japanese resistance forces in China. They were given training at the American-sponsored Military English Language School starting in December 1945, which the following year became the Constabulatory Officers' Candidate School. The army was established in November 1948. All male youths are required to undertake some form of military service. In 1981, South Korea had the world's sixth-largest armed forces, with some 600,000 personnel on active duty, augmented by 39,000 American troops.

Park Chung Hee studied at a Japanese military academy and served as a lieutenant in the Japanese Kwantung Army in northeast China during World War II. His demise and the takeover by Chun Doo Hwan marked the passing of a generation within the military elite. Chun, born in 1931, graduated in 1955 from the Korean Military Academy, the top school for military officers founded in 1950 on the model of West Point in the United States. Chun drew upon his fellow academy alumni for support during the months when he maneuvered himself into a position of power.

In contrast to the situation in the early 1960s, however, when South Korea lacked trained administrators and professionals and officers took over a broad range of functions, there is now a large, highly educated class of civil servants, technocrats, and managers with whom the military must cooperate in the national interest. Against such a backdrop, the process of South Korea's transition to democracy has taken place. Indeed, the election of Kim Young Sam, the first civilian president since 1961, and his successful purge of politicized military officers, who centered around the Chun Doo Hwan–controlled secret military society *Hanahoe* (literally, One Society) seem to signal the end of the prolonged military dominance of South Korean politics.

United States

The Republic of Korea's most important foreign relations have been with the United States. The United States has supported South Korea militarily and economically since before the outbreak of the Korean War, and a continued U.S. commitment to the peninsula has been seen both in Washington and in Seoul as essential to the country's security. During the administration of President Jimmy Carter, there was talk of a phased withdrawal of ground troops, the most visible sign of American commitment. But when intelligence reports in 1978 and 1979 revealed that North Korea had greater military strength than was previously estimated, this idea was dropped. Although the Reagan Administration's support of Korea's new military regime under the leadership of Chun Doo Hwan aroused significant anti-American feelings, especially among intellectuals and militant students during the 1980s, the continued presence of American troops undoubtedly has played an important role in keeping peace and stability intact. In the post–cold war era, the United States has reaffirmed its security commitments to South Korea as well as to Japan by deciding to maintain its present troop levels in the country. Although the United States policy toward North Korea has shifted from that of containment to positive engagement in light of North Korea's nuclear diplomacy and the resultant process of prolonged negotiations between Washington and P'yongyang, the United States remains the closest ally to South Korea.

Japan

The specter of 35 years of Japan's colonial rule over Korea still haunts the relations between Japan and South Korea. The years since 1965 have seen close cooperation between the two neighboring countries, particularly in the economic sphere. However, the rise of Japan's military capability and the gradual increase of its willingness to use its forces overseas in the post–cold war era cause concern to South Korea as well as to China. It is all the more the case given Japan's lack of reflection on its past militarism and such unresolved historical issues as Japan's textbooks and comfort women. There is no doubt that Japan remains South Korea's most important ally and partner, second only to the United States. But Japan's position on Korean unification seems to remain ambiguous, as it does not wish to see a unified, strong Korea.

China

While maintaining its traditional relations of comradeship with North Korea, China has been rapidly deepening its economic relations with South Korea, particularly since the establishment of diplomatic ties in 1992. The trade volume between the two countries reached about $20 billion by 1996, and one-quarter of South Korea's direct foreign investment went to China. China seems to seek closer links with prosperous South Korea because both nations fear the possibility of the rise of a Japan-

centered order in East Asia. Concerning the Korean unification issue, China clearly does not want to see the collapse of the North Korean regime and the consequent instability and trouble on its border, but it may not want to see Korea united soon either.

NATIONAL PROSPECTS

The Republic of Korea has come a long way in modernizing the country. Ever since its initial, if belated, efforts at modernization or Westernization were hijacked by Japan, the nation has suffered many traumatic experiences, including Japan's colonial rule, which systematically tried to degrade and destroy the Korean identity; the Korean War, which caused excruciating societal pain, dislocation, and turmoil; and the wrenching process of condensed, if desperate, economic development. To South Korea, which has found its own path to modernization and present prosperity and thereby regained some of its national confidence, the two issues that seem to be most critical and challenging are Korean identity and national reunification.

In the midst of growing globalization pressures that appear to drive the convergence of diverse political economies, Korea finds itself undergoing a crucial historical moment when it can and must make strategic, if *state-led*, choices on how to continue to modernize the country. The increasing influences that the American or neoclassical model exerts on policymakers are evident everywhere. Especially in light of the extraordinary performance of the U.S. economy in the 1990s, the American model of gaining productivity and competitiveness by deregulation and freer market competition appears tough to resist. It looks as if the market-rational American way is once again proving itself to be superior to both the democratic corporatist variant of German capitalism and the "plan-rational" Japanese political economy. It seems that Korea's future success depends on how well the state can accomplish the paradoxical task of executing the neoclassical vision of freeing the market mechanism. But the questions remain: Which social path do South Koreans want to pursue? What do they as people value most? The virtual collapse of the economy in 1997 makes answering these questions even more important.

The reunification problem is likely to pose the same question in a different way. Without orchestrating the cooperation from the United States, China, and to a lesser extent Japan, Korea's reunification may not take place. But the post–cold war international environment and South Korea's rising national strength have been enhancing South Korea's position in its relations with the great powers. In the end, reunification may well be a matter of time, given the nation's long history as a unified country and the people's strong desire for reunification. But what kind of country will unified Korea be? For instance, South Korea has as yet not solved the problem of regionalism and the relative deprivation that the honam region has experienced. How can North Koreans be sure that their fate would be any better if a national malintegration, Italian-style, transpires.

Further Reading

Amsden, Alice H. *Asia's Next Giant: South Korea and Late Industrialization.* Oxford: Oxford University Press, 1989.

Clifford, Mark L. *Troubled Tiger: Businessmen, Bureaucrats, and Generals in South Korea.* Armonk, N.Y.: M.E. Sharpe, 1994.

Eckert, Carter J., et al. *Korea Old and New: A History.* Seoul: Ilchokak, 1990.

The Economist. "Survey: South Korea." *The Economist,* June 3, 1995

The Economist Intelligence Unit Limited. *South Korea: EIU Country Profile, 1996–97.*

Henderson, Gregory. *Korea: The Politics of Vortex.* Cambridge, Mass.: Harvard University Press, 1968.

Koh, B.C. "South Korea in 1995." *Asian Survey* 36, no. 1 (January 1996).

———. "South Korea in 1996." *Asian Survey* 37, no. 1 (January 1997).

Lee, Hong Yung. "South Korea in 1992." *Asian Survey* 33, no. 1 (January 1993).

News Review, April 13, 1996, 6–8.

KUWAIT

(Dawlat Al-Kuwayt)

By Jill Crystal, M.A.
Revised by Ghassan Salame, Ph.D.
Revised by Curtis R. Ryan, Ph.D.

THE SYSTEM OF GOVERNMENT

Kuwait, a nation of nearly 2 million people at the northwest end of the Persian Gulf, is a semiconstitutional monarchy governed by an emir from the Sabah family who rules in conjunction with senior family members through an appointed Council of Ministers. Kuwait first emerged as a semiautonomous political unit in the early 18th century when it was settled by the Bani Utub branch of the Arabian Anazah confederation. The ascendancy of the Sabah family dates from about 1756, when the leading families appointed a Sabah sheikh to represent them in dealings with the Ottoman Empire. In the 19th century, Kuwaiti rulers, caught on the fringes of empires and fearing Ottoman, Persian, and Wahhabi incursions, acquiesced to the growing British influence in the Gulf region. In 1899, Sheikh Mubarak (founder of the current ruling line) negotiated a treaty with Great Britain that secured Kuwait's independence from the Ottomans in exchange for British control over its foreign relations. The association with Great Britain, which continued until independence in 1961, consolidated the Sabah family's control over domestic politics.

The Kuwaiti constitution was promulgated on November 11, 1962. In international politics, Kuwait's existence as an independent state remained tenuous. Its current borders were established at the 1922 Uqair Conference attended by Britain, Iraq, and Saudi Arabia. Kuwait remains threatened by its neighbors, however, particularly by Iraq, which laid claim to the sheikhdom's territory in a 1961 proclamation. That claim has been revived on many occasions and resulted, ultimately, in the August 2, 1990, Iraqi invasion and conquest of Kuwait. Following months of regional and international tension, the emirate was liberated by a U.S.-led coalition in the 1991 Gulf War.

Kuwait, originally a pearling and trading economy, became increasingly dependent on oil after World War II. In 1936 Sheikh Ahmad had granted a concession to the Kuwait Oil Company (jointly owned by British Petroleum and Gulf Oil). In 1973 Kuwait acquired a 25% share in the company and took over full ownership in 1976. Production rose to 1.076 billion barrels a year by 1972 but fell to 607 million barrels in 1980 in line with the state's conservationist policy following the 1973 price increases. Kuwait's current reserves are among the highest in the world and, at current production levels, will last for over a century. The consequences of a transformation to an oil-based economy were to give Kuwait one of the highest per capita incomes in the world (almost $20,000) and to increase its dependence on foreign trade and foreign laborers (who now constitute more than half the population). The large revenues, paid directly to the rulers, freed the Sabahs from much of their historical dependence on merchant allies and financed a large bureaucracy to administer new welfare and development projects and to redistribute wealth through state employment.

Executive

In accordance with the 1962 constitution, Kuwait's chief executive, the emir, is chosen from male descendants of Sheikh Mubarak. Since 1915, All but one of Kuwait's emirs have been chosen alternately from the Salim and Jabir branches of the Sabah family. The actual selection is made privately by senior family members. In this manner, Kuwait's present emir, Sheikh Jabir al-Ahmad al-Sabah (born 1928 in the Jabir line) was named heir apparent and crown prince in 1966. He acceded to power peacefully in December 1977 on the death of the emir Sheikh Sabah al-Salim al-Sabah (of the Salim line). The present crown prince (a Salim), appointed February 1978, is Sheikh Jabir's second cousin, Prime Minister Sa'ad Abdullah al-Salim al-Sabah.

The emir has very broad powers but governs within the informal constraints set by family consensus. Intrafamily disagreements are managed and family control assured by the direct recruitment of family members into the highest and most sensitive administrative posts. In the Council of Ministers appointed following the 1996 elections, 7 of the 16 ministers were Sabahs. Besides Prime Minister Sa'ad, these included the emir's brother Sheikh Sabah al-Ahmad al-Jabir al-Sabah (deputy prime minister and minister of foreign affairs) and Crown Prince Sa'ad's cousin Sheikh Salim al-Sabah al-Salim al-Sabah (minister of defense).

Legislature

Kuwait's National Assembly (*Majlis al-Umma*) was first elected in 1963. Subsequent elections were held in 1967, 1971, and 1975. In August 1976, the Assembly was dissolved and several articles of the constitution suspended by decree of the emir. The Assembly's functions were assumed by six appointed legislative committees under the Council of Ministers.

Several factors led to the suspension of the National Assembly in 1976. The Assembly had grown popular as a forum for public opinion and criticism of government policies. Debates over oil company agreements and production levels and over social policy (especially housing) sometimes included verbal attacks on members of the Sabah family. The government had become concerned about internal security problems precipitated by terrorist activity and the rise of a leftist opposition. The Assembly had also become an effective forum for Middle Eastern issues, of particular importance to the country's non-Kuwaiti majority, who at the time included 300,000 resident Palestinians. Just prior to its dissolution, the Assembly adopted pro-Palestinian resolutions condemning Syrian involvement in the Lebanese civil war, in opposition to the government's officially neutral position. The dissolution of the Assembly was accompanied by press curbs, the introduction of new censorship rules, the arrest of several leftists, and the dissolution or suspension of several newspapers, social clubs, and professional and trade unions.

In February 1981, new elections were held and the Assembly reconvened with new guidelines. The Assembly consists of 50 seats, 2 in each of 25 constituencies. Election is by simple plurality for four-year terms. The majority of seats were filled, as in previous elections, by conservative government loyalists and members of traditionally allied families. Within this group, some observers saw a shift in predominance from the established commercial elite toward tribal bedouin leaders (who took 23 of the 50 seats), toward younger technocrats (who took 13 seats), and toward Sunni Muslim "fundamentalists" (5 seats). The election was viewed as a defeat for more radical Arab nationalists who, under the leadership of Dr. Ahmad al-Khatib of the Arab Nationalist Movement, had held a third of the seats in the 1976 Assembly but won no seats in the 1981 election. It was also a defeat for the Shi'a Muslims, who ran several candidates but won only 4 seats.

This realignment was partly attributable to a redistricting that affected many previously radical and Shi'a areas. New elections were held on February 20, 1985. The results showed a reemergence of the secular Arab nationalist movement led by Dr. Ahmad al-Khatib (5 seats) and some erosion of the Islamic fundamentalist group, two of whose leaders were defeated.

Following the liberation of the emirate from Iraqi occupation, new Assembly elections were held in 1992 in which most of the new representatives were opponents—or at least critics—of the regime. This Assembly, and its successors, included a strong Islamist influence that has been demonstrated in a number of pieces of legislation. In 1994, 39 of the 50 delegates backed a request from the Assembly to the government to make the Shari'ah the only legal system in the emirate. This was promptly rejected by the government. But in 1996, an Islamist-sponsored proposal to introduce gender segregation in colleges and universities was passed in the National Assembly. The post–Gulf War Assemblies, in short, have given voice at least to male critics of the regime; but by 1997, women still could not vote or run for political office in Kuwait.

Judiciary

Kuwait's judicial system, as reorganized in 1980, has three levels. The highest court is the Supreme Court of Appeals, although the emir can act as a de facto final appeals court. There is the national Court of First Instance and summary courts in each administrative district. The legal code is drawn primarily from the Egyptian and Ottoman codes, with the constitutional stipulation that legislation not conflict with the Shari'ah (Islamic law). "Acts of Government" are outside the jurisdiction of the courts.

Regional and Local Government

Kuwait's administration is highly centralized. However, Kuwait City, Ahmadi, Jahra, and Hawalli are, administratively, provincial governates, with governors and municipal councils appointed by the emir. Smaller administrative divisions are the same as electoral constituencies.

THE ELECTORAL SYSTEM

Suffrage is restricted to adult (age 21), literate, male Kuwaiti citizens. Citizens are defined as persons whose families lived in Kuwait before 1921. Members of the police and armed forces cannot vote, nor can foreigners, some 60% of the population. In January 1982, the Assembly defeated a bill to enfranchise women. A popular women's suffrage movement was very active (and as fruitless) in the weeks preceding the 1985 elections and each of the elections in the 1990s. The electorate thus comprises less than 10% of Kuwait's total population. Of this group, less then half are registered to vote. But despite the legal prohibitions denying women the vote, the suffrage movement appeared to be gaining strength and momentum in the late 1990s.

Candidates run on individual platforms, since political parties are illegal. In the 1990s, however, despite the continuing ban on political parties, a number of political "tendencies" did emerge. These political tendencies, if not political parties, include two predominantly Sunni Muslim groupings: the Islamic Constitutional Movement and the Islamic Popular Group. The former is the more moderate of the two and may have ties to the Muslim Brotherhood in various Arab countries. Both the Islamic Constitutional Movement and the Islamic Popular Group have had some success in the 1992 and 1996 elections, and both have been represented in the Kuwaiti Council of Ministers. Other political tendencies include the Kuwaiti Democratic Forum, a secular liberal grouping pressing for an end to corruption and royal nepotism in political life, and the Islamic National Alliance, which is the main group organizing Kuwait's Shi'a Muslims.

Ruling-Family, Tribal, and Merchant Leaders

Kuwait has had more success than neighboring Gulf sheikhdoms in settling intrafamily disputes peaceably. Since the time of Mubarak, succession has been confined, relatively smoothly, to the Jabir and Salim lines. Personal ambitions within the family, loosely associated with either traditionalist or more modern points of view, are the primary sources of dispute.

Tribal and merchant families, whose input into the decision-making process has declined since the development of an oil economy, have not presented an overt challenge to the regime. Nonetheless, these somewhat overlapping groups may offer the greatest potential threat to regime stability. They have been mollified, economically, by the business opportunities associated with increased oil revenues. Politically, they have been partially co-opted into the state through the Assembly and ministerial posts. Still, their autonomous corporate existence, their own media, notably *Al-Qabas*, a daily newspaper, and historical claim to political participation could provide the basis for a loyal or disloyal opposition, especially in the new era of shrinking oil revenues. This became especially clear following the withdrawal of Iraqi forces from Kuwait in 1991. Kuwait's mercantile and technocratic elites in particular pushed for democratization in the emirate, many contesting the elections of the reconstituted National Assembly in 1992. In that first post–Gulf War election, critics of the regime took a majority of the new Assembly's seats.

OTHER POLITICAL FORCES

Military

The military is subject to firm, and personal, Sabah control. Disturbances have been reported in recent years within the police force and at the infantry school. There is some potential for a disenchanted prince within the military establishment to use his position in alliance with other groups to create opposition for the regime.

Shi'a Muslims

Estimates of the number of Shi'a in Kuwait vary. Some 10% of the total population may be Shi'a, while the number of Kuwaiti nationals who are Shi'a may be as high as 20%. Most of these latter are probably Persian in origin. While a small portion of the Shi'a community is influentially placed in commerce, the community's impact on policy has been slight and appeared to be diminishing as the power of Shi'a Iran grew throughout the 1980s and 1990s.

Nonnationals

The citizens of Kuwait remain a minority in the emirate, constituting at the most 45% of the population. That may be an overly generous statistic, however, as some observers have suggested that the Kuwait population in the latter 1990s included 1.3 million nonnationals out of a total population of nearly 2 million. Palestinians and Indians have historically formed the two largest groups of nonnationals. Crucial to the economy, these nonnationals, some now of several generations' standing, have few political rights and little chance of acquiring them through citizenship. They cannot organize independent trade unions; they cannot own property, stock in Kuwaiti businesses, or companies without a Kuwaiti partner. They enjoy only limited access to the benefits of the welfare state.

Nonnationals, however, have so far provided only sporadic opposition to the regime. Their capacity to organize is minimized by internal cleavages (language, culture, and occupation), fear of deportation, and self-interest in keeping lucrative if insecure jobs. Their long-term threat to the regime lies, first, in their potential nuisance value in alliance with other disaffected groups, and, second, in their contacts abroad. The Kuwaiti border with Iraq is difficult to close effectively against the movement of people, money, weapons, and ideas. Activities of the Palestine Liberation Organization, while financially supported by Kuwait outside its borders, have long worried the Kuwaiti regime, given the large Palestinian population in the emirate up until the 1991 Gulf War.

Kuwait's rulers are well aware of the trade-offs involved in having such a large nonnational population. In the months surrounding the constitutional crisis of 1976, the government deported thousands of foreign (primarily Arab) workers. New deportations (mainly Iranian this time) took place in 1985. At the same time, the government made some social services available to foreigners and opened a few loopholes for acquiring Kuwaiti citizenship.

The 1991 Gulf War, however, changed the situation for Palestinians in particular. Following Iraq's defeat and withdrawal, groups of Kuwaiti vigilante groups executed an unknown number of people accused of collaborating with Iraq, and many of those accused and executed were Palestinians. Upon reassuming power in Kuwait, the restored Sabah regime took vengeance on the Arab regimes and organizations it viewed as supportive of Iraq, such as Jordan, Yemen, and the PLO. Kuwait promptly expelled tens of thousands of Jordanian, Palestinian, and Yemeni guest workers (whose positions were largely filled by workers from other Arab states and from South Asia).

NATIONAL PROSPECTS

Thus far, Kuwait has maintained a high degree of political stability through a combination of cautious leadership, a cohesive ruling coalition, government largesse, and alliances with powerful external states—such as Britain and the United States. Domestically, merchant and tribal allies of the regime have profited from business ventures, while the bulk of the Kuwaiti population has benefited from the massive distribution of oil wealth in the form of direct transfer payments, guaranteed state employment (the state is Kuwait's largest employer), and free or subsidized housing, health care, and education. As extensive social services have become the norm, however, they may be seen less as examples of the rulers' largesse and more as rights that the individual, as a citizen, can claim from the state.

Kuwait's leaders also face possible trouble from the internalization of external threats. Iraqi claims to Kuwait and its oil had been a recurrent problem even before the 1990 invasion and could easily be revived by Saddam Hussein or any successor regime in Baghdad. The Arab-Israeli conflict, which insinuated itself into local politics most notably in the 1976 Assembly suspension, continues to be monitored closely by Palestinians and other Arabs. After the Iranian revolution and subsequent Iran-Iraq War (1980–88), Kuwait also had to contend with growing Shi'a unrest (manifested in demonstrations and bombing incidents) and with security problems associated directly with the war itself. Iran bombed Kuwaiti refineries and tankers several times during the war, as a warning against aid to Iraq.

This sensitivity to the regional political environment, coupled with potential internal threats, became much more evident after 1983. On December 12, 1983, a truck bomb exploded in the vicinity of the American Embassy and other bombs exploded at five other sites. Attempts against the life of the editors of two Kuwaiti newspapers (*Al-Anba* and *As-Siyassa*) followed, as did the assassination of an Iraqi diplomat. On May 25, 1985, the emir escaped an attack on his motorcade in which at least 4 people were killed. Six weeks later, bombs were planted in two popular cafés, killing 10 people and injuring 56.

Kuwaiti courts and government officials accused pro-Iranian Shi'a militants of having perpetrated these acts. Iran systematically denied any involvement, but Kuwait deported thousands of Iranians and Lebanese and Iraqi Shi'a from the Emirate.

These internal security concerns of the 1970s and 1980s, however, paled in comparison with the external security threat demonstrated in Iraq's invasion of Kuwait in 1990. But even after the U.S.-led coalition defeated and expelled Iraq from Kuwait, both domestic and regional security tensions remained very real for the Sabah regime. The Sabahs attempted to rectify any resurgent external threats by completing a string of alliances with major world powers—including military defense commitments from the United States, United Kingdom, France, and Russia and an agreement on military cooperation with the Peoples' Republic of China. In short, Kuwait had established military linkages to all five permanent members of the UN Security Council. In addition, since 1981, Kuwait has been a member of the Gulf Cooperation Council along with Bahrain, Oman, Qatar, Saudi Arabia, and the United Arab Emirates.

On the domestic front, the key issues appear to be conservative pressures from Islamist members of the National Assembly, on the one hand, and liberalizing pressures from groups supporting women's suffrage and political rights, on the other. A third key issue continues to be the conflict between reformers seeking to clean up public life and resisting members of the "old guard" of Kuwaiti politics. A June 1997 assassination attempt on Abdullah al-Naybari, a leading reformer in the National Assembly, served to underscore this line of tension. Naybari had led the first post–Gulf War investigations into charges of corruption and embezzlement within the government. Several Kuwaitis and Iranians were arrested for the attack, but many Kuwaiti democracy advocates took the attack to mean that the continuing investigations were coming too close to powerful government figures.

Thus Kuwait has had no shortage of domestic political troubles to focus on, while in regional affairs, tensions with Iraq flared repeatedly throughout the 1990s and the regime continued to regard warily the growing power of Iran. Kuwait's small size, vulnerable strategic location, and dependence on foreign labor all render it particularly susceptible to domestic unrest and especially to external disputes in the Persian Gulf region.

Further Reading

Al-Ebraheem, Hassan Ali. *Kuwait and the Gulf: Small States and the International System*. London: Croom Helm, 1984.

Crystal, Jill. *Oil and Politics in the Gulf: Rulers and Merchants in Kuwait and Qatar*, 2d ed. New York: Cambridge University Press, 1995.

Ismael, Jacqueline. *Kuwait: Social Change in Historical*

Perspective. Syracuse, N.Y.: Syracuse University Press, 1982.

Lesch, Ann M. "Palestinians in Kuwait." *Journal of Palestine Studies* 20, no. 4 (summer 1991).

Tetreault, Mary Ann. "Autonomy, Necessity, and the Small State: Ruling Kuwait in the Twentieth Century."

International Organization 45, no. 4 (autumn 1991).

———. "Civil Society in Kuwait: Protected Spaces and Women's Rights." *Middle East Journal* 47, no. 2 (spring 1993).

Winstone, Harry, and Zahra Freeth. *Kuwait: Prospect and Reality*. New York: Crane, Russak, 1972.

THE KYRGYZ REPUBLIC

(Kyrgyzstan)

By Eugene Huskey, Ph.D.

THE SYSTEM OF GOVERNMENT

Kyrgyzstan is a small, mountainous country in Central Asia. Bordered by China on the east, Uzbekistan on the west, Kazakstan on the north, and Tajikistan on the south, Kyrgyzstan has a population of 4.5 million persons (1993) living in a territory roughly the size of England.

The country takes its name from the indigenous ethnic group, the Kyrgyz, who account for almost 60% of the population. Historically a nomadic people, the Kyrgyz belong ethnically and linguistically to the Turkic world, whose members populate territories stretching from Manchuria and Siberia in the east to Bulgaria and Turkey in the west. Islam is the dominant religion among the Kyrgyz, though its influence is far more evident in the south than in the north of the country. Among the other ethnic groups in Kyrgyzstan are several indigenous Central Asian peoples, such as the Uzbeks (14%), as well as numerous European settlers, including Russians (18%), Ukrainians (2%), and Germans (1%). The European groups migrated to the region during the past century while the country was under Russian and later Soviet rule. Whatever their ethnic background, citizens of the country are known as Kyrgyzstanis.

One of the 15 former republics of the USSR, Kyrgyzstan claimed state sovereignty in August 1991, though complete independence arrived only with the final collapse of the Soviet Union in December 1991. Unlike several other Soviet republics, Kyrgyzstan had never experienced statehood before. Indeed, it acquired the status of a territory in the Soviet Union only in 1936. Although the Kyrgyz trace their roots as a people to the 1,000-year-old legendary figure of Manas, Kyrgyzstan's statehood is an unintended by-product of the Soviet colonial era.

In the transition from Communist rule, the political leadership of Kyrgyzstan has sought to establish a new identity for the country by abandoning the Soviet political inheritance and lessening Russian cultural influence. The indigenization of cultural policy, for example, led to the replacement of Russian place names with Kyrgyz counterparts. The country's name changed from Kirgizia (sometimes spelled Khirgizia) to Kyrgyzstan. The main street in the capital of Bishkek (formerly Frunze), which previously bore the name of the Soviet secret police chief, Dzerzhinsky, became Erkindik (Freedom) Prospect. To revive the Kyrgyz language, which had gone into decline in the Soviet era, the parliament of Kyrgyzstan passed a language law that favored Kyrgyz at the expense of Russian. These and other measures prompted such a large exodus of highly trained Russians and other Europeans that the president of Kyrgyzstan scaled back the indigenization campaign in 1994 to stem the tide.

Kyrgyzstan has moved quickly and surely since 1991 to replace Communist rule with a republican form of government. Like France and Russia, Kyrgyzstan has adopted semipresidential institutional arrangements, which divide executive authority between a directly elected president and an appointed prime minister who requires the confidence of the parliament. Thus, where the president is the head of state, the prime minister is the head of the government.

Executive

The Kyrgyzstan constitution of 1993, the first in the independence era, grants the president broad powers over the shaping and execution of domestic and foreign policy. He has the authority to appoint—with the consent of parliament—the leading figures in the Government and the judiciary, he may declare war or introduce a state of emergency, he has the right to submit issues to popular referendum, and he enjoys wide decree-making powers. After a referendum expressing a lack of popular confidence in the parliament, the president may dissolve the legislature and call new elections.

The president maintains a staff of approximately 100 officials to assist him in overseeing the work of the prime minister and his Government (Council of Ministers) and the regional authorities beneath them. In 1997, the Government was composed of 27 members besides the prime minister, among them several vice premiers, the chief procurator, the head of the State Property Fund, and 21 ministers. More than 17,000 civil servants work in the country's ministries and local administrations.

Like de Gaulle at the beginning of the Fifth French Republic, the first president of Kyrgyzstan, Askar Akaev, has helped to define the office of the presidency. A Kyrgyz physicist and computer specialist who spent his early adult life in Leningrad, Akaev has made the presidency the institutional engine of economic and political reform in Kyrgyzstan. At the same time, he has championed the politics of inclusion, serving as a mediator among various political, ethnic, and regional interests. As a result, in terms of its political power, the presidency now towers above the Government, parliament, and judiciary. At the national level, at least, there are no effective intragovernmental checks on presidential power in Kyrgyzstan.

Legislature

Based on provisions of the 1993 constitution and the October 1994 referendum, Kyrgyzstan replaced a 350-person legislature inherited from the Soviet era with a smaller bicameral parliament, known as the *Jogorku Kenesh*, in 1995. The lower house, the Legislative Assembly, has 35 deputies who are full-time lawmakers, while the 70 members of the upper house, the Chamber of People's Representatives, meet only a few times a year. The two houses have yet to establish a clear division of labor. In general, lawmaking responsibilities fall to the Legislative Assembly while the Chamber of People's Representatives confirms executive appointments. Because of the weak role of political parties in the parliament, considerable authority is vested in the Speaker, or *Toraga*. In the mid-1990s, the Speaker, Medetkan Sherimkulov, was instrumental in limiting tensions between the reformist president and the generally conservative parliament. A popular referendum passed in October 1998 promised to redefine relations between the two chambers and to alter their size.

Judiciary

Kyrgyzstan inherited from the Soviet era a variant of the Continental civil law system. Although president and parliament have remade the country's legislation in recent years through the issuance of new laws and decrees, they have left virtually intact the structure of legal institutions. Criminal proceedings as well as civil disputes between individuals are heard in courts of general jurisdiction, which operate at every administrative level, from the district and city courts at the bottom of the judicial hierarchy to the Supreme Court at the top. Economic disputes between enterprises or other juridical persons are heard in special *arbitrazh* courts, which exist at the regional and national levels.

Conflicts between branches or levels of government are matters for the new Constitutional Court in Bishkek, which has thus far been reluctant to challenge powerful political interests. There are also courts of elders (*aksakal*), designed to revive traditional Kyrgyz justice in less serious cases.

All judges are nominated by the president and confirmed by the Chamber of People's Representatives, though the justices on the country's highest courts are said to be "elected" by the upper house. Constitutional Court justices serve 15-year terms, while members of the Supreme Court and Supreme *Arbitrazh* Court have 10-year terms of office. All other judges serve 7-year terms after an initial probationary term of 3 years. Higher-court judges may be removed from office for high treason and other crimes by a two-thirds vote of the parliament, based on a finding of wrongdoing by the Constitutional Court. Lower-court judges enjoy no such security in office. They may be removed administratively for disreputable conduct or failing a performance evaluation or judicially on the basis of a conviction in a higher court.

Regional and Local Government

Kyrgyzstan is a unitary government divided into six regions (*oblasti*)—Osh, Jalal-Abad, Talas, Naryn, Chu, and Issyk-Kul (or Ysyk-Kol)—and the capital city of Bishkek. Each has its own governor, known as an *akim*, and a legislative assembly, or *kenesh*. Within the regions, there is an *akim* and *kenesh* in each rural district and major city as well as a *kenesh* in each village and settlement. Whereas the *kenesh* are popularly elected, an *akim* serves at the pleasure of the executive official at the next administrative level. Thus, President Akaev appoints the regional governors, and they in turn select the *akimy* in the cities and districts beneath them. Only in the case of Bishkek is the *akim* directly elected by the population, a novelty in all of Central Asia. In this executive-dominated system, the *akimy* wield almost unlimited power in their locales; the role of the *kenesh* is consultative at best.

Despite President Akaev's ability to appoint and dismiss the regional governors, he has not been able to impose a tight rein on local bureaucracies, an indication of the weakness of the state in Kyrgyzstan. With their own bases of local support as well as political allies among deputies and executive officials in Bishkek, the regional *akimy* have become key power brokers in Kyrgyzstani politics. Thus, the most effective check on presidential power comes not from the legislature or the courts but from the regional elites. Attempts by the president to restrain these "localist" tendencies by appointing political clients from outside the region as *akimy* have met with only limited success.

THE ELECTORAL SYSTEM

Members of both the Legislative Assembly and the Chamber of People's Representatives are elected every five years in single-member districts. Contests for parliamentary seats are decided by a two-round system similar to that governing presidential elections. Given the lower interest levels in some parliamentary races, especially at the second round, the 50% turnout requirement has forced "repeat elections" in numerous constituencies, which complicates the timely seating of a new parliament.

The most recent parliamentary elections in Kyrgyzstan, held in February 1995, were noteworthy on several counts. Only one-third of the deputies elected had party affiliations. Most of the newly elected legislators were linked instead to regional or business cliques. Compared with the previous parliament, the *Jogorku Kenesh* also had fewer women and ethnic minorities. The female share of the parliament declined from 8% to 5%, while the proportion of Russian deputies fell from 19% to 6%. Ethnic vote dilution was due in large part to the dramatic increase in the size of the constituencies. Rather than 350 electoral districts, many of which corresponded to areas of compact ethnic settlement, the country now had 70 districts electing members to the upper house and 35 districts returning deputies to the lower house.

The president of Kyrgyzstan is elected for a five-year term and may not hold the office for more than two terms in succession. However, in 1998 the Constitutional Court ruled—contrary to its Russian counterpart—that for electoral purposes the president's first term would not count because it commenced before the adoption of the constitution. Eligibility for the presidency is limited to Kyrgyz-speaking persons between the ages of 35 and 65 at the time of election. In addition, they must have lived in the country for not less than 15 years prior to nomination. To stand for the presidency, candidates must receive no fewer than 50,000 signatures from the electorate. If a candidate obtains an outright majority in the first round of the presidential election, he or she is declared the winner. If no candidate receives a majority, the top two vote getters proceed to the second round, where the candidate with the most votes wins. In both instances, elections are only valid if no less than half of the electorate has voted.

Direct presidential elections have taken place in Kyrgyzstan in October 1991 and December 1995. In the first election, Askar Akaev ran unopposed; in the second, he won with minimal opposition, garnering almost 72% of the vote. Prior to the 1995 contest, the president's desire to avoid the risks and unpleasantness of an election campaign led him to seek a second term a year early by popular referendum, which would have asked the electorate to vote "Yes" or "No" on extending his tenure for another five years. Facing parliamentary opposition to this unconstitutional move, Akaev accepted a compromise: he would stand in a contested election a year before the expiration of his first term. With his popularity buoyant in the fall of 1995, in part because of the national celebrations of the Manas millenium, Akaev did not wish to lose the political advantages of the moment, especially given the economic downtown that was expected the following year.

THE PARTY SYSTEM

Party development is still in its infancy in Kyrgyzstan. Of the 12 parties registered with the Ministry of Justice in 1996, most were groups of notables with little support outside the capital. Only one—the Communist Party—has a sizable membership (25,000 in 1997) as well as constituency organizations throughout the country. Led by Absamat Masaliev, the last party first secretary in the Soviet era, the Communist Party has not been able to translate its organizational advantages into parliamentary seats. Only 3 of the 105 members in the *Jogorku Kenesh* were elected on the Communist ticket. Like the Communist Party of the Russian Federation, Kyrgyzstan's Communists remain unreconstructed advocates of a command economy and collective, rather than individual, rights.

The most successful parliamentary faction is the Social-Democratic Party. Founded in December 1994, just in time to contest the 1995 parliamentary elections, the Social Democrats represent the interests of Kyrgyzstan's regional political elites and officialdom. They won 14 seats in the new parliament, far more than any of their rivals. Trailing the Social Democrats, with 4 seats each, were the "Unity of Kyrgyzstan" Party and the Party of National Renewal "Asaba" (Flag). The former, registered in June 1994, is a Westernizing party committed to "a decisive continuation of economic reform." Its leader is Amangel'dy Muraliev, appointed governor of the Osh region in 1996. Asaba, on the other hand, has championed the defense of ethnic Kyrgyz interests. Registered in the last days of the Soviet era, Asaba has pressed for the revival of Kyrgyz language and culture.

Another important political force is Erkin (Free) Kyrgyzstan, which enjoyed more success in its early days as a social movement than in its later incarnation as a party. Initially an umbrella group uniting diverse political clubs and factions, Erkin Kyrgyzstan was the first major organized opposition to the Communist Party in the waning months of Soviet rule. Now headed by a young politician, Tursunbai Bakir uulu, it is struggling to find a role for itself as a democratic party in opposition to the president. It won only 3 seats in the 1995 parliamentary elections. Although there are no explicitly Russian parties in Kyrgyzstan, the Slavic population—which is concentrated in the north of the country—has formed numerous politicocultural associations, the most important of which is *Soglasie* (Harmony).

Among the many factors retarding the development of strong national political parties is the choice of the electoral system—majoritarian rather than proportional representation—and the constitutionally mandated nonpartisanship of the president of Kyrgyzstan. Designed to inoculate the country against a revival of communism, under which the party apparatus controlled state positions, the requirement that the president "suspend his activity in political parties" for his term of office removed a natural rallying point for party formation. The only party to have sought to attach itself explicitly to the president, *Ata-Meken* (Fatherland), gained 3 seats in the 1995 elections.

NATIONAL PROSPECTS

During its first years of independence, Kyrgyzstan earned a reputation as an oasis of democracy in the authoritarian desert of inner Asia. The new state promoted a free press, private political associations, and a market economy and in so doing attracted the sympathy and financial assistance of the West. Yet the very openness and competitiveness of the new politics in Kyrgyzstan made the country difficult to govern at a time of declining economic production and increasing social stratification and ethnic tension.

In the mid-1990s, President Akaev resorted at times to authoritarian measures as a means of imposing discipline on an ever-more-fractured state and society. During the summer and fall of 1994, he closed two opposition newspapers and—in violation of the constitution—revised institutional arrangements by plebiscite and engineered the early dissolution of parliament. Although the new, and more corrupt, parliament elected in February 1995 did not contain a presidential majority, it was so divided that it presented only a weak challenge to presidential rule, which was further strengthened by the reelection of Akaev in December 1995 and the expansion of presidential powers by referendum in February 1996.

The major challenge now facing Kyrgyzstan is reviving the economy. An infusion of money and expertise from the IMF and other Western institutions has enabled Kyrgyzstan to introduce its own currency, tame inflation, and put in place part of the infrastructure of a market economy. Western mining companies have concluded agreements with Kyrgyzstan that may lead to significant export earnings from gold and other minerals in the near future. But as elsewhere in the former Soviet Union, large-scale corruption has accompanied the privatization of the economy, as business and bureaucratic interests conspire to protect their own ventures against competition. Moreover, without a renegotiation of the external loans received in the early and mid-1990s, servicing the national debt may force Kyrgyzstan to make deep, and politically dangerous, cuts in state spending on essential services such as health, education, and welfare. The question for the future is whether political democratization in Kyrgyzstan can survive the country's painful economic transition.

Further Reading

Edgeworth, Linda, William Fierman, and Chitra Tiwari. *Kyrgyzstan: Pre-Election Assessment*. Washington, D.C.: IFES, 1994.

Huskey, Eugene. "Kyrgyzstan: The Fate of Political Liberalization." In *Conflict, Cleavage, and Change in Central Asia and the Caucasus*. Ed. Karen Dawisha and Bruce Parrott. Cambridge: Cambridge University Press, 1997.

———. "Kyrgyzstan: The Politics of Demographic and Economic Frustration." In *New States, New Politics: Building the Post-Soviet Nations*. Ed. Ian Bremmer and Raymond Taras. Cambridge: Cambridge University Press, 1996.

———. "The Rise of Contested Politics in Central Asia: Elections in Kyrgyzstan, 1989–1990." *Europe-Asia Studies*, no. 5 (1995).

Imart, Guy. "Kirgizia-Kazakhstan: A Hinge or a Fault Line." *Problems of Communism*, no. 5 (1990).

Olcott, Martha. "Central Asia's Catapult to Independence." *Foreign Affairs*, no. 3 (1992): 108–30.

Pryde, Ian. "Kyrgyzstan's Slow Progress to Reform." *The World Today*, June 1995.

———. "Kyrgyzstan: The Trials of Independence." *Journal of Democracy*, no. 1 (1994).

LAO PEOPLE'S DEMOCRATIC REPUBLIC

(Sāthālanalat Paxāthipatai Paxāxon Lao)

By Martin Stuart-Fox, Ph.D.

THE SYSTEM OF GOVERNMENT

Laos, a nation of almost 4.5 million people on the Southeast Asian mainland, is a member state of the Association of Southeast Asian Nations (ASEAN). Only just over half the population are lowland ethnic Lao; the rest comprise more than 40 different mountain tribes (including upland Tai and Hmong). The present government seized power on December 2, 1975, when the forced abdication of King Savāngvatthanā brought the six-century-old Lao monarchy to an end.

Government is the monopoly of the Lao People's Revolutionary Party (LPRP), which directed the Lao Communist movement in its revolutionary struggle against both French colonial domination and the former Royal Lao regime. In this it was strongly supported by neighboring Communist North Vietnam.

Executive

The party controls all three arms of government, but under the Lao constitution, enacted in 1991, the state president wields more than just symbolic power. Elected by a two-thirds vote of the National Assembly, he or she issues decrees, appoints the prime minister, and decides on promotions in the judiciary and the military (as head of the armed forces). This position was first held by the powerful secretary-general (subsequently president) of the LPRP, Kaisôn Phomvihān. After Kaisôn's death, power was shared between the state president and the president of the party. Other powerful positions include the state vice president, the prime minister, and the president of the National Assembly.

Legislature

The National Assembly (*Saphāthaeng Xāt*) is the supreme legislative body. Elections to the 85-member Assembly take place every five years, the most recent being in December 1997. Members of government are not, however, drawn from the National Assembly; they are appointed by the prime minister. Most are members of the LPRP, though non–party members may be named in an acting capacity. The government is defined as "the administrative organization of the state" and is responsible for drafting laws, strategic development plans, and national budgets (in accordance with the policies of the party) for ratification by the National Assembly. Though some debate does take place, the National Assembly essentially provides a rubber stamp for party and government decisions. Five committees of the National Assembly oversee its work: law; economic planning and finance; social and cultural affairs and nationalities; and foreign affairs. A Standing Committee meets when the Assembly is not in session.

Judiciary

The president of the Supreme People's Court and the state prosecutor are appointed (and can be dismissed) by the National Assembly. Not until 1989, however, was a recognizable judicial system formally adopted and the Supreme People's Court separated from the Office of the State Prosecutor. Criminal and civil codes followed, and since 1993 all laws have been published in the trilingual judicial gazette (in Lao, English, and French). Thus a legal framework is painstakingly coming into being to replace the arbitrary use of state power in people's courts. Provincial and district courts function at those levels of administration, though there the new legal framework is less likely to be observed.

Regional and Local Government

From 1975 until 1991, people's councils in all 16 provinces and the municipality of Viang Chan (Vientiane) and at the district level were popularly elected, all candidates being "vetted" by the party. The new constitution, however, eliminated elected bodies at both these levels of administration. The reason for this appears to have been twofold: to strengthen central government control in the face of continuing regionalism; and to strengthen the "leading role" of the party. Province governors and district and village chiefs are appointed by the party, though not without some popular consultation. They have responsibility for implementing decisions taken at each higher level.

THE ELECTORAL SYSTEM

Elections are straightforward in the LPDR. They take place at the national level only in single-member constituencies. The winners are those who poll the largest number of votes. Not all candidates are members of the LPRP, but party endorsement is required through the Lao Front for National Construction. This ensures that only a limited number (usually two, no more than three) candidates contest any seat.

THE PARTY SYSTEM

Laos is a Communist state with a single legal political party, the Lao People's Revolutionary Party (*Phak Paxāxon Pativat Lao*). The party traces its history back to the Indochina Communist Party (the ICP) founded in 1930 by the veteran Vietnamese Communist Ho Chi Minh. With the breakup of the ICP in 1951, Lao members began organizing their own party, with Vietnamese assistance. In 1955 they formed the Lao People's Party, forerunner of the LPRP (the name adopted at the party's second congress in 1972). The party concealed its existence, however, behind the facade of the Lao Patriotic Front (*Naeo Lao Sang Xāt*), led by the charismatic Prince Suphanuvong. Real power meanwhile lay in the hands of the party secretary-general, Kaisôn Phomvihān, son of a Vietnamese father and a Lao mother.

Under the provisions of the 1954 Geneva Agreements that brought the First Indochina War (against French colonialism) to an end, two provinces were set aside for regroupment of Communist *(Pathēt Lao)* guerrillas. Not until 1959 was the country reunited through formation of a coalition government that included two Communist ministers. Such a coalition, in the context of the cold war, was not acceptable to the United States, which engineered its overthrow. Three years later, as the country descended into civil war, the incoming Kennedy administration agreed to the neutralization of Laos at another conference at Geneva that endorsed formation of a second coalition government in 1962.

Very soon, however, Laos became caught up in the Second Indochina (Vietnam) War. For a decade, until the cease-fire of 1973, the Pathēt Lao, directed by the LPRP and with the support of its North Vietnamese allies, fought the U.S.-supported Royal Lao regime. In 1974, a third coalition government was formed, this one with half the ministerial positions going to the LPRP (to reflect the fact that the Pathët Lao by then controlled fully two-thirds of the country, though less than half the population). Following Communist victories in Cambodia and Vietnam in April 1975, the LPRP moved to seize full power. Royal Lao bureaucrats and military officers were interned in reeducation camps, and in a bloodless coup on December 2, 1975, the LPRP declared formation of the Lao People's Democratic Republic.

From some 300 to 400 members in 1955, the LPRP grew to a membership of 25,000 by the time it seized power in 1975, and to 78,000 by 1997 (still accounting for less than 2% of the population). It is organized, as are other Communist parties, on a Leninist basis with cells at all administrative levels and throughout the bureaucracy, the military, and mass organizations. Party committees function at the local, district, and provincial levels, each electing members to the next higher committee. At the apex stands the central committee of 49 members elected at the 6th party congress in March 1996, who in turn elected the 9-member political bureau (politburo), where actual power within the party resides.

At the 6th party congress, the dominance of the army within the party became pronounced. Of the 9 politburo members, no fewer than 6 were generals and one was a colonel. Just as significant, 3 of the 9 members were from ethnic minorities and regions outside the capital were well represented in both the politburo and the central committee. Educational standards of members also improved, with a majority claiming postsecondary qualifications of one kind or another.

As of the 6th party congress, the president of the LPRP was General Khamtai Sīphandôn (concurrently prime minister), with General Samān Vinyakēt, president of the National Assembly, and General Chummalī Xainyasôn, defense minister, at numbers two and three. State president Nūhak Phūmsavan retired from the politburo, but Vice President Sīsavāt Kaeobunphan remained a member.

The LPRP claims to exercise power on behalf of the worker-peasant alliance (the Lao proletariat is minute) through the system of democratic centralism in the name of Marxism-Leninism. What this means in practice is that all decisions are made by the politburo and central committee and communicated down the party hierarchy to be implemented, not to ensure the victory of Marxist-Leninist ideology (which has been largely forgotten) but to ensure that the party retains its monopoly of political power.

To this end the party keeps as tight control over all the media as it can. There is no press freedom. The party publishes its own newspaper, *Paxāxon* (The People), as do some mass organizations and the army. An English-language paper, *The Vientiane Times*, appears twice a week, while the most popular magazine (*Vannasin*) features short stories and articles on Lao culture. The medium the party cannot control is television beamed into Laos from Thailand. Lao and Thai are closely similar languages; all

Lao understand Thai, and most Lao prefer Thai TV to their own rather dowdy single government channel.

OTHER POLITICAL FORCES

Mass Organizations

The principal mass organization is the Lao Front for National Construction (*Naeo Lao Sang Xāt*), which has branches all over the country and representatives from all ethnic and religious groups. Its purpose, along with that of other mass organizations, according to the constitution, is to "unite and mobilize" the people to build a new and modern Lao society as directed by the LPRP. This it does by developing political consciousness among all the multiethnic Lao people and among all social classes.

The other sanctioned mass organizations are the Federation of Trade Unions for the benefit of the Lao working class, the Lao Women's Union grouping women's organizations, and the People's Revolutionary Youth Union for young people.

Opposition

With the ending of the cold war and inclusion of both Laos and Vietnam in ASEAN, Thailand no longer supports armed opposition to the Lao regime. Lao refugee camps in Thailand have been closed down, with the exception of one for Hmong that is due to close. Only a handful of diehard Hmong continue to oppose the government from their mountain fastness south of the Plain of Jars.

Internal opposition surfaced briefly in the late 1980s when a group of intellectuals called for introduction of multiparty social democracy. Three ringleaders were arrested, charged with plotting against the government, and sentenced to 14 years' imprisonment. All calls for their release have been ignored, and one of the three has subsequently died.

Buddhism now flourishes in the LPDR, and it is not unusual to see members of the politburo on their knees as a mark of respect to Buddhist monks. Many temples have been repaired and refurbished, not least to encourage rapidly developing tourism. The modus vivendi that thus exists between Buddhism and the LPRP makes it most unlikely, therefore, that the Buddhist Sangha (monastic order) will become a vehicle for political opposition to the regime.

Many Lao refugees abroad who previously opposed the regime have since 1990 returned to visit their homeland. Some have invested money, and some have returned to live in Laos. The regime has generally welcomed returnees, providing they do not involve themselves in politics. What prevents more Lao returning is the "nationality law," which prohibits dual nationality: Lao who live abroad are most reluctant to relinquish their acquired nationalities. While many Lao abroad still detest the regime, more now seek to compromise with it rather than plot its overthrow.

NATIONAL PROSPECTS

Since 1989 when the last Vietnamese troops were finally withdrawn, Laos has resumed its traditional position as a neutral "buffer" state enjoying friendly relations with all its neighbors. While relations with Vietnam remain close, as fellow Communist states and wartime allies, relations with both Thailand and China have also become warm and friendly. Laos has also actively developed its relations with both Burma (Myanmar) and Cambodia.

As a member of ASEAN, Laos will inevitably develop ever-closer ties with its neighbors. In April 1994 the first bridge was opened across the Mekong River between Thailand and Laos, and three more are planned. Road and bridge building are priorities for the Lao government, and for foreign aid donors, as these will link Vietnam with Thailand and Thailand with southern China (Yunnan). A feasibility study has been carried out for a rail line from Thailand to Yunnan to pass through Laos.

This growing transport network will assist in integrating the states of mainland Southeast Asia into a single expanding market, linked to both the rest of ASEAN and to southern China. The strategic position of Laos makes it central to such a project, which holds out opportunities for future growth and development.

At present, however, Laos remains one of the UN's "Least Developed Nations," with an annual per capita income of only about US$350. The value of imports is double that of exports, and the country is heavily dependent on foreign aid and soft loans from the World Bank and the Asian Development Bank. Some light industry is in production (especially textiles), but the principal exports are hydropower and timber.

Laos has great potential as an exporter of electricity and has an ambitious program to build a series of huge dams on fast-flowing tributaries of the Mekong. Timber, minerals, and agriculture provide other opportunities for investment and development that promise to turn around the Lao trade deficit in the longer term.

In conclusion, therefore, the prospects are for steady if not spectacular economic growth and for continued political stability under the watchful eye of a party that is now Communist only in name.

Further Reading

Bourdet, Yves. "Laos: The Sixth Party Congress, and After?" *Southeast Asian Affairs 1997*. Singapore: ISEAS, 1997, 143–60.

Ireson, Carol J., and W. Randall Ireson. "Ethnicity and Development in Laos." *Asian Survey* 31 (1991): 920–37.

Ngaosyvathn, Mayoury, and Pheuiphanh Ngaosyvathn. *Kith and Kin Politics: The Relationship between Laos and Thailand*. Manila: Contemporary Asia Press, 1994.

Savada, A. M., ed. *Laos: A Country Study*, 3d ed. Washington, D.C.: Library of Congress, 1995.

Stuart-Fox, Martin. *Buddhist Kingdom, Marxist State: The Making of Modern Laos*. Bangkok and Cheney, N.Y.: White Lotus, 1996.

———. *A History of Laos*. Cambridge: Cambridge University Press, 1997.

———. "Laos 1995: Towards Regional Integration." *Southeast Asian Affairs* 1995. Singapore: ISEAS, 1995, 177–95.

———. *Laos: Politics, Economics and Society* . London: Frances Pinter, and Boulder, Colo.: Lynne Rienner, 1986.

Stuart-Fox, Martin, and Mary Kooyman. *Historical Dictionary of Laos*. Metuchen, N.J.: Scarecrow Press, 1992.

Zasloff, J.J., and L. Unger, eds. *Laos: Beyond the Revolution*. London: Macmillan, 1991.

LATVIA

(Latvijas Republika)

By Jeffrey K. Hass, Ph.D.

THE SYSTEM OF GOVERNMENT

On August 21, 1991, following the failed Soviet putsch, the Latvian Supreme Soviet declared Latvia independent of the Soviet Union, beginning the process of building democracy. Officially a republic (with a strong Parliament and weak president), Latvia is composed politically of 26 "counties" (*rajons*) and 7 municipalities.

Latvia, like its two Baltic neighbors, has enjoyed a happier transition to democracy and capitalism than other former Eastern bloc or Soviet republics. While disputes over policy, territorial boundaries, economic policy, and definition of citizenship have been problematic and while Latvia's economy bottomed out in 1992 and 1993, Latvia has enjoyed relative political calm and recent economic growth.

While it may perhaps be early to talk about a stable, never-changing political system, Latvia's polity has come closer to institutionalization than other post-Soviet states except Estonia.

With a total area of 64,000 square kilometers (roughly equal to that of West Virginia), Latvia is the "middle" Baltic nation, with Estonia to the north and Lithuania to the south; on the west Latvia is bordered by the Baltic Sea and shares its eastern border with Russia. The population of Latvia in 1996 was almost 2.5 million persons. Culturally Latvia is far from homogeneous—a potential political problem in the past, present, and future. According to official data, "Latvians" (ethnically defined) make up 51.8% of the population; Russians are 33.8% (a result of migration from other Soviet republics before 1991); Byelorussians make up 4.5%, Ukrainians 3.4%, and other ethnic groups 6.5%. Given the Germanic heritage of this region, the two dominant religions are Roman Catholicism and Lutheranism; Russian Orthodoxy is also prevalent. The official language is Lettish ("Latvian"); Lithuanian and Russian are prevalent as well.

Executive

The executive branch is headed by two figures, the president and the prime minister. The president, who sits for a three-year term (and who cannot sit for more than two consecutive terms), is the nominal head of state but is not a powerful figure in Latvian politics; the constitution holds the president as a figurehead who represents Latvia in the international arena and has circumscribed other powers. For example, no bill can come into force with a presidential signature alone; the prime minister must countersign bills. The constitution gives the president unilateral political power only in two cases: inviting a figure to become prime minister and form a government, and suggesting that the Parliament be dissolved. In the first case, the president can invite a prime minister to form a government only after the previous prime minister has resigned or failed to survive a parliamentary no-confidence vote. In the second case, the president may suggest that the *Saeima* (the Parliament) be dissolved; however, such a decision must go to a nationwide referendum. If the referendum receives a majority of votes cast, the *Saeima* is dissolved and new elections will be forthcoming. If, however, the referendum does not receive majority support and fails, then the president is dismissed from office and the *Saeima* elects a new president to serve out the remainder of the three-year term. Unlike some countries, such as Russia, where the president has the power to dissolve the legislature, the Latvian constitution makes such an action a double-edged sword, forcing the president not to take such action lightly.

In spite of such institutional obstacles to a strong presidency, the first president, Guntis Ulmanis, tried to move beyond his legal means—not confining himself to the presidential bully pulpit or his duties in the realm of diplomacy and foreign policy (including talks with Russia about removing troops and bringing Latvia closer to NATO and the European Union). In 1995 the *Saeima* was divided into two roughly equal groups to the right and to the left, making support for a prime minister and government difficult; Ulmanis attempted to play power broker to put in his favorite for prime minister but finally had to turn to a compromise candidate (Andris Skele) on the third try. The law gives only so much room for presidential maneuver.

The prime minister is the head of the government and as such answers to the *Saeima* for the progress and outcomes of policies and for problems within the government and Council of Ministers. In essence this makes the prime minister, rather than the president, the real executive authority. First, legislation becomes law only with the prime minister's cosignature. Second, by heading the ministries that form the apex of the government, the prime minister and the Council of Ministers have direct control over policy implementation and day-to-day operations (albeit at some bureaucratic distance). Third, in cases of urgent need occurring between sessions of the Parliament, the Council of Ministers has the right to issue temporary decrees with the force of law. However, the Council cannot issue such decrees on just any subject. For example, Council decrees cannot, among other issues, amend elections, judicial procedures, the state budget, or laws passed by the *Saeima* at that time in power.

The president and the prime minister are not only beholden to the Parliament to account for their actions; they owe their positions to parliamentary election. The prime minister must be approved and can lose office to a vote of no confidence. In Latvia, the president is not elected by direct popular vote but by the Parliament. Presidential "elections" were held in 1993 and 1995. In July 1993, at the convocation of the first pure post-Soviet Parliament, three individuals came forward as presidential candidates: Gunars Meirovics (Latvia's Way), Aivars Jerumanis (Christian Democratic Union), and Guntis Ulmanis (Latvian Farmers' Union). After two ballots, when no single candidate could obtain 51 votes, Ulmanis won on the third ballot; on July 8, 1993 he was officially inaugurated, and his first major action was to appoint Valdis Birkavs (Latvia's Way leader) to the post of prime minister. In June 1996, the second post-Soviet presidential election was held. Parties in the *Saeima*, not forgetting Ulmanis's attempts to play power broker and to prevent members of certain parties from obtaining ministerial positions, put up their own candidates to run against him: Saimnieks proposed Ilga Kreituse, the extremist party For Latvia put up Imants Liepa, and the Socialist Party nominated Alfreds Rubiks, the former first secretary of the Latvian Communist Party who was at that time serving an eight-year prison sentence for his role in the failed August 1991 putsch. (Interestingly, the only qualification for a presidential candidate is to be over 40 years old; hence, being in prison is not legally an obstacle to a presidential bid.) Ulmanis maintained a moderate policy program, and this helped him win 53 of 97 ballots in the first round of voting, returning Ulmanis to the presidency for a second term.

Legislature

The *Saeima*, or Parliament, is the locus of political power in Latvia. The *Saeima* is a unicameral body composed of 100 seats and is elected for a term of three years, except in a special case: if the *Saeima* is dissolved by referendum (see above), the *Saeima* elected in its place has a life of only two years, after which new elections for a three-year sitting are held again. When a newly elected Parliament meets for the first time, the deputies elect a board that acts as the organizing head of the *Saeima*. This board consists of a chairman, two deputy chairmen, and two secretaries; the chairman acts in the role of Speaker of Parliament. The *Saeima* also has 10 committees that make up 100 positions; thus, in theory every *Saeima* member can become a member of a parliamentary committee. These committees are one path for submitting legislation; if five or more members of a committee so act, they can present a bill for a vote in the Parliament. (A bill can also be brought up by the president, Cabinet of Ministers, or one-tenth of eligible voters.)

Parliament wields not only legislative power but ultimate political sovereignty. The president is selected by the *Saeima*, and the prime minister must answer to the Parliament. If the president dies, the next in line is not the prime minister, as in some countries (like Russia); power instead goes to the chairman of the *Saeima*. While the executive branch proposes and implements administrative policy, these policies are embedded in the legal framework formed by *Saeima* decisions. Parliamentary deputies enjoy not only immunity from criminal prosecution but also from recall: according to the constitution, deputies cannot be recalled from their office and can be disciplined only by the *Saeima* itself. (Only in the case of defamation or the revealing of defamatory information known to be false or revealing information about another's private life, can deputies become liable to prosecution.) Even in cases of criminal activity, a *Saeima* member cannot be prosecuted until the *Saeima* decides to sanction such prosecution.

Legislation is the primary duty of the *Saeima*. Laws pass if they receive a majority vote (51 votes). While the president can send legislation back to the *Saeima* for reconsideration, the *Saeima* can override the veto with a simply majority (51) a second time in support of the proposed bill. The president then cannot raise his initial objections a second time; that is, the president cannot veto a bill with the same objections twice. One-third of the *Saeima* can motion to suspend implementation of a law for two months or can request the president to suspend implementation. The law in question is then submitted to a nationwide referendum if one-tenth of the voters request it; otherwise, the law goes into force at the end of the two-month waiting period. If in the referendum a majority does not support the draft law, then it will not go into force.

Only laws and measures on the budget, on taxes and customs duties, on military service, on declaration of war or peace, on a state of emergence, and on foreign treaties cannot be subject to a nationwide referendum. Further, two-thirds of the *Saeima* may vote that a law is "urgent," which means that the president may not demand a second review of the law and a referendum cannot be called to judge it. Finally, the *Saeima* can amend the constitution if new articles are passed by a two-thirds majority after three readings; two-thirds of *Saeima* deputies must be present for such constitutional changes to be valid.

Judiciary

The judiciary is in the process of being reorganized. For the first half of the 1990s, Latvia used the system it inherited from its Soviet past, namely district, regional, and administrative courts, along with a newly created Supreme Court. Each level handles both criminal cases and civil cases (disputes), and appeals move up the chain to the Supreme Court, which is the final arbiter of legal conflict. The Supreme Court also has the right to determine the constitutionality or unconstitutionality of laws.

Only the Supreme Court has the power to review legislative acts, and then only in order to establish constitutionality (or lack thereof). Otherwise, Latvia follows a Continental judicial system, whereby the courts act merely to decide in conflicts and to apply the law, rather than to interpret the law (as is the case in the Anglo-American tradition). Further, precedent does not play a major role either in legal interpretation or in the process of judicial decisions; decisions are made for each individual case.

Regional and Local Government

At the local level, the highest political body is the local council, ranging from 15 to 120 members (depending on the region) and sitting for a five-year term. The council is run by a chairman and board elected by the council deputies. In local politics, members of the Latvian National Independence Movement have faired well and dominate, whereas candidates linked to the Communist Party have fared poorly.

THE ELECTORAL SYSTEM

The Latvian Constitution holds that election to the *Saeima* is through proportional means—that is, voters receive a list with parties and then vote for a party. Those parties receiving more than 5% of votes cast receive a number of seats equal to the percentage of votes they received out of the total votes cast for parties that overcame the 5% barrier; votes for parties that do not cross the 5% barrier are, therefore, wasted votes.

The first post-Soviet elections to the *Saeima* were held in 1993, when 20 parties or coalitions entered the fray. The winner of the 1993 elections was Latvia's Way (*Latvijas Cels*), which took 32.4% of the vote and 36 Parliament seats. In 1995 the left's *Saimnieks* ("man-

ager" in Latvian) achieved 15.1% of the vote and 18 seats to 15% and 18 seats for Latvia's Way; For Latvia was a close third with 14.9% and 16 seats. In 1998 the centrist People's Party (*Tautas Partija*) placed first with 20.9% and 24 seats to 18.2% and 21 seats for Latvia's Way.

1993 *Saeima* Election Results

Party	Seats
Latvia's Way	36
Latvian National Independence Movement	15
Harmony for Latvia	13
Latvian Farmers' Union	12
Ravnopraviye (Equal Rights)	7
Fatherland and Freedom Union	6
Christian Democratic Union	6
Democratic Center Party	5

Source: Estonia, Latvia, and Lithuania. Country Studies. (Washington, D.C.: Federal Research Division, Library of Congress).

Upon the convocation of the first post-Soviet *Saeima*, deputies elected Anatolijs Gorbunovs (Latvia's Way) as parliamentary chairman. To guarantee a majority vote on policy decisions, Latvia's Way formed a coalition encompassing other prodemocracy/promarket parties, including the Farmers' Union. However, after disputes over agricultural tariffs and distribution of ministerial portfolios, the Farmers' Union in July 1994 left the ruling coalition. As a result, Prime Minister Birkavs, seeing his power base ebb, resigned from office. His first appointed replacement, Andrejs Krastins (deputy chairman of the *Saeima* and head of the party Latvian National Independence Movement), could not obtain the necessary parliamentary support to form a new government. The next appointment, Maris Gailis (Latvia's Way), convinced the National Union of Economists—a group that emerged after a split within the ranks of the National Harmony Party—and the National Harmony Party to join Latvia's Way in forming a new ruling coalition and to support his bid as prime minister.

After the 1994 parliamentary elections Gailis had to step down, leading to another round of negotiations and politicking over the selection of a new prime minister. The rightist candidate (Maris Grinblats), proposed by President Ulmanis and supported by the right-of-center National Bloc and Latvia's Way, lost 51 to 49; the second nominee, Ziedonis Cevers of the left-of-center National Conciliation Bloc (see below) was denied confirmation by a 50-to-45 vote (5 abstentions). Andris Skele, a 37-year-old businessman, was proposed as a compromise candidate and was confirmed by the *Saeima* as prime minister.

1995 *Saeima* Election Results

Party	% Votes	Seats
Saimnieks	15.1	18
Latvia's Way (LC)	15.0	18
For Latvia	14.9	16
Fatherland and Freedom (TB)	11.9	14
Latvian National Conservative Party (LNNK) and Green Party	6.3	8
Latvian Unity Party	7.1	8
Farmers' Union/Christian Democratic Union (LKDS)/Latgale Democratic Party Coalition	6.3	7
National Harmony Party (TSP)	5.6	6
Latvian Socialist Party (LSP)	5.6	5

Source: David Arter, *Parties and Democracy in the Post-Soviet Republics* (Aldershot, England: Dartmouth, 1996), xvi, and *OMRI Daily Digest*, October 5, 1995.

The trends over time show a rise in the power of left-leaning groups, such as Saimnieks, and a decline in the progressive but promarket parties such as Latvia's Way. Latvia's Way and For Latvia, which has stronger nationalist rhetoric (and whose leader has been called "extremist" and "xenophobic") maintained their positions; the Fatherland and Freedom Party, also nationalist, increased its number in the *Saeima*. This trend suggests a polarization in Latvian politics away from the moderate nationalism and progressive market reform of Latvia's Way to the stronger nationalism of conservative parties or the weaker nationalism and rejection of rapid market reform of Saimnieks and other left-of-center parties.

In this case, the electoral results show how rural, poorer, and pension-age Latvians, hurt by the market reforms, have rejected the Latvian Way program and have opted for more radical parties—although Latvian parties do not seem to share the same degree of radical leftism or nationalism that many leftist or nationalist parties in Russia or Romania show. On the other hand, some observers think that the rise of stronger nationalist parties and leftist parties is a rejection of party-centered politics altogether, since the campaigns of Saimnieks, Latvia's Way, and the Latvian Unity Party focused not on the parties and their platforms but rather on their leaders and leaders' images.

THE PARTY SYSTEM

As in the other two Baltic countries and for many former Communist countries in general, talking about coherent "parties" is difficult. While there are formal party groupings, parties in Latvia may disappear and new parties sometimes are created, making the party landscape some-

what in flux. Further, the last few years have seen shifting coalitions of parties, who ally or merge in order to increase their potential electoral support and voting power in the *Saeima*. Finally, party organization and discipline do not always seem very strong, since candidates may run on their party's list in one district and on a list for a coalition in a district where that party is weaker. Hence, there may be a low correlation between the "rank and file" (which may be rather low—Latvia's Way has, according to one report, only 435 members), programmatic stance, positions of deputies in parliamentary debates, and leadership within one party.

The most prominent party has been Latvia's Way. Latvia's Way is promarket and prodemocracy and favors increased ties between the three Baltic countries; Latvia's Way is centrist in general and does not espouse a nationalist line. Further to the right are the Latvian National Independence Movement and Fatherland and Freedom party; they tend to be more nationalist and less likely to compromise with Russia over contentious issues. The For Latvia popular movement, led by Joachim Siegerist (considered by many to be an ultrarightist), has tended to side with more nationalist groups, although For Latvia did join left-leaning Saimnieks and the National Harmony Party in forming the ruling coalition "National Conciliation Bloc." (Other right-of-center groups did not want to work with Siegerist because of his extremism, and his candidacy as economics minister doomed the National Conciliation Bloc's first attempt to form a government in 1995. Only when the Latvian Unity Party was added to the coalition was a new government approved by the Saeima.)

To the left are Saimnieks, founded in 1994 by a former Komsomol leader and referred to as a party of "recycled Communists," the National Harmony Party, and the Latvian Socialist Party. In July 1996, the Republican Party and the Latvian Unity Party merged with Saimnieks. These parties tend to favor more gradual reform and compromise with Russia, although all also stress the inviolability of Latvian independence.

NATIONAL PROSPECTS

Latvia's economy was on the rise until banking crises hit; however, there is reason to believe that the groundwork for healthy economic growth is being laid. While politics is currently fractured between two roughly equal groups (right-of-center and left-of-center), such ideological differences are actually rather slight and not of the same intensity as in Russia, Romania, or other European countries. Most parties support some form of market reform, democracy, and further integration with the West.

Latvia at this time has two major political problems, those having to do with ethnic issues and those having to do with political gridlock. On the ethnic front, the problems are mainly between ethnic Latvians and Russians, who make up one-third of the Latvian population. While citizenship had been a thorny issue, it appears to have been solved for the present. While some groups claim political abuse, the actual abuse is not particularly abominable.

The second potential problem is political gridlock. With most parties hovering around a center ground, political disputes are more like those in the United States—conflicts between rival political ambitions rather than over different ideological views and policies. With the *Saeima* split in half, forging political coalitions and bold political policies may be difficult. However, if this is put in the context of the politics of other former Soviet nations, perhaps such political gridlock of the American variety is a sign that Latvia is in good shape.

Further Reading

Arter, David. *Parties and Democracy in the Post-Soviet Republics*. Aldershot, England: Dartmouth, 1996, xvi, and *OMRI Daily Digest*, October 5, 1995.

Iwaskiw, Walter R., ed. *Estonia, Latvia, and Lithuania*. Country Studies. Washington, D.C.: Federal Research Division, Library of Congress.

OMRI Daily Digest. Open Media Research Institute daily reports were issued until April 1997. Good concise information, which can be obtained at www.omri.cz.

Radio Free Europe/Radio Liberty Research Report. Can be accessed at www.rferl.org.

Transition. Began publication in January 1995 and covers the former Soviet Union and Eastern Europe. In practice a successor to Radio Liberty/Radio Free Europe Research Reports.

REPUBLIC OF LEBANON

(Al-Jumhuriyyah Al-Lubnaniyyah)

By As'ad Abukhalil, Ph.D.

THE SYSTEM OF GOVERNMENT

Lebanon is associated in the mind of the world with violence and mayhem; the protracted civil war (1975–90) erased the memory of the prewar country of relative peace and democracy in a region long known for stubborn dictatorships. Civil war has left Lebanon with a severely damaged economy, destroyed its infrastructure, fostered deep communal hatred, compromised sovereignty, and killed or injured at least a half million Lebanese. Furthermore, some 1 million Lebanese were displaced. While Lebanon is now being reconstructed, analysts will continue to argue whether the civil war is really over or whether Lebanon is now enjoying an extended period of truce.

This small but strategically located country has long served as a link between one region and another: in modern times it has linked the Arab world and the Mediterranean world. It consists of some 130 miles of coastline on the Mediterranean sea and comprises with its mountains some 4,000 square miles. It has been an integral part of the Arab East, or the Levant, for much of its recent history. Its location has shaped its history and society: its relatively isolated mountainous environment has allowed various sectarian groups from throughout the region to seek haven on its territory to avoid fear and persecution. This history of welcoming various peoples is probably responsible for the richly diverse composition of its population.

The last official census was conducted by the French in 1932, and successive governments have considered the sectarian distribution of the population a state secret that could potentially destabilize the country. In reality, the Christian establishment avoided conducting a new census because it did not want to confirm the fact that Muslims now form the overwhelming majority of the Lebanese population, contrary to the French figures in 1932. Population figures are important because the political posts of governments are still distributed along sectarian lines, with the Christians enjoying significant privileges, including the post of president of the republic.

Lebanon is a modern creation; it was fashioned from the legacy of the Ottoman Empire in part as a response to Christian demands for a Christian entity tied to the West. The League of Nations granted France mandate authority over Greater Syria, an area that included Lebanon. The French designed the political system of Lebanon and shaped the constitution, which was enacted in 1926. Lebanon was established as a republic, and the Christians were given supreme political positions. In 1932, the French announced the result of a comprehensive census that found the Christians to be the majority of the population. In response, political posts were divided according to an arithmetic formula of sectarian weights, to the advantage of the Maronites and of the Christians in general. Lebanon won its independence in 1943, and the Sunni and Maronite elites reached an understanding that become known as the National Pact. This unwritten agreement was essential for the operation of the political system from 1943 until the civil war in 1975.

According to the terms of the National Pact, the Christians were to promise not to seek foreign, i.e., Western Christian, protection and to accept Lebanon's Arab "face," a partial recognition of Lebanon's ties to its Arab surroundings and its gratitude to its Arab/Islamic heritage. In return, the Muslims were to agree to recognize Lebanon's independence and the legitimacy of the state with its 1920 boundaries and to renounce aspirations of a union with Syria or with any other Arab country. The Pact also reinforced the sectarian division of political powers: it specified that the Maronites will have the presidency, the Shi'ites the ceremonial Speakership of parliament, and the Sunnis the prime ministership. Other top security positions were also reserved for Maronites.

In 1975, a civil war broke out that was to last for at least 16 years. While the Lebanese government officially declared the end of the war, one can still disagree with the notion that all sources of conflict have been amicably resolved in that country. The war began as the product of acute socioeconomic injustices and as a result of the distribution of political power according to an outmoded formula of sectarian (im)balance. Shi'ites, among other groups, became increasing unhappy over their small share of power given their large demographic share of the population. Leftists battled rightists, and some Muslims battled some Christians, while outsiders (primarily Israel and Syria) intervened heavily on this side or that. The PLO in Lebanon also fought alongside the leftist/Muslim coalition of forces. Syrian troops intervened heavily in Lebanon in 1976 to crush the power of the PLO and its Lebanese leftist allies, while Israel intervened at several times and invaded the country in 1982 to install its ally Bashir Gemayyel as president and to expel PLO forces from Lebanon. The civil war caused significant damage to the national economy and the Lebanese currency and was marked by assassination, kidnappings, massacres, and mutilation of bodies.

In September 1989, the Lebanese parliament met in special sessions in the city of Ta'if in Saudi Arabia to discuss formulas and plans for constitutional and political reforms. These sessions were attended by 31 Christian and 31 Muslim deputies out of the 73 surviving members of the 1972 parliament. They met again in October 1889 in an effort to put an end to the civil war and to respond to popular demands for serious constitutional reforms.

The resulting agreement, known as the Ta'if Accord, shifted some powers from the president to the Council of Ministers and called for equal sectarian representation of Christian and Muslims in parliament. The agreement also promised to end "political sectarianism," although no firm timetable was specified. The agreement also included a comprehensive settlement of the Lebanese civil war, which entailed the dissolution of all militias in Lebanon. The identity of Lebanon was declared to be Arab and Lebanon's relations with Syria were officially and juridically characterized as "distinctive." The agreement included a promise of Syrian evacuation of troops from Lebanon. Thereafter, the administration of Ilyas Hrawi adopted the agreement and the parliament amended the constitution to incorporate those reforms. Observers still disagree whether the Ta'if agreement was actually implemented and whether those reforms are sufficient to end national discord in Lebanon.

Executive

The original constitution gives great powers to the president. He or she is commander in chief of the army and security forces; can appoint and dismiss the prime minister and Cabinet; promulgates laws passed by the parliament and may also propose laws, enact urgent legislation by decree, and veto bills; and can dissolve the parliament under certain circumstances. The president also has powers over the government bureaucracy.

The sectarian system, however, puts some constraints on the powers of the president because national concord requires mutual agreement among the various sects. The Ta'if agreement has transferred some of the powers of the president to the collective Council of Ministers, over

which he or she presides. Furthermore, the Maronite president has to try to obtain the support of the Sunni Muslim prime minister.

The president is elected by the parliament, and not by a direct vote from the public. This has facilitated corrupt practices such as bribery of the members of parliament. The president serves for a six-year term and may not succeed himself, although the constitution may be amended toward that end, as was the case with Bisharah Al-Khuri and recently with Ilyas Hrawi, who served for three years beyond his first term, which expired in 1995. A quorum of two-thirds of the deputies is required to hold a special session for the election of the president, and a two-thirds majority of deputies attending is required for the president to be elected on the first ballot. In the second round, a simple majority suffices.

The Ta'if agreement strengthened the powers of the Council of Ministers, which includes the president, the prime minister, and the ministers. The president consults with the deputies before naming a prime minister. The designated prime minister then conducts his own consultation before designating the ministers. Sectarian sensibilities and the terms of the National Pact are often more important criteria than specialization and merit. The prime minister is the highest Muslim official in the country and can bring great authority to the position, as has the current prime minister, the billionaire Rafiq Hariri, who was replaced by Salim al-Huss in 1998. The prime minister presides over the Council of Ministers and and is responsible for running the day-to-day affairs of the government. The powers of the prime minister, however, vary by personality. Some presidents have selected weak individuals with no power bases as subservient political tools.

The country is theoretically administered through the Council of Ministers, although the president, the prime minister, and the Speaker of the parliament often reach decisions in informal meetings without consulting with the Cabinet members. Ministers do not necessarily mind as long as they receive support for their pet projects and as long as they serve their own personal and political objectives.

Legislature

Legislative power is vested in a unicameral Chamber of Deputies, which has seldom exercised its legislative authority because the president, with or without the Council of Ministers, often legislates by special decree. The constitution gives the parliament powers for dealing with budgetary oversight and amendment of the constitution, but the president can easily manipulate the deputies through an exploitation of the sectarian system and through direct dealing with the sectarian political bosses, known as *zu'ama'*.

Deputies are elected every four years by popular vote,

but according to a strict sectarian formula that designates the sectarian affiliation of every candidate for every seat. The citizens are then forced to select according to sectarian/political considerations.

The civil war disrupted parliamentary life in Lebanon, and no election was held from 1972 until 1992. The credibility of the 1992 election was questioned by many because many Christians boycotted it in protest of Syrian influence in Lebanon. The 1996 elections, however, were more representative, although they too, were marred by fraud and irregularities. Party politics has played a small part in electoral politics because sectarian leaders dominate the list making and campaigning. The electoral system also discourages nonsectarian parties.

To be eligible for election, an individual has to be at least 25 years of age. The first woman served in parliament in 1960, but women were elected in the 1992 and 1996 elections. The number of seats in parliament accorded with to a 6-to-5 formula, to the advantage of Christians, but the formula is now 50-50, that is, 50% Muslim and 50% Christian.

Judiciary

The judicial system is supposed to mirror that of France; the Ministry of Justice has official authority over the judicial system. But the Supreme Council of Justice, an independent body appointed by the Council of Ministers, exercises actual jurisdiction over the various courts. There are 56 courts of first instance, with 17 in Beirut alone. Cases from these courts can be appealed to one of 11 courts of appeal, each of which has a three-judge panel. Above these are four courts of cassation, on which sit three judges each. Three of these courts adjudicate civil cases, and one hears criminal complaints.

Several other courts exist outside of this framework. There are, for example, an appeals court for administrative matters and the Judicial Council, which includes the most senior judge of the courts of cassation and four other judges appointed by the government and rules on cases of public security. Other specialized courts exist to deal with matters relating to the military, the press, and business affairs.

While the French legal system inspired the organization of the judiciary, personal status laws remain the domain of the sectarian religious leadership within each community. In issues dealing with marriage, divorce, burial, and inheritance, the state has given total control to the clerical establishment. Secularists and feminists regard this monopoly over personal status laws as harmful to the cause of equality and liberty; it also impedes the process of national construction of one identity. The clerical establishments encourage the perpetuation of sectarian identities, and they insist on commanding the loyalty of the various sectarian groups.

In a country known for sectarian loyalties, patronage,

and elite rivalries, political interference in judicial affairs is quite common. Judicial appointments, even in the era of the so-called second republic (in reference to post–civil war Lebanon), are the product of sectarian considerations. Informal meetings between the president, the prime minister, and the Speaker decide very crucial appointments, with each of them thinking about the interests of the sect. Thus, the judge in question is loyal to the individual leader who was responsible for his or her appointment. This minimizes the independence of the judiciary and makes it susceptible to political and sectarian pressures.

Local and Regional Government

The operation of the government in Lebanon has been highly centralized; citizens from outside the capital often complain that simple governmental transactions require a visit to the capital. The state has not tried to ease the burden by decentralizing its structure. The civil war heightened fears of partition of the country and demands by right-wing groups of decentralization intended to split the country into Christian and Muslim sectors. After the political defeat of the Maronite-oriented groups, the state has insisted on a unified Lebanon, which only weakens the operation of local governments.

The country is divided into six provinces, or governates (*muhafadhah*): Beirut, Al-Biqa‘, Mount Lebanon, the South, the North, and Jabal ‘Amil. The last one was created in the 1980s to satisfy Shi‘ite demands. All governates, except Beirut, are divided into districts (*qada‘*). The Ministry of Interior has oversight and fiscal responsibility over the local administrations. The governor, who is appointed by the Council of Ministers, is the highest-ranking official in each province. He or she must come from a region different from that of the region he or she is assigned to administer. The governor heads the Council of the Governorate, which includes a representative of the Ministry of Finance and the deputy governors (*qa‘immaqam*), who are also appointed by the Council of Ministers.

THE ELECTORAL SYSTEM

The study of Lebanese political parties is made difficult due to the fragmentation of the political culture into narrow, sectarian subcultures. Most Lebanese political parties and organizations, not to mention political leaders, mobilize members of a particular sectarian group. The explosion of the civil war in 1975 only reinforced sectarian political identities and marginalized those parties that championed secular reforms of the political system. This excessive fragmentation, which goes beyond the Muslim-Christian distinction to include denominations within each of the two religions, requires a typology of parties based on the type of sectarian identity promoted by the party and on the sectarian composition of party members.

THE PARTY SYSTEM

Origins of Lebanese political parties predate the founding of independent Lebanon in 1943: some existing political parties in Lebanon trace their roots to the 1920s and 1930s. This era witnessed the formation of small political identities following centuries of grand identities based on either Islam or pan-Arabism. To be sure, identities based on sectarian loyalties have been a feature of Lebanese society for centuries, but those identities were only channeled in modern political formations in this century. The formation of political parties reflected an attempt by sectarian leaders to adjust to the consequences of the creation of the Lebanese republic. They wanted to mask their sectarian agendas behind an ostensible national outlook encompassing the whole of Lebanon and its people. Also, the Lebanese electoral system sometimes required the election of a leader by a multisectarian constituency, although the narrow sectarian districts often served the interests of sectarian agitation and representation.

SHI'ITE-ORIENTED PARTIES AND ORGANIZATIONS

Amal Movement
(Harakat Amal)

The original name of this organization is *Harakat Al-Mahrumin* (Movement of the Disinherited), but its name after 1978 became known by the acronym of its military arm *Afwaj Al-Muqawamah Al-Lubnaniyyah* (Detachments of the Lebanese Resistance), or AMAL. The word also means "hope" in Arabic.

The history of this movement is closely associated with the role of its founder Imam Musa As-Sadr, who came to Lebanon from Iran in 1959 and organized the political movement of the Shi'ite community. Israeli bombardment of South Lebanon in the 1960s, when the Palestine Liberation Organization (PLO) was emerging as a political and military force in Lebanon, radicalized the community, which was—and is—the poorest community in the country. As-Sadr called on the Lebanese state to defend the villages of South Lebanon and to bring about economic improvement in the lives of Shi'ites. The role of As-Sadr was boosted in 1969 when he was elected chairman of the Higher Islamic Shi'ite Council. He founded the council to separate the demands of the Shi'ites from the political demands of other Muslims sects in the country; he wanted to assert an independent Shi'ite voice after decades of Sunni leadership of all Muslim sects in Lebanon. While As-Sadr did not call for a revolution, he supported "armed struggle" to fight back against Israeli forces in Lebanon.

The civil war did not help the cause of the movement: its role was marginalized as many Shi'ites flocked to Lebanese and Palestinian radical organizations that offered them arms and ideologies. In 1976, the movement was ejected from areas under the control of the PLO and its Lebanese allies because it supported Syrian military intervention in the country. The movement was dormant until 1978 when pro-Syrian As-Sadr "disappeared" while on an official visit to Libya. His supporters blamed the Libyan regime, while the regime denied responsibility. This coincided with two other important developments that affected the Shi'ite political culture: the PLO rule in South Lebanon was growing increasingly unpopular due to various acts of misconduct and thuggery (committed by both Lebanese and Palestinian gunmen), and the Islamic revolution in Iran was popularizing a form of religious-inspired mobilization. This propelled the movement again into prominence, and the Shi'ite sectarian identity became the cornerstone of the movement's ideology.

The movement's strong pro-Syrian orientations were confirmed and consolidated in 1980 when Nabih Birri assumed the leadership of the movement, which has been under his command ever since. The Israeli invasion of 1982 produced a split in the movement, but Birri succeeded in steering the organization away from Iranian hegemony. The movement launched a war against the Palestinian refugee camps in 1987, which dragged on for three years. Birri became a minister in 1984 and was elected to the Speakership of parliament (the highest Shi'ite post in the government) in 1992. The movement was disarmed along with other militias during the first administration of Ilyas Hrawi (1989–95). The movement won four parliamentary seats in the 1992 elections, and its list won overwhelmingly in the South in the 1996 parliamentary election, in which Amal and Hizb-ul-Lah unified their list.

Youths of 'Ali
(Fityan 'Ali)

This small organization split off from the Amal movement during the 1975–76 phase of the civil war. It was led by an extremist street leader, 'Ali Safwan, who was active with his followers on the Shiyyah front during the first phase of the war. It later went into oblivion, and Safwan has not been heard from since.

Brigades of As-Sadr
(Alwiyat As-Sadr)

This small and secretive organization was formed after 1978, when Imam Musa As-Sadr "disappeared" while on a state visit to Libya. It claimed responsibility for various violent acts, including hijacking, aimed at Libyan interests. It is believed that the Amal leader, Nabih Birri, succeeded in absorbing the organization within his movement.

Islamic Amal Movement
(Harakat Amal Al-Islamiyyah)

This movement was formed by Husayn Al-Musawi, who was a former leader of Amal, in the wake of the 1982 Israeli invasion of Lebanon. He split from the movement to protest Nabih Birri's decision to join the Salvation Committee, which the former president Ilyas Sarkis formed and which included, among other members, Bashir Gemayyel, who was a close ally of Israel in Lebanon. Islamic Amal also rejected what it considered the "secular" orientations of the Amal movement. Al-Musawi has kept the party under his strict control and has coordinated his activities closely with the Iranian regime. He often joins forces with the Hizb-ul-Lah (Party of God) but has refused Iranian efforts at uniting the two organizations, both of which share a vision of an Islamic republic in Lebanon. Al-Musawi has been linked in press reports to various anti-U.S. acts in Lebanon during the 1980s, although he denied any responsibility.

Islamic Movement in Lebanon
(Al-Harakah Al-Islamiyyah fi Lubnan)

This highly secretive and small organization first announced its existence in 1983. It is considered to be the most militant Shi'ite organization in Lebanon because it considers the Party of God to be moderate. It calls for the immediate establishment of an Islamic republic in Lebanon and for the election of a Muslim as president of the country. It is headed by Sadiq Al-Musawi, who has maintained close ties to the Iranian regime.

Democratic Socialist Party
(Al-Hizb Ad-Dimuqrati Al-Ishtiraki)

This is a mere vehicle for the followers of traditional *za'im* Kamil Al-As'ad, who held the Speakership of parliament from 1970 until 1984, when his relations with the Syrian regime worsened and the Amal movement marginalized his political movement and extinguished his influence among Lebanese Shi'ites. Al-As'ad founded the party in hope of competing with Lebanese and Palestinian leftist and nationalist organizations, which succeeded in mobilizing Shi'ite masses. His political journey came to an end in 1982 when he supported Bashir Gemayyel, reportedly after receiving a bribe from Gemayyel's political machine. He moved to Europe in 1984 and only returned before the 1992 elections, which marked his political obituary. He lost the election again in 1996. This party, notwithstanding its name, promotes a conservative antisocialist agenda and facilitates the authoritarian leadership of the As'ad family in South Lebanon.

Party of God
(Hizb-ul-Lah)

This party was officially established in the wake of the Israeli invasion of 1982, but its formation can be traced back to the 1960s, when militants Shi'ites expressed unhappiness with the moderate agenda of Imam Musa As-Sadr. The party was formed in opposition to the Amal movement, and the Islamic republic in Iran played a key role in its formation. The existence of the party was announced in 1984. Shaykh Muhammad Husayn Fadlallah, who has been considered the spiritual guide of the party, has played a major role in the party's history and in widening its appeal among Lebanon's Shi'ites. While the party stressed the need for an Islamic republic in Lebanon, it has been mostly known through press reports linking it to anti-American acts of violence in Lebanon, including the kidnapping of American hostages in Lebanon in the 1980s. The party has refused to disarm and continues to launch acts of national resistance against the Israeli occupation of South Lebanon. It has won seats in the 1992 and 1996 parliamentary elections.

Suicidal Forces of Husayn
(Quwwat Husayn Al-Intihariyyah)

This small organization participated in the fighting in the Shiyyah front in the 1975–76 phase of the Lebanese civil war. It has not been heard from in recent years.

MARONITE-ORIENTED PARTIES AND ORGANIZATIONS

Socialist Christian Democratic Party– The Action Party
(Al-Hizb Ad-Dimuqrati Al-Masihi al-Ishtiraki-Hizb Al-'Amal)

This party is associated with right-wing writer Walid Faris, who was until 1989 the head of the "immigrants' apparatus" of the command of the Lebanese Forces. He sided with Michel 'Awn during his "liberation war" and has joined the ranks of the "new" Lebanese Front, which mobilized supporters of 'Awn in East Beirut. The party combines a strong anti-Syrian stance with vague formulations about Christian socialism. Its leader now resides in the United States.

Guardians of the Cedar
(Hizb Hurras Al-Arz)

This extremist right-wing party was established in 1975 to urge the expulsion of all Palestinians from Lebanon. It has been closely associated with the Israeli army in

Lebanon, and its leader, Ityan Saqr (Abu Arz), is now wanted for collaboration with an enemy country of the state. Under the control of Arz, the party called for severing of Lebanon's ties with the Arab world, which it viewed as backward. The party participated actively during the civil war, and its fighters earned a deserved reputation for savagery and ruthlessness. The party was banned in 1990 when Syrian forces evicted General Michel 'Awn and his allies from East Beirut. Its leader, Abu Arz, suffered an injury and now resides in Israeli-occupied South Lebanon.

Lebanese Phalanges Party
(Hizb Al-Kata'ib Al-Lubnaniyyah)

One of the oldest parties in Lebanon, it was founded in 1936 by Pierre Gemayyel in imitation of Nazi youth organizations, which he observed in Germany. The party was formed to reject calls for uniting Lebanon with its neighbors and insisted on a special Christian identity for Lebanon. The party became a sophisticated political machine benefiting from its blatant sectarian agenda, which was useful during the 1958 sectarian civil war. The party's motto emphasized allegiance to "God, homeland, and family," and it has promoted a conservative political agenda that blamed Lebanon's problems on outsiders (Syrians, Egyptians, Iranians, Palestinians, and others). It has been recently revealed that the party had benefited from secret ties to Israel, which helped fund the party's electoral campaigns. It professed its dedication to democracy, private property, and the free-enterprise system, and it consistently expressed its detestation of communism and Arab nationalism. Members of the party have been predominantly Christians, and Maronites have led the party over the years.

It founded one of the early militias in Lebanon and succeeded in attracting members by provoking clashes with the PLO forces in the country. It was one of the main fighting forces on the right during the civil war, and the Lebanese army helped it in training and the supply of matériel. Pierre's son, Bashir, emerged as the main right-wing leader in Lebanon in the wake of the 1975–76 phase of the civil war. The 1982 Israeli invasion of Lebanon boosted the fortunes of the party, and the Israeli occupation army ensured the election of Bashir as president, although he was assassinated days after his election. He was succeeded by his brother Amin, who led Lebanon in one of the worst periods of its contemporary history. Many Lebanese still blame him for intensifying the conflict and for worsening Lebanon's economic problems. Pierre died in 1984, and the party never recovered. It was later headed by the former deputy George Sa'adah, who failed to reunite the party. Many former leaders and members formed their own organizations and refused to acknowledge the leadership of Sa'adah, who failed in the 1996 elections. He died in 1998.

Promise Party
(Hizb Al-Wa'd)

The Promise Party is a small, violent clique or gang comprising the followers of the former Lebanese Forces leader, Elie Hubayqah, who was ousted from his command in 1986 after he aligned himself with the Syrian regime. In return for unwavering loyalty to the regime, he has been consistently awarded ministerial posts, and he is now mentioned as a serious presidential contender. This party won seats in the 1992 and 1996 parliamentary elections.

National Liberal Party
(Hizb Al-Wataniyyin Al-Ahrar)

This party was founded in 1958 by the former Lebanese president Kamil Sham'un to compete with the well-organized Lebanese Phalanges Party. The party was an informal group, and it did not bother to publish a program until the 1960s. It stands for capitalism and opposes leftism and Arab nationalism. It served as a parliamentary bloc aided by the charismatic appeal of Sham'un among Christians in Lebanon. It calls for a close alliance with the West, and the leader of the party did exactly that in 1958 when as president he opposed Nasser's role in the region.

The party formed a militia called the Tigers and worked against the PLO in Lebanon. It participated in the civil war in 1975, but its role was quickly marginalized due to the influence of Bashir Gemayyel, who put all right-wing forces under his own command. Sham'un's two sons, Duri and Dani, served as party leaders, and Dani inherited the leadership of the party 1987 when Kamil died. Dani was assassinated by forces loyal to his Maronite rival Samir Ja'ja' in 1990, and his brother succeeded him. It continues to oppose the Syrian influence in Lebanon and is still aligned with General Michel 'Awn.

Lebanese Front
(Al-Jabhah Al-Lubnaniyyah)

This is a body that brings together all the important Maronite-oriented parties, organizations, and personalities in East Beirut. The front was founded (under a different name) in 1976 to "restore sovereignty" to Lebanon. It comprised the head of the Maronite Order of Monks, the National Liberal Party, the Lebanese Phalanges Party, the Organization, the Guardians of the Cedar, and right-wing personalities like Charles Malik and Sa'id 'Aql. It defended the free-enterprise system in Lebanon and called for the expulsion of Palestinians from Lebanon. The front was reorganized in 1977, and it emphasized the "eternal existence of the Lebanese entity" and affirmed the members' commitment to the preservation of Lebanon's "distinctive characteristics," which have become code words for Maronite political hegemony.

The emergence of Bashir Gemayyel as the imposed undisputed leader of Lebanese Christians in 1978 put the front under the command of the Lebanese Forces, which served as Bashir's own political and military tool. The front was used to legitimize decisions Bashir had made. In 1980, Bashir had eliminated all rival Christian groups, including the Tigers militia of the National Liberal Party. The death of Bashir in 1982 weakened the front and inaugurated its demise. Samir Ja'ja', who assumed the leadership of the Lebanese Forces in 1986, tried to revive the front and to expand its appeal, but he had to contend with the ambitious role of General Michel 'Awn, who tolerated no dissent in East Beirut and who launched an all-out war against his enemies. 'Awn arranged for the creation of a new front to oppose the Ta'if agreement, but it was seen as merely his tool. East Beirut suffered at the time from a vacuum of political leadership and from internecine wars and conflicts. The role of the front has ended, although there are occasional talks aimed at its revival under the guidance of General 'Awn, who remains in exile in France.

Lebanese Forces
(Al-Quwwat Al-Lubnaniyyah)

This coalition of right-wing militias was officially established in the summer of 1976 in the wake of the death of William Hawi, the head of the military apparatus of the Lebanese Phalanges Party. Bashir Gemayyel wanted to unify "the Christian rifle" to end the competition and wars between the various Christian militias in East Beirut. He also wanted to ensure utmost loyalty and obedience by Christian fighters. The role of the Forces gradually grew from that of a joint command of militias to that of a political-military apparatus with a large budget. It soon dominated the political leadership in East Beirut and marginalized the roles of other parties, organizations, and personalities. Bashir eliminated by force the presence of rival militias and arranged for the killing of rivals.

The Lebanese Forces was supported and financed by Israel and paved the way for the 1982 Israeli invasion of Lebanon. The election of Bashir to the presidency brought more prestige to the Forces, although his death brought about a decline in its effectiveness; previously dormant parties were revived and the leadership of the Christian camps was no longer monopolized by one man. The Lebanese Forces was tied to the massacres of Sabra and Shatila in 1982, which resulted in the death of innocent Palestinians residing in refugee camps. The Forces was briefly aligned with the Syrian regime under the leadership of Elie Hubayqah, but he was ousted and replaced by Samir Ja'ja' in 1986. Ja'ja' led the Forces through the difficult wars with General 'Awn, but he was arrested in 1994 for plotting the assassination of a rival and the bombing of a church. Like other militias, the Forces was disbanded but was then registered as a new political party. Ja'ja' remains in jail and the Lebanese Forces awaits the emergence of a new leader.

National Bloc Party
(Hizb Al-Kutlah al-Wataniyyah)

This vehicle of the Iddi *za'im* family was founded in the 1930s as an informal grouping of supporters of the former president Emile Iddi, who was the most subservient politician to French interests during the Mandate period. He was at odds with Bisharah Al-Khuri, who supported independence and called for Muslim-Christian understanding. Iddi, on the other hand, wanted Lebanon as a Christian entity aligned with the Jewish state. His version of ultranationalism and his rejection of identification with the Arab world alienated many Muslims from the party. Lebanese independence dealt a severe blow to Iddi's role and his party, although he transformed the bloc into a quasi-modern political party in 1946. It was his son Raymond, however, who revived the party and won it credibility when he assumed its leadership in 1949 following the death of his father.

The party became known as a moderately conservative party that supported the free-enterprise system and called for the defense of Lebanon's borders from Israeli military attacks. The party suffered in the 1960s due to Iddi's staunch opposition to Shihabism (the ideology of governance associated with General Fu'ad Shihab) and to the omnipotent role of the Lebanese army in Lebanese political affairs. Raymond Iddi was a serious and hard-working legislator whose accomplishment benefited the party. It was regularly represented in parliament. Iddi split from the right-wing camp in 1975 when he opposed the civil war and called for Muslim-Christian understanding. His opposition to Syrian military intervention in 1976 almost cost him his life, and he left Lebanon and settled in Paris. He refuses to return before the withdrawal of Syrian and Israeli forces from Lebanon.

Forces of Al-Maradah
(Quwwat Al-Maradah)

This militia belongs to the powerful *za'im* family of Franjiyyah of North Lebanon. It can be traced to the Zgharta Liberation Army, which was founded by the former president Sulayman Franjiyyah in 1968. It was renamed during the 1975–76 phase of the civil war and participated actively in the war on the Tripoli front against Lebanese and Palestinian militias. Bashir Gemayyel succeeded in marginalizing the Forces, but his death revived the group especially after the emergence of Sulayman Franjiyyah Jr., who wrestled control of the Forces from his uncle Robert. Sulayman Jr. was elected to parliament in 1992 and 1996, and he is one of the most prominent pro-Syrian Maronite leaders in the country.

SUNNI-ORIENTED PARTIES

Movement of the Independent Nasserists—Al-Murabitun
(Harakat An-Nasiriyyin Al-Mustaqillin–al-Murabitun)

This movement is closely associated with the personality of its founder and leader, Ibrahim Qulaylat. It was founded in 1958 to promote Egyptian President Gamal Nasser's policies in Lebanon and to express opposition to pro-Western policies in Lebanon. Qulaylat is a controversial figure who was tried in 1966 for responsibility in the assassination of the anti-Nasser editor Kamil Muruwwah. The movement was adopted by the Fath Movement during the civil war and actively participated in the first phase of the civil war (1975–76). Its militia, Al-Murabitun, became the name of the movement. It lacked a coherent program and spoke the language of Nasserism and Arab nationalism.

Between 1977 and 1982 Qulaylat was a key master of the streets of West Beirut, and Libya rewarded the movement with money and shipments of weapons. In 1984, the movement suffered a setback when the Amal Movement and the Progressive Socialist Party imposed their dominance over the city and gradually eliminated all rival Sunni militias in the city. Qulaylat was forced to flee the city in 1985, and his militia was disbanded. Qulaylat has lived in Europe ever since, and the movement plays no role in Lebanese political life. This party was once extremely influential and may be revived again if Syria leaves Lebanon.

Movement of the Pioneers of Reform
(Harakat Ruwwad Al-Islah)

This movement was founded by Tammam Salam, son of the former prime minister Sa'ib Salam, in 1973. The Salam family was concerned about leftist radical influence among Sunnis in Beirut and wanted to pretend that it too was interested in political reform. The militia of the movement did not participate in the 1975–76 phase of the war because many Sunnis joined other more credibly reformist organizations. Tammam Salam won a seat in the 1996 election.

Movement of Unionist Nasserists
(Harakat Al-Wihdawiyyin An-Nasiriyyin)

This small organization was founded by Ibrahim Qulaylat's former deputy, Samir Sabbagh. Sabbagh formed his group in 1982 to rebel against the autocratic tendencies of the head of Al-Murabitun. It has been aligned with Syria and the Socialist Progressive Party but has failed to establish a power base.

Islamic Community
(Al-Jama'ah Al-Islamiyyah)

This Sunni fundamentalist movement was founded in 1964 in Tripoli by the influential Sunni pamphleteer Fathi Yakan. It advocated the establishment of an Islamic society in Lebanon that would be based on Islamic laws. It argued for the need for armed struggle and formed its own militia, Al-Mujahidun, in 1976. It participated in the civil war. Yakan and two other members of the movement were elected to parliament in 1992.

Islamic Unification Movement
(Harakat At-Tawhid Al-Islami)

This Tripoli-based movement was founded by Shaykh Sa'id Sha'ban in 1982. It asserted its authority over the whole city in 1983 in defiance of Syrian political wishes. It recruited from the ranks of the lumpenproleteriat of Tripoli. Sha'ban, the prince of the movement, called for the strict application of Islamic laws in Lebanon, and he masterminded the massacre of Communists in the city in 1983. The Syrian army later intervened to weaken the influence of the movement, and Sha'ban, presumably under Iranian instructions, reconciled with Damascus. This is one of the most militant Sunni fundamentalist organizations in Lebanon. Sha'ban died in 1998.

October 24 Movement
(Harakat 24 Tishrin)

This small Tripoli-based party takes its name from the revolt of its leader, Faruq Al-Muqaddam, on October 24, 1969, when—with PLO help—it occupied the city's fortress to protest the government's policies toward the Palestinians in Lebanon and to draw attention to the plight of the poor. Al-Muqaddam ran for parliament in 1972 but lost, and he became an influential element of the Lebanese National Movement. It called for "armed struggle" and participated actively in the Lebanese civil war. The movement underwent mysterious changes in the late 1970s when Al-Muqaddam began to reconcile with right-wing groups in Lebanon and was closely tied to the Lebanese state and army. In the 1980s, he was aligned with the Lebanese Phalanges Party, and he relocated to East Beirut after alienating the Syrian will in Lebanon. He is said to have relocated to France in the 1990s.

Habashi Group, or The Society of Islamic Philanthropic Projects

This formerly small and secretive Sunni fundamentalist group has become one of the most organized and disciplined organizations in Lebanon. It is headed by, and named after, the eccentric former mufti from Ethiopia, known as al-Habashi, or the Abyssinian. One of its leaders was elected to parliament in 1992. After a period of tensions, the movement has become close to the Syrian government.

Helpers Party
(Hizb An-Najjadah)

This Sunni-oriented party was founded in 1936 to call for a pro-Arab orientation for Lebanon. It advocated Nasserism and participated in the 1958 civil war. Some of its members held parliamentary seats over the years, although it has become marginalized since 1975, when new political parties emerged in Lebanon. It also suffered from several splits, and the death of its veteran leader, 'Adnan Al-Hakim, further diminished its fortunes.

Arab Socialist Union
(Al-Ittihad Al-Ishtiraki Al-'Arabi)

There are several small, Sunni-oriented organizations that use this name. They all fight over the legacy of Gamal Abdel Nasser, who championed the cause of Arab nationalism. The main organization by this name was formed in 1975 and has received generous Libyan support over the years. It has been headed by 'Abdul-Rahim Murad and 'Umar Harb, although the two parted company in the 1990s, with each forming his own group and using the name Arab Socialist Union. Both factions are close to the Syrian regime. The union was a member of the Lebanese National Movement and has participated in the Lebanese civil war. Murad won a seat in the 1992 and the 1996 elections.

Arab Socialist Union (the Nasserist Organization)
(Al-Ittihad Al-'Arabi [at-Tandhim An-Nasiri])

This is a splinter group of the main Arab Socialist Union. It split from the mother organization in 1976 and has been led by Munir As-Sayyad, who is a local leader in the neighborhood of 'Ayn Al-Muraysah in Beirut. As-Sayyad ran for parliament in 1992 and lost.

Union of the Forces of the Working People—the Nasserist Organization
(Ittihad Qiwa Ash-Sha'b Al-'Amil [At-Tandhim An-Nasiri])

This organization was formed in 1969 during the turmoil caused by the clashes between the PLO and the Lebanese state. It was founded by Sunni student leader Kamal Shatila, who successfully recruited from public schools and the state-run Lebanese University. The movement achieved national fame when its Greek Orthodox candidate, Najah Wakim, won the Greek Orthodox seat in West Beirut in the 1972 parliamentary election. The movement partici-

pated timidly in the civil war and was militarily crushed in the spring of 1976, when forces loyal to the PLO and the Lebanese National Movement defeated all pro-Syrian forces in West Beirut. Shatila and the movement were then revived when Syria intervened militarily and imposed its will over much of Beirut in late 1976. Najah Wakim, who is now one of the most popular opposition figures in the country, left the movement in the late 1970s, and Syria forced Shatila out of the country and his movement was suppressed. Shatila remains in exile in Paris, and his followers operate under the name of the Lebanese Popular Congress, which was founded in 1981.

Nasser's Forces
(Quwwat Nasir)

This is a splinter and self-declared corrective movement of the Union of the Forces of the Working People–the Nasserist Organization. Its leader, 'Isam Al-'Arab, split off from the Union in 1974 to protest Kamal Shatila's support for Anwar Sadat's policies. Al-'Arab was a consistent supporter of the Libyan regime. This organization was active in the Lebanese civil war and was a member of the Lebanese National Movement, although it had a small membership. Al-'Arab was assassinated in the 1980s, and his movement no longer exists.

Popular Nasserist Organization
(At-Tandhim Ash-Sha'bi An-Nasiri)

This Sidon-based organization was founded by Ma'ruf Sa'd in 1970. Like many other Nasserist organizations in Lebanon, it appealed to Sunnis and championed Arab nationalism and support for the PLO in Lebanon. Sa'd was assassinated in 1975, and his assassination marks for many the beginning of the Lebanese civil war. He was succeeded by his son Mustafa, who modernized the organization's militia and received strong support from the PLO in Lebanon. Sa'd survived an assassination attempt in 1985, which left him blind. He is a main rival to Prime Minister Rafiq Hariri and won a seat in parliament in the 1992 and the 1996 elections.

DRUZE-ORIENTED PARTIES

Progressive Socialist Party
(Al-Hizb At-Taqaddumi Al-Ishtiraki; PSP)

This party was founded by the famed Druze leader Kamal Jumblat in 1949. He invited a group of multisectarian intellectuals to form the leadership, but the party quickly became a sectarian Druze party despite its secular agenda. It served as a political vehicle for this influential Druze *za'im*. Jumblat was a key parliamentary leader and played a crucial role in the 1958 civil war. By 1975, Jumblat had emerged as one of the most important opposition leaders in the country, and he founded and headed the Lebanese National Movement, which supported political reforms and the PLO in Lebanon. Jumblat wanted to defeat the Phalangist-led forces in Lebanon but was thwarted in his efforts by the Syrian regime. He was assassinated in 1977 and was immediately succeeded by his son Walid.

Walid quickly ended the feud with the Syrian regime and reorganized the PSP's militia in preparation for a major showdown with the Lebanese Forces. In the 1983–84 War of the Mountain, Jumblat consolidated his leadership within the Druze community and the party emerged as one of the most effective militias in the country. The party won seats in the 1992 and 1996 elections. The party does not serve as more than a tool for Walid Jumblat.

'ALAWITE PARTIES

Arab Democratic Party
(Al-Hizb Al-'Arabi Ad-Dimuqrati)

This small 'Alawite organization can be traced back to 1975, when 'Ali 'Id, a local 'Alawite leader from Tripoli, founded the Confrontation Front. The front was closely aligned with the Syrian army in Lebanon, and its militia was nicknamed the Pink Panthers. Its fighters were notorious for their thuggery. The front's name was changed in the mid-1980s to the Arab Democratic Party. 'Ali 'Id was elected to parliament in 1992 but failed to win a seat in the 1996 election.

ARAB NATIONALIST PARTIES

The Lebanese National Movement

This broad front of leftist and Muslim-oriented parties and organizations was first founded in 1964 under the name of the Front of the National and Progressive Parties, Bodies, and Personalities. It was reorganized in 1969 and renamed the Grouping of National and Progressive Parties. Kamal Jumblat was the founder and leader of this movement, which was renamed the Lebanese National Movement in 1975. It championed the right of the PLO to operate militarily outside of—and inside—Lebanon. In 1976, Jumblat established a structure for the movement and its leading council comprised representatives of the Progressive Socialist Party, the Lebanese Communist Party, the Communist Action Organization, the Syrian Social National Party, the Movement of Independent Nasserists (Al-Murabitun), the Arab Ba'th Socialist Party, the Lebanese Movement in Support of the Revolution, the Organization of the Social-

ist Arab Ba'th Party, the Popular Nasserist Organization, the Arab Socialist Union (the Nasserist Organization), Al-Afwaj Al-'Arabiyyah, Nasser's Forces, the Leftist Kurdish Party, the Socialist Arab Action Party-Lebanon, the Democratic Christians, and pro-Jumblat personalities, such as Albert Mansur, Usamah Al-Fakhuri, Muhammad Qabbani, 'Isam Nu'man, 'Izzat Harb, and Fu'ad Shbaqlu. The movement ceased to exist after the Israeli invasion of 1982.

ARAB SOCIALIST BA'TH PARTY
(Hizb Al-Ba'th Al-'Arabi Al-Ishtiraki)

This party emerged as an active player in radical Lebanese politics in the 1950s. The founding congress of this party was held in 1956 and suffered from many schisms that split the party primarily into pro-Syrian and pro-Iraqi branches. The split was formally set in 1964. The pro-Iraqi branch was far more popular and effective than the pro-Syrian branch (which adds the word "organization" to the full name of the party): a member of the former ('Abdul-Majid Ar-Rafi'i) was elected to parliament in 1972. The pro-Iraqi branch suffered a fatal setback in 1976 when the Syrian army intervened militarily in Lebanon and established Syrian political and military domination in Lebanon. The Syrian army forced all pro-Iraqi Ba'thists either to flee or to go underground. Many were assassinated. Only the pro-Syrian branch now operates in Lebanon, and it has representatives in parliament.

PAN-SYRIAN PARTIES

Syrian Social National Party
(Al-Hizb As-Suri Al-Qawmi Al-Ijtima'i)

This is one of the oldest parties in the country. It was founded by Antun Sa'adah in 1932 and quickly became one of the most influential parties in the entire Arab East, attracting scores of intellectuals and workers. The party advocated the unity of Greater Syria, which includes the Fertile Crescent and Cyprus. Sa'adah coined the slogan "Syria is for the Syrians and the Syrians form one nation" to summarize his vision. He opposed sectarianism and called for Christian-Muslim brotherhood within the context of Syrian nationalism. He strongly denounced the clerical establishment in Lebanon.

The party clearly reflected fascist organizations of the time: this can be seen in its ideology and organizational structure, which focuses on blind allegiance to the personality of the leader (Sa'adah). The party's ideology is virulently anti-Semitic, and Sa'adah understood nationalism in racial terms. Sa'adah declared an armed revolt against the Lebanese state, and he was executed without trial in 1949. The party recovered from the death of its founder and continued to expand in the region. It was originally right-wing and supported Kamil Sham'un in the 1958 revolt. The most serious crisis in the party's history was the coup attempt—the only one of its kind in Lebanon—launched by the party in 1961. The coup failed and the Shihabi regime led a brutal campaign against party members, which resulted in its temporary exclusion from Lebanese political life. While in jail, many party leaders decided to move the party in a more leftist direction and to express solidarity with Arab nationalist parties in Lebanon. Party leaders were released from jail in 1969, and they worked to revive party activity.

The party suffered from many splits in its history and from conflicting claims of allegiance to the personality of Sa'adah, and all party members are required to salute his picture before party meetings. The party participated in the Lebanese civil war as a member of the Lebanese National Movement and received aid from the PLO. A pro-Syrian branch of the party opposed the Lebanese National Movement, especially when the latter fought against the Syrian army in 1976. The two factions were temporarily reunited in 1978, but other splits continued to tear the party apart. There are now at least two parties that use the name of the party and both claim to be the authentic heirs of Sa'adah. The major party won six seats in the 1996 parliamentary election.

COMMUNIST PARTIES

Lebanese Communist Party
(Al-Hizb Ash-Shuyu'i Al-Lubnani; LCP)

This is one of the oldest parties in Lebanon. It was founded in 1920 by a group of workers and intellectuals. Historian Yusuf Ibrahim Yazbak and Fu'ad Shimali were two of the early founders of the party that was originally called the Lebanese People's Party. The USSR put the party under its strict control when the Stalinist Syrian Communist Khalid Bakdash became leader of the party, which was one common to both Lebanon and Syria. The two countries later split the two parties into a Syrian and a Lebanese one. Like other Communist Parties in the Arab world, it suffered from the consequences of Soviet recognition of Israel in 1948 and from its opposition to Arab unity. In the 1960s, the party associated itself closely with Arab nationalist and progressive struggles in the country, although it suffered a number of splits especially after the Sino-Soviet split and Soviet invasion of Czechoslovakia in 1968.

The party played a major role in organizing a broad coalition of leftist parties in the 1960s, and Kamal Jumblat, when he was serving as minister of interior, gave the movement a much-needed legitimacy by awarding it a license, along with other leftist parties and organizations. It participated actively in the civil war and managed to enjoy a unique multisectarian base. Its leadership had a diverse

group of intellectuals and workers from different sectarian backgrounds. The right-wing camp, however, evicted the party from Christian areas under its control, which hurt the party's recruitment campaigns among Christians. George Hawi, the party's secretary-general, was a close ally of Kamal Jumblat and a leading leftist spokesperson for much of the civil war. In recent years, Hawi resigned from all leadership positions amid charges of corruption. The party has been weakened and failed to win seats in the 1992 and 1996 elections. It held its 8th party congress in 1999 and restored Hawi to a ceremonial position.

Communist Action Organization
(Munadhdhamat Al-'Amal Ash-Shuyu'i)

This is the second-most-important Communist organization in Lebanon. It was born as a radical alternative to the Lebanese Communist Party (LCP) but soon became indistinguishable in its pronouncements and actions from that party. It was founded in 1969 by Muhsin Ibrahim, who was a leader of the Movement of Arab Nationalists. The founding congress was held in 1971, but its effectiveness was marred from the beginning by a series of defections and splits. By 1975, the organization had formed an alliance with the LCP and participated in the civil war. Yasir Arafat's friendship with Ibrahim provided the party with much-needed weapons and financial assistance. In recent years, the organization's relations with the LCP worsened and its role in Lebanese politics was marginalized.

Socialist Arab Action Party-Lebanon
(Hizb Al-'Amal Al-Ishtiraki Al-'Arabi-Lubnan)

This small Marxist-Leninist-Stalinist party was founded in 1969 from the Lebanese remnants of the Movement of Arab Nationalists. It presented itself as a radical revolutionary alternative to both the Lebanese Communist Party and the Communist Action Organization. It glorified "armed struggle" and called for a revolution in Lebanon. It was until the 1980s the Lebanese sister party of the Popular Front for the Liberation of Palestine (PLO). It participated actively in the civil war and was linked by a PLO official to the assassination of the American ambassador in Lebanon in 1976.

ARMENIAN PARTIES

Armenian Secret Army for the Liberation of Armenia

This is a small, secretive organization. It was founded in 1975 and has been responsible for acts of violence against Turkish interests around the world. It is dedicated to extract revenge for the massacre of Armenians in

Turkey early in this century. It has been closely associated with the Lebanese and Palestinian left, although the Turkish government forced the Syrian government to suppress its activities in the 1980s.

Dashnak Party

The Dashnak party was founded in 1890 in Tiflis in Russia to draw world attention to the plight of the Armenians living under Ottoman rule. It began as a revolutionary organization but later moderated its stance. The Lebanese Dashnak Party, which rejects the socialist ideology of the mother party, is the major political party for Armenians in Lebanon. It has been affiliated with the right-wing camp but avoided the bloody battles of the Lebanese civil war. Its leadership is indistinguishable from the Armenian political and economic elite in Lebanon. Most Armenian deputies and ministers have been either members of or sympathizers with this party. It won four seats in the 1992 elections.

Hunchak Party

This formerly Marxist-oriented party was founded in 1887 in Geneva but had to adjust its ideology to fit the political environment of Lebanon. It has avoided taking extreme positions in Lebanese politics for fear of jeopardizing the status of Armenians in Lebanon. It has maintained good ties with the Dashnak Party, although the two parties had engaged in bloody clashes in the 1950s. The party has been successful in recruiting in working-class Armenian districts, although intellectuals and professionals lead the party. One leader of the party was elected to parliament in 1992.

Ramgavar Party

This party was founded in 1921 as an organization of Armenian intellectuals who want to avoid the rivalry of the Dashnak and Hunchak Parties. It has emphasized the necessity of preserving Armenian culture and heritage in the diaspora. It was active in the 1960s in creating an opposition front against the political dominance of the Dashnak.

KURDISH PARTIES

Kurdish Democratic Party

This party was founded in 1960 by Jamil Mihhu, who was for years the most prominent Kurdish politician in Lebanon. It operated without a legal license until 1970. It espouses the cause of Kurdish nationalism and works on instilling Kurdish national consciousness among the Kurds in Lebanon. Jamil Mihhu ran for parliament in 1968 but lost. The party was closely affiliated with the

Iraqi regime, which only served to earn the enmity of the Syrian regime. The party was a member of the Lebanese National Movement during the civil war but was later replaced in the movement by its left-wing offshoot.

Kurdish Democratic Party-Provisional Leadership

In 1977 Muhammad Mihhu, son of Jamil Mihhu of the Kurdish Democratic Party, split off from his father's party to form his own. He was a very close ally of the Lebanese National Movement and the PLO.

Lebanese Kurdish Party
(Riz Kari)

This party was founded in 1975 by Faysal Fakhru to steer Kurdish party activity in Lebanon toward the Syrian regime. He objected to Iraqi influence over the Kurdish Democratic Party. This party also struggled to break the monopoly of the Mihhu family over Kurdish political life.

NATIONAL PROSPECTS

As Lebanon continues on the path of reconstruction and national conciliation, some people remain skeptical about its ability to end once and for all the national discord and sectarian hatred. The government of President Ilyas Hrawi is largely overshadowed by the prominent personality of his prime minister, Rafic Hariri. Hariri has emerged as the single most important architect of postwar Lebanon, and his international reputation has secured him a stable political status that few prime ministers have had in modern Lebanon history. His reconstruction plans, however, have earned him the hostility of advocates of the poor in Lebanon. It is widely believed that his plans for postwar Lebanon are based on the old economic formula for prewar Lebanon, which stressed the service sector of the economy at the expense of agriculture and industry, where most of the poor are employed. In addition, his plans do not address the problem of acute centralization that has characterized modern Lebanon. Poor Lebanese residing in remote areas of the country still depend on the services and government agencies centered in Beirut.

The formula of political reform known as the Ta'if Accord has also created resentment on the part of large segments of the Christian population, which feel that Syrian political dominance in Lebanon has caused a reduction of their political power. They especially criticize the marginalization of important opposition figures, such as General Michel 'Awn, who is in exile in France. Many Christian leaders have been hoping that the Syrian army would have been withdrawn from Lebanon by now, while Syrian leaders insist that its army is needed in Lebanon as long as the Lebanese government does not ask for its withdrawal and as long as Israel remains in occupation of part of South Lebanon.

Militias, like the Hizb-ul-Lah, continue to launch armed operations in Lebanon against Israeli occupation in South Lebanon. Negotiations between Israel and Lebanon, according to the terms of the Madrid conference, have been stalled, and there are no signs that the Israeli government of Netanyahu is planning a rejuvenation of the peace process. Lebanon, however, has improved its ties with the United States, and the American government has finally lifted its long-held ban on travel to Lebanon. Moreover, the country has finally been removed from the list of countries involved in major production of narcotics. The Lebanese people, after long years of savage war and bloodshed, remain hopeful although the difficult economic conditions and the widening gap between the rich and the poor pose serious threats to efforts of peace building.

Lebanon elected Emile Lahhud president in 1998, and he accepted the resignation of Prime Minister Rafiq Hariri. Lahhud promised to fight corruption.

Further Reading

AbuKhalil, As'ad. *Historical Dictionary of Lebanon.* Lanham, Md.: Scarecrow Press, 1998.

Ajami, Fouad. *The Vanished Imam.* Ithaca, N.Y.: Cornell University Press, 1986.

Beydoun, Ahmed. *Identite confessionelle et temps social chez les historiens libanais contemorains.* Beirut: Lebanese University, 1984.

Collings, Deirdre, ed. *Peace for Lebanon?* Boulder, Colo.: Lynne Reinner, 1994.

Gilmour, David. *Lebanon: The Fractured Country.* New York: St. Martin's Press, 1983.

Gordon, David. *Lebanon: The Fragmented Nation.* London: Croom Helm, 1980.

Goria, Wade. *Sovereignty and Leadership in Lebanon.* London: Ithaca Press, 1985.

Hanf, Theodor. *Coexistence in Wartime Lebanon.* Trans. John Richardson. London: I.B. Tauris, 1993.

Hudson, Michael. *The Precarious Republic: Political Modernization in Lebanon.* New York: Random House, 1968.

Khalaf, Samir. *Lebanon's Predicament.* New York: Columbia University Press, 1987.

Khalidi, Walid. *Conflict and Violence in Lebanon.* Cambridge, Mass.: Harvard University Press, 1979.

Norton, Augustus Richard. *Amal and the Shi'a.* Austin: University of Texas Press, 1987.

Owen, Roger. *Essays on the Crisis in Lebanon.* London: Ithaca Press, 1976.

Petran, Tabitha. *The Struggle over Lebanon.* New York: Monthly Review Press, 1987.

LESOTHO

By B. David Meyers, Ph.D.

THE SYSTEM OF GOVERNMENT

Lesotho, a nation of slightly fewer than 2 million people, is completely surrounded by South Africa. Most of the nation's GNP is provided by citizens working in South Africa.

Formerly the British territory of Basutoland, Lesotho received its independence in October 1966. Moshoeshoe II, the paramount chief of the Basotho, was recognized as king of a constitutional monarchy. In the last elections before independence, the Basotho National Party (BNP), helped by funds from South Africa, narrowly defeated the Basotho Congress Party (BCP), and the BNP's leader, Chief Leabua Jonathan, became the nation's prime minister.

Relations between Jonathan and King Moshoeshoe were often turbulent, and, by 1970, the king had once been placed under house arrest and, another time, sent overseas in the first of three periods of exile. When he returned from exile, the king agreed to respect the constitutional nature of the monarchy and to refrain from any political activities. Jonathan, meanwhile, further consolidated his own power. In January 1970, when the opposition BCP had seemingly won a majority of seats in elections to the National Assembly, Jonathan suspended the constitution, jailed his opponents, and established rule by decree.

In 1986, South Africa, angered that Lesotho had given sanctuary to antiapartheid African National Congress guerrillas, imposed a blockade on its tiny neighbor. The blockade sparked a military coup, led by General Metsing Lekhanya, who seized power from Jonathan and agreed to expel the guerrillas. In March 1990, following a power struggle between the king and the general, the military government again exiled Moshoeshoe. After seven months the king returned, but rather than refrain from politics, he insisted that military rule be ended and elections held. Lekhanya again deposed him, and the nation's senior chiefs put his son, Letsie III, who promised to keep out of politics, on the throne.

In 1991, another coup, led by Colonel Phisoane Ramaema, ousted Lekhanya and announced that the army would return to barracks following free elections. After a number of postponements, these elections were held in March 1993, and a new government took power.

This elected government, headed by Prime Minister Ntsu Mokhele, quickly ran into problems with the military as armed units fought one another, killed the deputy prime minister, and killed or abducted other Cabinet members. Intervention by neighboring Botswana, South Africa, and Zimbabwe was needed to diffuse these crises. In August 1994, after a series of such violent disturbances, King Letsie dissolved the parliament, dismissed the Mokhele government, and replaced it with one that included the leader of the opposition BNP. Intervention by leaders of the same neighboring states restored the elected government, forced Letsie to abdicate, and reinstated his father, Moshoeshoe.

On January 15, 1996, King Moshoeshoe was killed in an automobile accident and was, again, succeeded by Letsie. In February there was another unsuccessful coup attempt.

Violence again racked Lesotho in 1998 when, following general elections swept by the ruling party, opposition parties claimed the polling was rigged and thousands of angry people took to the streets. Reports of another attempted military coup followed by the arrest of a number of officers increased the widespread disorder. In September, South African and Botswanan soldiers who had entered Lesotho to quell the unrest fought pitched battles with members of the Lesotho Defense Force.

Executive

The Lesotho king is intended to reign as a ceremonial head of state with no executive power. In theory, such a constitutional monarch provides continuity and stability to a political system. To date, this has not been the case in Lesotho as both Letsie and his father, despite promises to the contrary, were politically active. The proper role, and even the continued existence of the monarchy, is often a topic of heated political difference.

Executive authority is vested in the Cabinet, which is headed by the prime minister. Dr. Ntsu Mokhehle, leader of the Basotho Congress Party and later its virtual successor, the Lesotho Congress for Democracy (LCD), served as prime minister from 1993 to 1998. The popular

Mokhehle was a survivor of jail, exile, and coup attempts. When he stepped down due to ill health, he was replaced by Pakalitha Mosisili.

Legislature

Lesotho has a bicameral legislature. There is an 80-member National Assembly whose members are elected from single-member districts at intervals of not more than five years. There is also a Senate, comprising the country's 22 principal chiefs and 11 members appointed by the governing party.

In March 1993 elections to the National Assembly the Basotho Congress Party won all of the seats. In 1998 the LCD captured 79 of the 80 National Assembly seats.

Judiciary

At the top of the judicial system is a High Court that has the power of judicial review of legislative acts. It heads a system of subordinate courts. In 1994, Chief Justice Khoela administered an oath of office to the short-lived government created by King Letsie. Some observers interpreted this as judicial support for this government and for the overthrow of the elected BCP government.

The legal system is based on English common law and Roman-Dutch law. There is a movement to change the Roman-Dutch legal system as it is thought to discriminate against women.

Regional and Local Government

The nation is divided into 10 administrative districts. Outside of the urban areas, the country is divided into numerous chiefdoms, whose traditional leaders fulfill many of the functions of local government.

THE ELECTORAL SYSTEM

Three major parties, nine minor parties, and numerous independent candidates contested the 1998 National Assembly elections. Although there was considerable discussion of major national and local issues, the final outcome was primarily a demonstration of popular affection for the LCD's former leader, Ntsu Mokhehle. The LCD won over 60% of the popular vote and captured a plurality in all but one electoral district. Immediately following the election, the major opposition parties claimed that the election had been fraudulent.

THE PARTY SYSTEM

Political parties in Lesotho began with the formation of the BCP in 1952, more than a decade before indepen-

dence. Lesotho's conservatives saw the BCP programs as radical and formed their own party, the BNP, to protect their positions and beliefs as the country moved toward independence. With the exception of the period of military rule when political activity was suspended, and despite the existence of a multiparty system, one or the other of these two parties or their virtual successor has always controlled the government.

LESOTHO CONGRESS FOR DEMOCRACY (LCD)

The Lesotho Congress for Democracy (LCD) was organized in June 1997 by Ntsu Mokhehle, who was at the time the nation's prime minister and the leader of the Basotho Congress Party (BCP). Mokhehle quit the BCP, which he had founded, in reply to a challenge launched by young, self-proclaimed "progressives," who wished to remove him from the party leadership. Almost half of the BCP's members of Parliament followed Mokhehle into the new party. Pakalitha Mosisili, who had been Mokhehle's deputy as both party leader and prime minister, was among those who made the switch. When age and ill health forced Mokhehle's retirement, Mosisili assumed both the government and the party offices.

The LCD supports the development of a socialist economy and favors the limitation or abolition of the governmental role of chiefs. In the most recent election it campaigned, as did the other major parties, on the promise of more jobs and a continued fight against poverty.

BASOTHO CONGRESS PARTY (BCP)

The Basotho Congress Party (BCP) was formed in 1952 under the leadership of Ntsu Mokhele. From the time of its founding, the party encouraged Lesotho's national independence and opposed the advancement of ties to neighboring South Africa. Party policies have also included the development of a socialist economy and have supported efforts to limit or abolish the governmental roles of the traditional chiefs.

The BCP won the 1960 elections but lost to the BNP in 1965, the last elections before independence. It was apparently winning in 1970, when Jonathan annulled the election results and arrested Mokhele and other BCP leaders. During the years of Jonathan's rule, the BCP temporarily split between those who chose to accept participation in his government of national unity and those who followed Mokhele into exile.

This so-called external faction of the BCP unsuccessfully tried to gain power through a coup in 1974. Throughout the 1970s and 1980s, the Lesotho Liberation Army (LLA), the military wing of the external BCP, conducted a sporadic campaign of violence against

Jonathan's government. Since the BCP's 1993 electoral victory, there have been efforts to integrate these LLA soldiers into the regular army.

The 1997 split left the party with a minority of its former members. In the 1998 elections the BCP came in third in the popular vote and captured no seats in the Assembly. The BCP is headed by Molapo Qhobela, a leader of the faction that ousted Mokhehle.

BASOTHO NATIONAL PARTY (BNP)

The BNP was formed in 1958 under the leadership of Leabua Jonathan, a minor chief. Originally much more conservative than its BCP rival, it supported the traditional chiefs, opposed communism, and sought good relations with South Africa. With the support of the chiefs and their followers and the Catholic Church, and with financial support from South Africa, BNP won the 1965 elections and led the country at independence. During the 1970s and early 1980s, the BNP dominated Lesotho politics. During this period, Jonathan became an opponent of South African apartheid and there were clashes between the two countries. The growing problems with South Africa and the rise in power of the BNP's radical Youth League were the major reasons for the 1986 military coup that removed the party and its leader from power. Jonathan died about a year later.

In the 1993 elections, the BNP, under the leadership of Evaristus Sekhonyana, received only 16% of the popular vote and won no seats. Its prospects were further damaged when Sekhonyana supported King Letsie's brief dismissal of the elected government in August 1994. It is widely believed that the BNP's leaders have been involved with numerous recent military efforts to overthrow the government.

The BNP remains the most conservative of Lesotho's major parties. In 1998 it received 24% of the popular vote but captured only one Assembly seat. The party is still lead by Evaristus Sekhonyana.

OTHER POLITICAL PARTIES

Lesotho has many other political parties, only one of which, Marematlou Freedom Party (MFP), once held a single seat in the National Assembly. The MFP, a royalist party, has, historically, been supported by some of the chiefs, and it may gain wider popular support if BNP falters. MFP is led by A. C. Manyeli.

OTHER POLITICAL FORCES

Within Lesotho, the 2,000-strong army has been, and seemingly remains, the most powerful political actor. The army's long distaste for the governing party comes originally from its years of bloody struggle against the BCP's armed wing, the LLA. In recent years the military leaders have opposed efforts to integrate LLA members into the regular forces and have mutinied over demands for a pay raise. The army has continually resisted the government's efforts to exert control and has killed some political leaders and held others captive. Only threats of South African intervention have prevented, pacified, or ended various army threats to, and actions against, the elected government.

During the 1960s, the Roman Catholic Church was politically powerful and was supportive of the BNP. More recently, church leaders have issued calls for internal peace and for holding a national conference on peace, democracy, and stability, but, in general, they appear peripheral to the ongoing crises and efforts to resolve them. Lesotho's labor unions have generally compounded the nation's problems with their own strikes and economic demands.

More than anything else, Lesotho's political fate continues to be decided in neighboring South Africa. South African decisions to use fewer foreign miners has hurt Lesotho's already-poor economy, while South African diplomatic and military power has diffused or decided its series of political crises. Since President Mandela took power in Pretoria in May 1994, the question of integrating Lesotho into South Africa has frequently been raised but appears unlikely in the foreseeable future.

NATIONAL PROSPECTS

Lesotho's major political institutions appear unable to provide the nation with any stability as the government, monarchy, and army lurch from crisis to crisis. No internal actor appears capable of ending this cycle.

The country has become increasingly dependent on its neighbors, particularly South Africa, for any semblance of security. There is no reason to expect change from this pattern of dependence.

Further Reading

Bardhill, John E., and James H. Cobbe. *Lesotho: Dilemmas of Dependence in Southern Africa*. Boulder, Colo.: Westview Press, 1985.

Kelso, B.J."An Uncertain Future." *Africa Report*, March–April 1993, 40–43.

THE REPUBLIC OF LIBERIA

By Elizabeth L. Normandy, Ph.D.

THE SYSTEM OF GOVERNMENT

Liberia is located in Western Africa. It lies between Sierra Leone and Côte d'Ivoire and borders the North Atlantic Ocean. It has a land area of 38,250 square miles, slightly larger than the state of Tennessee.

Liberia's population is estimated at 2.1 million people, excluding the approximately 1.4 million refugees residing in the surrounding countries of Côte d'Ivoire, Guinea, Ghana, Sierra Leone, and Nigeria. Approximately 160,000 Liberians have died between 1990 and 1997 as a result of the civil war. In addition, at least 7,000 refugees from Sierra Leone have fled into Liberia as the result of a May 1997 coup in Sierra Leone.

Indigenous African ethnic groups make up 95% of Liberia's population. These groups include the Kpelle, Bassa, Gio, Kru, Grebo, Mano, Krahn, Gola, Gbandi, Loma, Kissi, Vai, and Bella. Americo-Liberians, descendants of the African Americans who settled the territory in the 19th century, make up 5% of the population. Those who practice traditional African religions are 70% of the population, while 20% of the remainder are Muslim and 10% are Christian.

Liberia has a republican form of government established in 1847 and patterned after the United States. From 1877 to 1980, Liberia was ruled by the True Whig Party (TWP), which was dominated by the Americo-Liberian elite. Americo-Liberian domination of Liberian politics ended in April 1980 when a coup brought a military regime, led by Samuel K. Doe, to power. Doe was elected to the post of president in 1985, returning Liberia to a civilian republican form of government. An armed insurrection in 1989 resulted in the death of Doe and brought to power a series of interim governments that held office between 1990 and 1997 as an expanding array of rebel factions carried out a bloody struggle for control of the country. In July 1997, Charles Taylor, leader of the rebel faction that began the insurrection, was elected to the presidency in the first multiparty elections since 1985.

Executive

Under Liberia's constitution, approved by a national referendum in 1984, executive power is vested in a president who is head of state, head of government, and commander in chief of the armed forces. The president is elected through universal suffrage for a six-year term. The president appoints a 16-member Cabinet.

Following the death of Samuel Doe in 1990, Amos Sawyer was inaugurated as interim president. The Interim Government of National Unity (IGNU) was backed by ECOWAS, a regional organization of West African states that had put an 8,000-member peacekeeping force known as ECOMOG into the country. The Sawyer government entered into a cease-fire with the rebel forces, a truce that lasted for two years until October 1992. A July 1993 peace accord created a five-member transitional authority, the Liberian National Transitional Government (LNTG), to rule until elections were held. The council contained representatives of the three major factions in the war and two independent members agreeable to the principal factions. Presidential aspirants were barred from membership on the interim council, and transitional officeholders were prohibited from running for president.

Amid bickering over the composition and leadership of the transitional government, David Kpormikor was named chairman of the council. An amendment to the 1993 peace accord in December 1994 provided for the replacement of the transitional government and, in September 1995, Wilton Sankawulo became the head of the five-member council until elections could be held in August 1996. The council included representatives of at least three rebel factions in the civil war, and the leaders of the major factions influenced the selection of the Cabinet. Continued fighting prevented elections from being held, and, in August 1996, Ruth Perry was selected to serve as interim leader until elections in 1997. In July 1997, Charles Taylor defeated Ellen Johnson-Sirleaf and 11 other candidates to become president. Taylor's Cabinet includes some of his former adversaries.

Legislature

Liberia's 1984 constitution provides for a bicameral legislature. The 26 members of the upper house, the Senate, are elected for a nine-year term. Members of the 64-seat House of Representatives are elected for six-year terms. There is no limit on the number of terms a legislator may serve.

There are 2 seats for each of Liberia's 13 counties in the Senate and 1 representative for every 20,000 people in the House of Representatives. The passage of laws requires the approval of both houses and the president. The president has veto power, but a presidential veto can be overridden by a two-thirds majority of both houses.

Liberia does not have a strong tradition of legislative independence. Until the election of Samuel Doe, the True Whig Party dominated the executive and the legislative branches. Doe's party, the National Democratic Party of Liberia (NDPL), won 51 of the 64 seats in the House and 21 of the 26 seats in the Senate in the 1985 election. The Liberal Action Party (LAP) won 8 seats in the House and 3 seats in the Senate, while the Unity Party (UP) won 3 seats in the House and 1 seat in the Senate. The Liberian Unification Party (LUP) won 2 seats in the House and 1 in the Senate.

In March 1994, a unicameral Transitional Legislative Assembly was established. Members of the 35-seat body were appointed by the leaders of the major factions in the civil war. In July 1997, Charles Taylor's National Patriotic Party (NPP) captured a majority of the 90 seats in the bicameral legislature.

Judiciary

The constitution of Liberia provides for an independent judiciary with power vested in the People's Supreme Court and several lower courts. Magistrates' courts and circuit courts exist at the local level. The Supreme Court comprises a chief justice and four associate justices. They and the judges of the lower courts are appointed by the president and approved by the Senate. In March 1992, a five-member interim Supreme Court was established. Rebel leader Charles Taylor appointed the chief justice and two other justices. The remaining two justices were appointed by the interim president, Amos Sawyer.

Traditionally, Liberia has maintained a dual legal system: statutory law based on Anglo-American common law for the modern sector, and customary law based on unwritten tribal practices for the indigenous sector. Efforts to unify the legal system have not been successful.

Regional and Local Government

Liberia is divided into 13 counties administered by superintendents who are the direct representatives of the president. They are appointed by the president and approved by the Senate. Each county also has a county council. The capital city of each county is governed by a mayor and a city council. The counties are divided into districts administered by district commissioners. The districts are further divided into smaller units administered by paramount, clan, and town chiefs who are locally elected. Monrovia, the capital city, is administered by a city corporation that levies and collects taxes on real property within the city limits. Historically, local governments have had very little fiscal or administrative autonomy from the central government.

THE ELECTORAL SYSTEM

Liberia's constitution calls for a multiparty system and an Elections Commission to conduct and supervise all elections for public office. Election is by universal suffrage exercised by citizens 18 years of age or older. Citizenship is available only to people of black ancestry and is conferred by birth or naturalization.

Four parties participated in the 1995 elections: the National Democratic Party of Liberia (NDPL), led by Samuel K. Doe; the Liberia Action Party (LAP), led by Jackson F. Doe; the Unity Party (UP), headed by Edward B. Kesselly; and the Liberia Unification Party (LUP), headed by Gabriel Kpoleh. The NDPL captured the majority of the seats in the legislature, and Samuel Doe took the presidency with 50.9% of the vote. Jackson Doe of the LAP won 26.4% of the vote for president and other candidates received 22.7%. Reports of election irregularities were widespread.

In the 1997 elections, Charles Taylor defeated 12 other presidential candidates, receiving 75.3% of the approximately 700,000 votes. Taylor's closest challenger, Ellen Johnson-Sirleaf, a former head of the UNDP Regional Bureau for Africa running for the Unity Party, won 9.5% of the popular vote. Other candidates for president included Alhaji Kromah and George Bailey, leaders of two main factions in the civil war. Charles Taylor's party, the National Patriotic Party (NPP), captured 21 of 26 seats in the Senate and 49 of 64 seats in the House of Representatives.

Voter turnout in the 1997 elections, which were monitored by 500 international observers, was estimated at over 85%. A seven-member Independent Electoral Commission conducted the election. Taylor and his party conducted an aggressive and well-financed campaign that reached all parts of Liberia. Taylor's considerable name recognition was enhanced by his monopolization of the airwaves. International observers certified that the elections were free and fair.

THE PARTY SYSTEM

For more than a century, Liberia was effectively a one-party state dominated by the True Whig Party. In the years preceding the 1980 coup, the most significant opposition came from the Progressive Alliance of Liberia (PAL) and the Movement for Justice in Africa (MOJA). Headed by Gabriel Baccus Mathews, PAL was founded by Liberian students in the United States and began functioning in Liberia in 1978. In early 1980, PAL registered as a political party under the name Progressive People's Party (PPP). Formed in Liberia in 1973 as a campus-based intellectual movement, MOJA was a pressure group led by Drs. Togba Nah Tipoteh and Amos Sawyer from the faculty of the University of Liberia. It focused on labor grievances and endorsed industrial action.

The 1980 military coup resulted in the destruction of the True Whig Party. When the ban on political parties was lifted in 1984, the Americo-Liberians combined with indigenous Liberians to form the Liberian Action Party (LAP). In the 1985 elections, four parties, Doe's NDPL, the LAP, the Unity Party (UP), and the Liberia Unification Party (LUP), won seats. Two other parties and their leaders were banned. These were the Liberia People's Party (LPP) headed by Amos Sawyer and the United People's Party (UPP) headed by Gabriel Baccus Mathews.

By 1996, the political party system consisted of many of the same parties that had existed in 1985 plus the newly created party of Charles Taylor, the National Patriotic Party (NPP). These parties were the National Democratic Party of Liberia (NDPL), led by Augustus Caine and formerly the party of Samuel Doe; the Liberian Action Party (LAP), led by Emmanuel Kromah and formerly supported by Americo-Liberian elements; the Unity Party (UP), led by Joseph Kofa and preparing to run Johnson-Sirleaf for president in 1997; the United Peoples Party (UPP), led by Gabriel Baccus Mathews and banned in the 1985 election; and the Liberia People's Party (LPP), led by Dusty Wolokollie and formerly headed by Amos Sawyer, interim president of Liberia from 1990 to 1993.

THE POLITICAL PARTIES

Charles Taylor's party, the NPP, is an outgrowth of his rebel movement, the National Patriotic Front of Liberia (NPFL), which, in December 1989, launched an incursion from Côte d'Ivoire into Liberia in an attempt to oust Samuel Doe from power. The NPFL, which was dominated by the Gio and Mano ethnic groups, took on Doe's forces, the Armed Forces of Liberia (AFL), which were dominated by the Krahn ethnic group. ECOMOG troops, which arrived in Monrovia in 1990, succeeded in pushing NPFL forces out of Monrovia, obtaining a cease-fire among the three warring factions [the NPFL, the AFL, and the Independent National Patriotic Front of Liberia (INPFL), a Taylor splinter group], and installing an interim government. Taylor's forces controlled most of the territory outside of Monrovia.

In 1991, another rebel movement, the United Liberia Movement for Democracy (ULIMO) was formed from anti-Taylor, ex-AFL soldiers who had fled to Sierra Leone. This movement, which launched a successful incursion against the NPFL in 1992, was initially led by Raleigh Seekie and was dominated by the Krahn ethnic group. Taylor's forces ended the cease-fire in October 1992 by launching artillery and infantry attacks on ECOMOG forces in Monrovia. ECOMOG forces, heavily dominated by Nigerian troops, used Nigerian jets to bomb Taylor's headquarters.

As neighboring countries tried to broker a peace accord in 1993, rebel groups proliferated. ULIMO split into two groups, one led by Alhaji Kromah that was Mandingo-based and came to be known as ULIMO-K, and one eventually led by Roosevelt Johnson that was Krahn-based and known as ULIMO-J. By 1994, there were two wings of the NPFL, two wings of ULIMO, the AFL, the Lofa Defense Force, the Nimba Redemption Council, and a militia from the interim government (IGNU) contending for power. In addition, a new group, the Liberian Peace Council, was formed from elements of the AFL. Krahn-based, it was led by George Boley.

After more than a dozen peace conferences, three major peace accords, several broken cease-fires, and three interim governments, a new accord was signed in August 1996 that led to the installation of a new interim government and the disarming of all factions. Charles Taylor proceeded to transform the National Patriotic Front into the National Patriotic Party in preparation for the 1997 elections. Alhaji Kromah of ULIMO-K and George Boley of the Liberian Peace Council also prepared to contest the presidential election.

NATIONAL PROSPECTS

The new government of Liberia faces a number of formidable challenges. It must rebuild the economic infrastructure destroyed by the civil war. It must repatriate as many as 750,000 refugees and restore water, electricity, and social services. Housing, education, and employment are needed for the former rebels. It is unclear to what extent the international community, especially the United States, Liberia's traditional friend, will help this country, which has struggled for years with a large foreign debt.

Political challenges include the maintenance of order and stability in a country that has seen so much ethnic strife. The leadership must inspire confidence among the various ethnic groups and foster reconciliation to heal the wounds of war. It must demonstrate a respect for human rights and tolerate dissent without resorting to repressive measures. It must see to it that development and wealth creation are more evenly distributed throughout the nation than has been the case in the past. Charles Taylor won at the ballot box what he could not win on the battlefield. Whether or not he will be able to use the opportunity to make Liberia's future different from its past remains to be seen.

Further Reading

Clapham, Christopher. *Liberia and Sierra Leone: An Essay in Comparative Politics*. London: Cambridge University Press, 1976.

Dolo, Emmanuel. *Democracy versus Dictatorship: The Quest for Freedom and Justice in Africa's Oldest Republic—Liberia*. Washington, D.C.: University Press of America, 1996.

Dunn, D. Elwood, and Svend E. Holsoe. *Historical Dictionary of Liberia*. Lanham, Md.: Scarecrow Press, 1985.

Hlophe, Stephen S. *Class, Ethnicity and Politics in Liberia: A Class Analysis of Power Struggles in the Tubman and Tolbert Administrations from 1944–1975*. Washington, D.C.: University Press of America, 1979.

Jackson, Robert H., and Carl G. Rosberg. *Personal Rule in Black Africa: Prince, Autocrat, Prophet, Tyrant*. Berkeley: University of California Press, 1982.

Kieh, George K., Jr. *Dependency and the Foreign Policy of a Small Power: The Liberian Case*. Lewiston, N.Y.: Edward E. Mellen Press, 1992.

Liebnow, J. Gus. *The Evolution of Privilege*. Ithaca, N.Y.: Cornell University Press, 1969.

———. *The Quest for Democracy*. Bloomington: Indiana University Press, 1987.

Weller, Marc., ed. *Regional Peacekeeping and International Enforcement: The Liberian Crisis*. New York: Cambridge University Press. 1994.

SOCIALIST PEOPLE'S LIBYAN ARAB JAMAHIRIYA

(Al-Jamahiriya al-Arabiya al-Libiya al-Sha'abiya al-Ishtirakiya)

By Ronald Bruce St.John, Ph.D.
Revised by Curtis R. Ryan, Ph.D.

THE SYSTEM OF GOVERNMENT

The Socialist People's Libyan Arab Jamahiriya, a nation of 5.3 million people, is a unitary state governed by a unique organization of congresses and committees. This system of government evolved slowly after the Libyan Free Unionist Officers Movement, led by a Central Committee of 12 officers, executed a well-planned coup d'état on September 1, 1969, and overthrew the monarchy that had ruled the United Kingdom of Libya since independence in 1951.

The Central Committee soon renamed itself the Revolutionary Command Council (RCC), and on December 11, 1969, it replaced the 1951 constitution with a Constitutional Proclamation, which described the Libyan Arab Republic as a free Arab democratic republic constituting part of the Arab nation, with Islam as the religion of the state and Arab unity as its overall objective.

The RCC is designated the highest authority in the Libyan Arab Republic and exercises both executive and legislative functions. As such, it is empowered to take whatever measures it deems necessary to protect the regime or the revolution. Such measures may take the form of proclamations, laws, orders, or resolutions. The Constitutional Proclamation specifically gives the RCC power to declare war, conclude and ratify treaties, appoint diplomatic envoys and receive diplomatic missions, proclaim martial law, and control the armed forces.

The RCC is further empowered to appoint a Council of Ministers consisting of a prime minister and ministers; the Council's function is to implement the state's general policy as defined by the RCC. The RCC may also dismiss the prime minister and ministers; the prime minister's resignation automatically results in the resignation of the entire Council of Ministers.

The 1969 Constitutional Proclamation was to remain in force until the completion of the so-called nationalist democratic revolution, when it would be superseded by a permanent constitution. This has never occurred, and since Libya's political system has experienced continuous change since the overthrow of the monarchy, the system functioning today bears little resemblance to the one detailed in the proclamation. Moreover, there is some doubt as to whether the Constitutional Proclamation will ever be replaced by a constitution. The Green Book, the economic and political manifesto of Colonel Muammar al-Qaddafi, de facto ruler of Libya, describes human-made law, including constitutions, as illogical and invalid, concluding that the genuine law of any society is either tradition (custom) or religion.

Executive

Colonel Qaddafi, initially chairman of the RCC, is the head of state. The general secretary of the General People's Congress (GPC) is the chief executive, and the General Secretariat of the GPC is the chief executive's staff and advisory body. The General People's Committee (or General Popular Committee), comprised of a general secretary and 19 secretaries, serves as a Cabinet, replacing the former Council of Ministers, which was abolished in 1977.

Colonel Qaddafi was the general secretary of the GPC from 1977 until early 1979, when he relinquished the post to concentrate on what he described as "revolutionary activities with the masses." He has retained his position as de facto commander in chief of the armed forces and adopted the new title of leader of the revolution. During Qaddafi's tenure as general secretary of the GPC, the remaining members of the RCC initially formed its General Secretariat. They also resigned their posts in 1979 to focus on revolutionary activities. Regardless of position or title, Qaddafi and the former members of the RCC control and direct the Libyan government. Members of the General Secretariat of the General People's Congress are selected by them and serve at their convenience. Members of the General Secretariat, in turn, appoint members of the General People's Committee who serve three-year terms.

The objectives of the revolution have remained constant since the overthrow of the monarchy and can best be summarized within the major goal statements of freedom, socialism, and unity. The emphasis on freedom is the result of Libya's long history of foreign domination and exploitation. In practical terms, it means complete political and economic independence from any foreign direction or control. Through socialism, more often referred to as social justice, the revolution seeks to insure equal access to law and justice, to achieve a more equitable distribution of wealth, and to eliminate class differences. With the issuance of part two of Qaddafi's Green Book in 1977, the socioeconomic revolution in Libya became increasingly radical and pervasive. Unity is sought both domestically and internationally. On the national level, the objective is to unite society in purpose and effort by a centralized political authority. Internationally, the goal is overall Arab unity, and in pursuit of it, the government repeatedly has proposed mergers with neighboring Arab states.

Legislature

The national-level representative body is called the General People's Congress (GPC), which was created in 1976. Delegates to the GPC are usually the chairpersons of the basic people's congresses and the branch or municipal people's committees, as well as representatives from the university student unions and the national federation of unions and professional associations. The number of delegates varies from session to session but generally approximates 1,000.

Scheduled to meet annually, normally for two weeks in January or February, the GPC is the major arena in which the plans, programs, and policies of the government are discussed and ratified. Formal ratification carries with it the responsibility of implementation by the people's committees, people's congresses, and trade unions and associations. At its first session in 1976, the General Secretariat of the GPC began submitting major government policies and plans to the GPC for review and authorization. Both the general administrative budget and the 1976–80 development budget were submitted, for example, as well as several major domestic and foreign policy items. This practice was continued thereafter. At the fifth session of the GPC (January 1–6, 1980), for example, a progress report on the 1976–80 five-year plan and a draft of the 1981–2000 national socioeconomic plan were discussed, as were a wide range of other domestic policy and foreign policy questions ranging from an amendment to the social security law to the bilateral pacts that Libya had concluded with other states in 1979. Nevertheless, there are limits to the subjects the head of state will allow on the GPC agenda. Libya's intervention in Chad, for example, was not discussed at the sixth session of the GPC (January 3–7, 1981).

With the abolition of the RCC and the Council of Ministers in 1977, both executive and legislative power was theoretically vested in the GPC. In reality, the GPC has delegated much of its major responsibility to the General Secretariat and the General People's Committee. In December 1978, for example, the GPC authorized the General People's Committee to appoint ambassadors and the secretary of foreign affairs to receive the credentials of foreign diplomats.

The fourth session of the GPC (December 1978) illustrated some of the limits of its power and authority. In the first two days of the Congress, several representatives called for an increase in salaries, although the recently published second part of the Green Book had called for their abolition. Other representatives demanded an end to the military draft after the General Secretariat had announced universal conscription for all young people. As a result of these and similar actions, the meeting was adjourned on the third day, officially out of respect for the death of the president of Algeria. Unofficially, delegate independence convinced the general secretary and the General Secretariat that they had to reassert their control over the revolution. After the adjournment, several people's committees were told to select new members before the GPC reconvened, and mobile election teams representing the government were dispatched to monitor those reelections. Similarly, when the ninth session of the GPC (February 1984) opposed three key proposals put forward by Qaddafi, he criticized the reactionary nature of the body and later revised the delegate makeup to ensure that such opposition was not repeated.

While the General Secretariat closely supervises the activities of the General People's Congress, the GPC does serve as a clearinghouse and sounding board for the views of the Libyan people as transmitted by their representatives on the congresses, committees, and functional organizations. Moreover, for the first time in the nation's history, subnational government requires popular participation in the selection of local leadership and allows popular involvement in the local policymaking process. At the same time, it provides an effective organization for the national leadership to communicate its ideas and objectives to the people. In this regard, while Colonel Qaddafi and the former members of the RCC remain the primary decision makers, the current political system has produced a level of representation and participation hitherto unknown in Libya.

Judiciary

From the beginning, the RCC indicated that it intended to place the nation's entire juridical system in an Islamic context. On October 28, 1971, the RCC established a Legislative Review and Amendment Committee, composed of the leading legal experts in Libya, to make existing laws conform with the basic tenets of the Islamic code of law, the *Shari'ah*. Two years later, the RCC promulgated a law that merged the existing civil and *Shari'ah* courts into a single juridical system.

The revised court system consists of four levels: Partial Court, Court of First Instance, Appeals Court, and the Supreme Court. The Partial Court, existing in most villages and towns, is the primary level of the system. The Court of First Instance serves as a court of appeal for the Partial Court. In addition, it is the court of original jurisdiction for all matters involving more than 100 Libyan dinars. An Appeals Court sits in each of three cities: Tripoli, Benghazi, and Sabhah. As its name suggests, it hears cases referred from a Court of First Instance. The Appeals Court has no original jurisdiction except for cases involving felonies or high crimes. The Supreme Court sits in Tripoli and is composed of five chambers specializing in civil and commercial, criminal, administrative, constitutional, and personal matters. Each chamber consists of a five-judge panel with the majority establishing a decision. Before its formal abolition, the RCC appointed all judges; now, they are appointed by the GPC with the General Secretariat and the secretary of justice probably making the actual decision. With the exception of political cases, both judicial independence and due process of law generally appear to have been respected since 1969.

In addition to the regular court system, certain other bodies are involved in the administration or enforcement of justice. The Supreme Court for Judicial Authorities plays an administrative role, supervising and coordinating the various courts. The prime responsibility of the Council of State is to deliver advisory legal opinions for government bodies on draft legislation or other actions or regulations they are contemplating. A People's Court has been convened periodically to try crimes against the state. Plots and conspiracies against the state have also been referred to special ad hoc military courts convened for that purpose.

Regional and Local Government

There are three levels of subnational government in Libya: the zone, the municipality or branch municipality, and the national. At the lowest level, zone residents elect a zone people's committee (or popular committee) to administer the affairs of the zone. The zone does not include a congress or legislative body.

The next echelon of government is the municipality. In the case of Libya's larger urban areas, municipalities are divided into branch municipalities; Tripoli, for instance, is divided into five branches. There are approximately 190 municipalities or branch municipalities, although the total number fluctuates. All zones are components of either a municipality or a branch municipality. Each municipality or branch municipality elects a legislative assembly known as the basic people's congress (BPC). Meeting quarterly, the BPC makes recommendations or decisions on administrative matters within its jurisdiction, such as roads, sewage, water, and public clinics. The BPC also debates the agenda of the GPC in advance of its annual meeting. The BPC selects its own chairman as well as a five-member people's committee, which has day-to-day administrative responsibility. All voting in the BPC is public; it is either a show of hands or a division into yes-or-no camps.

In those instances where a municipality is divided into two or more branches, a municipal People's Leadership Committee is established to coordinate the activities of the branch people's committees. The municipal people's leadership committee is made up of the chairperson and deputy chair of the branch people's committees. They select one of their number to be chair, who is, effectively, the mayor of the municipality. In those municipalities not large enough to be divided into branches, the chair of the municipal people's committee serves as mayor of the municipality. In 1978, the General People's Committee at the national level was decentralized to include a similar structure at the municipal level. Municipal general people's committees are elected by the BPC for a term of three years. They are responsible for the coordination of activities between the General People's Committee and the BPC.

In addition to the zone and municipal committees and congresses, Libyan workers are organized into unions or professional associations. Each union or professional association elects its own people's committee (also known as popular committee) to administer its affairs. In turn, these People's Committees participate in the federation of unions at the national level. The national federation of unions and professional associations sends representatives to the GPC to address issues of special relevance to the unions, but these representatives are not allowed to vote on major policy issues. While the unions and professional associations bring necessary expertise to selected issues, Colonel Qaddafi has insisted that their views as citizens be represented through the people's committees and the BPCs.

Libyan universities are managed to a large degree by student unions. Under this system, each college or faculty in Libya's three universities (Tripoli, Benghazi, and Beida) elects a chairperson and a committee (also known as cabinet) to administer the college. Representatives of these committees form the university student union, which, along with the president of the university, is responsible for running the university. The president of the university serves at the pleasure of the members of the student union. Like unions and professional associations, university student unions attend the GPC in a nonvoting capacity.

A completely new echelon of subnational government, the revolutionary committee, was also established in 1979. Revolutionary committees now exist in virtually all government departments and agencies as well as within the BPCs, the people's committees of the union and professional associations, the university student unions, and the armed forces.

The revolutionary-committee system was established to raise the political consciousness of the people, especially in those areas that seemed to be influenced by traditional or petit bourgeois ideas or individuals. It was also expected to counter the growing tendency of BPCs to advocate parochial interests and concerns instead of taking a broader view of the nation's needs. Examples of this latter tendency were the excessive budgetary demands made by

BPCs at the Fourth General People's Congress and the reluctance of people's committees west of Tripoli to support the reallocation of coastal farming land.

Revolutionary committees report directly to Qaddafi. Colonel Qaddafi convenes the revolutionary committees both individually and en masse. Since all members are self-proclaimed zealots, the revolutionary committees have become the true cadres of the revolution. In the words of Colonel Qaddafi, "the People's Committees exercise administrative responsibilities while the Revolutionary Committees exercise revolutionary control."

THE ELECTORAL SYSTEM

The Declaration of the Establishment of the People's Authority declares that direct popular authority is the basis for the political system in the Socialist People's Libyan Arab Jamahiriya. The people exercise their authority through the people's committees, people's congresses, unions and professional associations, and the General People's Congress. Elections are direct, and all voting consists of a show of hands or a division into yes-or-no camps. Suffrage and committee/congress membership are open to all Libyan citizens 18 years of age or older in good legal and political standing.

In theory, the residents of each zone elect their own people's committee. Similarly, the residents of each branch municipality or municipality elect their own basic people's congress. The members of a BPC then elect a chairman and a five-member branch or municipal people's committee. The General People's Congress is made up of the chairmen of the BPC, the branch and municipal people's committees, and representatives of the people's committees for unions, professional associations, and student unions.

In reality, the revolutionary committees severely limit the democratic process by closely supervising committee and congress elections at the branch and municipal levels of government. Revolutionary committees scrutinize the professional and revolutionary credentials of all candidates for the basic people's congresses, professional people's committees, and the municipal General People's Committees; only approved candidates actually stand for election.

THE PARTY SYSTEM

The RCC has continued the monarchy's ban on the organization and operation of political parties. The only exception to this was the 1971 formation of the Arab Socialist Union (ASU) modeled after the Egyptian ASU under Nasser. But even by the mid-1970s, the ASU disappeared from the Libyan political scene. In effect, the December 1969 Decision on the Protection of the Revolution, the Penal Code, and Law No. 71 of 1972 render political party activity of any sort a crime and constitute a strict legal injunction against unauthorized political activity.

Like many Islamic thinkers, Colonel Qaddafi rejects the political party system. This is not because it is fundamentally incompatible with the Koran or the *Shari'ah* but rather because he is unfavorably impressed with party organization and competition. In the Green Book, he describes the political party as the modern dictatorial instrument of governing and the party system as an overt form of dictatorship.

Qaddafi's condemnation of the political party system is multifaceted. He argues that political parties, because they are generally made up of people of similar beliefs, represent and promote the interests of only a segment of society. Such segments form parties to attain their ends and impose their doctrines on society as a whole. Moreover, in such a system, competition between parties frequently escalates, often resulting in the dominant party or parties ignoring the rights and interests of minority-party members. In a final criticism, Qaddafi argues that political parties, in their struggle to gain power, often destroy the accomplishments of their predecessors, even if those accomplishments were for the general good. His solution to these dilemmas is the system of congresses and committees that he has established.

GENERAL PEOPLE'S CONGRESS SYSTEM

The development of Libya's current political system has been an evolutionary process that very likely is still incomplete. To understand this system and how it functions, it is necessary to trace its progress from the traditional, tribal-based monarchy, which the RCC overthrew in 1969, to the formal Declaration of the Establishment of the People's Authority in 1977.

The members of the Revolutionary Command Council shared similar backgrounds, motivations, and world views. Most were from lower- middle-class families and minor tribes and attended the Libyan military academy at a time when a military career offered opportunities for higher education and upward socioeconomic mobility. The language of the RCC was the language of Arab nationalism guided by the precepts of the Koran and *Shari'ah*, strengthened by a conviction that only the revolutionary government understood and spoke for the masses.

The September 1, 1969, coup d'état was completed without the participation of any organized civilian groups, and initially the RCC maintained the military character of the revolution. In the early days, it exercised both executive and legislative functions, enshrining its right to do so in the December 1969 Constitutional Proclamation. Later, the RCC appointed civilians to the Council of Ministers to help operate the government, but even then it reserved supreme authority in all fields for itself. It sat at the top of the pyramid, issuing proclamations, laws, and resolutions; insuring support of the armed forces; overseeing the activities of the government; and creating new institutions to promote the objectives of the revolution.

The RCC's chairman, Colonel Qaddafi, quickly became the dominant figure in the revolutionary government. While never given formal authority over his RCC colleagues, Qaddafi was able to impose his will through a combination of personality and argument. In theory, the RCC functioned as a collegial body with the members discussing issues and policies until enough of a consensus evolved to establish a unified position. In practice, as the revolution unfolded, Qaddafi increasingly exercised the final choice in major decisions and Libyans increasingly looked to his public statements to guide their own behavior. In late 1975, he issued part one of the Green Book, entitled "The Solution to the Problem of Democracy." Part two followed in the fall of 1977 and part three in early 1979.

The executive-legislative system comprised of the RCC and the Council of Ministers operated into 1977; however, on September 1, 1976, the seventh anniversary of the revolution, Colonel Qaddafi introduced a plan to reorganize the government. The key feature of his proposal was the creation of a new, national-level representative body called the General People's Congress (GPC) to replace the RCC as the supreme instrument of government. The details of the plan were included in the Declaration of the Establishment of the People's Authority issued on March 2, 1977, which fundamentally revised the governmental organization described in the 1969 Constitutional Proclamation. The March 1977 Declaration also changed the name of the country to the Socialist People's Libyan Arab Jamahiriya. *Jamahiriya* was a newly coined Arabic word with no official definition but unofficially has been translated as "people's power" or "state of the masses."

Colonel Qaddafi was designated general secretary of the GPC, and the remaining members of the now-defunct RCC made up the General Secretariat. A General People's Committee was also named to replace the Council of Ministers, whose 26 members were termed secretaries instead of ministers.

On June 11, 1971, Colonel Qaddafi announced the formation of the Arab Socialist Union (ASU), an official mass-mobilization organization patterned after the Egyptian counterpart of the same name. The ASU system was envisioned as an organization from local to national level that would provide the masses with an opportunity to participate in the establishment and execution of local policies; it also could function as a pervasive network of organizations throughout Libyan society capable both of monitoring citizens at all levels and of becoming a source of support for revolutionary policies.

The ASU was organized at the national, governate, and basic (local) levels. Both the basic and *muhafaza* units consisted of two main organizations: a congress (or conference) representing the general membership and a committee for leadership. Membership was based both on geography (places of residence) and function (occupation or workplace). Application for membership was made either where the individual lived (a *mudiriya* or *mahalat*) or at the workplace; however, the individual could not join the ASU at both levels. The basic committee consisted of 10 people elected by and from the basic congress to serve as its executive body. The governate congress consisted of two or more representatives elected from each basic unit, with the actual number elected depending on the size of the basic unit's membership. The governate committee consisted of 20 people elected by and from the congress members.

Membership in the ASU was open to any Libyan citizen of the working people who was 18 or more years of age, in good legal standing and sound mental health, and not a member of the royal family or associated with the previous monarchical government or specifically barred by the RCC. The charter of the ASU specified that 50% of all ASU members must be workers and farmers.

The ASU structure at the national level was the National General Congress (or Conference), a forerunner of the General People's Congress. The Congress was made up of 10, 14, or 20 representatives from each governate, as well as members of the RCC, the Council of Ministers, and delegates from the army, police, youth and women's organizations, professional associations, and trade unions. The term of the National General Congress, scheduled to meet every two years, was six years. The ASU was firmly controlled by the RCC with Qaddafi serving as president and the other members of the RCC designated the Supreme Leading Authority of the Arab Socialist Union.

By 1972, the ASU was dismantled, since the RCC's rigid direction and control stifled local initiative and suffocated local leadership. The former district and subdistrict divisions were abolished, thus reducing subnational administration to the governate and municipality. The principal organ of local government at both levels became the council, which had both executive and legislative powers. At the governate level, executive power was exercised by the governor; at the municipal level, by the mayor. Both governors and mayors were appointed by the RCC.

On April 15, 1973, Colonel Qaddafi proclaimed a popular revolution and called for the Libyan people to elect people's committees. Like the ASU, the people's committee structure was given both a geographical and a functional basis. Geographically, committees were formed at the zone, municipal, and governate levels. At the zone level, direct popular elections were used to fill the seats on the people's committee. Later in 1973, the RCC promulgated Law No. 78 to clarify the administrative responsibilities of the people's committees. The law transferred the functions and authority of the governate and municipal councils established in 1972 to the people's committees at the same levels. The chairs of the governate people's committees, in effect, became the governors and the chairs of the municipal people's committees became the mayors. The RCC also authorized the election of people's committees in public corporations, institutions, companies, and universities as well as in other sectors, such as hospitals, convalescent homes, and government printing plants.

The creation of the people's committee system was a significant stage in Libya's political evolution. For the first time in Libya's history, the subnational political system actively encouraged popular participation in the selection of local leadership and allowed substantial local involvement in the local policymaking process. With its formation, the RCC increased the political involvement and experience of the Libyan people and focused their attention on the issues of most importance to the local community.

Still not satisfied with the level of popular involvement and participation, Qaddafi at the 1974 National Congress called for a further refinement of the subnational administrative machinery. The Congress responded by stressing the primacy of the people's committees in administrative affairs and by recommending the elimination of the governates. In February 1975, the RCC issued a law abolishing the governates and reestablishing a Ministry of Municipalities. Within five years, another RCC law formally established the municipality as the single geographical and administrative subdivision in Libya.

OTHER POLITICAL FORCES

The Military

The September 1969 coup d'état was totally military in conception, planning, and execution. It was accomplished without the participation or even knowledge of organized civilian groups. In the early years the RCC insisted on maintaining the military direction of the revolution. Under attack from all facets of the former elite structure, the RCC worked to create a reliable coercive arm capable of sustaining the revolution.

To a certain degree, the military has become the most representative institution in the country; it now draws its membership from all strata of society. Recognizing this fact, Qaddafi has integrated the armed forces and sought to instill in them a spirit of unity, discipline, and professionalism. Within a year, the military establishment tripled in size, largely due to the merger of regional and specialized security forces; it continued to grow in quantity and quality throughout the 1970s. In May 1978, the government issued a conscription law making military service compulsory; in January 1979, it was announced that women would be conscripted along with men. Expenditures for equipment also increased dramatically throughout the decade, and Libya's armed forces entered the 1980s with the highest ratio of military equipment to manpower in the Third World.

Military opposition has grown as Qaddafi has increasingly advocated a people's militia to offset the power of a professional military organization. His insistence on compulsory military service for women, a measure opposed by the GPC in 1984, was especially unpopular in the military. Most observers agree that any significant challenge to the revolution will probably originate within the armed forces, particularly the army, as the military is the only group in the country with the required power and organization.

Qaddafi's strongest bases of support are the military and also the revolutionary youth committees designed to socialize youth into the Green Book principles and to guard these "revolutionary" principles zealously. But one of the paradoxes of Libyan politics is that just as the armed forces remain the strongest source of regime support, they are also the most likely source of any successful opposition. There have, indeed, been numerous coup attempts since the original 1969 coup d'etat itself. In 1975, groups of army officers rebelled against Qaddafi but were repressed. In 1984, army units linked to opposition Libyan exiles attacked Qaddafi's own military stronghold but were beaten back in a bloody fight. And most recently, in 1993, units revolted in several locations throughout the country, but they too were ultimately defeated by loyalist military forces.

Petit Bourgeoisie

After 1977, the regime followed an increasingly radical socioeconomic policy that included housing redistribution and currency exchange, leading to the state takeover of all import, export, and distribution functions by the end of 1981. The resultant widespread redistribution of wealth and power directly affected the economic well-being of different sectors of the population, activating dormant political opposition. Particularly affected were the members of the petit bourgeoisie, which had prospered after 1969 as the revolutionary government's emphasis on the service and housing sectors created lucrative opportunities in trade, real estate, and small consumer manufacture.

Opposition is not limited to a single socioeconomic group; it also includes farmers, the educated elite, and even middle-level and senior-level government officials. Outside the country, opposition exists among student groups and self-imposed exiles, with a number of organized opposition groups operating in Western Europe and the Middle East. The largest and most active of these groups is the National Front for the Salvation of Libya (NFSL), founded in Khartoum in 1981 and since then operating out of Egypt and the United States. The attempted military coup of 1984 was instigated by military officers sympathetic to the NFSL.

However, the opposition is badly fragmented and must

deal with the considerable support for the regime, especially among the younger, less well-to-do elements of society. This support has been generated by Qaddafi's charismatic leadership and the regime's distributive economic policies. Moreover, in recent years, Qaddafi had taken extraordinary and often violent measures to stifle opposition at home and abroad and to limit any collaboration between domestic and foreign opponents. The regime has in particular taken aim at Libya's growing Islamist movement. The regime began to reemphasize the role of the *Shari'ah* in Libyan political life in the 1990s while also cracking down on those suspected of having Islamist sympathies. In this regard, the Qaddafi regime may have been deeply influenced by the unrest and violence between government and Islamists in neighboring Algeria.

NATIONAL PROSPECTS

After almost 30 years in power, Colonel Muammar al-Qaddafi is one of the longest-established rulers in the Middle East. Assisted by oil revenues, which have generally accounted for some 99% of Libya's export earnings since the mid-1960s, he has implemented a series of radical policies that have drastically—and permanently—modified Libya's social, cultural, and material life. Regardless of changes in national leadership, the former socioeconomic and political system has been destroyed. But Qaddafi's political position today seems less secure than at any time in the last several decades. The large oil revenues that made most of his achievements possible have declined in recent years, undermining both his foreign and domestic policies. As a result, the regime is confronted by increasing challenges domestically and internationally.

In terms of its foreign relations, Libya continued to be regarded as a "rogue state" by Western powers, and particularly the United States, which accused Libya of supporting international terrorism and of developing chemical weapons. In 1986, in response to a terrorist attack that may or may not have been linked to Libya, the United States launched air strikes against Tripoli and Benghazi. By the 1990s, the central issue was the Qaddafi regime's refusal to extradite two Libyan agents accused of involvement in the 1988 bombing of a Pan Am airliner over Lockerbie, Scotland. The UN Security Council responded by issuing sanctions against Libya, and increased these in 1993 to include a freeze on Libyan overseas assets and a ban on arms as well as on equipment for the airline industry, effectively grounding Libyan Arab Airlines.

In regional relations, Qaddafi remained vigorously opposed to the Arab-Israeli peace process and was particularly critical of the 1994 Jordanian-Israeli peace treaty and of Israeli accords with the PLO (in 1993 and 1995). It was allegedly in response to these accords that Libya expelled thousands of Palestinians in 1995. Yet Sudanese guest workers were also expelled, leading many observers

to suspect that the real motives were economic constraints on the domestic job market coupled with Qaddafi's anger at the Khartoum regime's apparent support for Islamist opposition within Libya.

The Qaddafi regime had, however, managed to smooth over a number of long-standing conflicts and tensions with its other neighbors. In 1973, for example, the Libyan army had taken over the Aouzou Strip in northern Chad, leading to a lengthy confrontation with various Chadian governments. But by 1989, following a series of military defeats in 1986 and 1987, Libya and Chad signed a cease-fire agreement and turned the territorial dispute over to the International Court of Justice (ICJ). The ICJ subsequently awarded the Aouzou Strip to Chad in 1994, and the last Libyan troops withdrew.

In Arab affairs, Libya restored relations with Egypt, broken off in 1978 following the Camp David Accords and remaining problematic until 1990. Tensions among the Arab states of northwest Africa, or the Maghreb, were eased somewhat by the creation in 1989 of the Arab Maghreb Union (AMU) comprised of Libya, Algeria, Mauritania, Morocco, and Tunisia. Almost a decade later, however, the AMU had achieved little in the way of real political or economic cooperation.

Yet despite some foreign policy gains, for the Qaddafi regime the most pressing challenges remained from within. The regime has responded to its domestic insecurity (augmented by economic uncertainty) by alternating between apparent political liberalization and outright repression. In the late 1980s the regime embarked on a program of limited economic and political liberalization, softening the state's stranglehold of control over economic and political life. Yet despite the much-heralded program of "openness," the fact remained that the regime continued to tolerate no dissent, and indeed in the mid-1990s state violence against opponents seemed to be on the rise once again.

The state appeared to be lashing out against an increasingly strong Islamist movement in particular, as well as against democracy and human rights activists, dissidents within the armed forces, and even against the Libyan opposition in exile when possible. But this only underscores the insecurity of the regime itself. For opposition to Qaddafi's rule, both inside and outside of Libya, is increasing and may hasten the end of the regime.

Further Reading

Alexander, Nathan (Ronald Bruce St. John). "The Foreign Policy of Libya: Inflexibility amid Change." *Orbis* 24, no. 4 (winter 1981).

———. "Libya: The Continuous Revolution." *Middle Eastern Studies* 17, no. 2 (April 1981).

Allan, J.A. *Libya: The Experience of Oil.* London: Croom Helm, 1981.

Anderson, Lisa. *The State and Social Transformation in*

Tunisia and Libya, 1830–1980. Princeton, N.J.: Princeton University Press, 1986.

Davis, John. *Libyan Politics: Tribe and Revolution*. Berkeley: University of California Press, 1987.

Deeb, Marius, and Mary Jane Deeb. *Libya since the Revolution: Aspects of Social and Political Development*. New York: Praeger, 1982.

el-Fathaly, Omar I., and Monte Palmer. *Political Development and Social Change in Libya*. Lexington, Mass.: Lexington, 1980.

Haley, P. Edward. *Qaddafi and the United States since 1969*. Praeger, 1984.

al-Qaddafi, Muammar. *The Green Book, Part I: The Solution to the Problem of Democracy*. London: Martin Brian and O'Keefe, 1976.

St. John, Ronald Bruce. "The Ideology of Mu'ammar al-Qaddafi: Theory and Practice." *International Journal of Middle East Studies* 15, no. 4 (November 1983).

———. "Libya's Foreign and Domestic Policies." *Current History* 80, no. 470 (December 1981).

Vandewalle, Dirk. "Qadhafi's 'Perestroika': Economic and Political Liberalization in Libya." *Middle East Journal* 45, no. 2 (spring 1991).

Wright, John. *Libya: A Modern History*. Baltimore: Johns Hopkins University Press, 1982.

PRINCIPALITY OF LIECHTENSTEIN

(Fürstentum Liechtenstein)

By Valerie O'Regan

The Principality of Liechtenstein, located between Switzerland and Austria, is a 62-mile sovereign state with a population of approximately 31,000. In 1719, the Emperor Charles VI constituted the two counties of Schellenberg and Vaduz as the present principality; in 1815, it became part of the German Confederation, and, following the collapse of the Confederation, Liechtenstein declared its permanent neutrality in 1868. During the 1920s, the principality adopted the Swiss currency and joined a customs union with Switzerland, a union that continues to the present day. Over the years, Liechtenstein has become a member of the Council of Europe (1978), United Nations (1990), and European Free Trade Association (1991).

Liechtenstein is a hereditary constitutional monarchy ruled by the princes of the House of Liechtenstein; the sovereign executes legislative power in conjunction with the unicameral legislature (Diet). The reigning prince and head of state, Hans-Adam II (born 1945), assumed executive authority in 1984 and succeeded his father, Prince Franz Josef, to the throne upon his father's death in November 1989. The prince has the power to convene and dismiss parliament, approve legislation that is passed by the Diet, and make government appointments upon parliamentary recommendation. These appointed officials, who are responsible to both the sovereign and the Diet, include the head of government (from the majority party), the deputy head of government (from the leading minority party), and three government councillors.

The 1921 constitution provided for a 15-member Diet; membership was increased to 25 members by a 1988 amendment. Members serve four-year terms (subject to dissolution). Parties must win 8% of the vote to qualify for the distribution of legislative seats. Election to the Diet is by proportional representation in two constituencies; with the passage of female suffrage in 1984, all citizens over the age of 20 are eligible to vote in national elections. Voters may also directly participate in the legislative process through the use of the initiative and referendum.

In the February 1993 election, the FBP won the most parliamentary seats; however, the Diet was dissolved in September following a vote of no confidence in the head of government, Prime Minister Markus Böchel of the Progressive Citizen's Party (*Fortschrittliche Bürgerpartei*; FBP). During the October 1993 election, the Fatherland Union (*Vaterländische Union*; VU) won a 13-seat majority, and in December, Prime Minister Mario Frick of the VU formed a coalition government. The VU maintained its majority in the February 1997 election; the current deputy head of government is Michael Ritter of the FBP.

Liechtenstein's judicial system includes civil, criminal, and administrative divisions. For civil and criminal cases, the system consists of local, Superior, and Supreme courts. The administrative division involves an Administrative Court of Appeal that hears complaints regarding government actions and a State Court that determines questions of constitutionality.

The principality also consists of 11 communes with independent administrative bodies. The communes are responsible for administering local affairs and imposing additional taxes.

There are two dominant parties in Liechtenstein: the liberal Fatherland Union and the conservative Progressive Citizens' Party; government coalitions have been formed between these two parties since 1938. From 1938 to 1970 and 1974 to 1978, the VU held the junior partner position in the coalition with the FBP. The VU gained the senior position from 1970 to 1974 and again in 1978 until February 1993 when the FBP regained its senior position with a 12-seat plurality. However, by October 1993, the VU had once again secured the senior rank in the government. Both major newspapers in the principality are controlled by these two political parties; *Liechtensteiner Vaterland* is associated with the VU and *Liechtensteiner Volksblatt* is published by the FBP.

Besides the VU and FBP, only one other party has been successful in winning parliamentary seats. In February 1993, the Free List Party (*Freie Liste*; FL) secured 2 seats with 10.4% of the vote; the party retained 1 of the seats in the October 1993 election and returned to 2 seats in the 1997 elections.

Liechtenstein maintains a low rate of inflation (0.8% in 1996) and unemployment (1.1% in 1996). Although the principality's primary trading partner continues to be Switzerland, trade with the EU nations reached approximately 40% of total exports in 1994.

Further Reading

Banks, Arthur S., Alan J. Day, and Thomas C. Muller, eds. *Political Handbook of the World*. New York: CSA, 1995–96.

Europa World Yearbook. *Liechtenstein*. London: Europa, 1996.

LITHUANIA

(Lietuvos Respublika)

By Jeffrey K. Hass, Ph.D.

THE SYSTEM OF GOVERNMENT

The southernmost of the three Baltic nations, Lithuania borders Russia, Latvia, Belarus, and Poland and has an area roughly equal to that of West Virginia (65,200 square kilometers). Lithuania's borders are still under some dispute: with Russia (over the border line in the Nemen River), with Latvia (over a maritime border, a dispute primarily tied to oil exploration), and with Belarus. Lithuania's population in 1996 was approximately 3.65 million persons. Culturally, "Lithuanians" defined ethnically (knowledge of language and having pre-1941 Lithuanian ancestry) make up 80% of the population; Russians make up 8.6%, Poles 7.7%, and others 3.6%, making Lithuania much more homogeneous than the other Baltic (or post-Soviet) states. Roman Catholicism is the major religion, while Lutheranism also has a number of followers.

Formally Lithuania is a republic. With the capital in Vilnius, Lithuania is made up of 44 regions (*rajonai*) and 11 municipalities. The national government is composed of three branches—executive, legislative, and judiciary. Lithuania has a stronger presidency than the other Baltic countries and is referred to as a "presidential democracy" that has come to resemble the French system, where the president presides over policymaking and the Parliament (*Seimas*) is weakened by divisions between several parties and factions; however, this strength may be illusory for institutional reasons.

Executive

Lithuania did not initially have a president after independence from the Soviet Union; instead, the country had a prime minister and a Speaker of Parliament. Before 1993, the prime minister ran the government—essentially heading the bureaucracy and implementing policy—and was joined by the Speaker of Parliament (Vytautis Landsbergis in 1991–93) as head of state. However, Landsbergis felt himself to be a captive of the Parliament, which was particularly troublesome when the majority Sajudis coalition began to fragment. To free the figurative head of state from the Parliament, Landsbergis campaigned for

creation of a strong presidency that would head the executive branch, effectively taking the place of the prime minister; but a 1992 referendum on this question failed to receive a majority of votes cast nationwide. Instead, a presidential position was created in the 1992 constitution, which was passed by a national referendum in that year.

The president's powers are, relative to presidents in other countries, weak. As in other Eastern European countries, the president is a figurehead, representing Lithuania in the international arena. Along with this responsibility are the president's powers to appoint and dismiss diplomatic personnel. However, the president is not as weak as in Estonia or Latvia, and presidential powers do extend somewhat beyond diplomacy. When a new government must be created, the president selects the prime minister for approval in the *Seimas*. The president has the use of a weak veto to send legislation either back to the *Seimas* for reconsideration or to the Constitutional Court to check the constitutionality of laws; only with an absolute majority can the Parliament override the veto. Further, the president has the power to dissolve the *Seimas* in two situations: when the *Seimas* refuses to approve the governmental budget within a 60-day period, and when the Parliament passes a vote of no confidence in the prime minister and his government. Such power of threat over the Parliament is a double-edged sword, however, for the Parliament also holds the right to call early presidential elections; and a Parliament following in the footsteps of one dissolved by the president may decide to call early elections as punishment.

Formally the president is picked by popular election, except in 1993, when the *Seimas* chose the president. (This is the opposite of Estonia, where the Parliament elected the president except for 1992, when the first presidential election was by nationwide popular vote.) A president may serve only two terms in office. To be elected, a candidate (who must be at least 40 years old) must win more than 50% of votes cast, and 50% of registered voters must participate in the election. If fewer than 50% of voters cast ballots, then the candidate with the most votes (plurality) wins, unless the number of votes received is less than one-third of votes cast. If no candidate wins a majority (or more than one-third for a weak voter turnout), the two candidates who garnered the most votes move on to a second round held within two weeks, where the winner needs to receive only a plurality. For the 1993 election, Algirdas Brazauskas, the former Communist head of the Lithuanian Soviet Socialist Republic and a key player in Lithuania's drive toward independence under Gorbachev's reign, announced his candidacy and was faced by Stasys Lozoaitis, the ambassador to the United States and the Sajudis-backed candidate. Brazauskas won the election.

While the president is an important figure, he also is not, strictly speaking, the head of the executive. While he performs executive duties, he is almost above politics. The head of the executive branch (meaning the head of the state bureaucracy of police, ministries, and representatives of the federal government) is the prime minister, who is formally the head of the government. The prime minister is assisted in policy and administration by his deputy ministers and heads of ministries, who together make up the Council of Ministers.

Legislature

The legislative branch is headed by the Parliament (*Seimas*), a unicameral body that holds the majority of political power. As in the other two Baltic countries, the Parliament is the most important governmental body. The Parliament holds the most power of all three branches of government, it has the final say on legislative matters, and it both wields greater responsibilities than the executive and holds the power of accountability over the executive to a much greater degree than in most Eastern European countries.

The *Seimas* is made up of 141 seats, which come up for election every four years. Of these seats, 70 are reserved for party lists and 71 for single-member voting. That is, 71 deputies are chosen in single-mandate elections (where individuals campaign against each other and are chosen by local voters), and 70 are chosen on the basis of votes cast for political parties. For the single-mandate positions, a candidate must win more than 50% of votes cast; otherwise a runoff between the top two is held.

For the party lists, a party must receive 5% or more of the total votes cast (except for the 1992 elections, where the barrier was set at 4%); the barrier is 7% for coalitions of parties running together. Those parties or coalitions that do not overcome this barrier do not receive any of the 70 party-specified places; a party or coalition that *does* overcome the barrier receives a proportion of seats equal to the proportion of votes it received out of votes cast for parties that overcame the barrier. (This means that if some parties do not overcome the barrier, a successful party's seats will be a percentage of 70 greater than its percentage of total votes received; consequently,

a vote cast for a party that does not overcome the barrier is a wasted vote.) Finally, parties representing ethnic minorities do not need to overcome the 5% barrier.

Judiciary

Lithuania's judiciary follows the civil law tradition of Continental Europe; precedent does not play an important role in judicial review or in defining laws and policies. Instead, court decisions are made for individual cases of conflict or contestation. The three levels of courts, which are local, district, and the Court of Appeals, are the stages through which conflict between parties or prosecution of criminals moves. Local courts are the first stage, and appeals move up the judicial ladder. Above the Court of Appeals is the Supreme Court, whose decisions either on criminal cases or on arbitration between conflicting parties is the final judgment.

In general, only the Constitutional Court has the power to review legislation. Expressly created for this purpose and separate from the other courts, the Constitutional Court is based on the American model of the Supreme Court. In Lithuania, the Constitutional Court acts as a watchdog for rights and freedoms from a vantage point beyond the everyday political process. Other courts neither review nor interpret legislation. Courts act as arbitrators in cases of legal conflict, applying the law to individual cases (there is no precedent, as in Anglo-American common law), and mete out justice in the case of criminal trials.

Three of the nine members of the Constitutional Court and all members of the Supreme Court are nominated by the president and must be confirmed by the *Seimas*. According to the constitution, members of the Constitutional Court serve for a nine-year period, and every three years three judges must come up for reappointment.

Regional and Local Government

Local government consists of directly elected councils. These councils sit for a term of two years and upon convocation select an executive board, which acts as the head of the local-level executive—responsible for implementation of local policies and of national laws and policies handed down by the *Seimas*. Recently, local authorities have battled with the central authorities for more autonomy in decision making. Reminiscent of the Soviet era, the central government in Vilnius had increased its presence in localities, even with the prime minister appointing governors. Also, local officials have been unhappy with the Lithuanian tax system (which gives collection power to the central government) and with the dearth of funding coming the locals' way from Vilnius; because of the way taxes are collected, the lion's share goes to Vilnius and then is redistributed to the regions.

THE ELECTORAL SYSTEM

Before the 1992 elections, the important political players were the Lithuanian Communist Party and its successor, the Lithuanian Democratic Labor Party (LDLP), and *Sajudis*, the nationalist movement for liberation of Lithuania from Soviet domination. At the top of politics (in the Supreme Soviet), *Sajudis*, which is not a party but a movement of several nationalist partiers, was the most powerful, while the LDLP controlled political offices at the local level. *Sajudis* was headed by Vytautis Landsbergis, whose nationalist defiance of Mikhail Gorbachev set the tone for Lithuanian politics up to the failed August 1991 coup in the USSR.

Landsbergis and Sajudis attempted to pass a law denying office to any who had held some position within the Communist Party. Landsbergis's confrontational tactics, however, backfired; *Sajudis* suffered a surprising defeat in the 1992 parliamentary elections, and the LDLP went on to become the party of power in Lithuania. This change in power occurred for several reasons: because of Landsbergis's anti-Communist virulence; because the LDLP had a stronger presence in the localities; because conflicts within the movement had led to political paralysis and conflict in the *Seimas*; because of the negative effects of economic reform; and because the LDLP, while preferring more gradualist economic reforms and compromise and moderation with Russia, remained committed to Lithuanian independence and held a more moderate rhetorical line. A vote for LDLP was not a vote for return to the pre-1991 status quo but rather for a kinder, gentler Lithuania.

In 1992, Lithuanian voters gave the Lithuanian Democratic Labor Party (LDLP)—the heirs to the Lithuanian Communist Party—42.6% of all votes and hence a majority in the *Seimas* (73 of 141 seats). The *Sajudis* movement, formerly the party in power, received only 30 seats. Portraying themselves as a technocratic alternative

to *Sajudis*, LDLP went on to less than competent handling of the market transition (which suffered a severe banking crisis due to problems in regulation and corruption) and to turn a deaf ear to problems of corruption. The Central Union, a nationalist promarket party out of power after 1992, managed to play on these problems and its opposition status to return to power. As a result, the turn to the left in 1992 was countered by a turn to the right in 1996.

Parliamentary Elections: October 20, 1996
(runoff November 4, 1996)

Party	Seats	% Votes Received
Homeland Union/Conservatives of Lithuania	70	29.8
Lithuanian Christian-Democratic Party	16	12.2
Center Union	13	8.2
Democratic Labor Party	12	9.5
Social-Democratic Party	12	6.6
Polish Election Action	2	3.0
Lithuanian Democratic Party	2	2.1
National Party "Young Lithuanians"	1	3.8
Women's Party	1	3.7
Christian Democratic Union	1	3.1
Liberal Union	1	1.8
Peasant Party	1	1.7
Union of Political Prisoners and Deportees	1	1.5
Independent	4	—

Source: Department of Computing, Lithuanian *Seimas*.
Note: Due to low voter turnout (nullifying the election), four individual-mandate seats were not filled and awaited new elections in the first half of 1997. Also, deputies are chosen from individual mandates (71 places) and nationwide party lists (70), hence there will not be an exact correspondence between percentage vote received and places in the *Seimas*.

Parliamentary Elections: October 25, 1992
(runoff November 1992)

Party	Seats
LDLP	73
Conservative Party	30
Christian Democratic Party	17
Lithuanian Nationalist Union	8
Farmers' Union	4
Lithuanian Polish Union	4
Center Union	2
Others	3

Source: *CIA Factbook, 1996*. Washington, D.C.: Government Printing Office, 1996.

Both elections show that voters tend to reject parties in power, blaming them for economic misery and for political problems and scandals. In 1992, voters rejected the *Sajudis* movement and moderates in the Supreme Soviet for creating economic pain and for political infighting. Thus, in 1992 the LDLP (Lithuanian Democratic Labor Party), portraying itself as ideologically moderate and staffed by technocrats rather than bureaucrats or ideologues, became the first of many Eastern European socialist (formerly Communist) parties to return to power. However, by 1995, the LDLP had not improved the economy—although Lithuania's economy certainly has not slumped as those in Ukraine and Russia—and received much of the blame for the 1995 banking crisis, which stopped the slow economic growth and hurt the country once more. Further, between the two elections the conservative parties—Landsbergis's Conservatives and his allies the Christian Democrats, along with the more moderate Center Union—maintained anti-Communist rhetoric and focused on problems of government corruption and on slow economic reform.

The tendencies in voting in 1992 and 1996 can be interpreted in three ways. The first is that voters are still in search of a political program and set of policies that they can feel comfortable with and that they think will bring success. Economic reform in 1991 and 1992 did not bring immediate success, hence voters tried a new tack, moderate reform. With the failure of moderate reform, voters have returned to the conservatives (nationalist and promarket) for another try. The second interpretation of voting trends is that because Lithuania's economy has suffered slumps and setbacks, voters blame and vote out the majority of deputies and the majority party in the *Seimas*. If this is the case, then parties in power should learn the lesson of American Republican mishaps in 1995 (when Republican leadership misinterpreted voter backlash in 1994 against Congress and hence against the majority, the Democrats) as support for Republican programs.

However, voting for a party does not mean voting for a particular ideology or policy. This leads to the third interpretation—that Lithuanians do not vote for political programs but rather for the appealing personality at the moment of election. (Some observers claim that all Baltic peoples have been antiparty in the 1990s, ignoring party appeals and platforms.) As in the other two Baltic nations, parties in Lithuania are connected more to the personalities and characters of those leading them than to any political program, as is more the case in other Eastern European and former Soviet countries. Further, the 1996 election was marred by low voter turnout, which suggests disillusionment or fatigue with voting. Hence, the turn to the conservatives may have no real deepseated meaning whatsoever. The most probable interpretation is a combination of factors, such as a lack of concern with parties and parties' organization and platforms and a rejection of those in power because of economic problems and political scandals. (That voters rejected the LDLP's populist policies and voted for the Conservatives, who had switched from populist to monetarist policies, suggests that voters do consider political promises in light of events and experience.)

THE PARTY SYSTEM

To speak of stable parties is difficult in contemporary Lithuania, as parties are still forming and institutionalizing. The first major partylike structure was *Sajudis*, which was actually a movement formed by various embryonic parties acting together in a coalition. However, before 1992 the *Sajudis* coalition began to fragment. In April 1993 Landsbergis formed the "Union of the Fatherland (Conservative Party)," which claimed the mantle of the defunct *Sajudis*. The Conservative Party favors economic restructuring, subsidizing agricultural exports, fighting crime, and giving independence to the Central Bank (to ensure fiscal discipline). The Christian Democrats are more moderate than the Conservatives but share many of the same ideas: support for small and medium business, reform of the energy sector, fighting organized crime, and independence for the Central Bank.

The Center Union is, as the name implies, a party of moderates. While they oppose organized crime and support Central Bank autonomy, they also support targeted state investment for economic projects, such as special projects and export-oriented activities.

Left-of-center are the Social Democrats and the Lithuanian Democratic Labor Party. Both parties favor a more gradualist and populist approach to reform; for example, the LDLP supported a referendum calling for a restoration of savings lost to inflation. (The Conservatives also supported this populist plan at first but did not appear unhappy when the nationwide referendum on savings restoration failed.) Both parties have called for slower privatization and maintenance of a social safety net and have put social justice on a par with economic growth.

NATIONAL PROSPECTS

The Lithuanian government has pushed strong economic reform—both in privatization (more than two-thirds of industry and most housing) and fiscal discipline (reducing inflation from 1,100% in 1992 to 35% in 1995). GDP growth was 1% in 1995, as Lithuania's economy began to recover after a 1991–94 decline. While a banking crisis in 1995 hurt growth—the central bank was forced to use one-third of its reserves during this period—the base for real economic improvement may have been set already. Lithuania relies on imports for its raw materials and fuel and has focused on creating an export economy; at present, close to 40% of exports are with Russia (although this is down from 85% in 1991, a situation of trade dependence).

The first Soviet republic to challenge Soviet domination, Lithuania has undergone a bumpy transition to a democratic capitalist nation, although the transition here (as in the other Baltic states) has been smoother than in other former Soviet republics. While former Communists enjoyed a brief return to power (as in other Eastern European nations), they have since lost power to more nationalist promarket forces.

Further Reading

Bremmer, Bremmer, and Ray Taras, eds. *New States, New Politics: Building the Post-Soviet Nations.* Cambridge: Cambridge University Press, 1997.

CIA Factbook, 1996. Washington, D.C.: Government Printing Office, 1996.

Girnius, Saulinius. "The Parliamentary Elections in Lithuania." *RFE/RL Research Report* 1, no. 48 (December 4, 1992): 6–12.

Iwaskiw, Walter R., ed. *Estonia, Latvia, and Lithuania.* Country Studies. Washington, D.C.: Federal Research Division, Library of Congress, 1995.

Open Media Research Institute (OMRI). Found on the internet at http://www.omri.cz/.

Radio Free Europe/Radio Liberty (RFE/RL) Reports. Accessible through the web site www.rferl.org.

Transition. Put out by the Open Media Research Institute (OMRI), *Transition* is a biweekly collection of analyses on Eastern Europe and the former Soviet Union.

GRAND DUCHY OF LUXEMBOURG

(Grand-Duche de Luxembourg)

By William G. Andrews, Ph.D.

THE SYSTEM OF GOVERNMENT

Luxembourg (population 400,000) is a constitutional monarchy with a parliamentary form of government. The Grand Duchy was created in 1815 with the Dutch king as the first grand duke. Following Belgium's secession from the Netherlands (1830), part of the duchy became autonomous (1839), while the rest became the Belgian county of Luxembourg. Full independence came in 1867, and the present constitution dates from 1868. The present grand ducal family, the House of Nassau, ascended the throne in 1890.

Executive

The position of grand duke is hereditary and its powers primarily formal. Real executive power lies with the prime minister and Cabinet, who are responsible to the Chamber of Deputies.

Legislature

The 60-member Chamber of Deputies is the unicameral legislature. However, the constitution requires that it reaffirm legislation after three months, unless the Administrative Council of State waives that rule. In practice, the vast majority of bills are exempted from the second read-

ing. The Council of State, 21 members appointed for life by the grand duke, gives advisory opinions on all bills before they go to the Chamber and on any subsequent amendments. Also, the Chamber must consult one of six corporatist "chambers" on all bills that affect directly a trade or profession.

Judiciary

The highest court is the Superior Court of Justice. Its 16 full members are appointed for life by the grand duke on advice of the Superior Court itself. The Superior Court also nominates judges for the lower courts, whose members can be removed only by the Superior Court. The Superior Court, when sitting as a court of review, has jurisdiction over questions of law, but no general power to disallow legislation.

Regional and Local Government

Luxembourg is divided into 12 administrative districts (cantons). Below them are municipalities (communes) with councils elected for six-year terms and mayors (burgomasters) appointed by the councils. Politically, the larger communes are miniatures of the nation, with elections based on proportional representation and party

Elections to the Chamber of Deputies (1964–84)

	1964 %	1968 %	1974 %	1979 %	1984 %	1984 Seats	1989 %	1989 Seats	1994 %	1994 Seats
CSP	35.6	37.4	29.8	36.4	34.9	25	31.7	22	31.4	21
LSAP	35.9	30.9	26.9	22.5	33.6	21	27.2	18	24.8	17
DP	12.2	18.0	23.3	21.9	18.7	14	16.2	11	18.9	12
KPL	10.4	13.1	<8.7	<4.9	<5.0	<2	5.1	1	—	—
SDP	—	—	10.1	<6.4	<2.5	<0	—	—	—	—
Greens	—	—	—	—	—	—	8.4	4	10.9	5
ADR	—	—	—	—	—	—	7.1	4	8.2	5
Others	<5.9	—	—	<8.3	<5.4	<2	4.2	—	5.8	—

lists. As a result, interparty cooperation and coalition are essential. In smaller communes, council members are elected by simple majorities and personality is usually more significant than party affiliation.

THE ELECTORAL SYSTEM

The Chamber of Deputies has a five-year term but may be dissolved early if the prime minister chooses or if the government loses the confidence of the Chamber. However, no election has been called early since World War II. Seats are allocated from party lists in four electoral districts using proportional representation. Voting is compulsory for all citizens age 18 or older. Each voter has as many votes as that district has seats and may cast them all for a single party list or distribute them among candidates from several parties. The latter option, known as *panachage*, affects the representation of parties and the ranking of candidates on the party lists. This "personalization" benefits well-known politicians, thereby aiding bourgeois parties at the expense of the left.

THE PARTY SYSTEM

Origins of the Parties

The modern party system dates from the formation of the Socialist Workers' Party (LSAP) in 1902. Under electoral pressure from the LSAP, the previously unstructured personalist coalitions of bourgeois interests coalesced into the Party of the Right in 1914, and the oldest political formation in Luxembourg, the Liberals, followed suit.

The Parties in Law

The parties are not specifically mentioned in the constitution, although they are safeguarded by its general provisions. A series of electoral laws, beginning with the adoption of proportional representation in 1919, determines in detail the conduct and form of elections, especially the presentation of party lists. Otherwise, the parties are free concerning their internal organization and financing.

Party Organization

Parties are organized at both the communal and national levels. Party congresses (usually annual) constitute the primary authority. The strength of cantonal politics means that even the smaller parties are active locally. However, party membership is never very large, so activists tend to determine party policy. The parties' relationships with nonparty organizations—the Catholic Church and trade unions (separate confessional, secular, and salaried employee associations)—are very important.

Campaigning

Despite the coalition basis of politics, campaigns are hard fought. Partly, given the electoral system, competition is a matter of personality, but left and right have sharp ideological differences. Party newspapers play a significant part in campaigns.

Independent Voters

The influence of the Catholic Church and the organized labor movement ensures that party identification is high. However, because the voting system permits voters to cross party lines, they tend to give some votes to attractive candidates of parties not sharply opposed to their preferred party.

CHRISTIAN SOCIAL PARTY
(Chreschtlich-Sozial Partei; CSP)

Founded as the Party of the Right (*Partei der Rechten*) in 1914, the CSP took its present name in 1944. It has been the "natural" party of government for many years. It has been represented in every government since 1919 and has supplied every prime minister since 1945, except for a stint in the opposition in 1974–79. The LSAP and the Democratic Party (DP) alternate as junior coalition partners.

In an overwhelmingly Catholic country (94%), the CSP enjoys widespread support, fairly evenly distributed among all ages and classes throughout the country, although the party is affected adversely by urban encroachment and the declining importance of agriculture. Party membership (9,500) is higher than for the other parties. CSP finance depends partly on membership dues, but it also gets help from such organizations as the Christian trade union movement and benefits from its close association with the Catholic Church and from the support of the country's leading daily newspaper.

For decades, the party was dominated by Pierre Werner (prime minister 1959–74, 1979–84). He retired after the 1984 elections and was succeeded by Jacques Santer, who had been finance minister under Werner. When Santer became president of the European Commission in 1995, Jean-Claude Juncker, born 1955, his finance minister, took over.

The CSP's proven record in office and its unswerving antisocialist policy has helped, in the more conservative 1980s and 1990s, to counter a long-term decline in the social bases of its support. The CSP president is Erna Hennicot-Schoepges, and its general secretary is Claude Wiseler.

Party headquarters are located at 4 Rue de l'Eau, L-1449 Luxembourg.

DEMOCRATIC PARTY
(Demokratesch Partei; DP)

The Democratic Party was founded in 1945, based partly on the anti-German resistance movement. It was characterized by a strong anticlericalism that it inherited from its forerunner, the prewar Liberal Party. The DP is fully in the mainstream of European progressive liberalism and joined with the LSAP in 1974–79 to implement a program of social reform. The party appears to have a secure electoral base in the middle classes and among white-collar employees, especially in Luxembourg City. The party is also attractive to floating voters who make use of *panachage*. Party membership is only about 3,500, so finance from this source is low.

The party favors free enterprise and, in the liberal tradition, stands close to industry. The DP publishes its own daily newspaper. The DP leader until 1980 was the widely popular Gaston Thorn, born 1928, prime minister from 1974 to 1979. In 1981 he became president of the European Commission. His successor as DP leader was Colette Flesch, born 1937. The current president is Lydie Polfer, and the general secretary is Henri Grethen. By its character and its location on the political spectrum, the DP has become a sort of "party of government." In 1979, it switched alliances from the Socialists to the Christian Democrats and remained in the ministry. In 1984, it defied unsuccessfully the Luxembourg convention relegating to opposition parties that lose seats in an election. In any case, a DP–LSAP combination rarely has an overall majority in the assembly.

Party headquarters are located at 46 Grand'rue, L-1660 Luxembourg.

LUXEMBOURG SOCIALIST WORKERS' PARTY
(Letzeburger Sozialistisch Arbrechterpartei; LSAP)

Founded in 1902, the LSAP is determinedly "working class," with little sign of ideological weakening. The party has very close links with the trade union movement, especially the Independent Trade Union Federation of Luxembourg *(Onofhängege Gewerkscheftsbond Lëtzebuerg)*, the left wing of a union movement that is deeply divided ideologically and between Catholic and secular organizations. During the 1974–79 coalition, the LSAP promoted programs to increase the authority and unity of the trade union movement. Despite that stance, the LSAP has joined several coalition governments with the CSP, both before and after its 1974–79 partnership with the DP—not surprising given the affiliation of the Christian unions to the CSP. The party has overtaken the CSV in share of the vote only once (1964) but came within 1.3 percentage points in 1984.

Party support and membership comes largely from trade unionists, especially manual occupations. The LSAP has approximately 6,000 members. Party finance relies on membership dues and trade union support. The LSAP publishes a daily newspaper with a relatively large circulation. Unlike the CSP and the DP, the LSAP lacks a significant personality as leader, reflecting the nature of the party. Its present leader is Jacques F. Poos, foreign minister and a banker. The party president is Jean Asselborn, and the general secretary is Paul Bach.

Party headquarters are located at 16 rue de Crecy, L-1364 Luxembourg.

MINOR POLITICAL PARTIES

The Communist Party of Luxembourg
(Kommunistesch Partei vun Letzeburg; KPL)

The KPL was founded in 1921 as a breakaway from the LSAP. For many years the KPL was the most intransigent of all Communist Parties in Western Europe. It alone welcomed the 1968 Soviet invasion of Czechoslovakia. Subsequently, it became more critical, but its share of the vote has steadily declined since the "pre-Czechoslovakia" election of 1968. The KPL's strongest support comes from the area of heavy industry in south Luxembourg. Its president is Aloyse Bisdorff.

The Greens
(Dei Greng)

Environmental parties appeared on the Luxembourg scene in the late 1970s. The "Alternative List," a loose coalition favoring the "new politics" of environmental and antinuclear concerns, attracted only about 1% of the vote in 1979 but increased to 5.2% and two deputies in 1984. By 1994, they had 10.9% and five seats. The Greens are the more moderate wing of the movement, advocating grassroots democracy, social concerns, and increased foreign development aid, along with environmentalism. The Greens' leaders are Robert Garcia and Jean Huss.

Action Committee for Democracy and Pension Justice
(Aktiounskomitee fir Demokratie a Rentegerechtegkeet; ADR)

The ADR was founded in 1987 as a special-interest party to campaign for improved pensions for private-sector employees. Since then it has broadened its policy concerns somewhat but continues its emphasis heavily on economic equity for pensioners. In its first national electoral appearance, it polled 7.1% of the vote and won four seats in the 1989 parliamentary elections. Its share rose to 8.2% and five seats in 1994, and it emerged under the Juncker government as the most active opposition party. Roby Mehlen has been national president since 1991, and Fernand Greisen is general secretary. Both are also ADR members of Parliament.

Luxembourg also has had some ephemeral, special-interest minor parties. The Conscriptees movement ran a common list with independent socialists in 1979 that won 7% of the vote. However, its only MP defected to the CSP before the 1984 elections, and the party disappeared. It was an interest group for persons forcibly recruited into the German army during World War II.

NATIONAL PROSPECTS

Luxembourgers pride themselves on their stable, consensual politics. Governments rarely fall between elections, and all major parties are potential coalition partners. The general economic slump precipitated by the oil crises has been followed by unprecedented prosperity, making Luxembourg the wealthiest country in Europe. However, the low unemployment and relative prosperity attracted an influx of immigrants, who now constitute about 40% of the population. Perhaps the biggest question confronting the Grand Duchy is whether, with so many foreigners in residence, it can still live up to the national motto, "We want to be what we are."

Further Reading

Flesch, Colette. *The Luxembourg Chamber of Deputies: A Microcosmic Image of a Small Country*. Luxembourg: European Parliament, 1974.

Majerus, Pierre. *The Institutions of the Grand Duchy of Luxembourg*, rev. ed. Luxembourg: Grand Duchy of Luxembourg, 1995.

Weil, G.L. *The Benelux Nations: The Politics of Small Country Democracies*. New York: Holt, Rinehart and Winston, 1970.

Web Sites

General information: http://www.silis.lu and http://www.luxweb.lu

Government: http://www.etat.lu

Parliament: http://chd.lu

Action Committee: http://www.adr.lu

Christian Social Party: http://csj.lu/csj

Democratic Party: http://www.dp.lu

KPL: http://kpl.lu

Communist Party: http://ourworld.compuserve.dom/homepages/KPLLUX/

Socialist Party: http://socialistes.lu

REPUBLIC OF MACEDONIA*

(Republika Makedonija)

By Stephen Markovich, Ph.D.

THE SYSTEM OF GOVERNMENT

Macedonia is a small, landlocked country situated in the central part of the Balkan peninsula. Bordered by Serbia, Bulgaria, Greece, and Albania, it covers over 25,000 square kilometers and has 2.1 million people. Of these 2.1 million, approximately 67% are Macedonians, 23% Albanians, 4% Turks, 2% Romani, 2% Serbs, and 2% other, including Vlachs, Bulgarians, and Greeks. Though the Macedonians are the dominant people in the country, the Albanians constitute a substantial minority, substantial enough to spawn nationalist demands and autonomous movements that have complicated the political process in the new Macedonia.

Macedonia became an independent republic in 1991 and immediately declared that it was a democratic state. The development of democracy has been a difficult process. Internally, ethnic, political, and economic differences have hampered the firm establishment of a fundamental consensus in the country; externally, problems with all of its neighbors—Yugoslavia, Bulgaria, Greece, and Albania—have also slowed progressive development. (Even the awkward international name of the country, Former Yugoslav Republic of Macedonia, is due to Greek objections to the use of "Macedonia.") These differences and problems notwithstanding, some progress has been made. Simply keeping the domestic differences in the realm of political quarrels and quietly easing tensions with neighboring nations have been significant achievements. And promulgating a constitution that has served to institutionalize the government and promote free elections and competitive parties has added to these achievements.

Executive

Macedonia has a dual executive consisting of a president and a prime minister. The president is elected by the people for a term of five years, and the prime minister is the head of the party or coalition of parties that has a majority in parliament. Constitutionally, the president is the head of state and the prime minister is the head of government.

The constitution states that the president represents the republic, signs bills into laws, nominates the prime minister, appoints several governmental and judicial offices—usually in consultation with the government and with approval by parliament, grants decorations and honors, and serves as commander in chief. In signing bills into law, the president may veto a bill and send it back to the Assembly for reconsideration; if the Assembly reconsiders the bill and passes it by an absolute majority, then the president is obliged to sign it. Apart from this discretion on bills and possibly the role as commander in chief, the presidential powers collectively, as they are presented in the constitution, portray the president more as a formal head of state than as a political leader of the country.

In practice, however, in the early years of the new Macedonia, the first president, Kiro Gligorov, has been active in leading the country and therefore has been more than a formal head of state. An experienced politician with a strong sense of leadership, he has in fact achieved a revered status in Macedonia as the father of the new Macedonia and the symbol of political reform. This status has enabled him to win the parliamentary election for president in 1991 and the popular election for that office in 1994.

The stability of Gligorov's leadership has been particularly significant in light of the latent instability in the coalition governments that have run the country. The first coalition government, headed by Prime Minister Nikola Kljusev, lost a vote of confidence in 1992 and had to resign after a little more than a year in office. The second coalition government, headed by Branko Crvenkovski, survived a vote of confidence after several months in office and went on to run the country for several years. Still, to stay in office Crvenkovski had to manage broad coalitions that have to date been fragile partnerships; he not only had to balance his ministerial assignments among three or four parties but also had to placate the Albanian elements in his coalitions. For example, following the 1994 elections, Crvenkovski led a ruling coalition composed of Social Democrats, Liberals, Socialists, and Democratic Prosperity but 15 months later had to drop the Liberals because of political differences and reform his Cabinet from a three-

*Internationally recognized as: Former Yugoslav Republic of Macedonia (Poranesna Jugoslovenska Republika Makedonija).

party coalition. By 1998 his coalition could not withstand the vigorous challenge by an opposition led by IMRO-DPMU. As a result Crvenkovski had to resign as prime minister and was replaced by Ljubco Georgievski. In forming his first coalition government on November 30, Georgievski has been as inclusive as his predecessor; his Cabinet of 27 members includes 14 ministers from his own IMRO-DPMNU, 8 from the Democratic Alternative, and 5 from the coalition of Albanian parties.

Now, as long as a prime minister can maintain a stable Cabinet, he and his Cabinet are in a strong position to govern as the constitution gives them sufficient powers. Article 91 states that the government determines policies, introduces laws, proposes the budget, establishes relations with foreign nations, and appoints a series of officials including diplomatic officers and public prosecutors. For the government proposals to be enacted, they have to be passed by the Assembly, but this is usually pro forma in a parliamentary system when a majority party or coalition controls the legislature. While Macedonian governments have more often than not managed to keep in control, they have frequently had to do considerable maneuvering to maintain this control and sustain the support of the Assembly.

Legislature

The Macedonian legislature is a unicameral parliament called the Assembly (or *Sobranie*) and constitutionally composed of 120 to 140 representatives. Following the parliamentary elections of 1994, there were 120 representatives installed in the Assembly. Representatives who accept ministerial posts in the government must resign their legislative seats.

According to article 68 of the constitution, the Assembly can enact laws, adopt the budget, elect the government, elect judges and other officials, amend the constitution, ratify international agreements, and decide on war and peace. It can also reject the government through a vote of no confidence. So far the Assembly has forced one government to resign and forced another to defend itself against legislative challenges. In general the Assembly has taken all of its legislative powers seriously and has vigorously exercised them, and has consequently acted as a viable branch in the political system.

Judiciary

For regular judicial matters, the legislature has established 27 courts of first instance, three courts of appeal, and a Supreme Court. These courts cover all civil and criminal matters, the lower courts hearing original cases and the upper courts hearing appeals; in addition to considering appeals, the Supreme Court also monitors the uniform application of laws. A special Constitutional Court of Macedonia decides on the constitutionality of laws, on jurisdictional disputes between the branches of government, on conflicts between national and local governments, and on cases involving individual freedoms.

Judges for the regular courts are nominated for life terms by the Republican Judicial Council, a seven-member board of prestigious legal experts, and confirmed by a majority of the Assembly. The nine judges on the Constitutional Court are elected by the Assembly for nine-year terms and cannot be reelected.

Regional and Local Government

The provisions for local government are laid out in section V of the constitution and in the Law for Local Self-Government enacted in 1995. These provisions allow municipalities to be governed by elected mayors and councils, but their governing jurisdictions are limited to local matters and are subject to supervision by the national government. Until the 1995 law was passed, there was considerable tension between the national government and the municipal councils, particularly between national bodies and Albanian municipalities. What generated this tension were disputes over which languages could be officially used in municipal transactions. Once the law allowed the use of minority languages as well as Macedonian in municipalities that had substantial minority populations, the national-local tensions were reduced.

THE ELECTORAL SYSTEM

All citizens who have reached the age of 18 have the right to vote. On the national level this vote may be exercised in elections for president and parliament. In the 1990 parliamentary elections, the first free elections held in Macedonia prior to independence, over 80% of the voters turned out to cast their ballots for more than 20 parties. In the 1994 parliamentary and presidential elections, just under 80% turned out for the first round but less than 60% for the second round; this substantial drop in turnout was due to some parties' boycotting the second round on grounds that the first-round results were fraudulent. In the 1998 parliamentary elections, turnout reached 73% for the first round and dropped slightly to 70% for the second.

Under the new constitution the president of the Republic is elected directly by the people for a five-year term in a system that emulates presidential elections in France. That is, it is a system that employs a double ballot. In order for a candidate to be elected he or she must win a majority of the eligible votes on the first ballot; if no candidate wins a majority on this ballot, then a second ballot or runoff between the top two candidates is held two weeks later. In the presidential elections of October 1994, there was no need for a second ballot as the popular Kiro Gligorov, the incumbent president, garnered 78% of the votes cast, which translated into 52% of the eligible votes.

Elections in 1994 for the 120 seats in the Assembly also employed the double ballot system, but winning one of the seats in the first round proved to be a rarity. Of the 1,765 candidates competing for the 120 seats on October 16, only 10 managed to gain the required majority to escape a second-round runoff on October 30. Thus, over 90% of the seats had to be contested a second time to reduce the multitude of candidates to 120 representatives. The results of the election returned to power the incumbent coalition government led by the Social Democratic Union; the Union itself won 58 seats, the Liberal Party 29, the Party for Democratic Prosperity 10, the Socialist Party 8, and five minor parties and seven independent candidates split the remaining 15 seats. Despite some irregularities in the electoral process and despite the advantages that the incumbent government had with the media, international observers judged that the elections overall were free and fair and that they contributed significantly to democratic development in Macedonia.

The elections in 1998 were also considered free and fair, though they had to be repeated in seven districts due to irregularities, but both the electoral system and the results were different from 1994. In the 1998 election 35 of the seats were based on proportional representation and 85 seats were elected in individual districts. Only four parties shared the 35 proportional seats as small parties were eliminated by a 5% threshold and five parties shared the 85 district seats that were based on the majority principle. Of the 85 district seats, 23 were won in the first round, held on October 18, and 62 in the second round, held on November 1. The results gave the IMRO-DPMNU and its junior partner, the Democratic Alternative, 62 seats; the Social Democratic Union 27 seats; the coalition of Albanian parties 25 seats; the Liberal-Democratic Party 4 seats; and the Socialist Party 2 seats.

THE PARTY SYSTEM

Once Macedonia decided to end the one-party Communist monopoly and hold multiparty elections toward the end of 1990, several parties were formed. Of course, not all of them would be serious contenders and many of them would not even last long enough to register as official parties. By the time the first round of balloting took place, there were 20 parties registered, and 16 of these participated in the elections; when the elections were over, only 10 parties or party coalitions had gained legislative seats and only 4 of these had seats in double figures. In the 1994 elections, only 9 of 31 registered parties won any representation and only 3 of them won in double figures; and for the 1998 elections, 39 parties were registered, 17 parties/coalitions participated, and 5 won some seats—again only 3 in double figures. Today only the three in double figures can justifiably be labeled major parties,

namely, the Internal Macedonian Revolutionary Organization-Democratic Party of Macedonian National Unity (IMRO-DPMNU), the Social Democratic Union of Macedonia (SDUM), and the Party for Democratic Prosperity (DPD). A case may possibly be made for the Party of Democratic Prosperity of Albanians in Macedonia (PDPAM), but this party formed a close coalition with the PDP in 1998. A case could also be made for the Liberal Party based on its past electoral support, but it will have to recover from its weak showing in the 1998 elections to regain status as a major player.

INTERNAL MACEDONIAN REVOLUTIONARY ORGANIZATION–DEMOCRATIC PARTY OF MACEDONIAN NATIONAL UNITY (IMRO–DPMNU)
(Vnatresno-Makedonska Revolucionerna Organizacija–Demokratska Partija za Makedonsko Nacionalno Edinstvo)

The Internal Macedonian Revolutionary Organization (IMRO) was first founded in 1893 to promote Macedonian nationalism and became a legendary organization among Macedonians for its role in establishing a Macedonian identity. In promoting its goals, IMRO resorted to terrorist activities so frequently that it was usually referred to as a terrorist group. When today's IMRO–DPMNU was founded in 1990, its leaders assumed the goals of the original IMRO but not the means; that is, they established a legitimate a party that eschewed terrorist means yet remained stridently nationalistic.

The strident nationalism and legendary name of the party paid dividends in the 1990 elections but not in the 1994 elections. The success of the party in 1990 was surprising to everyone, including its own leaders, when it led all political parties with 38 seats. In 1994, however, the IMRO–DPMNU faltered. The party was ineffective in the first round of voting and pulled out of the second round because of alleged electoral irregularities. Moreover, its party leader, Ljubco Georgievski, gained only 22% of the vote to Gligorov's 78%. After pulling out of the political arena, the IMRO–DPMNU had had to convey its views and criticisms through public speeches and press releases, obviously a less effective way to further party interests. Nevertheless, since it had a solid organization and over 100,000 members, the party survived its self-imposed isolation and rebounded dramatically in the 1998 elections, winning 62 seats with its electoral partner, the Democratic Alternative (DA), and becoming the dominant partner in the new coalition government. Its success was due partly to its large membership and core support and partly to its shift to moderation and inclusiveness, an inclusiveness that accepted the Albanians in their government.

SOCIAL DEMOCRATIC UNION OF MACEDONIA (SDUM)
(Socijaldemokratski Sojuz Makedonije)

The Social Democrats are the successors to the reform Communists of Macedonia. In 1989, when Yugoslavia was still technically intact, they established their party as the League of Communists of Macedonia–Party of Democratic Transformation but later changed it to Social Democratic Union. As reform Communists they had to convince the people that they did in fact favor fundamental political and economic changes rather than cosmetic touch-ups of Titoism. To be convincing, therefore, they made firm commitments to democratic pluralism and a market economy, and then lived up to these commitments.

Though Kiro Gligorov was one of the original reform Communists, in his role as president he has clearly risen above party politics and serves the nation as an independent. As pluralism began to emerge in Macedonia, Gligorov began to drift from partisan positions and leave party politics to others. The first leader of the reform Communists was Petar Gosev, but he was supplanted by Branko Crvenkovski who became leader of the party in 1991 and prime minister of the country in 1992. While Crvenkovski's Social Democrats were not able to win a majority on their own, they were able to sustain themselves as the major centrist party and as the senior partner in the coalition governments that ruled Macedonia from 1992 to 1998. Certainly the party has been successful, successful enough to attract over 100,000 members in local organizations throughout the country and to convince voters and observers that their transformation from Yugoslav Communists to Macedonian democrats has been complete. By 1998, however, the voters wanted a change and consequently voted the Social Democrats out of office.

PARTY FOR DEMOCRATIC PROSPERITY (PDP)
(Partija za Demokratski Prosperitet)

The Party for Democratic Prosperity was founded in 1990 by Nevzat Halili, who wanted to protect Albanian interests within Macedonia. The main thrust of the party has been equality for Albanians. Its leaders have worked toward guaranteeing the rights of Albanians and other minorities, officially recognizing the Albanian language, accepting Albanian educational institutions, and ensuring that Albanian representation in government proportionally reflects its population. If such equality cannot be secured, claim the Albanians, then they will have to seek autonomy in order to protect their interests.

Just how much autonomy the PDP should seek became the subject of a divisive debate within the party. For the moderates, assurances of equality and some regional autonomy within a Macedonian framework were enough; for the radicals, more autonomy and possibly secession were the goals. When the two factions could not resolve their differences peacefully, the party split in 1994; as a result of the split, Abdurahman Aliti replaced Halili as leader of the PDP, now a party of 25,000 members, and the radicals, a small splinter group, left to form their own party, the Party for Democratic Prosperity of Albanians in Macedonia (PDPAM). By the 1998 elections, however, the two factions managed to reconcile their differences and, joined by a minor Albanian party called the People's Democratic Party (PDP), merged into a tripartite electoral coalition that won 25 seats and agreed to become a part of the coalition government.

Though the moderate PDP leaders have been firm in protecting Albanian interests, they have generally chosen to do this as a part of the ruling government, earlier as members of Crvenkovski's cabinet, at president as members of Georgievski government. As members of these ruking coalitions, they have worked positively to further the interests of the country as a whole. While they occasionally express complaints and apprehensions, sometimes to remind the government about their concerns and sometimes to placate their Albanian supporters, the PDP leaders clearly believe they are better off exerting influence within the government than they would be trying to pressure it from the outside.

LIBERAL DEMOCRATIC PARTY (LDP)
(Liberalno Demokratska Partija)

The Liberal Democratic Party was formed in 1997 through the merger of the Liberal and Democratic Parties in an attempt to stay the faltering fortunes of the once-successful Liberal Party. After the Liberal Party itself was created in 1991, it did very well as a small but influential party. Although it numbered about 10,000 members, most of these members were successful businesspeople who strongly supported the transformation to a market economy and heavily promoted privatization in the country. Their influence in the economic sector was nearly matched by their role in the government; as partners in coalition governments from 1992 to 1996, members of the party held important posts in both the Cabinet and the legislature, posts which allowed them some say in the policymaking process.

One of the important posts, president of the Assembly, was held by a party leader, Stojan Andov, for five years—from 1991 to 1996. From this post Andov could affect governmental policies and decisions and concomitantly, because of his governmental power, manage his party in a disciplined and authoritarian manner. Much of this power vanished when differences between Andov and Crvenkovski came to a head in 1996. Because of these differences Andov had to resign his position as Assembly president and his Liberal colleagues lost their ministerial posts in a Cabinet reshuffle engineered by Crvenkovski. Once they were removed from ruling posts, the Liberal's influence and support dropped precipitously. Whereas they won 24% of the popular vote and 29 parliamentary seats as the single Liberal Party in 1994, they won only 7% of the vote and 4 seats as the united Liberal Democratic Party in 1998. The new party will have to generate a dramatic comeback to repeat the earlier Liberal successes or, more pointedly, even to survive as a viable party.

MINOR POLITICAL PARTIES

In 1995, the Assembly passed a law that required a party to have 500 citizens signed as members before it could be registered. This law served to reduce the number of parties from about 60 proclaimed parties to 39 registered parties. Of the 39, only 3 can be acknowledged as major parties and only 5 have representation in the Assembly.

Currently the most significant minor parties are those that have joined major parties in coalitions. One of these, the Democratic Alternative (DA), is a socialist party that joined IMRO-DPMNU in a coalition and did its share in winning the 1998 election for the coalition and thereby earned its eight Cabinet posts in the government. The Party for Democratic Prosperity of Albanians in Macedonia (PDPAM) and the People's Democratic Party (NDP) are Albanian minority parties that have joined in a coalition with the PDP. The only other party with representation in parliament is the Socialist Party of Macedonia (SPM), a small party that gained influence by serving in Crvenkovski's coalition government following the 1994 elections; in that year it won over 7% of the vote and 8 seats as part of an electoral alliance, but in 1998 it got less than 5% of the vote and only 2 seats and its position as an influential small party has faded. There are many other parties that have registered, but their support in elections is diminishing rather than increasing, and consequently their prospects are not encouraging.

NATIONAL PROSPECTS

A cursory glance at Macedonia's problems could easily lead one to conclude that the country is facing insurmountable difficulties. Externally there are continuing problems with all of its neighbors, and internally there are ongoing ethnic, political, and economic problems. And yet, if one gives the situation more than a cursory glance, one finds there is some hope for the future. Though difficult problems with neighbors remain, relations are better now than they were when independence was declared.

Similar conclusions can be reached about Macedonia's internal situation. The government has made good-faith efforts to placate its Albanian population by being inclusive and by bringing them into the governing process as much as possible. This policy has led to the active participation in the work of the system by the major Albanian party, the PDP. Politically, too, the situation is better than it was initially. While there have been shifting coalitions in the Cabinet, the coalitions have survived and provided stability in running the government; and President Gligorov has been a towering figure for the country—an able and honored man who has provided sound and steady leadership in managing sensitive issues at home and abroad.

At present, economic questions pose the gravest threats to the country. In this critical area, progress has not been sufficient, and this weakness can ultimately undermine the achievements in other areas. If more progress can be made on economic issues, then Macedonia has a good chance to survive as a nation-state and develop as a new democracy.

Further Reading

Cohen, Lenard J. *Broken Bonds: Yugoslavia's Disintegration and Balkan Politics in Transition*, 2d ed. Boulder, Colo.: Westview Press, 1995.

Danforth, Loring M. *The Macedonian Conflict*. Princeton, N.J.: Princeton University Press, 1995.

Lampe, John R. *Yugoslavia as History: Twice There Was a Country*. New York: Cambridge University Press, 1996.

Poulton, Hugh. *Who Are the Macedonians?* London: Hurst, 1994.

Pribichevich, Stojan. *Macedonia: Its People and History*. University Park: Pennsylvania State University Press, 1982.

Singleton, Fred. *A Short History of the Yugoslav Peoples*. New York: Cambridge University Press, 1985.

REPUBLIC OF MADAGASCAR

By David B. Meyers, Ph.D.

THE SYSTEM OF GOVERNMENT

The Republic of Madagascar constitutes the large, southwestern Indian Ocean island of the same name. The population of approximately 14 million is divided between the *Merina*, persons of Malayo-Indonesian descent who make up about one-fourth of the population, and *cotiers*, coastal people of African descent who make up the majority. Malagasy, a language that resembles Malay and Indonesian, is spoken throughout the country.

During the late 19th century, Merina kings, who controlled the entire island, lost a series of wars to the French and, in 1896, Madagascar became a French colony. On June 26 1960, the country regained independence as the Malagasy Republic. Philibert Tsiranana, originally elected president in 1959, was reelected in 1965 and 1972. In 1972, Tsiranana, the only candidate, received 99.9% of the votes cast, but this bore little relation to the true state of political opinion.

In May 1972, the First Republic ended as popular discontent with inflation and continued French influence caused Tsiranana to resign in favor of a military government. The new, leftist government nationalized French holdings, closed French military bases and an American space-tracking station, and accepted foreign aid from a number of Communist states. The highly authoritarian, socialist, military government expelled foreigners, suppressed strikes, and arrested its opponents. In June 1975, Didier Ratsiraka, a naval officer of *cotier* background, became the fourth in a series of military leaders to head the government. Both in and out of power, he has remained Madagascar's dominant political figure.

In June 1975, in a popular referendum, 95% of the voters changed the name of the country to Madagascar, adopted a new constitution, proclaimed the Second Republic, and confirmed Ratsiraka as president. In 1977, Ratsiraka allowed parliamentary elections, and in 1982 and 1989, presidential elections, which he won. It is difficult to determine whether these elections reflected public opinion since they were conducted under a ban on opposition parties. During these years, Ratsiraka's unsuccessful attempts to effect a socialist revolution further damaged the country's already-troubled economy.

During 1990–91, Madagascar was marked by widespread civil unrest and a number of attempted military coups. On one occasion, during a general strike, the army fired into a crowd of protesters immediately outside of the president's palace. Failing to quell the unrest by force, Ratsiraka agreed to surrender some of his powers and to include opposition members in a new unity government.

In August 1992, Ratsiraka was forced to make further political concessions. A new constitution, which created the Third Republic, was quickly written and then endorsed by a national referendum. This constitution replaced Madagascar's presidential government with a parliamentary system. Under the constitution, the presidency, still held by Ratsiraka, became a largely ceremonial position, with governing power being exercised by a prime minister chosen by the National Assembly. In another liberalizing change there was a return to multiparty politics.

In national elections held in 1993, Ratsiraka's rule temporarily ended, as Albert Zafy was elected president. High hopes that Madagascar was on the path to becoming a successful parliamentary democracy were soon dashed as the new president got into a series of clashes with the National Assembly and the prime minister. In September 1995, Zafy called for, and won, a national referendum on a constitutional amendment that again allowed the president to appoint the prime minister. This action essentially returned the political system to presidential rule.

Zafy's success was short-lived as his constitutional maneuvers angered some members of the National Assembly who had previously supported him. In 1996, this discontent, by both long-term foes and former allies, climaxed. Zafy was impeached by the legislature and removed from office by the Constitutional Court. New presidential elections then became necessary.

Fifteen candidates, including both Ratsiraka and Zafy, filed for the vacant office. The first round of presidential elections, held on November 3, 1996, failed to achieve the required absolute majority but led to the elimination of 13 of the candidates. In the second polling, an aged and infirm Ratsiraka narrowly defeated Zafy and was returned to power.

The Madagascan political system was again altered in 1998, when a popular referendum narrowly accepted a new constitution, proposed by Ratsiraka. This created a federal system with a strong president and a weak legislature. Ratsiraka's position was further strengthened when his supporters won the majority of seats in the National Assembly.

Executive

The Madagascan political tradition has been one of strong presidential rule. The 1998 Constitution essentially provides a legal basis for the presidential regimes that have, in fact, already been the rule. Although the National Assembly demonstrated its power in the impeachment of President Zafy, it has not played any major, regular role in the nation's governance.

The president is elected popularly for a five-year term. If no candidate obtains a majority of the overall vote, a second round of voting takes place within 30 days of the publication of the results of the first ballot.

The 1996 presidential election was originally contested by 15 candidates. In the first round of balloting, Ratsiraka received 37% of the vote and Zafy 23%, thus setting up a direct rematch between the two former leaders. Only two other candidates, Herizo Razafimaleo, a minister and businessman who had served as an economic adviser to the government, and Norbert Ratsirahonana, the prime minister and interim president, received at least 10% of the vote, thus becoming eligible to have their deposits returned. Following the ballot counting, Razafimaleo announced his support of Ratsiraka, and Ratsirahonana announced for Zafy.

The second-round runoff was held on December 29. Turnout was only 50%. When the final counting was completed, Ratsiraka had won with 50.7% of the vote, a margin of slightly over 40,000 votes.

Under the new constitution the prime minister and Cabinet members are chosen by, and responsible to, the president. In July 1998, President Ratsiraka appointed Tantely Andrianarivo, a longtime, faithful supporter, as prime minister. The government also includes two deputy premiers, 21 ministers and two secretaries of state; 17 of the offices are held by members of the president's party, 3 by members of the major opposition. The government also represents an effort to reflect Madagascar's ethnic mix.

Legislature

The 1992 constitution provides for a unicameral legislature, the National Assembly, whose 150 members serve five-year terms. There are 82 single-member and 34 two-member constituencies. The single-member constituencies are chosen by simple majority vote, the two-member constituencies by party-list proportional representation.

Previously the National Assembly had 134 members, all of whom were chosen by proportional representation. Following the June 1993 elections, 25 political parties and a number of independents held seats. By 1996, following a series of breakaways and shifts of support, these parties had regrouped into three main coalitions based on their support for, or opposition to, then President Zafy. Asa Zafy broke with his original prime minister and moved toward more authoritarian rule, his support decreased, and in September 1996, the National Assembly voted to impeach him.

The impeachment vote aside, the Madagascan tradition of authoritarian presidents and fractious parties usually left the National Assembly powerless. Its debates might dramatize problems but seldom accomplished much toward their solution. The Assembly will probably be at least equally ineffective under the new constitution.

After a lengthy postponement, general elections under the new constitution were held in May 1998. A total of 3,500 candidates was provided by 151 parties, as well as numerous independents. The final results assured President Ratsiraka a comfortable majority in parliament as his party (AREMA) captured 63 seats, while allied parties, most importantly, Leader-Fanilo, which holds 16 seats, and a number of supportive independents won enough to assure control.

Distribution of National Assembly Seats, May 1998	
Vanguard of the Malagasy Revolution (AREMA)	63
Leader-Fanilo	16
Asa Vita Ifampitsanara (AVI)	14
Rally for Social Democracy (RSPD)	11
AFFA	6
Movement for Madagascar Progress (MFM)	3
AKFM-Renewal	3
GRAD-Iloafo	1
Fihaonana	1
Independents	32
Total	150

Judiciary

The apex of Madagascar's legal system is a Constitutional High Court comprised of seven judges who are elected by the National Assembly. The Court has the power of judicial review, in that it interprets the Madagascan constitution and rules on the constitutionality of new laws. Often it has served as the final arbiter of political differences including electoral disputes and conflicts between central and local authorities. The Court supported and, in effect, finalized, Zafy's impeachment in 1996 and certified Ratsiraka's extremely narrow comeback victory in 1997.

In addition to the Constitutional Court, there is a Supreme Court, a Court of Appeals, and a large number of local, lower courts, some of which have highly specialized jurisdiction.

The legal system is largely based on French legal codes and practices with the addition of some practices from traditional Malagasy law.

Regional and Local Government

Madagascar's poor communications and transportation have made it difficult for any regime to effectively link the capital to the outlying areas. A popular federalist movement received renewed momentum when, during the 1996 presidential elections, Ratsiraka promised that a national referendum on federalism would be held in the near future. In March 1998, a federal system was adopted as part of the new constitution. There are six autonomous provinces, each with an elected governor and legislative council. The provinces have great financial autonomy.

Local government Madagascar has been based on traditional village assemblies (fokonolona) and elected urban district councils (fokontany) headed by mayors.

THE ELECTORAL SYSTEM

Madagascans are universally enfranchised at 18 years of age. They vote in national elections for the president and members of the National Assembly, for regional and local leaders, and in recall elections and constitutional referendums. As illiteracy is widespread, ballots have usually been marked with party symbols and colors. Elections are often accompanied by claims of fraud. In May 1997, the National Assembly passed a law making an identity card necessary to register on voting lists and take part in elections.

Presidential candidates file with a deposit that is returned to candidates who receive at least 10% of the vote. If no candidate receives a majority on the first ballot, the two highest finishers compete in a runoff a month after the first-round results are officially announced.

Members of the National Assembly are chosen in elections that are separate from the presidential balloting. Members are chosen from either single- or two-member constituencies.

Most recent elections have been marked by low turnout. Some of this may be due to party leaders who call on followers to boycott the polls, but growing popular apathy and disillusionment with the political system are likely a greater cause.

THE PARTY SYSTEM

Political parties in colonial Madagascar were originally developed in the mid-1940s but were suppressed by the French following widespread violence in 1947. Parties reemerged in preparation for elections in 1958. As was typical in French Africa, most were affiliates of parties found within France. The most important of these parties was the Social Democratic Party (PSD) of Philibert Tsiranana, the nation's first president. PSD remained the governing party throughout the First Republic. Its major opposition was the Congress Party for the Independence of Madagascar (AKFM), which wanted complete independence rather than internal self-government within the French Community. In general, PSD support came from the coastal tribes, AKFM's from the *Merina*.

As one of the new, "revolutionary" institutions of the Second Republic, Ratsiraka created his own party, the Vanguard of the Malagasy Revolution (AREMA). AREMA was the nucleus of a fractious coalition called the National Front for the Defense of the Revolution (FNDR). Under the constitution, the FNDR was the only legal political organization. All political parties had to be within the Front, which offered a single list of candidates to the voters. Ratsiraka's efforts to create a viable one-party system were, however, thwarted by conflicts among the groups and individuals supposedly united within the Front.

In March 1990, the Ratsiraka government, recognizing the disintegration of the Front and faced with popular demands for democratic change, agreed to the resumption of multiparty politics. Quickly, a plethora of new parties emerged.

Over 120 political parties, as well as a large number of independent candidates, contested the June 1993 elections to the National Assembly, and 25 of these parties and a few independents were successful in winning seats. Although 151 parties contested the 1998 elections, only 9 of them won seats.

With a few exceptions, Madagascan parties frequently fracture and combine, change names, and disappear only to reappear again. In general, during the Third Republic, to date, the parties have tended to form broad, fluid coalitions that either support or oppose the nation's president.

Campaigning

Political and economic programs are often largely absent or meaninglessly vague in political campaigns. Candidates appeal to popular dissent and clamors for radical change. Ratsiraka's successful electoral comeback was partly the result of extensive personal campaigning that took him into even the smallest, remote communities. Some supporters believed he would be best able to secure foreign assistance; many simply voted against the former president, Zafy, under whom the economy had continued to worsen.

Only two political parties, AREMA and Leader-Fanilo, contested all National Assembly constituencies in 1998. Some opposition parties boycotted the polls. President Ratsiraka did not personally participate in the campaign.

VANGUARD OF THE MALAGASY REVOLUTION
(Avant-Garde de la Revolution Malagasy; AREMA)

AREMA was established by President Ratsiraka as one of the new revolutionary institutions of the Second Republic. It was the core group of the FNDR and served as the electoral instrument for the president, most members of the National Assembly, and the majority of elected local government officials. It included youth and women's groups and was closely tied to organized labor. Its ability to coordinate and govern was, however, continually compromised by internal factionalization. Its members held differing images of socialism, disagreed strongly about its application, and had differing reactions to the president's slide from socialist revolutionary toward reluctant free marketeer.

The party was temporarily dissolved following Ratsiraka's defeat in the February 1993 presidential elections. AREMA did not participate in the June 1993 elections to the National Assembly. By the mid-1990s, AREMA was reconstituted by Ratsiraka, and the party served as his vehicle in the successful 1996 presidential elections. The party's national strength was demonstrated in the 1998 National Assembly elections when it fielded candidates in every constituency and won four times as many seats as its closest rival.

Upon assuming the nation's presidency in 1996, Ratsiraka resigned his party leadership. At the party national congress in November, Pierrot Rajaonarivelo was elected as the new national secretary. AREMA members currently include the nation's prime minister and 17 Cabinet positions.

TORCH
(Leader-Fanilo)

Leader-Fanilo was organized in 1992 as a party of "nonpoliticians." Its founder and president is Herizo Razafimahaleo, a businessman who had previously served as an adviser to Ratsiraka. In the 1993 National Assembly elections, it captured 13 seats. The party was one of the more powerful members of the coalition of parties that regularly opposed then President Zafy.

The party leader and most of his top aides have maintained close ties to Ratsiraka. Razafimahaleo received 15% of the vote in the first round of the 1996 presidential balloting. In the second round he asked his supporters to back Ratsiraka. Razafimahaleo was subsequently chosen as a deputy prime minister, and three other party members received Cabinet portfolios.

In 1998, Leader-Fanilo was the only party other than AREMA to contest all of the National Assembly seats. It won 16 seats, making it the second-largest in the Assembly. The party was given three positions in the new government. For reasons that have not been explained, Razafimahaleo was not given a government position.

ASA VITA IFAMPITSANARA
(Work Finished by Solidarity; AVI)

AVI, a political party recently created by the former prime minister Norbert Ratsirhonana, will serve as the core of the moderate opposition in the National Assembly. Most of the party's popular strength is located in the national capital, Antananarivo.

RALLY FOR SOCIAL DEMOCRACY
(Rassemblement pour le Socialisme et la Democratie; RPSD)

The RPSD, which has roots going back to the former president Philibert Tsiranana's PSD, was established in 1993. A social-democratic party, it has often been critical of Ratsiraka's moves toward a market economy. The RPSD won 8 seats in the 1993 National Assembly elections and 11 in 1998. The party's leaders are Pierre Tsiranana, son of the former national president, and Evariste Marson, who was the party's candidate in the 1996 presidential election.

CONGRESS PARTY FOR MADAGASCAR INDEPENDENCE-RENEWAL PARTY
(Parti du Congres de l'Independence de Madagascar-Renouveau; AKFM-Renewal)

AKFM-Renewal was created by Reverend Richard Andriamanjato, who has long been active in Madagascar politics. Andriamanjato formed the party in 1989 after the original AKFM backed Ratsiraka for president. AKFM-Renewal gets most of its support in Madagascar's urban areas and has done well in some local elections.

In 1993 AKFM-Renewal won five National Assembly seats. The party joined Zafy's Living Forces Coalition, and Andriamanjato was chosen as prime minister. Following the break between the two leaders, Andriamanjato successfully led the movement to impeach the president.

In the first round of the 1996 presidential elections, Andriamamjato finished a disappointing fifth, with only 5% of the popular vote. In the 1998 National Assembly elections the party won only three seats. It remains a party of the extreme left.

NATIONAL UNION FOR DEVELOPMENT AND DEMOCRACY
(Union Nationale pour le Developpement et la Democratie; UNDD)

The UNDD was created by Albert Zafy in 1991 to oppose the Ratsiraka regime, which it denounced as despotic and corrupt. Its electoral slogan was simple: "Ratsiraka out." With support from Catholic and Protestant church groups it promised to effect a peaceful democratic revolution.

The UNDD became a core member of the anti-Ratsiraka Coalition of Living Forces. In May 1993, following his election as Madagascar's president, Zafy resigned as UNDD's president but accepted the title of "honorary president" and remained the party's leader.

Zafy's impeachment and subsequent loss in the presidential elections and the party's unsuccessful opposition to the 1998 constitution have left the party's future, at best, uncertain. The UNDD boycotted the 1998 National Assembly elections.

COMMITTEE FOR THE SUPPORT OF DEMOCRACY AND DEVELOPMENT IN MADAGASCAR
(Comite de Soutien a la Democratie et au Development de Madagascar; CSDDM)

The CSDDM was organized in December 1992 by the then deputy prime minister, Francisque Ravony, in support of Zafy's presidential bid. Although the party elected only two members in the June 1993 National Assembly elections, Ravony was, nevertheless, chosen as the country's prime minister. When relations between the president and prime minister soured, the CSDDM joined Zafy's opponents in the successful impeachment movement.

During the 1996 presidential election, Ravony unsuccessfully tried to forge an anti-Ratsiraka alliance that he claimed was necessary to prevent a return to dictatorship. More recent efforts to form such an alliance have been equally unsuccessful. CSDDM boycotted the 1998 elections, and the party faces an uncertain future.

OTHER POLITICAL FORCES

Christian Churches

Many of the nation's churches are organized in the politically active, staunchly democratic Federation of Christian Churches of Madagascar. During the early 1990s they supported Zafy and the movement for democratic reform. In 1998 they opposed the new constitution, which they claimed would create a presidential dictatorship. Their opposition is believed by many observers to be the major reason why the new constitution was adopted by only the slimmest majority of voters.

Military

Madagascar's military, including the regular army, gendarmes, and a presidential guard, have long been highly politicized. The military overthrew the First Republic and installed its own leaders, including Ratsiraka as president. During these years the military was responsible for internal security and frequently turned its guns on political protesters.

More recently, the military's role has been less overt, but if strife breaks out, it could again become the final political arbiter.

Student Groups

Student groups have often been troublesome for the Madagascan regimes. Student and other youth groups were highly involved in a series of deadly riots during the early 1980s. Their concerns included a broad mix of political and economic discontents.

During the 1990s, student actions have usually been more peaceful and more narrowly focused. The most frequent demand has been for an increase in the level of government-funded grants.

Ethnic Groups

Madagascar's multitude of ethnic groups usually play a relatively limited role in the political system. Although there is some correspondence between ethnicity and partisanship, political loyalties are as likely to be determined by economic interests and other factors that cut across ethnic lines. There was an effort to get an ethnic balance in the new government.

Newspapers

Press censorship has often been the rule in Madagascar. During the Third Republic, however, Madagascar has enjoyed a free press. Unfortunately, illiteracy, poverty, and the isolation of many communities has limited its readership.

NATIONAL PROSPECTS

Although Madagascar's usually tumultuous polity has, at least temporarily, been stabilized, it is hard to be optimistic concerning the country's future. Low voter turnouts, and the very thin margins of support for Ratsiraka in 1996, and the new constitution in 1998, suggest a weakness in public support for the current political system. AREMA's victory in the National Assembly elections may be either a positive sign or significant only of lack of realistic alternatives.

However slim, Ratsiraka's electoral successes may provide him sufficient legitimacy and support to pursue badly needed economic reforms. One signal of the importance to be given to the economy was provided when newly appointed Prime Minister Andrianarivo was also chosen to head the finance and economics ministry.

Any major improvement in the economy will be largely determined by external forces. In December 1996, the International Monetary Fund and the World Bank agreed to provide some aid to Madagascar. It is hoped that more aid will be forthcoming as the political system appears more stable and popular.

For the long term, underlying economic, social, and political problems make optimism difficult. Madagascar's deteriorating infrastructure, low world prices for its primary export crops, corruption, inflation, and population increase contribute to continued grinding poverty.

Further Reading

Allen, Philip M. *Madagascar: Conflicts of Authority in the Great Island*. San Francisco: Westview Press, 1995.

"Madagascar." In *Africa: South of the Sahara 1997*, 26th ed. London: Europa, 1997, 563–85.

Mukonoweshuro, Eliphas G. "Madagascar: The Collapse of an Experiment." *Journal of Third World Studies*, spring 1994, 336–68.

REPUBLIC OF MALAWI

By Tobias J. Lanz

THE SYSTEM OF GOVERNMENT

Malawi, a country of some 12 million people, is a multiparty republic and a unitary state. It was formerly the British protectorate of Nyasaland. In 1953 Malawi became part of the British-ruled Federation of Rhodesia (present-day Zimbabwe and Zambia) and Nyasaland. After a period of active native opposition to both the federation and colonial power, the former was dissolved in 1963. Six months later, the independent Republic of Malawi was created.

In 1966, Malawi became a republic and a one-party state under President Dr. Hastings Banda, who was named president for life in 1971. The political system of the nation was dominated by Banda and his Malawi Congress Party (MCP) until 1994, when internal pressures forced the regime to hold multiparty elections and adopt a new constitution. The rule of the Banda regime finally came to an end when the country elected Bakili Muluzi as president.

Executive

Executive power is exercised by the president. The president is both head of state and head of the government and is elected for a five-year term by universal adult suffrage. The government is comprised of the president, two vice presidents, and 24 Cabinet ministers. The current government is a coalition of the ruling party, the United Democratic Front (UDF), and the major opposition party, the Alliance for Democracy (AFORD). Two smaller parties, the Malawi National Democratic Party (MNDP) and the United Front for Multi-Party Democracy (UFMD), which worked to defeat Banda and the MCP, are also part of this coalition.

Legislature

The parliament is comprised of the president, two vice presidents, and the National Assembly. The National Assembly has 177 seats, which are elected for five-year terms. The Speaker is chosen from among the members of the Assembly. The Assembly also has the power to change the constitution with a two-thirds vote.

The president has the right to refuse the assent of any bill in the Assembly. In the event that a bill is resubmitted and passed within a six-month period, the president has the right to dissolve the legislature and call new elections. Both constitutionally and in the view of the party system, the legislature is dominated by the executive branch.

Judiciary

The court system in Malawi includes the Supreme Court of Appeal, the High Court, and magistrate's courts. Formally, the highest court is the Supreme Court, which hears appeals against decisions of the High Court. It is headed by the chief justice, who is a presidential appointee. The High Court has full jurisdiction over civil and criminal cases. It consists of a chief justice and five puisne judges. Magistrate's courts handle criminal and civil matters at the regional and local level. Traditional courts were established in 1970 by the Banda regime and were presided over by local chiefs. These were abolished by the 1994 constitution.

Regional and Local Government

Malawi is divided into three major areas, the Southern, the Central, and the Northern Regions. Each is represented in the national Cabinet by an appointed regional minister. The regions, in turn, are divided into a total of 24 districts, the cities of Blantyre and Lilongwe, the municipality of Zomba, and 7 towns. While local councils are elected, all are supervised by the Ministry of Local Government, which also controls the allocations of money to all levels.

The recent referendum and the subsequent national elections reveal regional and ethnic differences in the support of the major political parties. Bakili Muluzi (UDF) had his strongest showing in the heavily populated south, whereas former President Banda (MCP) maintained support in the center, and Chakufwa Chihana (AFORD) held the north.

THE ELECTORAL SYSTEM

Deputies to the National Assembly are directly elected in single-member districts. The ballot is secret, although the high level of illiteracy requires voters to show their preferences by placing slips of paper in a separate box for each candidate.

Elections in 1971 and 1976 were uncontested, but in 1978, 47 of 87 electoral districts were contested. Although all candidates were from the MCP, no fewer than 31 sitting MPs were replaced. President Banda stated that he would use the election to reshuffle his Cabinet and was pleased with the defeat of so many MPs. This was Malawi's first experiment in a competitive election. However, it was skeptically regarded by Western observers and opposition parties, since it provided Malawians a choice among competing personalities, not policies.

Elections held in 1981 and 1987 followed a similar pattern. In 1981, 75 of 101 seats were contested, and in 1987, 69 of 112 seats. Again, all candidates were MCP members. In 1983 and 1984 Banda appointed a number of additional members to the National Assembly, bringing the total to 124 seats. In 1992, elections took place for an enlarged legislature that now consisted of 141 seats; 91 were contested as 62 former members lost their seats. Banda also nominated 10 members. The government claimed voter turnout of 80%, but other observers gave much lower figures.

The most significant election in recent history was the national referendum on multiparty democracy in 1993. Although the government tried to disrupt the process and the activities of opposition groups, the measure passed with over 63% of the vote. Banda opposed the immediate creation of a government of national unity but agreed to establish a multiparty national executive council to oversee the transition to multiparty democracy and to draft a new constitution. Legislative elections were scheduled to take place in 1994. It is widely believed that the Banda regime agreed to the referendum after international donors cut economic aid in response to the government's human rights violations.

The country's first multiparty elections were held in May 1994. The elections brought almost 3 million Malawians to the polls and resulted in the election of Bakili Muluzi (UDF) as president with 1.4 million votes (47%). His party also captured 84 seats in the parliament. Dr. Hastings Banda and the MCP came in second with 1 million votes (33.5%) and 55 parliamentary seats, while Chakufwa Chihana (AFORD) came in third with 550,000 votes (18.6%) and 36 parliamentary seats. Elections in two of the legislative districts were invalidated but were later repeated to give the UDF and MCP 1 additional seat each.

Political Parties

Dr. Hastings Banda and the Malawi Congress Party ruled Malawi from 1964 to 1994, making both Banda and his party one of the most enduring political institutions in Africa. Between 1963 and 1993 all opposition parties to the MCP were banned. But with the coming of the multiparty system, eight major parties have been organized and authorized to participate in the nation's political system. In addition to the MCP, there are two other major political parties in Malawi: the Alliance for Democracy (AFORD) and the United Democratic Front (UDF). It was the UDF that emerged victorious in the 1994 elections and now heads the nation's government.

Despite the recent political changes in the country, it is important to place this event and the political future of the country in the context of the rule of Dr. Hastings Banda and the Malawi Congress Party.

MALAWI CONGRESS PARTY (MCP)

History

The MCP was established in 1959 under Banda's leadership to fight for the end of the federation with Rhodesia and for independence from British colonial rule. The party's early success stemmed from Banda's ability to secure independence and create successful programs of economic development. Since 1965, political opposition was virtually nonexistent until the recent elections.

Organization

The party was more of an organization for promoting support for the regime than a forum for debating policy issues. Officially, party policy was made by the annual party convention composed of party officials from national, regional, and district levels, members of parliament, some traditional chiefs, chairmen of the district councils, and representatives of other organizations.

In the past, the convention's role was at best advisory and at worst ceremonial. But, given the recent national election losses and the declining health of Dr. Banda, the party is likely to be reorganized in a more democratic fashion.

Policy

The policy of the MCP has basically been that of Banda. In foreign affairs, Malawi is distinguished from other Black Africa states by its willingness to remain on good terms with South Africa. Only in 1975, when a black government came to power in Mozambique, did Banda temporarily modify his friendship with Pretoria. Even then, the modification lasted less than two years.

Despite its relationship to South Africa, Malawi joined the South African Development Co-ordination Conference (SADCC) in 1980 to decrease its economic dependence on South Africa. Internally, Banda sought to encourage the growth of private industry, especially commercial agriculture and small-scale industrial development. These ventures were financed and promoted through foreign investment and by the Malawi Development Corporation (MDC), a state-owned development organization.

Membership

All Malawi adults were required to join the MCP, but few took an active part. It was a strictly disciplined organization that was reorganized several times to exclude threats to party integrity. Although recent political changes have reduced the size of the party, it remains a major political force and maintains a large following. No membership figures are available

Financing

During the era of the one-party state, much of the party's income appears to have come from the government itself.

Leadership

Hastings Banda was president of the party but took little interest in directing its internal affairs. It has been run by a number of ranking members in recent years. In 1982, Dick Tennyson Matenje became secretary general, replacing Elson Bakili Muluzi. After Matenje died in a car accident the following year, he was succeeded by Robson Chirwa, who was appointed as a caretaker administrative secretary.

In 1985, Banda dissolved his Cabinet and took over all posts himself, giving no explanation. The most important change was the appointment of Chakakala Chaziya as governor of the Reserve Bank, replacing John Tembo, one of the MCP's most powerful members. This clearly signaled that Banda did not want his power challenged by any other political leader.

In early 1994, Gwanda Chakuamba was named the MCP vice presidential candidate for the national election later that year. Some MCP officials had contemplated dropping Banda from the ticket, but it was feared that this would fragment the party and lead to failure in the national elections. Banda held political power to represent the MCP in the national elections of 1996, but the loss to Muluzi revealed a dramatic political shift in the country and an end to the political fortunes of Dr. Banda and the party.

Many observers now feel that Chakuamba, who spent 13 years as a political prisoner under Banda, may be the reformer and new voice for the MCP. In this sense, the party could separate itself from years of corruption and brutality under the "old" MCP and still retain positive vestiges of its legacy.

UNITED DEMOCRATIC FRONT (UDF)

History

The UDF was formed in September 1992 as an opposition group to the Banda government. The party was organized by Bakili Muluzi and other former MCP members who favored political and economic reforms. Together with the Alliance for Democracy (AFORD), the UDF was instrumental in promoting the referendum on multiparty democracy and constitutional reform in 1993 and the multiparty elections that followed in 1994.

Organization

The UDF is well financed and organized, advantages that derive from the fact that much of the party leadership consists of business leaders and former MCP government officials. The MCP links helped the party to establish an instant national foothold that carried it to victory in 1994. The party is especially strong in the south, but superior party organization and financing have also given it a solid presence in the traditional MCP stronghold of the Central Region.

Policy

One of the party's principal issues has been the promotion of democratic and political reforms. In this respect it differs little from AFORD. But since the party does have closer links to commercial interests, there is a greater emphasis on the role that the private sector plays in this process. The UDF has sought political and financial support from numerous European nations and solicited international organizations to help liberalize the economy. The party is fully in support of IMF policies of privatization, tariff cuts, and currency devaluations.

Membership

Party membership consists largely of individuals who formerly supported the MCP. As Banda's grip on the government and economy created intolerable conditions in the country, many MCP members moved to support the newly created UDF in 1992. Many of the party's members are younger people who felt that democratic reforms were the only alternative to the autocratic rule that was quickly coming to an end in Malawi and the rest of Africa. The UDF's support of economic liberalization has also made it popular among the business class, including most of the country's Asian population. No membership figures are available.

Financing

The party derives much of its support from its large membership, which includes many prominent Malawians in commerce and government. The party's strong political position and its promotion of internal reforms have also brought it international financial support from governments and institutions who are in sympathy with these policy positions.

Leadership

The party is headed by President Bakili Muluzi, who was a former government minister and chair of the Chamber of Commerce under Banda. Aleke Banda (no relation to the former president) is the party's current finance minister and previous vice presidential candidate. He was also a former MCP member and once headed the Malawi Young Pioneers (MYP), a widely feared paramilitary section of the MCP. Most senior positions in the party and government are held by UDF members who have had previous experience and association with the MCP.

ALLIANCE FOR DEMOCRACY (AFORD)

History

AFORD was formed in September 1992 under the leadership of Chakufwa Chihana shortly before the organization of the UDF. Together with the UDF it pressured the Banda regime into the political reforms that came to fruition in 1994. After the formation of the party in 1992, it absorbed the membership of the Malawi Freedom Movement (MAFREMO), another outspoken political opposition group.

Organization

The party is organized under the leadership and vision of Chihana, who seeks to create a truly national party. Although its strength lies mainly in the north, AFORD has brought many of its key members, including the party deputy, secretary-general, and treasurer, from the Central and Southern Regions. Despite these efforts, the party still suffers considerable organizational weakness due to financial and institutional deficiencies.

Policy

AFORD was originally organized around a platform that sought to implement multiparty democracy with a mixed economy. During the elections of 1994, the party also identified itself with moral issues such as human rights and political freedom. While AFORD supports IMF liberalization and donor aid programs, it retains stronger links to labor movements and hence a more social democratic vision of democracy than either of its rivals.

One of the important positions of the party with respect to the democratization process is that it sees itself as the true representative of democracy in Malawi. Unlike the MCP or the UDF, AFORD's members have always operated in opposition to the Malawian political system. This distinction led Chihana to attack the UDF as "recycled politicians" and members of the "Malawi Congress Party B" during the election campaign. This legacy also led to Chihana's refusal to unite with the UDF in a broad political coalition against the MCP. Yet, after a vitriolic campaign and the UDF victory, AFORD has joined the ruling party to resolve the country's many socioeconomic and political problems.

Membership

AFORD is distinct from the UDF and the MCP in that it has drawn its leadership from outside the Malawian political system. Its membership also reflects this, in that it appeals to those citizens who have been peripheral to the national political and economic system. As such, much of the party's membership is based on ethnic and regional affiliation with the more isolated north. Moreover, given Chihana's career as a trade union leader and the party's strident positions on human rights and political freedom, it has been popular in urban areas among workers, religious groups, students, intellectuals, and journalists. No membership figures are available.

Financing

Without strong links to the political and economic institutions of the country, AFORD has had greater difficulty in raising money than its competitors. Much of the party's funds seem to come from loyal supporters.

Leadership

AFORD is headed by Chakufwa Chihana. Under his leadership, the party emerged as one of the main opposition groups during the waning years of Banda's rule. Chihana is a popular political figure who is viewed as a champion of political change and human rights. He spent nine months in prison in 1992 for his outspoken demands for multiparty elections. Although he openly revealed his mistrust for the UDF during the election campaign, Chihana did reconcile with the new leadership by accepting a government Cabinet position after the election.

MINOR POLITICAL PARTIES

Malawi Democratic Union (MDU)

These are the smallest of the eight political parties authorized to participate in the 1994 elections. Their impact has been negligible.

United Front for Multi-Party Democracy (UFMD)

Both of these parties are part of the ruling coalition and were given one Cabinet position each for their role in promoting democratic change.

Congress for the Second Republic (CSR)

Malawi Democratic Party (MDP)

Malawi National Democratic Party (MNDP)

Little information is available on these parties.

OTHER POLITICAL FORCES

Forces outside of organized political movements have had a minimal role in shaping the nation's political system. The military has remained subservient to the state since all of its leaders are appointed by Banda. Although the country contains several ethnic groups, the only conflict to arise occurred when the capital was moved from Zombe to Lilongwe in 1975. This caused resentment among ethnic groups in the more prosperous Southern Region of the country. They saw the decision to move the capital to the center of the country as bias toward the Chewa people, whose language has become dominant throughout the country. The role of labor and religious factions in political matters has been virtually nonexistent.

NATIONAL PROSPECTS

Despite the claims of its opponents, the Banda regime was responsible for creating economic and political stability during its period of rule. For this reason it maintained fairly high levels of popular support. In recent years, however, internal and external factors significantly altered Malawi's political and socioeconomic situation. The political changes in South Africa affected Malawi's economic and security status in southern Africa. Also, as the charismatic Hastings Banda began to fade from the political scene, the creation of a competitive multiparty system became a logical next step.

The election of 1994 signaled a major watershed in Malawi's political history. The election of Bakili Muluzi as a freely elected president marks the beginning of a new era in Malawi in which the country struggles to create a new identity and direction after decades of one-party rule. Despite the massive political changes, the internal obstacles to political and socioeconomic transformation remain tremendous. Lack of infrastructure and massive poverty will undoubtedly plague all future regimes. The new government will also face the daunting task of rebuilding political and social institutions, many of which have collapsed or still operate under the distortions and corruption created by decades of Banda's influence.

Further Reading

McMaster, Carolyn. *Malawi: Foreign Policy and Development*. London: Julian Freedman Press, 1974.

Pachai, B. *Malawi: History of a Nation*. London: Longman, 1973.

Short, Philip. *The Rise of Nationalism in Central Africa*. London: Oxford University Press, 1974.

Williams, T. David. *Malawi: The Politics of Despair*. Ithaca, N.Y.: Cornell University Press, 1978.

MALAYSIA

By Peter Dawson
Revised by Carlo Bonura, Jr.

THE SYSTEM OF GOVERNMENT

Malaysia is a parliamentary federation comprising the 11 states of the Malay peninsula and the federal territory of Kuala Lumpur, the capital, which together make up West Malaysia, and the states of Sabah and Sarawak on the island of Borneo, which make up East Malaysia. The country has a population of 22 million (1998 estimate), of whom 57.7% are Malay and other indigenous, 25.4% Chinese, and 7.2% Indian. It achieved independence from British colonial rule on August 31, 1957, as the Malayan Federation, then consisting of the states of the peninsula only. In September 1963, Sabah, Sarawak, and Singapore joined the federation, but Singapore seceded on August 9, 1965. The federal territory of Kuala Lumpur was created in 1974. The present constitution has been effective from 1957, with only limited subsequent alterations. It provides for a parliamentary and cabinet system closely modeled on that of the United Kingdom.

Executive

The head of state is the *Yang di-Pertuan Agong* (or king), who serves for a term of five years. The office rotates according to precedence among the royal rulers of 9 of the 13 states of the federation, but accession to the office is confirmed by election among these 9 rulers. The office thus constitutes a unique combination of monarchic, rotational, and elective principles. Although formally the head of government, the king is in practice a constitutional monarch with only very limited discretionary powers. The effective head of government is the *Perdana Mentri* (prime minister), working with and through the *Juma'ah Mentri* (Cabinet). The king appoints as prime minister the member of the *Dewan Ra'ayat* (House of Representatives) likely to command the confidence of a majority in the House, normally the leader of the majority party. Members of the Cabinet are appointed by the king from either of the two houses of Parliament on the advice of the prime minister. The Cabinet is required by the constitution to be collectively responsible to the Parliament.

Legislature

The legislature consists of the king and the two *majlis* (councils): the *Dewan Negara* (Senate) and the *Dewan Ra'ayat* (House of Representatives). The king, however, takes no active part in the proceedings of Parliament. The Senate, which is the less powerful of the two houses, has 69 members. Each of the 13 state legislatures elects 2 members, while the king, acting on advice from the prime minister, appoints an additional 43, including 2 to represent the federal territory.

Senators serve for three years, their term being unaffected by a dissolution of the House of Representatives. Senators tend to be prominent older figures in public life, representative of occupational and ethnic groupings, although in recent years Senate seats have sometimes been used to groom younger, rising politicians. Despite the minority group of territorial representatives, the Senate has never been active in promoting states' rights against those of the federation.

The House of Representatives currently has 192 members (12 more than in the 1991 elections) directly elected from single-member constituencies by simple majorities. The minimum qualifying age for membership is 21. Dual membership of the two federal houses is forbidden as is simultaneous representation of two federal constituencies, but several federal legislators also hold seats or office in their state assemblies. The maximum life of the House of Representatives is five years, but it may be dissolved at any time by the king acting upon the request of the prime minister. The king does have the power, never used so far, to refuse such a request.

In recent years, Parliament has met for about 11 weeks in each year. A simple majority in both houses is sufficient to carry legislation. The Senate has a delaying power of one month over money bills and of one year over other bills. Most constitutional amendments require a two-thirds majority, while certain articles of the constitution cannot be amended without the consent of the *Majlis Raja Raja* (Conference of Rulers). The *Majlis Raja Raja*, which meets three or four times a year, comprises the 13 rulers of the states of the federation, including the

9 hereditary royal rulers and the governors of Penang, Malacca, Sabah, and Sarawak. It acts as a third house of the Parliament on amendments to certain sections of the constitution (especially Article 153, which protects the position of Malays), the extension of Islamic religious practices, and the making of certain major state appointments (such as judges of the Supreme Court), as well as on legislation affecting the position of rulers and the boundaries of states. The 9 royal rulers, sitting within the Conference of Rulers, are responsible also for the election of the king and his deputy.

Since independence, the government coalition, the National Front, dominated by the United Malays National Organization, has always held an absolute majority of the seats in the House of Representatives. In the 1995 general election, the Democratic Action Party (DAP) was able to win seats in the federal territory and in only four states, including Sabah and Sarawak. The Pan-Malaysian Islamic Party (PAS) won seats in only two states, while the independents were all elected in Sabah and Sarawak. The dominance of the National Front and the very limited territorial base of the opposition parties were confirmed by the results of the elections to state assemblies that were held at the same time.

Judiciary

The Supreme Court is the highest judicial authority in Malaysia with the power to interpret the constitution and to adjudicate in disputes between states or between any state and the federal government. It is also the highest court of appeal in criminal cases for the federation. Beneath the Supreme Court are two High Courts, one for West and one for East Malaysia, which have original jurisdiction in their areas in both civil and criminal cases as well as appeal from subordinate courts. The lord president, who heads the Supreme Court, is appointed by the king, who must act on the advice of the prime minister after consulting the Conference of Rulers. Other senior judges are similarly appointed with the lord president also being consulted. The independence of the judiciary is maintained by this means as well as by the stipulation of legal qualifications, a high security of tenure and remuneration, and restrictions on discussion of judicial conduct in the legislatures. In numerous cases, the judiciary have displayed a very high standard of independence from political influence.

Regional and Local Government

Each state is governed by a *Mentri Besar* (chief minister) responsible to a unicameral legislative assembly whose members are directly elected, except in Sabah, which retains a limited number of nominated members. The relations among the state ruler or governor, the chief minister, and the assembly are broadly similar to those that prevail at the federal level among the king, the prime minister, and the Parliament. But the powers of states are limited, being confined principally to land and natural-resource management and the oversight of local government. Sabah and Sarawak, however, enjoy some powers not available to the states of West Malaysia. The federal government is the main taxing authority and controls the borrowing powers of states so that apart from land revenue, states enjoy no significant sources of income. Since state legislatures are now dominated by political parties that are members of the governing coalition at the federal level, a further degree of state and federal harmonization is achieved.

THE ELECTORAL SYSTEM

All members of the House of Representatives are directly elected by a simple majority within each of the 192 single-member constituencies. Of the 69 members of the Senate, 26 are elected by their state legislatures. All citizens over the age of 21 (other than those detained as being of "unsound mind" or serving a prison sentence or who have been sentenced to death or imprisonment of more than 12 months) are eligible to vote by secret ballot in elections for the House of Representatives or legislative assemblies.

The Election Commission conducts elections and prepares and annually revises electoral rolls. It is also responsible every 8 to 10 years for reviewing and recommending changes to the boundaries of state and national constituencies. Registration of voters is neither automatic nor compulsory. The ballot paper in each constituency lists all the candidates and their party symbols; voters indicate their choice by marking an X. Votes are counted centrally within each constituency in the presence of candidates and their agents. Turnout is high, usually above 60 to 70%. The system is in the main fair and equitable, although various technical factors relating to voter registration and constituency delimitation together with the effects of the simple-majority method have produced in all national elections a highly disproportionate number of seats for the governing coalition.

THE PARTY SYSTEM

Origins of the Parties

The most distinctive feature of Malaysian political parties is that they are all communally based, but a second major feature is a tendency toward consolidation and coalition. The communal divisions are not only racial but are also reinforced by language, religion, culture, and, to a considerable extent, economic role. With Malays constituting more than half of the total population, Chinese approximately one-quarter, and people of Indian descent one-fourteenth, parties that represent the interests of these groups are assured of substantial support. The three major parties—the United Malays National Organization, Malayan Chinese Association, and Malayan Indian Congress (UMNO, MCA, and MIC)—all came into existence in the late 1940s specifically to defend their respective ethnic communities against threats perceived in the various constitutional proposals advanced by the colonial government. A coalition they had formed well before independence in 1957 was formally registered as the Alliance Party in 1958. The Alliance collapsed in the wake of communal rioting after the 1969 election, which had shown a growth in support for non-Alliance parties and thus an erosion of the claim by the Alliance to represent a national interest.

After a period of emergency rule, during which electoral and parliamentary activity was suspended, the coalition was reconstituted in 1971 as the National Front (BN). At the same time, it was broadened to include several smaller parties, previously in opposition, so that the Malay and Chinese communities were now represented by more than one party within the front. The United Malays National Organization (UMNO) has always been the dominant participant. With intercommunal harmony the overriding aim of government throughout Malaysia's history, the BN has achieved this aim by private interparty compromise. However, resentment among some sections of the population against this process of elite adjustment has sustained support for several opposition parties.

The Parties in Law

The constitution makes no reference to political parties, but under separate legislation (the Societies Act of 1966) all organizations seeking to contest elections must be formally registered. On a few occasions, the refusal of registration has effectively suppressed the activities of some smaller opposition parties. A 1981 amendment to the Societies Act requires all clubs, societies, and associations to register as either political or nonpolitical. This has been seen as limiting the capacity of pressure groups to campaign and lobby to secure changes in government policy. From time to time, security and sedition laws have been used to detain members of opposition parties either because of suspected communist links or because their activities were deemed to be subversive. Parties receive no direct, formal state support. Any qualified election candidate whose nomination has been properly made can be included on the ballot whether or not he or she is a representative of a political party.

Party Organization

Malaysian parties are too numerous, too different in size, and in several cases too limited to particular regions for many substantial generalizations to be possible. The par-

ties are permanent associations sustained by membership dues and private donations. Most maintain a three-tiered organization at the constituency, state, and national levels. They are identifiable principally by communal characteristics, although different parties drawing their membership from the same community may be distinguished by socioeconomic and, to a limited degree, ideological differences. The major support for the Democratic Action Party, for example, comes from the poorer stratum of Chinese, while the Malayan Chinese Association is more substantially supported by the better-off. The participation of the major parties in the National Front and the dependence of all—except the United Malays National Organization—on that membership for access to Cabinet office and the consequent benefits to their communities necessitate keeping close central control over subordinate levels. A major instrument of this control for parties within the National Front is the patronage exercised by the chief ministers of states. Although the principal parties hold annual conferences at which major policy issues are determined and national officers are chosen, these processes are usually closely and successfully regulated. Nevertheless, despite this consistent pattern of central and elite domination, some opportunity remains for local leaders to develop local support. For the wealthier, especially within Chinese and urban Malay communities, contributions to community projects, such as schools and places of worship, may generate prestige and power. For all aspirants to party office or candidacy, the role of broker representing constituents' interests within the multiple and many-layered processes of governmental bureaucracy is universally expected. Thus, education and experience of working within bureaucracies are important factors determining election at the local level.

Campaigning

Fear of threats to public order have led the government, in recent elections, to ban large public rallies by any party. The preferred method of campaigning has been to hold meetings within private houses at which a largely invited audience participates in a process akin to a seminar, with an address by a speaker followed by questions and discussion. This method, where it is used, permits issues to be presented in a way that is specific to particular areas or occupational groups. In addition, door-to-door canvassing occurs, and pamphlets and posters are widely distributed and displayed although their influence, if any, is difficult to assess. The press has an important role. Seven newspapers, published in vernacular languages as well as in English, have an influence that is generally felt to be substantial, their effect being usually to enhance support for candidates representing the ruling National Front.

It is difficult to determine accurately the full expenditure of parties during election campaigns. Local party branches are in all cases dependent on central party funds derived either from voluntary contributions or from levies on holders of well-paid posts that have been secured by party intervention. The larger parties, most of which are in the National Front, are by far the richer and can thus readily afford the costs of publicity, transport for party workers, and other necessary expenses.

There is usually no close national party control of local campaigns. With the larger parties, preexisting party cohesion encourages a uniformity of approach, although the fact that state assembly elections are held at the same time as those for the national legislature will often ensure that wholly local issues may be promoted in a manner that conflicts with the national party's line.

Independent Voters

The existence of the National Front as an electoral, as well as a governing, coalition may present some voters with a dilemma when the BN-endorsed candidate is not from their own ethnic community. In that event, if a candidate from their own community is standing for an opposition party, a conflict arises between the desire to vote for the coalition that almost inevitably enjoys a national majority and is regarded as the source of many material benefits and the wish to assert communal solidarity. There has been some evidence of differential voting for national and for state assemblymen.

NATIONAL FRONT
(Barisan Nasional; BN)

This interparty organization is broadly known by its Malay title, *Barisan Nasional*, or BN. Although registered for legal purposes as a political party, the BN is an electoral and governing coalition comprising 12 parties and has no organizational structure of its own. Its constituent parties (each of which has a separate entry) are (in order of number of parliamentary representatives) the United Malays National Organization, Malayan Chinese Association, United Traditional Bumiputra Party, Malayan Indian Congress, Gerakan, Sarawak United People's Party, Sarawak Dayak People's Party, Sarawak National Action Party, Sabah Progressive Party, Sarawak Malayan People's Party, People's Justice Movement, and Liberal Democratic Party.

UNITED MALAYS NATIONAL ORGANIZATION
(Pertubohan Kebangsaan Melayu Bersatu; UMNO)

HISTORY
The UMNO was founded in May 1946, with Dato Onn bin Jaafar as its first president, in order to resist the intro-

duction by the British colonial administration of a unitary form of government throughout Peninsular Malaya. This was seen by Malays and especially by their hereditary rulers as detrimental to Malay interests. The UMNO was not formally registered as a political party until April 1950. Throughout Malaysia's history, it has been the largest national party and the dominant party of government. All four of Malaysia's prime ministers since 1957 have been the leaders of UMNO. Data Onn's attempts in 1950 to widen UMNO membership to include non-Malays and to introduce other reforms were strongly opposed and led to his resignation and replacement as party president in 1951 by Tunku Abdul Rahman. An ad hoc coalition between UMNO and the MCA to fight the Kuala Lumpur municipal Malaysian Chinese Association elections in 1952 led to the establishment a year later of the Alliance coalition that also included the MIC. Tunku Abdul Rahman became prime Malaysian Indian Congress minister following the first general election in 1955 and led his country to independence in 1957. Throughout the 1960s, his attempts to hold the Alliance together and placate ultranationalist Malays in his own Alliance Party weakened his position. The decline in support both for UMNO and the Alliance revealed by the 1969 election results and the communal rioting that followed led to Rahman's resignation, both as prime minister and as party president, and his replacement by Tun Abdul Razak.

After a period of emergency rule during which Parliament was suspended, Razak was able to put together a wider governing coalition of nine parties, including some which had previously been in opposition. This Barisan Nasional was registered as a political party on June 1, 1974. In the parliamentary elections that followed, the front won 135 out of the 154 seats. Other major measures taken during the emergency period were the introduction of the New Economic Policy (NEP), which sought to promote substantially the economic advancement of the Malay population, and the passing of a constitutional amendment that declared seditious any questioning of Malay privileges, the status of Malay as the national language, and such issues as citizenship and the position of traditional rulers. Important controversies were thus barred from public debate, even in Parliament, and the grounds on which opposition parties might base their criticisms were denied to them.

The death of Tun Abdul Razak in 1976 and the succession of Datuk Hussein Onn was followed by a brief period of factional fighting within UMNO. In part, the conflict was between older members of the party who had been associates of Tunku Abdul Rahman and younger men, technocratically inclined, who had been brought to prominence by Tun Abdul Razak. The outcome involved the arrest of several of the latter group for alleged communist activities, although much of the evidence, including their confessions, appeared fragile. At the same time others of Tun Abdul Razak's protégés, untainted by any communist association, survived. Of this group, Dr. Mahathir bin Mohamad, who in 1970 had been expelled from the party's supreme council, was appointed to the deputy premiership over the heads of more senior men. A major casualty of this period was Datuk Harun, the chief minister of Selangor. His control over the massive patronage of his state and his support in the youth wing of the party constituted a threat to the leadership of Razak and then of Datuk Hussein Onn. He was charged with corruption in late 1975. Over the next two years, he was successively stripped of office, expelled from the party, and tried and sentenced to a term of imprisonment, thus demonstrating Hussein Onn's gathering control of the party. But in August 1982 he was granted a royal pardon and has since resumed party activity.

In July 1981, Hussein Onn was succeeded as prime minister by Dr. Mahathir Mohamad, who within a year led his party into a general election, the results of which reemphasized UMNO's continuing dominance in the political life of Malaysia. Since that time, the UMNO general assembly has reelected him five times as party president, and he plans to remain president of the party as well as prime minister until the year 2000. Prime Minister Mahathir's leadership, however, has not gone uncontested.

The largest threat to his tenure as party president came from within the party in 1986 and 1987. The beginnings of UMNO's "split" arose in the general assembly of 1984 when, as minister of education, Dutak Musa Hitam successfully defeated Tengku Razaleigh for the position of party deputy president. In late 1985, Prime Minister Mahathir chose to offer Tengku Tazaleigh the powerful position of minister of finance within the prime minister's Cabinet. Dutak Musa Hitam resisted the move and saw it as a direct affront to his status within UMNO. As the crisis progressed, both Dutak Musa Hitam and Tengku Razaleigh resigned their positions in the Cabinet to cooperate in opposing the reelection bid of the UMNO president, Mahathir, and his new selection for deputy president, Gafar Baba, at the 1986 general assembly. Mahathir and Baba successfully won the hotly contested election. This victory resulted in a legal challenge brought against UMNO by Musa and Razaleigh. In a surprising outcome, a judge sided in their favor and declared UMNO to be an illegal society under the Societies Act, which regulates the activities of all political parties. Old UMNO leadership's response was to reconstitute the party under the name New UMNO (UMNO *Baru*). In the wake of UMNO's quick recovery from its decertification as a party, Razaleigh three years later would form the party Semangat 46 and organize an oppositional coalition against the BN in the 1991 general elections.

During this time, Anwar Ibrahim, the finance minister, began to gain considerable respect and power within UMNO. Recruited by the UMNO president, Mahathir, in 1982 to join the party, Anwar left his activist leadership position in the Angkatan Belia Islam Malaysia (Malaysian Islamic Youth Movement). During the 1980s, Anwar's status within UMNO increased with considerable speed to the amazement of many and the dismay of some (such as Dutak Musa Hitam). After the 1995 election, the position of deputy prime minister was added to Anwar's finance portfolio. But in 1998, reflecting the East Asian financial crisis, the once-buoyant Malaysian economy contracted by an estimated 7%. Anwar and Mahathir had a bitter falling out over economic policy. In September, Mahathir dismissed Anwar from both his posts, provoking public demostrations of support for Anwar. Anwar was then arrested under the Internal Security Act, released, and almost immediately brought up on charges of corruption and sodomy, to which he pleaded complete innocence. A verdict in his trial was expected in early 1999.

ORGANIZATION

The UMNO is a cadre party, exclusively Malay in membership, which has succeeded through its extensive organization in every state and penetration to the village level in uniting Malay interests across region and class. As an exclusively Malay party, UMNO enjoys a high degree of homogeneity. It is distinguished also by being the only party with branches throughout the federation, including Sabah and Sarawak. It is relatively highly structured with a president, deputy president, and five vice presidents. The heads of the party's youth wing and its women's wing (*Wanita UMNO*) are automatically vice presidents, the remaining three being elected by the party's general assembly. Together with other appointed and elected members, including a secretary-general, treasurer, and publicity chief, they constitute the principal power center of the party.

The dual roles of party president and prime minister have been employed in a mutually enhancing manner by all four incumbents, whose positions have usually been supported by the senior party officers, who are also Cabinet ministers. The youth and women's wings enjoy a semiautonomous status, at times acting as pressure groups within the party. They have both performed vitally important functions during elections in organizing campaigns at the local level.

POLICY

The principal objectives of UMNO policy have consistently been UMNO dominance and Malay unity. The one is seen as reinforcing the other. These aims are secured by maintaining tight central control of the party while securing the widest possible electoral and governing coalition with Malay and non-Malay parties. These two strategies have at times been felt to conflict, leading to strains within the party, notably in 1969. Since 1991, the party has promoted the New Development Policy (NDP), successor to the New Economic Policy of 1971–91, which uses active discriminatory measures to advance the material well-being of Malays. This policy has coincided with a more strident assertion of economic nationalism that has led the government to buy its way into many of the large expatriate corporations, especially in the mining and plantation industries.

The NDP has been enacted in conjunction with Vision 2020 (*Wawasan 2020*), a development strategy that promises Malaysia accomplishment of full development by the year 2020. Determinedly anticommunist both at home and abroad, the party's and government's foreign policy has been characterized by active membership in the Association of Southeast Asian Nations, an increasing concern to promote cooperation among Islamic countries, very cautious relations with China, the assertion of ostensibly anti-British sentiment coupled with a more markedly amenable attitude toward Japan, and lately a more critical and outspoken diplomatic stance against the United States.

MEMBERSHIP AND CONSTITUENCY

No information is available on the size of the membership of UMNO. The party's supporters include most of the Malays of West Malaysia and many in Sabah and Sarawak. Only those Malays whose political views are most influenced by their Islamic faith support other parties in any appreciable number.

FINANCING

No information is available on UMNO financial sources or expenditures.

LEADERSHIP

Dr. Mahathir bin Mohamad (born 1925) is in firm control of the party. He is the first prime minister to have been educated locally (in medicine), and unlike his predecessors, he is not a member of a Malay royal house. Once identified with the radical right, he is thought by many observers to retain an inclination in that direction.

PROSPECTS

While the party's leadership remains acutely sensitive to any threat to its hegemony, especially from rival Malay parties, it is extremely difficult to envisage UMNO's being displaced as the governing party.

MALAYAN CHINESE ASSOCIATION (MCA)

The MCA was founded in 1949 to protect the interests of the Chinese people, approximately one-third of the population, in the face of what were regarded as markedly pro-Malay policies of the British colonial government. Officially registered as a party in 1952, the MCA cooperated with UMNO at an electoral level and, in 1953, became a member, together with the MIC, of the Alliance coalition. The MCA is again a member of the front, but the inclusion as well of Gerakan, a rival Chinese party, has reduced the MCA's standing, since it can no longer claim to be the sole representative of Chinese interests in the government. While it has a widespread organization throughout Malaysia, it does not control any state assembly—unlike Gerakan, which controls Penang. Although from its inception it attempted to be a mass-membership party, it is seen as representing the interests of the better-off among the Chinese community and is vulnerable to the more populist appeal of some of the opposition parties among the poorer Chinese. These difficulties as well as the party's overall dependence on UMNO leadership were reflected in a sharp factional struggle through the 1970s and 1980s between some of the older founding members of the party and younger and more radical elements. With 30 seats in the federal Parliament as of the 1995 election, it is the second-largest coalition partner, but its freedom to formulate policy is powerfully circumscribed by its membership in the front. In order to protect its position and that of its members, it must acquiesce in policies, especially with regard to Malay advancement, which cannot always be regarded as being in the immediate interest of its members.

Organizationally, the MCA is very similar to UMNO, with a powerful central committee comprising members elected by a general assembly or nominated by the party president. It has a strong state-level organization with subordinate levels down to ward branches.

UNITED TRADITIONAL BUMIPUTRA PARTY (Parti Pesaka Bumiputra Bersaut; PPBB)

The PPBB is a Sarawak-based party established in 1973 within the front. It obtained 10 seats in the 1995 federal election, making it the most powerful of BN parties in Sarawak. Its appeal is to the Malay and Melanau population of that state.

MALAYAN INDIAN CONGRESS (MIC)

From its inception in 1946, the MIC has been faced by the difficulty of sustaining unity in the face of divisions within the Indian community, which constitutes less than 10% of the population and is clustered in geographically scattered locations or thinly spread in urban centers. Although a member of the Alliance Party and subsequently of the Barisan Nasional, it cannot command the same electoral support as UMNO or the MCA. It won only 7 seats in the federal Parliament in 1995. Since the Indian population accounts for more than 25% of the voters in any constituency, without the constituencies and seats allocated to it by the front it could not hope to survive politically as a significant group.

MALAYSIAN PEOPLE'S MOVEMENT (GERAKAN)
(Parti Gerakan Rakyat Malaysia)

The party is universally known as Gerakan, but its full name can be loosely translated as Malaysian People's Movement. It was founded in 1968 by Dr. Lim Chong Eu and is pledged to a program of noncommunalism, moderate socialism, and democracy. It entered the BN in 1972. Despite the presence of Malays on the party committee, it is still seen as a Chinese party. Its power base is in Penang, where it controls the state government with the patronage that entails, but it also has a few branches elsewhere. It won 7 parliamentary seats in the 1995 election.

SARAWAK UNITED PEOPLE'S PARTY (SUPP)

The oldest Sarawak party in the front was founded in 1959. Its Barisan Nasional support is predominantly from the Chinese population. It has 7 seats in the federal Parliament.

SARAWAK DAYAK PEOPLE'S PARTY
(Parti Bansa Dayak Sarawak; PBDS)

Formed in July 1983 by federal MPs who had broken away from the Sarawak National Action Party, it successfully won 5 seats in 1995. Prior to the 1986 general election the PBDS left the BN to contest Sarawak's elections independently. In 1991, however, after it failed to win a majority of votes in the Sarawak state assembly, the party reentered the BN. Its major object is to represent the interests of the indigenous Dayak community.

SARAWAK NATIONAL ACTION PARTY (SNAP)

Founded in 1961 this Sarawak-based party, whose support comes mainly from the indigenous peoples of the state, joined the Barisan Nasional in 1976. In July 1983, three of its federal members resigned from the party. Together with three independent members they formed a new party, the Sarawak Dayak Party (PBDS), specifically to represent the interests of the Dayak community. In 1995, it won 3 federal parliamentary seats with its BN allies. This electoral performance indicates SNAP's political power has diminished somewhat since its peak in the 1980s.

MALAYSIAN ISLAMIC PEOPLE'S FRONT (BERJASA)
(Barisan Jama'ah Islamiah Semalaysia)

Most commonly known by its Malay acronym, Berjasa, the party's name can be translated as the Malaysian Islamic People's Front. It was formed in 1977 as a splinter group from the Pan-Malaysian Islamic Party and has served to weaken that party's electoral support within the state of Kelantan in which both are based. A more assertively Islamic party than UMNO, this religious-organized political bloc holds no seats in the federal Parliament but is represented in the Kelantan state assembly.

PEOPLE'S PROGRESSIVE PARTY OF MALAYSIA (PPP)

Originally founded in 1953 as the Perak Progressive Party, it changed to its present name in 1956. Its appeal is restricted mainly to non-Malays in the Ipoh area. It survives as a party within the Perak state assembly, where its appeal to poorer Chinese offsets some of the advantage that might otherwise accrue to the DAP, one of the two Democratic Action Party opposition parties in that state.

SABAH PEOPLE'S UNION
(Bersatu Rakyat Jelata Sabah; Berjaya)

Berjaya was founded in 1975 and from 1976 until its defeat in 1985 held an overwhelming majority of seats in the state assembly. In the wake of this defeat, which significantly changed the makeup of Sabah state politics, the party has lost considerable political power. It was regarded as one of the few multicommunal parties in Malaysia, but its 1985 defeat was largely the result of the belief, on the part of the majority Christian Kadazan population, that it had become more markedly pro-Muslim in its policies.

UNITED SABAH NATIONAL ORGANIZATION (UNSO)

Formed in 1969, the UNSO played a governing role in Sabah state politics until its severe losses in 1985 to the United Sabah Party (PBS). In 1990 it worked with UMNO to establish the first UMNO branch in Sabah. Following a political falling out with UMNO leadership, the party realigned itself with PBS in 1992. It has no federal representation.

OPPOSITION PARTIES

Democratic Action Party (DAP)

Founded in 1966 in the wake of Singapore's secession from the federation, the DAP was the Malayan version of the People's Action Party, Lee Kuan Yew's Singapore-based party. DAP's objective was and is to establish a democratic and socialist society in Malaysia. It analyzes Malaysian society in class rather than communal terms, and while its support comes mainly from urban, working-class Chinese, it retains an appeal for many disaffected non-Malays including some of the intelligentsia. Although it is efficiently organized, the competition from rival Chinese parties, MCA and Gerakan, and its inability to secure any substantial Malayan Chinese Association support in rural areas have denied it control of any state assembly and thus substantially limited its capacity to secure federal parliamentary seats. Although the DAP suffered major losses in the 1995 election, it remained in control of 9 parliamentary seats, still more than any other opposition party. The party chairman, Lim Kit Siang, serves as the opposition leader within the federal Parliament.

United Sabah Party
(Parti Bersatu Sabah; PBS)

The United Sabah Party emerged in 1975 out of defections from the BN party Berjaya. The party was established to represent both Kadazan and Chinese interests. PBS won a surprising victory in the 1985 state elections, which effectively ended BN-supported Berjaya and USNO control of Sabah. In 1986, PBS entered the BN, only to leave again in 1990 after the government detained several PBS leaders under the Internal Security Act. Although PBS won the majority of state seats in the assembly elections of 1994, major party defections caused the party to incur severe losses at the federal level.

Pan-Malaysian Islamic Party
(Partai Islam Se Malaysia; PAS)

Known variously by its English (PMIP) or Malay/Arabic acronym, PAS originated in the early 1950s as an Islamic promotional group within UMNO. In 1951, alienated by UMNO concessions to non-Malays, it was established as a separate party. A Malay nationalist party, its primary appeal is to poorer, especially rural, Malays. It seeks to combine Islamic traditions with a modernizing thrust and some elements of socialism. Islam is regarded as a force for national unity. Religious teachers are active in its campaigning, and religious themes are interwoven with political assertions. PAS may represent the only significant potential threat to UMNO's dominance, partly because the rural poor as a whole have derived the least benefit from the substantial economic changes since independence, partly because PAS may be ready to accommodate the interests of other racial groups, and partly because its appeal echoes the success of radical Islamic movements elsewhere. In 1973 PAS entered the BN for four years until it left again in 1977. Since 1982 the role of the Islamic "theocratic" element in the party has been greatly strengthened. Attacks by fundamentalist elements

on the party's president, Datuk Haji Mohamed Asri bin Haji Muda, led to his resignation in 1983. Four of the five federal MPs resigned with him to form a new party, Hamim. In 1991, it won a major victory in both the Kelantan state assembly and in national parliamentary elections. Under the leadership of Nik Aziz, PAS used its victory to consolidate its power and embark on a new policy of Islamicization. This statewide program included the introduction of Islamic legal codes into the Kelantan state court system. Subsequently, the BN has made a substantial effort to regain its lost influence in the state. In the 1995 general election, PAS lost some seats at both the state and federal levels, though it still retains control of the state assembly and has 7 seats in Parliament.

Malay Spirit of 46 Party
(Parti Melayu Semangat 46)

Known simply as "Semangat 46," the party was formed in 1989 by Tengku Razaleigh following his departure from UMNO after the UMNO split of 1986–87. The party quickly formed an oppositional coalition during the 1991 general election designed to contest the Malay vote. The coalition included PAS and the United Sabah Party. In 1991, Semangat 46 won major victories in collaboration with PAS in the states of Kelantan and Trengganu. The party suffered considerable losses, however, in 1995, and a year later its leader, Tengku Razaleigh, reentered UMNO. Razaleigh's departure brought with it hundreds of other defections from the party, which has since been dissolved.

Muslim Front; Hamim
(Parti Hisbul Muslimin Malaysia)

Formed in 1983 by Datuk Haji Mohamed Asri bin Haji Muda when he resigned from PAS. The simultaneous defection of four of his former party's five federal MPs, coupled with his own substantial political experience, makes Hamim a significant grouping but one that will have difficulty in straddling the divide between the fundamentalist Muslim appeal of PAS and the more avowedly modernistic stance of UMNO.

MINOR POLITICAL PARTIES

There are a number of very minor parties, most of which are active only in state assembly elections. Three small Barison Nasional–affiliated parties arose following the 1994 split of the United Sabah Party. These parties include the Liberal Democratic Party (LDP), Sabah Development Party (*Parti Maju Sabah*; SAPP), and the People's Justice Movement (*Angkatan Keadilan Raykat*; AKAR). Although all three won parliamentary seats (SAPP 2, LDP 1, and AKAR 1), very little information is available concerning their organization.

OTHER POLITICAL FORCES

Formal groups other than political parties are not of significance in Malaysian politics. The principal parties are capable of articulating within themselves and within the governing coalition many of the demands and pressures that would elsewhere find separate institutional expression. Traditional social structures within the main communal groups provide a further channel for meeting demands, while extensive networks of patronage and clientalism within and outside the public sector perform the same function. Another important factor inhibiting the rise of other political organizations has been the 1981 amendment to the Societies Act, which forbids political activity to groups not registered as political. This has severely inhibited overt political activities on the part of all nonparty groups. A similar tool for limiting oppositional activities exists in the Internal Security Act, which allows for detention without charge. In 1987, the Malaysian government carried out Operation Lalang, resulting in the detention of over 119 party leaders, academics, religious, and political activists. The ISA has been used over time to remove central figures within oppositional movements.

Organized Labor

Trade unions provide only a very limited exception to these generalizations. Their membership is drawn principally from the Chinese and Indian communities. Subject to strict government control, not affiliated with any political party, and with the joint holding of union and political party office forbidden, unions have had their role restricted to localized place-of-work bargaining with employers. They have no impact on national political activity.

Ethnic occupational groups also exist, such as the Chinese Chambers of Commerce or the United Chinese School Teachers' Association, but a largely overlapping membership with the Malayan Chinese Association ensures that collective interests are promoted within and through the party.

Briefly, during the early to mid-1970s, student organizations, notably the University of Malaya Students Union, were active in making political assertions, especially on behalf of poor peasant communities, but separate legislation making political activity on university campuses a punishable offense and the more general restraints referred to above have served to preempt any further student role in national or local parties.

NATIONAL PROSPECTS

Since 1969, Malaysia's political system has been remarkably stable and relatively peaceful, even though its party system is predominantly based on ethnic differences. The government and the unique political arrangement of the National Front have worked to maintain communal peace by any means necessary. The drastic impact of the global financial crisis and the destabilizing effects of Anwar Ibrahim's removal from office, his trial, and the resulting protest movement have robbed Malaysia of potentially positive prospects for the future. There have been considerable calls for democratic reforms that include the resignation of Prime Minister Mahathir and the limiting of UMNO's hegemonic position in Malaysian politics. Opposition parties, most notably PAS and DAP, have worked to foster new alliances and support during what seems to be a political "window of opportunity." In light of these developments, however, UMNO's crucial victory in the Sabah state election of March 1999 (in which it won 31 of 48 seats) demonstrates the prime minister's willingness to resist outspoken political pressure and UMNO's unhindered capability to provide Dr. Mahathir with electoral victories and legitimacy. These battles will certainly play themselves out toward the year 2000 national elections. The verdict in Anwar's trial, the relative success or failure of Malaysia's fledgling *Reformasi* movement, and the ability of Dr. Mahathir's government to reorient Malaysia's economy in light of its recent negative performance will all prove to be significant tests for the future stability of Malaysia's political system.

Further Reading

Crouch, Harold A. *Government and Society in Malaysia* . Ithaca, N.Y.: Cornell University Press, 1996.

Kahn, J.S., and L.K.F. Wah, eds. *Fragmented Vision* . Honolulu: University of Hawaii Press, 1992.

Khoo, Boo Teik. *Paradoxes of Mahathirism : An Intellectual Biography of Mahathir Mohamad*. New York : Oxford University Press, 1995.

Lee, R.L.M. "The State, Religious Nationalism, and Ethnic Rationalization in Malaysia." *Ethnic and Racial Studies* 13, no. 4 (1990): 482–501.

Means, G. P. *Malaysian Politics: The Second Generation.* Oxford: Oxford University Press, 1991.

Nagata, Judith A. *The Reflowering of Malaysian Islam : Modern Religious Radicals and Their Roots*. Vancouver: University of British Columbia Press, 1984.

Oo, Yu Hock. *Ethnic Chameleon : Multiracial Politics in Malaysia*. Petaling Jaya, Selangor Darul Ehsan, Malaysia: Pelanduk, 1991.

THE REPUBLIC OF MALDIVES

By Robert J. Griffiths, Ph.D.

The Republic of Maldives is a string of some 1,190 small islands stretching for approximately 500 miles in a north-south orientation southwest of India and Sri Lanka. The 198 inhabited islands have an estimated population of 280,391 (July 1997) and are divided for administrative purposes into 19 atolls. Islam is the state religion and most of the Maldives' inhabitants are Sunni Muslims. The government, although constitutional, has been dominated in recent decades by a small elite.

Executive power is vested in the president, who is designated by the *Majlis* and approved by popular referendum for a five-year term. The president appoints major government officials including those with the responsibility for overseeing the legal system. The president governs with the assistance of a Cabinet responsible to the *Majlis*. President Gayoom was reelected for a fifth term in October 1998.

Legislative authority resides in a 48-member legislature, the *Majlis*, which meets three times a year. Two members are elected from each of the country's 19 atolls, two from the capital, Mahe, and eight are appointed by the president. Their term of office is five years, with all candidates running as independents. The Maldives legal system is based on Islamic law.

The country is divided into 19 administrative districts, corresponding to the main atolls, plus the capital. Each atoll is administered by a presidentially appointed chief (*verin*) advised by an elected committee. Each island is administered by a headman (*kateeb*), a number of assistants, and a mosque representative.

The president is nominated by the *Majlis* and approved by popular referendum. Forty members of the *Majlis* are popularly elected by the 19 atolls and the capital, and eight are appointed by the president. As noted, all candidates for the *Majlis* run as independents. There are no political parties in the Republic of Maldives.

The president is Maumoon Abdul Gayoom, who is currently serving his fifth term in office. He has survived various coup attempts and a serious challenge, in 1993, to his presidency by his brother-in-law and minister of atolls administration, Ilyas Ibrahim. In October 1993, Gayoom was reelected for a fourth term in a national referendum; he received 92.8% of the vote.

In 1994, President Gayoom outlined further reforms including greater responsibility and autonomy for Cabinet officials, greater accountability for civil servants, democratic elections for island development and atoll committees, and formation of a law commission to reform the judicial system. The possibility of multicandidate presidential elections and constitutional reforms was discussed, but no action was taken. Optimism regarding political reform increased in 1995 when the president told the *Majlis* that he would introduce legislation to increase public confidence in the electoral system. Prompted by reports that the conservative Muslim Wahabi sect was gaining adherents, the government also promised measures to combat religious extremism. In 1996, the president reshuffled his Cabinet and reorganized government bodies, including the establishment of a Supreme Council for Islamic Affairs to advise the president. In 1997, Gayoom announced that the Citizens' Special *Majlis* had resolved to complete constitutional revision and implement the amended version by January 1, 1998.

Despite optimism generated by recent presidential actions regarding greater political liberalization, political parties remain prohibited. There is also some concern about the government's treatment of political opponents.

In October 1998, President Gayoom was reelected to a fifth term in office with 90.9% of the vote. This was the country's first election under its new constitution, adopted earlier in the year. In his inaugural speech, Gayoom emphasized the importance of strengthening national unity and identity, reinforcing family values, preserving social harmony and cultural traditions, and empowering women. He also announced plans to address the need for housing, safe drinking water, deepening the country's ports, and diversifying the economy.

Because the Maldives are low-lying islands, the country has been in the forefront of a movement of island nations, the Alliance of Small Island States (ASIS), concerned with rising sea levels attributed to global warming. In 1994, President Gayoom called for action to address what he termed a global problem. This issue remains an important one in the Republic of the Maldives.

Tourism has become the islands' largest source of foreign exchange, and infrastructure projects are under way to improve the islands' facilities. The most recent economic indicators showed improvement, with greater private-sector participation in the economy, more foreign investment, and continued expansion of tourism.

Web Site

Repulic of Maldives: www.Maldives-Info.com

REPUBLIC OF MALI

(République du Mali)

By Pascal James Imperato

THE SYSTEM OF GOVERNMENT

Mali, a country of 9 million people in the heart of West Africa, is a multiparty state with a civilian government. The present government was elected in Mali's first fully democratic elections in over 30 years, which were held in early 1992. These elections represented an important step in Mali's development of a democratic government following the ouster of General Moussa Traoré on March 26, 1991. Traoré came to power through a coup d'état on November 19, 1968, which ousted Mali's then one-party Marxist president, Modibo Keita.

Traoré initially ruled Mali with military colleagues through a Military Committee of National Liberation (CMLN). In 1979, this committee was dissolved, and Traoré ruled through a political party, the Democratic Union of Malian People (UDPM), in which the military held important posts. Although legislative elections were regularly held, the military continued to hold onto power through ministerial posts and the central committee of the UDPM.

During 1990 and 1991, prodemocracy groups in Mali placed increasing pressure on Traoré for multiparty democracy. He rejected their demands and insisted on the expression of politically diverse views within the context of the UDPM. Prodemocracy groups were then joined by students, trade unionists, and the unemployed in a series of violent demonstrations that culminated in an opportunistic coup d'état against Traoré by Lieutenant Colonel Amadou Toumani Touré and his military associates. Touré and his clique formed a Military Council of National Reconciliation (CRN). However, under pressure from prodemocracy groups and external donors, they quickly stepped aside and established a 25-member Transition Committee for the Health of the People (CTSP). This joint civilian-military committee guided Mali to multiparty elections in early 1992.

The government of Mali functions under the constitution of the Third Republic, which was adopted through a referendum held on January 12, 1992. This provides for a president elected for five-year terms by universal adult suffrage, a prime minister appointed by the president, a unicameral National Assembly whose 129 deputies are elected for five-year terms, and an independent judiciary.

Executive

Alpha Oumar Konaré is the president and presides over a civilian Cabinet. He was elected on April 26, 1992, with 69% of the vote. He was the candidate of the Alliance for Democracy in Mali–The African Party for Solidarity and Justice (ADEMA). ADEMA was a leading prodemocracy movement that became a political party in 1991, following the overthrow of General Traoré.

Under the terms of the 1992 constitution, the president is eligible for reelection only once. Konaré was reelected for a second term on May 11, 1997.

Legislature

Elections to the National Assembly were held on July 20 and August 3, 1997. ADEMA captured 130 seats; 8 seats went to the Party for National Renewal (PARENA), which in 1995 had split from the then second-leading party, the National Congress of Democratic Initiative (CNID). The remaining 9 seats were split among three smaller parties.

Judiciary

The 1992 constitution provides for an independent judiciary consisting of a Supreme Court, a Constitutional Court, a High Court of Justice, a Court of Appeals, and lower courts. The Supreme Court consists of three sections: judicial, administrative, and accounts. The Constitutional Court, comprised of nine members, rules on the constitutionality of laws. The High Court of Justice judges the president and ministers accused before the National Assembly of treason, crimes, or offenses committed in the course of discharging their responsibilities.

Local Government

Mali is divided into eight regions and the District of Bamako surrounding the capital. The regions in turn are divided into *cercles* (districts) comprised of smaller units known as *arrondissements*. Larger towns have elected councils and mayors while the *cercles* and *arrondissements* are headed by central government appointees. Each region is headed by a governor who reports to the minister of territorial administration and internal security. *Cercles* are administered by commandants and *arrondissements* by chiefs.

THE ELECTORAL SYSTEM

Candidates for local and national government positions are selected by individual political parties, of which there are close to 50 in Mali. The selection process varies greatly among these various political parties.

THE PARTY SYSTEM

Political parties were first organized in Mali in the immediate post–World War II era. The strongly anticolonial and Marxist Sudanese Union (*Union Soudanaise-Rassemblement Démocratique Africain*; US-RDA) was founded in 1946 by Mamadou Konaté and Modibo Keita. Its chief opponent was the Sudanese Progressive Party (*Parti Progressiste Soudanais*; PPS) established by Fily Dabo Sissoko the same year. It drew much of its support from traders and merchants. Faced with overwhelming popular support for the US-RDA, Sissoko and the PPS merged with the former in 1959. Following independence in 1960, the US-RDA was the only political party in the country. Under Modibo Keita, it pushed forward with radical Marxist domestic and foreign policies. In 1962, Keita moved to eliminate Sissoko by charging him with treason and attempting a coup during a July 20 riot in Bamako, the capital, by merchants protesting Mali's new nonconvertible currency. Sissoko was arrested, tried by a "popular tribunal," and later shot in a remote northern district of the country.

Keita launched a cultural revolution in 1967 during which he purged many party and government leaders and activated a Popular Militia that terrorized the population.

The 1968 military coup by Moussa Traoré and his associates ended all political activity in the country. The military initially ruled through a committee. However, in 1979, Traoré formally established a new political party, the Democratic Union of the Malian People (*Union Démocratique du Peuple Malien*; UDPM). The UDPM was structured along Marxist-Leninist lines. Although the party was organized down to the grassroots level, the military controlled it and the one-party National Assembly. The UDPM effectively served to give legitimacy to Traoré's military rule. While he used the party apparatus and the National Assembly to build consensus with regard to policy formulation, he and his military supporters remained firmly in control.

Traoré followed pragmatic domestic and foreign policies but remained heavily dependent for a long time on the Communist bloc, especially China and the Soviet Union. He also exploited cold war rivalries to the best advantage. France continued to subsidize the country's budget in return for trade preferences and other concessions. During the late 1980s, the collapse of Euro-Communism deprived Mali of many of its principal international sponsors, especially the Soviet Union. Simultaneously, the Traoré government came under increasing pressure from the World Bank, the International Monetary Fund, and France to restructure its finances, disband unprofitable state enterprises, and foster private enterprise. Initially, France supported democratic reforms within a one-party political system.

Ex-government employees, students, and graduates without hope of future government or private-sector employment and prodemocracy groups galvanized in 1990 to put increasing pressure on Traoré and the UDPM for political reform and an end to gross corruption. Continuous bloody demonstrations in March 1991 led to a military coup d'état and the disbanding of the UDPM. Traoré was sentenced to death for blood crimes and for embezzling 2 billion dollars, an amount equal to Mali's external debt. The sentence was not carried out.

ALLIANCE FOR DEMOCRACY IN MALI–THE AFRICAN PARTY FOR SOLIDARITY AND JUSTICE
(Alliance Pour La Démocratie au Mali–Parti Africain Pour La Solidarité et La Justice; ADEMA)

Mali functions under a multiparty system in which ADEMA controls the National Assembly and the presidency. This party was originally founded in 1990 as a prodemocracy movement by Alpha Oumar Konaré, who had also established Jamana, a cultural cooperative. ADEMA drew its political support from civil servants and the rural population and its financial support from groups in France. Konaré, who was first elected president in 1992, heads the party, which has a vocal left wing. Konaré himself in his earlier writings and speeches revealed strong Marxist views that he has muted since the demise of communism in Europe.

OTHER POLITICAL FORCES

Minor Political Parties

During most of the 1990s, two other political parties exercised significant influence in Mali. They are the National Congress of Democratic Initiative (*Congrès National d'Initiative Démocratique*; CNID) and the resuscitated US-RDA of Modibo Keita. The former has its roots among lawyers, while the latter draws its strength from old hard-line Marxists. However, internal conflicts in both during the latter part of the 1990s led to the formation of rival splinter parties. PARENA was formed in 1995 by dissidents from CNID. Further splits in the US-RDA in 1998 left the Patriotic Movement for Renewal (*Mouvement Patriotique pour le Renouveau*; MPR), the successor to Traoré's UDPM, the second-most-important party after ADEMA. In an environment of winner-take-all politics, a number of parties constitute a radical opposition that has assumed a confrontational and at times violent posture toward the ADEMA-dominated government.

Military

Mali's 7,000-man army is equipped primarily with Soviet arms. There were several attempted military coups during the Traoré regime, in 1969, 1976, 1978, and 1981, and finally a successful one in 1991. Hard-line officers opposed to the transition to multiparty rule and the loss of their special privileges organized a successful coup on July 15, 1991. The threat of strong internal popular opposition and external repercussions from donors serve to hinder the military from launching coups.

Bureaucracy

The Malian government is excessively bureaucratized, employing close to 40,000 people in the civil service and state-run companies. A Marxist legacy of the Keita and Traoré regimes, this bloated bureaucracy is politically powerful and defensive of its entitlements. Under World Bank and International Monetary Fund pressure, Traoré disbanded a number of unprofitable state companies and blocked entry into the civil service. The resulting layoffs created a large cohesive group of disgruntled unemployed people who joined students, trade unionists, and others in a common cause to topple Traoré and his government.

Organized Labor

Unions are federated in the National Union of Malian Workers (*Union Nationale des Travailleurs Maliens*; UNTM). The UNTM was sequentially controlled by the US-RDA and then later by the UDPM. However, as Traoré closed down access to civil service employment and reduced the size of the parastatals, the union increasingly criticized him and his government. The teachers' union, the National Union of Education and Culture (UNEC), proved especially thorny for Traoré, joining with students during the 1980s in a number of demonstrations and anti-government activities. Lagged salary payments, instituted with the support of the IMF, were a major focus of teacher discontent during the 1980s.

Under multiparty democracy, the UNTM is completely independent of any party control.

Students

Since the late 1970s, student groups have emerged in Mali as an independent and fairly powerful political force. Students were first politically galvanized when the Traoré government, responding to bilateral donor and IMF demands, sought to block what had been almost automatic entry into the civil service and parastatals. The government also intervened to stem the upward flow of students into higher levels by giving tougher examinations. Although students rallied around slogans praising scientific socialism, the real issue was future guaranteed government employment.

Student protests in 1979–81 were organized by an independent union, the National Union of Students and Pupils of Mali (*Union Nationale des Etudiants et des Elèves du Mali*; UNEEM). Although proscribed by the government, the union effectively boycotted classes and organized demonstrations. The union was finally broken in 1981 through concessions and hard-line retaliation.

In 1990, students banded together in another independent union, the Association of Pupils and Students of Mali (*Association des Elèves et Etudiants du Mali*; AEEM). Their leader, Oumar Mariko, an ardent Marxist, mobilized large numbers around the issue of perceived inadequate student entitlements and the government's refusal to agree to guaranteed future employment. During 1990 and early 1991, AEEM along with prodemocracy groups and the unemployed organized a number of demonstrations that eventually led to the fall of the Traoré regime.

The Konaré government has also had to deal with violent student protests. In March and April 1993, serious clashes took place as students rebelled over the government's austerity measures with regard to their stipends. They burned public buildings and attacked the state radio station. A month later, even more violent clashes took place as they attempted to burn the National Assembly building, the headquarters of ADEMA, and other government buildings. In this case, they were protesting the government's alleged attempt to impose a new leader on their union. This protest led to the resignation of Prime Minister Abdoulaye Sékou Sow. In the final analysis, AEEM succeeded in forcing the resignation of Konaré's first government. Student protests continued throughout 1994–96, during which government and foreign diplomatic facilities were attacked.

Malian student demands for government stipends and guaranteed state employment cannot be met by any government. Concessions around the periphery of these issues have served to defuse them for the short term. However, until Mali develops a free-market economy full of employment opportunities, students will continue to look to the government to guarantee their welfare. The prospects for greater private-sector employment are poor. Thus, students will continue to press their case and confront the government through violent means.

Ethnic Groups

Until recently, there was little ethnic rivalry among Mali's several ethnic groups. The Bambara, Dogon, Malinké, Minianka, Senufo, and Songhay are farmers; the Bozo and Sorko fishermen; the Peul and Tuareg herdsmen; and the Sarakolé merchants. Population growth and a stagnant economy have led to a breakdown in long-standing harmonious and complementary economic relationships. As increasing numbers of people compete for limited resources, they move into economic spheres once the traditional reserve of specific ethnic groups. Thus, the increased ethnic rivalry occurring in Mali is in many ways an expression of economic competition.

Mali's population is 70% Moslem. However, syncretic practices combining older indigenous religious beliefs and Islam are common. Indigenous religions have been in steady retreat before Islam for many decades. There are fewer than 100,000 Christians, of whom 20% belong to various Protestant groups; 80% are Catholic. Christians are actively discriminated against by the Moslem majority, especially in towns and the capital, Bamako.

The Berber Tuareg of the north have been the victims of government policies that have denied them access to education, health services, and development. Both the Keita and Traoré governments also persecuted the Tuareg in a variety of ways. Their livestock were often confiscated, and they were actively encouraged to migrate into Algeria during periods of drought. Government officials have often been vocal and public in claiming that a "white race" such as the Tuareg have no place in a black African state. This position has been strongly denounced by prodemocracy groups in the country. The Tuareg see themselves as the victims of racist government policies. Their armed rebellion of the 1990s forced the government to reverse long-standing policies and meet many of their demands.

NATIONAL PROSPECTS

By the end of 1998 Mali had made a remarkable political transition from three decades of one-party dictatorial rule to a multiparty democracy. President Alpha Oumar Konaré, respected for his integrity and honesty, has successfully built political consensus both within his own party and by reaching out to radical opposition groups. The country's major problems remain a weak economy highly dependent on agriculture and insecurity in the north where Tuareg splinter groups continue their military operations.

Agricultural output has grown in recent years, largely due to development schemes such as Mali Sud and Opération Haute-Vallée. However, annual production levels depend on rainfall. During the past two decades, weather cycles have included periods of severe drought that greatly affect food and cash crop production. Declines in food crops have also been influenced by conversion to cotton production in certain areas.

Official corruption was rampant during the years of the Traoré regime. This problem, while still present to some degree, has been vigorously addressed by Konaré's government, which is widely perceived as being honest. Like Traoré before him, Konaré has shown flexibility in following the requirements of major aid donors. He has held the line on public-sector employment and encouraged the development of a free-market economy as had his predecessor Moussa Traoré.

Manufacturing activity contributes about 8% to the gross domestic product. Most manufacturing meets national demands. Although there has been much investment in gold mining by foreign concerns in recent years, overall production is insufficient to alter Mali's basic dependence on agriculture and livestock raising. The construction of hydroelectric dams at Selingué and at Manantali during the 1980s has provided Mali with cheap electricity that could be harnessed in the future to support industrial development.

Konaré and his government face considerable discontent from students who continue to press demands for increased stipends and government employment. Civil servants are likewise unhappy with lagged salaries whose purchasing power has been eroded by inflation. The 50% devaluation of the CFA franc in January 1994 has further aggravated their financial distress. Rural populations, whose needs were often ignored in the Keita and Traoré eras, are now pressing for their fair share of services through their representatives in the National Assembly. The survival of multiparty democracy in Mali is very much dependent on the government's ability to build political consensus concerning major issues and to successfully address some of the country's pressing economic problems.

Further Reading

de Benoist, Joseph-Roger. *Le Mali*. Paris: Editions L'Harmattan, 1989.

Diarrah, Cheick Oumar. *Le Mali de Modibo Keita*. Paris: Editions L'Harmattan, 1986.

Gaudio, Attilo. *Le Mali*. Paris: Editions Karthala, 1987.

Imperato, Pascal James. *Historical Dictionary of Mali*, 3d ed. Lanham, Md.: Scarecrow Press, 1996.

———. *Mali; A Search for Direction*. Boulder, Colo.: Westview Press, 1989.

O'Toole, Thomas. *Mali . . . in Pictures*. Minneapolis: Lerner, 1990.

MALTA

(Repubblika ta' Malta)

By Kenneth E. Bauzon, Ph.D.

THE SYSTEM OF GOVERNMENT

Malta is an island country in the Mediterranean consisting of the inhabited islands of Malta, Gozo, and Comino as well as the tiny uninhabited islands of Cominotto and Filfla. It is one of the most densely populated countries in the world with a population of 360,000 and a total land area of 122 square miles. Its population is predominantly of Carthaginian and Phoenician background, and its culture is a mix of Arab, Italian, French, and English traditions. This population mix reflects Maltese history in which the country has been, throughout the centuries, under the control of the Roman and Byzantine Empires (212 B.C.E. and 870 C.E., respectively), the Normans (1020), the Knights of Malta (1523), the French (1798), and the British (1814). The major religion is Roman Catholicism, subscribed to by 98% of the Maltese population and, by law, the state religion. Official languages are Maltese and English, although Italian is also widely spoken. The seat of government is in the port city of Valletta, located on the island of Malta.

Until its political independence from Great Britain in September 1964, Malta was a constitutional monarchy with the queen of England as its titular head. In December 1964, the Malta independence constitution was proclaimed, transforming Malta into an autonomous liberal parliamentary democracy within the British Commonwealth. While maintaining the centralized character of the government, this new constitution provided safeguards for the human rights of citizens, guaranteed a degree of power separation among the branches of government, and ensured periodic elections based on universal suffrage. Under this constitution, the governor-general retained his power to appoint the prime minister and the Cabinet from among members of Parliament. In 1974, this constitution was revised to transform Malta into an independent republic. The amendment retained the Westminster model of government, which provided for the president—of Maltese citizenship—as the constitutional head of state, with a term of five years, to be indirectly elected through Parliament. The office of the president replaced the office of the governor-general, who, up to that time, represented the British royal crown as de jure head of state. In 1987, the constitution was once again amended to modify the electoral law so that the party garnering the majority in a popular election would have a parliamentary majority by being awarded additional parliamentary seats, if necessary.

Executive

Under the current constitution, the president is elected to a five-year term by the Parliament. The president wields formal executive authority and assents to bills, prorogues and dissolves Parliament, and acts on the advice of the prime minister. Dr. Ugo Mifsud Bonnici currently holds the office of the president. A member and former president of the Nationalist Party, Dr. Bonnici was elected to his position on April 4, 1994, after having served as minister of education and human resources.

The prime minister, who also serves a five-year term depending on parliamentary majority, is both the effective head of government and chief executive officer. The prime minister, as leader of the majority party in Parliament, exercises prerogative in filling ministry positions in the Cabinet, although the president formally appoints this body. Currently, Alfred Sant fills the office of the prime minister as leader of the Labour Party, which won majority seats in the legislative elections held on October 26, 1996.

Legislature

Under the present constitution, the legislature consists of a unicameral House of Representatives whose members are elected to five-year terms on the basis of proportional representation. The majority party forms a government consisting of the prime minister and a Cabinet formally appointed by the president. As provided for in an amendment to the constitution in 1987, the party with a majority of popular votes may be awarded additional seats in the House to ensure a legislative majority.

Members of Parliament are elected from electoral divisions. Each division is represented by at least five but not more than seven members, as determined from time to time by Parliament, to ensure equal and proportional representation of the divisions. The Speaker of the House is elected from among its members.

Unless Parliament is dissolved sooner, the current members of the legislature will serve their terms of five years (until the year 2001), after which elections are to be held.

Judiciary

The constitution provides for an independent judiciary. It consists of a Superior (or Constitutional) Court, which is the highest court, a Court of Appeals, a Criminal Court of Appeal, and lower courts. The Superior Court consists of a chief justice and nine other justices, who serve until age 65.

In March 1994, Parliament created the Commission for the Administration of Justice. Designed to be an independent body, it supervises the work of both the superior courts and the lower courts; formulates recommendations to be submitted to the minister of justice related to the operation, administration, and organization of the courts; provides advice to the president on appointments; draws up a code of ethics to govern the behavior of members of the judiciary, legal practitioners, and procurators; and draws attention to any judge or magistrate whose performance may be hampering the efficient and proper functioning of his office. The president, who serves as the chairman, heads the Commission.

Regional and Local Government

Prior to 1993, there were no local governments per se in Malta, with the exception of the island of Gozo, which was governed by a civic council. In 1993, however, through an act of Parliament, municipal councils in various localities throughout the country were created. Today, there are 67 such councils elected popularly, serving as local governments charged with the administration of the local police, post office, medical facilities, and other government programs. They also assist in the administration and enforcement of national laws. Ultimately, however, they are advisory in nature and depend for their budgetary allocation on, and are answerable to, the central government.

THE ELECTORAL SYSTEM

Malta's unusual electoral system, adopted in 1921, is based on the method called single transferable vote. Ireland is the only other country that uses this system.

The method seems complex but is not. At election time, voters, who must be at least 18 years of age and registered, are asked to rank numerically the candidates, regardless of political party affiliation, whose names appear on the ballot. To qualify for a parliamentary seat, a candidate must fill a specified "quota" in the electoral di-

vision or district in which he is a candidate. This quota is determined on the basis of the total number of valid votes cast divided by the number of seats allotted for that district, plus one. If in a particular district, for instance, five parliamentary seats are open to competition, and 12,000 votes have been cast (assuming they are all valid), then the quota of votes that a candidate must fill would be 12,000 divided by 6 (i.e., 5 + 1), or 2,000 votes.

Any candidate who meets the quota after the initial vote count is declared a winner. If that winning candidate has received votes in excess of the required minimum needed to meet the quota, as frequently happens, these excess votes are then transferred and added on to the votes of the next-highest-ranked candidate indicated by the voters. It is in this context that the method is called "transferable" because the excess or, more appropriately, the "surplus" votes are used to help the next-highest-preferred candidate attain the quota instead of being discarded.

THE PARTY SYSTEM

Malta's political party system has evolved from that of a multiparty to that of a dominant-two-party system. The two main parties have their origins in a dispute over the use of English in schools. Those who favored the use of English and acquired the distinction as liberals later formed the Malta Labour Party. On the other hand, those who supported the retention of Italian earned the label of conservatives and eventually formed the core of the Nationalist Party.

Although these two parties dominate political life, Malta is still a multiparty state. Political party competition in Malta is characterized by intense and vigorous partisanship. Their strong party loyalty and allegiance distinguish voters themselves. Even though the electoral system allows them to cross party lines, they rarely do so. Thus, crossover votes tend to be very small (about 1–2%) of the overall votes cast during any given election (or since the 1971 elections).

Despite sharp differences on issues, however, all political parties are agreed on the democratic premises of the Maltese constitution, primary of which is the parliamentary means to political power through competitive elections. There is no underground revolutionary movement seeking the overthrow of the political system. The Maltese Communist Party, unlike its counterparts elsewhere in the world, operates aboveground; in one attempt to participate in the electoral contest (in 1987), it received a mere 119 votes (or .05% of the votes cast).

THE MALTA LABOUR PARTY

Paul Boffa established the Malta Labour Party officially in 1921. Its unique structure explains in large measure its durability and cohesiveness. At the village level, it maintains a network of village committees. Members of these committees are elected annually by dues-paying party members. Each village committee in turn elects one representative to the district committee. The district committee is responsible for preparing campaign materials as well as organizing and mobilizing support for the national party within the district. At the national level sits an executive committee consisting of representatives from the various districts as well as from the Labor Youth League, incumbent members of Parliament who are party members, and representatives from the national party conference, which convenes annually. The national conference is composed of delegates from village committees nationwide.

The party platform of the Malta Labour Party envisions a socialist future. Throughout the years it has been in power, the Malta Labour Party has adopted policies oriented toward the equalization of social wealth. A key component of this orientation is the nationalization of key sectors of the Maltese economy, including banking, insurance, and shipping. With the assertion of the public sector in the economy, particularly through governmental and quasi-governmental corporations, it has increased the number of those employed in governmental departments and government-controlled corporations to nearly 40% of the overall labor force. It also has adopted progressive social policies with regard to social freedom, employment, and education. It has frequently complained about church intrusion into state affairs and has pushed for greater appropriation of church property.

With its recapture of the government in the October 1996 elections, the Malta Labour Party is in a position to reverse some of the policies instituted by the previous Nationalist-led government. It is also in a position to slide back into its habit of acting as a one-party dictator, due to almost complete control of access to governmental institutions and resources as well as to instruments of coercion. However, it has to be mindful always that it came to power through a razor-thin victory. The possibility of losing the next round of elections to its closest rival, the Nationalist Party, has to have a sobering and moderating effect on the way it exercises power. Additionally, it must contend with the influence of the Roman Catholic Church, especially at the grassroots level. It has little choice but to tread more gingerly on issues that are close to the heart of its church constituents.

THE NATIONALIST PARTY

The Nationalist Party, unlike the Malta Labour Party, has a loose national organization. It relies largely on the semi-autonomous organizations organized by its candidates, members, and supporters at the local level; these are usually prominent local personalities (mainly religious leaders, business entrepreneurs, or white-collar professionals) who have built up extensive clientelist support networks in their respective municipalities or districts. While the national party organization does not generally maintain permanent local committees, these are supplemented by the local or districtwide clientelist networks that designate representatives to form a sort of executive body at the national level; this body, in turn, serves to formulate policies and strategies for adoption by the party as a whole.

The party platform of the Nationalist Party may be described as conservative. It favors the retention of traditional Roman Catholic values in Maltese religious and social life. It is protective of the church's preeminent role in the country by deferring to its influence in the policymaking process, particularly in the area of education and in the matter of church property. While standing for liberal democratic beliefs of the Western European variety, it has particularly advocated electoral reforms that would achieve both "proportionality and governability" in obvious response to the 1981 election in which the Nationalist Party garnered more popular votes than the Malta Labour Party but failed to get a majority of parliamentary seats. In this reform effort, it succeeded only in achieving the proportionality segment of the reform package because, as Labour Party parliamentarians contended, inclusion as well of the governability segment would have allowed one-party dictatorship in government.

In economic matters, the Nationalist Party has always stood for the principle of free enterprise. In pursuit of this principle, it has dedicated efforts and resources to attract foreign investors into the country. It has promoted an investment code, officially adopted in October 1987, liberalizing rules on tariffs and repatriation of profits by foreign companies. These companies currently invest and generate employment in such areas as light engineering, footwear and clothing, automotive spare parts, electrical goods and devices, medical and health care–related products, among others. The long-term goal was to transform Malta into a center for overseas banking, insurance, and financial services; it also sought to make Malta a shipping capital in the Mediterranean. To help accomplish this, the Nationalist-led government retained the services of a United States–based financial institution, the Chase Manhattan Bank Corporation, in late 1987 as a consultant in the formulation of appropriate legislation.

So long as Malta's dominant-two-party system lasts, the prospects of the Nationalist Party's recapture of control of government in the next elections are as good as its main rival's ability to hold onto power. Given Malta's electoral history, the difference between victory and defeat has been so narrow that no winning party can really rest comfortably or afford to be complacent. In fact, it might be better if the Nationalist Party and the Malta Labour Party, for pragmatic reasons, simply agreed to share and alternate power between themselves until any of the third parties are able to send a significant number of their own candidates to Parliament.

MINOR POLITICAL PARTIES

Democratic Alternative

Founded only shortly prior to the 1992 elections, the Democratic Alternative advocates environmentalism. It managed to get a 1.7% share of the popular vote in the 1992 balloting but gained no parliamentary seat. It is led by Wenzu Mintoff as chairman and Saviour Balzan as coordinator.

Communist Party of Malta

The Communist Party of Malta is a legal, aboveground Marxist-oriented political party. It has adopted a pro-Soviet stance in the context of the cold war. Instead of fielding its own candidates to run in the elections of 1987 and 1992, it has deferred to Malta Labour Party candidates, presumably so as not to take away votes from the latter. In the 1996 elections, it did field a candidate who managed to get only a little over 100 votes altogether. Consequently, it has never secured any legislative seat. Its leaders are Charles Zammit as president and Anthony Vassallo as general secretary.

Malta Democratic Party

The Malta Democratic Party was founded in 1986 on the basis of the principles of environmentalism, administrative decentralization, and political pluralism. Although it has fielded candidates since the 1987 elections, it has never had significant grassroots support or any parliamentary representation. Michael Vella is its president while Lino Briguglio serves as its general secretary.

NATIONAL PROSPECTS

Malta's dominant-two-party system is well entrenched. Despite the appearance of third parties in recent years, these have not been significant enough to pose serious challenge to the hegemony of the Malta Labour Party and the Nationalist Party on the national political scene.

In terms of the balance of power among the executive, legislative, and judicial branches of government, it is obvious that the executive wields a disproportionate advantage over the two others. The president sets the agenda while the prime minister and the Cabinet serve the largely advisory and supervisory functions of day-to-day government operations. Parliament's independence seems under constant threat from the president's power to dissolve and the majority party's tendency to ratify and support the president's agenda. The judiciary, while relatively independent, wields no power of judicial review. Thus, in real terms, there is no system of checks and balances similar to that known in other Western parliamentary systems. The country's political condition has permitted this situation, which is highly unlikely to change drastically in the near future.

The current political arrangement in Malta has some advantages and disadvantages. The consolidation of political control between the Malta Labour Party and the Nationalist Party has a stabilizing effect on the country's political system but also signals the relative decline of the Parliament vis-à-vis the executive. This calls into question the future of democracy in Malta as presidentialism becomes the norm. Historical examples show that where the national executive plays a dominant role in national life, e.g., in Germany during the 1930s and in many Latin American countries in the 1960s and 1970s, liberal democracy becomes less stable. On the other hand, the Maltese Parliament, despite the ebb and flow of its power, has demonstrated the capacity to persist and survive. The two major political parties are aware of this parliamentary function and, thus, would be unlikely to initiate a political agenda that would veer too far in any direction from the center.

Further Reading

Flanz, Gisbert H., ed. *Constitutions of the Countries of the World: Malta Supplement*. Dobbs Ferry, N.Y.: Oceana, May 1995.

Frendo, Henry. *Malta's Quest for Independence*. Valletta: Valletta Publishing, 1989.

———, ed. *Maltese Political Development 1798–1964: Selected Readings*. Valletta: Ministry of Education and Human Resources, 1993.

Political Handbook of the World 1995–1996. Binghamton, N.Y.: CSA, 1996.

Thackrah, Richard. *Malta*. London: Oxford University Press, 1985.

Marshall Islands

By Eugene Ogan, Ph.D.

The Republic of the Marshall Islands (RMI) was one of the Pacific Island nations created in 1986 from what had been the United Nations Trust Territory of the Pacific (TTPI). It comprises 26 coral atolls, 19 inhabited, and five coral pinnacles, four occupied by humans. These form two roughly parallel chains, called *Ratak* (Sunrise) and *Ralik* (Sunset). Though the Marshall Islands spread over 1.95 million square kilometers of eastern Pacific Ocean, the combined land mass is just under 180 square kilometers. Population was estimated in 1997 at 60,000, almost all of whom are ethnically Micronesian.

These islands have a long colonial history. Beginning in 1885, they were successively administered by the Spanish, Germans, and Japanese; the last ruled under a Mandate of the League of Nations. World War II had a terrible impact on the islands as fighting killed many Marshallese while bombing devastated the landscape. After establishing military control in 1944, the United States regarded the islands as having strategic importance. This perspective shaped American administration when the United States became Trustee of TTPI and continues to affect political developments in the modern republic.

The Compact of Free Association that produced RMI was the result of long negotiation with Marshallese and others in the Trust Territory. In these negotiations, Marshallese chose by referendum to be a nation separate from the other TTPI groups. Although the Compact became effective in 1986, it is still subject to interpretation. This fact has not prevented Marshallese from establishing their own political institutions, which take the form of a modified parliamentary system with a distinctive element of traditional chiefly authority.

Executive authority lies with the Cabinet, whose members are collectively responsible to the legislature, or *Nitijela*. Thus the *Nitijela* is the key political institution. This unicameral chamber at present consists of 32 members who must be 21 years of age or older. They are elected to two-year terms by universal suffrage of Marshallese over the age of 18. They elect the president from among their number; he then vacates his legislative seat, which is filled by special election. The president appoints from 6 to 10 *Nitijela* members as Cabinet ministers. In contrast to a true presidential system, the Marshallese president can-not veto bills passed by the legislature. His only power in case of serious disagreement is to dissolve the *Nitijela*, forcing a general election.

Traditional Marshallese society was built around chiefs (*iroij*), some of whom were recognized as paramount in their islands (*iroijlaplap*). Their status is institutionalized in the Council of Iroij, technically an advisory body with special concern for Marshallese culture. Although the Council has no veto power, every bill passed by the *Nitijela* must be sent for its consideration. It is composed of 12 "eligible persons," 5 from the Ralik chain of islands, 7 from Ratak. Eligible persons are *iroij*, or equivalent, eligible to vote in general elections but not members of the *Nitijela*.

The constitution provides that the judiciary is independent of the executive and legislative branches. There is a Supreme Court, High Court, Traditional Rights Court, and a system of subordinate courts. The High Court is both a trial court and an appellate court for cases from lower courts; appeals from its decisions go to the Supreme Court, which may take appeals from lower courts. Judges of both courts are appointed by the Cabinet, acting on recommendation of the Judicial Service Commission and with *Nitijela* approval. Despite its name, the Traditional Rights Court does not have jurisdiction over such issues as composition of the Council of Iroij or the declaration of customary law and may be regarded as a body ancillary to the rest of the system.

Although RMI institutions, including named political parties, appear quite modern, actual practice remains dominated by conflicting chiefly interests. Amata Kabua, who served as president from the republic's inception until his death in 1996, was an *iroijlaplap* descended from the chief who signed the 1885 treaty with the Germans. He was succeeded by his kinsman, Imata Kabua, who enjoys similar chiefly status. Those from outside the ranks of *iroij* have yet to achieve the top positions in RMI politics.

Further Reading

Encyclopedia of World Cultures: Oceania. Boston: G.K. Hall, 1991.

ISLAMIC REPUBLIC OF MAURITANIA

(Al-Jumhuriyya al-Islamiyya al-Mawritaniyy)

By Isla MacLean
Revised by Deborah A. Kaple, Ph.D.

THE SYSTEM OF GOVERNMENT

Mauritania, which borders the north Atlantic Ocean, the disputed area of Western Sahara, Algeria, Mali, and Senegal, is a country of 2.4 million people (1997 estimate). It is very poor, and predominantly Islamic, and its main language is Arabic. The population is roughly one-third Beydane (Arabic for "white") Moors, descendants of northern Arabs and Berbers with an equal number of mixed-race people who have also adopted Berber customs. The most important black Africans in Mauritania are the tribal groups Toucouleur, the Fulani, the Sarakole, and the Wolof. Tensions between the groups continue to surface, with allegations of "arabization" efforts and even instances of black slavery, which, although illegal, allegedly is still in force.

Mauritania became a French colony in 1920 and an autonomous republic within the French community in 1958. On November 28, 1960, it became independent. Moktar Ould Daddah, who led the independence fight, set up one-party rule and governed for 18 years. In 1964, all political parties merged into the Ould Daddah's party to form the Party of the People of Mauritania (PPM). In 1978, after the Ould Daddah regime seized the southern part of Western Sahara, he was ousted in a bloodless coup by Lieutenant Colonel Mustapha Ould Salek. Ould Salek was replaced by Colonel Mohamed Khouna Ould Haidalla, who was then ousted in 1984 by Colonel Maaouiya Ould Sid'Achmed Taya in a bloodless coup. Taya established an authoritarian government.

In 1991, Mauritania promulgated a new constitution, which emphasizes a strong role for the president. It states that the president is continuously eligible for the post (of president), it provides for short regular sessions of Parliament, it allows the government to set the priorities of the parliamentary agendas, and it restricts votes of no confidence.

Executive

The chief of state is the president, who is elected for a six-year term by the people. According to the constitution, he must be a Muslim. The current president, Maaouiya Ould Sid'Achmed Taya, has been in office since December 1984. He presides over the Council of Ministers. He is also the supreme chief of the armed forces, and presides over the Superior National Defense Councils and Committees. The president is assisted by a High Islamic Council composed of five persons whom he appoints and whose role is vague. According to the 1991 constitution, the High Islamic Council "formulates opinions concerning the questions about which it has been consulted by the President of the Republic."

The head of government is the prime minister, who is also appointed by the president. The prime minister is Mohamed Lamine Ould Guig. Under the authority of the president, he defines the policy of the government and directs and coordinates the business of the government. He is responsible for dividing tasks among ministers.

Both the president and the prime minister belong to the ruling party, the Social and Democratic Republican Party (PRDS).

Legislature

The Parliament has two chambers. The National Assembly (*Al Jamiya al-Wataniyah/Assemblée Nationale*) has 79 members who are popularly elected for a five-year term in single-seat constituencies. The Senate (*Majlis al-Shuyukh/Sénat*) has 56 members, 53 of whom are elected for six-year terms by municipal leaders. Among these, 17 are up for election every two years. Mauritanians abroad elect 3 members.

The Parliament meets in regular session twice a year during the first two weeks of November, and again during the first two weeks of May. The length of each ordinary session may not exceed two months.

Judiciary

In 1980, Islamic law (*shari'ah*) was introduced and the Islamic Court of Justice was founded to try crimes against people and property and adjudicate in family matters. The first application of the *shari'ah* (a public execution and three hand amputations) was in September of that year. In June 1983, it was decided to apply the *shari'ah* in all domains. The Special (Military) Court of Justice was set up in 1980 to investigate and try cases that threaten the security of the government and state. In 1985, the court was reorganized to include civilian magistrates and the right of appeal in civilian and commercial cases.

The main courts include 3 courts of appeal, 10 regional tribunals, 2 labor tribunals and 53 departmental civil courts. There is also a revenue court for financial matters.

Regional and Local Government

Mauritania is divided into 12 regions administered by appointees of the central government. Nouakchott, the capital, is administered directly by the central government. Within these 13 regions, there are 208 districts. More traditional administrative structures (emirates) have all but disappeared. During Ould Daddah's presidency, it was decided that when an emir died his title would die with him.

In January and February 1994, Mauritania had its first multiparty municipal elections, in which the Taya's political party, the PRDS, took 172 of the 208 districts. Thus local government is dominated by the president's party.

THE PARTY SYSTEM

On July 12, 1991, a new constitution was promulgated that guaranteed "freedom of association" in Mauritania. This, along with later legislation, signaled the freedom to form political parties. However, politics continues to be tribally based, and one party in particular tends to dominate the political landscape. President Taya's party, the Social and Democratic Republican Party (PRDS), forms the present government. In the last presidential election, held in December 1997, the PRDS garnered 90.2% of the vote.

SOCIAL AND DEMOCRATIC REPUBLICAN PARTY

(Maaouiya Ould Sid'Achmed Taya; Parti Républicain Démocratique et Social; PRDS)

After the new constitution was promulgated in 1991, the PRDS was one of the first parties to be accorded official status. The PRDS is the official government party, and has been criticized by opposition groups for its close relationship with the state apparatus. For instance, in early January 1996, Taya appointed Cheikh Afia Ould Mohamed Khouna as the new prime minister, replacing Sidi Mohamed Ould Boubacar. Ould Boubacar then went on to be elected as secretary-general of the PRDS.

As the presidential nominee in the balloting that fol-

lowed the new constitution in 1992, Taya won by a large margin. The PRDS subsequently won a large majority in the National Assembly and Senate elections that followed.

In the October 1996 election for National Assembly members, 90% of the members elected were PRDS members. In the April 1996 elections to the Senate, the figure was 75%.

Parties in the Legislature, 1996 Elections		
Party	Assembly	Senate
Social and Democratic Republican Party (PRDS)	71	42
Action for Change (AC)	1	—
Union of Democratic Forces (UFD)	boycotted	
Others	—	11
Independents	6	11
Mauritanians Abroad	—	3
Total Number of Seats	79	56

Note: Senate elections took place in April 1996; National Assembly elections took place in October 1996

MINOR POLITICAL PARTIES

President Taya's political party, the PRDS, is seen by most observers as a tool of the president and of the state apparatus. While an opposition exists today in Mauritania, more often than not it is insignificant in elections or campaigns.

In the 1992 legislative elections, six opposition parties withdrew their candidates, alleging that certain election tactics were favorable to the PRDS. Therefore, Taya's party took 67 of the 79 available seats. In the Senate race in April 1992, only one successful party presented candidates at elections. In the 1996 legislative elections in October 1996, the PRDS again reaffirmed its dominance, winning 71 of the 79 seats. Only one opposition party, the Action for Change (*Action pour Changement*; AC) won a seat; the other six were taken by independent candidates. Several opposition parties contested the results of this election, saying that censorship in the period preceding the elections helped the PRDS to win. The Union of Democratic Forces (*Union des Forces Démocratiques*; UFD) boycotted the election altogether.

Action for Change
(Action pour le Changement; AC)

The AC was granted full legal status in 1995, and it became the "main opposition" party by virtue of the fact that it won the only legislative seat that did not go to the

PRDS. The AC has been described as including the most militant parts of Harratin (ex-slave) and black groupings.

Union of Democratic Forces
(Union des Forces Démocratiques; UFD)

The UFD was legalized in 1991. It comprised a diverse cross section of political groupings that were all united in the goal of ousting the Taya regime. Led by Ahmed Ould Daddah, the party has been highly critical of the government. In the municipal elections of 1994, the UFD garnered 17 of the country's 208 districts, but it boycotted the 1992 legislative elections. It also boycotted the 1996 legislative elections, claiming unfair political procedures.

OTHER POLITICAL PARTIES

Religious parties are not allowed under the constitution, and the Taya government has banned political speeches in places of worship. Those who admit to belonging to the illegal Islamic Movement are often detained and harassed by police. The government views such religious groups as vehicles for the influence of extremist foreign Islamic groups.

There are also some human rights parties, such as the unauthorized Mauritanian Human Rights Association (MHRA). In 1994, the leader of MHRA was detained by police for meeting with international human rights organizations on the issue of black slavery in Mauritania. Also, there is the African Liberation Forces of Mauritania (*Forces de libération africaine do Mauritanie*; FLAM), founded in 1983, which represents black Africans in Mauritania. In 1984, FLAM issued "The Manifesto of the Oppressed Black Mauritanian," which detailed persecution of blacks.

OTHER POLITICAL FORCES

Ethnic Groups

About 70% of Mauritanians are Arabic-speaking Moors of mixed Arab, Berber, and black Berber African stock. They are divided into numerous tribal groups and into the "white" Moors, the dominant class, and the "black" Moors, the ex-slaves, or Harratin. Some 30% of the population are black African and belong to the Peul, Toucouleur, Sonink, and Wolof ethnic groups. Their society is also highly stratified and traditionally permitted the ownership of slaves. The black Africans were traditionally settled farmers in the Senegal River basin on the southern border, while the Moors were traditionally nomadic pastoralists.

The dominant position occupied by "white" Moors in the past is being eroded. "Black" Moors now constitute a sizable portion of the free labor force and urban shantytown dwellers. The black African population is growing at a faster rate than the Moorish population. (The actual balance of numbers is disputed.) Black demands for greater representation and protests at the "arabization" of education have erupted periodically into violence. Periodically, organizations have been formed in the south to seek an independent black state.

The fragile unity of the country is maintained through a common adherence to Islam and, more importantly, an intricate power-balancing process. The government includes representatives of the various ethnic groups, although "white" Moors still predominate.

Organized Labor

The Mauritanian Workers' Union (*Union des Travailleurs Mauritaniens*; UTM) is the only organized force in the country aside from the army. Union militancy reached its height in the late 1960s and early 1970s. A series of strikes in support of nationalist demands forced the government's hand on revision of the cooperation agreement with France, creation of a national currency, and nationalization of the iron ore mines. Since then, the work of the UTM has been hampered by disagreement within the executive over the political role the trade union should play.

Religious Leaders

All Mauritanian nationals are Muslim, although not all practice their religion. The traditional religious figures, the *marabouts*, gain their position partly by inheritance and partly by their reputations for wisdom and piety. Most Mauritanians, black and Moor, are followers of one or another *marabout* and frequently consult that *marabout* on all matters. Given their dominant role in society, the *marabouts* are essentially a conservative political force. They favored introduction of the *shar'iah*, and many opposed the abolition of slavery on the grounds that the practice is sanctioned in the Koran.

Mauritania also has a small Catholic following in a single diocese in Nouakchott.

NATIONAL PROSPECTS

Although Mauritania now has a constitution that provides for multiparty elections and for some fundamental rights, the country continues to be dominated by President Taya and his political party, the PRDS. The first presidential election, in 1992, following the promulgation of the new constitution, saw President Taya elected by 63% of the votes. Later that year, his party won a majority of seats in the legislature. In the municipal elections in January–February 1994, the PRDS took 172 of the seats. In the 1996 legislative elections, the PRDS also dominated. While an opposition exists, it is small and not significant, and its leaders are harassed and detained regularly by police.

In September 1998, in preparation for the upcoming municipal elections, a campaign was launched to revise the voters' lists. Opposition parties (who boycotted the last presidential election) accused the government of managing the elections and have been indifferent to this recent measure.

Mauritania has also come under fire for alleged human rights violations, for the continuation of a system of black slavery that the Taya government claims is nonexistent.

Mauritania has faced extreme economic difficulties for many years, with growth over the past decade limited to an annual rate of 2%. Mauritania's per capita GNP is estimated at US$480 (1994), a high level for Africa, but nevertheless living conditions for most Mauritanians are still relatively difficult. The economy continues to show a sharp contrast between the modern sector, dominated by mining, industrial fishing, and irrigated agriculture, and the traditional subsistence sector. The majority of the population is employed in the traditional sector comprising livestock, agriculture, and services. The government's habit of engaging in battles over turf with neighbors has only drained monies toward this goal at the expense of improving people's lives. It remains to be seen how Mauritania will fare, since its economy still relies heavily on external borrowing and its vulnerability to drought and high population growth continue to make demands on resources.

Further Reading

Calderini, S., et al. *Mauritania.* World Bibliographic Series, vol. 141. Santa Barbara, Calif.: Clio Press, 1992.

CIA World Factbook. Washington D.C.: Government Printing Office, various years.

Diallo, Garba. *Mauritania—The Other Apartheid?* Current African Issues, no. 16. Uppsala, Sweden: Scandinavian Institute of African Studies, 1993.

Fleischman, Janet. *Mauritania's Campaign of Terror: State-Sponsored Repression of Black Africans.* New York: Human Rights Watch, 1994.

Ould-Mey, Mohameden. *Global Restructuring and Peripheral States: The Carrot and the Stick in Mauritania.* Lanham, Md.: Rowan and Littlefield, 1996.

A copy of Mauritania's 1991 constitution can be found on the Internet at:

http://www.uni-wuerzburg.de/law/mr00000_.html

MAURITIUS

By B. David Meyers, Ph.D.

THE SYSTEM OF GOVERNMENT

Most of Mauritius's 1 million citizens live on the Indian Ocean island of that name, while 35,000 reside, some 300 miles away, on the much smaller island of Rodrigues. Mauritius also claims Tromelin, an island held by France, and Diego Garcia, a strategically important, midocean atoll, administered by the United Kingdom.

This former French and, more recently, British, colony is an ethnically diverse society of religious, color, caste, class, and linguistic differences. A majority of the population is Hindu, descendants of persons brought from India to work the sugar plantations. Other ethnic communities include white Franco-Mauritians, Creoles (persons of mixed, white-African, descent), Africans, Muslims, and Chinese.

Since independence, Mauritius has successfully maintained a stable parliamentary democracy. Elections have been held regularly, and power has been transferred peacefully. Dr. Navin Ramgoolam, who took power in parliamentary elections in December 1995, is Mauritius's third prime minister since independence in 1968. He succeeded Sir Anerood Jugnauth, who had led the government since 1982, and Sir Seewoosagur Ramgoolam, who governed from 1968 to 1982.

In contrast with this stability, the multiparty system, which reflects the complexity of Mauritian society, is in constant turmoil. It demonstrates an ever-shifting pattern of consolidation, fragmentation, and reassembly.

Executive

The head of state is a ceremonial president, elected for a five-year term by a simple majority of the National Assembly. Executive power is vested in a prime minister, who leads the majority party or coalition in the legislature. Other members of the governing Council of Ministers are appointed by the president on the recommendation of the prime minister. The Council is responsible to the National Assembly.

The current prime minister, a relative newcomer to politics, is both a doctor and a lawyer, but, most importantly, he is the leader of the Labor Party and the son of the nation's first leader.

Legislature

Legislative authority is vested in a unicameral National Assembly presided over by a Speaker. Ordinary legislation requires a majority vote, constitutional amendments require the approval of three-quarters of the deputies.

Sixty members of the Assembly are elected by receiving the three highest vote totals in 20 three-member districts, two additional members are elected from Rodrigues, and four seats are allotted to "best losers," the unsuccessful candidates who have received the largest number of votes.

Judiciary

The legal system is based on French civil law together with some elements of English common law. There is a Supreme Court whose nine judges preside additionally in lower courts. The Supreme Court, which has the authority to find legislation unconstitutional, has been a powerful, independent institution.

Regional and Local Government

There are nine administrative districts on Mauritius and a resident commissioner for Rodrigues. There are elected town councils in the urban areas, and district and village councils in the rural areas.

ELECTORAL SYSTEM

Mauritian elections have involved over 40 political parties and many hundreds of candidates, only a few of whom have any chance of winning. As no one party has sufficiently broad appeal to win a majority in the National Assembly, elections have always been contested, and governments formed, by coalitions of two or more parties.

In the 1995 elections, Ramgoolam led such an alliance of his own Labor Party with the Mauritian Militant Movement, headed by Paul Berenger. Together they captured all 60 contested seats on Mauritius. Two seats on the island of Rodrigues were won by the Rodrigues People's Organization.

POLITICAL PARTIES

Three political parties, Labor, the Mauritian Militant Movement (MMM), and the Mauritian Socialist Movement (MSM), dominate the political system. The Labor Party, founded before independence, gets its support from within the Hindu community. Once strictly a supporter of free-market economic policy, it now promotes a mixed economy with widespread social welfare benefits. The MMM was founded by Paul Berenger, in 1969, as a noncommunal, socialist party focusing on issues of wages and employment. Its constituency is primarily found in the trade unions and urban areas. The MSM, originally a splinter from MMM, has also proved to be pragmatic, accepting a mix of free-market economics together with its socialist inclinations. Since its founding, it has been headed by Sir Anerood Jugnauth.

Thirty-nine other parties contested the 1995 election. Of these, the most important were the Rodrigues People's Organization, which represents the interests of that island, and the Mauritian Social Democratic Party, a once-powerful conservative party that draws support primarily from Creoles and whites concerned with Hindu dominance.

OTHER POLITICAL FORCES

The Mauritian press, subject to state censorship during the early 1970s, is now free and robust. Labor unions and communal groups are often politically active.

NATIONAL PROSPECTS

The Mauritian political system has remained stable and democratic while the economy has been transformed from one dependent solely on sugar plantations to a successful mix of agriculture, tourism, and manufacturing. This country has been, and will probably remain, one of the Third World's success stories.

Further Reading

Bowman, Larry W. *Mauritius: Democracy and Development in the Indian Ocean*. Boulder, Colo.: Westview Press, 1991.

UNITED MEXICAN STATES

(Estados Unidos Mexicanos)

By Dale Story, Ph.D.

THE SYSTEM OF GOVERNMENT

Mexico's constitution officially designates this nation as the "United Mexican States," indicating a federal republic in form. However, in practice Mexico remains a centralized or unitary republic with minimal powers granted to the states. The other major characteristic of the Mexican political system has been its domination by a hegemonic party. At the national level, the Institutional Revolutionary Party (*Partido Institucional Revolucionario*; PRI) has won every presidential election since the formation of political parties in the late 1920s, as well as almost all of the national legislators. Also, while a governor is popularly elected within each of the 31 states, the PRI had won in every state until 1989, when the historically major opposition party, the National Action Party (PAN) achieved the governorship of Baja California Norte. The president of Mexico unofficially selects all PRI gubernatorial candidates, guaranteeing the dominance of the national government. The constitution reserves for the federal government all authority over commerce, banking, land use, public health, labor laws, corporations, and licensing of professionals.

In the summer of 1994, this hegemonic party system faced its greatest challenge ever. On the heels of major economic reform (highlighted by the initiation of the North American Free Trade Agreement, or NAFTA), the popular demands for a truly competitive electoral system were mounting—both at home and abroad. Actually, the PRI's presidential candidate in 1988, Carlos Salinas de Gortari, had received the party's lowest vote total ever (just over 50% of the vote). The opposition claimed that Cuauhtémoc Cárdenas (former PRI governor and son of Lázaro Cárdenas, the PRI's most popular leader and president in the 1930s) had actually won the election. To bolster his legitimacy, Salinas began to open the political system. His efforts won widespread applause, but the presidential election year of 1994 brought even greater challenges to the PRI and its one-party system. First, a major peasant rebellion erupted in the southern state of Chiapas on January 1, 1994 (the day that NAFTA went into effect). While a truce was negotiated, the renewal of violence continually threatened the electoral process. Next, the PRI's presidential candidate, Luis Donaldo Colosio, was assassinated in March. The party selected his campaign manager (and former minister of programming and budget), Ernest Zedillo, as his successor. Zedillo's chief competitors were Diego Fernández de Cevallos of the PAN, and Cuauhtémoc Cárdenas (running under the banner of the Party of the Democratic Revolution (PRD).

Salinas attempted to ensure the fairest elections ever in Mexico. Electoral reforms adopted in May guaranteed the complete independence of the Federal Electoral Institute (*Instituto Federal Electoral*; IFE), appointed a special prosecutor to handle all violations, allowed for national observers and foreign visitors, and provided mechanisms to eliminate voter fraud. For the first time, the voter registration cards were laminated IDs with personal photographs, thumb prints, and individualized bar codes. The list of registered voters was audited by several independent organizations and certified as 97% accurate. Over 80,000 national observers and 2,000 accredited foreign "visitors" performed important watchdog functions. Transparent ballot boxes were used, and all voters had their registration cards punched and indelible ink affixed to their thumbs. The government had invested millions of dollars in a computerized system of counting the votes and allowed several independent "exit polls" and "quick counts" to provide validation for the official results.

On August 21, 1994, the Mexican citizens went to the polls in record numbers (estimated at over 75% turnout rate) in the most critical election yet in the evolution of the Mexican political system. Though the result was another victory for the PRI, the perception of fairness established by the electoral reforms was widely held. Zedillo garnered some 49% of the vote total, with the PAN's Fernández a distant second with 26% and Cárdenas a more distant third at 16%. Thus, the PRI's one-party dominance of the presidency remained unbroken.

National elections were next held on July 6, 1997, for all 500 members of the Chamber of Deputies (the lower house of the Mexican legislature), 32 seats in the Senate (one-quarter of the total number in this upper house of the Mexican legislature), six governors, and the mayor of Mexico City (undoubtedly the race receiving the most attention). Heralded as the most honest elections yet, they brought further erosion of the PRI's dominance. In the widely followed election of the Mexico City mayor, Cuauhtémoc Cárdenas (twice a loser in the presidential contest) finally won an election, outpacing the PRI candidate for mayor by an almost 2-to-1 ratio. Just as historic a breakthrough occurred in the vote for the Chamber of Deputies, where the PRI lost its long-held majority for the first time. Nationally, the PRI polled just 38% of the vote, which translated into only 238 deputies (of the total of 500, or less than 48%); the PAN received 26% of the vote and 121 deputies, and the PRD scored 25% of the vote and 126 deputies. Thus, together the two major opposition parties commanded a 9-vote lead over the PRI in the lower house.

Background: The Revolution

A better understanding of the evolution of Mexico's one-party and centralized system must begin with the concept of the Revolution of 1910. Prior to the Revolution, General Porfirio Díaz had ruled Mexico as a repressive dictator from 1876 to 1911. The army and police maintained order through force. Díaz took land from political opponents and peasant villages, concentrating large farm-ranch-plantations (called *haciendas*) among a ruling elite. A few hundred *hacienda* owners controlled half of the nation's arable area. Some 90% of the rural population spent their lives working on the *haciendas* at marginal pay, perennially in debt to their employers, virtually under feudal conditions.

The Revolution began in November 1910 as a reaction to the political and economic dominance of Díaz. Over the following 10 years more than a million lives were sacrificed—almost one-tenth of the population. Francisco Madero, the first Revolutionary president (1911–13), stressed a political agenda of "effective suffrage and no reelection." The peasant leader Emiliano Zapata emphasized the socioeconomic goals of "land and liberty." Venustiano Carranza spearheaded the writing of the 1917 constitution, which codified the aims of the Revolution (including the secularization of education, nationalization of subsoil rights and other assets, agrarian reform, and extensive labor rights). The 1920s consolidated the power of the "Revolutionary Family," which was institutionalized in the creation of the precursor to the PRI in 1929. The rest of the century has seen the continued dominance of the ruling party through the continual election of its presidential candidates to six-year terms.

The "no reelection" clause limits the president to one six-year term, with no second term ever, and prohibits members of Congress, state legislatures, and municipal councils from serving two consecutive terms. After an intervening term, these lesser officials can run again for the same office. Thus the Mexican political structure is a "musical chairs" system under which PRI leaders rotate horizontally as well as vertically from one government position to another.

With its population reaching 100 million, by 1998 Mexico had experienced nearly 70 years of relatively nonviolent government headed by a self-replenishing leadership that has used the PRI to win major elections. A dominant coalition of government, party, industrial, labor, and agrarian leaders has contributed to this political stability.

Executive

Executive power is vested in a president as head of government and head of state. The president must be a native-born Mexican of native-born parents, indicating the nationalism in the constitution, and at least 35 years of age. Unofficially, the president typically would have experience as a Cabinet minister and be able to mediate between the left and right wings of the dominant PRI. After consultations with the party's inner circle, the incumbent president of the country has chosen the party's next presidential nominee. During the last year of his six-year term, the incumbent strives to inculcate in his successor his personal concept of the ongoing Revolutionary goals. From 1913 to 1946, presidents had been army generals as well as civilian administrators; since 1946 every president has been a civilian. There is no vice president. In the event of the death or resignation of the president, the federal Congress elects an interim president.

Presidential powers are extensive and allow the chief executive to dominate the legislative branch. The president can introduce bills directly into both houses of Congress and can assign legislative priorities. The president can veto legislation; he has never had to do so, however, as no law opposed by him has ever been enacted. The president appoints the Cabinet ministers, diplomats, high-ranking officers of the armed forces, and all federal judges, with Senate confirmation. One-party dominance assures approval of his choices. The president can pardon anyone convicted of any felony, and chief executives have used this right freely in political matters to co-opt former opponents.

The constitution allows the chief executive to issue decree laws in most areas of public life. For example, the income tax was created by presidential decree, followed years later by congressional action. Presidential decrees have created Cabinet ministries, government corporations, major public-works projects, significant budget changes, and public policies ranging from family planning to nuclear energy, followed later by congressional legislation.

For years, the senior Cabinet officer was the *Secretaría de Gobernación* (minister of internal affairs), who controls federal-state-municipal relations, liaison with Congress, elections, voter and party registration, immigration and emigration, motion picture production and theaters, television and radio noncommercial air time, the federal police, and federal prisons. More recently the economic ministries of planning and budget, finance, and commerce and industrial development have risen to the forefront due to the primacy of economic policy. Ranking next is the minister of foreign relations, who helps the president conduct foreign policy.

Presidents Lázaro Cárdenas (1934–40) and Manuel Avila Camacho (1940–46) had been ministers of defense. Presidents Miguel Alemán (1946–52), Adolfo Ruiz Cortines (1952–58), Gustavo Díaz Ordaz (1964-70), and Luis Echeverría (1970–76) had been *Secretaría de Gobernación*. President Adolfo López Mateos (1958–64) had been minister of labor, and President José López Portillo (1976–82), minister of finance. Most recently, Presidents Miguel de la Madrid (1982–88), Carlos Salinas (1988–94), and Ernesto Zedillo (1994–2000) were ministers of planning and budget.

Legislature

The federal Congress consists of a Senate and a Chamber of Deputies. There are now 128 senators, essentially divided among the 31 states and the Federal District surrounding the national capital, Mexico City. A senator's term runs six years. Until 1988, the PRI had always won every Senate seat except one, in 1976, which went to a candidate of the opposition Popular Socialist Party (PPS) from the state of Oaxaca.

The Chamber of Deputies has 500 members, of which 300 are elected from congressional districts based on population. In each congressional district, the candidate with the most votes, plurality or majority, wins the seat. The remaining 200 seats are chosen on the basis of proportional representation. A deputy's term runs three years, with the full Chamber being elected every three years. The accompanying table illustrates the division (by percentages) of seats in the Chamber by party since 1976.

Party Representation in the Chamber of Deputies, 1976–97 (in percentages)

Year	PRI	PAN	FDN/PDR	Others
1976	82.0	8.5	—	9.5
1979	74.0	10.8	—	7.8
1982	74.8	12.5	—	12.7
1985	72.7	10.3	—	17.0
1988	52.0	20.2	27.6	—
1991	63.9	17.8	8.2	10.2
1994	60.0	23.8	14.2	2.0
1997	47.6	24.2	25.2	3.0

Sources: Howard Handelman, *Mexican Politics: The Dynamics of Change* (New York: St. Martin's Press, 1997); and *Instituto Federal Electoral.*

At least until 1997, the PRI dominated Congress regardless of slight shifts in the number of minority-party deputy seats. Since the legislative branch debates the form rather than the substance of new laws, changes in bills received from the executive branch have been generally cosmetic rather than substantive. Both houses put legislation in final form in committee hearings that follow the guidelines set down by the appropriate Cabinet ministry. Floor debate serves as an escape valve for frustration but has had little effect on legislation. With the loss of an absolute majority in the Chamber in 1997, the PRI was facing its first challenges ever in the legislature. Questions remained as to the development of alliances and coalitions, with the PRI obviously hoping to woo the PAN into a working majority coalition.

Sessions run from September 1 to December 31 annually. Each year, the president calls Congress into special sessions for two months or more sometime during a period in January to August. When Congress is not in session, each house furnishes half of the 30 members of the Congressional Commission (*Gran Comisión*), which functions in place of Congress, including the confirmation of presidential appointments. Without consecutive terms, senators and deputies cannot acquire seniority in Congress. Thus, committee, subcommittee, and house leaders have been chosen instead on the basis of party seniority.

Judiciary

Mexico's federal court system has exclusive authority for all important civil litigation, leaving to the court system of each state civil jurisdiction over minor sums of money and divorce cases. Suits involving contracts, finance and banking, labor-management relations, corporations, and interstate and intrastate commerce are handled by federal courts. In criminal law, federal courts handle bank robberies, kidnappings, and most major felonies. Murder cases, however, are heard in state courts.

The one major restraint on presidential power is judicial, specifically the writ of *amparo* (relief), which can be issued by any federal judge on behalf of a citizen claiming his constitutional rights have been violated by a government official. The *amparo* can be directed against a government official at any level but can be obtained only from a federal court. This writ stays the disputed governmental action until an appeal can be heard by the federal Supreme Court. The *amparo* combines some of the judicial powers found in the Anglo-Saxon writs of injunction, mandamus, and habeas corpus. It may halt official action, compel officials to carry out constitutional obligations, or force judges to tell a defendant the specific charges against him in a criminal case. Political disputes over elections and campaigns are excluded from the authority of *amparos*.

From 1917 to 1980, some 5,500 writs of *amparo* involved the president and his Cabinet ministers as defendants. In one-third of these cases, private citizens or groups won their Supreme Court appeal over presidential action.

However, the Court has never issued such a writ when political rights or economic policies were involved.

Reforms in 1994 reduced the size of the federal Supreme Court from 26 to 11 members and precluded individuals who have just left political office from being appointed to the Court. Supreme Court justices must be native-born Mexicans and be at least 35 years old. The president appoints them with Senate confirmation. A justice must retire at age 65 or at any time after age 60 if he or she has completed 10 years of service. Since 1929 every justice has been a member of the dominant party, the PRI.

The intermediate federal judicial level is circuit courts of appeal, of which there are six. The Supreme Court selects appellate judges from among federal district court judges to serve four-year terms. The president can grant an appellate judge tenure until age 65. Each of the 31 states has a state supreme court (*Supremo Tribunal de Justicia*), ranging in size from three to eight justices. The governor selects these justices for six-year terms.

Regional and Local Government

In each of the 31 states, a governor is popularly elected for a six-year term and can never serve a second term. From 1929 until 1989, every governor was a member of the PRI. Despite the formality of state party conventions, the dominant party's inner circle in Mexico City has selected the candidate most likely to carry out the national administration's wishes. Except in six states, gubernatorial terms do not coincide with the presidential term. Under Article 76 of the constitution, the president can have the Senate remove the governor of any state in which law and order cannot be maintained. The chief executive then designates an interim governor to finish the term. From 1917 to 1964, presidents have removed an average of one governor per year. Since 1964, presidents have averaged only one removal per presidential term. However, each chief executive has pressured one to three other governors to voluntarily resign when political crises got out of control.

Each state has a one-chamber legislature, with members elected for three-year terms, every other election coinciding with the election of the governor. State constitutions reserve most of the powers for the governor, making the legislature a rubber-stamp committee formalizing details of his programs. Legislatures vary from 9 to 25 members. In each state the legislature must approve all municipal budgets, which the governor's finance director coordinates. Mexico has 2,359 municipalities (*municipios*), which are like counties in the United States. Every town and city within the *municipio* is governed by the municipal council (*ayuntamiento*). Councils range in size from 5 to 11 members who serve three-year terms. Mayors (*presidente municipal*) have the constitutional powers to dominate the councils.

THE ELECTORAL SYSTEM

Elections at all levels of government are popular and direct and provide representation by a simple majority winner, except for the 200 seats in the federal Chamber of Deputies and 32 seats in the federal Senate, which are chosen by a system of proportional representation. Federal Chamber of Deputies districts and state legislative districts each have a single representative. For each senator and deputy, as well as state legislators and municipal council members, a substitute is also elected. This allows each party to reward its workers with nominations as substitutes. In the event of a vacancy between elections, the substitute immediately fills the post, obviating the need for a interim election.

With the PRI having dominated so many elections, voter apathy has characterized most elections. Half of the eligible voters historically do not go to the polls in presidential elections (however, the 1994 election saw a record turnout of 78%); in congressional or municipal races with strong minority-party candidates, the turnout may reach 70% of the registered voters. PRI leaders encourage PRI voter turnout with promises of continuing welfare programs and patronage.

THE PARTY SYSTEM

Origins of the Parties

After Mexico achieved independence from Spain in 1821, its party system consisted of several small parties, each a personalistic group following a strong leader. The real impetus for the institutionalization of parties and the end of more personalistic movements was the desire by the revolutionary leaders of the 1920s (particularly Plutarco Calles) to consolidate the victory of the revolutionary government in the context of an umbrella party—first known as the National Revolutionary Party (*Partido Nacional Revolucionario*; PNR).

The Parties in Law

The federal Law of Political Organizations and Electoral Processes (*Ley Federal de Organizaciones Politicas y Procesos Electorales*, or LOPPE) gives Congress the authority to set requirements for a party to qualify for a place on the ballot. The LOPPE has required a party to have a minimal number of members and to win a similarly minimal percentage of the total national vote to retain its legal status. The standards have been interpreted loosely in order to promote the image of a multiparty system. Typically, as many as eight minority parties have participated as registered parties.

Party Organization

The LOPPE requires each party to maintain a permanent national headquarters and a national executive committee. At least six months before an election, a party must hold a national convention to publicly announce its candidates for all offices it intends to contest. In practice, the standard procedure has been for each party's inner circle to choose its candidates. National officers of each party dominate state and local committees. The only party with active municipal committees throughout the republic is the dominant PRI, which maintains them with government patronage and informal, extralegal use of contingency funds from federal and state budgets.

Campaigning

Electoral reforms through the 1980s and 1990s were directed at creating a more independent Federal Electoral Institute and providing a more level playing field for all parties to contest elections. While considerable progress has been made in equalizing the resources available to parties, the PRI undoubtedly maintains a distinct advantage through its years of domination of the political system. For example, the PRI continues to garner a disproportionate share of media attention. A variety of factors contribute to the PRI's dominance of both television and print coverage. The ruling party enjoys a symbiotic relationship with the major networks and several newspapers. Even in cases of journalistic independence, the fact that the PRI dominates the newsmaking events explains its overwhelming lead in coverage.

The Spectrum of Mexican Political Parties

In 1997, the Federal Electoral Institute listed a total of eight registered parties. The proliferation of parties has been a clear objective of the PRI in an effort to divide-and-conquer. However, to the benefit of the opposition, since 1988 the political spectrum of Mexican political parties has been concentrated in a triumvirate with the PAN on the right, the PRI in the center, and the PRD on the left. We will discuss these three principal parties first, then conclude with some of the remaining fringe parties.

INSTITUTIONAL REVOLUTIONARY PARTY
(Partido Revolucionario Institucional; PRI)

HISTORY

The dominant party of Mexico, the PRI, was founded as the National Revolutionary Party (*Partido Nacional Revolucionario*; PNR) by the former Mexican president Plutarco Calles on March 4, 1929, in Querétaro. At this point in history, Calles can be credited for making two in-

fluential decisions. First, he announced in his state of the union address that he would not seek another term in office—thereby solidifying the concept of no reelection. Second, he outlined and enacted the plan to create a new national party to encompass all the revolutionary factions and to institutionalize the succession of power. After three "puppet" presidents between 1928 and 1933, Calles endorsed Lázaro Cárdenas as the presidential candidate of the PNR for the 1934 election. The decision proved as pivotal as that of creating the party. Cárdenas immediately began to shape the landscape of Mexican politics for decades to come. The new president demonstrated the powers of the office, declaring his independence from previous administrations and even sending Calles into exile in the United States. Fulfilling many of the aims of the Revolution, Cárdenas redistributed land to peasants at levels unparalleled before or after his administration, organized more of the working class than ever before, and nationalized the petroleum and railroad industries. Finally, Cárdenas solidified the concept of the six-year presidential term, the unilateral selection of the next presidential candidate by the incumbent, and also the recognized independence and autonomy of the succeeding president.

The party's national assembly changed the name to the Institutional Revolutionary Party in 1946 to emphasize the continuing social and economic reforms to which it is committed. The renamed PRI was also organized along the corporate lines of economic sectoral representation. In this case, the PRI focused on bringing together three major sectors: labor, the peasantry, and the "middle class." The umbrellas for both organized labor, the Confederation of Mexican Workers (*Confederación de Trabajadores de México*; CTM), and the peasantry, the National Peasant Confederation (*Confederación Nacional Campesina*; CNC), were already in place by the 1940s. Than President Manuel Avila Camacho in 1943 created the National Federation of Popular Organizations (*Confederación Nacional de Organizaciones Populares*; CNOP) as the sector for bureaucrats, professionals, housewives, merchants, and others of the growing middle class. These three groups became the institutional and organizational backbone of the party, with the CNOP subsequently becoming a dominant force in the party, overshadowing the labor and agrarian sectors in policymaking.

In a significant initiative in 1963, the party created an Institute of Political, Economic, and Social Studies (*Instituto de Estudios Políticos, Económicos, y Sociales*; IEPES) to research national needs and policy priorities. The IEPES coordinates PRI and government policy formulation. In 1964, the PRI elected as its president an attorney, Carlos Madrazo, former governor of Tabasco. He convinced the PRI to adopt a policy of party primaries to open nominations for state and local offices to those not tied to political cliques. Madrazo arranged party primaries in two states, Baja California Norte and Chihuahua. However, since its 1929 founding, the PRI has relied on an elite inner circle to select nominees. The inner circle, therefore, got the party's national executive committee to cancel the policy of primaries and forced Madrazo to resign in a major defeat to internal party reform efforts. While many other aspects of the political scene have been liberalized and reformed, the PRI has continued to use a closed system of selecting nominees.

ORGANIZATION

At the apex of the PRI's organization is the national executive committee (*Comité Ejecutivo Nacional*; CEN). The "inner circle" of the CEN includes the party president; the secretary-general; secretaries for agrarian, labor, and popular action; and two secretaries of political action (always one federal deputy and one senator). The CEN has 13 additional secretaries, who are designated by the inner circle. The next level is the national council, which has at least 60 representatives from each of the agrarian, labor, and popular sectors, plus the heads of the state committees from the 31 states and the Federal District. The CEN dominates the council. The council guides state and municipal PRI assemblies and reports on them to four staff officers of the CEN: the director of administrative services, the director of adjudication, the director of electoral action, and the director of social activities. The lowest nationwide entity is the national assembly, in which about 2,000 representatives chosen from both the sectoral and regional divisions of the party represent the general PRI membership. National assemblies meet every three or four years and merely ratify CEN policies. In addition, the PRI convenes a national convention every six years to formally ratify the presidential candidate whom the CEN already has announced.

As mentioned earlier, the agrarian sector is dominated by the National Confederation of Peasants, which grew from state-organized peasant leagues. The labor sector includes 8 confederations, 7 federations, and 19 independent unions, all under the umbrella of the Congress of Labor. The largest and most influential of these labor groups is the Mexican Confederation of Labor. The popular sector is headed by the National Confederation of Popular Organizations, with government employees being the dominant force.

POLICY

PRI's domestic policy stresses "no reelection," the Revolutionary ban on continuation in one office. The party supports (some would say controls) the right to strike, even for those working for the government in essential services (except for the military). PRI economic policies have initiated many important social programs: minimum wages for all trades and for unskilled labor, social security, basic health care for the poor, public housing for workers, communal or individual farms for peasants, and profit sharing for private-sector workers. Yet the party has done much to placate the private sector, particularly in creating a stable economic environment and courting business confidence. PRI's foreign policy stresses Mexico's independence from the United States, the Soviet Union, and Europe. It favors cooperation with the Organization of American States to promote Latin American regional common markets and has consistently sympathized with left-of-center and even revolutionary Latin American governments.

A key to the success of the PRI has been its ability to maintain a sense of balance and equilibrium. Presidential administrations oscillate between leftist and rightist perspectives to mollify various constituencies. A perceived probusiness domestic bent in economic policy has been balanced with a perceived leftist favoritism in foreign policy.

MEMBERSHIP AND CONSTITUENCY

PRI members have held all executive government posts from minister down through middle-level bureaucrats, all federal judgeships, and most governorships, Senate seats, and congressional district deputy seats. Civil service merit systems are only token, with the PRI's political patronage being the rule in public life. Government jobs are filled on the basis of the political clique (*camarilla*) system. A successful PRI politician's entourage is horizontal among peers who were classmates in school and vertical among rising administrators and their trusted assistants. Since a *camarilla* is based on close friendships and loyalty, as a camarilla leader rises in the PRI and in government, he has his associates promoted into higher-level offices. Among rank-and-file PRI members, extended family relationships form clusters within the party, based on lifelong friendships within each age group, class, and community.

FINANCING

Bureaucrats pay party dues equal to three days' pay a year. Other members pay token dues or are given credit for dues by performing various services for the party. Prominent politicians fund banquets and entertainment within their own cities and states, and at every level of government, unaudited government contingency funds have long been suspected as financing for PRI activities.

LEADERSHIP

The current PRI president is Mariano Palacios Alcocer. He was born in Querétaro and received a law degree from the National University. He has served in various party posts, as well as a president of the University of Querétaro, mayor of his home city, and both a federal deputy and senator. The PRI secretary-general is Socorro Díaz Palacios, a former senator and deputy from the state of Colima and former general director of the newspaper *El Día*. However, Ernesto Zedillo, the president of Mexico, is the real leader of the party. Zedillo has both master's and Ph.D. degrees in economics from Yale University. He has taught at *El Colegio de México* and worked in the *Banco de México* in the early 1980s. Between 1988 and 1992, Zedillo served as secretary of programming and budget and briefly as secretary of public education in 1992.

PROSPECTS

The PRI has run the government since 1929 and dominates most facets of public life. In the 1960s and the 1970s, communist guerrilla kidnappings and killings did selective damage to the PRI in a few cities. The most serious challenge to the PRI in this period came in 1968 when student demonstrators protested political repression, hoping to force the government to cancel the Olympics. Such a cancellation might have discredited the PRI enough to drive it from power, but the demonstrators were repressed violently by the government in the infamous Tlatelolco Massacre.

The late 1980s, however, saw the onset of a steady erosion of PRI electoral and popular support. Economic decline forced the PRI to yield ground in terms of political liberalization and also to lose political support to opposition parties. As described above, in presidential elections in 1988 and 1994 and in national congressional elections (particularly those of 1997), the ruling party's margin of victory has steadily declined to below 50%. Having already lost control of the Chamber of Deputies, the PRI, some commentators are speculating, could possibly lose its first-ever presidential race in the year 2000.

NATIONAL ACTION PARTY

(Partido de Acción Nacional; PAN)

HISTORY

The political party seen as the chief opposition to the PRI in the postwar years has been the conservative National Action Party. The PAN was founded on September 14, 1939, by Manuel Gómez Morín, on a platform of Catholic social principles within the framework of the institutionalized Revolution. Gómez Morín (1897–1972) was dean of the law school of the National University of Mexico and university president. The party's roots can be traced to a number of earlier political and social movements, although its initial leaders were primarily motivated by reactions against the anticlericalism of the 1920s and the perceived radicalism of the Cárdenas regime in the 1930s. The early *panistas* wanted to restore to the church many of its pre-Revolutionary powers, especially in the areas of religious education and political participation. When the PAN ran its first candidate in 1940, it marked the first time since 1914 that a conservative party could fully participate in Revolutionary Mexico. In 1946, the

PAN won four deputy seats in Congress and its first two municipal governments. In 1947, the PAN won its first seat in a state legislature in Michoacan. The national vote for the PAN has steadily increased from around 8% in the early 1950s to 15% in the 1980s and rose dramatically to 28% in the 1994 presidential election.

ORGANIZATION

The party president and secretary-general direct the national executive committee, which has secretaries for political action, public relations, finance, recruitment, and campaigning. The committee guides state and municipal chairmen. In 1958, PAN presidential candidate Luis H. Alvarez introduced into Mexico the first open party convention—an obvious contrast to the PRI's inner-circle selection of candidates. PAN's subsequent conventions also have been open contests. In 1976, the necessary 80% of delegates could not agree to nominate Pablo Emilio Madero, nephew of the father of the 1910 Revolution, Francisco Madero. The party then voted not to offer a 1976 presidential candidate.

POLICY

On economic and social issues the PAN in recent years has not perfectly fit the model of a conservative party favoring free enterprise over economic justice and growth over equity. Certainly the party's philosophy has been probusiness and oriented toward private ownership. But at least since the 1960s the PAN has also stressed social consciousness. In an important document issued at the close of the party's 20th national convention in 1969, the PAN advocated a third path of development between capitalism and socialism: "*solidarismo*," or, as described by one author, "political humanism." Private property is viewed as positive so long as it also contributes to the society at large.

MEMBERSHIP AND CONSTITUENCY

The PAN has claimed upwards of 500,000 members, a majority undoubtedly being from the middle class and upper class. A base of strength has always been northern Mexico, where an independent and conservative spirit has served as a fertile base for the PAN. However, the PAN has achieved successes in other regions of Mexico as well. Key early victories came in 1967 when the PAN took over local government in two state capitals, Hermosillo in Sonora and Merida in Yucatan. As of 1998, the PAN controlled 4 governorships, 25 federal senators, 121 federal deputies, and a myriad of municipal mayors and state deputies.

FINANCING

Three-fourths of the members pay voluntary, locally set dues. Political officeholders often contribute a portion of their salaries to the party. Catholic Action groups make contributions, as do many wealth entrepreneurs. The party holds fund-raising raffles, dances, and concerts to enhance its financial coffers and is well known for its past refusal to accept government financing as a sign of its fierce independence.

PROSPECTS

While recognized as the historically most significant opposition party in Mexico, the PAN is currently constrained from achieving a majority role by its close identification with many current policies of the PRI and recent administrations. Most succinctly, the party is hard-pressed to establish itself as a true alternative to PRI economic ideology.

PARTY OF THE DEMOCRATIC REVOLUTION
(Partido de la Revolución Democrática; PRD)

HISTORY

The political left in Mexico has had a long and torturous history of divide-and-rule control exercised by the PRI. Only in the last decade, with the onset of the PRD (essentially as a splinter from the PRI), has the left achieved any considerable electoral success.

The history of today's PRD begins with the creation of the Communist Party of Mexico (*Partido Comunista de México*; PCM). Francisco Cervantes López, publisher of a weekly socialist newspaper, and Manabendra N. Roy, a Marxist from India, founded the PCM at a Mexico City socialist conference in September 1919. In 1920, the PCM began publishing its official organ, *Vida Nueva*, twice a month. In 1921, the party launched its Communist youth of Mexico group, sent delegates to the third comintern congress in Moscow, and held its own first party congress.

In 1922, the famous painters Diego Rivera and David Siqueiros joined the PCM and began its magazine, *El Machete*. However, from 1930 to 1935, the party was outlawed for its violence against the government. The Hitler-Stalin nonaggression pact in 1939 cost the PCM many members; and in 1940 the PCM helped the French Stalinist Jacques Mornard assassinate the Soviet dissident Leon Trotsky in Mexico City. In 1978 the PCM applied for conditional registration after 30 years of being denied legal status. Allied with three small parties, the PCM gained legal registration after the 1979 elections in which it won 5.4% of the vote and 18 proportional representation seats in the Chamber of Deputies. At a national party convention in November of 1981, the PCM officially dissolved itself; and a few days later the Unified Socialist Party of Mexico (*Partido Socialista Unificado de México*; PSUM) was created by the union of the old PCM and the other smaller parties. However, the PSUM did not fare any better in the 1982 presidential election, receiving less than 5% of the national vote.

Frustrated with the economic decline and the slow pace of political reform, in late 1985 a group of dissident *priista* leaders began to foment change, particularly in terms of a more open process of selecting nominees within the PRI. This group became known as the "Democratic Current" and was led by the key PRI leaders Cuauhtémoc Cárdenas and Porfirio Muñoz Ledo. The split within the PRI escalated throughout 1986 and 1987, culminating with Cárdenas and Muñoz Ledo leaving the PRI and Cárdenas accepting the presidential banner of a small opposition party. In January of 1988, the National Democratic Front (FDN) was constituted as a coalition of leftist parties to support the *Cardenista* candidacy. While Cárdenas struck a very popular chord throughout Mexico, the PRI candidate (Carlos Salinas) won the presidency in July with just over 50% of the vote. The following year, the FDN dissolved—replaced by the PRD as the leading political party on the left. The PRD ran Cárdenas again for president in 1994 and won considerable electoral gains in the congressional (and Mexico City mayoralty) elections of 1997.

ORGANIZATION

The PRD defines itself as a union of three political movements:

(1) The Democratic Current splinter from the PRI

(2) The "Socialist Left

(3) The "Socialist Left" descending from the Mexican Socialist Party (PMS), the Mexican Worker's Party (PMT), the PSUM, the PCM, the Coalition of the Left, and the Movement of Popular Action

(4) The "Social Left" composed of independent worker, peasant, and civic action groups

The PRD was formed in and has been chiefly directed by national party congresses, of which there have been three (in 1990, 1993, and 1995).

POLICY

The traditional domestic policy of the PCM called for expropriation of all privately owned businesses, industries, and services under a Marxist government; party ownership of all media; and abolition of nonsocialist schools. Its foreign policy was anti–United States and pro–Soviet Union—supporting Cuba, the Sandinista government in Nicaragua, and the Democratic Revolutionary Front in El Salvador. The new reincarnation under the format of the PRD, however, has produced a much more moderate left and more successful electoral outcomes. While the party openly sympathizes with revolutionary movements, such as the Zapatistas, its domestic policies principally focus on moderate reforms, exemplified by efforts to reduce the value-added tax.

MEMBERSHIP AND CONSTITUENCY

Somewhat akin to the dilemma of the PAN, the Mexican left has been challenged to find a significant electoral base in the Mexican political spectrum. With the PRI monopolizing the imagery of the Mexican Revolution and dominating the organizational bases of both labor and peasants, the left has had little room in which to operate. However, with the economic decline of the 1980s and the resulting political misfortunes of the PRI, the more moderate leftist split from the PRI has come together in the PRD to represent a formidable alternative and challenge to the PRI. The remarkable increases in congressional representation in 1997 and the election of Cárdenas as mayor of Mexico City marked an apex in electoral success for leftists in Mexican history.

LEADERSHIP

Both the administrative and political leadership of the PRD has been dominated by the powerful personages of Cárdenas and Muñoz Ledo. Both have served as key party leaders as well as top nominees and candidates for various elected offices.

AUTHENTIC PARTY OF THE MEXICAN REVOLUTION
(Partido Auténtico de la Revolución Mexicana; PARM)

HISTORY

The PARM was founded in 1954 by General Jacinto B. Trevino, former minister of industry. Over the years, it has served an illustrative role as a prototypical appendage of the PRI. The PARM elected its first 2 deputies to the federal Congress in 1958; adding seats each three years thereafter, it elected 12 deputies in 1979. The party usually wins from 2% to 2.5% of the total congressional vote in each federal election. But in 1982 it did so poorly (1.36%) that it won no seats and lost its status as a recognized party. The PARM regained conditional registration in 1985 and even won 2 of the 300 congressional district seats along with 9 minority-party seats. Besides deputy seats, its only other officeholders have run a few municipal governments since 1958. Essentially, it has served the role as a right-of-center satellite of the PRI—never challenging the dominant party while providing it with more democratic legitimacy.

PROSPECTS

PARM's resurrection as a party in 1985 was primarily due to the PRI's desire to have another surrogate party. It remained weak at the national level, and its greatest claim to influence was serving as the initial standard-bearer of the *Cardenista* candidacy in late 1987. Today, the IFE does not even list the PARM as a registered party.

POPULAR SOCIALIST PARTY
(Partido Popular Socialista; PPS)

HISTORY

The PPS has served as the other classical satellite party of the PRI, albeit on the left of the political continuum. On September 25, 1947, labor leader Vicente Lombardo Toledano founded the Popular Party (PP). In 1948, he added "Socialist" to its name, trying to unite Marxists and noncommunist leftists. A union organizer, Lombardo Toledano had been ousted as head of the Mexican Federation of Labor in 1940 because he organized the communist-oriented Latin American Workers Federation. He was the unsuccessful PPS presidential candidate in 1952 and a PPS deputy in Congress from 1964 to 1967. He died in 1968.

Since 1958 the PPS has supported the PRI presidential candidate but fields its own candidates for Congress and for state and local office.

POLICY

The PPS has advocated a payment moratorium on Mexico's enormous international debt, and its foreign policy supports all leftist and Marxist developing nations and is strongly anti-imperialist. However, this ideology is purely rhetorical, and in reality the PPS has supported the mainstream PRI domestic and foreign policies.

MEMBERSHIP AND CONSTITUENCY

PPS has claimed as many as 300,000 members. While always a small party, it has seen some success in the states of Oaxaca, Nayarit, and the Federal District. In 1968 Jorge Cruickshank, without opposition in the state of Oaxaca, became the first PPS senator, breaking the 39-year PRI monopoly on Senate seats. However, his victory was a shallow one, since it was widely and correctly construed as a PRI reward for opposing a potential PPS gubernatorial victory in Nayarit. Every three years from 1964 through 1976, the PPS won from 5 to 10 deputy seats in Congress. In 1979 it won 2.9% of the total congressional vote and 11 deputy seats. In 1982 and 1985, its share of the vote was consistent at 1.9% and it won 10 and 11 seats, respectively. However, by 1997 its vote share had declined to a negligible 0.34% and its future was in considerable doubt.

MEXICAN DEMOCRAT PARTY
(Partido Demócrata Mexicano; PDM)

HISTORY

In the city of Irapuato on May 23, 1971, Juan Aguilera Aspeitia founded the right-wing PDM. Aguilera, a business executive in the state of Guanajuato, is head of the Sinarquista National Union (*Union Nacional Sinar-*

quista; UNS), a fascist group that began in Guanajuato in 1937. In addition to UNS members, he assembled other rightists who wanted parochial education to replace public schools.

The PDM gained conditional registration in 1978 and full registration in 1979. Campaigning under its ideology emphasizing the Catholic Church, the family, the individual, and private party, the PDM acquired 10 proportional deputies in 1979 and 12 in both 1982 and 1985. Its share of the vote has consistently fluctuated around 2%. It is particularly strong in the west (the so-called *Bajío* region where conservative Catholics and the UNS have been concentrated) and the center-north of Mexico. Its best states in terms of the 1982 vote were Guanjuato (where it once controlled the town of Guanajuato), Tlaxcala, San Luis Potosí, and Jalisco.

POLICY

The PDM's domestic policy calls for a reduction of state-owned enterprises, reduction of welfare programs, an end to PRI cronyism in government, and a "union of Church and State." Its foreign policy favors alliances with anticommunist nations.

PROSPECTS

PDM's chances for growth are almost nil. Catholic lay leaders favor the National Action Party, and the PDM has no other base of major support. Its national electoral support level had declined to 0.66% by 1997.

REVOLUTIONARY PARTY OF THE WORKERS
(Partido Revolucionario de los Trabajadores; PRT)

HISTORY

The PRT was founded in September 1976 as the first Trotskyite party in Mexico. It received conditional registration in 1981 and full registration with the election of 1982.

POLICY

The PRT declared itself to be in "service to the proletariat" and committed to the socialist revolution to construct a socialist democracy.

MEMBERSHIP AND CONSTITUENCY

The PRT became significant as a tool for protesting political repression, especially after the selection of Rosario Ibarra de Piedra as its 1982 presidential candidate. As the first woman candidate in Mexican history, mother of a political prisoner, and well-known leader of a human rights group, her campaign attracted considerable attention. Though the PRT won no federal deputies in 1982, Ibarra de Piedra polled 1.76% of the presidential vote and thus

the party gained its full registration. In 1985 the PRT received 1.25% of the vote and six minority-party deputies.

PROSPECTS

Though organized as a new ideological tool of the Marxist left in Mexico, the PRT proved to be little more than a vehicle for the popular message of Ibarra de Piedra against political repression. Without an identifiable base, the PRT was essentially subsumed by the PRD in the 1990s and is not currently listed as a registered party.

MEXICAN WORKERS' PARTY
(Partido Mexicano de los Trabajadores; PMT)

HISTORY

The PMT was established in September 1974 by a distinguished group of Mexican leftists who had been involved in the railroad strike of 1959 and the student protests of 1968. The PMT chose not to participate in elections prior to 1985, because it believed they were not fair or democratic. It finally gained conditional registration in 1984 and fielded its first candidates in 1985.

POLICY

The PMT proposed to socialize the means of production and to produce a just and egalitarian society without discrimination or privileges.

LEADERSHIP

The dominant force in organizing the party was Heberto Castillo, who was born in the state of Veracruz and is a civil engineer by profession. He was a private secretary to Lázaro Cárdenas and participated in various leftist movements in the 1960s. He was jailed after the 1968 student protests and upon his release became one of the most respected opponents of the Echeverría and López Portillo administrations.

PROSPECTS

In the months leading up to the July 1988 presidential election, Castillo was persuaded to withdraw his candidacy and support Cárdenas. That decision effectively ended the PMT, which was essentially subsumed into the PRD.

OTHER POLITICAL FORCES

Organized Management

Under a 1941 law, every retail store or commercial company must join the local chamber of commerce. These chambers in turn must unite in the Confederation of National Chambers of Commerce (*Confederación de Cá-*

maras Nacionales de Comercio; CONCANACO). It has an executive council, holds annual general assemblies, and assesses dues on a scale based on annual sales.

Under that 1941 law, every manufacturer, wholesaler, and distributor within a nationwide industry must belong to that industry's national chamber. For example, every shoe manufacturer must belong to the National Chamber of the Shoe Industry; every radio and television station must belong to the National Chamber of Broadcasters, and so on. These industrywide chambers in turn must unite in the Confederation of Industrial Chambers (*Confederación de Cámaras Industriales*; CONCAMIN). It, too, has an executive council, holds an annual general assembly, and assesses dues on a scale based on annual sales.

Neither CONCANACO nor CONCAMIN are part of the PRI, but individual business and industrial executives may join the PRI. CONCAMIN and CONCANACO have full-time staffs of economists, lawyers, and other specialists who draft suggested policies, regulations, and procedures. They then lobby directly with the highest appropriate level of government concerned. These private-sector groups are widely recognized as the most autonomous and potentially the most powerful political organizations in Mexico.

Organized Bureaucracy

All federal government employees below the top five levels of administrators belong to unions. Thirty-one unions have members throughout the agencies and departments of the executive branch and among staff employees of the judicial and legislative branches. Since 1936, these unions have been united in the Federation of Unions of Workers in the Service of the State (*Federación de Sindicatos de los Trabajadores en el Servicio del Estado*; FSTSE). It has 1 million members.

The FSTSE dominates the popular sector of the PRI and helps formulate major government policies. Its well-disciplined members turn out for political rallies, campaign speeches, and elections. The FSTSE has its own Social Security Institute, which provides better pensions and health services than the social security system for workers in the private sector.

Organized Labor

The largest group of unions is the Confederation of Mexican Workers (CTM), which helps formulate labor policy for the PRI and the government. Other federations less politically powerful have been the Revolutionary Federation of Workers and Peasants (*Confederación Revolucionario de Obreros y Campesinos*; CROC) and the

National Workers Federation (*Confederación Nacional de Trabajadores*; CNT). The Railroad Workers, Petroleum Workers, and Telephone Workers Unions are semiautonomous, having loose links to the CTM but operating independently. All federations and autonomous unions meet annually in the Congress of Labor, whose key committees articulate organized labor's needs and goals.

NATIONAL PROSPECTS

Ernesto Zedillo came to power on the heels of two major challenges to the political stability of Mexico: the Zapatista uprising in Chiapas and the assassination of the former PRI candidate Luis Donaldo Colosio. The losses of the first elected mayor of Mexico City and of the majority in the Chamber of Deputies were further blows to the power and prestige of the PRI. For the first time in its history, the PRI is facing the very real possibility of even losing the presidency in the elections of 2000. That year could prove to be not only a calendar milestone but the demarcation of a new political era in modern Mexico.

Further Reading

Bailey, John. *Governing Mexico: The Statecraft of Crisis Management*. New York: St. Martin's Press, 1988.

Bruhn, Kathleen. *Taking on Goliath: The Emergence of a New Left Party and the Struggle for Democracy in Mexico*. University Park: Pennsylvania State University Press, 1997.

Camp, Roderic Ai. *Politics in Mexico*. New York: Oxford University Press, 1993.

Centeno, Miguel Ángel. *Democracy within Reason: Technocratic Revolution in Mexico*. University Park: Pennsylvania State University Press, 1994.

Handelman, Howard. *Mexican Politics: The Dynamics of Change*. New York: St. Martin's Press, 1997.

Johnson, Kenneth F. *Mexican Democracy: A Critical View*, 2d ed. New York: Praeger, 1978.

Levy, Daniel, and Gabriel Székely. *Mexico: Paradoxes of Stability and Change*. Boulder, Colo.: Westview Press, 1987.

Meyer, Michael C., and William L Sherman. *The Course of Mexican History*. New York: Oxford University Press, 1995.

Needler, Martin C. *Mexican Politics: The Containment of Conflict*. New York: Praeger, 1982.

Padgett, L. Vincent. *The Mexican Political System*, 2d ed. Boston: Houghton Mifflin, 1976.

Russell, Philip L. *Mexico under Salinas*. Austin, Tex.: Mexico Resource Center, 1994.

Story, Dale. *The Mexican Ruling Party: Stability and Authority*. New York: Praeger, 1986.

FEDERATED STATES OF MICRONESIA

By Eugene Ogan, Ph.D.

The Federated States of Micronesia (FSM) is an island republic that developed out of the former United Nations Trust Territory of the Pacific. It was administered by the United States from 1947 to 1982, when a Compact of Free Association was signed between the two nations. FSM is made up of some 607 islands, including a number of tiny coral atolls, that were charted on the map as the Caroline Islands. (Another Caroline Island group now constitutes the Republic of Palau.) The total land area of 271 square miles contains a population estimated in 1998 at 115,000.

The Caroline Islands had a complicated colonial history, as they were administered successively by Spain, Germany, and Japan before the United States became Trustee. During the long series of negotiations that reconstituted the UN Trust Territory as separate nations, four island groups decided to remain in a confederation to form the FSM. These are the present states of Kosrae, Pohnpei, Yap, and Chuuk. This history, combined with the islanders' general distrust of centralized authority, has produced a distinctive structure for a polity of such small size.

FSM has a national government, but each state has its own constitution, designating executive, legislative, and judicial powers. Each state differs in some detail from the others constitutionally. The national government is headed by a president who is both chief executive and head of state. He and his vice president must be from different states within the federation. They are chosen from the members of Congress by majority vote of that body; they must then resign their congressional seats, which are filled by special election. They cannot serve more than two consecutive terms of four years each.

The FSM Congress is unicameral, but the constitution provides for two kinds of members, with different terms of office. One member is elected at large from each state for a four-year term. Members are elected for two-year terms from congressional districts within each state that are based on population. There must be at least one such district within each state, and Congress must reapportion itself into districts at least every 10 years. In the first Congress, in addition to the 4 at-large members, there were 10 elected on the basis of population—1 from Kosrae, 1 from Yap, 3 from Pohnpei, and 5 from Chuuk. Any citizen at least 18 years of age may vote, but a member of Congress must be at least 30 years old.

Each state places executive authority in a popularly elected governor who serves for a four-year term. State legislatures vary in form, though all try to deal with the problem of balancing representation according to population numbers with appropriate attention to geographic and social configurations. Only Chuuk's legislature is bicameral. Yap is the only state with constitutionally established councils of traditional leaders, one from Yap Island, the other from the outer islands. These councils have the power to veto legislation; otherwise, they are primarily advisory bodies.

National judicial authority is vested in a Supreme Court, with both trial and appellate divisions. The chief justice and no more than five associate justices are appointed by the president with the approval of two-thirds of Congress. Justices serve during good behavior. State judiciaries vary. Unique to Yap are municipal courts in which presiding judges are the traditional leaders representing the municipality in one or the other council of traditional leaders.

The Compact of Free Association between the FSM and the United States maintains to a degree the relationship established after the Second World War. However, financial support provided by America will not continue at the levels operating during its Trusteeship. It remains to be seen if an economy based largely on gardening and fishing, in which government is almost the sole employer paying monetary wages, will sustain the present political system. Under the Compact, citizens of the FSM can migrate to the United States without being subject to the usual immigration procedures. It is possible that increasing numbers will take advantage of this opportunity and, like migrants from other Pacific Island nations, maintain a system of monetary remittances to support those who remain at home.

Further Reading

Levy, Neil M. *Micronesia Handbook*, 4th ed. Chico, Calif., Moon, 1996.

MOLDOVA

By William Crowther, Ph.D.

THE SYSTEM OF GOVERNMENT

The Republic of Moldova, which was established on August 27, 1991, is a parliamentary democracy with a unicameral legislature. Moldova is a relatively small country, with a territory of approximately 13,000 square miles and a population of approximately 4,4000. Located in southeastern Europe, it is bordered on the north, east, and south by Ukraine, and on the west by Romania.

Moldova's political circumstances are largely consistent with those found in other former Soviet republics. Paralleling developments in the Baltic republics, Moldavian nationalists participated in the campaign for election to the Soviet Congress of People's Deputies of the USSR in 1989 and formed the nationalist-oriented Moldavian Popular Front. The Soviet Republic of Moldavia's first partly democratic elections for the Supreme Soviet, in February 1990, produced a majority of delegates aligned with the Popular Front. Four further competitive national elections have been held since independence: for the president of the republic in 1991 and 1996; and for an entirely new post-Soviet Parliament in February 1994 and March 1998. Each of these elections was scrutinized by forigin observers.

Among the key factors complicating the republic's current situation is its ethnic diversity. Ethnic Moldovans are in the majority, making up 64.5% of the total population, with other groups of Slavic origin, including Ukrainians (13.8%), Russians (13%), Bulgarians (2.0%), and the Turkic-origin Gagauz community (3.5%). Moldova's sovereignty was challenged by two active separatist efforts, one on the left bank of the Dniester (the "Dniester Republic") the other in southern Moldova, (the "Gagauz Republic"). While the Gaguaz crisis was successfully resolved in 1995 through negotiation, the Transdniestrian controversy remains ongoing as of early 1999.

Executive

The head of state of Moldova is the president of the republic. Under constitutional arrangements prevailing at the time of the 1990 national elections, the president was elected by the members of the Parliament. New provisions were introduced in 1991 called for direct presidential elections. Moldova's first president was Mircea Snegur. Snegur gained the position at the time of the transition to independence with the support of Popular Front delegates in the Parliament. He retained it through winning the first popular election to the post in 1991, which he contested unopposed.

The president is described by the Moldovan constitution as the chief of state and under the terms of the 1994 constitution is elected by direct universal vote for a term of four years. His election is validated by the Constitutional Court. He is charged with guaranteeing the independence and unity of the republic and overseeing the efficient functioning of public authorities. The president may be impeached by vote of two-thirds of the total number of deputies elected to Parliament. His case is then heard by the Supreme Court of Justice. The president can take part in meetings of the Government and presides when he does so. He also can take part in the work of the Parliament and is called upon to deliver to the Parliament messages concerning issues of national concern. He names the prime minister following consultation with the parliamentary majority and names the Government on the basis of a vote of confidence by the Parliament. The president can dissolve Parliament if it fails to form a government for a period of 60 days. This can be done only once in one year, not during the last six months of the life of a Parliament, and not during a state of emergency or war.

The Government (or Cabinet) of Moldova is made up of a prime minister, two deputy prime ministers, and approximately 20 ministers. This leadership directs the activities of 20 functionally organized ministries and seven departments of state. Members of the Government are nominated by the president but must be confirmed by the Parliament before taking office. Once selected by the president, the prime minister selects a Government and establishes a program that is then submitted to Parliament for a vote of confidence. The Government must submit to parliamentary questioning, if requested. Parliament is given the power to dismiss the Government or an individual member thereof through a vote of no confidence by a majority vote of the members.

Moldova's most recent presidential elections pitted sitting president Mircea Snegur against two prominent leaders with power bases in the legislative branch: the Socialist Party leader, Petru Luchinschi (president of the Parliament), and the Agrarian Democrat Andrei Sangheli (prime minister). Despite earlier cooperation with the Agrarians and the Socialist Party, Snegur found himself at a disadvantage to his former partners in vying for the support of moderate Moldovans and Russian-speakers in presidential elections.

Forming his own political organization, the Party of Revival and Conciliation in Moldova, Snegur campaigned aggressively during late 1995 and early 1996. After launching a series of attacks on his opponents for failure to carry out necessary reforms, he argued for the formation of a "Presidential State." Despite obvious efforts to capture the pro-Romanian nationalist support formerly directed to the Popular Front, Snegur failed to attract widespread support. In first-round balloting on November 17, President Snegur led the electoral pack, with 38.71% of the vote, ahead of parliamentary Speaker Luchinschi, with 27.869% and the Communist leader Vladimir Voronin with 10.26%. Prime Minister Andre Sangheli polled 9.5% of the vote, coming in a disappointing fourth place in the election, in which overall turnout was approximately 67%. But in the second round, leftist forces united behind Luchinschi, giving him 54% of the vote over Mircea Snegur's 47%.

Legislature

Moldova's legislative branch is a unicameral body referred to as the Parliament of Moldova (*Parlamentul Moldovei*). It is described in the constitution as the supreme representative body of the republic and is made up of 104 deputies elected to four-year terms by means of direct universal vote. It elects a president of the Parliament by secret majority vote of the deputies and may remove him by a two-thirds vote. Leadership of the Parliament is vested in the president of the Parliament, two vice presidents, and a standing bureau of nine members (the preceding three officers are ex officio members). Parliament meets in four-month sessions, twice a year, and may be called into extraordinary session by the president of the republic, the president of the Parliament, or a two-thirds vote of the deputies. The Parliament passes laws, may call for referenda, and exercises control over the executive as called for in the constitution. Permanent commissions consider legislation in the following areas: legal affairs and immunity; economy industry and privatization; budget and finance; state security and public order; foreign relations; human rights and national minorities; culture, science education, and mass media; social and health protection and ecology; control and petitions.

Results of the (February 27, 1994) legislative election marked a sharp reversal from the politics of the early post-Communist transition. Turnout for the election was 79.3%. A total of 13 electoral blocs, political parties, and social political formations, as well as 20 independent candidates, contended for 104 legislative positions; 4 parties won seats. The greatest beneficiaries of the election were the Agrarian Democrats, who won 43.2% of the vote and 56 of the 104 seats, providing them with an absolute majority. Another 28 seats were won by the Socialist Bloc, allies of the Agrarians, which captured 22% of the vote. The nationalist pro-Romanian parties suffered a massive defeat, while more moderate pro-Romanian parties fared somewhat better. The Bloc of Peasants and Intellectuals won 9.2% of the vote and 11 seats, while the Popular Front Alliance won 7.5% of the vote and 9 seats. None of the other 9 parties and blocs that campaigned surpassed the threshold required for participation in the national legislature.

A second round of legislative elections in March 1997 pitted a reconstituted Communist Party against parties on the political center and the right. In this contest, three parties and one electoral alliance, the Democratic Convention of Moldova, bringing together the former president Mircea Snegur's Party of Revival and Accord in Moldova and the Christian Democratic Popular Front, surpassed the 5% threshold for entry into Parliament. The Communist Party of Moldova emerged with a substantial plurality: 30.1% of the national vote and 40 out of 104 parliamentary seats. The Bloc for a Democratic and Prosperous Moldova, strongest of the center parties, polled 18.1% of the vote and garnered 24 seats in Parliament. On the political right, the Democratic Convention of Moldova won 19.4% of the vote and 26 parliamentary seats. Finally, Valeriu Matei's center-right Party of Democratic Forces attracted 8.8% of the vote and won 11 seats in the legislature. Strikingly, the Agrarian Democratic Party, which overwhelmingly dominated the previous election, could attract only 3.6% of the vote and was not able to enter Parliament.

Judiciary

The Moldovan judicial system consists of a Supreme Court of Justice, a Court of Appeals, subordinate tribunals, the Superior Council of the Magistracy, the Procuracy, and a Constitutional Court. The Superior Council of the Magistracy is made up of judges chosen by the Parliament for five-year terms and is responsible for discipline in the judicial system. The Constitutional Court comprises nine deputies, three chosen by the president and six by the Parliament. It is named as the sole authority with constitutional jurisdiction in the republic and is described as entirely independent, subordinated only to the constitution itself. The Procuracy, which is headed by a procurator and a collegium, directs investigations, orders arrests, and administers the prosecution of criminal cases. It is also charged with administration of the justice system and insuring the legality of government actions. Below the national level the judicial system is based on a network of local courts, and higher-level appeals courts.

Regional and Local Government

Below the central government Moldova is divided administratively into 40 districts (*raiony*), each of which is governed by a locally elected council. District councils elect executive committees from among their members. The heads of these executive committees are the chief executive officers of the districts. City and village governments have institutions similar to those at the district level. In addition to the capital, Kishinev, nine other cities are, according to law, subordinated directly to the national government. These include Balti, Cahul, Dubasari, Orhei, RibniÛa, Soroca, Tighina (Bender), Tiraspol, and Ungheni.

THE ELECTORAL SYSTEM

The law on Moldovan legislative elections was passed on October 19, 1993. It called for the formation of a new national Parliament that differed significantly from its initial legislature. In a key shift, it was decided that Moldova's first entirely post-Communist legislature would comprise 104 delegates. After years of deadlock, republican leaders hoped that this smaller body would be more manageable than the 380-member Soviet institution, in which it was often difficult even to achieve a quorum. Rules governing the electoral mechanism were also fundamentally altered. Under the new system, delegates were elected on the basis of proportional representation from closed party lists. A 4% threshold for participation in the legislature was established in order to avoid excessive fragmentation. In a move that distinguished it from the vast majority of proportional representation systems, the Moldovans adopted a single national electoral district for the 1994 elections. While not ensuring participation in the separatist region, this mechanism allowed elections to go forward, selecting a body of delegates whose constituency was the entire republic, regardless of their individual places of residence. Transdniestrian leaders refused to allow voting in their region but did agree to permit those who wished to cross over into Moldovan territory in order to participate in the elections. Some 6,000 people took advantage of this opportunity to cross the Dniester and vote in specially established west bank polling places.

As established in the 1994 constitution, the president is chosen through a two-round popular election, with a requirement that more than 50% of the vote must be gained for victory in the first round. If no candidate achieves such a majority, a runoff between the top two candidates determines the outcome in the second round.

THE PARTY SYSTEM

The Communist Party of Moldavia (CPM) dominated the political life of the republic from its inception in 1944 until 1990. During that period CPM officials monopolized all politically significant positions. However, the party's power disintegrated with remarkable swiftness once democratic elections were held. The Communist Party was formally abolished in 1991, following the abortive August 1991 coup attempt in Moscow. But the CPM continued to operate in the region on the left bank of the Dniester (Transdniestria), which refused to recognize the legitimacy of the government of Moldova.

The character of party politics in Moldova after independence reflected the relatively recent emergence of competitive politics in the republic, the legacy of communism, and the existence of deeply divisive ethnic and linguistic issues. Party competition has focused on proreform/antireform and pro-CIS/pro-Romania orientations. For a short time the dominant party was the Popular Front of Moldova, which was formed in June of 1989.

Several new parties were organized in the period between Moldova's declaration of independence in August 1991 and the parliamentary elections of February 1994. The most significant of these were the Agrarian Democratic Party, the Socialist Party, Edinstvo ("Unity"), and the Congress of the Intellectuals. The Agrarian Democratic Party was formed in 1991 by collective farm leaders and other agricultural sector managers. The Socialist Party is a successor of the Communist Party, and it has significant support among urban workers and pensioners. Edinstvo was originally formed as a movement of Russian workers during the ethnic strife of 1989, and the Congress of Intellectuals was formed in April 1993 by defectors from the Popular Front.

A number of smaller parties have emerged in the post-Communist period as well. Among the most significant of these has been the Social Democratic Party of Moldova. Most of the Social Democrats' leaders originally participated in the Popular Front, then formed their own political organization in response to what they perceived as an increasingly nationalistic evolution in the Front's political position. While the Social Democrats are as a matter of principle committed to becoming a broad-based multinational party, their membership is largely Moldovan.

Several smaller parties representing a wide range of less influential interest were also formed. Both the Republican Party and the Party of Reform advocate economic reforms, but they differ on unification with Romania, the Republicans being for independence and the Reform Party being for unification. The Social Democratic Party formed in 1990 is a moderate proindependence party, ideologically in line with European social democratic parties and opposed to ethnic extremism. Its leaders are drawn primarily from the state technocrats and urban intelligentsia.

In 1991–92 the strongest of the Gagauz political organizations was *Gagauz-Halki* ("Gagauz People"), which sought independence for the southern region, where the Gagauz population is concentrated. Its influence has since waned. For the 1994 elections the *Gagauz Halk Partisi* ("Gagauz People's Party") was organized. It advocated participation in an independent Moldovan republic.

Following the 1994 legislative campaign, electoral competition shifted to the plane of presidential politics. With the Christian Democratic Popular Front forces effectively marginalized, President Snegur formed his own political organization, the Party of Revival and Conciliation in Moldova, in order to contest presidential elections with the leaders of the Agrarian Democratic and Socialist Parties.

COMMUNIST PARTY OF MOLDOVA

The Communist Party of Moldova is a direct successor of the Soviet-era Communist Party. It was outlawed until late 1994 and thus did not compete in the February 1994 parliamentary elections. After the party reentered political activity, it formed a parliamentary faction from among deputies who migrated to it from other left-wing party factions. It has since established itself as a powerful electoral force in the country.

THE CONGRESS OF THE INTELLECTUALS
(Congresul Intelectualitatii)

The Congress of Intellectuals is a centrist party and was established in April 1993 by defectors from the Popular Front. Its members include many prominent intellectuals who helped set up the Popular Front but later became disenchanted with the front's increasingly radical pro-Romanian unionist stance. The Congress is pro-Romanian in orientation but advocates a longer-term program for unification.

CHRISTIAN DEMOCRATIC POPULAR FRONT
(Frontul Popular Crestin si Democrat)

The Christian Democratic Popular Front originated from the Popular Front of Moldova, which was formed in June of 1989. The Popular Front emerged as an advocate of increased autonomy from the Soviet Union and of the rights of the ethnically Moldovan population of the republic. Following the Popular Front's success in 1990 elections, delegates were able to dominate proceedings in the national legislature and secure government support of its agenda. The Popular Front is well organized nationally but is strongest in the capital and in the areas of the country most heavily populated by Moldovans. At its

third congress, in February 1992, the Popular Front became explicitly committed to unification with Romania and changed its name to the Christian Democratic Popular Front. Popular reaction against the party's increasingly nationalist orientation led to defections of moderate party leaders and significant decline in popular support in the period leading up to the 1994 legislative elections.

The party's strongest support is found among ethnic Moldovan nationalists. The party is led by Iuri Rosca. On June 19, 1997, the Christian Democratic Popular Front joined with the Party for a Democratic and Prosperous Moldova to form the Democratic Convention of Moldova in an effort to unite right -wing forces.

BLOC FOR A DEMOCRATIC AND PROSPEROUS MOLDOVA
(Pentru Moldova Democratica si Prospera)

The Movement for a Democratic and Prosperous Moldova was established on February 8, 1997, by supporters of President Luchinschi in the Moldovan Parliament to promote his legislative agenda. It is led by the deputy parliamentary Speaker, Dumitru Diacov.

SOCIALIST UNITY/EDINSTVO
(Unitatea Sociulisla/Edinstvo)

Edinstvo was formed in 1989 as one of the "interfront" organizations that emerged among workers in many of the former Soviet republics in order to oppose the anti-Soviet independence movements. In the early transition it was politically conservative in the sense of supporting the status quo of the pre-1990 period, and it is strongly pro-Russian. It has strong sympathies for the separatist movement among Russian speakers on the left bank of the Dniester. Edinstvo's main base of support is found in the ethnic Russian urban population. It is positively inclined toward the Commonwealth of Independent States (CIS) and special status for Transdniestria. In the 1994 elections it campaigned with the Socialist Party.

COMMUNIST PARTY OF THE REPUBLIC OF MOLDOVA
(Partidul Communist Republica Moldovei)

A successor of the Soviet-era Communist Party, the Communist Party of Moldova has strong support among industrial workers and Russian-speakers. It is pro-CIS and cautious on reform and favors compromise with the leadership of Transdniestria. The party is led by Vladimir Voronin, who gained 10.3% of the 1996 presidential vote.

DEMOCRATIC AGRARIAN PARTY OF MOLDOVA
(Partidul Democrat Agrar din Moldova)

The democratic Agrarian Party was originally formed by deputies in the transition legislature elected in 1990. The Agrarians were able to maintain a remarkable degree of cohesion throughout the disruption that occurred within the Parliament from 1990 through 1993, and they emerged as a powerful electoral force. Their success was attributable to a variety of factors. The Agrarian deputies were, for the most, associated with the republican agroindustrial complex, either as village mayors or collective farm managers. Hence they shared substantial common material interests, with respect to both reform and resource allocation issues. Many held a common ideological orientation, as reform Communists. The party maintained a very strong electoral base among rural Moldovans. It takes a moderate position on ethnic relations. The Agrarians are cautious on reform issues in general and oppose complete privatization of agricultural land.

THE PARTY OF DEMOCRATIC FORCES
(Partidul Fortii Democratice)

The Party of Democratic Forces is a center-right party, formed on October 16, 1995, from the opposition movement, the United Democratic Congress. It is led by Valeriu Matei.

PARTY FOR REVIVAL AND ACCORD OF MOLDOVA
(Partidul Pentru Renastere si Conciliere din Moldova)

The Party of Renaissance and Accord of Moldova was formed in July 1995 as an electoral vehicle through which the then incumbent president, Mircea Snegur, sought a second term in office in November 1996. The Party of Renaissance and Conciliation's original membership was drawn from defectors from the Agrarian Democratic Parliamentary Deputies. The party sought to attract support from former constituents of the Popular Front, whose following had declined since the early 1990s. Its platform was moderately pro-Romanian and proreform. The party's leader is the former president Mircea Snegur. On June 19, 1997, it joined with the Christian Democratic Popular Front to form the Democratic Convention of Moldova.

THE UNITED SOCIAL DEMOCRATIC PARTY OF MOLDOVA
(Partidul Social Democrat Unificat din Moldova)

The United Social Democratic Party of Moldova was formed on March 29, 1997, as an effort to unite the center-left in anticipation of the upcoming parliamentary elections. It brings together several smaller parties, including the Social Democratic Party, the Party for Social Progress, the Republican Party, and the Party of Economic Rebirth. The United Social Democratic Party of Moldova is led by Anatol Tarcanu and Eugin Sobor.

MINOR POLITICAL PARTIES

Since its inception, the new Moldova has seen the formation of several minor political parties. These include Alianta Civica "Furnica" (Civic Alliance "Ant"), Gagauz People's Party, League of Christian Democratic Women, National Liberal Party, National Peasant Party, National Christian Party, National Youth League, New Forces Movement, Party of Social and Economic Rights, Popular Democratic Party, and the United Liberal Party of Moldova.

NATIONAL PROSPECTS

The political party environment has been volatile in Moldova since independence. The interaction of ethnic conflict and proreform versus antireform political cleavages has complicated the process of party formation. A second negative factor has been the disjunction between elite political competition and mass-level politics. Individual leaders have both repeatedly abandoned their party affiliation and formed parties as vehicles for the pursuit of their individual ambitions. Both of these practices decrease the ability of the electorate to vote on the basis of stable expectations concerning leaders' behavior, and have hence undermined party institutionalization.

On the positive side, some parties, particularly those on the center-left, have remained stable despite these conditions. Moldova has carried out a series of competitive elections that have exhibited the peaceful change in power in both the legislative and executive branches. While substantial fragmentation remains, the Republic of Moldova thus appears to be moving in the direction of stable competitive politics, with the institutionalization of some parties and the effective marginalization of antidemocratic parties.

Further Reading

Crowther, William. "The Construction of Moldovan National Consciousness." In *Beyond Borders: Remaking Cultural Identities in the New Eastern and Central Europe.* Ed. Laszlo Kurti and Juliet Langman. Boulder, Colo.: Westview Press, 1997.

——. "Nationalism and Political Transformation in Moldova." In *Studies in Moldavian: The History, Culture, Language and Contemporary Politics of the People of Moldova.* Ed. Donald Dryer. Boulder, Colo.: East European Monographs, 1996.

——. "The Politics of Democratization in Postcommunist Moldova." In *Democratic Changes and Authoritarian Reactions in Russia, Ukraine, Belarus, and Moldova.* Ed. Karen Dawisha and Bruce Parrott. London: Cambridge University Press, 1997.

Dima, Nicholas. *From Moldavia to Moldova: The Soviet Romanian Territorial Dispute.* Boulder, Colo.: East European Monographs, 1991.

Dryer, Donald. "Nationalism and Political Transformation in Moldova." In *Studies in Moldovan: The History, Culture, Language and Contemporary Politics of the People of Moldova.* Ed. Donald Dryer. Boulder, Colo.: East European Monographs, 1996.

MONACO

(Principaute de Monaco)

By Kenneth E. Bauzon, Ph.D.

The sovereign country of Monaco is situated in Western Europe, facing the Mediterranean Sea, and bordered on three sides by the Alpes-Maritimes department of France. It has a population of 30,000 (1990) and occupies a total land area of 1.95 square kilometers. It is home to French, Italians, Swiss, and Belgians and native Monegasques, who make up 15% of the population and speak their own language, Monegasque, a cross between Italian and French. Roman Catholicism is the official religion, adhered to by 95% of the population.

Monaco's government is a constitutional monarchy. A prince who keeps the title chief of state along with at least 20 other titles rules it. In this system, actual political power rests with the prince, and all powers vested with the legislature and the judiciary are derived from him.

Executive authority is exercised jointly by the prince and the four-member Council of Government, which consists of three state councilors and the minister of state, who is head of the Council. The Council of Government derives its authority from the prince and is answerable to the prince. Further, two other bodies—the Council of State and the Council of the Crown—are also established for the purpose of providing advice to the prince.

Legislative authority rests with a unicameral body, the National Council, which consists of 18 members who each serve a term of five years. These legislators are elected through a competitive electoral process based on universal adult suffrage. Eligibility for election to this body includes Monegasque citizenship and at least 25 years in age.

The judicial branch consists of the Supreme Court (or Supreme Tribunal), the Court of High Appeal, the Court of Appeal, the Criminal Court, and the Court of First Instance. Two other courts were established in 1946 and 1948, namely, the Industrial Court and the Higher Court of Arbitration of Collective Labor Disputes, respectively.

Monaco's electoral system is currently based on universal direct adult suffrage at age 21, and women have had the right to vote since 1963.

The political party system in Monaco may be classified as a dominant-party system comparable with that of Mexico. The National Democratic Union (Union Nationale et Democratique; UND) has dominated the political scene for decades, but its control is not absolute and it has been successfully challenged on occasion by minority parties. Today, the UND exists mainly to articulate and support the wishes of the monarchy and the prince.

In 1973, 2 of the 18 seats in the National Council were shared between two minor political parties, and again, in the January 31, 1993, elections, 3 seats were shared. Another minor political party, the Monegasque Socialist Party (Parti Socialiste Monegasque; PSM) has been in existence but has never succeeded in electing a candidate to the National Council.

The most important functions of Monaco's political party system have been to secure and maintain the country's political stability and to validate and legitimize the monarchy. Although most people do not engage in political activity, the party system gives a semblance of democratic choice and participation. However, the perception of a foreordained outcome of any election does deter many. Also, dissenting political parties, particularly those of Marxist orientation, have had little luck in Monaco. Visitors and citizens alike are always reminded of the ever-presence of the police and how it safeguards the tiny principality from any disorder and the royalty from any criticism.

The economic prosperity and political stability of Monaco may be attributed generally to the strict disciplinarian and conservative style with which the principality has been ruled. Propitious international conditions may also be credited, in particular, its protected status with France, which obviated the necessity of raising an army. Its conscious promotion as a tax haven has attracted significant businesses, e.g., perfumes, pharmaceuticals, and ceramics, enough to transform it into an international business center. Also, the entire principality is a free trade zone without actually becoming a member of the European Union. Although long known for its gambling casinos, raceways, and pleasure-seeking visitors, Monaco has striven to diversify its image and enhance its international status.

The domestic political and administrative institutions show no sign of weakening or discontinuity. Barring any unlikely radical shift in both domestic and international conditions, or extinction of the clan, the Grimaldi family may yet reign in Monaco for another 700 years.

Further Reading

Bibliography of Monaco. New York: St. Martin's Press, 1971.
Conniff, Richard. "Monaco." National Geographic 189 (May 5) 1996: 80, 82–94.

MONGOLIA

By Paul Hyer, Ph.D.

THE SYSTEM OF GOVERNMENT

Mongolia, formerly the Mongolian People's Republic (MPR) until 1992, is a nation of 2.2 million people. A Communist state until the collapse of the Soviet Union, it is rapidly moving toward democracy and a free-market system. Political institutions are still in a flux, so some points of analysis must be tentative. For 70 years Mongolia was characterized as a satellite of the Soviet Union; indeed, it was the prototype of the satellite system that later emerged in the Soviet bloc in Eastern Europe. Now it is the first Communist state of Asia to move toward democracy.

Mongolia was under the control of China's Manchu-Ching dynasty from 1691 to 1911, when it declared itself an independent monarchy under a traditionally powerful "reincarnated" Buddhist lama. Mongolia's Communist revolution (1924) was the first in Asia when, with Soviet aid, it revolted against a continuing Chinese threat and declared itself a People's Republic in 1924. From that time most Mongols believed that their independence from China required a strong link to the Soviet Union.

Mongolian politics were historically characterized by fragmented political power in the hands of a hereditary nobility paralleled and complemented by a powerful monastic clergy of lamas (Tibetan Buddhist monks). Politics was dominated by these elites, and the people had no active role.

The move for independence in 1911 was followed by a decade of nationalistic fervor and continued political turbulence. In January 1920 radical Mongolian nationalists, encouraged by the victory of the Bolsheviks in Russia, organized the vanguard of a revolutionary party (Mongolian People's Revolutionary Party; MPRP). Support from the Soviet political cadre and the Red Army consolidated the party's dominance.

After gaining power in 1921 this party controlled Mongolia's political life for the next 70 years. It looked to the Soviet Union for direction and institutions to revolutionize the nation. Its political control was insured by Moscow as a satellite of the Soviet Union.

During the 1920s there were great internal divisions among left-wing radicals, moderates, and conservatives. The nobility and clergy were neutralized if not liquidated, and covert competition for personal power continued within the party for many years. The late 1920s and the 1930s saw violent purges and forced collectivization of the countryside.

In 1939, Khorloogin Choibalsan, a dominating personality with a Stalinist approach to politics, emerged as the strongman. He ran the government with virtually no consultation with formal government bodies. Yumjhagiin Tsedenbal succeeded Choibalsan on his death in 1952. His administrative style was much more moderate and conventional; Tsedenbal remained in power until 1984, the eve of reforms.

As a prelude to the cataclysmic changes of the 1990s, Mongolia saw the rise of a younger, nationalistic generation, anathema to Moscow and a worry to Marxist governmental leadership. There were occasional purges—no executions but simply removal from office. Despite this, there was considerable stability in government structure, dynamics, and personnel, accompanied by a fair amount of mobility or "changing of the guard." All this made the 1990s bloodless revolution a much less painful process.

The former Communist leaders clung to power in the 1990 election but failed to make any serious changes. Consequently, in the June 30, 1996 election, they were surprisingly swept out as the democratic opposition won 50 of the 76 seats in the State Great Hural (the parliament).

Executive

Mongolia's president is the head of state, the commander in chief of the armed forces, and the head of the National Security Council. Previously the president was elected by the Hural, which was manipulated by the Communist Party. Now he is popularly elected by a majority, for a four-year term and is limited to two terms. He is empowered to nominate a prime minister who must be confirmed by the parliament. The president may initiate legislation and veto all or part of the same. He may issue decrees and call for the government's dissolution. He directs foreign affairs and national defense and maintains public order through the police. In the absence, incapacity, or resignation of the president, the chairman of the State Great Hural exercises presidential power until the inauguration of a newly elected president.

The Presidential Office includes the following services

in suboffices: organization, correspondence, information services, an economic adviser, a legal adviser, a National Defense Council secretary, and an adviser on public order.

The prime minister is nominated by the president and confirmed by the parliament for a four-year term. He chooses a Cabinet also subject to parliamentary approval. Decrees issued by the parliament become effective when signed by the president. In 1994, the prime minister, Puntsagiyn Jasray, moved to combine or abolish many ministries in a radical change to reduce governmental expenses and bureaucratic agencies. This move had long been discussed and was supported by many groups including independent economists.

The top political leadership, the governmental elite, generally reflects the ethnic divisions of the country. About 80% are from the Khalkha Mongolian ethnic group, which makes up about 76% of the population. Most of the rest of officialdom comes from two other closely related Mongolian ethnic groups, about 13% of the population.

Kazakhs, the largest single minority in the country, making up only 2% of the population, are represented in officialdom and are not a source of friction. Chinese, a negligible fraction of the urban population, have no power and no impact on politics. The concerns with the Chinese are in international relations, not internal politics.

Legislature

The State Great Hural, or parliament, is the supreme state authority. It is a democratic parliament organized in 1992 as a new unicameral legislature. Previously there was a bicameral assembly that simply rubber-stamped Communist Party policy and decisions. Seventy-six members are popularly elected for a four-year term. Meeting twice annually this assembly elects a chairman and a vice chairman to serve four-year terms. Its constitutional role is to enact and amend laws, determine domestic and foreign policy, ratify international agreements, and declare a state of emergency if necessary. The Great Hural can override a presidential veto by a two-thirds majority vote. It may issue decrees that become effective with the president's signature. A dissolution of the government occurs if the prime minister resigns, if half the Cabinet resigns, or if it votes to dissolve itself.

Judiciary

The constitution inaugurated in January 1992 marked a new historical era for the country; it is more an expression of hope and aspiration than a reflection of the political realities of the country. Moreover, it resulted from some two years of intense debate over the proposition of transforming the country from a Communist Party dictatorship to a pluralistic democracy and from a command economy to a free-market system. In addition to establishing Mongolia as an independent, sovereign republic the constitution guarantees a number of rights and freedoms. The new political structure of Mongolia mirrors Western democracies.

For some 70 years Mongolia's legal system was a blend of Mongolian, Russian, and Chinese elements and there was no provision for an independent judicial review of legislation. Now the 1992 constitution provides for an independent judiciary on the model of those found in democratic societies. The highest judiciary body is the Supreme Court. A General Council of Courts is empowered to nominate justices, who are then confirmed by the State Great Hural.

The Supreme Court is mandated to examine all lower court decisions upon appeal, and it is empowered by the constitution to interpret all laws except the constitution. This last function is reserved to a special Constitutional Court of nine members, including a chairman, appointed for terms of six years. Its sole function is to interpret the constitution.

THE ELECTORAL SYSTEM

Until 1990 the Communist Party controlled elections to the Hural; voting was usually by single candidate election lists. But now there is a plurality of parties and free, open elections. Suffrage is universal for all over 18 years of age. In recent national elections almost 95% of the electorate was reported to have voted.

THE PARTY SYSTEM

A number of political parties have arisen in the 1990s, including a National Democratic Party, a Social Democratic Party, a Mongolian People's Party, and a Party of National Progress. None was so radically inclined as to threaten disruption of the society. Nevertheless, later in the 1996 election the democratic opposition in a surprise defeat of the MPRP took over the national assembly.

The first multiparty elections in Mongolia's history were held July 26, 1990, and the MPRP, with the advantages of preparation time and organization, gained 85% of the seats in the State Great Hural and took the presidency. But representatives of the major opposition parties were appointed to top positions in the new government.

Free parliamentary elections were held in June 1992 with a 92.7% turnout and a Communist Party landslide. It won 72 of 76 seats in the new parliament. One reason given for this rout is that the people had lost confidence in the opposition leaders due to their lack of experience and bungling. It should be emphasized, however, that the "Communists" elected were *not* old party "hard-liners" but a young, pragmatic, competent generation.

A reorganized Mongolian People's Revolutionary Party

continued to rule through the early 1990s, but organized dissent that emerged with the decline of communism and disintegration of the Communist bloc continued to grow.

President Punsalmaagiyn Ochirbat, elected in the 1993 presidential election, had switched from the former MPRP/Communist Party and ran as a candidate for the opposition. This was the first defeat for the Mongolian People's Revolutionary Party.

THE MONGOLIAN PEOPLE'S REVOLUTIONARY PARTY (MPRP)

The MPRP, the former Communist Party with a new perspective, is still a very important force in Mongolian politics, particularly in view of the inexperience and blunders of the democratic forces. The party's membership and influence have decreased and the current composition of the party is unclear, but prior to the recent political changes, its membership was about 4% of the population, of which 50% consisted of government employees and a so-called intelligentsia, a term commonly stretched to include the working intelligentsia, who are really not well educated. Another 30% was made up of urban workers, and the remaining 20% consisted of members who work with livestock. The party elite are virtually all true intelligentsia— bureaucrats, officials, and professionals.

No information is available on party finances.

OTHER POLITICAL FORCES

Mongolia between China and Russia

Seventy years of dependence on the USSR, until the recent collapse of the Soviet empire, was crucial in both internal politics and foreign policy. Policy for decades was anti-Chinese but has now moderated, and Soviet troops stationed in Mongolia along the border with China have been withdrawn.

Mongolia now pursues an independent, nonaligned foreign policy. Previously, policy decisions of Moscow were invariably echoed in Ulanbator. Mongolia frequently reminds itself and others that due to its landlocked position, it is essential to have good relations with both large neighbors. Long-term, fairly cooperative relations with Russia continue. Relations with China are more complex and are now of prime importance. During the period of Sino-Soviet confrontation Mongolia initially tried to maintain a neutral position. But in 1966, with the onset of China's Cultural Revolution and the dangers it posed, Mongolia signed agreements introducing large-scale Soviet ground forces in a buildup on the Mongolia-China frontier. As relations worsened, Mongolia began expelling the 7,000 ethnic Chinese contracted in the 1950s as construction workers.

In the above moves Mongolia was motivated by its historical enmity for the Chinese; Chinese statements suggesting a desire to reannex Mongolia; continued border tension in spite of the 1964 demarcation agreements; Mongolia's heavy dependence on Soviet economic aid; and Russia's historical role in counterbalancing Chinese influence.

With the demise of the Soviet Union, Mongolia is particularly concerned with its relations with China, because its strategic trade access to the sea is via China; and China is now the prime source, directly or indirectly, of foodstuffs and consumer goods. With its new options in the late 1980s Mongolia reached consular agreements with China and cross-border trade is expanding. In 1989 Mongolia and China exchanged foreign minister visits. In 1990 Mongolia's head of state visited China, and in 1991 China's president, Yang Shangkun, visited Ulanbator. Contacts have been established between a number of Mongolian and Chinese ministries, local areas, and private firms and their Chinese counterparts. Soviet troop withdrawals from Mongolia's China border began in 1987 and were completed in 1992.

Meanwhile, Mongolia has maintained close relations with Russia, including agreements for bilateral trade and cooperation, exemption of Mongolian exports from Russian customs duties, and the establishment of a commission to speed up important trade exchanges. Mongolia's debt to Russia, however, is still problematical. Also, the Mongols are naturally critical of any trend toward the rise of a radical Russian nationalism such as seen in the Russian Liberal Democratic Party's Vladimir Zhirinovsky.

FUTURE PROSPECTS

Of all former Soviet satellites Mongolia is making the smoothest transition to new, more democratic institutions, and there is good cause to be optimistic for its political development in the future. The United States and Japan have been working closely with international organizations to assist Mongolia's transition. Numerous donor group meetings have been held and have coordinated considerable financial and development assistance.

These efforts are naturally working from a background of many decades of communism and a traditionally nomadic society. Mongolia's earlier political system was totalitarian in intent but less so in practice. The nomadic spirit of freewheeling independence remained alive in Mongolia. The slow development of education, and problems of communication and transportation, made the classic formula for Communist control difficult to apply. Dedicated, capable leaders complained that bureaucratic incompetence and inefficiency were endemic. Party policy was often not carried out, less because of deliberate opposition than because of the ineptitude and lethargy of those who had to deal directly with the people and the problems.

The Mongolian people have great vitality and potential, but they also face the great challenges of an inhospitable environment. Their agenda to change to an industrial and agricultural society has proceeded rapidly but is by no means complete. The majority of the people are less than a generation removed from a pastoral-nomadic society.

A positive pattern is that recent decades have seen a major increase in the percentage of the population involved in the political life of the country. It is the consensus of specialists that a higher percentage of the Mongolian people are represented in the power structure of Mongolia than in any other Communist nation—or indeed in most other Asian nations. This trend is increasing with the current move to democratization. Progress is due in part to Mongolia's sparse and relatively homogeneous population; but it also reflects improvements in education, communications, and transportation—developments that are essential in Mongolia's institutionalization of democracy, the rule of law, and the modernization of the nation.

Further Reading

Bawden, Charles R. *The Modern History of Mongolia*. New York: Praeger, 1968.

Jagchid, Sechin, and Paul Hyer. *Mongolia's Culture and Society*. Boulder, Colo.: Westview Press, 1980.

Milivojevic, Marko. *The Mongolian Revolution of 1990: Stability or Conflict in Inner Asia?* Conflict Studies, no. 242. London: Research Institute for the Study of Conflict and Terrorism, 1990.

Rupen, Robert A. *How Mongolia Is Really Ruled*. Stanford, Calif.: Hoover Institution Press, Stanford University, 1979.

Sanders, Alan J.K. "Mongolia 1990: A New Dawn." *Asian Affairs* 22, no. 2 (June 1991): 158–66.

Shirendev, B., and M. Sanjdorj. *History of the Mongolian People's Republic*. Trans. and annot. William A. Brown and Urgunge Onon. Cambridge, Mass.: Harvard University Press, 1977.

KINGDOM OF MOROCCO

(Al-Mamlaka al-Maghrebia)

By David Seddon, Ph.D.
Revised by Deborah A. Kaple, Ph.D.

THE SYSTEM OF GOVERNMENT

The Kingdom of Morocco, in northern Africa, borders the North Atlantic Ocean and the Mediterranean Sea and lies between Algeria and Western Sahara. With a population of nearly 30.4 million (1997 estimate), it is a traditional monarchy, with the crown being hereditary and passed to the eldest son. Although all three of Morocco's postindependence constitutions (adopted in 1962, 1970, and 1972) enhanced rather than limited the king's power, the 1992 and 1996 constitutional revisions gave the prime minister more power, broadened the authority of the legislature, and cstablished new constitutional councils.

Morocco has often come under the sway of various occupying powers in its history, but not until the 7th century when Islam made its appearance did any of them have an impact on Morocco's population. Since that time, both Arab and Berber peoples have united around Islam. Morocco was independent until 1912, when France and Spain made it a "protectorate." During this time, the foreign "protectors" endowed the sultan with enhanced powers so as to better control and rule through him. When they left in 1956, giving Morocco its independence, the sultan emerged as the sovereign figure in Moroccan politics. This created a tension that still exists today between the monarchy and political parties.

In the 1990s, the king, who has ruled for 37 years, has attempted to liberalize Morocco: he released many political prisoners, reduced censorship and curbed the power of the security services, initiated a new constitution, helped to force Morocco's 17 political parties into three main blocks, and called new elections for November and December 1997.

The center-left government that took over in March 1998 has been praised for setting the foundations of a civil society. The press has been a critical force, an active opposition has been allowed, and there have even been revelations about extrajudicial killings. In a year of political surprises, the king shocked everyone by choosing Abderrahmane Youssoufi, a well-known opposition socialist and a former political prisoner, to be prime minister. Youssoufi's party, the Socialist Union of Popular Forces (USFP), controls about a third of the parliamentary seats, and the seven-party coalition Cabinet is seen as fragile, though hopeful.

The Monarchy

The pivotal role of the monarch is spelled out in the 1996 amended constitution: "The King, Commander of the Faithful, shall be the Supreme Representative of the nation and the Symbol of its unity thereof. As defender of the Faith, he shall ensure respect for the Constitution." While the latest version of the constitution rather obliquely mentions the word "faith" and the previous ones mentioned that the king "ensures the observance of Islam and the Constitution," Article 6 states that "Islam shall be the state religion."

The constitutional powers of the king are wide-ranging. He appoints and dismisses the prime minister and the other ministers. He has the right to address the parliament: "The messages shall be read out before both Houses and shall not be subject to any debate." He is commander in chief of the armed forces and appoints the senior military officers. He controls the judiciary by virtue of his powers to appoint the judges and preside over the Supreme Council of Magistracy.

The king has the right to dissolve the two houses of parliament by decree and exercise its legislative powers until new elections, which must be held within three months. However, by virtue of Article 35 of the constitution, the king may declare a state of exception under which he may rule by decree for an indefinite period. Hassan II first invoked this right in 1965. The state of exception lasted almost five years, until the promulgation of the 1970 constitution. Hassan II was able once again to rule by decree without any elected legislative body between 1972 and 1977 simply by refusing to call general elections after the adoption of the 1972 constitution.

Constitutional revision, which can be initiated by the king without reference to the parliament, requires approval in a referendum, but the constitution specifies that "Neither the state system of monarchy nor the prescriptions related to the religion of Islam may be subject to a constitutional revision."

The king claims a divine right to rule, as *Amir al-Muminin*, or Commander of the Faithful; and it is this presumption to both the spiritual and temporal leadership of his subjects that sanctions his claim to ultimate control over the nation's political life. A rule of primogeniture is established in the constitution. If the king dies or abdicates before his successor reaches the age of 16, the king's powers are exercised by a regency council, composed primarily of royal appointees. Until the heir reaches his 20th birthday, it acts as a consultative body.

Executive powers are delegated by the king to the Council of Ministers, which is headed by the prime minister. Although its influence on the process of decision making is considerable, the Council of Ministers is subordinate and responsible to the king, who personally makes the most important policy decisions. The king is advised by a small, influential royal Cabinet, a group of four or five royal counselors headed by a director-general, who are among the king's most trusted political allies.

Legislature

From 1977, when the first parliamentary elections were held under the 1972 constitution, until the constitutional revisions of 1996, Morocco had a unicameral legislature, known as the Chamber of Representatives (*Majlis al-Nuwab*). The 1996 constitution established a bicameral legislature, which was effected by adding a lower house, the Chamber of Councillors (*Majlis al-Mustasharin*).

Members of the Chamber of Representatives are elected for six-year terms by direct, universal suffrage; there are 325 members. For three-fifths of its 270 seats, members of the Chamber of Councillors are elected in each region by electoral colleges made up of elected members of local councils, and two-fifths of them are elected by the people. The parliament meets for two sessions a year.

The parliament's legislative competence is relatively narrow. The constitution bars the parliament from adopting bills or amendments that reduce the state's revenue or raise public expenditure. If, by December 31, the parliament has not approved the following year's budget, the government can simply proceed as if the budget had been approved. The deputies have the right to vote on the development plan but cannot amend it. With regard to the broad objectives of economic, social, and cultural policy, the parliament can pass *lois cadres* (framework laws), but the details of such laws and all other subjects not specified as falling within the parliament's competence are considered to come under the government's administrative authority. The government is entitled to reject any legislative proposal passed by the parliament that it deems to be outside its legislative competence. In the

event of a disagreement between the parliament and the government in such a case, a ruling is made by the Constitutional Council of the Supreme Court.

Judiciary

Although formally independent of the executive and the legislature, the judiciary is under the strong influence of the king, who appoints the judges and presides over the Supreme Council of Magistry, which supervises the judicial system. In political trials, sentences often appear to be predetermined by the Ministry of Justice; and Amnesty International has claimed that political prisoners frequently are not given a fair trial, often subjected to torture, and may be held incommunicado for months or years.

The court system includes communal and district courts for minor offenses, 30 tribunals of first instance, nine appeal courts, a Supreme Court (with criminal, civil, administrative, social, and constitutional chambers), social courts for labor cases, the High Court for crimes committed by ministers in the exercise of their public functions, the Special Court of Justice for crimes committed by civil servants, and the Court of Justice, which judges serious state security and political cases.

Regional and Local Government

According to the constitution, local government consists of 49 provinces and prefectures, with further subdivision into regions and rural communes. In each of these, local assemblies are democratically elected, and it is these assemblies that are responsible for managing the region. However, the governors, who "shall carry out decisions by provincial, prefectoral and regional assemblies in accordance with the conditions set by the law," are also there to represent the state and "see to it that the law is enforced" and that government decisions are implemented. The king appoints all of the governors.

The King

Hassan II (born 1929) has displayed remarkable skill in defending the monarchy's grip on power, which he codified when he finally drew up the country's first constitution in 1962. Like his father, he has tried to undermine the National Union of Popular Forces (UNFP) and the Istiqlal Party (which was forced to leave the government in 1963) by building up rival ultraroyalist movements. These royalist groups, such as the Popular Movement (MP) and a royalist coalition, the Front for the Defense of Constitutional Institutions (FDIC), were formed to contest the first general elections, in 1963. Although the FDIC itself was short-lived, royal support for such loyalist movements has been a constant theme of Hassan II's political strategy. Thus, it was the MP and the "independents" who received the palace's support in the 1977 elections.

In the 1983 and 1984 elections, the newly formed Constitutional Union (UC), which held its founding congress in April 1983, clearly had the support of the palace in its objective of creating a new conservative "center" for Moroccan politics. In the 1997 parliamentary elections, this party still garnered 50 seats of the 325 in the Chamber of Councillors and 28 out of 270 in the Chamber of Representatives.

It has been in the countryside, where the king still enjoys considerable religious prestige and the Ministry of the Interior's *caids* (Muslim tribal chiefs) can prevent effective penetration by the opposition parties, that the king has been able to rely on solid electoral support for these loyalist movements. Hassan's control of state resources, including radio and television, is an important political advantage of which he makes full use. The educational system is also used to inculcate loyalty to the monarchy, which textbooks portray as the country's bastion against foreign rule.

The king also uses his powers of appointment and patronage to buy support and placate critics. Indeed, favoritism and corruption are an integral part of his strategy of rule. He is also a renowned master of creating and exploiting divisiveness, a political juggler who has successfully orchestrated the political system by playing up the rivalries and mutual suspicions of the country's main factions—political parties, trade unions, and the armed forces—and so diminished the threat to the throne from each.

Additionally, he has been careful to include "safety valves" in the political system—outlets for the expression of grievances and protest that, although circumscribed, discourage most opposition politicians from dropping out of the established system altogether and engaging in more radical forms of opposition. Thus, within certain bounds, political parties are allowed to exist legally, publish newspapers, and, from time to time, contest elections and express their views in parliament. This does not, however, prevent the king from repressing his political opponents or curbing civil liberties when he finds it opportune or necessary to defend his rule.

An additional weapon in the king's armory is his populism. After narrowly thwarting two military coups in 1971 and 1972, for example, he rallied popular support by ordering the Moroccanization of the remaining French landholdings, sending troops to fight in the October 1973 Middle East war, and, above all, launching his great campaign to annex Spanish-ruled Western Sahara. Spain's cession of its desert colony in 1976 allowed the king to recoup his lost popularity, neutralize the opposition parties, and so permit a relative liberalization, which culminated in the calling of the 1977 general elections. However, as the enthusiasm generated by the "recovery"

of Western Sahara gave way to renewed mass agitation over the country's chronic domestic problems, the king resorted once again to the stick. In June 1981, he ordered the army to suppress riots in Casablanca sparked by huge rises in food prices. More than 600 are believed to have been killed and 2,000 arrested. More than 200 leaders of the Socialist Union of Popular Forces and its trade unions received jail terms in a series of political trials, and the party's newspapers were shut down. In January 1984, after the introduction of austerity measures—including a reduction in the subsidies on basic foodstuffs in the second half of the previous year—riots in Marrakesh and in several towns in the north of the country were subdued with violence by the state security forces. As many as 400 may have died during the two weeks of disturbances. Only when Hassan appeared on television to announce the restoration of subsidies did the demonstrations cease.

During his two decades of rule, King Hassan generally has aligned his foreign policy with the West's. He has maintained especially close relations with France and the United States. While condemning Zionism, he has tended to favor détente between Israel and the Arab world and met with the prime minister of Israel in 1986. He has allied with the most pro-Western regimes in Africa and sent troops to help crush the Shaba uprisings in Zaire in 1977 and 1978. In the Maghreb (North Africa, excluding Egypt), he abandoned Morocco's traditional claims to Mauritania and the Algerian Sahara in 1969 to 1972, but maintained the claim to Western Sahara. Since 1975, the war against the Western Saharan nationalist guerrillas of the Polisario Front has been his major preoccupation. Domestically, he favors retaining an important place for private business and foreign investment in the economy, though many large industries, including the key phosphate mines, are in public hands. A pragmatic and flexible politician, King Hassan is, above all, committed to the maintenance of his rule and the survival of his dynasty. The fate of many monarchies in the Third World suggests that eventually the Alawite dynasty will be overturned. The progressive urbanization and modernization of Moroccan society bring greater questioning of the monarch's claim to a divine right to rule. His religious prestige is lowest in the urban areas, where 44% of Moroccans now live (compared with only 14% at the time of independence).

THE ELECTORAL SYSTEM

Suffrage is universal for Moroccan citizens age 21 and over. The parliament, made up of two houses, the Chamber of Representatives and the Chamber of Councillors, holds various elections at which citizens may vote. Elections for the 325 members of the Chamber of Representatives are held every five years. The Chamber of Councillors' 270 members are elected for nine-year terms. One-third of the Chamber of Councillors is renewed every three years. three-fifths of the Councillors are elected by local councils, and two-fifths of them by the people.

Elections to the Chamber of Representatives, November 1997

Bloc/Party	325 Members
Democratic Bloc:	
Socialist Union of Popular Forces (USFP)	57
Independence Party (IP)	32
Party of Renewal and Progress (PRP)	9
Organization of Action for Democracy and the People	4
National Entente:	
Popular Movement (MP)	40
Constitutional Union (UC)	50
National Democratic Party (PND)	10
Center:	
National Assembly of Independents (RNI)	46
Democratic and Social Movement (MDS)	32
National Popular Movement (MNP)	19
Other:	26

Elections to the Chamber of Councillors, December 1997

Democratic Bloc:	
Socialist Union of Popular Forces (USFP)	16
Independence Party (IP)	21
Party of Renewal and Progress (PRP)	7
Organization of Action for Democracy and the People	—
National Entente:	
Popular Movement (MP)	27
Constitutional Union (UC)	28
National Democratic Party (PND)	21
Center:	
National Assembly of Independents (RNI)	42
Democratic and Social Movement (MDS)	33
National Popular Movement (MNP)	15
Other:	60

THE PARTY SYSTEM

Parties first emerged in Morocco as a consequence of the nationalist struggle against French and Spanish rule, which began under the leadership of French-educated intellectuals and religious reformists (*Salafis*) and reached a mass scale in the late 1930s. In 1943, Ahmed Balafrej and other nationalists founded the Independence Party (*Istiqlal*), which was to spearhead the struggle for independence under the leadership of Allal el-Fassi.

The Istiqlal Party formed a close alliance with Sultan Mohammed V, whose Alawite dynasty had been forced to accept a Franco-Spanish "protectorate" in 1912. After about 1946, he refused to cooperate with the French authorities, who retaliated by exiling him to Madagascar in 1953. This step only fanned the flames of nationalist revolt. An Army of Liberation began guerrilla attacks in 1955, and France, which was already facing a rebellion in Algeria, decided to come to terms with the Moroccan nationalists. Mohammed V returned to Morocco as a national hero, and, in 1956, France and Spain ended their protectorate.

In granting Morocco independence, France and Spain returned full sovereignty to the sultan, who acquired the title of king. A struggle for primacy then ensued between the monarch and the more radical factions of the nationalist movement. The king retained all legislative powers and refused to hold elections or allow a constitution to be drafted. He also encouraged the emergence of royalist political movements. The king's enormous prestige stood him in good stead in this contest, as did the practical support of France, which helped to build up the king's Royal Armed Forces (FAR) and provided many of his government's civil servants for several years. Between 1956 and 1959, the irregulars of the Army of Liberation were gradually forced to hand over their arms, join the FAR, or disband. Though the Istiqlal Party was included in the postindependence government, the king tried to weaken it by giving Cabinet posts to royalist independents and the small Democratic Independence Party (*Parti Démocratique de l'Indépendance*; PDI) and by encouraging the Berber-based MP after its creation in 1957. As little more than a loose alliance of factions united in support of independence, the Istiqlal Party was unable to check Mohammed V's tightening grip on power. In 1959 the party split, the more radical nationalists setting up the National Union of Popular Forces (*Union Nationale des Forces Populaires*; UNFP). By the time of Hassan II's ascent to the throne, in 1961, upon Mohammed V's death, the monarchy was well entrenched in power.

Multipartism is an essential characteristic of the current Moroccan political system. Today there are several political parties, most of which belong to one of the major groupings: the Democratic Bloc (*Bloc Démocratique*), the National Entente (*Entente Nationale*), and Center.

DEMOCRATIC BLOC
(Bloc Démocratique)

Founded in May 1992 to promote democracy within the framework of a constitutional monarchy, the Democratic Bloc currently includes the Socialist Union of Popular Forces (*Union Socialiste des Forces Populaires*; USFP), the Independence Party (*Istiqlal*), the Party of Renewal and Progress (*Parti du Renouveau et du Progrés*), and the

Organization of Democratic and Popular Action (*Organisation de l'Action pour Démocratie et Peuple*). Since its formation, it has tried to ensure that all political actions are legal and that elections are free and fair. In the 1997 parliamentary elections, the Democratic Bloc won 31% of the seats (102 of 325 available seats) in the Chamber of Representatives and 16% of the seats (44 of 270 seats) in the Chamber of Councillors.

SOCIALIST UNION OF POPULAR FORCES
(Union Socialiste des Forces Populaires; USFP)

HISTORY

Founded in 1974, the USFP emerged from a split in the National Union of Popular Forces (UNFP) in 1972. The UNFP had itself split from the Istiqlal Party in 1959. Led by the more radical Istiqlal leaders, among them Mehdi Ben Barka, the UNFP was immediately harassed by the palace—first by its expulsion from the government in 1960, then by the mass trial of UNFP leaders in 1963. Two years later, Ben Barka was assassinated.

The loss of the party's most radical leaders led to the emergence of a more compromise-prone leadership, while the uneasy relations between the UNFP and Moroccan Union of Labor (UMT) leaders led to a party split in 1972. One faction, led by Abderrahim Bouabid, broke ranks with a rival faction led by Abdallah Irbahim and the UMT's leader, Mahjoub Ben Seddik. Bouabid's "Rabat wing" of the UNFP was briefly banned in 1973 and 1974 but was relegalized as a result of the liberalization initiated by the king in 1974 changing its name to the *Union Socialiste des Forces Populaires* the same year. The party accused the government of fixing many of the results in the 1977 elections and has since remained in opposition. It was severely repressed after the June 1981 Casablanca riots and massacre. Its newspapers were immediately suppressed and had still not been allowed to restart publication a year later. Some 200 leaders of the party and its allied Democratic Labor Confederation (*Confederation Démocratique du Travail*; CDT) were jailed. Abderrahim Bouabid and two other members of the party's political bureau were imprisoned between September 1981 and March 1982. In May 1983, the king pardoned 22 of the imprisoned USFP and CDT members, and the USFP decided to participate in the local and national elections. In November 1983, Abderrahman Bouabid, leader of the party, was included in the government as a minister of state.

Although it won a sizable number of seats in the 1993 legislative elections, USFP ultimately rejected the king's invitation to participate in a coalition government. In April 1995, the king again tried to convince leftist groups to join the government, but USFP declined. In the 1997 parliamentary elections, USFP garnered 57 seats, the largest number of seats of any party, in the Chamber of Representatives, and 16 seats in the Chamber of Councillors. In March 1998, the king appointed the prominent socialist USFP member Abderrahmane Youssoufi to be prime minister.

POLICY

The USFP's political outlook is, broadly speaking, social democratic. It advocates reform of the constitution, civil liberties, and the liberation of political prisoners. It calls for the nationalization of the principal means of production, transport, exchange, and credit; land reform on the basis of "land to the tiller"; large-scale housing programs and the control of urban rents and property speculation; anticorruption measures; and wage increases.

MEMBERSHIP AND CONSTITUENCY

Primarily urban-based, the USFP draws most of its members from the educated middle class. It is particularly strong among students, teachers, and lower-level civil servants, but it also recruits through the trade unions affiliated with the CDT, which it controls. In elections, it enjoys wide support in the cities from workers, the unemployed poor, students, and the middle class.

FINANCING

The USFP has been liberally supported by its wealthier adherents.

LEADERSHIP

Its leaders include Noubir el-Amaoui, Mohamed el Yazghi, and Abdelwaheb Radi. Fathallah Oulaalou is the party's first secretary.

PROSPECTS

As the major left-wing party, the USFP seems to be growing in strength and influence. Although the repression it suffered off and on since June 1981 seriously handicapped the party and prevented it from capitalizing effectively on its political opportunities, it still has managed to garner an impressive number of seats in the current parliament. Now, with the appointment of USFP's Abderrahmane Youssoufi as prime minister, the party's stock will certainly rise.

Independence Party (IP)
(Istiqlal)

HISTORY

Founded in 1943, the Istiqlal Party led the struggle for independence, in close alliance with Sultan Mohammed V. As a broad alliance united in pursuit of independence, it enjoyed overwhelming popular support, but it had no agreed program of policies for independent Morocco. It was unable to offer effective resistance to the consolidation of political power in the hands of the monarch. The party was greatly weakened by the split with the National Union of Popular Forces (*Union Nationale des Forces Populaires*; UNFP) in 1959, as well as by the palace's encouragement of ultraloyalist factions. In 1963 it was forced out of the government, in which it had participated since 1956, and it remained in opposition until 1977, when it reentered the government with eight Cabinet posts. It continued to maintain an important involvement in government after November 1983, when the new Cabinet was formed, although its strength has been somewhat reduced.

In the 1993 elections it was already allied with the Socialist Union of Popular Forces (USFP) into the newly formed Democratic Bloc. The bloc, a coalition of center-left opposition groups, garnered 99 parliamentary seats. In the 1997 elections, Istiqlal won 32 of 325 Chamber of Representatives seats and 21 of 270 Chamber of Councillors seats.

Organization

Between party congresses, which are held every two or three years with over 5,000 delegates attending, the party is headed by a 510-member national council. Day-to-day leadership is provided by the much smaller executive committee. The party publishes two daily newspapers, *Al-Alam* in Arabic and *L'Opinion* in French.

Policy

Party policy is strongly nationalist. In the immediate postindependence years, it championed the idea of "Greater Morocco"—the incorporation into Morocco of Western Sahara, Ifni, Mauritania, the Algerian Sahara, and northwestern Mali. The party objected strongly to King Hassan's recognition of Mauritania and to the de facto border with Algeria in 1969 to 1972. Istiqlal would be the most resistant to concessions to the Polisario Front in Western Sahara. The party has been noted for supporting full Arabization of education, strict adherence to Islamic principles, rejection of birth control, and denigration of "foreign ideologies" like Marxism.

Once proroyalist, the party now is more reformist and only supports the king on a few issues. In fact, it has challenged the monarchy on human rights abuses and has begun to rally for improving living standards in Morocco.

Membership and Constituency

The party is primarily urban and middle class and enjoys the support of much of the country's religious officialdom. It is weak among students and unionized workers, though it has a very small student organization and a labor organization.

Financing

Istiglal's funding traditionally has come from prominent bourgeois families. This support, however, has declined significantly since the early 1960s.

Leadership

Mohamed Douri is the party leader, and Mohamed Boucetta is the secretary-general.

Prospects

Because of its participation in the Democratic Bloc, Istiqlal has changed its focus to one of reform and therefore garnered a sizable support in the last parliamentary elections. It received 32 seats in the Chamber of Representatives and 21 seats in the Chamber of Councillors. Its biggest challenge may be the tensions within the party between the aging members and the younger, more reform-minded members.

National Entente
(Entente Nationale)

The National Entente is made up of the Popular Movement (*Mouvement Populaire*), the Constitutional Union (*Union Constitutionelle*), and the National Democratic Party (*Parti National-Démocrate*). It is a center-right coalition whose parties had leading roles in the government in the 1985 to 1992 period. In 1993 when King Hassan tried (and failed) to entice other, more left-leaning parties to participate in the government, Entente parties were named to form the Cabinet in 1995. In the 1997 parliamentary elections, Entente parties garnered 31% of the Chamber of Representatives seats (100 of 325) and 28% of the Chamber of Councillors seats (76 of 270).

Popular Movement
(Mouvement Populaire; MP)

Created in 1957 and legalized in 1959, the MP exploited local rural grievances that lay behind rural rebellions in 1957 to 1959. It presented itself in the Berber-populated mountainous regions as a Berber alternative to the Arab-dominated, urban-based Istiqlal Party. It received encouragement from the palace, which saw the movement as a useful counterweight to the urban parties. It gave loyal support to the king and joined the FDIC in the sixties. It received four posts in the government after the 1977 elections and was third-ranked after the 1984 and 1993 elections.

The MP's distinctive features are its royalism and Berberism. In 1986 an extraordinary party congress removed its founder and then secretary-general, Mahjoubi Aherdane (born 1921). In the 1997 parliamentary elections, as part of the National Entente, the MP garnered 40 Chamber of Representatives seats and 27 Chamber of Councillors seats.

Constitutional Union
(Union Constitutionnelle; UC)

HISTORY

This party was founded in April 1983 under the leadership of the former prime minister M. Maati Bouabid after extensive preparation during the preceding three months. Between January and April 1983, M. Bouabid toured the country and held innumerable meetings with local officials, dignitaries, and other influential persons, with a view to constructing a broad-based popular yet conservative and loyalist political alliance. The new alliance received support from the palace and was able to command very considerable electoral support both in the local elections of June 1983 and the national elections of September–October 1984. In electoral terms it was the most popular party of all—in all stages of the elections— garnering more seats, both in the rural and municipal commune councils and in the Chamber of Representatives, than any other party. In the 1997 parliamentary elections, as part of the National Entente, the UC garnered 50 Chamber of Representatives seats and 28 Chamber of Councillors seats.

POLICY

The UC declares that it is faithful to the country's constitutional traditions and to the monarchy. It seeks to mobilize a new alliance centered around a program "quite distinct from the demagogy of imported ideologies and destructive forces." Its major stated concern is to move beyond the politics of the immediate postindependence period and to develop a new "centrist" grouping. It is weak on specific economic and social policy.

MEMBERSHIP AND CONSTITUENCY

Party members are drawn generally from the wealthy and middle classes, both urban and rural; landowners, industrialists, and business interests are represented, as are the professional middle classes. The electoral base is predominantly, but by no means exclusively, rural.

FINANCING

The financial support of its broad constituency covers the UC expenses. It may also have support from the palace.

LEADERSHIP

The founder, Maati Bouabid, former prime minister, died in 1996. Current leaders are Abdellatif Semlali and Jalal Essaid.

PROSPECTS

As the major conservative, loyalist political grouping, with evident electoral support and the approval of the palace, the UC is no longer as popular and powerful as it once was. The death of founder Maati Bouabid in 1996 appears to have weakened the party's former internal unity.

National Democratic Party
(Parti National-Démocrate; PND)

HISTORY

Registered as a parliamentary group in April 1981 and as a political party a few weeks later, the National Democratic Party is a breakaway from the National Assembly of Independents (*Rassemblement National des Independents*; RNI). In the November 1981 Cabinet reshuffle, it increased its number of ministerial posts from three to five, while the RNI rump left the government. In the Cabinet of November 1983 its number of ministerial posts was back to three, while the RNI also obtained a ministerial presence. The PND continues to attract electoral support, although to a significantly lesser extent than does the RNI. In the 1997 parliamentary elections, as part of the National Entente, the PND won only 10 Chamber of Representatives seats and 21 Chamber of Councillors seats.

POLICY

Like the RNI, the PND is strongly proroyalist. It is antisocialist, prowestern in foreign policy, and supportive of private business. But whereas the RNI rump tends to represent the interests of industry and commerce, the PND is supported by many of the large landowners and therefore supports policies favorable to the development of large-scale commercial farming. Nevertheless, it presents itself as the defender of the interests of the small farmer and peasant, claims to be progressive, and condemns those political tendencies and ideologies that encourage the division into left and right.

MEMBERSHIP AND CONSTITUENCY

The leaders of the PND are generally wealthy and are often large landowners. Their electoral base is overwhelmingly rural.

FINANCING

The financial support of its wealthy constituency covers most expenses.

LEADERSHIP

Abdelhamid Kassimi is the party leader, and Arsalane el-Jadidi is the party's secretary-general.

PROSPECTS

Although for a while, between 1981 and 1983, it seemed as though the PND would emerge as the favored conservative, loyalist grouping, its position has been seriously undermined by the Constitutional Union. The PND has as its mandate to remain loyal to the monarchy, yet to be a counterweight to the "old" parties. It is probable that its strongly rural base will weaken its claim to be a broad and unifying party.

Center
(Centre)

Center consists of the National Assembly of Independents (*Rassemblement National des Indépendents*), the Democratic and Social Movement (*Mouvement Démocratique et Social*), and the National Popular Movement (*Mouvement Nationale Populaire*).

In the 1997 Chamber of Representatives elections, Center parties took approximately 30% of the votes. In the 1997 Chamber of Councillors elections, Center parties garnered 90 of the 270 seats.

National Assembly of Independents
(Rassemblement National des Indépendents; RNI)

HISTORY

Founded in October 1978, the RNI was initially a loose coalition of the royalist "independents" who won the 1977 general elections. It had much in common with the earlier FDIC, the bloc of proroyalist forces that held half the seats in the 1963–65 parliament, although, unlike the FDIC, it did not include the MP. Like the FDIC, the RNI was soon beset by internal squabbles. Two rival factions emerged in 1980; and, in April 1981, 59 of the RNI's deputies announced that they were forming a new parliamentary group, known as the Democrat Independents. The RNI rump then suffered a serious setback when its six members in the government lost their ministerial posts in a Cabinet reshuffle in November 1981. The Cabinet formed in November 1983, however, once again contained RNI ministers. However, its parliamentary representation fell to 41 in 1993.

In the 1997 parliamentary elections, as part of the Center, the RNI won 46 Chamber of Representatives seats and 42 Chamber of Councillors seats.

POLICY

The RNI is strongly proroyalist. It is supportive of private business, strongly antisocialist, and pro-Western in foreign policy.

MEMBERSHIP AND CONSTITUENCY

The party's top leaders come mainly from the wealthiest strata of Moroccan society. Many have important commercial or industrial interests or have served as senior technocrats in successive governments. The party enjoys support from members of the chambers of commerce and industry and such bodies as the employer's General Economic Confederation of Morocco (*Confederation Generale Economique du Maroc*; CGEM). Its electoral support is primarily rural.

FINANCING

The RNI is supported by the personal funds of its leading members.

LEADERSHIP

Ahmed Osman is the RNI's president. He is a brother-in-law of King Hassan and was prime minister from 1973 to 1979.

PROSPECTS

Despite continuing difficulties, the party maintains a presence in the government and commands considerable support among the electors. It is rumored that deep divisions exist in the RNI and that a new generation of party leaders is rising to challenge the charismatic Osnan.

OTHER POLITICAL FORCES

Opposition Parties

Morocco's multipartism has traditionally not extended to include Islamist parties, which have no legal basis for existing. Justice and Welfare (*Adl wal Ihsan*), founded in 1980, is the country's leading Islamic fundamentalist organization. Its leader, Abd Assalam Yasine, has served several prison sentences, has been placed under house arrest, and has been under police protection since the 1970s. Other Islamist parties include Movement for Reform and Renewal, To the Future, and Islamic Youth.

These Islamist organizations denounce what they see as a decline in moral values and Morocco's deviation from the Muslim faith. They have not advocated violence, but their presence is a reminder to the king that his religious authority could be challenged.

Organized Labor

Though French unions had had affiliates in Morocco for some years, the first Moroccan labor federation, the Moroccan Union of Labor (*Union Marocaine du Travail*; UMT) was founded in 1955 by supporters of the Istiqlal Party. Under Mahjoub Ben Seddik, the federation supported the UNFP's split from the party in 1959; but from

1962, relations between the UMT and the UNFP were strained. The UMT, which was subsidized by the government, was generally unwilling to back the UNFP's political campaigns and concentrated on narrow trade union matters.

After the split in the UNFP in 1972, Ben Seddik retained links with the rump led by Abdallah Ibrahim. In consequence, the larger faction, which went on to form the USFP in 1974, set about building a rival trade union movement. From the beginning it had the support of the National Education Union (*Syndicat National de l'Enseignement*; SNE), which had been independent of the UMT since its creation in 1965, and the postal workers' union, which had split from the UMT in 1963. In 1978, eight USFP-led unions, representing teachers, phosphate workers, postal workers, health employees, sugar and tea workers, water and electricity workers, petroleum and gas workers, and some railwaymen, founded the Democratic Labor Confederation (*Confédération Démocratique du Travail*; CDT). By 1979 there were three more affiliates, representing workers in the tobacco industry, agriculture, and municipal administration; and although the UMT retained some of its traditional strength in basic industries, notably the railway and the electricity-generating industries, the CDT had become the more powerful of the two federations by 1981.

Morocco owes its profusion of trade unions to its pluralism of political parties. However, according to some observers, trade unions are still linked to the regime or to political parties, which means that patronage, clientelism and power sharing still exist, thus undermining their power and role in society.

NATIONAL PROSPECTS

The 1990s in Morocco were a time of drastic change for this traditional monarchy–led Muslim country. Beginning with the political reforms that have led to the latest coalition government in March 1997, Morocco appears on its way to democratizing and reforming. However, critics are quick to point out that King Hassan II still maintains supreme power in his country's political and economic matters.

Indeed, one of the country's main selling points is stability in a largely unstable Middle East, and King Hassan's grip on power so far assures that. On the economic front, beginning in December 1989, Morocco dropped its state-centrist economic policy in favor of privatization. Now the country has begun to call for more reliance on private entrepreneurship and investment as tools for future economic growth. Debt has dropped, and inflation is decreasing. A new Moroccan middle class has appeared, and the privatization program has attracted foreign investment.

With all the political and economic reforms, however, the king still has the political legitimacy of descending from a dynasty and the religious legitimacy of descending from a prophet. As long as he is able to hold on to those and, at the same time, oversee even limited economic and political reform, Morocco will be a bright spot of stability in the Middle East.

Further Reading

Bendourou, Omar. "Power and Opposition in Morocco." *Journal of Democracy* 7, no. 3 (1996).

CIA World Factbook. Washington, D.C.: Government Printing Office, various years.

The Economist, London, various issues.

Hammoudi, Abdellah. *Master and Disciple: The Cultural Foundations of Moroccan Authoritarianism*. Chicago: University of Chicago Press, 1997.

Henry, Clement M. *The Mediterranean Debt Crescent: Money and Power in Algeria, Egypt, Morocco, Tunisia, and Turkey*. Gainesville: University Press of Florida, 1996.

Hoisington, William A., Jr. *Lyautey and the French Conquest of Morocco*. New York: St. Martin's Press, 1995.

Islam, Roumeen. "Growing Faster, Finding Jobs: Choices for Morocco." World Bank Middle East and North Africa Economic Studies. Washington, D.C.: World Bank, 1996.

Joffé, George. "Elections and Reform in Morocco." In *Mediterranean Politics*, vol. 1. Ed. Richard Gillespie. Cranbury, N.J.: Association of University Presses, 1994.

Khosrowshahi, Cameron. "Privatization in Morocco: The Politics of Development." *The Middle East Journal* 51, no. 2 (spring 1997).

Park, Thomas Kerlin. *Historical Dictionary of Morocco*. African Historical Dictionaries Series, no. 71. New York: Scarecrow Press, 1996.

Pazzanita, Anthony G. *Western Sahara*. World Bibliographical Series, vol. 190. Santa Barbara, Calif.: ABC-Clio, 1996.

Shahin, Emad Eldin. "Under the Shadow of the Imam." *Middle East Insight* 11, no. 2 (January/February 1995). Washington, D.C.: International Insight, Inc., 1995.

Waltz, Susan Eileen. *Human Rights and Reform: Changing the Face of North African Politics*. Berkeley, Calif.: University of California Press, 1995.

REPUBLIC OF MOZAMBIQUE

By Robert J. Griffiths, Ph.D.

THE SYSTEM OF GOVERNMENT

The Republic of Mozambique is located on the southeast coast of Africa with a population of 15,740,000 according to the 1997 census, although estimates have it as high as 18 million. After 17 years of single-party rule, Mozambique became a multiparty democracy with the October 1994 elections. The current president is Joachim Chissano.

Mozambique became independent on June 25, 1975, following more than a decade of guerrilla war against Portuguese colonial rule. The independence war was waged by the Front for the Liberation of Mozambique (Frelimo). The Portuguese Revolution of 1974 led to a cease-fire and independence agreement on September 7. The agreement transferred power to a transitional government led by the then prime minister, Joaquim Chissano, and composed of Portuguese officers and representatives of Frelimo. The country became fully independent on June 25, 1975. After independence, Mozambique adopted a presidential system with Samora Machel as president and Chissano as foreign minister.

In 1977, the country was proclaimed a people's republic, with Marxism-Leninism as its official ideology and Frelimo as the only legal party. After achieving independence, Frelimo shifted its focus onto Mozambique's pressing economic and social problems. Frelimo's efforts to improve the nation's economy were complicated by its support for the nationalist movement in Rhodesia. In 1976, Mozambique closed its borders with Rhodesia in response to the international boycott of the Ian Smith regime. This boycott was extremely costly to Mozambique. The United Nations estimated that between 1976 and 1980 Mozambique lost $550 million in trade. In addition, the Rhodesians had trained and financed a counterrevolutionary movement, the Mozambican National Resistance (MNR, more popularly known as Renamo).

By 1980, Mozambique faced two major problems: a serious drought, which extended from Ethiopia to South Africa, and increased tension within South Africa. After independence, Frelimo was left with an economy that had been almost completely destroyed by the war and the attendant loss of the middle class. Also, the Mozambican economy was still dependent on income from migrant workers in South Africa and fees from South African goods exported from the Mozambican ports of Maputo and Beira. Drought compounded the country's difficulties. Second, rising conflict within South Africa led Pretoria to implement a destabilization campaign against neighboring countries from which antiapartheid forces were operating. Part of this campaign involved increased support for guerrilla groups in bordering countries. Although Renamo had lost its foreign support with the fall of the Smith regime and the independence of Zimbabwe in 1980, it began to receive aid from South Africa and waged a campaign of economic destruction, kidnapping, and killing of the civilian population.

Renamo activities increasingly escalated after 1980. No longer able to sustain the economic and human losses, Machel concluded the Nkomati Accords with South Africa on March 16, 1984. The Accords were a nonagression treaty in which Mozambique agreed to bar the African National Congress (ANC) from its territory and South Africa agreed to end its support for Renamo. The Nkomati Accords were controversial. The treaty was widely criticized as a concession to the white South African government. Machel's optimism about Mozambique's ability to make accommodations with South Africa proved to be ill founded. By December 1984, ANC operations were no longer conducted from Mozambique, but Renamo operations had, in fact, increased and were receiving support from South African army personnel.

In October 1985, Mozambique conducted a joint military operation with Zimbabwe against Renamo. The government was able to overrun the rebel headquarters, and captured documents revealed that South Africa had continued to support Renamo in violation of the Nkomati Accords. Relations between Mozambique and South Africa worsened with President Samora Machel's death in an October 1986 plane crash. There was speculation that South Africa was involved, although this was never confirmed. Frelimo appointed the foreign minister, Joaquim Chissano, Machel's successor as president.

Relations between South Africa and Mozambique improved in 1987 with an agreement to jointly investigate a massacre allegedly carried out by Renamo. In 1988, the two countries agreed to revive the Nkomati Accords and reestablish the Joint Security Commission. Meetings between Chissano and the then South African president, P. W. Botha, produced further cooperation between Maputo and Pretoria.

In July 1989, Frelimo renounced its exclusive commitment to Marxism-Leninism, opened party membership to all citizens of the country, and adopted more pragmatic policies. In 1990, the government announced that it would present a new constitution to the Popular Assembly, and the document was adopted in November.

In the meantime, fighting between the government and Renamo continued. Efforts to find a negotiated settlement began with face-to-face talks in Rome in July 1990. The talks continued in December when a Joint Verification Commission was established and a partial cease-fire took effect. Several more rounds of talks took place before a General Peace Agreement (GPA) was finally signed on October 4, 1992. The agreement called for a cease-fire, demobilization of soldiers on both sides, and multiparty elections.

The United Nations sent approximately 8,000 peacekeepers to oversee the agreement. The UN operation (UNOMOZ) faced the difficult task of demobilizing soldiers on each side prior to elections. This was essential to avoid a repeat of the situation in Angola, another former Portuguese colony, where failure to demobilize the warring factions led to renewed fighting after democratic elections failed in 1992.

Executive

The 1990 constitution provides for a popularly elected president who can serve a maximum of two consecutive five-year terms. The president is the head of government and the state, as well as commander in chief of the armed forces. The Council of Ministers is headed by the prime minister, who is selected by the president. The prime minister assists and advises the president and puts forth the government's budget and programs to the legislature.

Legislature

The national legislature, the Assembly of the Republic, consists of 250 deputies elected on a multiparty basis according to a system of proportional representation. The deputies are elected for a five-year term, but the Assembly can be dissolved by the president before its term expires. The Assembly meets for two sessions each year.

Judiciary

Under the terms of the 1990 constitution, Mozambique has an independent judiciary. The Supreme Court is at the top of the system of courts provided for by the law on the judiciary. The courts are subordinate to the Assembly of the Republic.

Regional and Local Government

Mozambique is divided into 11 provinces. The capital, Maputo, has provincial status and unlike the other provinces, is administered by a city council chairman. The other 10 provinces are presided over by a provincial governor, appointed by the president. Local assemblies are directly elected and choose representatives to district assemblies, which, in turn, select members of the provincial assemblies. Decisions of these bodies may be annulled by the president.

THE ELECTORAL SYSTEM

Democratic elections in Mozambique were originally scheduled to take place within a year of the General Peace Accord. The run-up to Mozambique's first multiparty elections was long and complicated, and the election date had to be postponed. Troop demobilization was delayed as both sides tried to maintain a military advantage in case of a breakdown in the peace accord. Renamo stalled while it tried to transform itself from a guerrilla movement into a political party and sought to gain assurances that it would play a role in governing the country, whatever the outcome of elections.

The 1994 Elections

Elections were finally scheduled for October 27–28, 1994. Renamo's leader, Afonso Dhlakama, threatened to boycott the elections just one day before they began, but international pressure forced Renamo to reconsider. Western diplomats also encouraged Mozambique's president, Joachim Chissano, to form a government of national unity with Renamo in order to avoid the winner-take-all formula that contributed to electoral failure in Angola, but President Chissano resisted this pressure.

The elections were the culmination of the two-year process that began with the General Peace Accord of 1992. The UN-monitored process cost an estimated $1 billion and elections were judged to be substantially free and fair with over 80% voter turnout. Renamo received a surprising 38% of the popular vote, giving it 112 seats in the 250-seat parliament. Its greatest strength was in the central and northern regions. Frelimo got 48% of the popular vote and 129 seats in parliament. The remaining 9 seats went to the Democratic Union party. Renamo also won a majority of the popular vote in 5 of the 11 provinces in the country. Renamo's leader, Afonso Dhlakama, was less successful in the presidential poll, receiving only 34%, compared with President Joachim Chissano's 53%. On the strength of the Frelimo's electoral victory, Chissano appointed a government made up entirely of his Frelimo supporters, assuring continued political divisions.

FRONT FOR THE LIBERATION OF MOZAMBIQUE
(Frente de Liberacao de Mozambique; Frelimo)

Frelimo was created on June 25, 1962, when Dr. Eduardo Mondlane unified three different movements headquartered in Dar es Salaam: Udenamo (National Democratic Union of Mozambique), Manu (Mozambican-Makonde Union), and Unami (National African Union of Independent Mozambique). He was then chosen as president of the umbrella group Frelimo but was subsequently assassinated in 1969. Frelimo pursued a Marxist-Leninist ideology in 1977 but retreated from this philosophy at its 1989 party congress, adopting a more pragmatic, free-market orientation.

MOZAMBIQUE NATIONAL RESISTANCE
(Resistencia Nacional Mocambicana; MNR, Renamo)

Renamo was established in the early 1970s by the Rhodesian government as an intelligence network to keep track of its opponents operating out of Mozambique. With the independence of Zimbabwe in 1980, South Africa took over as Renamo's patron and the organization engaged in a bloody, widespread guerrilla war against the Frelimo government. Locked into a stalemate with the government and under increasing pressure to negotiate with the government, Renamo finally agreed to the General Peace Accord in October 1992. Renamo then set about to recast itself as a political party in order to contest the 1994 elections.

DEMOCRATIC UNION OF MOZAMBIQUE
(Unido Democratica de Mocambique, Udemo)

This party was formerly the military wing of the Mozambiquan National Union (Unamo), established as a splinter group of Renamo. This was the only party other than Frelimo and Renamo to win legislative seats in the 1994 elections.

MINOR POLITICAL PARTIES

There are several other parties active in Mozambique, but their support is limited. They include the National Convention Party, the Democratic Union, the Patriotic Alliance, the United Salvation Front, the Mozambiquan National Union, the Social, Liberal, and Democratic Party, the Labor Party, the Democratic Renewal Party, United Front of Mozambique–Democratic Convergence Party, Mozambique Democratic Party, Independent Congress of Mozambique, Mozambique Internationalist Democratic Party, and the Mozambique Communist Party.

OTHER POLITICAL FORCES

Armed Forces

A critical component of the peace process was the demobilization of combatants and the creation of a new armed forces. According to the General Peace Accord (GPA), troops from both sides were to assemble at separate designated areas. Those who wanted to enlist in the new armed forces were evaluated and processed, while those who wished to return to civilian life were demobilized. The new army was to be composed of equal numbers of soldiers from both sides for a total troop strength of 30,000. A commission was established consisting of representatives of Frelimo, Renamo, and the UN to oversee the creation of the new military. Demobilization and the formation of the Forcas Armadas de Defesa de Mocambique (FADM) was slow because of delays in deploying UN personnel, dissatisfaction on both sides over conditions in the camps, and mutual suspicion. The FADM came into existence in August 1994, but at well below the 30,000 troops envisioned. Although the GPA called for each side to contribute 15,000 troops, by the time the Cease Fire Commission issued its final report in December 1994, a combined total of only 11,579 troops had enlisted in the FADM. In 1995, the government announced that it would introduce legislation to increase troop strength by 4,500 and that government policy, not the figure specified in the GPA, would determine troop strength. The armed forces are also contending with reduced budgets and continued dissatisfaction in the ranks.

NATIONAL PROSPECTS

Despite the success of Mozambique's first multiparty, democratic elections, the country continues to face formidable obstacles. In 1993, the per capita GNP was only $80, making Mozambique one of the poorest countries in the world. The 16-year civil war decimated the economy and infrastructure. Mozambique has also been plagued by substantial external debt, high inflation, lack of a coherent economic policy, and corruption in the bureaucracy. Although the 1987 Economic and Social Rehabilitation Program supported by the IMF and the World Bank helped reduce the deficit and curb inflation, the country still depends heavily on foreign aid. The lack of economic opportunity, particularly for demobilized soldiers, and the presence of large numbers of weapons left over from the war have contributed to rising crime rates. On a more positive note, Mozambique does stand to benefit from regional peace and good relations with

South Africa, which has increased its investment in the country. In 1997, the country managed an impressive 8% growth rate in GDP and is looked upon favorably by the international financial institutions.

Political tensions between Frelimo and Renamo continue. At the first session of the new parliament, Renamo and UD members of parliament temporarily walked out in a dispute about the election of a parliamentary chairman. Political parties have proliferated, and an alliance of smaller parties that lack parliamentary representation formed to try to influence policy. Despite these deep political divisions, however, a return to war is not likely. The peace process was fueled by a weariness of war, and peace remains popular.

There are major legacies of the civil war to be overcome. By 1992, there had been approximately 1 million casualties, some 1.7 million refugees had fled the country, and another 2 to 3 million were displaced by the war. Repatriation has been both slow and expensive. A further legacy of the long civil war is the presence of an estimated 2 million land mines scattered throughout the country that threaten civilians and complicate vital agricultural production.

Further Reading

Finnegan, William. *A Complicated War: The Harrowing of Mozambique*. Berkeley: University of California Press, 1992.

Haines, Richard, and Geoffrey Wood. "The 1994 Election and Mozambique's Democratic Transition." *Democratization* 2, no. 3 (autumn 1995): 362–76.

Issacs, Dan. "Fulfilling a Dream." *Africa Report* 40, no.1 (January–February 1995): 13–21.

Vines, Alex. *Angola and Mozambique: The Aftermath of Conflict*. London: Research Institute for the Study of Conflict and Terrorism, 1995.

———. *Renamo: Terrorism in Mozambique*. London: Centre for Southern African Studies, 1991.

Wurst, Jim. "Mozambique: Peace and More." *World Policy Journal* 11, no. 3 (fall 1994): 79–83.

UNION OF MYANMAR

(Pyihtaungsu Myanmar Naingngandaw)

By Mary P. Callahan, Ph.D.

THE SYSTEM OF GOVERNMENT

The Union of Myanmar has been ruled by a military junta since the September 18, 1988, coup d'état, which brought a definitive end to 26 years of military-dominated, socialist rule. This junta, now called the State Peace and Development Council (*Naingngandaw Ayechanthayaye Nint Phwinphyotothetye Counci*), is made up of 19 senior military officers, most of whom also serve as members of the government's Cabinet. Soon after taking power, the junta changed the name of the country from "Burma" to "Myanmar."

The largest country in mainland Southeast Asia, Myanmar encompasses 261,228 square miles and shares 4,016 miles of land borders with Thailand, Laos, China, India, and Bangladesh. Its coastline in the south rests along the Bay of Bengal and the Andaman Sea. The people of Myanmar are ethnically diverse, with minority groups estimated to make up at least one-third of Myanmar's total population of 45 million. The majority ethnicity are the Burmans, who reside mainly in the central agricultural valleys and in the southern coastal and delta regions. Although an accurate census of the minority regions has not been attempted since 1931, most government and scholarly sources estimate that the ethnic makeup is as follows: 65% Burman, 10% Shan, 7% Karen, 4% Rakhine, 3% Chinese, 2% Mon, 2% Indian, along with small numbers of Assamese and Chin minority peoples. The official language of the state is Burmese, although other languages such as Karen, Chin, Shan, and Kachin are spoken in ethnic-minority regions. Theravada Buddhism is practiced by 87% of the population. Within Myanmar, there are also Christians (5% of the population), Muslims (4%), animists (3%), and Hindus (1%).

The territory that came to be known as "Burma" with the advent of British rule had never before been fully integrated or controlled by a single, central state. It was not until the late 18th century that a Burman king, Alaungpaya, was able to establish authority reaching out to many parts of the land that would come to be known as "Burma."

In the 19th century, Britain began a gradual, three-stage takeover of all territory today considered part of Myanmar. The conquest was completed in 1886, when the last Burman king was deposed and Burma became a province of India. The colonial regime divided the country into two administrative zones. The central area was called "Ministerial Burma" and was home to most of the ethnic-majority Burmans, while the "Frontier Areas" were located in the territory along the newly drawn borders and were populated mainly by other ethnic groups. The Frontier Areas were were left largely untouched by the British rulers. In Ministerial Burma, the more intrusive, direct colonial rule sparked the emergence of an ethnic-Burman-dominated nationalist movement (the Dobama Asiayone) in the 1920s and 1930s, demanding complete independence from Britain. The agitation by nationalist leaders including Aung San along with the wartime collapse of the British regime eventually led to the granting of independence on January 4, 1948.

From independence until 1958 and again from 1960 to 1962, the Union of Burma had civilian rule with a parliamentary form of government. Former nationalist leader U Nu served as prime minister during most of this period. Political life was dominated by one party: the Anti-Fascist People's Freedom League (AFPFL). The early years of independence were characterized by a number of serious threats to survival, including internal ones (Communist and separatist ethnic rebellions) and external ones (the U.S.-backed Kuomintang incursions into Burma, where they prepared to stage an assault to retake mainland China from the Chinese Communists). Due to AFPFL infighting that threatened to aggravate the civil war and also due to poor economic performance, the military (in Burmese, the *tatmadaw*) stepped in to govern as a Caretaker Government in 1958, and then again more permanently in March 1962 when the army again took power. Under the leadership of its commander in chief, General Ne Win, the coup group formed a Revolutionary Council of military officers to replace the Cabinet and parliament. The Council suspended the 1947 constitution, established the Leninist-style Burma Socialist Program Party (BSPP), and outlawed all other political parties. Under its Burmese Way to Socialism, the BSPP attempted to impose a central, command economy and to eliminate foreign control over business in Burma.

In 1974, a new constitution was promulgated, providing for a highly centralized, civilian, single-party form of government. The constitution vested state power in the unicameral People's Assembly, the State Council, the Council of Ministers, and the Council of People's Justice. At the national, state, township, and village levels, government administration was greatly influenced by the BSPP, which stepped up its efforts to build a mass following across the country. Most party and government leadership positions came to be occupied by the same military officers who had held them before 1974, although they shed their ranks and their uniforms. As chairman of the State Council and party chairman, General Ne Win continued his hold on power into the 1980s.

In September 1987, following a series of unexpected demonetization measures that devastated the economy and wiped out the savings of most Burmese people, student demonstrations erupted in Rangoon and continued sporadically into the following year. The police used harsh tactics to put down the demonstrations, including one incident that led to the suffocation deaths of 41 students in a police van. Public outcry over the incident led to further demonstrations, some of which began attracting participants from other walks of life. This led to the convening of an extraordinary BSPP congress in July, during which Ne Win and San Yu resigned from the party leadership. Nationwide demonstrations continued until September 18, when the army leadership took power directly and established the State Law and Order Restoration Council under the chairmanship of the army commander and Ne Win follower General Saw Maung.

The SLORC suspended the 1974 constitution and abolished the presidency, State Council, Council of Ministers, and People's Assembly. Under SLORC's orders, the crack troops of the armed forces put an abrupt end to the popular prodemocracy demonstrations, killing thousands of unarmed civilians in the process. The SLORC distributed Cabinet portfolios to senior military officers, with General Saw Maung assuming the responsibility of prime minister and defense minister. Saw Maung, who was replaced in April 1992 in a palace coup by the SLORC vice chair, General Than Shwe, had little education and no real power within the regime. Most observers consider that Brigadier General Khin Nyunt, secretary-1 of the SLORC and head of the ominous Directorate of Defense Services Intelligence, has been in charge of the regime; many are convinced that his longtime mentor—the aging General Ne Win—is in fact responsible for major policy decisions from his home along Inya Lake. In November 1997, the junta renamed itself the State Peace and Development Council.

Executive

After suspending the 1974 constitution, the SLORC took over executive authority in Myanmar in September 1988.

Executive power is vested in the junta chair, Senior General Than Shwe, who also serves as prime minister, commander in chief of the defense services, and defense minister. At present, there are no legal provisions that limit executive power. In 1997, there were 21 members of the junta; all were active-duty, senior military officers. Many, though not all, of the members also held ministerial positions. Beginning in 1992, the junta began appointing some civilians to the Cabinet; in 1997, 27 portfolios were held by military officers, 8 by civilians. Below the Cabinet level, the executive is dominated by military or recently retired military officers who hold numerous director general and subordinate posts as well as crucial positions in economic ministries.

With apparently unlimited power, SPDC rules with an authoritarian fist in its pursuit of what it calls the "three main causes": nondisintegration of the Union, nondisintegration of the national solidarity, and perpetuation of national sovereignty.

Upon assuming the chairmanship of the junta in 1992, Than Shwe called for a national convention to meet and draw up a new constitution. Opening on January 9, 1993, the National Convention (*Amyotha Nyilagkan*) consisted of 702 handpicked delegates. Although the Convention witnessed sporadic dissension in its ranks, the discussions were tightly controlled by the regime and the proposed constitution that emerged continued to shore up the power of the military. The Convention arrived at a number of principles. It promised "a genuine multiparty democracy" but stressed the "basic principle" that the military would be guaranteed a "leading role" in national politics. The president would be chosen by an electoral college but would be required to have military as well as political experience. The military was to be represented at every level of the executive. Finally, the draft included a provision that anyone "under acknowledgement of allegiance" to a foreigner or who had received any type of assistance from a foreign source would be disqualified from participating in the government; this provision was clearly aimed at the popular opposition figure, Aung San Suu Kyi, who is married to a British subject.

Legislature

Under the present regime, there is no legislative branch of government. After abolishing the People's Assembly in September 1988, SLORC continued to allow political parties to prepare for the coming May 1990 elections, although the government banned all public gatherings of more than four individuals. Nonetheless, 223 parties were legalized and registered in 1989, the most significant of which were the National League for Democracy (led by Daw Aung San Suu Kyi, daughter of the national martyr Aung San) and the National Unity Party (the progovernment successor to the BSPP). In the remarkably free and fair election for the legislative assembly held on May 27, 1990, the NLD secured 392 of the 485 seats available (more than 80% of the vote), while the junta's NUP gained a miniscule 10 seats (2.1%). Since that election, SLORC set aside the results and disqualified, arrested, or drove into exile many of the elected candidates. Since 1990, 216 of the 485 elected deputies have been disqualified, have resigned under protest, have been detained, have gone into exile, or have died.

The draft constitution before the National Convention established a bicameral legislature in which 25% of the seats of each house would be held by military appointees.

Judiciary

The judiciary in Myanmar functions as an appendage to the executive junta. SPDC appoints justices to the Supreme Court, and they in turn appoint lower court judges with the approval of SPDC. Courts are located at the national, state, division, and township levels of government. Although there are remnants of the British colonial-era legal system formally in place, in actual practice there is pervasive corruption that undermines the impartiality of the judiciary. In its most recent annual report on human rights in Myanmar, the U.S. State Department noted that in 1996, there was "ongoing unprofessional behavior by some court officials, the misuse of overly broad laws, and the manipulation of the courts for political ends."

Regional and Local Government

The regional configuration of states and divisions established under the 1974 constitution has been maintained under SPDC. There are seven states and seven divisions; the term "state" refers to an ethnic minority region, while "division" refers to a region in central Myanmar largely populated by ethnic Burmans. Each regional unit is governed by a state or division Peace and Development Council (PDC), which is dominated by locally based, senior military officers. Below the state level, there are district, township, and village PDCs—also under the leadership of active-duty or recently retired military officers—which administer local affairs. In most cases, the PDCs at all subnational levels simply were grafted onto the administrative structures left behind by the BSPP; in fact, in many cases, the same military officers who ran local-level BSPP administrative bodies or local party councils were reassigned to the PDCs of that same locality or region.

THE ELECTORAL SYSTEM AND THE PARTY SYSTEM

No elections have been held in Myanmar since the May 1990 election noted above. Because of the suspension of the 1974 constitution, there is neither an "electoral system" nor a "party system" enshrined in a constitution,

government decree, or law. These aspects of the draft constitution have not been revealed at this writing.

NATIONAL LEAGUE FOR DEMOCRACY
(Amyotha Democracy Apwehgyoke)

Despite the uninstitutionalized nature of party and electoral politics, two political organizations dominate the political landscape of Myanmar. Founded in September 1988, the National League for Democracy (*Amyotha Democracy Apwehgyoke*) is the only viable opposition political party in Myanmar. The party is led by Aung San Suu Kyi (de facto leader and spokeswoman), Brigadier General (ret.) Aung Shwe (chairman), and General (ret.) Tin Oo. Despite the disqualification and detention of its two national leaders (Suu Kyi and Tin Oo) and many of the local leadership as well, the NLD won a landslide electoral victory in the May 1990 legislative elections. After the release of Tin Oo (March 1995) and Suu Kyi (July 1995), the NLD has attempted unsuccessfully to force the junta into a dialogue on future political arrangements. Frustrated with the conduct of the National Convention, the NLD boycotted the constitution-writing assembly in November 1995, and the government subsequently banned all its representatives from any future participation in the Convention. The NLD continues to attract support in Rangoon and other parts of the country, despite ongoing attempts by the regime to harass and frustrate the party leadership.

UNION SOLIDARITY DEVELOPMENT ASSOCIATION
(Pyihtaungsu Kyankhainyeh Pwinphyotothetyeh Athin)

Although not registered as a political party, the Union Solidarity Development Association (*Pyihtaungsu Kyankhainyeh Pwinphyotothetyeh Athin*) has emerged as the government's heir apparent to the collapsed BSPP and the NUP (repudiated in the May 1990 election). According to the junta, the USDA was formed on September 15, 1993, to help the army fight against threats to the nation. In late 1996, the organization claimed 5 million members. Geared toward the mobilization of youths throughout the country, the USDA resembles a scout organization, stressing patriotism and good character. Additionally, the USDA has vast economic holdings throughout the country. But its most prominent characteristic is its mobilization of huge public rallies numbering in the hundreds of thousands, held to support government policies. While there is strong evidence that attendance at these rallies is coerced by local PDC officials, it is clear that the regime is preparing to develop a political party for the postjunta era. As the scholar David Steinberg notes, "Since the SLORC had promised that there would be a multiparty political system in place at some indefinite date in the future, . . . the SLORC may have considered the need for some mass organization that could propagate the views of the military when the time came, as eventually it will, for the promulgation of the new constitution."

OTHER POLITICAL FORCES

In the 1990s, rebel activity throughout Myanmar greatly diminished, in part because of the 1989 collapse of the Communist Party of Burma and in part because of the effort of the regime to reach cease-fire agreements with ethnic-minority insurgent groups. By 1997, the regime had attained such agreements with 17 of the 21 largest armed opposition movements in the country. The remaining rebel groups do not pose a serious threat to the regime. Nevertheless, as many observers have noted, the cease-fires have broken down in a number of regions. Additionally, the agreements have provided ethnic groups with the authority to hold onto their arms, to police their territory, and to use their former rebel armies as private security forces to protect both legal and illegal business operations. This authority, however, is due to run out when the junta's handpicked National Convention completes its new constitution. At that point, it is difficult to imagine that SPDC will be able to convince ethnic warlords to turn in their weapons peacefully.

After the September 1988 and post–1990 election crackdowns on the popular prodemocracy movement, many of the participants fled to the Thai border region where they linked up with the ethnic-minority groups who had set up rebel headquarters in the region. This alliance led to the formation of a parallel government, the National Coalition Government Union of Burma (NCGUB). Led by Prime Minister Sein Win, the NCGUB has campaigned in international arenas to bring pressure upon SPDC to respect the results of the 1990 election and to transfer power to elected officials.

NATIONAL PROSPECTS

The opposition, led by the charismatic Aung San Suu Kyi, continues to attract widespread popular support both within and outside the country. Nonetheless, after nine years in office, the military officers in SPDC show no inclination to step out of the political realm and back to their barracks or to discuss a possible transfer-of-power scenario with the NLD. Furthermore, the military's extensive involvement in the newly marketized economy has given it an added incentive to hold onto the political power that can protect their economic holdings.

Further Reading

Lintner, Bertil. *Outrage*. Hong Kong: Review Publishing, 1989.

Maung Maung (former brigadier). *Burmese Nationalist Movements: 1940–1948*. Honolulu: University of Hawaii Press, 1990.

Silverstein, Josef. *The Political Legacy of Aung San*, 2d ed. Ithaca, N.Y.: Cornell Southeast Asia Program, 1993.

Smith, Martin. *Burma: Insurgency and the Politics of Ethnicity*. London: Zed, 1991.

———. *Ethnic Groups in Burma: Development, Democracy and Human Rights*. London: Anti-Slavery International, 1994.

Steinberg, David I. "The Union Solidarity and Development Association." *Burma Debate*, January–February 1997.

Taylor, Robert H. *The State in Burma*. London: C. Hurst, 1987.

U.S. Department of State. "Burma: Report on Human Rights Practices for 1996," January 1997.

REPUBLIC OF NAMIBIA

By Richard Dale, Ph.D.

THE SYSTEM OF GOVERNMENT

The current political system of Namibia is the product of nearly a quarter century of a war of independence (1966–89) that pitted the government of the Republic of South Africa against the internal and external wings of the South West Africa People's Organization of Namibia (SWAPO). Originally the country had been a German colony (1885–1915) conquered primarily by South African forces (and, to a lesser extent, by Southern Rhodesian forces in the northeast) during the early part of the First World War.

From 1920 until 1966 Namibia was a League of Nations Mandate, administered by South Africa, whose political leaders refused to accede to numerous international requests to transform the Mandate into a United Nations Trusteeship Territory. The United Nations General Assembly and the Security Council asked the International Court of Justice on several occasions to determine the international standing of the territory. In 1966, the General Assembly declared the anomalous League Mandate to be ended, and the United Nations itself became the administrator of the Territory, a position South Africa challenged.

Both the South African regime and its SWAPO opponents (often relying upon the United Nations Council for Namibia) claimed to be the sole legitimate authority in the territory; the legitimacy gap was characterized by the different names for the country, with the African nationalists terming it Namibia and the South Africans calling it South West Africa. The South Africans employed both their police and defense forces in the bush war against the People's Liberation Army of Namibia (PLAN), which was SWAPO's army, and armed confrontations usually took place in the northern reaches of the territory and even in the southern parts of neighboring Angola, which served as a sanctuary for PLAN after the 1974 Portuguese coup d'état.

This war was fought on diplomatic, economic, and military battlefields and had a noticeable impact upon the domestic politics of South Africa. There was a small, albeit important, fallout among the English-speaking whites in South Africa, a number of whom took up the cause of conscientious objection with respect to the South African Defense Force (SADF). In the final stages of the war, concern about the number of white SADF casualties in Namibia was an important consideration, as was the dire combat state of the South African Air Force, which bore much of the brunt of international arms sanctions. The war became increasingly localized by the use of South West African units, known as the South West Africa Territorial Force (SWATF), as well as internationalized when PLAN was able to take advantage of Cuban forces, aircraft, and Soviet and East bloc military advisers. International negotiation involving the Cubans, the Angolans, and the South Africans, under the aegis of the United States (and, to a much smaller extent, the Soviet Union) brought the hostilities to an end, with the Cuban forces vacating Angola and the SADF leaving Namibia. Military and civilian components of the United Nations oversaw, and legitimated, the 1989–90 phase of international decolonization ending in independence on March 21, 1990.

Executive

The executive branch in Namibia includes the head of state (the president), the head of government (the prime minister), the Cabinet, and the civil service. In the Namibian case, the president is no mere figurehead, as sometimes occurs in nations with a dual executive. Shafilsona Samuel (known as Sam) Nujoma, the current incumbent, embodies the victory of SWAPO in the quest for independence. His legitimacy stems in large measure from his (external) leadership of SWAPO, and he has been elected as president twice now. In 1990, the Constituent Assembly selected him as the first president of Namibia, but in 1994 the election of the president changed from a legislative to a popular vote: Nujoma garnered 76.3%.

The president serves a five-year term and is limited to two terms. The duties of the president include the appointment of the prime minister and Cabinet ministers as well as six special, nonvoting members of the National Assembly, and the president serves as commander in chief of the Namibian Defense Force (NDF). In addition, the president enjoys a veto power with respect to legislation and can use certain circumscribed powers in a declared national emergency. There is, however, a constitutional provision for the impeachment of the president.

Legislature

Effectively Namibia has a unicameral system embodied in a National Assembly, although in early 1993 a second chamber, known as the National Council, became operational. The 26 National Council members, who have six-year terms, represent the 13 different elected regional councils, and hence its members are indirectly elected. This Council can be seen as an institutional mechanism to reflect local diversity without adopting a federal system. The National Assembly, which includes 72 elected and 6 nonvoting members appointed by the president, is the senior legislative body, with the National Council playing a secondary role, although it can turn down a bill passed by the National Assembly. It did so for the first time in 1996. As in the Westminster (British) model, the National Assembly, whose members enjoy five-year terms, has the customary question period and provides a forum for the criticism (and defense) of government policies through departmental budget debates and various types of motions. Parliamentary debates are conducted in English, the newly adopted official language.

Judiciary

The president of Namibia is responsible for appointing judges and the ombudsman pursuant to the recommendations of a Judicial Service Commission. The judicial system includes both a Supreme Court and a High Court, along with lower courts, such as traditional courts and magistrates' courts. There is demonstrable concern for human rights in the Namibian political system that reflects not only many Namibians' revulsion against the authoritarian aspects of the preindependence regime, which were exacerbated during the war of independence, but also international concern about the treatment of individuals once majority rule took effect. Observers have generally been satisfied with the quality of the constitution and of its implementation.

Regional and Local Government

Namibia has a unitary system of government, which is a reflection of the African nationalists' desire for a unified, rather than a fragmented, state. These nationalists were reacting to the earlier German and South African policies of dividing the country into African and non-African areas and controlling the movement of Africans into what was called the Police Zone (that is, the area occupied by the white inhabitants in the central and southern part of Namibia). Under the system of apartheid (prac-

ticed in fact by the Germans and in law by the South Africans) there were exclusive African areas, particularly in the north, which served as catchment areas for African migrant workers for the white-owned farms and mines in the central and southern portions of Namibia. As apartheid came to be applied more systematically in the 1960s under the Odendaal Plan, some of these areas, especially in the north, were granted self-government in the name of separate development, and they became employment havens for civil servants, many of whom were posted to the country from metropolitan South Africa.

The bicameral legislature with its regionally oriented 26-member National Council has become an institutional device for taking into consideration the geographic and ethnic diversity of this generally thinly settled land without adopting a federal system. Ethnic balancing and arithmetic come into play in the Namibian Cabinet, as they also do, for instance, in the Cabinet (rather than in the parliament) of the Canadian federal system.

THE ELECTORAL SYSTEM

Elections in Namibia are held for local, regional, and national offices, and in 1992 elections at the first two levels were held, while the postindependence national elections, with international monitors as in the 1989 Constituent Assembly elections, took place in 1994. In the elections for the National Assembly, the system of party lists is combined with a system of proportional representation. In 1996 a select committee of the National Assembly proposed that the state underwrite the political parties, which would benefit both SWAPO and the DTA (Democratic Turnhalle Alliance), but not the smaller political parties. This recommendation was a reflection of the distaste for foreign bankrolling of political parties.

THE PARTY SYSTEM

The political party system can be dated back to the early period of the League of Nations Mandate system when the Pretoria government (following the German precedent) granted the white inhabitants of the territory a limited system of self-government. The principal lines of cleavage were between the German-speaking inhabitants (who were granted South African citizenship) and the South African (primarily Afrikaans-speaking) inhabitants; the former looked to Berlin for civic protection and the latter to Pretoria for cultural comfort and public goods. During the Second World War, many German-speakers were placed in South African internment camps, and once the war ended, some were slated for deportation to Germany.

Following the accession of the National Party to power in the 1948 South African general elections, the Afrikaner government of Dr. Daniel F. Malan demonstrated its concern for these Germans because of their fundamental Anglophobia, dating back to the 1899–1902 Anglo-Boer War. Thereafter the Germans in the territory aligned themselves with the local National Party, which held a hegemonic position in the Legislative Assembly in Windhoek.

Political parties catering to African, rather than to white, needs developed much later. A political protoparty organization termed the Ovamboland People's Congress (OPC) was formed by expatriate Namibian workers and students in Cape Town in 1958. The next year, the OPC changed its name to the Ovamboland People's Organization (OPO). Also in 1959, the South West Africa National Union (SWANU) began. Some of SWANU's founding members also had been involved in the OPC. By 1960, OPO had evolved into yet another political grouping called the South West Africa People's Organization (SWAPO), which served as the foremost mobilizing agent for the majority African population. It was able to capitalize on the Africans' grievances against the migrant labor system, which had its greatest and most deleterious impact upon the Ovambo people, the largest single ethnic cluster in the country.

SOUTH WEST AFRICA PEOPLE'S ORGANIZATION OF NAMIBIA (SWAPO)

In many postcolonial nations, the premier nationalist party attempts to wrap itself in the mantle of legitimacy and to portray itself as the herald and protector of independence. Such behavior is also characteristic of SWAPO, which was able to secure recognition from the United Nations General Assembly (but not the Security Council) as the authentic, as well as sole, representative of the Namibian people, a status it was loath to lose. As part of the international understanding worked out between South Africa and the Western Contact Group (composed of diplomats from Canada, France, the Federal Republic of Germany, the United Kingdom, and the United States), SWAPO forfeited its position of nationalist and symbolic hegemony and its access to United Nations funding in the United Nations–monitored 1989 elections for the Constituent Assembly. This assembly, whose members drafted the constitution of Namibia, was reconstituted as the National Assembly. In the 1989 election, SWAPO won 57.3% of the votes (and 41 of the 72 legislative seats) but failed to achieve the two-thirds majority that would have permitted it to write its own version of the constitution.

One particular reason why SWAPO did not secure electoral paramountcy had to do with unanswered allegations that it had mistreated quite a number of Namibians who fled to SWAPO enclaves in Angola. This maltreatment stemmed from wartime concern that South African spies and agents had infiltrated refugee groups,

and SWAPO was concerned about its own security and vulnerability. These charges were ventilated both in the 1989 electoral campaign and in the National Assembly, where passions ran high on the issue. Five years later, in the 1994 general election, SWAPO improved its standing with the electorate and secured 73.9% of the votes and 53 of the 72 legislative seats. Currently SWAPO holds 19 of the 26 seats in the National Council.

MINOR POLITICAL PARTIES

Namibia has historically been characterized by centrifugal, rather than centripetal, political tendencies that may be explained in part by the policy of apartheid or separate development, as it was later called. Panethnic movements were not commonplace, and the tendency was for party alignments along ethnic lines. The National Party in the territory tended to be the political home of the German- and Afrikaans-speaking whites (the English-speaking white community was quite small and politically quiescent), while SWAPO attempted to serve as a panethnic community for African nationalists. Once separate development was institutionalized and the Pretoria regime began to woo Africans with the litany of self-determination, political vehicles of various ethnic groups began to emerge. In 1975 these groups met in Windhoek in a refurbished German gymnasium (known as the Turnhalle) in order to craft an alternative, more conservative view of the political future of Namibia. Subsequently, this cluster of particularistic ethnically based parties became known as the Democratic Turnhalle Alliance (DTA); this anti-SWAPO coalition contained both African and non-African elements, although the white ultraconservatives remained apart in the National Party. The DTA performed credibly in the 1989 Constituent Assembly elections, winning 28.6% of the votes cast and 21 of the 72 legislative seats. Although the South African authorities were able to minimize the material and symbolic support the United Nations proffered to SWAPO, they in turn quietly funded the DTA in the 1989 elections. This created a significant backlash among SWAPO MPs, who capitalized on the South African electoral slush funds in the National Assembly debates. In the 1994 National Assembly elections, the DTA lost some of its staying power, winning 20.8% of the vote and 15 of the 72 seats. In addition, DTA holds 7 of the 26 seats in the National Council.

OTHER POLITICAL FORCES

As is the case with Botswana, transnational mining corporations are influential political players in the political economy of Namibia. Foreign public aid donors, especially Germany and the Scandinavian states, are significant, the former because of its historic links with its erstwhile colony and the latter because of their support for SWAPO during the war for independence. The current government has been actively courting foreign private investors, and it has signed agreements with the United States, Switzerland, and Germany to create an attractive investment climate. Job creation in the private sector is vital, and some argue that the public sector is demonstrably overstaffed. The NDF, which the country created with British military assistance, is an amalgam of former enemies in PLAN and the SWATF. As yet it is not an intrusive force in Namibian politics, but it might become one in future, as have the armed forces in neighboring states.

NATIONAL PROSPECTS

The prospects for a viable democratic order in this southern African Commonwealth state seem rather good, in part because of the international interest that the nation generated. Slowly the nation is developing a civic culture built around the concept of national reconciliation between the foes in the war of independence. The issue of SWAPO detainees in Angola has not been resolved to the satisfaction of all, nor has there been sufficient transparency in the personal finances of some of the Cabinet ministers, which provides grist for the opposition mill. Provided that political corruption can be reduced, land and job hunger assuaged, and the fragile ecology of this desert republic protected, a civil society can emerge to sustain democratic aspirations and declarations.

Further Reading

Carpenter, Gretchen. "The Namibian Constitution: *ex Africa Aliquid Novi* after All?" *South African Journal of International Law* (Pretoria) 15 (1989–90): 22–64.

Cliffe, Lionel, with Ray Bush, et al. *The Transition to Independence in Namibia.* Boulder, Colo.: Lynne Rienner, 1994.

Diescho, Joseph. *The Namibian Constitution in Perspective.* Windhoek: Gamsberg Macmillan, 1994.

Dreyer, Ronald. *Namibia and Southern Africa: Regional Dynamics of Decolonization, 1945–90.* New York: Kegan Paul, 1994.

du Pisani, André. *SWA / Namibia: The Politics of Continuity and Change.* Johannesburg: Jonathan Ball, 1985.

Groth, Siegfried. *Namibia, The Wall of Silence: The Dark Days of the Liberation Struggle.* Trans. Hugh Meyer. Wuppertal, Germany: Peter Hammer Verlag, 1995, distributed by David Philip, Claremont, South Africa.

Grotpeter, John. *Historical Dictionary of Namibia.* African Historical Dictionaries, no. 57. Metuchen, N.J.: Scarecrow Press, 1994.

Kaela, Laurent C.W. *The Question of Namibia.* New York: St. Martin's Press, 1996.

Leys, Colin, and John Saul, with contributions by Susan Brown et al. *Namibia's Liberation Struggle: The Two-Edged Sword.* Athens: Ohio University Press, 1995.

Lush, David. *Last Steps to Uhuru: An Eye-Witness Account of Namibia's Transition to Independence.* Windhoek: New Namibia, 1993.

Sparks, Donald L., and December Green. *Namibia: The Nation after Independence.* Boulder, Colo.: Westview Press, 1992.

Tötemeyer, Gerhard. "The Regional Reconstruction of the State: The Namibian Case." *Politikon* (Florida, South Africa) 19, no. 1 (December 1991): 66–82.

NAURU

By Eugene Ogan, Ph.D.

The island republic of Nauru gained its independence in January 1968. Because of its rich phosphate deposits, the island had been governed by outsiders for the preceding 80 years. Initially annexed by Germany, Nauru came under the joint administration of Australia, New Zealand, and Britain as a League of Nations Mandate after the First World War. This changed to a United Nations Trusteeship, administered by Australia on behalf of the other two trust powers, after World War II.

Nauru is a single raised atoll with an area of 8 square miles. Nauruans are ethnically Micronesian, but it is difficult to establish accurate population figures for the nation. On the one hand, of some 10,000 island residents, more than 2,000 are there temporarily as contract officers and laborers. These include Europeans, Filipinos, Indians, and other Pacific Islanders. On the other, the wealth enjoyed by indigenous Nauruans permits them to migrate and travel widely.

At independence, Nauru's constitution established the nation as a republic with a parliamentary system of government. The president is de facto head of state as well as head of government. He is elected by Parliament from among its elected members and is the most important authority in the system, since legislation tends over time to vest more power in that office. He appoints and removes the four or five ministers who make up the Cabinet. The Cabinet is collectively responsible to Parliament, which can remove them along with the president by a no-confidence vote of at least half its members. If it fails to choose a new president within seven days, Parliament itself is dissolved.

The unicameral Parliament consists of 18 members. They are elected from eight constituencies for three-year terms, unless Parliament is dissolved earlier. Seven of the constituencies elect two members each, except Ubenide, which is made up of four smaller districts and elects four members of Parliament. Voting is compulsory for all Nauruan citizens over the age of 20. Parliament elects one of its members to preside as Speaker; the Speaker cannot at the same time be a member of the Cabinet.

Judicial authority is vested in a Supreme Court with a chief justice (and other judges, if any) appointed by the president. A Supreme Court judge must have been entitled to practice as a barrister or solicitor in Nauru for at least five years and must retire at the age of 65. The Courts Act also establishes a District Court headed by a resident magistrate with the same qualifications as a Supreme Court judge. He too is appointed by the president, after consultation with the chief justice. A family court also operates.

Because of successful legal battles that eventually won control of phosphate revenues, Nauru has the highest per capita income of any Pacific Island nation and one of the highest in the world. In 1985 it was estimated at more than US$8,000 per Nauruan. (This wealth and the changing lifestyle it affords may be connected to the extraordinarily high incidence of diabetes from which Nauruans suffer.)

The Nauru Local Government Council was originally responsible for matters relating to land ownership and the provision of public services, and chiefly represented customary politics. However, after independence it took over ownership and control of many of the country's numerous enterprises and investments, including a national air line and extensive real estate holdings in Australia and Hawaii. The Local Government Council was abolished in 1992, and the Nauru Island Council was formed to handle these functions.

The economy and politics of Nauru are thoroughly intertwined since it has been common for individuals to hold seats in both the Parliament and the Council. For more than a decade, Hammar DeRoburt, Nauru's first president, remained in that office while serving as head chief of the Local Government Council. Electoral politics has had more to do with kin relationships and personal factions than with issues or formal political parties. Furthermore, the performance of Nauruan business interests affects electoral outcomes, especially recently when business decisions have been criticized and accusations of corruption raised. The president in 1998 is Bernard Dowiyogo, who served two previous terms.

Further Reading

Macdonald, Barrie. *In Pursuit of the Sacred Trust: Trusteeship and Independence in Nauru.* Wellington (New Zealand), 1988.

KINGDOM OF NEPAL

(Nepal Adhirajya)

By Kanak Mani Dixit, M.A.
Revised by N. Koirala
Revised by Deborah A. Kaple, Ph.D.

THE SYSTEM OF GOVERNMENT

Nepal, a nation of nearly 23 million people (1997 estimate) in the Himalaya Mountains north of India, has been a monarchy since the present king's 10th ancestor unified the country two centuries ago. There have been extended periods when the king was merely a figurehead while the country was ruled by various oligarchs, the last of whom was ousted in 1951. King Mahendra initiated a brief experiment in parliamentary democracy in 1959 but terminated it in December 1960. In 1990 several political parties and coalitions exerted pressure on the government to introduce multiparty elections and to end its age-old system of government. After a very rocky few years, the king accepted the draft of a new basic law that provided for multiparty elections. As of November 9, 1990, Nepal has been a parliamentary democracy.

The Demise of the Panchayat System

In 1961, King Mahendra developed the *panchayat* system of guided "partyless democracy" to facilitate his direct involvement in national politics. The *panchayat* system was based on the king's vehement objections to party politics. Parties were said to foster factionalism, and their internecine feuds were thought to distract the national consciousness from the tasks of development. The *panchayat* system was initially a four-tiered structure (later reduced to three) leading up from village assemblies to a national legislature of indirectly elected and appointed members representing localities, the king, and class and professional organizations (of women, peasants, and ex-servicemen). Party alignments of any form were prohibited. In 1975 the system was further restricted when the class and professional organizations were disbanded and all candidates for the national legislature were selected by a government body.

In May 1979, King Birendra, King Mahendra's son, who ascended the throne in 1972, announced a national plebiscite that gave the people a choice between a "suitably reformed" *panchayat* system and a multiparty system of government. The announcement followed large-scale agitation in Katmandu, the capital, and in other towns. In 1980, the majority (54.7%) of the 6 million eligible voters opted for the *panchayat* system. The monarchy's close association with the *panchayat* system to a large extent explains the outcome of the plebiscite. Despite his bold step in announcing the exercise, King Birendra failed to disassociate himself from the issues. As a result, the "multiparty" proponents were pitted not only against the *panchayat* status quo but also against kingship.

In February 1990, thousands of Nepalese took to the streets to demand an end to the *panchayat* system. Later that year, the king announced a new constitution that basically replaced the *panchayat* system with a mostly elected bicameral legislature and a multiparty system of government. In the 1991 general elections, the country's first multiparty general election since 1959, the Nepalese Congress Party (NCP) won control of the House of Representatives with 110 seats. The other main political party, the Communist Party of Nepal–Unified Marxist Leninists (UML), which was a merger of the Communist Party of Nepal-Marxist and the Communist Party of Nepal-Leninists, won 69 seats. Girija Prasad Koirala was elected prime minister.

Since 1991, there have been tensions between the two leading political parties, as the Communists constantly suspect the government of colluding with the NCP in order to keep Communists out. The radical left continues to hold strikes and protests in Kathmandu against price rises, water shortages and corruption. In response, the NCP has become more authoritarian in its internal party politics and has helped facilitate the government's rehabilitation of old *panchayat* officials. In the 1994 elections, the Communists garnered the largest number of seats (88), while the NCP received 83. The coalition governments that have formed and re-formed since this election have been troubled by the seemingly inescapable ideological differences between these two major parties.

Executive

According to the 1990 constitution, executive power of the Kingdom of Nepal is vested in King Birendra Bir

Bikram Shah Dev (born 1945) and the Council of Ministers. The powers of the king are exercised upon the recommendation and advice and with the consent of the Council of Ministers. Such recommendation, advice, and consent are submitted through the prime minister. The king appoints the leader of the party that commands a majority in the House of Representatives as the prime minister, and he chairs the Council of Ministers. In addition, the king, on the recommendation of the prime minister, appoints state ministers from among the members of Parliament.

Legislature

The constitution provides for a Parliament (*Sansad*) that has two chambers. The House of Representatives (*Pratinidhi Sabha*) has 205 members who are elected by popular vote for five-year terms in single-seat constituencies. The House of States (*Rashtriya Sabha*) has 60 members, 35 of whom are elected by the House of Representatives, 15 elected by an electoral college, and 10 appointed by the king. One-third of the members are elected every two years to serve six-year terms.

The king must summon a session of Parliament within one month after the elections to the House of Representatives are held. Thereafter, he can summon other sessions as he sees fit, provided that the interval between two consecutive sessions is not more than six months. The king may also dissolve the House of Representatives on the recommendation of the prime minister. If the king dissolves the House, then he must specify a date within six months for new elections to the House of Representatives.

In the most recent parliamentary elections, which took place in November 1994, the Communist Party of Nepal-Unified Marxist-Leninists (UML) and the Nepalese Congress Party (NCP) took the majority of the seats.

Elections to the House of Representatives, November 1994	
Party	**Seats**
Communist Party of Nepal/ Unified Marxist-Leninists (UML)	88
Nepalese Congress Party (NCP)	83
National Democratic Party (RPP)	20
Nepalese Workers' and Farmers' Party (NMKP)	4
Nepalese Goodwill Council (NSP)	3
Nonpartisans	7

Judiciary

According to the 1990 constitution, courts in the Kingdom of Nepal consist of the following three tiers: the Supreme Court, the Appellate Court, and the District Court.

The Supreme Court is the highest court in the judicial hierarchy. All other courts and judicial institutions of Nepal, other than the Military Court, are under the Supreme Court. The Supreme Court may inspect, supervise, and give directives to its subordinate courts and other judicial institutions. The Supreme Court also functions as a Court of Record. It may initiate proceedings and impose punishment in accordance with law for contempt of itself and of its subordinate courts or judicial institutions. In addition to the chief justice, there is a maximum of 14 other judges.

The king appoints the chief justice of Nepal on the recommendation of the Constitutional Council and appoints other judges of the Supreme Court on the recommendation of the Judicial Council. (This council makes recommendations and gives advice concerning the appointment of, transfer of, disciplinary action against, and dismissal of, judges and concerning other matters related to judicial administration.)

The tenure of office of the chief justice is seven years from the date of appointment. On the recommendation of the Judicial Council, the king also appoints any chief judge and judges of the appellate courts and any judges of the district courts of the Judicial Council.

Regional and Local Government

Nepal is divided into 14 zones and subdivided into 75 districts. Zonal commissioners are appointed by the king and serve as executive heads within the zones. Central district officers, who are assigned from the Home Ministry of Katmandu, handle individual districts.

THE ELECTORAL SYSTEM

According to the constitution, elections to the national legislature are direct and based on universal adult (age 18) suffrage. The Election Commission, which conducts, supervises, directs, and controls the elections to Parliament and local elections in villages, towns, and districts, consists of a chief election commissioner and others. The chief election commissioner, who is the chairman of the Election Commission, is appointed by the king. The term of office of the chief election commissioner and other election commissioners is six years from the date of appointment.

In the 1994 national parliamentary elections, 61.9% of the electorate turned out to vote for candidates.

THE PARTY SYSTEM

Political parties made their debut in the late 1940s and early 1950s and were strongly influenced in policy and structure by the parties of neighboring India, which gained independence from the British in 1947. While the Indian parties were preoccupied with shedding colonialism, the Nepali parties were engaged in ousting the Rana family, whose oligarchy finally collapsed in 1951.

Prior to the royal coup of 1960, there was a host of minor parties that existed primarily as personal vehicles for ambitious individuals. With the banning of parties, these groups disappeared as the leaders began to bargain individually with the king for ministerial positions. The exceptions were the Congress Party and the Communist Party, which continued to maintain a shadowy existence as their leaders either went underground or into exile in India.

Party alignments continued as pervasive undercurrents under the *panchayat* system, and party ideologies emerged whenever free elections were allowed. For example, student union voting and elections for the graduate constituency and the various class and professional organizations were consistently marked by party rhetoric and positions. The graduate constituency consisted of four seats in the legislature reserved for university graduates, predominantly from Nepal's only university. This "graduate" group of legislators proved consistently irksome to the political elite, so the second amendment of the Nepali constitution abolished this constituency and with it the special representation of the other class organizations. In the 1981 elections, the main party units, still smarting under the plebiscite defeat, refused to take part, though some independent candidates did gain grudging support from the organizations. Some Communists also ran as independents.

A total of 70 parties applied for registration to run in the parliamentary elections of November 1994. Of these, 60 parties were recognized as "national parties," meaning that they had garnered a minimum vote share of 3% in the last election. The two dominant parties in Nepal are the Communist Party of Nepal-Unified Marxist-Leninists (UML) and the Nepalese Congress Party (NCP).

COMMUNIST PARTY OF NEPAL–UNIFIED MARXIST LENINISTS (UML)

Formed in January 1991 as a merger of Communist Party of Nepal-Marxist and Communist Party of Nepal-Leninists, this party is an amalgamation of various Communist and Socialist parties. In May 1991, Man Mohan Adhikari, the party leader, was elected to the Parliament and became the leader of the opposition, but he resigned in September 1994. In November 1994, he was reelected parliamentary leader but was obliged to resign in September 1995 after losing a no-confidence vote.

In the November 14, 1994, parliamentary elections, UML garnered 88 of the 205 seats. Despite its name, the UML advocates social democracy and had called for an end to the absolute monarchy in Nepal. The Communists are committed to economic liberalization and advocate land reform to break up large landholdings. Man Mohan Adhikari remains the party president.

NEPALESE CONGRESS PARTY (NCP)

The Nepalese Congress Party originated in the late 1940s as a movement against the feudalistic Rana oligarchs in Nepal. The party won an absolute majority in the first general elections of 1959. With the dissolution of parliamentary democracy in December 1960, Congress activists were prosecuted under the *panchayat* system as they provided the most potent threat to the newly established *panchayat* regime.

The party weathered several decades underground or in exile and the defection and the co-option of some of its leaders to emerge as a still-viable entity. It abandoned its confrontationist policy with the king when its leader, B. P. Koirala, called for national reconciliation and returned to Nepal from exile in India. Although constitutionally banned, the party was allowed to function in a semilegal fashion.

In the November 14, 1994, parliamentary elections, this party garnered 83 seats of the 205. The NCP's head is Girija Prasad Koirala, who is also Nepal's current prime minister.

NATIONAL PROSPECTS

Nepal is one of the poorest and least-developed countries in the world, and in 1993, heavy monsoon rains left homeless and caused the deaths of thousands of its people. Its economy is largely agricultural, engaging about 80% of the Nepalese population. Around 60% of the population live below the poverty line. Although the government in the 1990s has been trying to encourage foreign investment and trade to bolster its economy, Nepal's landlocked and remote location and its susceptibility to natural disasters do not bode well for foreign investment and economic reform.

Nepal has made the transition from constitutional to parliamentary democracy in the 1990s and now can boast over 60 political parties. However, this parliamentary democracy has engendered much squabbling and fighting between parties and even within parties, making governing the country extremely difficult. Also, the monarchy still maintains a great deal of power in Nepalese government. The 1990s have witnessed numerous government reshufflings, allegations by the UML of improprieties in the untimely death of its party leader in 1993, resignations of prime ministers, and parliamentary motions of no confidence in the government. In addition, the radical left continues to plague the government with its strikes and violent clashes with police.

Further Reading

Blaike, Piers, John Cameron, and David Seddon. *Nepal in Crisis*. London: Oxford University Press, 1980.
Gurung, Harka. "The Sociology of Elections in Nepal, 1959–1981." *Asian Survey* 22, no. 3 (March 1982).
Hutt, Michael, ed. *Nepal in the Nineties*. SOAS Studies on South Asia. New Delhi: Oxford University Press, 1993.
Laksman, Bahadur K.C. *Recent Nepal*. Niral Series-24. New Delhi: Nirala, 1993.

Web Site

Nepal's constitution can be found on the Internet at: http://asnic.utexas.edu/asnic/countries/nepal/nepalconstitution.html.

KINGDOM OF THE NETHERLANDS

(Koninkrijk der Nederlanden)

By William G. Andrews, Ph.D.

THE SYSTEM OF GOVERNMENT

The Netherlands (present population about 15.6 million) as a unified State dates to the late 16th century, especially with the institutionalization of the States General in 1579. That system was replaced in 1815 with the adoption of a new constitution and the accession to the throne of William of Orange-Nassau as monarch of the north and south Netherlands. The fragile union was broken when the south seceded and became the independent state of Belgium in 1831.

The king ruled as a constitutional monarch through representation by estates until direct, but limited, suffrage was introduced in 1849. Adult suffrage became universal in 1919. Until very recently, Dutch politics and government were based very solidly on a system of four highly articulated subcultures: Catholic, Protestant, socialist, and liberal. Most Netherlanders carried out all social activities within organizations, institutions, and enterprises of one of those groups. Public policymaking was largely a carefully modulated balancing act among them. However, that so-called pillarization has declined significantly in recent years, and the cultures no longer monopolize Dutch political life.

Executive

The House of Orange is a hereditary monarchy in a unitary State. Since 1890, three successive queens have reigned, Wilhemina (1890–1948), Juliana (1948–80), and Beatrix (1980–). Following the Napoleonic tradition of strong central administration, the Netherlands emphasizes executive authority. Until 1849, the king was the dominant executive. Thereafter, the principle of government responsibility has been recognized and the scope for active intervention by the monarch gradually diminished. Effective executive authority now resides with the prime minister and Cabinet, though the monarch still plays a key role in the process of forming a government and sometimes exerts effective influence over Cabinet policy in private. The prime minister is more a Cabinet coordinator than a true chief executive.

The government is formally responsible to both houses of the bicameral States General (*Staten-Generaal*), but in practice only the directly elected lower house, the Second Chamber, wields that authority. Once a government is formed, it becomes distinct from the legislature and ministers must relinquish their seats in the States General on appointment. Also, government ministers may be nonpolitical experts or public officials, but over the years, parliamentary recruitment has become paramount. Dutch government is distinctive by the degree to which it incorporates interest-group representatives into the policymaking and implementing processes—an extreme form of "corporatism."

After an election, the monarch appoints an *informateur* to identify the combination of parties that can provide the basis for a governing majority in the Second Chamber. Those parties negotiate a formal policy agreement as a sort of governmental contract. After the government is formed, the agreement becomes its policy program. Such accords have become increasingly long and detailed, resulting in longer periods of governmental paralysis but greater Cabinet stability. Between 1971 and 1982, three prime ministers headed six governments with six different sets of coalition partners, but from 1982 to 1994, only one prime minister led three governments with two different coalitions and the prime minister (Wim Kok) and government that took office in August 1994 was still there through 1998. The four most recent parliaments averaged nearly four years in length, with only one government each. That stability was accentuated until 1994 by the presence in every government since 1917 of one party (Catholic) that had also provided most prime ministers.

Legislature

Legislative power is shared between the First and Second Chambers, but the popularly elected Second Chamber with 150 members has primary authority. The First Chamber with 75 members has general veto power but cannot initiate legislation or propose amendments. Its

Elections to the Second Chamber of the States General

Party	1977 %	1981 %	1982 %	1986 %	1986 Seats	1989 %	1989 Seats	1994 %	1994 Seats	1998 %	1998 Seats
Christian Democratic Appeal (CDA)[a]	31.9	30.8	29.3	34.6	54	35.3	54	22.2	34	18.4	29
Labor Party (PvdA)	33.8	29.3	30.4	33.3	52	31.9	49	24.0	37	29.0	45
Liberal Party (VVD)	18.0	17.3	23.1	17.4	27	14.6	22	19.9	31	24.7	38
Democrats 66 (D66) (ex DS'70)	5.4	11.0	4.3	6.1	9	7.9	12	15.5	24	9.0	14
Socialist Party	0.7	0.6	0.4	—	—	—	—	1.3	2	3.5	5
Political Reformed Party (SGP)	2.1	2.3	1.9	1.7	3	1.9	3	—	2	1.8	3
Reformational Polit. Feder. (RPF)	—	1.2	1.5	0.9	1	1.0	1	4.8	3	2.0	3
Reformed Political Union (GPV)	1.0	0.8	0.3	1.0	1	1.2	2	—	2	1.3	2
Farmers' Party (BP)	0.8	0.2	0.3	—	—	—	—	—	—	—	—
Senior Alliance (AOV)[b]	—	—	—	—	—	—	—	3.6	6	0.5	—
Pacifist Socialist Party (PSP)[c]	1.0	2.1	2.3	1.2	1	—	—	—	—	—	—
Communist Party (CPN)[c]	1.7	2.0	1.8	0.6	—	—	—	—	—	—	—
Radical Political Party (PPR)[c]	1.7	2.0	1.7	?	2	—	—	—	—	—	—
Green Left[c]	—	—	—	—	—	4.1	6	3.5	5	7.3	11
Center Party/Center Democrats	—	—	—	0.4	—	0.9	1	2.5	3	0.6	—
Union 55+[b]	—	—	—	—	—	—	0.9	1	—	—	—
Others	1.5	1.6	2.3	1.5	—	1.2	1.8	—	—	1.4	—

Note: The May 1995 elections to the First Chamber produced the following results in vote percentage and seats: PvdA 17.1, 14; CDA 22.9, 19; VVD 27.2, 23; D66 9.2, 7; Senior Alliance 5.2, 2; Green Left 5.4, 4; Calvinists 6.7, 4; SP 2.1, 1; Greens —, 1.

[a]The CDA was formed in 1977. The share of the 1977 vote won by the three parties that later formed the CDA has been aggregated.

[b]AOV and Unio 55+ merged for the 1998 elections as AOV–U55+.

[c]The CPN, PPR, PSP, and Evangelical People's Party formed an electoral alliance and merged in 1991 as the Green Left.

principal function is to review bills for constitutionality and proper legislative form. Also, only the Second Chamber exercises significant administrative oversight.

The government initiates most legislation, which it submits to the Second Chamber after review by the independent administrative Council of State for consistency and compatibility with existing law. Normally, the government's legislative program prevails. The deputies adhere closely to party discipline in voting on bills, though recent years have seen a marked increase in the number of private member's bills and amendments to government bills. Nevertheless, disagreements are much more likely among government parties than within them. For proposed constitutional changes to be adopted, elections must be held for the Second Chamber and the revisions passed thereafter by a two-thirds majority in both houses. A 1995 amendment permits popular referendums to reverse parliamentary laws.

The two chambers can disagree but rarely do because their party composition is similar. The First Chamber is chosen for four-year terms by an electoral college composed of all members of the provincial assemblies voting by proportional representation. The Second Chamber is elected for four years by direct, universal adult suffrage but may be dissolved early. Second Chamber members are full-time, meeting in plenary session Tuesdays, Wednesdays, and Thursdays, whereas the First Chamber is a part-time institution, meeting only on Tuesdays.

Judiciary

The Supreme Court, with 20 judges appointed for life (in practice, the retirement age is 70), is the ultimate court of appeal. It cannot review a law or treaty for constitutionality. This limitation places the onus for protecting basic rights on the States General and the government, with the judiciary concerned solely with correct application of the law. Lower courts include five courts of Appeal, 19 district courts of justice, and 62 cantonal courts. A separate court system handles administrative litigation.

Regional and Local Government

Dutch local government consists of 12 provinces and about 636 municipalities, the latter grouped into 62 "co-operation districts." The municipal level is the more important, though both may be controlled closely by the national executive. Provinces and municipalities have elective councils serving four-year terms. Both types of council elect executive committees from among their members. Commissioners for provinces and mayors for municipalities are appointed by the central government to preside over both the executives and the councils at both levels.

Mayors are career officials serving more or less permanently. However, in making appointments the central government gives due weight to local factors—especially religious and political-party considerations. Local party collaboration is fairly close, for one party rarely has an absolute majority on a council and executive committees are usually coalitions. Moreover, the mayors lack formal political attachment, helping to ensure partisan neutrality.

THE ELECTORAL SYSTEM

The Dutch electoral system is one of the "purest" examples of proportional representation, as each party obtains precisely the same share of seats in the Second Chamber as it received of popular votes. Exact proportionality is achieved by treating the country as a single constituency, so that a party's representation depends entirely on its aggregated national vote. The electoral quotient—the number of votes needed to win a seat—is calculated by dividing the number of votes cast in the election by the number of seats in the Second Chamber (150). Thus, each party that polls at least 0.67% of the national vote (about 60,000 votes) is represented. The Netherlands does not require parties to reach a threshold (say, 5% of the total vote) to qualify for parliamentary seats. As a result, minor parties always win seats and multipartism is a permanent feature of Dutch political life.

Voting is entirely by party lists, whose preparation is controlled closely by the party leaders. Voters may change the presented order but rarely do. The country forms 19 electoral districts. Parties offer lists in as many districts as they wish, and the nominees may vary by district. However, such variations do not affect the principle of national proportionality. Seats are first allocated on a regional level and then nationally. A 1995 constitutional amendment provided that half the members are elected on regional lists and half on national lists. Seats that are unallocated in the first distribution are allotted on the basis of the "highest average," that is, to the parties with the highest averages of votes to seats already won.

One consequence of the Dutch electoral system is that deputies represent the nation at large, rather than being attached to regional or local interests. Interest in elections is considerable, with turnout exceeding 70%, a decline from the level before compulsory voting was abolished in 1970.

THE PARTY SYSTEM

Origins of the Parties

Before the franchise was expanded in 1887, only about 3% of the population could vote, Conservatives and Liberals held political power, and parties were very loosely organized. The modern party system began emerging in the 1880s, taking shape around the complex, especially religious, cleavages in Dutch society. One line of separation lay between Protestants (Calvinists) and Roman Catholics, and another divided the religious from the secular forces in society. The latter in turn were split between the anticlerical, bourgeois liberals, and the organized working-class movement.

Various factors prevented the system from fragmenting. One was the absence of a single state church, so that religious pluralism fostered political pluralism. A second reason was the 1917 fundamental compromise on the "schools issue": denominational schools thereafter received state subsidies, removing a contentious issue for the religious parties. A third reason was that no single political grouping constituted a majority, requiring alliances and accommodation. This conciliatory impulse has remained a hallmark of Dutch political life.

Five parties were dominant from 1919 until recently, providing the pattern of governing coalitions and accounting for up to 90% of the popular vote. Three were religious parties; the others were the Liberals (later the People's Party for Freedom and Democracy) and the Social Democrats (now the Labor Party). Despite the number of parties—no fewer than 54 parties contested the 1933 election—the inherent stability of Dutch parliamentary democracy was never in doubt.

Two changes have become evident since the 1960s. One is the long-term decline of the religious parties, a development that led to the amalgamation of the three major ones in 1980. A second, possibly related change has been the growth of parties that oppose the lack of electoral influence on the formation of the government. The direction of voting frequently has little influence on the composition of the governing coalition that ultimately results. Parties that lose voting strength often increase their governmental strength.

The Parties in Law

Very little restricts the formation and operation of Dutch parties. The electoral law is the main regulator by penalizing very small parties: those that fail to win 75% of the national electoral quotient lose their deposits of 25,000 guilders ($12,500) each. During election campaigns the parties have access to the public broadcasting media; the parliamentary blocs in the States General receive assistance for their parliamentary work. The executive has an important restrictive power, in that it can ban extremist parties without involving the Supreme Court, though it has been more tolerant than the parliamentary majority.

Party Organization

The large number and range in the size of the parties have produced wide variations in organization. At the local level, all major parties have district associations that are active for local, provincial, and parliamentary elections. Typically, an annual delegate congress is the supreme party organ to which an executive committee is responsible and a party council exercises the authority of the congress between its sessions. Dutch parties are membership parties, but their size has declined since the mid-1960s. The larger ones number fewer than 100,000 members, while the smaller ones represented in the States General count perhaps 10,000. On average, the ratio of members to voters is rather low and declining. However, an important contribution to the vitality of the parties is made by a political "infrastructure" of social organizations: the churches, church-related organizations, and the trade unions.

All parties represented in parliament receive government subsidies proportionate to their respective shares of the popular vote. Most parties also rely heavily on membership dues and contributions and assessments on party members who hold salaried public office. The Liberals receive substantial income from gifts, but the other parties do not. Research and educational foundations affiliated with parties receive modest subsidies from the government. The CDA and PvdA have annual outlays of around 7 million guilders (about $3.5 million), the Liberals about 2 million, and D66 about 1 million, which are rather modest expenditures, not counting the indirect state support. The parties spend similar amounts on each parliamentary election campaign. Declining membership has inevitably given the parties major financial problems.

Campaigning

Election campaigns in the Netherlands are relatively short, since polling takes place 43 days after the nomination of candidates. Television and radio broadcasting is relied on heavily, and the leaders of the larger parties are the major contestants. Campaign expenditure is not very high: the total for all parties in 1981 amounted to about 8 million guilders ($4 million). Most parties can also rely on the support of at least one national daily newspaper, although official party publications are weeklies or magazines and journals. Campaigning concentrates on mobilizing support among adherents, since structural and historical factors determine party loyalties and these are not weakened in the course of a single campaign. Moreover, elections are primarily about the choice of parties rather than a choice of government. As a result, party leaders are regarded primarily as party representatives rather than potential national leaders. This emphasis may be changing, since even if recent elections have been indeterminate in their outcome, increasingly the parties have been forced to spell out their coalition preferences during the election campaign.

Independent Voters

The best single predictor of voting behavior remains religion, and practicing members of the Protestant and Catholic churches tend to support one or another of the religious parties. But since the end of "pillarization" in the 1960s, such connections have declined significantly. In 1956, for instance, 95% of practicing Catholic voters cast their ballots for the Catholic party, but the corresponding figure in 1989 was only 72. The scale of the decline of the main confessional parties—from about 50% of the vote in the 1950s to 30–35% in the 1970s and 1980s and 23% in 1998—indicates that party identification has weakened considerably. Nor is it safe to rely on social-class variables, since parties tend to be interclass in their appeal. Thus, while the Dutch Labor Party attracts about half the working-class vote, the Christian Democratic Appeal takes about a third. A third variable, urban-rural differences, also reveals less than might be supposed, for although the religious parties tend to fare better in rural communities and the Liberals and Labor in the cities and suburbs, all the major parties are strongly competitive in all types of communities.

These factors all point to considerable flux in electoral behavior now that the formerly strong segmentation of Dutch society with its "spiritual families" is in decay. Evidence of the growing volatility is seen in the rise of "protest" parties, the most important of which is Democrats66. They are particularly attractive to younger voters and draw support from all sections of the electorate.

CHRISTIAN DEMOCRATIC APPEAL (CDA)
(Christen Democratisch Appel)

HISTORY

The CDA was formed as a unified party in 1980. It amalgamated the three main religious parties—the Catholic People's Party (KVP) and two Protestant groups, the

Anti-Revolutionary Party (ARP) and the Christian-Historical Union (CHU). The ARP, founded in 1879, was the oldest Dutch party; the CHU was formed in 1908; and the Catholic party was based on the League of Roman Catholic Voters' Clubs established in 1904. The KVP, the largest of the three, was formed in 1946 as the successor to the more exclusive Roman Catholic State Party (founded in 1926). It was consistently the strongest single party in the States General until the 1970s, when the three parties all experienced a downturn in membership and in their electoral appeal. The first moves to create the CDA began in the early 1970s, and the three parties fought the 1977 election as a loose federation.

ORGANIZATION

After the full merger in 1980, the constituent parties gradually harmonized their structures, which are now fully integrated. The basic units (municipal, district, or village departments) may be organized by any 10 CDA members and exist in almost every municipality (589 in 1997). The departments are grouped in 12 areas, corresponding to the provinces. The sovereign body at the national level is the party congress, which meets at least biennially. Its authority is exercised in the interim by the party council, which meets twice a year. A 30-member party executive manages the political and organizational activities and delegates 11 of its members as an executive board, responsible for day-to-day management. An "Informal Management Bureau," consisting of the president, the two vice presidents, the secretary-treasurer, and the director, meets weekly. The party's affiliated organizations include women's and youth groups, an association of local councillors, a research institute and educational institute, and a foreign outreach foundation. Party headquarters are at Antwoordnemmer 1700, 2501 WB The Hague.

POLICY

The CDA is a center party, advocating the application of Christian principles to political life and professing that its "political creed is established in a constant dialogue with the Bible." Its basic concepts are legal and social justice; domestic and international solidarity; differentiated responsibility to give individuals, families, and organizations specific duties; and personal stewardship. The party favors orthodox financial and economic management and economic austerity, especially curbs on social security expenditures. Its 1994–98 "Action Program" focused on three issues: reducing unemployment and, thereby, strengthening the social security system; improving environmental protections; and crime prevention. The CDA supports NATO and is a leader in the construction of the European Union.

MEMBERSHIP AND CONSTITUENCY

With a membership of 91,000 the CDA is much the largest party in the Netherlands. Its most loyal supporters are professed Christians who are independent tradespeople and farmers, but it draws nearly equal support from all social classes. The CDA is strongest in smaller towns and rural areas. In 1998, the ratio of members to valid votes was about 1:17.

FINANCING

The party depends on membership dues for 90% of its income. Annual expenditures probably do not exceed 7 million guilders ($3.5 million), not counting campaign expenses.

LEADERSHIP

Ruud Lubbers, born 1939, millionaire businessman and economist, CDA leader and prime minister 1982–94 elections; Andries Van Agt, born 1931, prime minister 1977–82; Elco Brinkman, born 1948, Protestant, Lubbers's successor as party leader, resigned after 1994 election defeat; Hans Helgers, current party president; Jaap de Hoop Scheffer, born 1948, parliamentary leader; L. M. van Leeuwen, born 1933, First Chamber parliamentary leader; Cees Bremmer, general secretary. The Catholic wing being the largest element in the CDA, the leader is usually of that faith.

PROSPECTS

Lubbers's dynamic leadership reinvigorated the CDA and made him much the most popular politician in the country. The party's solid organization and basis of support in the religious communities were other valuable assets, despite the declining intensity of religious commitment in the Dutch population. Lubbers's skillful handling of major policy problems maintained his party's position as a nearly essential member of all governmental coalitions. However, Brinkman was not as adept. Lubbers used with great success a "Jericho" solution to political problems: walk around them seven times and they will fall down. This has not worked for his heirs. Until they find an effective replacement for Lubbers and for that approach, the role of the CDA will be in doubt. It lost nearly half its voters from 1989 to 1998 and has fallen behind both the Labor and the Liberal Parties. This raises serious questions as to its ability to remain one of the major Dutch political forces.

DEMOCRATS66 (D66)
(Democraten 66)

HISTORY

A long tradition of "free-thinking democratic" political organizations led to the formation of D66 in 1966 as a constitutional reform party. As a pragmatic, modernizing, reformist party, it contributed significantly to the decline of "pillarization." After initial successes the party lost momentum but grew again in three successive elections from 1986 to a peak of 15.5% of the vote in 1994, before declining again in 1998. It has served in the government since 1994.

ORGANIZATION

The party structure is very open and democratic. All members can attend the annual national congress and vote on all issues. Elected officials and local units are not bound by those decisions so long as their positions conform to the party's basic policy program. Between congresses, the party is run by a chairman and a 21-member national board elected for two-year terms by the congress. The executive, formed by 9 board members, is responsible for day-to-day management. The other 12 represent the board to the regions. The party chairman has organizational but not political responsibilities. Party headquarters: Noordwal 10, 2513 EA The Hague.

POLICY

A liberal-radical party, D66 finds a natural ally in the PvdA. The party argues that the political system fails to alter governments to reflect the wishes of the voters. It advocates the abolition of proportional representation and the direct election of the prime minister. It also wants the parties to set forth their coalition commitments before elections so the voters can choose clearly among potential governments. The party also actively promotes an environmental protection program. The party's social policies are progressive, but its economic policies fit the CDA better than the Labor Party.

MEMBERSHIP AND CONSTITUENCY

The D66 is predominantly an urban party with a strong base in Amsterdam. Its staunchest supporters tend to be younger than average, upwardly mobile, and relatively well educated. Membership is about 13,500, making the 1998 ratio of members to valid votes 1:57.

FINANCING

With its small membership, D66 is financially hard pressed and depends more on small contributions and volunteer effort than most parties.

LEADERSHIP

The party's founders were Jan Terlouw, born 1931, physicist and writer, deputy premier and economics minister 1981–82, and Hans A. F. M. O. van Mierlo, born 1931, journalist, deputy prime minister and foreign affairs minister 1994–98. The top leaders have been Mierlo 1966–73 and 1986–98, Terlouw 1973–82, and Laurens Brinkhorst 1982–86. The president is Wim Vri-jhoef, and parliamentary leaders are Thom de Graff and Eddy Schuyer, born 1940.

PROSPECTS

Despite its 1998 setback, D66 remains among the top four Dutch parties. It seems to be established as the main partisan expression of the professional, urban, middle class and the dominant voice of liberalism, despite its inability to secure adoption of the constitutional reforms it wants. Its pivotal place on the political spectrum and its electoral growth enable it to arbitrate among its larger rivals and maximize its influence.

LABOR PARTY (PvdA)
(Partij ven de Arbeid)

HISTORY

The PvdA was founded in 1946, succeeding the Social Democratic Workers' Party, which had begun in 1894 as an orthodox Marxist organization. During the interwar period, it became reformist, and it reorganized under its present name as a more broadly based movement to include progressive Christians and members of resistance groups. The PvdA served in various coalitions, always with the KVP until 1994, and has provided prime ministers Willem Drees (1948–58), Joop Den Uyl (1973–77), and Wim Kok (1994–). The PvdA benefited from the gradual weakening of the religious parties, becoming the largest single party in the Second Chamber in 1971. Elections since then have given the party approximate parity with the CDA and, most recently, with the VVD.

ORGANIZATION

Although unusually susceptible to schisms, the PvdA is the best-organized Dutch party, with some 500 local committees and the full panoply of regional and national organizations. The annual congress decides policy, formulates the party's election platform, selects the parliamentary candidates, and elects biennially the 23-member national board executive, which oversees party management between congresses. Party headquarters are at Harrengracht 54, 1015 BN, Amsterdam.

POLICY

The PvdA advocates a "personal socialism" that emphasizes religious and humanist commitments to socialism. Between 1966 and 1986, the party was strongly influenced by a New Left movement that turned it sharply to the left. Some of the moderate old guard left to form the Democratic Socialists in 1970. Since 1986, it has become more moderate, seeking to create a new, modern form of social democracy without the ideological baggage of the past. The PvdA stresses a search for solutions within the free-market system to the persistent unemployment and reform and protection of the social security system. Internationally, it supports European integration but wants more emphasis on social cohesion and less on purely economic matters. It promotes a strong United Nations and increased international development aid. It has switched from main critic to reluctant supporter of economic austerity programs, combined with extra measures to improve the Dutch infrastructure, environmental protection, and suppression of crime.

MEMBERSHIP AND CONSTITUENCY

The move to the left cost the party heavily in membership, and its return toward the center has not stemmed the decline. It has fallen from about 120,000 in the early 1980s to about 80,000 in 1992, and 60,000 in 1997. It has lost its second-place status to the VVD. Its supporters come from all sectors of the population, but its most faithful members tend to be urban working-class people without religious ties and middle-class professionals. It also draws heavily on white-collar workers. Support for the party is fairly evenly spread through all age groups. Its ratio of members to valid votes in 1998 was 1:42.

FINANCING

The party is considerably better financed than the others. Most of the party's income derives from government subsidies and income-based membership dues of a maximum of 2% of gross annual income. Expenditures probably exceed $1.5 million, not counting campaign costs.

LEADERSHIP

Joop Den Uyl led the party until he died in 1987. He was succeeded by trade union leader Wim Kok, born 1938, deputy prime minister in the Lubbers government and prime minister 1994– . National board chair is Marijke van Hees, and vice chairs are Ruud Vreemens and J. M. Wiersma. Parliamentary leaders are A. Melkert, born 1946, and Ria Jearama, born 1947.

PROSPECTS

The PvdA is at a disadvantage in comparison with other European socialist parties in that the structure of Dutch politics and parties, particularly the religious ones, operates against a purely class-based party, so that the PvdA lags in growth despite the disappearance of the Communist Party. At the same time, the party, with its natural alliance partners, D'66 and the VVD, does not produce a parliamentary majority. Therefore, until 1994, the PvdA could only come to office in coalition with the CDA, a combination not likely to produce the legislation the PvdA most wanted to see enacted. Nevertheless, the party's solid organization and membership base are likely to ensure that it will continue to claim nearly a third of the vote and will remain a major force in parliament. Its

present prospects depend very heavily on its success in leading the coalition it brought into office in 1994.

PEOPLE'S PARTY FOR FREEDOM AND DEMOCRACY (VVD)
(Volkspartij voor Vrijheid en Democratie)

HISTORY

The Liberals dominated Dutch politics from the 1848 beginning of constitutional rule until the 1917 extension of the franchise and adoption of proportional representation. Then they went into partial eclipse. The original Liberal movement, loosely organized in several parties, was decidedly anticlerical. In 1948, a single Liberal party emerged and took its present name. Until 1972, the party hovered around 10% of the vote. Under Hans Wiegel's leadership it shed its anticlerical image, became more progressive while remaining middle-class, and reemerged as a major party, usually drawing votes in the 15–20% range. It was the largest party in the 1995 local elections with 27% of the vote and second-largest in the 1998 parliamentary elections with 25%.

ORGANIZATION

The VVD is fairly decentralized, especially for candidate selection, over which the party congress has some say. The party is also notable for limiting the influence of parliamentary deputies on the party executive. Otherwise, the VVD's organization is similar to that of the other parties. The general assembly is the supreme authority, but the smaller national executive committee elected by the assembly has more practical day-to-day influence on the party executive. Party headquarters are at Koninginnegracht 57, 2514 AE The Hague.

POLICY

On many counts, the VVD is the most conservative Dutch party. However, it advocates worker participation in profits and management. It supports the social security programs in principle but advocates cutting benefits to help get control of the budget. The VVD represents a moderately polarizing force in the Dutch context, particularly in its attachment to free enterprise and to a restrictive view of government economic intervention. Its secular orientation has not prevented the VVD from cooperating with the religious parties in governing coalitions, but it now serves in a Labor-led coalition. The party supports the European Union and NATO strongly.

MEMBERSHIP AND CONSTITUENCY

The VVD doubled its membership in the 1970s but has declined again from more than 100,000 members to about 53,000 in 1998. It remains the third-largest party in membership and is now second in share of the vote. Its primary appeal is to the upper and middle classes, but it also draws support from white-collar workers. Like the PvdA, the party attracts the support of those with no religious attachment. Its ratio of members to voters in the 1998 elections was 1:40.

FINANCING

To a greater extent than any other party the VVD can depend on substantial contributions from business and industry and therefore does not rely as much on government subsidies and membership dues. Annual expenditures, not counting campaign costs, run in the neighborhood of $1.3 million.

LEADERSHIP

The president since 1994 is W. K. Hoekzema, and parliamentary leaders are Frits Bolkestein, born 1933, and L. Ginjaar, born 1928. D. W. Zwart is director of the general secretariat.

PROSPECTS

The decline of the religious parties over the years has probably contributed to the VVD's success. That trend is likely to continue, though perhaps at a slower pace than recently. For many years, the party's conservative policies make it unacceptable as a coalition partner to the PvdA, but the latter's evolution toward the center made possible the 1994 coalition. The CDA is ambivalent toward it. Van Agt favored it as a coalition partner, but Lubbers was less enthusiastic. Nevertheless, its electoral strength and central location on the political spectrum give it a continuing role in most Dutch governments.

MINOR POLITICAL PARTIES

Green Left (Groen Links); The Greens (De Groenen)

Four leftist parties that had suffered declining influence in the preceding elections—the Communist Party of the Netherlands (CPN), the Evangelical People's Party (EPP), the Radical Political Party (RPP), and the Pacifist Socialist Party (PSP)—merged in 1989 as the Green Left. The CPN was a traditional Marxist-Leninist party that had broken away from the predecessor of the PvdA and adopted a more moderate Eurocommunist stance in the 1960s. The EPP was formed by leftist dissidents of the major Christian parties when they merged in 1980. The RPP were young, activist, antinuclear Catholics who defected from the KVP during the widespread student disorders in 1968. The PSP was formed in 1957 by radical, pacifist leftists who objected to the moderate positions of the PvdA. Green Left won six seats in 1989, five in 1994,

and 11 in 1998 and claimed about 12,000 members in 1999. Its 1998 ratio of members to valid votes was about 1:52. It is the leading environmentalist party in the Netherlands, takes leftist positions on most social issues, and is the only Dutch party to oppose privatization. The president is H. Harrewijn, and the parliamentary leaders are P. Rosenmöller, born 1956, and Wim Th. de Boer, born 1938. Headquarters are located at Oude Gracht 312, Postbus 8008, 3503 RA Utrecht. The Greens, a more moderate environmentalist party, won 1.7% of the 1994 vote and a single seat but were wiped out in 1998. Its president is Kirsten Kuipers.

Reformational Political Federation (RPF) (Reformatorische Politieke Federatie)

The RPF is the newest of the three very small Calvinist parties represented in the States General. It was formed in 1975 by the National Evangelical Association, largely as a splinter off the Anti-Revolutionary Party, arguing that Calvinist teachings should be more directly applied to political and social problems. It usually wins one or two seats but picked up a third seat in the 1994 and the 1998 elections. It claimed about 12,128 members in 1997. Its president is A. van den Berg, and its parliamentary leader is Leen van Dijke, born 1955. Headquarters are located at POB 302, 8070 AH Nunspeet.

Reformed Political Association (Gereformeerd Politiek Verbond; GPV)

The GPV, founded in 1948, is a fundamentalist religious party that looks back to the national Calvinism of the 17th century for its political doctrine, holding that the Anti-Revolutionary Party diluted these ideas with liberalism and socialism. It favors severe governmental restrictions on immoral social behavior, supports NATO and a strong defense policy, but opposes supranationalism. The GPV has a small but consistent following and is usually represented in the Second Chamber with two seats. It claimed 14,650 members in 1996. Its president is S. J. C. Cnossen, and its parliamentary leader is Gert J. Schutte, born 1939. Headquarters are located at Berkenweg 46, POB 439, 3800 AK Amersfoort.

State Reform Party (Staatkundig Gereformeerde Partij; SGP)

The State Reform Party (SGP) is the oldest and largest of the Calvinist parties and like the others was a split (in 1918) from the Anti-Revolutionary Party. The SGP is ultraconservative in outlook, drawing its support mainly from fundamentalist members of the Dutch Reformed Church. It has the distinction of having banned female members in 1993. The party consistently wins about 2%

of the vote and two or three seats in parliament. It claimed 24,000 members in 1996. Its president is the Rev. D. J. Budding, and its parliamentary leader is B. J. van der Vlies, born 1942. Headquarters are located at Laan van Meerdervoort 165, 2517 AZ, The Hague.

Center Democrats
(Centrumdemocraten; CD)

The Center Democrats (formerly Center Party) is a right-wing, nationalist, anti-immigrant organization, the successor to the Dutch People's Union (NVU) of the 1970s. It won 3 seats in 1994 but lost them both in 1998. It claims about 1,500 members. It was fined 6,000 guilders ($3,000) after the 1994 election for encouraging racial hatred and discrimination. Its president and parliamentary leader is Johannes J. H. Janmaat, born 1934, and its secretary is W. B. Schuurman, born 1943. Headquarters are located at POB 84 2501 CB The Hague.

General Union of the Elderly
(Algemeen Ouderen Verbond; AOV)
and Unie 55+

These are really interest groups for the elderly that formed to protest governmental proposals to freeze state pensions. They first appeared in national elections in 1994 but had split into three squabbling groups by 1997. The Elderly party won six seats and Unie 55+ one in 1994, but they lost them all in 1998. The founding Elderly party leader was Jet Nijpels, born 1947, who defected to form her own splinter group, Seniors 2000, in 1995 and was succeeded by Will J. Verkerk, born 1938. In 1999, the AOV leader was M. C. Battenberg and the U55+ leader was Bert Leerkes, born 1922.

Socialist Party (SP)
(Socialistische Partij)

The SP was founded in 1972 by social democrats opposed to the leftward drift of the PvdA. It claims 25,000 members in 100 local branches, five members of parliament, and 3.5% of the 1998 vote. J. G. C. A. Marijnissen, born 1952, is its president and parliamentary leader. Headquarters are located at Vijverhofstraat 65, 3032 SC Rotterdam.

NATIONAL PROSPECTS

The Dutch party and political systems can best be described as being "in transition." The "pillarization" of society has been giving way to secularization. This became especially evident in the negotiations following the 1994 elections, in which the three leading parties (Labor, Liberal, and D66) excluded the CDA from the government for the first time since 1918 by forming a "purple," or secular, coalition. This suggests, also, that the "clubbiness" of the past may have broken down definitively.

At the electoral level, on the other hand, there are signs of polarization between left and right. The disjunction between voting shifts and eventual makeup of coalition governments is clearly shown in the difficulties surrounding coalition building in recent elections. It has become normal that the voting results give no clear guide to the coalition outcome and that interparty negotiations take several months. Although such an impasse is serious, it also serves to underline the stability of Dutch politics: in spite of serious problems with government cohesion, a high degree of tolerance and social consensus holds the system together and diffuses political tension.

Several specific problems have plagued the Dutch political scene in recent years. Most intractable has been the general economic situation, especially persistent unemployment, a low growth rate, high wage costs, and an increasing budget deficit. The last named has been largely a result of heavy social security payments, that reached as high as 31% of GDP. The Kok governments, based on the so-called purple coalition (Labor, VVD, and D66), took a consensus approach to the problems. As a result, it has been largely successful in cutting public expenditure, restraining labor costs, deregulating business, and shifting social security contributions from employers to employees. Unemployment, taxes, the budget deficit, and the national debt were all cut, and the Netherlands met the criteria for entry into the European Monetary Union, on January 1, 199.

Further Reading

Andeweg, R.B. *Dutch Government and Politics.* Basingstoke, England: Macmillan, 1993.

Bryant, Christopher G.A., and Edmund Mokrzycki, eds. *Democracy, Civil Society and Pluralism in Comparative Perspective: Poland, Great Britain and the Netherlands.* Warsaw: IFIS, 1995.

Daalder, Hans, and Galen A. Irwin, eds. *Politics in the Netherlands: How Much Change?* Totowa, N.J.: F. Cass, 1989.

Deth, Jan W. van. *Dutch Parliamentary Election Studies Data Source Book 1971–1989.* Amsterdam: Steinmetz Archive/SWIDOC, 1993.

Gladdish, Ken. *Governing from the Center: Politics and Policy-Making in the Netherlands.* DeKalb: Northern Illinois University Press, 1991.

Lijphart, J. *The Politics of Accommodation: Pluralism and Democracy in the Netherlands.* Berkeley: University of California Press, 1975.

Middendorp, C. P. *Ideology in Dutch Politics: The Democratic System Reconsidered, 1970–1985.*

Assen/Maastricht: Van Gorcum, 1991.

Snellen, I. Th. M. *Limits of Government: Dutch Experiences*. Amsterdam: Kobra, 1985.

Tash, Robert C. *Dutch Pluralism: A Model in Tolerance for Developing Countries*. New York: P. Lang, 1991.

Web Sites

Dutch government and politics: http://www.overheid.net

Government Information Service: http://www.postbus51.nl

Central Statistics Bureau: http://www.cbs.nl

Parliament: http://www.parlement.nl/ and

http://www.dds.nl/overheid/pdc/

CDA—English: http://www.cda.nl/english/7.htm

D'66—English: http://www.d66.nl/english

PvdA—English: http://www.pvda.nl/partij/index_eng.html

Green Left—English: http://www.dds.nl/~groen-l/groenl/english/index.html

VVD: http://www.vvd/nl/

SP: http://www.sp.nl

RPF: http://rpf.nl;wsc@rpf.nl

GPV: http://www.gpv.nl;bureau@gpv.nl

NEW ZEALAND

(Aotearoa)

By Peter Aimer M.A., Ph.D

THE SYSTEM OF GOVERNMENT

New Zealand (*Aotearoa*) is a small, South Pacific unitary state, with a population in 1997 of 3.7 million people. Of this, more than half a million claim descent from the indigenous population, the Maori. Much smaller non-European minorities reflect patterns of immigration by different Pacific Island peoples since 1950, and more recently from Asia. Most European settlement dates from the 19th century, and Britain claimed New Zealand as a colony after a negotiated treaty with a number of Maori chiefs in 1840. The Treaty of Waitangi is an important document within the framework of the modern New Zealand constitution. The core of the constitution is contained in the Constitution Act of 1986, which codifies the basic institutions and practices associated with a Westminster model of parliamentary democracy. New Zealand's colonial status gave way to dominion status in 1907, and complete autonomy was achieved in 1947. New Zealand is currently one of the community of sovereign states making up the Commonwealth of Nations.

Executive

New Zealand is a constitutional monarchy, its formal head of state being the British monarch, represented by a governor-general appointed by the monarch on the advice of the New Zealand government, usually for a term of five years. All governors-general since the 1970s have been resident New Zealanders. Among them, the first Maori to hold office was Sir Paul Reeves (1985–90), and the first woman was Dame Catherine Tizard (1990–96). The present incumbent, His Excellency, the Right Honourable Michael Hardie Boys, began his term in March 1996. The governor-general's constitutional duties include assenting to bills, appointing and dismissing High Court judges and Cabinet ministers, dissolving or opening Parliament, and attending meetings of the Executive Council, consisting of Cabinet ministers. The governors-general perform these duties on the advice of ministers. The head of state's reserve powers over the appointment and dismissal of ministers and the dissolution of Parliament remain vague and unused.

Effective executive power resides in a single or multi-party Cabinet headed by the prime minister. The Cabinet functions according to the convention of collective responsibility. Only elected members of Parliament may hold portfolios in the Cabinet of 15 to 20 or outer ministry of 5 or 6. A government remains in office as long as it has the confidence of a majority of elected members of Parliament and can secure the passage through Parliament of the necessary supply (money) bills. The business of government is conducted by public servants organized in departments of state headed by nonpartisan chief executive officers appointed by the State Services Commission.

Legislature

Parliament has been unicameral since the abolition of the appointed Legislative Council in 1950. The 120-member House of Representatives is elected for a maximum term of three years. The prime minister may advise the calling of a snap election at any time. It is usual, however, for Parliaments to run their full term with elections normally being held in October or November.

Parliament's principal presiding officer is the Speaker, usually, though not necessarily, elected from one of the governing parties. Once elected, the Speaker is expected to be nonpartisan. Cabinet ministers continue to sit as elected members of Parliament. MPs sit in party blocks, with government ministers and senior opposition spokespersons occupying their respective parties' front benches.

Parliament is required to meet within six weeks of the return of the writs following a general election. The parliamentary year normally runs from February to December, with sittings usually on three days a week (Tuesday through Thursday) for three weeks out of four. Regular Cabinet meetings are scheduled for Mondays, and party caucuses customarily meet on Tuesday mornings, when Parliament is in session.

Most legislation is introduced by ministers as part of government business. Provision is also made for a limited number of members' bills to be introduced. Passage of these and other nongovernmental bills depends, however, on the leave of a majority of members of Parliament. As well as being debated in detail, bills are sent to select committees, enabling public submissions and possible amendment of the original bill. Since the passage of the Bill of Rights Act in 1990, all draft legislation must be scrutinized for consistency with the basic civil and political rights of citizens specified in that act.

Legislative power, while formally located in the plenary sessions of Parliament, effectively flows from the Cabinet and from the parliamentary select committees. Cabinet collective responsibility, combined with strict party discipline, normally ensures the passage of government-sponsored legislation, with minimal legislative influence by opposition parties.

Elections since 1987 have been marked by a weakening of the two-party system and the growing share of the vote dispersed among minor parties. This trend was accelerated by the adoption of proportional representation in 1996, when six parties won seats in the legislature. The single-party, National or Labour, majority governments manufactured by the plurality electoral system gave way under proportional representation to coalition or minority government. Another result of the introduction of proportional representation was an increase in the representation of women (to 29% in 1996) and Maori (to 12.5%, almost equivalent to the Maori proportion of the total population).

Since 1993, citizens have been able to initiate referenda on submission of a petition to Parliament supported by at least 10% of eligible electors. The result of such a referendum, however, is not binding on the government.

Judiciary

The judicial branch of government is derived from the British system, and is still linked to it, insofar as appeals to the Judicial Committee of the Privy Council are still permitted. Most civil matters involving interpretation of the law are handled at the level of the lowest tier of the judiciary, the district court and associated specialist courts—the family court, youth court, environment court, Maori land court, and employment court. More serious cases, including appeals from the district courts, are determined in the High Court. Appeals against the High Court are dealt with by the Court of Appeal. Further recourse—to the Judicial Committee of the Privy Council in the United Kingdom—is both rare and costly. The question of abolition of appeals to the Privy Council is frequently debated.

Appointments to the judiciary are formally made by the executive, after a process of consultation. Such appointments are not regarded as being influenced by partisan considerations, and judges may be removed only by a directive to the governor-general from Parliament.

Since 1962, ombudsmen have been appointed as officers of Parliament, independent of the executive. The ombudsmen function as intermediaries between citizens and the various branches of government administration, offering citizens the possibility of redress of grievances and making procedural recommendations. The office of the ombudsmen received nearly 3,000 complaints in the 1994–95 year. The success of the institution has led to the establishment of private-sector ombudsmen in the consumer-sensitive areas of banking and insurance.

Other quasi judicial watchdog bodies dealing with the rights of citizens are the Human Rights Commission, which includes a separate privacy commissioner and race relations conciliator, and a parliamentary commissioner for the environment. All are independent of the executive and report annually to Parliament.

A distinctive and highly significant statutory body is the Waitangi tribunal, which takes its name from the Treaty of Waitangi (1840), the founding document of modern New Zealand history. The Waitangi tribunal was enacted in 1975 to hear and recommend on grievances relating to Maori land and resources. The Treaty of Wai-

1996 Election Results						
	Party Vote (%)	Change 1993–96 (%)	Electorate Seats	List Seats	Total	Change 1993–96 (%)
National	33.8	−1.3	30	14	44	−13.8
Labour	28.2	−6.5	26	11	37	−14.7
New Zealand First	13.4	+5.0	6	11	17	+12.2
Alliance	10.1	−8.1	1	12	13	+8.8
ACT	6.1	+6.1	1	7	8	+6.6
Christian Coalition[a]	4.3	+2.3	0	0	0	
United	0.9	+0.9	1	0	1	+0.8
Others	3.3	+1.7	0	0	0	

[a] Christian Heritage in 1993.

tangi broadly ceded sovereignty to the British Crown in return for a guarantee to the Maori of the retention and use of their land and legal equality between Maori and immigrant settlers. Subsequently, however, much land was alienated from the Maori by illegal and often violent means. The tribunal has significant power in relation to state land and assets on the land and has been an important catalyst in the negotiation of settlements of several major grievances between the state and the Maori. The Waitangi tribunal has established itself as a central institution in the politics of race relations in New Zealand.

Regional and Local Government

New Zealand is constitutionally a unitary state. Subnational units of government exist on the basis of statutes passed by the central government. The Local Government Act was amended in 1989 to create a radically restructured system of local government, reducing the number of local authorities and ad hoc bodies to 12 regional authorities, 74 city and district authorities, and 154 community boards. All three levels are directly elected by citizens on the general electoral roll and residents within the boundaries of the authority concerned. Terms of office are for three years, and mayors of the city and district authorities are elected directly and separately from councillors.

Political parties may stand tickets of candidates, but the partisan patterns and allegiances of national politics are only loosely if at all replicated in the arena of local government. Participation rates in local elections fall well below those in national elections, leading some local authorities to introduce postal voting in elections. City and district authorities perform a wide range of regulatory and service functions close to the daily life of citizens, levying rates on property in order to finance the supply and maintenance of such basic utilities as local roads, water supply, sewerage, libraries, and recreational facilities.

Regional councils are primarily concerned with the planning and management of natural resources over larger geographic areas. Community boards have little power, and function as channels for parochial interests, linking citizens with their larger elected territorial authority.

THE ELECTORAL SYSTEM

In 1996, after more than 80 years of first-past-the-post (winner-take-all) elections, New Zealand switched to a form of proportional representation, modeled on the German system, and known in New Zealand as mixed-member proportional (MMP). MMP had been recommended by a Royal Commission in 1986 and after much controversy was affirmed by 54% of the voters in a referendum in 1993.

MMP combines single-member electorate representation with party list representation. Under MMP, the number of territorial electorates was reduced from 99 to 65, while the total number of members of Parliament was increased from 99 to 120, consisting of 65 electorate MPs and 55 party list MPs. The 65 territorial electorates include 5 Maori electorates and 60 general electorates. Under MMP, registered electors have two votes, one for an electorate MP, the second for a political party on the nationwide list of parties. Electors vote by attending a designated polling place in their local community on election day, traditionally a Saturday, and ticking a circle opposite the chosen candidate or party. Provision is made for electors who cannot visit a polling place to cast a special vote.

Electorate MPs are elected by first-past-the-post contests in each electorate. Proportional representation in Parliament is achieved by calculating the total number of parliamentary seats each party is eligible for on the basis of its nationwide party vote, using the St. Lague formula for this purpose. Party candidates who have won electorate contests are automatically elected to Parliament. If necessary, this number is then topped up from candidates on the parties' ranked lists until each party's rightful share is reached.

To qualify for a proportional allocation of seats in Parliament a party is required to win either one electorate or 5% of the total party vote. Only registered political parties are eligible to compete for party votes. To register, a party must satisfy the Electoral Commission, the overseeing body, that it has at least 500 financial members. Independent (nonparty) and unregistered party candidates may contest electorates only. In 1996, there were 21 registered parties on the party ballot paper and a further 11 unregistered parties nominated candidates in one or more electorates. However, only 7 parties secured more than 1% of the valid party vote, and only 5 of these crossed the 5% threshold of eligibility for seats in Parliament, while a 6th gained representation in Parliament by winning an electorate.

The age of eligibility to vote in general and local elections is 18 years. Registration is required by law, though it is not rigorously enforced. Rather, publicity campaigns are used to encourage newly eligible citizens to register. In 1996 it was estimated that 91.5% of the age-eligible population had registered. Maori (being defined as people of Maori descent who identify as Maori) may choose to register on either the general roll or the separate Maori roll. This Maori option is revised every five years. Since 1993, the number of Maori electorates, formerly fixed at four, has been determined by the number of Maori registering on the Maori roll. As a result, the number of Maori electorates increased to five in 1996, rising again to six as a result of the 1997 Maori option, when 54% of people of Maori descent registered on the Maori roll.

Electorate boundaries are redrawn after every fifth-yearly census, to take account of changes in population distribution. This is the task of a seven-member, largely nonpartisan Representation Commission. Boundaries are drawn, having regard for specified community, geographic, and demographic criteria, and the maximum permissible population variance among electorates is 5%. The number of South Island electorates is pegged at 16. The population of the South Island is divided by 16 to identify the population quota for general electorates. Following the 1996 census, the population quota for general electorates was 54,105.

Turnout in general elections is between 80 and 90% of registered electors. Election campaigns are normally four to six weeks in duration. Legal limitations on the parties' electoral expenses are, however, calculated over a period of three months before election day. The maximum expenditure permitted for registered parties is $1 million, plus an additional $20,000 for every electorate candidate nominated by the party. While there is no direct state funding of political parties, broadcasting time and money are allocated on the basis of defined criteria, the object being to provide greater equality of access to powerful mass media.

THE PARTY SYSTEM

Origins of the Parties

The left-right dimension remains the predominant organizing principle of the party system, reflecting the historical cleavage between advocates of an active versus a diminishing economic and social role for the state. Rural sectionalism has for long been absorbed into a broad coalition of the right. Religious cleavages have not contributed significantly to party divisions. Since the 1970s, this rather simple pattern of conflict has been only slightly blurred by the emergence of a postmaterialist dimension in the form of environmentalism and by the development of a clearer ethnic cleavage based on Maori political interests. The main influence on political thinking and practice since the 1970s has been the upsurge of neoliberal doctrines. The resulting greater political pluralism and the advent of proportional representation have together transformed party politics from two-party dominance to a moderate multiparty format in the 1990s.

Labour and National, the traditional adversaries of the left and right, remain the main political actors under MMP and the anchors of the left and right blocks, respectively. The two parties converge in terms of ideology and political objectives, competing for the so-called moderate center ground of New Zealand politics. Both parties experience internal tensions between those who favor a central tendency and those who advocate either a stronger pursuit of free-market policies (in National) or social democratic policies (in Labour). Both parties suf-

fered splits in the transition to proportional representation, as MPs weighed their future prospects under the restructured electorate boundaries and reassessed their relations with their parties in the light of their own ideological leanings.

State funding of parties has been recommended, but since it has been resisted by some parties and is widely unpopular, no state funding formula has yet been adopted. Instead, all parties rely on internal sources of finance and donations from sympathetic interest groups, some of which donate to more than one party. The law requires public disclosure of national donations of more than $10,000 and single electorate donations of more than $1,000.

Party Organization

All parties broadly follow the same principles of organization, with a loosely defined membership organized into local branches and electorate or regional structures lying between the grassroots and the central party executives. Party membership has tended to decline over the years. To register and compete for a proportional share of the seats in Parliament, however, a party must provide evidence to the Electoral Commission that it has at least 500 financial members. Parties are also expected to select and rank their lists of candidates in a manner compatible with democratic practices, and to avoid conflict and damaging publicity it is in their interests to do so. This means that candidates must be either directly selected by the party membership or by selection committees that themselves have been democratically selected by members. The parties used different selection procedures and ranking criteria in the first MMP election. The resulting lists evoked sufficient controversy within and outside the parties to ensure reviews of their practices before the second MMP election.

Among all parties, the most representative and constitutionally authoritative unit of organization is the annual conference. As the conferences have tended to become the public showpieces for the parties, so their agendas and proceedings have become more structured and managed by the party leadership. Nevertheless, the conferences remain vital arenas for the interaction of the party hierarchies with their grass roots and of the members of Parliament with the active members of the organization. Conferences set the direction of party policies, thus binding the party leadership to varying degrees, but the linkage between party policy and conference remits has loosened, especially in the Labour Party in recent years. Party conferences also have the important function of electing the powerful party executives and the officers of the organization. Organizational leaders are not precluded from also being MPs, but such role duplication is rare. Parliamentary leaders are chosen by and from the respective party caucuses.

The main parties all have a central office serviced by a small body of paid clerical staff answerable to the chief executive or general secretary. The larger parties also maintain regional offices and depending on the state of their finances, employ a small number of field staff or organizers. In addition, parties represented in Parliament qualify for state-funded research staff and clerical assistance, as well as printing and postage entitlements.

Campaigning

Party campaigns are fought at both the electorate and the national levels. Electorate campaigns are organized locally by active party members or personal supporters of the candidate and consist of public meetings, door-to-door canvassing, the distribution of leaflets to households, and other candidate-centered activities. Except in the case of unusual contests, little media attention is given to individual electorates. The main media focus is on the national level of the campaign, centered on the party leaders. To the extent that the parties' resources permit, their campaign themes and tactics are adjusted to the results of public-opinion polls, private party polling, or focus group research and the advice of professional agencies. One or two televised leaders' debates have become a normal feature of campaigns and, as in 1996, may have a significant influence on the fortunes of individual party leaders and parties. It is expected that under MMP, party resources will focus even more on the national campaigns, with less concentration on the few key marginal electorates, which determined election outcomes under the previous winner-take-all electoral system. However, the strength of the leading parties' local organizations in the marginal electorates will act as a check on the centralization of the campaign and will ensure that some local contests will continue to be vigorously fought.

Independent Voters

In survey research, around 40% of electors decline to identify themselves as "usually" aligned to one party or another. Nevertheless, people vote for parties and party candidates. The 28 independent candidates contesting electorates in 1996 together attracted less than 1% of the total electorate votes.

LABOUR PARTY

History

The New Zealand Labour Party (NZLP) was formed in 1916 at a conference of delegates from trade unions and radical and moderately reformist political groups. It contested its first general election in 1919. By 1922 it had captured a large share of the urban wage earners' vote and that of miners and timber workers in more rural electorates. A more moderate image and program under the leadership of Michael Joseph Savage after 1933 and the widespread effects of the world depression brought the Labour Party to power in 1935. The first Labour government greatly expanded the welfare state with innovative polices in housing, public works, social welfare, public health, and price support for farm commodities. Labour retained its electoral popularity in 1938 but lost votes and seats in the 1940s, its problems compounded by the death of the popular Savage and bitter internal conflict. Amid a mood of rejection of continued wartime state controls and restrictions, Peter Fraser lost the 1949 election, which was the beginning of a long period of National political dominance in New Zealand politics.

In 1957, the second Labour government, under Walter Nash, was elected, but with only a one-seat majority. Faced with a severe balance-of-payments crisis, the government introduced the infamous "Black Budget," which raised taxes on beer and cigarettes and deeply antagonized many Labour supporters. The Nash government was voted out in 1960. The third Labour government (1972–75), led by Norman Kirk, similarly faced severe economic problems associated with the world oil crisis. It was further destabilized by Kirk's sudden death in 1974 and by the highly effective attack mounted by the pugnacious leader of the opposition National Party, Robert Muldoon. Labour was heavily defeated in 1975. Although it recovered to receive more votes than National in 1978 and 1981, under the first-past-the-post electoral system it failed to attain a parliamentary majority. In 1984, however, in a rare snap election, a largely new generation of tertiary-educated and professional Labour politicians, led by David Lange, won in a landslide rejection of the National government. Lange's fourth Labour government stunned its traditional supporters by commencing a program of radical economic reform involving financial deregulation, increased competition, a removal of rural subsidies, public-service restructuring, and micropolitical reforms more consistent with a neoliberal than a social democratic agenda. Although Labour was returned in 1987, its natural constituency was already eroding and rapidly declined further in the face of a deep split in the Cabinet between supporters of the treasurer, Roger Douglas, who wished to continue the program of economic reform, and Lange, who advocated a slowing of the pace. The party split extended through caucus and into the party organization. In 1989 Lange resigned as party leader and PM. He was replaced by his deputy, Geoffrey Palmer, who in turn stepped down in 1990 in favor of Mike Moore. The change of leadership could not save the government, which was swept from office in the 1990 election.

Organization

The formal structure of the party is based on branches, defined as at least 10 eligible persons. Reflecting the party's historical origins, unions may affiliate with the party. The resulting voting power of union affiliates, formerly a contentious issue, has declined in recent years, owing to declining union membership and disaffiliation of some unions. Besides general branches there is provision for special branches associated with women, youth, Maori, Pacific Islanders, and the universities. Branches appoint delegates to electorate committees, which coordinate election campaigns at the local level. Groups of electorates may be designated as a region, and regions may combine to hold conferences whose policy remits are channeled to the party's central annual conference. The supreme governing body, with formal jurisdiction over constitutional and policy matters, is the annual conference of delegates representing all constituent sections of the party. Executive power within the party is held by the New Zealand Council of 15 members. Another powerful group is the policy council, which prepares policies for inclusion in the party's election manifesto. Elected members of Parliament are influential at all levels of organization, have speaking and voting rights at the annual conference, and are represented on the New Zealand Council and the policy committee.

Membership and Constituency

Party membership is secret. The long-term trend has been a decline in both affiliated and dues-paying members. Numbers fluctuate according to the party's political circumstances, declining after periods of unpopular government, as in 1957–60 and 1987–90, and rising again as the party's political fortunes revive, as in 1997, when dues-paying membership was said to be about 6,500. Although historical patterns of class voting have blurred in the postwar period, Labour retains its electoral base among manual occupations and also receives disproportionate support among state-sector white-collar occupations, Maori, and Pacific Island voters, welfare beneficiaries, and low-income earners.

Policy

Official party policy is contained in the election manifesto. The manifesto evolves within an elaborate framework of policy committees, the policy council, and the annual conference. Labour governments are expected to make progress on implementing the manifesto. Departures from policy are reported by the policy council to the annual conference. Although party policy is presented in the name of democratic socialist principles, this must be interpreted in practice in the context of a modern, competitive, capitalist, largely deregulated, and globally influenced economy. The party not only eschews socialism but is now associated with the radical neoliberal reforms of the fourth Labour government. As a self-designated center-left party, it proposes a moderately more redistributive tax policy than center-right and right parties, greater expenditure on health, housing, education, and welfare, and employment policies offering more protection to the wage earner, along with a stronger commitment to achieving gender equality in the workforce. Labour's distinctive antinuclear policy has been adopted by other parties. Its post–cold war foreign policy stresses regional alignments, especially with Australia, in the South Pacific and Southeast Asia, participation in multilateral peacekeeping roles, a continued liberalization of international trade and investment, and a more vigorous pursuit of international environmental protection programs.

Financing

Like membership, the party's finances are secret. Intraparty and union sources have declined as a share of the total party income. Also like membership, income fluctuates with the political environment. In 1987, for example, the private financial sector gave generously in acknowledgment of the fourth Labour government's deregulative and generally probusiness policies. By 1990, both these and party sources had contracted again, leaving the party in debt after the election.

Leadership

The party president is elected by the annual conference. The present incumbent is Michael Hirschfeld. Caucus elects the parliamentary party leader and deputy leader, usually with some regard to a North Island-South Island spread of leadership. After narrowly losing the 1993 election, Mike Moore was successfully challenged by his deputy, Helen Clark, the party's first woman leader, a graduate in political science, and former university lecturer, who represents an Auckland electorate. Her deputy, Dr. Michael Cullen, also a former academic, represents a Dunedin (South Island) electorate.

Prospects

During the transition to proportional representation and the lead-up to the 1996 election, Labour's electoral status according to opinion polls fell to a historic low level, due largely to internal tensions following the change of leadership. Labour's dominance of the center-left was at this time under challenge by the Alliance and New Zealand First parties. The 1996 election turned both the party's and the leader's fortunes around. Labour is guaranteed to be the dominant center-left party in the new MMP-based multiparty system for the foreseeable future. Nevertheless, its governing prospects are contingent on the aggregate strength of the center-left block, leading to either a Labour-led majority coalition or Labour minority government.

NATIONAL PARTY

History

After Labour's electoral success in 1935, the two non-Labour parliamentary opposition parties—Reform and United—merged to form the National Party in 1936. They were joined by a newer grouping, the Democrats, to create the foundations of a single conservative party spanning rural and wealthier city interests. The formation of National marked also the beginning of a long period of two-party dominance in parliamentary politics, which, although weakening after the 1970s, lasted effectively until the transition to proportional representation after 1993. National remained in opposition under its first leader, Adam Hamilton, but began to make electoral advances under S. G. Holland in the 1940s, first winning back the rural electorates it had lost to Labour in 1935 and 1938 and finally attaining a parliamentary majority in 1949. By 1999, National will have governed alone or in coalition for nearly 40 of the last 50 years. This parliamentary dominance owed much to the first-past-the-post electoral system, which enabled the party to achieve clear parliamentary majorities despite only once, in 1951, winning a majority of votes. A second reason for National's disproportionate tenure of office was its pragmatic moderation in government, administering a regulated mixed economy strongly tied to the protected British commodity market until the 1970s and maintaining the welfare state developed by the first Labour government. Thirdly, National benefited from the stable, effective leadership associated with Sir Keith Holyoake (1957–72) and Sir Robert Muldoon (1974–84). Out of office for only two separate single terms, 1957–60 and 1972–75, National's dominance was finally undermined not only by the Labour opposition but from within the party by those who had begun to subscribe to the free-market, small-state thinking in the late 20th century. Attacked from the right and the left, National was defeated in 1984, only to return in a landslide win in 1990. Since then it has proceeded along the path of economic reform and restructuring initiated by the fourth Labour government. After the first MMP election in 1996, National continued to govern in a majority coalition with New Zealand First.

Organization

Members, defined as those eligible to vote who pay a subscription to the party, are organized in geographical branches of at least 20 members within electorates. The electorate committees, consisting of representatives of branches, are, however, the basic effective units of the grassroots level of organization. National's regional organization is more developed and influential than Labour's. National's five regional divisions model the overall party organization, holding annual conferences, electing officers, dealing with policy matters, and, since 1996, rank-ing list candidates from within the region. The activities of the divisions are initiated and coordinated by elected divisional councils and executives. The party's annual conference comprises representatives of the electorate and divisional levels of organization. The conference elects the officers of the party, considers selected policy remits, and ratifies any constitutional changes. It is not as influential in policy matters as Labour's conference. Paralleling the general organization at electorate, divisional, and central levels are separate structures for women, youth, Maori, and in the Auckland division, Pacific Islanders. Parliamentary members participate primarily at divisional and central levels. The powerful central organs of the party consist, first, of the national management board, comprising the organizational and parliamentary leaderships, women's, youth's, and Maori vice presidents, and divisional representatives, and, second, five committees of the board, dealing with strategy, rules, policy, Maori advice, and the executive of the youth branch (Young Nationals).

Membership and Constituency

National has been more successful than Labour in mobilizing and maintaining a mass membership. As for Labour, however, the long-term trend is one of erratic decline, from a high of 246,000 to the present figure of approximately 40,000. National's constituency is strongest in rural regions and among the self-employed, higher-income groups, private-sector employees, and churchgoers and is slightly stronger among men than women.

Policy

In its own statement of principles, National emphasizes its belief in an "open, competitive economy, driven by the private sector and valuing individual effort and initiative." In the social sphere it identifies the traditional family unit as the source of norms of "personal and family responsibility" and the values of hard work and enterprise. In government, National has accelerated the policies of the previous Labour government in relation to privatization of state assets, market liberalization, managerialist practices throughout the public service, including the health sector, moves toward a flatter income tax regime, a tight rein on welfare costs and benefit levels, and a high priority on reduction of the level of the national debt. Once heavily influenced by a powerful rural lobby, National is now more closely aligned with business interests. In a major policy reversal in 1989, National adopted Labour's domestic and military antinuclear stance. There is little practical difference between National's and Labour's foreign policies.

Financing

Sources and amounts are secret. However, National has usually been the wealthier of the two major parties, sustained by personal contributions and fund-raising among its substantial membership, along with donations from business and wealthy supporters.

Leadership

The party has had only eight leaders since its formation, four of whom held the office for more than 10 years each. Caucus dissatisfaction with the 1996 campaign performance of the leader and prime minister, Jim Bolger, and unease over the coalition government's falling popularity, led to his replacement in December 1997 by Jenny Shipley, who thus became the first woman to lead National and New Zealand's first woman prime minister. The party president is elected by the annual conference, the present incumbent being John Slater.

Prospects

National has survived the transition to proportional representation to become the dominant party of the center-right block, but with its future governing status dependent on the parliamentary strength of potential coalition partners or parties prepared to support a minority National government. Its electoral and parliamentary presence is contingent also on its ability to check the development of an assertive free-market party to its right, while at the same time maintaining the support of its more moderate, pragmatic constituency.

MINOR POLITICAL PARTIES

Alliance

The Alliance is itself a coalition of minor parties (New Labour, Greens (until 1997), Mana Motuhake, Democrats, Liberals). It is a grouping forged before the 1993 election in an attempt to surmount the disadvantages of small parties under the then first-past-the-post electoral system. The Alliance's share of the vote reached 18% in 1993, before contracting again to 10% in 1996, thus dashing its chance of replacing Labour as the main opposition party to National under MMP. Alliance stands for more traditional social democratic egalitarian values and state interventionist policies. Under MMP, the Alliance is seen as Labour's most likely coalition partner or support party.

NewLabour, the dominant component of the Alliance, is a splinter party formed in 1989 by Jim Anderton, a former Labour MP and president of the party, who split from Labour in protest at the direction and social consequences of the fourth Labour government's policies. Anderton has been the driving force behind first NewLabour and subsequently the Alliance. Their electoral support owed much to his popularity.

The Green party originated in 1972 as the Values party. It was re-formed as the Aotearoa Green party to contest the 1990 election and, benefiting from a large protest vote against the Labour government, attained nearly 7% of the vote. It contested the 1993 and 1996 elections as part of the Alliance. However, in November 1997, the party withdrew from the Alliance, preferring to take its chance again as a separate party in the new MMP environment.

Mana Motuhake, a Maori party, was formed in 1979 by Matiu Rata, a former Labour Cabinet minister, to advance the social and economic status of Maori and to argue for greater self-determination for Maori in New Zealand society. Mana Motuhake threatened Labour's hold on the Maori seats in 1981, but its vote declined after that. Under the Alliance umbrella in 1993 and 1996, Sandra Lee, the deputy leader and for a time leader of the Alliance, became Mana Motuhake's first and only MP.

The Democratic party is descended from the Social Credit Political League, which contested its first general election in 1954. Over the years, the distinctive social credit doctrines of monetary reform have been reduced in significance. Joining the Alliance in 1992, the Democrats brought with them few potential voters but a useful core of party workers and a source of funds.

The Liberal party's presence in the Alliance is of little significance. The party was formed in 1992 by two National MPs in protest of their government's policies of economic liberalization and social retrenchment.

New Zealand First

The party is synonymous with its founder and leader, Winston Peters, a Maori and a long-standing National MP, who, after a short, stormy period as minister of Maori affairs, was dismissed from the Cabinet in 1991 and expelled from the caucus in 1992; he finally split from his party in 1993 by resigning from Parliament and forcing a by-election in his seat of Tauranga. Peters, whom polls identified as the country's most popular politician, easily won the by-election and founded his own party, New Zealand First, in July 1993. The party won 8.4% of the vote in the general election a few months later, and Peters was again returned to Parliament. In the unstable transition to MMP between 1993 and 1996, Peters capitalized on his continuing personal standing, his espousal of populist issues, and a widespread sense of discontent with the major parties to place his party electorally in a pivotal balance-of-power position between Labour and National. New Zealand First won 13.4% of the vote in 1996. In a historic realignment of Maori partisanship, New Zealand First candidates won all five Maori electorates. After prolonged negotiations with both Labour and National, Peters entered into a majority coalition with National, securing for himself the roles of treasurer and deputy prime minister and a further eight ministerial positions for his party. Within months his and the party's ratings had slumped to very low levels. Although New Zealand First was able to slow the pace of National's economic liberalization program, a majority of New Zealand First voters had expected Peters to help end the National government, not join it. The image of New Zealand First was also damaged by the inexperience of its ministerial members and the aggressive performance of the Maori MPs. In 1998 the coalition with National was dissolved and half the New Zealand First MPs left the party.

United New Zealand

In the transition to MMP, some saw a need for a party of the center to mediate between Labour and National. In 1995, three Labour or ex-Labour and five National MPs left their parties to form United, undertaking at the same time not to destabilize the incumbent National government. United won less than 1% of the vote in the 1996 election, therefore qualifying for no list MPs. National, however, did not contest the seat held by one United MP, Peter Dunne, who thus became United's sole MP after 1996.

ACT New Zealand

ACT is evidence of the deep impact on the partisan structure of New Zealand politics of neoliberal thinking and the move to proportional representation. ACT began as a lobby group advocating further market liberalization and small state politics. Roger Douglas, the reforming treasurer of the fourth Labour government, was a founding member. He was joined by people from both Labour and National backgrounds, including Richard Prebble, a former Labour Cabinet minister who became party leader in 1996, and Derek Quigley, a former National minister, forced from the Cabinet for his free-market advocacy in 1982. Generously funded from business sources, ACT outspent all other parties during the 1996 election campaign and won 6.1% of the vote. Located on the right of the political spectrum, ACT provides a potential coalition partner or support party for National.

Christian Democrats

In the period of transition to MMP, the Christian Democrats formed around an ex-National Cabinet minister, Graeme Lee, in support of Christian and family-based values and against social and sexual permissiveness. A more fundamentalist Christian Heritage Party had contested the 1990 and 1993 elections. In 1996, the two Christian parties combined as the Christian Coalition and fell only a fraction short of the 5% threshold for seats in Parliament. In 1997, the coalition dissolved, and the Christian Democrats emerged as the more politically robust of the two.

NATIONAL PROSPECTS

The party system has not yet settled to a stable post-MMP, multiparty format. It is not clear that there is a viable constituency in the center of the political spectrum for any other party between Labour and National. The balance between the center-left and right blocks, respectively, depends largely on the electoral performance of minor parties. New Zealand First is unlikely to survive beyond the 1999 election in its present form. Its possible future is as a vehicle for Maori politics, on the basis of the six Maori electorates, though only if Maori voters do not realign back to their traditional support for Labour. The withdrawal of the Greens from the Alliance weakens that party electorally, and therefore possibly the overall parliamentary strength of the center-left block, which has implications for Labour's status as a potential governing party. National, in turn, will rely for support on ACT and the Christians, if they surmount the threshold. Public disappointment with the functioning of the first post-MMP coalition may lead to modifications to the electoral system. Cutting the number of party list MPs to produce a smaller Parliament is a popular option.

Further Reading

Boston, J., S. Levine, E. McLeay, and N. Roberts. *New Zealand under MMP: A New Politics?* Auckland: Auckland University Press, 1996.

Bush, Graham. *Local Government and Politics in New Zealand*, 2d ed. Auckland: Auckland University Press, 1995.

Miller, Raymond, ed. *New Zealand Politics in Transition.* Auckland: Oxford University Press, 1997.

Mulgan, Richard. *Politics in New Zealand*, 2d ed. Auckland: Auckland University Press, 1997.

Palmer, Geoffrey, and Matthew Palmer. *Bridled Power: New Zealand Government under MMP.* Auckland: Oxford University Press,1997.

Rice, G.W., ed. *The Oxford History of New Zealand*, 2d ed. Auckland: Oxford University Press, 1992.

Vowles, Jack, and Peter Aimer. *Voters' Vengeance. The 1990 Election in New Zealand and the Fate of the Fourth Labour Government.* Auckland: Auckland University Press, 1993

Vowles, J., P. Aimer, H. Catt, J. Lamare, and R. Miller. *Towards Consensus? The 1993 Election in New Zealand and the Transition to Proportional Representation.* Auckland: Auckland University Press, 1995.

Vowles, J., P. Aimer, S. Banducci, and J. Karp, eds. *Voters' Victory? The First MMP Election in New Zealand.* Auckland: Auckland University Press, 1998.

REPUBLIC OF NICARAGUA

(República de Nicaragua)

By John A. Booth, Ph.D.

THE SYSTEM OF GOVERNMENT

The Republic of Nicaragua (1998 population approximately 4.5 million) spans the Central American isthmus between Honduras and Costa Rica. From the 1970s through the early 1990s Nicaragua experienced repeated economic crises, two civil wars, and a massive foreign intervention as it passed from rightist dictatorship through Marxist-led revolution to electoral democracy. The Somoza dynasty ruled Nicaragua (1936–79) using the National Guard and the Liberal Nationalist Party as its instruments of control. A violent 1978–79 insurrection toppled the Somozas and brought to power a revolutionary coalition dominated by the Sandinista National Liberation Front (FSLN). The Marxist-Leninist FSLN, led by its national directorate, dominated the new regime and revolution and promoted extensive sociopolitical change. Opposition grew and some FSLN allies broke with the revolution. Various forces encouraged and backed by the United States rebelled against the regime. The resulting counterrevolutionary ("contra") war of the 1980s disrupted the economy and polarized Nicaraguans as the Sandinista government mobilized to defend the revolution.

Until 1984 the FSLN governed de facto through a multimember junta guided by the FSLN national directorate. Despite Sandinista dominance of public policy, other parties participated in the junta, Cabinet, and bureaucracy. Opposition parties existed openly. In 1984 the revolutionary government held a national election in which FSLN candidate Daniel Ortega Saavedra won the presidency (Table 1) and the FSLN captured about 60% of the new National Assembly (Table 2). The Assembly drafted a new constitution, effective in 1987. It established a republican, presidential government with a strong executive but with some checks and balances.

The counterrevolutionary war, the antagonism of the Reagan and Bush administrations (including an economic embargo and diplomatic opposition), economic problems aggravated by the war, embargo, and revolutionary policies, and restrictions on civil liberties deepened polarization and discontent. Pursuant to the 1987 Central American Peace Accord, the government forged

TABLE 1
Presidential Election Results (Leading Candidates), Nicaragua, 1984, 1990, and 1996

Party	Candidate	%
A. 1984 Election		
FSLN	Daniel Ortega	67
Democratic Conservative	Clemente Guido	14
Independent Liberal	Virgilio Godoy	10
Others		9
B. 1990 Election		
UNO	Violeta Chamorro	55
FSLN	Daniel Ortega	41
C. 1996 Election		
Liberal Alliance	Arnoldo Alemán	51
FSLN	Daniel Ortega	38
Christian Way	Guillermo Osorno	4
Conservative Party of Nicaragua	Noel Vidaurre	2
Others		5

Sources: Consejo Supremo Electoral; Latin American Studies Association, *The Electoral Process in Nicaragua: Domestic and International Influences* (Austin, Tex., November 19, 1984), Table 3; Latin American Studies Association, *Electoral Democracy under International Pressure* (Pittsburgh, March 15, 1990), table 3; and "How Nicaraguans Voted," *Envío* 15, nos. 185–86 (December–January 1996–1997): 40.

a cease-fire with the contras in 1989. It also imposed draconian economic stabilization measures in the late 1980s, but to little avail. In the 1990 election, 20 opposition parties formed the U.S.-backed Nicaraguan Opposition Union (UNO) coalition that nominated Violeta Barrios de Chamorro for the presidency. Winning 54% of the vote, Chamorro defeated incumbent Ortega, and the Sandinistas relinquished power.

Chamorro settled the war, demobilized the contras, and dramatically trimmed the armed forces. Her government liberalized the economy and shrank the public sector to curtail inflation, but conflict over property confiscated during the revolution blocked economic recovery. The UNO coalition in the National Assembly collapsed, leaving President Chamorro to legislate by forging transitory alliances with other parties, often including the FLSN.

In the 1996 election the Liberal Alliance (AL) led by the former Managua mayor Arnoldo Alemán Lacayo won the presidency with 51% of the vote, handing Daniel Ortega of the Sandinistas his second successive defeat (Table 1). Nicaragua's third national election since the overthrow of the Somozas and second peaceful exchange of power from an incumbent to the opposition definitively signaled the end of the Sandinista revolution.

Executive

The 1987 constitution vested great executive authority in a reelectable presidency with a six-year term. The president had a virtual monopoly of budgeting and enjoyed decree authority. Combined with the strong FSLN majority in the National Assembly, these powers weakened formal constitutional checks upon executive authority. The FSLN's defeat in 1990 triggered a long struggle to curtail presidential power. Reform efforts, resisted by President Chamorro, sparked a protracted legislative-constitutional crisis. Legislation and constitutional amendments trimming executive authority finally passed in 1996.

Nicaragua's president now serves for five years, may not seek immediate reelection, and has a two-term maximum. (The next presidential election is in 2001.) The president appoints Cabinet ministers and ambassadors and shares both the appointment of the Supreme Court and Supreme Electoral Council and budgeting and fiscal authority with the National Assembly. The 1996 reforms divide presidential military and decree powers with the National Assembly, which also won new powers to hold executive officials accountable.

Restructured by the revolution in the 1980s and again by UNO in the 1990s, the Nicaraguan executive branch has experienced dramatic alterations in its size and mission. The revolution dramatically expanded government's size and scope with new economic and welfare functions. Neoliberal reforms begun in the late 1980s and extended by the Chamorro government radically retrenched the public sector, curtailing services, state economic regulation and ownership, and the government's budget and payroll. The government slashed spending, privatized hundreds of stated-owned firms, and ended its banking monopoly. The military and police, dominated by the FSLN during the revolution, were depoliticized. The police were civilianized and the army's forces cut 80%.

Legislature

Nicaragua's legislature is the unicameral National Assembly (Asamblea Nacional). In 1996 the Assembly's term of office increased to five years, with the next election scheduled for 2001. The Assembly has 90 regular seats for deputies (diputados), plus one additional seat for the losing presidential candidate of each party winning over 1.5% of the presidential vote.

Nicaraguans elect deputies from two lists: the 20-seat national list is allocated among the parties in proportion to their share of the national list vote; 70 regular departmental seats are elected from party slates from each of the 15 departments and two autonomous regions, apportioned by population. Distribution of winning seats within each department/region is in proportion to party vote share. Table 2 contains recent Assembly election results.

TABLE 2
Seats in Nicaraguan National Assembly, 1984–2001

Party[a]	1984–90	1990–96	Nat'l	1996–2001 Dept'l	Total[b]
FSLN	61	39[c]	8	27	36
PDC	14				
PLI	9				
PPSC	6				
UNO		51[d]			
AL			9	33	42
CC			1	2	4
PCN			1	1	3
PN			1	1	2
Others	6	2		6	6
Total Seats	96	92	20	70	93

Sources: Consejo Supremo Electoral; Latin American Studies Association, *The Electoral Process in Nicaragua: Domestic and International Influences* (Austin, Tex.: November 19, 1984), table 3; Latin American Studies Association, *Electoral Democracy Under International Pressure* (Pittsburgh: March 15, 1990), table 4; and "How Nicaraguans Voted," *Envío* 15, nos. 185–86 (December–January 1996–97): 40 (with corrections by the author), and "Split Down the Middle, *Barricada Internacional*, no. 403 (December 1996): 8–9.

[a]Party names: FSLN = Sandinista National Liberation Front; PDC = Democratic Conservative Party; PLI = Independent Liberal Party; PPSC = Popular Social Christian Party; UNO = Nicaraguan Opposition Union; AL = Liberal Alliance; PCN = Conservative Party of Nicaragua; CC = Christian Way; PN = National Project.

[b]Total seats for 1996 include an extra seat each for losing presidential candidates for three parties (FSLN, Christian Way, and the PCN).

[c]Split ca. 1995 between 7 hard-line FSLN deputies led by D. Ortega and 31 MRS-identified deputies led by S. Ramírez.

[d]Fragmented ca. 1990–91 into various factions.

The National Assembly is presided over by a president, secretary, and other officers elected by the membership. Subject-area committees handle legislation; their makeup is distributed in rough proportion to parties' shares of deputies. The larger parties' caucuses shape legislation through committee action and maintaining voting discipline. The FLSN caucus has sometimes boycotted Assembly sessions to block a quorum and thus prevent legislation.

Few clear trends have emerged in the two legislative elections since 1990. President Alemán's Liberal Alliance coalesced with other conservative parties in 1996 to forge a legislative majority excluding the FSLN. The AL caucus and its coalition in the 1996–2001 Assembly appeared more coherent and likely more stable than those of UNO during the 1990–96 term.

The executive-legislative power balance tilted strongly away from the Assembly until 1996. The fractious Assembly of 1995–96 attempted to limit executive power, provoking a political crisis eventually mediated by international brokers. The resulting reforms shifted power toward the National Assembly.

Because the Assembly may amend the constitution by a 60% vote, the legislative-executive balance of power (indeed, constitutional provisions in general) may remain unstable.

Judiciary

Nicaragua's legal system follows the civil law tradition, based upon legislated codes. The judiciary established under the 1987 constitution includes a Supreme Court (*Tribunal Supremo*) and civil and criminal lower courts. The Supreme Court's 12 magistrates (appointed by the National Assembly) sit as members of four specialized benches (criminal, civil, constitutional and administrative). Under the 1987 constitution, the president submitted a list of candidates from which the Assembly had to choose, but 1996 reforms freed the Assembly to appoint magistrates not among the president's nominees. The Assembly also won the power to remove judges for diverse motives, including vaguely defined inappropriate moral or political conduct. The reforms also extended magistrates' terms of office from five to seven years, gave the Court jurisdiction over disputes among the branches of government, and doubled the judiciary's share of the national budget to 4%. The president of Nicaragua formerly designated the Court's president, but since 1996 the magistrates themselves annually elect their president.

Prior to 1996, critics viewed the Court as too subservient to the presidency and the FSLN, largely unchecked by the legislature, and underfunded. The reforms rectified those problems but now raise concerns that the Court's dependency upon the National Assembly permits legislative manipulation of the courts.

Regional and Local Government

Nicaragua's political subdivisions consist of 15 departments and two autonomous regions. Departments per se have very limited functions, serving mainly as subdivisions for the election of the 70 departmental list members of the National Assembly and some administrative responsibilities for the national government. The autonomous regions of the Atlantic coast, formed during the revolution, have more functions than departments. Responding to disaffection among ethnic and racial groups of the Atlantic zone, the revolutionary government gave the autonomous regions quasi-federal status. Each has an elected regional council with certain legislative and administrative authority and resources beyond those of the departments.

Departments are subdivided into 145 municipalities (*municipios*—analogous to counties), each headed by an elected mayor (*alcalde*) and councils. Municipal councils vary in size according to local population, ranging from Managua's 16 members down to four members for municipalities of under 30,000. The mayor, elected separately, chairs the municipal council. The 1966 electoral reforms set municipal office terms at four years, with the next election scheduled in 2000.

Municipalities have local authority, including modest powers to tax, regulate, and promote development. Traditionally underfunded because of limited taxing authority, municipalities receive additional funding from the national government.

THE ELECTORAL SYSTEM

Nicaragua employs direct elections for all offices. The voting age is 16. The presidential–vice presidential ticket requires a 45% plurality to avoid a runoff between the top two candidates. Mayors win by simple plurality votes. Seats in the National Assembly (both national and departmental lists), the Central American Parliament, and on all municipal councils are distributed among the contending parties by proportional representation. Citizens vote for slates of candidates nominated by parties on both Assembly and municipal ballots.

Nicaragua has a fourth governmental branch that administers elections. Established in 1984, the five member Supreme Electoral Council (*Consejo Supremo Electoral*; CSE) is appointed by the National Assembly. The CSE handles voter registration, election organization and administration, and resolution of electoral disputes.

In the early 1990s the CSE began developing national civil registry functions, including issuing to all citizens a national identity card (*cédula*) that doubles as a voter registration document. Unable to complete this process prior to the 1996 general election, the CSE employed two ad hoc strategies to register voters. Despite multiple systems, the CSE successfully registered voters and delivered documents.

Until 1995 a majority of CSE magistrates and staff came from FSLN ranks. Despite its partisan cadres, the CSE earned a reputation for technical competence and nonpartisanship during the 1984 and 1990 elections. Reforms undertaken by the National Assembly in 1996, however, reorganized the CSE and caused numerous flaws in the 1996 general election:

(1) New elections were added (the Assembly's national list, the Central American Parliament, and mayors) to those for president, Assembly, and municipal councils, doubling the number of ballots.

(2) Departmental list Assembly seats were reorganized using the departments and autonomous regions as the districts represented (formerly nine administrative regions).

(3) Appointment of departmental and local electoral staff was revamped, with party nominees replacing selection by the CSE. This transformed the CSE from a predominantly technical bureaucracy into a multiparty-penetrated one with inexperienced personnel. As the election approached, the parties delayed their nominations for local polling officials, snarling the electoral apparatus.

(4) The number of polling places (*juntas receptoras de votos*; JRVs) was doubled over 1990, to almost 9,000.

(5) Despite these changes the National Assembly funded the CSE at the same level as in 1990. Mariano Fiallos, CSE president since 1984, resigned to protest the disruptions and poor funding.

These problems led to difficulty preparing and delivering election materials, JRV operational errors on election day, inaccurate early count reports, and delayed final counting. Revelations of anomalies delayed the final count and audit of the vote. Ultimately the CSE discarded the results of over 5% of the JRVs—mainly from Managua, Jinotega, and Matagalpa. Nevertheless, Liberal candidate Alemán's victory margin was sufficient that not even all the disallowed votes having gone to Ortega would have caused a runoff. Less clear, however, is whether the irregularities had similarly negligible impact upon legislative and municipal races. In those, seats were allocated by proportional representation, giving small numbers of votes considerable potential marginal impact.

THE PARTY SYSTEM

Origins of the Parties

Nicaragua's party system retains traits that originated in the late colonial era. Factions of promonarchy Conservatives from around Granada and proindependence Liberals from the León area evolved into extended clans with regional bases that survive today. Independence from Spain (1821) and inclusion into the Central American Republic (1823) eventually pitted Liberals and Conservatives in a nearly continuous violent competition that hardened regional partisan identification and cyclical political violence. By the early 20th century, most Liberal-Conservative ideological differences had vanished, but violent civil clashes persisted.

The United States intervened heavily in Nicaraguan politics after 1909 to protect its transisthmian canal monopoly in Panama. U.S. Marines occupied Nicaragua for most of the period from 1909 to 1925 in support of Conservative governments. A Liberal revolt in 1926 led to another U.S. occupation and a truce between the combatants that let the Liberals assume power in 1932. One Liberal general, the anti-interventionist revolutionary Augusto Sandino, rejected the truce and waged a six-year guerrilla struggle against the U.S.-trained Nicaraguan National Guard. Without defeating Sandino, the United States withdrew its troops in 1933.

The legacy of U.S. occupation included weakened political institutions, anti-American resentment, and the National Guard. At the head of the Guard was Anastasio Somoza García, a Liberal who had Sandino assassinated in 1933 and in 1936 seized ruling power. Somoza García took over the Liberal Party (renamed Liberal Nationalist) as a tool to control government and distribute graft. He employed the Guard to repress opponents and manipulated U.S. ties to bolster his power. Beginning in 1948, Somoza García countered prodemocracy sentiment by co-opting Conservatives into the government with a share of offices and spoils. These arrangements continued after his 1956 assassination; his sons Luis and Anastasio Somoza Debayle succeeded him in control of the presidency, National Guard, and PLN.

Several parties arose to protest Somocista National Liberalism and collaborationist Conservatism; others were ideological movements. The Independent Liberal Party (*Partido Liberal Independiente*; PLI) split from the PLN in the 1940s. The pro-Soviet Nicaraguan Socialist Party (*Partido Socialista Nicaragüense*; PSN) appeared in the 1940s, and the Christian democratic-aligned Social Christian Party arose in the 1950s, each developing a significant base in the labor movement.

This century's most important new political movement has been the Sandinista National Liberation Front, formed in 1961 as a Marxist guerrilla group drawing members from the disaffected of other parties and anti-Somoza movements. FSLN rule dramatically altered the party spectrum. The Sandinista party dominated politics during the 1980s and has survived its electoral defeats of 1990 and 1996 able to marshal a large minority vote.

The revolution shattered the old party system. It outlawed the PLN and collaborationist Conservative splinters but permitted other political parties to develop and contend for power. Older anti-Somocista parties like the PLI, Social Christians, and some Conservatives took part in the FSLN-led coalition government of 1979–84, as did several new parties—the latter typically personalistic rather than ideological. Outside of Nicaragua, ex-PLN and National Guard figures, dissident Sandinistas, and alienated former FSLN collaborators from other parties formed new parties or revived old ones in opposition to the FSLN. One expression of this anti-Sandinism was the U.S.-backed contras, who emphasized guerrilla insurgency. The contras (several coalitions of divergent interests and personalities) failed to form a coherent political movement after the 1989 cease-fire and had fragmented into and among various parties by the 1990 election.

The other major anti-Sandinista movement was the several new internal opposition parties that appeared in the late 1980s. Many received support from the United States or from social democratic, liberal, and Christian democratic party international organizations. In the 1990 vote the United States labored assiduously to defeat the FLSN. It encouraged 20 ideologically diverse parties, old and new, to form the Nicaraguan Opposition Union (*Unión Nicaragüense Opositora*; UNO) and nominate Violeta Barrios de Chamorro for president. Although victorious, Violeta Chamorro's UNO coalition soon fragmented.

The 1990 election law provided for disbanding unsuccessful parties, but liberal rules governing party formation permitted a multiplication of groups by the 1996 election, eventually contested by over 40 parties and coalitions. The FSLN retained about 38% of the national vote. The reformist Sandinista splinter MRS fared poorly, as did Conservatives (Tables 1 and 2). The big news was the resurgence of the Liberals behind Arnoldo Alemán. A coalition of Alemán's Liberal Constitutionalists and other groups, the Liberal Alliance attracted back to Nicaragua many exiled Liberals, including personalities once associated with the Somozas' PLN.

Party Organization

Great organizational differences exist between the FSLN and other parties. The FSLN is a mass-based, ideological party with an elaborate bureaucratic structure. During the revolution it had large ancillary organizations among women, youth, communities, labor, and peasants. Since the FSLN's 1990 electoral defeat it has effectively lost most such groups. Long dominated by its original revolutionary directorate, the FLSN added new members to the DN in the early 1990s. Despite reforms, various moderates led by the former vice president Sergio Ramírez Mercado defected to form the MRS, which failed to woo many votes away from the FSLN in 1996. Out of power, the FSLN not only lost mid-level leadership to the MRS and to disenchantment but also developed funding problems.

Except for the Liberals and Conservatives, other parties tend to be small and formed around an ideology (Socialists, Social Christians, Independent Liberals), interest group, or personality. From this amalgam, two big anti-Sandinista coalitions have arisen to dominate postrevolutionary politics. In 1990, UNO rallied behind the unifying personality of Violeta Chamorro, a Conservative by background but nominally and recently a member of the new Social Democratic Party. Chamorro headed an extended clan that ran all of Nicaragua's main newspapers: the FSLN's *Barricada*, pro-FSLN *El Nuevo Diario*, and the opposition *La Prensa*. In 1996, Arnoldo Alemán pulled several Liberal factions, some unions, and some Conservatives into the AL.

Campaigning

Before 1979, campaigns were ritualistic; the regime so manipulated results that it was unaffected by campaigns. When the opposition campaigned effectively, the National Guard usually disrupted the activity. Since the 1980s, with outcomes more in doubt, campaigning by the FSLN and its major opponents has become more open, civil, organized, and modern.

Nicaragua's 1984, 1990, and 1996 elections were among the most highly and systematically monitored votes ever conducted anywhere. In 1984 the revolutionary government invited hundreds of journalists, scholars, and foreign governmental representatives as election observers in hopes of improving the regime's legitimacy. Registered, legally participating parties campaigned without problems, but progovernment crowds disrupted events of the Democratic Coordinating Committee, an anti-Sandinista, U.S.-backed coalition that did not contest but sought to disrupt the election. Press and civil liberties restrictions stemming from the contra war were lifted to permit open campaigning, but opinion polling was not allowed. Outside observers characterized the election as flawed by the weakness of the FSLN's opponents and by U.S. efforts to disrupt the vote but fair in terms of the opposition's freedom to campaign and media access.

In 1990, with even more external observation, the FSLN confronted a stronger, better financed, and more unified opponent, UNO. Campaigning was open and intense. External observer missions of the United Nations, Organization of American States, and Carter Center facilitated the campaign and mediated disputes. Parties had access to subsidized mass media, and both the FSLN and UNO received considerable external funding and technical advice. Both UNO and the Sandinistas used public-opinion polling and sophisticated advertising. Despite a violent clash between UNO and FSLN partisans at a rally in Nandaime and other lesser incidents, external observers helped cool the acrimonious environment. The opposition's win bore witness to the fairness of the 1990 campaign and election.

In 1996, a reduced external observer contingent took part, but several thousand domestic observers from nongovernmental organizations (NGOs) and tens of thousands of party poll watchers scrutinized the process. The largest NGO involved was Ethics and Transparency (*Etica y Transparencia*; ET), a broad civil society coalition that fielded several thousand observers. Compared with 1984 and 1990, 1996 was less tense (the war having ended and partisan acrimony marginally diminished). Larger parties and the press polled extensively. The FSLN and the AL smeared each other enthusiastically by referring to ugly aspects of prior regimes, but otherwise interparty relations were generally civil.

Three other forces have played significant roles in recent Nicaraguan election campaigns—the Catholic Church, foreign political parties, and foreign governments. The church has often expressed its distaste for the Sandinistas. For example, during the final days of the 1996 campaign Cardinal Miguel Obando y Bravo, a harsh critic of the FSLN both during and after the revolution, held a televised mass that encouraged citizens to vote against the FSLN.

Foreign political parties have supported ideologically similar Nicaraguan parties with funding and technical assistance during recent campaigns.

Foreign governments have played diverse roles. Spain and the Nordic countries have provided technical assistance to the Supreme Electoral Council (CSE) to facilitate the conduct of the election. U.S. intervention has varied according to whether the FSLN held power and the prospects of the Sandinistas' opponents. In 1984 the United States denounced the CSE and tried to disrupt the election. In 1990 the United States both criticized the CSE and the campaign as unfair while heavily backing UNO. In 1996 the United States provided extensive technical assistance to the CSE, a new role. Meanwhile the U.S. embassy in Managua proclaimed formal neutrality, but the State Department in Washington made clear it hoped the FSLN would lose.

Independent Voters

Identifying independent voters in Nicaragua is difficult given the instability of voting patterns since 1984. The FSLN's share of the vote fell from 67% in 1984 to 38% in 1996. The party system and allegiance are fragmented and personalistic, somewhat masking patterns of support for parties other than the FSLN. A large shift in party support occurred from 1990 to 1996, and UNO and AL consisted of different party coalitions.

In addition to the numerous loyal FSLN identifiers there are contingents (of size unknown) of strong identifiers with other parties—especially Liberals and Conserv-

atives—and small nuclei of Independent Liberals, Social Christians, and Socialists. Outside these core identifiers, however, a substantial but indeterminate portion of Nicaraguans appeared to vote in 1990 and 1996 on the basis of candidate personality, ideology, or policy preference. Opinion polling so far offers scant insight into the phenomenon because of the recent great shifts in party support. Ultimately, shifting party identification and voting per se constitute voter independence.

SANDINISTA NATIONAL LIBERATION FRONT
(Frente Sandinista de Liberación Nacional; FSLN)

Carlos Fonseca Amador founded the FSLN in 1961 to pursue a revolutionary guerrilla struggle against the Somoza regime. A Marxist-Leninist, he had abandoned the Nicaraguan Socialist Party because it rejected armed struggle. Fonseca's cofounders were Tomás Borge Martínez, a former Independent Liberal activist, and Silvio Mayorga—both also Marxists. All three were from Matagalpa (a region once loyal to Sandino), had been student activists at the National University, and had suffered imprisonment for their antiregime efforts.

Until the mid-1970s the Sandinistas operated as a guerrilla force in the mountainous northern jungles and grew very slowly. Limited support from Cuba and urban and university groups developed despite major military reversals in 1963 and 1967. In the mid-1970s growing public opposition to the Somoza regime evoked escalated repression. This drove disaffected elites, repressed civil society, and many ordinary citizens into the arms of the FSLN, the only armed challenger of the regime. The FSLN divided into three "tendencies" over tactics in the mid-1970s, a schism resolved by the spontaneous popular uprisings of 1978. The FSLN grew rapidly in late 1978 and 1979, drawing civil society into an anti-Somoza coalition and recruiting as many as 5,000 troops. After its final offensive defeated the Guard, the FSLN assumed leadership of the rebel coalition that took power on July 19, 1979. Within months the Sandinistas consolidated control of the revolutionary government.

ORGANIZATION

The FSLN developed a complex nationwide structure supported by ancillary organizations of students, women, peasants, workers, and neighborhood organizations. Until the 1990s, a nine-member national directorate (*Dirección Nacional*; DN) of top military commanders from the insurrection headed the party. DN members served on the junta through 1984 and held key Cabinet and military portfolios until 1990. Throughout the revolutionary era the armed forces and police were fused with the FSLN. FSLN cadre penetrated the government bureaucracy.

By the late 1980s hard times had eroded or alienated the FSLN's ancillary organizations. The electoral defeat of 1990 dealt the party several further blows. The FSLN lost control of the police. The military (albeit retaining Sandinista officers) was dramatically downsized and its party links severed. The Chamorro administration began reversing revolutionary policies. Feeling its way as an opposition party in the National Assembly, the FSLN struggled to salvage what it could of its policy legacy. The party debated its political errors and sought a strategy for the long term. Party congresses in 1991 and 1994 sought to regroup and revise its charter. The 1991 congress reorganized the party, but the DN blocked important democratization initiatives. The party congress became the FSLN's highest authority. An elected (by secret ballot among members) party assembly would govern between congresses. A new party secretary-generalship was established, to which the congress elected the old guard's Daniel Ortega.

Major fissures appeared in the FSLN's leadership, in part because harder-line, old-guard leaders resisted certain intellectuals' reform proposals. Social democratic "renovationists" led by the former vice president Sergio Ramírez Mercado pushed for further reforms. The Sandinista bench in the National Assembly split, most of the deputies aligning with the renovationists. Rebuffed and punished by the 1994 congress, key reformers bolted the party and established the splinter Sandinista Renovation Movement. However, the "democratic left" old guard remained united behind Daniel Ortega. The 1994 congress enacted deeper reforms: new members on the DN (including the first women), the election of party leadership, primary elections for party nominees for public office, and assigning women 30% of legislative slates. Despite such efforts, Daniel Ortega's leadership of the party became more powerfully entrenched in the late 1990s. Party rank and file rallied around him in 1998 when his stepdaughter publicly accused him of sexually molesting her when she was an adolescent.

POLICY

Although Marxist-Leninist, the FSLN experimented widely and pragmatically with its goals and policies. Early objectives included eliminating the Somoza dictatorship, improving popular living standards and participation in decision making, progressive socialization of the economy, and reducing U.S. influence over Nicaragua. Once in power the FSLN openly pursued many of these policies. It greatly expanded government participation in the economy, redistributed agricultural land and firms owned by the Somozas and their allies to cooperatives of peasants and workers, and established a panoply of new health, education, and welfare services. The FSLN's pragmatism stood out in several arenas: In concession to its geopolitical context and the dominant

U.S. regional role, the revolutionary regime retained a private sector, permitted opposition parties and independent media and civil society, held elections, and remained formally unaligned with the Soviet bloc.

Economic and geopolitical strains forced the FSLN to improvise and change just to salvage the revolution during the mid- and late-1980s. Capital flight, a U.S. economic embargo, revolutionary policy blunders, and the contra war demolished the economy. To finance military mobilization and the war, the government curtailed public services. Political and civil liberties decreased when the contra war intensified, and increased around elections.

The 1990 electoral defeat and the demise of Soviet bloc economic support forced further FSLN policy changes. The outgoing FSLN-dominated National Assembly in 1990 approved a widespread distribution of government and confiscated private property to party leaders and members. This shameful "*piñata*" embarrassed on the party and exacerbated the byzantine complexity of property ownership disputes generated by the revolution. After 1990 the FSLN generally embraced the role of loyal opposition but never definitively renounced recourse to violence. In effect the party behaved moderately, oscillating between two tactics: (1) using its remaining mobilizational capacity to challenge rollbacks of revolutionary policies, and (2) using its National Assembly votes to cooperate ("cogovern") with the Chamorro government in exchange for concessions.

MEMBERSHIP AND CONSTITUENCY

The FSLN drew its first members from the insurgent forces of the 1960s and 1970s. During the revolution it brought in tens of thousands of new members by recruiting from support groups and the armed forces. Since losing power, the FSLN has become an even more broadly based membership organization, claiming 350,000 members in 1996 despite the defection of the MRS. Current FSLN support comes disproportionately from León, Estelé, and Managua and from the middle class.

LEADERSHIP

Major Sandinista leaders come primarily from middle-class backgrounds, many recruited out of Liberal and Conservative families into the armed struggle through student opposition to the Somozas or as victims of repression. National directorate membership remained unchanged until 1991, consisting exclusively of the nine men on the body in 1979. New members have been added and some removed since 1991. Among the key DN members since 1979 have been:

- **Tomás Borge Martínez**, born in 1930 of middle-class parents affiliated with the Independent Liberals. He studied law and owned a bookstore before cofounding the FLSN in 1961. The only surviving FSLN founder, he was imprisoned twice and tortured during the Somoza regime, and the National Guard also killed his wife. From 1979 through 1990 Borge served as minister of interior.

- **Daniel Ortega Saavedra** was born in 1945 in Chontales to a middle-class family and quit the university for the FLSN. He spent several years in guerrilla combat and several more in prison for subversion. He represented the DN on the revolutionary junta from 1979 through 1984 and in 1984 was elected president of Nicaragua. Although defeated in his 1990 and 1996 reelection bids, Daniel Ortega became party secretary-general in 1991. Long regarded as a policy pragmatist, in defense of a harder party line he fended off the reformist challenge of 1994–95.

- **Humberto Ortega Saavedra**, younger brother of Daniel, lost his right hand in combat. A student of politics and guerrilla tactics, he was the insurrection's main strategist. As commander in chief of the Sandinista Popular Army (later the Nicaraguan Army) from 1979 until his retirement from that post in 1995, Humberto Ortega was the architect of Nicaragua's successful military strategy during the contra war. He resigned from the DN in 1990 to retain his military command.

- **Jaime Wheelock Román**, born in 1946 in Managua to an upper-class family, is an intellectual, theorist, and author of two books on Nicaraguan political economy. Although without combat experience, he served as minister of agrarian reform and agriculture (1979–90).

The FSLN's 1990 election defeat, subsequent internecine organizational and leadership debates, and the increasing dominance of Daniel Ortega and his allies raised problems for the party. Many loyal and experienced middle-level FSLN leaders and intellectuals quit over the party's increasing personalism and lack of ideological change. While the party retained a substantial base of loyal followers and voters, its pool of talented middle-level leaders (many veterans of the insurrection and years in power) had diminished sharply by the late 1990s.

PROSPECTS

Popular early on, the FSLN easily won its first election, but a deteriorated economy, the contra war, repression, and conflict with the United States eventually alienated many supporters. The FSLN remains strong, but its prospects for recapturing power—even with its large base—appear limited for several reasons: its depleted leadership ranks, its persistent demonization by other actors for its policy failures, Marxism, repression, and the *piñata* undermine the Sandinistas' image. The end of the cold war and loss of socialist bloc support limit resources, especially given the old guard's refusal to fully renounce violent methods. Perhaps most importantly, most other parties and many voters tend to form a working anti-Sandinista coalition for elections.

THE LIBERAL PARTIES

A cluster of parties arising from the Liberal clans has the greatest capacity to challenge the Sandinistas, as evidenced by the Liberal Alliance's 1996 national election victory.

Liberal Constitutionalist Party (Partido Liberal Constitucionalista; PLC)

The PLC first surfaced within the Somocista PLN in the late 1960s as a mildly reformist faction known as the Liberal Constitutionalist Movement (MLC). The movement distanced itself from Somoza and reconstituted itself as a party. The PLC stayed for the civic struggle within Nicaragua during the revolution and took part in government. Its economic policies follow rightist classical liberalism (favoring a small state, private property, and unfettered markets). With U.S. support and progressively antagonistic toward the FSLN and revolutionary economic policies, the PLC joined the Democratic Coordinator (*Coordinadora Democrática*; CD) that boycotted the 1984 election.

In 1990 the PLC joined UNO, and attorney Arnoldo Alemán Lacayo won the mayorship of Managua. Alemán adopted a mixture of urban populism and fierce anti-Sandinism. He leveraged the Managua municipality's patronage power, development projects, his confrontational style, and intense criticism of President Chamorro's cooperation with the FSLN to become a leading presidential contender for 1996. Having partly relegitimized Liberalism, Alemán and the PLC attracted support from the wealthy Liberal exile community in the United States. During the early 1990s the party organized nationwide, eventually claiming 150,000 members. The PLC forged the Liberal Alliance in 1995 with two other small Liberal splinter parties, some former PLN elements, and a PLI splinter, some ex-contras, and anti-Sandinista unions. Also pulled into the AL was a powerful private-sector organization known as the Superior Council of Private Enterprise (COSEP), whose former president Enrique Bolaños became the AL's vice presidential candidate. The AL campaigned for neoliberal economic policies similar to Chamorro's, judicial reform, and a reopening of the contentious property conflicts stemming from the revolution.

The PLC's and the Liberal Alliance's prospects are mixed. Having pulled together the AL and winning the presidency could strengthen the party and coalition should the economy eventually improve. However, because actually governing Nicaragua and its disastrous economy is extremely difficult, the record of the FLSN and UNO as governing parties recommends caution here. Much of the PLC/AL's success derives from Arnoldo Alemán's charisma. Unless the constitution is amended to permit reelection of the president, holding the coalition together or winning without Alemán may prove very difficult. The AL adopted a tendentious posture toward the FSLN in the National Assembly in 1997. Left critics have denounced the AL's election as the "restoration" of Somocista Liberalism.

Independent Liberal Party
(Partido Liberal Independiente; PLI)

A liberal splinter established in 1944, the PLI struggled against the Somozas and allied with the FLSN in the insurrection and the revolutionary government until 1984. Led since the late 1970s by Virgilio Godoy Reyes, a former labor minister (1979–84), the PLI entered formal opposition to the Sandinistas when it contested the 1984 election.

The PLI joined UNO in 1990, winning Godoy the vice presidency, but the party quickly broke with UNO and the Chamorro government and thereafter decried the UNO–FSLN cooperation of the mid-1990s. The PLI eschewed the AL in 1996 and finished catastrophically, with no seats in the National Assembly. Originally social democratic in ideology, the PLI's more recent image has been dominated by Godoy's anti-Sandinism.

Other Liberal Parties

The Neo-Liberal Party (*Partido Neo-Liberal*; PALI) formed in 1989, as did the Liberal Party of National Unity (*Partido Liberal de Unidad Nacional*; PLIUN). A handful of Liberals took up the Liberal Nationalist (PLN) label again in 1994. All three joined the Liberal Alliance in 1996; their prospects as independent parties appear dim.

CONSERVATIVE PARTIES

Another cluster of parties arose from the Conservative clans. The Conservative Party of Nicaragua (*Partido Conservador de Nicaragua*) dominated Nicaraguan politics for most of the 19th century but was displaced by the Liberals in 1890. U.S. military intervention (1909–28) put in power Conservatives willing to guarantee the U.S. canal monopoly in Panama, but Conservaties lost ascendancy in the 1930s in a U.S.-brokered pact. Afterward Conservatives took two approaches to

the Somoza Liberals: earnest opposition and co-opted collaboration. While the latter discredited the movement, the principled opposition of Conservatives like Fernando Agüero Rocha and martyred *La Prensa* publisher Pedro Joaquín Chamorro earned them repression and exile. Their example inspired many to oppose the dictatorship, and numerous Sandinista leaders came from Conservative backgrounds. Many Conservatives have tended toward class reconciliation orientation and support government social welfare responsibilities. The Conservatives fragmented in the late 1970s and 1980s over questions of social welfare, the revolution, whether to seek exile, and personalities.

Democratic Conservative Party
(Partido Conservador Democrático; PCD)

An independent, anti-Somoza Conservative splinter, the PCD was led by Rafaél Córdoba Rivas, a member of the governing junta, and represented in the Council of State until 1984. The party ran Clemente Guido for president in 1984. Guido advocated negotiations with the contras, an end to the state of emergency, and separating the Sandinista party from the state. The PCD captured 14% of the 1984 vote, running best in traditional southwestern Conservative strongholds. In 1990 the PCD opted out of UNO, contested the election alone, and won only 0.3% of the vote. In 1992 the PCD merged with the Social Conservatism Party (PSOC) to form the Conservative Party of Nicaragua (PCN).

Popular Conservative Alliance
(Alianza Popular Conservadora; APC)

Led by Miriam Argüello Morales, a follower of Fernando Agüero Rocha, the APC formed part of the revolution's domestic civic opposition. The APC joined the nonparticipating Democratic Coordinator in the 1984 election. The party was formally constituted in 1989 after a factional dispute over leadership within the PCN. The APC then joined UNO for the 1990 election but broke away from the governing coalition.

Social Conservatism Party
(Partido Social Conservador; PSOC)

Fernando Agüero Rocha, leader of a 1960s Conservative challenge to the Somozas, went into exile in the early years of the revolution. Eventually returning in the late 1980s seeking to recapture the leadership of the Conservatives, Agüero clashed with his former ally Miriam Argüello. Agüero founded the PSOC, which won only 0.4% of the 1990 vote. The PSOC merged into the reconstituted PCN in 1992.

National Conservative Party
(Partido Nacional Conservador; PNC)

The PNC split from the Democratic Conservatives in 1984, took an intransigent anti-FSLN position, and proclaimed sympathy to the United States and to the contras. It constituted part of UNO in 1990 (with three deputies in the National Assembly) and remained loyal to the Chamorro government throughout. The PNC merged with the PSOC and PDC into the reformed PCN in the early 1990s.

Conservative Party of Nicaragua
(Partido Conservador de Nicaragua; PCN)

This party formed in 1992 when the PDC, PNC, and PSOC merged. It reclaimed the traditional Conservative Party name. Fernando Agüero Rocha became its leader. Demonstrating some residual Conservative voter loyalty despite years of fragmentation, the PCN won three seats in the National Assembly in 1996.

Conservative National Action
(Acción Nacional Conservadora; ANC)

Originally descended from the anti-Somoza movement led by *La Prensa* editor Pedro Joaquín Chamorro, the ANC initially supported the Sandinista-led revolutionary government and held five of seven Supreme Court seats in the early years of the revolution. Later the ANC formed part of UNO and had three representatives in the National Assembly, a Cabinet post, and ambassadorships.

OTHER POLITICAL PARTIES

Christian Way
(Camino Cristiano; CC)

This new party arose from the Assemblies of God congregations of Nicaragua in the 1996 election. Its presidential candidate, Guillermo Osorno, is an Assembly of God pastor. He won 4% of the 1996 presidential vote. Osorno and three other CC deputies serve in the 1996–2001 National Assembly.

National Project
(Proyecto Nacional; PN)

Founded around 1995 by Antonio Lacayo, son-in-law and minister of the presidency to President Violeta Chamorro, the centrist PN originally appeared to be a vehicle for Lacayo's presidential candidacy. Other parties reformed the constitution with antinepotism rules that blocked his bid in 1996. The PN won two seats in the National Assembly.

Sandinista Renovation Movement
(Movimiento de Renovación Sandinista; MRS)

The Renovationists arose within the FSLN after its 1990 election loss. A reformist group headed by former vice president and DN member Sergio Ramírez and others challenged old-guard leaders to moderate the FSLN's policies. The FSLN delegation in the National Assembly sided heavily with the renovationists in 1995. When Ramírez and allies were dropped from the DN, some of them formed the new MRS that contested the 1996 election with Ramírez as its presidential candidate. Despite having attracted many FSLN intellectuals, the MRS fared poorly at the polls and captured only one Assembly seat.

Social Christian Parties

The **Social Christian Party (Partido Social Cristiano Nicaragüense; PSCN)** was founded in 1957, led the 1960s electoral movement against the Somoza dynasty, and introduced Christian democratic politics to Nicaragua. It established Christian labor unions and participated actively in university student politics in the 1960s. The more left-leaning **Popular Social Christian Party (Partido Popular Social Cristiano; PPSC)** broke away from the PSCN during the 1970s. During the revolution the PPSC supported the FSLN early on but contested the presidency in 1984 and won six seats in the National Assembly. Meanwhile, the more conservative PSCN increasingly identified with the opposition. The PPSC joined UNO in 1990, but the PSCN ran separately and won only one Assembly seat. By 1990 both the PPSC and PSCN had faded badly.

Nicaraguan Socialist Party
(Partido Socialista Nicaragüense; PSN)

The PSN was a pro-Soviet Communist party from its inception in the 1940s. It collaborated with the dictatorship from 1944 to 1948 but was later banned and repressed. It had close ties to the General Confederation of Workers (CGT) for several decades. The PSN opposed the Sandinista insurrection until its final months. In 1984 the PSN won two National Assembly seats. In 1990 with the cold war over and the revolution in trouble, the PSN joined UNO.

Nicaraguan Communist Party
(Partido Comunista de Nicaragua; PCdeN)

The was PCdeN was begun by a PSN schism in 1967. Like the PSN, the PCdeN followed Moscow's line, supported the insurrection only late, frequently criticized the FSLN during the revolution, and joined UNO in 1990.

OTHER POLITICAL FORCES

Military

The National Guard (*Guardia Nacional*; GN) was the Somozas' main instrument of political control. The FSLN's guerrilla army destroyed the Guard in 1979, though GN remnants formed the early nucleus of the contras. FSLN forces were reorganized into a new Sandinista Popular Army (*Ejército Popular Sandinista*; EPS), air force, and militia and the Sandinista Police (*Policía Sandinista*). Top FLSN leaders commanded these forces, and officers were FSLN cadre.

After the cease-fire with the contras in 1989, the 1990 election defeat of the FLSN, and the negotiated end of the contra war, the military underwent drastic changes. President Chamorro retained General Humberto Ortega as defense minister until 1995 to allay Sandinista fears of persecution of the party, although he relinquished his DN post. Troop strength was slashed 80%, the draft abolished, militias disbanded, and party identification of the police and military were dropped.

Critics feared military disloyalty to the regime after 1990, but both army and police have enforced order against labor and popular protesters and against rearmed former contra and Sandinista/EPS combatants alike.

Organized Labor

Freed from Somocista repression, the labor movement expanded greatly to encompass 250,000 workers by 1990. Before 1979, myriad unions and labor confederations existed: the General Workers Confederation (*Confederación General de Trabajadores*; CGT), the Independent General Workers Confederation (*Confederación General de Trabajadores-Independiente*; CGTI), the Social Christian Nicaraguan Workers Confederation (*Confederación de Trabajadores de Nicaragua*; CTN), and the AFL-CIO-linked Council for Union Action and Unity (*Consejo de Acción y Unidad Sindical*; CAUS). There were various associations of public employees. During the revolution independent labor lost ground to the rapidly growing FSLN-linked Sandinista Workers Confederation (*Central Sandinista de Trabajadores*; CST).

During the late 1980s the CST restrained workers in support of the FSLN government's harsh austerity programs, but this opened FSLN-CST fissures. After 1990 the FLSN lost much of its influence over the CST, which struck frequently against party wishes and formed new labor alliances such as the National Workers Front (*Frente Nacional de Trabajadores*; FNT). These strikes protested Chamorro and Alemán administration reversals of revolutionary policy gains, public-sector layoffs, and public-sector privatization. Labor confrontation won some concessions (shares for workers in privatized firms), but despite labor efforts public payrolls shrank and wages eroded.

The Association of Rural Workers (*Asociación de Trabajadores del Campo*; ATC), an FSLN-linked peasant union, arose in the 1970s. The union helped shape agrarian policy in the 1980s, winning land for many peasants and giving rise to the small landowners group UNAG (see below). Government austerity programs eventually undermined ATC loyalty to the FSLN, and the ATC in the 1990s struggled to defend peasants' shares and rights during agrarian reprivatization.

Business Groups

Private-sector interests find expression through several national chambers (e.g., commerce, industry) and through the Superior Council of Private Enterprise (*Consejo Superior de la Empresa Privada*; COSEP). COSEP and other business groups eventually opposed the Somozas in the late 1970s, then held some influence in the early revolutionary government (especially Cabinet positions). Most capitalists and such groups as COSEP soon broke with the revolution. Many joined the CD opposition coalition in 1984. By 1990 business groups became deeply committed to UNO but found themselves frustrated with the Chamorro administration's economic policies, especially the failure to resolve property claims in favor of former owners. Business interests hoped for better from the AL in 1996 because former COSEP leader Enrique Bolaños was Alemán's vice president.

One private-sector group that sprang from the revolution was the National Farmers and Cattleman's Association (*Unión Nacional de Agricultores y Ganaderos*; UNAG). The Sandinistas' ATC began as a rural labor union but gradually came to include small property holders, especially those created by agrarian reform. The interests of landless peasants and smallholders diverged enough that the UNAG separated from ATC. UNAG became an important voice for rural smallholders and increasingly independent of the FSLN. Since 1990 UNAG has worked to assist and to reconcile former Sandinsta and contra combatants who received land in the demobilization.

Former Combatants

The contra war settlement demobilized several tens of thousands of ex-combatants from the counterrevolutionary forces and EPS. Settlement terms promised land and other benefits to help them reintegrate into the economy. These programs often failed to meet ex-combatants' needs. Many then remobilized into armed groups. Rearmed groups practiced banditry to support themselves and confronted the government to win further benefits in exchange for laying down their arms anew. This turbulence persisted into the late 1990s, disrupting voter registration for the 1996 election and forcing new government concessions.

Various organizations, including small parties, arose from among the ranks of the ex-contras but have had little lasting independent effect on politics or policy. The traditional parties absorbed most ex-contra activists.

Atlantic Coastal Zone and Ethnic Minorities

Once isolated in the Atlantic coastal zone, a heterogenous population of indigenous peoples (Miskito, Sumu, Rama) and English-speaking blacks (together 10% of Nicaragua's population) was thrust into national politics by the revolution. When the Sandinista regime attempted to integrate them into the revolution and to isolate the indigenous from the contras operating from nearby Honduras, many Miskitos joined the counterrevolutionaries.

After several years of war the government in 1987 passed laws and constitutional provisions that conceded limited autonomy to the peoples of the region. This dampened Miskito resistance and the area's refugees began to return. Autonomy established two 45-member elected regional councils: the Northern Atlantic Autonomous Region (*Región Autónoma del Atlántico Norte*; RAAN) and the Southern Atlantic Autonomous Region (*Región Autónoma del Atlántico Sur*; RAAS). YATAMA, a Miskito opposition group originating among contra elements, has contested RAAN and RAAS elections with the FSLN, UNO, and the Liberals. Strong at first, in successive elections YATAMA has lost ground to these national parties and coalitions.

Religious Groups

The Roman Catholic hierarchy opposed the Somoza regime during the 1970s, influenced by social Christian doctrines and activist clergy. Many Catholics and some clergy joined or assisted the revolutionary forces and after the insurrection collaborated with the revolution. The hierarchy, however, soon swung right and opposed the FSLN-led regime. Headed by Archbishop (later Cardinal) Miguel Obando y Bravo and increasingly supported by the Vatican, the Nicaraguan church often collaborated with the revolution's domestic and armed foreign opponents. Despite a pretense of political neutrality, the church rather openly sided with UNO in the 1990 election and with the Liberal Alliance in 1996. Since 1990 the church has supported conservative shifts in national social, family, and education policy.

Much of the small Protestant community, growing quickly since the 1980s, supported the Sandinista insurrection and the revolution. Over time Protestant support for the revolution became divided. The Assembly of God–based Christian Way party, a newcomer to national politics, won four seats in the National Assembly in 1996.

NATIONAL PROSPECTS

With its 1996 election Nicaragua took another step beyond its divisive, economically devastating revolution and civil wars. The Liberal government enjoyed prospects for good U.S. relations and a chance to resolve outstanding property claims. These could stimulate economic recovery by attracting back flight capital and by encouraging foreign investment and assistance. On the other hand, the historic links between the Liberal Alliance and the Somoza-era PLN, combined with the 1996 election irregularities, recall for many a time of fraudulent elections and dictatorship.

The FSLN eventually accepted the 1996 election despite its flaws and retained its role as the leading opposition party in the National Assembly. If the FSLN continues to perform as a loyal opposition and if the electoral system can be repaired, Nicaragua may continue to consolidate its democracy. Early signs from the FSLN and AL suggested that polarization and rancor could continue. Prospects for the FSLN to win a national election seem limited while its revolutionary-era old guard, headed by Daniel Ortega, leads the party.

Nicaragua's party system appears likely to remain not only polarized but highly fragmented. Elite political culture is division-prone, election rules encourage new party formation, and independent voters remain unpredictable. The 2001 election may eventually reveal whether 1996 reestablished dominant Liberalism or was merely another temporary electoral coalition of anti-Sandinista forces. Nicaraguan democracy seems likely to remain turbulent in the middle run.

In October 1998, hurricane Mitch devastated parts of Nicaragua with floods and mudslides that killed thousands, left hundreds homeless, devastated roads and bridges, and destroyed most domestic and export crops. Despite foreign relief efforts, heavy infrastructure damage appeared likely to set economic development back badly. The catastrophe's political implications remained to be played out, but the gravity of relief and recovery needs confronted the Alemán government and Liberal Alliance Party with enormous political risks.

Further Reading

Arnove, Robert F. *Education as Contested Terrain: Nicaragua, 1979–1993.* Boulder, Colo.: Westview Press, 1994.

Booth, John A. *The End and the Beginning: The Nicaraguan Revolution.* Boulder, Colo.: Westview Press, 1985.

Booth, John A., and Patricia Bayer Richard. "The Nicaraguan Elections of October 1996." *Electoral Studies* 16 (September 1997): 386–93.

Booth, John A., and Thomas W. Walker. *Understanding Central America*. Boulder, Colo.: Westview Press, 1993.

Everingham, Mark. *Revolution and the Multiclass Coalition in Nicaragua*. Pittsburgh: University of Pittsburgh Press, 1996.

Latin American Studies Association. *Electoral Democracy under International Pressure*. Pittsburgh, March 15, 1990.

———. *The Electoral Process in Nicaragua: Domestic and International Influences*. Austin, Tex., November 19, 1984.

Merrill, Tim L., ed. *Nicaragua: A Country Study*. Washington, D.C: Federal Research Division, Library of Congress, 1994.

Prevost, Gary, and Harry E. Vanden, eds. *The Undermining of the Sandinista Revolution*. New York: St. Martin's Press, 1997.

Spalding, Rose J. *Capitalists and Revolution in Nicaragua: Opposition and Accommodation, 1979–1993*. Chapel Hill: University of North Carolina Press, 1994.

Walker, Thomas W. *Nicaragua: The Land of Sandino*. Boulder, Colo.: Westview Press, 1986.

———, ed. *Nicaragua in Revolution*. New York: Praeger, 1981.

———. *Nicaragua: The First Five Years*. New York: Praeger, 1985.

———. *Nicaragua without Illusions: Regime Transition and Structural Adjustment in the 1990s*. Wilmington, Del.: Scholarly Resources, 1997.

REPUBLIC OF NIGER

(République du Niger)

By Christopher J. Lee, M.A.

THE SYSTEM OF GOVERNMENT

Previously a part of French West Africa, Niger is a unitary republic maintaining a constitutional government within a multiparty political system. It achieved independence on August 3, 1960. It is the largest country in West Africa, covering an area of approximately 1,267,000 square kilometers. Proportionately, its population is relatively small at 8,361,000 (mid-1993 estimate), primarily due to arid conditions. Two-thirds of Niger's territory is Saharan desert. Hausas form the largest demographic group at 53% (1988 estimate), with the Djerma Songhai at 22%, Peuhls at 10%, and Tuaregs at 10%. Islam is practiced by an estimated 90% of the population. Roughly 0.5% practice Christianity and the rest traditional beliefs. Niger's capital is Niamey.

Executive

Executive authority is vested exclusively in the president as dictated by the constitution of the Fourth Republic, promulgated on May 22, 1996. National policy emanates from this authority. The prime minister has the responsibility of implementing the president's agenda. As of July 1996, the president is Brigadier General Ibrahim Baré Maïnassara. The prime minister is Ibrahim Maiyaki.

Since independence executive power has experienced significant fluctuations. Hamani Diori, leader of the Niger Progressive Party (PPN), was the first to have executive authority and followed a policy of maintaining close links with France. In April 1974, Diori was overthrown by a military coup on the basis of corruption charges. A Supreme Military Council (*Conseil Militaire Supreme*; CMS) was set up, headed by Lieutenant Colonel Seyni Kountché. Political parties were outlawed.

Nevertheless, political activism existed, and tensions within the CMS existed as well. In 1981 Kountché began to increase civilian representation in the CMS. In January 1984, a commission was established to write a "national charter." A draft was completed in 1986 and approved by a national referendum in June 1987 by 99.6% of the voters. This charter provided for nonelected, consultative bodies at local and national levels. Kountché died in November 1987.

The military chief of staff, Colonel Ali Saïbou, succeeded Kountché as head of state. In a national referendum in 1989, a constitutional motion to support continued military involvement in the government was approved. The new government was to be referred to as the Second Republic. In December 1989, Saïbou was elected to a seven-year term as president. The position of prime minister was abolished. Economic unrest in 1990 prompted an announcement of further political reform along the lines of a more pluralist system.

In July 1991, a national conference was convened to address Niger's political problems. The constitution was suspended and the government dissolved. Saïbou remained in office for an interim period, though his position was largely ceremonial. Amadou Cheiffou was appointed prime minister in October. A 15-member interim legislature was convened as well. In December 1992, a new constitution was approved by a national referendum. A presidential election followed, consisting of two rounds. In March 1993 Mahamane Ousmane, leader of the Democratic and Social Convention-Rahama (CDS-Rahama), won the election with 55.4% of the vote (approximately 35% of the total electorate voted).

Ousmane's succession brought the Third Republic. Further labor unrest developed during his administration. Moreover, a political challenge came from the National Movement for a Society of Development Nassara (MNSD-Nassara). A lack of confidence also developed within the National Assembly with Ousmane eventually dissolving this body in October 1994. This action provoked further criticism and unrest. New elections in January 1995 resulted in a MNSD-Nassara majority. Ousmane initially rejected the MNSD-Nassara's choice for prime minister, Hama Amadou, but later relented. In July 1995, tensions between the president and prime minister reached a new peak with foreign mediation from Mali,

Benin, and Togo. This tension was only temporarily resolved. Labor unrest and student protest further exacerbated political conditions.

A military coup ended the Third Republic on January 27, 1996. Led by Colonel Ibrahim Baré Maïnassara, the Council of National Health; (CSN), consisting of 12 members, was formed. The constitution was suspended, and the National Assembly was dissolved. Political parties were banned as well. The CSN aimed to reform the government and to improve economic conditions. Boukary Adji was appointed the prime minister of a transitional government. A national forum for government reform was convened in April 1996. A plan was outlined with greater power being conferred on the president. Constitutional reforms were approved by a referendum held on May 12, 1996. A presidential election was held on July 7, 1996. Political rivalries among the five candidates instigated controversy during the election.

Maïnassara won with 52.2% of the vote. The Fourth Republic was ushered in on August 7, 1996. Legislative elections were held in November 1996 with opposition parties, despite having wide support, boycotting the elections. Maïnassara supporters gained control of 52 out of 83 seats. In December 1996 the CSN was dissolved, and a new government was established.

Since 1996, tensions between Maïnassara and opposition forces, collectively existing as the Front for the Restoration and Defense of Democracy (DRDD), have continued. Social protests by various unions have taken place, as well as an attempted coup in January 1998 and a military mutiny in February 1998.

Legislature

Legislative authority is vested in a National Assembly consisting of 83 members as dictated by the 1996 constitution. Elections to this body are conducted on the basis of universal adult suffrage within a multiparty system.

Judiciary

The judicial system consists of several levels of courts. There is a Supreme Court that provides a forum for matters of national importance. The High Court of Justice was created with the sole function of indicting political officials, including the president, for matters such as treason. The Court of State Security serves as a court for martial law. Below these courts is a national court of appeal, and below this, criminal courts, courts of first instance, and labor courts handle matters at the local level.

THE ELECTORAL SYSTEM

The most recent legislative elections were held in November 1996. Candidates are chosen by universal adult suffrage. Opposition parties, united as the Front for the Restoration and Defense of Democracy, boycotted the elections despite signs of having wide support. As a result, Maïnassara supporters gained control of 52 out of 83 seats. These results held despite calls for a new election. Party activity is in decline with the government tightening control over the media and public gatherings.

The most recent presidential election was held in July 1996. The president is also elected by universal adult suffrage. Maïnassara won with 52.2% of the vote. The next pair of legislative and presidential elections will occur in 2001.

THE PARTY SYSTEM

Niger has a history of instability regarding its party system. This history has been characterized primarily by tensions between military leaders and opposition parties rather than conflicts solely on the basis of expressed ideological differences. The party system remains in jeopardy to this day.

Beginning in 1959, Niger was a one-party state with the Niger Progressive Party (PPN). In 1974 legislation was enacted that further abolished alternate political groups. In August 1988 this ban on other political organizations was slightly lifted with Saïbou forming a new party, the National Movement for a Society of Development (MNSD; later it would be renamed the National Movement for a Society of Development Nassara (MNSD- Nassara). However, Saïbou was against establishing immediately a multiparty system. In July 1991, a national conference attended by 1,200 delegates was convened to address Niger's political problems. The constitution was suspended.

In December 1992, a new constitution was approved by a national referendum, and in February 1993, elections for a new 83-member national assembly were held. The MNSD-Nassara, the previously ruling party, won the most seats at 29, though a coalition of other parties, the Alliance of Forces of Change (AFC), took a majority with 50 seats. The AFC consisted of six parties, though its main members were the Democratic and Social Convention-Rahama (CDS-Rahama), the Nigerian Party for Democracy and Social Progress-Tarayya (PNDS-Tarayya), and the Nigerian Alliance for Democracy and Social Progress-Zaman Lahiya (ANDPS-Zaman Lahiya).

Following the military coup of January 1996, political parties were suspended. After a new constitution was approved in May 1996, political parties were reinstated. Shortly after Maïnassara's election, an opposition coalition formed consisting of eight parties, notably the MNSD-Nassara, CDS-Rahama, and the PNDS-Tarayya. This front was named the Front for the Restoration and Defense of Democracy (FRDD). In reaction, a coalition in support of Maïnassara was formed called the Front for Democracy and Progress.

MINOR POLITICAL PARTIES

Several other parties were in existence prior to the 1996 coup. These include Niger Democratic Front-Mountounchi (FDN-Mountounchi); Niger Progressive Party–African Democratic Rally (PPN–RDA); Republican Party for the Liberty and Progress of Niger-Nakowa (PRLPN-Nakowa); Niger Social-Democratic Party-Alheri (PSDN-Alheri); Party for National Unity and Development-Salama (PUND-Salama); Union for Democracy and Progress-Amici (UDP-Amici); Union for Democracy and Social Progress-Amana (UDPS-Amana); Union of Popular Forces for Democracy and Progress-Sawaba (UFPDP-Sawaba); and Union of Democratic and Progressive Patriots-Shamuwa (UPDP-Shamuwa).

OTHER POLITICAL FORCES

The Tuaregs

In the late 1980s, an influx of Tuareg nomads arrived from Libya and Algeria. They were primarily returnees, having left Niger approximately a decade earlier because of drought conditions. Nevertheless, their large numbers caused tensions to develop in the north.

In May 1990, a Tuareg attack in Tchin Tabaraden based on political grievances met a violent military response that attracted international attention. The governments of Niger, Mali, and Algeria met to try to resolve the problem by agreeing to expedite the return of persons to their places of origin. In 1991, further Tuareg attacks occurred. In 1992, the government recognized formally a rebellion in the north consisting of a Tuareg movement, the Liberation Front of Aïr and Azaouad (FLAA). The FLAA was led by Rissa Ag Boula. It sought not independence but a federal system of government in which it would be able to practice a form of self-administration.

A truce was agreed to in 1992, though it was later broken with both sides assigning blame to the other. A major government military offensive was launched in August 1992. However, a government commission recommended in November a plan of decentralizing authority to the local level as a compromise with the FLAA's federalist plan. Still, further attacks conducted by the Tuaregs occurred in early 1993. In March a temporary truce was reached. A more formal accord was signed in June in Paris that called for demilitarizing the north and further political negotiations. France pledged to help financially the process of Tuareg resettlement.

Tuareg resistance to this agreement developed, however. A new Tuareg group, the Revolutionary Army of Liberation of Northern Niger (ARLN) rejected the agreement. The FLAA split into factions with the Liberation Front of Tamoust (FLT) supporting the truce while Boula and his supporters rejected it. Shortly thereafter, the ARLN, FLAA, and FLT formed a negotiating body known as the Coordination of Armed Resistance (CRA) to deal with future negotiations. However, negotiations failed to take place. The French withdrew from their mediating role. Incidents of violence originating from both sides began anew.

In January 1994, a new Tuareg movement was organized known as the Patriotic Front of Liberation of the Sahara (FPLS). With the CRA, they demanded regional autonomy along with greater participation in the national government and military. The Niger government meanwhile sought a more general program of political decentralization. In June, an agreement was reached in Paris for the establishment of a regional system of government for local ethnic groups, though greater Tuareg participation at the national level was not decided upon. Further unrest developed in late summer and early fall.

A new accord was signed on October 9. Months after, Boula formed a new group, the Organization of Armed Resistance (ORA), in early 1995 as a protest against the delayed implementation of the October 1994 accord. In April 1995, a more formal agreement was reached with an affirmation of the principles laid out in October. A period of disarmament would take place with general amnesty being granted to all parties involved in the conflict. Development in the north was to take place along with a process of political decentralization.

However, this agreement met a new set of national problems. Unrest developed in the east and south near Lake Chad between Toubous and Peuhls. Refugees from Chad, primarily Toubou, created insecure border conditions with Chad. Moreover, a movement known as the Democratic Front of Renewal (FDR) formed in October 1994 with demands for political autonomy in this region. Implementation of a peace agreement was slow with incidents of violence continuing to occur. In March 1996, the CRA and FDR both recognized the April 1995 agreement.

Since Maïnassara's election, efforts at disarmament and repatriation have continued, despite occasional incidents of violence. Financing and implementing the peace process are ongoing issues that have necessitated continued international coordination for approaching resolution.

NATIONAL PROSPECTS

Brigadier General Ibrahim Baré Maïnassara appears to be secure in power. Despite criticisms from such organizations as Amnesty International, he has achieved a level of legitimacy within the international community. The government has been trying to tighten control over oppositional political activity, particularly through limiting freedom of the press. Despite these efforts, students and workers remain a significant factor for political unrest. Whether economic reform will succeed in appeasing these and other domestic forces remains to be seen.

Further Reading

Baier, Stephen. *An Economic History of Central Niger.* Oxford: Clarendon Press, 1980.

Charlick, Robert. *Niger Personal Rule and Survival in the Sahel.* Boulder, Colo.: Westview Press, 1991.

Charlick, Robert, and James Thompson. *Niger.* Boulder, Colo.: Westview Press, 1986.

Decalo, S. *Historical Dictionary of Niger.* Metuchen, N.J.: Scarecrow Press, 1989.

Keenan, J. *The Tuareg.* London: Allen Lane, 1978.

FEDERAL REPUBLIC OF NIGERIA

By Naomi Chazan, Ph.D.
Revised by Terry M. Mays, Ph.D.

THE SYSTEM OF GOVERNMENT

Nigeria, a country of perhaps as many as 100 million people, is at present governed by a military junta composed of General Abdulsalami Abubakar and the officers of the Provisional Ruling Council. The exact population of the largest country in Africa is in question. The official 1991 census counted 88,500,000 people before being annulled by the government amid charges of undercounting. Nigeria, a federal state, obtained its independence from Great Britain on October 1, 1960.

Nigeria emerged at independence with over 200 ethnic groups living in the country's three regions—a Western region dominated by the Yoruba; a Northern region dominated by the Hausa/Fulani; and an Eastern region dominated by the Ibo. The Hausa/Fulani, the largest ethnic group in the country, represented approximately 30% of the population while the Yoruba were 20% and the Ibo were 17% of the total Nigerian population. Today, the country consists of 36 states in an attempt to dilute the political power of these groups.

With independence Abubakar Tafawa Balewa (a Northerner) became prime minister and Nnamdi Azikiwe (an Easterner) became governor general under a British-style parliamentary system of government. Independence intensified the campaign by many Nigerians, particularly among the country's minority ethnic groups, for greater autonomy. On January 15, 1966, the military, led by General Johnson Ironsi, ended the First Republic by means of a coup. Most Nigerians welcomed the demise of a regime hopelessly compromised by corruption, rampant patronage, sectionalism, factionalism, and election fraud. On May 24, the Federal Military Government (FMG) abolished the regions of the country and introduced a unitary state. Because the leader of the FMG was an Ibo, the move was not seen as a step toward national unity but as a device to break the powerful grip of the Northerners on the country. Violent protests in the North resulted in great loss of life and property, primarily among Ibos settled there.

On July 26, 1966, a second military coup replaced Ironsi with General Yakubu Gowon. However, Southerners were not satisfied with the change. On May 27, 1967, the FMG divided the country into 12 states in an attempt to settle regional divisions within the country. Nevertheless, three days later, the former Eastern Region, renamed Biafra, seceded. A bitter 30-month civil war followed, with some 600,000 military and civilian deaths. The defeat of Biafra and the exile of its leader, Lieutenant Colonel Odumegwu Ojukwu, reaffirmed the continuation of a federal system rather than the confederal one Ojukwu had proposed.

General Gowon presided over the relatively enlightened reintegration of the Ibo people into Nigeria. However, he failed to prepare to return the country to civilian rule. He was overthrown on July 29, 1975, by Brigadier Murtala Muhammed. By October, Muhammed had appointed the 50-member Constitution Drafting Committee to prepare a constitution to be submitted to a constituent assembly for debate, amendment, and approval before October 1978. Four months later Muhammed decreed the establishment of 7 new states, raising the total to 19. He also introduced a plan to move the capital from Lagos, a Yoruba stronghold, to a federal capital territory in the ethnically mixed center of the country. Muhammed, a popular leader among average Nigerians, was assassinated in February 1976, but his transition timetable was carried out by his deputy, Olusegun Obasanjo.

On October 1, 1979, the Second Republic came into being under democratically elected civilians led by Shehu Shagari. The civilian government survived one complete term in office but fell early in its second term, on December 31, 1983, to another military coup, which brought into power a mixed military-civilian government headed by General Muhamadu Buhari. General Ibrahim Babangida toppled Buhari's regime on August 27, 1985. Babangida planned a slow transition to a democracy because of domestic and international pressure. However, his government refused to announce the results of a presidential election, apparently won by Moshood Abiola, on June 12, 1993. Babangida established a civilian government under Chief Ernest Shonekan and stepped down from power on August 26, 1993.

Shonekan's government quickly collapsed following a coup led by General Sani Abacha on November 17,

1993. After assuming power in Nigeria, Abacha dismantled the various elements of the democratic process developed under the Babangida regime and arrested Abiola. Domestic and international pressure forced Abacha to pledge a return to civilian government in 1998. The execution of Ken Saro-Wiwa, the leader of the Movement for the Survival of the Ogoni People, and others on November 10, 1995, led to international condemnation. The British Commonwealth suspended Nigeria's membership, and several Western states recalled their ambassadors for consultation. Various forms of mild international sanctions were also imposed on Nigeria.

General Abacha legalized five new political parties, and each nominated him as its presidential candidate in an obvious sham of a democratization pledge. However, Abacha died suddenly on June 8, 1998, and was replaced by General Abubakar while many questioned the circumstances behind Abacha's death. The new Nigerian leader faced considerable internal and external pressure to return the country to civilian rule. Abiola died of a heart attack in prison on July 7, 1998—only one month after Abacha's death. Within months of assuming power, General Abubakar announced that he would return the country to civilian rule. He legalized political parties and established a transition timetable with local elections set for December 1998, state elections in January 1999, and national elections in February 1999.

Executive

The chief executive of Nigeria is President Abdulsalami Abubakar, who came to power in June 1998 following the death of Abacha. Abubakar is Nigeria's head of state and commander in chief of the military. The Provisional Ruling Council is the highest decision-making executive body of the government. Real power in the Nigerian government resides in this body, which consists of military officers. In addition, the government includes a civilian Cabinet known as the Federal Executive Council, which conducts the day-to-day operations of the government. This body consists of progovernment military officers, ethnic leaders and chiefs, and academics. Abubakar serves as chairman of both the Provisional Ruling Council and the Federal Executive Council.

Executive authority has rested with military officers for most of Nigeria's postindependence history. During the period of Nigeria's Second Republic, between 1979 and 1983, the executive branch of government consisted of a democratically elected president, Shagari, and a civilian Cabinet. The military returned to power following a coup on December 31, 1983. General Ibrahim Babangida assumed the reigns of executive power and became the first military officer to assume the title of president. Babangida's government established the Armed Forces Ruling Council, which exercised the real governmental power. General Babangida served as the chairman of this Council of senior military officers. The National Council of Ministers conducted the day-to-day operations of the government under Babangida.

In 1992, Babangida announced the establishment of the National Defense and Security Council to replace the Armed Forces Ruling Council as the country moved toward a transition to civilian government. At the same time, Babangida discussed the transformation of the Council of Ministers into the all-civilian Transitional Council. The new executive bodies became effective on January 4, 1993.

Presidential balloting was held on June 12, 1993, with Moshood Abiola, a very wealthy Muslim Yoruba, winning the election according to most sources. However, the Babangida regime refused to announce the official election results and called for new balloting without the participation of the two previous presidential candidates. Babangida, under domestic and international pressure for invalidating Nigerian presidential election results, appointed Chief Ernest Shonekan, the chairman of the Transitional Council, to assume the executive powers in Nigeria on August 26, 1993.

Shonekan maintained the two councils until overthrown by General Abacha of the National Defense and Security Council on November 17, 1993. Many observers contend that Abacha was the true power behind both the Babangida and Shonekan governments. After coming to power, Abacha replaced the National Defense and Security Council with the Provisional Ruling Council, while the new Federal Executive Council replaced the Transitional Council. Abacha's attempts to integrate opposition elements into his government included the appointment of Abiola's vice presidential running mate, Babagana Kingibe, as minister of the interior in the Federal Executive Council.

General Abubakar assumed the chief executive's office following the death of Abacha and within months announced presidential elections for February 1999 and a complete transition to civilian rule by May 1999. Olusegun Obasanjo of the People's Democratic Party emerged from the February 1999 elections as Nigeria's first democratically selected president in 16 years.

Legislature

A National Assembly has represented the legislative branch of government in Nigeria during two periods since the first military coup in 1966. After 13 years of military rule, Nigerians elected representatives to a bicameral National Assembly in July 1979. Like the United States, the Nigerian legislature consisted of a Senate and a House of Representatives.

The military coup on December 31, 1983, that ousted President Shagari also dissolved the National Assembly.

During the transition to civilian rule under President Babangida, Nigerians elected members to each house of the National Assembly, on July 4, 1992, to serve terms of four years. The Social Democratic Party dominated both houses and the new members of the National Assembly met for the first time on December 5, 1992. At this time, the National Assembly officially functioned as the legislative branch of government but in reality wielded very little power in the military government. The Abacha regime dismissed the legislators after the military coup, in November 1993. General Abubakar announced that the country would conduct elections for a new legislature during February 1999. The People's Democratic Party dominated both houses following February 1999 legislative elections; 74 of the 109 Senate seats and 273 of the 360 House of Representatives seats were filled in this election. (The remaining seats will be filled in a future election.) The People's Democratic Party won 58% of the Senate seats and 56% of the House seats. The Alliance For Democracy secured 24% of the Senate seats and 26% of the House seats. Nigeria's third-strongest political organization, the All People's Party, recieved 18% of the Senate seats and 17% of the House seats.

Judiciary

The Supreme Court is the highest court in Nigeria. The president appoints the chief justice at his discretion, while the other judges on the Supreme Court, no more than 15, are appointed by the president on the advice of the Judicial Service Commission. The Supreme Court is the final court of appeal and has original jurisdiction in disputes between the federal government and a state or between states. The Supreme Court is duly constituted by 5 judges in most cases but requires 7 judges in cases that require constitutional interpretation or involve questions of civil or human rights. The Supreme Court can be seen as an arm of the military regime rather than an independent branch of government.

The Federal Court of Appeal, consisting of no fewer than 15 judges, is headed by a president appointed by the president of the republic on advice from the Judicial Service Commission. The other members of the Court are appointed by the president of the republic on the recommendation of the Commission. The Court of Appeal is duly constituted by 3 judges. In cases of appeals from state *sharia* (Islamic law) courts or state customary law courts, the Court of Appeal judges must be experts in those fields.

State courts consist of a high court with appellate and supervisory functions as well as original jurisdiction. States with a large Islamic population also have *sharia* courts of appeal and/or customary courts of appeal. These courts deal with appeals from lower *sharia* and customary courts, which handle personal and family matters on the basis of Islamic or traditional law. Judges may be removed only for disability or misconduct.

Regional and Local Government

Nigeria emerged at independence with 3 regions but currently consists of 36 states in a federal system. The original 3 regions were split into 12 states in 1967, 21 states in 1987, 30 states in 1991, and then 36 states under General Abacha. Nigeria also has a Federal Capital Territory similar to the District of Columbia in the United States or the Federal District in Brazil. The large number of states within the border of Nigeria is an attempt to dilute the power wielded by ethnic groups and local leaders.

Most groups support the establishment of additional states. Minority ethnic groups view new and smaller states as opportunities for greater autonomy, while the Nigerian workforce recognizes new states, during periods of civilian rule, as opportunities for additional political offices and government jobs.

A hotly debated issue in Nigerian politics is that of revenue allocation from the federal to the state and local governments. During the Second Republic, after months of debate over the amount to go to the state governments and whether the allocation to local governments should go directly to them or through state offices, the National Assembly finally agreed, in 1982, that the federal government would keep 55% of the revenues, distribute 35% to the states, and pass 10% directly to the local governments. The amount of the shares of each state and local government also causes great controversy. A few states, particularly the oil-rich ones, produce large numbers of petroleum-based jobs. However, many individuals within the states argue that they do not receive their fair share of petroleum income from the federal government. Other states are not as wealthy and/or have larger populations. Individuals in these states believe that they should receive increased funds from the federal government as compensation for the lack of lucrative mineral resources.

In the past, the Nigerian government has attempted to allocate federal funding of the states based upon population. As a result, states have tended to inflate their population reports as a means of increasing their percentage of funds. Due to this factor and the sensitivity of religious differences, census taking has been a heavily criticized activity within the state. For two decades, Nigeria operated with a continuing series of estimations added to its 1963 census. The 1973 census count was not trusted by states and ethnic groups. The 1991 census counted over 88,000,000 people, far below the estimated population of over 105,000,000. Some observers attributed the 1991 census count to overreporting by states in search of funds, while others view the count as inaccurate and an underreporting of the true population of Nigeria.

Southerners fear the population growth of the Islamic North could increase the latter's participation in a democratic government and share of federal funds. On the other hand, the North would like to keep Southerners divided in order to prevent any possible attempt to dominate a democratic government. The Abacha regime temporarily settled the question by annulling the 1991 census count in 1994.

The structure of state government has usually paralleled that of the federal government. During the Second Republic each state had a governor and vice governor of the same party elected statewide to a four-year term as well as a state legislature. Under military rule the states are administered by military governors who have powers at a state level similar to those of the president at the federal level.

Local government represents the only political unit below that of the state. Elections for local government positions were last held in December 1998 during the democratic transition process under General Abubakar. Traditional chiefs and religious leaders still carry considerable influence in many local areas.

THE ELECTORAL SYSTEM

The electoral register consists of all Nigerians 18 years of age or over. Prior to the 1979 elections, nearly 50 million voters were registered in a house-to-house campaign, but voter turnout was very low. The Babangida regime established a National Election Commission (NEC) in 1989 to help prepare the country for the 1990–91 elections and the transition to civilian government. The first elections since the 1983 coup occurred on December 8, 1990, when voters selected local officials. Elections at the state level were conducted in January 1999.

The elections in 1990 and 1991 were controversial due to the nature of the balloting. Rather than secret balloting, the Nigerian elections involved open voting. All Nigerian voters reported to the polling stations at the same time and openly lined up behind a picture of one of the two authorized political parties. Poll officials then counted the number of people in each line. Many Nigerians refused to vote due to this open process. Heads of families, village leaders, and other individuals tended to intimidate individuals into voting in accordance with their preferences. The open-balloting system allowed these individuals to observe anyone who dared to challenge their authority.

Local elections in December 1998 and state elections in January 1999 produced a lower-than-expected voter turnout but have been declared fairly free by international observers.

THE PARTY SYSTEM

Origins of the Parties

Political activity by Africans appeared in the South, especially in Lagos, as early as the 1880s. It was largely a consequence of the spread of European-style education brought by Christian missionaries, as well as a natural continuation of Southern Nigerian patterns of participation in government. In the North, where the British indirectly ruled a feudal society from which missionaries were banned, popular political activity was rare until the 1950s.

The first political parties were formed to contest limited indirect elections to a Southern advisory legislative council in 1922. Herbert Macauly, of Yoruba–Sierra Leonean descent, founded the Nigerian National Democratic Party (NNDP) in Lagos prior to those elections. The NNDP dominated Southern politics until 1934 when students founded the Nigerian Youth Movement (NYM). Although based in Lagos and largely Yoruba in membership, the NYM made efforts to be a national party and replaced the NNDP as the dominant political party in 1938.

As World War II drew to a close, political activity became more intense in Nigeria. In 1944, Nnamdi Azikiwe founded the National Council of Nigeria and the Cameroons (NCNC). Azikiwe, an American-educated Ibo, worked for national unity in spite of the fact that the NCNC was largely Ibo in membership. In 1951, Chief Obafemi Awolowo founded the Action Group as an outgrowth of a Yoruba cultural preservation society. Awolowo, in contrast to Azikiwe's goal, argued that the sharp ethnic divisions in Nigeria made it unrealistic to expect the populace to suddenly abandon their ethnic identifications and adopt a vague national one. Instead, he advocated that ethnic identities be protected and enhanced as the first step in a process of developing a pluralistic national polity. Also in 1951, the Northern People's Congress (NPC) was founded by Ahmadu Bello, the sardauna of Sokoto, heir apparent to the Fulani sultan of Sokoto, the most important political and religious position in the North.

The first government of independent Nigeria in 1960 emerged as a coalition between the NPC and the NCNC (which in 1961 changed its name to the National Convention of Nigerian Citizens). The Action Group became the formal opposition party. Awolowo and Azikiwe shifted their focus to the national level, with Azikiwe becoming the governor-general and later president. The sardauna concentrated his efforts on the Northern Region and became premier of this area. Abubakar Tafawa Balewa, the sardauna's representative in Lagos, became Nigeria's first prime minister.

In 1962, a splinter of the Action Group formed the Nigerian National Democratic Party under the leadership of S. L. Akintola. Shortly thereafter, Awolowo and many other Action Group leaders were arrested and tried on controversial charges of conspiracy to overthrow the government. Most, including Awolowo, were released in 1966 in the aftermath of the military takeover. The NCNC and the Action Group boycotted the elections of 1964, which were won overwhelmingly by an NPC–NNDP alliance. Azikiwe, as president, tried to force new national elections but failed. New elections were held in the Western Region in October 1965, and after a particularly violent campaign, the NNDP won openly rigged elections and Akintola became Nigerian National Democratic Party premier of the region.

When the army took over in January 1966, the constitution was suspended, regional governments were dissolved, and political-party activity was banned. The coup was particularly bloody as evidenced by the murders of Balewa, Akintola, the Ahmadu Bello Sardaunas, and other politicians. Ten senior army officers, most of them Northerners, were also killed.

When political parties were allowed to reform on September 21, 1978, most of the new organizations could trace their roots directly to the precoup parties. Azikiwe and Awolowo reappeared as major political party leaders. In the attempt to reduce regional and ethnic loyalties, political parties had to prove they operated offices in at least 13 of Nigeria's 19 states. Candidates for the presidency had to receive at least 25% of the vote in at least 13 states to claim victory. Five political parties participated in the 1979 elections for the new office of president and a national legislature. The parties included the Nigerian People's Congress, Great Nigeria People's Party, United Party of Nigeria (led by Awolowo), People's Redemption Party, and the Nigeria's People's Party (led by Azikiwe).

The Nigerian People's Congress, led by Shehu Shagari, received a majority in the national elections. Shagari became Nigeria's first elected national leader since Balewa in October 1979. The collapse of the national economy and charges of corruption were followed by a military coup on December 31, 1983. When General Buhari assumed power in Nigeria on January 3, 1984, he banned all political parties in the country.

After another military coup, General Babangida announced in September 1987 that he planned to guide Nigeria toward democratic elections. University representatives recommended the establishment of only two political parties in an attempt to eliminate regional and ethnic tensions during an election process. The Armed Forces Ruling Council of the Babangida regime accepted the plan and called for the establishment of two national political parties. After May 1989, 50 organizations sought recognition as legal political parties and 13 were able to meet the strict requirements imposed by the government. Of the 13 organizations, 6 were nominated to the Armed Forces Ruling Council. However, the Babangida government disqualified all 13 parties. In their places, Babangida established 2 new parties, the Social Democratic Party (SDP) and the National Republican Convention (NRC), on October 7, 1989. The parties were the Democrats and Republicans, and each received government funding.

The SDP tended to dominate the election process during local and national balloting. Abiola, the SDP's candidate, won the election for the presidency according to most observers. However, Babangida disqualified Abiola and his opponent while calling for new elections. Following Babangida's departure and Abacha's overthrow of the Shonekan government, political parties were, again, banned, on November 18, 1993. The government arrested Abiola on June 23, 1994.

In 1995, General Abacha allowed political parties to form under a complicated guideline that led to only pro-military parties being recognized by the government and able to participate in future elections. After the deaths of Abacha and Abiola, General Abukabar legalized mass political parties, resulting in the establishment of nine organizations in October 1998. Following local elections in December 1998, only three of these parties could garner enough popular support to qualify for state and national elections in 1999. These organizations were the People's Democratic Party, the All People's Party, and the Alliance for Democracy.

PEOPLE'S DEMOCRATIC PARTY

The People's Democratic Party (PDP), a coalition of smaller parties, is the strongest political organization in Nigeria. The organization, consisting of many former opponents of General Abacha, cut across ethnic and geographical boundaries and is the closest thing to a national party in Nigeria. Leadership within the PDP includes General Olusegun Obasanjo, a popular figure among many Nigerians for returning the country to democratic rule in 1979, and the former vice president Alex Ekwueme. The party won over 60% of the seats in the December 1998 local elections, over 50% of the gubernatorial seats in January 1999, and over 55% of the seats in both houses of the national legislature in February 1999. The party nominated Obasanjo to run for the national presidency. Obasanjo recieved 63% of the popular vote in the February 1999 contest to become Nigerian president. Obasanjo is scheduled to be installed in May 1999.

ALL PEOPLE'S PARTY

The All People's Party (APP) is chaired by Mahmud Waziri and garners much of its popular support from the Northern and Central areas of Nigeria. Many Nigerians refer to the APP as the "Abacha People's Party" due to the large number of former supporters of General Abacha who hold membership in the organization. The APP won approximately 25% of the local government seats in the December 1998 election and over 17% in both national legislative houses in the February 1999 elections. The APP and the Alliance For Democracy united under a single presidential candidate, Olu Falae, to challenge the popularity of Olusegun Obasanjo of the People's Democratic Party. Falae received 37% of the popular vote in a hotly contested election in February 1999.

ALLIANCE FOR DEMOCRACY

The Alliance For Democracy (AFD) is a Yoruba-based party with its strength in the Southwestern part of the country. The AFD is led by Bola Ige, a former governor of

Oyo state, and includes many former supporters of Abiola. The party won less than 15% of the local seats in December 1998 and 6 gubernatorial seats in January 1999, but it received approximately 25% of the seats in both national legislative houses. The AFD united with the All People's Party under a single presidential candidate, Olu Falae, to counter the People's Democratic Party canadidate, Olusegun Obasanjo. Falae received 37% of the popular vote in the February 1999 election.

OTHER POLITICAL FORCES

Military

The Nigerian military, numbering close to 77,000 in 1998, can also be seen as a political party/movement within Nigeria due to its history of manipulation and coups since independence. Although all ethnic groups are represented in the military, the Hausa tend to dominate the senior officer ranks.

Organized Labor

Labor unions have also participated in the Nigerian political scene. Labor organizations tend to cut across ethnic and regional lines in order to concentrate on basic issues of workers' welfare such as minimum wages, fringe benefits, and a variety of special subsidies. These groups are major champions of the demands of government employees. Oil unions were among the most instrumental in organizing the strikes in support of Abiola following his arrest by the government. The Provisional Ruling Council replaced the union leaders with individuals more sympathetic to the government, thus ending much of the union-based political resistance.

The expansion of Nigeria's system of higher education during the 1970s, which brought a university to every state in the federation, increased the political importance of the students, who have consistently been an invaluable indicator of public opinion in the country. During the Shagari and Buhari administrations, students were vociferous in opposition to the government. As educational institutions expanded, these student forces have become important factors on the Nigerian political, economic, and social scene. The government tends to base special riot control police units near Nigerian universities as a quick response to protesting students. Frequently in recent years, the government has shut down the country's universities for entire semesters to relieve the boiling political tensions on campus. Professionals, journalists and intellectuals have also emerged to speak for a broad array of public interests.

Ethnic Groups

The various major ethnic groups that make up modern Nigera are important forces in the national political arena. Depending on the definitions used, there are between 250 and 350 distinct ethnic groups in Nigeria with different customs, social structures, and languages or dialects. Aside from the three major groups, most of these groups are very small, and most are in the "middle belt," an uneven swath that stretches across the country from Kwara state in the West to Gongola state in the East.

North of the "middle belt," the Hausa-Fulani dominate, although Fulani concentrations can be found in the eastern section of the "belt." Conservative and strictly Islamic, the Fulani are descended from nomadic peoples, partly of Berber origin. Some Fulani still lead a seminomadic life in the Far North. Settled Fulani are the aristocrats of the North, leaders of a stratified feudal society whose emirs wield great political and Hausa-Fulani social authority. That society includes the Hausa, who had established several city-states and the feudal system in the North before the founding of the Sokoto state in the early 19th century. Hausa is the lingua franca of the North. The Kanuri are another major people of the North. Nearly all the peoples of the North are Muslim and together make up at least half of Nigeria's population.

The Yoruba of the Southwest are probably the largest single ethnic group. Yoruba society is structured in communal groups based on large extended families. Yorubas, in nearly equal numbers, profess Islam and Protestant Christianity. The obas, or chiefs, continue to exercise effective social, and often political, control, and the alafin of Oyo is still the preeminent traditional political ruler.

The Ibos of the Southeast are known over much of Africa for their individualism, energy, and personal enterprise. They are largely Roman Catholic with few vestiges of traditional religion. Among the minority ethnic groups, the Tiv are perhaps the most numerous and live in the North. The Nupe, most of whom are Muslim, are concentrated in the North and exhibit a hierarchic society. The Edo, who predominate in the Midwest, have much in common with the Yoruba, while the Ibibio in the East have been influenced by Ibo culture. The Ijaw of the East are probably of mixed origin, a product of the social disruptions caused by the former slave trade.

NATIONAL PROSPECTS

Nigeria is at a political and economic crossroads. Many Nigerians viewed arrested president-elect Moshood Abiola as one of the few men who could unite the various elements of Nigerian society and lead the country into a period of democracy. Not only was Abiola a Yoruba, but he was also a Muslim, two characteristics alone that could have united much of the country. Abiola's wealth was also viewed positively by many Nigerians. It had been suggested in many circles that Abiola was so wealthy that he would not have needed to continue the corruption that characterized the regimes preceding him and so could have concentrated on rebuilding Nigeria.

True or not, the idea helped unite many Nigerians behind him. General Obasnjo has emerged as a possible national alternative to the late Abiola. Obasanjo is widely respected for his return of the government to civilian rule in 1979. He is a Yoruba from Southwest Nigeria but is trusted by many of the Hausa/Fulani of the North. Opposition party charges of massive fraud following the February 1999 presidential contest did not receive concurrence from the many election observers in the country. Obasanjo received an impressive 63% of the national popular vote but overwhelmingly lost in the Yoruba-dominated states of the Southwest, where he is seen by many as being too pro-Hausa/Fulani. The future will determine whether the Yoruba Southwest will settle into accepting Obasanjo as a truly national leader.

The Abubakar government has pledged to allow a democratic transition to civilian government in May 1999 following the February 1999 elections for a national president. However, earlier pledges have been broken by a string of military governments. The Obasanjo regime is the only Nigerian military-led government, prior to 1999, to have returned to the barracks and allowed a democratically elected civilian government to assume power in the country. On the basis of the African experience, one can identify four possible scenarios. First, Abubakar could carry out his promise to step down and allow a civilian regime to assume power. However, if this occurs, will the military remain in the barracks or will another general emerge to take his turn at Nigeria's helm? Second, Abubakar could change his plans and stall on the transition to democracy. Third, another military officer could step in, with or without Abubakar's tacit approval, and take over the government to "save the country" and pledge future elections. Fourth, and the least probable option, the military could declare that they are the only ones who can preserve a united Nigeria and refuse to return the country to a democratically elected civilian government.

Nigeria's unpopular participation in the Economic Community of West African States Monitoring Group's peacekeeping operation in Liberia since 1990 and Sierra Leone since 1993 also plagues the country. Nigeria's providing the lion's share of manpower and financing of this organization has been a drain on the country and its population. Involvement has been not only unpopular in Nigeria but also used as an example of a political failure by the military governments of Babangida, Abacha, and Abubakar.

Nigeria is also facing an economic crisis. Years of rampant corruption and mismanagement have taken a terrible toll on the national economy. Half-completed construction projects have been abandoned across the entire country due to the skimming of funds by officials. The money disappears while the projects and buildings are never completed. The economic growth of the 1970s based on high petroleum prices has stagnated with the drop in the cost of oil in the 1980s and 1990s. Rising foreign debt and inflation add to the economic problems facing Nigeria.

Since 1984, successive governments have undertaken self-imposed austerity measures, which included the retrenchment of employees in the civil service, the floating of the national currency, and the divestment or closure of a large number of state corporations and agricultural marketing boards. Nigeria's military governments have often refused to abide by International Monetary Fund preconditions for the opening of credit facilities and attempted, instead, to design their own programs for economic resuscitation. The challenges of restructuring the public arena, establishing a strong democratic leadership, and developing effective channels of participation are central to the governability of this large and potentially prosperous country. The steps toward economic stabilization are hence tied to political reforms within the state.

Further Reading

Awolowo, Obafemi. *The Strategy and Tactics of the People's Republic of Nigeria.* London: Macmillan, 1970.

Diamond, Larry, Anthony Kirk-Greene, and Oyeleye Oyediran, eds. *Transition without End: Nigerian Politics and Civil Society under Babangida.* Boulder, Colo.: Lynne Rienner, 1997.

Dudley, B. J. *Instability and Political Order: Politics and Crisis in Nigeria.* Ibadan: Ibadan University Press, 1973.

———. *An Introduction to Nigerian Government and Politics.* London: Macmillan, 1982.

Graf, William D. *Elections, 1979.* Lagos: Daily Times Publications, 1979.

———. *The Nigerian State.* Portsmouth, N.H.: Heinemann, 1988.

Herskovits, Jean. *Nigeria: Power and Democracy in Africa.* Headline Series, no. 257. New York: Foreign Policy Association, 1982.

Kirk-Greene, A.M.H. *Nigeria since 1970: A Political and Economic Outline.* London: Hedder and Stoughton, 1981.

Mackintosh, John P. *Nigerian Government and Politics.* London: Allen and Unwin, 1966.

Nnoli, Okwudiba. *Ethnic Politics in Nigeria.* Enugu, Nigeria: Fourth Dimension Press, 1978.

Ojiako, James O. *Thirteen Years of Military Rule.* Lagos: Daily Times Publications, 1980.

Oluleye, General James J. *Military Leadership in Nigeria 1966–1979.* Ibadan: University Press Limited, 1985.

Schwartz, Frederick, and August Otto. *Nigeria: The Tribes, the Nation, or the Race: The Politics of Independence.* London: Cambridge University Press, 1965.

KINGDOM OF NORWAY

(Kongeriket Norge)

By John T. S. Madeley, Ph.D.
Revised by Robert S. Kadel

THE SYSTEM OF GOVERNMENT

The kingdom of Norway, a nation of just over 4.2 million people, is a parliamentary democracy headed by a constitutional monarchy. Norway adopted its constitution on May 17, 1814, a date on which the Norwegian people declared independence from the Danish crown that had ruled them for four centuries. The Norwegian constitution has remained in force since this date, making it the oldest constitution still in force in Europe. However, Norway remained subject to the Swedish crown (by cession from Denmark) until 1905.

When Norway finally achieved complete independence, the people decided by referendum to reinstate the ancient Norwegian monarchy. The Danish Prince Carl Frederick was invited to ascend to the Norwegian throne; he assumed the name Haakon VII and thus began Norway's contemporary monarchy. The Crown makes up the executive branch of government, while the constitution makes provisions for a legislative branch (vested in the *Storting*, the primary legislative and budgetary authority) and a judiciary power centered in a Supreme Court. The official language of Norway is Norwegian with two dialects, Bokmål (Book Standard) and Nynorsk (New Norwegian). The official state religion of Norway is Evangelical-Lutheran.

Executive

Executive power is formally vested in the Crown, which, prior to 1990, was hereditary in the male line. On May 29, 1990, the constitution was amended to provide for gender equality in succession rights to the throne, having effect only for anyone born after this date. The present king is Harald V, who acceded to the throne in 1991. The Crown is responsible for appointing all officials and authorizes all legislative and administrative acts.

The king is the head of the Church of Norway and must profess the Evangelical-Lutheran faith. He may issue and repeal ordinances relating to commerce, customs tariffs, all economic sectors, and the police, although he is bound by the laws of the constitution and the *Storting*. The king is responsible for collecting taxes and duties imposed by the *Storting*. Furthermore, he is the commander in chief of the Norwegian armed forces. Since the introduction of parliamentarism in 1884, the Crown's performance of all of these duties is subject to the *Storting*. Like many contemporary monarchies, then, the function of the Norwegian monarchy is now almost entirely ceremonial. In an inconclusive election, the king may be called upon to decide, with the advice of the *Storting*, which party leader will form a government.

For all intents and purposes, executive power rests with the prime minister and other ministers in the Council of State (Cabinet). The ministers are appointed by the king, but only after approval from the majority party or parties in the *Storting*. Prime Minister Thorbjørn Jagland formed a new Norwegian minority government on October 25, 1996. On that date, Gro Harlem Brundtland, one of the most influential Norwegian politicians of the 20th century, retired from her 10-year-long term as prime minister. Since October 17, 1997, the prime minister has been Kjell Magne Bondevik, who heads a coalition government.

Legislature

The *Storting* is the primary legislative and budgetary authority in Norway. It consists of 165 members, 157 of whom are elected from the 19 counties in Norway. An additional 8 representatives are elected at large. Elections occur at regular four-year intervals, with no provision in the constitution for the dissolution of parliament. A system of alternates, or deputy representatives, ensures immediate replacement for any unoccupied seat in the *Storting*. The *Storting* begins each year's session on the first weekday of October; however, there is no formal end of session. The *Storting* is required to remain in session as long as is deemed necessary and terminates its proceedings only when it has concluded its business.

The entire *Storting* is elected as a single body. Once elections have taken place, members of the *Storting* nominate one-fourth to constitute the *Lagting*, or upper division, the remaining three-fourths constituting the *Odelsting*, or lower division. The *Storting* attempts to balance power between the two divisions via the specific members nominated to the *Lagting*. If a disagreement over legislation does arise between the two divisions, the entire Storting acts to resolve the issue, a two-thirds vote being necessary for a measure to pass. Constitutional amendments also require a two-thirds majority, as well as a general election, before any proposed amendment can be enacted.

Each division and the *Storting* as a whole is responsible for electing its own presidents, deputy presidents, and secretaries (two representatives in each position). These officers make up a presidium with the president of the *Storting* as chair. The presidium acts as a steering committee responsible for the smooth operation of the legislature, the order of business, management of the *Storting*, and so on. Thirteen standing committees, which correspond to the government ministries, perform much of the budgetary, legislative, and managerial functions of the government. Caucuses of the political parties in the *Storting* make decisions about the membership of the presidium and the standing committees. For the most part, the parties function smoothly with one another on the basis of strict rules of internal party discipline and interparty relations. However, and very rarely, a government will receive a motion of no confidence—the last time in 1963 when two Socialist People's Party representatives withdrew their support for a minority Labor government.

Judiciary

The Norwegian Constitution establishes a court system divided into four sections, with the *Hoiesterett* (Supreme Court of Justice) at the top. The members of the *Hoiesterett* are appointed by the king and can only be removed after due process. The courts practice the process of judicial review in constitutional matters and may declare a law unconstitutional. However, the courts generally defer to the *Storting* in matters related to the constitution, so it is rare for the courts to declare unconstitutionality. The *Hoiesterett* consists of a president and at least four other members. The High Court of the Realm (the Court of Impeachment) is drawn from the permanent members of the *Lagting* (two-thirds) and the permanently appointed members of the Supreme Court (one-third). Impeachment trials, however, are rare.

Regional and Local Government

Norway is divided into 19 counties and 435 municipalities. The counties vary in size and range in population from about 80,000 to 450,000. Populations of the municipalities range from a mere 5,000 to around 50,000. Each local body elects its own governing council, the *Kommunestyret* in the municipalities and the *Fylkesting* in the counties. Elections to these councils are held every four years, although they are staggered so that county elections do not take place at the same time as municipality elections.

There is no hierarchy of control between the two, i.e., the municipalities are not subordinate to the counties. Each has its own specific function for its inhabitants. The municipalities are responsible for kindergartens, child care, elementary schools, libraries, various cultural provisions for municipal residents, social welfare, sewer systems and treatment, and so on. The counties' primary responsibilities revolve around high schools, hospitals, and other special health services, care for substance abusers, county roads and transportation, and large-scale cultural enterprises, such as museums.

Storting Election Results, 1981–93

	1981 Vote %	1981 Seats	1985 Vote %	1985 Seats	1989 Vote %	1989 Seats	1993 Vote %	1993 Seats	1997 Vote %	1997 Seats
Labor	37.2	66	40.8	71	34.3	63	36.9	67	35.0	65
Conservative	31.7	53	30.4	50	22.2	37	17.0	28	14.3	23
Christian People's	8.9	15	8.3	16	8.5	14	7.9	13	13.7	25
Center	4.2	11	6.6	12	6.5	11	16.7	32	7.9	11
Socialist Left	4.9	4	5.5	6	10.1	17	7.9	13	6.0	9
Liberal	3.2	2	3.1	—	3.2	—	3.6	1	4.5	6
Progress	4.5	4	3.7	2	13.0	22	6.3	6	15.3	25
Red Electoral Alliance	0.7	—	0.6	—	—	—	1.1	1	1.7	—
Communist	0.3	—	0.2	—	—	—	—	—	—	—
Others	4.2	—	0.7	—	2.2	1	3.7	—	1.6	1
Total	100.0	155	100.0	157	100.0	165	100.0	165	100.0	165

Source: Norwegian Ministry of Foreign Affairs.

Note: Percentages rounded to the nearest 10th.

THE ELECTORAL SYSTEM

The *Storting*'s 165 members are chosen by direct election in multimember constituencies. All citizens who are at least 18 years of age, or will have their 18th birthday by the end of an election year, are eligible to vote. The electoral register is drawn up in the summer months immediately preceding an election; thus, voter registration is consistently up-to-date. Each of the 19 counties elects a number of representatives to the *Storting* in proportion to its population. The largest representation can be found in the county of Oslo (Oslo) and the county of Hordaland (Bergen), each of which elects 15 members to parliament. Finnmark and Aust-Adger counties receive the lowest number of representatives, 4 apiece. The numbers of representatives for all other counties lie somewhere between. Within each constituency, each party will have a list of candidates with at least as many names as there are seats for the county. Thus a voter may vote for none or all from one party. The voter is also allowed to cross out names on one list and write in names from another party list; however, this has had only a minuscule effect on election outcomes in the past. Of the *Storting*'s 165 members, 157 are elected in this manner, with a proportional system devised to translate the party list votes into seats. The remaining 8 *Storting* members are elected at large, drawing on the proportion of votes for their party from the entire realm. This system was established prior to the 1993 election to ensure a greater degree of proportionality among the parties.

Voter turnout is generally high in Norway, with usually more than 82% of the population active in *Storting* elections and about 10% less for local elections.

THE PARTY SYSTEM

Just over a century has elapsed since the introduction of political parties in Norway. Before this time, groups existed that did have political links to activities in the Norwegian government; however, there were no formally organized parties. The year 1884 saw the onset of parliamentarism and, shortly afterward, the creation of the first official political party, the Liberals. Only six months had passed when the opposition to this party formed their own party, the Conservative Party. In 1914, the Labor Party emerged as a major electoral force and was joined shortly after World War I by the Agrarian League. The addition of the Christian People's Party in the 1930s completed the basic framework of parties in Norway. Meanwhile, smaller parties also emerged, such as the Communist Party in the 1920s and the Socialist People's Party in the 1960s. Members of these groups joined forces in 1973 to form the basis for the Socialist Left Party. On the other side of the political spectrum, the right-wing Progress Party also formed in 1973.

The Labor, Conservative, and Agrarian/Center Parties all represent their traditional economic interests: worker, business, and farming, respectively. Formally each party, with the exception of the Labor Party, has adopted a position of neutrality with respect to interest-group organizations. However, voting patterns indicate that there are strong ties between each party and interest groups.

Ideologically, the groups fall fairly clearly along the traditional political spectrum: Labor on the left, Conservative on the right, Agrarian/Center Party in the center, with the smaller groups in their respective positions (e.g., the Communists further to the left and the Progress Party further to the right). Pragmatically, the split is mostly between the socialists and nonsocialists and is borne out in the alternation of parliamentary control between these two blocs.

There are other important factors in the party divisions and the vote. In particular, center-periphery, urban-rural, environmental, and cultural divisions exist. Such factors have been particularly important in the development of the Christian People's Party, the Liberal Party, and the newly formed Green Party. These parties' identities are not formed necessarily along economic lines but involve other social forces.

Highly articulated systems of party discipline and interparty relations ensure that these ideological differences are translated into action by party representatives in the *Storting*.

Party Organization

Each of the Norwegian political parties is of the mass-branch type with relatively high levels of dues-paying membership. Overall the proportion of members to voters for the different parties has been around 20%, with the Center and Labor Parties, in that order, having somewhat higher proportions. The Labor Party alone allows for collective membership, e.g., among trade union branches. This exception does not affect the basic fact that all Norwegian parties share the same type of structure; their party constitutions resemble one another to a remarkable degree.

The basic unit in all parties is the local association, which includes all dues-paying members in a particular locality. Associations are joined together at municipal, county, and national levels. An important feature is that the municipal and county party organizations have complete power to nominate candidates for elective office. This means, in particular, that central party organs have no formal power to affect the composition of party lists, even at the level of the *Storting*. This decentralized structure of power in the matter of nominations is reinforced by the existence of residential qualifications for *Storting* candidates. The nominating conventions of the constituency organizations usually take pains to include on the party list representatives of a range of groups (whether by locality, sex, or interest group) in order to attract the widest possible support consistent with the (local) party's political line.

The highest governing body in each party is the national conference, usually held every two years. Delegates to the conference are elected by constituency organizations but also include government ministers (where a party has any), members of the *Storting*, and representatives of the party's women's and youth organizations. The principal business of a conference is usually the discussion and adoption of the party program on the basis of a draft circulated to and debated by local parties in advance. In addition, the conference elects party leaders and rules on general matters of organization and discipline. The principal party leader is generally the national chairman, who in most cases is also the leader of the party in the *Storting*.

The national chairman presides over the national committee, which is elected by the conference and includes members from all constituent organizations. The national chairman also presides over the executive committee, which is in charge of the day-to-day activities of the party. The national committee, which meets much less frequently than the executive committee, possesses the highest authority in the party between conferences. The chairman is assisted by the party general secretary, who heads the party's administrative apparatus.

At the municipal, county, and national levels the party's elected officeholders (*Storting* deputies and county or municipal council members) frequently meet in caucus with the appropriate level of party leaders. These caucuses ensure a high degree of internal party agreement and discipline. The national or local party membership organizations, through their representatives in conference, are accorded final authority in the party constitutions, but conflicts between them and the caucuses of elected representatives are rare.

Campaigning

Election campaigns are rarely colorful or exciting affairs because the electoral system ensures that the decisive contest lies between disciplined parties rather than between individual candidates. Much of the press is bound to particular parties, and few newspapers in Norway can be considered nonpartisan, so voters are generally presented with news and views that only confirm their initial predispositions. Since 1960, however, television has tended to supersede the press as the citizens' principal source of information, and the press and party rallies have become less important. Although the electronic media generally have exposed the public to a wider spectrum of political debate and have doubtless contributed to the recent increase in electoral volatility, this new element of drama has been restricted by the absence of political commercials. (There is no commercial advertising on radio or television.) Meanwhile, all parties are allotted equal exposure.

Independent Voters

Party identification in Norway has been an important factor underpinning the remarkable stability of the electorate until recent years. Over the 20 years after 1945, a substantial majority of voters regularly identified with one of the major parties. Until the 1970s, the reflection of social and economic cleavages in the party system further reinforced this stability. However, since the issue of Norway's membership in the European Economic Community (EEC) became a major concern, the country has experienced a wave of electoral volatility unprecedented since the 1930s. During the stable years, it was unusual for individual parties to vary by as much as 3% in electoral support from one election to another. Since the post-EEC referendum election of 1973, however, a substantial floating vote, perhaps as high as 25% of voters, has made its impact felt in marked changes of electoral strength. These changes, however, have occurred principally among parties that make up the socialist and nonsocialist blocs themselves. The 1970s and 1980s saw a distinct electoral shift away from the socialist parties. However, this nonsocialist turn has waned in recent elections, returning toward the left end of the political spectrum.

CENTER PARTY
(Senterpartiet; SP)

HISTORY

The Center Party was founded in 1920 as the Agrarian League. The following year it changed its name to Farmers' Party; the Center Party name was adopted in 1959. From the start it was an agrarian-interest party closely associated with the farmers' organizations. In the postwar period, it has joined in government coalitions with nonsocialist parties in 1963, 1965 to 1971, 1972–73, and since 1983. Looking out for its members' economic interests, the party continues to campaign against membership in the European Union (EU), as the EEC was renamed in 1994.

ORGANIZATION

The Center Party shares the mass-branch structure described above. It maintains auxiliary organizations for women and youth and conducts a variety of educational programs, particularly in rural areas. Its primary publication is *Informasjon* (Information), a quarterly journal of opinion, but it also receives important support from the daily newspaper *Natiuonen* (The Nation). National headquarters are at Arbeidergate 4, Egertorget, Oslo 1. As of 1997, Anne Enger Lahnstein chaired the party.

MEMBERSHIP AND CONSTITUENCY

The Center Party reported a membership of 50,000 in 1990, a decline of about 10,000 members over 10 years. A great majority of the membership belongs to the various agrarian-interest associations. By and large, the party draws more support from the larger landowners than from owners of small farms. Regionally, the party's greatest strength is in the *Trøndelag*.

POLICY

The Center Party's principal aim has been to promote the interests of those engaged in agriculture by securing favorable credit, marketing, and pricing arrangements. Despite this advocacy of government intervention and support in agriculture, the party is firmly nonsocialist.

The party changed its name in 1959 in an attempt to make up for the decline of the agricultural sector by appealing to all centrist voters, regardless of their occupation or residence. This attempt has largely failed, even though the party has adopted a range of environmental and decentralist policies that have modified its traditional political stance.

In foreign policy, the party continues its firm stance against membership in the EU, a policy that placed it in sharp contrast with the other nonsocialist parties and was largely responsible for the collapse of the center-right coalition in 1971. In other respects, the party's foreign policy is orthodox—pro-West, pro-NATO—and favors a strong defense establishment.

FINANCING

As is the case with all Norwegian parties, the exact breakdown of sources of finance is not publicly known. While the government subsidy is almost certainly the largest single source of funds, important contributions are received from the agricultural organizations, and membership dues make up the balance.

LEADERSHIP

In the late 1970s, the party underwent something of a leadership crisis. In early 1977, the party chairman, who had supported close cooperation with the Conservative Party, resigned; his replacement, a clergyman, signally failed to provide the kind of strong leadership that might have avoided electoral defeat later that year and was subsequently replaced in 1979. Anne Enger Lahnstein is the current chairman of the party.

PROSPECTS

The Center Party has seen a decline in votes recently, as low as only 11.8% in the 1995 local elections and 7.9% in the 1997 national election. Some of this reduction in popularity is due to a number of Center Party issues being coopted by the Conservatives. Nonetheless, the Center Party became a part of the coalition government with the Christian People's Party and Liberals after the 1997 election when Labor stepped down from power.

CHRISTIAN PEOPLE'S PARTY
(Kristelig Folkeparti; KrF)

HISTORY

The party was founded in 1933 by a group of religious temperance activists after one of their main leaders was dropped from the Liberal Party list for the *Storting* election that year. It emerged as a national party in 1945 and since then has advanced to become the third-largest party in the system. It attracts support principally from religious activists both within and outside the state church, in particular from those who are members of the numerous organizations for home and foreign missions. It joined government coalitions with the other nonsocialist parties in 1963, 1965 to 1971, and 1972–73 (when it also provided the prime minister, Lars Korvald), 1986–89, with the Conservative and Center Parties following the 1989 general election, and with the Center and Liberal Parties in 1997, when it again provided the prime minister, Kjell Magne Bondevik.

ORGANIZATION

The Christian People's Party shares the mass-branch structure described above and also maintains auxiliary organizations for women and youth. Unlike the other major parties, it receives no direct support from a major national newspaper, although two nonpartisan Christian papers give it generally sympathetic treatment. The party's own principal organs are *Folkets Framtid* (The People's Future), published twice weekly, and *Ide* (Idea), a quarterly journal. National headquarters are at Rosenkrantzgt. 13, Oslo 1.

MEMBERSHIP AND CONSTITUENCY

The party has for most of the postwar period had a relatively weak membership base. This is compensated for by its ability to borrow strength from the religious and temperance organizations, despite the fact that the party has no formal connections with them. Its principal stronghold is still in those areas, particularly in the south and west of the country, where these organizations maintain an important, if declining, strength. In 1990, the party reported a membership of approximately 62,000, an increase of about 2,000 members since 1980.

POLICY

From its inception the party has been committed to the promotion and defense of fundamentalist Christian values, including temperance. The party has distinguished itself from all others through its stands on moral and religious issues. Since the late 1960s the most controversial of these stands has been the party's strong opposition to the liberal abortion law espoused and then introduced by the Labor Party. The party's inability in recent years to persuade the Conservative Party to adopt an equally strong position led directly to the failure of attempts to form a majority nonsocialist coalition after the 1981 election. When it finally joined the Conservative and Center Parties in government in 1983, it firmly reserved its position on this issue.

In economic policy, the party is nonsocialist, although in the area of social welfare it has often been closer to Labor than the other nonsocialist parties. In foreign affairs, it is strongly pro-NATO, but the EEC question in the early 1970s caused severe internal divisions.

FINANCING

Unlike the other major parties, the Christian People's Party does not receive support from the major economic-interest organizations. Nor does it receive funds from the politically neutral religious organizations. Consequently, membership dues, private contributions, and the government subsidy account for almost all of the party's finances.

LEADERSHIP

For most of the 1970s the main leader of the Christian Democrats was Lars Korvald, who was opposed to EEC entry and strongly against any compromise on the abortion issue. The disagreement over these issues led to strong party infighting. Korvald disputed the EEC and abortion issues heavily with Kaare Kristiansen, who took over as party leader during the 1980s. However, the disagreements have subsided for the most part. Valgerd Svarstad Haugland is the current party chair.

PROSPECTS

The Christian People's Party reached a peak of popular support in the 1997 election with 13.7% of the vote. A majority of the party's supporters are known to favor the formation of a majority nonsocialist government despite the inability to agree on the repeal of the existing abortion law. Guided by Christian and moral principles, this remains one of the central arguments of the party's platform. Such changes may now be possible as the Christian People's Party makes up the largest part of the current coalition government (with the Center and Liberal Parties).

CONSERVATIVE PARTY
(Høyre; "The Right")

HISTORY

The Conservative Party was founded in 1884 to oppose Liberals' demands that the royal veto should be defied and the rules of parliamentarism be adopted. For most of this century it has aspired to be the principal national party of all those opposed to socialism. It constituted a major element in the nonsocialist coalitions of 1963 and 1965 to 1971. Despite being the largest of the nonsocialist parties, in most of the post-1945 period, it usually took only about 18% of the votes. After 1973, however, it enjoyed a remarkable growth of support, taking as much as 31.7% of the vote in 1981. This support has waned in recent elections, dropping to 17% of the vote in the 1993 general election.

ORGANIZATION

Like the other major parties, the Conservative Party has a mass-branch type of organization with women's and youth wings. In the 1970s the organization was reformed and greatly expanded after a successful membership recruitment drive. The party receives indirect support from a number of important national regional daily newspapers.

National headquarters are at Høyres Hus, Stortingsgate 20, Oslo 1.

MEMBERSHIP AND CONSTITUENCY

Around the turn of the century, the party changed from being the party of the old class of officials, which had administered the state for centuries, to being the party of the rising class of those in business and higher professionals. Because of the survival of the other nonsocialist parties, the party failed to become a national party appealing to all classes and regions, remaining instead a largely urban-based party of high-income earners. Its recent membership drive has broadened this base somewhat. Membership in 1990 stood at around 170,000, a steady figure since 1980, but more than 50% greater than that of the mid-1970s.

POLICY

The party's opposition to socialism has been associated with the championship of private enterprise and initiative in the context of a free market. Like the other nonsocialist parties, however, it has come to accept the most central aspects of the country's highly developed welfare state. In recent years it has called for the deregulation of the economy and the reduction of taxes, claiming that such a strategy would generate new economic growth and so leave the welfare state intact.

In foreign policy the Conservatives have been strongly pro-NATO and pro-EEC. Their support for the EEC in the early 1970s, when the country voted by referendum not to join, led to a relative decline in the party's fortunes. In the 1980s, a period with less EEC concern among Norwegians, the Conservatives attracted growing support for their economic programs. However, the EEC (now EU) issue has arisen again in the 1990s and still looms large in the rhetoric of the Conservative Party.

FINANCING

The party receives large contributions from private business organizations, although, as in the case of the other parties, exact figures are unknown. The party claims that membership subscriptions and the government subsidy nonetheless account for the lion's share of party finances.

LEADERSHIP

Since the early 1970s the party has benefited from the services of an able and generally harmonious leadership. The main political figure in the 1980s was Kare Willoch (born 1928), who served as prime minister after the 1985 general election. A young and dynamic general secretary and chairman from the north of the country was primarily responsible for the organizational rejuvenation of the party in the 1970s. The current chair of the party is Jan Petersen.

PROSPECTS

The party's successes in the regional strongholds of the centrist parties and among the young and the better-paid (and more highly taxed) workers support its claim to have become at last the "progressive, liberal-conservative, and moderate" party of the country—and the worthy counterpart and opponent of the long-dominant Labor Party. Together with the Center Party, the Conservatives provided a strong challenge to Labor's long-standing rule in parliament. However, the party was not a part of the coalition government formed when Labor stepped down after the 1997 election. The Conservative Party will continue to argue for deregulation, lower taxes, and membership in the EU, as market forces, it believes, can solve most of the country's problems.

LABOR PARTY
(Det Norske Arbeiderparti; DNA)

HISTORY

Founded in 1887, the party did not become an important electoral force until after the introduction of manhood suffrage in 1898. It was from the first closely associated with trade unions, which experienced considerable membership growth in the industrial takeoff period immediately before the First World War. In 1918 the party was taken over by a radical new leadership that soon brought it into the Communist International, thereby precipitating a number of splits. When the party was reunited in the late 1920s, it immediately established itself as the largest electoral force in the system, a status it has been able to maintain with ease throughout most general and local elections.

In 1935 Labor began a term of office that was to last for 30 years, interrupted only by the German occupation and the two-month nonsocialist coalition of 1963. From 1945 to 1961 it enjoyed an absolute majority in the *Storting*. In 1971 the party again formed a minority government committed to negotiating Norwegian entry into the EEC. When this policy was rejected in the September 1972 referendum, the government resigned. In the 1973 election, the party suffered its heaviest loss of votes since 1930 but was able to form a minority government by relying on the support of the Socialist Electoral. For eight years thereafter it clung to office on the strength of a single-seat majority for the parties of the socialist bloc, finally being defeated in the election of 1981. The Labor Party regained its dominance in the late 1980s and has retained its position since.

ORGANIZATION

Like the other major parties, Labor has a mass-branch type of organization with important women's and youth sections. Its close association with the trade unions is institutionalized in a system of collective membership; i.e., trade union locals are members of the party at the local level. This feature lends the party organization great depth and penetration. The party is involved in the management of the main national daily newspaper of the labor movement, *Arbeiderbladet* (Workers' Paper), and some 40 other regional and local newspapers.

Party headquarters are at Youngstorgt 2, Oslo 1.

MEMBERSHIP AND CONSTITUENCY

The party has traditionally been supported by the industrial working class, which is highly unionized, but also by workers in primary industry and smallholders in agriculture. It is the urban-rural basis of support that accounts for the party's historic strength. Membership in 1990 was reported to be 180,000, an increase of about 20,000 members since 1980. More than half of the party's members come from collective trade union affiliation.

POLICY

As the natural party of government since the mid-1930s, Labor has abandoned its early policies of radical social and economic change, opting instead for gradual reform aimed at maintaining full employment and the development of a welfare state in a mixed economy. In contrast to the nonsocialist parties, it is committed to a relatively high degree of government planning and intervention in the economy.

In foreign policy, the party adopted a firmly pro-NATO position in the late 1940s. It has generally maintained this stance ever since, but it has been opposed to the stationing of foreign troops and the installation of nuclear weapons in Norway. During the 1980s the Labor Party committed itself to the introduction of a nuclear-free zone in the Nordic area. From the early 1960s, the party was for a decade also strongly pro-EEC, but the defeat of the policy in the 1972 referendum led it to abandon this commitment.

FINANCING

Substantial financial support is received from the trade unions, but membership dues and the government subsidy still account for a major proportion of party finance.

LEADERSHIP

Labor's electoral fortunes were undermined in the mid-1970s by tensions between the party's radical and moderate wings. It attempted to accommodate the two sides by dividing the leadership between a moderate prime minister and a more radical chairman. The experiment failed to resolve the tensions, and in early 1981 the two functions were reunited in the person of Gro Harlem Brundtland (born 1939), the country's first female prime minister and perhaps the most prolific Norwegian prime minister of the latter 20th century. Despite Conservative rule of the *Storting* in the 1980s, Brundtland returned to the office of prime minister in 1985. She resigned her position in 1989 but returned after one year when the nonsocialist government resigned over internal differences on the EEC. Brundtland has since retired, and the current Labor Party chair is Thorbjørn Jagland.

PROSPECTS

Labor's 1981 electoral performance, although not as bad as that of 1973 when it suffered a hemorrhage of support to its left, was approximately 10% below its average vote in the 1950s and 1960s. Regaining some power in 1985, Labor enjoyed a resurgence of support as it campaigned successfully on social welfare issues. The resurgence was insufficient to return it to office, however, even with the increased support for the Socialist Left Party, and the continuing loss of support among the young and the higher-paid workers in the more prosperous parts of the country remained as warning signs for the future. Labor enjoyed increased support in the early 1990s, but with the defeat of the 1994 referendum on EU membership and subsequent political attacks on the party, Labor has again lost some of its support. Even though the party received the largest proportion of the vote in the 1997 election, the Labor government stepped down stating that it would not remain in power because it had not received at least as much of the popular vote in 1997 as it did in the 1993 election.

MINOR POLITICAL PARTIES

Communist Party of Norway
(Norges Kommunistiske Parti; NKP)

The Communist Party of Norway was founded by left-wing members of the Labor Party when it disaffiliated from the Third (Communist) International in 1923 after a short period of membership. In the interwar period it declined to the status of an insignificant political sect, but it enjoyed a strong revival (taking almost 12% of the vote) in 1945 after a period of active involvement in the resistance to the German occupation. From that high point it again declined, losing its last *Storting* seat in 1961. In 1973 it joined the Socialist Electoral League (see under Socialist Left Party below) and shared in the success of that organization as it capitalized on the strong wave of mobilization against the EEC. Two years later, however, die-hard elements refused to go along with the decision to merge with other left-socialist elements in the new Socialist Left Party.

In the years after 1945 the Communist Party purged itself of "bourgeois-nationalist," "Trotskyite," and "Titoist"

elements and reverted to being a strict Stalinist, Moscow-aligned party. With the exception of the EEC referendum episode, it has largely remained within this mold and is now again a party of almost no electoral importance.

Liberal Party
(Venstre; literally "The Left")

Founded in the early 1880s on the basis of a coalition of peasants and urban intellectuals committed to the introduction of parliamentarism, the Liberal Party's history since then has been very checkered. Until the First World War it remained the predominant party of government despite two serious splits on the right. In the period since then, however, it was first overtaken by Labor as the principal party of social reform and then lost support to the Farmer's and Christian Democrat Parties in the center of the political spectrum. Its remaining support was based on an uneasy alliance of diverse groups: temperance, religious, and language activists; secularist libertarians; and low-salaried workers.

Unlike other parties it had no single social or economic constituency and was sustained by little more than a common commitment to rather vague liberal ideas and the party's historic traditions. As such it joined the other nonsocialist parties in the 1963 and 1965–71 coalitions. The EEC issue found the party badly divided, however, and it split into two soon after, the faction opposed to the EEC retaining the old party label. The Liberal Party since the 1973 election has not been able to take more than two seats in the *Storting*. In 1985 it declared its willingness to lend support to a socialist government in exchange for the adoption of its environmentalist policies, but in the election it failed to gain any representation for the first time in its long history. The party returned to regain one *Storting* seat in the 1993 election. In the 1995 local election, the Liberal Party made a stronger showing, taking 4.7% of the vote. Finally, in 1997, the Liberals formed a coalition government with the Christian People's Party and the Center Party after Labor relinquished its control of the government.

Liberal People's Party
(Det Liberale Folkepartiet; DLF)

When the Liberal Party split in 1972, the pro-EEC faction, which included 9 of the 13 members of the old Liberal *Storting* group, broke away to form the Liberal People's Party. In the 1973 election it fared even worse than the remaining Liberals, taking only a single seat, which it lost in 1977 and has since been unable to regain. With less than 1% of the vote the party is clearly moribund with little or no prospect of resuscitation.

Progress Party
(Fremskrittspartiet)

The Progress Party was founded in 1973 under the name Anders Lange's Party for Substantial Reduction in Taxes, Duties, and Governmental Interference. Anders Lange was a well-known political maverick. In 1973 the party took 5% of the vote and four seats. After Lange's death a year later the party was torn by internal strife, for which it paid in 1977 with the loss of its *Storting* representation, despite the shift to its present name. At the 1981 election it rode the conservative wave of popular resentment against high taxes and returned to the *Storting* with four members. In 1985, although its representation was halved, it was placed in the position of holding the balance of power. It has since regained some strength, gaining six seats in parliament in 1993. Since both government and opposition are pledged not to negotiate with it, the party seems unlikely to be able to exert much leverage. It has, instead, cast itself in the role of watchdog for the right, alert to any slips or sellouts on the part of, in particular, the Conservative Party.

Socialist Left Party
(Sosialistisk Venstreparti; SV)

In 1961, a Socialist People's Party was founded by a group of anti-NATO activists who had been expelled from the Labor Party. In the election of the same year they deprived Labor of its overall *Storting* majority by taking 2 seats, which they managed to hold for eight years, to 1969. With the success of the anti-EEC referendum campaign in 1972, the party enjoyed a revival that was strengthened by cooperation with other anti-EEC and anti-NATO groups (including the Communist Party and a further splinter from Labor known as the Workers' Information Office) in the Socialist Electoral League. In the 1973 election, it took 11.2% of the vote and 16 seats. Two years later, the League was converted into the Socialist Left Party. The process was attended by considerable internal disagreement; the Communist Party die-hards eventually refused to merge into the new party. In the 1980s, SV failed to sustain the 1973 level of support for its radical socialist and neutralist policies. With the Labor Party in opposition there is the danger it might shift leftward and undercut the Socialist Left Party, but the Conservative and Labor Parties' continued support for NATO and EU issues are likely to leave adequate space for the party to the far left of the party spectrum.

Red Electoral Alliance
(Rød Valgallianse; RV)

In 1973, a Maoist party was formed by the merger of a number of extreme-left splinter groups, the largest of which had split in 1968 from the Socialist People's Party's youth section. The party took the name Workers' Communist Party Marxist-Leninist (*Arbeidernes Kommunist parti Marxist-Leninistene*; AKPML). Since 1971, the party has fought the *Storting* elections under the name Red Electoral Alliance, failing to gain representation. Despite internal problems connected with attitudes toward China, the party will doubtless continue to exist, but its prospects for achieving anything but the most marginal electoral support must be meager.

OTHER POLITICAL FORCES

Economic-Interest Groups

Like neighboring Sweden, Norway has a very highly developed system of interest-group representation that plays an important role within the overall political system. Despite the overwhelming ethnic and confessional homogeneity of the population (the Lapps in the far north account for less than 1%, and over 90% of Norwegians remain members of the Lutheran state church), the earliest voluntary associations to develop were those that articulated emergent cultural differences. In the middle and late 19th century, movements associated with religious revivalism, temperance or prohibition, and the promotion of an alternative linguistic standard (New Norwegian) based on rural dialects gave rise to organizations that have continued to have a significant political impact. In particular these three "countercultural" movements with their disproportionate strength in the south and west of the country provided the historic basis for the viability of the centrist parties with their opposition to the industrialism and secularism of the Labor and Conservative Parties.

It is the economic-interest organizations—founded around the turn of the century to defend and promote the interest of workers, employers, and farmers—that have had the greatest impact on the style and content of political decision making. Through a system of regular consultation with government in a wide range of ad hoc and regular committees, commissions, and boards, they have provided a second channel of popular representation alongside that of the *Storting*. The system has been called one of corporate pluralism, and decisions made within it have regularly affected central questions of economic and social policy. The existence of this second tier of decision making or representation helps to explain the high level of policy consensus and general political stability in a system that for 20 years after the war was dominated by one party, the Labor Party, to the exclusion of all others. The standing of the main interest groups is enhanced by extremely high levels of membership within their respective economic constituencies and a degree of centralization, not least among the trade unions, that has enabled group leaderships to deliver binding agreements.

The major interest-group organizations are the Norwegian Employers' Association (*Norsk Arbeidsgiverforening*; NAF), the Norwegian Trades Union Federation (*Landsorganisasjonen i Norge*; LO), and the Norwegian Farmers' Union (*Norges Bondelag*). No other groups are nearly so important, but two small groups do have some role; they are the Norwegian Smallholders' Union (*Norsk Bonde-og Smabrukarlag*) and the Norwegian Fisherman's Union (*Norges Fiskarlag*).

NATIONAL PROSPECTS

Although full-employment policies are usually associated with high inflation, Norwegians have, of late, staved off many of the negative consequences of full employment. This has not always been the case. In the 1980s, traditional industries such as shipping, wood processing, and textiles required massive financial support from the Norwegian government to remain economically healthy and competitive. At the same time, the Norwegian government–led *Statoil* (the state-run oil industry) required large loans to continue the development of North Sea oil projects. The 1990s have seen great economic returns on these investments. The Labor government maintained full employment policies while a now-healthy Norwegian economy sees strong wage growth with relatively low inflation rates.

Politically, Labor is no longer in charge of the *Storting*, and it is unclear what effect this change will have on the Norwegian economy. Entering the 1997 election, Labor's popularity was waning. Having supported membership in the European Economic Community for a number of years, Labor saw the 1994 referendum on membership voted down by a slim margin: 52.2% of the population. Prime Minister Thorbjørn Jagland announced before the election that the Labor Party would step down if it failed to receive 36.9% of the vote (the same amount it received in 1993's election). Labor's 35% of the vote in 1997,

while still the largest proportion of the total, was not enough to meet this self-imposed demand of the voters' show of confidence.

Thus the Labor Party relinquished its control over the *Storting*, making way for a coalition government among the Christian People's, Center, and Liberal Parties. However, this change in power did not take place until after Labor submitted its 1998 fiscal budget. The coalition government could make only minor changes to this budget, and it remains to be seen what major economic, political, and social changes the new government will make when the 1999 fiscal budget is implemented.

Further Reading

Arter, David. *The Nordic Parliaments*. London: C. Hurst, and New York: St. Martin's Press, 1984.

Berglund, Sten, and Ulf Lindstrom. *The Scandinavian Party System(s)*. Lund, Sweden: Studentlitteratur, 1978.

Cerny, Karl H., ed. *Scandinavia at the Polls*. Washington, D.C.: American Enterprise Institute for Public Policy Research, 1977.

Eckstein, Harry. *Division and Cohesion in Democracy: A Study of Norway*. Princeton, N.J.: Princeton University Press, 1966.

Rokkan, Stein. "Norway, Numerical Democracy and Corporate Pluralism." In *Political Oppositions in Western Democracies*, Ed. Robert Dahl. New Haven, Conn.: Yale University Press, 1966.

Storing, James A. *Norwegian Democracy*. Boston: Houghton Mifflin, 1963.

Valen, Henry, and D. Katz. *Political Parties in Norway*. Oslo: Universitetsforlaget, 1964.

Valen, Henry, D. Katz, and Stein Rokkan. "Norway: Conflict Structure and Mass Politics in a European Periphery." In *Electoral Behavior: A Comparative Handbook*. Ed. Richard Rose. London: Collier Macmillan, and New York: Free Press, 1974.

Web Site

Official Documentation and Information from Norway (ODIN; central web server for Norwegian government, the office of the prime minister, and the ministries): http://odin.dep.no/html/english

INDEX

A

Abacha, Sani, 816–817, 818, 820, 822, 984

Abashidze, Aslan, 393, 397

Abbas, Abul, 850

Abbas, Chetti Ali, 193

Abbas, Farhat, 17

Abboud, Ibrahim, 1041, 1044, 1046, 1047

Abdallah, Ahmed, 232

Abdallah, Ali Hamisi, 1092

Abdildin, Serkbolsyn, 606, 608, 609

Abdul Aziz, 961, 962, 963, 964, 965, 967

Abdul Aziz bin Fahd, 963

Abdul Aziz bin Salman, 963

Abdullah, 604, 962, 963

Abdullah, David, 1115

Abdullah, Farooq, 499

Abdullah, Mohammed, 499

'Abdullah, 919

Abdullah al-Sulayman, 964

Abdullojonov, Abdumalik, 1086, 1088, 1089

Abdul Muhsin, 963

Abdul Rahman, 962, 963

Abessole, Paul M'Ba, 387, 389

Abinader, José Rafael, 307

Abiola, Moshood, 816, 817, 820, 821, 822

Abubakar, Abdulsalami, 817, 818, 819, 820, 822

Abuhatzeira, Aharon, 550

Abybajarm Abdyksakanu, 816

Achakzai, Mahmud Khan, 844

Acheampong, I. K., 414

Action Committee for Democracy and Pension Justice (Aktiounskomitee fir Demokratie a Rentegerechtegkeet; ADR) (Luxembourg), 687–688

Action Committee for Renewal (Comite d'Action pour la Renou-veau; CAR) (Togo), 1110–1111

Action for Change (Action pour le Changement; AC) (Mauritania), 725–726

Action for the Republic (Acción de la República) (Argentina), 36

Action Front for Renewal and Development (FARD) (Benin), 109, 110

Action Group for Democracy (Grupo de Acción por la Democracia; GAD) (Dominican Republic), 310

Action of Social Democrats (Croatia), 258

ACT New Zealand, 798

Adalberto Rivera, Julio, 335

Adams, David, 1180

Adams, Gerry, 1177

Adams, Grantley, 91

Adams, John Michael Geoffrey "Tom," 91

Adams, Tom, 430

Adelsohn, Ulf, 1063

Adenauer, Konrad, 252, 404, 405, 406

Adiahenot, Jacques, 388

Adji, Boukary, 813

Adjovi, Severin, 110

Adolat Social Democratic Party of Uzbekistan, 1213

Advani, L. K., 489, 490

Afäwärk'i, Issaias, 341

Afghanistan, 1–8

Afghan National Liberation Front (Jabba-ye-Milli-ye-Afghanistan), 2

Aflaq, Michel, 527, 1073, 1076

African Christian Democratic Party (ACDP) (South Africa), 1018–1019

African Democratic Rally (Rassemblement Démocratique Africain; RDA) (Ivory Coast), 575

African Forum for Reconstruction (Forum Africain pour la Reconstruction; FAR) (Gabon), 389

African Independence Party (Parti Africain de l'Independence; PAI) (Senegal), 975

African Liberation Forces of Mauritania (Forces de libération africaine do Mauritanie; FLAM), 726

African National Congress (ANC) (South Africa), 1010, 1011, 1012, 1013, 1014–1016, 1018, 1019, 1020, 1047

African National Congress (Zambia), 1257

African National Congress (Zimbabwe), 1264

African National Union (Zimbabwe), 1265

African Party for the Independence of Cape Verde (Partido Africano da Independência da Guiné e Cabo Verde; PAICV), 186, 187

African Party for the Independence of Guinea and Cape Verde (PAIGC) (Partido Africano da Independência da Guiné e Cabo Verde) (Guinea-Bissau), 187, 443, 444, 445

African People's League for Independence (Ligue populaire africaine pour l'independence; LPAI) (Djibouti), 301

African Rally for Progress and Democracy, 110

Afro-Shirazi Party (ASP) (Tanzania), 1093

Agboyibo, Yaovi, 1110, 1111, 1112

Agenda for Zambia, 1259

Agondjo-Okawé, Pierre Louis Agondjo, 389

Agrarian/Center Party of Norway, 825

Agrarian Democratic Party (Moldova), 744, 745

Agrarian Labor Party (Panama), 855

Agrarian League (Norway), 826

M

Q

Sinn Féin (SF) (We Ourselves) (Northern Ireland), 1171, 1173, 1175—1177, 1182

Sinn Féin (We Ourselves) (Ireland), 533, 536—537, 539, 540

Sinowatz, Fred, 61, 67

Sinzoyiheba, Firmin, 157

Siphandôn, Khamtai, 642

Siqueiros, David, 737

Sirag al-Din, Fuad, 328

Sissoko, Fily Dabo, 716

Sisulu, Walter, 1014

Sithole, Ndabaningi, 1262, 1267

Siwar al-Dahab, Abd al-Rahman, 1041

Sjursen, Jann, 297

Skaarup, Peter, 291

Skarphédinsson, Össur, 481

Skate, Bill, 864

Skele, Andris, 647

Skifte, Daniel, 299

Skokov, Iurii, 938

Sládek, Miroslav, 280

Slater, John, 797

Slavonian-Baranian Party (Croatia), 258

Slovak Democratic Coalition (SDK), 996

Slovak Freedom Party (Czech Republic), 277

Slovakia (The Slovak Republik), 992—1001

Slovak National Coalition (SDK), 1000

Slovak National Party (Slovenská narodná strana; SNS), 998—999

Slovak Party of Entrepreneurs and Traders (SPZ), 1000

Slovak Renaissance Party (Czech Republic), 277

Slovene National Party, 1006

Slovene People's Party (Slovenska Ljudska Stranka; SLS), 1004, 1005

Slovenia, Republic of (Republika Slovenija), 1002—1006

Slovenian Christian Democrats (Slovenski Krscanski Demokrati; SKD), 1005

Smallwoods, Raymond, 1180

Smart, John K., 981

Smarth, Rosny, 451, 454

Smith, F. G., 91

Smith, Gerald, 1267

Smith, Ian Douglas, 1262, 1267

Smith, John, 1164

Smith, William, 1180

Snegur, Mircea, 742, 743, 745, 746

Snoh Tienthong, 1104, 1105, 1106

Soares, Mario, 902, 904, 905, 906

Sobchak, Anatolii, 940

Sobor, Eugin, 746

Social, Liberal, and Democratic Party (Mozambique), 764

Social Action Party (Kit Sanghom) (Thailand), 1099

Social and Democratic Republican Party (Maaouiya Ould Sid'Achmed Taya; Parti Républicain Démocratique et Social; PRDS) (Mauritania), 724, 725, 726

Social Christian Movement (Ecuador), 319

Social Christian Party of Ecuador (Partido Social Cristiano; PSC), 314, 317, 318, 319

Social Christian Party of Guatemala (Partido Social Cristiano; PSC), 436, 437

Social Christian Party of Nicaragua (Partido Social Cristiano Nicaragüense; PSCN), 802, 803, 808

Social Christian Unity Party (Partido Unidad Social Cristiana; PUSC) (Costa Rica), 246, 247, 248—249

Social Conservatism Party (Partido Social Conservador; PSOC) (Nicaragua), 807

Social Credit Party (Canada), 175

Social Democracy Party (SODEP) (Turkey), 1125

Social Democratic Alliance (Alianza Social Democrática) (Dominican Republic), 307

Social Democratic Alliance (Iceland), 480, 482

Social Democratic and Labour Party (SDLP) (Northern Ireland), 1171, 1173, 1174, 1177—1178

Social Democratic Center of Angola, 27

Social Democratic Center of Spain (Center Democrático y Social; CDS), 1026, 1028—1029

Social Democratic Front (SDF) (Cameroon), 163, 166

Social Democratic Institutional Block (Bloque Institutional Social Demócrata; BIS) (Dominican Republic), 310

Social Democratic League of Workers and Small Farmers (TPSL) (Finland), 363

Social Democratic Party Estonia, 347

Social Democratic Party of Angola, 27

Social Democratic Party of Austria (Sozialdemokratische Partei Österreichs; SPÖ), 61, 62, 63, 65, 66—67

Social Democratic Party of Bahamas (SDP), 78

Social Democratic Party of Benin (PSD), 110

Social Democratic Party of Bosnia, 124, 126

Social Democratic Party of Brazil (Partido Democrático Social; PDS), 132, 133, 136, 137, 138, 139, 141

Social Democratic Party of Costa Rica, 248

Social Democratic Party of Croatia (Socijal Demokratska Partija Hrvatske; SDP), 256—257

Social Democratic Party of Czech, 278

Social Democratic Party of Denmark (Socialdemokratiet; SD), 283, 287, 288, 290, 292, 293, 294, 299

Social Democratic Party of Finland (SDP) (Suomen Socialidemokraattinen Puolue), 355, 356, 361, 362—363, 364

Social Democratic Party of France (PSD), 381

Social Democratic Party of Germany (Sozialdemokratische Partei Deutschlands; SPD), 399, 401, 402, 403, 404, 405, 406, 408, 409, 410, 411—412, 460

Social Democratic Party of Guatemala (Partido Socialista Democrático; PSD), 433, 435, 436—437

Social Democratic Party of Guinea-Bissau (Partido Social Democratico; PSD), 445

Social Democratic Party of Iceland (SDP) (Althyduflokkurinn), 474, 475, 477, 479, 480—481

Social Democratic Party of Japan (SDP) (Shaminto), 590, 591, 592, 593—594, 595

Social Democratic Party of Kenya, 614

Social-Democratic Party of Kyrgyzstan, 639

Social Democratic Party of Madagascar (PSD), 696, 697

Social Democratic Party of Moldova, 744, 746

Social Democratic Party of Mongolia, 750

Social Democratic Party of Nicaragua, 803

Social Democratic Party of Nigeria (SDP), 818, 820

LIST OF ACRONYMS AND ABBREVIATIONS

AAFU–see Anti-Communist and Anti-Imperialist Front of Ukraine

AAPO–see All-Amhara People's Organization (Ethiopia)

ABVP–see All-India Students Organization

AC–see Action for Change (Mauritania)

ACDP–see African Christian Democratic Party (South Africa)

ACLM–see Antigua Caribbean Liberation Movement (Antigua and Barbuda)

AD–see Democratic Alliance (Guatemala)

AD–see Alleanza Democratica (Italy)

AD–see Democratic Action (Venezuela)

ADA–see Democratic Alliance of Angola

ADEMA–see Alliance for Democracy in Mali-The African Party for Solidarity and Justice

ADERE–see Democratic and Republican Alliance (Gabon)

ADFL–see Alliance of Democratic Forces for Liberation of Congo/Zaire (D. Rep. Congo)

ADM-19–see M-19 Democratic Alliance (Colombia)

AND–see Nationalist Democratic Action (Bolivia)

ADP–see Alliance for Democracy and Progress (Benin)

ADP–see Assembly of People's Deputies (Burkina Faso)

ADP–see Alliance for Democracy and Progress (Central African Republic)

ADP–see Arab Democratic Party (Israel)

ADR–see Action Committee for Democracy and Pension Justice (Luxembourg)

ADS–see Alternative for Democracy and Socialism (France)

ADSR–see Alliance of Democrats of the Slovak Republic

AEEM–see Association of Pupils and Students of Mali

AEPA–see All-Ethiopian Peasants Association

AETU–see All-Ethiopian Trade Union

AFC–see Alliance of Forces of Change (Niger)

AFD–see Alliance of Free Democrats (Hungary)

AFD–see Alliance For Democracy (Nigeria)

AFKM–see Congress Party for the Independence of Madagascar

AFKM-Renewal–see Congress Party for Madagascar Independence-Renewal Party

AFL–see Armed Forces of Liberia

AFL-CIO–see American Federation of Labor-Congress of Industrial Organizations (U.S.A.)

AFORD–see Alliance for Democracy (Malawi)

AFPFL–see Anti-Fascist People's Freedom League (Myanmar)

AFRC–see Armed Forces Revolutionary Council (Sierra Leone)

Agaleu–see Ecologist Parties (Belgium)

AGP–see Assam Peoples Council (India)

AIADMK–see All-India Anna-Dravida Munnetra Kazhagam

AICC–see All-India Congress Committee

AICP–see All-India Communist Party

AID–see Agency for International Development (U.S.A.)

AIS–see Islamic Salvation Army (Algeria)

AKAR–see People's Justice Movement (Malaysia)

AKEL–see Progressive Party of the Working People (Cyprus)

AKPML–see Workers' Communist Party Marxist-Leninist (Norway)

AL–see Awami League (Bangladesh)

AL–see Liberal Alliance (Nicaragua)

AL–see Awami League (Pakistan)

ALF–see Arab Liberation Front (Palestinian Authority)

ALN–see National Liberation Army (Algeria)

ALO–see Austrian Alternative List

ALP–see Australian Labor Party

ALP–see Antigua Labour Party (Antigua and Barbuda)

AMAL–see Detachments of the Lebanese Resistance

AMP–see Association for Muslim Professionals (Singapore)

AMU–see Arab Maghreb Union (Libya)

AMU–see African Mineworker's Union (Zambia)

AN–see Alleanza Nationale (Italy)

ANAGAN–see National Association of Ranchers (Panama)

ANAPO–see National Popular Alliance (Colombia)

ANC–see Conservative National Action (Nicaragua)

ANC–see African National Congress (South Africa)

AND–see National Democratic Group (Andorra)

ANDDS-Zaman Lahiya–see Nigerian Alliance for Democracy and Social Progress-Zaman Lahiya (Niger)

ANDI–see National Association of Industrialists (Colombia)

ANDM–see Amhara National Democratic Movement (Ethiopia)

ANL–see National Liberating Alliance (Brazil)

ANM–see Armenian National Movement

ANP–see Alliance for New Politics (Philippines)

AOV and UNIE 55+–see General Union of the Elderly (Netherlands)

AP–see Popular Action (Peru)

AP–see Popular Alliance (Spain)

AP5–see Popular Alliance 5 (Guatemala)

APAI–see Israel Workers Party

APC–see Popular Conservative Alliance (Nicaragua)

APC–see All People's Congress (Sierra Leone)

APED–see Alliance for Ecology and Democracy (France)

APEDE–see Panamanian Association of Business Executives

APK–see Worker Party Communists (Sweden)

APMU–see All-Popular Movement of Ukraine

APNI or AP–see Alliance Party of Northern Ireland

APP–see All People's Party (Nigeria)

APRA–see American Popular Revolutionary Alliance (Peru)

APRC–see Alliance for Patriotic Reorientation and Construction (Gambia)

APRE–see Ecuadorian Popular Revolutionary Action

APU–see United Peoples Alliance (Portugal)

ARD–see Democratic Resistance Alliance (D. Rep. Congo)

AREMA–see Vanguard of the Malagasy Revolution (Madagascar)

ARENA–see National Renovating Alliance (Brazil)

ARENA–see Nationalist Republican Alliance (El Salvador)

AREV–see Red and Green Alternative (France)

ARF–see Armenian Revolutionary Federation

ARLN–see Revolutionary Army of Liberation of Northern Niger

ARMM–see Autonomous Region of Muslim Mindanao (Philippines)

ARP–see Anti-Revolutionary Party (Netherlands)

ASD–see Dominican Social Alliance Party

ASEAN–see Association of Southeast Asian Nations

ASI–see Federation of Labor (Iceland)

ASIS–see Alliance of Small Island States (Maldives)

ASP–see Afro-Shirazi Party (Tanzania)

ASU–see Arab Socialist Union (Egypt)

ASU–see Arab Socialist Union (Libya)

ATC–see Association of Rural Workers (Nicaragua)

ATLU–see Antigua Trades Labour Union (Antigua and Barbuda)

AV/MRDN–see And Jeff: Revolutionary Movement for the New Democracy (Senegal)

AVI–see Work Finished by Solidarity (Madagascar)

AWARE–see Association of Women for Action and Research (Singapore)

AWS–see Solidarity Electoral Action (Poland)

AYD–see Alliance of Young Democrats (Hungary)

AZADHO–see Zairian Association for the Defense of Human Rights (D. Rep. Congo)

BAKSAL–see Bangladesh Krishak Sramik Awami League

BAMCEF–see All-India Backward and Minority Communities Employees Federation

BBB–see Bulgarian Business Bloc

BCP–see Basotho Congress Party (Lesotho)

BDF–see Botswana Defense Force

BDG–see Gabonese Democratic Group

BDP–see Bahamian Democratic Party

BDP–see Botswana Democratic Party

BDS–see Senegalese Democratic Bloc

BIP–see Citizen's Initiative Parliament (Austria)

BIS–see Social Democratic Institutional Block (Dominican Rep.)

BITU–see Bustamante Industrial Trade Union (Jamaica)

BJP–see Bhanatiya Jawata Party (India)

BKU–see Bhanasiya Kisan Union, Punjab (India)

BKU–see Bhanatiya Kisan Union, Uttar Pradesh (India)

BLDP–see Buddhist Liberal Democratic Party (Cambodia)

BLP–see Barbados Labour Party

BN–see National Front (Malaysia)

BNA Act–see British North America Act (Canada)

BNF–see Botswana National Front

BNG–see Galician Nationalist Bloc (Spain)

BNP–see Bangladesh National Party

BNP–see Basotho National Party (Lesotho)

BPC–see Basic People's Congress (Libya)

BPF–see Belarusian Popular Front "Adrazennie"

BPP–see Bechuanaland People's Party (Botswana)

BQ–see Bloc Quebecois (Canada)

BRA–see Bougainville Revolutionary Army (Papua New Guinea)

BSB–see Burkina Socialist Bloc

BSP–see Bulgarian Socialist Party

BSP–see Bhutan Samas Party (Party of Society's Maturity) (India)

BSPP–see Burma Socialist Program Party (Myanmar)

C–see Center Party (Sweden)

C90–see Change 90 (Peru)

CAC–see Argentine Chamber of Commerce

CACIF–see Coordinating Committee of Commercial, Industrial, and Financial Associations (Guatemala)

CADE–see Annual Conference of Business Executives (Panama)

CAFPDE–see Council of Alternative Forces for Peace and Democracy (Ethiopia)

CAN–see Authentic Nationalist Central (Guatemala)

CAP–see Convention for a Progressive Alternative (France)

CASC–see Autonomous Confederation of Christian Syndicates (Dominican Rep.)

CAUS–see Council for Union Action and Unity (Nicaragua)

CC–see Christian Way (Nicaragua)

CC–see Canarian Coalition (Spain)

CCD–see Christian Democratic Center (Italy)

CCD–see Democratic Constituent Congress (Peru)

CCE–see Central Elections Council (El Salvador)

CCF–see Co-operative Commonwealth Federation (Canada)

CCM–see Concerned Citizens Movement (Saint Kitts)

CCM–see Revolutionary Party (Tanzania)

CCOOs–see Worker's Commissions (Spain)

CCP–see Chinese Communist Party

CD–see Center Democrats (Denmark)

CD–see Democratic Convergence (El Salvador)

CD–see Center Democrats (Netherlands)

CD–see Democratic Coordination (Nicaragua)

CD–see Democratic Change (Panama)

CD–see Democratic Center (Spain)

CDA–see Christian Democratic Appeal (Netherlands)

CDJ–see Congress for Democracy and Justice (Gabon)

CDP–see Congress for Democracy and Progress (Burkina Faso)

CDP–Convention of Democrats and Patriots (Senegal)

CDPA–see Democratic Convention of African People (Togo)

CDPP–see Christian Democratic People's Party (Hungary)

CDRs–see Committees of the Defense of the Revolution (Burkina Faso)

CDRs–see Committees for the Defense of the Revolution (Ghana)

CDS–see Social Democratic Center (Angola)

CDS–see Center of Social Democrats (France)

CDS–see Social Democratic Center Party (Portugal)

CDS–see Party of the Social Democratic Center (Portugal)

CDS–see Social Democratic Center (Spain)

CDS-Rahama–see Democratic and Social Convention-Rahama (Niger)

CDT–see Democratic Labor Confederation (Morocco)

CDU–see Union of Christian Democrats (Italy)

CDU–see United Democratic Coalition (Portugal)

CDU–see Unified Democratic Coalition (Portugal)

CDU/CSU–see Christian Democrats (Germany)

CEA –see Argentine Episcopal Conference

CEC–see Central Executive Committee (Singapore)

CEMC–see Central Election Management Committee (South Korea)

CEN–see National Executive Committee (Mexico)

CEN–see National Executive Committee (Venezuela)

CES–see Convergence Ecology Solidarity (France)

CETU–see Confederation of Ethiopian Trade Unions

CFD–see Coordination of Democratic Forces (Burkina Faso)

CFN–see Coordination of New Forces (Togo)

CFP–see Concentration of Popular Forces (Ecuador)

CG–see Galician Centrist (Spain)

CGEM–see General Economic Confederation of Morocco

CGT–see General Confederation of Labor (Argentina)

CGT–see General Confederation of Labor (France)

CGT–see General Confederation of Workers (Nicaragua)

CGTI–see Independent General Workers Confederation (Nicaragua)

CGTP–see General Central of Workers of Panama

CGUP–see Guatemalan Committee of Patriotic Unity

CHU–see Christian-Historical Union (Netherlands)

CIA–see U.S. Central Intelligence Agency

CIDOB–see Indigenous Confederation of the East, Chaco, and Amazonia of Bolivia

CIPRODEH–see Center for the Investigation and Promotion of Human Rights (Honduras)

CIS–see Commonwealth of Independent States

CiU–see Convergence and Union (Spain)

CLC–see Canadian Labor Congress

CLR–see Convention of Reformist Liberals (Gabon)

CLSTP–see Liberation Committee of Sao Tome and Principe

CM–see Council of Ministers (Cuba)

CMC–see Central Military Commission (China)

CMEA or COMECON–see Council for Mutual Economic Assistance (Vietnam)

CMLN–see Military Committee of National Liberation (Mali)

CMRPN–see Military Committee of Redressment for National Progress (Burkina Faso)

CMS–see Supreme Military Council (Niger)

CMSS–see Czech-Moravian Party of the Center (Czech Rep.)

CN–see National Convention (CAR)

CNC–see National Peasant Confederation (Mexico)

CND–see National Development Council (Rwanda)

CNDF–see Congress of National Democratic Forces (Ukraine)

CNE–see National Electoral Council (Venezuela)

CNI–see National Center of Independents and Peasants (France)

CNID–see National Congress of Democratic Initiative (Mali)

CNIR–see Inter-Regional National Council (France)

CNJ–see National Council of the Judiciary (El Salvador)

CNOP–see National Federation of Popular Organizations (Mexico)

CNR–see National Council of Revolution (Burkina Faso)

CNS–see Sovereign National Council (Chad)

CNS–see National Unity Commission (Rwanda)

CNT–see National Workers Federation (Mexico)

CNTP–see National Worker's Central of Panama

CNU–see Cameroon National Union

COB–see Confederation of Bolivian Workers

COD–see Coalition of Democratic Opposition (Togo)

CODE–see Democratic Coordinator (Peru)

CODEH–see Committee for the Defense of Human Rights in Honduras

COFADEH–see Committee of the Families of the Detained and Disappeared in Honduras

COMELEC–see Commission on Elections (Philippines)

CONAIE–see Confederation of Indigenous Nationalities of Ecuador

CONAPRODEH–see National Commission for the Protection of Human Rights (Honduras)

CONCAMIN–see Confederation of Industrial Chambers (Mexico)

CONCANACO–see Confederation of National Chambers of Commerce (Mexico)

CONCLAT–see National Coordination of the Working Class (Brazil)

CONDEPA–see Conscience of the Fatherland (Bolivia)

CONEP–see National Council of Private Enterprise (Panama)

CONFENIAE–see Confederation of Indigenous Nationalities of the Amazon (Ecuador)

COPAZ–see National Commission for Consolidation of Peace (El Salvador)

COPCON–see Continental Operations Command (Portugal)

COPE–see Committee on Political Education (U.S.A.)

COPEI–see Christian Social Party (Venezuela)

COSATU–see Congress of South African Trade Unions

COSEP–see Superior Council of Private Enterprise (Nicaragua)

COSU–see Coordination of the United Senegalese Opposition

COTU–see Central Organization of Trade Unions (Kenya)

CP–see Popular Coalition (Spain)

CPBM–see Communist Party of Bohemia and Moravia (Czech Rep.)

CPC–see Central People's Committee (North Korea)

CPCC–see Chinese People's Consultative Conference

CPD–see Citizens for Democracy (Guatemala)

CPDM–see Cameroon People's Democratic Movement

CPI–see Communist Party of India

CPIB–see Coordinator of the Indigenous Peoples of Beni (Bolivia)

CPM–see Communist Party of India (Marxist)

CPM–see Communist Party of Moldavia (Moldova)

CPML–see Communist Party of India

CPN–see Communist Party of the Netherlands

CPP–see Cambodian People's Party

CPP–see Communist Party of the Philippines

CPP–see Convention People's Party (Ghana)

CPRF–see Communist Party of the Russian Federation

CPSA–see Conservative Party (South Africa)

CPSU–see Communist Party of the Soviet Union (Tajikistan)

CPSU–see Communist Party of the Soviet Union (Turkmenistan)

CPT–see Communist Party of Tajikistan

CPT–see Communist Party of Turkmenistan

CPU–see Communist Party of Ukraine

CPUz–see Communist Party of Uzbekistan

CRA–see Argentine Rural Confederations

CRA–see Coordination of Armed Resistance (Niger)

CRM–see Citizens Rights Movement (Israel)

CRN–see Council of National Reconciliation (Mali)

CROC–see Revolutionary Federation of Workers and Peasants (Mexico)

CRP–see Circle for Renewal and Progress (Gabon)

CS–see Council of State (Cuba)

CSDDM–see Committee for the Support of Democracy and Development in Madagascar

CSE–see Supreme Electoral Council (Nicaragua)

CSL–see Czech People's Party

CSN–see Council of National Health (Niger)

CSP–see Council of Health of the People (Burkina Faso)

CSP–see Christian Social Party (Luxembourg)

CSR–see Congress for the Second Republic (Malawi)

CSS–see Czech Socialist Party

CSSD–see Czech Social Democratic Party

CST–see Higher Transitional Council (Chad)

CST–see Sandinista Workers Confederation (Nicaragua)

CSTC–see Trade Union Confederation of Colombian Workers

CSU–see Christian Social Union (Germany)

CSUTCB–see United Syndical Confederation of Bolivian Peasant Workers

CTC–see Confederation of Colombian Workers

CTM–see Confederation of Mexican Workers

CTN–see Social-Christian Nicaraguan Worker's Confederation

CTP–see Republican Turkish Party (Cyprus)

CTRP–see Confederation of Workers of the Republic of Panama

CTSP–see Transition Committee for the Health of the People (Mali)

CTV–see Confederation of Venezuelan Workers

CUAS–see Chief of Army Staff (Pakistan)

CUF–see Civic United Front (Tanzania)

CUG–see Citizen's Union of Georgia

CUT–see Central Union of Workers (Brazil)

CVP–see Civic United Front (Tanzania)

CVP–see Christian Democratic People's Party of Switzerland

CVP–see Christian Democratic Parties (Belgium)

CWC–see Congress Working Committee (India)

CWC–see Ceylon Workers Congress (Sri Lanka)

CYL–see Congress Youth League (South Africa)

D66–see Democrats 66 (Netherlands)

DA–see Democratic Renewal (Greece)

DA–see Democratic Alternative (Macedonia)

DAC–see Democratic Action Congress (Trinidad & Tobago)

DAP–see Democratic Action Party (Malaysia)

DC–see Democratic Arrangement (Dominican Rep.)

DC–see Democratic Convergence (Guatemala)

DC–see Christian Democratic Party (Italy)

DC–see Deputy Commissioner (Pakistan)

DC–see Christian Democracy (Spain)

DCG–see Christian Democrats (Guatemala)

DDCs–see District Development Councils (Sri Lanka)

DDLP–see Dominican Democratic Labor Party (Dominica)

DEMOS–see Democratic Opposition of Slovenia

DEMYC–see Democratic Youth Community of Europe

DEPOS–see Democratic Coalition of Serbia (Yugoslavia)

DF–see Danish People's Party

DFLP–see Democratic Front for the Liberation of Palestine

DFP–see Democratic Freedom Party (Dominica)

DFPE–see Democratic Front For Peace and Equality (Israel)

DIKKI–see Democratic Social Movement (Greece)

DIKO–see Democratic Party (Cyprus)

DISK–see Confederation of Revolutionary Workers' Unions (Turkey)

DISY–see Democratic Rally (Cyprus)

DJAMA–see Masses (Guinea)

DJP–see Democratic Justice Party (South Korea)

DL–see Liberal Democracy (France)

DLF–see Liberal People's Party (Norway)

DLP–see Democratic Labour Party (Barbados)

DLP–see Dominican Labour Party (Dominica)

DLP–see Democratic Liberal Party (South Korea)

DM–see District Minister (Sri Lanka)

DMC–see Democratic Movement For Change (Israel)

DMK–see Dravidian Progressive Federation-Dravida Munnetra Kazhagam (India)

DMLP–see Democratic Movement for the Liberation of Eritrea

DMOs–see Democratic Mass Organizations (Tanzania)

DN–see National Directorate (Nicaragua)

DNA–see Labor Party (Norway)

DOLA–see Department of Local Administration (Thailand)

DOP–see Declaration of Principles (Israel)

DP–see Democratic Party (Cyprus)

DP–see Popular Democracy (Ecuador)

DP–see Democratic Party (Kenya)

DP–see Democratic Party (Uganda)

DP–see Democratic Party (Luxembourg)

DP–see Democratic Party (Seychelles)

DP–see Democratic Party (Zimbabwe)

DP–see Democratic Party (South Africa)

DPJ–see Democratic Party of Japan

DPP–see Democratic Progressive Party (Taiwan)

DPS–see Movement for Rights and Freedoms (Bulgaria)

DPSCG–see Democratic Party of Socialists of Montenegro (Yugoslavia)

DPT–see Democratic Party of Tajikistan

DPT–see Democratic Party of Turkmenistan

DPU–see Democratic Party of Ukraine

DRC–see Democratic Republic of Congo

DRP–see Democratic Republican Party (South Korea)

DRY–see Democratic Republic of Yemen

DS–see Democratic Party (Slovakia)

DS–see Socialist Democracy (Spain)

DS–see Democratic Party (Yugoslavia)

DTA–see Democratic Turnhalle Alliance (Namibia)

DUP–see Democratic Unionist Party (Sudan)

DUP–see Democratic Unionist Party (Northern Ireland)

DUS–see Democratic Union of Slovakia

DVU–see German People's Union (Germany)

DZJ–see Pensions for Secure Living (Czech Rep.)

EA–see Basque Solidarity (Spain)

Ecolo–see Ecologist Parties (Belgium)

ECOMOG–see Economic Community of West African States Cease-Fire Monitoring Group

ECOWAS–see Economic Community of West African States

ECZ–see Church of Christ in Zaire (D. Rep. Congo)

EDEK–see Unified Democratic Union of the Center (Cyprus)

EDP–see Erk "Will" Democratic Party (Uzbekistan)

EDU–see European Democratic Union

EE–see Basque Left (Spain)

EEA–see European Economic Agreement

EEC–see European Economic Community

EGLE–see Every Ghanian Living Everywhere

EGP–see Guerrilla Army of the Poor (Guatemala)

EL–see Euroleft Coalition (Bulgaria)

ELF–see Eritrean Liberation Front

EMU–see Economic and Monetary Union

ENIP–see Estonian National Independence Party

EOP–see Executive Office of the President (U.S.A.)

EP–see European Parliament

EPLF–see Eritrean People's Liberation Front

EPP–see Evangelical People's Party (Netherlands)

EPRDF–see Ethiopian Peoples' Revolutionary Democratic Front

EPRLF–see Eelam Peoples' Revolutionary Liberation Front (Sri Lanka)

EPS–see Sandinista Popular Army (Nicaragua)

ERC–see Catalonian Republican Left (Spain)

ERC–see Catalan Republican Left (Spain)

ERTU–see Egyptian Radio and Television Union

ESNS–see Coexistence (Slovakia)

ET–see Ethics and Transparency (Nicaragua)

ETA–see Basque Nation and Liberty (Spain)

EU–see European Union

EVP–see Protestant People's Party (Switzerland)

FAA–see Angolan Armed Forces

FAR–see African Forum for Reconstruction (Gabon)

FAR–see Rebel Armed Forces (Guatemala)

FAR–see Royal Armed Forces (Morocco)

FAR–see Front of Associations for Renewal (Togo)

FARC–see Revolutionary Armed Forces of Colombia

FARD–see Action Front for Renewal and Development (Benin)

FATAs–see Federally Administered Tribal Areas (Pakistan)

FAZ–see Armed Forces of Zaire (D. Rep. Congo)

FBP–see Progressive Citizen's Party (Liechtenstein)

FC–see Civic Forum (CAR)

FCC–see Federal Communications Commission (U.S.A.)

FCD–see Civic Democratic Front (Guatemala)

FD–see Democratic Force (France)

FDA–see Angolan Democratic Forum

FDCs–see Forces Defence Committees (Ghana)

FDF–see French-Speaking Democratic Front (Belgium)

FDIC–see Front for the Defense of Constitutional Institutions (Morocco)

FDN–see National Democratic Front (Mexico)

FDNG–see New Guatemalan Democratic Front

FDN-Mountounchi–see Nigerian Democratic Front-Mountounchi (Niger)

FDP–see Democratic and Patriotic Forces (Rep. of Congo)

FDP–see Free Democratic Party (Germany)

FDP–see Radical Democratic Party of Switzerland

FDR–see Democratic Front of Renewal (Niger)

FDU–see United Democratic Forces (Rep. of Congo)

FEDECAFE–see National Federation of Coffee Growers (Colombia)

FEDEMU–see Federal Democratic Movement of Uganda

FENALCO–see National Federation of Merchants (Colombia)

FESE–see Federation of Secondary Students of Ecuador

FEUE–see Federation of University Students of Ecuador

FEUU–see Federation of Uruguayan University Students

FF- see Front of Democratic Forces (Djibouti)

FFS–see Socialist Forces Front (Algeria)

FI–see Forward Italy

FIDA–see Palestinian Democratic Union Party

FIM–see Independent Clean Government Front (Peru)

FIS–see Islamic Salvation Front (Algeria)

FL–see Free List Party (Liechtenstein)

FLAA–see Liberation Front of Air and Azaouad (Niger)

FLAM–see African Liberation Forces of Mauritania

FLEC–see Front for the Liberation of the Cabinda Enclave (Angola)

FLING–see Front for the Liberation and Independence of Guinea

FLN–see National Liberation Front (Algeria)

FLOSY–see Front for the Liberation of Occupied South Yemen

FLQ–see Quebec Liberation Front (Canada)

FLT–see Liberation Front of Tamoust (Niger)

FMG–see Federal Military Government (Nigeria)

FMLN–see Farabundo Marti National Liberation Front (El Salvador)

FN–see National Front (Belgium)

FN–see National Front (France)

FN–see National Front (Spain)

FNC–see Federal National Council (United Arab Emirates)

FNDR–see National Front for the Defense of the Revolution (Madagascar)

FNJ–see National Front for Justice (Comoros)

FNLA–see National Front for the Liberation of Angola

FNM–see Free National Movement (Bahamas)

FNP–see National Progressive Force (Dominican Rep.)

FNR–see National Reconstruction Front (Ecuador)

FNT–see National Worker's Front (Nicaragua)

FNTC–see National Front of Workers and Peasants (Peru)

FO–see Worker's Force (France)

FORD–see Forum for Restoration of Democracy-Kenya-Asili

FP–see Popular Front (Burkina Faso)

FP–see Patriotic Front (D. Rep. Congo)

FP–see Progress Party (Denmark)

FP–see Progressive Federation (Spain)

FP–see Federal Party (Sri Lanka)

FP–see Liberal Party (Sweden)

FPD–see Front for Democracy (Angola)

FPD–see Free Democrats (Germany)

FPI–see Ivorian Popular Front (Ivory Coast)

FPLS–see Patriotic Front of Liberation of the Sahara (Niger)

FPO–see Freedom Party (of Austria) or Freedomites (Austria)

FPP–see Patriotic Front for Progress (Central African Republic)

FPR–see Rwanda Patriotic Front

FPT–see Ivorian Popular Front (Ivory Coast)

FRA–see Afarist Radical Front (Ecuador)

FRAP–see Popular Action Front (Chile)

FRD–see Forum for the Restoration of Democracy (Comoros)

FRDD–see Front for the Restoration and Defense of Democracy (Niger)

FRDD–see Front for the Restoration and Defense of Democracy (Niger)

FRDE–see Front for the Restoration of Right and Equality (Djibouti)

Frelimo–see Front for the Liberation of Mozambique

Frepaso–see Front for a Country in Solidarity (Argentina)

FRG–see Guatemalan Republican Front

FRODEBU–see Burundi Democratic Front

FROLINAT–see Chad National Liberation Front

FRUD–see Front for the Restoration of Unity and Democracy (Djibouti)

FSB–see Bolivian Socialist Falange

FSB–see Federal Security Council (Russia)

FSLN–see Sandinista National Liberation Front (Nicaragua)

FSN–see National Salvation Front (Romania)

FSTMB–see Bolivian Mineworkers Syndical Federation

FSTSE–see Federation of Unions of Workers in the Service of the State (Mexico)

FTC–see Federal Trade Commission (U.S.A.)

FUDR–see United Front for Democracy and the Republic (Burkina Faso)

FULRO–see United Front for the Struggle of Oppressed Races (Vietnam)

FUN–see National Unity Front (Guatemala)

FUNCINPEC–see National United Front for an Independent, Neutral, Peaceful and Cooperative Cambodia

FUR–see United Revolutionary Front (Guatemala)

FUSA–see United Front for the Salvation of Angola

FUT–see Unitary Workers Front (Ecuador)

GA–see Green Alternatives (Austria)

GAD–see Action Group for Democracy (Dominican Rep.)

GAD–see Grand Alliance for Democracy (Philippines)

GAO–see General Accounting Office (U.S.A.)

GDF–see Guyanese Defense Force

GDK Azat–see Freedom Civil Movement of Kazakhstan "Azat"

GDP–see Guyana Democratic Party

GE–see Ecological Generation (France)

GGG–see Good and Green Georgetown (Guyana)

GIA–see Armed Islamic Group (Algeria)

GMMLU–see Grenada Manual and Mental Labourer's Union

GN–see National Guard (Nicaragua)

GNP–see Gross National Product

GPA–see General Peace Agreement (Mozambique)

GPC–see General People's Congress (Libya)

GPC–see General People's Congress (Yemen)

GPRA–see Provisional Government of the Republic of Algeria

GPS–see Green Party of Switzerland

GPV–see Reformed Political Association (Netherlands)

GRCs–see Group Representation Constituencies (Singapore)

GST–see Goods and Service Tax

GULP–see Grenada United Labour Party

GURN–see Government of Unity and National Reconciliation (Angola)

GURN–see Government of Unity and National Reconciliation (Palestinian Authority)

HAMAS–see Movement for an Islamic Society (Algeria)

HB–see United People (Spain)

HBP–see People's Unity Party (Uzbekistan)

HCR–see High Council of the Republic (Togo)

HCR-PT–see High Council of the Republic-Transitional Parliament (D. Rep. Congo)

HD–see Grand National Party (South Korea)

HDF–see Hungarian Democratic Forum

HDP–see People's Democratic Party (Uzbekistan)

HDZ–see Croatian Democratic Union

HDZ–see Croatian Democratic Union (Bosnia and Hercegovina)

HFP/PFH–see Humanist Feminist Party (Belgium)

HNS–see Croatian People's Party

HSD-SMS–see Movement for Autonomous Democracy of Moravia and Silesia (Czech Rep.)

HSLS–see Croatian Social Liberal Party

HSP–see Hungarian Socialist Party

HSP–see Croatian Party of Rights

HSS–see Croatian Peasant Party

HZ–see Farmer's Movement (Slovakia)

HZDS–see Movement for a Democratic Slovakia

I–see India National Congress

IAF–see Islamic Action Front (Jordan)

ICJ–see International Court of Justice

ICP–see Indochinese Communist Party (Vietnam)

ID–see Democratic Left Party (Ecuador)

IDF–see Israeli Defense Force

IDH-RH–see Institute for Research, Documentation and Human Rights (Dominican Rep.)

IDN–see National Democratic Initiative (Andorra)

IDS–see Istrian Democratic Assembly (Croatia)

IEC–see Independent Electoral Commission (South Africa)

IEPES–see Institute of Political, Economic and Social Studies (Mexico)

IFE–see Federal Electoral Institute (Mexico)

IFES–see International Foundation for Election Systems

IFLB–see Islamic Front for the Liberation of Bahrain

IFLRY–see International Federation of Liberal & Radical Youth

IFP–see Inkatha Freedom Party (South Africa)

IGNU–see Interim Government of National Unity (Liberia)

IKL–see People's Patriotic League (Finland)

ILO–see International Labor Organization

IMF–see International Monetary Fund

IMRO-DPMNU–see Internal Macedonian Revolutionary Organization-Democratic Party of Macedonian National Unity

INCRA–see National Institute for Colonization and Agrarian Reform (Brazil)

INF–see National Front of Iran

INLA–see Irish National Liberation Party (Northern Ireland)

INPFL–see Independent National Patriotic Front of Liberia

INTU–see Indian National Trade Union Congress

IP–see Independence Party (Iceland)

IP–see Independence Party (Morocco)

IPD–see Impulse to Progress and Democracy (Benin)

IRA–see Provincial Irish Republican Army (Northern Ireland)

IRP–see Islamic Renaissance Party (Uzbekistan)

IRPT–see Islamic Renaissance Party of Tajikistan

IRSP–see Irish Republican Socialist Party (Northern Ireland)

ISP–see Independent Smallholders' Party (Hungary)

IU–see United Left (Bolivia)

IU–see United Left (Peru)

IU–see United Left (Spain)

IZG–see Independent Zimbabwe Group

JADP–see Jordanian Arab Democratic Party

JAPBP–see Jordanian Arab Progressive Ba'th Party

JASBP–see Jordanian Arab Socialist Ba'th Party

JCP–see Japan Communist Party

JCP–see Jordanian Communist Party

JD–see People's Party (India)

JDPUP–see Jordanian Democratic Popular Unity Party

JI–see Islamic Assembly (Bangladesh)

JI–see Islamic Assembly (Pakistan)

JLP–see Jamaica Labour Party

JNE–see National Board of Elections (Peru)

JP–see Jatiya Party (Bangladesh)

JRM–see Society of Combatant Clergy (Iran)

JRV–see Vote Receiving Commitees (Ecuador)

JRV–see Polling Places (Nicaragua)

JSC–see Judicial Service Commission (Sri Lanka)

JTI–see Islamic Assembly (Student Wing) (Pakistan)

JUDP–see Jordanian United Democratic Party

JUI–see Conference of ULEMA of Islam (Pakistan)

JUL–see Yugoslav United Left

JUP–see Conference of ULEMA of Pakistan

JVP–see People's Liberation Front (Sri Lanka)

KADU–see Kenya African Democratic Union

KAMPI–see Supporters of the Free Philippines

KANU–see Kenya African National Union

KAU–see Kenyan African Union

KBL–see New Society Movement (Philippines)

KCIA–see Korean Central Intelligence Agency (South Korea)

KD–see Christian Democrats (Sweden)

KDH–see Christian Democratic Movement (Slovakia)

KDS–see Christian Democratic Party (Czech Rep.)

KDU–see Christian Democratic Union (Czech Rep.)

KF–see Conservative People's Party (Denmark)

KF–see Cooperative Movement (Sweden)

KKE–see Communist Party of Greece

KKE-Interior–see Greek Communist Party of the Interior

KMT–see Nationalist Party (Taiwan)

KNDP–see Kamerun National Democratic Party (Cameroon)

KNUT–see Kenya National Union of Teachers

KPA–see Korean People's Army (North Korea)

KPB–see Party of Communists of Belarus

KPD–see Communists (Germany)

KPK–see Communist Party of Kazakhstan

KPL–see Communist Party of Luxembourg

KPO–see Communist Party (Austria)

KPRP–see Kampuchean People's Revolutionary Party (Cambodia)

KPU- see Kenya People's Union

KRF–see Christian People's Party (Denmark)

KrF–see Christian People's Party (Norway)

KRO–see Congress of Russian Communities

KRRS–see Karnataka State Farmers' Association (India)

KSCM–see Communist Party of Bohemia and Moravia-Left Bloc (Czech Rep.)

KSOOR–see "Republic" Coordinating Council of Public Associations (Kazakhstan)

KSP–see Farmer's and Worker's Party (Bangladesh)

KSS–see Communist Party of Slovakia

KTPI–see Indonesian Party of High Ideals (Suriname)

KUP–see Catholic People's Party (Netherlands)

KWP–see Korean Workers' Party (North Korea)

LA–see Leftist Alliance (Finland)

LAA–see Local Administration Bill (Zambia)

LABAN–see People's Force (Philippines)

LAKAS-NUCD–see People's Power-National Union of Christian Democrats (Philippines)

LAMMP–see Fight of the Free Filipino Masses Party

LAP–see Liberal Action Party (Liberia)

LC–see Latvia's Way

LCD–see Lesotho Congress for Democracy

LCP–see Lebanese Communist Party

LCR–see Revolutionary Communist League (France)

LCR–see The Radical-Cause (Venezuela)

LCs–see Local Councils (Uganda)

LCS–see League of Communists of Yugoslavia (Slovenia)

LD/MPT–see Democratic League/Popular Labor Movement (Senegal)

LDLP–see Lithuanian Democratic Labor Party

LDP–see Democratic Filipino Struggle

LDP–see Liberal Democratic Party (Japan)

LDP–see Liberal Democratic Party (Macedonia)

LDP–see Liberal Democratic Party (Malaysia)

LDPR–see Liberal Democratic Party of Russia

LDS–see Liberal Democracy of Slovenia

LdU–see Alliance of Independents (Switzerland)

LF–see Liberal Forum (Austria)

LIPAD–see Patriotic League for Development (Burkina Faso)

LIPE–see Guinean League for the Protection of the Environment

LKDS–see Farmer's Union/Christian Democratic Union/Latgale/Democratic Party Coalition (Latvia)

LLA–see Lesotho Liberation Army

LMI–see Liberation Movement of Iran

LN–see Northern League (Italy)

LNNK–see Latvian National Conservative Party and Green Party

LNTG–see Liberian National Transitional Government

LO–see Norwegian Trades Union Federation

LO–see Swedish Confederation of Trade Unions

LOPPE–see Law of Political Organizations and Electoral Processes (Mexico)

LP–see Liberal Party (Philippines)

LP–see Labor Party (Saint Kitts)

LPAI–see African People's League for Independence (Djibouti)

LPP–see Law of Popular Participation (Bolivia)

LPP–see Liberia People's Party

LPRP–see Lao People's Revolutionary Party (Laos)

LRF–see National Farmer's Association (Sweden)

LSAP–see Socialist Workers' Party (Luxembourg)

LSP–see Latvian Socialist Party

LSP–see Liberal Socialist Party (Egypt)

LSSP–see Ceylon Equal Society Party (Sri Lanka)

LSU–see Liberal Social Union (Czech Rep.)

LTTE–see Liberation Tigers of Tamil Eelam (Sri Lanka)

LU–see Liberal Union (Andorra)

LUP–see Liberian Unification Party

M–see Moderate Party (Sweden)

M.G.R.–see M.G. Ramachaudran (India)

MA–see Melanesian Alliance (Papua New Guinea)

MAC–see Christian Authentic Movement (El Salvador)

MAFREMO–see Malawi Freedom Movement

MAKI–see Israel Communist Party

MAPAM–see United Workers Party (Israel)

MAS–see Solidarity Action Movement (Guatemala)

MAS–see Movement toward Socialism (Venezuela)

MAUDR–see Angolan Democratic Unity Movement for Reconstruction

MBL–see Movement for a Free Bolivia

MBPM–see Maurice Bishop Patriotic Movement (Grenada)

MCA–see Malayan Chinese Association

MCDDI–see Congolese Movement for Democracy and Comprehensive Development (Rep. of Congo)

MCP–see Malawi Congress Party

MCPC–see Central African People's Liberation Movement

MCs–see Municipal Councils (Sri Lanka)

MDA–see Movement for Democracy in Algeria

MDB–see Brazilian Democratic Movement

MDC–see Malawi Development Corporation

MDC–see Citizen's Movement (France)

MDD–see Movement for Democracy and Development (Central African Republic)

MDN–see National Democratic Movement (Guatemala)

MDP–see Malawi Democratic Party

MDP–see Portuguese Democratic Movement

MDP–see Movement for Democracy and Progress (Cameroon)

MDP–see Movement for the Defense of the Republic (Cameroon)

MDP–see Democratic Popular Movement (Senegal)

MDR–see Democratic Republican Movement (Rwanda)

MDREC–see Movement for Democracy, Renaissance and Revolution in Central Africa

MDS–see Movement of Social Democrats (Tunisia)

MDS–see Democratic and Social Movement (Morocco)

MDU–see Malawi Democratic Union

MEI–see Independent Ecology Movement (France)

MEP–see People's Electoral Movement (Venezuela)

MESAN–see Movement of Social Evolution in Black Africa (Central African Rep.)

MFA–see Armed Forces Movement (Portugal)

MFDC–see Movement of Democratic Forces of Casamance (Senegal)

MFP–see Marematlou Freedom Party (Lesotho)

MHRA–see Mauritanian Human Rights Association

MIC–see Malayan Indian Congress

MILF–see Moro Islamic Liberation Front (Philippines)

MINUGUA–see UN Verification Mission (Guatemala)

MIR–see Movement of the Revolutionary Left (Bolivia)

MIRT–see Movement for the Islamic Revival of Tajikistan

MISK–see Confederation of Nationalist Labor Unions (Turkey)

MK–see Member of Knesset (Israel)

MKDH–see Hungarian Christian Democratic Movement (Slovakia)

ML–see Liberty Movement (Peru)

MLA–see Martial Law Administrator (Pakistan)

MLN–see National Liberation Movement (Uruguay)

MLN–see National Liberation Movement (Guatemala)

MLPC–see Central African People's Liberation Movement

MLSTP–see Liberation Movement of Sao Tome and Principe

MMD–see Movement for Multiparty Democracy (Zambia)

MMM–see Mauritanian Militant Movement

MMP–see Mixed-Member Proportion (New Zealand)

MNDP–see Malawi National Democratic Party

MNLF–see Moro National Liberation Front (Philippines)

MNPP–see New Country Movement (Ecuador)

MNR–see Nationalist Revolutionary Movement (Bolivia)

MNR–see National Movement of Revolution (Republic of Congo)

MNR–see National Revolutionary Movement (El Salvador)

MNR–see Mozambique National Resistance

MNR/Renamo–see Mozambique National Resistance

MNSD–see National Movement for Solidarity and Democracy (Cameroon)

MNSD-Nassara–see National Movement for a Society of Development-Nassara (Niger)

MNU–see Movement for National Unity (Saint Vincent and the Grenadines)

Modin–see Movement for Dignity and National Independence (Argentina)

MOJA–see Movement for Justice in Africa (Liberia)

MOLIRENA–see Liberal National Republican Movement (Panama)

MOPOCO–see Colorado Popular Movement (Paraguay)

MORENA–see National Renovation Movement (Panama)

MORENA-B–see Movement for National Regeneration-Woodcutters (Gabon)

MOTION–see Movement For Social Transformation (Trinidad & Tobago)

MOVERS–see Movement for Responsible Public Service (Philippines)

MP–see Member of Parliament

MP–see Popular Movement (Morocco)

MP–see Motherland Party (Turkey)

MP–see Ecology Party (Sweden)

MP's–see Members of Parliament

MpD–see Movement for Democracy (Cape Verde)

MPD–see Democratic Popular Movement (Ecuador)

MPF–see Movement for France

MPLA-PT–see Popular Liberation Movement of Angola (Labor Party

MPR–see Popular Movement of the Revolution (D. Rep. Congo)

MPR–see Patriotic Movement for Renewal (Mali)

MPRP–see Mongolian People's Revolutionary Party

MPS–see Patriotic Salvation Movement (Chad)

MQM–A–see Mutahida Qaumi Movement (Altaf) (Pakistan)

MQM–H–see Mutahida Qaumi Movement (Haqiqi) (Pakistan)

MRD–see Movement for the Restoration of Democracy (Pakistan)

MRG–see Left Radical Movement (France)

MRM–see Assembly of Combatant Clerics (Iran)

MRND–see National Revolutionary Movement for Development (Rwanda)

MRNDD–see National Republican Movement for Democracy and Development (Rwanda)

MRP–see Popular Republican Movement (France)

MRS–see Senegalese Republican Movement

MRS–see Sandinista Renovation Movement (Nicaragua)

MRTA–see Tupac Amaru Revolutionary Movement (Peru)

MRTKL–see Tupak Katari Revolutionary Liberation Movement (Bolivia)

MSC–see Social Christian Movement (Ecuador)

MSI–see Italian Social Movement

MSM–see Mauritian Socialist Movement

MSN–see National Salvation Movement (Colombia)

MSP–see Movement for a Peaceful Society (Algeria)

MST–see Landless Peoples' Movement (Brazil)

MTD–see Togolese Movement for Democracy

MTDP–see National Revival Democratic Party (Uzbekistan)

MTI–see Islamic Tendency Movement (Tunisia)

MUN–see Mission of National Unity (Panama)

MUZ–see Mine Workers Union of Zambia

MVR–see Fifth Republic Movement (Venezuela)

MYP–see Malawi Young Pioneers

NA–see New Alliance (Slovakia)

NABR–see National Alliance for Belizean Rights

NAF–see Norwegian Employers' Association

NAFTA–see North American Free Trade Agreement

NAP–see National Awami Party (Bangladesh)

NAP–see New Aspiration Party (Thailand)

NAP–see Nationalist Action Party (Turkey)

NAR–see National Alliance for Reconstruction (Trinidad and Tobago)

NATO–see North Atlantic Treaty Organization

NBM–see New Beginnings Movement (Jamaica)

NCC–see Our Common Cause(Benin)

NCCR–see National Convention for Constitutional Reform (Tanzania)

NCF–see Nordic Youth Center Association

NCGUB–see National Coalition Government Union of Burma (Myanmar)

NCMPs–see Non-Constituency Members of Parliament (Singapore)

NCNC–see National Council of Nigeria and the Cameroons (Nigeria)

NCNP–see National Council for New Politics (South Korea)

NCP–see National Constitutional Party (Jordan)

NCP–see National Convention Party (Ghana)

NCP–see Nepalese Congress Party

NCP–see National Conservative Party (Finland)

ND–see New Democracy (Andorra)

ND–see New Democracy (Greece)

ND–see New Democracy (Yugoslavia)

NDA–see National Democratic Aliance (Sudan)

NDC–see National Democratic Convention (Ghana)

NDC–see National Democratic Congress (Grenada)

NDC–see National Defense Commission (North Korea)

NDF–see Namibian Defense Force

NDM–see National Democratic Movement (Jamaica)

NDP–see National Democratic Party (Antigua and Barbuda)

NDP–see New Democratic Party (Canada)

NDP–see National Democratic Party (Egypt)

NDP–see New Development Policy (Malaysia)

NDP–see National Democratic Party (Saint Vincent and the Grenadines)

NDP–see National Development Party (Trinidad and Tobago)

NDP–see Nationalist Democracy Party (Turkey)

NDP–see New Democratic Party (South Korea)

NDP–see New Democratic Party (Suriname)

NDP Zheltoksan–see December National Democratic Party (Kazakhstan)

NDPL–see National Democratic Party of Liberia

NDRP–see New Democratic Republican Party (South Korea)

NDS–see National Democratic Party (Slovakia)

NDU–see National Democratic Union (Argentina)

NEC–see National Election Commission (Nigeria)

NEP–see New Economic Policy (Malaysia)

NERP–see New Economic Recovery Program (Zambia)

NF–see National Front (UK of Great Britain)

NFD–see New Democratic Force (Colombia)

NFP–see New Frontier Party (Japan)

NFSL–see National Front for the Salvation of Libya

NGOs–see Non-Governmental Organizations (India)

NIF–see National Islamic Front (Sudan)

NIO–see Northern Ireland Office

NIP–see National Independence Party (Ghana)

NJAC–see National Joint Action Committee (Trinidad and Tobago)

NJM–see New Jewel Movement (Grenada)

NKK–see People's Congress of Kazakhstan

NKP–see Communist Party of Norway

NKP–see New Korea Party (South Korea)

NLD–see National League for Democracy (Myanmar)

NLF–see National Liberation Front (Yemen)

NLM–see National Labour Movement (Saint Lucia)

NM–see New Majority (Peru)

NMPs–see Nominated Members of Parliament (Singapore)

NNDP–see Nigerian National Democratic Party

NNLC–see Ngwane National Liberatory Congress (Swaziland)

NNP–see New National Party (Grenada)

NORAID–see Irish Northern Aid Committee (Northern Ireland)

NP–see Nacionalista Party (Philippines)

NP–see National Party (South Africa)

NPA–see New People's Army (Philippines)

NPC–see National People's Congress (China)

NPC–see Northern People's Congress (Nigeria)

NPC–see National People's Coalition (Philippines)

NPD–see National Democratic Party (Germany)

NPF–see National Policy Forum (UK of Great Britain)

NPFL–see National Patriotic Front of Liberia

NPH–see New Party Harbinger (Japan)

NPP–see New Patriotic Party (Ghana)

NPP–see National Patriotic Party (Liberia)

NPS–see Suriname National Party

NPUP–see National Progressive Unionist Party (Egypt)

NRA–see National Resistance Army (Uganda)

NRC–see National Resistance Council (Uganda)

NRC–see Nuclear Regulatory Commission (U.S.A.)

NRC–see National Republican Convention (Nigeria)

NRM–see National Resistance Movement (D. Rep. Congo)

NRM–see National Resistance Movement (Uganda)

NRP–see National Reconciliation Party (Gambia)

NRP–see National Religious Party (Israel)

NRP–see Nevis Reform Party (Saint Kitts)

NRP–see Nevis Reformation Party (Saint Kitts)

NSC–see National Security Council (Tunisia)

NSC–see National Security Council (U.S.A.)

NSP–see National Solidarity Party (Singapore)

NSS–see Nature Society of Singapore

NTC–see National Transition Council (Algeria)

NUCD–see National Union for Christian Democrats (Philippines)

NUP–see National Union Party (Sudan)

NUP–see National Unity Party (Myanmar)

NUPRG–see New Ulster Political Research Group (Northern Ireland)

NVU–see Dutch People's Union (Netherlands)

NWFP–see Northwest Frontier Province (Pakistan)

NWU–see National Workers' Union (Jamaica)

NYM–see Nigerian Youth Movement

NZLP–see New Zealand Labour Party

OAAB–see Austrian Association of Workers and Employees

OAPEC–see Organization of Arab Petroleum Exporting Countries

OAS–see Organization of American States

OAU–see Organization of African Unity

OBB–see Austrian Farmer's Association

OBCs–see Backward Castes (India)

ODA–see Civic Democratic Alliance (Czech Rep.)

ODP/MT–see Organization for Popular Democracy/Labor Movement (Burkina Faso)

ODS–see Civic Democratic Party (Czech Rep.)

ODU–see Civic Democratic Union (Slovakia)

OECD–see Organization for Economic Cooperation and Development

OHR–see Our Home Is Russia

OIRA–see Official Irish Republican Army (Northern Ireland)

OLF–see Oromo (Ethiopia)

OMB–see Office of Management and Budget (U.S.A.)

OMUG–see Organizations for the Exploitation of the Gambia River (Guinea-Bissau)

OMUS–see Organizations for the Exploitation of the Senegal River (Guinea-Bissau)

ONA-JPU–see Uruguayan National Organization of Retirees' and Pensioners' Associations

ONM–see National Organization of Veterans (Algeria)

ONR–see Organization for National Reconstruction (Trinidad and Tobago)

ONUSAL–see United Nations Observer Mission in El Salvador

OPC–see Ovambolamo People's Congress (Namibia)

OPDO–see Oromo People's Democratic Organization (Ethiopia)

OPEC–see Organization of Petroleum Exporting Countries

OPG–see Official Parliamentary Group (Pakistan)

OPL–see Lavalas Political Organization (Haiti)

OPL–see Organization of the Struggling People (Haiti)

OPP–see Organ of People's Power (Cuba)

ORA–see Organization of Armed Resistance (Niger)

ORPA–see Armed People's Organization (Guatemala)

OSCE–see Organization for Security and Cooperation in Europe

OUP–see Official Unionist Party (Northern Ireland)

OVP–see Austrian People's Party

OWB–see Austrian Economic Association

OYAK–see Army Mutual Assistance Foundation (Turkey)

PA–see Palestinian Authority

PA–see People's Alliance (Iceland)

PA–see Arnulfista Party (Panama)

PA–see People's Alliance (Sri Lanka)

PAC–see Civilian Self-Defense Patrol (Guatemala)

PAC–see Pan-Africanist Congress (South Africa)

PACIA–see Angolan Party of African Identity Conservative

PACs–see Political Action Committees (U.S.A.)

PAD–see People's Party for Democracy and Development (Ghana)

PAGS–see Socialist Vanguard Party (Algeria)

PAI–see Angolan Independent Party

PAI–see African Independence Party (Senegal)

PAICV–see African Party for the Independence of Cape Verde

PAIGC–see African Party for the Independence of Guinea and Cape Verde (Guinea-Bissau)

PAIS–see Open Politics for the Social Country (Argentina)

PAJOCA–see Party of the Alliance of Youth, Workers, and Farmers of Angola

PAL–see Progressive Alliance of Liberia

PAL–see Angolan Liberal Party

PALA–see Labor Party (Panama)

PALI–see Neo-Liberal Party (Nicaragua)

PALIPEHUTU–see Party for the Liberation of the Hutu People (Burundi)

PALU–see United Lumumbist Party (D. Rep. Congo)

PAM–see Peoples Action Movement (Saint Kitts)

PAMSCAD–see Program of Action to Mitigate the Costs of Adjustment (Ghana)

PAN–see National Advancement Party (Guatemala)

PAN–see National Action Party (Mexico)

PAP–see People's Action Paarty (Papua New Guinea)

PAP–see People's Action Party (Sierra Leone)

PAR–see Aragonese Regionalist Party (Spain)

PARENA–see Party for National Renewal (Mali)

PARM–see Authentic Party of the Mexican Revolution

PAS–see Pan-Malaysian Islamic Party

PASOC–see Socialist Action Party (Spain)

PASOK–see Pan-Hellenic Socialist Movement (Greece)

PATAs–see Provincially Administered Tribal Areas (Pakistan)

PAV–see Public Against Violence (Slovakia)

PAVN–see People's Army of Vietnam

PBDS–see Sarawak Dayak People's Party (Malaysia)

PBS–see United Sabah Party (Malaysia)

PC–see Progressive Conservative Party of Canada

PC–see Conservative Party (Ecuador)

PC–see Center Alliance Party (Poland)

PC–see Carlist Party (Spain)

PCB–see Brazililian Communist Party

PCB–see Communist Party of Benin

PCB–see Bolivian Communist Party

PCB–see Belgian Communist Party

PCC–see Colombian Communist Party

PCC–see Cuban Communist Party

PCD–see Liberal Democratic Party (Angola)

PCD–see Party for the Democratic Convergence (Cape Verde)

PCD–see Democratic Conservative Party (Nicaragua)

PcdeN–see Nicaraguan Communist Party

PcdoB–see Communist Party of Brazil

PCE–see Spanish Communist Party

PCF–see French Communist Party

PCI–see Italian Communist Party

PCL–see Plenary of Legislative Commissions (Ecuador)

PCM–see Communist Party of Mexico

PCML–see Maoist Marxist-Leninist Communist Party (Ecuador)

PCMR–see Presidential Council for Minority Rights (Singapore)

PCN–see Conservative Party of Nicaragua

PCN–see Party of National Reconciliation (El Salvador)

PCP–see Palestine Communist Party

PCP–see Portuguese Communist Party

PCP–see Communist Party (Paraguay)

PCS–see San Marino Communist Party

PCT–see Congolese Workers' Party (Republic of Congo)

PCT–see Tunisian Communist Party

PCV–see Venezuelan Communist Party

PD–see Democratic Party (Ecuador)

PD–see Democratic Party (Romania)

PDA–see Angolan Democratic Party

PdA–see Swiss Labor Party

PDB–see Party of German-Speaking Belgians

PDB–see Democratic Bolivian Party

PDC–see Christian Democrat Party (Argentina)

PDC–see Christian Democratic Party (Brazil)

PDC–see Christian Democratic Party (Burundi)

PDC–see Christian Democratic Party (Chile)

PDC–see Christian Democratic Party (El Salvador)

PDC–see Christian Democrat Party (Honduras)

PDC–see Peace and Development Council (Myanmar)

PDC–see Christian Democratic Party (Panama)

PDC–see Christian Democratic Party (Paraguay)

PDC–see Christian Democratic Party (Rwanda)

PDCI–see Democratic Party of Ivory Coast

PDCN–see Democratic Party of National Cooperation (Guatemala)

PDCs–see People's Defence Committees (Ghana)

PDCS–see Christian Democratic Party (San Marino)

PDG–see Gabonese Democratic Party

PDGE–see Democratic Party of Equatorial Guinea

PDG-RDA–see Democratic Party of Guinea-African Democratic Assembly

PDI–see Institutional Democratic Party (Dominican Rep.)

PDI–see Democratic Independence Party (Morocco)

PDL–see Liberal Democratic Party (Spain)

PDLA–see Angolan Democratic Liberal Party

PDM–see Mexican Democrat Party

PDM–see People's Democratic Movement (Papua New Guinea)

PDOIS–see People's Democratic Organization for Independence and Socialism (Gambia)

PDP–see Filipino Democratic Party

PDP–see Pakistan Democratic Party

PDP–see Progressive Democratic Party (Argentina)

PDP–see Party for Democracy and Progress (Burkina Faso)

PDP–see Party for Democratic Prosperity (Macedonia)

PDP–see People's Democratic Party (Nigeria)

PDP–see Popular Democratic Party (Spain)

PDP–see People's Democratic Party (Sudan)

PDP–see Party for Democracy and Progress (Tanzania)

PDP–see Moral Force Party (Thailand)

PDPA–see Angolan Democratic Party for Peace

PDPAM–see Party for Democratic Prosperity of Albanians in Macedonia

PDP-ANA–see Democratic Party for Progress-Angolan National Alliance

PDRU–see Party of Democratic Rebirth of Ukraine

PDRY–see People's Democratic Republic of Yemen

PDS–see Senegalese Democratic Party

PDS–see Democratic Social Party (Brazil)

PDS–see Party of Democratic Socialism (Germany)

PDS–see Democratic Party of the Left (Italy)

PDSH–see Democratic Party of Albania

PDSR–see Social Democratic Party of Romania

PDT–see Democratic Labor Party (Brazil)

PDT–see Democratic Worker's Party (Brazil)

PdvA–see Party of Labor (Belgium)

PEC–see Provisional Electoral Council (Haiti)

PF–see Patriotic Front (Zimbabwe)

PFB–see Popular Front in Bahrain

PFDJ–see Popular Front For Democracy and Justice (Eritrea)

PFE–see Spanish Feminist Party

PFL–see Party of the Liberal Front (Brazil)

PFLOAG–see Popular Front for the Liberation of Oman and the Arab Gulf (Bahrain)

PFLOAG–see Popular Front for the Liberation of Oman and the Arab Gulf (United Arab Emirates)

PFLP–see Popular Front for the Liberation of Palestine

PGP–see Gabonese Progress Party

PGP–see Guinea Progress Party (Guinea)

PGT-LN–see Guatemalan Labour Party-National Leadership Nucleus

PH–see Humanist Party (Spain)

PHP–see People's Heritage Party (Ghana)

PID–see Democratic Institutionalist Party (Guatemala)

PIL–see Public Interest Litigation (India)

PINU–see Party of Innovation and Unity (Honduras)

PIP–see Puerto Rican Independence Party

PIT–see Ivorian Workers Party (Ivory Coast)

PIT–see Independence and Labor Party (Senegal)

PIT-CNT–see Interunion Workers' Assembly-National Workers Convention (Uruguay)

PKMAP–see National Peoples' Pathan Brotherhood Party (Pakistan)

PKMS–see Singapore National Malay Organization

PL–see Liberal Party (Brazil)

PL–see Liberal Party (Panama)

PL–see Liberal Party (Paraguay)

PL–see Liberal Party (Rwanda)

PL–see Liberal Party (Spain)

PLA–see People's Liberation Army (China)

PLA–see Authentic Liberal Party (Panama)

PLAN–see People's Liberation Army of Namibia

PLB–see Communist Party (Belgium)

PLC–see Liberal Constitutionalist Party (Nicaragua)

PLD–see Liberal Democratic Party (Central African Republic)

PLD–see Dominican Liberation Party (Dominican Rep.)

PLE–see "The Structure" Liberal Party (Dominican Rep.)

PLH–see Honduras Liberal Party

PLI–see Independent Liberal Party (Nicaragua)

PLIUN–see Liberal Party of National Unity (Nicaragua)

PLM–see Progressive Labour Movement (Antigua and Barbuda)

PLN–see National Liberation Party (Costa Rica)

PLN–see Liberal Nationalist Party (Nicaragua)

PLN–see National Liberal Party (Panama)

PLO–see Palestine Liberation Organization

PLO–see Palestine Liberation Organization (Israel)

PLOTE–see People's Liberation of Tamil Eelam (Sri Lanka)

PLP–see Progressive Liberal Party (Bahamas)

PLP–see Progressive List For Peace (Israel)

PLP–see Progressive Labour Party (Saint Lucia)

PLP–see People's Liberation Party (Senegal)

PLR–see Liberal Republican Party (Panama)

PLR–see Liberal Radical Party (Paraguay)

PLRA–see Liberal Radical Authentic Party (Paraguay)

PLRE–see Radical Liberal Party (Ecuador)

PLS–see Liberal Party (Switzerland)

PLT–see Liberal Teete Party (Paraguay)

PMAC–see Ethiopian Provisional Military Administrative Council (Eritrea)

PMC–see Military-Peasant Pact (Bolivia)

PMDB–see Party of the Brazilian Democratic Movement

PML–see Pakistan Muslim League

PML-N–see Pakistan Muslim League-N (Pakistan)

PMP–see Party of the Filipino Masses

PMT–see Mexican Workers' Party

PN–see National Project (Nicaragua)

PNA–see Pakistan National Alliance (Pakistan)

PnB–see People's Party (Philippines)

PNC–see Palestinian National Council

PNC–see People's National Convention Party (Ghana)

PNC–see People's National Congress (Guyana)

PNC–see National Conservative Party (Nicaragua)

PND–see National Democratic Party (Djibouti)

PND–see National Democratic Party (Morocco)

PNDA–see Angolan National Democratic Party

PNDC–see Provisional National Defense Council (Ghana)

PNDS-Tarayya–see Nigerian Party for Democracy and Social Progress-Tarayya (Niger)

PNEA–see Angolan National Geological Party

PNEK–see Party of People's Unity of Kazakhstan

PNH–see National Party of Honduras

PNM–see People's National Movement (Trinidad and Tobago)

PNP–see Pakistan National Party

PNP–see Peoples National Party (Jamaica)

PNP–see New Progressive Party (Puerto Rico)

PNR–see National Renewal Party (Guatemala)

PNR–see National Revolutionary Party (Mexico)

PNU–see Basque Nationalist Party (Spain)

PNV–see No Sellout Platform (Guatemala)

PNV–see Platform Ninety (Guatemala)

PNVC–see National Party of Veterans and Civilians (Dominican Rep.)

POC–see Joint Opposition Party (Eq. Guinea)

POEs–see Party-Owned Enterprises (Taiwan)

POLA–see Political Spring (Greece)

PP–see Popular Party (Brazil)

PP–see Progressive Party (Brazil)

PP–see Progressive Party (Iceland)

PP–see People's Party (Portugal)

PP–see Popular Party (Spain)

PP–see Populist Party (Turkey)

PPA–see Public Prosecutions Administration (South Korea)

PPB–see Brazilian Progressive Party

PPB–see Progressive Reform Party (Brazil)

PPBB–see United Traditional Bumiputra Party (Malaysia)

PPC–see Christian People's Party (Dominican Rep.)

PPC–see Popular Christian Party (Peru)

PPD–see Djibouti People's Party

PPD–see Doctrinaire Panamenista Party

PPD–see Party for Democracy (Chile)

PPD–see Popular Democratic Party (Puerto Rico)

PPDF–see Popular Party for French Democracy

PPE–see Papa Egoro Party (Panama)

PPI–see Italian People's Party

PPM–see Party of the People of Mauritania

PPM–see Popular Monarchist Party (Portugal)

PPN–see Niger Progressive Party

PPN-RDA–see Niger Progressive Party-African Democratic Rally

PPOs–see Primary Party Organizations (Kazakhstan)

PPP–see People's Progressive Party of Malaysia

PPP–see Palestine People's Party

PPP–see People's Progressive Party (Gambia)

PPP–see People's Progressive Party (Guyana)

PPP–see Pakistan People's Party (Pakistan)

PPP–see People's Progress Party (Papua New Guinea)

PPP–see People's Power Party (Philippines)

PPP–see People's Progressive Party (Saint Lucia)

PPP–see People's Political Party (Saint Vincent and the Grenadines)

PPR–see Progressive Republican Party (Brazil)

PPS–see Popular Socialist Party (Brazil)

PPS–see Popular Socialist Party (Mexico)

PPSC–see Popular Social Christian Party (Nicaragua)

PPT–see People's Party of Tajikistan

PPT–see Country for All (Venezuela)

PQ–see Parti Quebecois (Canada)

PQ–see Democratic Quisqueyan Party (Dominican Rep.)

PR–see Proportional Representation

PR–see Revolutionary Party (Guatemala)

PRB–see Party of the Rebirth of Benin

PRC–see Cuban Revolutionary Party

PRC–see Central African Republican Party

PRC–see Civic Renewal Party (Panama)

PRD–see Democratic Renewal Party (Angola)

PRD–see Democratic Renewal Party (Benin)

PRD–see Party of Democratic Renewal (Djibouti)

PRD–see Dominican Revolutionary Party (Dominican Rep.)

PRD–see Party of the Democratic Revolution (Mexico)

PRD–see Revolutionary Democratic Party (Panama)

PRD–see Democratic Renewal Party (Portugal)

PRD–see Democratic Reformist Party (Spain)

PRDS–see Social and Democratic Republican Party (Mauritania)

PRE–see Roldosista Party of Ecuador

Pref–see Reformist Party (Dominican Rep.)

PRF–see Revolutionary Febrerist Party (Paraguay)

PRI–see Italian Republican Party

PRI–see Independent Revolutionary Party (Dominican Rep.)

PRI–see Institutional Revolutionary Party (Mexico)

PRL–see Liberal Parties (Belgium)

PRLPN-Nakowa–see Republican Party for the Liberty and Progress of Niger-Nakowa

PRM–see Party of Greater Romania

PRN–see Party of National Reconstruction (Brazil)

PRN–see National Republican Party (Costa Rica)

PRP–see Popular Revolutionary Party (D. Rep. Congo)

PRP–see Party of Renovation and Progress (Guinea)

PRP–see Party of Renewal and Progress (Morocco)

PRP–see People's Reform Party (Philippines)

PRPB–see Popular Revolutionary Party of Benin

PRS–see Social Renewal Party (Angola)

PRS–see Radical Socialist Party (France)

PRS–see Social Renovation Party (Guinea-Bissau)

PRSC–see Reformist Social Christian Party (Dominican Rep.)

PRSD–see Social Democratic Radical Party (Chile)

PRT–see Revolutionary Party of the Workers (Mexico)

PS–see Portuguese Socialist Party

PS–see Socialist Parties (Belgium)

PS–see Socialist Party (Chile)

PS–see Socialist Party (France)

PS–see Solidarity Party (Panama)

PS–see Socialist Party (Senegal)

PSA–see Socialist Party of Andalucia (Spain)

PS–see Brazilian Socialist Party

PSB–see Burkina Socialist Party

PSC–see Christian Democratic Parties (Belgium)

PSC–see Social Christian Party (Ecuador)

PSC–see Social Christian Party (Guatemala)

PSCN–see Social Christian Party (Nicaragua)

PSD–see Social Democratic Party (Angola)

PSD–see Social Democratic Party (Benin)

PSD–see Social Democratic Party (Brazil)

PSD–see Democratic Socialist Party (Central African Rep.)

PSD–see Social Democratic Party (France)

PSD–see Social Democratic Party (Guatemala)

PSD–see Social Democratic Party (Guinea-Bissau)

PSD–see Social Democratic Party (Portugal)

PSD–see Social Democratic Party (Rwanda)

PSDA–see Angolan Social Democratic Party

PSDB–see Brazilian Social Democratic Party

PSDN-Alheri–see Niger Social-Democratic Party-Alheri

PSE–see Basque Socialist Party (Spain)

PSI–see Italian Socialist Party

PSL–see Polish Peasant Party

PSM–see Monegasque Socialist Party

PSN–see Nicaraguan Socialist Party

PSN–see National Solidarity Party (Portugal)

PSOC–see Social Conservatism Party (Nicaragua)

PSOE–see Spanish Socialist Workers' Party

PSP–see Popular Socialist Party (Cuba)

PSP–see Progressive Socialist Party (Lebanon)

PSP–see Pacifist Socialist Party (Netherlands)

PSs–see Regional Councils (Sri Lanka)

PSS–see San Marino Socialist Party

PSSH–see Socialist Party of Albania

PSUC–see Unified Socialist Party of Catalonia (Spain)

PSUM–see Unified Socialist Party of Mexico

PT–see Workers' Party (Brazil)

PTA–see Angolan Labor Party

PTB–see Brazilian Worker's Party

PTB–see Brazilian Labor Party

PTD–see Dominican Worker's Party

PTP–see Togolese Progressive Party

PUD–see Democratic Unification Party (Honduras)

PUDEMO–see People's United Democratic Movement (Swaziland)

PUND-Salama–see Party for National Unity and Development-Salama (Niger)

PUNR–see Romanian National Unity Party

PUNT–see National Workers' Party (Eq. Guinea)

PUP–see People's United Party (Belize)

PUP–see Popular Unity Party (Tunisia)

PUP–see Party of Unity and Progress (Guinea)

PUR–see Republican Union (Ecuador)

PUSC–see Social Christian Unity (Costa Rica)

PUU–see Party of Liberty and Progress (Belgium)

PvdA–see Labor Party (Netherlands)

PVE–see Spanish Green Party

PW–see Walloon Party (Belgium)

PWP–see Peasants and Workers Party (India)

PYO–see Progressive Youth Organization (Guyana)

RAAN–see Northern Atlantic Autonomous Region (Nicaragua)

RAAS–see Southern Atlantic Autonomous Region (Nicaragua)

RAKAH–see New Communist List (Israel)

RATZ–see Citizens Right Movement (Israel)

RC–see Communist Refoundation (Italy)

RCC–see Revolutionary Command Council (Ecuador)

RCC–see Revolutionary Command Council (Iran)

RCC–see Revolutionary Command Council (Libya)

RCD–see Rally for Culture and Democracy (Algeria)

RCD–see Congolese Rally for Democracy (D. Rep. Congo)

RCs–see Resistance Committees (Uganda)

RDA–see African Democratic Assembly (Burkina Faso)

RDA–see African Democratic Rally (Ivory Coast)

RDL–see Rally of Liberal Democrats (Benin)

RDP–see Rally for Democracy and Progress (Gabon)

RDP–see Reunification and Democracy Party (South Korea)

RDR–see Rally of Republicans (Ivory Coast)

Renamo–see Mozambique National Resistance

RF–see Republican Front (Ivory Coast)

RGB-MB–see Guinea-Bissau Resistance-Bah Fatah Movement

RMC–see Revolutionary Military Council (Grenada)

RN–see National Renovation (Chile)

RNB–see National Woodcutters Rally (Gabon)

RND–see National Democratic Rally (Algeria)

RND–see National Rally for Development (Comoros)

RND–see National Democratic Assembly (Senegal)

RNI–see National Assembly of Independents (Morocco)

ROAD–see Citizens' Movement for Democratic Action (Poland)

RP–see Republic Party (Trinidad and Tobago)

RPF–see Rwandan Patriotic Front

RPF–see Rally for the French People

RPF-SEE–see Reformational Political Federation (Netherlands)

RPG–see Assembly of the Guinean People

RPI–see Republican Party of India

RPP–see Popular Rally for Progress (Djibouti)

RPP–see Radical Political Party (Netherlands)

RP–see Republican People's Party (Turkey)

RPR–see Rally for the French Republic

RPSD–see Rally for Social Democracy (Madagascar)

RPT–see Rally of Togolese People

RSF–see Rhodesian Security Forces

RSFSR–see Russian Soviet Federated Socialist Republic

RSP–see Socialist Progressive Rally (Tunisia)

RSS–see Agrarian Party of Slovakia

RSS–see National Volunteer Organization (India)

RUC–see Royal Ulster Constabulary (Northern Ireland)

RUF–see Revolutionary Front (Sierra Leone)

RV–see Radical Liberals (Denmark)

RV–see Red Electoral Alliance (Norway)

S–see Janata Dal (India)

S or SAP–see Social Democratic Party (Sweden)

SAC–see Cabinet of the State Administration Council (North Korea)

SACP–see South Africa Communist Party

SAD–see Shiromani Akali Party (India)

SADC–see Southern African Development Council (Zimbabwe)

SADCC–see South African Development Coordination Conference (Malawi)

SADF–see South African Defense Force

SAP–see Structural Adjustment Program

SAP–see Social Action Party (Thailand)

SAPP–see Sabah Development Party (Malaysia)

SAR–see Special Administrative Region (China)

SBPF–see Sind-Baluch Pakhtoun Front (Pakistan)

SD–see Social Democrats (Denmark)

SDA–see Party of Democratic Action (Bosnia and Hercegovina)

SDF–see Social Democratic Front (Cameroon)

SDK–see Slovak Democratic Coalition

SDL–see Party of the Democratic Left (Slovakia)

SDLP–see Social Democratic and Labour Party (Northern Ireland)

SDP–see Social Democratic Party of Croatia

SDP–see Singapore Democratic Party

SDP–see Social Democratic Party (Bahamas)

SDP–see Social Democratic Party (Finland)

SDP–see Social Democratic Party (Iceland)

SDP–see Social Democratic Party (Japan)

SDP–see Social Democratic Party (Nigeria)

SDP–see Social Democratic Party (United Kingdom)

SdRP–see Social-Democratic Party of Poland

SDS–see Serb Democratic Party (Bosnia and Hercegovina)

SDS–see Union of Democratic Forces (Bulgaria)

SDSS–see Social Democratic Party of Slovenia

SDSS–see Social Democrat Party of Slovakia

SDUM–see Social Democratic Union of Macedonia

SEC–see Securities and Exchange Commission (U.S.A.)

SED–see Socialist Unity Party of Germany

SEPDF–see Southern Ethiopian Peoples' Democratic Front

SF–see Socialist People's Party (Denmark)

SF–see Sinn Fein (Northern Ireland)

SGP–see State Reform Party (Netherlands)

SHAS–see Sephardi Torah Guardians (Israel)

SIN–see Coalition of the Left and Progress (Greece)

SIP–see Industrial Union of Panama

SJKH–see National Council for New Politics (South Korea)

SJP–see Samajwadi Janata Party (India)

SKD–see Slovenian Christian Democrats

SKDL–see Finnish People's Democratic League

SKNLP–see St. Kitts & Nevis Labour Party

SKOI–see Standing Conference of the Civic Institute (Slovakia)

SKP–see Finnish Communist Party

SLD–see Democratic Left Alliance (Poland)

SLFP–see Sri Lanka Freedom Party

SLP–see St. Lucia Labour Party

SLP–see Socialist Labor Party (Egypt)

SLPP–see Sierra Leone People's Party

SLS–see Slovene People's Party

SMK–see Hungarian Coalition (Slovakia)

SMP–see Sipah-I-Muhamund (Pakistan)

SMS–see Great Council of Sinhalese (Sri Lanka)

SNAP–see Sarawak National Action Party (Malaysia)

SNC–see Supreme National Council (Cambodia)

SNE–see National Education Union (Morocco)

SNP–see Scottish National Party (UK of Great Britain)

SNS–see Slovak National Party

SNS–see Serb National Alliance (Bosnia and Hercegovina)

SNS–see Serbian People's Party (Croatia)

SNTVs–see Single Nontransferable Votes (Taiwan)

SODEP–see Social Democracy Party (Turkey)

SOP–see Party of Civic Understanding (Slovakia)

SP–see Socialist Parties (Belgium)

SP–see Samajwadi (Socialist) Party (India)

SP–see Samata Party (India)

SP–see Socialist Party (Netherlands)

SP–see Center Party (Norway)

SPA–see Supreme People's Assembly (North Korea)

SPD–see Social Democrats (Germany)

SPDC–see State Peace and Development Council (Myanmar)

SPK–see Socialist Party of Kazakhstan

SPLM–see Sudan People's Liberation Movement

SPO–see Social Democratic Party (Austria)

SPO–see Serbian Renewal Movement (Yugoslavia)

SPP–see Singapore People's Paarty

SPPF–see Seychelles People's Progressive Front

SPS–see Socialist Party of Serbia (Yugoslavia)

SPS–see Social-Democratic Party of Switzerland

SPU–see Socialist Party of Ukraine

SPZ–see Slovak Party of Entrepreneurs and Traders

SRA–see Argentine Rural Society

SRS–see Serbian Radical Party (Yugoslavia)

SRV–see Socialist Republic of Vietnam

SSIM–see Southern Sudan Independence Movement

SSP–see Sipah-i-Sahaba (Pakistan)

SSR–see Uzbek Soviet Socialist Republic

SSU–see Sudan Socialist Union

STV–see Single Transferable Vote (Ireland)

SUPP–see Sarawak United People's Party (Malaysia)

SV–see Socialist Left Party (Norway)

SVLP–see St. Vincent Labour Party

SVP–see Swiss People's Party/Democratic Center Union

SWAPO–see Southwest Africa People's Organization

SWAPO–see South West Africa People's Organization of Namibia

SWATF–see South West Africa Territorial Force (Namibia)

SZ–see Green Party (Czech Rep.)

SZS–see Green Party in Slovakia

TAIP–see Taiwan Independence Party

TAMI–see Movement for Jewish Tradition (Israel)

TANU–see Tanganyikan African National Union

TB–see Fatherland and Freedom (Latvia)

TC–see Tamil Congress (Sri Lanka)

TDP–see Telegu Desam Party (India)

TELO–see Tamil Eelam Liberation Organization (Sri Lanka)

TEU–see Maastricht Treaty of European Union

TGC–see Constitutional Tribunal (Ecuador)

THM–see Tapia House Movement (Trinidad and Tobago)

TI–see Struggle Movement (Pakistan)

TKP–see Communal Liberation Party (Cyprus)

TMC–see Tamil Maanila Congress (India)

TNP–see National Party (Grenada)

TPEs–see Provisional Electoral Tribunals (Ecuador)

TPLF–see Tigray People's Liberation Front (Ethiopia)

TPP–see True Path Party (Turkey)

TPSL–see Social Democratic League of Workers and Small Farmers (Finland)

TSE–see Supreme Electoral Tribunal (Ecuador)

TSE–see Supreme Electoral Tribunal (El Salvador)

TSP–see National Harmony Party (Latvia)

TTPI–see United Nations Trust Territory of the Pacific (Marshall I.)

TUC–see Trade Union Congress (Bahamas)

TUC–see Trade Union Congress (Zambia)

TULF–see Tamil United Liberation Front (Sri Lanka)

TUSIAD–see Turkish Industrialists and Businessmen's Association

TVS–see Tamil Nadu Agriculturalists' Association (India)

TWP–see True Whig Party (Liberia)

UBC–see Unified Buddhist Church (Vietnam)

UBP–see Party of National Unity (Cyprus)

UC–see Constitutional Union (Morocco)

UCC–see Center-Center Union (Chile)

UCD–see Union of the Democratic Center (Spain)

Ucede–see Union of the Democratic Center (Argentina)

UCN–see National Civic Union (Dominican Rep.)

UCN–see National Center Union (Guatemala)

UCP–see United Convention Party (Ghana)

UCR–see Radical Civic Union (Argentina)

UCRP–see Ukrainian Conservative Republican Party

UCs–see Urban Councils (Sri Lanka)

UCS–see Civic Solidarity Union (Bolivia)

UD–see Democratic Unity Party (Dominican Rep.)

UD–see Democratic Union (Guatemala)

UD–see Democratic Union (Poland)

UDA–see Ulster Defense Association (Northern Ireland)

UDC–see Cameroon Democratic Union

UDD–see Djibouti Democratic Union

Udemo–see Democratic Union of Mozambique

UDF–see Union for French Democracy

UDF–see United Democratic Front (Malawi)

UDI–see Independent Democratic Union (Chile)

UDI–see Independent Democratic Union (Panama)

UDI–see Unilateral Declaration of Independence (Zimbabwe)

UDJED–see Democratic Union for Justice and Equality in Djibouti

UDLP–see United Dominica Labor Party (Dominica)

UDM–see United Democratic Movement (South Africa)

UDN–see National Democratic Union (Brazil)

UDN–see National Democratic Union (El Salvador)

UDP–see United Democratic Party (Belize)

UDP–see Popular Unity Coalition (Bolivia)

UDP–see United Democratic Party (Gambia)

UDP–see United Democratic Party (Tanzania)

UDP–see Ulster Democratic Party (Northern Ireland)

UDP–see United Democratic Party (Zambia)

UDP-Amici–see Union for Democracy and Progress-Amici (Niger)

UDPE–see Union of the Spanish People

UDPM–see Democratic Union of Malian People

UDPS–see Democratic Republic of Congo

UDPS–see Union for Democracy and Social Progress (D. Rep. Congo)

UDPS-Amana–see Union for Democracy and Social Progress-Amana (Niger)

UDR–see Ulster Defense Regiment (Northern Ireland)

UDSG–see Gabonese Democratic and Social Union

UDS-R–see Senegalese Democratic Union

UDU–see Unionist Democratic Union (Tunisia)

UDV–see Volta Democratic Union (Burkina Faso)

UF–see United Force (Guyana)

UFA–see United Farmers of Alberta (Canada)

UFC–see Union of Forces of Change (Togo)

UFD–see Union of Democratic Forces (Mauritania)

UFM–see Uganda Freedom Movement

UFMD–see United Front for Multi-Party Democracy (Malawi)

UFPDP-Sawaba–see Union of Popular Forces for Democracy and Progress-Sawaba (Niger)

UFRI–see Union of Federalists and Independent Republicans (Democratic Republic of Congo)

UGEMA–see General Union of Algerian Muslim Students

UGT–see General Union of Workers (Spain)

UGTA–see General Union of Algerian Workers

UGTT–see General Union of Tunisian Workers

UIA–see Argentine Industrial Union

UIRP–see Uganda Islamic Revolutionary Party

UJD–see Union for Justice and Democracy (Togo)

UKUP–see United Kingdom Unionist Party (Northern Ireland)

ULCR–see Union of Reconstructed Communists (Burkina Faso)

ULD–see United Liberal Democrats (South Korea)

ULF–see United Labour Front (Trinidad and Tobago)

ULI–see Union of Independent Liberals (Togo)

ULIMO–see United Liberia Movement for Democracy

ULP–see United Labour Party (Saint Vincent and the Grenadines)

UM–see Union for Change Coalition (Guinea-Bissau)

UMA–see Union of the Arab Maghrib (North Africa)

UML–see Nepal-Unified Marxist Leninists

UMNO–see United Malays National Organization

UMOA–see West African Monetary Union

UMT–see Moroccan Union of Labor

UNA–see Ukrainian National Assembly

UNAG–see National Farmer's and Cattleman's Association (Nicaragua)

UNAMO–see Mozambican National Union

UNAVEM–see UN Angola Verification Mission

UNC–see United National Congress (Trinidad and Tobago

UNC–see Uganda National Congress

UND–see National Democratic Union (Monaco)

UNDC–see National Union for Democracy (Comoros)

UNDD–see National Union for the Defense of Democracy (Burkina Faso)

UNDD–see National Union for Development and Democracy (Madagascar)

UNDP–see United National Democratic Party (Antigua and Barbuda)

UNDP–see National Union for Democracy and Progress (Cameroon)

UNEC–see National Union of Education and Culture (Mali)

UNEEM–see National Union of Students and Pupils of Mali

UNFA–see National Union of Algerian Women

UNFP–see United National Federal Party (Zimbabwe)

UNFP–see National Union of Popular Forces (Morocco)

UNIDO–see United Democratic Opposition (Philippines)

UNIP–see United National Independence Party (Zambia)

UNITA–see National Union for the Total Independence of Angola

UNLDDA–see National Union for the Light of Democracy and Development in Angola

UNO–see Nicaraguan Opposition Union

UNOMOZ–see UN Operation Mozambique

UNP–see National Union for Prosperity (Guinea)

UNP–see United National Party (Sri Lanka)

UNPA–see National Union of Algerian Peasants

UNPP–see National People's Party (Sierra Leone)

UNR–see Union for the New Republic (Guinea)

UNS–see Sinarquista National Union (Mexico)

UNSO–see United Sabah National Organization (Malaysia)

UNTAC–see United Nations Transitional Authority in Cambodia

UNTM–see National Union of Malian Workers

UNZA–see University of Zambia

UP–see Patriotic Union (Colombia)

UP–see Unity Party (Liberia)

UP–see Union of Labor (Poland)

UPADS–see Pan-African Union for Social Democracy (Republic of Congo)

UPC–see Union of Cameroon Populations

UPC–see Ugandan People's Congress

UPDM–see Uganda People's Democratic Movement

UPDP–see Ukrainian Peasant Democratic Party

UPDP-Shamuwa–see Union of Democratic and Progressive Patriots-Shamuwa (Niger)

UPG–see Gabonese Peoples Union

UPG–see Union for the Progress of Guinea

UPM–see United Peoples Movement (Antigua and Barbuda)

UPM–see Ugandan Patriotic Movement

UPN–see Navarrese Peoples' Union (Spain)

UPO–see Union of the People of Ordino (Andorra)

UPP–see Union for the Progress of Chile

UPP–see Union for Peru

UPP–see United Progressive Party (Antigua and Barbuda)

UPP–see United Peoples Party (Liberia)

UPRONA–see Union for National Progress (Burundi)

UPV–see Volta Progressive Union (Burkina Faso)

URD–see Union for Democratic Renewal (Republic of Congo)

URNG–see Guatemalan National Revolutionary Unity

URP–see Ukrainian Republican Party

URS–see Social Reformist Union (Guatemala)

USC–see Cameroon Social Union

USC–see Ulster Special Constabulary (Northern Ireland)

USDA–see Union Solidarity Development Association (Myanmar)

USFP–see Socialist Union of Popular Forces (Monaco)

USG–see Union for Gabonese Socialism

US-RDA–see Marxist Sudanese Union (Mali)

UT–see United Togolese Committee

UTC–see Union of Colombian Workers

UTD–see Togolese Union for Democracy

UTJ–see United Torah Judaism (Israel)

UTM–see Mauritanian Workers' Union

UTO–see United Tajik Opposition

UUP–see Ulster Unionist Party (Northern Ireland)

UUUC–see United Ulster Unionist Council (Northern Ireland)

UV–see Valencian Union (Spain)

UVDB–see Union of Greens for the Development of Burkina

UW–see Freedom Union (Poland)

UWP–see United Workers Party (Dominica)

UWP–see United Workers' Party (Saint Lucia)

V–see Danish Liberal Party

V–see Left Party (Sweden)

VA–see Voter's Association (Finland)

VB–see Flemish Bloc (Belgium)

VBC–see Vietnam Buddhist Church

VCP–see Vietnam Communist Party

VGO–see United Green Party of Austria

VHP–see Progressive Reform Party (Suriname)

VLD–see Liberal Parties (Belgium)

VRD–see Democratic Republican Union (Venezuela)

VSI–see Federation of Employees (Iceland)

VU–see People's Union (Belgium)

VU–see Fatherland Union (Liechtenstein)

VVD–see People's Party for Freedom and Democracy (Netherlands)

WCPDM–see Women's Organization of Cameroon People's Democratic Movement

WDCs–see Worker's Defense Committees (Ghana)

WP–see Welfare Party (Turkey)

WP–see Worker's Party (Singapore)

WPA–see Working People's Alliance (Guyana)

WPO–see Women's Progressive Organization (Guyana)

WTP–see Progress of the Fatherland Party (Uzbekistan)

YAR–see Yemen Arab Republic

YATAMA–see Miskito Opposition Group (Nicaragua)

YCPDM–see Youth Organization of Cameroon People's Democratic Movement

YSP–see Yemeni Socialist Party

ZANC–see Zambian African National Congress

ZANLA–see Zimbabwe African National Liberation Army

ZANU–see Zimbabwe African Nationalist Union

ZANU-N–see Zimbabwe African National Union-Ndongo

ZANU-PF–see Zimbabwe African National Patriotic Front

ZAPU–see Zimbabwe African People's Union

ZCTU–see Zambia Congress of Trade Unions

ZDC–see Zambia Democratic Congress

ZDP–see Zambabwe Democratic Party

ZIPRA–see Zimbabwe People's Revolutionary Army

ZLA–see Zimbabwe Liberation Army

ZLSD–see United List of Social Democrats of Slovenia

ZNF–see Zimbabwe National Front

ZPA–see Zimbabwe People's Army

ZRC–see Zanzibar Revolutionary Council (Tanzania)

ZRS–see Worker's Association of Slovakia

ZS–see Agrarian Party (Czech Rep.)

ZUM–see Zimbabwe Unity Movement

ZUPO–see Zimbabwe United Peoples Organization